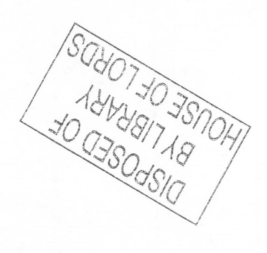

Human Rights and Civil Practice

AUSTRALIA
LBC Information Services Sydney
Sydney

CANADA and USA
Carswell
Toronto—Ontario

NEW ZEALAND
Brookers
Auckland

SINGAPORE and MALAYSIA
Sweet & Maxwell Asia
Singapore and Kuala Lumpur

Human Rights and Civil Practice

General Editor

Leigh-Ann Mulcahy

M.A. (Cantab.) LL.M. (Osgoode)
Dip. E.C. Law (London)
Barrister, 4 New Square

LONDON
SWEET & MAXWELL
2001

Published in 2001 by
Sweet & Maxwell Limited of
100 Avenue Road London NW3 3PF
http:/www/sweetandmaxwell.co.uk
Typeset by Interactive Sciences Ltd, Gloucester
Printed in England by
MPG Books Ltd, Bodmin, Cornwall

A CIP catalogue record for this book is available
from the British Library

ISBN 0421 709901

No natural forests were destroyed to make this
product, only farmed timber was used and
re-planted.

General Editor

Leigh-Ann Mulcahy
M.A. (Cantab.) LL.M. (Osgoode) Dip. E.C. Law (London)
Barrister, 4 New Square

Contributors

Scott Allen
M.A. (Oxon.)
Barrister, 4 New Square

Kieron Beal
M.A. (Cantab.) LL.M. (Harvard)
Barrister, 4 Paper Buildings

Anneliese Day
M.A. (Cantab.)
Barrister, 4 New Square

Francis Fitzpatrick
M.A., B.C.L. (Oxon.)
Barrister, 11 New Square

Michael Ford
LL.B., (Hons), M.A., Visiting Fellow, L.S.E.
Barrister, Doughty Street Chambers

Margaret Gray
B.A., B.C.L. (Oxon.) LL.M. (Bruges)
Barrister, Brick Court Chambers

Alex Hall Taylor
B.A. (Hons) (Bristol) Dipl. Law (London)
Barrister, 11 Old Square

Samantha Knights
B.A. (Hons) (Oxon.)
Barrister, 3–4 South Square

Jonathan Peacock Q.C.
M.A. (Oxon.)
Barrister, 11 New Square

Anya Proops
M.A. (Cantab.) Ph.D. (London)
Barrister, 11 Kings Bench Walk

Keir Starmer
LL.B. (Hons), B.C.L. (Oxon.)
Barrister, Doughty Street Chambers

Foreword

By the Rt. Hon. The Lord Phillips of Worth Matravers

It is now nearly a year since the entry into force of the Human Rights Act 1998 made the European Convention of Human Rights part of our law. I am one of those who believe that this is the most notable development of our constitutional law since the Bill of Rights of 1689. The terms of the Act preserve the supremacy of Parliament, but they make a dramatic change to the manner in which the Courts are to determine the will of Parliament. No longer is it the primary task of the Court to attempt to ascertain and apply the natural and ordinary meaning of the words used in a Statute, having regard to the relevant context. No longer is the Court required to ensure that the interpretation of a Statute accords to its language a meaning which the words are reasonably capable of bearing—see the speech of Lord Steyn in *R. v. A* [2001] UKHL 25. Section 3 of the Act requires the Court to find an interpretation of a Statute that is compatible with human rights so far as it is possible to do so, and Section 2 requires the Court to take account of Strasbourg jurisprudence. *In extremis*, Section 4 requires the Court to declare that primary legislation is incompatible with a Convention right.

Some forecast that the Human Rights Act would have minimal impact on our law, on the basis that respect for human rights was already the foundation of our common law. Others forecast that it would lead the judiciary to invade territories that should properly be the reserve of the legislature or the executive. A year on there is already sufficient case material to justify the production of a text book which assesses the impact that the Human Rights Act is having on our domestic law.

Leigh-Ann Mulcahy and her co-authors have done much more than this. They have produced a work which should prove of great value to all who practise civil law, and particularly to those who specialise in a number of fields that have been given individual treatment.

There is much that is novel both about the approach and the content of this book. Unusually, it considers human rights in the context of different topics rather than analysing the application of each of the Articles of the Convention in turn. The first part of the book deals comprehensively with the background to human rights law and the second part with the impact of human rights on practice and procedure. The final part consists of contributions on the effect of human rights on eight important areas of civil law, provided by practitioners who specialise in them.

The book is crafted throughout to cater for the needs of the practitioner, with chapters giving practical guidance on how to make use of human rights arguments at every stage and in relation to every aspect of the new civil procedure. This work will also be welcomed by the Judge, for it will help all who use it to place good human rights arguments before the Court and to avoid the ritual invocation of human rights where they have, in truth, nothing to add.

Preface

The Human Rights Act 1998 came into force on October 2, 2000. Nine months on, over 195 decisions in total, of which 142 are civil cases, have already been handed down by the higher courts in England & Wales.[1] These demonstrate some of the ways in which the Act is already affecting civil practice. The book includes reference to relevant domestic cases up to July 1, 2001.

The 1998 Act gives effect in domestic law to the majority of the fundamental human rights laid down in the European Convention on Human Rights 1950 so that parties in domestic proceedings can directly rely on these rights without recourse to the European Court of Human Rights in Strasbourg, save in the last resort. The Act has an extremely broad application both to litigation involving public authorities and to litigation between private individuals.

The purpose of this book is:

(1) to detail the implications of the Human Rights Act for some key areas of civil or commercial practice. These chapters are written by specialist practitioners in those fields;

(2) to provide a comprehensive analysis of the impact of the Human Rights Act on the Civil Procedure Rules and evidence;

(3) as far as possible, to adopt a subject-based analysis, rather than a right-by-right based approach;

(4) to provide straightforward, practical guidance to the practitioner and advocate about pleading, arguing and responding to human rights claims or issues and available remedies for violations of the Human Rights Act;

(5) to provide an introduction to relevant non-Convention sources of human rights law including:

(a) constitutional rights already protected by domestic common law;
(b) fundamental rights protected by European Community law;
(c) international human rights instruments;
(d) the human rights experience of other common-law jurisdictions.

The book is divided into three parts: Part I—The Background to Human Rights Law; Part II—Practice and Procedure; Part III—Applications for Civil Practice.

---

[1] The figure is taken from Lawtel's reported cases. In the last decade, some 1,289 domestic cases (including Scotland) involving human rights have been reported by Lawtel.

Part I provides an overview of the Human Rights Act and an introduction to the Convention. It then details the general principles of European human rights law and their application within domestic courts. Further, it identifies the protection given to human rights by other legal regimes including the common law and equity, European Community law, international law and other common law jurisdictions. A full analysis of each Article of the Convention is beyond the scope of this book and the reader is referred to one of the many detailed "rights-based" texts in this regard.[2]

Part II explains the practical aspects of litigation involving issues of human rights and the remedies available for violations of Convention rights. It then analyses the effect of the Human Rights Act on the Civil Procedure Rules and on the rules of evidence. Finally, it considers the right of access to a court and its implications for alternative proceedings such as arbitration and alternative dispute resolution and for the provision of legal aid.

Part III discusses the application of the Human Rights Act for key areas of civil practice. The focus is on fields that tend to be regarded as part of "commercial" civil law rather than those which form part of administrative or family law. The chapters in Part III are written by specialist practitioners in the fields in question. They consist of:

- employment law (Chapter 13);
- companies and financial services (Chapter 14);
- insolvency (Chapter 15);
- property, planning and environmental law (Chapter 16);
- professional liability and negligence (Chapter 17);
- taxation (Chapter 18);
- consumer protection and advertising (Chapter 19);
- civil disciplinary proceedings (Chapter 20).

Appendices C to K contain the major United Nations human rights instruments together with the bills of rights or major constitutional instruments of other common-law jurisdictions.

To avoid confusion, throughout this book unless otherwise stated, the following terminology will be adopted:

- The Human Rights Act 1998 will be abbreviated to "the HRA";
- The European Convention on Human Rights and Fundamental Freedoms 1950 will be referred to as "the Convention" or, in Chapter 7, "the ECHR";

---

[2] See particularly, Simor & Emmerson, *Human Rights Practice* (Sweet & Maxwell, 2000); Lester & Pannick, *Human Rights Law and Practice* (Butterworths, 1999); Tomlinson & Clayton, *The Law of Human Rights* (Oxford, 2000); Grosz, Beatson & Duffy, *Human Rights, The 1998 Act and the European Convention* (Sweet & Maxwell, 2000).

- The International Covenant on Civil and Political Rights 1966 will be referred to as "the ICCPR";

- The European Court of Human Rights will be referred to as the "European Court";

- The European Commission of Human Rights will be referred to as the "European Commission";

- The Court of Justice of the European Communities will be referred to as the "European Court of Justice" (or as the "ECJ").

- The Commission of the European Communities will be referred to as such.

All shorthand references to "he" should be taken to include "she" and "him" to include "her".

Stop Press

As this book goes to press, we learn that in *Ferrazzini v. Italy*, Application No. 44759/98, the ECtHR held by a majority decision that tax disputes fall outside the scope of Article 6 on the ground that individuals' civil rights are not engaged. In the United Kingdom the probable consequence of this decision is that Article 6 will not apply to appeals against tax assessments, whether of direct or indirect tax. However, Article 6 does apply where a tax penalty is a criminal charge within Article 6, and applies where a tax-payer's civil rights are engaged (for example where a taxpayer makes a claim for damages or restitution against the tax authorities).

Acknowledgments

I wish to acknowledge and thank my original co-author, Conn MacEvilly, who conceived the idea for this book but whose professional circumstances unfortunately forced him to retire from further involvement.

As general editor, I wisk to thank the specialist contributors to the book for taking time from their busy practices to provide chapters which are of the highest quality and which I believe benefit enormously from the specialist expertise of their authors. This work is the product of a cross-chambers venture, drawing together a number of civil and commercial practitioners from leading chambers who each had a keen interest in writing about the impact of the Human Rights Act on their fields. The contributors are (in chapter order):

Kieron Beal of 4 Paper Buildings and Margaret Gray of Brock Court Chambers who contributed Chapter 6, European Community Law and Human Rights.

Scott Allen of 4 New Square who is the primary author of Chapter 7, International Sources of Human Rights Law.

Anya Proops of 11 King's Bench Walk who contributed Chapter 13, Employment.

Samantha Knights of 3–4 South Square who contributed Chapter 14, Companies and Financial Services and Chapter 15, Insolvency.

Alex Hall Taylor of 11 Old Square who contributed Chapter 16, Property, Planning and Environment.

Anneliese Day of 4 New Square who contributed the medical law section for Chapter 17, Professional Liability and Negligence.

Jonathan Peacock Q.C. and Francis Fitzpatrick of 11 New Square who contributed Chapter 18, Taxation.

Michael Ford and Keir Starmer of Doughty Street Chambers who contributed Chapter 20, Civil Disciplinary Proceedings.

Every book in a developing field owes a debt to the books that have gone before. As civil and commercial practitioners prior to developing expertise in human rights law, the contributors and I have been much assisted by the excellent leading texts on European human rights law in guiding us to the human rights case-law relevant to our individual subjects. Jointly, we wish to gratefully acknowledge the assistance we have derived from such texts as Lester & Pannick, *Human Rights Law & Practice* (Butterworths: 1999):

Grosz, Beatson & Duffy, *Human Rights: The 1998 Act and the European Convention* (Sweet & Maxwell: 2000), Simor & Emmerson, *Human Rights Practice* (Sweet & Maxwell: 2000), Starmer, *European Human Rights Law* (Legal Action Group: 1999), Clayton & Tomlinson, *The Law of Human Rights* (Oxford: 2000) and Coppel, *The Human Rights Act 1998* (Wiley: 1999) and Reid, *A Practitioner's Guide to the European Convention of Human Rights* (Sweet & Maxwell: 1998).

We are also grateful to the Alexander Maxwell Law Scholarship Trust who generously provided a grant that helped to defray some of the expenses incurred in writing this book.

Several people have generously given of their time to provide valuable comments on draft chapters of the book. I would like to thank in particular Keir Starmer, Marion Simmons Q.C., Elizabeth Haggett, Lisa Tomas, Matthew Abraham and Jeremy Croft.

I am indebted to Siân Mirchandani for her valuable input into the immunities section of Chapter 17, Jason Coppel for his general advice and Richard Liddell for his enthusiastic assistance with research for the books. Others from whom I have gratefully received help with research and proof reading include Arash Amel, Stephen Cottrell, Steve Innes and above all, Darren Mulcahy, who gave up weeks of his time to assist me (and thanks also to TLT Solicitors who generously seconded him to me). I have very much appreciated the interest and support shown by my head of chambers Justin Fenwick Q.C., Lizzy Wiseman, and all of my colleagues at 4 New Square whilst I was writing this book. I would particularly like to thank Nick Bryant, my clerk, who patiently and repeatedly juggled my practice commitments to allow me to meet impending writing deadlines, and Joyce Lester for all her help with typing and formatting.

The current and former team at Sweet & Maxwell were tremendously helpful and efficient throughout the writing and publishing process. Whilst company policy prevents me from identifying the individuals concerned, I cannot praise too highly the service that I and the other authors have received. I should also like to thank my very good friend, Ruth Pratten, for her sound advice on the publishing aspects.

I am very grateful to Lord Phillips, the Master of the Rolls, who kindly agreed to spare time from his busy schedule to write an excellent foreword for the book.

Finally, on a personal note, I would like to thank above all my husband and parents who (as with everything I do) provided unwavering support and encouragement throughout this writing project.

Leigh-Ann Mulcahy
4 New Square
Lincoln's Inn
London WC2A 3RJ

July 18, 2001

Contents

APPENDICES

TABLE OF CASES

TABLE OF STATUTES

TABLE OF STATUTORY INSTRUMENTS

TABLE OF CONVENTIONS

The Background to Human Rights Law

CHAPTER 1

Introduction

1. THE IMPACT OF THE HUMAN RIGHTS ACT ON CIVIL PRACTITIONERS

Pre-incorporation. The European Convention on Human Rights   **1.01**
1950 is an agreement between the governments of the Contracting
States. It imposes obligations in international law on the United Kingdom
as a signatory. In English law, international treaties are not self executing,[1]
and prior to incorporation, do not give rise to rights enforceable by individuals in domestic courts. Accordingly, prior to the Human Rights Act 1998
("the HRA"), the role of the European Convention on Human Rights was
limited. It was a principle of interpretation of primary and secondary
legislation in case of ambiguity that there was a presumption that the law
conformed to the United Kingdom's treaty obligations.[2] Further, it was
possible to have recourse to the Convention in relation to ambiguity in the
common law.[3] However, the courts stopped short of finding that administrative discretion conferred on the executive must be exercised within
Convention limits.[4]

Post–HRA. The effect of the HRA has been to root the Convention   **1.02**
firmly into domestic law. As the Lord Chancellor expressively stated in
Parliamentary debates on the Human Rights Bill:

> "Convention rights are our magnetic north and our law must point
> towards them."[5]

---

[1] *J.H. Rayner Ltd v. Department of Trade* [1990] 2 A.C. 418, *per* Lord Templeman at
476G–477A. But see the recent decisions in the Privy Council set out at para. 7.02.
[2] In *R v. Home Office, ex p. Brind* [1991] 1 A.C. 696, Lord Bridge stated " . . . it is already well
settled that, in construing any provision in domestic legislation which is ambiguous in the
sense that it is capable of a meaning which either conforms to or conflicts with the Convention the courts will presume that Parliament intended to legislate in conformity with the
Convention, not in conflict with it."
[3] *Derbyshire County Council v. Times Newspapers Ltd* [1993] A.C. 534, HL.
[4] Although the Court of Appeal refined the *Wednesbury* unreasonableness test to take
greater cognisance of the Convention in *R. v. Ministry of Defence, ex p. Smith* [1996] Q.B.
517 at 554 " . . . in judging whether the decision-maker has exceeded this margin of
appreciation the human rights context is important. The more substantial the interference
with human rights, the more the court will require by way of justification before it is satisfied
that the decision is reasonable . . . "
[5] H.L. Deb., February 5, 1998, col. 840.

1.03 The Act has "incorporated" the majority of the Convention rights into domestic law by four key methods:

(1) By section 6, it has created a new statutory tort, making it unlawful for a "public authority" to act incompatibly with the Convention. Public authority is defined to include courts and tribunals and any person or body who exercises a "public function". The court's duty arising from section 6 means that the Convention has effect on both the common law and equity;

(2) By section 7, it empowers a "victim" of a violation of Convention rights to bring proceedings against a "public authority" guilty of such a violation or raise the violation in any legal proceedings;

(3) By section 3, it has created a strong interpretive obligation to construe all past and future legislation compatibly with the Convention, "so far as it is possible to do so";

(4) By section 2, it has placed a duty on courts to "take into account" Strasbourg jurisprudence whenever a Convention issue arises.

1.04 The entry into force of the HRA has also raised the prospect of the fused practical application of no fewer than four streams of human rights law and jurisprudence:

(1) domestic "human rights law", both at common law and under the HRA[6];

(2) human rights law derived from the European Convention on Human Rights ("the Convention");[7]

(3) 'human rights' recognised as general principles of law under the jurisprudence of the Court of Justice of the European Communities ("the ECJ") and in other sources of Community law;[8]

(4) international law relating to the protection of fundamental rights.[9]

2. DOMESTIC CASES FOLLOWING OCTOBER 2, 2000

1.05 The Lord Chancellor's Department set aside £60 million for anticipated legal costs arising from the Human Rights Act,[10] which provided some indication of the anticipated importance of the Act. The sheer number of cases raising Convention points since the Act has come into effect has borne this out,[10A] although the Lord Chancellor has stated that there has

---

[6] As the Lord Justice General, Lord Rodger of Earlsferry noted in *Her Majesty's Advocate v. Montgomery* (2000) S.L.T. 122 at 127A-B: "it would be wrong to see the Convention rights as somehow forming a wholly separate stream of jurisprudence."
[7] See further Chapter 3.
[8] See further Chapter 6.
[9] See further Chapter 7.
[10] £39 million in respect of legal aid and £21 million for extra court sittings.
[10A] See Preface.

been no significant impact on the length or complexity of hearings.[11] The impact on the Legal Services Commission is not yet possible to predict.[12]

It can be seen that on occasion (*e.g. Marcic v. Thames Water Utilities*)[12A] **1.06** an action may now succeed before domestic courts using the Human Rights Act when it would have failed under pre-existing domestic law. Further, the approach of the European Court of Human Rights in *Z v. United Kingdom*[12B] may provide an added incentive to litigants to frame tortious claims based on pre-October 2000 acts or omissions additionally as a breach of a Convention right so that if they do not succeed before the English courts, they can argue for a remedy in Strasbourg based on breach of the State's obligation to provide an effective remedy for the Convention violation under Article 13. However, of the cases raising human rights points, very few have been successful based on the Convention arguments alone. This is very similar to the Scottish experience following the introduction of the Scotland Act 1998 which permitted challenges to be made to Scottish legislative and executive acts using the Convention. Whilst the Convention has had a direct impact on many areas including striking out, committal proceedings, use of self-incriminatory evidence and civil disciplinary proceedings, the real impact of the Human Rights Act is, in general terms, rather subtler. Whilst there have certainly been landmark decisions such as *R. v. Director of Public Prosecutions, ex p. Kebilene* (pre-HRA coming into force) which addressed the margin of appreciation and reverse onuses of proof,[13] *Stott (Procurator Fiscal, Dunfermline) & anr v. Brown*,[14] which considered the right against self-incrimination in relation to a provision of the Road Traffic Act 1988 and *Douglas v. Hello! Ltd*[15] which recognised expressly a right of privacy in English law, the HRA can more usually be seen to modify the approach taken as a matter of ordinary domestic law. Sometimes, the Convention argument might be argued to have given rise to a rather different decision as a matter of domestic law that might otherwise have been anticipated, thereby making it unnecessary for the Convention point to be decided.[16] Whilst the effect of the HRA has often been overstated, nonetheless it is having a significant impact and its influence in all areas of civil practice can safely be predicted to increase over time.

---

[11] Lord Chancellor's Department Press Release, March 20, 2001. See http://www.open. gov.uk/lcd.
[12] *ibid.*
[12A] *The Independent*, July 9, 2001, HHJ Havery Q.C.
[12B] Application No. 29392/95, [2001] 2 F.C.R. 246. See further paras 17.19 *et seq.* below.
[13] [1999] 3 W.L.R. 972, HL.
[14] [2001] 2 W.L.R. 817; *The Times*, December 6, 2000, PC.
[15] [2001] 2 W.L.R. 817; *The Times*, January 16, 2001, CA (Judgment handed down on December 21, 2000).
[16] See *e.g.*, *Phelps v. Hillingdon London Borough Council*, [2000] 3 W.L.R. 776, HL (claims in negligence against educational psychologists not struck out); *Daniels v. Walker* [2000] 1 W.L.R. 1382, CA (parties allowed to call own expert in addition to single joint expert under the CPR) and *Arthur J.S. Hall v. Simons* [2000] 3 W.L.R. 543, HL (abolition of advocates' immunity for *both* civil and criminal proceedings).

CHAPTER 2
The Human Rights Act 1998

1. LEGISLATIVE BACKGROUND AND APPLICATION

Legislative Background

2.01 The Human Rights Act 1998[1] ("the HRA") was introduced by the Government as a Bill in the House of Lords on October 23, 1997 and eventually
received the Royal Assent on November 9, 1998.[2]

2.02 The Human Rights Bill was preceded by a Consultation Paper (December
1996) produced whilst the Labour Party were in opposition and a White
Paper entitled "Rights Brought Home: The Human Rights Bill"[3] (October

---

[1] c.42.

[2] The Parliamentary stages were as follows: First Reading (H.L.) October 23, 1997; Second
Reading (H.L.) November 3, 1997; Committee stage (H.L.) November 18, 1997; Committee
stage (H.L.) November 24, 1997; Committee stage (H.L.) November 11, 1997; Report Stage
(H.L.) January 19, 1998; Third Reading (H.L.) February 2, 1998; Second Reading (H.C.)
February 16, 1998; Committee Stage (H.C.) May 20, 1998; Committee Stage (H.C.) June 3,
1998; Committee Stage (H.C.) June 17, 1998; Committee Stage (H.C.) June 24, 1998;
Committee Stage (H.C.) July 2, 1998; Report Stage and Third Reading (H.C.) October 21,
1998; Commons Amendments (H.L.) October 29, 1998; Royal Assent November 9, 1998.
The debates can be accessed on the internet through the Lord Chancellor's Department
web-site: www.open.gov.uk/lcd/humanrights/parlfr.htm. See also Cooper & Owers, *The
Human Rights Bill. The Debate in Parliament* (Hart, 2000).

[3] Cm. 3782 (October 1997).

1997)[4] when in government. In the White Paper, the purpose of the Bill is stated as follows:

> "Our aim is a straightforward one. It is to make more directly accessible the rights which the British people already enjoy under the Convention. In other words, to bring those rights home."

Apart from section 18 (the provisions relating to the appointment of judges), section 20 (powers of ministers to make orders under the HRA) and section 21(5) (substitution of other sentences for the death penalty) which came into force on the passing of the HRA,[5] and section 19 (statements of compatibility) which came into force on November 24, 1998,[6] the main provisions came into force on October 2, 2000.[7]   **2.03**

Application of HRA

Prior to the HRA coming into force, although reference was increasingly made to the Convention in judicial decisions, the House of Lords made it clear that it did not have retrospective effect: *R. v. DPP, ex p. Kebilene*.[8] However, the operation of section 22(4) of the HRA permits some limited retrospective effect.[9] This section enables an individual to rely on his Convention rights when defending proceedings, including an appeal, brought by or at the instigation of a public authority, even where an alleged breach of those rights occurred before the HRA came into force.[10] In addition, it seems that the principles of interpretation of primary and secondary legislation contained in section 3 of the HRA can be relied on in an appeal which is heard after the Act came into force, even though the appeal is against an order made by the court below before the Act came into force.[11]   **2.04**

The sentiments expressed in the White Paper were reiterated by the Secretary of State for the Home Department, Mr Jack Straw, when introducing the Bill into the House of Commons. He stated: **2.05**

> "The Bill will guarantee to everyone the means to enforce a set of basic civil and political rights, establishing a floor below which standards will not be allowed to fall. The Bill will achieve that by giving further effect in our domestic law to the fundamental rights and

---

[4] There have been several attempts to incorporate the Convention by Private Members' Bills. The most recent attempts were by a Conservative M.P., Sir Edward Gardner q.c., who introduced a Bill into the House of Commons in 1987 and a Liberal Democrat Peer, Lord Lester of Herne Hill q.c., introduced Bills into the House of Lords in 1994 and 1996.

[5] HRA, s.22(2).

[6] The Human Rights Act 1998 (Commencement) Order 1998, S.I.1998 No. 2882 (C.71).

[7] The Human Rights Act 1998 (Commencement No.2) Order 2000, S.I.2000 No.1851 (C.47). The application to Scotland, Wales and Northern Ireland is addressed below. The HRA does not extend to the Isle of Man and the Channel Islands, although the Isle of Man intends to introduce its own legislation.

[8] [1999] 3 W.L.R. 972; but see also the comments of Lord Woolf C.J. in *R. v. Lambert* [2001] 1 All E.R. 1014, CA at 1024.

[9] See para. 2.30, below.

[10] *R. v. Director of Public Prosecutions, ex p. Kebilene* [1999] 3 W.L.R. 972 at 982. See also the Division Court judgment [1999] 3 W.L.R. 175 at 187, adopted in *R. v. Benjafield*, [2001] 3 W.L.R. 75, CA and *R. v. Lambert* [2001] 1 All E.R. 1014 at 1024.

[11] *J.A. Pye (Oxford) Ltd v. Graham Ltd*, [2001] 2 W.L.R. 1293, CA.

freedoms contained in the European convention on human rights."[12]

2.06   The primary motivations behind the HRA were as follows:

(1) to permit the domestic legal system to protect individuals from acts or omissions of public bodies which harm them in a way which is incompatible with their human rights under the Convention[13];

(2) to obviate the delay and cost involved in pursuing an application before the European Court of Human Rights[14];

(3) to influence the development of case law on the Convention by the European Court of Human Rights on the basis of familiarity with domestic laws and customs and sensitivity to practices and procedures in the United Kingdom[15];

(4) to enable closer scrutiny of the humans rights implications of new legislation and new policies.[16]

2. THE CONVENTION IN SCOTLAND, WALES AND NORTHERN IRELAND

2.07   **Devolution.**   The Convention was given indirect effect in Scotland,[17] Wales[18] and Northern Ireland,[19] prior to the coming into force of the HRA, through the individual devolution provisions. The gap in timing resulted from the speedier progress of the devolution Acts through Parliament and the delay in the coming into force of the HRA to allow sufficient time for preparation. The devolution provisions differ from, but overlap with, the HRA. Since October 2, 2000, in relation to questions which arise as to whether the devolved legislatures or executives have acted or are proposing to act in a way that is incompatible with any of the Convention rights, these may be resolved as devolution issues[20] or under the HRA 1998. The devolution systems seek to achieve uniformity in the determination of issues arising under the Convention throughout all parts of the United Kingdom by reserving to the Judicial Committee of the Privy Council the power of final decision. The impact of the Convention on the competencies

---

[12] H.C. Deb., February 16, 1998, col. 769.

[13] The Lord Chancellor referred to the 50 cases in which the European Court of Human Rights had found a violation of the Convention by the United Kingdom, more than any other country except Italy. More than half of those violations were since 1990: H.L., Deb., November 3, 1997, col. 1228.

[14] In 1998, the average time from notification of complaint to hearing was five years and the average cost was £30,000.

[15] White Paper, para. 1.18.

[16] White Paper, para. 1.18.

[17] Scotland Act 1998 (c.46): see particularly ss. 29, 57 and 126(1).

[18] Government of Wales Act 1998 (c.38): see particularly Sched. 8.

[19] Northern Ireland Act 1998 (c.47): see particularly ss. 9–11, 13, 14 , 71.

[20] For procedural matters involving devolution issues arising under the devolution statutes, see also the Court of Appeal Practice Direction: Devolution Issues (and Crown Office Applications in Wales) issued on June 30, 1999.

of the national legislatures and executives pursuant to their devolution provisions is briefly summarised below. A more detailed consideration of the inter-relationship between individual devolution statutes and the HRA is beyond the scope of this book. However, the reader is referred to Grosz, Beatson & Duffy, *Human Rights: The 1998 Act and the European Convention*,[21] Chapter 7 and Lester & Pannick, *Human Rights Law & Practice*,[22] Chapters 5 (Scotland), 6 (Northern Ireland) and 7 (Wales) for a fuller description.

Scotland. In Scotland, the position with regard to Acts of the West- **2.08** minster Parliament is the same as in England and Wales. If a statute or statutory instrument is found to be incompatible,[23] the Court of Session (provided that it is not sitting as a trial court) or the High Court can make a declaration of incompatibility, but this does not affect the validity of the provision. On the other hand, unlike the Westminster Parliament, the Scottish Parliament has no power to legislate in a way which is incompatible with the Convention. A legislative measure can therefore be judicially challenged on the ground that the Scottish Parliament incorrectly exercised its powers, and be declared invalid by the courts if it is incompatible with the Convention. Similarly, the Scottish Executive has no power to act (including omitting to act) in a way that is incompatible with the Convention. Most of the early Scottish cases concerned the position of the Lord Advocate, who is a member of the Executive but also (together with his deputies) responsible for prosecuting crime. There is a right of appeal to the Judicial Committee of the Privy Council in devolution matters that have properly arisen within the meaning of Schedule 6 to the Scotland Act.[24]

Wales. In Wales, the Welsh Assembly has no power to make sub- **2.09** ordinate legislation which is incompatible with the Convention and the Welsh Executive has no power to act incompatibly with the Convention. Again, it is possible to challenge such legislation and Executive acts or omissions in the courts.

Northern Ireland. In Northern Ireland, the position in relation to **2.10** Acts of the Westminster Parliament is the same as in England and Wales. Further, Orders in Council made under section 38(1)(a) of the Northern Ireland Constitution Act 1973, or the corresponding provisions of the Northern Ireland Act 1998, are included in the definition of "primary legislation" under the HRA, preventing challenge on the grounds of incompatibility with the Convention. By contrast, Acts of the Parliament of Northern Ireland, Measures of the Assembly established under section 1 of the

---

[21] Sweet & Maxwell, 2000
[22] Butterworths, 1999.
[23] See declarations of incompatibility discussed at para. 2.44, below.
[24] The Privy Council does not have jurisdiction in relation to England, but only to the devolved administrations. For consideration of the jurisdiction of the Privy Council in Scottish devolution matters, see *Hoekstra v. H. M. Advocate*, [2000] 3 W.L.R. 1817, PC (an appeal could only be brought, or a reference made to the Judicial Committee under the Scotland Act 1998, Sched. 6, if it raised a devolution issue. The Judicial Committee declined jurisdiction because it did not have power to review interlocutors of the High Court of Justiciary). See also *Stott (Procurator Fiscal, Dunfermline) v. Brown* [2001] 2 W.L.R. 817, PC where the Judicial Committee accepted jurisdiction. The court of last resort in relation to appeals under the HRA is the House of Lords.

Northern Ireland Assembly Act 1973, and Acts of the Northern Ireland Assembly are included in the definition of "subordinate legislation" under the HRA and can be challenged in the courts on the ground of incompatibility.[25]

3. THE HUMAN RIGHTS ACT

General

General effect of the HRA

2.11   The HRA has the following general effects:

(1) it obliges the domestic courts to use the Convention as an aid to the construction of primary and secondary legislation (whenever enacted), even in the absence of any ambiguity;

(2) where primary legislation is incompatible with the Convention, the higher courts can make a declaration of incompatibility;

(3) where it is impossible to construe subordinate legislation in a way which is compatible with the Convention, the courts can disapply or strike down subordinate legislation (provided that the legislation is not incompatible solely by reason of the parent primary legislation)[26];

(4) it makes it unlawful for public authorities, including all courts and tribunals and "any person certain of whose functions are functions of a public nature", to act or omit to act in a way which is incompatible with the Convention and confers a new cause of action on those who can show that they are victims of such an unlawful act or omission;

(5) it adds to the criteria upon which administrative discretion is scrutinised: courts are obliged to determine, not only its *Wednesbury* reasonableness or rationality, but also in appropriate cases,[26A] whether it is a response to a pressing social need and whether it satisfies the requirements of proportionality and fair balance;

(6) it permits the courts to use Convention rights to shape and develop the common law;

(7) it determines the way in which judicial powers and discretions are to be exercised.

The Convention rights protected

2.12   The HRA's preamble states that it is intended to give *"further effect"* to the Convention in domestic law. The Lord Chancellor explained that this was

---

[25] s. 21(1).

[26] It is arguable that inferior courts cannot strike down such legislation: *Pardeepan v. Secretary of State for the Home Department*, unreported, October 5, 2000, IAT. However they may disapply it as *ultra vires* subordinate legislation.

[26A] See further paras 4.26 *et seq.* and para. 10.152.

because, in domestic law, the Convention can, and is, already applied in a variety of different circumstances.[27] Further, it is clear from this use of language that the Convention is not imported wholesale into English law. It does not provide *"full effect"*. For example, Article 1 (the obligation on Convention States to secure Convention rights)[28] and Article 13 (the right to an effective remedy)[28A] are not incorporated by the HRA, although the jurisprudence of the court on Article 13 may be referred to by the courts as a result of the operation of section 2.[29]

The rights protected under the HRA are those set out in Articles 2 to 12 and 14 of the Convention, Articles 1 to 3 of Protocol 1 and Article 1 of Protocol 6 as read with Articles 16 to 18 of the Convention. These rights are subject to any designated derogation or reservation entered by the United Kingdom.[30] They include: **2.13**

    (1) the right to life (Article 2);

    (2) freedom from torture and inhuman or degrading treatment or punishment (Article 3);

    (3) freedom from slavery and forced or compulsory labour (Article 4);

    (4) the right to liberty and security of the person (Article 5);

    (5) the right to a fair trial (Article 6);

    (6) freedom from retrospective criminal offences (Article 7);

    (7) the right to respect for private life, family, home and correspondence (Article 8);

    (8) the right to freedom of thought, conscience and religion (Article 9);

    (9) the right to freedom of expression (Article 10);

    (10) the right to freedom of association and assembly (Article 11);

---

[27] See *e.g.* H.L. Deb., January 29, 1998, col. 421. Further, U.K. litigants have been able to enforce Convention rights extra-domestically, in Strasbourg, since the right of individual petition was granted in 1966. The Lord Chancellor specifically decried the use of the word "incorporation", stating:

> "As I have said before, the Bill as such does not incorporate Convention rights into domestic law, but in accordance with the language of the long title, it gives further effect in the United Kingdom to Convention rights by requiring the courts in Section 3(1) so far as it is possible to do so to construe . . . primary legislation and subordinate legislation in a way which is compatible with the Convention rights. This is an interpretative principle . . . I have to make the point absolutely plain. The European Convention on Human Rights is not made part of our law. The Human Rights Bill gives the European Convention on Human Rights a special relationship which will mean that the courts will give effect to the interpretative provisions to which I have already referred, but it does not make the Convention directly justiciable as it would be if it were expressly made part of our law. I want there to be no ambiguity about that . . . "

[28] See para. 2.15, below.
[28A] See para. 2.17, below.
[29] See para. 2.19, below.
[30] s.1(2). See further paras 2.54 *et seq.*, below.

(11) the right to marry and found a family (Article 12);

(12) freedom from discrimination (Article 14);

(13) the right to peaceful enjoyment of possessions (Article 1 of Protocol No. 1);

(14) the right to education (Article 2 of Protocol No. 1);

(15) the right to free and fair elections (Article 3 of Protocol No. 1);

(16) the abolition of the death penalty in peacetime (Articles 1 and 2 of Protocol No. 6).

During the passage of the Bill, the Government indicated that it intended to sign and ratify Protocol 7 (which requires, *inter alia*, procedural safeguards relating to the expulsion of aliens, the right not to be tried or punished twice and the right to equality between spouses) once certain property legislation had been amended to bring it into line with the right to spousal equality. A more detailed overview of the Convention rights protected is set out in Chapter 3.

Excluded Articles

Article 1

2.14 Article 1 of the Convention states:

"The High Contracting Parties shall secure to everyone within their jurisdiction the rights and freedoms defined in Section 1 of this Convention."

2.15 Article 1 obliges Contracting States to "secure" Convention rights to "everyone within their jurisdiction". Whilst it is in one sense an inter-state obligation, it also forms the basis for the doctrine of positive obligations.[31] State responsibility is engaged under Article 1 if the violation of a Convention right or freedom arises as the result of the state's failure to secure that right or freedom in its domestic law.[32] A state may satisfy Article 1 by ensuring, in whichever way it chooses, that its laws and practice secure the rights and freedoms set out in the Convention.[33] It does not confer enforceable rights on individuals to complain of a breach, although one Contracting State may complain of a breach of Article 1 by another state, pursuant to Article 33 of the Convention. However, the obligation to "secure" rights and freedoms to everyone in its jurisdiction essentially imposes a positive obligation on a Contracting State to secure Convention rights to individuals.[34] It is arguable that a parallel approach may be adopted in relation to the obligation of the courts under the Act to secure the protection of Convention rights in proceedings between private individuals.[35]

---

[31] See further paras 5.27 *et seq.*, below.
[32] *Costello-Roberts v.United Kingdom* (1995) 19 E.H.R.R. 112, para. 26.
[33] *Ireland v.United Kingdom* (1980) 2 E.H.R.R. 25, paras 238–240.
[34] Subject to a margin of appreciation when considering breach of the Article.
[35] See para. 5.38, below.

The Lord Chancellor rationalised the exclusion of Article 1 on the basis that the HRA gives effect to Article 1 by securing to people in the United Kingdom the rights and freedoms of the Convention.[36] In any event, it seems unlikely that the exclusion of Article 1 will relieve the courts from taking into account the duty to secure Convention rights when they develop the common law.[37]

2.16

Article 13

Article 13 of the Convention states:

2.17

> "Everyone whose rights and freedoms as set forth in this Convention are violated shall have an effective remedy before a national authority notwithstanding that the violation has been committed by persons acting in an official capacity."

Article 13 provides that anyone whose Convention rights are violated should have an effective remedy before a national authority. The European Court has held that Article 13 independently exists as a substantive right, the application of which does not depend on the existence of a violation of another right or freedom in the Convention.[38] However, for Article 13 to be applicable, the claim that another Convention right or freedom has been breached must be "arguable". The scope of the obligation under Article 13 varies depending on the nature of the complaint under the Convention. States are afforded a discretion as to the manner in which they conform to their obligations under Article 13. However, the remedy must be "effective" in practice as well as in law and its exercise must not be hindered by acts or omissions of the state.[39]

2.18

The Lord Chancellor stated that it was unnecessary for Article 13 to be incorporated because the HRA establishes a scheme under which Convention rights can be raised and their breach remedied.[40] He indicated that if the concern was to ensure that the Act provides an exhaustive code of remedies for those whose Convention rights have been violated, the Government believed that section 8 already achieved this end and nothing further was needed.[41] However, by section 2(1) of the HRA, courts are obliged to take account of Strasbourg jurisprudence, including that relating to Article 13. Accordingly, courts and practitioners need to be aware of and have regard to Article 13, particularly when considering issues of remedies under section 8(1) of the HRA.[42] Article 13 is considered in more detail in relation to remedies in Chapter 9.[42A]

2.19

---

[36] H.L. Deb., November 18, 1997, col. 475.
[37] *Per* Brooke L.J. in *Douglas v. Hello! Ltd* [2001] 2 W.L.R. 992, para. 91, CA and transcript at para. 91.
[38] *Boyle and Rice v. U.K.* [1988] 10 E.H.R.R. 425.
[39] See *e.g. Aksoy v.Turkey* (1997) 23 E.H.R.R. 553, para. 95.
[40] H.L. Deb., November 18, 1997, cols. 466–481 at col.475.
[41] H.L. Deb., November 18, 1997, col.475. The Lord Chancellor also raised a concern that expressly incorporating Article 13 might lead to the courts fashioning completely new remedies, though this was not the primary justification given for its exclusion: H.L. Deb., November 18, 1997, col. 477.
[42] H.L. Deb., November 18, 1997, col. 476.
[42A] See para. 9.06.

Protocol No. 12

2.20 On November 4, 2000, a new Protocol to the Convention, conferring a free-standing prohibition on discrimination, was opened for signature and ratification. Article 1 of Protocol 12 gives effect under the Convention to the fundamental right in Article 26 of the International Covenant on Civil and Political Rights to the equal protection of the law without discrimination.[43] The United Kingdom Government has indicated that it has no present intention to sign it.

New Legislation

Statements of compatibility

2.21 Any new legislation after November 24, 1998,[44] must comply with the procedure laid down in section 19 of the HRA which provides:

> "(1) A Minister of the Crown in charge of a Bill in either House of Parliament must, before Second Reading of the Bill—
>
> > (a) make a statement to the effect that in his view the provisions of the Bill are compatible with the Convention rights ("a statement of compatibility"); or
> > (b) make a statement to the effect that although he is unable to make a statement of compatibility, the government nevertheless wishes the House to proceed with the Bill.
>
> (2) The statement must be in writing and be published in such manner as the Minister making it considers appropriate."

2.22 The statement is to be included alongside the explanatory and financial memorandum that accompanies a Bill when it is introduced into each House of Parliament.[45] The intention behind the obligation to make this statement is to ensure that all Ministers and their departments and officials fully appreciate their human rights obligations. To date, the Government has strongly resisted calls for stating their reasoning in the section 19 compatibility statements.

Incompatible legislation

2.23 It clearly remains open to Parliament to pass legislation that is incompatible with the Convention in the future.[46] However, if this occurs intentionally, the Minister in charge of the Bill will be expected to explain the reasons for doing so to Parliament during the course of its passage.

---

[43] See further para. 7.15, below.
[44] The Human Rights Act 1998 (Commencement) Order 1998, S.I.1998 No. 2882 (C.71).
[45] White Paper, para. 3.2. Since the ministerial statement of compatibility applies only to a Government Bill before second reading, it is possible that new clauses may be subsequently introduced which are not compatible with human rights. This situation occurred in *R. v. Pora*, December 20, 2000, New Zealand Court of Appeal. The New Zealand Parliament had inadvertently, through a late amendment proposed by a back-bench M.P., enacted legislation which amounted to a retrospective penalty contrary to both an earlier Criminal Justice Act and the New Zealand Bill of Rights Act 1990, s.23. See further, A.Bradley, "Conflicting Statutory Provisions—The Impact of Fundamental Rights", [2001] N.L.J. 311.
[46] *ibid.*

The reservation of the power to introduce or pass incompatible legislation is echoed in section 6(2) of the HRA where the Houses of Parliament and "a person exercising functions in connection with proceedings in Parliament" are expressly omitted from the definition of a "public authority".[47] Further, the failure to introduce in or lay before Parliament a proposal for legislation or to make any primary legislation or remedial orders is not an "act" within the meaning of the section.[48] Whilst the introduction or making of incompatible subordinate legislation by Ministers (or other public officials with power to promulgate subordinate legislation), which is not required to be incompatible by reason of primary legislation, is an unlawful "act" under section 6(1), it is unclear whether the failure to pass secondary legislation is an "act" for the purposes of the Act. The effect of these provisions is to grant immunity from legal action to Parliament from passing, and any Minister from introducing, primary legislation or failing to pass or introduce primary (and possibly subordinate) legislation in breach of Convention rights.[49] However, there will no doubt be significant political pressure on a government that seeks to justify legislation that infringes fundamental rights.

2.24

The Duty on Public Bodies

Section 6 HRA duty

A key effect of the HRA is to make it unlawful for a public authority to act in a way which is incompatible with a Convention right, pursuant to section 6(1) of the HRA. A "public authority" is defined as including "a court or tribunal" and "any person certain of whose functions are functions of a public nature".[50] It does not include either House of Parliament or any person exercising functions in connection with proceedings in Parliament.[51] Accordingly, central and local government departments and other "obvious" public authorities must comply with the Convention in relation to all their acts or omissions both public and private. In addition, any hybrid body that exercises public functions must comply with the Convention, save in relation to a purely private act.[52] The use of a function-based definition means that the scope of the section 6 duty is potentially very broad. Some examples of hybrid bodies referred to by the Government during debates include the privatised utilities such as Railtrack, the Press Complaints Commission, the Churches, the BBC, the Advertising Standards Authority and the Jockey Club. However, ultimately, it is for the courts to interpret the definitions of "public authority" and "public function".[53] An "act" also includes a failure to act, but does not include a failure to:

2.25

---

[47] s.6(3).
[48] s.6(6).
[49] See further para. 8.25 *et seq.* and in relation to subordinate legislation para. 5.10 *et seq.*
[50] s.6(3).
[51] *ibid.*
[52] s.6(3), (5).
[53] See further paras 8.15 *et seq.*, below, and H.L. Deb., November 24, 1997, cols 809–816 at 810.

(1) introduce in, or lay before, Parliament a proposal for legislation; or

(2) make any primary legislation or remedial order.[54]

Proceedings for Breach of the Duty

Section 7(1) HRA

2.26 Section 7(1) of the HRA provides that a person who claims that a public authority has acted, or proposes to act, in a way which is rendered unlawful by section 6(1) may either:

(1) bring proceedings against the public authority under the HRA in the appropriate court or tribunal[55]; or

(2) rely on the Convention right or rights concerned in any legal proceedings, but only if he is (or would be) a victim of the unlawful act.[56]

2.27 The effect of section 7(1)(a) is to create a new statutory cause of action for breach of a Convention right. Proceedings for breach of a Convention right at first instance may only be brought in the "appropriate court or tribunal" determined by the rules: section 7(2). The Civil Procedure Rules[57] permit such proceedings to be brought by way of:

(1) judicial review under existing procedures;

(2) in the county court or in the High Court where a claim for damages is made, by proceedings under Part 7 CPR by way of a claim or counterclaim (unless this is associated with a claim for judicial review). The normal jurisdictional limits apply. County courts are not empowered to make declarations of incompatibility under section 4;

(3) in the county court or in the High Court following a finding of unlawfulness under section 7(1)(b) in some other court or tribunal which did not have the power to award damages or compensation, for example a magistrates' court or Crown Court. In this situation, the party seeking a civil remedy may rely upon the finding of unlawfulness in the other court as prima facie evidence that the defendant acted unlawfully.[58] It is open to the defendant to refute the finding on factual or legal grounds pursuant to Civil Procedure Act 1997, Schedule 1, paragraph 4.

Nothing in the HRA creates a criminal offence.[59]

---

[54] s.6(6).

[55] s.7(1)(a). Proceedings in this section include a counterclaim or similar proceeding (s.7(2)). See further paras 8.04 *et seq.*

[56] s.7(1)(b). See further paras 8.40 *et seq.*

[57] CPR 7.11 (inserted by the Civil Procedure (Amendment No.4) Rules 2000, S.I. 2000 No. 2092 (L.16)).

[58] The previous finding of unlawfulness is treated in the same way as a conviction is treated in civil proceedings under the Civil Evidence Act 1968, s.11.

[59] s.7(7).

Proceedings in respect of judicial acts

Section 9(1) provides that proceedings brought against a court or tribunal **2.28** under section 7(1)(a) in respect of a judicial act may be brought only (a) by exercising a right of appeal; (b) on an application for judicial review[60]; or (c) in such other forum as may be prescribed by rules.[61] Where a judicial act is done in good faith, damages may not be awarded otherwise than to compensate a person to the extent required by Article 5(5) of the Convention.[62] The Crown Court cannot award damages where it has found a breach of Article 5(5) and the question of damages must be referred to the High Court. The Lord Chancellor must be joined to section 9 cases. An applicant must state in the notice of appeal or application for judicial review if he is seeking damages under Article 5(5) in respect of a judicial act. The Lord Chancellor must be notified (except where the appeal is to the Crown Court in which case the Lord Chancellor will only be notified if and when a breach is found).[63] The duty to notify is placed on the courts. However, there will usually be a transfer to the Administrative Court.[64]

Limitation

Proceedings under section 7(1)(a) are subject to a limitation period of one **2.29** year beginning with the date on which the act complained of took place[65] or such longer period as the court or tribunal considers equitable having regard to all the circumstances.[66] However, this is subject to any rule imposing a stricter time limit in relation to the procedure in question,[67] for example the three-month time limit for judicial review proceedings. The discretion to extend time is intended to be used flexibly where there is a good reason for delay.[68] There is no time limit imposed where an individual relies upon breach of a Convention right in any legal proceedings under section 7(1)(b) of the HRA. "Legal proceedings" in this subsection includes but is not limited to:

(1) proceedings brought by or at the instigation of a public authority[69]; and

(b) an appeal against the decision of a court or tribunal.[70]

Section 22(4) provides that: **2.30**

"Paragraph (b) of subsection (1) of section 7 applies to proceedings brought by or at the instigation of a public authority whenever the act

---

[60] Subject to any rule of law which prevents a court from being the subject of judicial review.
[61] No other forum has yet been prescribed.
[62] Article 5(5) of the Convention provides that "Everyone who has been the victim of arrest or detention in contravention of the provisions of this Article shall have an enforceable right to compensation." See further paras 2.36–2.37 and 9.44 *et seq.*, below.
[63] CPR Part 19 PD, para. 6.6.
[64] CPR Part 30 PD, para.7.
[65] s.7(5)(a). See further paras 8.36 *et seq.*
[66] s.7(5)(b).
[67] s.7(5).
[68] H.L. Deb., October 29, 1998, col. 2095.
[69] s.7(6)(a).
[70] s.7(6)(b).

in question took place; but *otherwise that subsection does not apply to an act taking place before the coming into force of that section."* (emphasis added)

2.31 This section is important because it provides that section 7(1)(b) applies to proceedings brought by or at the instigation of a public authority "whenever the act in question took place". Accordingly, acts of a public authority prior to the HRA coming into force, which are unlawful within the meaning of section 6(1) of the HRA, may be relied upon by an individual after the Act has come into force, in defending first instance proceedings against him by or at the instigation of the public authority or in the course of a subsequent appeal.[71] However, acts which took place before October 2, 2000 cannot be relied upon to found a cause of action under s.7(1)(a) in either self-standing or existing proceedings by reason of the words underlined above.[72]

Challenges to incompatible legislation

2.32 The HRA confers no power to challenge either Parliament or a Minister of the Crown or any other person exercising functions in connection with proceedings in Parliament for either introducing a proposal for primary legislation or making primary legislation in a way that is incompatible with Convention rights.[73] The same applies to a failure to introduce a proposal for primary legislation or to make any primary legislation or a remedial order where to fail to do so is unlawful within the meaning of section 6 of the HRA.[74] A Minister or other public official (but not Parliament) introducing or making subordinate legislation after October 2, 2000, which is incompatible with Convention rights but is not required to be incompatible by reason of primary legislation, does act unlawfully within the meaning of section 6(1). It is unclear whether a Minister or public official's failure to introduce subordinate legislation after October 2, 2000, where this is incompatible with the Convention, is unlawful pursuant to section 6(1). Section 6(6)(a) is ambiguous in that it confers immunity for "a failure to . . . introduce in, or lay before, Parliament, a proposal for *legislation*". The term "legislation" is broad enough to include a failure to introduce in, or lay before, Parliament subordinate legislation. However, not all subordinate legislation is required to be laid before Parliament and if such a construction were upheld, the making of subordinate legislation which is required to be laid before Parliament would not be unlawful, whereas the making of subordinate legislation which is not required, would be unlawful.[75]

---

[71] s.7(6).
[72] See also *R. v. Secretary of State for the Home Department, ex p. Mahmood (Amjad)*, [2001] 1 W.L.R. 840, CA (administrative decision made before October 2, 2000 but which came into effect after that date could not be challenged under the HRA). See also *Biggin Hill Airport Ltd v. Bromley London Borough Council, The Times*, January 9, 2001, Nicholas Strauss Q.C. See also Court of Appeal decision, unreported, July 11, 2001. See further paras 8.36 *et seq.*, below.
[73] s.6(3), (6).
[74] Above.
[75] See further paras 8.26 *et seq.* and particularly para. 8.31.

Standing

To have standing to bring proceedings for breach of a Convention right **2.33**
under section 7(1)(a) of the HRA, an applicant must be a "victim" of the
unlawful act (section 7(7)). The test is the same as that under Article 34 of
the Convention. An individual only has standing if he is *actually and
directly affected* by the act or omission which is the subject of complaint,
although he may also be a victim if he could *potentially* be affected by the
act or omission.[76] Both natural and legal persons may sue, although there
are some limitations in relation to legal persons, for example a company
has not yet been regarded by the European Court as having a right to
respect for private life under Article 8.

Claims by action or interest groups are excluded, although they may apply **2.34**
to, or be invited to, intervene in a type of *amicus curiae* role and some
representative actions are permitted.[77] Further, there is nothing preventing
interest groups assisting individuals who might bring proceedings or making their views known to the Crown.[78] The Crown can intervene if there is
a possibility of a declaration of incompatibility.[79] The Crown is entitled to
notice of the possibility of a declaration of incompatibility so that it can
decide whether it wishes to intervene.[80] The issue of standing is considered further in Chapter 8.[80A]

Remedies

Section 8(1) of the HRA provides that a court which finds that any act (or **2.35**
proposed act) of a public authority is (or would be) unlawful under section
6(1) of the HRA may grant such relief or remedy, or make such order,
within its powers, as it considers just and appropriate. This obviously
includes granting a declaration that there has been a violation of a Convention right and the grant of an injunction to prevent an act that would
infringe Convention rights. Damages may only be awarded by a court or
tribunal which has power to award damages[81] or to order the payment of
compensation in civil proceedings.[82] The court cannot make any award of
damages unless, taking account of all the circumstances of the case,
including:

---

[76] See, *e.g. Dudgeon v. United Kingdom* (1982) 4 E.H.R.R. 149.
[77] See further Keir Starmer, *European Human Rights Law* (Legal Action Group, 1999), para.
2.31. Unincorporated bodies such as professional associations, non-governmental organisations or trade unions can act on behalf of their members if they can identify those members
directly affected by the measure in question and have authority to represent them: *Confederation des Syndicats Medicauz Francais v. France* (1986) 47 D.R. 225; *Zentralrat
Deutscher Sinti und Roma and Rose v. Germany* (1997) 23 E.H.R.R. C.D. 209. An unincorporated association may also be a "victim" within the meaning of Article 41: *Christians
Against Racism and Fascism v. United Kingdom* (1980) 21 D.R. 138. Claims may also be
brought in a representative capacity where the victim lacks legal capacity: *X v. Sweden*
(1979) 16 D.R. 105; *SD, DP & T v. United Kingdom* (1996) 22 E.H.R.R. CD 148.
[78] H.L. Deb., October 29, 1998, col. 2094.
[79] s.5(2).
[80] s.5(1). Notice may be given at any time during the proceedings: s.5(3). See also CPR
19.4A(1) and CPR Part 19 PD, para. 6.1.
[80A] See paras 8.35 *et seq.*
[81] s.8(6).
[82] s.8(2).

(1) any other relief or remedy granted, or order made, in relation to the act by that or any other court; and

(2) the consequences of any decision of that or any other court in respect of that act,

the court is satisfied that the award "is necessary to afford just satisfaction to the person in whose favour it is made". The test for making an award of damages is identical to that applied by the European Court of Human Rights in relation to an award of compensation under Article 41 of the Convention, and a domestic court is obliged to take into account the principles applied by the European Court of Human Rights in exercising its power to award damages.[83] Remedies are considered in further detail in Chapter 9.

Preservation of judicial immunity

2.36 Section 9 of the HRA provides an enforceable right to compensation for breaches of Article 5 (the right to liberty and security) by judicial acts.[83A] This is a requirement imposed by Article 5(5), namely that everyone who has been the victim of arrest or detention in contravention of the provisions of Article 5 shall have an enforceable right to compensation. When a complaint is made that Article 5 has been breached as a result of a judicial act or omission, it is necessary first to establish whether the judicial act complained of was unlawful, then to rule on whether the aggrieved person is entitled to compensation under Article 5(5) and then to determine the amount of compensation. In determining those questions, the court must take into account the Strasbourg jurisprudence on unlawful detention and on the award of damages, as required by sections 2 and 8 of the Act. There is an interface with domestic law remedies, for example, in relation to the tort of false imprisonment.[84] Section 9(1) requires that proceedings under section 7(1)(a) in respect of a judicial act may be brought either:

(1) by exercising a right of appeal;

(2) on an application for judicial review; or

(3) in such other forum as may be prescribed by the rules.

Any award of damages is made against the Crown.[85]

2.37 Section 9(2) preserves judicial immunity[86] generally for judicial acts undertaken by judges, magistrates, tribunal members and court staff performing judicial functions acting on behalf of the judge or on the instructions of the judge.[87] Where a judicial act is done in good faith, damages may not be

---

[83] s.8(4).
[83A] A "judicial act" means a judicial act of a court and includes an act done on the instructions, or on behalf, of a judge: s.9(5). A "judge" includes a member of a tribunal, a justice of the peace and a clerk or other officer entitled to exercise the jurisdiction of the court: s.9.5.
[84] See further paras 9.46 and 9.61 *et seq.*, below.
[85] s.9(4).
[86] See, *e.g. Sirros v. Moore* [1975] 1 Q.B. 118; [1974] 3 W.L.R. 459.
[87] See s.9(5) definition of "judge" and "judicial act" set out above.

awarded otherwise than to compensate a person to the extent required by Article 5(5) of the Convention.[88] Where a judicial act is done in bad faith, section 9(3) does not apply.

Contribution

Under section 8(5)(b) of the HRA, a public authority against which dam- **2.38**
ages are awarded is to be treated, for the purpose of the Civil Liability (Contribution) Act 1978, as liable in respect of the same damage suffered by the person to whom the award is made. Accordingly, a claim can be brought by or against a public authority as tortfeasor in Part 20 or contribution proceedings under the 1978 Act.

Interpretative Obligation

Construction of legislation

Section 3 of the HRA provides: **2.39**

> "(1) So far as it is possible to do so, primary legislation and subordinate legislation must be read and given effect in a way which is compatible with the Convention rights.
> (2) This section—
>
> (a) applies to primary legislation and subordinate legislation whenever enacted;
> (b) does not affect the validity, continuing operation or enforcement of any incompatible primary legislation; and
> (c) does not affect the validity, continuing operation or enforcement of any incompatible subordinate legislation if (disregarding any possibility of revocation) primary legislation prevents removal of the incompatibility."

By section 3 of the HRA, primary[89] and subordinate[90] legislation must be **2.40**
read and given effect to in a way which is compatible with Convention rights "so far as it is possible to do so".[91] This is a principle of interpretation which goes considerably further than the pre-existing use of the Convention to resolve ambiguities in legislation. The courts are required to interpret legislation so as to uphold Convention rights unless the legislation is so clearly incompatible with the Convention that it is impossible to do so.[92]

[88] s.9(3). See further paras 9.44 *et seq.*
[89] See s.21 for definition of "primary legislation" which includes, *inter alia*, any public general Act, local and personal Act, private Act, Order in Council made in exercise of Her Majesty's Royal Prerogative and any order or other instrument made under primary legislation to the extent that it operates to bring one or more provisions of that legislation into force or amends any primary legislation.
[90] See s.21 for definition of "subordinate legislation" which includes, *inter alia*, any Order in Council (other than one made in exercise of the Royal Prerogative), Act of the Scottish Parliament, Act of the Parliament or Assembly of Northern Ireland, orders, rules, regulations, scheme, warrant, byelaw or other instrument made under primary legislation (except to the extent to which it operates to bring one or more provisions of that legislation into force or amends any primary legislation).
[91] s.3(1). See further paras 5.02 *et seq.* for a detailed analysis of the interpretative obligation under s.3 of the HRA.
[92] White Paper, Cm. 3782, (1997), para. 2.7.

The interpretative obligation applies whenever the legislation was enacted.[93] It also applies to any relevant issues of construction of the HRA itself. Whilst the obligation in section 3 principally falls on the courts, it is a general mandatory principle of interpretation that is not limited to the courts and appears to apply to all concerned with interpreting legislation, including the Executive and administrators.

No power to disapply or strike down primary legislation

2.41 Where a court finds it impossible to read primary legislation or subordinate legislation, (where its parent primary legislation prevents removal of the incompatibility[94]) in such a way as to make it compatible, the courts cannot strike down or declare such legislation invalid.[95] This rule is intended to preserve Parliamentary sovereignty.

Legislation of devolved legislatures

2.42 As stated earlier,[96] legislative measures of the Westminster Parliament are treated differently from those of the Scottish Parliament, the Welsh Assembly and the Northern Ireland Assembly, which each lack the power to legislate in a way which is incompatible with the Convention. Equally, the Scottish, Welsh and Northern Ireland Executives have no power to make subordinate legislation or to take executive action which is incompatible with the Convention. Accordingly, in these jurisdictions, it is possible for the courts to hold that such legislation or executive action is unlawful, in effect, striking it down.

2.43 Challenges to legislation or executive action in Scotland, Wales and Northern Ireland may be made either:

> (1) under their individual devolution provisions, from which a preliminary reference procedure or appeal lies to the Judicial Committee of the Privy Council[97];

> (2) under the HRA 1998, where the court of last resort is the House of Lords.[98]

Declarations of incompatibility

2.44 Under the HRA, although primary legislation which is incompatible with the Convention (and secondary legislation which is incompatible solely because of primary legislation) cannot be struck down, an appropriate court which finds an incompatibility may make a declaration that the legislation is incompatible with a Convention right.[99] Section 4 provides that:

---

[93] s.3(2).
[94] s.3(2)(c).
[95] s.3(2)(b). See also para. 5.06.
[96] See paras 2.07 et seq., above.
[97] See para. 2.08, above.
[98] For procedural matters, see also the Court of Appeal Practice Direction: Devolution Issues (and Crown Office Applications in Wales) issued on June 30, 1999.
[99] s.4. See further paras 9.07 et seq.

"(1) Subsection (2) applies in any proceedings in which a court determines whether a provision of primary legislation is compatible with a Convention right.

(2) If the court is satisfied that the provision is incompatible with a Convention right, it may make a declaration of that incompatibility.

(3) Subsection (4) applies in any proceedings in which a court determines whether a provision of subordinate legislation, made in the exercise of a power conferred by primary legislation, is compatible with a Convention right.

(4) If the court is satisfied—

> (a) that the provision is incompatible with a Convention right, and
> (b) that (disregarding any possibility of revocation) the primary legislation concerned prevents removal of the incompatibility, it may make a declaration of that incompatibility."

Power to make declaration of incompatibility

2.45 Only the House of Lords, Judicial Committee of the Privy Council, Court of Appeal, High Court Courts-Martial Appeal Court and the High Court of Justiciary[1] and Court of Session in Scotland have the power to make declarations of incompatibility.[2] County courts, coroners' courts and tribunals have no procedure to declare legislation incompatible with the Convention. Notice must be given to the Crown prior to the making of a declaration of incompatibility.[3]

Fast track remedial procedure

2.46 A Minister of the Crown may take remedial action to amend the legislation and remove the incompatibility, using a fast track procedure created by section 10 and Schedule 2 to the HRA. Whilst a remedial order includes a power to amend or repeal primary legislation other than that which contains the incompatible provision, it was Parliament's intention that the power to make incidental, supplementary and consequential changes to primary legislation should be limited to those deemed necessary to correct the incompatibility.[4] A remedial order may have retrospective effect.[5]

2.47 Whilst there is no sanction in domestic law for failing to introduce remedial legislation, there will be political pressure on a government to do so.[6] Further, as Lord Cooke pointed out during the course of debates on the Bill, where expeditious remedial steps do not follow this will amount to a plain invitation to take the matter to Strasbourg.[7]

2.48 What is not yet clear under the HRA, but will present a practical problem, is what course of action a court or tribunal should take in relation to proceedings where it has made a declaration of incompatibility but it

---

[1] Other than when sitting as a trial court.
[2] s.4(5). See para. 9.08, below.
[3] CPR 19.4A(1) and CPR Part 19 PD, para. 6.1. See further paras 8.35 and 8.58, below.
[4] H.L. Deb., January 29, 1998, col. 402.
[5] Sched. 2, para. 1(1)(b).
[6] The Government envisaged that a declaration of incompatibility would "almost certainly" prompt legislative change: White Paper, para.2.9; see also H.L. Deb., November 3, 1997, col.1230 (Lord Chancellor).
[7] H.L. Deb., November 3, 1997, col. 1272.

cannot be certain whether the legislation will be amended or if it is, whether it will have retrospective effect. Some commentators take the view that a court is *functus* (has no further jurisdiction) following a declaration. Others assume that it is possible for the court to adjourn proceedings for a remedial order to be made. It is submitted that the courts probably can, and should, adjourn proceedings for a sufficient period of time in order to see whether retrospective legislation has been or is intended to be introduced before making final orders determining the rights of the parties and determining where the costs burden shall fall.[8]

Reference to Case Law

Strasbourg jurisprudence

2.49   Section 2(1) of the HRA provides that a court or tribunal determining a question which has arisen in connection with a Convention right must *take into account* any:

(1) judgment, decision, declaration or advisory opinion of the European Court of Human Rights;

(2) opinion of the Commission given in a report adopted under Article 31 of the Convention[9] (opinion on the merits);

(3) decision of the Commission in connection with Article 26[10] (exhaustion of domestic remedies) or 27(2)[11] (admissibility) of the Convention; or

---

[8] See further paras 9.12 *et seq.*, below.
[9] The references in paragraphs (a) and (b) of s.2(1) to Articles are to Articles of the Convention as they had effect immediately before the coming into force of the Eleventh Protocol (HRA, s.21(2)). The Convention has been amended by the coming into force of Protocol 11 on November 1, 1998 resulting in the re-numbering of its Articles. Art. 31, prior to amendment and as referred to in the HRA 1998, provided as follows:

"(1) If the examination of a petition has not been completed in accordance with Article 28(2), 29 or 30, the Commission shall draw up a Report on the facts and state its opinion as to whether the facts found disclose a breach of the State concerned of its obligations under the Convention. The individual opinions of members of the Commission on this point may be stated in the Report.
(2) The Report shall be transmitted to the Committee of Ministers. It shall also be transmitted to the States concerned, who shall not be at liberty to publish it.
(3) In transmitting the Report to the Committee of Ministers the Commission may make such proposals as it thinks fit."

[10] Art. 26, prior to amendment by Protocol 11 and as referred to in the HRA 1998, provided as follows:

"The Commission may only deal with the matter after all domestic remedies have been exhausted, according to the generally recognised rules of international law, and within a period of six months from the date on which the final decision was taken."

The present provision, following amendment by Protocol 11, is now set out at Art. 35(1).
[11] Art. 27(2), prior to amendment by Protocol 11 and as referred to in the HRA 1998, provided as follows:

"The Commission shall consider inadmissible any petition submitted under Article 25 which it considers incompatible with the provisions of the present Convention, manifestly ill-founded, or an abuse of the right of petition."

The present provision concerning the court's power to declare an application inadmissible is at Art. 35(3).

(4) decision of the Committee of Ministers taken under Article 46 of the Convention[12];

whenever made or given, so far as, in the opinion of the court or tribunal, it is relevant to the proceedings in which the question has arisen.[13] Accordingly, every court or tribunal concerned with an issue that is connected with a Convention right is obliged to take into account the Strasbourg jurisprudence so far as it is relevant. This jurisprudence is not, however, binding on the court or tribunal in question, and the obligation is less than an obligation to "adopt" or "apply" the relevant decisions.[14] Further, where it is taken into account, the protection conferred by the Strasbourg authorities represents a minimum, not maximum, standard and domestic courts are free to provide additional protection to an individual's fundamental rights if appropriate. It should be noted that if a relevant decision or group of decisions of the European Court of Human Rights has been examined by the House of Lords or the Court of Appeal, the lower courts are bound by the reasoning of the superior courts and are not permitted to re-examine the decisions in order to ascertain whether the conclusion of the superior courts might be inconsistent with those decisions, or susceptible to a continuing gloss: *R. v. Central Criminal Court, ex p. Bright*.[15] Evidence of any judgment, decision, declaration or opinion is to be given in proceedings before any court as set out in CPR Part 39 PD paragraph 8.1 or, in relation to tribunals, rules made for the purposes of section 2.[16] Citations of reports from other than the prescribed sources may only be used with the permission of the court.[16A] Any party wishing to cite Strasbourg jurisprudence is required to give the court and any other party a list of authorities and copies of the reports from which they are to be cited not less than three days before the hearing.[17]

---

[12] Art. 46, prior to amendment by Protocol 11, related to recognition by Contracting States of the jurisdiction of the Court. It is likely that the Article which was intended to be referred to was Art. 32 which, prior to amendment, provided as follows:

"(1) If the question is not referred to the Court in accordance with Article 48 of this Convention within a period of three months from the date of the transmission of the Report to the Committee of Ministers, the Committee of Ministers shall decide by a majority of two-thirds of the members entitled to sit on the Committee whether there has been a violation of the Convention.
(2) In the affirmative case the Committee of Ministers shall prescribe a period during which the High Contracting Party concerned must take the measures required by the decision of the Committee of Ministers.
(3) If the High Contracting Party has not taken satisfactory measures within the prescribed period, the Committee of Ministers shall decide by the majority provided for in paragraph (1) above, what effect shall be given to its original decision and shall publish the Report.
(4) The High Contracting Parties undertake to regard as binding on them any decision which the Committee of Ministers may take in application of the preceding paragraphs."

[13] s.2(1).
[14] *R. v. Rowe,Davis and Johnson, The Times*, July 25, 2000. See also *R. v. Secretary of State for the Home Department, ex p. Anderson and Taylor, The Times*, February 27, 2001, QBD; [2001] E.W.H.C. Admin. 181 at paras. 36, 52.
[15] [2001] 1 W.L.R. 662, QBD.
[16] s.2(3). See, *e.g.* the Practice Direction issued by the President of the VAT and Duties Tribunals and the Presiding Special Commissioner, October 31, 2000.
[16A] See paras 8.59 *et seq.*
[17] CPR 39 PD, para. 8.1(2). See para. 8.60.

2.50 It should be noted that the interpretation of human rights law relies on the concept of the Convention being a "living instrument which . . . must be interpreted in light of present day conditions".[18] Accordingly, the doctrine of precedent in human rights law is of considerably less importance than in domestic law and older cases must be treated with some caution. This is dealt with in more detail in Chapter 4 below.[19]

Other jurisprudence

2.51 The HRA does not specify the status of other human rights jurisprudence, such as that of common law jurisdictions like New Zealand, Canada and the USA, and other European signatories to the Convention. However, it is likely that courts or tribunals will also take such case law into account for the following reasons:

(1) section 2 of the HRA refers to determination of "a question which has arisen in connection with a Convention right". Convention rights are fundamental rights that are themselves informed by international human rights standards, and the Strasbourg Court has on occasion adverted to them;

(2) domestic courts are not limited to having regard only to Strasbourg jurisprudence. The jurisprudence of other contracting European states that have already incorporated the Convention will be relevant to interpretation of the Convention, particularly where no Strasbourg decision yet exists. Further, the jurisprudence of other common law jurisdictions like New Zealand, Canada, Ireland, USA, South Africa, Hong Kong and India is also likely to be a fruitful guide to interpretation of Convention rights in the context of common law legal systems which have given helpful answers to analogous questions.[20]

(3) since the HRA is based on the New Zealand Bill of Rights Act 1990, New Zealand case law in particular is likely to be a very useful resource in interpreting the provisions of the 1998 Act itself.[20A]

Special Provisions for Freedom of Expression and Freedom of Thought

2.52   **Freedom of expression.**   Section 12 of the HRA makes special provision for cases where the court is asked to consider granting any relief which, if granted, might affect the exercise of the Convention right to freedom of expression. It provides that no relief should be granted against

---

[18] *Tyrer v. United Kingdom* (1980) 2 E.H.R.R. 1, paras 31 and 38; *Marckx v. Belgium* (1980) 2 E.H.R.R. 330, para. 41.
[19] At paras 4.17 *et seq.*, below.
[20] See, *e.g.* the comments of the Lord Chief Justice, Lord Bingham at H.L. Deb., November 3, 1997, col. 1247, and the consideration of the human rights case law of New Zealand, Canada, the USA and South Africa by the Privy Council in *Stott (Procurator Fiscal, Dunfermline) v. Brown*, [2001] 2 W.L.R. 817.
[20A] For an overview of the principal case-law of other common law jurisdictions, see paras 7.44 *et seq.*

a respondent who is not present nor represented unless the court is satisfied that the applicant has taken all practicable steps to notify the respondent[21] or that there are compelling reasons why the respondent should not be notified.[22] Further, no interim relief is to be granted so as to restrain publication before trial unless the court is satisfied that the applicant is likely to establish that publication should not be allowed.[23] Section 12(4) obliges a court or tribunal to have particular regard to the importance of the Convention right to freedom of expression and, where the proceedings relate to material which the respondent claims, or which appears to the court, to be journalistic, literary or artistic material, to the extent to which the material has (or is about to) become available to the public or it is in the public interest for the material to be published[24] and to any relevant privacy code.[25] The section was a response to concerns by the press that the right to private life under Article 8 of the Convention might override the counter-balancing right to freedom of expression under Article 10.

Freedom of thought. Section 13 obliges a court or tribunal to have   **2.53**
particular regard to the importance of the Convention right to freedom of thought, conscience and religion where it is determining any question arising under the HRA which might affect the exercise by a religious organisation of that right. The section was included as a response to the concerns of the Churches and other religious organisations that sought a firm guarantee of their continued doctrinal independence.

Derogations and Reservations

Derogations

Provision is made by Article 15 for derogations from the Convention: **2.54**

> "(1) In time of war or other public emergency threatening the life of the nation any High Contracting Party may take measures derogating from its obligations under this Convention to the extent strictly required by the exigencies of the situation, provided that such measures are not inconsistent with its obligations under international law. (2) No derogation from article 2, except in respect of deaths resulting from lawful acts of war, or from articles 3, 4(paragraph 1) and 7 shall be made under this provision."[26]

The United Kingdom has one derogation in place at present in relation to   **2.55**
Article 5(3) of the Convention concerning pre-trial detention under prevention of terrorism legislation. The terms of the derogation are contained in Schedule 3, Part I of the HRA. Section 1(2) of the Act provides that any

---

[21] s.12(2)(a).
[22] s.12(2)(b).
[23] s.12(3).
[24] s.12(4)(a).
[25] s.12(4)(b).
[26] Nothing in the Convention shall be construed as limiting or derogating from any of the rights or freedoms which may be ensured under the United Kingdom's domestic laws or international obligations: Art. 53.

derogation will have effect in domestic law because Convention rights are subject to designated derogations. If a designated derogation is amended or replaced, it ceases to be a designated derogation.[27] Future derogations become designated derogations by means of an order laid before Parliament by the Secretary of State.[28] If an order is not approved by resolution passed by each House within 40 days, it ceases to have effect.[29] Designated derogations cease to have effect after five years, unless renewed.[30]

Reservations

2.56 Article 57 of the Convention permits a state to enter a reservation when it ratifies the Convention or when depositing its instrument of ratification, to the extent that any law then in force in its territory is not in conformity with a Convention right or freedom. Reservations of a general character are not permitted. The United Kingdom has made a reservation in respect of Article 2 of Protocol 1 to the Convention (the right to education) to the effect that that principle is affirmed only in so far as it is compatible with the provision of efficient instruction and training, and the avoidance of unreasonable public expenditure. Under the HRA, this reservation and any future reservations designated by order made by the Secretary of State have effect in domestic law[31] but they are not subject to the requirement of periodic renewal.

Safeguard for Existing Human Rights

Section 11 HRA

2.57 Section 11 of the HRA makes clear that a person's reliance on a Convention right does not restrict:

(1) any other right or freedom conferred on him or under any law having effect in any part of the United Kingdom; or

(2) his right to make any claim or bring any proceedings which he could make or bring apart from sections 7 to 9 of the HRA.

2.58 In essence, this means that a claimant may be able to rely on related or overlapping rights under domestic law, under the Convention and under E.C. law in the same set of proceedings or simultaneously mount several claims in different sets of proceedings. The HRA is intended to improve upon and supplement existing rights. Further, in the words of Jack Straw, quoted above at paragraph 2.05, Convention rights imported by the HRA form a "floor" below which protection will not be allowed to fall, and are not intended to be a "ceiling". Accordingly, Parliament and the courts will be free to impose a higher level of protection for fundamental rights where appropriate.

---

[27] s.14(3).
[28] s.14(1)(b).
[29] s.14(4)(a); s.16(3), (4).
[30] s.16(1), (2).
[31] s.1(2).

Further, there is nothing to prevent an individual taking a case to Stras- **2.59**
bourg, provided that all relevant domestic remedies are exhausted in
accordance with Article 35 of the Convention, including those remedies
created by the HRA.[32]

Rules of Court Relating to Human Rights

Civil Procedure Rules. The HRA promised rules of court relating to **2.60**
the citation of authority of Strasbourg jurisprudence under section 2,
notice and joining of the Crown to proceedings where the court is considering making a declaration of incompatibility under section 5 and the
identification of appropriate courts and tribunals where free-standing proceedings may be brought under sections 7 and 9. The additional Civil
Procedure Rules and additions to Practice Directions relating to HRA
claims came into effect on October 2, 2000. The provisions are as follows:

(1) citation of human rights material: Part 39 (Hearings) Practice
Direction, para. 8.1.

(2) declarations of incompatibility and joining a Minister: CPR 19.4A
(Parties and Group Litigation); CPR Part 19 PD, para. 6; CPR
30.3(2)(g) (transfers); CPR Part 30 PD, para. 7; CPR Part 54 PD
para. 8.2.

(3) claims against a public authority under section 7: CPR 7.11;
CPR Part 16 (Statements of Case) PD, para.16.1; CPR 33.9
(Evidence); CPR Part 40 (Judgments and Orders) PD, para.
14.4; CPR Part 52 (Appeals) PD, paras 5.1A and 5.1B;

(4) claims against courts or tribunals: CPR 7.11; CPR Part 16 PD,
para.16.1.[33]

Human Rights Commission

Joint Parliamentary Committee. On December 14, 1998, the **2.61**
Leader of the House of Commons announced that a Joint Parliamentary
Committee on Human Rights would be appointed to conduct inquiries on
a range of human rights issues in relation to the Convention, to examine
draft legislation where there is a doubt about its compatibility and to
consider the case for establishing a Human Rights Commission. The
Committee was established in January 2001. It is not within the Committee's terms of reference to get involved in individual cases.[34]

Human Rights Commission. The establishment of a Human **2.62**
Rights Commission was mooted prior to the introduction of the Human
Rights Bill but did not form part of the published Bill because the Govern-
ment was not convinced that it was necessary to create a United Kingdom

---

[32] H.L. Deb., January 28, 1998, col. 398.
[33] The procedural aspects of bringing or defending a HRA claim are discussed in detail in
Chap. 8.
[34] For further information on the Committee, see http://www.parliament.uk/commons/selcom/
hrhome.htm.

Human Rights Commission (unlike the Northern Ireland Human Rights Commission set up under section 68 of the Northern Ireland Act 1998) and wanted to consider how a Human Rights Commission would work with existing bodies such as the Equal Opportunities Commission, the Commission for Racial Equality and the Disability Rights Commission with a view to resolving issues over its functions and structure. The issue apparently remains open for further consideration in the future. Indeed, at the first meeting of the reconstituted Joint Committee in July 2001, it re-affirmed the previous Committee's decision to establish an inquiry into the case for a Human Rights Commission for the United Kingdom.[35]

---

[35] Press Notice, July 20, 2001.

CHAPTER 3

An Overview of the European Convention on Human Rights

1. Introduction

3.01 This chapter aims to provide an introduction to the key principles relating to each of the Convention rights and freedoms which are protected in domestic law as a result of the coming into force of the HRA. It is intended to outline the scope and effect of each Article in a general way. The individual rights are considered in context in Part III on a subject-by-subject basis. For a more comprehensive analysis of the jurisprudence of the Convention on an Article-by-Article basis, the reader is invited to consult one of the many general texts on the law and practice of the Convention.[1]

2. History of Convention

Origin of Convention

3.02 On November 4, 1950, the European Convention for the Protection of Human Rights and Fundamental Freedoms was opened for signature by Member States of the Council of Europe at Rome. It was ratified by the United Kingdom in March 1951 and entered into force on September 3, 1953. It has been amended on several occasions since 1950.[2] The Convention's origin may be found in the Congress of Europe held at The Hague in May 1948 convened by the International Committee of Movements of European Unity. The Council of Europe was founded on May 5, 1949 with the aim of achieving greater unity amongst its members and the maintenance and further realisation of human rights and fundamental freedoms.[3]

Civil and Political Rights

3.03 The Convention is primarily a statement of civil and political rights (rather than social and economic rights) that is loosely based on the United Nations Universal Declaration of Human Rights 1948. It was born out of a collective desire by the States of Western Europe to respond to the human rights abuses of the Second World War and also to strengthen political democracy in the face of the rise of communism. The Preamble to the Convention sets out the aims of its founders:

> "Considering that the aim of the Council of Europe is the achievement of greater unity between its members and that one of the methods by which that aim is to be pursued is the maintenance and further realization of human rights and fundamental freedoms;

---

[1] See para. 8.81 for a list of reference books.
[2] By Protocol No.2 and Protocol No. 3, both of which entered into force on September 21, 1970; by Protocol No. 5, which entered into force on December 20,1971; by Protocol No. 8, which entered into force on January 1, 1990 and by Protocol No. 11 which entered into force on November 1, 1998 and replaced Articles 19–56 and Protocol No.2 with new Articles 19–51 and repealed Protocol No.9.
[3] Statute of the Council of Europe, Art. 1. See generally J.Simor & B. Emmerson q.c., *Human Rights Practice* (London: Sweet & Maxwell: 2000), Chap. 1, Section 1.

Reaffirming their profound belief in those fundamental freedoms which are the foundation of justice and peace in the world and are best maintained on the one hand by an effective political democracy and on the other by a common understanding and observance of the human rights upon which they depend;
Being resolved, as the governments of European countries which are like minded and have a common heritage of political traditions, ideals, freedom and the rule of law, to take the first steps for the collective enforcement of certain of those rights stated in the Universal Declaration [of Human Rights]."

Prior to the introduction of the HRA 1998, all the signatory countries, **3.04** except the United Kingdom and the Republic of Ireland (which has its own constitution), had incorporated the Convention into their domestic law. Further, there had been more adverse findings against the United Kingdom in relation to the Convention than any other Contracting State except Italy.[3A]

3. NATURE OF OBLIGATIONS

State obligations. The Convention imposes obligations on states, **3.05** not on individuals.[4] The Convention cannot be relied upon to bring an action against a private person before the Strasbourg institutions. However, under Article 1, states have a positive obligation to secure protection of fundamental rights between individuals. An individual whose fundamental rights have been breached (or threatened to be breached) by a private body or individual may be able to secure effective action by public authorities to protect him or her.

4. THE STRASBOURG INSTITUTIONS

Enforcement of the Convention

In addition to laying down civil and political rights, the Convention also set **3.06** up a system of enforcement of the obligations entered into by the Contracting States. Three institutions had responsibility for enforcement: the European Commission of Human Rights which was set up in 1954, the European Court of Human Rights which was set up in 1959 and the Committee of Ministers of the Council of Europe which was composed of the Ministers for Foreign Affairs of the Contracting States or their representatives.
Contracting States, and where the State at issue had accepted the right of **3.07** individual petition, individual applicants, could lodge complaints against Contracting States for alleged violations of Convention rights. The right of

---

[3A] See para. 2.06, above.
[4] Although see the Home Secretary in relation to the corresponding duties of the citizen, University College London Constitution Unit Annual Lecture, October 27, 1999 at http://www.homeoffice.gov.uk/hract/cuspeech.htm.

individual petition greatly strengthened the effectiveness of the Convention in securing protection for fundamental rights. On January 14, 1966, the United Kingdom lodged a declaration with the Secretary-General of the Council of Europe in which it accepted the right of individuals to bring a petition before the European Commission in accordance with (what was then) Article 25. The acceptance was limited to petitions in relation to any act or decision occurring or any facts or events arising subsequent to January 13, 1966. A declaration pursuant to what was then Article 46 of the Convention, recognising the European Court's jurisdiction subject to similar conditions, was filed on the same day.

Pre-November 1998 Procedure

3.08   Until November 1998, complaints under the Convention were the subject of a preliminary examination by the Commission which made a decision regarding their admissibility. Where an application had been declared admissible and no friendly settlement had been reached, the Commission drew up a report establishing the facts and expressing an opinion on the merits of the case. The report was transmitted to the Committee of Ministers. Where the respondent state had accepted the compulsory jurisdiction of the European Court, the Commission and/or any Contracting State concerned could within three months following the transmission of the report to the Committee of Ministers bring the case before the Court for a final, binding adjudication. Individuals were not entitled to bring their cases before the Court. If a case was not referred to the Court, the Committee of Ministers decided whether there had been a violation of the Convention and, if appropriate, awarded just satisfaction to the victim. The Committee of Ministers also had responsibility for supervising the execution of the judgments of the Court.

Post-November 1998 Procedure

3.09   On November 1, 1998, a full time Court was established, replacing the original two-tier system of a part time Commission and Court.[5] On October 31, 1998, the old Court ceased to function. The Commission continued for a further year until October 31, 1999, to deal with cases which had been declared admissible before November 1, 1998. The Court is composed of a number of judges equal to that of the Contracting States who are elected by the Parliamentary Assembly of the Council of Europe for a term of six years. Judges sit in their individual capacities and do not represent any state. Any state or individual application is now lodged directly with the Court and its admissibility is dealt with by a Committee or Chamber of the Court. Once admitted, this is followed by a procedure on the merits and then a provisional judgment by a Chamber. Unless a party requests referral to the Grand Chamber within a period of three months following judgment on the ground that it raises a serious question of interpretation or application or a serious issue of general importance, the judgment

---

[5] This resulted from the coming into force of Protocol No. 11 to the Convention, which has substantially revised the Convention.

becomes final and binding on the respondent state concerned. Responsibility for supervising the execution of judgments remains with the Committee of Ministers. The Court may, at the request of the Committee of Ministers, also give advisory opinions on legal questions concerning the interpretation of the Convention.[5A]

5. ARTICLES INCORPORATED BY HRA

The Rights Incorporated

The Articles of the Convention which are incorporated into domestic law by   **3.10**
the Act are as follows[5B]:

Article	Right/freedom
Article 2	Right to life
Article 3	Freedom from torture
Article 4	Freedom from slavery
Article 5	Freedom from arbitrary arrest and detention
Article 6	Right to a fair trial
Article 7	Freedom from retrospective penalties
Article 8	Right to respect for privacy, family life, home and correspondence
Article 9	Freedom of thought, conscience and religion
Article 10	Freedom of expression
Article 11	Freedom of assembly and association
Article 12	Right to marry and found a family
Article 14	Freedom from discrimination
Article 16	Restrictions on political activity of aliens
Article 17	Prohibition on abuse of rights
Article 18	Limitation on use of restrictions on rights
Protocol 1, Article 1	Right to peaceful enjoyment of possessions
Protocol 1, Article 2	Right to education
Protocol 1, Article 3	Right to free elections
Protocol 6, Article 1	Abolition of death penalty
Protocol 6, Article 2	Death penalty in time of war

Classification of Rights

The rights in the Convention and Protocols are either derogable or non-   **3.11**
derogable rights. Non-derogable rights allow for no limitation or derogation, even in time of war or public emergency. Articles 2, 3, 4(1) and 7 are non-derogable rights.[6] Derogable rights permit derogation by the state in

---

[5A] See http://www.echr.coe.int, General Information, Historical background, organisation and procedure.
[5B] For a discussion of the excluded Art. 1, see paras 2.14 *et seq.* and Art. 13, see paras 2.17 *et seq.*
[6] However, Art. 15 provides that deaths arising from lawful acts of war will not violate Art. 2.

times of public emergency but only to the "extent strictly required by the exigencies of the situation": Article 15(1). There is also a "hierarchy" of rights in that some rights can be characterised as absolute rights where no limitation is, as a matter of principle, permissible. Such rights include Article 2, Article 3 and the right to a fair trial in Article 6. In practice, however, the *scope* of absolute rights has been limited by way of interpretation by the European Court. Other rights are expressly qualified in that state interference with such rights may be justified in pursuit of expressly stated aims, provided that the interference is in accordance with the law and necessary in a democratic society (for example Articles 8 to 11).[7] Where rights have been implied into the Convention, such as the right of access to a court, limitations are generally permitted under prescribed conditions (for example that the restriction satisfies a legitimate aim, does not impair the very essence of the right and is proportionate).[7A]

3.12 There are various Protocols to the Convention which the United Kingdom has not yet signed or ratified. The Secretary of State may amend the Act by order to give effect to rights contained in any Protocols that are ratified in the future, subject to the approval of both Houses of Parliament.

3.13 The rights will each be reviewed in turn below. The Convention rights of widest application from the standpoint of most civil and commercial practitioners are Articles 6, 8, 10 and Article 1 of Protocol 1 and these are considered in slightly greater detail. Nonetheless, the other rights merit familiarity and consideration, as they are will arise in the civil context depending on the subject area concerned.

Article 2 (Right to Life)

3.14 Article 2 of the Convention provides:

> "(1) Everyone's right to life shall be protected by law. No one shall be deprived of his life intentionally save in the execution of a sentence of a court following his conviction of a crime for which this penalty is provided by law.
>
> (2) Deprivation of life shall not be regarded as inflicted in contravention of this article when it results from the use of force which is no more than absolutely necessary:
>
> a. in defence of any person from unlawful violence;
> b. in order to effect a lawful arrest or to prevent the escape of a person lawfully detained;
> c. in action lawfully taken for the purpose of quelling a riot or insurrection."

3.15 Article 2 provides for the protection of human life. The right to life is expressed in mandatory terms and in peace-time; it is not possible for a state to derogate from Article 2. This Article does not prohibit the death penalty where this has been provided for by law. However, a prohibition on

---

[7] See also Art. 1 of Protocol No. 1.
[7A] *Golder v. United Kingdom* (1979) 1 E.H.R.R. 524, para. 38. See generally Keir Starmer, *European Human Rights Law* (Legal Action Group, 1999) Chap. 4 at pp. 155–156.

the death penalty is contained in the optional Protocol 6, which the United
Kingdom ratified on January 27, 1999.

Article 2 imposes two duties on the state (and so, through the HRA, on   **3.16**
public authorities):

(1) not to take a person's life save in the limited circumstances set
out in Article 2(2);

(2) to take reasonable measures to protect life.

The duty to take reasonable measures to protect life is a positive duty.[8]   **3.17**
Article 2 is "one of the most fundamental provisions in the Convention".[9]
It includes a primary duty to put in place "effective criminal law provisions
to deter the commission of offences against the person backed up by law-
enforcement machinery for the prevention, suppression and sanctioning
of breaches of such provisions": *Osman v.United Kingdom.*[10]

Article 2(2) sets out limited exceptions to the right to life, namely: **3.18**

(1) defence from unlawful violence;

(2) in order to effect a lawful arrest or prevent the unlawful escape
of a person lawfully detained;

(3) in quelling a riot or insurrection.

The fundamental nature of Article 2 means that the exceptions set out in
Article 2(2) are "exhaustive" and must be "narrowly construed".[11] Even
when the use of force is permitted under Article 2(2), it must be "no more
force than is absolutely necessary". Force is "absolutely necessary" if it is
"strictly proportionate to the achievement of the permitted purpose".[12] To
assess whether the use of force is strictly proportionate, regard must be
had to:

(a) the nature of the aim pursued;

(b) the dangers to life and body inherent in the situation; and

(c) the degree of risk that the force employed might result in the loss
of life.[13]

All the circumstances must be closely scrutinised, especially where intentional force is used. The Court has stated that in making its decision, it will
take into consideration, not only the actions of the organs of state which

---

[8] *X v. United Kingdom* (1978) 14 D.R. 31, Application No. 7154/75.
[9] *McCann v. United Kingdom* (1996) 21 E.H.R.R. 97, para. 197.
[10] (2000) 29 E.H.R.R. 245, para.115. See also *Keenan v. United Kingdom*, Application No.
27229/95, April 3, 2001, para.88.
[11] *Stewart v. United Kingdom* (1985) 7 E.H.R.R. 453; *McCann v. United Kingdom* (1996) 21
E.H.R.R. 97.
[12] *Stewart v. United Kingdom* (1985) 7 E.H.R.R. 453.
[13] *ibid.*

administer the force, but also the surrounding circumstances such as the "planning and control of the actions under examination".[14]

3.19 Although regarded as an absolute right, as stated above, Article 2 does not extend to every situation where life is taken or death is not prevented. In *X v.United Kingdom*,[15] a husband who was separated from his wife, tried to prevent her from having an abortion. The Commission ruled that the abortion of a 10 week old foetus did not violate Article 2 and held that Article 2 generally only applied post-natally. The Court has not yet ruled on this issue.[16]

3.20 Under Article 2, there is a positive obligation on the investigating authorities of a state to carry out an effective investigation into deaths arising out of circumstances involving the security forces.[17] Further, there is an obligation on the state to provide an effective, independent system for establishing the cause of death of an individual under the care and responsibility of health professionals and any liability on their part.[18]

3.21 Article 2 also has potential application to life-threatening hazards (particularly in the environmental context), so far as these hazards may be attributed to the state. In *LCB v.United Kingdom*,[19] a woman who had been diagnosed with leukaemia brought a claim under Article 2 against the United Kingdom on the basis that this had been caused by her father's exposure to radiation while serving with the Royal Air Force during the nuclear tests conducted on Christmas Island in the late 1950s. She could not challenge the exposure to radiation because this occurred prior to the United Kingdom granting the right of individual petition. However, she alleged that the state owed a duty to warn and advise her parents and to monitor her health prior to the diagnosis of leukaemia, which it had breached. The European Court dismissed the claim on the basis that there was insufficient evidence of causation between the father's exposure to radiation and the daughter's leukaemia. The Court stated that the test to be applied is:

> "whether, given the circumstances of the case, the State did all that could have been required of it to prevent a life from being avoidably put at risk."[20]

---

[14] *McCann v. United Kingdom* (1996) 21 E.H.R.R. 97. See also *Andronicou & Constantinou v. Cyprus* (1998) 25 E.H.R.R. 491, and *Jordan v. United Kingdom*, (2001) 31 E.H.R.R. 201 (applicant's son killed in Northern Ireland by officers of the Royal Ulster Constabulary—application that son deprived of his life in violation of Art. 2 declared admissible).

[15] (1980) 19 D.R. 244.

[16] See also *A National Health Service Trust v. D* [2000] 2 F.L.R. 677; [2000] Lloyd's Rep. Med. 411; *The Times*, July 19, 2000, Cazalet J. (where it was held that it was not a breach of Art. 2 not to resuscitate a child with severe disabilities). See further paras 17.69 *et seq.*

[17] *Kaya v. Turkey* (1999) 28 E.H.R.R. 1; *Tankrikulu v. Turkey* (2000) 30 E.H.R.R. 950.

[18] *Powell (William and Anita) v. United Kingdom*, Application No. 43505/99, May 4, 2000. See also in relation to Art. 13 *Keenan v. United Kingdom*, Application No. 27229/95, April 3, 2001, para.122 (given the fundamental importance of the right to the protection of life, Art. 13 requires, in addition to the payment of compensation where appropriate, a thorough and effective investigation capable of leading to the identification and punishment of those responsible for the deprivation of life, including effective access for the complainant to the investigation procedure). See also *Kaya v. Turkey* (1999) 28 E.H.R.R. 1, para.107.

[19] (1999) 27 E.H.R.R. 212. See also *Guerra v. Italy* (1998) 26 E.H.R.R. 357.

[20] *LCB, ibid.*, para 36. The right to respect for private and family life under Art. 8 of the Convention may also be relevant in this context.

The Court accepted that the state might have been required to take steps to warn and advise if it appeared likely at the relevant time that the father's exposure to radiation might endanger the health of any future children. This case has fairly wide-ranging implications for government action when addressing potential health risks such as, for example food safety, the use of weapons in the armed forces and the regulation of medicines.[20A] However, it is likely that a fairly wide discretion will be granted to the state in deciding what steps to take to regulate the hazard in light of the known risks.

In *Osman*, the Court took account of the public policy considerations and resource issues in holding that "not every claimed risk to life can entail for the authorities a Convention requirement to take operational measures to prevent that risk from materialising".[21] The scope of the positive obligation must be interpreted in a way which does not impose an impossible or disproportionate burden on the authorities.[22] The Court stated for a violation of Article 2 to be found, it must be established to its satisfaction that "the authorities knew or ought to have known at the time of the existence of a real and immediate risk to the life of an identified individual or individuals from the criminal acts of a third party and that they failed to take measures within the scope of their powers which, judged reasonably, might have been expected to avoid that risk".[23] The Court rejected the Government's contention that the failure to perceive the risk to life in the circumstances known at the time, or the failure to take preventative measures to avoid that risk, must be tantamount to gross negligence or wilful disregard of the duty to protect life and held that: **3.22**

> "it is sufficient for an application to show that the authorities did not do all that could reasonably have been expected of them to avoid a real and immediate risk to life of which they have or ought to have knowledge. This is a question which can only be answered in the light of all the circumstances of any particular case".[24]

Article 3 (Freedom from Torture)

Article 3 of the Convention states: **3.23**

> "No one shall be subjected to torture or to inhuman or degrading treatment or punishment."

Like Article 2, Article 3 is an absolute right and pursuant to Article 15, no derogation is permitted even during war or public emergency. Everyone is entitled to the protection of Article 3, regardless of his own conduct.   **3.24**

[20A] See further in relation to product liability, paras 19.70 *et seq.*
[21] At para. 116. Such public policy considerations included the difficulties of policing modern societies, the unpredictability of human conduct and the operational choices which must be made in terms of priorities and resources.
[22] *ibid.* See also *Keenan v. United Kingdom*, Application No. 27229/95, April 3, 2001, para.89 (death in prison custody).
[23] *ibid.*
[24] *ibid.*

3.25 Article 3 encompasses three types of treatment or punishment, categorised by the European Court in *Ireland v.United Kingdom*[25] to mean:

(1) torture: deliberate inhuman treatment causing very serious and cruel suffering;

(2) inhuman treatment: treatment or punishment that causes intense physical and mental suffering;

(3) degrading treatment: treatment or punishment that arouses in the victim a feeling of fear, anguish and inferiority capable of humiliating and debasing the victim and possibly breaking his or her physical or moral resistance.

3.26 Conduct must "attain a minimum level of severity" before Article 3 is breached.[26] Whether this level is reached depends on all the circumstances of the case, including the duration of the treatment or punishment, its physical or mental effects and the sex, age and state of health of the victim. In the *Ireland v. United Kingdom* case, the Court reviewed interrogation techniques used by the British Government in relation to alleged terrorists, including depriving them of food, drink and sleep, forcing them to stand against a wall in an uncomfortable position, hooding and subjecting them to loud constant noise. The Court did not find that these practices amounted to torture but found that they constituted degrading treatment and were therefore in violation of Article 3.[27] In *Aksoy v.Turkey*,[28] the Court for the first time used the term "torture" to describe the conduct of state officials in stringing the naked applicant up by his arms and electrocuting him, causing him to lose the movement of his arms and legs. In *Selmouni v. France*,[29] the Court was satisfied with the applicant's evidence of torture whilst in police custody consisting of beating him with a baseball bat, urinating on him, lighting blowlamps under his feet and inserting a truncheon into his anus. One of the important factors was that the ill-treatment had been carried out in order to obtain a confession. The Court reiterated the principle that where an individual is taken into police custody in good health, but found to be injured at the time of release, the state must provide a plausible explanation of how those injuries were caused. However, the classification of ill-treatment as torture, inhuman or degrading is not fixed and should reflect contemporary standards.[30]

3.27 In *Keenan v. United Kingdom*,[31] the Court stated that whilst the severity of suffering, physical and mental, attributable to a particular measure has been a significant consideration in many of the cases decided by the Court under Article 3, there are circumstances where proof of the actual effect on the person may not be a major factor.[32] Where a person is deprived of his liberty, recourse to physical force not made strictly necessary by his own conduct diminishes human dignity and is in principle an infringement of

[25] (1980) 2 E.H.R.R. 25.
[26] *Ireland v. United Kingdom* (1980) 2 E.H.R.R. 25, para.162.
[27] *ibid.*, paras 167–168.
[28] (1997) 23 E.H.R.R. 553.
[29] (2000) 29 E.H.R.R. 403.
[30] *Selmouni v. France* (2000) 29 E.H.R.R. 403, para.101.
[31] Application No. 27229/95, April 3, 2001.
[32] *ibid.*

Article 3.[33] Further, treatment of a mentally-ill person may be incompatible with Article 3, even though that person may not be able, or capable of, pointing to any specific ill-effects.[34] In the *Keenan* case, the Court held, in the case of a death by hanging in prison custody of a psychiatrically-ill prisoner, the lack of effective monitoring and informed psychiatric input in the medical care provided to a mentally-ill person, known to be a suicide risk, into his psychiatric condition and the imposition on him in those circumstances of a serious disciplinary punishment involving segregation from other prisoners, constituted inhuman and degrading treatment and punishment within the meaning of Article 3.[35]

3.28 Article 3 has also been applied in the context of deportation and extradition, founded on a positive obligation on a state to prevent extra-territorial breaches of Article 3. In *Chahal v.United Kingdom*,[36] the Court found that a deportation could violate Article 3 because of the positive obligation within the Article to prevent torture, as Mr Chahal, a Sikh separatist leader, faced a real risk of being subjected to ill-treatment if deported to India. In *Soering v.United Kingdom* ((1989) 11 E.H.R.R. 439), Mr Soering was being extradited to America to face a murder trial. The Court found that this could mean that he would be held on death row pending execution for long periods. To permit Mr Soering to be extradited to America would constitute a violation of the Article by the United Kingdom because it would expose him to a real risk of "treatment going beyond the threshold of Article 3". Where removal of an applicant would entail loss of vital medical treatment and thereby reduce his life expectancy, there may be a violation of Article 3: *D v. United Kingdom*.[37]

3.29 Article 3 has also arisen in the context of corporal punishment, which has been held to violate Article 3: see *Tyrer v. United Kingdom*[38] (judicial corporal punishment by birching); *A v. United Kingdom*[39] (stepfather beating child with a stick).[40]

3.30 The subjecting of a child to punitive detention of indeterminate length following conviction for a serious crime does not amount to inhuman and degrading treatment: *V v. United Kingdom*.[41]

---

[33] *Ribitsch v. Austria* (1996) 21 E.H.R.R. 573, para.38.
[34] *Keenan v. United Kingdom*, Application No. 27229/95, April 3, 2001, para.112.
[35] *ibid.*, para.115.
[36] (1997) 23 E.H.R.R. 413.
[37] (1997) 23 E.H.R.R. 423. See also *R. v. Chief Immigration Officer, ex p. Njai*, unreported, December 1, 2000, Admin. Ct.
[38] (1980) 2 E.H.R.R. 1. The Court held that judicial corporal punishment was institutionalised violence and was an attack on the integrity and dignity of the applicant. Although it was not severe enough to constitute inhuman treatment or torture, the circumstances of the punishment attained a level of humiliation (even if only in the applicant's own eyes) which constituted degrading treatment.
[39] (1999) 27 E.H.R.R. 611.
[40] See also *Costello-Roberts v. United Kingdom* (1995) 19 E.H.R.R. 112 (corporal punishment of child consisting of slippering by headmaster) and *Regina v. H* (*Reasonable chastisement*) *The Times*, May 17, 2001, CA (after consideration of Article 3, the Court concluded that the defence of reasonable chastisement remained available but a jury considering such a defence had to be given supplementary directions).
[41] And *T v. United Kingdom* (2000) 30 E.H.R.R. 121. *cf. Hussain v. United Kingdom* (1996) 22 E.H.R.R. 123 (Court doubted whether sentence of detention during Her Majesty's pleasure for juvenile was compatible with Art. 3). Mandatory life sentences imposed following convictions for murder do not violate Article 3 (or Article 5): *R. v. Secretary of State for the Home Department, ex p. Lichniak & Pyrah, The Times*, May 16, 2001; *The Independent*, June 11, 2001, CA.

3.31 Where an individual has an arguable claim against the state in relation to torture under Article 3, Article 13 imposes, without prejudice to other remedies available, an obligation on the state to carry out a thorough and effective investigation of incidents of torture capable of leading to the identification and punishment of those responsible.[42] In *Price v. United Kingdom*,[42A] the European Court held that detention of a severely disabled person in conditions where she was dangerously cold, risked developing sores because her bed was too hard or unreachable and was unable to go to the toilet or keep clean without the greatest of difficulty constituted degrading treatment within the meaning of Article 3. The standard of proof for Article 3 is discussed at para. 4.50 below.

Article 4 (Freedom from Slavery and Forced Labour)

3.32 Article 4 of the Convention states:

"(1) No one shall be held in slavery or servitude.

(2) No one shall be required to perform forced or compulsory labour.

(3) For the purpose of this article the term "forced or compulsory labour" shall not include:

    a. any work required to be done in the ordinary course of detention imposed according to the provisions of Article 5 of this Convention or during conditional release from such detention;

    b. any service of a military character or, in case of conscientious objectors in countries where they are recognised, service exacted instead of compulsory military service;

    c. any service exacted in case of any emergency or calamity threatening the life or well-being of the community;

    d. any work or service which forms part of normal civil obligations."

3.33 The prohibition on slavery or servitude is an absolute right from which no derogation is possible pursuant to Article 15. However, derogation is permissible from Article 4(2) (freedom from forced or compulsory labour).

3.34 Slavery is not defined but would appear to require ownership of a person by another. In *Van Droogenbroeck v. Belgium*,[43] the applicant was a habitual thief who, at the end of a custodial sentence, was placed at the disposal of the government for a period of 10 years. He argued that this amounted to "servitude". The Court rejected this claim as there was no serious denial of freedom. Accordingly, servitude requires a serious denial of freedom, but it is not clear what further specific conditions are required.

3.35 Forced or compulsory labour is work for which the individual in question has not volunteered, which is exacted under threat of a penalty. An

---

[42] *Aksoy v. Turkey* (1997) 23 E.H.R.R. 553, paras 98–99.
[42A] Application No. 33394/96, July 10, 2001.
[43] (1982) 4 E.H.R.R. 443.

obligation to work will only violate Article 4(2) if it is excessive or disproportionate in the circumstances.

The Court has held that: 3.36

(1) an obligation on a professional to exercise his profession in a
    particular part of a country for a limited period which was well-
    remunerated[44];

(2) an obligation to carry out legal aid work[45]; and

(3) an obligation on a pupil advocate to undertake free legal repre-
    sentation for poor defendants[46] do not breach Article 4(2). In *Van
    der Mussele v. Belgium,*[47] the Court held that labour could com-
    prise non-manual work, and that it is forced if there is a degree
    of compulsion on an individual to carry it out.

Further, Article 4(3)(a) permits forced or compulsory labour where it is in   3.37
the ordinary course of detention and complies with Article 5[48] or during
conditional release. It is irrelevant that the detained person's conviction is
later quashed.[49]

Article 4(3)(b) permits states who recognise conscientious objectors to   3.38
military service to impose some substitute service for them.[50]

Article 4(3)(c) permits service exacted in the case of an emergency   3.39
threatening the life or well-being of the community.

Article 4(3)(d) is intended to include all civic obligations including, for   3.40
example an employer's obligation to deduct tax from his employees'
income,[51] a lessor's obligation to maintain his building[52] or compulsory fire
service.[53]

Article 5 (Right to Liberty and Security)

Article 5 of the Convention states: 3.41

"(1) Everyone has the right to liberty and security of person. No one
shall be deprived of his liberty save in the following cases and in
accordance with a procedure prescribed by law:

a. the lawful detention of a person after conviction by a competent court;
b. the lawful arrest or detention of a person for non-compliance
   with the lawful order of a court or in order to secure the
   fulfillment of any obligation prescribed by law;
c. the lawful arrest or detention of a person effected for the
   purpose of bringing him before the competent legal authority

---

[44] *Iversen v. Norway* (1963) 6 Y.B. 278.
[45] *X and Y v. Germany* (1976) 10 D.R. 224.
[46] *Van der Mussele v. Belgium* (1984) 6 E.H.R.R. 163.
[47] *ibid.*
[48] *De Wilde, Ooms and Versyp v. Belgium* (1979) 1 E.H.R.R. 373.
[49] *X v. Austria* (1969) 12 Y.B. 206.
[50] *Grandrath v. Germany* (1965) 8 Y.B. 324; 10 Y.B. 626, Application No.2299/64.
[51] *Four Companies v. Austria* (1976) 7 D.R. 148, Application No. 7427/76.
[52] *X v. Austria* (1973) 45 C.D. 113.
[53] *Schmidt v. Germany* (1994) 18 E.H.R.R. 513, para. 22.

on reasonable suspicion of having committed an offence or when it is reasonably considered necessary to prevent his committing an offence or fleeing after having done so;

d. the detention of a minor by lawful order for the purpose of educational supervision or his lawful detention for the purpose of bringing him before the competent legal authority;

e. the lawful detention of persons for the prevention of the spreading of infectious diseases, of persons of unsound mind, alcoholics or drug addicts or vagrants;

f. the lawful arrest or detention of a person to prevent his effecting an unauthorised entry into the country or of a person against whom action is being taken with a view to deportation or extradition.

(2) Everyone who is arrested shall be informed promptly, in a language which he understands, of the reasons for his arrest and of any charge against him.

(3) Everyone arrested or detained in accordance with the provisions of paragraph 1.c of this article shall be brought promptly before a judge or other officer authorized by law to exercise judicial power and shall be entitled to trial within a reasonable time or to release pending trial. Release may be conditioned by guarantees to appear for trial.

(4) Everyone who is deprived of his liberty by arrest or detention shall be entitled to take proceedings by which the lawfulness of his detention shall be decided speedily by a court and his release ordered if the detention is not lawful.

(5) Everyone who has been the victim of arrest or detention in contravention of the provisions of this article shall have an enforceable right to compensation."

3.42 Article 5 (1) guarantees liberty and security of the person. The underlying principle is to ensure that no one is deprived of his personal liberty in an "arbitrary fashion".[54] The concepts of liberty and security are very closely linked and "security" does not refer to physical or bodily integrity independent of liberty.[55]

3.43 A state may only derogate from Article 5 in war-time or other public emergency threatening the life of the nation, pursuant to Article 15. The United Kingdom has derogated from Article 5(3), in relation to the Prevention of Terrorism (Temporary Provisions) Act 1984, by preserving the power to extend detention of suspected terrorists in connection with Northern Ireland for a total of up to seven days.

3.44 Article 5(1) provides a list of circumstances in which a person may be lawfully deprived of his liberty:

(1) detention following conviction (Article 5(1)(a));

---

[54] *Engel v. Netherlands* (1979) 1 E.H.R.R. 647, para. 58.
[55] *East African Asians v. United* Kingdom (1981) 3 E.H.R.R. 76. Issues of bodily or physical integrity fall to be considered under other provisions such as Art. 3 (freedom from torture, etc.) or Art. 8 (right to respect for privacy).

(2) detention for non-compliance with court orders or to secure compliance with a legal obligation (Article 5(1)(b));

(3) arrest on reasonable suspicion (Article 5(1)(c));

(4) detention of minors for the purpose of educational supervision or to be brought before the competent legal authority (Article 5(1)(d));

(5) detention for the prevention of the spreading of infectious diseases, persons of unsound mind, alcoholics, drug addicts or vagrants (Article 5(1)(e));

(6) detention in connection with unauthorised immigration, deportation or extradition (Article 5(1)(f)).

The definition in Article 5(1) of the circumstances in which a person may **3.45** be lawfully deprived of his liberty is exhaustive[56] and is to be narrowly interpreted.[57] Further, any detention must be (1) lawful in accordance with both domestic law and the Convention; and (2) carried out "in accordance with a procedure prescribed by domestic law".[58] A margin of appreciation[59] has been afforded by the European Court to national authorities to interpret and apply domestic law. However, the European Court retains a supervisory jurisdiction to determine whether Article 5 has been violated.[60] The Court has been reluctant to accept contentions that an individual may waive the right to liberty under Article 5.[61]

The exception for lawful detention of a person after conviction by a **3.46** competent court permitted by Article 5(1)(a) is concerned only with the fact of detention and not with the conditions of detention. In order to be "lawful", a competent court must justify the detention and lawful procedures must be followed to effect the detention. Any decision of a court would have to comply with the provisions of Article 6 (the right to a fair hearing).

A person who has failed to observe a court order or obligation may be **3.47** detained under Article 5(1)(b). The requirements for application of Article 5(1)(b) are that:

(1) the order or obligation must be clear;

(2) the person detained must have a reasonable opportunity to comply with the order or obligation; and

(3) the detention must be the only reasonable way to secure the fulfilment of the order or obligation.

---

[56] *Ireland v. United Kingdom* (1980) 2 E.H.R.R. 25, para. 194.
[57] *Winterwerp v. Netherlands* (1980) 2 E.H.R.R. 387, para. 37.
[58] *Amuur v. France* (1996) 22 E.H.R.R. 533, para. 50. Detention may become unlawful by a subsequent declaration of the law by the courts, causing breach of Art. 5 even though respondent acted in accordance with law as it was understood at the time: *R. v. Governor of Brockhill Prison, ex p. Evans* [2000] 3 W.L.R. 843.
[59] See paras 4.22 *et seq.*, below.
[60] *Benham v. United Kingdom* (1996) 22 E.H.R.R. 293.
[61] *De Wilde, Ooms and Versyp v. Belgium* (1971) 1 E.H.R.R. 373, at para. 65; *Amuur v. France* (1996) 22 E.H.R.R. 533, para. 48.

3.48 Under Article 5(1)(c), a person may be lawfully arrested only where:

> (1) he is reasonably suspected of committing a crime;
>
> (2) it is reasonably considered necessary to prevent him committing a crime; or
>
> (3) it is sought to prevent him absconding after committing a crime.

The test of reasonable suspicion is objective.[62] An arrest is only lawful under this Article if its purpose is to bring the detained person before a competent legal authority.[63]

3.49 Article 5(1)(d) permits the detention of minors for the purpose of educational supervision or juvenile detention on remand.

3.50 Article 5(1)(e) permits the detention of those with infectious diseases, persons of unsound mind, alcoholics, drug addicts and vagrants. In *Guzzardi v. Italy*,[64] the European Court stated that these categories of person are listed because they have to be considered as occasionally dangerous for public safety and because their own interests may necessitate their detention. Article 5 governs the regime for detention of persons suffering from mental illness.[65]

3.51 Article 5(1)(f) relates to detention for immigration, deportation and extradition purposes. The lawfulness of the detention depends only on whether the intention behind the detention is the deportation of the detainee.[66]

3.52 Article 5(2) to (5) sets out procedural rights for detainees:

> (1) the right to be informed of the reasons for arrest or detention[66A];
>
> (2) right to release pending trial[67];
>
> (3) the right to take proceedings by which the lawfulness of detention can be decided speedily and release ordered if it is unlawful (*habeas corpus*)[68];
>
> (4) compensation for unlawful detention.

---

[62] *Fox v. United Kingdom* (1991) 13 E.H.R.R. 157.

[63] *Brogan v. United Kingdom* (1989) 11 E.H.R.R. 117.

[64] (1981) 3 E.H.R.R. 333.

[65] See, *e.g.*, *Winterwerp v. Netherlands* (1980) 2 E.H.R.R. 387; *Johnson v. United Kingdom* (1997) 27 E.H.R.R. 296; *R. v. Camden and Islington Health Authority, ex p. K*, unreported, February 21, 2001, CA; *R v. East London and City Mental Health NHS Trust, ex p. Brandenburg*, unreported, February 21, 2001, CA.

[66] *Zamir v. United Kingdom* (1983) 5 E.H.R.R. 242.

[66A] See, *e.g. H.B. v. Switzerland*, Application No. 26899/95, April 5, 2001.

[67] See, *e.g.*, *Caballero v. United Kingdom* (2000) 30 E.H.R.R. 643.

[68] *Winterwerp v. Netherlands* (1980) 2 E.H.R.R. 387 (violation of Art. 5(4) since Netherlands law did not permit psychiatric patient to bring judicial proceedings to determine the lawfulness of his detention). See also *Anderson v. Scottish Ministers & Attorney-General for Scotland*, unreported, June 16, 2000, Inner House, Ct of Sess. In *R (C) v. Mental Health Review Tribunal, The Times*, July 11, 2001, CA, it was held that a practice of routinely listing applications for hearing eight weeks after the date of the application contravened Article 5(4) which required the lawfulness of the detention to be decided speedily by a court.

Article 6 (Right to a Fair Trial)

Article 6 of the Convention states: **3.53**

"(1) In the determination of his civil rights and obligations or of any criminal charge against him, everyone is entitled to a fair and public hearing within a reasonable time by an independent and impartial tribunal established by law. Judgment shall be pronounced publicly but the press and public may be excluded from all or part of the trial in the interests of morals, public order or national security in a democratic society, where the interests of juveniles or the protection of private life of the parties so require, or to the extent strictly necessary in the opinion of the court in special circumstances where publicity would prejudice the interests of justice.
(2) Everyone charged with a criminal offence shall be presumed innocent until proved guilty according to law
(3) Everyone charged with a criminal offence has the following minimum rights.

(a) to be informed promptly, in a language which he understands and in detail, of the nature and cause of the accusation against him;
(b) to have adequate time and facilities for the preparation of his defence;
(c) to defend himself in person or through legal assistance of his own choosing or, if he has not sufficient means to pay for legal assistance, to be given it free when the interests of justice so require;
(d) to examine or have examined witnesses against him and to obtain the attendance and examination of witnesses on his behalf under the same conditions as witnesses against him;
(e) to have the free assistance of an interpreter if he cannot understand or speak the language used in court."

Article 6(1) applies to both criminal and civil proceedings, including all **3.54** proceedings between private individuals. Article 6(2) and 6(3) apply only to criminal proceedings and represent irreducible minimum guarantees. Article 6 is the most invoked Article of the Convention.

Civil Proceedings

Apart from criminal proceedings, Article 6(1) applies only to the determina- **3.55** tion of "civil rights and obligations". This is a broad phrase which is likely to cover issues arising under many aspects of law. The concept of "civil rights and obligations" has an autonomous meaning which is not derived from classifications in domestic legal systems[69] but which only includes rights which exist under domestic law. It is sufficient for an applicant to show that there are at least arguable grounds which point to the recognition of the right at issue under domestic law.[70] In the final analysis, it is for

---

[69] *Feldebrugge v. Netherlands* (1986) 8 E.H.R.R. 425.
[70] *Fayed v. United Kingdom* (1994) 18 E.H.R.R. 393, para. 65.

the European Court, in the exercise of its supervisory jurisdiction and on the basis of Convention criteria, to rule on whether the applicant has shown this to be the case.

"Civil rights and obligations"

3.56 Whilst there exist several advocates for the adoption of a broad inter-pretation to the phrase "civil rights and obligations" so that it means any non-criminal matter which comes before a national court[71] or a right "recognised in the national legal system as an individual right within the sphere of general individual freedom",[72] the European Court has to date preferred to adopt a narrower, incremental approach to its meaning.

3.57 Issues arising in contract, tort,[73] commercial law, insurance law, real and personal property, intellectual property,[74] restitution,[75] planning,[76] educa-tion, family law and succession are generally regarded as matters to which Article 6(1) applies. Preliminary investigative procedures, such as a DTI investigation, are not determinative of a civil right.[77] Pure "public" law rights are not generally regarded as "civil rights", for example the entry and removal of immigrants.[78] Matters concerning public employment are generally regarded as "public rights".[79] Further, proceedings regarding political rights are not within Article 6(1).[80] The European Court has focused on identification of a pecuniary right or interest in determining whether a right was a "civil" right: *Editions Périscope v. France*.[81] How-ever, in *Ferrazzini v. Italy*[81A] the Court stated that merely showing that a dispute was "pecuniary" in nature was not in itself sufficient to attract the applicability of Article 6(1). There might exist "pecuniary" obligations vis-à-vis the State or its subordinate authorities which were, for the purpose of the Article, to be considered as belonging exclusively to the realm of public law. Apart from fines imposed by way of "criminal sanction", this would be the case in particular where an obligation which was pecuniary in nature derived from tax legislation or was otherwise part of the normal civic duties in a democratic society. Whilst acknowledging that the Court had increas-ingly found that procedures classified under national law as being part of "public law" could come within the purview of Article 6 under its "civil"

---

[71] P. van Dijk, "The Interpretation of 'Civil Rights and Obligations' by the European Court of Human Rights—one more step to take" in Franz Matscher and Herbert Petzold (eds), *Protecting Human Rights: the European Dimension*—Studies in Honour of Gerard J. Wiarda, Köln (Carl Heymanns Verlag KG 1988) pp. 131–143.
[72] See concurring opinion of Judge Jambrek in *Osman v. United Kingdom* (2000) 29 E.H.R.R. 245. See also the dissenting opinions of Judge Melchior and Judge Frowein in *Benthem v. Netherlands* (1986) 8 E.H.R.R. 1.
[73] A pending negligence claim is a possession within the meaning of Art. 1 of the First Protocol (*Pressos Compania SA v. Belgium* (1996) 21 E.H.R.R. 301) and will therefore attract Art. 6. See also *Osman v. United Kingdom* (2000) 29 E.H.R.R. 245.
[74] *British American Tobacco Co. Ltd v. Netherlands* (1996) 21 E.H.R.R. 409.
[75] *Krcmár v. Czech Republic*, Application No. 35376/97 (3.3.00).
[76] *Allan Jacobbson v. Sweden (No 2)*, Application No. 16970/90, Judgment February 19, 1998, para. 39.
[77] *Fayed v. United Kingdom* (1994) 18 E.H.R.R. 393.
[78] *Uppal v. United Kingdom* (1981) 3 E.H.R.R. 391.
[79] *Koseck v. Germany* (1987) 9 E.H.R.R. 328; *Neigel v. France* [1997] E.H.R.L.R. 424; *Argento v. Italy* (1999) 28 E.H.R.R. 719.
[80] *Pierre-Bloch v. France* (1998) 26 E.H.R.R. 202.
[81] (1992) 14 E.H.R.R. 597, para. 40.
[81A] Application No. 44759/98, July 12, 2001.

head if the outcome was decisive for civil rights and obligations,[81B] this was not the case in tax disputes, despite the pecuniary effects which they necessarily produced for the taxpayer.

The term "civil right" in Article 6 is not necessarily co-extensive with what **3.58** domestic law would classify as a civil right[82] or a private law right. For example, an application for judicial review may amount to litigation about a "civil right or obligation" and proceedings relating to certain contributory welfare benefits also amount to civil rights by falling within the scope of "property" in Article 1 of the First Protocol.[83] However, public law rights such as the categorisation of prisoners[84] or decisions concerning the admission or exclusion of immigrants[85] are not defined as "civil rights". In *Rasmussen v. Denmark,*[86] despite an element of public interest, a paternity suit was considered civil in nature. In *McMichael v. United Kingdom,*[87] where a father had not taken steps to obtain legal recognition of his status as father, care proceedings involving his child did not involve the determination of his "civil rights". Decisions regarding public employment have not generally been held to concern "civil rights",[88] save possibly where breach of another Convention right is in play. In *Vogt v. Germany,*[89] the European Court held that a civil servant's complaint relating to dismissal from civil service employment could amount to a civil right in the context of freedom of expression.[90] The European Court sought to end the uncertainty surrounding the application of Article 6(1) to disputes between States and employees in the public sector over their conditions of service *Pellegrin v. France.*[90A] It established an autonomous interpretation of the term "civil service" which would make it possible to afford equal treatment to public servants performing equivalent or similar duties, irrespective of the domestic system of employment and, in particular, whatever the nature of the legal relation between the official and the administrative authority. In so doing, it adopted a functional criterion based on the nature of the employee's duties and responsibilities. It held that the only disputes excluded from the scope of Article 6(1) are those which are raised by public servants whose duties typify the specific activities of the public service insofar as the latter is acting as the depositary of public authority responsible for protecting the general interests of the State or other public authorities (*e.g.* the armed forces or police).[90B] In practice, the Court will ascertain in each case whether the applicant's post entails—in the light of the nature of the duties and responsibilities pertaining to it—direct or indirect participation in the exercise of powers conferred by public law and duties designed to safeguard the general interests of the State and/or

---

[81B] See further para. 3.58 below.
[82] *James v. United Kingdom* (1986) 8 E.H.R.R. 123.
[83] *Gaygusuz v. Austria* (1997) 23 E.H.R.R. 364.
[84] *Brady v. United Kingdom* (1981) 3 E.H.R.R. 297.
[85] *Uppal v. United Kingdom* (1981) 3 E.H.R.R. 391.
[86] (1985) 7 E.H.R.R. 371, para.32.
[87] (1995) 20 E.H.R.R. 205.
[88] *Koseck v. Germany* (1987) 9 E.H.R.R. 328; *Neigel v. France* [1997] E.H.R.L.R. 424; *Balfour v. United Kingdom* [1997] E.H.R.L.R. 665.
[89] (1996) 21 E.H.R.R. 205.
[90] See also *Neigel v. France* (2000) 30 E.H.R.R. 310.
[90A] (2001) 31 E.H.R.R. 651.
[90B] At para. 66.

other public authorities. In so doing, the Court will have regard, for guidance, to the categories of activities and posts listed by the E.C. Commission in its Communication of March 18, 1988 and by the European Court of Justice.[90C] Disputes concerning pensions all come within the ambit of Article 6(1) because on retirement employees break the special bond between themselves and the authorities.[90D] However, private employment rights are generally "civil" in character. In *Helle v. Finland*,[91] the applicant and his employer, a parish, were in dispute over his claim to have held a full-time post and to be entitled to the remuneration and related financial benefits associated with such a post. The rights invoked by the applicant were pecuniary in nature and fell within the category of "civil" rights, despite the administrative nature of the proceedings in issue. The European Commission which is part of the E.C. Institutions has held that directly effective Community rights are not civil rights and obligations because a general treaty provision providing for freedom of movement is of a "public law nature, having regard to the origin and general nature of the provision, which lacks the economic or individual aspects which are characteristic to the private law sphere".[91A] This decision is surprising and perhaps open to question.

3.59 Civil rights and obligations include matters outside the sphere of courts or tribunals. Licensing and withdrawal of licenses or permits by regulatory authorities,[92] the granting or refusal of planning permission, decisions about social security, welfare benefits and pensions may all amount to determinations concerning civil rights and obligations. Professional disciplinary proceedings regulating the right to practice a profession concern civil rights and must conform to Article 6(1) of the Convention.[93]

"Determination"

3.60 Article 6(1) also requires a *"contestation"* or dispute concerning the particular civil right or obligation in question. Such a dispute may include preliminary issues, issues of liability or quantum and issues solely as to costs. Proceedings are not determinative of a civil right or obligation if they merely constitute a preliminary investigative stage[94] or form part of an administrative process.[95] The requirement that there be a dispute (contestation) over a civil right in order to bring Article 6(1) into play has been construed to cover not only disputes concerning the scope of a right but also its very existence under domestic law.[96] In *Aït-Mouhoub v. France*,[97]

[90C] *ibid.*
[90D] At para. 67.
[91] (1998) 26 E.H.R.R. 159.
[91A] *Adams and Benn v. United Kingdom* (1997) 23 E.H.R.R. CD160 at 165.
[92] See, *e.g. Håkansson and Sturesson v. Sweden* (1991) 13 E.H.R.R. 1, Application No. 11855/85, February 21, 1990; *Pudas v. Sweden* (1988) 10 E.H.R.R. 380 (dispute over revocation of taxi licence subject to Art. 6); *Benthem v. Netherlands* (1986) 8 E.H.R.R. 1.
[93] *Konig v. Germany* (1980) 2 E.H.R.R. 170; *Wickramsinghe v. United Kingdom* [1998] E.H.R.L.R. 338; *Gautrin v. France* (1999) 28 E.H.R.R. 196. See further para. 17.106 and Chap. 20.
[94] *Fayed v. United Kingdom* (1994) 18 E.H.R.R. 393.
[95] *R v. Lord Chancellor, ex p. Lightfoot* [2000] 2 W.L.R. 318, CA; [1999] 2 W.L.R. 1126, Laws J.
[96] *Ashingdane v. United Kingdom* (1985) 7 E.H.R.R. 528.
[97] (2000) 30 E.H.R.R. 382.

in determining the applicability of Article 6(1), the court asked itself whether there was a dispute over a "civil right" which could be "said, at least on arguable grounds to be recognised under domestic law" and whether the proceedings were "directly decisive" of that right.[98]

Article 6(1) "does not in itself guarantee any particular content for the **3.61** 'rights and obligations' in the substantive law of the Contracting States". A civil right or obligation only attracts Article 6(1) when it is "recognised" by national law. In *Powell and Rayner v. United Kingdom*,[99] the applicant residents of property near Heathrow did not have a substantive right under domestic law to obtain relief for exposure to aircraft noise where the aircraft conformed with reasonable height requirements and navigation regulations, as a result of an express exclusion of liability for nuisance and trespass by statute. In *Fayed v. United Kingdom*[1] the European Court acknowledged that it is:

> "not always an easy matter to trace the dividing line between procedural and substantive limitations of a given entitlement under domestic law. It may sometimes be no more than a question of legislative technique whether a limitation is expressed in terms of the right or its remedy."

Further, a rule may be characterised either as one which initially defines the scope of a substantive right, which would fall outside the scope of Article 6(1) or alternatively as a rule which seeks to limit a substantive right.[1A]

The Article 6(1) rights

The procedural rights expressly conferred by Article 6(1) are: **3.62**

    (1) the right to a fair hearing;

    (2) the right to a public hearing except to the extent that (a) it is strictly necessary where publicity would prejudice the interests of justice or in the interests of (b) morals (c) public order (d) national security (e) juveniles or (f) the protection of the private life of the parties;

    (3) the right to a hearing within a reasonable time;

---

[98] By contrast Judge de Meyer argued that anyone who believes, rightly or wrongly, that he is entitled to assert a right must be able to put his case before a court, even if only to be told that he is mistaken. See also *R. v. Secretary of State for Education and Employment, ex p. B, T & C, The Times*, June 8, 2001, QBD (Article 6 not applicable to a school independent appeal panel's exclusion proceedings because they were not directly decisive of the civil law right to the enjoyment of reputation).

[99] (1990) 12 E.H.R.R. 355. See also *W v. United Kingdom* (1988) 10 E.H.R.R. 29: Art. 6(1) "extends only to contestations over (civil) 'rights and obligations' which can be said, at least on arguable grounds, to be recognised under domestic law: it does not in itself guarantee any particular content for (civil) 'rights and obligations' in the substantive law of the contracting states."

[1] (1994) 18 E.H.R.R. 393, para. 67.

[1A] See further the discussion of *Osman v. United Kingdom* (2000) 29 E.H.R.R. 245 and *Z v. United Kingdom*, Application No. 29392/95, May 10, 2001 at paras 10.29 *et seq.*

(4) the right to an independent and impartial tribunal established by law;

(5) public judgment.

3.63 The rights set out above are considered in detail in relation to civil procedure in Chapter 10.

3.64 The European Court has held that the object and purpose of Article 6 is "to enshrine the fundamental principle of the rule of law" and it is accordingly to be given a broad and purposive construction: *Delcourt v. Belgium*[2]; *Moreira de Azevedo Portugal*.[3] Accordingly, the European Court has extended Article 6 to encompass the following implied rights:

(1) the right of effective access to a court;

(2) the right to equality of arms;

(3) the right to effective participation in a hearing.

3.65 In the case of *Golder v. United Kingdom*,[4] the European Court held that the right of access to a court (*i.e.* the right to institute proceedings before a court in civil matters) was inherent in the notion of Article 6. This right has become an important source of Strasbourg case-law in relation to civil procedure. By implication, the right of access to a court requires regulation by the state.[5] A limitation must not restrict or reduce the access left to the individual in such a way or to such an extent that the very essence of the right is impaired. Furthermore, a limitation will not be compatible with Article 6(1) unless (1) the aim of the limitation is legitimate and (2) there is a reasonable relationship of proportionality between the means employed and the aim sought to be achieved.[6]

3.66 Legitimate restrictions on the right of access include restrictions on access to the courts by, for example prisoners[7] or the mentally ill[8] and limitation periods.[9] A fuller discussion of the impact of Article 6 on civil procedure is set out at Chapter 10, on evidence at Chapter 11 and on other forms of dispute resolution at Chapter 12.

3.67 In *Airey v. Ireland*,[10] the European Court considered whether the right of access to domestic courts included the existence of civil legal aid and held that Article 6 may sometimes compel the state to provide for the assistance of a lawyer when such assistance proves indispensable for an effective access to the court, either because legal representation is rendered compulsory, as is done by the domestic law of certain Contracting States, or by reason of the complexity of the procedure of the case. The

---

[2] (1979) 1 E.H.R.R. 355, para. 25.
[3] (1991) 13 E.H.R.R. 721, para. 66.
[4] (1979) 1 E.H.R.R. 524.
[5] *Stubbings v. United Kingdom* (1997) 23 E.H.R.R. 213.
[6] *Ashingdane v. United Kingdom* (1985) 7 E.H.R.R. 528. See also *Omar v. France* (2000) 29 E.H.R.R. 210.
[7] *Golder v. United Kingdom* (1979) 1 E.H.R.R. 524.
[8] *Winterwerp v. Netherlands* (1980) 2 E.H.R.R. 387.
[9] *Stubbings v. United Kingdom* (1997) 23 E.H.R.R. 213.
[10] (1980) 2 E.H.R.R. 305.

Court found that Mrs Airey needed provision of free legal representation to enable her to properly present her case in an emotionally charged and legally complex judicial separation dispute, involving issues of child custody.[11]

In *Fayed v. United Kingdom*,[12] where it was alleged that publication of a   **3.68** report by DTI investigators had resulted in determination of civil rights without access to a civil court, the European Court stated[13]:

" . . . it would not be consistent with the rule of law in a democratic society or with the basic principle underlying Article 6(1) if a State could without restraint remove from the jurisdiction of the courts a whole range of civil claims, or confer immunities from civil liability on large groups or categories of persons."

This quotation reveals the expansive approach of the European Court to protection of the right of access to a court.

In *Osman v. United Kingdom*,[14] the European Court of Human Rights   **3.69** found that the application of the domestic principle of law that it was not fair, just and reasonable to impose liability on the police for negligence arising in the investigation and suppression of crime[15] where foreseeability and proximity were established was a disproportionate limitation on the applicant's right of access to a court. The European Court expressly resiled from this position in *Z v. United Kingdom*,[16] conceding that the striking out of the cases where it was not fair, just and reasonable to impose a duty of care was a matter of substantive domestic law and did not violate Article 6(1). However, it notably did not overrule *Osman* and went on to find that, following the striking out of the claim, there was a violation of Article 13 in that no effective remedy existed for a breach of the applicants' Convention rights.[17] Article 6(1) also has ramifications for any domestic law that confers an immunity or operates as a general exclusionary rule in relation to a particular type of claim.[18]

The right to "equality of arms" requires a fair balance between the parties   **3.70** and applies to both civil and criminal proceedings.[19] In *Dombo Beheer BV v. Netherlands*,[20] the European Court of Human Rights stated:

---

[11] See further paras 12.27 *et seq.* on legal aid.
[12] (1994) 18 E.H.R.R. 393.
[13] At para 65.
[14] (2000) 29 E.H.R.R. 245.
[15] Often termed "public interest (or policy) immunity", derived from *Hill v. Chief Constable of West Yorkshire* [1989] A.C. 53, HL.
[16] Application No. 29392/95, May 10, 2001; *The Times*, May 31, 2001. See also *T.P. and K.M. v. United Kingdom* Application No. 28945/95, May 10, 2001; *The Times*, May 31, 2001.
[17] See further paras 10.43 *et seq.* and para. 17.
[18] See also *Tinnelly & Sons Ltd and McElduff v. United Kingdom* (1999) 27 E.H.R.R. 249 where the issue by the Secretary of State for Northern Ireland of certificates under the Fair Employment (Northern Ireland) Act conclusively certifying that the decision not to grant the applicants tender contracts was an act done for the purpose of safeguarding national security or the protection of public safety or order had the effect of preventing a judicial determination on the merits of the applicants' complaints and the limitation was disproportionate to the aim to be achieved. See further paras 17.41 *et seq.*, below.
[19] *Neumeister v. Austria* (1979) 1 E.H.R.R. 91.
[20] (1994) 18 E.H.R.R. 213, para. 33.

" . . . equality of arms implies that each party must be afforded a reasonable opportunity to present his case—including his evidence—under conditions that do not place him at a substantial disadvantage vis-à-vis his opponent."[21]

3.71 The right to participate effectively in proceedings extends not only to the right to be present but also to the right to hear and follow the proceedings: *Stanford v. United Kingdom.*[22]

Legal certainty and Article 6(1)

3.72 There is no general principle under Article 6(1) that changes in civil law should not operate retrospectively. While certainty of law is required, absolute certainty is not required and the European Court stated in *Sunday Times v. United Kingdom*[23]:

" . . . a norm cannot be regarded as 'law' unless it is formulated with sufficient precision to enable the citizen to regulate his conduct: he must be able—if need be with appropriate advice—to foresee, to a degree that is reasonable in the circumstances, the consequences which a given action may entail.

. . . whilst certainty is highly desirable, it may bring in its train excessive rigidity and the law must be able to keep pace with changing circumstances. Accordingly, many laws are inevitably couched in terms which, to a greater or lesser extent, are vague and whose interpretation and application are questions of practice."[24]

3.73 The European Court decided that the change in the law made by the House of Lords, even though it applied with retrospective effect in the proceedings before the Court, did not in itself infringe the European Convention.

3.74 Changing the law retrospectively was held to be a breach of Article 6(1) in the case of *Stran Greek Refineries v. Greece*[25] where the Greek Government legislated so as to render an arbitral award in favour of the applicant invalid. However, in *National Provincial Building Society v. United Kingdom*[26] the European Court refused to find a breach of Article 6 where legislation retrospectively remedied a tax loophole and the applicants were seeking to take advantage of a technicality. In *Zielinski v. France,*[26A] the European Court stated that while in principle the legislature is not precluded in civil matters from adopting new retrospective provisions to regulate rights arising under existing laws, the principle of the rule of law

---

[21] See further paras 10.81 *et seq.*, below.
[22] Application No. 16757/90, February 23, 1994. See also paras 10.79 *et seq.*
[23] (1980) 2 E.H.R.R. 245.
[24] At para. 47.
[25] (1995) 19 E.H.R.R. 293.
[26] (1998) 25 E.H.R.R. 127.
[26A] (2001) 31 E.H.R.R. 532.

and the notion of fair trial enshrined in Article 6 preclude any interference by the legislature—other than on compelling grounds of the general interest—with the administration of justice designed to influence the judicial determination of a dispute.[26B]

Waiver of Article 6(1) rights

A litigant may be held to have waived certain of his Article 6(1) rights, and in particular, the right to a public hearing,[27] the right to a determination of all issues of fact as well as law[28] and (possibly) the right to an independent and impartial tribunal.[29] The European Court has held that to be effective, a waiver must be made in an unequivocal manner, without undue compulsion[30] and "must not run counter to any important public interest".[31] Where an implied waiver is alleged, the issue to be addressed is whether it was reasonable to expect the litigant to have taken his complaint up at an earlier stage.[32]   **3.75**

Criminal proceedings

The rights guaranteed by Article 6(1) apply to proceedings which involve the determination of a criminal charge. The classification of proceedings in domestic law as criminal is conclusive. If proceedings are classified as civil in nature, this is not determinative. Proceedings may be found to involve the determination of a criminal charge by reference to three criteria: **3.76**

(1) the classification in domestic law;

(2) the nature of the offence or conduct in question; and

(3) the severity of any possible penalty.[33]

If a domestic court can impose imprisonment, this will generally be sufficient to define the proceedings as "criminal" unless the "nature, duration   **3.77**

[26B] At para. 57.
[27] *Le Compte, Van Leuven and De Meyere v. Belgium* (1982) 4 E.H.R.R. 1; *Albert and Le Compte v. Belgium* (1983) 5 E.H.R.R. 533; *Pauger v. Austria* (1998) 25 E.H.R.R. 105; *H v. Belgium* (1988) 10 E.H.R.R. 339; *Håkansson and Sturesson v. Sweden* (1991) 13 E.H.R.R. 1.
[28] *Air Canada v. United Kingdom* (1995) 20 E.H.R.R. 150, para. 61.
[29] *Oberschlick v. Austria (No.1)* (1995) 19 E.H.R.R. 389, *Håkansson and Sturesson v. Sweden* (1991) 13 E.H.R.R. 1 (loss of right to object to a particular tribunal); *cf. Pfeifer and Plankl v. Austria* (1992) 14 E.H.R.R. 692 (the Court doubted whether it would ever be possible for a defendant to waive the fundamental right to an independent and impartial tribunal); and *Bulut v. Austria* (1997) 24 E.H.R.R. 84 (Court considered that it had to decide whether tribunal was impartial regardless of whether applicant had unequivocally waived his rights under Art. 6).
[30] *Pfeifer and Plankl v. Austria* (1992) 14 E.H.R.R. 692, para. 37.
[31] *Håkansson and Sturesson v. Sweden* (1991) 13 E.H.R.R. 1, Application No. 11855/85, February 21, 1990, para. 66, see also para. 3.152.
[32] *McGonnell v. United Kingdom*, Application No. 28488/95, February 8, 2000, para. 44, ECHR.
[33] *Engel v. Netherlands* (1979) 1 E.H.R.R. 647.

or manner of execution of the imprisonment" is not "appreciably detrimental".[34] So, for instance, prison disciplinary proceedings[35] and contempt proceedings[36] have been held to be criminal proceedings for the purpose of Article 6, notwithstanding their domestic designation. Income tax penalty assessments[36A] and the imposition of a civil evasion penalty in respect of VAT or excise duty[36B] have been held to amount to criminal charges within Article 6(1). However, condemnation and forfeiture proceedings under section 139 Customs and Excise Management Act 1979 were not.[36C] The interview and interrogation of a suspect prior to formal charge does not amount to a criminal charge for the purpose of Article 6(1).[36D] In *R. v. Securities and Futures Authority, ex parte Fleurose*[36E] a decision of the Securities and Futures Authority Disciplinary Appeal Panel was held to be civil, rather than criminal, in nature. Although the SFA rules had punitive features, in that an individual in breach might be liable for an unlimited fine or disqualification, the SFA disciplinary system was not applicable to the public at large, there was no risk of imprisonment and no state involvement.

3.78 The same express rights set out at paragraph 3.62 above equally apply to criminal proceedings. If an applicant is unable to participate effectively in criminal proceedings, there will be a violation of the right to a fair hearing in Article 6(1).[37]

Right against self-incrimination

3.79 Although there is no express reference to the privilege against self-incrimination in relation to criminal proceedings, the European Court has implied this right into Article 6(1). In *Saunders v. United Kingdom*,[38] the Court held that the right not to incriminate oneself was a generally recognised international standard which lay at the heart of the notion of a fair trial under Article 6. The right, together with the right to silence, presupposed that the prosecution must prove its case without resorting to evidence obtained through methods of coercion and oppression of the accused. In *Funke v. France*,[39] the Court held that by attempting to compel the applicant to produce incriminating evidence, namely bank statements relevant to investigations into customs offences that might have been committed by him, the applicant's right to silence and right not to incrimi-

---

[34] *Engel v. Netherlands* (1979) 1 E.H.R.R. 647, para. 82.
[35] *Campbell & Fell v. United Kingdom* (1985) 7 E.H.R.R. 165; cf. *McFeeley v. United Kingdom* (1981) 3 E.H.R.R. 161. See also *Greenfield v. Secretary of State for the Home Department, The Times*, March 6, 2001, DC; *R. v. Carroll, ex p. Secretary of State for the Home Department*, unreported, February 16, 2001, Admin Ct (adjudications relating to prisoners not legal proceedings but disciplinary proceedings).
[36] *Harman v. United Kingdom* (1984) 38 D.R. 53, Application No. 10038/82. See also *Benham v. United Kingdom* (1996) 22 E.H.R.R. 293 in relation to committal proceedings.
[36A] *King v. Walden (HMIT) The Times*, June 12, 2001, Ch.D.
[36B] *Han & Yau v. Customs & Excise Commissioners, The Independent*, July 5, 2001, CA.
[36C] *Goldsmith v. Customs & Excise Commissioners, The Times*, June 12, 2001, DC.
[36D] *Attorney-General's Reference (No. 2 of 2001), The Times*, July 12, 2001, CA.
[36E] *The Times*, May 15, 2001, Admin. Ct.
[37] *V v. United Kingdom and T v. United Kingdom* (2000) 30 E.H.R.R. 121.
[38] (1997) 23 E.H.R.R. 313.
[39] (1993) 16 E.H.R.R. 297.

nate himself had been infringed.[40] The right only applies to the self-incrimination in *criminal* proceedings.[41]

Article 6(2) presumption of innocence

The presumption of innocence enshrined in Article 6(2) affects issues such **3.80** as pre-trial publicity, the burden and standard of proof in criminal cases,[42] adducing evidence of previous convictions and costs in criminal cases. Article 6(2) requires that, when carrying out their duties, the members of a court should not start with the preconceived idea that the accused has committed the offence charged. The burden of proof is on the prosecution and any doubt should benefit the accused: *Barbara, Messegue and Jabardo v. Spain.*[43] Article 6(2) continues to apply until the end of any appeal proceedings against conviction. It deals only with proof of guilt and does not apply to either trial or appellate proceedings in so far as they concern sentencing of a convicted person: *Engel v. Netherlands.*[44]

The presumption of innocence may be violated not only by a judge or **3.81** court, but also by other public authorities (*Allenet de Ribemont v. France*),[45] and by legislators (*Salabiaku v. France*).[46] However, under the HRA 1998 which incorporates the majority of the rights and freedoms in the Convention into domestic law, the passing of primary legislation or the failure to pass legislation is not "unlawful" under section 6(1) of the Act or actionable under the new statutory cause of action against public authorities who act incompatibly with Convention rights created by section 7 of the Act (see section 6(1), (3), (6)).

Presumptions of fact or law

Presumptions of fact or of law are not prohibited in principle under Article **3.82** 6(2) of the Convention since they operate in every legal system. However,

[40] See also *Serves v. France* (1999) 28 E.H.R.R. 265; *Heaney and McGuinness v. Ireland*, Application No. 34720/97, December 21, 2000. Note that the ECJ has distinguished between factual information that is accessible from elsewhere (*e.g.* public records) or is pre-existing and information which does not pre-exist and might be treated as a confession, regarding the latter as self-incriminating: *Case 374/87, Orkem SA v. Commission* [1989] E.C.R. 3283; [1991] 4 C.M.L.R. 502, ECJ. The ECHR has adopted a similar approach to real evidence such as intimate samples—see further paras 11.22 *et seq.*, below. However, in *Funke* above, it appears to have regarded the obligation to compel production of incriminating documents as contrary to the right against self-incrimination. The case-law on this point is not consistent. See further para. 11.20 below.

[41] *Abas v. Netherlands* [1997] E.H.R.L.R. 418.

[42] See, *e.g.*, *R. v. Director of Public Prosecutions, ex p. Kebilene* [1999] 3 W.L.R. 972, HL; *Stott (Procurator Fiscal, Dunfermline) v. Brown* [2001] 2 W.L.R. 817, *The Times*, December 6, 2000, PC. See also *Telfner v. Austria* Application No. 33501/96, March 20, 2001 (violation of Article 6(2) where conviction for causing injury by negligence during a road traffic accident. The domestic courts had relied on a police report that the applicant was the main user of the car and that he had not been home on the night of the accident but the victim of the accident had not been able to identify the driver). In *R. v. Lambert* [2001] UKHL 37, July 5, 2001, the House of Lords held that if section 28(2) Misuse of Drugs Act 1971 which placed a burden on the accused to prove that he did not know that he was in possession of a controlled drug would infringe Article 6(2) if it imposed a legal burden. However, the section could and should be read, if necessary under s.3(1) HRA, as imposing merely an evidential burden and the words "to prove" should be read instead as "to give sufficient evidence".

[43] (1989) 11 E.H.R.R. 360, para. 77.

[44] (1979) 1 E.H.R.R. 706, para. 90.

[45] (1995) 20 E.H.R.R. 557, para. 36.

[46] (1991) 13 E.H.R.R. 379.

the Convention does require Contracting States to confine presumptions in the criminal law context:

> "within reasonable limits which take into account the importance of what is at stake and maintain the rights of the defence."[47]

3.83 In *Salabiaku v. France*,[48] the applicant had been caught with 10kg of cannabis in his luggage at an airport and claimed to have no knowledge of the drugs. He was convicted under French law, which contained a presumption that a person who is in possession of drugs in such circumstances was presumed to be guilty of smuggling unless he proved that it was impossible for him to have known that they were in his possession. The European Court found that the presumption did not breach Article 6(2). However, the court had concluded from the evidence, regardless of the presumption, that the applicant knew what was contained in his luggage.[49] The factors that the Court is likely to take into account in determining whether a presumption of fact or law is in violation of Article 6(2) are:

(1) whether the presumption was rebuttable;

(2) whether the court resorted automatically to the presumption or diligently assessed the matter on the basis of all the evidence before them including looking for evidence that might rebut the presumption;

(3) the strength of the case against the accused, leaving aside the presumption;

(4) whether the accused is afforded a defence or means of exculpating himself;

(5) whether the presumption is so widely worded as to amount to a presumption of guilt either in form or in substance and effect;

(6) whether the subject-matter of the presumption is peculiarly within the knowledge of the accused and is accordingly difficult for the prosecution to prove to the required standard of proof;

---

[47] *Salabiaku, ibid.* para.28.
[48] (1991) 13 E.H.R.R. 379.
[49] See also *X v. United Kingdom* (1972) 42 C.D. 135, where the European Commission upheld a rebuttable presumption that a man proved to be living with or controlling a prostitute was living off immoral earnings. The Commission noted that a presumption must not be so widely or unreasonably worded as to amount to a presumption of guilt. In *G v. Malta*, Application No. 16641/90, December 10, 1991, the European Commission held that a presumption that a company director was guilty of an offence committed by the company unless he proved that the offence was committed without his knowledge and that he exercised all due diligence to prevent the commission of the offence was not inconsistent with Art. 6(2). The Commission attached importance to the fact that the applicant was provided under the legislation with the possibility of exculpating himself. See also *Phillips v. United Kingdom*, Application No. 41087/98, November 30, 2000 (complaint under Article 6(2) relating to presumption in Drug Trafficking Act 1994 that property held by defendant since conviction was received as a benefit of drug trafficking declared admissible). Domestic decisions include *R. v. Director of Public Prosecutions, ex p. Kebilene* [1999] 3 W.L.R. 972, HL; *R. v. Lambert; R. v. Ali; R. v. Jordan, The Times*, September 5, 2000, CA.

(7) the standard of proof on the defence in rebutting the presumption.

Article 6(3)

Article 6(3) sets out a number of specific guarantees in criminal pro- **3.84**
ceedings:

(1) information about the charge;

(2) adequate time and facilities to prepare a defence;

(3) the right to legal aid and legal representation where the interests of justice so require;

(4) the right to call and cross-examine witnesses;

(5) the right to interpretation.

Article 6(3)(a) guarantees prompt, intelligible notification of charges in a **3.85**
language the accused can understand, so that he knows the case against
him.[50]

Article 6(3)(b) requires that the accused have adequate time and facilities **3.86**
to be able to properly prepare his defence.[51]

Article 6(3)(c) confers the right to legal representation of the accused's **3.87**
choosing and legal aid in criminal proceedings if the accused is without
sufficient means and the interests of justice so require.[52] However, a
person also has the right to defend himself if he so chooses.

Article 6(3)(d) protects the right to attendance of witnesses and their **3.88**
examination. Article 6(3)(e) guarantees the right to an interpreter in the
accused's native language where he does not speak or cannot understand
the language used by the court or tribunal. The assistance of an interpreter
should be provided free without the payment of the costs incurred being
claimed back from the accused.[53]

Article 7 (No Punishment Without Law)

Article 7 of the Convention provides: **3.89**

"(1) No one shall be held guilty of any criminal offence on account of
any act or omission which did not constitute a criminal offence under
national or international law at the time when it was committed. Nor

---

[50] *Brozicek v. Italy* (1990) 12 E.H.R.R. 371; *Pelissier and Sassi v. France* (2000) 30 E.H.R.R. 715.
[51] See *Jespers v. Belgium* (1981) 27 D.R. 61, Application No. 8403/78; *Pelissier and Sassi v. France* (2000) 30 E.H.R.R. 715.
[52] See *Benham v. United Kingdom* (1996) 22 E.H.R.R. 293; *Murray v. United Kingdom* (1996) 22 E.H.R.R. 29; *Granger v. United Kingdom* (1990) 12 E.H.R.R. 469; and *Daud v. Portugal* (2000) 30 E.H.R.R. 400. See also *R. v. Commissioner of Police for the Metropolis, ex p. M & Leon La Rose*, unreported July 13, 2001, Div. Ct (there was no breach of Article 6(3)(c) where the lack of a consultation room at every police station and facilities for private phone calls to be made for legal consultations did not result in a denial of adequate facilities for the preparation of the defence).
[53] *Akdogan v. Germany*, Application No. 11394/85, July 5, 1988.

shall a heavier penalty be imposed than the one that was applicable at the time the criminal offence was committed.

(2) This article shall not prejudice the trial and punishment of any person for any act or omission which, at the time when it was committed, was criminal according to the general principles of law recognised by civilized nations."

3.90   The meaning of "criminal offence" under Article 7 is consonant with the meaning of "criminal charge" under Article 6.[53A] Save in relation to the classification of civil proceedings as criminal, for example contempt of court proceedings, Article 7 has no application in civil cases.

3.91   Article 7(1) enshrines two principles:

> (1) A prohibition on the retrospective application of criminal law: the law in question must have existed at the time of the act which is the subject of the offence is based for the conviction to be based on it;

> (2) No heavier penalty for the infringement of the law may be imposed than was in force at the time the act was committed.

Article 7 embodies, *inter alia*, the principle that only the law can define a crime and prescribe a penalty and the principle that the criminal law must not be extensively construed to an accused's detriment, for instance by analogy. It follows that an offence and the sanctions for it must be clearly defined in the law.[53B] When speaking of "law", Article 7 alludes to the same concept as that to which the Convention elsewhere refers when using that term, a concept which comprises statutory law as well as case law and implies qualitative requirements, notaby those of accessibility and foreseeability.[53C]

3.92   The second principle above was breached in *Welch v. United Kingdom*[54] where a new provision of the Drug Trafficking Offences Act 1986 relating to confiscation orders (which was classified as a penalty) came into effect after the applicant's arrest. In *Gough & Smith v. Chief Constable of Derbyshire*,[54A] the Divisional Court held that court should follow the guidance in *Welch* in applying Article 7 and as to the nature of a penalty under Article 7(2).

3.93   Article 7(2) is intended to exclude laws which were passed at the end of the Second World War to punish war crimes and treason.

Article 8 (Right to Respect for Private and Family Life, Home and Correspondence)

3.94   Article 8 of the Convention states:

> "(1) Everyone has the right to respect for his private and family life, his home and his correspondence.

[53A] See paras 3.76 *et seq.* above.
[53B] *Baskaya and Okçuoglu v. Turkey* (2001) 31 E.H.R.R. 292, para. 36. See also paras 4.43 *et seq.* below.
[53C] *ibid.*
[54] (1995) 20 E.H.R.R. 247.
[54A] unreported, July 13, 2001, Div. Ct.

(2) There shall be no interference by a public authority with the exercise of this right except such as is in accordance with the law and is necessary in a democratic society in the interests of national security, public safety or the economic well-being of the country, for the prevention of disorder or crime, for the protection of health or morals, or for the protection of the rights and freedoms of others."

Article 8 protects the right to a person's private and family life, home and **3.95** correspondence.[54B] The right is engaged in a wide range of contexts from surveillance of an individual to use of confidential information, from the right to practice one's sexuality to the right to protection from a noise nuisance. The essential effect of Article 8 is to protect the individual from arbitrary action by state authorities: *Kroon v. Netherlands.*[55]

Article 8 has vertical effect in that it restrains infringements of privacy by a **3.96** public authority. It does not *prima facie* apply between individuals.[55A] However, the Court has held that Article 8 imposes not just a negative obligation to refrain from interference but also a positive obligation to secure an effective respect for private life.[56]

In *Niemietz v. Germany,*[57] the European Court held that the concept of **3.97** "private life" went beyond the right to live one's own personal life as one chooses and encompassed the right to establish and develop relationships with other human beings. Private life also encompasses the right to protect one's physical and moral integrity,[58] the right to determine one's identity (including one's name,[59] dress[60] and sexual orientation), the right to prevent intrusion or revelations about one's private life[61]; the right to personal or private space[62] and the right to respect for sexual identity, orientation[63] and relations.[64] The storage and use of data relating to the "private life" of an individual also falls within the application of Article 8(1).[65]

The meaning of "family life" is a question of fact and depends upon "the **3.98** real existence in practice of close personal ties".[66] It extends beyond

---

[54B] See also paras 16.20 *et seq.*
[55] (1995) 19 E.H.R.R. 263.
[55A] See discussion of vertical and horizontal effect at paras 5.15 *et seq.*
[56] *X & Y v. Netherlands* (1986) 8 E.H.R.R. 235, para. 23; *Johnston v. Ireland* (1987) 9 E.H.R.R. 203, para. 55. See the protection given to the right to respect for private life in English law post-HRA set out in *Douglas v. Hello ! Ltd* [2001] 2 W.L.R. 992, CA, especially the judgment of Sedley L.J. See also paras 5.28 *et seq.* on positive obligations.
[57] (1993) 16 E.H.R.R. 97.
[58] *Costello-Roberts v. United Kingdom* (1995) 19 E.H.R.R. 112 (corporal punishment by school—insufficiently adverse to amount to violation of Art. 8); *A v. United Kingdom* (1998) 5 B.H.R.C.137 (corporal punishment by stepfather with cane—violation of Art. 8)
[59] *Gaskin v. United Kingdom* (1990) 12 E.H.R.R. 36; *Burghartz and Burghartz v. Switzerland* (1994) 18 E.H.R.R. 101.
[60] *McFeeley v. United Kingdom* (1980) 20 D.R. 44, para. 91.
[61] *Winer v. United* Kingdom (1986) 48 D.R. 154, Application No. 10871/84; *Earl Spencer and Countess Spencer v. United Kingdom* (1998) 25 E.H.R.R. CD 105. See also *Sheffield and Horsham v. United Kingdom* (1999) 27 E.H.R.R. 163 (inquiries about pre-operative status of transsexual).
[62] *Niemietz v. Germany* (1993) 16 E.H.R.R. 97.
[63] *Dudgeon v. United Kingdom* (1982) 4 E.H.R.R.149; *Sutherland v. United Kingdom* [1998] E.H.R.L.R. 117 (homosexuals); *Cossey v. United Kingdom* (1991) 13 E.H.R.R. 622; *Sheffield & Horsham v. United Kingdom* (1999) 27 E.H.R.R. 163 (transsexuals).
[64] *Dudgeon, ibid. Jaggard & Brown v. United Kingdom* (1997) 24 E.H.R.R. 39, para.36.
[65] *Amann v. Switzerland* (2000) 30 E.H.R.R. 843, paras 65–71.
[66] *K v. United Kingdom* (1986) 50 D.R. 199, para. 207, Application Nos. 11468/85.

husband and wife and parent and (biological or adopted[67]) child to co-habiting adults[68] and step-parents, grandparents and grandchildren[69] and other relatives, provided sufficiently close ties can be shown. A foster family relationship may potentially constitute "family life".[70] A homosexual[71] or transsexual[72] relationship may also come within "family life". Article 8 does not give a right to create a family by the conception of a child through artificial insemination.[73]

3.99 The "home" has been construed to cover a range of accommodation provided that a sufficient degree of connection and permanence is established.[74] In *Niemietz*,[75] the Court also held that the protections granted by Article 8 may extend to certain business or professional activities. The right to respect for a "home" also involves the ability to live freely in it and enjoy it, not merely possess it.[76] This has implications for the tort of nuisance,[77] property, planning and environmental law.[78]

3.100 "Correspondence" includes other communications and Article 8 may be breached if a public authority keeps an individual under surveillance,[79] taps his telephone,[80] reads or intercepts correspondence[81] or collects and maintains information about him or her.[82] It extends to both private and some business communications.[83] Communications between an individual and his legal advisers attracts a high degree of protection.[84]

3.101 The rights conferred by Article 8 may be expressly limited or restricted on the grounds set out in Article 8(2), namely:

    (1) national security;

    (2) public safety;

    (3) the economic well-being of the country;

    (4) the prevention of disorder or crime;

---

[67] See *Söderbäck v. Sweden* (2000) 29 E.H.R.R. 95; *McMichael v. United Kingdom* (1995) 20 E.H.R.R. 205.
[68] See, *e.g. Kroon v. Netherlands* (1995) 19 E.H.R.R. 263.
[69] See *Bronda v. Italy*, Application No.22430/93, June 9, 1998.
[70] *Gaskin v. United Kingdom* (1990) 12 E.H.R.R. 36.
[71] *B v. United Kingdom* (1990) 64 DR 278, Application No. 16106/90.
[72] *X, Y & Z v. United Kingdom* (1997) 24 E.H.R.R. 143. See also *Bellinger v. Bellinger & HM Attorney-General*, unreported, July 17, 2001, CA (the law did not allow the court to declare a transsexual marriage as valid and subsisting).
[73] *R. (Mellor) v. Secretary of State for the Home Department* [2000] 2 F.L.R. 951.
[74] *Gillow v. United Kingdom* (1989) 11 E.H.R.R. 335.
[75] (1993) 16 E.H.R.R. 97.
[76] *Lopez Ostra v. Spain* (1995) 20 E.H.R.R. 277; *Guerra v. Italy* (1998) 26 E.H.R.R. 357.
[77] See paras 16.148 *et seq.*, below.
[78] See, *e.g. Guerra v. Italy* (1998) 26 E.H.R.R. 357; *Lopez-Ostra v. Italy* (1995) 20 E.H.R.R. 277.
[79] *Klass v. Germany* (1980) 2 E.H.R.R. 214. See also paras 19.52 *et seq.*
[80] *Malone v. United Kingdom* (1985) 7 E.H.R.R. 14.
[81] See, *e.g. Campbell v. United Kingdom* (1993) 15 E.H.R.R. 137.
[82] See, *e.g. Murray v. United Kingdom* (1995) 19 E.H.R.R. 193.
[83] *Halford v. United Kingdom* (1997) 24 E.H.R.R. 523.
[84] *Golder v. United Kingdom* (1979) 1 E.H.R.R. 524; *Campbell v. United Kingdom* (1993) 15 E.H.R.R. 137; *Silver v. United Kingdom* (1983) 5 E.H.R.R. 347. See further on legal confidentiality and privilege, paras 11.64 *et seq.*

(5) the protection of health or morals;

(6) the protection of the rights and freedoms of others.

If a limitation does fall within one of the Article 8(2) categories, the interference must also be

(a) "in accordance with the law",

(b) necessary in a democratic society (*i.e.* a response to a pressing social need), and

(c) proportionate to that aim (*i.e.* the interference goes no further than necessary to achieve the intended aim). Article 8(2) has been held to justify a policy of allowing babies to remain in prison with their mothers until the age of 18 months but not thereafter.[84A] The impairment of the right to family life was a consequence of the deprivation of liberty which prison involved. Promoting the welfare of prisoners' children was constrained by considerations of punishment and the need for the efficient running of and the maintenance of good order and discipline within prisons. Article 8 rights interrelate with the rights and freedoms of others particularly under Article 10 (right to freedom of expression).

Article 8 has particular relevance substantive law areas like lawyer/client **3.102** confidentiality,[85] property[86] and employment law.[87] It is also relevant to procedural issues such as search orders and injunctions,[88] and the use of evidence obtained by enquiry agents.[89]

Article 9 (Freedom of Thought, Conscience and Religion)

Article 9 of the Convention states: **3.103**

"(1) Everyone has the right to freedom of thought, conscience and religion; this right includes freedom to change his religion or belief and freedom, either alone or in community with others and in public or private, to manifest his religion or belief, in worship, teaching, practice and observance.

(2) Freedom to manifest one's religion or beliefs shall be subject only to such limitations as are prescribed by law and are necessary in a democratic society in the interests of public safety, for the protection

---

[84A] *R. (on the application of L) v. Secretary of State for the Home Department*, [2001] EWHC Admin 357, May 17, 2001, Div. Ct.
[85] See paras 11.64 *et seq.*, below.
[86] See Chap. 16 (Property, Planning and Environment).
[87] See Chap. 13 (Employment).
[88] See paras 10.61 *et seq.*, below.
[89] See paras 11.48 *et seq.*, below.

of public order, health or morals, or for the protection of the rights and freedoms of others."

3.104 Article 9 protects freedom of thought, conscience and religion. It also protects the freedom to manifest religion or belief. However, the latter right is expressly qualified by Article 9(2). Article 9 issues have arisen in relation to religious practice, prisoners' rights and pacifism.

3.105 A broad definition has been adopted to freedom of thought, conscience and religion. The right has been extended to the Muslim religion,[90] Jehovah's Witnesses,[91] the Krishna movement,[92] the Church of Scientology,[93] the Pentecostal Church,[94] Druidism,[95] pacifism[96] and veganism.[97] It includes the right of reinterment of remains in a cemetery of the deceased's faith.[98] However, the protection conferred by Article 9 does not extend to the espousal of purely idealistic or political goals, such as those of a prisoners' support group[99] or IRA prisoners claiming "special category status".[1] Protection for such groups is more squarely within Article 10 (freedom of expression). The role of State authorities is to ensure that competing religious groups tolerate each other, not to remove causes of tension where a community becomes divided by eliminating pluralism.[1A]

3.106 Freedom of religion includes freedom to change one's religion.[2] However, the maintenance of an established church is not, of itself, a violation of Article 9.[3] In relation to manifestation of religion or belief, the European institutions have sought to distinguish between conduct which directly expresses religion or belief and conduct which is only motivated by religion or belief. The former is protected. The latter is not.

3.107 The rights conferred by Article 9 may be exercised by an individual, by a church body or by an association with religious and philosophical objects, but can only be enforced by a "victim".[4] However, it may be harder for a church body or association than for an individual to establish that its activities amount to a manifestation of religion or belief.[5]

3.108 Conscientious objection to military service has been challenged under Article 9. However, such complaints have been rejected on the basis that Article 4 specifically envisages compulsory military service.[6]

---

[90] *Ahmad v. United Kingdom* (1982) 4 E.H.R.R. 126.
[91] *Kokkinakis v. Greece* (1994) 17 E.H.R.R. 397.
[92] *Iskcon v. United Kingdom* (1994) 76A D.R. 90, Application No. 20490/92.
[93] *X and Church of Scientology v. Sweden* Application No. 7805/77 (1979) 16 D.R. 68; Application No. 8282/78, (1980) 21 DR 109.
[94] *Larissis v. Greece* [1998] E.H.R.L.R. 505.
[95] *Chappell v. United Kingdom* (1987) 53 D.R. 241, Application No. 12587/86.
[96] *Arrowsmith v.United Kingdom* (1978) 19 D.R. 5, Application No. 7050/75.
[97] *X v. U.K.*, Commission, February 10, 1993, unreported.
[98] *Re Durrington Cemetery, The Times*, July 5, 2000, Consistory Ct.
[99] *Vereniging Rechtswinkels Utrecht v. Netherlands* (1986) 46 D.R. 200, Application No. 11308/84.
[1] *McFeeley v. United Kingdom* (1980) 20 D.R. 44.
[1A] *Serif v. Greece* (2001) 31 E.H.R.R. 561, para. 53.
[2] *Angelini v. Sweden* (1986) 51 D.R. 41, Application No. 10491/83.
[3] *Darby v. Sweden* (1991) 13 E.H.R.R. 774.
[4] *Chappell v. United Kingdom* (1987) 53 D.R. 241, Application No. 12587/86.
[5] *Church of X v. United Kingdom* (1969) 12 Y.B. 306.
[6] See, *e.g. Autio v. Finland* (1991) 72 D.R. 245, Application No. 17086/90.

A restriction on Article 9 rights will be compatible with the Convention only   **3.109**
if it is aimed at protecting one or more of the interests set out in Article 9(2),
namely, public safety, public order, health or morals or the rights and
freedoms of others. The list is exhaustive and each interest is to be
narrowly construed. Like Article 8, any restriction must be "prescribed by
law" and must be "necessary in a democratic society". In *McGuinness
(Martin) v. United Kingdom*,[7] the applicant was elected M.P. for a con-
stituency in Northern Ireland but refused to take the oath of allegiance to
the British monarch that M.P.s were required to swear as a condition of
taking a seat in parliament. He alleged that the requirement to swear the
oath in circumstances where the monarch was prohibited from being or
marrying a Roman Catholic was in breach of Articles 9,10 and 13. The
Court ruled the application inadmissible stating, in relation to Article 9, that
it was decisive that the applicant was not required to swear or affirm
allegiance to a particular religion, nor was he required to change his
political views or not pursue them in the House of Commons.[8]

Article 10 (Freedom of Expression)

Article 10 of the Convention states: **3.110**

"(1) Everyone has the right to freedom of expression. This right shall
include freedom to hold opinions and to receive and impart information and ideas without interference by public authority and regardless
of frontiers. This article shall not prevent States from requiring the
licensing of broadcasting, television or cinema enterprises.
(2) The exercise of these freedoms, since it carries with it duties and
responsibilities, may be subject to such formalities, conditions, restrictions and penalties as are prescribed by law and are necessary in a
democratic society, in the interests of national security, territorial
integrity or public safety, for the prevention of disorder or crime, for the
protection of health or morals, for the protection of the reputation or
rights of others, for preventing the disclosure of information received
in confidence, or for maintaining the authority and impartiality of the
judiciary."

Article 10 protects the "freedom to hold opinions and to receive and impart   **3.111**
information and ideas without interference by public authority and regardless of frontiers". It has given rise to a considerable amount of jurisprudence. "Expression" is not defined in Article 10. It clearly covers words,
pictures, cinema, video and conduct intended to convey an idea or information.[9] It extends to a wide range of types of expression including

---

[7] Application No. 39511/98, June 8, 1999.
[8] *cf. Buscarini v. San Marino* (2000) 30 E.H.R.R. 208 (requirement to take oath on the
Gospels in order to hold parliamentary office violation of Art. 9).
[9] *Stevens v. United Kingdom* (1986) 46 D.R. 245, Application No. 11674/85.

political,[10] journalistic,[11] artistic[12] and commercial expression[12A] (in particular advertising).[13]

3.112 In *Handyside v. United Kingdom*,[14] the European Court stated that:

"Freedom of expression constitutes one of the essential foundations of . . . a [democratic] society, one of the basic conditions for its progress and for the development of every man. Subject to paragraph 2 of Article 10, it is applicable not only to "information" or "ideas" that are favourably received or regarded as inoffensive or as a matter of indifference, but also to those that offend, shock or disturb the State or any sector of the population. Such are the demands of that pluralism, tolerance and broadmindedness, without which there is no 'democratic society'."

3.113 Article 10 protects the freedom to both receive and impart "information" and "ideas".[15] No limit is placed on the definition of "information and ideas". Article 10 does not impose any general duty on the state to provide information. Further, it does not protect individuals from being compelled to disclose information.[16] Licensing the means of broadcasting, television or cinema is permitted by Article 10(1) and does not need to be justified under Article 10(2).[17] Licensing of information is not permitted. A prohibi-

---

[10] *Bowman v. United Kingdom* (1998) 26 E.H.R.R. 1 (distribution of political pamphlets before an election); *Nilsen and Johnsen v. Norway* (2000) 30 E.H.R.R. 878 (statements by representatives of police associations about a government appointed expert in context of a public debate about police brutality); *Incal v. Turkey* (2000) 29 E.H.R.R. 449 (participation in decision to distribute leaflet criticising government). See also *Jerusalem v. Austria* Application No. 26958/95, February 27, 2001.
[11] *Goodwin v. United Kingdom* (1996) 22 E.H.R.R. 123 (refusal of journalist to disclose sources); *Bladet Tromsø and Stensaas v. Norway* (2000) 29 E.H.R.R. 125 (defamation judgment against newspaper for article alleging breaches of seal hunting regulations); *Thorma v. Luxembourg* Application No. 38432/97, March 29, 2001 (a general requirement for journalists to distance themselves formally from a quotation which might insult or provoke a third party is not reconcilable with the press's role of providing information on current events, opinions and ideas and violated Article 10). In *HM Attorney-General v. Punch Ltd and Steen*, [2001] 2 W.L.R. 1713, CA, the Court held in light of Article 10 that where a court ordered that specified material was not to be published, a third party who with knowledge of the court order published the specified material would only commit a contempt of court if the third party thereby knowingly defeated the purpose for which the order was made.
[12] *Wingrove v. United Kingdom* (1997) 24 E.H.R.R. 1 (refusal by British Board of Film Classification to grant certificate to video on grounds of blasphemy); *Müller v. Switzerland* (1991) 13 E.H.R.R. 212 (prosecution of artist displaying sexually deviant pictures at public exhibition).
[12A] See paras 19.93 *et seq.* on commercial free expression.
[13] *Barthold v. Germany* (1985) 7 E.H.R.R. 383 (veterinarian surgeons' advertising); *Colman v. United Kingdom* (1994) 18 E.H.R.R. 119 (doctors' advertising). See paras 19.98 *et seq.* on advertising.
[14] (1979) 1 E.H.R.R. 737.
[15] *Open Door Counselling and Dublin Well Woman v. Ireland* (1993) 15 E.H.R.R. 244. *cf. R. v. Shayler* unreported, May 16, 2001, QBD (the provisions of the Official Secrets Act 1989 which do permit a defence to a charge of imparting protected information that the disclosure of documents or information without lawful authority was in the public interest do not violate Article 10).
[16] *Goodwin v. United Kingdom* (1996) 22 E.H.R.R. 123.
[17] *Groppera Radio AG v. Switzerland* (1990) 12 E.H.R.R. 321; *Tele 1 Privatfernsehgesellschaft mbH v. Austria*, Application No. 32240/96, September 21, 2000.

tion on setting up and operating a radio or television station will usually breach Article 10.[18]

A restriction on the rights conferred by Article 10 (other than a licensing **3.114** restriction) will be compatible with the Convention only if its aim is to protect one of the interests set out in Article 10(2), namely, national security, territorial integrity, public safety, the prevention of disorder or crime, the protection of health or morals, the protection of the rights of others, preventing the disclosure of information received in confidence or maintaining the authority and impartiality of the judiciary. Like Article 9, this list is exhaustive and the interest is to be narrowly construed.[18A] Further, like Articles 8 and 9, the restriction must be "prescribed by law", "necessary in a democratic society" and proportionate. Injunctions or convictions arising out of newspaper articles that interfere with the outcome of legal proceedings do not violate Article 10.[19]

Freedom of expression has a special position under the Convention and **3.115** the European Court has required a strong justification for interference with the right.[20]

Article 11 (Freedom of Assembly and Association)

Article 11 of the Convention states: **3.116**

"(1) Everyone has the right to freedom of peaceful assembly and to freedom of association with others, including the right to form and to join trade unions for the protection of his interests.

(2) No restrictions shall be placed on the exercise of these rights other than such as are prescribed by law and are necessary in a democratic society in the interests of national security or public safety, for the prevention of disorder or crime, for the protection of health or morals or for the protection of the rights and freedoms of others. This article shall not prevent the imposition of lawful restrictions on the exercise of these rights by members of the armed forces, of the police or of the administration of the State."

Article 11 protects the right to freedom of peaceful assembly and to **3.117** freedom of association with others. The rights are expressly qualified by Article 11(2). The limitation "for the protection of the rights and freedoms of others" set out in Article 11(2) means that it is necessary to balance Article 11 rights with rights under other Articles of the Convention.[21] States

---

[18] *Informationsverein Lentia v. Austria* (1994) 17 E.H.R.R. 93; *Autronic AG v. Switzerland* (1990) 12 E.H.R.R. 485. See further paras 19.110 *et seq.*

[18A] For example, there is little scope under Article 10(2) for restrictions on political speech of debate on questions of public interest and the limits of permissible criticism are wider with regard to the Government than in relation to a private citizen or a politician: *Arslan v. Turkey* (2001) 31 E.H.R.R. 264.

[19] *Worm v. Austria* (1998) 25 E.H.R.R. 454; *cf. Sunday Times v. United Kingdom* (1980) 2 E.H.R.R. 245.

[20] *Sunday Times (No.2) v. United Kingdom* (1991) 14 E.H.R.R. 229, para.50.

[21] See, *e.g. Pendragon v. United Kingdom* (1999) 27 E.H.R.R. CD 179 (application by druid who was prevented from holding a summer solstice service at Stonehenge under Art. 11 declared inadmissible by the European Commission because restriction was necessary and legitimate in the interests of preventing the disorder which had occurred in previous years, it was a proportionate response and the restriction was not discriminatory against a particular group.)

may place limitations on the exercise of Article 11 rights by, for example members of the armed forces, police or members of the administration of the State.[22]

3.118 Article 11 contains a positive obligation for authorities to protect the exercise of the rights contained in it. In *Young, James & Webster v. United Kingdom*,[23] Article 11 was held to include the right *not* to join a trade union. The United Kingdom violated Article 11 by failing to prevent "closed shop" practices where refusal to join a trade union led to a threat of dismissal involving loss of livelihood. In *Plattform 'Ärzte für das Leben' v. Austria*,[24] the European Court held that the state had a duty to protect the participants in a peaceful demonstration from disruption by a violent counter-demonstration.

3.119 The term "association" has an autonomous meaning under the Convention and the classification in national law is only a starting point.[25] The right to freedom of association protects the right to form or join trade unions and other associations. Professional regulatory bodies set up by statute to regulate a profession do not fall within the definition of an "association" and compulsory membership does not violate Article 11.[26] However, a taxi drivers' association does fall within Article 11.[27] An organisation may have a right to exclude from its membership persons whom it thinks in good faith are likely to damage its objectives.[28]

3.120 Article 11 also protects both the right to strike[29] and the right to demonstrate,[30] provided that these are peaceful.

Article 12 (Right to Marry and Found a Family)

3.121 Article 12 of the Convention states:

> "Men and women of marriageable age have the right to marry and to found a family, according to the national laws governing the exercise of this right."

3.122 The right to marry under Article 12 is "a right to form a legal relationship, to acquire a status", the essence of which is "the formation of a legally binding association between a man and a woman".[31] Article 12 does not confer a right to divorce.[32]

3.123 The right to marry under Article 12 is subject only to the requirement that (1) individuals seeking to marry are of "marriageable age" and (2) they comply with marriage rules in domestic law.

---

[22] *Council of Civil Service Unions v. United Kingdom* (1987) 50 D.R. 228, Application No. 11603/85; *Rekvényi v. Hungary* (2000) 30 E.H.R.R. 519.
[23] (1982) 4 E.H.R.R. 38.
[24] (1991) 13 E.H.R.R. 204.
[25] *Chassagnou v. France* (2000) 29 E.H.R.R. 615.
[26] *Le Compte v. Belgium* (1982) 4 E.H.R.R. 1.
[27] *Sigurdur A. Sigurjonsson v. Iceland* (1993) 16 E.H.R.R. 462.
[28] *Royal Society for the Prevention of Cruelty to Animals v. Attorney-General, The Times,* February 13, 2001, Lightman J.
[29] *Schmidt v. Sweden* (1979) 1 E.H.R.R. 632.
[30] *G v. Germany* (1989) 60 D.R. 256, Application No. 13079/87.
[31] *Hamer v. United Kingdom* (1982) 4 E.H.R.R. 139.
[32] *Johnston v. Ireland* (1987) 9 E.H.R.R. 203.

The right to found a family encompasses the right to live together.[33] In **3.124** *Abdulaziz, Cabales and Balkandali v. United Kingdom*,[34] the European Court held that "family" comes into existence upon lawful marriage.

Domestic law can lay down the procedural requirements for legally valid **3.125** marriages, but must not impair the very essence of the right to marry. The European Court has held that a prohibition of homosexual or transsexual marriage does not breach Article 12.[35]

Article 14 (Freedom from Discrimination)

Article 14 of the Convention states: **3.126**

> "The enjoyment of the rights and freedoms set forth in this Convention shall be secured without discrimination on any ground such as sex, race, colour, language, religion, political or other opinion, national or social origin, association with a national minority, property, birth or other status."

Article 14 does not provide a general free-standing right to freedom from **3.127** discrimination, unlike Protocol No. 12. It can only be invoked in relation to one of the other Convention rights set out in Articles 2 to 12 and the First Protocol. Whilst it is not necessary to establish breach of another Convention right, the facts in issue must "fall within the ambit" of one or more of the other Convention provisions for Article 14 to be engaged.

In order to establish discrimination, the individual must show that he or she **3.128** has been treated differently to someone in a similar situation.[36] The issue in determining whether a difference in treatment is discriminatory is whether a "reasonable and objective justification" can be shown for the difference in question.[37] Whilst a margin of appreciation[38] is granted when determining whether a difference in treatment can be justified, "very weighty reasons" are needed to justify discrimination on grounds of sex or race.[39] In *Cornwell v. United Kingdom*,[40] the Court declared admissible a claim by a widower that he had been discriminated against on the ground of sex in breach of Article 14 in conjunction with Article 8 and Article 1 of the First Protocol since he was not allowed to claim social security benefits payable only to widows and widowed mothers. The Government later reached a friendly settlement.

The word "sex" in Article 14 can also cover discrimination based on sexual **3.129** orientation.[41]

---

[33] *Abdulaziz, Cabales and Balkandali v. United Kingdom* (1985) 7 E.H.R.R. 471, para. 62. Article 12 does not entitle a prisoner to inseminate his wife by artificial means: *R (Mellor) v. Secretary of State for the Home Department* The Times, May 1, 2001, [2001] EWCA Civ 472, CA.

[34] *ibid.*

[35] *Cossey v. United Kingdom* (1991) 13 E.H.R.R. 622.

[36] *Van der Mussele v. Belgium* (1984) 6 E.H.R.R. 163; *Fredin v. Sweden* (1991) 13 E.H.R.R. 784, para. 60.

[37] *Belgian Linguistics Case* (1979) 1 E.H.R.R. 241; *Chassagnou v. France* (2000) 29 E.H.R.R. 615. See also K. Monaghan, "Limitations and Opportunities: A Review of the Likely Domestic Impact of Article 14 ECHR" [2001] E.H.R.L.R. 167.

[38] See paras. 4.22 *et seq.*, below.

[39] *Van Raalte v. Netherlands* (1997) 24 E.H.R.R. 503.

[40] Application No. 36578/97, April 25, 2000. See also *Leary v. United Kingdom*, Application No. 38890/97, April 25, 2000.

[41] *Salguerio da Silva Mouta v. Portugal*, Application No. 33290/96, December 21, 1999.

3.130 If a difference in treatment is justified, it must nevertheless be proportionate to the legitimate aim pursued.[42]

Article 1 of Protocol No. 1 (Right to Peaceful Enjoyment of Possessions)

3.131 Article 1 of Protocol No. 1 to the Convention states:

> "Every natural or legal person is entitled to the peaceful enjoyment of
> his possessions. No one shall be deprived of his possessions except
> in the public interest and subject to the conditions provided for by law
> and by the general principles of international law.
> The preceding provisions shall not, however, in any way impair the
> right of a State to enforce such laws as it deems necessary to control
> the use of property in accordance with the general interest or to
> secure the payment of taxes or other contributions or penalties."

3.132 Article 1 of Protocol No. 1 encompasses three principles[42A]:

(1) the right to peaceful enjoyment of possessions;

(2) the right not to be deprived of possessions except in the public
interest and in accordance with the law;

(3) the state's right to exercise control over possessions in accordance with the general interest or to secure the payment of taxes
or other contributions or penalties.

3.133 Article 1 of Protocol No. 1 protects economic rights. Possessions include
all movable and immovable property, contractual rights including leases,
orders for possession of property,[43] judgment debts,[44] shares,[45] goodwill[46]
and even a claim for compensation in tort.[47] Both natural and legal
persons are expressly conferred with rights under this Article.

3.134 The European Court has shown a tendency to assimilate the assessment
of all interferences with the peaceful enjoyment of possessions under a
single test of fair balance: any interference must not place a disproportionate burden on the individual owner or result in discriminatory treatment. It has in general seen the availability of an effective remedy and the
provision of compensation[48] as a necessary element in preserving a fair
balance, whether the interference involves the deprivation of property or
the control of its use. In relation to compensation, Article 1 of Protocol No.

---

[42] *Belgian Linguistics Case* (1979) 1 E.H.R.R. 241.
[42A] See further paras 16.43 *et seq.*
[43] *Immobiliare Saffi v. Italy* (2000) 30 E.H.R.R. 756.
[44] *Agneessens v. Belgium* (1988) 58 D.R. 63, Application No. 12164/86.
[45] *Bramelid and Malmstron v. Sweden* (1982) 5 E.H.R.R. 249.
[46] *Van Marle v. Netherlands* (1986) 8 E.H.R.R. 483.
[47] *Pressos Compania Naviera SA v. Belgium* (1996) 21 E.H.R.R. 301.
[48] See, *e.g.*, *Holy Monasteries v. Greece* (1995) 20 E.H.R.R. 1.

1 requires payment of an amount reasonably related to the value of the property, but does not guarantee a right to full compensation in all circumstances.[49] Delay in paying compensation may also upset the fair balance between protection of property and the requirements of general interest.[50]

Deprivation of property is permitted only if it is in the "public interest" and in accordance with the principles of domestic and general international law. The European Court has held that the public interest requires that **3.135**

(1) any deprivation of property must be for a legitimate purpose and

(2) the achievement of that purpose must strike a "fair balance" between the demands of the general interest of the community and the need to protect individual rights.[51]

Where the state is exercising control over property: **3.136**

(1) the measure in question must not be "manifestly without reasonable foundation" and

(2) there must be a reasonable relationship of proportionality between the means employed and the achievement of that aim.

Where a measure does not amount to either deprivation or control, it is **3.137** necessary to consider whether a "fair balance" has been struck between the demands of the general interest and the protection of the individual. A fair balance will not exist where the measure imposes "an individual and excessive burden" on those affected.[52]

Article 1 of Protocol No. 1 has particular relevance to companies,[53] taxa- **3.138** tion[54] and property law.[55]

The retrospective effect of a judicial decision does not necessarily infringe **3.139** Article 1 of Protocol No. 1. Even where an individual has a legitimate expectation that a certain state of affairs will prevail, Article 1 of Protocol

---

[49] *Papachelas v. Greece* (2000) 30 E.H.R.R. 923, para. 48 (legitimate objectives of "public interest" may call for less than reimbursement of full market value).
[50] *Akkus v. Turkey* (2000) 30 E.H.R.R. 365.
[51] *James v. United Kingdom* (1986) 8 E.H.R.R. 123.
[52] *Spörrong and Lonroth v. Sweden* (1983) 5 E.H.R.R. 35, para. 69; *Immobiliare Saffi v. Italy* (2000) 30 E.H.R.R. 756, para. 49.
[53] See Chap. 14 (Companies and Financial Services).
[54] See Chap. 18 (Taxation). A form of taxation which operates entirely arbitrarily will not meet the conditions required by Article 1 of Protocol No. 1: *Aston Cantlow and Wilmcote with Billesley Parochial Church Council v. Wallbank and another* [2001] 3 All E.R. 393, CA at para. 45.
[55] See Chap. 16 (Property Planning and Environment).

No. 1 does not necessarily protect such an expectation from the retrospective effect of the court's decision: *Antoniades v. United Kingdom.*[56]

Article 2 of Protocol No. 1 (Right to Education)

3.140   Article 2 of Protocol No. 1 states:

> "No person shall be denied the right to education. In the exercise of
> any functions which it assumes in relation to education and to teach-
> ing, the State shall respect the right of parents to ensure such educa-
> tion and teaching in conformity with their own religious and
> philosophical convictions."

3.141   Article 2 of Protocol No. 1 does not oblige the state to provide education.
It requires the state to respect the right of parents to ensure that their
children are educated in accordance with their religious and philosophical
convictions.

3.142   The United Kingdom has entered a reservation in relation to the right to
educations, affirming the principle in the second sentence of Article 2 of
Protocol No. 1 but:

> " . . . only in so far as it is compatible with the provision of efficient
> instruction and training, and the avoidance of unreasonable public
> expenditure."[57]

3.143   There are implied limitations on the right to education.[58] The right is
generally concerned with primary and secondary education. A state may
limit further education to those who will benefit from it.[59] Failure to allocate
resources to particular educational provisions is unlikely to be contrary to
Article 2 of Protocol No. 1. This is relevant in the context of special needs
education, where the HRA is unlikely to provide a remedy. The obligation
to respect religious and philosophical convictions is not confined to the
content of educational instruction, but includes the organisation and
financing of public education, the supervision of the educational system in
general and questions of discipline.[60] A requirement that education be
given in a particular language does not come within the concept of "philosophical convictions" for the purposes of Article 2 of Protocol No. 1.[61] The

---

[56] (1990) 64 D.R. 232, Application No. 15434/89. See also *Heil v. Rankin* [2000] 2 W.L.R.
1173, where the Court of Appeal retrospectively altered the tariff for general damages in
personal injury cases. The Court rejected the defendants' arguments that for the change in
the tariff to operate retrospectively would infringe the Convention.
[57] HRA, Sched.3, Pt II. The reservation was made on March 20, 1952.
[58] *Belgian Linguistic Case (No 2)* (1979) 1 E.H.R.R. 252.
[59] *X v. United Kingdom* (1980) 23 D.R. 228.
[60] *Campbell v. United Kingdom* (1982) 4 E.H.R.R. 293. See also *R. v. Head Teacher of
Alperton Community School, The Times,* June 8, 2001, QBD (the School Standards and
Framework Act 1998 did not breach Article 2 of Protocol No. 1 or other provisions of the
European Convention in respect of school admissions and exclusions).
[61] *Belgian Linguistics Case (No 2)* (1979) 1 E.H.R.R. 252.

Convention does not confer a right to education in any particular country.[62]

Article 3 of Protocol No. 1 (Right to Free Elections)

Article 3 of Protocol No. 1 states: **3.144**

"The High Contracting Parties undertake to hold free elections at reasonable intervals by secret ballot, under conditions which will ensure the free expression of the opinion of the people in the choice of the legislature."

Article 3 of Protocol No. 1 only applies to election of the "legislature". In **3.145** *Matthews v. United Kingdom*,[63] the European Court held that the European Parliament also bears the characteristics of a "legislature" for the purpose of the Article. However, Article 3 of Protocol No. 1 does not apply to local elections.[64]

In *Mathieu-Mohin and Clerfayt v. Belgium*,[65] the European Court set out **3.146** the following principles:

(1) the importance of free elections is such as to impose positive measures on the state to "hold" democratic elections[65A];

(2) the rights protected are the right to vote and the right to stand for election to the legislature[65B];

(3) these rights are not absolute and can be subject to implied limitations, so long as any such limitations do not impair the very essence of the rights and deprive them of their effectiveness.[65C]

Article 3 of Protocol No. 1 does not oblige states to introduce any particular **3.147** electoral system. In *Lindsay v. United Kingdom*,[66] the Commission held that proportional representation with a single transferable vote was not contrary to the Convention.

In *Bowman v. United Kingdom*[67] the Court considered the amount of **3.148** money spent by unauthorised persons on publications during an election in the context of electoral laws. The Court weighed Article 10 against Article 3 of Protocol No. 1 and found the domestic legal limits to be a disproportionate infringement on the right of free speech. This was not outweighed by the need to hold free elections.

---

[62] *R. (Holub) v. Secretary of State for the Home Department* [2001] 1 W.L.R. 1359, CA.
[63] (1999) 28 E.H.R.R. 361.
[64] *Cherepkov v. Russia*, Application No. 51501/99, January 25, 2000.
[65] (1988) 10 E.H.R.R. 1.
[65A] At para. 50.
[65B] At para. 51.
[65C] At para. 52. See Keir Starmer, *European Human Rights Law* (Legal Action Group, 1999) p. 151. See also *R. (Pearson and another) v. Secretary of State for the Home Department, The Times*, April 17, 2001, [2001] EWCH Admin 239, April 4, 2001, Admin Ct. (disqualification of prisoners from voting at local and general elections was lawful and not in contravention of the Convention).
[66] Application No. 8364/78; (1979) 15 D.R. 247.
[67] (1998) 26 E.H.R.R. 1.

Articles 1 and 2 of Protocol No. 6 (Abolition of the Death Penalty)

3.149   Article 1 of Protocol No. 6 states:

> "The death penalty shall be abolished. No one shall be condemned to such penalty or executed."

3.150   Article 2 of Protocol No. 6 states:

> "A State may make provision in its law for the death penalty in respect of acts committed in time of war or of imminent threat of war; such penalty shall be applied only in the instances laid down in the law and in accordance with its provisions."

3.151   No derogations[68] or reservations[69] from the provisions of Protocol No. 6 are permitted. This Article, which forms part of an optional Protocol, provides for abolition of the death penalty, save in times of war or threat or war. The United Kingdom ratified Protocol No. 6 on January 27, 1999.

6. WAIVER AND CONTRACTING OUT OF CONVENTION RIGHTS

Waiver

3.152   The European Court has not yet formulated a coherent doctrine of waiver. It has held that some rights may not be waived because this would be contrary to the public interest and would undermine the role of the protection of individual rights in safeguarding a democratic society.[70] The Court has been reluctant to accept an argument that an individual has waived his right to personal liberty under Article 5.[71] On the other hand, it has held that a litigant can waive certain of his Article 6(1) rights, including the right to a public hearing,[72] the right to a hearing in his presence,[73] and the right to a determination of all issues of fact as well as law.[74] It is not clear whether the right to an independent and impartial tribunal can be waived. In *Pfeifer and Plankl v. Austria*,[75] the Court doubted whether it would ever be possible to waive the right to an independent and impartial tribunal. In

---

[68] Protocol 6, Art. 3.
[69] Protocol 6, Art. 4.
[70] *Albert and Le Compte v. Belgium* (1983) 5 E.H.R.R. 533, para. 35.
[71] *De Wilde, Ooms and Versyp v. Belgium* (1979) 1 E.H.R.R. 373, para. 65.
[72] *Le Compte, Van Leuven and De Meyere v. Belgium* (1982) 4 E.H.R.R. 1; *Albert and Le Compte v. Belgium* (1983) 5 E.H.R.R. 533; *Pauger v. Austria* (1998) 25 E.H.R.R. 105; *H v. Belgium* (1988) 10 E.H.R.R. 339, ECHR; *Ginikawana v. United Kingdom* (1988) 55 D.R. 251 at 260; *Austin Hall Building Ltd v. Buckland Securities Ltd* (2001) C.I.L.L. 1734; (2001) EGCS 155. See also para. 10.93 below.
[73] *Colozza v. Italy* (1985) 7 E.H.R.R. 516, para. 29 (however, the state must have acted diligently to secure the attendance of the accused, and he must be able to obtain a fresh determination of the merits of the charge if he did not know but later learns of the proceedings).
[74] *Air Canada v. United Kingdom* (1995) 20 E.H.R.R. 150, para. 61. See also para. 3.75 above.
[75] (1992) 14 E.H.R.R. 692, paras 38–39.

Millar v. Dickson,[75A] the Privy Council held that defendants could not be regarded as having tacitly waived their right to trial before an independent and impartial tribunal by having failed to object to the use of temporary sheriffs at the time of the hearing. However, in *Deweer v. Belgium*,[76] the Court suggested that it is possible to waive the right to a trial by the settlement of proceedings freely and unequivocally entered into.[76A] When considering an argument regarding waiver, it is necessary to determine:

(1) the extent to which it is possible as a matter of law to waive specific Article 6(1) rights; and

(2) whether in an individual case, a party has in fact done so either expressly or tacitly.

The European Court has held that to be effective, a waiver must be made: **3.153**

(1) in an unequivocal manner;

(2) without undue compulsion[77]; and

(3) "must not run counter to any important public interest".[78]

Where an implied waiver is alleged, the court must look at whether it was reasonable to expect the litigant to have taken his complaint up at an earlier stage.[79]

Contracting Out

In principle, the Convention would appear to permit contractual obligations which limit (and possibly, remove Convention rights) provided that they are freely entered into by the individual concerned. In *Rommelfanger v. Germany*,[80] the European Commission upheld as within the Convention a provision in an employment contract limiting an employee's freedom of expression. The applicant was a doctor employed by a Catholic hospital who had entered into a contract of employment accepting a duty of loyalty towards the Catholic Church, thereby waiving his freedom to make statements contrary to his duty of loyalty. The applicant signed a letter to the editor of a magazine containing anti-abortion views and was dismissed as a result. He complained that his dismissal violated Article 10. The Commission held the complaint to be manifestly ill-founded.[81]   **3.154**

[75A] *The Times*, July 27, 2001, PC.
[76] (1980) 2 E.H.R.R. 439.
[76A] See further para. 10.120 below.
[77] *Pfeifer and Plankl v. Austria* (1992) 14 E.H.R.R. 692, para. 37.
[78] *Håkansson and Sturesson v. Sweden* (1991) 13 E.H.R.R. 1, para. 66.
[79] *McGonnell v. United Kingdom* (2000) 30 E.H.R.R. 289, para. 44.
[80] Application No. 12242/86; (1989) 62 D.R. 151.
[81] See further paras 13.33 *et seq.* for an analysis of contracting out in the employment context and generally.

CHAPTER 4
General Principles of European Human Rights Law

1. INTRODUCTION

This chapter considers the general principles governing the approach of **4.01**
the European Court and Commission to the interpretation of the Convention and the application of these principles by the domestic courts under
the HRA. The principles of interpretation of domestic legislation under
section 3 of the HRA are discussed in Chapter 5.[1]

2. INTERPRETATION OF THE CONVENTION

International Treaty

The European Convention on Human Rights is an international treaty and **4.02**
should be interpreted in accordance with Articles 31 to 33 of the Vienna
Convention on the Law of Treaties 1969. Whilst the Vienna Convention
does not have retrospective effect, the European Court has stated that it
enunciates generally accepted principles of international law.[2] Article
31(1) of the Vienna Convention states that a treaty:

> "shall be interpreted in good faith in accordance with the ordinary
> meaning to be given to the terms of the Treaty in their context and in
> the light of its objects and purpose."

This is the basis for the purposive or teleological interpretation that the **4.03**
European Court has taken in relation to the Convention discussed
below.

The Court has had recourse to the text of the Convention, its preamble, **4.04**
related Conventions and instruments of the Contracting Parties in interpreting the Convention. It has on different occasions employed the following various principles of interpretation[3]:

(1) a literal interpretation based on the text of the Convention[4];

(2) a grammatical interpretation, involving a comparison between
the English and the French texts[5];

(3) a systematic interpretation, whereby the meaning of a provision
is ascertained by examining its place within the Convention and
its relation to other provisions[6];

(4) an historical interpretation, with reference to the *travaux pré-
paratoires*[7];

---

[1] At paras. 5.02 *et seq.*, below.
[2] *Golder v. United Kingdom* (1979) 1 E.H.R.R. 524, paras. 29–30.
[3] See generally, Lawson & Schermers, *Leading Cases of the European Court of Human
Rights* (Ars Aequi Libri, 1997).
[4] See, *e.g. Lawless v. Ireland* (1979) 1 E.H.R.R. 15, para. 28; *Johnston v. Ireland* (1987) 9
E.H.R.R. 203, para. 52.
[5] See, *e.g. Golder v. United Kingdom* (1979) 1 E.H.R.R. 524, para. 32; *Niemietz v. Germany*
(1993) 16 E.H.R.R. 97, para. 30.
[6] See, *e.g. Engel v. Netherlands* (1979) 1 E.H.R.R. 647, para. 59; *Klass v. Germany* (1980)
2 E.H.R.R. 214, para. 68.
[7] See, *e.g. Johnston v. Ireland* (1987) 9 E.H.R.R. 203, para. 52; *James v. United Kingdom*
(1986) 8 E.H.R.R. 123, para. 64.

(5) a teleological and purposive interpretation, in light of the objects and purpose of the Convention[8];

(6) a dynamic or evolutive interpretation.[9]

Purposive or Teleological Approach

4.05 The Court does not merely look at the text of a provision of the Convention and give it an objective meaning. It interprets the provision in the light of the objects and purposes of the Convention and gives it a meaning consistent with those objects. This differs significantly from the traditional literal approach of the domestic courts to construction of a statute, although it is not wholly new to domestic courts, particularly in light of the development of Community law.[10]

Objects and Purpose of the Convention

4.06 The objects and purpose of the Convention have been said to be the protection of individual human rights[11] and the maintenance and promotion of the ideals and values of a democratic society. The latter includes:

(1) "pluralism, tolerance and broad-mindedness"[12];

(2) "the rule of law" encompassing effective control by the judiciary of executive interference with individual rights[13];

(3) the fair and proper treatment of minorities[14];

(4) the separation of powers[15];

(5) freedom of expression and political debate[16]; and

---

[8] See, *e.g. Airey v. Ireland* (1980) 2 E.H.R.R. 305, para. 24; *Loizidou v.Turkey* (1997) 23 E.H.R.R. 513, para. 72; *cf. Van der Mussele v. Belgium* (1984) 6 E.H.R.R. 163, para. 49.
[9] See, *e.g. Young, James & Webster v. United Kingdom* (1982) 4 E.H.R.R. 38, para. 32; *Sigurjónsson v. Iceland* (1993) 16 E.H.R.R. 462, para. 35.
[10] See, *e.g. Pickstone v. Freemans plc* [1989] A.C. 66 and *Litster v. Forth Dry Dock and Engineering Co Ltd* [1990] 1 A.C. 546. Further in *Minister of Home Affairs v. Fisher* [1980] A.C. 319 at 328G-H, Lord Wilberforce noted that a constitutional provision in the Constitution of Bermuda called for a "generous interpretation avoiding what has been called 'the austerity of tabulated legalism', suitable to give to individuals the full measure of the fundamental rights and freedoms referred to". See also *Attorney-General of Hong Kong v. Lee Kwong-kut* [1993] A.C. 951 at 966B-E, PC; *R. v. Big M Drug Mart Ltd* (1985) 18 D.L.R. (4th) 321 at 360 Sup Ct of Canada; *Ministry of Transport v. Noort* [1992] 3 N.Z.L.R. 360 at 371, N.Z. CA; and *Matinkinca v. Council of State, Ciskei* [1996] 1 C.H.R.D. 61, January 13, 1994, Sup Ct, Ciskei General Division, S.A. In *Pointu v. Minister of Education and Science* [1996] 1 C.H.R.D., October 27, 1995, Sup Ct, Mauritius, it was held that a constitution, and most particularly that part of it which embodies fundamental rights, should be interpreted in light of history, its sources and, whenever applicable, pronouncements on similar provisions either by national courts or by international institutions.
[11] *Soering v. United Kingdom* (1989) 11 E.H.R.R. 439.
[12] *Handyside v. United Kingdom* (1979) 1 E.H.R.R. 737, para. 49.
[13] *Klass v. Germany* (1980) 2 E.H.R.R. 214, para. 55.
[14] *Young, James & Webster v. United Kingdom* (1982) 4 E.H.R.R. 38, para. 63.
[15] *Klass v. Germany* (1980) 2 E.H.R.R.214.
[16] *Lingens v. Austria* (1986) 8 E.H.R.R. 407, paras 41–42 (freedom of political debate is described as "the very core of the concept of a democratic society which prevails throughout the Convention").

(6) access to the courts.[17]

The preamble to the Convention sets out its objects, stating in particular,   **4.07**
that fundamental freedoms are the foundation of peace and justice in the
world and are best maintained by a political democracy and a common
understanding and observance of the rights on which such freedoms
depend. It provides:

> "The governments signatory hereto, members of the Council of
> Europe,
> *Considering* the Universal Declaration of Human Rights proclaimed
> by the General Assembly of the United Nations on 10th December
> 1948;
> *Considering* that this Declaration aims at securing the universal and
> effective recognition and observance of the Rights declared;
> *Considering* that the aim of the Council of Europe is the achievement
> of greater unity between its members and that one of the methods by
> which that aim is to be pursued is the maintenance and further
> realisation of human rights and fundamental freedoms;
> *Reaffirming* their profound belief in those fundamental freedoms
> which are the foundation of justice and peace in the world and are
> best maintained on the one hand by an effective political democracy
> and on the other by a common understanding and observance of the
> human rights on which they depend;
> *Being resolved*, as the governments of European countries which are
> like-minded and have a common heritage of political traditions, ideals,
> freedom and the rule of law, to take the first steps for the collective
> enforcement of certain of the rights stated in the Universal Declara-
> tion, have agreed as follows . . . ".[18]

In *Soering v. United Kingdom*,[19] the Court required interpretation of Con-   **4.08**
vention rights to be consistent with "the general spirit of the Convention"
and its aim of promoting the ideals and values of a democratic society:

> "[A]ny interpretation of the rights and freedoms guaranteed has to be
> consistent with 'the general spirit of the Convention, an instrument
> designed to maintain and promote the values of a democratic soci-
> ety' . . . ".[20]

Practical and Effective Rights

The European Court has stated that: **4.09**

> "the Convention is intended to guarantee not rights that are theoret-
> ical or illusory but rights that are practical and effective."[21]

---

[17] *Golder v. United Kingdom* (1979) 1 E.H.R.R. 524, para. 34.
[18] See further S. Marks, "The European Convention on Human Rights and its Democratic
Society" (1995) 66 B.Y.I.L. 209 (including an analysis of the aims of the Convention as
expressed in the *travaux préparatoires*).
[19] (1989) 11 E.H.R.R. 439.
[20] At para. 87.
[21] *Airey v. Ireland* (1980) 2 E.H.R.R. 305, para. 24. See also *Soering v. United Kingdom*
(1989) 11 E.H.R.R. 439, para. 87.

The Court has relied upon this principle of effectiveness of rights in relation to, for example, considering the scope of a state's positive obligations under the Convention[22] and the right to effective assistance from a lawyer.[23]

Substance not Form

4.10   The interpretation of the Convention is concerned with substance, not form, and categorisation in domestic law is not determinative.[24] The European Court will:

> "look behind the appearances and investigate the realities of the procedure in question."[25]

Common Approach

4.11   The existence or absence of a "generally shared approach" in other Contracting States is relevant to the interpretation and application of Convention rights as a guide to social norms.[26] This is sometimes known as the "consensus principle".[27] However, uniformity of approach is not required,[28] particularly in relation to conceptions of morality.[29] In the absence of consistent Contracting State practice, the Court will often leave national authorities a wide margin of appreciation.[30]

International Agreements

4.12   The European Court sometimes uses other international agreements and decisions of international courts to clarify the meaning of certain Convention provisions.[31] The general rules of international law are also taken into account.[32] The importance and content of international human rights standards are considered in more detail in Chapter 5[33]–[34] and Chapter 7.

Fair Balance between Individual Rights and General Interest

4.13   In interpreting the Convention, the European Court gives effect to the general principle:

> "inherent in the whole of the Convention . . . [to strike a] fair balance between the demands of the general interest of the community and

---

[22] *Soering v. United Kingdom* (1989) 11 E.H.R.R. 439, para. 90. See further Chapter 5, paras 5.28 *et seq.*, below.
[23] *Artico v. Italy* (1981) 3 E.H.R.R. 1, para. 33. See also para. 12.45 below.
[24] *Campbell and Fell v. United Kingdom* (1985) 7 E.H.R.R. 165, para. 71.
[25] *Deweer v. Belgium* (1980) 2 E.H.R.R. 439, para. 44.
[26] *X, Y and Z v. United Kingdom* (1997) 24 E.H.R.R. 143, para. 52.
[27] *Öztürk v. Germany* (1984) 6 E.H.R.R. 409, para. 53.
[28] *Sunday Times v. United Kingdom* (1980) 2 E.H.R.R. 245, para. 61.
[29] See, *e.g. Müller v. Switzerland* (1991) 13 E.H.R.R. 212, para. 35.
[30] See, *e.g. Abdulaziz, Cabales and Balkandali v. United Kingdom* (1985) 7 E.H.R.R. 471, para. 67; *Rees v. United Kingdom* (1987) 9 E.H.R.R.56, para. 37.
[31] See, *e.g. Sigurjónsson v. Iceland* (1993) 16 E.H.R.R. 462, para. 35.
[32] See, *e.g. Abdulaziz, Cabales and Balkandali v. United Kingdom* (1985) 7 E.H.R.R. 471, para. 67.
[33]–[34] At paras 5.69 and 5.71, below.

the requirements of the protection of the individual's fundamental rights."[35]

The doctrine of proportionality, discussed below, is central to the principle of a "fair balance".

General Domestic Interpretation of Convention

Whilst the principles applied by the European Court for the interpretation of the Convention will be heavily influential on the interpretation of the HRA, the Act also gives room for judges to exercise independent judgment and develop a domestic interpretation for the Convention, provided that they do not provide less protection for fundamental rights than the European Court.[36] The courts are now required expressly to consider the requirements of a democratic society and to weigh and assess the importance of particular legislative aims and the extent to which restrictions on individual rights are permitted. Since this is traditionally the role of the legislature, to the extent that the judiciary engage in this process, it represents a new departure.[37]

4.14

However, in *Stott (Procurator Fiscal, Dunfermline) v. Brown*,[38] Lord Bingham advocated a cautious, rather than expansive, approach to interpretation. He stated that:

4.15

"In interpreting the Convention, as any other treaty, it is generally to be assumed that the parties have included the terms which they wished to include and on which they were able to agree, omitting other terms which they did not wish to include or on which they were not able to agree. Thus, particular regard must be had and reliance placed on the express terms of the Convention, which define the rights and freedoms which the contracting parties have undertaken to secure. This does not mean that nothing can be implied into the Convention. The language of the Convention is for the most part so general that some implication of terms is necessary and the case law of the European Court shows that the Court has been willing to imply terms into the Convention when it was judged necessary or plainly right to do so. But the process of implication is one to be carried out with caution, if the risk is to be averted that the contracting parties may, by judicial interpretation, become bound by obligations which they did not expressly accept and might not have been willing to accept.

As an important constitutional instrument, the Convention is to be seen as a 'living tree capable of growth and expansion within its natural limits'—*Edwards v. Attorney-General for Canada* [1930] A.C.

---

[35] *Spörrong and Lonnroth v. Sweden* (1983) 5 E.H.R.R. 35, para. 69.
[36] Speaking on behalf of the Government, Lord Irvine conceded that there was scope for judges to exercise independent judgment: H.L. Deb., January 19, 1998, col.1271.
[37] See, *e.g.* G. Marshall "Patriating Rights with Reservations—The Human Rights Bill 1998" in J. Beatson, C. Forsyth and I. Hare (eds), *Constitutional Reform in the United Kingdom: Practice and Principles* (Hart Publishing, 1998), p. 79
[38] (2001) 2 W.L.R. 817; *The Times*, December 6, 2000, PC.

124 at 126 per L.Sankey L.C.—but these limits will often call for very careful consideration."

4.16 In the same case, Lord Steyn considered that on the first real test of the Act, it was opportune to stand back and consider the basic aims of the Convention in a way which could provide a framework for consideration of future claims under the HRA. He found assistance in the words of the preambles to the Convention and identified that the two principal objectives as follows:

(1) to maintain and further realise human rights and fundamental freedoms.

(2) to foster effective political democracy.

Lord Steyn noted that, in relation to the maintenance and further realisation of human rights, the framers of the Convention recognised that it was not only morally right to promote the observance of human rights but that it was also the best way of achieving pluralistic and just societies in which all can peaceably go about their lives. In relation to the fostering of political democracy, he stated that this aim necessarily involved the creation of conditions of stability and order under the rule of law, not for its own sake, but as the best way to ensuring the well-being of the inhabitants of the European countries. The inspirers of the Convention realised that from time to time the fundamental rights of one individual may conflict with the human rights of others. The fundamental rights of individuals are of supreme importance but are not unlimited since individuals live in communities of individuals who also have rights. He noted that the Convention is the direct descendant of the Universal Declaration of Human Rights 1948 which in Article 29 expressly recognised the duties of everyone to the community and the limitation on rights in order to secure and protect respect for the rights of others.

3. PRECEDENT AND THE CONVENTION AS A "LIVING INSTRUMENT"

No Doctrine of Precedent

4.17 There is no formal doctrine of precedent in European human rights law. Whilst the Strasbourg institutions have generally sought to arrive at conclusions consistent with previous judgments, the European Court has famously stated that:

"the Convention is a living instrument which must be interpreted in light of present day conditions".[39]

---

[39] *Tyrer v. United Kingdom* (1980) 2 E.H.R.R. 1, para. 31.

In *Tyrer v. United Kingdom*,[40] the Court took account of developments in penal policy to find that judicial corporal punishment violated the Convention.

Dynamic Interpretation

The Court adopts a dynamic or evolutive approach and will depart from its **4.18** earlier decisions where it deems this appropriate in the light of changing social conditions and priorities.[41] Thus, a decision made several years ago could be decided differently today if the social norms common to all or many of the Contracting States have changed from those in place when the Convention was drafted or at the time an earlier decision was reached. In *Loizidou v. Turkey*, the Court stated that the provisions of the Convention:

" . . . cannot be interpreted solely in accordance with the intentions of their authors as expressed more than forty years ago . . . at a time when a minority of the present Contracting Parties adopted the Convention."[42]

However, the Court will not use a dynamic approach to read in rights which were deliberately excluded from the Convention at the outset, for example, the right to divorce.[43] The disadvantage of the evolutive approach is the inevitable uncertainty it creates in predicting the outcome of future cases.

In *Stott (Procurator Fiscal, Dunfermline) v. Brown*,[44] Lord Clyde recog- **4.19** nised that the Convention is "plainly a living instrument" which is open to new applications as society develops and changes. However, he stated that it is also to be remembered that:

"it is dealing with the realities of life and it is not to be applied in ways which run counter to reason and common sense."[45]

Focus on Individual Facts

The European Court is principally concerned with the facts and circum- **4.20** stances of the individual case before it in considering the application of the Convention. Whilst this allows it to flexibly adapt to respond to do justice in a particular case, giving effect to factual differences and recognising

---

[40] *ibid*. See also the transsexual rights case where social developments in Contracting States were expressly considered: *Cossey v. United Kingdom* (1991) 13 E.H.R.R. 622; *Sheffield and Horsham v. United Kingdom* (1999) 27 E.H.R.R. 163.

[41] *Marckx v. Belgium* (1980) 2 E.H.R.R. 330, para. 41; *Soering v. United Kindom* (1989) 11 E.H.R.R. 439, para. 102;

[42] See para. 71.

[43] *Johnston v. Ireland* (1987) 9 E.H.R.R. 203.

[44] (2001) 2 W.L.R. 817; *The Times*, December 6, 2000, PC.

[45] This statement echoes that of Lord Woolf in *Attorney-General of Hong Kong v. Lee Kwong-kut* [1993] A.C. 951 at 975B-C (the issues "should be approached with realism and good sense, and kept in proportion"). See also *R v. Grayson and Taylor* [1997] 1 N.Z.L.R. 399 at 409, N.Z.CA.

differences of degree, on occasion has led to inconsistency in the application of Convention rights between one case and another.

Domestic Law of Precedent in Interpretation of Convention Rights

4.21   Whilst the European Court does not apply any strict doctrine of precedent in relation to its interpretation of the Convention, domestic law rules of precedent will continue to be effective in relation to domestic law decisions relating to human rights issues. If a relevant decision or group of decisions of the European Court of Human Rights has been examined by the House of Lords or the Court of Appeal, the lower courts are bound by the reasoning of the superior courts and are not permitted to re-examine the decision of the Strasbourg court in order to ascertain whether the conclusion of the House of Lords or Court of Appeal might be inconsistent with those decisions or susceptible to a continuing gloss: *R v Central Criminal Court, ex p. Bright*.[46] In practice, it is likely that a body of HRA decisions from the House of Lords and Court of Appeal will build up which will be followed by lower courts in the absence of clearly distinguishing facts.

4. The Margin of Appreciation

The Doctrine of Margin of Appreciation

4.22   In interpreting and applying Convention principles, the European Court has often recognised that a measure of discretion, labelled the "margin of appreciation", should be left to the Contracting States. This is in effect an application of the principle of "subsidiarity", that is, that the machinery of protection established by the Convention is subsidiary to the national systems safeguarding human rights.[47] It is grounded in the premise that state authorities are often in a better position to assess in particular cases the need for measures that adversely affect Convention rights.[48] The doctrine is a reflection of the supervisory jurisdiction of the European Court as an international court, remote from local conditions. However, where appropriate, the Court does indeed exercise its supervisory role.[49]

4.23   The doctrine of margin of appreciation is classically stated in *Handyside v. United Kingdom*,[50] which concerned the publication of a schoolbook condemned as obscene in the United Kingdom. The European Court stated:

> "In particular, it is not possible to find in the domestic law of the various Contracting States a uniform European conception of morals. The view taken by their respective laws of the requirements of morals

---

[46] [2001] 1 W.L.R. 662.

[47] *Handyside v. United Kingdom* (1979) 1 E.H.R.R. 737, para. 48. See also Singh, Hunt & Demetriou, "Is there a Role for the 'Margin of Appreciation' in National Law after the Human Rights Act?" [1999] E.H.R.L.R. 15 at 17, and R. Ryssdall, "The Coming of Age of the European Convention on Human Rights" [1996] E.H.R.L.R. 18 at 24.

[48] *Sunday Times v. United Kingdom* (1980) 2 E.H.R.R. 245; *Buckley v. United Kingdom* (1997) 23 E.H.R.R. 101, para. 75.

[49] *Handyside v. United Kingdom* (1979) 1 E.H.R.R. 737, para. 49.

[50] (1979) 1 E.H.R.R. 737.

varies from time to time and from place to place, especially in our era which is characterised by a rapid and far-reaching evolution of opinions on the subject. By reason of their direct and continuous contact with the vital forces of their countries, State authorities are in principle in a better position than the international judge to give an opinion on the exact content of these requirements as well as on the 'necessity' or a 'restriction' or 'penalty' intended to meet them . . . Consequently Article 10(2) leaves to the Contracting States a margin of appreciation."[51]

The European Court seeks to ensure a uniform approach to the Convention whilst, at the same time, recognising the democratic mandate of the individual Contracting States. The margin of appreciation is, perhaps, an inevitable side-effect of this stance. The Court explained the margin of appreciation in *Jersild v. Denmark*,[52] a case relating to the Court's approach to Article 10, as follows: **4.24**

"The Court's task, in exercising its supervisory jurisdiction, is not to take the place of the competent national authorities but rather to review under Article 10 the decisions they delivered pursuant to their power of appreciation. This does not mean that the supervision is limited to ascertaining whether the respondent State exercised its discretion reasonably, carefully and in good faith; what the Court has to do is to look at the interference complained of in the light of the case as a whole and determine whether it was 'proportionate to the legitimate aim pursued' and whether the reasons adduced by the national authorities to justify it are 'relevant and sufficient': *Sunday Times v. United Kingdom* (1992) 14 E.H.R.R. 229, para.50. In so doing, the Court has to satisfy itself that the national authorities applied standards which were in conformity with the principles embodied in Article 10 and, moreover, that they based their decisions on an acceptable assessment of the relevant facts."[53]

A Variable Margin

The margin of appreciation varies according to the context. Relevant factors include: **4.25**

(1) the nature of the Convention right in issue;

(2) its importance for the individual;

(3) the nature of the activities concerned.[54]

The margin of appreciation permitted has been narrower in relation to certain Convention rights than in relation to others. For example, it is very narrow when considering freedom of expression (particularly political expression) under Article 10 or in relation to discrimination on grounds of

---

[51] *ibid.*, para. 48.
[52] (1995) 19 E.H.R.R. 1.
[53] *ibid.*, para. 37.
[54] *Buckley v. United Kingdom* (1997) 23 E.H.R.R. 101, para. 74.

sex or race.[55] In these circumstances, the Court sometimes shifts the burden of proof to the respondent state to show "very weighty reasons" for the interference.[56] On the other hand, it is fairly broad in the following circumstances[57]:

(a) when considering interference with property rights under Article 1 of Protocol No. 1, which involves consideration of social and economic policy[58];

(b) in relation to moral issues generally[59];

(c) in relation to the more intimate aspects of private life[60];

(d) where considerations of national security and the prevention of crime exist[61];

(e) where there is little European consensus[62];

(f) where the Court has found that the Convention imposed positive obligations[63];

(g) where a sovereign right is in issue.[64]

---

[55] *Abdulaziz, Cabales and Balkandali v. United Kingdom* (1985) 7 E.H.R.R. 471. See also *Burghartz v. Switzerland* (1994) 18 E.H.R.R.101, para. 28; *Marckx v. Belgium* (1980) 2 E.H.R.R. 330, para. 41.

[56] See, *e.g. Abdulaziz, Cabales and Balkandali v. United Kingdom* (1985) 7 E.H.R.R. 471, para. 78.

[57] See generally Y. Arai, "The Margin of Appreciation Doctrine in the Jurisprudence of Article 8 of the European Convention on Human Rights", Netherlands Quarterly of Human Rights, Vol.16/1, 41–61, 1998.

[58] See, *e.g. James v. United Kingdom* (1986) 8 E.H.R.R. 123, paras. 46–47 (the Court will respect a national legislature's judgment as to what is in the public interest when implementing social and economic policies, unless that judgment is "manifestly without foundation"). See also *Lithgow v. United Kingdom* (1986) 8 E.H.R.R. 329, para. 122.

[59] *Handyside v. United Kingdom* (1979) 1 E.H.R.R. 737.

[60] See, *e.g.* in relation to the age of consent for homosexuals: *X v. United Kingdom* (1978) 19 D.R. 66, paras 147–148, or the question of whether a homosexual couple are entitled to family life: *X and Y v. United Kingdom,* Application No. 9369/81, (1983) 32 D.R. 220. The national courts are better placed to assess the particular culture, morals and religion in their state's society.

[61] See, *e.g. Klass v. Germany* (1980) 2 E.H.R.R. 214.

[62] See, *e.g.* in relation to transsexual issues: *Rees v. United Kingdom* (1987) 9 E.H.R.R.56, para. 37; *Cossey v. United Kingdom* (1991) 13 E.H.R.R. 622, para. 40; *X, Y and Z v. United Kingdom* (1997) 24 E.H.R.R. 143, para. 44; and in relation to paternity proceedings *Rasmussen v. Denmark* (1985) 7 E.H.R.R. 371 , para. 41. By contrast, where there is consensus in the majority of Contracting States, this may justify recourse to an evolutive interpretation.

[63] See, *e.g. Johnston v. Ireland* (1987) 9 E.H.R.R. 203. The Court stated (at para. 55):

"Although the essential object of Article 8 is to protect the individual against arbitrary interference by the public authorities, there may in addition be positive obligations inherent in an effective 'respect' for family life. However, especially as far as those positive obligations are concerned, the notion of 'respect' is not clear-cut: having regard to the diversity of the practices followed and the situations obtaining in the Contracting States, the notion's requirements will vary considerably from case to case. Accordingly, this is an area in which the Contracting Parties enjoy a wide margin of appreciation in determining the steps to be taken to ensure compliance with the Convention with due regard to the needs and resources of the community and of individuals."

[64] See, *e.g.* in relation to immigration: *Amuur v. France* (1996) 22 E.H.R.R. 533, para. 41.

Extent of Margin of Appreciation Granted by Domestic Courts

The rationale for the doctrine of "margin of appreciation", *i.e.*, that an **4.26** international court exercising a supervisory jurisdiction is not in the best position to assess the substantive merits of a decision, does not apply in the domestic context as judges do have knowledge of, and the ability to judge, the position in a national or local area.[65] On the other hand, domestic courts have traditionally allowed public authorities a certain margin of appreciation or discretion in relation to their particular spheres of competence, though with a sliding scale of review. In formulating a heightened test of *Wednesbury* unreasonableness,[66] where Convention rights were in issue prior to the HRA, in *R. v. Ministry of Defence, ex p. Smith*,[67] Sir Thomas Bingham M.R. held that:

"The more substantial the interference with human rights, the more the court will require by way of justification before it is satisfied that the decision is reasonable in the sense outlined above."[68]

Nonetheless, the domestic concept of *Wednesbury* unreasonableness is **4.27** not the same as the doctrine of margin of appreciation, since it falls short of the level of scrutiny applied by the European Court even on the heightened test.[69] In the case of *R v. Director of Public Prosecutions, ex p. Kebilene*,[70] the House of Lords considered the applicability of the doctrine of margin of appreciation to the domestic context. Lord Hope stated as follows:

"The doctrine is an integral part of the supervisory jurisdiction which is exercised over state conduct by the international court. By conceding a margin of appreciation to each national system, the court has recognised that the Convention, as a living system, does not need to be applied uniformly by all states but may vary in its application

---

[65] See, *e.g.* The Honourable Sir John Laws, "The Limitations of Human Rights" [1998] P.L. 254 at 258. See also *R. v. Secretary of State for the Environment, ex p. National and Local Government Officer Association* (1993) 5 Admin L.R. 785 at 801 *per* Neill L.J.
[66] *Associated Provincial Picture Houses v. Wednesbury Corporation* [1948] 1 K.B. 223.
[67] [1996] Q.B. 517.
[68] *ibid.*, at 554. See also *R v. Lord Saville of Newdigate, ex p. A* [1999] 4 All E.R. 860 at 872; *R. v. Secretary of State for the Home Department, ex p. Launder* [1997] 1 W.L.R. 839 at 867. This approach recognises that a fundamental right is engaged and the court insists in consequence that this be respected by the decision maker, who is required to demonstrate either that his proposed action does not in truth interfere with the right, or if it does, that considerations exist which might reasonably be accepted as amounting to a substantial justification for the interference: see *R. v. Secretary of State for the Home Department, ex p. Mahmood (Amjad)*, [2001] 1 W.L.R. 840, CA and *R. v. Secretary of State for the Home Department, ex p. Mehmet Sezek*, unreported, December 21, 2000, expressly approving *ex p. Mahmood* and stating that the decision maker retains the ultimate decision but bears the burden of proving he has not violated human rights.
[69] This is illustrated by the fact that the Court of Appeal was unable to provide a remedy to the armed forces applicants who had been investigated and discharged from employment by reason of their homosexuality in *ex p. Smith*. However, the European Court found violations of the Convention: *Smith & Grady v. United Kingdom* (2000) 29 E.H.R.R. 493. See also *R. v. Ministry of Defence, ex p. Smith* [1996] Q.B. 517 at 558–559 (*per* L. Bingham M.R.); at 564 (*per* Henry L.J.) and at 565 (*per* Thorpe L.J.)
[70] [1999] 3 W.L.R. 972, HL.

according to local needs and conditions. This technique is not available to the national courts when they are considering Convention issues arising within their own countries. But in the hands of the national courts also the Convention should be seen as an expression of fundamental principles rather than as a set of mere rules. The questions which the courts will have to decide in the application of these principles will involve questions of balance between competing interests and issues of proportionality.

In this area difficult choices may have to be made by the executive or the legislature between the rights of the individual and the needs of society. In some circumstances it will be appropriate for the courts to recognise that there is an area of judgment within which the judiciary will defer, on democratic grounds, to the considered opinion of the elected body or person whose act or decision is said to be incompatible with the Convention. This point is well made at p.74, para.3.21 of *Human Rights Law and Practice* (1999), of which Lord Lester of Herne Hill and Mr. Pannick are the general editors, where the area in which these choices may arise is conveniently and appropriately described as 'the discretionary area of judgment'. It will be easier for such an area of judgment to be recognised where the Convention itself requires a balance to be struck, much less so where the right is stated in terms which are unqualified. It will be easier for it to be recognised where the issues involve questions of social or economic policy, much less so where the rights are of high constitutional importance or are of a kind where the courts are especially well placed to assess the need for protection."[71]

4.28 The Privy Council also considered the margin of appreciation in *Stott (Procurator Fiscal, Dunfermline) v. Brown*.[72] Lord Bingham stated:

"While a national court does not accord the margin of appreciation recognised by the European Court as a supra-national court, it will give weight to the decisions of a representative legislature and a democratic government within the discretionary area of judgment accorded to those bodies."[73]

Lord Steyn also addressed the margin of appreciation:

"Under the Convention system the primary duty is placed on domestic courts to secure and protect Convention rights. The function of the ECHR is essential but supervisory. In that capacity it accords to domestic courts a margin of appreciation, which recognises that national institutions are in principle better placed than an international court to evaluate local needs and conditions. That principle is logically

---

[71] *ibid.*, at 993H–994D.
[72] (2001) 2 W.L.R. 817, PC.
[73] The Privy Council endorsed the argument set out in Lester & Pannick, *Human Rights Law & Practice* (Butterworths, 1999), pp. 73–76. See also Singh, Hunt & Demetriou, "Is there a Role for the 'Margin of Appreciation' in National Law after the Human Rights Act?" [1999] E.H.R.L.R. 15 and D. Pannick, "Principles of interpretation of Convention rights under the Human Rights Act and the discretionary area of judgment" [1998] P.L. 545.

not applicable to domestic courts. On the other hand, national courts may accord to the decisions of national legislatures some deference *where the context justifies* it: see *R v. Director of Public Prosecutions, ex parte Kebilene* [1999] 3 W.L.R. 972 *per* Lord Hope of Craighead at 993–994 . . . ".[74]

The domestic approach is, therefore, that the margin of appreciation does **4.29** not apply to domestic litigation. However, in areas which involve a balancing exercise between the rights of the individual and the interests of society or where questions of social and economic policy are at issue, it may be appropriate for the courts to defer to the considered opinion of the elected body or person whose act or decision is being challenged. Particular facts to which the court will have regard will be the importance of the right in issue both to the individual and more generally, and the court's own expertise in relation to the subject-matter in question.

It remains to be fully worked out in practice how much leeway the courts **4.30** will allow to the legislature or decision maker when assessing the necessity for restrictions on Convention rights. Since the court is itself exercising a primary judgment and must conduct an adequate examination of the facts on which a decision is based,[75] the "margin of appreciation" granted must inevitably be significantly less than under the traditional irrationality or *Wednesbury* unreasonableness test and therefore be more generous to the applicant or claimant. Greater deference will generally be given to the legislature or where the authority being reviewed is elected or otherwise accountable to the electorate.[76] The approach demonstrated by *R. v. Secretary of State for the Home Department, ex p. Mahmood (Amjad)*,[77] and *R. v. Secretary of State for the Home Department, ex p. Mehmet Sezek*,[78] is to hold that the decision maker retains the ultimate decision but bears the burden of proving he has not violated Convention rights. In *Mahmood*, Lord Phillips M.R. stated:

> "When anxiously scrutinizing an executive decision that interferences with human rights, the court will ask the question, applying an objective test, whether the decision-maker could reasonably have concluded that the interference was necessary to achieve one or more of the legitimate aims recognised by the Convention. When considering the test of necessity in the relevant context, the court must taken into account the European jurisprudence in accordance with section 2 of the 1998 Act."[78A]

---

[74] See also Sir John Laws, "The Limitation of Human Rights" [1998] P.L. 254 at 261, who argues that the difference between the margin of appreciation and the *Wednesbury* approach is only one of degree.

[75] *Vogt v. Germany* (1996) 21 E.H.R.R. 205

[76] See also *Libman v. Attorney-General of Quebec* (1998) 3 B.H.R.C. 269 at 289.

[77] [2001] 1 W.L.R. 840, CA.

[78] Unreported, December 21, 2000, Admin Ct expressly approving *ex p. Mahmood*. See also *R. (Sezek) v. Secretary of State for the Home Department*, *The Times*, June 20, 2001, CA.

[78A] At para. 40.

Mahmood was followed by the Court of Appeal in *R. (Isiko) v. Secretary of State for the Home Department*[78B] and by Thomas J. in *R. (Samaroo) v. Secretary of State for the Home Department.*[78C] In *Nasser v. United Bank of Kuwait,*[78D] the Court of Appeal stated that the task for an English court was to decide what was a justifiable and proportionate exercise of discretion in the domestic context.

The test adopted by Lord Phillips M.R. in *Mahmood* was further considered and refined by the House of Lords in *R. (Daly) v. Secretary of State for the Home Department.*[78E] Lord Steyn noted that the observations were couched in language reminiscent of the *Wednesbury*[78F] ground of review and in particular the heightened scrutiny test formulated in *R. v. Ministry of Defence, ex p. Smith.*[78G] Lord Steyn noted that there is a material difference between the *Wednesbury* and *Smith* grounds of review and the approach of proportionality applicable in respect of review when Convention rights are at stake. He stated that:

"The starting point is that there is an overlap between the traditional grounds of review and the approach of proportionality. Most cases would be decided in the same way whichever approach is adopted. But the intensity of review is somewhat greater under the proportionality approach . . . . First, the doctrine of proportionality may require the reviewing court to assess the balance which the decision maker has struck, not merely whether it is within the range of rational or reasonable decisions. Secondly, the proportionality test may go further than the traditional grounds of review inasmuch as it may require attention to be directed to the relative weight accorded to interests and considerations. Thirdly, even the heightened scrutiny test developed in *R. v. Ministry of Defence, ex p. Smith* [1996] Q.B. 517, 554 is not necessarily appropriate to the protection of human rights . . . . In other words, the intensity of review, in similar cases, is guaranteed by the twin requirements that the limitation of the right was necessary in a democratic society, in the sense of meeting a pressing social need, and the question whether the interference was really proportionate to the legitimate aim being pursued."[78H]

Lord Steyn stated that the differences between the traditional grounds of review and the proportionality approach may sometimes yield different results and it is therefore important that cases involving Convention rights are analysed in the correct way. He emphasized that this approach did not mean that there had been a shift to merits review. The respective roles of judges and administrators remain distinct. To this extent the general tenor of the observations in *Mahmood* are correct. Accordingly, the court does not substitute its own decision for that of the administrative decision-

---

[78B] *The Times*, February 20, 2001, CA.
[78C] Unreported, December 20, 2000.
[78D] [2001] EWCA Civ 556, April 11, 2001, CA.
[78E] [2001] 2 W.L.R. 1622. See also *R. v. S. Borough Council and W. Borough Council, ex p. The Independent*, June 18, 2001, QBD.
[78F] *Associated Provincial Picture Houses Ltd v. Wednesbury Corpn* [1948] 1 K.B. 223.
[78G] [1996] Q.B. 517 at 554.
[78H] At 1635–1636, para. 27.

maker. However, the degree of scrutiny is greater than a heightened *Wednesbury* test and the requirements of proportionality must be expressly considered. As Laws L.J. emphasised in *Mahmood*, the intensity of review will depend on the subject matter at hand.[78I]

Giving Reasons for Judicial Deference

A court should comply with its own duty under section 6 of the HRA to apply the principles of the Convention and to identify and justify the scope of review,[79] giving reasons for any deference shown to the legislature or executive.   **4.31**

Reconsideration of Strasbourg Decisions

It is possible that United Kingdom laws or decisions which have previously been upheld by the European Court as within the margin of appreciation can now be reconsidered for compatibility under the HRA.   **4.32**

5. PERMITTED RESTRICTIONS ON RIGHTS

Articles 8 to 11 each contain permitted restrictions upon, or justifications for interferences by, public authorities with the exercises of the rights they contain. They may be contrasted with the absolute rights contained in the Convention (for example the right to life in Article 2 and the prohibition on torture in Article 3) upon which no restrictions are permitted. Restrictions on the Article 8 to 11 rights falling within the above categories are permitted only on condition that such restrictions are: **4.33**

    (1) prescribed by law (or are "in accordance with the law")[80]; and

    (2) necessary in a democratic society[81] for the protection of certain
        specified interests. These interests include, *inter alia*:

        (a) national security;
        (b) prevention of disorder or crime;
        (c) public safety;
        (d) the protection of health or morals;
        (e) the protection of the rights and freedoms of others.[81A]

The categories of justification are exhaustive.[82] Further, exceptions to the rights contained in these Articles are to be narrowly interpreted.[83] Any limitation or restriction on a fundamental right must not be discriminatory under Article 14.

[78I] [2001] 1 W.L.R. 840 at 847, para. 18 approved by Lord Steyn in *Daly* at page 1636, para. 28.
[79] See further Singh, Hunt & Demetriou, "Is there a Role for the 'Margin of Appreciation' in National Law after the Human Rights Act?" [1999] E.H.R.L.R. 15 at 21.
[80] See paras 4.43 *et seq.*, below.
[81] See paras 4.34 *et seq.*, below.
[81A] Reference should be made to the individual Articles for the categories of justification permitted in each case.
[82] Convention, Art. 17.
[83] *Sunday Times v. United Kingdom* (1980) 2 E.H.R.R. 245, para. 65.

6. WHAT IS "NECESSARY IN A DEMOCRATIC SOCIETY"?

4.34   As stated above,[84] the European Court has held that important features of a "democratic society" are "pluralism, tolerance and broadmindedness", "the rule of law", access to the courts, freedom of expression including particularly freedom of political debate, and the protection of any "most intimate aspect of private life".

4.35   The test of what is "necessary in a democratic society" involves considering:

> (1) whether the interference corresponds to a "a pressing social need";
>
> (2) whether it is proportionate to the legitimate aim pursued; and
>
> (3) whether the reasons given by the national authorities to justify it are relevant and sufficient.[85]

The "pressing social need" test requires evaluation of the severity of the social need, which must be evaluated in light of the nature and extent of the problem. The concept of "necessity" is not synonymous with "indispensable"; neither has it the flexibility of such expressions as "desirable" or "reasonable".[86] The Contracting State has a certain margin of appreciation in assessing whether such a need exists, but it goes hand in hand with a European supervision and the European Court is therefore empowered to give the final ruling.[87]

International Context

4.36   The concept of "necessary in a democratic society" is paralleled by Article 22 of the International Covenant on Civil and Political Rights 1966 and section 1 of the Canadian Charter of Rights and Freedoms. In *R. v. Oakes*,[88] the Supreme Court of Canada considered the values and principles by which the Canadian Charter of Rights and Freedoms is to be interpreted. Section 1 of the Charter states that rights and freedoms are guaranteed "subject only to such reasonable limits prescribed by law as can be demonstrably justified in a free and democratic society". Dickson C.J. stated:

> "[T]he values and principles essential to a free and democratic society . . . embody, to name but a few, respect for the inherent dignity of the human person, commitment to social justice and equality, accommodation of a wide variety of beliefs, respect for cultural and group identity, and faith in social and political institutions which enhance the participation of individuals and groups in society."

---

[84] See para. 4.06, above.
[85] *Sunday Times v. United Kingdom* (1980) 2 E.H.R.R. 245, para. 62.
[86] *Silver v. United Kingdom* (1983) 5 E.H.R.R. 347, para. 97; *Handyside v. United Kingdom* (1979) 1 E.H.R.R. 737, para. 48.
[87] *Jersild v. Denmark* (1995) 19 E.H.R.R. 1, para. 37. See paras 4.22 *et seq.* above.
[88] [1986] S.C.R. 1; (1986) 26 D.L.R. (4th) 200.

In Australia, which has no bill of rights, the notion of representational **4.37**
democracy underlies the constitution. A freedom will be implied where it is
an indispensable incident of the system of representative government
created by the constitution.[89]

7. PROPORTIONALITY

The majority of Convention rights are qualified rights allowing in appro- **4.38**
priate cases interference with or restrictions of that right in the general or
public interest. The legitimate application of such rights involves a balancing of the right of the individual against the general interest of the community as a whole or the rights of another individual or section of the
community.[90] The principle of proportionality is a component part of determining the necessity of restrictions upon Convention rights. It features
particularly in Article 6 (subject to the absolute nature of the overall right)
and Articles 8 to 11.

Proportionality essentially means that a restriction on a Convention right **4.39**
must go no further than absolutely necessary to satisfy the legitimate aim
to be achieved (for example in relation to the implied rights in Article 6(1))
or what is necessary in a democratic society (for example in Articles 8 to
11). A restriction on a Convention right must be "proportionate to the
legitimate aim pursued".[91] Put another way, there must be "a reasonable
relationship of proportionality between the means employed and the legitimate objectives pursued by the contested limitation".[92] Determining the
proportionality of a measure will require consideration of the following:[93]

(1) whether relevant and sufficient reasons have been advanced for
the interference[94];

(2) whether there is a less restrictive alternative[95];

(3) whether there are effective safeguards against abuse[96];

(4) whether there is procedural fairness, ensuring that individual
rights affected by the measure are taken into account.[97]

If the restriction destroys the very essence of the right in question, the **4.40**
interference will not generally be proportionate.[98] The proportionality test

---

[89] *Lange v. Australian Broadcasting Corporation* (1997) 189 C.L.R. 520; (1997) B.H.R.C. 513.
[90] *Sporrong & Lönnroth v. Sweden* (1983) 5 E.H.R.R. 35, para. 69; *Sheffield & Horsham v. United Kingdom* (1999) 27 E.H.R.R. 163, para. 52. See also *R. v. Oakes* (1986) 26 D.L.R. (4th) 200 at 227–228, Canadian Sup Ct; *Ross v. New Brunswick School District No. 15* [1996] 1 S.C.R. 825 at 872, Canadian Sup Ct.
[91] *Handyside v. United Kingdom* (1979) 1 E.H.R.R. 737, para. 49.
[92] *Fayed v. United Kingdom* (1994) 18 E.H.R.R. 393, para. 71.
[93] See Keir Starmer, *European Human Rights Law* (Legal Action Group, 1999) who advanced this list of relevant factors at para. 4.42.
[94] *Vogt v. Germany* (1996) 21 E.H.R.R. 205, para. 52.
[95] *Campbell v. United Kingdom* (1993) 15 E.H.R.R. 137.
[96] *Klass v. Germany* (1980) 2 E.H.R.R. 214.
[97] *Buckley v. United Kingdom* (1997) 23 E.H.R.R. 101.
[98] *Stubbings v. United Kingdom* (1997) 23 E.H.R.R. 213; *F v. Switzerland* (1988) 10 E.H.R.R. 411, para. 40.

echoes that applied by the European Court of Justice when applying Community law which requires that:

(1) a measure is intended to achieve a legitimate objective;

(2) it is the least restrictive means of achieving that objective;

(3) it does not have an excessive or disproportionate effect on the interests of affected persons.[99]

In *R. v. A*,[99A] Lord Steyn directly introduced the E.C. law concept of proportionality into the HRA. He stated that the criteria for determining the test of proportionality have been analysed in similar terms in the case-law of the European Court of Justice and the European Court of Human Rights. He observed that it was not necessary to re-invent the wheel. In *de Freitas v. Permanent Secretary of Ministry of Agriculture, Fisheries, Land and Housing*.[99B] Lord Clyde adopted a precise and concrete analysis of the criteria. In determining whether a limitation is arbitrary or excessive, a court should ask itself whether:

(i) the legislative objective is sufficiently important to justify limiting a fundamental right;

(ii) the measures designed to meet the legislative objective are rationally connected with it; and

(iii) the means used to impair the right or freedom are no more than is necessary to accomplish the objective.

The critical matter is the third criterion. Lord Steyn again repeated this test in *R. (Daly) v. Secretary of State for the Home Department*.[99C].

4.41 The principle of proportionality focuses in particular on the effects of interferences on the rights of the individual. In *B v. Secretary of State for the Home Department*,[1] Sedley L.J. identified the principle of proportionality in this way:

" . . . a measure that interferes with a Community or human right must not only be authorised by law but must correspond to a pressing social need and go no further than is strictly necessary in a pluralistic society to achieve its permitted purpose; or, more shortly, must be appropriate and necessary to its legitimate aim."

4.42 A public authority exercising a discretion must consider all of the available methods of meeting the aim to be achieved and select the least restrictive of individual Convention rights. If the decision or act is challenged before the domestic courts, the court must make its own determination of whether

---

[99] See, *e.g.* Case C–331/88 *R. v. Ministry of Agriculture, Fisheries and Food, ex p. Fedesa* [1990] E.C.R. 4023, para. 13; [1991] 1 C.M.L.R. 507, ECJ. There is also a parallel with the Canadian approach of "minimum impairment" or "least drastic means": *R. v. Oakes* [1986] S.C.R. 103; (1986) 26 D.L.R.(4th) 200.

[99A] [2001] 2 W.L.R. 1546; [2001] 3 All E.R. 1, HL.

[99B] [1999] 1 A.C. 69, PC.

[99C] [2001] 2 W.L.R. 1622, HL at para. 27.

[1] [2000] 2 C.M.L.R. 1086, CA.

the decision or act was proportionate. It must make a *primary* judgment based on the facts which formed the basis for the decision or act in question. It is not conducting merely a secondary review function,[2] although it will no doubt carefully consider the manner in which the decision was reached by the authority in question. In *R v. Secretary of State for the Home Department, ex p. Javed*,[3] Turner J. recognised that although the courts have been historically reluctant to evaluate evidence when reviewing decisions of the Executive, since the HRA the court has a positive duty to give effect to the Convention and to ensure that there is an effective remedy in cases of suspected breach of Convention rights so that, where an executive decision needs to be reviewed on the facts, the court can carry out this exercise once the relevant material is before it.

8. THE RULE OF LAW

The rule of law is inherent in the Convention as a whole. Interference with or restriction of a Convention right must be lawful for it to be justified. The legality principle is expressly contained in Articles 2, 5, 6 and 8 to 11 and Article 1 of Protocol No. 1. For example, in Article 8(2) an interference by a public authority with the right to respect for private life can only be justified if it is "in accordance with the law". In Article 10(2), a restriction on the right to freedom of expression can only be justified if it is "prescribed by law". Article 1 of Protocol No. 1 only permits deprivation of possessions "subject to the conditions provided for by law and by the general principles of international law".   **4.43**

An act may be lawful if it has "some basis in domestic law" whether pursuant to statutory authority, the common law,[4] European Community law,[5] or other sufficient source of guidance.[6] The rule of law as interpreted by the European Court effectively requires a positive legal basis for the act in question. This contrasts with the traditional Diceyan approach adopted by the domestic courts premised on the theory that an act is lawful unless it is prohibited. However, the legal source must additionally be both clear and accessible for it to be compatible with the rule of law.[7]   **4.44**

Clarity or Legal Certainty

Interferences with Convention rights and freedoms are not permitted unless there is a clear legal basis for doing so. Similarly, an individual should be able to predict with reasonable certainty when, and under what conditions, such interferences may occur. A norm will not be regarded as a "law" unless it is formulated with sufficient precision to enable the citizen   **4.45**

---

[2] *R. v. Ministry of Defence, ex p. Smith* [1996] Q.B. 517 at 541, *per* Simon Brown L.J.
[3] *The Times*, February 9, 2001, QBD, Turner J.
[4] *SW & CR v. United Kingdom* (1996) 21 E.H.R.R. 363, para. 46; *Sunday Times v. United Kingdom* (1980) 2 E.H.R.R. 245, para. 47.
[5] *Groppera Radio AG v. Switzerland* (1990) 12 E.H.R.R. 321, paras. 67–68.
[6] *Silver v. United Kingdom* (1983) 5 E.H.R.R. 347, para. 86.
[7] This is to ensure a measure of protection in domestic law against arbitrary interferences by public authorities: *Malone v. United Kingdom* (1985) 7 E.H.R.R. 14, para. 67.

to regulate his conduct.[8] The level of precision required of a domestic law depends to a considerable degree on the content of the instrument in question, the field it is designed to cover and the number and status of those to whom it is addressed.[9] In this regard, the Court gives a margin of appreciation to the national authorities who interpret and apply domestic law.[10] The mere fact that a legal provision is capable of more than one construction does not necessarily mean that it does not meet the requirement implied in the notion "prescribed by law".[11] Further, the fact that a person has to consult a lawyer in order to properly understand a provision does not breach the requirement. The existence of a discretion in a person or body responsible for implementing the measure is not fatal provided that there is, in the measure or supplementary to it, a sufficient indication of the circumstances in which the discretion will be exercised.[12] A progressive change in the common law by way of interpretation will not breach the principle of legal certainty provided that the development of the law is reasonably foreseeable (with the assistance of appropriate legal advice if necessary).[13]

Accessibility

4.46   The law must be publicly and reasonably available so that an individual affected or potentially affected by the provision is enabled:

> "if need be with appropriate advice—to foresee, to a degree that is reasonable in the circumstances, the consequences which a given action may entail. Those consequences need not be foreseeable with absolute certainty: experience shows this to be unattainable. Again, whilst certainty is highly desirable, it may bring in its train excessive rigidity and the law must be able to keep pace with changing circumstances. Accordingly, many laws are inevitably couched in terms which, to a greater or lesser extent, are vague and whose interpretation and application are questions of practice.[14]

4.47   In *De Geouffre de la Pradelle v. France*,[15] the European Court found that a statutory procedure for challenging a decree which affected the status and use of the applicant's property violated Article 6(1), because the extreme complexity of the procedure was likely to create legal uncertainty as to the exact nature of the decree in question and as to calculating the time limit for bringing a legal challenge. The system was not "sufficiently coherent and clear".[16]

---

[8] *Sunday Times v. United Kingdom* (1980) 2 E.H.R.R. 245, para. 49.
[9] *Vogt v. Germany,* (1996) 21 E.H.R.R. 205, para. 48.
[10] *ibid.*
[11] *ibid.*
[12] *Silver v. United Kingdom* (1983) 5 E.H.R.R. 347, para. 88. See also *Malone v. United Kingdom* (1985) 7 E.H.R.R. 14, para. 67.
[13] *SW and CR v. United Kingdom* (1996) 21 E.H.R.R. 363, para. 48.
[14] *Sunday Times v. United Kingdom* (1980) 2 E.H.R.R. 245, para. 49.
[15] Application No. 12964/87, November 24, 1992.
[16] *ibid.*, para. 35.

Regulatory Provisions

The European Court has, however, recognised that regulatory provisions **4.48** do involve a measure of administrative discretion and interpretation in their application.[17]

Interference with Judicial Determinations

Interference by the legislature or Executive with the judicial determination **4.49** of a dispute may also be contrary to the rule of law.[18]

9. BURDEN AND STANDARD OF PROOF

Once the interference with a Convention right has been established, the **4.50** burden of proof is on the defendant or respondent to justify the interference. The standard of proof is that the justification for the interference must be "convincingly established".[19] The Court has stated that, in the case of an interference with an intimate aspect of private life, "particularly serious reasons" for justifying the interference must be shown,[20] and in cases involving discrimination on the ground of sex or race, the defendant or respondent must show "very weighty reasons" to justify differences in treatment.[21] This might be contrasted with the civil burden of proof, which is usually borne by the claimant or applicant in relation to all aspects of the claim, and the application of the civil standard of proof, that is the "balance of probabilities" test. However, it is not clear that the Court will require a significantly higher standard of proof than the balance of probabilities test in all such cases. In assessing evidence under Article 3, the Court has applied a standard of proof "beyond reasonable doubt". However, this co-existed with strong presumptions of fact where a person was injured during custody by state authorities.[21A]

10. ABUSE OF RIGHTS

Article 17 of the Convention provides: **4.51**

> "Nothing in this Convention may be interpreted as implying for any state, group or person any right to engage in any activity or perform any act aimed at the destruction of any of the rights and freedoms set forth herein or at their limitation to a greater extent than is provided for in the Convention."

Article 17 prevents the state, or its citizens, from invoking a Convention right in order to engage in an activity or perform an act which is aimed at

---

[17] *Ahmed v. United Kingdom* (2000) 29 E.H.R.R. 1.
[18] *Benthem v. Netherlands* (1986) 8 E.H.R.R. 1, para. 40; *cf. National & Provincial Building Society v. United Kingdom* (1998) 25 E.H.R.R. 127.
[19] *Barthold v. Germany* (1985) 7 E.H.R.R. 383, para. 58.
[20] *Dudgeon v. United Kingdom* (1982) 4 E.H.R.R. 149, para. 52.
[21] *Abdulaziz, Cabales and Balkandali v. United Kingdom* (1985) 7 E.H.R.R. 471, para. 78.
[21A] *Altay v. Turkey*, Application No. 22279/93, May 22, 2001.

destroying or limiting the Convention rights of others (to a greater extent than is permissible by the Convention). This Article prevents the state from relying on a defence to an interference with a Convention right other than one authorised by the Convention. In relation to groups or individuals relying on Convention rights to deprive others of their rights, the European Court stated in *Lawless v. Ireland (No. 3)*[22] that:

" . . . the purpose of Article 17, in so far as it refers to groups or individuals, is to make it impossible for them to derive from the Convention a right to engage in any activity, or perform any act aimed at destroying any of the rights and freedoms set forth in the Convention. Therefore no person may be able to take advantage of the provisions of the Convention to perform acts aimed at destroying the aforesaid rights and freedoms."[23]

---

[22] (1979) 1 E.H.R.R. 15.
[23] *ibid.*, para. 7.

CHAPTER 5

General Principles of Human Rights Law In Domestic Courts

1. INTRODUCTION

This chapter considers some of the particular issues that arise in the **5.01** domestic setting. First, the interpretative obligation imposed by section 3 of the HRA in relation to legislation is considered in more detail. Secondly, the effect of human rights law between private individuals is considered. The extent to which the courts will permit the development of the horizontal effect of the Convention on litigation between private parties is obviously highly significant to the impact of European human rights law on many areas of commercial and civil practice. Thirdly, attention is drawn to sources of human rights jurisprudence other than the European Convention. These include domestic common law constitutional rights, rights protected in European Community law and international human rights law. The rights derived from the common law are considered at paragraphs 5.72 *et seq.*, below. The protection given to fundamental rights under

European Community law is potentially of enormous significance since such rights will be supreme in domestic law over incompatible primary legislation pursuant to section 2(2) of the European Communities Act 1972 and this is discussed in Chapter 6. Various sources of international human rights law are identified and discussed in Chapter 7.

2. THE INTERPRETATIVE OBLIGATION IN SECTION 3, HRA

Introduction

5.02 The HRA imposes a duty to interpret primary and subordinate legislation compatibly with the Convention. This is a key element in the Act.[1] Section 3 of the HRA provides:

> "(1) So far as it is possible to do so, primary legislation and subordinate legislation must be read and given effect in a way which is compatible with the Convention rights.
> (2) This section—
>> (a) applies to primary legislation and subordinate legislation whenever enacted;
>> (b) does not affect the validity, continuing operation or enforcement of any incompatible primary legislation; and
>> (c) does not affect the validity, continuing operation or enforcement of any incompatible subordinate legislation if (disregarding any possibility of revocation) primary legislation prevents removal of the incompatibility."

5.03 Pursuant to section 3(1), primary and subordinate legislation must be read and given effect to in a way which is compatible with Convention rights "so far as it is possible to do so". This is a very strong principle of interpretation that goes considerably further than the pre-existing use of the Convention to resolve ambiguities in legislation. The courts are required to interpret legislation so as to uphold Convention rights unless the legislation is so clearly incompatible with the Convention that it is impossible to do so.[2] The interpretative obligation applies whenever the legislation was enacted.[3] It also applies to any relevant issues of construction of the HRA itself. Whilst the obligation in section 3 principally falls on the courts, it is a general mandatory principle of interpretation that is not limited to the courts and appears to apply to all concerned with interpreting legislation, including the Executive and administrators. The section 3 principle of interpretation may be relied on in an appeal heard after the HRA came into force even though the appeal is against an order made before that date.[3A]

---

[1] *R. v. Director of Public Prosecutions ex p. Kebilene* [1999] 3 W.L.R. 972 at 987B, *per* Lord Cooke.
[2] White Paper, Cm. 3782 (1997), para. 2.7.
[3] s.3(2).
[3A] *J. A. Pye (Oxford) Ltd v. Graham* [2001] 2 W.L.R. 1293, CA.

As Francis Bennion points out,[4] section 3(1) requires two types of inter-   **5.04**
pretation:

(1) the construction of the Convention right in issue; and

(2) the construction of the statutory provision being tested by reference to that right.

In determining the former, the court must take into account the Strasbourg
interpretative approach and case law on the content and scope of the
right. In relation to the latter, section 3(1) probably requires a substantial
change from historic methods of interpretation (which focus on (a) deciding on an "informed" basis whether or not there is a real doubt about the
legal meaning of the enactment and (b) if there is, resolving that doubt by
looking at all the admissible surrounding circumstances before starting to
construe the enactment[5]) to a more purposive interpretative method
based on legislative intention plus Convention compatible construction,
even where this differs from the literal meaning.[6] The primary effect of
section 3(1) will be seen in relation to pre-HRA legislation where Parliament's original intention can no longer be decisive.[7] By contrast, subsequent legislation passed since November 24, 1998, can safely be
presumed in light of the HRA to have been intended by the legislature to
be compatible with the Convention, in the absence of clear evidence of an
intention to the contrary.[8] The nature and content of the interpretative
obligation in section 3(1) in relation to pre-HRA legislation is being developed by the courts post-HRA, although the case-law is not entirely consistent. In *R. v. Offen*,[8A] the Court of Appeal was required to determine
whether section 2 of the Crime (Sentences) Act 1997 which requires the
imposition of a mandatory life sentence where a defendant is convicted of
a second serious offence unless there are "exceptional circumstances" for
not doing so was compatible with Articles 3 and 5 of the Convention. Lord
Woolf C.J. analysed the requirements of Articles 3 and 5 and found that
both prohibited arbitrary detention and since it was possible to interpret
section 2 to avoid that result, the HRA required such an interpretation.[8B] In
*Poplar Housing and Regeneration Community Association Ltd v.
Donoghue*,[8C] the Court of Appeal questioned *obiter* whether a mandatory
duty to make possession orders in certain housing cases could be

---

[4] "What interpretation is 'possible' under s.3(1) of the Human Rights Act?" [2000] P.L. 77 at
86.
[5] Francis Bennion labels this the "global" method of interpretation (*ibid.*), pp. 78–80, 89.
[6] The "developmental" method of interpretation (*ibid.*), pp. 80–82, 91.
[7] In the Parliamentary debates on the Human Rights Bill, the Lord Chancellor spoke of a
deemed intention that pre-HRA legislation should be compatible with the Convention: H.L.
Deb., November 18, 1997, col. 353.
[8] The s.19 statement of compatibility by the Minister responsible for introducing the bill
enforces the intention underlying the HRA that all subsequent legislation is to be compatible
with the Convention, unless expressly stated otherwise (and justified to Parliament). Section
19 was brought into force on November 24, 1998 by the Human Rights Act 1998 (Commencement) Order 1998, S.I. 1998 No. 2882 (C. 71).
[8A] [2001] 2 All E.R. 154, CA.
[8B] This was a departure from pre-HRA law in *R v. Kelly (Edward)* [2000] Q.B. 198, CA.
[8C] [2001] EWCA Civ. 595, April 27, 2001, CA.

interpreted to add a requirement that it must also be reasonable to make possession orders. The Court stated:

(1) unless the legislation would otherwise be in breach of the Convention, section 3 can be ignored and so courts should always first ascertain whether, absent section 3, there would be any breach of the Convention;

(2) if the court has to rely on section 3, it should limit the extent of the modified meaning to that which is necessary to achieve compatibility;

(3) section 3 does not entitle the court to *legislate*. Its task is still one of *interpretation*, but interpretation in accordance with the direction contained in section 3;

(4) the views of the parties and of the Crown as to whether a "constructive" interpretation should be adopted cannot modify the task of the court. If s.3 applies, the court is required to adopt the s.3 approach to interpretation;

(5) the most difficult task which the courts face is distinguishing between legislation and interpretation. Here, practical experience of seeking to apply section 3 will provide the best guide. However, if it is necessary in order to obtain compliance to radically alter the effect of the legislation, this will be an indication that more than interpretation is involved.[8D]

The effect of the Court's approach in *Poplar* is to give effect to Convention rights only where this does not involve judge's legislating and where it does not defeat Parliament's "original objective".[8E] This issue is, at its heart, concerned with sensitivity over the role of judges taking over the role of the legislature in the context of the HRA which was expressly designed to preserve Parliamentary sovereignty. On the other hand, the courts must act in accordance with the interpretative obligation which the legislature has prescribed in section 3(1) HRA. As can be seen below, when considering pre-HRA legislation, judges differ in their views on whether the interpretative obligation in section 3(1) obliges the judiciary to give a legislative provision a meaning compatible with the Convention compatible meaning where this conflicts with the language of the provision and with Parliament's original intention. In *R. v. A*,[8F] the majority of the House of Lords reached a high water mark in the decisions so far in relation to their willingness to override Parliament's original intention if that was incompatible with Convention rights in order to comply with the section 3 interpretative obligation. Lord Steyn considered that it would sometimes be necessary to arrive at a linguistically strained construction and that a declaration of incompatibility must be avoided unless it was plainly impossible to do so, for example where a clear limitation on

---

[8D] Para. 75.
[8E] Para. 77. See also dissenting judgment of Lord Hope in *R. v. A.* [2001] 2 W.L.R. 1546, HL.
[8F] [2001] 2 W.L.R. 1546; [2001] 3 All E.R. 1, HL.

Convention rights was stated in terms. This definition of the obligation suggests that unless there is an *express* prohibition on giving effect to the Convention, section 3(1) requires that the Convention compatible construction be applied. He stated that:

" . . . the interpretative obligation under section 3 of the 1998 Act is a strong one. It applies even if there is no ambiguity in the language in the sense of the language being capable of two different meanings. It is an emphatic adjuration by the legislature: *R. v. Director of Public Prosecutions, ex p. Kebilene* [2000] 2 A.C. 326, per Lord Cooke of Thorodon, at p. 373F; and my judgment, at p. 366B. The White Paper made clear that the obligation goes far beyond the rule which enabled the courts to take the Convention into account in resolving any ambiguity in a legislative provision: see 'Rights Brought Home: The Human Rights Bill' (1997) (Cm 3782) para. 2.7. The draftsman of the Act had before him the slightly weaker model in section 6 of the New Zealand Bill of Rights Act 1990 but preferred stronger language. Parliament specifically rejected the legislative model of requiring a reasonable interpretation. Section 3 places a duty on the court to strive to find a possible interpretation compatible with Convention rights. Under ordinary methods of interpretation a court may depart from the language of the statute to avoid absurd consequences: section 3 goes much further. Undoubtedly, a court must always look for a contextual and purposive interpretation: section 3 is more radical in its effect. It is a general principle of the interpretation of legal instruments that the text is the primary source of interpretation: other sources are subordinate to it . . . Section 3 qualifies this general principle because it requires a court to find an interpretation compatible with Convention rights if it is possible to do so . . . In accordance with the will of Parliament as reflected in section 3 it will sometimes be necessary to adopt an interpretation which linguistically may appear strained. The techniques to be used will not only involve the reading down of express language in a statute but also the implication of provisions. A declaration of incompatibility is a measure of last resort. It must be avoided unless it is plainly impossible to do so. If a *clear* limitation on Convention rights is stated *in terms*, such an impossibility will arise: *R. v. Secretary of State for the Home Department, ex p. Simms* [2000] 2 A.C. 115, 132A–B per Lord Hoffmann."

The majority held that although the statutory provision under consideration—section 41 of the Youth Justice and Criminal Evidence Act 1999—which excluded evidence of a sexual relationship between a defendant and a complainant without the permission of the court, was incompatible with the defendant's right to a fair trial under Article 6, it was permissible to read an implied provision into the section using section 3 that evidence or questioning which was required to ensure a fair trial under Article 6 should not be treated as inadmissible. In *R. v. Lambert* [8G] Lord Hope supported by the majority returned to a theme he had discussed in

---

[8G] July 5, 2001, HL.

his dissenting judgment in *R. v. A.* (echoing the more restrictive approach in *Poplar*) stating that the section 3(1) obligation is inherently limited by the words "so far as it is possible to do so". He observed that resort to s.3(1) will not be possible if the legislation contains provisions, either in the words or phrases which are under scrutiny or elsewhere, which expressly contradict the meaning which the enactment would have to be given to make it compatible. The same consequences will follow if legislation contains provisions which have this effect by necessary implication. Section 3(1) preserves the sovereignty of Parliament. It does not give power to the judges to overturn decisions which the language of the statute shows have been taken on the very point at issue by the legislature. Lord Hope's approach stops short of applying the Convention compatible meaning where there are *implied* limitations on such a meaning. The majority held that the express limitation provisions in section 22(4) made it impossible to interpret section 6 HRA so as to give a wider retrospective effect.[8H]

5.05 Support for a purposive, rather than literal, approach where fundamental rights and freedoms are in issue may be derived from a dictum of Lord Hope in *R. v. Director of Public Prosecutions, ex p. Kebilene*.[9] He stated:

> "In *Attorney-General of Hong Kong v. Lee Kwong-kut* [1993] A.C. 951, 966 Lord Woolf referred to the general approach to the interpretations of constitutions and bills of rights indicated in the previous decisions of the [Privy Council], which he said were equally applicable to the Hong Kong Bill of Rights Ordinance 1991. He mentioned Lord Wilberforce's observation in *Minister of Home Affairs v. Fisher* [1980] A.C. 319, 328 that instruments of this nature call for a generous interpretation suitable to give to individuals the full measure of the fundamental rights and freedoms referred to, and Lord Diplock's comment in *Attorney-General of The Gambia v. Momodou Jobe* [1984] A.C. 689, 700 that a generous and purposive construction is to be given to that part of a constitution which protects and entrenches fundamental rights and freedoms to which all persons in the state are to be entitled. The same approach will now have to be applied in this country when issues are raised under the Act of 1998 about the compatibility of domestic legislation and of acts of public authorities with the fundamental rights and freedoms which are enshrined in the Convention."[10]

5.06 Where a court finds it impossible to read primary legislation, or subordinate legislation whose parent enabling legislation prevents removal of the incompatibility,[11] in such a way as to make it compatible, the courts cannot strike down or declare such legislation invalid.[12]

[8H] For a detailed and helpful analysis of the approach to section 3(1) of the HRA in recent cases, see F. Klug and K. Starmer, "Incorporation through the 'front door': the first year of the Human Rights Act?" P.L. (Autumn 2001 edition).
[9] [1999] 3 W.L.R. 972.
[10] *ibid.*, at 988E-H.
[11] HRA, s.3(2)(c).
[12] HRA, s.3(2)(b).

To the extent that the Convention affects the meaning of a legislative **5.07** provision passed prior to the HRA, it means that settled interpretations may be reopened.[13] Further, the historic approach of searching for legislative intent is now secondary to the search for an interpretation that is consistent with the Convention.

Primary Legislation

Section 21 of the HRA defines "primary legislation" to include, *inter alia*, **5.08** any public general Act, local and personal Act, private Act, Order in Council made in exercise of Her Majesty's Royal Prerogative and order or other instrument made under primary legislation to the extent that it operates to bring one or more provisions of that legislation into force or amends any primary legislation.

The position in relation to primary legislation is, in theory, straightforward. **5.09** All primary legislation, whenever passed, must be construed compatibly with the Convention unless it is clearly impossible to do so. However, this simple formulation belies the difficulties in determining in practice whether an interpretation, albeit strained,[14] is "possible" or whether it is clearly "impossible" to construe the statute compatibly with the Convention. Since the declaration of incompatibility is intended to be a remedy of last resort, it is likely that judges will endeavour to give a statute a meaning consistent with the Convention, even if this means straining the words to do so.[14A]

Subordinate Legislation

Section 21 of the HRA defines "subordinate legislation" to include, *inter* **5.10** *alia*, any Order in Council (other than one made in exercise of the Royal Prerogative), Act of the Scottish Parliament, Act of the Parliament of Northern Ireland, Act of the Northern Ireland Assembly, orders, rules, regulations, scheme, warrant, byelaw or other instrument made under primary legislation (except to the extent to which it operates to bring one or more provisions of that legislation into force or amends any primary legislation).

The position in relation to challenges to subordinate legislation is con- **5.11** ceptually more complex than in relation to challenges to primary legislation. This complexity arises from the structure and interrelationship between sections 3, 4, 6, 7 and 22(4) of the HRA, the effect of the obligation to construe legislation compatibly with the Convention whenever it was passed, and the strictures of the traditional theory underpinning the *ultra vires* doctrine. The *ultra vires* doctrine permits a court to strike down subordinate legislation where it is outside the enabling or parent primary legislation. The theoretical difficulty is this: since making legislation incompatible with the Convention was not outside Parliament's rule-

---

[13] See I. Leigh and L. Lustgarten, "Making Rights Real: The Courts, Remedies and the Human Rights Act" [1999] C.L.J. 509 at 511; F. Bennion, "What interpretation is 'possible' under s.3(1) of the Human Rights Act?" [2000] P.L. 77 at 89.

[14] Francis Bennion defines a strained meaning as any meaning other than the enactment's literal meaning: "What interpretation is 'possible' under s.3(1) of the Human Rights Act?" [2000] P.L. 77 at 85.

[14A] See further para. 5.04 above.

making powers prior to the introduction of the HRA, can the doctrine be used to retrospectively imply that incompatible legislation was *ultra vires* on the ground that it was incompatible with the Convention (where it was not required to be so by reason of primary legislation), even though it was valid and within the rule-making power at the time of its formation?

5.12 The problem and the likely approach is probably best set out in a perceptive article by Dan Squires entitled "Challenging Subordinate Legislation under the Human Rights Act" from which the following analysis is drawn.[15] Where subordinate legislation is *intra vires* its enabling legislation but incompatible with the Convention, and that incompatibility is required by primary legislation, the only recourse would appear to be to make a declaration of incompatibility under section 4 of the HRA. Where the subordinate legislation is *intra vires* its enabling legislation but incompatible with the Convention where the incompatibility is not required by primary legislation, there would appear to be no power to make a declaration of incompatibility: see section 4(3), (4) of the HRA. However, there is a potential power to strike down or disapply[15A] subordinate legislation on the basis of either:

(1) a reformulated definition of the traditional doctrine of *ultra vires* to retrospectively make legislation which is incompatible with the Convention outside the rule-making power; or

(2) a new separate power to strike down implicitly created by section 6(1) of the HRA.

If there is no power to strike down or disapply subordinate legislation or to declare it incompatible with the Convention, it seems that the subordinate legislation can only be left intact.

5.13 Where subordinate legislation is *ultra vires* its enabling legislation and is incompatible with Convention, the position will differ depending on when the legislation was passed. In relation to legislation passed after October 2, 2000, it should be possible to strike it down (or in the case of the inferior courts, to disapply it)[15B] on the basis of the *ultra vires* doctrine as subsequently modified by the HRA—*i.e.* that there is no longer any power to make subordinate legislation which is incompatible with the Convention, unless required by reason of incompatible primary legislation. Further, there exists a section 7(1)(a) HRA remedy for the making of incompatible subordinate legislation (assuming that section 6(3) of the HRA is *not* intended to apply to a Minister promulgating subordinate legislation). In relation to subordinate legislation passed prior to October 2, 2000, the courts can simply strike down such legislation using the traditional *ultra vires* ground. There exists no section 7(1)(a) remedy in relation to the passing of incompatible legislation before the HRA came into force by reason of the operation of section 22(4) of the HRA, although it is arguable

---

[15] [2000] E.H.R.L.R. 116.
[15A] See further para. 2.11 above at sub-para. (3).
[15B] See further para. 2.11 above at sub-para. (3).

that there might be a claim for failure to revoke the incompatible legislation,[15C] or for acting on such incompatible legislation where a Minister or official was not required to do so, at a time subsequent to October 2, 2000.

Royal Prerogative

Section 3 of the HRA also enables the judicial review of the royal prerog- **5.14**
ative.[16] Although the royal prerogative is not exercised under a power derived from statute, the drafters of the HRA have treated Orders in Council made under the prerogative as "primary legislation". Other exercises of the prerogative directly by Ministers or central government departments are not so classified and will not therefore attract the protection given by the designation of "primary legislation" for the purpose of the HRA. The prerogative remains an important source of executive power, for example, in the regulation of the civil service and armed services, the issuing of passports and the expulsion of aliens, and its exercise has since 1985 been subject to judicial review.[17] However, the classification of Orders in Council made under the prerogative as primary legislation means that an exercise of the prerogative of this kind will not be struck down if it is incompatible with the Convention. However, it remains open to the court to make a declaration of incompatibility under section 4 of the HRA.

3. EFFECT OF THE HRA BETWEEN PRIVATE INDIVIDUALS—VERTICAL AND HORIZONTAL EFFECT

General

The concepts of "vertical effect" and "horizontal effect" are very important **5.15**
to an understanding of the HRA. The issue of who can be sued in domestic courts for breach of Convention rights is one that arises directly from a transposition of the Convention into domestic law, since only Contracting States can be the subject of a complaint to Strasbourg. The effect of the Convention between private individuals is termed "horizontal effect".[18] The Human Rights Act is primarily intended to protect individuals against abuses of their fundamental rights by government and public bodies. The Human Rights Act makes no express reference to obligations upon private individuals or companies to act compatibly with the Convention. The effect of the Convention between individual and State is known as "vertical effect".[19] Nevertheless, the European Court has on occasion used the Convention to protect the rights of private individuals from interference by other private individuals, albeit through the medium of the

---

[15C] See *e.g. Marcic v. Thames Water Utilities, The Independent*, July 9, 2001, HHJ Havery Q.C.
[16] See D. Squires, "Judicial Review of the Prerogative after the Human Rights Act", (2000) 116 L.Q.R. 572.
[17] *Council of Civil Service Unions v. Minister for the Civil Service* (the *G.C.H.Q.* case) [1985] A.C. 374.
[18] Otherwise known as *Drittwurkung*, a term derived from German law.
[19] The terms vertical and horizontal effect are also used in relation to the principle of "direct effect" in European Community law.

State. Further, section 6(3)(a) of the HRA includes "courts and tribunals" within the definition of "public authorities". Accordingly, courts and tribunals are obliged to act compatibly with the Convention in the exercise of judicial functions in all disputes, including those between purely private parties. The Lord Chancellor emphasised, in the course of the Parliamentary debates, that courts would be able and obliged to adapt and develop existing causes of action to provide effective protection of rights guaranteed, not only in cases involving other public authorities but also in developing the common law when deciding cases between individuals.[20] It would therefore seem that the HRA does not have solely vertical effect. It seems likely that the HRA will also have a degree of horizontal effect, though where along the spectrum from solely vertical effect to full horizontal effect it sits is not yet clear.[21] The academic vertical/horizontal effect debate has been extensive and forceful. Whilst the issue still awaits full judicial consideration, it is clear from the treatment of the right to respect for private life in Article 8 in *Douglas v. Hello! Ltd*[22] that the HRA will have some degree of horizontal effect through the medium of sections 2 and 6 of the Act. Sedley L.J. stated:

> " . . . equity and the common law . . . [and] the Human Rights Act 1998 . . . now run in a single channel because, by virtue of s.2 and s.6 of the Act, the courts of this country must not only take into account jurisprudence of both the Commission and the European Court of Human Rights which points to a positive institutional obligation to respect privacy; they must themselves act compatibly with that and the other Convention rights."[23]

5.16 The early resolution of the important issue of the extent of the HRA's horizontal effect is clearly desirable. In the meantime, it is helpful to be aware of the arguments on each side and draw attention to the relevant provisions and European case law which are marshalled in support.

Vertical (Private/Public) Effect

5.17 Section 6 creates a three-fold classification of "body" for the purposes of the HRA:

> (1) public authorities which will have to act compatibly with the Convention in relation to all of their functions, both public and private;
>
> (2) hybrid bodies or individuals which are private but exercise some "public functions" and will have to act compatibly with the Convention in relation to their public functions only;

---

[20] H.L. Deb., November 24, 1997, col. 771.
[21] See M.Hunt, "The 'Horizontal Effect' of the Human Rights Act" [1998] P.L. 423, who developed the concept of a spectrum of vertical through to horizontal effect by reference to different common law jurisdictions.
[22] [2001] 2 W.L.R. 992, CA (judgment handed down on December 21, 2000).
[23] At para. 111.

(3) purely private bodies or individuals, which are under no express duty to act compatibly with the Convention.

Using the above classification, there will be vertical effect in relation to category (1) public authorities in the performance of all their functions and in relation to category (2) hybrid bodies in the performance of their public functions only. Hybrid bodies do not have to act compatibly with the Convention in relation to purely private acts. Accordingly, any application of Convention rights to a hybrid body in relation to its private acts will fall to be considered in relation to horizontal effect below together with category (3) private bodies and individuals.   **5.18**

Definition of Public Authority

It is unclear precisely what bodies or individuals will be treated as public or hybrid authorities[24] though this will determine the vertical effect of the HRA. Beyond the limited guidance in section 6(3), the HRA deliberately does not define a public authority on the basis that it was thought better to have a principle rather than an exhaustive list.[25] Hybrid bodies have to act compatibly with Convention rights in relation to their public functions.[26] It is not stated what private individuals or companies will fall within the definition of "any person certain of whose functions are of a public nature" within section 6(3) of the HRA with the corresponding duty to act compatibly with the Convention in relation to any public functions. The adoption of a function test is intended to overcome inconsistency in the situation where a nationalised utility has been privatised but remains a state-regulated private monopoly or a state function has been contracted-out (for example the transporting of prisoners).   **5.19**

What is clear is that it was intended that the category of public authority and hybrid authority should be broad in order to: **5.20**

" . . . provide as much protection as possible for the rights of individuals against misuse of power by the state".[27]

The Lord Advocate, Lord Hardies, explained, during debates on the Human Rights Bill, that section 6 is:

" . . . designed to invite the civil courts of the United Kingdom, as far as possible, to treat as a 'public authority' those bodies which the Strasbourg institutions would treat as bodies whose acts engage the responsibility of the state."[28]

Similar comments were made by the Home Secretary, Mr Jack Straw M.P., in which he indicated that the Government had tried to do its best in terms   **5.21**

---

[24] See paras 8.16 *et seq.*, below, for a list of illustrative examples of true public authorities.
[25] Lord Chancellor, H.L. Deb., November 24, 1997, col. 796.
[26] See para. 8.17, below, for an illustrative list of possible hybrid bodies identified in the White Paper and in debates on the Human Rights Bill.
[27] Lord Chancellor, H.L. Deb., November 24, 1997, col. 808.
[28] H.L. Deb., February 5, 1998, col. 794.

to replicate in domestic proceedings those bodies in respect of whose actions the United Kingdom Government were answerable in Strasbourg by taking into account whether a body is sufficiently public to engage the responsibility of the state.[29] The process of judicially defining what would constitute a public authority was commenced by the Court of Appeal in *Poplar Housing and Regeneration Community Association Ltd v. Donoghue*[29A] discussed in Chapter 8 at paragraph 8.17 below.

Horizontal (Private/Public) Effect

5.22   One of the most widely debated issues on the HRA was (and still is) the extent to which the Act will apply as between private individuals or companies. The key questions which arise are as follows:

(1)   whether private individuals or companies can enforce their Convention rights directly against other private individuals or companies in a new HRA cause of action which can be raised in addition to any existing domestic law cause of action or independently;

(2)   whether private individuals or companies can rely on Convention rights to bolster and develop an existing domestic law cause of action;

(3)   the nature and extent of the court's own duty under section 6(1) and (3) of the HRA to act compatibly with the Convention;

(4)   the relevance of the Convention to the development of the common law.

5.23   As commentators have noted, the extent of the reach of human rights legislation into private relations is ultimately a political and philosophical issue.[30] It involves deciding whether human rights guarantees are only concerned with the protection of the individual from arbitrary or unlawful interference by the organs of the state, or whether the individual is to be protected from interferences with his rights (whether the source of that interference is public or private)? Whilst traditionally, human rights protection has been concerned with interference by the state, there has been an increasing recognition on the international level that the interests protected by fundamental rights guarantees may also be encroached upon by private individuals and that governments are under an obligation to prevent or respond to such violations.

5.24   There are three sources of support for those who argue that the HRA has either a degree of horizontal effect or full horizontal effect:

---

[29] H.C. Deb., June 17, 1998, cols 406, 432, 433.
[29A] [2001] EWCA Civ. 595, April 27, 2001, CA.
[30] See, *e.g.* J. Cooper, "Horizontality: The Application of Human Rights Standards in Private Disputes" in *An Introduction to Human Rights and the Common Law* (Oxford: Hart: 2000); N. Bamforth, "The Application of the Human Rights Act 1998 to Public Authorities and Private Bodies", [1999] C.L.J. 159 at 170; A. Clapham, *Human Rights in the Private Sphere* (Oxford: Clarendon: 1993), Chap. 5. See also G. Davies, "The 'horizontal' effect of the Human Rights Act" (2000) 150 N.L.J. 839.

(1) the pre-HRA approach of domestic courts to the use of the Convention in private law matters;

(2) the Strasbourg approach to protection of rights from interference by private individuals; and

(3) the construction of the HRA and Parliamentary intention.

These are considered in turn.

Pre-Human Rights Act

Prior to the introduction of the HRA, courts in the United Kingdom have, on occasion, had recourse to the European Convention in order to develop private law. In an insightful article published in 1996, Michael Beloff q.c. and Helen Mountfield analysed the then existing effect of the Convention in the domestic courts.[31] Interestingly, they took the view that:

    " . . . in the field of private law, the courts are more likely to be expansive as to the relevance of the Convention since the constitutional tensions are less close to the surface".[32]

suggesting that there is perhaps more scope for development of the Convention in the private context. They identified that domestic courts were paying heed to the Convention in private litigation in several different ways including:

(1) the resolution of uncertainty in the common law or to supplement certain, but incomplete, common law: *e.g. Derbyshire County Council v. Times Newspapers*[33];

(2) the buttressing of principles already found in the common law: *e.g. Broome v. Cassell & Co Ltd*[34]; *R. v. Secretary of State, ex p. Anderson*[35]; *John v. Mirror Group Newspapers Ltd*[36];

(3) as a source of public policy: *e.g. Balthwayt v. Cawley*[37];

(4) as a measuring rod, by which to judge the efficacy of the common law: *e.g., Attorney-General v. Guardian Newspapers (No 2)*[38]; *Derbyshire County Council v. Times Newspapers*[39]; *R. v. Board of Visitors of Maze Prisoners ex parte Hone*[40]; *Wynne v. Secretary of State for Home Department*[41];

5.25

---

[31] "Unconventional Behaviour? Judicial Uses of the European Convention in England and Wales" [1996] E.H.R.L.R. 467. See also M. Hunt, *Using Human Rights in English Courts* (Oxford: Hart: 1998).
[32] See page 474.
[33] [1992] 1 Q.B. 770, CA; [1993] A.C. 534, HL.
[34] [1972] A.C. 1027 at 1113 (scope of exemplary damages in libel).
[35] [1984] Q.B. 778.
[36] [1996] 2 All E.R. 35.
[37] [1976] A.C. 397, HL, *per* Lord Wilberforce.
[38] [1990] 1 A.C. 109.
[39] [1993] A.C. 543.
[40] [1988] A.C. 379.
[41] [1993] All E.R. 174.

(5) in the case of Article 10, in the determination of whether to grant an interlocutory injunction or when the scope of the common law or equitable duty of confidence is uncertain: for example *Attorney-General v. Guardian Newspapers Ltd (No. 2)*[42]; *Derbyshire County Council v. Times Newspapers*[43]; *R. v. Secretary of State for the Home Department, ex p. NALGO.*[44]

5.26 In *R. v. Lord Chancellor, ex p. Witham*,[45] Laws J. stated that the common law provided no lesser protection of the right of access to a court than might be vindicated in Strasbourg.[46] On the basis that it infringed a common constitutional law right of access to a court, he struck down as *ultra vires* a new order prescribing court fees payable on issue of a writ which repealed provisions relieving litigants in person in receipt of income support from the obligation to pay fees and permitting the Lord Chancellor to reduce or remit the fee in any particular case on the ground of undue financial hardship. In *Derbyshire County Council v. Times Newspapers*,[47] the House of Lords held that a public authority did not have standing to sue for libel in order to vindicate its reputation since this "must inevitably have an inhibiting effect on freedom of speech" which was contrary to the public interest. Whereas the Court of Appeal had reached its conclusion on the basis of the Convention, Lord Keith stated that the common law provided no less protection to freedom of speech than the Strasbourg institutions,[48] relying on a previous statement to that effect by Lord Goff in *Attorney-General v. Guardian Newspapers (No. 2)*.[49] In *Rantzen v. Mirror Group Newspapers Ltd*,[50] the Court of Appeal held that Article 10 was relevant to its statutory powers to review jury awards of libel damages that inhibited free speech. In *R. v. Sultan Khan*,[51] the House of Lords stated that Article 6 jurisprudence had a valuable role to play in considering common law and statutory discretionary powers in the context of fair trial procedures. Accordingly, it can be seen that the Convention was relied upon in private law as well as other proceedings to develop the common law prior to the introduction of the HRA, though its further development was inhibited by judicial recognition that the Convention was not part of English law.[52]

The Strasbourg Approach

5.27 The European Court and the European Commission have developed two primary methods by which they have given protection to rights from interference by other private bodies or individuals. One is the development of a doctrine of "positive obligation" on the part of a state to protect

---

[42] [1990] 1 A.C. 109.
[43] [1993] A.C. 534.
[44] [1993] Admin.L.R. 785, *per* Neil L.J.
[45] [1997] 2 All E.R. 779.
[46] *ibid.*, at 787.
[47] [1993] A.C. 534.
[48] *ibid.*, at 551.
[49] [1990] 1 A.C. 109, HL.
[50] [1994] Q.B. 670.
[51] [1997] A.C. 558, HL; *The Times*, July 5, 1996.
[52] See, *e.g. R. v. Secretary of State for the Home Department, ex p. Brind* [1991] 1 A.C. 696, HL. See further on common law constitutional rights, paras 5.72 *et seq.*

individual rights from interference by other individuals. The jurisdiction for this has been found in Article 1 (the inter-state obligation on a Contracting State to secure rights and freedoms to everyone in their jurisdiction). The other is by treating domestic courts as part of the state and imposing liability on the state for failure by the courts to act compatibly with the Convention in proceedings involving private parties.

Positive obligations

The Convention creates rights and freedoms enforceable by individuals and the Contracting States are obliged by Article 1 of the Convention to secure these rights and freedoms to everyone within their jurisdiction. An individual can only assert those rights before the Strasbourg institutions against a national government. A complaint cannot be made against an individual and such complaints as have been made have been dismissed.[53] However, the European Court has nevertheless given some protection to private individuals by developing a doctrine of positive obligations. It has held that the Convention does not merely confer negative obligations to refrain from infringing Convention rights and freedoms but also confers certain positive obligations. Thus, a State has a positive duty to secure effective protection for Convention rights under Article 1, even where infringement is by other private individuals. The Court has applied Article 1 in conjunction with other Convention rights to create positive duties on the State to protect individuals in the private sphere.[54] For example, a State has a positive duty to take appropriate steps to safeguard the lives of those within its jurisdiction, including the provision of information concerning life-threatening risks to those potentially affected pursuant to Article 2: *LCB v. United Kingdom*.[55] In *A v. United Kingdom*,[56] the applicant complained that the State had failed to protect him from a violent beating by his stepfather, who was acquitted in criminal proceedings on the basis of a defence of "reasonable chastisement", contrary to Article 3. The Court found the conduct to have reached the level of severity required for a violation to be established and that the State, by failing to provide adequate legal protection against that conduct, became responsible for it under Article 1. In *Costello-Roberts v. United Kingdom*,[57] the State bore responsibility for a violation by a private school of Article 3 by engaging in corporal punishment of children. The European Court clearly considered education to be a function that is properly the responsibility of the State and stated that:

5.28

> "[T]he state cannot absolve itself from responsibility by delegating its obligations to private bodies or individuals".

---

[53] P. van Dijk & G.J.H. van Hoof, *Theory and Practice of the European Convention on Human Rights*, p. 119.
[54] For a useful and fuller discussion of the European Court's approach to protection of infringements by private actors, see A. Clapham, *Human Rights in the Private Sphere* (Oxford: Clarendon: 1993), Chap. 7.
[55] (1999) 27 E.H.R.R. 212.
[56] (1999) 27 E.H.R.R. 611.
[57] (1995) 19 E.H.R.R. 112.

5.29 In relation to Article 8, the European Court held in *Marckx v. Belgium*,[58] that:

> "the object of the Article is essentially that of protecting the individual against arbitrary interferences by the public authorities. Nevertheless, it does not merely compel the State to abstain from such interference: in addition to this primarily negative undertaking, there may be positive obligations inherent in an effective 'respect' for family life: *X and Y v. Netherlands.*"[59]

Under Article 11, the European Court held that the state provided insufficient protection for demonstrators who were attacked and intimidated by counter-demonstrators, in violation of their right to free assembly: *Plattform "Arzte fur das Leben" v. Austria.*[60] Further, in *Young, James and Webster v. United Kingdom*,[61] the applicants complained that their dismissal by British Rail for refusing to join a trade union had been an interference with their freedom of association under Article 11. It was conceded by the Government that the ability to dismiss applicants without liability for unfair dismissal flowed directly from national legislation concerning closed shop agreements. The European Court found that the legislation failed to secure the protection under Article 11 that Article 1 required of national governments. On a broad reading, it is arguable that the European Court accepts the possibility that the actions of a private party may comprise a violation of rights.[62]

5.30 One of the difficulties of relying on the European Court's approach in asserting Convention rights in domestic litigation is the deliberate non-inclusion of Article 1 in Schedule 2 to the HRA. However, since the exclusion of Article 1 was explained to be merely on the technical, not substantive, basis that Article 1 was an inter-state obligation to secure protection for human rights within a national jurisdiction, which the United Kingdom was satisfying by passing the HRA, the omission may not preclude the application of positive obligations in the domestic setting. A further difficulty is in determining how far the concept of positive obligations extends. On a narrow approach, the concept is well suited to transposition into the private setting where a public authority has regulatory functions involving the conduct of private individuals. In such a situation, a public authority may be liable for its failure to satisfy a positive Convention obligation where this has the effect of permitting an infringement of Convention rights of one private individual by another. For example, a local authority may arguably be in violation of Article 8 (right to respect for private life) or Article 1 of the First Protocol (right to peaceful enjoyment of possessions) where it fails to exercise its powers or duties under environmental health legislation to prevent serious noise nuisance to one private

---

[58] (1980) 2 E.H.R.R. 330.
[59] (1986) 8 E.H.R.R. 235. The European Court stated in this case that the State's obligations "may involve the adoption of measures designed to secure respect for private life even in the sphere of the relations of individuals between themselves".
[60] (1991) 13 E.H.R.R. 204. The result was reached with the assistance of Art. 1.
[61] (1982) 4 E.H.R.R. 38.
[62] See, *e.g.* G. Davies, "The 'horizontal' effect of the Human Rights Act" (2000) 150 N.L.J. 839.

individual by another. This approach would provide an indirect form of protection for Convention rights where the source of the interference is another private individual or body. It should be noted that a failure to legislate in order to protect the private sphere cannot be unlawful in light of section 6(1), (6) of the HRA or actionable in proceedings under section 7(1) HRA. In this situation, an individual will continue to have recourse to the European Court of Human Rights.

Courts as public authority

The European Court has also recognised the national courts as an organ   **5.31**
of the state and held the failure of national courts to secure rights for private individuals to constitute a failure of the Contracting State under Article 1. In *Markt Intern and Beermann v. Germany*,[63] the applicant complained that an injunction issued by a court against him under German fair trading laws on the application of a competitor represented a breach of Article 10. The European Court held that the injunction was an interference by a public authority and violated Article 10. In *Sunday Times v. United Kingdom*,[64] the European Court found that the domestic court had violated Article 10 by granting an injunction. In *Tolstoy-Miloslavsky v. United Kingdom*,[65] the level of the jury's award of damages for libel was disproportionate to the wrong suffered, so as to infringe the applicant's right to freedom of expression under Article 10. In *Goodwin v. United Kingdom*,[66] the issue of a contempt order for a journalist's refusal to disclose his sources was a breach of the applicant's right under Article 10. In *Rommelfanger v. Germany*,[67] the European Commission recognised the duty of the courts in some cases to protect the Convention rights of private individuals before the courts. A court or tribunal is clearly an organ of the state even when deciding proceedings between private parties. Accordingly, a court or tribunal will have to heed and uphold Convention rights in the exercise of judicial discretion whether to make orders and in the exercise of its own role in litigation regardless of the identity of the parties.

The Human Rights Act

The HRA

Subsequent to October 2, 2000, the HRA determines the application of   **5.32**
human rights to state and non-state organs in the United Kingdom (subject of course to other legal sources of rights or recourse to Strasbourg on additional grounds not provided by the HRA). There is no express provision in the HRA that purely private bodies or individuals, or hybrid bodies in relation to their private functions must act compatibly with the Convention. It would therefore appear that they are free to act in a manner contrary to the Convention. There is, however, a duty on a court or tribunal under section 6(1) of the HRA to act compatibly with the Convention in

---

[63] (1990) 12 E.H.R.R. 161.
[64] (1980) 2 E.H.R.R. 245.
[65] (1995) 20 E.H.R.R. 442.
[66] (1996) 22 E.H.R.R. 123.
[67] (1989) 62 D.R. 151, Application No. 12242/86.

relation to its own acts which may influence the application of the Convention to *proceedings* involving private parties.[67A] However, the content and extent of the court's duty in this regard is as yet uncertain. It is helpful to consider first, Parliamentary expressions of intention as to the horizontal effect of the HRA and secondly, the construction of the HRA itself.

Parliamentary intention

5.33 In accordance with the principle in *Pepper v. Hart*,[68] recourse may be had to the Parliamentary statements by Ministers responsible for introducing a bill, in order to determine Parliament's intention. The main statements about the application of the HRA were as follows. The Lord Chancellor, Lord Irvine stated that:

> " . . . a provision of this kind [Section 6 of the HRA] should only apply to public authorities, however defined, and not to private individuals. That reflects the arrangements for taking cases to the Convention institutions in Strasbourg. The Convention had its origins in a desire to protect people from the misuse of power by the state, rather than from the actions of private individuals . . . [Section] 6 does not impose a liability on organisations which have no public function at all." [69]

and further,

> "we have not provided for the Convention rights to be directly justiciable in actions between private individuals. We have sought to protect the human rights of individuals against the abuse of power by the state, broadly, defined, rather than to protect them against each other."[70]

5.34 These statements suggest that the Government did not intend the HRA to be enforceable directly against private individuals for breach of Convention rights (which would be a full or direct form of horizontal effect). The intention is that the operation of section 6 be primarily vertical in effect, though with potential for a broad definition of the term "public authority". It further suggests that the intention is to mirror the position in Strasbourg as far as possible. However, it was not Parliament's intention to exclude all possible horizontal effect. In opposing a proposed amendment by Lord Wakeham to expressly exclude private individuals from the effect of the Act, the Lord Chancellor stated the Government's position:

> "We . . . believe that it is right as a matter of principle for the courts to have the duty of acting compatibly with the Convention not only in cases involving other public authorities but also in developing the common law in deciding cases between individuals. Why should they not? In preparing this Bill, we have taken the view that it is the other course, that of excluding Convention considerations altogether from

---

[67A] See M. Hunt, "The 'Horizontal Effect' of the Human Rights Act" [1998] P.L. 423.
[68] [1993] A.C. 593.
[69] H.L. Deb., November 3, 1997, cols 1231–1232.
[70] H.L. Deb., February 5, 1998, col. 840.

cases between individuals, which would have to be justified. We do not think that that would be justifiable; nor indeed, do we think that it would be practicable."[71]

The HRA must, therefore, have at least some horizontal effect. A live issue **5.35** in Parliament was whether the HRA created, or would enable the courts to create, a new tort of privacy, in other words, did the Act create a statutory tort applicable even between private actors? The Lord Chancellor stated:

"In my opinion, the court is not obligated to remedy the failure by legislating via the common law either where a Convention right is infringed by incompatible legislation or where because of the absence of legislation—say privacy legislation—a Convention right is left unprotected. In my view, the courts may not act as legislators and grant new remedies for the infringement of Convention rights unless the common law itself enables them to develop new rights and remedies. I believe that the true view is that the courts will be able to adapt and develop the common law by relying on the existing domestic principles in the laws of trespass, nuisance, copyright, confidence and the like, to fashion a common law right to privacy."

It can be seen that the intention was that a domestic court should not **5.36** create new remedies for infringement of Convention rights, although it is free to adapt and develop the common law to protect Convention rights by relying on existing domestic causes of action at common law and in equity. On this basis, the courts potentially have considerable freedom to invoke Convention rights to buttress existing causes of action and to develop the common law in new directions. However, if there is no common law or equitable remedy which can be developed, Parliament did not intend that the courts step into the breach and create a wholly new tort, solely on the basis of the HRA.

Construction of the HRA

The HRA has not restricted actions for breach of Convention rights solely **5.37** to government or state action. Whilst the HRA does not expressly create a cause of action against a private party, neither does it expressly exclude it.

Section 6—The court as public authority

Courts and tribunals are true public authorities with a duty to act compat- **5.38** ibly with the Convention under section 6(1), (3). The extent of the duty on the court is not yet settled. It may confer either a duty or a power to apply the Convention to disputes involving private parties. The court's section 6

---

[71] H.L. Deb., November 24, 1997, col. 783.

obligation is the principal justification invoked for arguments in favour of horizontal effect and is discussed further at para. 5.43 below.

Section 3—Obligation to interpret legislation compatibly

5.39 The obligation to interpret legislation compatibly with the Convention in section 3(1) of the HRA is not restricted to proceedings involving a public authority. Accordingly, wherever statutory law is in issue, the Court must construe it to so as to give effect to Convention rights, even in proceedings between private parties.

Section 7—Proceedings between private parties

5.40 The primary area of uncertainty is the impact of the HRA in relation to the common law and equity in proceedings between private individuals and exercises of judicial discretion in civil proceedings. The position may be relatively straightforward in relation to the exercise of a judicial discretion such as the granting of an injunction, where the court would take account of Article 10 in deciding whether to make the order sought. Further, where there is uncertainty or ambiguity in the common law, there is no difficulty about having recourse to the Convention, as was the position prior to the introduction of the HRA.

5.41 What is not clear is whether, when the common law is settled, the HRA requires it to be reopened if, on examination, that position is incompatible with a Convention right? The primary example is a law of privacy. Before the introduction of the HRA, some courts had ruled that there is no right to privacy in English law and that it was for Parliament to remedy the situation if so desired.[72] Post-HRA, there were three theoretically possible approaches. Either (1) a court was obliged to create a new cause of action although previously it would have been bound by Court of Appeal authority; or (2) no new cause of action could be created but the court's role was to develop the common law or equity consistently with the Convention; or (3) the court was not entitled to change its approach, the HRA having insufficient horizontal effect to allow the courts to develop the law in this way. As outlined above,[73] Parliamentary intention clearly appeared to favour the second approach above in that it would enable the courts to develop a privacy law through the development of existing causes of action.[74] This approach was also consistent with the approach in *Spencer v. United Kingdom*,[75] where the applicants, Earl and Countess Spencer, complained about the taking and publication of a photograph of Lady Spencer in the garden of a clinic for the treatment of eating disorders. The European Commission declared the application inadmissible on the ground that the applicants had not exhausted domestic remedies, it being open to the courts to develop the law of breach of confidence to protect

---

[72] See, *e.g. Kaye v. Robertson* [1991] F.S.R. 62 at 71, *The Times*, March 21, 1990, CA; *R. v. Broadcasting Complaints Commission, ex p. Barclay* [1997] E.M.L.R. 62 at 69.

[73] See paras 5.33 *et seq*, above.

[74] See also Parliamentary Under-Secretary of State for the Home Department, Mr Mike O'Brien M.P., who stated that newspapers would not be public authorities and could not be proceeded against directly under the Act but that an Art. 8 point could be raised in proceedings for harassment or libel. H.C. Deb., July 2, 1998, col. 561.

[75] (1998) 26 E.H.R.R. CD 212.

against invasion of privacy.[76] On this approach, it is, however, not possible for a court to create a wholly new cause of action where there is no existing cause of action to develop. The domestic courts have now had an opportunity to consider the issue of privacy in light of the Convention. In *Douglas v. Hello!*,[77] the Court of Appeal stated that English law does now recognise a right of privacy, grounded in the equitable doctrine of confidence. Accordingly, the Court followed the second approach. Post HRA, the courts have clearly proceeded on the basis that their duty under Article 6(1) extended to applying the Convention to the common law. In *R. v. Lambert*,[77A] Lord Hope observed that in applying and developing the common law, the courts have a duty under section 6(1) to act compatibly with the Convention. He stated that:

> "A decision which is based on the application and development of the common law also is an act by the court, so I think it must follow that this too is subject to the prohibition in section 6(1)."[77B]

In *Venables v. News Group Newspapers Ltd*,[77C] Butler-Sloss P. having referred to *Douglas v. Hello!*[77D] stated that she was under a duty to act compatibly with Convention rights in adjudicating upon existing common law causes of action and applying Article 10:

> "That obligation on the court does not seem to me to encompass the creation of a free standing cause of action based directly upon the Articles of the Convention . . . The duty on the court, in my view, is to act compatibly with Convention rights in adjudicating upon existing common law causes of action, and that includes a positive as well as a negative obligation."[77E]

Accordingly, she granted an injunction to avoid publication of identity of two convicted murderers in the interests of their safety.

Section 7(1)(b) also provides that Convention rights may be relied upon by a victim of an unlawful act or omission "in *any* legal proceedings". This will permit a collateral challenge to any unlawful act by a victim in any legal proceedings, even those between private individuals. **5.42**

Academic arguments

The academic arguments over the meaning of the HRA range from asserting full horizontal effect to only very limited horizontal effect. In his excellent article, "Horizontal Rights, The Human Rights Act and Privacy: **5.43**

---

[76] But *cf. Winer v. United Kingdom*, Application No. 10871/84 (1986) 48 D.R. 154, where the Commission regarded the law relating to breach of confidence to be too uncertain to require the applicant to use it and concluded that the absence of an actionable right to privacy under English law constituted a lack of respect for private life and home.
[77] [2001] 2 W.L.R. 992, CA.
[77A] [2001] UKHL 37, July 5, 2001, HL.
[77B] Para. 114.
[77C] [2001] 2 W.L.R. 1038, QBD.
[77D] [2001] 2 W.L.R. 992, CA.
[77E] At para. 27.

Lessons from the Commonwealth?",[78] Professor Ian Leigh identified six potential types of horizontal effect under the HRA. The classification provides a valuable framework for distinguishing between the possible levels of application of the HRA to private proceedings and is gratefully adopted as a way of summarising the debate.

5.44   **Direct statutory horizontality.** Professor Leigh defines this as arising through interpretation of statutes applying between private individuals in accordance with the interpretative duty to give effect wherever possible to Convention rights. Section 3(1) of the HRA requires a court to interpret legislation compatibly with the Convention and applies regardless of the identity of the parties to the proceedings. The HRA therefore establishes direct statutory horizontality. Nicholas Bamforth has suggested that the true "horizontal effect" of the HRA is likely to be felt under section 3 of the Act rather than under section 6.[79]

5.45   **Public liability horizontality.** This arises through an enlarged definition of "public authority" where bodies or persons for which the state would not be liable under the Convention machinery are treated as public authorities for the purpose of the HRA. Public liability horizontality is already well established in Convention jurisprudence through a broad definition of the "state". This is mirrored by the "public function" test in section 6(3) of the HRA and the Parliamentary intention that the definition of "public authority" should be broadly construed.

5.46   **Intermediate horizontality.** This is where the right is claimed against a public authority for its failure to take action to protect one person against infringements of his or her Convention rights emanating from another private person. There is a solid basis in Convention jurisprudence for the application of intermediate horizontality by transposition of the principle of state responsibility and positive obligations into domestic law as set out at para. 5.28 above.

5.47   **Remedial horizontality.** This arises through the effect of section 6(3)(a) of the HRA on the discretionary and procedural actions of the courts. Remedial horizontality by means of a duty on a court or tribunal in relation to discretionary and procedural actions is well-established in Convention jurisprudence as set out at para. 5.31 above.

5.48   **Indirect horizontality.** This arises by "informing" the development of the common law as it applies between private parties. Whilst most commentators agree that the HRA will have indirect horizontal effect, there are differences as to the likely extent of indirect horizontality. For example, Murray Hunt suggested that the Convention may be regarded as applying to all law and therefore as potentially relevant in private proceedings, but would not confer any new private causes of action against individuals for breach of Convention rights.[80] On this approach, the Act would have an

---

[78] (1999) 48 I.C.L.Q. 55.
[79] (2001) 117 L.Q.R. 34–41.
[80] M. Hunt, "The 'Horizontal Effect' of the Human Rights Act" [1998] P.L. 423.

indirect horizontal effect with a mandatory obligation on the courts to develop the common law in a manner compatible with the Convention pursuant to section 6(1) and (3) HRA.[81] By contrast, Gavin Phillipson[82] argued that the most plausible reading of the HRA as a whole is that it would generate indirect horizontality at the weaker level. The courts would be obliged to have regard to the values represented by the rights in their development and application of the common law and the general application of the Convention would be to those situations where the ingredients of the common law are broad and open to a variety of interpretations. The issue of how much weight Convention rights have in the private sphere would be difficult in light of the wide discretion given to the courts.[83] At the weakest end of the scale, Richard Buxton,[84] a Lord Justice of Appeal, argued that it was clear that the HRA did nothing to create private law rights and that whilst the HRA and decisions of the European Court, such as *Osman v. United Kingdom*,[85] might have a more tangential effect on private law litigation, the English judge would need to proceed with great caution in drawing such conclusions from the Convention in all but the clearest case. He further rejected the notion that "values" could be extracted from the Convention and applied to the private setting on the ground that they:

"remain stubbornly values whose content lives in public law. To transpose those values into private law would require an exercise in analogy: an analogy that while it might be illuminating in general terms is very difficult to justify from the provisions of the HRA".

He expressed the hope that these substantial limitations would be appreciated at an early stage of the life of the HRA and that the courts would thus be freed to devote their attention to the very important task of working out the effect of the HRA in the sphere of public law where it, and the Convention, properly belonged.

Full or direct horizontality. This arises through a broad reading of sections 6(1) and 6(3) of the HRA so as to require the courts to create appropriate rights and remedies by revising the common law to protect Convention rights subject only to the limitation that a clear statute must prevail. Professor Sir William Wade argues that the HRA creates private law rights in the same terms as the Articles of the Convention which the English courts will be bound to enforce in litigation between private individuals, since the courts are public authorities with a duty to act compatibly with the Convention. If a Convention point arises, a court will be unable to **5.49**

---

[81] See also D. Pannick and A. Lester, "The Impact of the Human Rights Act on Private Law: The Knight's Move" (2000) 116 L.Q.R. 380 at 381.
[82] G. Phillipson, "The Human Rights Act, 'Horizontal Effect' and the Common Law: a Bang or Whimper?" (1999) M.L.R. 824.
[83] At pp. 843–844.
[84] R. Buxton, "The Human Rights Act and Private Law" (2000) 116 L.Q.R. 48.
[85] (2000) 29 E.H.R.R. 245. See further paras 10.29 and 17.09 *et seq*. For recent developments regarding *Osman*.

give a lawful judgment except in accordance with the Convention right.[86] He submits that a judge trying a case must give effect to the Convention right of privacy in a case against a private defendant such as a newspaper, where there may be no such right at common law.[87] In other words, he argues for a form of almost full or direct horizontality.[88] This view is not widely held.

Comparative Approach

5.50   A comparative perspective on the approach taken to vertical and horizontal effect given to fundamental rights in various other common law jurisdictions illustrates the spectrum of positions. However, it must always be borne in mind that the attitudes of each jurisdiction are shaped by both the mechanism whereby fundamental rights are brought into its domestic law and by the general nature of the domestic constitution, which differ from country to country. Any attempted comparison must therefore identify any special legal or constitutional features that have led to a particular legal approach.

Canada

5.51   Section 32 of the Canadian Charter of Rights and Freedoms 1982 states that the Charter only applies to the Parliament and Government of Canada and to the provincial legislatures and Governments. In Canada, the courts have rejected any direct cause of action based on the Canadian Charter of Rights and Freedoms between private individuals. Equally, they have rejected the stricter state action test adopted in the U.S.[88A] *Retail Wholesale and Department Store Union Local 580 et al v. Dolphin Delivery Ltd*[89] concerned an interlocutory injunction against a trade union to prohibit it from picketing business premises. The trade union acted for employees of a company named Purolator which had locked out its employees in a labour dispute. The trade union threatened to picket the premises of Dolphin Delivery, another courier company which had done business with Purolater before the lock-out and which was doing business with a connected company, Supercourier, subsequent to the lock out, if it did not cease to do business with Supercourier. Dolphin Delivery applied for an injunction to restrain the picketing. The application was granted at first instance with the judge finding that the proposed picketing involved the tort of inducing breach of contract or the tort of civil conspiracy. The union appealed, arguing that the common law principles applied by the judge infringed its Charter rights to freedom of expression and freedom of association. The Court of Appeal held that neither freedom of association nor freedom of expression could be invoked to protect the proposed

---

[86] See W. Wade, "The United Kingdom's Bill of Rights", in J. Beatson, C. Forsyth and I. Hare (eds), *Constitutional Reform in the United Kingdom: Practice and Principles* (Oxford: Hart, 1998); W. Wade, "Horizons of Horizontality" (2000) 116 L.Q.R. 217.

[87] Letter to *The Times* "Paradoxes in Human Rights Act", September 1, 2000.

[88] Although Sir William Wade's thesis is generally considered to be arguing for direct horizontality, Sir William Wade argues that Murray Hunt's thesis is in fact very similar to his own: "Horizons of Horizontality" (2000) 116 L.Q.R. 217.

[88A] See para. 5.56 below.

[89] (1985) 33 D.L.R. (4th) 174 at 573.

picketing activity. The union appealed to the Supreme Court on the basis of freedom of expression only. The Supreme Court of Canada held that the picketing in question involved the exercise of the right to freedom of expression (Beetz J. dissenting) but dismissed the appeal on the ground that the case involved private litigation under the common law. Although the court held that the Charter applied to the common law pursuant to Article 52(1) of the Constitution Act 1982[89A] (which gave the Charter priority over any inconsistent law), and the judiciary should apply and develop the principles of the common law in a manner consistent with the fundamental values enshrined in the Convention, it stated that the Charter did not apply where an individual attempted to found an action against another individual on the basis of the Charter. If private litigation is divorced from any connection with the government due to the lack of reliance on legislation or an executive act, the Charter is excluded. Accordingly, it is usually only if an act is based on legislation which is incompatible with the Charter that the necessary element of state action is present and the Charter can have application to private parties. The court will, however, take account of the values enshrined in the Charter.[90] The court was influenced by section 32 of the Charter concluding that the word "government" referred to the legislative, executive or administrative branches of government. The Charter applies to those branches of government in both public and private litigation, regardless of whether the action depends on statute or the common law. However, in an otherwise private action, "a more direct and more precisely-defined connection between the element of government action and the claim advanced must be present before the Charter applies." An order of the court granting an injunction was insufficient to amount to governmental action since if it were it would make subject all litigation to the application of the Charter. Where a party brings a case against another relying on the common law and no act of government is involved, the Charter is inapplicable. However, the Charter is still relevant since the judiciary will apply the principles of the common law "in a manner consistent with the fundamental values enshrined in the Convention".[91] The exclusion of the common law from the direct application of the Charter is not in practice as significant as might appear since the courts are prepared to give indirect application through the Charter "values".

In *Re Blainey and Ontario Hockey Association*,[92] the Ontario Court of Appeal applied the Charter to the rules of a private sports association. A young girl, Justine Blainey, wanted to play as a full member of an ice hockey team where all the other members were boys. However for a team to participate in the league, every member of the team had to be a member of the Ontario Hockey Association whose regulations required that members be male. The girl's mother complained on behalf of her daughter of sex discrimination to the Ontario Human Rights Commission. Section 1 of the Ontario Human Rights Code gave every person a right to equal

5.52

[89A] See Appendix F.
[90] See also *Re Blainey & Ontario Hockey Association* (1986) 26 D.L.R. (4th) 728.
[91] See also *McKinney v. University of Guelph* [1990] 3 S.C.R. 229 at 262; *Vriend v. Alberta* (1998) 4 B.H.R.C. 140 at 159.
[92] (1986) 26 D.L.R. (4th) 728.

treatment with respect to services, goods and facilities, without discrimination because of, *inter alia*, sex. However, section 19(2) of the Code stated that the right under section 1 to equal treatment was not infringed where membership in an athletic organisation or participation in an athletic activity is restricted to persons of the same sex. Mrs. Blainey successfully challenged the constitutionality of section 19(2) under the Charter. The Court of Appeal upheld the restriction in section 19(2) as unconstitutional since it denied Justine Blainey the protection of section 1 of the Code which she would otherwise have had. The existence of legislation permitting discrimination provided the necessary element of government action to allow the Charter to be applicable to a private body. The importance of *Re Blainey* is the *indirect* application of the Charter to a private action. However, this was attempted unsuccessfully in *McKinney v. University of Guelph* where the provisions relating to mandatory retirement challenged were saved by section 1 of the Code.

5.53 In *Hill v. Church of Scientology of Toronto*,[93] a Crown attorney sued the church for comments made at a press conference. Cory J. stated that:

> "[p]rivate parties owe each other no constitutional duties and cannot found their cause of action upon a Charter right. The party challenging the common law cannot allege that the common law violates a Charter right because, quite simply, Charter rights do not exist in the absence of state action. The most that the private litigant can do is to argue that the common law is inconsistent with Charter values."

The Supreme Court considered the common law of defamation in light of the values underlying the Charter, concluding that on the merits of the case, there was no need to modify the common law.

5.54 Examples of applicability or inapplicability more generally include the following:

(1) Once the state provides a benefit, it is obliged to do so in a non-discriminatory manner: *Eldridge v. British Columbia (Attorney-General)*[94];

(2) The Charter is inapplicable to the issue of age discrimination in mandatory retirement: *McKinney v. University of Guelph*[95];

(3) The Charter applies to a college because it is a government agency: *Douglas/Kwantlen Faculty Association v. Douglas College*[96];

(4) The Charter is inapplicable to a father stopping an abortion because it does not regulate private actions: *Tremblay v. Daigle*.[97]

---

[93] [1995] 2 S.C.R. 1130 at 1171–1171, *sub nom. Manning v. Hill* (1995) 129 D.L.R. (4th) 157.
[94] (1997) 151 D.L.R. (4th) 577, [1997] 3 S.C.R. 624, 35 C.R.R.(2d) 187n.
[95] [1990] 3 S.C.R.229. See also *Stoffman v. Vancouver General Hospital* (1988) 49 D.L.R. (4th) 727, [1988] 2 W.W.R. 708, 21 B.C.L.R. (2d) 165, CA, reversed on other grounds, 1991 C.L.L.C. para.17,003, SCC.
[96] [1990] 3 S.C.R. 570.
[97] [1989] 2 S.C.R. 530.

Other jurisdictions

New Zealand. The application clause in the New Zealand Bill of 5.55
Rights Act 1990[97A] is similar to the HRA. Section 3 provides that the Bill of
Rights applies only to acts done "(a) by the legislative, executive, or
judicial branches of the government of New Zealand; or (b) by any person
or body in performance of any public function, power, or duty conferred or
imposed on that person or body by or pursuant to law." There has not yet
been an authoritative judicial decision on the horizontal scope of section 3.
In *Lange v. Atkinson*,[98] Elias J. was prepared to concede that since section
3 bound the judiciary, the Act could therefore apply to the common law, but
in light of the defendant's concession that the Act was a "guiding principle"
for development of the common law, she found the argument was of no
real significance.

USA. The U.S. Constitution[98A] requires there to be governmental 5.56
action for the constitutional rights protections to apply.[99] Governmental
action may be found in relation to private bodies which have government
resources or other sufficient nexus with the state[1] or are in a position of
monopoly.[2] There is no state action through mere omission or acquies-
cence,[3] though facilitation of a violation may constitute state action.[4]
However, the courts are included within the concept of state action.[5]

South Africa. Section 7 of Chapter 3 of the Interim Constitution 5.57
provided that:

"(1) This Chapter shall bind all legislative and executive organs of
state at all levels of government. (2) This Chapter shall apply to all law
in force and all administrative decisions taken and acts performed
during the period of operation of this Constitution."

In *Du Plessis v. De Klerk*,[6] a company brought an action for defamation
against a newspaper. The newspaper argued that publication had not
been unlawful by reason of the protection given to freedom of speech
contained in the Bill of Rights in Chapter 3 of the Interim Constitution
(1993). The claimant argued that the Constitution did not have horizontal
effect and that the constitutional right to free speech could not be invoked
as a defence to an action for damages for defamation. The majority of the
South African Constitutional Court concluded that the Bill of Rights in

---

[97A] See Appendix G.
[98] [1997] 2 N.Z.L.R. 22; affirmed on appeal (1998) 4 B.H.R.C. 573, N.Z.C.A.
[98A] See Appendix I.
[99] For an overview, see A. Clapham, *Human Rights in the Private Sphere* (Oxford: Clarendon: 1993) pp. 150–163.
[1] *Kerr v. Enoch Pratt Free Library* 149 F. 2d. 212 (4th Cir.) (1945), 326 U.S. 721 (1945);
Burton v. Wilmington Parking Authority 365 U.S. 715 (1961); cf. *Dorsey v. Stuyvesant Town
Corporation* 299 N.Y. 512, 87 N.E. 2d. 541 (1949), 339 U.S. 981 (1949).
[2] *Jackson v. Metropolitan Edison Company* 419 U.S. 345 (1974).
[3] *Flag Bros v. Brooks* 436 U.S. 149 at 164 (1978).
[4] *Brown v. Socialist Workers '74 Campaign Committee* 103 S.Ct.416 (1982).
[5] *Shelley v. Kraemer* 334 U.S. 1 (1947); *The New York Times v. Sullivan* 376 U.S. 254
(1963).
[6] 1996 (3) S.A. 850 at 900.

Chapter 3 did not have "general direct horizontal application" but that it might have an influence on the development of the common law as it governs relations between individuals.[7] Constitutional rights could only be invoked against an organ of government. The Court found that the Constitution was intended to bind only the legislative and administrative organs of the state and was not intended to create a duty on the courts. Kentridge A.J. stated that a litigant may contend that a statute or executive act relied upon by another private litigant is invalid as being unconstitutional and that the court should have regard to the values in the Constitution when developing the common law. The majority approach was very similar to the Canadian approach. In *Du Plessis*, Kreigler J. powerfully dissented, arguing that the Chapter governed not only the relationship between the state and the individual but also governed "all law" including that applicable to private relationships. The *Du Plessis* decision resulted in a change to the Bill of Rights in Chapter 2 of the Final Constitution (1993),[7A] section 8(2) provides that:

> "a provision of the Bill of Rights binds a natural or juristic person if, and to the extent that, it is applicable, taking account of the nature of the right and the nature of any duty imposed by the right."

Section 8(3) requires the development of the common law if legislation does not protect the right in question. The common law may also be developed to limit rights if this is reasonable and justifiable within the meaning of section 36(1).

5.58   **Ireland.**   Ireland has recognised a cause of action against private parties for breach of some constitutional rights: *Lovett v. Grogan.*[8]

5.59   **Hong Kong.**   In Hong Kong, the courts have interpreted section 7(1) of the Bill of Rights Ordinance 1991[8A] as having no application in a dispute between private individuals. Section 7(1) provides that the Bill of Rights Ordinance binds only "(a) the Government and all public authorities; and (b) any person acting on behalf of the Government or a public authority". The original draft of Clause 7 of the Bill provided that it would bind "the Government and all authorities and persons, whether acting in a public or private capacity". The clause was amended due to opposition from sectors of the business community.[9] In *Tam Hing-yee v. Wu Tai-wai,*[10] the Hong Kong Court of Appeal held that a pre-existing ordinance pursuant to which an order had been made prohibiting a judgment debtor from leaving

---

[7] See at 887.
[7A] See Appendix H.
[8] [1995] 1 I.L.R.M. 12. See also *Parsons v. Kavanagh* [1990] I.L.R.M. 560; *Meskell v. Coras Iompair Eireann* [1973] I.R. 121.
[8A] See Appendix J.
[9] See A. Byrnes, "The Hong Kong Bill of Rights and Relations Between Private Individuals", Public Law and Human Rights: A Hong Kong Source Book, eds A. Byrnes and J. Chan (Butterworths, 1993).
[10] [1992] 1 H.K.L.R. 185.

the jurisdiction, should not be reviewed for consistency with the Bill of Rights Ordinance in litigation between private parties. In *Hong Kong Polytechnic University v. Next Magazine Publishing Ltd* [1996] 2 H.K.L.R. 260, the Hong Kong High Court interpreted the "government" in section 7(1) to include the legislative, executive and judicial organs of the state. It held that the Hong Kong Polytechnic University was a "public authority" given the nature of its functions and its public funding. The Bill of Rights Ordinance 1991 was deliberately limited to government action in the course of drafting.

Germany. The German Constitutional Court has long adopted the approach of *Drittwirkung* or the indirect horizontal application of human rights. Although the German Basic Law is not available in private law disputes, it permeates relationships between individuals. Unlike the USA, it is not necessary for state action to be involved.   **5.60**

Conclusion on Horizontal Effect

There are several practical arguments in favour of a greater than minimal degree of horizontal effect. One is the difficulty of maintaining a distinction between the public and the private spheres. Professor Dawn Oliver discusses many of the difficulties posed by a public/private divide in a well written and interesting book entitled *Common Values and the Public-Private Divide*,[11] in which she grounds her thesis that the traditional distinction between public and private law is artificial in that both are concerned with controlling exercises of power (whether by the state or private bodies), both are concerned to protect vital interests of individuals and public interests against abuses of state and private power and both kinds of law have a similar philosophical underpinning.   **5.61**

Further, courts tend to strive for consistency in the legal principles applicable to similar cases. A strict vertical interpretation of section 6 with limited effect between private parties is likely to lead to inconsistencies between legal proceedings with a similar subject-matter where the inconsistency is solely derived from the identity of the parties. For example, a public authority which is a defendant in, say a road traffic case, in a vicarious capacity will be subject to a duty to act compatibly with the Convention in the conduct of its defence such as in the obtaining of surveillance evidence, whilst a private motorist or private employer (or his/its insurers) will have no duty to so act. The question of admissibility of such evidence is considered at paras 11.48 *et seq.* below. It may rightly be said that this is an inconsistency that derives from the terms and intention behind the Convention itself and not the subsequent transposition into domestic law. However, it will remain an inconsistency between two identical sets of proceedings which turns solely on the identity of the parties to the litigation. A court might mitigate the effects of such inconsistency, in the example given above, by developing the rules on admissibility of evidence   **5.62**

---

[11] (London: Butterworths: 1999)

so as to exclude evidence obtained by any party in breach of a Convention right. Nevertheless, a litigant whose right to privacy has been violated will have a new cause of action under section 7(1)(a) of the HRA against the public authority defendant but will not against the private defendant.

5.63   A similar situation of inconsistency has been engendered in European Community law by the doctrine of vertical direct effect of Directives and this has given rise to various forms of legal manoeuvring by the European Court of Justice in order to achieve consistency of treatment between individuals in a domestic setting where a Directive has not been properly implemented by the Member State, even where an individual is seeking to rely on the Directive in proceedings between private individuals. For example, a wide definition was given to an emanation of the state in Case 152/84 *Marshall v. Southampton and South-West Hampshire Area Health Authority*[12] and Case C–188/89 *Foster v. British Gas plc*[13]; a principle of interpretation of legislation in conformity with a parent Directive in the case of ambiguity was formulated in Case 14/83 *Von Colson and Kamann v. Land Nordrhein-Westfalen*[14] and Case C–106/89 *Marleasing SA v. La Comercial Internacionale de Alimentacion SA*[15] and state liability in damages for non-implementation of a Directive was introduced in Cases C–6/90 and C9/90 *Francovich and Bonafaci v. Italy.*[16] These mechanisms have given a form of indirect horizontal effect to Directives in domestic law, the full scope of which remains uncertain.

5.64   As to the degree of horizontal effect likely to be given by the courts, the approach suggested by Murray Hunt of indirect horizontality is probably the most soundly based on a true construction of the HRA and the most likely to be upheld in practice when this issue comes to be fully judicially determined. The Hunt thesis, which is partially founded on Kreigler J.'s dissenting judgment in the South African case of *Du Plessis v. De Klerk*,[17] is that the Convention can be regarded as applying to all law and therefore as potentially relevant in private proceedings with a mandatory obligation on the courts under section 6 to develop the common law in a manner compatible with the Convention, but will not confer any new private causes of action against individuals for breach of Convention rights.[18] It is more unlikely that Professor Wade's thesis of full horizontal effect will meet with

---

[12] [1986] E.C.R. 723.

[13] [1990] E.C.R. I–3313, [1991] 1 Q.B. 405.

[14] [1984] E.C.R. 1891.

[15] [1990] E.C.R. I–4135. See also Case C–168/95 *Criminal Proceedings Against Luciano Arcaro* [1996] E.C.R. I–4705, Case C–194/94 *CIA Security International SA v. Signalson SA and Securitel SPRL* [1996] E.C.R. I–2201.

[16] [1991] E.C.R. I–5357. See also Cases C–46/93 and C–48/93 *Brasserie du Pecheur SA v. Germany; and R v. Secretary of State for Transport, ex p. Factortame Ltd* [1996] E.C.R. I–1029; Case C–392/93 *The Queen v. H.M.Treasury, ex p. British Telecommunications plc* [1996] E.C.R. I–1631 [1997] Q.B. 259; Cases C–178/94, C–179–94, C–188/94, C–189/94 and C–190/94 *Erich Dillenkofer v. Federal Republic of Germany* [1996] E.C.R. I–4845; Cases C–283/94, C–291/94 and C–292/94 *Denkavit Internationaal BV v. Bundesamt für Finanzen* [1996] E.C.R. I–5063; *R. v. Secretary of State for Transport, ex p. Factortame (No. 5)* [2001] A.C. 524; *R. v. Secretary of State for Transport, ex p. Factortame (No. 7)* [2001] 1 W.L.R. 942.

[17] 1996 (3) S.A. 850 at 900.

[18] D.Pannick and A.Lester agree with this view: "The Impact of the Human Rights Act on Private Law: The Knight's Move" (2000) 116 L.Q.R. 380 at 381.

judicial approval, because it appears to conflict with the careful structure of the HRA which read as a whole is constructed in a way which avoids imposing obligations on private individuals to act compatibly with the Convention.

The initial approach of the courts has been to treat themselves as under **5.65** an obligation to apply and develop the common law in accordance with the Convention.[18A] Accordingly, the HRA is undoubtedly having some degree of horizontal effect, the full extent of which will become clear over time.

4. OVERLAPPING RIGHTS ARGUMENTS

Sources of human rights law. There are four primary sources of **5.66** human rights law: the European Convention on Human Rights; E.C. law; the domestic common law; and international conventions. It is not uncommon for similar rights to arise under two or more of these sources. A good illustration of this is the case of *General Mediterranean Holdings v. Patel.*,[19] where Toulson J considered arguments regarding legal professional privilege and lawyer/client confidentiality under domestic law, E.C. law and the Convention. Accordingly, practitioners need to be familiar with other sources of fundamental rights law in addition to the Convention. Whilst there are clear overlaps between different sources of rights law, they are not usually identical and it is important to understand the legal effect of each rights source in the domestic courts.

Domestic law. The primary reason given for not incorporating the **5.67** European Convention into English law for nearly 50 years was that the rights and guarantees in the Convention were already protected in domestic law. The common law is, therefore, an important additional source of rights jurisprudence that has been under-utilised to date. The primary decisions regarding the rights which arise most frequently in civil practice are discussed at paragraphs 5.72 *et seq.*, below.

European Community law. Similarly, the "fundamental principles" **5.68** of E.C. law are another fruitful source of fundamental rights law. E.C. law has the major advantage of "trumping" any inconsistent primary or subordinate legislation by virtue of section 2(2) of the European Communities Act 1972.[20] Accordingly, it is a more powerful source of rights law than the HRA, which has carefully preserved Parliamentary sovereignty. The Charter of Fundamental Rights of the European Union may become a powerful source of rights law that will reduce the importance of the HRA with all of its inherent restrictions, particularly those limiting the courts from striking down incompatible legislation. Since it currently has only declaratory

---

[18A] See para. 5.41 above.
[19] [1999] 3 All E.R. 673.
[20] *R. v. Secretary of State for Transport, ex p. Factortame* [1990] 2 A.C. 85, [1991] 1 A.C. 603.

status, its importance will depend on its development by the European Court of Justice and the Court of First Instance.[20A]

5.69   **International conventions.**   International conventions to which the United Kingdom is a signatory state also provide a further source of fundamental rights. There are several United Nations Conventions which provide further rights that are relevant in a civil or commercial context and which share similar concepts with the European Convention. Two important United Nations conventions which have been signed and ratified by the United Kingdom are the International Covenant on Civil and Political Rights 1966[21] and the International Covenant on Social and Economic Rights 1966.[22] The main supervisory body for U.N. human rights conventions is the United Nations Human Rights Committee. The international conventions are summarised in Chapter 7.[22A] Whilst international instruments are not part of domestic law until expressly incorporated, a court may have regard to them in so far as they are relevant to a matter before the court. Further, the reporting requirements placed on the Government in relation to the U.N. conventions means that such rights are taken into account in the formulation of policy.

5.70   **Other European signatory states.**   The jurisprudence of other European signatory states that have incorporated the Convention is likely to be a useful reference source, particularly in relation to points which have not yet been determined by the European Court. In *Stott (Procurator Fiscal of Dunfermline) v. Brown,*[23] Lord Hope of Craighead stated, in relation to the use of materials from other signatory countries to the Convention, that references in the preamble to the Convention to these countries' common heritage of political traditions, ideals, freedom and the rule of law and by the European Court to the fact that generally recognised international standards lie at the heart of Article 6 encourage resort, as a check, to a comparative exercise based on the use of such materials. A good starting point for a comparative study is Conor Gearty (ed.), *European Civil Liberties and the European Convention on Human Rights: A Comparative Study.*[24] Sweet & Maxwell's *Current Law* is a reference source for the case law.

5.71   **Other common law jurisdictions.**   The case-law of other common law jurisdictions, including New Zealand, Canada, South Africa, India, Hong Kong and the United States, is another good reference source, which has the added attraction of being firmly rooted in common law traditions. The constitutions or bills of rights of these jurisdictions are usually derived from or based on the International Covenant on Civil and Political Rights. Care does, however, need to be taken in identifying the issue that a particular court is addressing and its general approach. It will not necessarily be possible to simply read across the relevant principles if

[20A] See further paras 6.159 *et seq.*
[21] See App. D.
[22] See App. E.
[22A] See paras 7.88 *et seq.*
[23] (2001) 2 W.L.R. 817, *The Times*, December 6, 2000, PC.
[24] M. Nijhoff, The Hague (1997).

the approach is dissimilar to that which has been adopted by the European Court and the European Commission.[25] The main parallels with the European Convention are discussed in Chapter 7.[25A]

5. COMMON LAW CONSTITUTIONAL RIGHTS

General

Despite the incorporation of the Convention into United Kingdom law and **5.72** its attendant status as the main source of human rights within the jurisdiction, it ought not to be forgotten that the domestic common law and equity both have something to contribute to the development of the Convention rights as enjoyed in domestic law, especially given that ratification of the Convention by the United Kingdom took place as long ago as 1951. The United Kingdom Government was involved in the drafting of the Convention and one of the justifications put forward in the past for the non-incorporation of the Convention prior to the HRA was that the Convention rights were already protected by domestic law. It follows that the rules fashioned by the common law and equity are compatible with and complementary to many of the rights protected under the Convention, and the common law position on any given area should not be relegated to a mere supporting role. Indeed in some cases (for example the rules as to the impartiality of tribunals), domestic law may arguably go further in its protection than Strasbourg. The Convention is now the "floor" of protection given to fundamental rights in domestic law. However, it is not necessarily the "ceiling" and domestic law may well confer additional protection to particular rights.

In the face of increasing argument from counsel prior to the HRA as to how **5.73** the Convention impacted upon English law, some courts were prepared to state that certain of the rights enshrined in the Convention have no less a home in the common law or equity. Although the Convention is now officially part of domestic law, and the courts should, strictly speaking, have no need of added encouragement to apply Convention principles on their own merit, on occasion it may be tactically advantageous for the practitioner to draw attention to the way in which a right has been traditionally protected by common law or equity as well as under the Convention. As the Court of Appeal pointed out in *R. v. Secretary of State for the Home Department, ex p. Togher*,[26] in those pre-incorporation days the courts tended to take greater notice of the Convention when it was presented as a *reflection* of the principles of the common law. The Court of Appeal stated in *R. v. Secretary of State for the Home Department, ex p. Brind*,[27] that one would have to look "long and hard" before it would be possible to detect *any* difference between the common law and the principles enshrined in the Convention. There are indeed a variety of more specific

---

[25] See, *e.g. R. v. Bow County Court, ex p. Pelling* [2001] U.K.H.R.R. 165, Admin Ct, where the court held that citation of American authority did not illuminate application of the European Convention to the case because the law relating to the First and Fourteenth Amendments of the U.S. Constitution differed in many respects from that applicable to Art. 10.

[25A] See paras 7.44 *et seq.*

[26] Unreported, February 1, 1995.

[27] [1991] A.C. 696.

cases in which the common law has been declared to encompass the same principles as a provision of the Convention. It is hoped that the following brief summary of domestic case law will represent an additional rights reference source as well as illustrating that pre-HRA rights law lends itself fairly well to evolution into the post-HRA landscape.[28]

Summary of Domestic Case Law

5.74   **Freedom of expression (Article 10).** There have been far more judicial statements as to the common law protection of freedom of expression than on any other equivalent Convention right. There exists considerable House of Lords dicta on the topic, with the most forceful being that of Lord Goff in *Attorney-General v. Guardian Newspapers (No. 2)*[29] to the effect that as far as the issue of free speech was concerned, there was no difference in principle between Article 10 of the Convention and the common law. This was re-iterated in *Derbyshire County Council v. Times Newspapers Ltd,*[30] *Lord Advocate v. The Scotsman Publications Ltd,*[31] and *Spring v. Guardian Assurance Plc.*[32] In the *Derbyshire County Council case,*[33] the House of Lords held that a public authority did not have standing to sue for libel in order to vindicate its reputation since this "must inevitably have an inhibiting effect on freedom of speech" which was contrary to the public interest. Whereas the Court of Appeal had reached its conclusion on the basis of the Convention, Lord Keith stated that the common law provided no less protection to freedom of speech than the Strasbourg institutions, relying on a previous statement to that effect by Lord Goff in *Attorney-General v. Guardian Newspapers (No. 2).*[34] A slightly more equivocal but potentially helpful nonetheless is the declaration by Lord Kilbrandon in *Broome v. Cassell & Co. Ltd*[35] that freedom of speech is a "constitutional right", and that of Lord Templeman in *Brind v. Secretary of State for the Home Department*[36] that freedom of expression is a principle of every democratic constitution. Court of Appeal authority of note on the same subject includes *John v. MGN Ltd,*[37] *Watts v. Times Newspapers,*[38] and *Associated Newspapers Group Ltd v. Wade.*[39] In *Rantzen v. Mirror Group Newspapers Ltd,*[40] the Court of Appeal held that Article 10

---

[28] The following summary of case law is primarily drawn from M. Hunt, *Using Human Rights Law in the Domestic Courts* (Oxford: Hart, 1998). Reference should be made to this excellent book for further detail on the protection given to human rights in English law prior to the HRA. See also "Unconventional Behaviour? Judicial Uses of the European Convention in England and Wales" [1996] E.H.R.L.R. 467 and R.Clayton & H.Tomlinson, *The Law of Human Rights* (Oxford: 2000) who discuss in considerable detail the pre-HRA position in relation to each Article of the Convention.
[29] [1990] 1 A.C. 109.
[30] [1993] A.C. 534 at 550E—551G, *per* Lord Keith.
[31] [1990] 1 A.C. 812. See also the speech of Lord Templeman.
[32] [1995] A.C. 296 at 326G-H and 352E-G, *per* Lord Lowry and Lord Woolf.
[33] [1993] A.C. 534.
[34] [1990] 1 A.C. 109, HL.
[35] [1972] A.C. 1027 at 1133A.
[36] [1991] A.C. 696.
[37] [1997] Q.B. 586.
[38] [1997] Q.B. 650.
[39] [1979] 1 W.L.R. 697.
[40] [1994] Q.B. 670.

was relevant to its statutory powers to review jury awards of libel damages that inhibited free speech.

Fair Trial (Article 6).   Various procedural guarantees under Article 6   **5.75** have been found to be in accordance with the English common law. In *Hamilton v. Naviede (Re Arrows Ltd (No. 4))*,[41] the House of Lords held that the privilege against self-incrimination was a basic freedom secured by English law regardless of the provisions of the Convention. A similar line was taken by the House of Lords in relation to natural justice—in *R. v. Board of Visitors of Her Majesty's Prison The Maze, ex p. Hone*,[42] the common law was held not to be incompatible with Article 6 of the Convention as it had been applied and interpreted by the European Court. In *Raymond v. Honey*,[43] in the context of an appeal against committal for contempt of court the House of Lords held that an individual in English law had a constitutional guarantee that their legal rights would be determined by a court. The question of access to a court arose again in *R. v. Lord Chancellor's Department, ex p. Witham*.[44] In holding that the Lord Chancellor could not introduce a minimum fee of £120 for issuing a writ, Laws J found that the right of access to a court was a common law constitutional right which could not be abrogated in the absence of a specific provision in an Act of Parliament. He further stated that the common law provided no lesser protection of the right of access to a court than might be vindicated in Strasbourg.[45] He reviewed the existing authorities supporting the existence of a common law right of access to a court including *Bremer Vulkan Schiffbau und Maschinenfabrik v. South India Shipping Corporation*,[46] *R. v. Secretary of State for the Home Department, ex p. Leech*,[47] and *R. v. Secretary of State for the Home Department, ex p. Wynne* (express reference to Article 6).[48] In *Science Research Council v. Nasse*,[49] it was held that the right to a fair hearing was the driving common law principle behind the rules on discovery and inspection in civil litigation. In *Reid v. Chief Constable of Merseyside Police*,[50] the Court of Appeal held that the European case law on Article 6(1) showed that the test of bias propounded by Lord Goff in *R. v. Gough*[51] was in all respects compatible with the Convention. In *R. v. Sultan Khan*,[52] the House of Lords acknowledged that Article 6 jurisprudence had a valuable role to play in considering common law and statutory discretionary powers in the context of fair trial procedures. Importantly, the Civil Procedure Rules have as their overriding obligation at Part 1.1 the obligation to act "justly", central to which is the notion of fair trial and equality of arms.

---

[41] [1995] 2 A.C. 75.
[42] [1988] A.C. 379.
[43] [1983] 1 A.C. 1.
[44] [1998] Q.B. 575.
[45] *ibid.*, at 787.
[46] [1981] A.C. 909, HL.
[47] [1994] Q.B. 198.
[48] [1992] Q.B. 406.
[49] [1978] 3 W.L.R. 754.
[50] *The Times*, February 5, 1996.
[51] [1993] A.C. 646.
[52] [1997] A.C. 558; *The Times*, July 5, 1996.

5.76   **Privacy and family life (Article 8).**   A tentative common law right to privacy was recognised in broad terms by the House of Lords in *Morris v. Beardmore*[53] in the shape of a presumption that Parliament could not be taken as having intended to authorise tortious conduct without a very clear indication of this fact. In *R. v. Brown*[54] Lord Slynn seemed prepared to accept that a right to privacy existed in the common law equivalent to that under the Convention, although in his opinion no privacy point fell to be decided in that case. The Court of Appeal had earlier warmed to this theme in *R. v. Inland Revenue Commissioners, ex p. T. C. Coombes & Co.*,[55] in which the court proclaimed that the protection of privacy was of great concern to both the common law and the Convention. Similarly in *Schering Chemicals Ltd v. Falkman Ltd*[56] the Court of Appeal declared that the Convention and the common law both protected the fundamental right of an individual to privacy. However, in *Kaye v. Robertson*,[57] the Court of Appeal stated that no self-standing right to privacy existed in English law (although no reference was made to the equitable law of confidence in that case). Post-HRA, the domestic courts have finally recognised a domestic law right to privacy grounded in the equitable doctrine of confidence: *Douglas v. Hello! Ltd.*[58] In *General Mediterranean Holdings v. Patel*,[59] Toulson J. considered domestic law principles of legal professional privilege and confidentiality as well as the protection given to lawyer/client confidentiality by Article 8 and European Community law.

5.77   In relation to the right to family life, this has been discussed primarily in the immigration law context, when a party argues that to deport either himself or his children is a denial of the fundamental right to family life. It has also been raised in the family law contexts of custody and adoption hearings. In all cases the English law has been said to conform with that of the Convention and examples include: *Re D (Minors)(Adoption Reports: Confidentiality)*[60] where the House of Lords, in the context of an application for adoption, found that the principles of English law were consonant with those of the Convention and *Re KD (a Minor) (Ward: Termination of Access)*[61] where a similar statement was made by the House of Lords in the context of an appeal against termination of access. An example in the immigration context is *Dibia v. Chief Immigration Officer, Heathrow Airport.*[62]

5.78   **No retrospective penalties (Article 7).**   This principle of natural justice is undoubtedly part of the common law. As Lord Reid pointed out in *Waddington v. Miah*,[63] the principle that there should be no retrospective

---

[53] [1981] A.C. 446.
[54] [1994] 1 A.C. 212.
[55] [1989] S.T.C. 520.
[56] [1982] Q.B. 1 at 21C (*per* Lord Denning M.R.). See also *Morris v. Beardmore* [1981] A.C. 446 at 464C (*per* Lord Scarman) and *Attorney-General v. Guardian Newspapers (No. 2)* [1990] Q.B. 109 at 255.
[57] [1991] F.S.R. 62; *The Times*, March 21, 1990, CA.
[58] [2001] 2 W.L.R. 992, CA.
[59] [2000] 1 W.L.R. 272, [1999] 3 All E.R. 673.
[60] [1996] A.C. 593.
[61] [1988] A.C. 806.
[62] Unreported, October 19, 1995, CA.
[63] [1974] 1 W.L.R. 683.

penalties is so engrained in our legal and political system that it was "hardly credible" that Parliament would ever promote or pass retrospective criminal legislation. This was a reiteration of what Stephenson L.J. had strongly asserted in the Court of Appeal below, namely that there was indisputably a common law presumption against retrospectivity.[64] Sir Thomas Bingham M.R. was clear in *L'Office Cherifien des Phosphates v. Yamashita-Shinnihon Steamship Co. Ltd*[65] that there was a "fundamental and longstanding rule" against retrospectivity in criminal offences; and similar sentiments were expressed by a Divisional Court of the Queen's Bench Division in *Budd v. Colchester BC.*[66] As yet, there have been no English decisions on whether the principle applies as strictly to penalties imposed in a non-criminal setting.

Freedom of Association (Article 11).   In *UKAPE v. ACAS,*[67] the   **5.79** Court of Appeal stated that Article 11 of the Convention was merely declaratory of the same right to be found enshrined in the common law. This pronouncement was repeated by Lord Scarman when the case subsequently went to the House of Lords,[68] and also by a later Court of Appeal decision in *Cheall v. APEX.*[69]

Right to life (Article 2).   The right to life under Article 2 of the   **5.80** Convention was said by the House of Lords in *Airedale NHS Trust v. Bland*[70] to form not only part of English law but that of most if not all civilised societies around the world.

Freedom of religion (Article 9).   In *R. v. Commissioners of English*   **5.81** *Heritage, ex p. Chappell,*[71] the Court of Appeal held that there was no significant difference between the freedom of religion guaranteed by Article 9 of the Convention and that protected by the common law.

---

[64] Above, at 690H—691A.
[65] [1993] 3 W.L.R. 266, CA; [1994] 2 W.L.R. 39, HL.
[66] Unreported, July 29, 1996, DC; *The Times*, April 4, 1999, CA.
[67] [1979] 1 W.L.R. 570.
[68] [1981] A.C. 424.
[69] [1983] Q.B. 126.
[70] [1993] A.C. 789.
[71] Unreported, June 19, 1986, CA.

CHAPTER 6
European Community Law and Human Rights

1. OUTLINE OF THE CHAPTER

The purpose of this chapter is to examine the application of human rights **6.01** law in the context of Community law. The entry into force of the Human Rights Act 1998 ("the HRA 1998") has raised the prospect of the fused practical application of no fewer than three separate legal regimes offering protection to an individual's rights: (1) domestic "human rights" law, both at common law and under the HRA 1998; (2) human rights law derived from the European Convention on Human Rights ("the Convention"); and (3) "human rights" recognised as general principles of law under the jurisprudence of the Court of Justice of the European Communities ("the ECJ") and in other sources of Community law.

Each of these regimes has developed "substantive" principles designed to **6.02** safeguard the procedural rights of both natural and legal persons. These rights may be invoked where a decision is taken by a public body which affects or is capable of affecting an individual's interests. It is therefore important for practitioners to appreciate which of the various regimes is applicable to their case. Schiemann L.J. (extra-judicially) has referred to the protection afforded under each of the three regimes as a "toolkit". Practitioners must understand which tool is most appropriate for the task at hand.

The importance of such human rights as are recognised under Community **6.03** law should not be underestimated. It is now well established that Community law is "supreme", which means that Community law "trumps" domestic law when the two are in conflict. This is so, even if it means disapplying inconsistent domestic law or even overturning an Act of Parliament.[1] In so far as Community law recognises the same or greater rights than the Convention (and *a fortiori* the HRA 1998), Community law should generally be the preferred tool. The reasons are briefly summarised here and dealt with in more detail below.

> (1) Community law "human rights" will be given direct effect in the law of England and Wales. These rights are not dependent on an interpretative method being adopted and the court's review may be broader in scope than with purely Convention rights

---

[1] See in particular the *Factortame* litigation in its various stages: Cases C–213/89 *R. v. Secretary of State for Transport, ex p. Factortame Ltd (No. 2)* [1991] 1 A.C. 603, ECJ and HL (interim relief); and C–221/89 *Factortame (No.3)* [1992] Q.B. 680, ECJ (substantive finding that the Merchant Shipping Act infringed Community law); Case C–48/93 *Factortame and Brasserie du Pêcheur* [1996] E.C.R. I–1029, ECJ (right to damages); *Factortame (No. 5)* [2000] 1 A.C. 524, HL (sufficiently serious breach established to trigger right to damages); and finally, the judgment of His Honour Judge Toulmin o.c. in *Factortame (No. 6)* [2001] 1 W.L.R. 942 (setting out domestic principles applied to claims for breach of Community law).

    (2) Community rights may, in certain circumstances, provide for an enhanced measure of review[2]

    (3) Further, in accordance with the established case law of the ECJ,[3] they require an adequate remedy to be granted for their breach, notwithstanding the fact that Article 13 of the Convention has not been incorporated into domestic law via the HRA 1998. The remedy will not be restricted to a declaration of incompatibility. Full force and effect must be given to the Community rights

    (4) Their breach may well give rise to a claim for damages. This may give a more generous measure of loss than the "just satisfaction" granted by the European Court of Human Rights. The case law on the assessment of damages under Community law is more developed than its domestic counterpart under the HRA 1998.

6.04 This chapter will therefore look at how "human rights" are recognised in Community law, what protection is given to them and how far they may be used in a domestic context. Given the advantages identified above of rights recognised under Community law, specific attention is paid to the method by which Community and domestic courts have determined whether Community rights are called into play. This chapter will examine in particular:

    (1) the origins and development of the protection of human rights in E.C. law;

    (2) the present content of the "fundamental principles" of E.C. law, highlighting any differences in the content of rights under E.C. law compared with those under the Convention;

    (3) the European Charter of Fundamental Rights;

    (4) the interaction between E.C. law, Strasbourg case law and the HRA 1998 together with any strategic implications arising from the interplay between those regimes.

---

[2] *Per* Forbes J. in *R. v. MAFF, ex p. Bell Lines Limited* [1984] 2 C.M.L.R. 502 at 511; *per* Popplewell J. in *R. v. MAFF, ex p. Roberts* [1991] 1 C.M.L.R. 555 at 576; but see Case C–120/97 *Upjohn Ltd v. Licensing Authority* [1999] E.C.R. I–223, where the ECJ held that Member States did not need to ensure that national reviewing courts carry out their own assessment on the facts. It could confine itself to making sure that there had been no obvious error or misuse of power and that the public authority had not exceeded its discretion in making the decision. *Quaere* the extent to which this approach may need to be reconsidered in the light of the judgment of the European Court of Human Rights in *Kingsley v. United Kingdom, The Times,* January 9, 2001.

[3] See Case 106/77 *Amministrazione delle Finanze dello Stato v. Simmenthal SpA (II)* [1978] E.C.R. 629, para. 21; Case 33/76 *Rewe-Zentralfinanz eG and Rewe-Zentral AG v. Landwirtschaftskammer für das Saarland* [1976] E.C.R. 1989 at 1998, para. 5; Case 199/82 *Amministrazione delle Finanze dello Stato v. SpA San Giorgio* [1982] E.C.R. 3595 at 3612, para. 12; Case C–213/89 *Factortame (No. 2)* [1990] E.C.R. I–2433, paras 20 to 23; Case C–6 and 9/90 *Francovich and Bonafaci v. Italy* [1991] E.C.R. I–5357, paras 38–39 of the Opinion of Advocate General Mischo.

2. THE ORIGINS AND DEVELOPMENT OF HUMAN RIGHTS IN COMMUNITY LAW[4]

Absence of Specific Rights in the Treaties

The notion of protecting human rights was not contained in the founding 6.05
treaties of the European Communities.[5] It has been said that the protection of fundamental rights was discussed by the drafters, but that the idea of including provisions for the purpose was rejected.[6] It was believed that the Council of Europe would guard against violations of fundamental rights. The Council of Europe had only recently undertaken the task of drafting the European Convention on Human Rights and establishing the European Court of Human Rights in Strasbourg. Moreover, it may have been thought that the development of the Communities based on a process of economic integration did not involve the risk of infringements of fundamental rights.[7]

The ECJ was keen from the start to protect the rights of individuals,[8] but 6.06
anxious not to overstep the boundaries of its competence or risk the application of purely domestic law to areas properly subject to Community law. In some of the early cases before it, the ECJ rejected any suggestion that the protection of fundamental rights formed part of a Community "common law".[9] Indeed, in the case of *Geitling v. High Authority* the Court went so far as to state that "Community law does not contain any general principle, express or otherwise, guaranteeing the maintenance of vested rights".[10]

Pressure for the Recognition of Human Rights in Community Law

Nonetheless, with the emergence of the twin concepts of the supremacy 6.07
of Community law and its direct effect in the national legal orders of

---

[4] See generally Professor J. Schwarze, *European Administrative Law* (Sweet & Maxwell, 1992); de Smith, Woolf & Jowell's *Principles of Judicial Review* (Sweet & Maxwell, 1999); Schwarze, "Developing Principles of European Administrative Law" [1993] P.L. 229; Professor T. Tridimas, *The General Principles of EC Law* (Oxford University Press, 1999); Murray Hunt, *Using Human Rights Law in English Courts* (Hart, 1998), Chap. 7.

[5] These are: (1) the Treaty of Paris, signed in April 1951 establishing the European Coal and Steel Community ("ECSC" Treaty); (2) the Treaty of Rome, signed in March 1957, establishing the European Economic Community ("EEC" Treaty); and (3) the Treaty of Rome, signed in March 1957 establishing the European Atomic Energy Community ("EAEC" or "EURATOM" Treaty). These Treaties have been amended and modified by the Single European Act 1986; the Treaty on European Union, signed at Maastricht in February 1992; and the Treaty of Amsterdam, which entered into force on May 1, 1999.

[6] See Betten and Grief, *EU Law and Human Rights*, (1st ed., Longman, London and New York, 1998) p. 53.

[7] See G.F. Mancini, *The Making of a Constitution for Europe* (1989) C.M.L. Rev., p. 595–614 at p. 609.

[8] See, *e.g.* Case 6/60 *Humblet v. Belgium* [1960] E.C.R. 559 at 572, where the ECJ held that a provision establishing guarantees for the protection of individual's rights cannot be interpreted in a restrictive manner to the detriment of the individual.

[9] See Case 1/58 *Stork v. High Authority* [1959] E.C.R. 17, para. 4(a), which stated that the High Authority's decisions were not open to challenge on the grounds of breach of a Member State's constitutional law; Joined Cases 36–38 and 40/59 *Geitling v. High Authority* [1960] E.C.R. 423 at 439; and Case 40/64 *Sgarlata v. Commission* [1965] E.C.R. 215 at 227, in which the ECJ would not look to the "fundamental principles governing all the Member States" when construing the Treaty.

[10] *ibid* at 438–439.

Member States, the case for the recognition of core, fundamental rights became more pressing. In *van Gend en Loos*,[11] the ECJ held that the Community constituted a "new legal order of international law, for the benefit of which the states have limited their sovereign rights, albeit within limited fields." The subjects of this new legal order were not simply the Member States, but their individual nationals as well. Furthermore, Treaty provisions that were sufficiently clear and unconditional did not need any legislative intervention on the part of Member States, before they produced "direct effects in the legal relationship between Member States and their subjects." The ECJ rejected the suggestion that the existence of infringement procedures initiated by either the Commission or Member States (under Articles 169 and 170 of the E.C. Treaty, now Articles 226 and 227 EC)[12] meant that the Treaty conferred no direct rights on individuals. The Court found that if rights of recourse were so restricted, it would "remove all direct legal protection of the individual rights of their nationals."[13]

6.08 In *Costa v. ENEL*,[14] the ECJ considered that by creating a Community of unlimited duration, with its own institutions, its own personality, its own legal capacity and with real powers, Member States had effected a transfer of power from those states to the Community. They had accordingly limited their sovereign power, albeit within limited fields. By doing so, the Member States had created a body of law binding on themselves and their nationals. Further, the ECJ found that:

> "The transfer by the States from their domestic legal system to the Community legal system of the rights and obligations arising under the Treaty carries with it a permanent limitation on their sovereign rights, against which a subsequent unilateral act incompatible with the concept of Community law cannot prevail."

6.09 Direct effect and supremacy therefore transferred permanently a degree of constitutional power from the Member States to the Community. The constitutional courts of certain Member States, such as Germany and Italy, were reluctant to accept these principles without an assurance that human rights would be protected at a Community level.[15] This reluctance manifested itself in a number of ways. First, in October 1967, the Constitutional Court of the Federal Republic of Germany declared that the Community order, lacking as it did any protection for human rights, had no lawful democratic basis. Any transfer of powers from Germany to the Community could not therefore deprive German citizens of the protection they received from the German Constitution. The Constitutional Court ruled

---

[11] Case 26/62 *Van Gend en* Loos [1963] E.C.R. 1 at 12–13.
[12] The E.C. and E.U. Treaties were consolidated, reorganised and renumbered pursuant to Article 12 of the Treaty of Amsterdam. The citation system for Treaty Articles adopted above is intended to conform with the uniform citation system set out in *Practice Notes (ECJ: Treaty Citation) (No. 1) and (No. 2)* [1999] All E.R. (E.C.) 481; [1999] All E.R. (E.C.) 646. The letters following the Arabic numerals use "C.S." for references to the ECSC Treaty; "EA" for the Euratom Treaty; "EC" for the E.C. Treaty and "EU" for the E.U. Treaty.
[13] See *Van Gend en Loos* (note 11 above), at 13.
[14] Case 6/64 *Costa v. ENEL* [1964] E.C.R. 585 at 593.
[15] See J.H.H Weiler, *Fundamental Rights and fundamental boundaries*, in *The Constitution of Europe* (Cambridge, 1999), pp. 107–108.

that Community law had to be examined domestically to ensure its compatibility with national, constitutional provisions.[16] Secondly, German and Italian appellants before the ECJ challenged decisions of Community institutions on the grounds that they were in conflict with fundamental rights guaranteed by their respective constitutions.[17] In the words of a former judge of the ECJ, these objections were;

> "a brutal blow, a blow jeopardizing not only the supremacy but the very independence of Community law. Something had to be done and the Court did it, both for fear that its hard-won conquests might vanish and because of its own growing awareness that a 'democratic deficit' had become apparent in the management of the Community."[18]

The Development of a Doctrine of "Fundamental Rights" by the ECJ

The opportunity for the ECJ to respond came first in the case of *Stauder*.[19]   **6.10**
A Commission decision in February 1969 authorised Member States to allow certain categories of consumer who were beneficiaries under a social welfare scheme to buy butter at a reduced price. The Federal Republic of Germany, pursuant to the authorisation, issued coupons for the butter. Under the German scheme, in order to be valid, the coupon had to give the name and address of the beneficiary. Mr Stauder complained that the requirement to give one's name in order to prove his entitlement infringed his fundamental rights under the German Constitution. The ECJ held that, on its proper construction, the Commission decision neither required nor prohibited the identification of the beneficiaries by name. More importantly, the Court considered, albeit by way of *obiter dicta*, that "interpreted in this way the provision at issue contains nothing capable of prejudicing the fundamental human rights enshrined in the general principles of Community law and protected by the Court."[20]

The ECJ called upon the "general principles of Community law" the   **6.11**
following year in the seminal case of *Internationale Handelsgesellschaft*.[21]
The German Administrative Court referred certain questions to the ECJ for a preliminary ruling under Article 177 of the E.C. Treaty (now Article 234 EC). The national court took the view that various provisions relating to export licences in the Community organised cereal market offended certain principles of German constitutional law. In particular, Council Regulation No. 129/67 on the common organisation of the market in cereals[22]

---

[16] Order of the *Bundesgerichtshof* dated October 18, 1967, BverGE, 1967 at 223.
[17] See generally A. Clapham, *Human Rights and the European Community: A Critical Overview* (Nomos: Baden-Baden, 1991).
[18] G.F. Mancini, *op. cit.* (note 7, above) at pp. 609–610.
[19] Case 29/69 *Erich Stauder v. City of Ulm* [1969] E.C.R. 419.
[20] *ibid.*, para. 7.
[21] Case 11/70 *Internationale Handelsgesellschaft mbH v. Einfuhr- und Vorratsstelle für Getriede und Futtermittel* [1970] E.C.R. 1125, often known more simply as the "IHG" case.
[22] [1967] O.J. L204/16.

mandated that deposits paid for obtaining export licences might be forfeited if the licence were not used within the required period of time. The national court considered that such a provision offended the German constitutional principle of proportionality. The ECJ reiterated that it was not open to the national court to question the validity of measures adopted by Community institutions by reference to legal rules or concepts of national law.[23] They could only be judged in the light of Community law. Otherwise the uniformity and efficacy of Community law would be jeopardised. Indeed, the Court warned that Community law could not, by its very nature, be overridden by rules of national law, of whatever nature, without the legal basis of the Community itself being called into question.[24] It followed that:

> " . . . the validity of a Community measure or its effect within a Member State cannot be affected by allegations that it runs counter to either fundamental rights as formulated by the constitution of that State or the principles of a national constitutional structure."

6.12 Lest this were too bitter a pill to swallow, the ECJ went on to examine whether "an analogous guarantee inherent in Community law" had been disregarded by the Regulation. In the light of the doubts expressed by the German Administrative Court, the ECJ felt compelled to ascertain whether the system of deposits infringed "rights of a fundamental nature, respect for which must be ensured in the Community legal system."[25] This obligation arose because:

> "In fact, respect for fundamental rights forms an integral part of the general principles of law protected by the Court of Justice. The protection of such rights, whilst inspired by the constitutional traditions common to the Member States, must be ensured within the framework of the structure and objectives of the Community."

On the facts of the case, the ECJ found that the licence provisions were both necessary and proportionate to the aims to be achieved.

6.13 This open recognition of respect for fundamental rights within Community law represented a dramatic change of tack for the ECJ. It has been suggested that the rationale for adopting the terminology of fundamental rights was a purely defensive one. The ECJ was anxious to defend the supremacy of Community law in the face of threats from the constitutional courts of the Member States. It wanted to avert the risk that the latter

---

[23] See (n. 21, above), at para. 3 of the judgment.
[24] This argument has been referred to by G.F. Mancini as the "or else" argument. See *The making of a Constitution for Europe* (note 7, above), at p. 600. Non-acceptance by Member States of the supremacy of E.C. law would have led to a "rapid erosion of the Community; and this was a possibility that nobody really envisaged, not even the most intransigent custodians of national sovereignty."
[25] See (n. 21, above) at para. 4 of the judgment.

would opt for the supremacy of their own constitutional provisions.[26] There is almost certainly an element of truth in this. The ruling in *Internationale Handelsgesellschaft* paved the way for the Court to reject expressly the suggestion that Community law was capable of being challenged by constitutional requirements of domestic law. In *Hauer*[27] the Court determined that the question of possible infringement of fundamental rights by a measure of the Community institutions could *only* be judged in the light of Community law itself. The idea of a challenge to Community measures being sustained on domestic grounds risked damaging the "substantive unity and efficacy of Community law". The Court feared that it would lead "inevitably to the destruction of the unity of the Common Market" and would jeopardise the cohesion of the Community.[28]

Nonetheless, the suggestion that the ECJ was exclusively or principally **6.14** motivated by a desire to protect the supremacy of Community law perhaps overlooks the Court's concern for the rights of the individual. Such a concern was already latent in the existing case law. It is also somewhat ironic that, if it were the rationale, it did not have the desired, defensive effect. The constitutional courts of Germany, Italy and France continued to proclaim for some years that Community law that fell foul of their respective constitutions would not necessarily be accorded supremacy.[29]

Regardless of the motivation for the adoption of the terminology of "funda- **6.15** mental rights", the practical effect was to enable the ECJ to indulge in a degree of judicial activism and to develop "general principles of law" along common law lines.[30] While this level of "creative jurisprudence" has been questioned,[31] as Professor Tridimas has validly pointed out, which Member State would have ratified a Treaty that was capable of violating the fundamental rights protected by its own constitution?[32]

---

[26] See Jason Coppel and Aidan O'Neill "The European Court of Justice: Taking Rights Seriously?" (1992) 29 C.M.L. Rev. 669–692 at p. 669. The authors' contentions were subjected to unusually detailed scrutiny in Professor J.H.H. Weiler and N.J.S. Lockhart, "'Taking Rights Seriously' Seriously: The European Court of Justice and its Fundamental Rights Jurisprudence" (1995) C.M.L. 32 Rev. 51 and 579.

[27] Case 44/79 *Liselotte Hauer v. Länd Rheinland-Pfalz* [1979] E.C.R. 3727, para. 14.

[28] *ibid.*, at para. 14 of the judgment. Professor Tridimas (note 4, above), at p. 206) adds: "Once it is accepted that human rights form part of the Community legal order and bind the Community institutions, their protection must be ensured within the four corners of the Community polity. It would simply not be possible to apply mechanically human rights as recognised in one or another national legal system without taking into account the specific qualities of Community law."

[29] See the judgments of the German Federal Constitutional Court in *Internationale Handelsgesellschaft (Solange I)* [1974] 2 C.M.L.R. 540; the Italian Constitutional Court in *Costa v. ENEL* [1964] C.M.L.R. 425, *Frontini v. Ministero delle Finanze* [1974] 2 C.M.L.R. 372 and, more recently, in *SpA Fragd v. Amministrazione delle Finanze*, Decision No. 232 of April 21, 1989; and the Conseil d'Etat in *Semoules* [1970] C.M.L.R. 395. The area has been revisited by the German Federal Constitutional Court more recently in its judgment of October 12, 1993 on the Maastricht Treaty [1993] 1 C.M.L.R. 57, where it reserved to itself the right to declare Community acts inapplicable if they breached fundamental norms of the German Constitution. See Professor J.H.H. Weiler, "Does Europe need a Constitution? Demos, Telos and the German Maastricht Decision" (1995) 1 E.L.J. 219.

[30] See Tridimas, *General Principles* (n. 4, above), p. 205, who notes that the *Internationale Handelsgesellschaft* case "marks a distinct development" and "is a testament to the Court's creative jurisprudence". Nonetheless, it was "not a paradigm of unwarranted judicial activism".

[31] Charges of "naked law-making" have been periodically levelled against the ECJ in this area. For a summary of such accusations, see Professor Tridimas, "The European Court of Justice and Judicial Activism" (1996) 21 E.L. Rev. 199.

[32] See Tridimas, *General Principles* (n. 4, above), p. 206.

The Role of the European Convention on Human Rights

6.16 The Court continued its development of the fundamental rights doctrine in subsequent cases. In *Nold*[33] the ECJ made its first express reference to the Convention. The Court was faced with a challenge to a decision of the Commission which the applicant contended violated its right to the free pursuit of business activity. The applicant alleged that such a right was protected not only by the German Constitution but also by: "various international treaties, including in particular the Convention for the Protection of Human Rights and Fundamental Freedoms of 4 November 1950 and the Protocol to that Convention of 20 March 1952." The ECJ reiterated that fundamental rights formed an integral part of the general principles of law. It also developed its reference to the "common constitutional traditions" as a source of inspiration and concluded that the Court was thereby precluded from upholding measures which were incompatible with fundamental rights recognised and protected by the constitutions of the Member States. The ECJ was, however, prepared to go further and hold that:

"... international treaties for the protection of human rights on which the Member States have collaborated or of which they are signatories, can supply guidelines which should be followed within the framework of Community law."

The Court then examined the substance of the right to property and found that it was usually subject to limitations laid down in accordance with the public interest. It could not be extended to protect mere commercial interests from uncertainties that formed part of ordinary economic activity.

6.17 The ECJ expressly considered the actual content of the Convention for the first time in *Rutili*.[34] Mr Rutili was an Italian national who challenged a French decision to restrict his right of residence in France, ostensibly because of his political activity and involvement with trade unions. The ECJ was called upon, in a reference for a preliminary ruling, to consider the scope of the justification of measures restricting free movement of workers on the grounds of public policy. In doing so, the ECJ noted that limitations placed on Member States in respect of the control of aliens were:

"... a specific manifestation of the more general principle, enshrined in Articles 8, 9, 10 and 11 of the [Convention] ... that no restrictions in the interests of national security or public safety shall be placed on the rights secured by the above-quoted articles other than such as are necessary for the protection of those interests 'in a democratic society'."

---

[33] Case 4/73 *J. Nold v. Commission of the European Communities* [1974] E.C.R. 491, paras 12 and 13.
[34] Case 36/75 *Rutili v. Minister for the Interior* [1975] E.C.R. 1219, para. 32.

Fundamental rights as recognised in Community law were therefore seen   **6.18**
as equivalent or analogous to the "human rights" protection afforded both
under the domestic laws of the Member States and under international
treaties which Member States had ratified. As a result, the Court was,
before long, considering the practical application of "common constitutional precepts" derived from the Member States, side by side with the
rights derived from the Convention.[35] This was so even if the rights drawn
from the Member States were different in nature or extent to those protected by the Convention, for example the right to pursue trade or professional activities protected by the German Constitution.

Fundamental Rights Recognised by Community Law are not Co-extensive with Rights under the Convention

It was precisely because the ECJ refused simply to apply Convention   **6.19**
rights or principles in the context of Community law—because the two sets
of rights were not co-extensive—that there was scope for the fundamental
rights recognised by Community law to go beyond those "human rights"
afforded protection under the Convention. Indeed, the Community courts
were also able to take into account the terms of other multilateral conventions concluded by the Member States, such as the European Social
Charter of November 18, 1961; Convention No. 111 of the International
Labour Organisation of June 25, 1958 concerning discrimination in
respect of employment and occupation[36]; and the International Covenant
on Civil and Political Rights of December 19, 1966.[37]

This potential for a broader interpretation, and its application to Member   **6.20**
States, was first recognised in *Watson and Belmann*.[38] The ECJ was
asked on a preliminary reference from the Pretura di Milano whether the
prohibition of discrimination between nationals of Member States constituted a "fundamental principle which the Court will enforce?" The facts of
the case were that Miss Watson was staying for a while in Italy with Mr
Belmann, an Italian national. Miss Watson disappeared in mysterious
circumstances and Mr Belmann reported her missing to the local police.
The police discovered that she had not registered herself as a foreign
national upon arriving in Italy and ultimately commenced proceedings
against her for violation of the relevant domestic law. The Pretura di Milano
also raised questions relating to Article 8 of the Convention (the right to
privacy) and whether, in the event of conflict, fundamental principles of
Community law prevailed over national laws. The ECJ found that it was
able, on the facts, to give judgment on the issues raised without specifically answering the above questions. It nonetheless concluded that the

---

[35] See, *e.g.* the judgment of the ECJ in *Hauer* (n. 27, above), paras. 18, 22 and 32; Case
136/79 *National Panasonic v. Commission* [1980] E.C.R. 2033, para. 18; and Joined Cases
46/87 and 227/88 *Hoechst AG v. Commission* [1989] E.C.R. 2859, para. 13, where the ECJ
pointed out that the Convention was of "particular significance".
[36] Case 149/77 *Defrenne v. Sabena (III)* [1978] E.C.R. 1365, para. 28.
[37] *United Nations Treaty Series*, vol. 999, p. 171 cited with approval in Case 374/87 *Orkem
v. Commission* [1989] E.C.R. 3283, para. 18, ECJ. See also Case C–249/96 *Grant v. South
West Trains* [1998] E.C.R. I–621, para. 44.
[38] Case 118/75 *Lynne Watson and Alessandro Belmann* [1976] E.C.R. 1185 at 1187.

prohibition of all discrimination on the grounds of nationality was a common thread to the Treaty provisions on the free movement of workers, the right of establishment and the free provision of services.[39] The full Court did not address the question (raised by the United Kingdom Government in its observations) as to the extent to which Community law guaranteed fundamental rights not recognised by the Convention.[40] Nonetheless, the issue was dealt with by the Advocate General. He noted that:

" . . . without impinging upon the jurisdiction of other courts, this Court too, can look into an infringement of a fundamental right by a State body if not to the same extent to which it could do so in reviewing the validity of Community acts, at least to the extent to which the fundamental right alleged to have been infringed may involve the protection of an economic right which is among the specific objects of the Treaty."[41]

6.21   Other examples of the Court recognising non-Convention rights quickly arose. The ECJ thus came to recognise the principle of non-discrimination on grounds of sex as a "fundamental right". In *Defrenne*, the Court had no doubt that the elimination of discrimination based on sex formed part of the fundamental personal human rights recognised under Community law.[42] This perhaps represents a broader statement of principle than is to be found in Article 14 of the Convention. In *Pinna* the Court stated that the principle of equal treatment prohibited not only overt discrimination on grounds of nationality but also "all covert forms of discrimination which, by applying other distinguishing criteria, in fact achieve the same result."[43] This prohibition of discrimination has been said to be merely a specific enunciation of the general principle of equality, itself one of the fundamental principles of Community law.[44] The Court has also recognised that the fundamental right to pursue an economic activity (if appropriate through a company) is derived from the Treaty freedoms.[45]

6.22   As the Court increasingly came to apply human rights principles derived either from the Convention or from the common constitutional concepts of Member States, so cross-fertilisation of Convention principles became

---

[39] *ibid.*, para. 9 of the judgment. The establishment of non-discrimination as a fundamental principle of Community law was confirmed in Case 63/83 *Kirk* [1984] E.C.R. 2689, para. 14.

[40] Interestingly, the other arguments raised by the U.K. Government in its observations (summarised at 1190–1191 of the judgment) foreshadow many of the subsequent issues raised in the development of the fundamental rights doctrine in Community law. Examples include the jurisdictional interplay of the Convention and Community institutions and the scope of application of Community fundamental rights to domestic law.

[41] *Watson and Belmann* (n. 38, above), at 1207, *per* Advocate General Trabucchi. The Advocate General went on to note (at 1208) that the principle of proportionality, *e.g.* was a general principle applied to public authorities, Community or national, within the Community legal order.

[42] See (n. 36, above), paras 26 and 27.

[43] Case 41/84 *Pinna v. Caisse d'allocations familiales de la Savoie* [1986] E.C.R. 1, para. 23.

[44] Joined Cases 201 and 202/85 *Klensch v. Secrétaire d'État à l'Agriculture et à la Viticulture* [1986] E.C.R. 3477, para. 9.

[45] Case 246/89R *Commission v. United Kingdom* [1989] E.C.R. 3125, para. 30.

more apparent. In *Testa*,[46] for example, the Court recognised that the competent services and institutions of the Member State might "enjoy a wide discretion" in the national implementation of Community measures, subject to the obligation to take into account the general principle of proportionality. Indeed, it has been suggested that the "margin of appreciation" recognised by Strasbourg case law is analogous to the Community principle of proportionality.[47] Moreover, in assessing the proportionality of measures affecting fundamental rights, Community law will naturally take into account the case law of the European Court of Human Rights on the issue. [48]

The Developing Scope of Application of Fundamental Rights

One significant long-running issue has been the extent to which the fundamental rights recognised by Community law would take effect not only as against acts of the Community institutions, but also at a domestic level. A variation on this theme is the extent to which those principles should take precedence (in accordance with the doctrine of supremacy of Community law) over domestic measures that were incompatible with them. The possibility of the application of Community fundamental rights to Member State's measures became apparent with the Opinion of Advocate General Trabucchi in *Watson and Belmann*.[49] He noted that "fundamental principles governing the protection of the rights of man . . . may, within the sphere of application of Community law, also be of importance in determining the legality of a State's conduct in relation to a freedom which the Treaty accords to individuals." **6.23**

A somewhat different position was taken in *Cinéthèque*.[50] There, the ECJ held that it had no power to examine the compatibility with the Convention of "national legislation which concerns, as in this case, an area which falls within the jurisdiction of the national legislator." This was the case even though (at paragraph 24 of its judgment) the Court had indicated that legislation protecting the French cinematographic industry fell outside the scope of Article 30 of the Treaty (now Article 28 EC) only if it satisfied the test of proportionality. A nuanced approach was adopted in *Demirel*.[51] The Court accepted that it had no power to examine the compatibility with the Convention of national legislation lying outside the scope of Community law. What then defined the scope of Community law? The ECJ considered that if national rules were not passed to implement a provision of Community law, it had no jurisdiction to assess whether they infringed fundamental rights. The application of the human rights jurisprudence up until this point had been largely limited in the scope of its application to purely **6.24**

---

[46] Joined Cases 41, 121 and 796/79 *Testa, Maggio and Vitale v. Bundesanstalt für Arbeit* [1980] E.C.R. 1979, para. 21.
[47] Case C–159/90 *Society for the Protection of Unborn Children Ireland Ltd v. Grogan* [1991] E.C.R. I–4685 at 4726, *per* Advocate General Van Gerven. See also *Hauer* (n. 27, above), para. 22; and the express reference to "margin of appreciation" at para. 22 of the ECJ's judgment in Case 5/88 *Wachauf v. Germany* [1989] E.C.R. 2609.
[48] See at 4726 of the Advocate General's Opinion in *Grogan*, above.
[49] See (n. 38, above) at 1207.
[50] Joined Cases 60/84 and 61/84 *Cinéthèque v. Fédération nationale des cinemas français* [1985] E.C.R. 2065, para. 26.
[51] Case 12/86 *Demirel v. Stadt Schwäbisch Gmünd* [1987] E.C.R. 3719, para. 28.

Community measures.[52] A former Judge of the ECJ, G.F. Mancini, felt able to say in 1989 that "the Court's efforts to safeguard the fundamental rights of the Community citizens stopped at the threshold of the national legislations."[53]

6.25 In the latter stages of 1989, however, there was yet a further shift in the approach of the Court to the exercise of its human rights jurisdiction in various respects. First, the Court expressly noted that the content of Community fundamental rights need not coincide with the protection offered by Strasbourg. As a by-product of this, the Court started considering the fundamental rights it recognised in a Community context and in relation to their "social function".[54] Human rights under Community law were steeped in Community considerations, which would not necessarily tally with the emphasis placed on competing rights by Strasbourg. *Hoechst*[55] saw the Court, for the first time, indicate that rights recognised under the Convention might well "be concerned with the development of man's personal freedom" and not necessarily extend to a business (or Community) context, especially in the absence of case law from Strasbourg on the issue. This approach represented a retrenchment on the Court's previously more expansive statements on the recognition given to the inviolability of business premises.[56] While the method adopted still concentrated on an examination both of the constitutional protections offered by the Member States and of the terms of the Convention, it is submitted that the Court tempered its desire to give protection to fundamental rights with a consideration of the practicalities of the situation.[57]

6.26 In *Orkem*,[58] the ECJ also had in mind the need to preserve the "useful effect" of the provisions in Regulation 17, by which the Commission enforced the competition provisions, in particular, those provisions that required an undertaking to provide information and disclose documents even if they might be used to establish anti-competitive conduct. The Court considered Article 6 of the Convention did not establish (in this context) a privilege against self-incrimination. It considered that proceedings in such an "economic sphere" could not be equated with criminal

---

[52] Examples of domestic implementation of Community law being assessed for compatibility with Community fundamental rights can be seen earlier than 1989 in Case 222/84 *Johnston v. RUC* [1986] E.C.R. 1651; Joined Cases 201 and 202/85 *Klensch* (n. 44, above); Case 222/86 *UNECTEF v. Heylens* [1987] E.C.R. 4097, para. 14; and arguably in *Kirk* (n. 39, above). In the latter case, another view might be that the Community Regulation was directly applicable and simply took immediate effect through the expiry of the transitional period in question. Up until that point, the U.K. legislation did not contravene E.C. law only because it took effect through a derogation valid for the transitional period.

[53] Mancini (n. 7, above), p. 611.

[54] See *Wachauf v. Germany* (n. 47, above), para. 18.

[55] Joined Cases 46/87 and 227/88 *Hoechst AG v. Commission* [1989] E.C.R. 2859, para. 18. The case concerned a German company that, in the words of Advocate General Mischo at 2876, "categorically refused to submit to the investigation" by the Commission. See also Case 85/87 *Dow Benelux NV v. Commission* [1989] E.C.R. 3137, paras 28–30.

[56] For a description of this case law, see para. 6.128, below.

[57] The Advocate General was anxious not to limit unduly the powers of the Commission to investigate businesses and seek blatant evidence of anti-competitive activity—"the smoking gun". He acknowledged (at 2884) that the measures to be adopted had to permit Commission officials to gain access to crucial documents before the undertaking could "have time to cause them to disappear". If the Commission's actions were excessive, an application could be made to the Court, the investigation declared void and thereafter any documents obtained excluded from consideration.

[58] Case 374/87 *Orkem v. Commission* [1989] E.C.R. 3283.

proceedings for the purposes of the presumption of innocence found in Article 6(2) of the Convention.[59] Advocate General Darmon went further. In his view, the Court was able to adopt an interpretation of the Convention which "does not coincide exactly with that given by the Strasbourg authorities, in particular the European Court of Human Rights."[60] The Court was not obliged systematically to take into account the interpretation of the Convention given by Strasbourg, when analysing its fundamental rights jurisprudence. Moreover, where, as in that case, the Strasbourg Court had not given an authorised interpretation of the Convention, there was no obligation to read into Community fundamental rights a privilege against self-incrimination in competition law matters that might be raised under Article 6(2) of the Convention.

Further, fundamental rights recognised by the Court are not absolute.   **6.27**
They do not amount to "unfettered prerogatives".[61] In keeping an eye on the practicalities of the situation, the ECJ has noted that[62]:

> " . . . restrictions may be imposed on the exercise of those rights, and in particular in the context of a common organisation of a market, provided that those restrictions in fact correspond to objectives of general interest pursued by the Community and do not constitute, with regard to the aim pursued, a disproportionate and intolerable interference, impairing the very substance of those rights."

It follows that the fundamental rights recognised by the Community will be tailored to fit any specific Community situation. Fundamental rights will not necessarily be given the same range or priority as the Strasbourg Court has set.[63]

Secondly, it is arguable that as from 1989 the ECJ extended the scope of   **6.28**
application of its fundamental rights jurisprudence.[64] In *Wauchauf*[65] the claimant was a tenant dairy farmer. He leased the land upon which he farmed, but brought to it all other features of his dairy production. Upon the expiry of his tenancy he sought compensation for "definitive discontinuance of milk production" pursuant to a German law. That legislation was based on a power contained in a Community Regulation governing the common organisation of the market in milk. The national court was concerned that, on a proper construction of the Community rules, the tenant farmer would be deprived of compensation for giving up his reference quantity of milk quota and the lessor (previously unconnected with milk production) would benefit from it. The tenant would thereby be deprived of the fruits of his labour without compensation, which might well offend

---

[59] *ibid.*, at paras 28–31. The ECJ nonetheless found that the requirement to answer certain questions infringed the fundamental principle of "the rights of the defence" and partially annulled the contested Commission decisions on that basis.
[60] *ibid.*, paras 140–141, *per* Advocate General Damon.
[61] Case 265/87 *Hermann Schräder HS Kraftfutter GmbH v. Hauptzollamt Gronau* [1989] E.C.R. 2237, para. 15; and Case C–62/90 *Commission v. Germany* [1992] E.C.R. I–2575, para. 23.
[62] See *Wachauf v. Germany* (n. 47, above), para. 18.
[63] See also Case C–62/90 *Commission v. Germany* (n. 61, above).
[64] Another view would be that the Court was recognising explicitly what should have been implicit since the Advocate General's Opinion in *Watson and Belmann*.
[65] Case 5/88 *Wachauf v. Germany* [1989] E.C.R. 2609.

German constitutional rights. On a preliminary reference from the domestic court, the ECJ held[66] that the fundamental rights, which had to be respected by Community measures, were also binding on the Member States when they implemented Community rules. It followed that Member States must, as far as possible, apply Community rules in accordance with those requirements. Thus, on the facts of the case, the Community measures in question left the competent national authorities a sufficiently wide margin of appreciation to enable them to apply the milk quota rules in a manner consistent with fundamental rights protected by Community law. That entailed either giving the tenant the opportunity to keep all or part of the reference quantity, or giving him compensation.[67]

6.29   Thereafter in *ERT*,[68] the Court reiterated that it did not have the power to examine (for compatibility with the Convention) national rules that did not fall within the scope of Community law. Nonetheless, where such rules did fall within the scope of Community law, the Court was obliged, on a reference for a preliminary ruling, to "provide all the criteria of interpretation needed by the national courts to determine whether those rules [were] compatible with the fundamental rights" recognised in Community law. More significantly, the Court held that the justification of any restriction on the freedom to provide services had to be interpreted in the light of general principles of law. Member States could rely on the derogations provided by Articles 56 and 66 of the E.C. Treaty (now, after amendment, Articles 46 and 55 EC) only if their national rules were compatible with the fundamental rights developed by the ECJ. It was for the national court to assess whether or not its national rules complied with the rules of Community law, "including freedom of expression, as embodied in Article 10 of the [Convention]."[69] It was implicit in the judgment, therefore, that in derogating from the Treaty freedoms, Member States would still be treated as acting within the scope of Community law.[70]

6.30   This principle was applied by the ECJ in a direct action brought by the Commission against the Netherlands in relation to a Dutch law relating to television and media.[71] The Netherlands argued that certain restrictions placed on television and radio programmes were justified in the public interest of preserving a pluralist and non-commercial audio-visual system. The ECJ examined this cultural policy justification by taking into account, *inter alia*, the freedom of expression recognised by Article 10 of the Convention.

6.31   A more controversial consideration of the same principles was found in *Grogan*.[72] Various members of students associations in Ireland distributed

---

[66] *ibid.*, paras 17–19.
[67] *ibid.*, para. 22.
[68] Case C–260/89 *Elliniki Radiophonia Tileorassi AE v. Dimotiki Etairia Pliroforissis and Sotirios Kouvelas* [1991] E.C.R. I–2925, paras 42 and 43.
[69] *ibid.*, para. 45.
[70] The judgment, to this extent, ran contrary to the finding of the Court in *Cinéthèque* which related to "rule of reason" exceptions based on "mandatory" or "imperative requirements" (not Treaty derogations) to fundamental Treaty provisions. This conflict was implicitly recognised by Advocate General Van Gerven in *Grogan* (n. 47, above), at 4723.
[71] Case C–353/89 *Commission v. Netherlands* [1991] E.C.R. I–4069, para. 30.
[72] Case C–159/90 *Society for the Protection of Unborn Children Ireland Ltd v. Grogan* [1991] E.C.R. I–4685. For commentary see D.R. Phelan, "Right to life of the Unborn v. Promotion of Trade in Services: the European Court of Justice and the Normative Shaping of the European Union" (1992) 55 M.L.R. 670.

information relating to the availability of abortions in the United Kingdom. The Society for the Protection of Unborn Children ('SPUC') requested the officers of the respective associations to undertake not to publish the information, on the basis that it contravened aspects of the Irish prohibition on abortion. When such an undertaking was not given, SPUC brought proceedings seeking a declaration that the students' conduct was unlawful under Irish law and injunctive relief. The ECJ held that the distribution of leaflets by the students was not done on behalf of economic operators (clinics) in the United Kingdom, but was rather a manifestation of freedom of expression.[73] As such, there was no question of the students exercising any Community freedom to provide services. As the national legislation accordingly fell outside the "field of application" of Community law the Court had no jurisdiction to examine its compatibility with the fundamental rights doctrine.[74]

The judgment was considered to be controversial because of the logical **6.32** consequences that stemmed from the finding. Had the leaflets been distributed by abortion clinics in the United Kingdom, it seems implicit in the Court's judgment that it would have assessed the Irish prohibition (on assisting abortion) for compatibility with the fundamental principles recognised by the Court. This would have entailed an assessment of the extent to which the right to free expression (as enshrined in Article 10 of the Convention) and perhaps of the right to life of the mother (as embodied in Article 2 of the Convention) was outweighed by the right to life of the foetus.[75] The assessment would have been made by the ECJ under Community law. It was seen, in some quarters, as a clear incursion by the Community into areas normally reserved to national legislatures.[76]

Nonetheless, such a possibility follows naturally from the twin concepts of **6.33** the supremacy and direct effect of Community law. Once the ECJ had developed a doctrine of respect for fundamental rights, it followed that Community law would be assessed for compatibility with those rights. As Community law may be applied at a domestic level, fundamental rights would also have to be considered (to like extent) at a domestic level. Community law consists not only of positive obligations derived from the treaties and subsidiary Community legislation, but also a requirement not to derogate from those provisions except as permitted by Community

---

[73] *ibid.*, para. 26.

[74] *ibid.*, para. 31.

[75] Advocate General Van Gerven considered that the prohibition of distribution of leaflets did fall within the scope of Art. 59 of the Treaty (now Art. 49 EC). Consequently, he went on to carry out exactly this sort of assessment. He nonetheless acknowledged that it was a very delicate matter involving an assessment of two fundamental rights as sensitive as freedom of expression and the right to life. It followed that in the absence of a uniform European conception of morals, a wide margin of discretion would be afforded to Member States. See at 4723 to 4729 of his Opinion.

[76] Others saw it as leading to enforcement of the Convention "by the back door". See Coppel and O'Neill, *op. cit.* (n. 26, above), p. 691; and Lord Browne-Wilkinson "The Infiltration of a Bill of Rights" [1992] P.L. 397 at 401. Coppel and O'Neill considered that "it would be increasingly difficult for national courts to resist the application, within domestic law, of the whole range of . . . human rights developed and applied by the ECJ." Indeed, the Irish Government, following the decision, attached a Protocol to the Treaty on European Union which stated that nothing in the Treaties shall affect the application in Ireland of the relevant provisions of its Constitution. An addendum subsequently added that the Protocol would not limit the freedom of travel between Member States or the freedom to provide information on services lawfully available in other Member States.

law.[77] Any derogations must therefore be assessed for compatibility with general principles of law recognised by the ECJ, be they the principles of proportionality, equality or respect for human rights.[78] Otherwise a derogation might be invalidly operated by a Member State to the detriment of the uniformity and supremacy of Community law. National legislation must be so scrutinised because it is impossible to disassociate the exercise of a derogation from the positive principle from which an exception is being claimed.[79]

6.34   An even wider scope of review has been claimed by some of the Advocates General, but not endorsed by the full Court. On one reading, Advocate General Van Gerven in *Grogan* suggested that the Community doctrine of fundamental rights might be applied to any national rule which no longer falls within the exclusive jurisdiction of the national legislature.[80]

6.35   Moreover, in *Konstantinidis*[81] Advocate General Jacobs set out the principles established thus far and asked whether, if a Member State's treatment of a national of another Member State was not discriminatory (and so fall to be justified by way of derogation) it would not infringe Article 52 of the Treaty (now Article 43 EC) even if it infringed his fundamental rights? The Advocate General concluded that whenever a Community worker exercised his free movement rights, he would also be entitled to assume that he would be treated in accordance with a common code of fundamental values, in particular those laid down in the Convention. In other words, "he is entitled to say '*civis europeus sum*' and to invoke that status in order to oppose any violation of fundamental rights."[82] The Advocate General dismissed as "untenable" the suggestion that a Member State should be able to violate the fundamental rights of nationals of other Member States, provided it treats its own nationals in the same way.

6.36   As will be seen in more detail below, the Community Courts have refrained from endorsing the development suggested by Advocate General Jacobs in *Konstantinidis*. Another Advocate General has described such a development as "too far-reaching".[83] Indeed, the Opinion of Advocate General

---

[77] See Case C–62/90 *Commission v. Germany* (n. 61, above), para. 23, where the ECJ held that as the justification permitting derogation was itself provided by Community law, it had to be interpreted in the light of the general principles of law and in particular fundamental rights.

[78] As happened in Case C–353/89 *Commission v. Netherlands* (n. 71, above), paras 15–19.

[79] Case C–2/92 *Bostock* [1994] E.C.R. I–955 at 971, *per* Advocate General Gulmann.

[80] See the Advocate General's Opinion in *Grogan* (n. 72, above), at 4723. Coppel and O'Neill (n. 26, above), p. 681 comment that: "the only Member State actions which the Court might decline to vet on human rights grounds are, therefore, those which occur in an area of exclusive Member State jurisdiction." In fact, the Advocate General was dealing with the issue of assessing the compatibility of derogations from the fundamental provisions of the Treaty. There will be areas of shared competence (or jurisdiction) where national rules do not implement directly effective Community law or where no derogation from directly effective Community law is sought where no "Community" human rights review will necessarily be available.

[81] Case C–168/91 *Konstantinidis v. Stadt Altensteig* [1993] E.C.R. I–1191.

[82] *ibid.*, at 1212. See now Art. 17 E.C. by which every national of a Member State is also a citizen of the European Union. The Treaty of Amsterdam amended the former Art. 8 (introduced by the TEU) to make clear that citizenship of the Union shall complement and not replace national citizenship.

[83] Case C–2/92 *R. v. Ministry of Agriculture, Fisheries and Food, ex p. Dennis Clifford Bostock* [1994] E.C.R. I–955, *per* Advocate General Gulmann.

Jacobs probably represents the high-water mark of the recognition of fundamental rights in Community law. Thereafter, most notably in *Bostock*, the ECJ has refrained from extending any further the scope of application of Community fundamental rights. In *Bostock*, the applicant was a dairy farmer who brought an action against the United Kingdom Government for their failure to provide for compensation to be paid to him upon the surrender of his milk quota.[84] Community Regulations in force at that time left to the Member States the issue of whether, and to what extent, protection should be given to the economic interests of a tenant surrendering his milk quota. The United Kingdom's domestic legislation at the material time made no provision for a landlord to pay his tenant compensation for the transfer to him of his "Reference quantity" upon surrender of the tenancy. Mr Bostock argued that the general principles of law (including respect for property, unjust enrichment and non-discrimination) should have been given effect within the domestic legislation, because the quota system as a whole was derived from Community law. National schemes for compensation (although not implementing a Community scheme for compensation) should therefore follow the same principles. In the words of Advocate General Gulmann, the question was whether: "a positive duty may be derived from the Community law principles on the protection of fundamental rights for Member States to protect the economic interests of tenants when a tenancy comes to an end."[85]

6.37 The ECJ found that Community law (including the general principles of Community law) did not require a Member State to introduce a scheme for compensation for an outgoing lessee by the lessor or confer directly on the lessee a right to like effect. In reaching its decision, the Court sought to distinguish *Wachauf* on the basis that the *Wachauf* case involved a question from the national court as to whether the Community Regulation precluded the application of fundamental principles of law. The ECJ held that it did not. But this did not mean, on the contrary, that a positive obligation could be derived from general principles of law. Grounds of distinction between the *Wachauf* case and *Bostock* may appear to be thin.[86] It seems that the only clear difference is that German law provided for compensation for Herr Wachauf whereas English law provided no obligation to compensate Mr Bostock.[87]

6.38 One way of reconciling the decisions would be to recognise that the duty to comply with the general principles (as set out in *Wauchauf*) arose when Member States implement rules on the basis of express enabling provisions in Community law. If that enabling provision is not used, no duty to compensate could be extracted from the general principles alone. But interestingly, the Court did not adopt such a route. The most that can be said is that the ECJ did not state that fundamental principles fell to be

---

[84] In fact, not at the time of actual surrender, but only after learning of the ECJ's judgment in *Wachauf*.

[85] See (n. 83, above), at 964, para. 16, of the Opinion.

[86] Grounds are nonetheless set out in the Advocate General's Opinion in *Bostock* at 966.

[87] This difference was almost certainly crucial. There was no general duty incumbent on Member States under the Community legislation at the time to provide compensation in the circumstances before the Court. The legislation gave Member States a discretion whether to do so. One (perhaps unattractive) way of reconciling the two decisions would be to find that if the discretion was exercised, then the principles of compensation would fall within the scope of Community law. If it was not exercised, they would not.

applied as a result of the dispute arising simply in a Community "context": that is, from rules governing the common organisation of a market. In refraining from doing so, the extension of the field of application of Community fundamental rights came to an uncertain stop. As will be seen below, the present scope of the field of application of fundamental rights remains unclear. It is therefore very much a live issue before the national courts of England and Wales.[88]

Institutional Support for the Development of the Fundamental Rights Doctrine

6.39   While it is correct that the development of the protection of fundamental rights under Community law has been driven by the case law of the Community courts, it would be misleading to view this development solely as an example of the Community courts engaged in a frolic of their own.[89] In seeking to protect fundamental rights under Community law, the courts have derived assistance from the ambiguous text of certain provisions of the Treaty of Rome. For example, Article 230 EC (ex Article 173 of the E.C. Treaty) provides for judicial review of Community acts by the ECJ. Under Article 230(2) EC, grounds of review include: "lack of competence, infringement of an essential procedural requirement, infringement of this Treaty or of any rule of law relating to its application, or misuse of powers." The four grounds for annulment,[90] drawn from French constitutional law, are necessarily silent as to what the given procedural requirements might be in any given case; and as to what "law" might be applied. This plea of infringement of the "Treaty or of any rule of law relating to its application" is accordingly open-ended in scope.[91] In a similar vein, Article 215 of the E.C. Treaty (now Article 288 EC) permits non-contractual liability of the Community to be determined in accordance with "the general principles common to the laws of the Member States". Finally, Article 164 of the E.C. Treaty (now Article 220 EC) mandates the ECJ to ensure that "the law" is observed.[92]

6.40   Further, the courts have also received timely fillips from the political arena.[93] Not long after the judgment in *Nold* was handed down, the nascent fundamental rights jurisprudence was recognised (and thereby

---

[88] See paras 6.195 *et seq.*, below.

[89] See, *e.g.* the commentary on this issue given by Professor Cappelletti in *The Judicial Process in Comparative Perspective* (Oxford Clarendon, 1989), p. 149. He referred, at the end of the 1980s, to "thirteen little men unknown to most of the 320 million Community citizens, devoid of political power, charisma and popular legitimation" doing "what the framers did not even think of doing, and what the political branches of the Community do not try and undertake".

[90] All measures taken by the Community institutions that are designed to have legal effect are subject to the same power of review: Case 22/70 *Commission v. Council (Re European Road Transport Agreement)* [1971] E.C.R. 263, para. 39.

[91] The applicant relied upon this plea expressly in Case 4/73 *Nold* (n. 33, above), para. 6.

[92] This was relied upon by Advocate General Gulmann in *Bostock* (n. 83, above), at 971 to support the contention that the ECJ must ensure that fundamental rights are respected by Community institutions.

[93] See Grainne de Bùrca "The Language of Rights in European Integration" in J. Shaw and G. More (eds) *New Legal Dynamics of European Union* (OUP, 1995) p. 29. De Bùrca considers that the institutional endorsement of the Court's case law arose from a recognition that the general principles could assist integration and promote the democratic legitimacy of the Community.

tacitly approved) by the Joint Declaration of the European Parliament, the Council and the Commission of April 5, 1977.[94] The Joint Declaration referred both to the rights guaranteed by the constitutions of the Member States and to the Convention. It stated that the European Parliament, the Council and the Commission attached "prime importance" to the protection of fundamental rights. The institutions declared that in the exercise of their powers and in pursuing the aims of the Treaty, they would "respect and continue to respect these rights". Other non-binding declarations of support for fundamental rights have followed with time. These include the European Council's Declaration on Democracy in 1978[95] and the European Parliament's Declaration of Fundamental Rights and Freedoms.[96] The fundamental rights doctrine was also recognised in the preamble to   **6.41** the Single European Act 1986 (the "SEA"). The preamble to the SEA[97] noted the determination of the Member States to:

> "work together to promote democracy on the basis of the fundamental rights recognised in the constitutions and laws of the Member States, in the Convention for the Protection of Human Rights and Fundamental Freedoms and the European Social Charter, notably freedom, equality and social justice."

In the Treaty on European Union, which entered into force on November 1, 1993,[98] the Member States reaffirmed their commitment to the democratic protection of human rights. Article F of the Treaty provided as follows:

> "1. The Union shall respect the national identities of its Member States, whose systems of government are founded on the principles of democracy.
> 2. The Union shall respect fundamental rights, as guaranteed by the European Convention for the protection of Human Rights and Fundamental Freedoms signed in Rome on 4 November 1950 and as they result from the constitutional traditions common to the Member States, as general principles of Community law.
> 3. The Union shall provide itself with the means necessary to attain its objective and carry through its policies."

In addition, Article J.1(2) stated that one of the objectives of the common   **6.42** foreign and security policy of the Union would be "to develop and consolidate democracy and the rule of law, and respect for human rights and fundamental freedoms." Article K.2(1) required the Member States to have

---

[94] [1977] O.J. C103/1.
[95] E.C. Bulletin, 3–1978, p. 5.
[96] [1989] O.J. C120/51.
[97] At Recital 3 (Cmnd. 9758).
[98] [1992] O.J. C191.

regard to the Convention when pursuing policies in their common interest in the field of justice and home affairs. Nonetheless, the principles were not inserted into the E.C. Treaty itself. Consequently, by virtue of Article L of the Treaty on European Union, the ECJ was not empowered to adjudicate on matters falling within Article F(2) which were not otherwise justiciable under the E.C. Treaty. It has been suggested that the Member States thereby sought to avoid the incorporation of the Convention (in relation to matters falling within the scope of the E.C. Treaty) by the back door.[99]

6.43 The Treaty of Amsterdam made certain amendments to the provisions found in the Treaty on European Union. Article 6 EU reiterated the contents of Article F(2) of the Treaty on European Union and modified Article F(1) so that it now provides that:

> "1. The Union is founded on the principles of liberty, democracy, respect for human rights and fundamental freedoms, and the rule of law, principles which are common to the Member States."

6.44 The Treaty of Amsterdam also granted the Community power to take action against any Member State that fails to comply with the principles set out in Article 6(1) EU. Article 7 EU enables the Council acting on a unanimous vote of all other Member States to make a finding that there has been a "serious and persistent breach" of those principles. After such a finding has been made, the Council acting by a qualified majority may decide to suspend certain rights for the infringing Member State. Contrary, perhaps, to expectations, these provisions have not proved to be a dead letter. In February 2000, they were used by the Community to impose sanctions on Austria following the election to (shared) power of the far right Freedom Party. In September 2000, a panel of "wise men" (appointed to examine Austria's observation of the fundamental principles of human rights and "common European values") filed a report, which cleared the coalition government of any unacceptable conduct.[1] Sanctions were thereafter withdrawn.[2]

6.45 The Treaty of Amsterdam has also made it a condition precedent to the enlargement of the Community that acceding states comply with Article 6(1) EU. Article 49 EU now provides that only states that respect these principles may apply to become a Member State of the Community. The ECJ has been granted competence to consider and exercise its powers over matters falling within Article 6(2) EU by Article 46 EU. However, this competence is expressed to be limited to: "the acts of the institutions, insofar as the Court has jurisdiction under the Treaties establishing the European Communities and under this Treaty." It might therefore be

---

[99] Jacobs and White, *The European Convention on Human Rights* (2nd ed., Clarendon, Oxford, 1996) p. 412. See also L. Krogsgaard, "Fundamental Rights in the EC after Maastricht" [1993] L.I.E.I. 99.

[1] *The Times*, September 9, 2000 "EU ready to bring Austria in from cold".

[2] *The Times*, September 13, 2000 "Austria is brought back into EU fold". Also reported in the *Financial Times*, September 13, 2000 and *The Independent*, September 13, 2000. At the time of writing, the threat of sanctions is being raised against Italy for its election of a far-right political party. See *The Sunday Times*, March 11, 2001.

wondered whether this could be interpreted as no more than a re-statement of the pre-existing position. Article 13 EC now empowers the Council, acting unanimously on a proposal from the Commission and after consulting the European Parliament, to "take appropriate action to combat discrimination based on sex, racial or ethnic origin, religion or belief, disability, age or sexual orientation."

These Treaty amendments re-affirm the commitment of the Member   **6.46** States to the continuing Community recognition of fundamental rights. It also provides a degree of democratic ratification for the ECJ's perceived activism. Professor Tridimas has pointed out that: "despite what ephemeral political rhetoric may suggest, where the Member States acting in a sovereign capacity decide to amend the founding Treaties, they look on the Court as a source of inspiration rather than an aberrant institution whose powers should be curtailed."[3]

The Question of Accession by the Community to the European Convention on Human Rights

Although each of the Member States (which have, at present, acceded to   **6.47** the European Communities and to the E.U. Treaty) is also individually a signatory to the European Convention on Human Rights, the Community collectively is not a signatory. References to the Convention in the early case law of the ECJ meant that it was not long before the question of accession by the Community was raised. The possibility was first considered in 1976 in a report of the European Commission of February 4, 1976 submitted to the European Parliament and the Council of Ministers.[4] The report concluded that accession was unnecessary because the rights enshrined in the Convention were already binding in Community law and that no additional constitutive act was necessary to achieve this. The Commission referred to the judgment of the Court of Justice in *Nold*. It did not, however, adhere faithfully to the text of the judgment, which simply acknowledges that international treaties such as the Convention "can supply guidelines". It nonetheless concluded that the protection of human rights could be strengthened through a declaration of respect for human rights on the part of the Community institutions. In 1977, as stated above, the European Commission, the Council and the European Parliament published a non-binding joint declaration.[5] In 1979, following requests by the European Parliament to the Commission for a follow-up report, the European Commission published a memorandum in which it favoured accession by the European Community to the Convention.[6]

It was, however, the Member States (through the Council) who requested   **6.48** the ECJ to consider whether the Community had competence to accede to the European Convention on Human Rights. In April 1994, pursuant to

[3] See *Tridimas* (n. 4, above), p. 5.
[4] Report of the European Commission of February 4, 1976, E.C. Bulletin, Supp. 5/76.
[5] [1977] O.J. C103/1.
[6] *Accession of the Communities to the European Convention for the Protection of Human Rights and Fundamental Freedoms,* April 4, 1979, E.C. Bulletin, Supp. 2/79.

Article 300(6) EC (ex Article 228(6) of the E.C. Treaty), the Council asked the ECJ for an Opinion on the following question: "Would the accession of the European Community to the Convention on Human Rights and Fundamental Freedoms of 4 November 1950 be compatible with the Treaty establishing the European Community?"[7] The request raised two legal issues:

(1) The legal basis of accession.

(2) The compatibility of accession with the E.C. Treaty.

6.49   A report of the observations of the Member States and the institutions, and the judgment of the ECJ is found in *Opinion 2/94*.[8] In their written observations and at the oral hearing, the parties were divided. The Community institutions and the governments of Austria, Belgium, Denmark, Finland, Germany, Greece, Italy and Sweden considered that, in the absence of specific enabling provisions, Article 308 EC (ex Article 235 of the E.C. Treaty) could serve as the legal basis for accession, and that accession, in particular, submission of the Community to the legal system of the Convention, would not be contrary to Article 220 EC (ex Article 164 of the E.C. Treaty) and Article 292 EC (ex Article 219 of the E.C. Treaty). In contrast, the French, Spanish and Portuguese governments, Ireland and the United Kingdom argued against any application of Article 308 EC. They denied that accession would be compatible with the Treaty.

6.50   In its Opinion, the ECJ ruled that no Treaty provision conferred on the Community institutions any general power to enact rules on human rights or to conclude international conventions in this field.[9] It continued:

"Respect for human rights is therefore a condition of the lawfulness of Community acts. Accession to the Convention would, however, entail a substantial change in the present Community system for the protection of human rights in that it would entail the entry of the Community into a distinct international institutional system as well as integration of all the provisions of the Convention into the Community legal order."[10]

6.51   Such a modification of the system for the protection of human rights in the Community, with equally fundamental institutional implications for the Community and for the Member States, would be of constitutional significance and would therefore be such as to go beyond the scope of Article 235. It could be bought about only by way of Treaty amendment.[11] The

---

[7] [1994] O.J. C174/8. The purpose of Art. 300(6) is to forestall complications which would result from legal disputes concerning the compatibility with the Treaty of international agreements binding on the Community.
[8] *Opinion 2/94 of the Court* [1996] E.C.R. I–1759.
[9] *ibid.*, para. 27.
[10] *ibid.*, para. 34.
[11] *ibid.*, para. 35.

ECJ therefore concluded that: "as Community law now stands, the Community has no competence to accede to the Convention."

The debate over such competence has not gone away. Attempts have **6.52** since continued on a political level to incorporate within Community law a "Charter of Fundamental Rights and Freedoms". The recent developments involving the Charter are set out in Section 4, below. Furthermore, some authors have argued that there is yet scope for saying that the Convention should be given direct effect in Community law, possibly to the point of actually trumping conflicting principles of Community law.[12] This argument is based on Article 307 EC (ex Article 234 of the E.C. Treaty). This Article provides that "the rights and obligations arising from agreements concluded before the entry into force of this Treaty between one or more Member States on the one hand, and one or more third countries on the other, shall not be affected by the provisions of this Treaty."

The ECJ held very early on that the purpose of Article 307(1) EC was to **6.53** make clear, in accordance with the principles of international law, that the application of the Treaty did not affect the commitment of Member States to respect the rights of non-member countries under earlier agreements. Member States had to comply with their earlier obligations.[13] Consequently, in order to determine whether a Community rule may be deprived of effect by an earlier international agreement, it is necessary to examine whether that agreement imposes, on the Member States concerned, obligations whose performance may still be required by third countries which are party to it.[14] To override a Community provision on this basis, two conditions must be fulfilled: (1) the agreement must have been concluded before the entry into force of the Treaty; and (2) the third country concerned must derive from it rights which it can require the Member States concerned to respect.[15]

The Convention was adopted on November 4, 1950 and entered into force **6.54** on September 3, 1953. The European Coal and Steel Community was established on April 18, 1951, at a time when the Convention existed but was not yet in force. The other Communities were established after the Convention had entered into force. An argument could be made for saying that once Member States had committed themselves *vis-à-vis* third countries, such as Norway and Iceland, to guarantee the respect for human rights in their respective territories, the Member States could not transfer to the Communities the possibility of infringing those rights.[16] The consequences would be that the Communities were bound by the Convention because the Member States were bound when they created the Communities.

---

[12] Richard Gordon Q.C. and Tim Ward *Judicial Review and the Human Rights Act* (Cavendish, 2000), p. 224.

[13] Case 10/61 *Commission v. Italy* [1962] E.C.R. 1.

[14] Case C–324/93 *R. v. Secretary of State for the Home Department, ex p. Evans Medical Ltd* [1995] E.C.R. I–563, para. 27; Case C–124/95 *R. v. H.M. Treasury and Bank of England, ex p. Centro-Com* [1997] E.C.R. I–81, paras. 56 and 57; Joined Cases C–364 and 365/95 *T. Port v. Hauptzollamt Hamburg-Jonas* [1998] E.C.R. I–1023, para. 60.

[15] Joined Cases C–364 and 365/95 *T. Port, ibid.*, para. 61.

[16] A point raised by Professor H.G. Schermers in his case note on the *Matthews* decision of the European Court of Human Rights in (1999) 36 C.M.L. Rev. 673–681 at 673. Professor Schermers did not discuss the issue in the context of Article 307 E.C.

6.55 There are certain potential difficulties with this argument. First, the Member States would seemingly only be bound *vis-à-vis* third states. It might be questioned whether, even after the incorporation of the Convention in the United Kingdom, any rights of redress were thereby conferred on individual British citizens. Further, Article 307 EC operates as an exemption from the requirement to comply with Community law. In *Levy*,[17] the director of a charcuterie factory was prosecuted for breaking a French law which prohibited the employment of women for night work. The French law was adopted in pursuance of an International Labour Organisation Convention which provided that women should not be employed to work at night in an industrial undertaking. The defendant argued that the French law was contrary to Community provisions on equal treatment of men and women. On a preliminary ruling, the ECJ held that national judges should apply E.C. law on equal treatment between men and women by disapplying conflicting national provisions, except in so far as the application of contrary national provisions was necessary to meet obligations under agreements with third countries that predated the EEC Treaty and were still in force. Where such agreements were incompatible with the EEC Treaty, Member States had to take appropriate steps to eliminate such incompatibilities.

6.56 This latter obligation was based on the terms of Article 307(2) EC, which provides that to the extent that such pre-existing agreements are not compatible with the E.C. Treaty, the Member States concerned "shall take all appropriate steps to eliminate the incompatibilities established". Member States are to assist one another to this end and to adopt a common attitude. The Court in *Levy* also held[18] that the key issue was whether the international agreement imposed on the Member State concerned obligations whose performance may still be required by non-member countries which are parties to it. It was left to the national court to make this assessment.

6.57 It might therefore be open to individuals to argue that domestic legislation should comply with the Convention in preference to Community law in cases where the rights of non-Member States, which are party to the Convention, might otherwise be affected. But it remains a moot point whether a Community measure could be impugned (rather than an existing domestic measure upheld) on the basis of a Member State's pre-existing accession to the Convention. An analogous argument was raised but rejected in the *T. Port* case.[19] The Court held that the domestic proceedings were concerned solely with bananas from Ecuador. As Ecuador was not a party to the General Agreement on Tariffs and Trade ("GATT") at the material time, the applicant could not rely on the alleged incompatibility between a Commission Regulation and GATT (which would have affected other third countries party to GATT) to deprive the Regulation of its effect in Germany.

---

[17] Case C–158/91 *Ministère public et direction du travail et de l'emploi v. Levy* [1993] E.C.R. I–4287.

[18] *ibid.*, at para. 13. The ECJ also found at para. 17 that the fundamental principle of equal treatment could not be relied upon to "evade performance of the obligations which are incumbent on a Member State . . . under an earlier international agreement and observance of which is safeguarded by the first paragraph of Article 234 of the Treaty."

[19] Joined Cases C–364 and 365/95 *T. Port* (n. 14, above), para. 65.

In *International Fruit*[20] the ECJ was asked on a reference from the Nether- **6.58**
lands whether various Commission Regulations restricting the import of
apples into the Community were invalid because they were contrary to a
rule of international law. It was suggested that they infringed an Article of
GATT. The ECJ referred expressly to Article 234 of the E.C. Treaty (now
Article 307 EC) and found that the Member States could not, simply by
concluding the Treaty of Rome, withdraw from their obligations to third
countries. The Court nonetheless ruled that "before the incompatibility of
a Community measure with a provision of international law can affect the
validity of that measure, the Community must first of all be bound by that
provision."[21] On the facts of the case, the Community had assumed the
powers previously exercised by the Member States under GATT, and so
the provisions of the agreement had the effect of binding the Community.
Nonetheless, where the invalidity was relied on before a national court, it
was necessary that the provision of international law should also be
capable of conferring rights on citizens which they can invoke before the
courts. GATT was found not to confer rights enforceable before the
domestic courts.[22]

This position was refined in *Germany v. Council*.[23] The ECJ found that the **6.59**
same features of GATT precluded the Court from taking its provisions into
account, in order to assess the lawfulness of a Regulation in an action to
annul brought by a Member State under Article 173 of the E.C. Treaty (now
Article 230 EC). The GATT rules were not unconditional. Accordingly, "an
obligation to recognise them as rules of international law which are directly
applicable in the domestic legal systems of the contracting parties cannot
be based on the spirit, general scheme or terms of GATT." It was only if the
"Community intended to implement a particular obligation entered into
within the framework of GATT, or if the Community act expressly refers to
specific provisions of GATT, that the Court can review the lawfulness of the
Community act in question from the point of view of the GATT rules."

The difficulty in a human rights context is that the ECJ has ruled out **6.60**
accession to the Convention. It has also found that the Convention is a
guide, but is not determinative, of Community human rights law.[24] It is not
bound to follow the terms of the Convention. It seems unlikely that the
Court would find that the Convention was therefore binding on the Community for these purposes. Moreover, the Convention could not be relied
upon in matters concerning two or more Member States with no third state
connection. If all parties to the earlier agreement had concluded a subsequent agreement which was incompatible with its predecessor, the ECJ

---

[20] Case 21/72 *International Fruit Co. NV v. Produktschap voor Groenten en Fruit (No.3)*
[1972] E.C.R. 1219.
[21] *ibid.*, para. 7. See also Case C–69/89 *Nakajima All Precision Co. Ltd v. Council of the
European Communities* [1991] E.C.R. I–2069, para. 31, where the ECJ reviewed a Community measure which was adopted to comply with international obligations for compatibility
with the provisions of that international obligation; and Case T– 256/97 *Bureau Europeen des
Unions de Consommateurs (BEUC) v. Commission* [2000] 1 C.M.L.R. 542, CFI.
[22] *International Fruit*, (n. 20, above), para. 27.
[23] Case C–280/93 *Germany v. Council* [1994] E.C.R. I–4973, paras 109–111.
[24] Indeed, in so far as the ECJ "applies" Strasbourg case law, it is careful to do so only "by
analogy". See Case C–185/95P, *Baustahlgewebe GmbH v. Commission* [1999] 4 C.M.L.R.
1203, para. 29.

in *Levy* considered that, in the light of Article 59(1)(b) of the Vienna Convention on the Law of Treaties of March 21, 1986, the earlier agreement might then be deprived of its binding effect.

3. THE PRESENT SCOPE AND CONTENT OF THE "FUNDAMENTAL RIGHTS" RECOGNISED BY E.C. LAW

The Scope of Application of Community Fundamental Rights

6.61   It is now settled that fundamental rights form part of the general principles of Community law recognised by the Community courts.[25] But how and when will these principles be applied? The answer depends on whether Community law is being applied at a Community or at a national level.[26]

Fundamental rights applied to Community measures and decisions

6.62   According to one of the Advocates General, two conclusions may be drawn from the judgment of the ECJ in *Internationale Handelsgesellsh-caft*:

> "First the respect for fundamental rights is a limitation on all Community acts: any measure whereby the powers of the Community institutions are exercised is subject to that limitation and in that sense the entire structure of the Community is under an obligation to observe that limitation. Secondly where directly applicable Community measures exist (by the effect of the Treaties or secondary legislation) they must be interpreted in a manner which accords with the principle that human rights must be respected."[27]

6.63   Community institutions must therefore have regard to fundamental rights in applying and interpreting Community law.[28] In *Opinion 2/94*[29] the ECJ held that respect for human rights is a condition of the lawfulness of Community acts. Fundamental rights accordingly provide grounds for review of Community acts before the Community courts. There have now been many examples of the Community courts examining measures and decisions of the Community institutions for compatibility with fundamental

---

[25] The distinction between fundamental rights and other general principles of law is not an easy one to draw. Advocate General Léger in *Baustahlgewebe* (n. 24, above), at 1216, fn. 23, endorsed the extra-judicial view of Judge Puissochet that: "by comparison with general principles, the term fundamental rights is reserved for 'human rights'."

[26] See, *e.g.* the Opinion of Advocate-General Capotorti in *Defrenne* (n. 36, above) at 1385. He found that the significance of the protection of fundamental rights on a Community plane is not the same as on the plane of national law.

[27] See the Opinion of Advocate General Capotorti in *ibid.*, at 1385.

[28] Case 265/87 *Schräder v. Hauptzollamt Gronau* [1989] E.C.R. 2237, paras 13–14; Case C–260/89 *ERT* (n. 68, above), para 41; *Opinion 2/94* (n. 8, above), para. 33.

[29] See (n. 8, above), para 34.

rights.[30] Thus in *Codorniu v. Council*[31] the ECJ annulled a Council Regulation which restricted the use of the term "crémant" to sparkling wine originating in France and Luxembourg. The Court found that it had infringed the principle of non-discrimination in that it deprived the Spanish applicant of the possibility of continuing to use the term "cremant" in its branding.

Council and Commission Regulations.   The litigation surrounding   **6.64** the "Banana Regulation" provides a ready case study. Council Regulation (EEC) No. 404/93 of February 13, 1993 on the common organisation of the market in bananas[32] introduced common arrangements for the importation of bananas ("the Basic Regulation"). It substituted a common organisation of the market for the various national regimes previously in force. The national regimes that had previously existed were divided into two camps. Laws in France, Spain and the United Kingdom favoured bananas produced either within national territory or in African, Caribbean and Pacific (ACP) States.[33] In Germany, Belgium and the Netherlands, however, there were no quantitative restrictions on the import of Latin-American bananas. Importers in those countries had therefore established their banana branding on the basis of Latin-American bananas. The Basic Regulation introduced a distinction between bananas produced in the Community; third country bananas produced by countries other than ACP States; and traditional and non-traditional ACP bananas. It provided for import quotas for third country and non-traditional ACP bananas. In addition, third country bananas imported within the quota would have a Community levy of 100 ECU per tonne imposed. Non-traditional ACP bananas would be subject to a zero duty. The Basic Regulation divided the quota between various categories (A to C) of operator depending upon their trading activities and the date on which they commenced operating. No such quota was put upon either Community bananas or traditional ACP bananas.

The Latin-American banana producing countries were not pleased with   **6.65** this development and opened consultations under GATT. Following various negotiations, the Community reached agreement with those countries as to import levels of bananas ("the Framework Agreement"). In April 1994, the Community and Member States concluded the final act of the Uruguay Round, including an agreement establishing the Word Trade Organisation Agreement ("WTO Agreement"). The Framework Agreement was annexed to the WTO Agreement. In December 1994, the Council unanimously adopted Decision 94/800 concerning the conclusion on behalf of the European Community, as regards matters within its competence, of the agreements reached in the Uruguay Round multilateral

---

[30] Whether on a preliminary reference from a national court, as in Case C–27/95 *Woodspring District Council v. Bakers of Nailsea* [1997] E.C.R. I–1847, para. 17; or in a direct action brought by a Member State to annul a Community measure under Article 230 E.C., as in Case C–150/94 *United Kingdom v.* Council [1999] 1 C.M.L.R. 367, para. 97. For an example of grounds for reviewing national acts, see Case C–15/95 *EARL de Kerlast v. Unicopa* [1997] E.C.R. I–1961, para. 36.

[31] Case C–309/89 *Codorniu SA v. Council* [1994] E.C.R. I–1853.

[32] [1993] O.J. L47/1.

[33] These were the countries with which the Community had concluded the Lomé Convention.

negotiations.[34] This included approval of the Framework Agreement. The Council adopted an amending Regulation[35] and the Commission thereafter adopted a further Regulation laying down measures for the implementation of the Framework Agreement.[36] That Regulation required an export licence (in addition to an import licence) to be obtained by Category A and C operators in respect of bananas originating from certain third countries. No export licence requirement was imposed on Category B operators.

6.66 Prior to the adoption of the Basic Regulation, Germany was entitled to import an annual quota of bananas free of customs duty. The Basic Regulation abolished the special rules relating to Germany. The introduction of the quota system therefore specifically affected banana importers in Germany, who commenced a number of actions both at a domestic level and before the Community courts on the grounds that the Regulations and Framework Agreement infringed their fundamental rights. The German Government also objected to the Basic Regulation and its implementing legislation. It brought a number of cases before the ECJ, in various guises. Its first action was to seek to annul the Basic Regulation. Germany challenged the introduction of the global tariff quota, which it said unfairly discriminated against third country imports in favour of traditional imports from ACP states. In particular, Category B operators were now entitled to a share of the third country market, whereas Category A and C operators had found their entitlement to third-country bananas restricted.

6.67 This application was determined by the ECJ on October 5, 1994 in *Germany v. Council*.[37] The ECJ was prepared to scrutinise the Basic Regulation to see whether it complied with the fundamental principle of non-discrimination (in this case against traders in third-country bananas).[38] The complaint of discrimination was rejected on the facts.[39] It was inherent in any common organisation of the market that a balance had to be struck between the various categories of economic operators. These operators would be in different situations prior to the integration of previously compartmentalised markets. The common organisation arising from that integration was designed to guarantee disposal of Community production and traditional ACP production, for the purposes of the common agricultural policy.[40] The Court also examined whether the Basic

---

[34] [1994] O.J. L336/1.
[35] Council Regulation (E.C.) No. 3290/94 of December 22, 1994, on the adjustments and transitional arrangements required in the agriculture sector in order to implement the agreements concluded in the Uruguay Round of multilateral trade negotiations: [1994] O.J. L349/105.
[36] Commission Regulation (E.C.) No. 478/95 of March 1, 1995 on additional rules for the application of Regulation No. 404/93 as regards the tariff quota arrangements for imports of bananas into the Community and amending Regulation No. 1442/93: [1993] O.J. L49/13. This implementation was now permanent. The Commission had previously also adopted Regulation (E.C.) No. 3224/94 laying down transitional measures for the implementation of the Framework Agreement on Bananas concluded as part of the Uruguay Round of multilateral trade negotiations: [1994] O.J. L337/72.
[37] Case C–280/93 *Germany v. Council* [1994] E.C.R. I–4973.
[38] *ibid.*, para. 69.
[39] *ibid.*, para. 75. The Court also held that the Council in adopting the Basic Regulation had properly complied with the objectives of the common agricultural policy in Art. 39 of the E.C. Treaty (now, Art. 33 EC).
[40] *ibid.*, para. 74.

Regulation infringed the fundamental right to property or the right to pursue a trade or business. It concluded that it did not and held:

> "The right to property of traders in third-country bananas is not called into question by the introduction of the Community quota and the rules for its sub-division. No economic operator can claim a right in property in a market share which he held at a time before the establishment of a common organisation of the market, since such a market share constitutes only a momentary economic position exposed to the risks of changing circumstances."[41]

Further, at paragraph 87, the Court held that any restriction on freedom to trade corresponded to an objective of general Community interest and did not impair the very substance of that right.

In April 1995, Germany commenced a further action to annul a Community   **6.68** measure, this time the Council Decision approving the Framework Agreement. Supported by Belgium, it argued that the Framework Agreement impaired the fundamental rights of Category A and C operators. Their freedom to pursue a trade or business and their rights to property were infringed and they were discriminated against when compared with Category B operators. Their ability to import bananas from third countries was limited and they had been deprived of the inherent value in brand names based on the country of origin of the bananas. Further, they had been forced to undertake an expensive exercise to diversify their sources of supply. Germany also maintained that Category B operators were unfairly privileged by virtue of the export licence requirement.

In *Germany v. Council*,[42] the ECJ ruled on these objections. It held[43] that   **6.69** there was no general principle of Community law which obliged the Community, in its external relations, to accord third countries equal treatment in all respects. It followed that different treatment of traders was objectively justified if it was based on, or the "automatic consequence" of the different treatment of non-Member States.[44] The restrictions on import opportunities placed on Category A and C traders were simply the result of quotas being imposed on certain third countries. The export licence requirement was, however, to be viewed differently. The difference in treatment arose among Community operators, all of whom had entered into commercial relations with third countries. The difference arose because among this cohort, some were required to obtain export licences and others were exempt.[45] This difference in treatment was not objectively justified. The effect of the Framework Agreement was to increase the quota available to all operators and to reduce the import levies for each. There was therefore no question of Category B operators needing exemption to restore any

---

[41] *ibid.*, para. 79.
[42] Case C–122/95 *Germany v. Council* [1998] ECR I–973. See also Joined Cases C–364 and 365/95 *T. Port GmbH & Co. v. Hauptzollamt Hamburg-Jonas* [1998] E.C.R. I–1023, in which the ECJ gave a near identical ruling under Art. 234 EC on a preliminary reference from the Finance Court in Hamburg.
[43] *ibid.*, para. 56.
[44] *ibid.*, para. 64, the ECJ also reiterated its findings in its previous judgment in Case C–280/93 *Germany v. Council* (n. 37, above).
[45] *ibid.*, para. 60.

imbalance against them specifically.[46] The ECJ accordingly annulled part of the Council Decision to the extent that it exempted Category B banana operators from the export licence requirement imposed on Category A and C operators. It did so on the basis of an infringement of the fundamental principle of non-discrimination. Cases have subsequently been brought (and rejected) for compensation from the Community for that infringement.[47]

6.70 The ECJ has held that, where general legislation requires implementing measures, the implementing measures may be found to be invalid if the general legislation infringes fundamental rights. It has conversely held that a finding by it that a Community legislative act is valid in terms of fundamental rights, also covers the case of the specific and individual application of that measure. If the measure has been reviewed for compatibility with fundamental rights by the ECJ, it cannot then be called into question when it is applied in specific cases.[48]

6.71 **Council and Commission Decisions.** Other areas where fundamental principles of Community law are frequently invoked to challenge Community measures, especially against the Council and the Commission, are competition and anti-dumping cases. While the Commission in the application and enforcement of E.C. competition law is not a "tribunal" for the purposes of Article 6 of the Convention,[49] various procedural safeguards and guarantees have been afforded to persons affected by its procedures, based in part upon the rights conferred by the Convention.[50] In *Hoechst*,[51] the Court ruled that the Commission's decision to launch an investigation of business premises (in a "dawn raid") did not violate the fundamental right to the inviolability of an individual's home. It also reviewed the decision against the rights conferred under Article 8 of the Convention. The Commission's recruitment policies and procedures have also been reviewed for compatibility with Article 8.[52]

6.72 **The Parliament.** The actions of the other institutions of the Community have not escaped scrutiny on fundamental rights grounds. In *Dufay v.*

---

[46] *ibid.*, para. 69.
[47] See Case T–1/99 *T. Port GmbH & Co. KG v. Commission*, judgment of the CFI of February 1, 2001 (n.y.r.). The applicant brought a claim for damages against the Commission under Art. 215(2) of the E.C. Treaty (now Art. 288(2) EC). It claimed for the loss it was said to have sustained in obtaining export licences for certain imports from Costa Rica and for the cost of financing the purchase of those export licences. Its claim was rejected by the CFI on the basis that the applicant had not adduced sufficient evidence of its loss. See also Case T–30/99 *Bocchi Food Trade International GmbH v. Commission*, judgment of the CFI of March 20, 2001 (n.y.r.); and the related judgments of the CFI of the same date in Case T–18/99 *Cordis Obst und Gemüse Grosshandel GmbH v. Commission* and Case T–52/99, *T. Port GmbH & Co. KG v. Commission*.
[48] Case C–104/97P *Atlanta AG v. Council and Commission* [2001] 1 C.M.L.R. 20, paras 43, 45.
[49] See Joined Cases 209 to 215 and 218/78 *Van Landewyck v. Commission (FEDETAB)* [1980] E.C.R. 3125, para. 81; Joined Cases 100 to 103/80 *Musique Diffusion Française v. Commission (Pioneer)* [1983] 1825, para. 7; Case T–11/89 *Shell v. Commission* [1992] E.C.R. II–757, para. 39.
[50] See *Orkem* (n. 58, above); Case 27/88 *Solvay v. Commission* [1989] E.C.R. 3355; Case T–34/93 *Société Générale v. Commission* [1995] E.C.R. II–545, CFI.
[51] Joined Cases 46/87 and 227/88 *Hoechst AG v. Commission* (n. 55, above), para. 18
[52] In Case C–404/92P *X v. Commission* [1994] E.C.R. I–4737, para. 17, concerning the refusal by a job applicant to undergo an AIDS test required by the Commission.

European Parliament[53] the Court examined certain provisions of the Parliament's Conditions of Employment for compatibility with Article 6 of the Convention and for compliance with the principle of non-discrimination.

The Community courts. In *Huls v. Commission*[54] the ECJ was prepared to examine whether the procedures before the CFI granted applicants a fair hearing. It held that the CFI had not erred in law (in breach of the right to a fair hearing) in refusing to re-open the oral hearing or order measures of organisation and inquiry. It did not consider that a request for re-opening the oral procedure or for further inquiry (after the procedure was closed) would have had a decisive influence on the outcome of the case. In *Baustahlgewebe GmbH v. Commission*[55] the appellant appealed against a judgment of the CFI partially annulling the Commission's decision on the "structural crisis cartel" for German producers of welded steel mesh and reducing some of the fines imposed. It contended that the CFI had infringed its right to a hearing within a reasonable time under Article 6 of the Convention. The ECJ held that it was a general principle of Community law (inspired by the Convention) that everyone is entitled to fair legal process. Within the context of proceedings brought against the decision of the Commission to impose a fine under the competition rules, there is a right to legal process within a reasonable period. In this case, the proceedings before the CFI had lasted for five years and six months. When examined in the light of the facts of the case, it was found that there had been an infringement of the appellant's right to a hearing within a reasonable period of time. In the absence of any indication that the delay had affected the outcome of the proceedings in any way, this did not however entitle the ECJ to set aside the judgment in its entirety.[56] Instead, it reduced the fine by 50,000 ECUs. 6.73

Indeed, the ECJ has even been prepared to consider whether its own procedures are compatible with the Convention. In *Emesa Sugar*[57] the applicant argued that the refusal of the ECJ to allow it to make representations to the Court in the light of the Advocate General's Opinion infringed its right to a fair hearing under Article 6(1) of the Convention. It also relied upon a decision of the European Court of Human Rights in *Vermeulen v. Belgium*[58] in which the Strasbourg Court was asked to adjudicate on the role of the Procureur General at the Belgium Court of Cassation. It found that his role involved delivering an opinion which was objective and reasoned in law, but which had the ultimate intention of influencing the Court. The European Court of Human Rights found that a refusal to allow Vermeulen to reply to the opinion before the end of the hearing infringed Article 6(1) of the Convention. 6.74

The ECJ distinguished the *Vermeulen* case on the basis that the Advocate General's Opinion brought the oral proceedings to an end and did not form part of the proceedings, but rather instigated the Court's deliberations. The 6.75

---

[53] Case 257/85 *C. Dufay v. European Parliament* [1987] E.C.R. 1561, paras 9, 12.
[54] Case C–199/92P *Huls AG v. Commission* [1999] 5 C.M.L.R. 1016, para. 127, ECJ.
[55] Case C–185/95P *Baustahlgewebe GmbH v. Commission* (n. 24, above), paras 20, 21.
[56] *ibid.*, paras. 47–49.
[57] Case C–17/98 *Emesa Sugar (Free Zone) NV v. Aruba (No.1)* [2000] E.C.R. I–0665.
[58] Reports of Judgments and Decisions, 1996 I 224. See also *JJ v. Netherlands* (1999) 28 E.H.R.R. 169.

role, therefore, was integral to the Court rather than originating from an external authority. This role differed fundamentally from that of the Procureur, and the Convention was therefore not relevant. The ECJ noted that there already existed a safeguard in the form of procedures to re-open the oral proceedings at the request of the Advocate General, or the parties themselves under the Rules of Procedure of the Court of Justice.

Fundamental Rights applied at a domestic level

6.76   The Community is the legal creation of its founding treaties. It is only certain defined areas that fall within Community competence. As the ECJ stated in *van Gend en Loos*: " . . . the Community constitutes a new legal order of international law for the benefit of which the states have limited their sovereign rights, *albeit within limited fields*" (emphasis added).[59] In *Opinion 1/91 EEA Agreement (No. 1)*, the ECJ described the Community Treaties as having "established a new legal order for the benefit of which the States have limited their sovereign rights, in ever wider fields."[60] Nonetheless, the ECJ has (unsurprisingly) never suggested that the transfer of competence to the Community has approached a total transfer of competence across the board.

6.77   As fundamental rights are of direct effect, they can be relied on directly by individuals in the national legal order as grounds of review not only of Community acts, but also of national acts that fall within the scope of Community law. At a national level, Member States, when acting within the scope of Community law, must do so in accordance with the fundamental rights recognised by Community law.[61] As the Community has bounded competence, Community courts do not have jurisdiction to examine whether national legislation that falls outside the field of application of Community law is compatible with fundamental rights.[62] The crucial question is therefore "what defines the scope of Community law?"[63] As Advocate General Gulmann stated in *Bostock*:

> "The issue is of fundamental significance because it is determinative for the division of powers between the Court of Justice and national courts as regards the protection of basic rights and the question is a difficult one to answer. The issue lies within an area where the Court must tread carefully. Similar questions may arise in the most diverse situations and it is important that the Court develop its case law in the light of the cases that are submitted to it."

6.78   **Cases that fall outside the scope of Community law.** Where there is a situation "unconnected with any of the situations contemplated

---

[59] See (n. 11, above) at 12.

[60] *Opinion 1/91 EEA Agreement (No. 1)* [1991] E.C.R. I–6079, para. 21.

[61] See *Wachauf* (n. 65, above), paras 17–19; *ERT* (n. 68, above), paras 41–45; *Bostock* (n. 83, above), para. 16; Case C–351/92 *Graff v. Hauptzollamt Köln-Rheinau* [1994] E.C.R. I–3361, para. 17.

[62] In addition to the cases cited above, see *Cinéthèque* (n. 50, above), paras 25–26; and *Demirel* (n. 51, above), para. 28.

[63] See Weiler and Lockhart, in *Taking Rights Seriously* (n. 26, above) p. 63, who state that "notions of 'the field of application' or 'the scope of' or 'the field of' Community law are, like the 'duty of care', say, in Scots law, open-textured and their parameters, as a matter of positive law and/or legal realism (what the law is, what we predict the Court will do) can only be stated by taking into account judicial praxis as well."

by Community law", there is no scope for fundamental principles of Community law to be applied. This is often equated with the concept of Community law having no application to a "purely internal situation".[64] This will often (but not always) be the case where there has been no transfer of competence from the Member States to the Community. Indeed, the ECJ has expressly stated that although fundamental rights form an integral part of the general principles of law and therefore of the legality of Community acts, they cannot have the effect of extending the scope of Treaty provisions beyond the competences of the Community.[65]

In *Kremzow*[66] the applicant was a retired Austrian judge who confessed to **6.79** the murder in Austria of an Austrian lawyer. He was sentenced to 20 years' imprisonment in an institution for the mentally ill. The applicant appealed against his sentence, but did not attend the appeal hearing. The appellate court changed his sentence to life imprisonment in an ordinary prison. The European Court of Human Rights held that in light of the seriousness of the matter, Mr Kremzow should have had the opportunity to defend himself in person.[67] After that judgment, the applicant applied for an award of damages and a reduction of his sentence. In the course of that action, the national court referred to the ECJ by way of a preliminary reference the question of whether the national court was bound by the decision of the Strasbourg Court. On the reference, the applicant contended that the Court of Justice had jurisdiction to answer a number of questions concerning Articles 5 and 6 of the Convention because he was a citizen of the E.U. enjoying the right to freedom movement, and a Member State which infringes that fundamental right guaranteed by Community law by executing an unlawful penalty of imprisonment must be held liable in damages by virtue of Community law.[68]

The ECJ found that the situation of the appellant was not connected with **6.80** any of the situations contemplated by the Treaty provisions on the free movement of persons. A purely hypothetical prospect of exercising the right does not establish a sufficient connection with Community law to justify the application of Community provisions.[69] Moreover, the appellant was sentenced for murder and for the illegal possession of a firearm under provisions of national law which were not designed to secure compliance with the rules of Community law.

---

[64] Case C–132/93 *Volker Steen v. Deutsche Bundespost (No. 2)* [1994] E.C.R. I–2715, para. 9, and in the Order of the Court. In Case C–332/90 *Volker Steen v. Deutsche Bundespost* [1992] E.C.R. I–341, para. 9, the ECJ held that a national of a Member State which has never exercised the right of free movement within the Community could not rely on Arts 7 or 48 of the E.C. Treaty to challenge a situation purely internal to that Member State. The German court referred a question to the ECJ a second time, as it was clearly worried by the concept of "reverse discrimination"—that is, a Member State treating its own nationals less favourably than those of other Member States.
[65] Case C–249/96 *Grant v. South West Trains* [1998] E.C.R. I–621, para. 45.
[66] Case C–299/95 *Kremzow* [1997] E.C.R. I–2629, para. 13.
[67] *Kremzow v. Austria* (1994) 17 E.H.R.R. 322, ECHR
[68] *ibid.*, para. 13. See also Case 180/83 *Moser v. Land Baden-Württemberg* [1984] E.C.R. 2539, para. 18, where the Court held that a purely hypothetical prospect of being employed in another Member State did not establish a "sufficient connection" with Community law. The ECJ defined a "purely internal situation" as being one where there is "no factor connecting them to any of the situations envisaged by Community law": para. 15.
[69] *ibid.*, para. 16.

6.81 Other examples of situations found not to fall within the scope of Community law include:

(1) A national rule which requires a victim of a criminal offence who wishes to bring suit as a civil party in criminal proceedings to grant his representative a special power of attorney, even when the law of the Member State of which the victim is a national does not lay down such a formality. In *Criminal proceedings against Gianfranco Perfili*[70] Italian legislation governing the procedure for bringing suit as a civil party in criminal proceedings was found to affect the ability of Lloyd's of London to defend its interests under civil law in Italy and had to be examined in the light of Articles 52 and 59 of the Treaty (now, Articles 43 and 49 EC). Those provisions, however, were not concerned with any disparities in treatment which may result between Member States. The national legislation did not fall within the scope of the Community law, and the Court of Justice had no jurisdiction to assess its compatibility with Article 6 of the Convention.[71]

(2) A national procedural rule prohibiting, *inter alia*, the sale of food products whose use-by date has expired.[72] In *Maurin*, in the course of criminal proceedings, the defendant argued that a police report was void because it had not been signed by the person concerned with the investigation contrary, *inter alia,* to Convention provisions concerning the observance of the rights of the defence and of the adversarial nature of the proceedings. The relevant community legislation was Directive 79/112 which provides that the date by which a product had to be used must be indicated on the labelling of foodstuffs. However, it did not regulate the sale of foodstuffs complying with its requirements, and did not impose any obligation on Member States where there is a sale of products whose use-by date had expired.[73]

(3) National legislation prohibiting the planting of an orchard in a national park.[74] In *Annibaldi*, Mr Annibaldi owned land that fell within a national park, created to help protect the environment in the Lazio region. He applied for permission to plant a small orchard within the park, but the municipality refused. On a preliminary reference to the ECJ, Mr Annibaldi argued that his right to property had been infringed without compensation and that the measure was in breach of the rule of non-discrimination set out in Article 40(3) of the E.C. Treaty (now Article 34(3) EC). The Court reiterated that where national legislation fell within the scope of Community law, the ECJ was obliged on a preliminary ruling to give the national court all the guidance necessary to

---

[70] Case C–177/94 *Criminal proceedings against Gianfranco Perfili* [1996] E.C.R. I–161.
[71] *ibid.*, para. 20.
[72] Case C–144/95 *Criminal proceedings against Jean-Louis Maurin* [1996] E.C.R. I–2909.
[73] *ibid.*, para. 11.
[74] Case C–309/96 *Daniele Annibaldi v. Sindaco del Comune di Guidonia and Presidente Regione Lazio* [1997] E.C.R. I–7493.

enable it to assess the compatibility of that legislation with fundamental rights. However, the ECJ had no such jurisdiction with
regard to legislation lying outside the scope of Community law.[75]
The Court found on the facts that national legislation which
established a nature and archaeological park applied to "a situation which does not fall within the scope of Community law".

Unlike in *Bostock*, the ECJ in *Annibaldi* not only decided that the national **6.82**
legislation did not have to comply with the fundamental principles of
Community law, but also considered that the Court had no jurisdiction over
the issues raised in the preliminary reference.[76] Of further interest in
Annibaldi are the factors which the ECJ took into account in declining to
give guidance on Community fundamental principles relating to property.
These were[77]:

(1) the fact that there was nothing to suggest that the domestic
legislation "was intended to implement a provision of Community
law either in the sphere of agriculture or in that of the environment or culture";

(2) even if the domestic law was "capable of affecting indirectly the
operation of a common organisation of the agricultural markets",
it was not in dispute that the legislation in issue pursued objectives other than those covered by the common agricultural policy. Further the domestic legislation itself was general in
character;

(3) given the absence of Community rules on expropriation of property, and the fact that a common organisation of a market had no
effect on systems of agricultural property ownership, it followed
from Article 222 of the E.C. Treaty (now Article 295 EC) that the
domestic legislation concerned an area which fell within the
purview of Member States.[78]

The ECJ in *Annibaldi* has therefore given some indication of the matters **6.83**
which may be examined in assessing whether a given subject falls within
the scope of Community law. In none of the above cases, however, has
the Court formed a convenient test for determining why the measure or
decision in question falls outside the scope of Community law. While an ad
hoc approach enables the Court to deal with each case on its merits, the
disadvantage is that national courts may struggle with the concept of

---

[75] *ibid.*, para. 13.
[76] *ibid.*, para. 25.
[77] As set out in paras 21–23 of the judgment.
[78] Advocate General Cosmas at 7502, para. 23, reached the same conclusion on the basis
that the domestic legislation was not adopted on the basis of a Community provision; was not
intended to ensure compliance with the rules of Community law; and involved no foreign
element.

whether a given piece of national legislation falls to be reviewed by reference to the fundamental principles of Community law. This may impede the ability of national courts effectively to apply and enforce Community law.[79]

6.84   **No single test is determinative of whether a case falls within the scope of Community law.** Nor can any definitive test be discerned from cases where Community law obligations have been triggered. The circumstances in which Member States must observe the general principles of Community law have not been the subject of comprehensive analysis by the ECJ. Evidently there must be some nexus between the national measure and Community law in order for the general principles to apply. However, it is not clear how strong the nexus must be. The development of a form of review based on a breach of principles of fundamental rights has been gradual and the ECJ has taken a case-by-case approach to the question.[80] There remains room for debate over what types of national measures may be challenged on grounds of breach of fundamental rights principles, including the Convention principles. Given the supremacy of Community law, it must ultimately be the ECJ that determines whether the subject matter of a particular dispute or decision falls within the scope of Community law.[81] The difficulty is that the Community courts have not given definitive guidance on how such an assessment is made.

6.85 This difficulty in making the assessment was highlighted by Advocate General Gulmann in *Bostock*. Mr Bostock's claim undoubtedly fell within a "Community law" context, because it arose out of a common organisation of the market. Nonetheless, Advocate General Gulmann considered that as Community law was largely silent on the specific legal issue (namely the respective interests of landlord and tenant upon surrender of such a tenancy) it was up to the Member States to strike the appropriate balance in accordance with their own national traditions.[82] The Advocate General concluded that there were good grounds for leaving that task to the legal systems of the Member States. The fact that the legal difficulty arose from the adoption of Community rules did not mean that the national authorities necessarily had to respect fundamental rights recognised in Community law. There was no difficulty in leaving the issue to the Member States since each was governed by the rule of law and was obliged to respect the fundamental rights laid down in the Convention.[83]

---

[79] The Community is keen for national courts to play this role. There have been suggestions that the ECJ would prefer to see fewer preliminary references from national courts. See also the Notice on Cooperation between Member States and Commission ([1993] O.J. C39/05) and the Notice on Cooperation between National Competition Authorities and the Commission ([1997] O.J. C313/3).

[80] See Craig and de Búrca, *EC Law: Text, cases and materials* (2nd ed., Oxford, 1998) p. 318. See also M. Demetriou, "Using Human Rights Through European Community Law" [1999] E.H.R.L.R. 484 at 487.

[81] See *Booker Aquaculture Ltd v. Secretary of State for Scotland* [2000] Eu. L.R. 449.

[82] See *Bostock* (n. 83, above) at 972, para. 33 of the Opinion.

[83] *ibid.*, at 972, para. 33. Indeed, it was precisely because the fundamental rights recognised in Community law were derived from the constitutional traditions of the Member States, which meant that the use of Community law was less suited to assess the legality of rules adopted by individual Member States.

The Court, however, adopted a different approach. It is not altogether easy **6.86** to see what its approach was.[84] The *ratio decidendi* of the case was that Community fundamental rights did not import a duty to give compensation to Mr Bostock. This could have been for one of two reasons. First, because the domestic legislation did not implement any provision of Community law and nor was the domestic law reliant upon a derogation from a Treaty provision. Accordingly, the domestic legislation fell outwith the scope of Community law for the purposes of a review based on fundamental rights. Alternatively, on the facts of the case it was arguable that no such duty arose (substantively) from the fundamental rights recognised by Community law. Unfortunately, it is not clear which of these two reasons was ultimately the rationale for rejecting the alleged duty to compensate. The ECJ did not simply follow the Advocate General and conclude that the issue was one for the domestic law of Member States alone. Instead, it recalled its earlier decisions in *Wachauf* and *ERT* to the effect that: "the requirements flowing from the protection of fundamental rights in the Community legal order are also binding on Member States when they implement Community rules." However, it also noted that the Court's function was to give the national court guidance on the interpretation of Community general principles of law by which national legislation fell to be assessed. It therefore decided it would have to examine the fundamental rights relied upon by Mr Bostock, in order to assist the national court to adjudicate on their compatibility with Community law.[85] It could well be said to be implicit within this finding that the domestic legislation was required to comply with the fundamental rights recognised in Community law.[86] Otherwise no substantive examination would have been necessary.

The Court went on to find that the right to property recognised as a general **6.87** principle of Community law did not, as a matter of substantive law, require a Member State to introduce a scheme for payment of compensation. Nor was such a right to compensation conferred directly on the tenant under Community law. In contrast, the principle of non-discrimination was not applicable because it could not bring about retroactive modification of relations between parties to a lease. Further, the Court held that legal relations between lessees and lessors were governed by national law and not Community law. Any consequences of unjust enrichment of the lessor upon expiry of the lease were not a matter for Community law.

Some might consider that the Court's reasoning betrays a fundamental **6.88** difference of opinion among the individual judges of the Court as to where to draw the line. This, however, would be to ignore the Court's concern about its function on a preliminary reference. The better view is probably that the ECJ felt obliged to give guidance to the national court as to the

---

[84] A point made by Laws J. in *R. v. Ministry of Agriculture, Fisheries and Food, ex p. First City Trading Ltd* [1997] 1 C.M.L.R. 250 at 266. His Lordship respectfully described the reasoning as "a little Delphic".
[85] Judgment of the Court in *Bostock*, (n. 83, above), paras 16 and 17.
[86] This view was put forward by counsel for the applicant in *First City Trading* and rejected by Laws J. on the basis that the Court did not seem to be implying a wider principle than that fundamental principles bind Member States only when they implement Community law. See *ex p. First City Trading Ltd* (n. 84, above) at 266, para. 36.

content of the fundamental rights relied upon by the applicant, in case the national court decided that the issue fell to be determined under Community law.[87] The Court's judgment has caused some difficulties for national courts seeking to determine what the appropriate test is.[88]

6.89 Clearly some form of overriding test or guidance would be of assistance. Attempts to find a unifying test have been made, in particular, by some of the Advocates General. Advocate General Gulmann in *Bostock* phrased his proposed test in this way: "is the domestic legislation under review so closely connected with Community law as to fall within its scope."[89] In *Kremzow*,[90] Advocate General La Pergola also stated that the "interpretative task" imposed on the Community by its recognition of fundamental rights "came into play and may be carried out only in regard to provisions connected with Community law, of which the Court is the supreme interpreter according to the Treaty". Such an approach has some support in related case law of the Court, albeit that such case law concerns the application of Article 12 E.C. (the prohibition of discrimination on the grounds of nationality). The Article is a useful comparator because it contains an express reference to matters "within the scope of applications of this Treaty". The potential for applying the case law on Article 12 E.C. by analogy is examined below.[91]

6.90 Another attempt to find a unifying test was made by Advocate General Cosmas in *Annibaldi*.[92] He concluded that: "the extent to which the Member States are bound by fundamental rights under Community law matches the extent of the jurisdiction of the Court to give a ruling on questions of interpretation of those rights." But such an approach ignores the fact that the Court has previously found (in *Demirel*) that it had jurisdiction to consider an issue and yet refused to apply to the measure in question the case law on fundamental rights. Further, if the question of whether a measure or decision falls within the scope of Community law is ultimately a matter of Community law, then the answer to the question posed (unless *acte clair*) will always be capable of being referred to the ECJ under Article 234 EC.

6.91 The only other unifying approach would also be extremely broad in scope. It would follow the "*civis europeus sum*" argument of Advocate General Jacobs in *Konstantinidis*. Rudimentary elements of support for this broad approach in the recent judgment of the ECJ in *Krombach v. Bamberski*.[93] The preliminary reference to the ECJ concerned the enforcement of a judgment of a French court in Germany, pursuant to the Brussels Convention. The ECJ held that a national court may, when considering whether to decline to enforce a judgment on public-policy grounds set out in Article

---

[87] This is only a partial explanation, given that ultimately the ECJ must determine whether or not domestic legislation falls within the scope of Community law.
[88] See paras 6.195 *et seq.*, below.
[89] See *Bostock* (n. 83, above) at 972 of his Opinion.
[90] See *Kremzow* (n. 66, above) at 2635.
[91] See paras. 6.105 *et seq.*, below.
[92] See (n. 74, above) at 7501, para. 19 of his Opinion.
[93] Case C–7/98 *Dieter Krombach v. André Bamberski*, *The Times*, March 30, 2000. Judgment of the Court of March 28, 2000. See also Case C–38/98 *Régie Nationale des Usines Rénault SA v. Maxicar SpA* [2000] E.C.D.R. 415, ECJ.

27(1) of the Brussels Convention,[94] take account of the fact that the court of the state of origin refused to allow the defendant to have his defence presented unless he appeared in person.[95] Depriving an individual of the right to have his defence presented in his absence constituted a fundamental breach of the right to a fair trial. This was an essential element of the legal order of the state, which had been enshrined in constitutional traditions common to all Member States. As such it was also a fundamental principle of Community law, which must be guaranteed even in the absence of any rules governing the proceedings in question.[96] Significantly, the Court found that recourse to the public-policy clause must be regarded as being possible in exceptional cases where the guarantees laid down in the legislation of the state of origin and in the Brussels Convention itself have been insufficient to protect the defendant from a manifest breach of his right to defend himself before the court of origin, as recognised by the Convention.

Nonetheless, the *Krombach* judgment may more properly be viewed as an example of the ECJ permitting Member States to derogate from the Brussels Convention only on grounds that are compatible with fundamental rights. Moreover, as was pointed out above, the Court has so far declined to follow the lead set by Advocate General Jacobs. In terms of predictive tests, the most that can therefore be said is that where a decision or dispute falls within certain pre-existing categories, one may safely assume that the ECJ will determine that the fundamental principles of Community law should be respected. In practical terms, various categories can be identified where Community fundamental rights will come into play. The categories are: **6.92**

(1) where Member States implement Community measures;

(2) where Member States act pursuant to a Treaty derogation;

(3) where directly effective Community law is invoked before the national courts of the Member States.

These categories are now examined in turn. It should be pointed out, however, that, on the basis of the case law of the ECJ, there exists the potential for a residual category of cases to be defined. The potential for development of this residual category, and the possibility for applying Article 12 EC by analogy, are examined thereafter. **6.93**

Category 1: where Member States implement Community measures. First, at a Community level, fundamental rights will be used to assess the validity of Community measures, the acts of Community institutions and as a guide to interpretation of Community legislation. Member States act as agents of the Community when implementing Community **6.94**

---

[94] The ECJ has jurisdiction to rule on the interpretation of the Brussels Convention through the Protocol on the Interpretation of the Convention on Jurisdiction and the Enforcement of Judgments in Civil and Commercial Matters, [1990] O.J. C No. 189 of July 28, 1990.

[95] See the *Krombach* judgment (n. 93, above), para. 45.

[96] *ibid.*, paras 42–44. Para. 39 of the judgment cites jurisprudence of the Court of Human Rights in support of the principle that an accused person does not forfeit entitlement to such a right simply because he is not present at the hearing.

law. Consequently, they must comply with the fundamental rights recognised by the ECJ when implementing Community law either by primary or secondary legislation, or by administrative measures.[97] This is the case whether the national measure was specifically enacted for the purpose of implementing a Community act taken under the authority of the European Communities Act 1972, or whether it was enacted prior to the Community act but purports to give effect to that Community act upon its coming into force. In short, the general principles of Community law are binding on all authorities entrusted with the implementation of Community provisions.[98]

6.95   The requirement that a Member State must comply with the Convention when implementing Community law must also be met when the Community legislation confers a discretion on the Member State as to implementation.[99] When faced with a range of measures for implementing Community legislation where some are Convention compatible and others are not, the Member State is obliged by Community law to select a measure which is Convention compatible. One common sub-set of such an area of application relates to the direct implementation by a Member State of a common organisation of agricultural markets.[1] Fundamental principles may also be used as an aid to interpretation of Community measures when they come to be applied domestically. In *Commission v. Germany*,[2] for example, the ECJ construed Regulation 1612/68, as applied in the case, in the light of the requirement of respect for family life set out in Article 8 of the Convention. The use of the fundamental rights doctrine as an aid to interpretation has been recognised by the House of Lords.[3]

6.96   By way of recent example, in *P v. S & Cornwall County Council*[4] a transsexual was dismissed from his employment for a reason related to a gender reassignment. The ECJ held that the objective pursued by the Equal Treatment Directive was simply the expression of the principle of equality, one of the fundamental principles of Community law, and included the equal treatment of transsexuals. It found that the Sex Discrimination Act 1975 did not properly implement the Equal Treatment

---

[97] See *Rutili* (n. 34, above); Case 249/86 *Commission v. Germany* [1989] E.C.R. 1263; Case C–63/93 *Duff* [1996] E.C.R. I–569, para. 29; Case C–351/92 *Graff* [1994] E.C.R. I–3361, para. 17.

[98] Joined Cases C–31/91 to C–44/91 *Alois Lageder SpA v. Amministrazione delle Finanze dello Stato* [1993] E.C.R. I–1761, para. 33.

[99] See *Wachauf* (n. 65, above), para. 19; *Bostock* (n. 83, above) at 971, *per* Advocate General Gulmann. See also *Booker Aquaculture Ltd v. Secretary of State for Scotland* [2000] Eu. L.R. 449, where the Scottish Court held that the implementation of a Directive by the U.K. required compliance with the fundamental rights protected by Community law. This might well include a requirement to provide compensation in order to protect the right to property. The Scottish Court referred to the ECJ the "fundamental question" of whether the implementing Regulations and the matter of compensation were governed by E.C. or national law.

[1] See *Klensch* (n. 44, above), paras 8, 9.

[2] Case 249/86 *Commission v. Germany* [1989] E.C.R. 1263, para. 10.

[3] In *R. v. Hertfordshire County Council, ex p. Green Industries Ltd* [2000] 2 WLR 373 at 380, *per* Lord Hoffmann who stated that: "[t]here is no dispute that since the Act of 1990 gives effect to a Directive, it must be interpreted according to principles of Community law, including its doctrines of fundamental human rights."

[4] Case C–13/94 *P v. S & Cornwall County Council* [1996] E.C.R. I–2143. At para 16 the ECJ referred to the decision of the Court of Human Rights of October 17, 1986 in *Rees v. United Kingdom*, para. 38, Series A, No. 106.

Directive, as it did not contain a prohibition on discrimination against transsexuals. The Act therefore had to be disapplied to prevent a breach of the fundamental principles recognised by Community law.

Category 2: Where Member States act pursuant to a derogation from a Treaty provision. When a Member State acts pursuant to powers conferred on it by Community law to derogate from rights granted, for example, under the E.C. Treaty or by a Directive, such derogation must comply with general principles of Community law, including Convention rights.[5] It is true that in its judgment in *Cinéthèque*[6] the ECJ, when faced with the question of whether the national legislation (enacted pursuant to a mandatory requirement) was in breach of Article 10 of the Convention, answered as follows: **6.97**

> "Although it is true that it is the duty of this Court to ensure observance of fundamental rights in the field of Community law, it has no power to examine the compatibility with the European Convention of national law which concerns, as in this case, an area which falls within the jurisdiction of the national legislator."

As was seen above, at paragraph 6–25, this judgment does not represent the last word on the issue of compatibility of Treaty derogations with fundamental rights. The more orthodox view can be gleaned from the Opinion of Advocate General Slynn in *Cinéthèque*, who stated that[7]:   **6.98**

> "It is clear from Case 4/73 *Nold*, and Case 44/79 *Hauer* that the Convention provides guidelines for the Court in laying down those fundamental rules of law which are part of Community law, though the Convention does not bind, and is not part of the law of the Community as such . . . In my opinion it is right, as the Commission contends, that the exception in Article 30 should be construed in the light of the Convention."

This approach has been followed more recently in cases such as *Demirel*, *ERT* and *Grogan*.[8] In *Commission v. Germany*,[9] the ECJ confirmed that where a Member State relies on the provisions of the Treaty in order to justify national rules which are likely to obstruct the exercise of a freedom guaranteed by the Treaty, such justification provided by Community law must be interpreted in the light of the general principles of law, and, in particular, fundamental rights. The ECJ also held that such rights did not constitute "unfettered prerogatives" and therefore could be restricted: "provided that the restrictions in fact correspond to objectives of general interest pursued by the Community and that they do not constitute a   **6.99**

---

[5] See *R. v. Ministry of Agriculture, Fisheries and Food, ex p. Bell Lines* [1984] 2 C.M.L.R. 502, where a restriction on the importation of milk contrary to Art. 28 EC (ex Art. 30 of the E.C. Treaty) was held disproportionate and incapable of justification under Art. 30 EC (ex Art. 36).

[6] See n. 50, above.

[7] *ibid.*, at 2616.

[8] See *Demirel* (n. 51, above); *ERT* (n. 68, above); and *Grogan* (n. 72, above).

[9] Case C–62/90 *Commission v. Germany* [1992] E.C.R. I–2575, para. 23.

disproportionate and intolerable interference which infringes upon the very substance of the rights guaranteed." The same principles also apply to derogations on the grounds of public policy from the Brussels Convention.[10]

6.100   **Category 3: Where directly effective Community law is engaged before national courts.**   A further category might be said to exist where national courts enforce directly effective Community law. This is most often the case when an individual seeks before a national court to rely upon a Treaty freedom. There have been many examples of a natural or legal person in such circumstances seeking not only to rely upon directly effective Community law, but also to rely upon fundamental rights as a necessary adjunct to the Treaty or other provision. The ECJ has occasionally held that national courts are obliged, in such circumstances, not only to apply the Treaty or other provision, but also to take into account fundamental rights recognised under Community law. The Court has often stated that a certain provision of the Treaty is merely a "specific enunciation" of a more general principle which must also be recognised.[11] If this is the case, then the application of a given Treaty provision within a Member State may carry with it an obligation to review the actions of a Member State for compatibility with the fundamental rights recognised by Community law, even if it does not seek to rely upon a derogation.

6.101   This is hardly surprising. If the national court considers Community fundamental rights when a derogation is relied upon, it would be odd if Community fundamental rights did not also fall for consideration where no derogation was or could be relied upon and the only issue was how a Treaty provision applied. Powers retained by Member States must, in certain circumstances, be exercised in a manner consistent with Community law,[12] which may include compliance with Community fundamental rights. This situation arises because of the requirement on Member States to comply with the fundamental freedoms and other Treaty provisions which are binding on them, save to the extent that a derogation may lawfully be relied upon. If no derogation is, in fact, relied upon by a Member State, it must still be open to Community and domestic courts to assess whether the Member State's actions infringe the fundamental freedoms or other Treaty provisions.[13] This category would, in fact, normally be seen as a corollary of category 2 and might ordinarily be safely elided with it. It is hard to think of a situation where a Member State would not seek to rely on a derogation to defend an allegation that it had failed to comply with directly effective Community law. Further, if the plea of such

---

[10] See the *Krombach* and *Rénault* cases (n. 93, above).
[11] Joined Cases 117/76 and 16/77 *Rucksdeschel v. Hauptzollamt Hamburg-St. Annen* [1977] E.C.R. 1753, para. 7; Case C–177/90 *Kühn v. Landwirtshaftskammer Wser*–Ems [1992] E.C.R. I–35, para. 18; Case C–98/91 *Herbrink v. Minister van Landbouw* [1994] E.C.R. I–223, para. 27; Case C–280/93 *Germany v. Council* [1994] E.C.R. I–4973, para. 67.
[12] See for a related point, Case C–124/95 *R. v. H.M. Treasury and Bank of England, ex p. Centro-Com* [1997] E.C.R. I–81, paras 24–27. The ECJ held (para. 25) that the powers retained by a Member State must be exercised in a manner consistent with Community law.
[13] In the words of Professor Tridimas, "the effect of *ERT* is that considerations of human rights are part of the inquiry which the Court performs in order to assess whether a national measure which interferes with one of the fundamental freedoms is permitted under Community law." See (n. 6, above), p. 230.

an infringement were made out, it might be thought that an additional plea of failure to observe fundamental rights would add little, if anything, of value. If, after examination of the issues, the Treaty provisions are found not to apply, there can be no scope for a free-standing review on fundamental rights grounds.[14]

However, in *Konsumentombudsmannen v. Gourmet International*[15] Advocate General Jacobs considered that a restriction on the sale of commercial advertising space for alcoholic drinks in Sweden would fall within Article 59 of the E.C. Treaty (now Article 49 E.C.). He referred to arguments that had been raised in relation to freedom of expression under Article 10 of the Convention and stated: **6.102**

> "Nonetheless, the existence of any encroachment on advertisers' fundamental right to freedom of expression (which may be justified on grounds analogous to those which may be invoked in relation to a restriction on freedom to provide services) can only mean that the incompatibility with Article 59 of the E.C. Treaty must be viewed with particular seriousness."

It therefore seems that by combining a complaint of infringement of a Treaty provision with a complaint that the Convention has also been infringed, an applicant may persuade the Court to adopt a more rigorous investigation both of the infringements themselves and the justifications provided for them (if any). What is controversial, perhaps, about such a field of application is the lack of Treaty basis.[16] Nonetheless, were the ECJ in this category of case applying the Treaty provision and no more, any reference to the fundamental rights doctrine would be otiose. The matter could be examined from the point of view of the Treaty Article alone. The express, additional reference to fundamental rights is usually made after the Community "nexus" has been secured by the invocation of a Treaty Article.   **6.103**

A residual category? What is more interesting is the potential scope the ECJ's case law leaves for further development of the threshold at which a domestic situation will be found to fall within the scope of Community law. The definitions used by the Court in a number of cases do not necessarily mean that the "scope of Community" law is restricted to the two/three identified categories above. Thus, the test to be drawn from *Volker Steen v. Deutsche Bundespost (No. 2)*[17] was whether the national measure under review was "unconnected with any of the situations contemplated by Community law". Similarly, in *Moser*,[18] the Court talked in   **6.104**

---

[14] See Case C–177/94 *Criminal proceedings against Gianfranco Perfili* [1996] E.C.R. I–161, where the ECJ concluded that because the application of Art. 49 EC was not raised on the facts of the case, there was no need to consider the application of Art. 6 of the Convention.

[15] Case C–405/98 *Konsumentombudsmannen v. Gourmet International Products Aktiebolag*, Opinion of Advocate General Jacobs of December 14, 2000 (n.y.r.), para. 74.

[16] A point made by Laws J. in *First City Trading* (n. 84, above) at 267–269 who found no need for general principles to be applied co-extensively with the application of Treaty provisions to the acts or omissions of Member States.

[17] See (n. 64, above), para. 9.

[18] See (n. 68, above), paras. 16, 18 respectively.

terms both of factors "connecting" the domestic decision to "any of the situations envisaged by Community law" and also of the need to establish a "sufficient connection with Community law". The expression used in *Kremzow*[19] was whether the national measure or decision in issue was "connected with any of the situations contemplated by the Treaty provisions" on the free movement of persons. Advocate General Gulmann in *Bostock* examined whether the domestic provisions was "so closely connected with Community law" as to fall within its scope.[20] Each of these formulations leaves the way open for arguing that fundamental rights have a "deeper bite"[21] than has been recognised in Categories 1 to 3 set out above.

6.105   **The scope of Community law defined by analogy with Article 12 E.C.?**   The possibility of a residual category also raises the prospect of arguments being run by analogy with the case law on Article 12 EC.[22] Indeed, the application of fundamental rights as an "adjunct" to Treaty freedoms resembles the application of Article 12 EC. Article 12 EC provides as follows:

"(1) Within the scope of application of this Treaty, and without prejudice to any special provisions contained therein, any discrimination on grounds of nationality shall be prohibited.

(2) The Council, acting in accordance with the procedure referred to in Article 251, may adopt rules designed to prohibit such discrimination."

6.106   In *Cowan*,[23] for example, Mr Cowan was a British citizen who was assaulted outside a Metro station in Paris. He was on a brief visit to the city as a tourist. His attacker was never arrested, so he applied to the French equivalent of the Criminal Injuries Compensation Authority (the Commission d'indemnisation des victimes d'infraction) for compensation for injuries suffered. The Commission argued that Mr Cowan was not a French national, did not hold a residence permit and did not come from a country with whom France had concluded a reciprocal agreement for compensation. Mr Cowan relied upon the prohibition of discrimination contained in what is now Article 12 EC. The French courts referred the question of the applicability of the Treaty to the ECJ. The Court held that the principle of non-discrimination contained in Article 12 EC was given "concrete form" in specific situations envisaged by the Treaty, such as the provisions governing the free movement of workers, the right of establishment and the

---

[19] See *Kremzow* (n. 66, above), para. 16. Advocate General La Pergola found that fundamental rights only "came into play" with regard to provisions connected with Community law. See at 2635.

[20] See (n. 83, above) at 972 of the Advocate General's Opinion.

[21] To paraphrase Laws J.'s observations in *First City Trading* (n. 84, above) at 261 who stated that the "deep question" of the scope of application concerned "the depth of Community law's bite".

[22] See generally Marie Demetriou, "The Principle of Equality and the Scope of Community law", Conference Paper for the Bar European Group, May 2000, shortly to be published by Richard Hart.

[23] Case 186/87 *Cowan v. Trésor public* [1989] E.C.R. 195.

freedom to provide services.[24] The French Government had argued that as compensation fell within domestic criminal procedure, it did not fall within the scope of the Treaty. The Court rejected that argument and stated:

> "Although in principle criminal legislation and the rules of criminal procedure, among which the national provision in issue is to be found, are matters for which the Member States are responsible, the Court has consistently held . . . that Community law sets certain limits to their power. Such legislative provisions may not discriminate against persons to whom Community law gives the right to equal treatment or restrict the fundamental freedoms guaranteed by Community law."

In the *Phil Collins* case[25] the British singer and composer brought pro-   **6.107**
ceedings in Germany relating to the marketing of a compact disc of a recording of a concert given in Germany, made without his consent. The German Copyright Act 1965 protected German performers in that position, but did not protect foreign performers. There were no Community provisions harmonising national laws governing the protection of literary and artistic property. The ECJ was asked for guidance from the German courts as to the extent to which such legislation fell within the "scope of application of the Treaty", for the purposes of Article 12 EC (ex Article 6 of the E.C. Treaty). The ECJ was also asked to consider whether the general principle of non-discrimination applied to those rights. The ECJ found that copyright and related rights had particular effects on intra-Community trade in goods and services and on competitive relationships within the Community. They would therefore fall "within the scope of application of the Treaty", notwithstanding that they were governed by national legislation. The Court therefore found that such rights were necessarily subject to the general principle of non-discrimination as set out in Article 12 E.C.[26] This was the case without there even being any need to connect them with the specific provisions of the Treaty.[27]

A similar line was taken by the ECJ in *Schumacker*.[28] This was a case   **6.108**
concerning the impact of domestic income tax legislation on the free movement of workers. The Court held that although in the present state of Community law direct taxation did not fall within the purview of the Community, nonetheless the powers retained by the Community had to be exercised consistently with Community law. Similar statements have been made in relation to the domestic application of criminal law, an area where competence is again retained by the Member States themselves.[29]

---

[24] *ibid.*, para. 14.
[25] Joined Cases C–92/92 and C–326/92 *Phil Collins v. Imtrat Handelsgesellschaft mbH* [1993] E.C.R. I–5145.
[26] *ibid.*, para. 22.
[27] *ibid.*, para. 27. See also Case C–172/98 *Commission v. Belgium* [1999] E.C.R. I–3999, para. 12.
[28] Case C–279/93 *Finanzamt Koln- Allstadt v. Schumacker* [1995] E.C.R. I–225, paras 21–22. See also Case C–107/94 *Asscher v. Staatssecretaris van Financien* [1996] E.C.R. I–3089, where the ECJ reiterated that although direct taxation fell within the competence of the Member States, that competence had to be exercised so as to avoid discrimination on nationality grounds.
[29] In Case C–348/96 *Criminal Proceedings against Calfa* [1999] 2 C.M.L.R. 1138.

6.109   It might be argued that in both *Phil Collins* and *Schumacker*, the applicant had by his situation or conduct triggered the application of a directly effective principle of Community law.[30] In contrast, in cases such as *Kremzow* or *Annibaldi*, the Treaty freedoms were latent or "hypothetical" but had not been directly engaged. The effect of engaging a directly effective Treaty provision is to justify a domestic court's review (or the ECJ's review on a preliminary reference) of the contested decision, measure or conduct for compatibility with either Article 12 E.C. or the Community fundamental rights doctrine. There are considerable difficulties with such an argument. The first is the absence of any Treaty basis invoked by the Court in the *Phil Collins* case. The national provision there in issue appeared to involve one of the "rare occasions" when a specific provision of the Treaty did not apply. Nonetheless the ECJ held[31] that copyright was in principle subject to Treaty provisions on free movement of goods and services and the competition rules. The absence of anything more than a potential link did not prevent the application of Article 12 E.C. A further difficulty with such an approach is that it elevates principles developed by the ECJ to a comparable status with actual Treaty provisions.[32] Indeed, if *Phil Collins* were followed by analogy, fundamental rights might end up as a freestanding ground for review of a domestic measure, dispensing with the need for a Treaty "peg".

Content

6.110   The Community Treaties do not set out a code of rights that will be protected under Community law. The rights that are recognised therefore depend on the incremental development of the case law.[33] One difficult theoretical question has been whether it is sufficient for a right to be safeguarded by the constitution of any one of the Member States for it to qualify for protection as a fundamental right. This "maximalist" approach has been sanctioned by Advocate General Warner in *IRCA*,[34] and by various academic commentators.[35] The alternative, "minimalist" approach would see the ECJ protect only those core values recognised by each of the Member States.[36] The approach of the Court has been to cut a path

---

[30] Thus *Phil Collins* involved the cross-border trade in goods and services and *Schumacker* involved the free movement of workers. Contrast *Steen v. Deutsche Bundespost* (n. 64, above), where the applicant had not exercised his latent free movement rights.

[31] *ibid.*, paras 19 *et seq.* See also Case C–43/95 *Data Delecta and Forsberg* [1996] E.C.R. I–4661, para. 13. The ECJ examined domestic provisions relating to security for costs and nationality requirements for compatibility with Art. 12 E.C., without there being any need to connect the specific case to particular provisions of the Treaty.

[32] In *First City Trading* (n. 84, above) at 267, Laws J. stated: "it is to my mind by no means self-evident that the contextual scope [of Community fundamental rights] must be the same as that of Treaty provisions relating to discrimination or equal treatment, which are statute law taking effect according to their express terms."

[33] Or, as Professor Tridimas has put it, "the accidents of litigation." (n. 4, above), p. 209.

[34] Case 7/76 *IRCA v. Amministrazione delle Finanze dello Stato* [1976] E.C.R. 1213 at 1237.

[35] H. Schermers, "The European Community bound by Fundamental Human Rights" (1990) 27 C.M.L. Rev. 249.

[36] See J.H.H. Weiler, "Fundamental Rights and Fundamental Boundaries: On the conflict of standards and values in the protection of Human Rights in the European Legal Space" (n. 15, above).

between these two extremes.[37] It has decried the possibility of analysing Community law by reference to any given constitutional provision or indeed by sole reference to the Convention itself.[38] In ensuring that fundamental rights are treated as a uniquely Community concept, the ECJ has sought to avoid damage to the substantive unity and efficacy of Community law.[39]

As Community law need not coincide exactly with the law derived from the **6.111** Convention, it is unsurprising that certain discrepancies have arisen from time to time. While the Luxembourg and Strasbourg Courts do meet occasionally to discuss trends in their case law, there is no formal procedure for reference between them.[40] Clearly each Court strives to avoid inconsistency.[41]

Article 2 (Right to Life)

In *Commission v. Germany*[42] the ECJ reiterated that "the health and life of **6.112** humans rank foremost among the property or interests protected by Article 36 of the Treaty" (now Article 30 EC). Further, a justification for a derogation from a Treaty freedom could be based on the protection of public health and human life. Moreover, in *Grogan*[43] the ECJ recognised that the right to life enshrined in the Irish Constitution was a fundamental right which fell to be balanced against competing rights, such as freedom of expression.[44]

Article 3 (Protection from torture, etc.)

Some authors have suggested that *Adoui*[45] displays an example of the **6.113** ECJ considering the principles contained in Article 3 of the Convention.[46]

---

[37] See the Opinion of Advocate General Slynn in Case 155/79 *AM & S Europe Ltd v. Commission* [1982] E.C.R. 1575 at 1649, who cited with approval the extra-judicial view of Judge Kutscher that: "when the Court interprets or supplements Community law on a comparative basis it is not obliged to take the minimum which the national solutions have in common, or their arithmetic mean or the solution produced by a majority of the legal systems as the basis of its decision. The Court has to weigh up and evaluate the particular problem and search for the best and most appropriate solution."

[38] See paras. 6–23 *et seq.*, above.

[39] Case 44/79 *Liselotte Hauer v. Länd Rheinland-Pfalz* [1979] E.C.R. 3727, para. 14.

[40] Advocate General Warner in Case 130/75 *Prais v. Council* [1976] E.C.R. 1589, was of the view that some form of preliminary reference system either from the ECJ, or from national courts, to the European Court of Human Rights would be desirable.

[41] Concern about conflict between Strasbourg and the ECJ was also expressed by Advocate General Jacobs in Case C–168/91 *Konstantinidis v. Stadt Altensteig* [1993] E.C.R. I–1191 at 1213.

[42] Case C–62/90 *Commission v. Germany* [1992] E.C.R. 2575, para. 10.

[43] See n. 72, above.

[44] See also *R. v. Secretary of State for the Home Department, ex p. McQuillan* [1995] 4 All ER 400. The applicant was a former member of the Irish Republican Socialist Party. An exclusion order was made against him. He argued that his right to life would be infringed if he were prevented (by the exclusion order) from working and settling in the U.K. Sedley J. stayed the case pending the outcome of two existing references to the ECJ concerning the compatibility of an exclusion order with rights of free movement as an E.C. citizen. The existing reference in *ex p. Adams* was not eventually heard. See *R. v. Secretary of State for the Home Department, ex p. Adams* [1995] All E.R. (EC) 177, QBD and *ex p. Adams (No. 2)* [1995] C.O.D. 426, QBD.

[45] Joined Cases 115/81 and 166/81 *Rezguia Adoui and Dominique Cornuaille v. Belgian State* [1982] E.C.R. 1665.

[46] See R. Gordon q.c. and T. Ward, (n. 12, above), p. 229.

Ms Adoui and Ms Cornuaille were French nationals resident in Belgium who had submitted applications for residence permits. Their applications were rejected, and expulsion orders were made against them, on the basis that their personal conduct was undesirable in that they worked in a bar of dubious moral standing. Each of them challenged the decisions before the Belgian courts, which referred no fewer than 14 questions to the ECJ. The eighth question wondered whether an expulsion of a national of another Member State might, in certain circumstances, become so serious that it constituted inhuman treatment.[47] In both their written and oral submissions, the applicants referred to Article 3 of the Convention and its prohibition of cruel or inhuman treatment. The Belgian Government contended that the issue was of academic interest only, as the main proceedings concerned "a young person in good health who lives 'by her charms'".[48] The Court dealt with a number of the questions together. It held that expulsion of a national of another Member State could only be based on the existence of a genuine and sufficiently serious threat to one of the fundamental interests of society. Although no uniform scale of values was to be applied, conduct could not be considered to be a sufficiently serious threat if the expelling Member State did not adopt for its own nationals "repressive measures or other genuine and effective measures intended to combat such conduct".[49]

6.114 In contrast, Advocate General Capotorti dealt with the Article 3 point in terms. He found that the:

> "principle has nothing to do with measures restricting freedom of entry into and residence in a particular State. Even if, on occasion, measures of that kind may have serious consequences regarding the circumstances of the person to whom they are addressed, it would be an abuse of the language to say that those consequences are as serious as those of treatment, such as torture, which is not only injurious to the physical integrity and human dignity of the victims but, as far as those who engage in it are concerned, is also an inexcusable disgrace."[50]

6.115 The issue was raised before the English Divisional Court in *ex p. McQuillan*.[51] The applicant challenged an exclusion order made against him on the basis that, given evidence of a real and persistent threat by terrorism to his life, he would be at risk of cruel and inhuman treatment were he required to remain in Northern Ireland. Sedley J. accepted that: "through the jurisprudence of the Court of Justice, the principles, though not the text, of the Convention now inform the law of the European Union."[52] His Lordship also accepted that, on the basis of the applicant's evidence before him, the further consequence of the exclusion order would be to

---

[47] *ibid.*, at 1672–1673. The national court thought this might be the case where the expelled person was a father or mother of a large family, a spouse or parent, minor or a person who risked (on the grounds of age or ill-health) failing to re-adjust to life in another country.
[48] *ibid.*, at 1684.
[49] *ibid.*, paras. 8, 9.
[50] *ibid.*, at 1721.
[51] See n. 44, above.
[52] *ibid.*, at 422.

subject him to the "inhuman treatment of being for all practical purposes confined to the one part of the United Kingdom where his life and his family's safety are most at risk".[53] He considered that it might eventually have to be decided whether a derogation by the United Kingdom from a Community right of free movement (as a result of European citizenship) could bring the Convention principles into play. A potential reference was nonetheless stayed pending the outcome of a reference made in a related case.[54]

This is an area that is likely to receive more attention from the ECJ now   **6.116** that asylum and immigration are matters that (for the majority of the Member States) have been brought within the justiciable scope of Community law under Title IV of the E.C. Treaty (Articles 61 to 69 EC).[55] Further, where proceedings concern extradition between two Member States,[56] it seems likely that principles derived from cases such as *Soering*[57] can theoretically have effect through Community law. The scope for their application may be limited in practice.

Article 5 (Right to liberty/security)

This principle was implicitly recognised as a fundamental right for the   **6.117** purposes of Community law in *Kremzow*.[58] The facts of the case have been set out above.[59] The ECJ accepted that any deprivation of liberty might impede the person concerned from exercising a right to free movement, but declined jurisdiction to examine the matter because there was an insufficient connection with Community law on the facts of the particular case.

Article 6 (Right to a fair hearing)

There have been numerous examples of the Community courts accepting   **6.118** that fundamental rights incorporate protections akin to those found in Article 6 of the Convention. Community law has developed a number of principles of administrative fairness founded on the "rights of the

---

[53] *ibid.*, at 423.

[54] *Ex p. Adams* (n. 44, above).

[55] By Art. 69 EC, the provisions of Title IV are subject to the Protocol on the position of the United Kingdom and Ireland. Two separate Protocols retain the United Kingdom's right to exercise immigration control and provide an optional "opt in" to measures otherwise adopted (without its participation) under Title IV.

[56] Community law does not govern extradition of an individual from a Member State to a non-Member State. A Council Act of March 10, 1995 drew up a Convention on simplified extradition procedure between the Member States of the European Union: see [1995] O.J. C78/1. The preamble notes that the European Convention on Extradition 1990 remains applicable for all matters not covered by the Convention. The European Convention on Extradition, established under the auspices of the Council of Europe, is not an instrument of Community law. A Convention relating to extradition between Member States of the European Union has been drawn up: [1996] O.J. C313/11. It goes further than the simplified procedure Convention. There is an explanatory report at [1997] O.J. C191/13.

[57] *Soering v. United Kingdom* (A/161) (1989) 11 E.H.R.R. 439, ECHR. See also *Cruz Varas v. Sweden* (A/201) (1992) 14 E.H.R.R. 000, ECHR; *Vilvarajah v. United Kingdom* (A/215) (1992) 14 E.H.R.R. 248, ECHR; *Chahal v. United Kingdom* (1997) 23 E.H.R.R. 413, ECHR; *Ahmed v. Austria* (1997) 24 E.H.R.R. 278, ECHR.

[58] See n. 66, above.

[59] See para. 6–79, above.

defence".[60] The rights of the defence must be respected, not only in proceedings before the courts, but also in preliminary inquiry procedures and investigations by the Commission.[61] Article 6 of the Convention was expressly recognised as guiding the content of fundamental rights in *Johnston v. RUC*.[62] There the ECJ held that the requirement of effective judicial control has long been acknowledged to be a general principle of law, underlying the constitutional traditions common to the Member States. A certificate signed by the Secretary of State could not constitute conclusive evidence of an act having been done for the purpose of safeguarding national security. It was also referred to in *UNECTEF v. Heylens*[63] in support of a Community principle that individual effective protection had to be afforded to any fundamental right conferred by the Treaty. The ECJ has also expressly stated that a right to a fair hearing is a fundamental right of Community law. It follows that close attention should be paid to procedural guarantees designed to protect the individual.[64] It will be recalled that the ECJ was prepared to assess the compatibility of its own procedures with Article 6 in the *Emesa Sugar* case.[65]

6.119   The ECJ recognised from an early date the right for an individual to be heard in matters affecting his interests.[66] This includes a requirement that an individual is afforded the opportunity during an administrative procedure of making known his views on the truth and relevance of the facts, charges and circumstances relied upon by the Community decision maker. He must be given an opportunity to make his views known on documents used by the decision maker in support of any decision made.[67] Further, the ECJ in *Adoui*[68] recognised the right to an independent tribunal and in *Van der Wal*[69] it found that the principle of procedural autonomy of national courts was in part derived from Article 6(1) of the Convention. The

---

[60] In Case 322/81 *Michelin v. Commission* [1983] E.C.R. 3461, para. 7, *e.g.*, the ECJ stated that: "the necessity to have regard to the rights of the defence is a fundamental principle of Community law which the Commission must observe in administrative procedures which may lead to the imposition of penalties under the rules of competition laid down in the Treaty. Its observance requires *inter alia* that the undertaking concerned must have been enabled to express its views effectively on the documents used by the Commission to support its allegation of an infringement." See also Case C–315/99P *Ismeri Europa Srl v. Court of Auditors*, judgment of the ECJ dated July 10, 2001 at para. 28.

[61] Joined Cases 46/87 and 227/88 *Hoechst* (n. 55, above) paras 12, 13

[62] Case 222/84 *Johnston v. Chief Constable of the Royal Ulster Constabulary* [1986] E.C.R. 1651, para. 18.

[63] Case 222/86 *UNECTEF v. Heylens* [1987] E.C.R. 4097, para. 14.

[64] Case C–49/88 *Al-Jubail Fertilizer Co. (SAMAD) v. Council* [1991] E.C.R. I–3187, paras 15, 16.

[65] See n. 57, and para. 6.74 above.

[66] A right to a hearing was first confirmed in relation to disciplinary proceedings against officials. See Case 32/62 *Alvis v. Council* [1963] ECR 49 at 55. See also the Opinion of Advocate-General Warner in Case 136/79 *National Panasonic v. Commission* [1980] E.C.R. 2033 at 2068; and, more recently, the judgment of the CFI in Joined Cases T–33/98 and T–34/98 *Petrotub SA and Republica SA v. Council* [1999] E.C.R. II–3837 especially para. 185.

[67] Case 85/76 *Hoffmann-La Roche AG v. Commission* [1979] E.C.R. 461, para. 11, ECJ; Case T–65/96 *Kish Glass & Co. Ltd v. Commission* [2000] E.C.R. II–1885. The right to be physically present before a disciplinary board and to hear and cross-examine witnesses was recognised in Case 141/84 *De Compte v. European Parliament* [1985] E.C.R. 1951, para. 17.

[68] See (n. 45, above), para. 16.

[69] Joined Cases C–174/98P and C–189/98P *Netherlands and Van der Wal v. Commission* [2000] E.C.R. I–0001.

requirement to ensure "equality of arms" has been used to justify disclosure of documents from the Commission in a number of competition cases.[70]

Nonetheless, the rights protected by the Convention and E.C. fundamental rights are not coterminous. The ECJ in *Orkem*[71] and *Solvay*[72] examined whether, in the absence of a right to silence embodied in Regulation 17/62, the general principles of Community law recognised a right of a person not to supply information capable of being used to establish an infringement of the competition rules against him. The ECJ observed that the domestic laws of Member States in general granted such a right only to natural persons charged with criminal proceedings. In general, no similar right was accorded to legal persons in relation to infringements in the economic sphere, especially infringements of competition law. The Court therefore concluded that[73]:   **6.120**

> "As far as Article 6 of the European Convention is concerned, although it may be relied upon by an undertaking subject to an investigation relating to competition law, it must be observed that neither the wording of that article nor the decisions of the European Court of Human Rights indicate that it upholds the right not to give evidence against oneself."

The Court also took into account Article 14 of the International Covenant on Civil and Political Rights of December 19, 1966,[74] which upholds the presumption of innocence and the privilege against self-incrimination. The Article was not followed, however, on the grounds that the presumption of innocence of an accused in criminal proceedings had "no bearing on investigations in the field of competition law".[75] Nonetheless, recognition of certain rights of the defence meant that the Commission could not compel an undertaking to provide the Commission with answers which might involve an admission of an infringement which it was incumbent on the Commission to prove.[76]   **6.121**

Subsequently, in various cases before the European Court of Human Rights the privilege against self-incrimination has been accepted to be an   **6.122**

---

[70] Case 51/69 *Bayer v. Commission* [1972] E.C.R. 745, para. 7; Cases 100–103/80 *Musique Diffusion Française v. Commission* [1983] E.C.R. 1825, para. 14; Case T–30/91 *Solvay SA v. Commission* [1995] E.C.R. II–1775, para. 57; Case T–36/91 *ICI plc v. Commission* [1995] E.C.R. II–1825, para. 93.

[71] Case 374/87 *Orkem v. Commission* [1989] E.C.R. 3283, paras 28, 29.

[72] Case 27/88 *Solvay & Cie v. Commission* [1989] E.C.R. 3355. The grounds of the judgment do not differ from the judgment in *Orkem* and were not separately set out in the Report.

[73] *ibid.*, para. 30.

[74] *United Nations Treaty Series*, vol. 999, p. 171.

[75] *Orkem* judgment (n. 71, above), para. 31.

[76] *ibid.*, para. 34. See also Joined Cases T–305–307, 313–16, 318, 325, 328–329 and 335/94 *Re the PVC Cartel No. II* [1999] E.C.R. II–0931, paras. 444, 445, CFI. The Court of First Instance was, however, anxious to prevent rights of the defence being "irremediably impaired during preliminary inquiry procedures" which may be decisive in providing evidence of unlawful conduct. An absolute right to silence would go beyond what was necessary to preserve the rights of the defence. It would constitute an unjustified hindrance to the Commission's task of ensuring compliance with the competition rules.

incident of Article 6 protection. Thus in *Funke v. France*,[77] the Court of Human Rights concluded that the applicant's conviction for failure to provide documents had been obtained by French customs authorities in an attempt to compel him to provide evidence of other offences he had allegedly committed. His conviction was an infringement of his right to stay silent and not to incriminate himself, which was a right protected by Article 6(1) of the Convention. It follows that at present there is a divergence between the E.C. and Strasbourg case law on the issue of the privilege against self-incrimination. The Strasbourg authority of *Ozturk*[78] was cited in *Orkem*, but was not explicitly followed. This seems to have been because it was not considered that the Convention did expressly confer a privilege against self-incrimination. The ECJ found no authority of the European Court of Human Rights which construed Article 6 to confer such a right. The Advocate General in *Orkem* also cited the European Commission of Human Right's reaction to *Funke*, but it was clearly not yet subject to a determination by the European Court of Human Rights itself.[79]

6.123 When the CFI was faced with the potential conflict between the two lines of case law in the *PVC Cartel No. II* case,[80] it declined to depart from the ECJ's case law on the subject. Nonetheless, when the ECJ recently re-examined a related issue in *Baustahlgewebe*,[81] there were signs in the Advocate General's Opinion that the Court might be prepared to reconsider this issue in the light of the developments in the Strasbourg jurisprudence.

6.124 In other areas, conversely, E.C. fundamental rights confer more protection on individuals than would be available under the Convention. In *Hoechst*,[82] the ECJ held that the investigative powers of the Commission in competition cases: "cannot be interpreted in such a way as to give rise to results which are incompatible with the general principles of Community law and in particular with fundamental rights." Thus fundamental rights are respected before the matter has even come before a court. The Commission must operate procedures which are Article 6 compliant even though it is well established that it is not a court or tribunal for the purposes of that Article.[83]

6.125 Notwithstanding the judgment of the ECJ in *Orkem*, it seems probable that the terms of Article 6(2) and (3) will in future be applicable to competition proceedings brought by the Commission. The Commission has now acknowledged that such proceedings are equivalent to a criminal cause or matter for the purposes of Article 6. One of the Advocates General[84] has

---

[77] *Funke v. France*, A Series 256–A; (1993) 16 E.H.R.R. 297. See also *Saunders v. United Kingdom* (1997) 23 E.H.R.R. 313, ECHR; *Murray v. United Kingdom (Right to Silence)* (1996) 22 E.H.R.R. 29, ECHR; *Serves v. France* (1999) 28 E.H.R.R. 265, ECHR.

[78] *Ozturk v. Germany* (Series A/73) (1984) 6 E.H.R.R. 409, ECHR.

[79] See (n. 71, above), para. 133 of the Opinion.

[80] See (n. 76, above), paras 429, 444–447.

[81] See (n. 24, above and para. 6.60), paras. 29–36, *per* Advocate General Léger.

[82] See (n. 55, above), paras 12, 13.

[83] Joined Cases 209–215 and 218/78 *Heintz Van Landewyck Sarl and Fédération Belgo-Luxembourgeoise Des Industries du Tabac Asbl (FEDETAB) v. Commission* [1980] E.C.R. 3125; Case 100/80 *Musique Diffusion Française SA v. Commission* [1983] E.C.R. 1825.

[84] Case C–185/95P, *Baustahlgewebe GmbH v. Commission* (n. 24, above), para. 31, *per* Advocate General Léger, who noted that it could not be disputed "and the Commission does not dispute" that Art. 6(2) may be invoked.

stated that it cannot be disputed that proceedings brought by the Commission for infringements of E.C. competition law and the imposition of fines are matters involving a "criminal charge" for the purposes of Article 6(2) of the Convention.[85] The case for re-considering the Community's position on self-incrimination and the right to silence may therefore need to be re-visited.

Article 7 (non-retroactivity)

The ECJ recognised this principle in *Kirk*.[86] Captain Kirk, the master of a **6.126** Danish fishing vessel, was prosecuted by the British authorities for unlawfully fishing within British coastal waters. He appealed against his conviction on the basis that the Sea Fish (Specified United Kingdom Waters) (Prohibition of Fishing) Order 1982 was contrary to a general principle of non-discrimination found in Community law. The Commission contended that such measures were authorised, retrospectively, by a Community Regulation promulgated in 1983. The ECJ held that the principle that penal provisions could not have retrospective effect was common to all the legal orders of the Member States and was enshrined in Article 7 of the Convention. It therefore constituted a general principle of law protected by the Court.[87] The 1983 Regulation could not therefore be used to validate domestic measures which were otherwise invalid.

A similar, and related, principle is derived from the case of *Pretore di Salò* **6.127** case.[88] A Directive cannot, of itself and independently of a national law adopted by a Member State for its implementation, have the effect of determining or aggravating the liability in criminal law of persons who act in contravention of the provisions of a Directive.

Article 8 (Right to family life)

The Court made its first (oblique) reference to the inviolability of private **6.128** premises in *Acciaieria di Brescia v. High Authority*.[89] The case concerned an Italian company with an iron and steel division and an engineering division. The High Authority carried out an inspection in which it required various documents to be disclosed to it. The company refused to show accounts relating to the engineering division, on the basis that it fell outwith the remit of the High Authority under the Coal and Steel Treaty. Article 86 of that Treaty gave officials such rights and powers as were granted by the laws of a Member State to its own revenue officials. The Court held that the effect of this provision was only to make available to the High Authority the compulsory powers afforded by national revenue laws

---

[85] He relied in part on the Opinion of the European Commission of Human Rights in *Société Stenuit v. France* (1992) 14 E.H.R.R. 509. The Commission found that fines imposed for infringements of French competition law would constitute a criminal charge for the purposes of the Convention. The Court did not rule on the issue, because the applicant withdrew its application.
[86] Case 63/83 *Kirk* [1984] E.C.R. 2689, para. 22.
[87] See to the same effect Case C–331/88 *R. v. MAFF, ex p. FEDESA* [1991] E.C.R. I–4023, para. 42.
[88] Case 14/86 *Pretore di Salò v. Persons Unknown* [1987] E.C.R. 2545.
[89] Case 31/59 *Acciaieria di Brescia v. High Authority* [1960] E.C.R. 71.

for the direct and compulsory execution by its own officials of inspections "capable of affecting the area of individual liberty and of departing from the principle of the inviolability of private premises".

6.129   In *National Panasonic*,[90] Advocate General Warner referred to the *Brescia* case and concluded that the right to privacy had to extend to business premises, whether those of a company or of an individual. The reason was that a public authority could not, in a democratic society, be permitted to invade private property save under a specific power conferred by law. The Court in *National Panasonic* recognised that the application of Article 8, in so far as it applied to legal persons, would be subject to the proviso that interference with those rights might be necessary in a democratic society in the interests of national security, public safety or for the economic well-being of the country, for the prevention of disorder or crime, for the protection of health and morals, or for the protection of the rights and freedom of others.[91] The ECJ held, on the facts of the case, that the ability of the E.C. Commission to carry out competition investigations without prior notification did not infringe the rights of the applicant company.[92]

6.130   Nonetheless, in *Hoechst*,[93] the Court retreated somewhat from this position. It held that while the existence of a fundamental right to the inviolability of the home was recognised in Member States in respect of the private dwellings of natural persons, the same could not be said for the business premises of undertakings. This was because there were considerable divergences between the legal systems of the Member States with regard to the nature and degree of protection afforded to business premises. The Court further noted that Article 8 of the Convention was concerned with the development of "man's personal freedom". It could not be extended to business premises. The Court noted that there was no case law from Strasbourg on the issue. The ECJ did, however, accept that it was a general principle of Community law that undertakings would be protected against arbitrary or disproportionate intervention.[94]

6.131   This finding puts Community law somewhat at odds with that under the Convention. In *Niemietz v. Germany*[95] the Court of Human Rights was asked to rule on the compatibility with the Convention of a search of premises carried out by German police. The premises searched were the offices of Mr Niemietz, a lawyer, and the search was conducted pursuant to a search warrant granted by a court. The warrant had been obtained in an effort to disclose the identity and possible whereabouts of a third party, who was the subject of a criminal investigation. The applicant argued that the search had infringed his right to respect for his private life, home and correspondence and thus infringed Article 8. The Court found that the infringement was made out. It considered that certain professional or

---

[90] Case 136/79 *National Panasonic v. Commission* [1980] E.C.R. 2033 at 2068.
[91] *ibid.*, paras 17, 18.
[92] See also Case 5/85 *AKZO Chemie BV v. Commission* [1986] E.C.R. 2585, paras 25, 27.
[93] See (n. 55, above), paras 18, 19.
[94] *ibid* at para. 19.
[95] *Niemitz v. Germany* (A/251B) (1993) 16 E.H.R.R. 97, ECHR. See also *Rotaru v. Romania* (2000) 8 B.H.R.C. 449, ECHR.

business activities or premises would fall within the ambit of "private life" and "home".

In *The PVC Cartel No. II* case,[96] the applicants challenged the validity of the ECJ's judgment in *Hoechst* on the basis that it had been overtaken by the judgment of the European Court of Human Rights in *Niemietz*. The CFI saw no reason to depart from the existing ECJ case law. At paragraph 420 of its judgment, the CFI stated that the case law of the ECJ: **6.132**

> "is, moreover, based on the existence of a general principle of Community law, as referred to above, which applies to legal persons. The fact that the case law of the European Court of Human Rights concerning the applicability of Article 8 [of the Convention] to legal persons has evolved since *Hoechst*, *Dow Benelux* and *Dow Chemical Iberica* therefore has no direct impact on the merits of the solutions adopted in those cases."

In short, the discrepancy between Strasbourg and Luxembourg on this issue remains.

The Community courts have also examined Article 8 from other perspectives. In *X v. Commission*[97] the applicant had applied for a job with the Commission. He was required to undergo a medical examination, but refused to be tested for HIV. The medical officer nonetheless conducted other blood tests (on lymphocyte counts), which revealed that the applicant had full-blown AIDS. His application for employment was therefore rejected. The applicant sought annulment of that decision before the ECJ on the basis that his right to privacy, enshrined in Article 8 of the Convention, had been infringed. The ECJ accepted that Community institutions could not be obliged to take the risk of recruiting a job applicant who, after being properly informed, withheld his consent to a test which the medical officer considered necessary in order to determine his suitability for the post for which he had applied. It was accepted that a pre-recruitment medical examination would serve a legitimate interest. However, that interest did not justify carrying out a test against the will of the person concerned. Since X had expressly refused to undergo an HIV screening test, the right to private life under Article 8 of the Convention precluded the administration from carrying out any test liable to point to, or establish, the existence of that virus or the AIDS illness. The right to respect for private life required a person's refusal to undergo medical tests to be respected in its entirety.[98]   **6.133**

In *Konstantinidis*,[99] Advocate General Jacobs was prepared to adopt a broad interpretation of Article 8 so as to encompass the right of an individual to oppose unjustified interference with his name. The right to respect for private life has been invoked to justify the requirement to protect patient confidentiality for doctors or pharmacists.[1] The right to   **6.134**

---

[96] *supra* note 76 at paras. 398, 419 and 420.
[97] Case C–404/92P *X v. Commission* [1994] E.C.R. I–4737, para. 17.
[98] *ibid.*, at paras 20–23.
[99] Case C–168/91 *Konstantinidis v. Stadt Altensteig* [1993] E.C.R. I–1191.
[1] Case C–62/90 *Commission v. Germany* [1992] E.C.R. I–2575, para. 23.

respect for family life has also been seen to be a feature of Community law derived from Article 8.[2]

Article 9 (Freedom of thought, conscience and religion)

6.135   In *Prais*,[3] the applicant relied on Article 9(2) of the Convention in support of her challenge to the refusal by the Council to allow her to sit an examination on a day which was not within the Jewish feast of Shavuot. The ECJ rather elliptically noted that the Council "did not seek to suggest that the right of freedom of religion as embodied in the European Convention does not form part of the fundamental rights recognised in Community law."

6.136   There was a further reference to Article 9 in *Rutili*.[4] Mr Rutili was an Italian national married to a French national who, until 1968, had been the holder of a French residence permit. Seemingly as a result of his participation in various trade union activities, the French authorities thereafter sought to impose upon him requirements as to where he could live within metropolitan France. The ECJ referred to Community secondary legislation by which the entry and residence of nationals of other Member States might be controlled. It held that the limitations imposed on Member States with regard to the control of aliens were but a specific manifestation of the more general principle enshrined, *inter alia*, in Article 9 of the Convention. No restrictions in the interests of national security or public safety could be placed on the rights of free movement other than such as were necessary for the protection of those interests in a democratic society.[5]

Article 10 (Freedom of expression)

6.137   Freedom of expression, as guaranteed by Article 10 of the Convention, has been acknowledged to be a specific manifestation in Community law of a more general principle which must be respected by Community institutions. The general principle of freedom of expression has been said to be embodied in Article 10 of the Convention.[6] Specific examples of the protection of freedom of expression may be found in the Community case law. The Community is prepared to safeguard the maintenance of pluralism as a cultural policy, it being connected with freedom of expression protected under Article 10 of the Convention.[7] The case of *Commission v. Netherlands*[8] concerned an action brought by the Commission against the Netherlands under Article 226 EC (ex Article 169 of the E.C. Treaty) for a failure to fulfil its obligations under the Treaty. Specifically, the Commission challenged the compatibility with the Treaty of Dutch legislation that

---

[2] Case 236/87 *Bergemann v. Bundesanstalt fur Arbeit* [1988] E.C.R. 5125 at 5137, *per* Advocate General Lenz, and, more recently, the judgment of the ECJ in Joined Cases C–122/99 and C–125/99P *D and Kingdom of Sweden v. European Council* [i], judgment of May 31, 2001 (n.y.r.).
[3] Case 130/75 *Prais v. Council* [1976] E.C.R. 1589, para. 8.
[4] Case 36/75 *Rutili v. Minister for the Interior* [1975] E.C.R. 1219, para. 32.
[5] *ibid.*, para. 32.
[6] Case C–260/89 *ERT* [1991] E.C.R. I–2925, para. 45 of the judgment and at 2948 of the Opinion of Advocate General Lenz.
[7] See Case C–288/89 *Stichting Collectieve Antennevoorziening Gouda v. Commissariaat voor de Media* [1991] E.C.R. I–4007, para. 23.
[8] Case C–353/89 *Commission v. Netherlands* [1991] E.C.R. I–4069, para. 30.

restricted certain television programmes and advertising from other Member States. The domestic legislation was reviewed under the Treaty provisions on the freedom to provide services. The Netherlands sought to justify its domestic law by reference to its interest in maintaining a pluralist and non-commercial television network. The ECJ held that a cultural policy of maintaining pluralism could constitute an overriding requirement relating to general interest which would justify a restriction on the freedom to provide services. Nonetheless, the Netherlands legislation went beyond the objective pursued, namely freedom of expression.[9]

The Court has also been willing to accept that commercial advertising **6.138** comes within the scope of Article 10 of the Convention.[10] Indeed, Advocate General Jacobs in the *Gourmet International* case[11] accepted that any encroachment on the advertiser's freedom would fall to be justified under Article 10(2) only on grounds analogous to those provided for under Article 46 EC (ex Article 56 of the E.C. Treaty).

Nonetheless, in this field too, certain discrepancies have emerged **6.139** between the Luxembourg and Strasbourg case law. The European Court of Human Rights was asked to rule on the compatibility of the Irish ban on dissemination of information about abortion clinics in the United Kingdom in *Open Door Counselling Ltd and Dublin Well Woman Centre v. Ireland.*[12] The facts were that a complaint was made by the Society for the Protection of the Unborn Child to the Irish authorities about counselling services that advised on the availability of abortion in the United Kingdom. Acting on that complaint, the Irish Attorney General applied for an injunction to prevent two counselling organisations from assisting clients to have abortions in England. The injunction was sought on the basis that the organisations' conduct infringed the Irish Constitution, which protects the unborn child's right to life. The counsellors challenged the injunction in so far as it specifically prevented them from giving information that might help clients contact abortion clinics. The Strasbourg Court found that the injunction infringed the organisations' rights under Article 10 of the Convention. It was accepted that because the constitutional protection reflected majority opinion about abortion, the legal basis of the injunctions was the protection of morals. Nonetheless, although states had a wide discretion in this area, they could not necessarily take any actions they saw fit. The right to freedom of expression included the right to disseminate information that offended the majority of the population. The ban was too general, allowing as it did for no exception.

In contrast, in *Grogan,*[13] the ECJ itself declined to consider the arguments **6.140** on Article 10 of the Convention on the basis that as Article 59 of the E.C. Treaty (now Article 49 EC) did not apply, the Court had no jurisdiction to consider the application of Community fundamental rights. Advocate General Van Gerven reached a different conclusion on the applicability of the freedom to provide services. He therefore carried out an appraisal of the

---

[9] *ibid.*, para. 31.
[10] See Case C–405/98 *Konsumentombudsmannen v. Gourmet International Products Aktiebolag*, para. 74, Opinion of Advocate General Jacobs of December 14, 2000 (n.y.r.).
[11] *ibid.*, paras 73, 74.
[12] *Open Door Counselling Ltd and Dublin Well Woman Centre v. Ireland* (1993) 15 E.H.R.R. 244, ECHR.
[13] See n. 72, above.

national rules in the light of Community fundamental rights.[14] He considered that such an appraisal required a balancing of the right to life and the freedom of expression. He recognised that the rules at issue infringed Article 10(1) and therefore examined whether they could fall within Article 10(2), as necessary in a democratic society for the protection of health, morals or the rights of others. He acknowledged that the European Commission of Human Rights had by then indicated that Article 10(2) could not be relied upon prior to the judgment of the Supreme Court, as the prohibition had not been sufficiently "prescribed by law". Nonetheless, such a conclusion had been overtaken by the fact that the judgment of the Supreme Court itself constituted a sufficient statement of legal principle. The Advocate General allowed the Member State a "fairly considerable margin of discretion", as the issue concerned an ethical value judgment. Applying this margin, and in the absence of a uniform European conception of morals, he concluded that a Member State was entitled to maintain the general prohibition in question.[15]

Article 11 (Freedom of assembly/association)

6.141   This principle was also recognised by the ECJ in *Rutili*.[16] In *Bosman*,[17] the applicant raised a challenge before his domestic courts to the transfer rules and nationality clauses prevalent under the various football associations in the Member States. He argued that they had restricted his right to free movement as a worker within the Community. The various Associations sought to justify the transfer system by reference, *inter alia*, to the freedom of assembly protected under Article 11. The ECJ accepted that:

> "[I]t must be recognised that this principle, enshrined in Article 11 of the [Convention] and resulting from the constitutional traditions common to the Member States, is one of the fundamental rights which, as the Court has consistently held and as is reaffirmed in the preamble to the Single European Act and in Article F(2) of the Treaty on European Union, are protected in the Community legal order."

The ECJ nonetheless held that the rules laid down by sporting associations could not be seen as necessary to ensure enjoyment of that freedom by the football associations, by the clubs or by the players.

Article 12 (Right to marry)

6.142   Advocate General Lenz considered the scope of Article 12 of the Convention in the *Bergemann* case.[18] The preliminary reference to the ECJ concerned the rejection by the German authorities of Mrs Bergemann's

---

[14] *ibid.*, at 4724–4730 of the Opinion.
[15] *ibid.*, at 4729.
[16] See (n 4. above) para. 32. See also the Opinion of Advocate General Capotorti in *Adoui* (n. 45, above) at 1718.
[17] Case C–415/93 *Union Royale Belge des Sociétés de Football Association ASBL v. Jean-Marc Bosman* [1995] E.C.R. I–4921, para. 79.
[18] Case 236/87 *Bergemann v. Bundesanstalt fur Arbeit* [1988] E.C.R. 5125, para. 27, of the Advocate General's Opinion.

claim for unemployment benefit. Mrs Bergemann had been employed in the Netherlands and was a Netherlands national. She married her German husband and they lived together after that in Germany. She did not return to her job in the Netherlands. The German authorities refused her claim for unemployment benefit on the basis that she was not a frontier worker. The ECJ, while recognising the legitimacy of a worker transferring her residence for family reasons, did not expressly rule on the applicability of Article 12.[19] It was, however, cited by the Advocate General. He noted that Article 12 of the Convention laid down the right to marry and to found a family. That right also included respect for the unity of the family and life together.[20]

The Court has also examined a claim for discrimination on the basis of sexual orientation by reference to Article 12 of the Convention. The ECJ has taken note of the fact that the European Court of Human Rights has construed Article 12 as only applying to the traditional marriage between two persons of opposite biological sex.[21] It concluded that in the present state of law in the Community: "stable relationships between two persons of the same sex are not regarded as equivalent to marriages or stable relations outside marriage between persons of the opposite sex." It followed that an employer was not required by Community law to treat a person in a stable relationship with a partner of the same sex in the same manner as a married person.   **6.143**

Article 13 (Right to an effective remedy)

Community law has also adopted the right to an effective remedy as a fundamental principle. In *UNECTEF v. Heylens*[22] the ECJ held that effective judicial review required that a court should be able to examine the legality of reasons given by an authority whose decision was being or might be challenged. Individual effective protection of Community rights conferred on individuals by the Treaty entailed the existence of a remedy of a judicial nature against any decision of an authority refusing the benefit of that right.   **6.144**

There is now a long line of case law that mandates effective protection for rights conferred on individuals by Community law. The cases of *Comet*[23] and *Rewe*,[24] explain that the principle flows from Article 5 of the Treaty of Rome (now, Article 10 EC). The duty of co-operation in Article 10 EC means that it is "the national courts which are entrusted with ensuring the legal protection which citizens derive from the direct effect of the provisions of Community law".[25] Thus in the absence of Community rules or   **6.145**

---

[19] *ibid.*, para. 21.
[20] *ibid.*, at 5137, para. 27.
[21] Case C–249/96 *Grant v. South West Trains Ltd* [1998] E.C.R. I–621, paras 34, 35. See also Joined Cases C–122/99P and C–125/99P *D and the Kingdom of Sweden v. European Council* [i], judgment of the ECJ dated May 31, 2001 (n.y.r.).
[22] Case 222/86 *UNECTEF v. Heylens* [1987] E.C.R. 4097, paras 14, 15.
[23] Case 45/76 *Comet v. Produktschap voor Siergewassen* [1976] E.C.R. 2043.
[24] Case 33/76 *Rewe-Zentralfinanz eG and Rewe-Zentral AG v. Landwirtschaftskammer für das Saarland* [1976] E.C.R. 1989.
[25] See *Rewe*, para. 5.

harmonisation on the subject, it is for the national legal systems of Member States to ensure the implementation and enforcement of rights generated at a Community level. Any claim to protect a right provided by Community law must: "be sought only within the framework of the conditions as to both substance and form laid down by the various national laws applicable thereto."[26] Any conditions imposed by national law (as to that protection of Community rights) cannot be less favourable than those relating to similar actions of a domestic nature (the principle of non-discrimination). In addition, under no circumstances may they be so adapted as to make it impossible in practice to exercise the rights which the national courts are bound to protect (the principle of effectiveness).

6.146   Moreover, the ECJ in *Factortame*[27] held that:

> "any provision of a national legal system . . . which might impair the effectiveness of Community law by withholding from the national court having jurisdiction to apply such law the power to do everything necessary at the moment of its application to set aside national legislative provisions which might prevent, even temporarily, Community rules from having full force and effect are incompatible with those requirements, which are the very essence of Community law."

In *Francovich*,[28] the ECJ restated that "the national courts whose task it is to apply the provisions of Community law in cases within their jurisdiction must ensure that those rules have full effect and protect the rights which they confer on individuals". Community law creates rights as well as obligations which form part of individuals' legal patrimony. More radically, the Court also found that:

> " . . . the full effectiveness of Community rules would be impaired and the protection of the rights which they grant would be weakened if individuals were unable to obtain redress when their rights are infringed by a breach of Community law for which a Member State is responsible."

The Court deemed that a right to compensation arose directly from Community law. National courts in safeguarding Community rights had an obligation to make reparation available.[29]

Article 14 (non-discrimination)

6.147   The principle of non-discrimination on grounds of nationality is actually protected within the Treaty itself, under Article 12 E.C. It provides that:

---

[26] Case 199/82 *Amministrazione delle Finanze dello Stato v. SpA San Giorgio* [1983] E.C.R. 3595, para. 12.
[27] Case C–213/89 *R. v. Secretary of State for Transport, ex p. Factortame Ltd (No. 2)* [1990] E.C.R. I–2433, para. 20.
[28] Case C–6 and 9/90 *Francovich and Bonafaci v. Italy* [1991] E.C.R. I–5357, paras 32–35.
[29] *ibid.*, para. 42. Since *Francovich* a number of cases have re-affirmed the Community right to an effective remedy. The most instructive is probably Case C–46/93 *Brasserie du Pecheur SA v. Germany* joined with Case C–48/93 *R. v. Secretary of State for Transport, ex p. Factortame Ltd (No.4)*. Both judgments are reported in [1996] Q.B. 404, ECJ.

"within the scope of application of this Treaty, and without prejudice to any special provisions contained therein, any discrimination on grounds of nationality shall be prohibited." Examples of the application of Article 12 E.C. have been set out above in paragraphs 6–105 *et seq.*

The ECJ has also found that the elimination of discrimination based on sex **6.148** forms part of the fundamental rights recognised in the Community.[30] The prohibition of discrimination is a specific expression of the general principle of equality, which itself is one of the fundamental principles of Community law.[31] The principle requires that comparable situations are not treated in a different manner unless the difference in treatment is objectively justified.[32] Equal treatment of men and women constitutes a fundamental right recognised by the Community legal order.[33] Discrimination against transsexuals is discrimination on the grounds of sex and is not permitted,[34] but there is (at present) no prohibition of discrimination on the grounds of sexual orientation.[35] Positive discrimination may be contrary to the Treaty, except where two candidates for a post are of equal merit and there is no other manner of distinguishing between them or where women were under-represented and positive discrimination was a way of removing the imbalance.[36] The ECJ has held that it is important to ensure that all candidates, irrespective of sex, were subject to an objective assessment taking account of all personal qualities and strengths.

Article 1 of Protocol 1 (Right to property)

In *Hauer*[37] Mrs Hauer applied for authorisation under German law to plant **6.149** new grape vines on her land. Her application was refused on the grounds that her land was not suitable for wine growing. She appealed against that refusal. Her appeal was refused partially on the basis that, in the meantime, the Community had adopted a Regulation which prohibited all new planting of vine varieties for her area. On a subsequent appeal, the local authority relented on their initial contention about the suitability of the land and relied solely on the effect of the Regulation. Mrs Hauer argued that her application had been made prior to the entry into force of the Regulation and could not therefore be applied to her. This argument was dismissed by the ECJ as a matter of construction of the Regulation. Nonetheless, the applicant also challenged the Regulation on the basis that it contravened her rights, enshrined in the German constitution. These rights were to

---

[30] Case 149/77 *Defrenne v. Sabena* [1978] E.C.R. 1365, para. 27
[31] Case C–177/90 *Kühn v. Landwirtshaftskammer Wser-Ems* [1992] E.C.R. I–35, para. 18; Case C–98/91 *Herbrink v. Minister van Landbouw* [1994] E.C.R. I–223, para. 27; Case C–280/93 *Germany v. Council* [1994] E.C.R. I–4973, para. 67.
[32] Joined Cases 201/85 and 202/85 *Klensch* [1986] E.C.R. 3477, para. 9; Joined Cases C–267/88 to 285/88 *Wuidart v. Laiterie Coopérative Eupenoise* [1990] E.C.R. I–435, para. 13.
[33] Case C–158/91 *Ministère public et direction du travail et de l'emploi v. Levy* [1993] E.C.R. I–4287, para. 16.
[34] Case C–13/94 *P v. S & Cornwall County Council* [1996] E.C.R. I–2143.
[35] Case C–249/96 *Grant v. South West Trains* [1998] E.C.R. I–621.
[36] Case C–407/98 *Abrahamsson v. Fogelqvist* [2000] E.C.R. I–5539, ECJ; Case C–158/97 *Re Badeck's Application* [2000] E.C.R. I–1875.
[37] Case 44/79 *Liselotte Hauer v. Länd Rheinland-Pfalz* [1979] E.C.R. 3727.

property and freely to pursue trade and professional activities. The ECJ held that:

> "The right to property is guaranteed in the Community legal order in accordance with the ideas common to the constitutions of the Member States, which are also reflected in the first Protocol for the Protection of Human Rights."

6.150 The Court found on the facts that the Regulation undoubtedly restricted the use to which Mrs Hauer could put her property. The ECJ nonetheless recognised, having examined the constitutional rules and practices of the (then) nine Member States, that Article 1 to the first Protocol permitted restrictions to be imposed on the use of property to the extent to which they were deemed necessary in the general interest. It noted that all wine-growing countries in the Community had restrictive legislation (to some degree) on the planting of vines. It followed, applying those common constitutional precepts, that the Regulation's restrictions on the planting of vines could not be challenged as a matter of principle.[38] The ECJ went on then to examine the second limb. That is, whether the restrictions in fact constituted a "disproportionate and intolerable interference with the rights of the owner" so as to impinge upon the very substance of the right to property. After a relatively detailed examination of the rationale behind the Regulation, the ECJ concluded that the substance of the right to property was not infringed.[39]

6.151 In contrast, in *Wachauf*[40] the ECJ considered that restrictions on the right to property might not be permitted where they were such a disproportionate and intolerable interference that the very substance of the right was impaired. This would be the case where, for example, Community rules deprived a lessee without compensation of the very fruits of his labour and of the investment in his tenanted land. In subsequent case law, the Court has stated on a number of occasions that the right to property does not include the right to dispose, for profit, of an advantage (such as a reference quantity of a quota product under a common organisation of a market) which does not derive from the assets or occupational activity of the person concerned.[41] The Court has also, to some extent, assimilated the requirements of the second limb of Article 1 of the first Protocol to the general Community law principle of proportionality.[42]

Article 2 of Protocol 4 (liberty of movement within territory of Contracting State)

6.152 Rights of free movement are one of the fundamental freedoms recognised in the Treaty itself. Article 18 EC (ex Article 8a of the E.C. Treaty) now provides that:

---

[38] *ibid.*, [i], paras 21, 22.
[39] *ibid.*, paras 23–30.
[40] Case 5/88 *Wachauf v. Germany* [1989] E.C.R. 2609, paras 18, 19.
[41] Case C–44/89 *Von Deetzen v. Hauptzollamt Oldenberg* [1991] E.C.R. I–5119, para. 27; Case C–2/92 *Bostock* [1994] E.C.R. I–955, para. 19.
[42] Joined Cases 41, 121 and 796/79 *Testa, Maggio and Vitale v. Bundesanstalt für Arbeit* [1980] E.C.R. 1979, para. 21.

"every citizen of the Union shall have the right to move and reside freely within the territory of the Member States, subject to the limitations and conditions laid down in this Treaty and by the measures adopted to give it effect."[43]

As has been set out above, the ECJ acknowledged in *Rutili*[44] that nationals of other Member States are entitled to freedom of movement and residence within the Community, subject only to exclusions or exceptions available under Community secondary legislation.[45] The ECJ in *Rutili* confirmed that the limitations placed on the powers of Member States in respect to the control of aliens were no more than a specific manifestation of the more general principle enshrined, *inter alia*, in Article 2 of Protocol 4.[46]   **6.153**

Article 3 of Protocol 4 (Prohibition of expulsion of nationals)

The Court has consistently recognised that Member States have no authority to expel their own nationals from their territory or deny them access to it.[47] The prohibition under Community law extends to the expulsion of nationals of another Member State, except on certain, narrowly construed, public policy grounds. In *Calfa*,[48] the ECJ was asked to consider the effect of an expulsion order made by Greece against an Italian national. Ms Calfa was charged with the possession and use of prohibited drugs while staying as a tourist in Crete. She was convicted of the charge and sentenced to three months' imprisonment. She was also ordered to be expelled for life from Greek territory. She appealed exclusively against the exclusion order to the Greek Supreme Court of Cassation. There was no equivalent penalty imposed on Greek nationals under domestic law. The ECJ accepted that this was because the Member State had no power to expel its own nationals.[49]   **6.154**

On a preliminary reference, the ECJ held that although in principle criminal legislation is a matter for which Member States are responsible, such legislation may not restrict the fundamental freedoms guaranteed by Community law. The penalty of expulsion for life from the territory of a Member State clearly constituted an obstacle to the freedom to provide services to   **6.155**

---

[43] The rights afforded by European citizenship under Art. 18 EC have been discussed in Case C–378/97 *Criminal Proceedings against Wijsenbeek* [1999] E.C.R. I–6207; and Case C–192/99 *R. v. Secretary of State for the Home Department ex p. Kaur*, The Times, March 8, 2001.

[44] See (n. 4, above), paras 18, 28. The Court specifically held that restrictions could not be imposed on the right of a national to enter the territory of another Member State, to stay there and to move within it unless his presence or conduct constitutes a genuine and sufficiently serious threat to public policy.

[45] See Regulation No. 1612/68 of the Council of October 15, 1968; Council Directive No. 68/360 of October 15, 1968 (O.J. Eng. Sp. Ed. 1968 (II) pp. 475 and 485); and Council Directive No. 64/221 of February 25, 1964 on the co-ordination of special measures concerning the movement and residence of foreign nationals which are justified on grounds of public policy, public security or public health (O.J. Eng. Sp. Ed. 1963–64 p. 117).

[46] See (n. 4, above), para. 32.

[47] Case 41/71 *van Duyn v. Home Office* [1974] E.C.R. 1337, paras 22, 23; *Adoui* (n. 45, above), para. 7; Joined Cases C–65/95 and C–111/95 *Shingara and Radiom* [1997] E.C.R. I–3343, para. 28.

[48] Case C–348/96 *Criminal Proceedings against Calfa* [1999] E.C.R. I–0011.

[49] *ibid.*, para. 20.

Ms Calfa (a recipient of those services), since it was the very negation of that freedom. It was open to Member States to justify derogations from the fundamental freedoms under Article 46 EC. Nonetheless, an exclusion order could only be made against Ms Calfa if her personal conduct (besides the drugs conviction) created a genuine and sufficiently serious threat affecting one of the fundamental interests of society. Legislation under which expulsion for life followed automatically as a result of a criminal conviction, without any account being taken of the personal conduct of the offender or of the danger that person represented for the requirements of public policy, would not fulfil the conditions laid down by Directive 64/221. Such legislation could not therefore be justified under the public policy derogation.[50]

6.156   Further, Member States may not deprive their nationals of the right to enter their territory, or discourage them from leaving and returning. The latter principle can be seen in the case of *Surinder Singh*.[51] Mr Singh was an Indian national who married a British national in 1982. He and his wife went to work in Germany before starting a business in the United Kingdom. Mr Singh was granted limited leave to remain in the United Kingdom as a spouse of a British national. The couple subsequently divorced and the United Kingdom Immigration Service curtailed his limited leave to remain and obtained a deportation order against him. Mr Singh appealed against the deportation order on the basis, *inter alia*, that he had a right of residence under Community law as the spouse of a British citizen who herself had a Community law right to set up in business in the United Kingdom. The ECJ accepted that a national entered and resided in his national Member State as a result of national law and not Community law. In this regard, the ECJ noted that, as provided in particular "by Article 3 of the Fourth Protocol to the [Convention], a State may not expel one of its own nationals or deny him entry to its territory." It nonetheless went on to find that a national of a Member State had the right, under Community law, to be accompanied by his spouse under the same conditions as to freedom of movement as applied to nationals of other Member States. Otherwise a national of a Member State might be deterred from leaving his country of origin to pursue an economic activity in another Member State.[52]

Miscellaneous rights recognised by Community law

6.157   The Court has recognised the right to trade, the right to pursue a profession and the right to pursue economic activity generally as a fundamental right.[53] But the right to trade does not include a right to a specific market share, as a market share constitutes only a momentary economic position exposed to the risks of changing circumstances.

---

[50] *ibid.*, paras 24–28.
[51] Case C–370/90 *R. v. Immigration Appeal Tribunal and Singh (Surinder), ex p. Secretary of State for the Home Department* [1992] E.C.R. I–4265.
[52] *ibid.*, para. 19.
[53] Case C–280/93 *Germany v. Council* [1994] E.C.R. I–4973, para. 78; Case C–124/95 *R. v. H.M. Treasury and Bank of England, ex p. Centro-Com* [1997] E.C.R. I–81, para. 65, *per* Advocate General Jacobs. Advocate General Jacobs doubted whether there was a fundamental right to export goods as such.

In the last few years, the Community courts have also fleshed out a **6.158** nascent right to open government. In 1993, the Council and Commission approved a Code of Conduct concerning public access to Council and Commission documents.[54] It sets out the principles upon which access to the institutions' documents will be granted. The Code expressly provides that the public should have the widest possible access to documents held. To give effect to that commitment, the Council adopted Decision 93/731 of December 20, 1993 on public access to Council documents[55] and the Commission adopted Decision 94/90 on public access to Commission documents.[56] The Community courts have furthered any nascent right by limiting the public policy exceptions to applications for disclosure of public documents,[57] and also by concentrating on the principle of transparency.[58] The Court decisions have prompted one commentator to note that "[i]nstead of Strasbourg, it is now Luxembourg that leads the way in open government, at least in providing an example of how it could be done if not in requiring it."[59]

4. THE EUROPEAN CHARTER OF FUNDAMENTAL RIGHTS

Introduction

The Charter of Fundamental Rights of the European Union ("the Char- **6.159** ter")[60] was solemnly proclaimed by the European Parliament, the Council of Ministers and the European Commission at Nice on December 18, 2000. The Charter consists of a Preamble which states that the Union is founded on the indivisible, universal values of human dignity, freedom, equality and solidarity and is based on the principles of democracy and the rule of law. It also states that the Union respects regional diversity, ensures the free movement of persons, goods, services and capital, and the freedom of establishment, and that, in a developing society, it is necessary to strengthen the protection of fundamental rights by "making them more

---

[54] [1993] O.J. L340/41 as amended by [1993] O.J. L23/34.
[55] [1993] O.J. L340/43, as amended by Decision 96/705/Euratom, ECSC, EC of December 6, 1996 [1996] O.J. L325/19.
[56] Commission Decision 94/90/ECSC,EC,Euratom of February 8, 1994 on public access to Commission document: [1994] O.J. L46/58.
[57] See Case C–58/94 *Netherlands v. Council* [1996] E.C.R. I–2169, ECJ; Case T–194/94 *Carvel and Guardian Newspapers v. Council* [1995] E.C.R. II–2765, CFI; Case T–105/95 *WWF v. Commission* [1997] E.C.R. II–313, CFI; Case T–174/95 *Svenska Journalistförbundet v. Council* [1998] E.C.R. II–2289, CFI; Case T–124/96 *Interporc v. Commission* [1998] E.C.R. II–231, CFI; Case T–188/97 *Rothmans International BV v. Commission* [1999] E.C.R. II–2463, CFI; Case T–309/97 *Bavarian Lager Company v. Commission* [1999] E.C.R. II–5217; Joined Cases C–174/98P and C–189/98P *Netherlands and Van der Wal v. Commission* [1998] E.C.R. II–0545; Case T–188/98 *Aldo Kuijer v. Council* [2000] E.C.R. II–1959.
[58] In Case T–188/97 *Rothmans International BV v. Commission* [1999] E.C.R. II–2463, paras 54–55, the CFI held that exceptions to the "general principle of transparency" were to be construed narrowly so that the application of the "general principle" was not frustrated. See also Case T–203/96 *Embassy Limousines & Services v. European Parliament* [1998] E.C.R. II–4239, CFI.
[59] James Michael, "Freedom of Information comes to the European Union", [1996] P.L. 31 at 31.
[60] [2000] O.J. C364/8. The text of the Charter can be found at fundamental.rights@consi lium.eu.int.

visible in a Charter".[61] The rights, freedoms and principles set out in the body of the Charter are recognised by the Union.

6.160   The Charter consists of 54 numbered Articles which fall under seven Chapters headed as follows: Dignity (Chapter I); Freedoms (Chapter II); Equality (Chapter III); Solidarity (Chapter IV); Citizen's Rights (Chapter V); Justice (Chapter VI); and General Provisions (Chapter VII). At present, the Charter is a freestanding solemn proclamation and therefore a non-binding instrument. It was not included in the draft Treaty amendments concluded at Nice and a conscious decision was taken to exclude it from having Treaty status. Its legal status will be reviewed in 2004. Until then, it is unclear to what extent it may be relied on by Member States and individuals to protect and enforce the rights, freedoms and principles that it contains. The Charter may be of little or no real additional value to the existing fundamental rights protection provided for in Community law, or it may come to be drawn upon by Community or national courts as a source of fundamental rights to define the scope of the general principles of Community law.

The Charter Initiative

6.161   The impetus for a Charter came from the Cologne European Council[62] which on June 3 and 4, 1999 concluded that a Charter should be established to consolidate fundamental rights applicable at Union level and to make "their overriding importance and relevance more visible to the Union's citizens". The Charter was to include the fundamental rights and freedoms and the basic procedural rights guaranteed by the Convention and derived from the constitutional traditions common to Member States, as well as the fundamental rights that pertain only to the Union's citizens. It was to take account of economic and social rights as contained in the European Social Charter and the Community Charter of the Fundamental Social Rights of Workers, referred to in Article 136 of the E.C. Treaty, in so far as those rights do not merely establish objectives for action by the Union. A draft Charter was to be elaborated by a body of representatives ("the drafting body")[63] that would present a draft document in advance of the European Council in December 2000. The composition, method of work and practical arrangements for the drafting body were set out in the conclusions of the Tampere European Council on October 15 and 16, 1999. Its members consisted of 15 representatives of the Heads of State

---

[61] The Preamble also states that "[t]his Charter reaffirms, with due regard for the powers and tasks of the Community and the Union and the principle of subsidiarity, the rights as they result, in particular, from the constitutional traditions and international obligations common to the Member States, the Treaty on European Union, the Community Treaties, the European Convention for the Protection of Human Rights and Fundamental Freedoms, the Social Charters adopted by the Community and by the Council of Europe and the case-law of the Court of Justice of the European Communities and of the European Court of Human Rights."

[62] The European Council (not the Council of Ministers) describes the summit meetings of the Heads of State or of Governments of the Member States and the President of the Commission which are to take place at least twice a year under the chairmanship of the Head of State or Government of the Member State which holds the Presidency of the Council (see Art. 4 E.U. (ex Art. d of the TEU)).

[63] Rather confusingly, the drafting body was named "the Convention". The drafting body had an inner core of members named "the Praesidium".

or Government of Member States,[64] one representative of the President of the Commission, 16 members of the European Parliament, and 30 members of national Parliaments.[65] The drafting body set up a web site from which its progress could be monitored and documents submitted to it could be accessed.[66] From December 17, 1999 to December 18, 2000 the drafting body met regularly and received over 300 written observations from a wide range of parties.

The Initiative at a National Level

An inquiry into the Charter was carried out by the House of Lords Select **6.162** Committee on the European Union Sub-Committee E (Law and Institutions) under the chairmanship of Lord Hope of Craighead.[67] Its Report was ordered to be printed on May 16, 2000.[68] The Sub-Committee sought views, in particular, on the questions of the need for and purpose of a Charter, the legal status of the Charter, and the scope and content of the Charter. Written and oral evidence was given by 31 parties.[69] On the national level, as on the European level, there was a wide variety of views and expectations as to the status of the Charter.[70] The Bar Council International Relations Committee, Bar Human Rights Committee and Bar European Group in their written evidence identified five purposes which might be served by the Charter: (1) publicising existing rights; (2) guaranteeing new rights; (3) cementing the supremacy of E.U. over national law; (4) providing the basis for an E.U. constitution; and (5) "Bringing Rights Home" from Strasbourg to the E.U.

In its Opinion, the Sub-Committee warned that in drafting the Charter it **6.163** would be dangerous to tamper, by paraphrase or other means, with language accepted as universally applicable in international human rights instruments. As the Convention rights were common to all Member States, they should form the core of the Charter. Further, if economic and social rights were to be included, consideration must be given to ensuring their incorporation would not enlarge the competence of the Union or the Community by the backdoor. The Sub-Committee concluded that although the potential significance of the Charter, both politically and legally, is very great, the extent of its usefulness would depend on the status it is to have and the purpose it is intended to serve. It took the opportunity to reopen the debate on, and argued strongly in favour of, accession by the Community to the Convention[71]:

---

[64] Lord Goldsmith Q.C. represented the Prime Minister of the United Kingdom.
[65] Mr Win Griffiths M.P. and Lord Bowness represented the Parliament of the United Kingdom.
[66] http://db.consilium.eu.int.
[67] Other members of the Sub-Committee included Lord Goodhart, Lord Lester of Herne Hill and Lord Wedderburn of Charlton.
[68] EU Charter of Fundamental Rights, 8th Report 1999–2000, H.L. Paper 67.
[69] Parties who gave evidence to the inquiry included the British Institute of Human Rights, the Confederation of British Industry, ETUC, Advocate General Jacobs, JUSTICE, Liberty and Professor H. G. Schermers. The evidence, written and oral, is printed with the Report.
[70] For a detailed account of the case for and against a Charter, and an examination of the nature of the rights to be protected, aspects of enforceability, and implications of a Charter for the Treaties, see Fredman, McCrudden and Freedland, "An EU Charter of Fundamental rights" [2000] P.L.178.
[71] EU Charter of Fundamental Rights, 8th Report 1999–2000, H.L. Paper 67, p. 39, para. 154.

"A declaration by the European Council of rights already existing and protected in E.C. law might provide a list of rights that would be clear and accessible to the public and reinforce the protection of ECHR rights as an integral part of Community law. But a political act of that kind would close none of the gaps that currently exist in Community law in protection of fundamental rights within the EU. While skilful drafting might side-step question of potential conflict with the ECHR and European Court of Human Rights, a non-binding Charter would not prevent alternative rights or interpretations of ECHR rights being adopted by the Community courts. Accession to the ECHR remains the crucial step required if the gap is to be closed. Accession of the EU to the ECHR, enabling the Strasbourg Court to act as an external final authority in the field of human rights, would go a long way in guaranteeing a firm and consistent foundation for fundamental rights in the Union. It would secure the ECHR as the common code for Europe. The question of accession by the Union to the ECHR should be on the agenda for the IGC."

The Initiative at a European Level

6.164   During the year of negotiations at European level, the drafting body had 29 separate meetings at which the content of the Charter was debated. Predictably, one of the major topics of debate was the relationship between the Charter and the Convention. Some participants held the view that the Charter should not seek to re-write or compete with the Convention; others considered the drafting process to be an opportunity to reform the Convention, which was thought to be outdated. The Council of Europe was clearly concerned about which instrument and system for human rights protection would take priority. Observations submitted in January 2000 by the Parliamentary Assembly stated that: "the existence of the two systems of human rights protection in Europe would . . . run the risk of inconsistency between their case-law, weaken the European Court of Human Rights, and be detrimental to legal certainty." Further observations of the Council of Europe representatives[72] highlighted the fact that their primary concern "is to ensure that the rights taken by the Charter from the European Convention on Human Rights (ECHR) are not interpreted in inconsistent or even contradictory ways depending on whether it is the European Court of Human Rights or the Court of Justice in Luxembourg that is construing them", but also noted that the text of the Charter amply deals with that concern.

Content of the Charter

6.165   A final text was agreed and published on December 18, 2000, representing the most comprehensive statement of fundamental rights protection by the Union. Six of the seven chapters of the Charter deal with substantive freedoms, rights and principles, and can be grouped under three main headings: civil and political rights (derived from Convention rights); citizenship rights (derived from Treaty rights); and social and economic rights

---

[72] Observations of the Council of Europe representatives on the draft Charter proposed by the Praesidium (Convent 45), Strasbourg, August 22, 2000.

(derived largely from the European Social Charter and also from Treaty rights). The Charter is wide in coverage.[73] The rights protected by it range from respect for certain principles in the field of biomedicine (Article 3), the freedom to choose an occupation and engage in work (Article 15), the right to asylum (Article 18), cultural, religious and linguistic diversity (Article 22), rights of the child (Article 24) and the elderly (Article 25), healthcare (Article 35) and environmental protection (Article 37).

The Relationship with the Convention

Article 52(3) states that in so far as the Charter contains rights which **6.166** correspond to rights guaranteed by the Convention, the meaning and scope of those rights shall be the same as those laid down by the Convention. The provision shall not, however, prevent Union law providing more extensive protection. For 12 of the rights protected by the Charter, both their meaning and scope are the same as the corresponding Articles in the Convention. In addition, there are a number of Articles where the meaning is the same as the corresponding Articles of the Convention, but the scope is wider: Article 9 (right to marry and found a family) covers the same field as Article 12 of the Convention, but its scope may be extended to other forms of marriage if these are established by national legislation. Article 12(1) (freedom of assembly and of association) corresponds to Article 11 of the Convention, but its scope is extended to Union level. Article 14 (right to education) corresponds to Article 2 of the First Protocol to the Convention, but is extended to cover access to vocational and continuing training. Article 47(2) and (3) corresponds to the right in Article 6(1) of the Convention to a fair trial, but is not limited to the determination of civil rights and obligations. Article 50 (right not to be tried or punished twice in criminal proceedings for the same criminal offence) corresponds to Article 4 of the Seventh Protocol to the Convention, but its scope is extended to European Union level between the courts of the Member States. Finally, as citizens of the European Union must not be considered as aliens in the scope of the application of Community law, the limitations provided for by Article 16 of the Convention as regards the rights of aliens therefore do not apply to them in this context.

Scope of Application

Article 51 reads as follows: **6.167**

> "1. The provisions of this Charter are addressed to the institutions and bodies of the Union with due regard to the principle of subsidiarity and to the Member States only when they are implementing Union law. They shall therefore respect the rights, observe the principles and promote the application thereof in accordance with their respective powers.
> 2. This Charter does not establish any new power or task for the Community or the Union, or modify powers and tasks defined by the Treaties."

---

[73] There are 54 Articles in the Charter, of which 50 are substantive, compared with 24 Articles in the Convention, of which 14 are substantive.

6.168 Article 51 is an important limitation. It emphasises that the Charter does not extend the competences of the Community or the Union. However, in so far as the Charter applies to Member States *only when they are implementing Union law*, the scope of application is arguably narrower than the scope of application of the fundamental rights principles guaranteed in Community law (see paragraphs 6–61 *et seq.*, above).

The Status of the Charter

6.169 It was originally intended that the Charter would be a non-binding declaration. As the drafting body itself could not alter the status of the instrument, it remains a non-binding declaration.[74] The Charter does not extend the jurisdiction of the ECJ, nor does it create a new and independent right of complaint that a Community or national act is contrary to a provision contained in it. Although not legally binding, the ECJ is entitled to refer to it and it may become a familiar statement of fundamental rights, and a useful resource. The extent to which parties will be able to rely upon the Charter will therefore depend on the status attributed to it by the ECJ. The first reference to the Charter was made in Case C–173/99 *BECTU v. Secretary of State for Trade and Industry*[75] which concerned the guarantee of four weeks' paid annual leave by the Working Time Directive. In his Opinion, Advocate General Tizzano noted that:

> "... in proceedings concerned with the nature and scope of a fundamental right, the relevant statements of the Charter cannot be ignored; in particular, we cannot ignore its clear purpose of serving, where its provisions so allow, as a substantive point of reference for all those involved—Member States, institutions, natural and legal persons—in the Community context. Accordingly, I consider that the Charter provides us with the most reliable and definitive confirmation of the fact that the right to paid annual leave constitutes a fundamental right."

Subsequently, in the Opinion of Advocate General Geelhoed at para. 59 in Case C–413/99 *Baumbast and R v. Secretary of State for the Home Department* delivered on July 5, 2001 (n.y.r.), Article 7 of the Charter which enshrines respect for family life was pointed to. The Advocate General stated, however, "as Community law currently stands, that Charter has no binding force."[75A]

---

[74] At the UCL-Herbert Smith Lecture on February 27, 2001, "The EU Charter of Fundamental rights: Constitution or Consolidation?" Lord Lester of Herne Hill compared the drafting body to a guild of elegant, and in some cases, unpaid tailors, fashioning for the Emperor a suit of clothes which would never be worn.

[75] Opinion of February 8, 2001 and judgment of June 26, 2001 (n.y.r.).

[75A] The Charter has also been referred to in the Opinion of Advocate General Jacobs at para. 197 in Case C–377/98 *Netherlands v. Parliament and Council* delivered on June 14, 2001 (n.y.r.), where reference was made to Articles 1 and 3(2) of the Charter. See also the Opinion of Advocate General Tizzano at para. 22 in Case C–133/00 *J. E. Bowden and Others v. Tuffnells Parcel Express Ltd* delivered on May 8, 2001.

5. THE INTERACTION BETWEEN E.C. LAW, CONVENTION LAW AND DOMESTIC LAW UNDER THE HRA 1998

Resolving Potentially Conflicting Jurisdictions

As mentioned at the beginning of this Chapter, the fused implementation **6.170** of three separate regimes for protecting human rights raises the possibility of jurisdictional conflicts. These potential conflicts are between:

(1) Community law and Strasbourg case law;

(2) Community law and domestic English law, including the HRA 1998.

In addition, although it does not represent a conflict over jurisdiction as such, there is also the possibility of domestic law and Community law arriving at differing interpretations on the subject of fundamental rights. Discrepancies could arise not only as to the specific content of fundamental rights, but also over what measures or decisions "fall within the scope of Community law".

While these potential fault lines are of considerable academic interest, the **6.171** practitioner is perhaps more concerned to know what the practical chances of conflict are, what to do in the event of a conflict, and what tactical considerations come into play when selecting any given "tool" from Schiemann L.J.'s "toolkit". The three areas are addressed in turn.

Community law and Strasbourg case law

As has been seen above, there are certain areas where the rights recog- **6.172** nised under Community law depart from the equivalent rights recognised under the Convention. Indeed, it is apparent from cases such as *Hoechst*, *Orkem* and *PVC Cartel (No. II)*[76] that the Community courts are not obliged systematically to take into account the interpretation of the Convention given by Strasbourg, when analysing the fundamental rights jurisprudence. It is precisely because Community fundamental rights have an autonomous existence that the Community courts will not necessarily simply follow the Strasbourg jurisprudence. In the event of conflict, which is to take precedence? The answer, as a matter of Community law, is straightforward. The Community is not a party to the Convention. Accession has been ruled out. It follows that Community law is supreme in areas which fall within the scope of Community law and must be applied regardless of the content of either the Convention or the constitutional requirements of a particular Member State.[77]

Moreover, in areas falling within the scope of Community law, it is the ECJ **6.173** and not the Court of Human Rights which must ultimately pronounce upon the nature and extent of fundamental rights recognised in Community law. This follows clearly from the terms of Article 220 EC (ex Article 164 of the

---

[76] See nn. 55, 71 and 76, above.
[77] See paras 6–07 et seq., above.

E.C. Treaty) which requires the ECJ to ensure that "the law" is observed. It has been said that the ability of the ECJ to carry out this mandate would be seriously impaired if another court, such as the Court of Human Rights, were to claim a co-extensive jurisdiction.[78] Nonetheless, as Advocate General Jacobs has observed:

" . . . the possibility of conflicting rulings on the interpretation of the Convention . . . has existed ever since the Court of Justice recognised that the Convention may be invoked under Community law. Such a possibility does not seem to have caused serious problems. It would in any event be paradoxical if the existence of the Convention and the system established under the Convention were to reduce the protection available in national law or in Community law."[79]

6.174 The answer from Strasbourg to the question of pre-eminence has proved interesting. In *Matthews v. United Kingdom*,[80] a resident of Gibraltar, Mrs Matthews, applied in 1994 to register to vote in the elections to the European Parliament. Her application was refused by the Electoral Registration Officer. Gibraltar was not included in the United Kingdom's franchise for those elections. She applied to the Court in Strasbourg, claiming that there had been a breach of her right to participate in elections to choose the legislature contrary to the Article 3 of the First Protocol to the Convention. Gibraltar is a dependent territory of the United Kingdom. Executive power is vested in a Governor (who acts in right of the Crown) and also in a Chief Minister of a Government that is elected to a domestic House of Assembly. Article 299(4) EC provides that the Treaty shall apply to European territories for whose external relations a Member State is responsible. While the territory of Gibraltar falls outside the Common Customs Territory, it is otherwise within the scope of the Treaty. Article 138(3) of the EEC Treaty provided that the European Parliament was to draw up proposals for elections. Pursuant to Council Decision 76/787, the Member States formulated an "Act concerning the Election of the Representatives of the European Parliament by Direct Universal Suffrage of 27 September 1976". The United Kingdom did not include Gibraltar in an Annex to that Act which governed direct elections to the European Parliament. By a declaration dated October 23, 1953, the United Kingdom extended the territorial scope of the Convention to Gibraltar. Protocol No. 1 applies to Gibraltar by virtue of a Declaration made under Article 4 of the First Protocol on February 25, 1988. The Court found that the following questions were raised by the application before it:

---

[78] N. Reich, "Judge-made 'Europe à la carte': Some remarks on Recent Conflicts between European and German Constitutional Law provoked by the Banana Litigation", (1996) 7 E.J.I.L. 103 at 110–111. See also para. 50 of Advocate General Jacob's Opinion in *Konstantinidis* (n. 83, above). He considered that the Court of Human Rights was prepared to accept that its role was largely a procedural and subsidiary one, with the Convention being enforced largely through national authorities and national courts in the Contracting States.
[79] Advocate General Jacob's Opinion in *Konstantinidis* (n. 83, above), para. 51.
[80] *Matthews v. United Kingdom* (1999) 28 E.H.R.R. 361, ECHR.

(1) Whether the United Kingdom could be held responsible under the Convention for the lack of elections to the European Parliament in Gibraltar;

(2) whether Article 3 of Protocol 1 was applicable to the European Parliament;

(3) whether the European Parliament had the characteristics of a legislature in Gibraltar;

(4) whether the absence of elections to the European Parliament in Gibraltar was compatible with Article 3 of the Protocol?

The Court found that acts of the Community as such could not be chal- **6.175** lenged before the Court of Human Rights, because the Community was not a Contracting Party. The Convention did not preclude the transfer of competences to international organisations, provided that Convention rights were still "secured". It was the responsibility of Member States to secure that those rights continued to be protected even after such a transfer.[81] Thus the United Kingdom was responsible for the consequences of both the Annex to the 1976 Act and also the Maastricht Treaty, entered into after the application of the First Protocol to the Convention had been extended to Gibraltar. As Community legislation affected the Gibraltarian population in the same way as domestic legislation, there was no reason why the United Kingdom should not secure the population's rights under Article 3 of Protocol No. 1. The suggestion that matters were now beyond the United Kingdom's control was rejected on the basis that the United Kingdom had chosen to make Gibraltar part of the Community by extending, or agreeing to the extension of, the territorial scope of the Treaties to it.

The Court also considered that "legislature" in Article 3 of Protocol No. 1 **6.176** did not necessarily refer only to national parliaments. As the Convention was a "living instrument", it had to be construed in the light of the constitutional arrangements of the state. The fact that the European Parliament was a supranational, rather than a domestic, representative organ did not justify it being excluded from the scope of Article 3. Additional powers and competences granted to the European Parliament by the Maastricht Treaty had transformed it into a "a body with a decisive role to play in the legislative process of the European Community".[82] The Court examined the various procedures by which Community legislation was passed, and the role of the European Parliament in them. In its view, the European Parliament represented the principal form of democratic, political accountability in the Community system. As such, in order to secure "effective political democracy" under the Convention, it fell to be construed as a legislature for the purposes of Article 3. It followed that the applicant had been completely denied any opportunity to express her opinion in the choice of members for the European Parliament, in violation of her right under Article 3 of Protocol No. 1.

---

[81] *ibid.*, para. 32.
[82] *ibid.*, para. 50.

6.177   This was the first case before the European Court of Human Rights directly concerning the European Community.[83] The European Commission on Human Rights had previously held that Member States could not be held responsible for infringements of the Convention by the Community. In the *M and Co. v. Germany* case, the Commission had held that "the transfer of powers to an international organisation is not incompatible with the Convention provided that within that organisation fundamental rights will receive an equivalent protection".[84] As the Community protected fundamental rights, it had been considered that Member States would not be responsible for the implementation of Community acts.

6.178   The significance of the *Matthews* judgment can be seen in the terms of the dissenting judgment of Judges Sir John Freeland and Jungwiert. They considered that: "a particular restraint should be required of the Court when it is invited . . . to pronounce on acts of the European Community or consequent to its requirements, especially when those acts relate to a matter so intimately concerned with the operation of the Community as elections to one of its constitutional organs."[85] In addition, they had some difficulty ascribing the infringement to the United Kingdom alone, when it arose out of a multi-lateral international agreement which, at the time, complied with the obligations imposed by the Convention.[86] The judges also recognised that, given the dispute over the sovereignty of Gibraltar with Spain and the need for unanimity in Treaty amendment, there was little in terms of *real politic* that the United Kingdom would be able to do to change the situation. It is perhaps for that reason that the Court of Human Rights (at para. 33) found that the United Kingdom, together with all the parties to the Masstricht Treaty, were responsible for ensuring that the rights granted by Protocol No. 1 were maintained.

6.179   The majority judgment of the Court therefore represents a strong signal from the Court of Human Rights that Member States cannot escape their obligations under the Convention, even if they are constrained by the actions or dynamic of the Community. In the view of the Court of Human Rights, rules of Community law should accord with the Convention. The Court will supervise the proper application of the Convention by the Community. While the actions of the Community itself cannot be directly challenged, they will, where appropriate, be scrutinised for compatibility

---

[83] All other attempts to bring cases against the Community had been declared to be manifestly ill-founded by the European Commission of Human Rights with the result that they were rejected at the admissibility stage. The *Matthews* case came before the revamped Court after the Commission's role as filter had been abolished, although the Commission had by then already given an Opinion that the claim was admissible but that an infringement was not made out. See Professor Schermers, *Case Note*, (1999) 36 C.M.L. Rev. 673–681.The length of time for an Art. 177 (now, Art. 234 E.C.) reference had come before the Court of Human Rights in *Parfitis v. Greece* (1999) 27 E.H.R.R. 566, ECHR. There the Court had declined to take into account the period of two and one-half years for a preliminary reference when considering whether proceedings had been heard in a reasonable time, for the purposes of Art. 6(1). The Court held that this period could not be taken into consideration since to do so would adversely affect the system of justice instituted by the preliminary reference system.

[84] Application No. 13258/87 *M and Co. v. Germany,* European Commission of Human Rights, Dec. 9.2.90, 64 Decisions and Reports 138 at 145.

[85] See at 405 of the judgment.

[86] *ibid.,* at 407. The pre-Maastricht powers of the European Parliament were not such as to bring it within the scope of Art. 3 of Protocol No. 1 and that Protocol had not been extended to Gibraltar at the time.

with the Convention. The enforcement mechanism will be via holding the Member States accountable. It is therefore well arguable that in the event the Community fails to secure for an individual the protection of a Convention right, a complaint will lie to Strasbourg against such a failure. The complaint would be made against the national's Member State, or possibly against all Member States.

It should also be noted that there will be areas, outside the scope of **6.180** Community law, where the application of the case law of the Court of Human Rights will continue to be paramount. This is because the doctrine of the supremacy of Community law only exists in so far as the subject matter falls within the scope of Community law. In cases such as *Kremzow* and *Annibaldi*, for example,[87] the ECJ declined any jurisdiction to apply fundamental rights as a matter of Community law. The complainants in each case would have had to rely upon protection afforded by the Convention or by their domestic law. In addition, even if Community law is applicable, there would appear to be no reason why the Convention or its incorporating domestic law could not be applied, provided that doing so did not impair the supremacy or effectiveness of Community law. Precisely because the Convention is not part of Community law, a finding by a national or Community court that there has been no breach of a Community fundamental right does not preclude the application thereafter of the Convention. For the reasons given by Advocate General Jacobs above, the scope for such a residual application may, in practice, be limited.

Community law and English domestic law, including the HRA 1998

There is a potential for conflict between the provisions of the HRA 1998, **6.181** by which the Convention was incorporated into domestic law, and the European Communities Act 1972, which incorporated the EEC Treaty. For example, section 2(1) of the HRA 1998 requires English courts or tribunals to take into account any judgment, decision, declaration or advisory opinion of the Court of Human Rights. Conversely, section 3(1) of the European Communities Act 1972 provides that the meaning or effect of Community law shall be determined in accordance with the principles laid down by any relevant decision of the ECJ.

Nonetheless, as a matter of Community law, were an actual conflict to **6.182** arise on the facts of any case, it is apparent that so long as the subject-matter falls within the scope of Community law, the Community construction must be preferred. This is so regardless of the nature of the domestic provision relied upon, be it statute, common law or obligation imposed by a subsequent international Treaty.[88] It is also no answer to say that the HRA 1998 was the Act of Parliament which came later in time.[89] The result of the doctrine of supremacy of Community law is, once again, that

---

[87] See nn. 66, 74, above.
[88] Case 11/70 *Internationale Handelsgesellschaft* [1970] E.C.R. 1125, para. 3, where the ECJ held that the law stemming from the Treaty cannot by its very nature be overridden by rules of national law, howsoever framed; and Case 22/70 *Commission v. Council (Re European Road Transport Agreement)* [1971] E.C.R. 263, para. 31.
[89] Case 6/64 *Costa v. ENEL* [1964] E.C.R. 585 at 593, where the ECJ held that a subsequent, unilateral national act could not prevail over Community law.

Community fundamental rights will "trump" any conflicting domestic measure or interpretation of human rights. Conversely, in areas that do not fall within the scope of Community law, there is nothing to prevent the domestic application of either the HRA 1998 or of common law principles designed to ensure procedural and administrative fairness.

6.183 The potential for conflict is therefore more apparent than real.[90] This can best be seen, perhaps, in a concrete example. In domestic proceedings involving alleged anti-competitive behaviour within the United Kingdom, a national court would be potentially obliged to consider both E.C. competition law and the provisions of the Competition Act 1998.[91] Section 60(1) and (2) of that Act provide that a national court is required to take into account Treaty principles and Community case law with a view to ensuring there is no inconsistency between the application of domestic competition law and the application of E.C. competition law. Imagine that a defendant wishes to exclude evidence before the court which was obtained in a "dawn raid". It raises an argument that the evidence was obtained in violation of the undertaking's right to inviolability of business premises, as recognised by Article 8 of the Convention and by the Court of Human Rights in *Niemietz*.[92] The competing argument would be that the ECJ in *Hoechst* and the CFI in *PVC Cartel (No. II)* did not recognise a fundamental right to protection of business premises.[93] Which argument should succeed? The answer depends on whether the anti-competitive conduct and, in particular, the "dawn raid" fell within the scope of Community law or not. If it did, then it would seem that Community law, being supreme, must be applied to exclude any conflicting principle of national law. If the investigation and the anti-competitive conduct related to a "purely internal situation", then there would be no room for fundamental rights to be applied. Section 2(1) of the HRA 1998 is in mandatory terms. Section 60(1) of the Competition Act 1998 requires Community law to be taken into account so far as is possible. It would therefore seem, as a matter of construction, that in the latter situation, the national court would be obliged to apply the Strasbourg case law to the issue.[94]

6.184 The English courts have, by and large, been prepared to accept that Convention rights may now be analysed through the filter of Community law. In *R. v. Hertfordshire County Council, ex p. Green Environmental Industries*,[95] for example, the House of Lords was faced with a defendant who sought to invoke a privilege against self-incrimination on the basis that the relevant legislation being applied against him had implemented a Community Directive. The House of Lords considered and distinguished the Article 6 line of cases[96] on the basis that they were anchored to the fairness of the trial and not with extra-judicial inquiries. Lord Hoffmann

---

[90] In practice, the divergence in any event between the Strasbourg case law and Community law is small.

[91] Arts 81 and 82 EC have been transmogrified in a domestic context into the Chapter I and Chapter II prohibitions in the Competition Act 1998.

[92] See n. 95, above.

[93] See nn. 55, 76, above.

[94] A nice issue would arise if the investigation was carried out by national authorities as agents for the Commission under E.C. competition law, but that the findings revealed that the conduct fell to be dealt with under the domestic provisions.

[95] [2000] 2 W.L.R. 373; [2000] Eu.L.R. 414, HL.

[96] *Funke, Serves* and *Saunders* (n. 84, above).

applied the test adopted by the ECJ in *Orkem*[97] and concluded that the requests for information did not, on the facts, invite an admission of wrongdoing.[98]

In *R. v. Secretary of State for Culture, Media and Sport, ex p. Danish Satellite Television*[99] the Court of Appeal was asked to consider the effect of Article 10 in the context of the United Kingdom relying on a derogation from Community law. The Secretary of State made a proscription order under section 177 of the Broadcasting Act 1990 against Danish Satellite Television's ("DST") foreign television service. The grounds for doing so were that DST broadcast explicit pornography. The United Kingdom relied upon a derogation permitted under Article 22 of the "Television without Frontiers" Directive.[1] Article 22 required Member States to ensure that material was not broadcast by persons under their jurisdiction which might seriously impair the moral development of minors. The E.C. Commission issued an opinion in which they considered the proscription order to be compatible with Community law. When DST sought judicial review of the order, the Court of Appeal examined the circumstances giving rise to the Order and concluded on the facts that the Secretary of State was entitled to regard DST's service as being in grave and serious breach of Article 22 of the Directive. Laws L.J. considered that it would consequently be very difficult for the applicant to contend that the proscription order was not justified under Articles 8(2) or 10(2) of the Convention or by the derogations excepting compliance with Article 49 E.C. There have also been recent examples of the English courts considering Article 8 of the Convention in the light of Community law.[2]

6.185

English courts have expressed a willingness to refer questions concerning fundamental rights to the ECJ where appropriate.[3] Indeed, Sedley L.J. has even advocated acceptance of cross-fertilisation of principles. He has stated that: "once it is accepted that the standards articulated in the Convention are standards which both match with those of the common law and inform the jurisprudence of the European Union, it becomes unreal and potentially unjust to continue to develop English public law without reference to them."[4]

6.186

---

[97] See n. 60, above.

[98] See also the judgment of the Divisional Court in *R. v. Central Criminal Court, ex p. Bright* [2001] 1 W.L.R. 662, QBD. The willingness to review domestic measures for compliance with fundamental rights extends even to statutory tribunals. See *Hodgson v. Commissioners of Customs and Excise* [1997] Eu. L.R. 116 at 130–134, *per* Stephen Oliver Q.C. in the VAT Tribunal.

[99] [1999] 3 C.M.L.R. 919, CA.

[1] Council Directive 89/552 of October 3, 1989 on the co-ordination of certain provisions laid down by law, regulation or administrative action in Member States concerning the pursuit of television broadcasting activities ([1989] O.J. L298/23), as amended by E.P. and Council Directive 97/36 of June 30, 1997 ([1997] O.J. L202/60).

[2] See *U v. W.* [1997] 2 C.M.L.R. 431, *per* Wilson J.; and *R. v. Secretary of State for the Home Department, ex p. Barrow (Buba)* [2000] Imm. A.R. 370, CA.

[3] *R. v. Secretary of State for the Home Department, ex p. Kaur* [1999] Eu.L.R. 554, QBD, *per* Lightman J., who considered that a reference to the ECJ on the issue of whether Articles 17 and 18 E.C. (ex Articles 8 and 8a of the E.C. Treaty) created directly enforceable rights for persons was "extremely important" from a fundamental rights perspective.

[4] See the judgment of Sedley J. (as he then was) in *ex p. McQuillan* [1995] 4 All E.R. 400 at 422. His Lordship cited with approval the extra-judicial arguments of Laws J. in "Is the High Court the Guardian of Fundamental Constitutional Rights" [1993] P.L. 59.

Tactical Considerations involved in the Interaction of the Regimes

6.187 There are also certain advantages to relying on Community law as a source of fundamental rights. Despite the fact that national measures may now be challenged directly under the provisions of the HRA 1998, the question of whether Community law can be used as a means of relying on the Convention is still important. This is because of certain Community law enforcement mechanisms which are at least equal to, and, in some respects, are superior to those provided under the HRA 1998. Where appropriate, an applicant should claim under the two alternative routes, as it may be more advantageous for him to enforce Convention rights indirectly via Community law.

6.188 The supremacy of Community law means that primary and subordinate national legislation which is declared incompatible with a directly effective Community law right, and therefore invalid, must be disapplied or struck down by national courts.[5] Fundamental rights are directly effective. Primary or subordinate domestic legislation that contravenes those rights protected by Community law must be disapplied by national courts and subsequently repealed or amended by legislation. By contrast, section 3(2)(b) and (c) of the HRA 1998 provide that the validity, continuing operation or enforcement of primary legislation (and of subordinate legislation where primary legislation prevents the removal of the incompatibility), which cannot be read or given effect in a way which is compatible with the Convention, is not affected. Section 4 of the HRA 1998 allows courts simply to make a declaration of the incompatibility of primary legislation with a Convention right. This is likely to be of little practical use to the applicant: a declaration itself does not affect the validity, continuing operation or enforcement of the provision in respect of which it is given.[6] It is not binding on the parties to the proceedings in which it is made.[7] It is not required to be retrospective and potentially therefore may not provide any relief to the applicant before the court.[8] Indeed one commentator has suggested that it is more likely to be prayed in aid by respondents, anxious to avoid an interpretative obligation under section 3 of the HRA 1998.[9] Where a declaration of incompatibility has been made, the power to take remedial action is limited. A Minister of the Crown may consider that there are compelling reasons to make such amendments to the legislation in question as he considers necessary to remove the incompatibility.[10]

6.189 Further, the remedies available under Community law may well have more teeth.[11] The general principles of effectiveness and equivalence dictate that effective protection must be given to the national and Community protection of E.C. fundamental rights. Article 10 EC (ex Article 5 of the E.C.

---

[5] See *R. v. Secretary of State for Employment, ex p. Equal Opportunities Commission* [1995] 1 A.C. 1 at 26E—27F, HL.
[6] HRA 1998, s.4(6)(a).
[7] HRA 1998, s.4(6)(b).
[8] See generally C. Neenan, "Is a Declaration of Incompatibility an effective remedy?" [2000] J.R. 247.
[9] G. Marshall "Two kinds of incompatibility: more about section 3 of the Human Rights Act 1998" [1999] P.L. 377, who describes a declaration of incompatibility as a species of "booby prize".
[10] HRA 1998, s.10(2), (3).
[11] See generally paras 6–144–6–146, above.

Treaty) obliges national courts to ensure the legal protection of rights which individuals derive from Community law.[12] Such protection by national courts in accordance with national procedural rules[13] is subject to two overriding principles. First, national rules that apply to Community law actions must not be discriminatory or less favourable than those governing analogous domestic actions (the principle of equivalence). Secondly, national rules must not make practically impossible the exercise of Community law rights which must be accorded effective protection (the principle of effective protection).

There are also advantages to proceeding under Community law in terms of the standing of applicants. A challenge to a legislative or administrative act alleging infringement of Community law rights is often most appropriately brought by judicial review.[14] Where a claimant has a sufficient interest in the matter to which the claim relates, the courts will grant permission for him to make an application for judicial review.[15] Recently, an increasingly liberal approach to standing has been developed by the courts. Claims are often made by public interest groups established to campaign on particular issues or to represent specific interests.[16] This must be contrasted with section 7(1) of the HRA 1998 pursuant to which a person who claims that a public authority has acted (or proposes to act) in a way incompatible with Convention rights may bring proceedings against the authority "only if he is (or would be) a victim of the unlawful act". The "victim test" is clearly a more restrictive approach.[17] **6.190**

A further tactical consideration arises from the question of damages. First, under Community law, an applicant may challenge a failure by a Member State to legislate, where that omission maintains in effect a situation contrary to Community law. Given the general principle of the effective protection of Community rights, and the right to reparation now acknowledged as a corollary of that principle, damages may be awarded for a failure to legislate.[18] The HRA 1998, on the other hand, expressly excludes the right to an award of damages as a result of such a failure. **6.191**

Further, under the *Francovich* test laid down by the ECJ and applied by the national courts, an applicant may claim damages against a Member State in respect of serious breaches of Community law. In order to make good a claim for loss, three conditions must be satisfied: **6.192**

---

[12] Case 33/76 *Rewe v. Landwirtschaftskammer Saarland* [1976] E.C.R. 1989, para. 5; Case C–213/89 *Factortame (No. 2)* [1990] E.C.R. I–2433, para. 19; Case C–2/88 *Zwartveld* [1990] E.C.R. I–3365, para. 18; Case C–312/93 *Peterbroeck v. Belgium* [1995] E.C.R. I–4599, para. 12.

[13] Joined Cases C–430/93 and C–431/93 *Van Schijndel v. SPF* [1995] E.C.R. I–4705, para. 29, *per* the Opinion of Advocate General Jacobs.

[14] The Supreme Court Act 1981, s.31 and the Civil Procedure Rules, Pts 8 and 54, deal with the rules applicable to judicial review.

[15] Supreme Court Act 1981, s.31(3).

[16] See N. Plemming q.c., "The Contribution of Public Interest Litigation to the Jurisprudence of Judicial Review" [1998] J.R. 63; and the judgment of Maurice Kay J. in *R. v. Secretary of State for Trade and Industry, ex p. Greenpeace Ltd (No. 2)* [2000] Eu.L.R. 196.

[17] For a more detailed consideration of the requirements of the HRA 1998, s.7(1), see Chapter 8 herein.

[18] Joined Cases C–6 and 9/90 *Francovich and Bonifaci v. Italy* [1991] E.C.R. I–5357. The failure must amount to a sufficiently serious breach of Community law which has directly caused loss to the individual concerned. See Case C–48/93 *Factortame and Brasserie du Pêcheur* [1996] E.C.R. I–1029, ECJ; *Factortame (No. 5)* [2000] 1 A.C. 524, HL for an example of a sufficiently serious breach.

(1) the rule of law infringed must have been intended to confer rights on individuals;

(2) the breach must be sufficiently serious;

(3) there must be a direct causal link between the breach of the obligation resting on the state and the damage sustained by the injured parties.[19]

6.193   Therefore, an applicant who has suffered damage as a result of the United Kingdom implementing Community legislation in a manner which is in breach of fundamental principles, including the Convention, may be able to sustain a damages claim, if the breach is sufficiently serious. The ECJ has held that a breach will be sufficiently serious where a Member State had manifestly and gravely disregarded the limits on its legislative powers. Furthermore, where a Member State was not called upon to make any legislative choices and had only a considerably reduced (or even no) discretion, the mere existence of an infringement of Community law may establish a sufficiently serious breach.[20] As set out above, damages must constitute an effective remedy and provide adequate compensation. In contrast, the HRA 1998 provides that the level of damages awarded under section 8(4)(b) are to be guided by the decisions of the Commission and the Court of Human Rights. These decisions, often based on the issue of whether or not a finding of an infringement gives "just satisfaction", are arguably more restrictive than their Community counterparts. Awards are likely to be smaller than those available under the *Francovich* test.

6.194   The scope of the sources of rights is also wider under E.C. law. Community law draws not only on the Convention as a source of fundamental rights, but also on other international treaties for the protection of human rights of which the Member States are signatories or on which they have collaborated.[21] The Court of Justice has referred to a number of international human rights instruments including the European Social Charter of November 18, 1961,[22] Convention No. 111 of the International Labour Organisation,[23] and the International Covenant on Civil and Political Rights of December 19, 1966.[24] A claim pursuant to the HRA 1998 requires consideration only of the Convention and jurisprudence of the Strasbourg institutions.

---

[19] *ibid.*, and also Case C–392/93 *R. v. H.M. Treasury, ex p. British Telecommunications plc* [1996] E.C.R. I–1631, para. 38; Case C–5/94 *R. v. Ministry of Agriculture, Fisheries and Food, ex p. Hedley Lomas* [1996] E.C.R. I–2553, para. 24; Joined Cases 178–179 and 188–190/94 *Dillenkofer v. Germany* [1996] E.C.R. I–4845, para. 20; Case C–127/95 *Norbrook Laboratories v. Ministry of Agriculture, Fisheries and Food* [1998] E.C.R. I–1531, paras 106, 107.

[20] See *Norbrook, ibid.*, para. 109.

[21] Case *Nold v. Commission* [1974] E.C.R. 491, paras 12–14; Case C–260/89 *ERT* [1991] I–2925, paras 41–45; Case 11/70 *Internationale Handelsgesellschaft* [1970] E.C.R. 1125, paras 3–4.

[22] Case 149/77 *Defrenne v. Sabena* [1978] E.C.R. 1365, paras 25–28.

[23] *ibid.*

[24] Case 374/87 *Orkem v. Commission* [1989] E.C.R. 3283, paras 18, 31; Case C–168/91 *Konstantinidis* [1993] E.C.R. I–1191, *per* the Opinion of Advocate General Jacobs.

Differences between Domestic Law and Community Law Interpretations of What Measures or Decisions "Fall within the Scope of Community Law"

It will be apparent from this section that the issue of "the scope of Community law" is an important one. Upon its construction will turn the availability of an enhanced scheme of protection for fundamental rights. It was seen above, in paragraphs 6–61 *et seq.*, that the Community courts have had some difficulty in establishing a bright-line test as to which domestic measures will fall within the scope of Community law. In most cases, that assessment will (at least initially) fall to be made by the national court, subject only to the possibility of a preliminary reference to the ECJ if it cannot determine the issue with "complete confidence".[25]

6.195

The English courts have considered the issue of whether national measures fall within the scope of Community law in a number of recent cases. In *ex p. Hamble Fisheries*[26] the measure under consideration was a licensing policy adopted by MAFF in relation to the fishing quota system adopted under the common fisheries policy of the Community. The applicant sought to argue that a change in that policy had frustrated its legitimate expectations and caused it loss. It sought to rely upon various decisions of the ECJ relating to legitimate expectation. The respondent argued that the relevant law was entirely domestic. Sedley J. rejected that submission as "unreal". He added:

6.196

> "It may no doubt be said that the immediate exercise is the formulation of policy within a discretion conferred entirely by domestic legislation. But the purpose of legislation and policy alike is to permit the respondent under the principle of subsidiarity to exercise its powers for the purpose of implementing the common agricultural policy of the European Community. If each Member State were governed in carrying out its part of this joint exercise by no jurisprudence but its own domestic law, a major objective of the policy would be frustrated. The availability of eventual recourse to the Court of Justice from and against all the Member States in relation to the carrying out of the common agricultural policy must require domestic courts to have full regard to the jurisprudence of the Court of Justice."

A narrower approach was adopted in *First City Trading Ltd.*[27] The domestic measure in issue was a MAFF aid package for beef exporters who were also slaughterers or cutters. The Government notified the aid to the European Commission as a state aid. It was adopted in the aftermath of the BSE crisis and the European Commission's ban on the export of beef from the United Kingdom. Exporters who were not slaughterers or cutters challenged their exclusion from the aid on the basis that it was contrary to the Community law principle of equal treatment. The court was faced with a number of questions relating to whether or not the aid scheme depended

6.197

---

[25] *R. v. Stock Exchange, ex p. Else (1982) Ltd* [1993] Q.B. 534.
[26] *R. v. Ministry of Agriculture, Fisheries and Food, ex p. Hamble Fisheries* [1995] 2 All E.R. 714 at 724–725.
[27] *R. v. Ministry of Agriculture, Fisheries and Food, ex p. First City Trading Limited* [1997] 1 C.M.L.R. 250, QBD. The correct counsel in the case are identified in [1997] Eu.L.R. 195.

for its legality on compliance with general principles of Community law and, if so, whether the principle of equality or non-discrimination had been infringed on the facts of the case.

6.198   Laws J. (as he then was) recognised that fundamental principles of Community law included a principle of equal treatment. The issue was whether such fundamental rights fell to be applied to the facts of the case. Counsel for the applicant relied upon the *Phil Collins* judgment of the ECJ[28] and the decision of Sedley J. in *Hamble Fisheries*[29] in support of the argument that fundamental rights were engaged in the Community context which was before the Court. Laws J. considered that such a test essentially sought to apply the same test as is set out in Article 7 of the E.C. Treaty (now Article 12 EC) by analogy. Counsel for the respondent contended that a narrower test for the scope of fundamental principles applied, based on the judgment of the ECJ in *Klensch*.[30] The judge then proceeded to examine in detail the ECJ judgments in *Volker Steen*, *Wachauf*, *Bostock* and *Schumacker*.[31] He concluded that if the fundamental principles of Community law had a co-extensive scope of application to Article 12 EC, they had to apply to the aid scheme in issue.[32] The real issue thus became whether or not fundamental principles had a narrower reach than Article 12 EC.

6.199   Laws J. held that the fundamental principles of Community law were not provided for on the face of the Treaty of Rome, but had been developed by the ECJ. They were akin to a "common law" of the Community. It was therefore not self-evident that "their contextual scope must be the same as that of Treaty provisions relating to discrimination or equal treatment", which were statute law taking effect through their express terms. His Lordship then drew a crucial distinction between two different types of situation[33]:

> "On the one hand, a Member State may take measures solely by virtue of its domestic law. On the other a Community institution or Member State may take measures which it is authorised or obliged to take by force of the law of the Community. In the former situation I contemplate a measure which is neither required of the Member State nor permitted to it by virtue of Community Treaty provisions. It is purely a domestic measure. Even so, it may affect the operation of the Common Market and accordingly be held to be 'within the scope of application' of the Treaty. This was the *Phil Collins* case. It is of the first importance to notice that its falling within the Treaty's scope is by no means the same thing as it being done under powers or duties conferred or imposed by Community law. The second situation primarily includes (so far as Member States are concerned) measures which Community law requires, such as, for example, law which is made to give effect to a Directive. It includes also an act or decision done or taken by a Member State in reliance on a derogation or permission granted by Community law: as where for instance a

---

[28] See n. 25, above.
[29] See n. 26, above.
[30] See n. 44, above.
[31] See paras 6–76 *et seq.*, above.
[32] See judgment of Laws J. (n. 27, above), para. 38.
[33] *ibid.*, para. 39.

restriction on imports or exports is sought to be justified by reference to Article 36 of the Treaty. In the first situation, the measure is in no sense a function of the law of Europe, although its legality may be constrained by it. In the second, the measure is necessarily a creature of the law of Europe. Community law alone either demands it, or permits it."

The court distinguished fundamental principles from other Treaty provisions. The learned Judge found that principles of public law developed by the Court itself could not be deployed "in a case where the measure in question, taken by a Member State, is not a function of Community law at all".[34] The ECJ could legitimately require that the Treaty was adhered to, when domestic measures fell within the scope of the Treaty's application. The same could not be said of the fundamental principles developed by the Court. To require the same scope of application for them would be to condition or moderate the internal law of a Member State without that being authorised by the Treaty. It followed that: **6.200**

" . . . precisely because the fundamental principles elaborated by the Court of Justice are not vouchsafed by the Treaty, there is no legal space for their application to any measure or decision taken otherwise than in pursuance of Treaty rights or obligations. This is as true of a case such as *Phil Collins* as it is of a domestic measure having no connection whatever with the law of the Community. No court can expand the Treaty provisions."

To do otherwise, considered the court, would be to re-write the Treaty by finding that Article 12 EC prohibited breach of all fundamental principles within the scope of the Treaty, and not just the prohibition of discrimination on the grounds of nationality. It followed that in the first situation described, there was no room for the application of fundamental principles of Community law. The position was altogether different where a measure was adopted *pursuant* to Community law. Then, the internal law of the ECJ would apply.[35] According to Laws J., *pursuant* to Community law involved either the measure having been adopted in order to implement a Community provision, or because in promulgating it, the United Kingdom was necessarily relying on a permission or derogation granted by Community legislation, but for which it would have been in breach of Community law.[36] He found that cases such as *Phil Collins*, *Volker Steen*, *Schumacker*, *etc.* were all cases falling within the first of the situations he described. They were examples of Article 12 E.C. being applied within the scope of the application of the Treaty provisions. On the facts of the case, although the MAFF aid package had been occasioned by the Commission ban on beef; had been notified to the Commission as a state aid; and made reference to aspects of Community law, it was not required by Community law. The government had not had to rely on any Community permission in order to **6.201**

---

[34] *ibid.*, para. 42.
[35] *ibid.*, para. 43.
[36] *ibid.*, para. 43 of the judgment.

implement it. It did not constitute a measure taken pursuant to Community law and the principle of equal treatment did not therefore apply.[37]

6.202   The approach in *First City Trading* was approved by the Divisional Court in *Lunn Poly*.[38] The applicants challenged a decision made by H.M. Customs and Excise to impose differential insurance premium tax rates on various suppliers of insurance, depending on the nature of the goods and services supplied with it. They sought a declaration that the statutory provisions giving effect to the differential tax rates were contrary to the general Community principles of non-discrimination and proportionality. Counsel for the applicants identified four circumstances where national measures fell to be tested against such principles:

    (1) where national authorities implement Community law by fulfilling an obligation to act, for example, implementing a Directive;

    (2) where national authorities implement Community law by acting within the scope of a Community enabling provision or authorisation;

    (3) where national authorities rely upon a Community derogation to justify a measure which restricts one of the fundamental freedoms protected by the Treaty;

    (4) where there is otherwise a sufficient Community context for the general principles to apply.

It was acknowledged that (3) might be a sub-category of (2) and that (4) was controversial.

6.203   Maurice Kay J. considered the judgment of Laws J. in *First City Trading*. He concluded with approval that Laws J. had accepted categories (1), (2) and (3), eliding (2) and (3), but rejected category (4). On the facts, the applicants failed to show any specific enabling provision of Community law upon which the insurance premium tax had been based. They consequently failed to come within categories (1) to (2)/(3). He also rejected an attempt to apply fundamental rights under category (4). That, in his judgment, would be "a wholly unwarranted encroachment on sovereign powers". There was accordingly no basis for applying the prohibition of non-discrimination to the facts of the case.

6.204   That, however, is not the end of the story. In *British Pig*,[39] a further challenge was mounted to certain financial assistance given in an agricultural sector governed in part by a common organisation of the market ("COM"). This time the BSE support measures had been granted to the beef and sheep industries and pig farmers claimed that they had not

---

[37] Laws J. also rejected an argument, based on *Klensch*, which confirmed that Article 34(3) E.C. is but a specific enunciation of a more general principle. His Lordship found (para. 53) that the fact that proposition X exemplified principle Y did not mean that X and Y had the same range of application. In any event, it was found that the scheme did not fall within the scope of Article 34(3) E.C.

[38] *R. v. H.M. Customs and Excise, ex p. Lunn Poly* [1998] Eu.L.R. 438 at 444–446. The case went on appeal to the Court of Appeal on the state aid ground only: see [1999] 1 C.M.L.R. 1357, CA.

[39] *R. v. Ministry of Agriculture, Fisheries and Food, ex p. British Pig Industry Support Group and Ward* [2000] Eu. L.R. 724 at 745H–747E.

received equal treatment by comparison. The applicants contended that the state aids granted in the present case fell within the second situation envisaged by Laws J. in *First City Trading*. That argument was rejected on the facts. The alternative submission, that *First City Trading* was wrongly decided, met with greater success before Richards J. It was suggested that where the adoption of national measures was circumscribed by a COM and dependent upon authorisation from the Commission, a Member State was acting within the scope of Community law and was obliged to comply with the fundamental principles of Community law. It was also said that Laws J.'s distinction between Treaty law and judge-made law was not a valid one, citing *Klensch*.

Richards J. accepted that a challenge based on fundamental rights could **6.205** theoretically have been lodged against Community support measures specifically adopted under the relevant COMs.[40] He went on to find that the COM context was as relevant in the *First City Trading* case as it was here, so that case could not simply be distinguished. Richards J. found that the distinction between the two situations described by Laws J. was not an easy one to apply. The court held that a state aid notified to the Commission had features of both situations. Any state aid was prohibited by Community law unless it was notified to and approved by the Commission. Its validity was therefore ultimately dependent upon a specific permission under Community law. Richards J. expressed "real doubts" about the correctness of *First City Trading* and *Lunn Poly* and concluded that:

> "Thus, although the grant of state aid cannot in my view be said to amount to 'implementation' of the COM or to be done 'pursuant' to Community law, I think it is well arguable that the grant of aid by a Member State falls within the scope of Community law to the extent that the fundamental principles of Community law apply to it. I also see some substance in Miss Sharpston's challenge to the validity of the distinction drawn in *First City Trading* between Treaty law and the fundamental principles of Community law as developed in the case law of the ECJ."

Rather than ordering a reference on the point to the ECJ, his Lordship went on to examine (and dismiss) the applicants' case on the facts, assuming in their favour that the principle of non-discrimination could be applied.

It is apparent that the test to be applied by English courts is consequently **6.206** in a state of uncertainty. This is not surprising, given the difficulties in the ECJ case law identified above. In neither *First City Trading* nor *British Pig* was a reference made to the ECJ. In both cases, the courts found that the applicants would not have succeeded on the merits in any event. The ECJ has not yet had a chance to rule on the various competing arguments. The two separate strands of the judgment of Laws J. in *First City Trading* continue to merit scrutiny. They are that (a) Treaty provisions have a different range of application before domestic courts than fundamental rights; and (b) that only categories (1) and (2) above[41] fall within the scope

---

[40] *ibid.*, para. 61.
[41] See para. 6–202, above.

of Community law for the purposes of applying fundamental rights to
domestic measures. In the light of the judgment of Richards J., it is
arguable that neither of these propositions is consistent with the ECJ
jurisprudence. It therefore remains to be seen what definitive test the
national courts will adopt, under section 3(1) of the European Communities Act 1972, to determine whether a domestic measure falls within the
scope of Community law. What ultimately falls to be determined is the
regime of protection of human rights by which domestic measures in
England and Wales fall to be assessed.

CHAPTER 7
International Sources of Human Rights Law

1. INTRODUCTION

The purpose of this chapter is to provide an overview of the various **7.01** international sources of human rights law, setting out the rights, explaining how they differ from the European Convention on Human Rights and identifying leading cases that will hopefully provide an entry point into the relevant case law for the domestic civil practitioner. Appendices [C] to [E] to this book contain the principal United Nations treaties on fundamental rights and Appendices [F] to [K] contain the bills of rights of various common law jurisdictions discussed in this chapter, which include New Zealand, Canada, South Africa, the United States of America, Hong Kong and India.

The rights in the European Convention represent important safeguards to **7.02** human dignity and natural justice, but they are not the only source of human rights with potential effect in the United Kingdom. For many years the United Kingdom has been a signatory to and has ratified numerous international treaties that have purported to secure various rights and freedoms for its citizens. Although such treaties are not of direct effect in United Kingdom law, there is now a rule of statutory interpretation, which dictates that where a statute is capable of bearing a meaning that is in accordance with Parliament's international obligations, that interpretation is to be preferred.[1] This recognition of the importance of international human rights obligations represents an expansion of the more restrictive, albeit *obiter*, formulation of the position by the House of Lords in *J.H. Rayner v. Department of Trade*.[2] Recently, the Privy Council has adopted a more flexible approach in relation to international human rights obligations and it is now, it seems, fairly well established that legislation should, so far as possible, be construed so as to give effect to such obligations.[3]

7.03   Arguments based upon the content of these treaties are therefore available to United Kingdom lawyers, and the heightened awareness of human rights cultivated by the Act is likely to lead to a greater willingness to pray these treaties in aid of rights based contentions in the future. Paragraphs 7.08–7.43 below list the most important of these treaties along with the sources which are most helpful in interpreting the United Kingdom's obligations under them.

7.04   Whilst treaties have no direct effect in English law, requiring an Act of Parliament to incorporate them into domestic law, international customary law suffers from no such defect. When a norm acquires the status of international custom, that is to say, when it has become general practice amongst nations and has sufficient *opinio juris*, or belief that such conduct is *obligatory*, to constitute an international legal principle, it automatically becomes part of the common law of the United Kingdom.[4]

7.05   Human rights law is an international phenomenon, with many states signing up to numerous treaties, and there is a growing argument that much of the content of these treaties has by now become international customary law directly binding on all nations, whether signatories to the treaties or not. In particular, it is now widely accepted among international jurists that the "core rights" contained within the Universal Declaration of Human Rights (1948) have become part of customary law, and many go further and assert that the entire Declaration is binding customary law.[5] Section 702 of the Third Restatement of the Foreign Relations Law of the United States identifies the norms which the United States believes to

---

[1] On this topic see the speech of Lord Bingham in the House of Lords legislative chamber in which he identified this and other areas in which international treaties affect U.K. law. Those other areas included a similar principle of interpretation whenever the common law is unclear; the fact that court discretion should, whenever possible, be exercised in accordance with international obligations; and that the dictates of public policy, when investigated by the courts, could legitimately be expanded to include consideration of treaty obligations. (574 H.L. Official Report (5 series) col. 1465 (July 3, 1996)).

[2] [1990] 2 A.C. 418—see in particular the judgment of Lord Oliver at 511–513. On the subject of reference to treaties in statutory interpretation in English law, see Chap. 4.2(a) of Hunt, *Using Human Rights in English Courts*, (1997).

[3] *Matadeen v. Pointu* [1999] 1 A.C. 98; *Lewis v. Attorney-General of Jamaica* [2000] 3 W.L.R. 1785.

[4] See *West Rand Central Gold Mining Co. v. R.* [1905] 2 K.B. 391; *Trendtex Trading Corporation v. Central Bank of Nigeria* [1977] 1 All E.R. 881; *1 Congreso del Partido* [1983] 1 W.L.R. 244. See App. 1 of Hunt, above, for a chronological table of all the English cases in which judicial reference has been made to unincorporated international human rights law.

[5] See, *e.g.*, J. Humphrey, "*The International Bill of Rights: Scope and Implementation*" 17 Wm & Mary L. Rev 527 (1976); McDougal, Lasswell and Chen, *Human Rights and World Public Order* (1980), pp. 273–274, 325–327; D'Amato, *International Law: Process and Prospect* (1986), pp. 123–147.

have acquired customary status.[6] There are increasing calls that all of the so-called "International Bill of Rights", that is to say the Universal Declaration of Human Rights (1948), the International Covenant on Civil and Political Rights (1966) and the International Covenant on Economic, Social and Cultural Rights (1966), have become customary norms. Whilst this argument is perhaps not yet fully justified it may only be a matter of time before it could legitimately prevail, and all practitioners with an eye to human rights arguments should carefully monitor the situation.

In any event, the international rights jurisprudence can be of great assistance to the practitioner. Many of the rights secured by the International Covenant on Civil and Political Rights (ICCPR) are largely indistinguishable in substance from those under the European Convention (referred to throughout this chapter as the "ECHR" to avoid confusion), and several of the countries who have bills of rights entrenched within their domestic systems have expressly declared that those bills of rights are the recognition of their commitments under the ICCPR, for example New Zealand, Canada and Hong Kong. In these jurisdictions amongst others, there are numerous instances of judicial dicta which make clear the value of comparative jurisprudence in the development of these rights, both between various jurisdictions and with regard to the regular reports and comments of the United Nations Human Rights Committee. This approach finds support in the pronouncements of numerous commonwealth jurists in the Bangalore Principles,[7] the key principles of which are: **7.06**

> "4. In most countries whose legal systems are based upon the common law, international conventions are not directly enforceable in national courts unless their provisions have been incorporated by legislation into domestic law. However, there is a growing tendency for national courts to have regard to these international norms for the purpose of deciding cases where the domestic law—whether constitutional, statute or common law—is uncertain or incomplete.
>
> 7. It is within the proper nature of the judicial process and well-established judicial functions for national courts to have regard to international obligations which a country undertakes—whether or not they have been incorporated into domestic law—for the purpose of removing ambiguity or uncertainty from national constitutions, legislation or common law."

These principles were "warmly endorsed" by the Harare Declaration,[8] and by the predominantly West African participants in the Banjul Affirmation.[9] **7.07**

---

[6] Section 702 identifies genocide; slavery; murder or "causing the disappearance" of individuals; torture or other cruel, inhuman or degrading treatment or punishment; prolonged arbitrary detention; systematic racial discrimination; and "consistent patterns of gross violations of internationally recognised human rights" as violations of customary international law.

[7] Commonwealth Secretariat, *Developing Human Rights Jurisprudence: The Domestic Application of International Human Rights Norms* (Judicial Colloquium in Bangalore, February 24–26, (1988) 14 *Commw L. Bull* 1196.

[8] Commonwealth Secretariat, *Developing Human Rights Jurisprudence (Vol. 2); A Second Judicial Colloquium on the Domestic Application of International Human Rights Norms* (Judicial Colloquium in Harare, April 19–22, 1989).

[9] The Banjul Affirmation: African Judges Adopt Human Rights Principles (1990) 5 *Interights Bulletin* No. 3, p. 39.

Comparative jurisprudence is an accepted and widely encouraged facet of the international human rights scene, and it is hoped that this chapter will aid civil practitioners seeking to begin a comparative exercise.

2. INTERNATIONAL HUMAN RIGHTS TREATIES

Universal Declaration of Human Rights

7.08 The Universal Declaration of Human Rights (1948) was an aspirational treaty, promulgated as a common standard of achievement for all civilised nations, and including:

> (1) Rights and freedoms without distinction—Article 2.
>
> (2) Right to life, liberty and security of the person—Article 3.
>
> (3) Equality and equal protection of law and freedom from discrimination—Article 7 .
>
> (4) Right to an effective remedy for violation of rights—Article 8.
>
> (5) No retrospective penalties—Article 11.
>
> (6) No arbitrary interference with privacy, family, home, correspondence and reputation—Article 12.
>
> (7) Freedom of movement—Article 13.
>
> (8) Right to property—Article 17.
>
> (9) Freedom of thought, conscience and religion—Article 18.
>
> (10) Freedom of opinion and expression—Article 19.
>
> (11) Freedom of association—Article 20.
>
> (12) Right to work—Article 23.
>
> (13) Right to Education—Article 26.

7.09 Although as mentioned above there is an increasingly respectable argument that the Universal Declaration is now part of international customary law and therefore part of United Kingdom law, binding upon domestic courts, there are difficulties in application of broadly drafted aspirational rights without any specific guidance as to their application as part of domestic law. It is more likely that treaty rights will need to be considered in conjunction with developed jurisprudence of their content and application.

The International Covenant on Civil and Political Rights (ICCPR)

7.10 At the present time, 140 countries have agreed to be bound by the ICCPR. As mentioned above, the ICCPR forms the basis of the Bills of Rights of Canada, New Zealand and Hong Kong, amongst others. The rights protected in the Covenant include:

(1) The entitlement to rights without distinction and equality before and equal protection of law—Articles 2(1) and 26.

(2) The right to life—Article 6.

(3) The right to liberty and security of person—Article 9.

(4) Liberty of movement—Article 12.

(5) Equality before the courts and a right to a fair and public hearing—Article 14(1).

(6) Protection of privacy, family, home, correspondence, honour and reputation—Article 17.

(7) Freedom of opinion and expression—Article 19.

(8) Right of peaceful assembly—Article 21.

(9) Freedom of association—Article 22.

(10) Right to participate in public life—Article 25.

7.11 Article 28 establishes the Human Rights Committee (HRC) to fulfil the function of treaty monitoring body. The committee consists of 18 independent experts who comment upon the reports submitted to it by the states parties, and adjudicates upon any state versus state or individual complaints.[10] As mentioned above, the HRC can issue either specific comments in response to a state's report, or it can issue general comments, which are meant to summarise the HRC's experience with states' reports. The subject-matters for these general comments can be:

> "the implementation of (a) the reporting obligation; (b) the obligation to guarantee the rights set forth in the covenant; (c) the application and content of its individual articles, and (d) suggestions for state co-operation in Covenant matters."[11]

Subject (c) is, of course, the heading most likely to contribute to the content of human rights law in a substantive way. Of the 26 general comments thus far made, 19 have fallen within this category. Of interest to exclusively civil practitioners are likely to be:

(1) General Comment Number 4 (Equality—Article 3 ICCPR);

(2) General Comment Number 10 (Freedom of expression—Article 19 ICCPR);

(3) General Comment Number 13 (Right to a fair trial—Article 14 ICCPR);

(4) General Comment Number 16 (Respect for privacy, family, home and correspondence—Article 17 ICCPR);

---

[10] See generally Boerefijn, *The Reporting Procedure under the Covenant on Civil and Political Rights—Practice and Procedures of the Human Rights Committee*, (1999); and Opsahl, *The Practice of the Human Rights Committee under the ICCPR* in J. Chan and Y. Ghai (Eds), *The Hong Kong Bill of Rights: A Comparative Approach* (1993), p. 429.

[11] As summarised by Opsahl, *op cit.*, at p. 434. The full descriptions of these subjects can be found in a 1980 Committee "Statement on the Duties of the Human Rights Committee under Article 40 of the Covenant" Report 1981, Annex IV, littera (c).

     (5) General Comment Number 18 (Non-Discrimination—Article 26 ICCPR).[12]

7.12   The United Kingdom, which ratified the ICCPR in 1976, reports to the HRC every five years. The reporting requirement ensures that the rights protected by the ICCPR are never far from Government policy-maker's minds, and in this sense, the ICCPR has demonstrable influence. In its most recent comments on the United Kingdom's performance, the HRC concentrated solely on matters within the criminal and immigration sphere,[13] which are outside the ambit of this book. The individual complaint mechanism under the ICCPR (mentioned below in connection with the *Toonen* case)[13A] can only be utilised by individuals within those states that have signed up to the First Optional Protocol and thereby conferred jurisdiction upon the HRC in this area. The United Kingdom has chosen not to accede to this Protocol No. 13 and there are consequently no decisions under this mechanism which directly affect the United Kingdom, although their comparative value is undiminished (see analysis below of similarities between ICCPR and ECHR rights).[14] For individuals in states that have acceded to the First Optional Protocol, the procedure for making a complaint consists of two stages. First, the HRC must determine whether the complaint is admissible, *i.e.* whether the complainant has exhausted all domestic remedies. If this is the case, the HRC, secondly, goes on to consider the merits of the complaint and whether any of the rights guaranteed under the Covenant have been infringed. Suggestions may be made as to how the infringement may be rectified, but any such suggestions have moral force only as against the infringing state.

Comparison of ICCPR Rights and ECHR Rights

7.13   The aim of this section is to demonstrate the similarities and differences between the key provisions of the two instruments as they relate to civil practitioners, and to demonstrate that in all key areas a comparative perspective would be of potential assistance to the English lawyer in interpreting and applying the ECHR under the HRA.

Articles 2(1) and 26 ICCPR—Entitlement to rights without distinction and equality before and equal protection of law (Article 14 ECHR and Protocol No. 12)

7.14   Article 2 ICCPR states:

     "Each State Party to the present Covenant undertakes to respect and to ensure to all individuals within its territory and subject to its jurisdiction the rights recognised in the present Covenant, without distinction

---

[12] General comments can be located thus: Nos 1–22, I.H.R.R. Vol. 1, No. 2 [1994] 1; No. 23, I.H.R.R. Vol. 1, No. 3 [1994] 1; No. 24 I.H.R.R. Vol. 2, No. 1 [1995] 10; No. 25, I.H.R.R. Vol. 4, No. 1 [1997] 1; No. 26, I.H.R.R. Vol. 5, No. 2 [1998].

[13] See I.H.R.R. Vol. 3, No. 1 [1996] 180.

[13A] At paras 7.43 and 7.113.

[14] The Home Secretary announced on March 3, 1999 that the U.K. Government had undertaken a review of the United Kingdom's obligations under various international treaties and would look again at the question of accepting a right of individual petition to the HRC after the Human Rights Act 1998 had been fully implemented.

of any kind, such as race, colour, sex, language, religion, political or other opinion, national or social origin, property, birth or other status."

Article 26 ICCPR states: **7.15**

"All persons are equal before the law and are entitled without any discrimination to the equal protection of the law. In this respect, the law shall prohibit any discrimination and guarantee to all persons equal and effective protection against discrimination on any ground such as race, colour, sex, language, religion, political or other opinion, national or social origin, property, birth or other status."

The nearest equivalent in the ECHR is Article 14, which reads as follows.

"The enjoyment of the rights and freedoms set forth in this Convention shall be secured without discrimination on any ground such as sex, race, colour, language, religion, political or other opinion, national or social origin, association with a national minority, property, birth or other status."

ECHR Article 14 then refers only to non-discrimination as regards "the **7.16** enjoyment of the rights and freedoms set forth in this Convention" and is not therefore a guarantee in its own right of equality of treatment before the law. The provisions in the ICCPR are wider than the current ECHR provision. On November 4, 2000, Protocol No. 12 to the ECHR was opened for signature and ratification. It will enter into force when it has been ratified by 10 Council of Europe states. Protocol No. 12 will give effect in European human rights law to the fundamental right in Article 26 ICCPR to the equal protection of the law without discrimination and would greatly strengthen the parasitic guarantee in Article 14. Article 1 of Protocol No. 12 provides as follows:

"(1) The enjoyment of any right set forth by law shall be secured without discrimination on any ground such as sex, race, colour, language, religion, political or other opinion, national or social origin, association with a national minority, property, birth or other status.

(2) No one shall be discriminated against by any public authority on any ground such as those mentioned in paragraph 1."

The United Kingdom Government has stated that it has "no plans at **7.17** present" to sign Protocol No. 12,[15] although over 30 Contracting States have signed or indicated an intention to sign it. Whether Article 26 applied only to Covenant rights was a question that effectively arose before the HRC in *Aumeeruddy-Cziffra et al v. Mauritius*,[16] and in further cases

---

[15] Justice Bulletin, Autumn 2000.
[16] No. 35/1978, Report 1983.

involving the Netherlands,[17] in which it is made clear that Article 26 applies to all areas in which the state party has legislated and is not limited to the rights secured by the ICCPR. Regard to the jurisprudence of the HRC under these provisions may well prove useful in ensuring that the common law under the HRA develops in accordance with the United Kingdom's wider responsibility to ensure non-discrimination under the ICCPR. Regard should be had to HRC General Comment 18,[18] in which several observations were made on the meaning of the word "discrimination": the fact that such action was expressly prohibited in any area of public authority operational ambit; and that not all distinctions will constitute discrimination, especially where the purpose of such distinction is recognised as a valid one under the Covenant.[19]

Article 14 ICCPR—Right to a fair trial (Article 6 ECHR)

7.18　Article 14 ICCPR states:

> "(1) All persons shall be equal before the courts and tribunals. In the determination of any criminal charge against him, or of his rights and obligations in a suit at law, everyone shall be entitled to a fair and public hearing by a competent, independent and impartial tribunal established by law. The press and the public may be excluded from all or part of a trial for reasons of morals, public order (ordre public) or national security in democratic society, or when the interest of the private lives of the parties so requires, or to the extent strictly necessary in the opinion of the court in special circumstances where publicity would prejudice the interests of justice; but any judgement rendered in a criminal case or in a suit at law shall be made public except where the interest of juvenile persons otherwise requires or the proceedings concern matrimonial disputes or the guardianship of children."

7.19　The relevant article under the ECHR is Article 6 (right to a fair trial):

> "(1) In the determination of his civil rights and obligations or of any criminal charge against him, everyone is entitled to a fair and public hearing within a reasonable time by an independent and impartial tribunal established by law. Judgment shall be pronounced publicly but the press and public may be excluded from all or part of the trial in the interests of morals, public order or national security in a democratic society, where the interests of juveniles or the protection of the private life of the parties so require, or to the extent strictly necessary

---

[17] No. 172/1984, *SWM Brooks v. Netherlands*; No. 180/1984, *L.G. Dinning v. Netherlands*; and No. 182/1984, *FH Swan-de Vries v. Netherlands, Report 1987.*

[18] See n. 13, above. For a good summary of the findings of the HRC up to July 1986 see de Zetas, Muller and Opsahl, *Application of the International Covenant on Civil and Political Rights under the Optional Protocol by the Human Rights Committee*, 28 German Yearbook of International Law (1985) (published 1987).

[19] For comment on the formulations in General Comment 18, see Edie and Opsahl, *Equality and Non-Discrimination* (Norwegian Institute of Human Rights, Oslo, Publication No. 1/1990).

in the opinion of the court in special circumstances where publicity would prejudice the interests of justice."

7.20 Despite the two provisions appearing at first glance to be similar in substance, questions have been raised as to whether "civil rights and obligations" are the same thing as "rights and obligations in a suit at law"? Unfortunately, the HRC has as yet been unable to clarify the situation: in General Comment 13 the related question was left unanswered as to how far the right to a fair hearing extends beyond criminal cases to disputes about "rights and obligations in a suit at law", and it is to be hoped that future reports and views of the HRC on this area may be of more assistance in ECHR interpretation. In *Y L v. Canada*[20] the HRC did give limited assistance by stating that:

> " . . . the concept of a 'suit at law' or its equivalent in the other language texts is based on the *nature of the right* in question rather than on the status of one of the parties . . . or else on the particular forum in which individual legal systems may provide that the right in question is to be adjudicated upon, especially in common law sys-. tems when there is no inherent difference between public law and private law, and where the Courts normally exercise control over the proceedings, either at first instance or on appeal specifically provided by statute or else by way of judicial review. In this regard, each communication must be examined in the light of its particular features."[21]

Article 17 ICCPR—Protection of privacy, family, home, correspondence, honour and reputation (Article 8 and 10 ECHR)

7.21 Article 17 ICCPR states:

> "(1) No one shall be subjected to arbitrary or unlawful interference with his privacy, family, home or correspondence, nor to unlawful attacks on his honour and reputation.
> (2) Everyone has the right to the protection of the law against such interference or attacks."

7.22 The ECHR equivalent is Article 8, plus Article 10(2) (restrictions on freedom of expression).

7.23 Article 8 ECHR (right to respect for private and family life) provides:

> "(1) Everyone has the right to respect for his private and family life, his home and his correspondence.
> (2) There shall be no interference by a public authority with the exercise of this right except such as is in accordance with the law and is necessary in a democratic society in the interests of national security, public safety or the economic well-being of the country, for

---

[20] Communication No. 112/1981, *Selected Decisions of the Human Rights Committee under the Optional Protocol* (1990), Vol. 2, p. 28.
[21] Above, at p. 30, para. 9.2.

> the prevention of disorder or crime, for the protection of health or morals or for the protection of the rights and freedoms of others."

7.24 Article 10(2) ECHR (freedom of expression) provides the justifications for interference with the right to freedom of expression in Article 10(1):

> "(2) The exercise of these freedoms, since it carries with it duties and responsibilities, may be subject to such formalities, conditions, restrictions or penalties as are prescribed by law and are necessary in a democratic society, in the interests of national security, territorial integrity or public safety, for the prevention of disorder or crime, for the protection of health or morals, for the protection of the reputation or rights of others, for preventing the disclosure of information received in confidence, or for maintaining the authority and impartiality of the judiciary."

7.25 Although the ICCPR provision is drawn in somewhat wider terms than the ECHR equivalents, the import of the two is not significantly different. Reference to the privacy jurisprudence of states that have effectively incorporated the ICCPR (see below) would be a useful aid to the interpretation of the ECHR right in accordance with its global cousin.

Article 14(3)(g) ICCPR—Privilege against self-incrimination (Article 6(1) ECHR)

7.26 Article 14(3)(g) provides:

> "In the determination of any criminal charge, everyone shall be entitled to certain minimum guarantees including a right not to be compelled to testify against himself or to confess guilt."

7.27 The privilege against self-incrimination is not found in the text of the ECHR since the right was omitted from Articles 10 and 11(1) of the Universal Declaration of Human Rights on which the ECHR is based. In *Saunders v. United Kingdom*,[22] the European Court expressly relied upon Article 14(3)(g) ICCPR in stating that the right not to incriminate oneself is a generally recognised international standard that lies at the heart of the notion of a fair procedure under Article 6(1).

Article 19 ICCPR—Freedom of expression (Article 10 ECHR)

7.28 Article 19 ICCPR provides:

> "1. Everyone shall have the right to hold opinions without interference.
> 2. Everyone shall have the right to freedom of expression; this right shall include freedom to seek, receive and impart information and ideas of all kinds, regardless of frontiers, either orally, in

---

[22] (1997) 23 E.H.R.R. 313.

writing or in print, in the form of art, or through any other media of his choice.

3. The exercise of the rights provided for in paragraph 2 of this article carries with it special duties and responsibilities. It may therefore be subject to certain restrictions, but these shall only be such as are provided by law and are necessary:

    (a) For respect of the rights or reputations of others;

    (b) For the protection of national security or of public order (ordre public), or of public health or morals.

The ECHR equivalent is to be found in Article 10 (plus the restrictions in Article 10(2), see above).

Article 10(1) ECHR (Right to freedom of expression) provides: **7.29**

"(1) Everyone has the right to freedom of expression. This right shall include freedom to hold opinions and to receive and impart information and ideas without interference by public authority and regardless of frontiers. This Article shall not prevent States from requiring the licensing of broadcasting, television or cinema enterprises."

Again, despite a difference in wording, the import of the two is the same,   **7.30**
and it is not difficult to see how an examination of ICCPR jurisprudence on the topic would aid ECHR interpretation—see HRC General Comment 10 and the international decisions on freedom of expression in an ICCPR context.

For those provisions of potential interest to the civil practitioner not listed   **7.31**
in detail above, the main sections to compare are as follows:

Right	ICCPR Provision	ECHR Equivalent
Right to life	Art. 6(1)	Art. 2
Right to liberty and security of the person	Art. 9	Art. 5
Right to liberty of movement	Art. 12	Art. 2, Protocol No. 4
Right to peaceful assembly	Art. 21	Art. 11
Right to freedom of association	Art. 22	Art. 11
Right to marriage and family	Art. 23	Art. 12
Right to participate in public life	Art. 25	Art. 3, Protocol No. 1

Additional sources when invoking human rights argument are: the *travaux*   **7.32**
preparatoires of the instrument in question which will show the historical context in which it was negotiated and the progression of the negotiations themselves[23]; the Inter-American Commission on and Inter-American Court of Human Rights under the American Convention on Human Rights

---

[23] For the ICCPR see M. Bossuyt, *Guide to the 'Travaux Preparatoires' of the International Covenant on Civil and Political Rights* (1987).

(1969), the African Commission on Human Rights and Peoples' Rights under the African Charter (1981).

7.33   Perhaps the most fruitful source of comparative rights jurisprudence is the decisions of courts in commonwealth and other jurisdictions in their domestic application of human rights instruments and these are considered below.[24]

Other U.N. Conventions

7.34   Alongside the International Bill of Rights mentioned above, the most important International Human Rights Treaties are:

> (1) Convention on the Elimination of All Forms of Racial Discrimination (1965).
>
> (2) Convention on the Elimination of All Forms of Discrimination Against Women (1980).
>
> (3) Convention Against Torture and Other Cruel, Inhuman or Degrading Treatment or Punishment (1984).
>
> (4) Convention on the Rights of the Child (1989).

7.35   The rights protected in the more specific treaties are to a large degree expansions upon rights to be found in the core "International Bill", in particular within the Universal Declaration and the ICCPR, and for the purposes of this work the latter instrument will form the main focus of analysis. The other treaties listed above, and the Convention on Economic, Social and Cultural Rights are, it is submitted, unlikely to be relevant to the general civil practitioner, and are dealt with only briefly below. Those with a specific interest in any of these areas are directed to other works more focused upon these particular rights.[25]

7.36   The Convention on the Elimination of All Forms of Racial Discrimination is monitored by the Committee on the Elimination of Racial Discrimination (CERD) to which the United Kingdom reports every two years. CERD issues comments on the individual state's performances as well as more general recommendations. There is an obligatory inter-state complaints mechanism and an optional system of individual complaint, to which the United Kingdom has not acceded.

7.37   The Convention on the Elimination of All Forms of Discrimination Against Women is monitored by the Committee on the Elimination of Discrimination Against Women (CEDAW), and to which the United Kingdom submits regular reports. The reporting system is the only means of monitoring this Convention. The Committee issues both specific and general reports.

7.38   The Convention against Torture and Other Cruel, Inhuman or Degrading Treatment or Punishment is monitored by the Committee Against Torture (CAT) to which the United Kingdom reports every four years. There is an inter-state complaint mechanism to which the United Kingdom has acceded, and an individual complaint mechanism to which it has not.

---

[24] A table at the end of this chapter shows which of the constitutionally guaranteed rights in the jurisdictions mentioned below accords with equivalent or similar rights in the ECHR.
[25] e.g. Lester and Pannick, *Human Rights Law and Practice* (Butterworths, 1999) Chap. 8 (International Human Rights Codes and United Kingdom Law).

Finally, the Convention on the Rights of the Child is monitored by the   **7.39**
Committee on the Rights of the Child to which the United Kingdom submits
regular reports. There are no other mechanisms to monitor or enforce this
treaty.

United Nations Human Rights Treaties can be "enforced" in potentially   **7.40**
three ways: reporting procedures; state versus state complaints; and
individual complaints against states. The latter two are only applicable to
those states which have expressly agreed to be bound by these procedures.

Reporting involves countries making periodic reports to a committee—   **7.41**
usually the United Nations Human Rights Committee—alongside information supplied by non-government organisations such as Amnesty International. In response to these reports, the committee will from time to time
issue comments upon the performance of the various states parties.
These comments will be either specifically directed towards an individual
state's performance as regards a particular provision of the treaty; or the
comment will be of a more general declaratory nature, highlighting the
committee's understanding of what states generally are required to do to
honour their obligations to secure the various treaty rights.

State versus state complaints as yet exist in certain treaties and between   **7.42**
certain state parties in theory only—no such complaint has ever been
made.

Individual complaints against states are a more fruitful source of human   **7.43**
rights standards. A good example of this is the case of *Toonen v. Australia*[26] in which the complainant alleged that Tasmania's laws which
criminalised male homosexuality "violate Australia's obligations under the
ICCPR to respect the author's privacy and equality rights". The HRC
agreed that the impugned laws did constitute a violation of the complainant's right to privacy and opined that the appropriate remedy was a repeal
of those laws. After some considerable debate and delay, the Tasmanian
Parliament did abolish the offending law in April 1997. This decision of the
HRC clearly has important ramifications for rights or privacy the world
over, and is just one example of the way in which international human
rights norms can have application to domestic law, both in a direct way to
the individual state concerned and in an indirect manner by analogy to all
other states who claim to protect their citizens' right to privacy.

3. INTERPRETATION OF HUMAN RIGHTS PROVISIONS IN OTHER JURISDICTIONS

Introduction

Both prior to and subsequent to the HRA coming into force, the Scottish   **7.44**
courts[27] and the Privy Council[28] have been referred to and relied upon

---

[26] (1994) Communication No. 488/1992, U.N. Document CCPR/C/50/D/488/1992.
[27] See, *e.g. Brown v. Procurator Fiscal, Dunfermline, The Times*, February 14, 2000. Appeal
Court, JC. The court relied heavily on certain Canadian decisions in coming to its conclusion.
[28] See, *e.g. Stott (Procurator Fiscal, Dunfermline v. Brown* [2001] 2 W.L.R. 817, PC. The
Privy Council focused particularly on the U.S. position: see, *e.g.* the speech of Lord Bingham.

case law from other common law jurisdictions, although Lord Hope of Craighead warned in relation to this approach that:

> "care needs to be taken in the context of the Convention to ensure that the analysis by the [other jurisdiction's] courts proceeds upon the same principles as those which have been developed by the European Commission and the European Court".[29]

If there are signs of a dissimilar approach, caution should be exercised in relation to the reliability of such case law as a guide to the European context.

New Zealand

7.45   The New Zealand Bill of Rights Act 1990 came into force on September 25, 1990 and was enacted to "affirm, protect and promote human rights and fundamental freedoms" and to "affirm New Zealand's commitment to the International Covenant on Civil and Political Rights". The incorporation of the ECHR into United Kingdom domestic law was based upon the New Zealand model, in which parliamentary sovereignty is maintained—by section 4 of the New Zealand Act the courts may not declare any enactment:

> "to be impliedly repealed or revoked, or to be in any way invalid or ineffective; or decline to apply any provision of the enactment by reason only that the provision is inconsistent with any provision of this Bill of Rights".

Any interpretation of an enactment that is consistent with the Bill of Rights is, by virtue of section 6, to be preferred; and the Attorney General is to report to Parliament whenever any bill appears to be inconsistent with the Bill of Rights (section 7).

7.46   The rights conferred by the Bill have only vertical effect—they apply only to government or judicial action or to "any person or body in the performance of any public function, power or duty conferred or imposed on that person or body by or pursuant to law" (section 3), and they are subject "only to such reasonable limits prescribed by law as can be demonstrably justified in a free and democratic society" (section 5).

7.47   In addition to the rights secured by the Bill of Rights there has been subsequent bolstering legislation, for example the HRA 1993 which added new grounds of discrimination to those already contained within section 19 of the original Bill, and the Privacy Act 1993 which has added a new express right to information privacy and given rise to much litigation of its own, and makes New Zealand a key jurisdiction for United Kingdom practitioners to turn to whenever an information privacy point arises.

7.48   Despite the early years of the New Zealand Bill of Rights jurisprudence being perhaps disproportionately occupied with criminal law and matters of the admissibility of certain kinds of evidence, New Zealand has by now given rise to a veritable wealth of decisions with human rights aspects to

---

[29] Above. Speech of Lord Hope under heading *Comparative Material*.

them. These are helpfully collated into a single publication, *The Human Rights Reports of New Zealand* (HRNZ) and are thus extremely easy to research. The following is a very brief selection of some of the more interesting cases of recent years of relevance for present purposes.

Privacy (Information)—Privacy Act 1993 (Article 8 ECHR)

The Privacy Act is a detailed statutory scheme containing over 130 sec-   **7.49**
tions, all of which are directed towards the protection of information privacy. A privacy commissioner is established by sections 12 to 26 to investigate any complaints under the Act, and is instructed to uphold those which:

> "in the opinion of the commissioner . . . i) has caused, or may cause, loss, detriment, damage or injury to that individual; or ii) has adversely affected, or may adversely affect, the rights, benefits, privileges, obligations or interests of that individual; or iii) has resulted in, or may result in, significant humiliation, significant loss of dignity, or significant injury to the feelings of that individual."(section 66(b)).

A complaint may be made against any information holding "agency", which is defined by section 2 as meaning:

> "any person or body of persons, whether corporate or incorporate, and whether in the public sector or the private sector; and, for the avoidance of doubt, includes a (Government) Department."

There then follows a list of excepted bodies and activities, including any "news activity" or "news medium".

Since its inception the Privacy Act has been used for many different   **7.50**
challenges, to denials of access to information and to its unauthorised dissemination to others; to delays in providing information; to the ways in which information is compiled in the first place, in areas ranging from hospital records,[30] bank records,[31] social welfare records,[32] records of school trustee board meetings[33] and video surveillance techniques,[34] to name but a few. In common with the United Kingdom, this is a fertile and rapidly developing area of law. Despite the fact that the above cases are based on a detailed statutory scheme and not on a broadly drafted right within a Bill, the New Zealand Privacy Act was brought into force on the understanding that it complied with New Zealand's international obligations to protect the privacy of its citizens, and accordingly it is believed that the Privacy Act case law is therefore of some relevance to United Kingdom lawyers endeavouring to develop rights of privacy under the ECHR.

---

[30] See, *e.g. M. v. Ministry of Health* 4 H.R.N.Z. 79; *L. v. Complaints Assessment Committee* 5 H.R.N.Z. 647; *L.v. J* 5 H.R.N.Z. 616; *Ilich v. Accident Rehabilitation and Compensation Insurance Corporation* 5 H.R.N.Z. 636.
[31] See, *e.g. C. v. A.S.B. Bank Ltd* 4 H.R.N.Z. 306.
[32] *W. v. Director-General of Social Welfare* 5 H.R.N.Z. 580.
[33] *Mayes v. Owairaka School Board of Trustees* 4 H.R.N.Z. 312.
[34] *Smits v. Sante Fe Gold Ltd* 5 H.R.N.Z. 586.

7.51   **Privacy generally.**   As mentioned above, there is no general right to privacy in the Bill of Rights, but the concept has played a major part in the development of the section 21 right against unreasonable search and seizure. Most of the jurisprudence in this area is beyond the scope of this book (although arguably it could have some relevance to the future legality of search orders in the United Kingdom). However, given the increasingly prolific use of video surveillance techniques in personal injury actions, it may be of interest to civil practitioners to note that the legality of these techniques in New Zealand depends upon the expectation of privacy attaching to the venue in which any complainant was filmed or otherwise recorded.[35]

7.52   **Discrimination—Section 19 NZBORA 1990 (Article 14 ECHR).**
Like Articles 2(1) and 26 of the ICCPR, Section 19 of the New Zealand Bill is a free-standing guarantee of the right to non-discrimination, and has been invoked in cases involving sex and sexual orientation,[36] race[37] and level of qualification,[38] again to name just a few. A more detailed discussion is beyond the scope of this book.

7.53   **Freedom of expression—Section 14 NZBORA 1990 (Article 10 ECHR).**   Much of the jurisprudence concerning freedom of expression has focused upon reporting restrictions at criminal trials and on censorship issues. Some of the more interesting cases in the latter category include *Re "Penthouse (US)"* Vol 19, No. 5 and others[39] in which it was considered whether an age restriction was a justified limitation on freedom of expression (on age restriction see also the case of *Re High Times Nos. 250, 251 and 252 (Film and Literature Board of Review)*[40] in which a publication describing the cultivation of marijuana was given an "R18" rating); *News Media Ltd v. Film and Literature Board of Review*[41] and *Moonen v. Film and Literature Board of Review,*[42] cases involving determination of the level of censorship that was in accordance with the applicants' rights under the Bill. In general terms the restrictions that may be placed upon an individual's section 5 freedom of expression must be tested in New Zealand according to the *Oakes* test in Canada (see below)—*Ministry of Transport v. Noort.*[43] Cases of interest have involved the compliance with the Bill of Rights of restriction upon the right to protest—*Bracanov v. Moss*[44]; the right to express offensive views—*Zdrahal v. Wellington City Council*[45]; and the question of whether the

---

[35] See *R. v. Peita* 5 H.R.N.Z. 250, and *R. v. Fraser* 2 NZLR 442.
[36] See, *e.g. Quilter v. A-G* 4 H.R.N.Z. 170, on whether restricting marriage to different sex couples amounted to discrimination on either sex or sexual orientation grounds.
[37] See, *e.g. Bhana v. Bay of Plenty (Rotorua) Indian Association Inc.* 5 H.R.N.Z. 515 whether sports club membership limited by age and race discriminatory.
[38] See, *e.g. Lal v. Residence Appeal Authority* 5 H.R.N.Z. 11; *Wheen v. Real Estate Agents Licensing Board* 2 H.R.N.Z. 481.
[39] 1 N.Z.B.O.R.R. 429.
[40] 4 H.R.N.Z. 437.
[41] 4 H.R.N.Z. 410.
[42] 5 H.R.N.Z. 224.
[43] 3 N.Z.L.R. 260.
[44] 2 H.R.N.Z. 319.
[45] 2 H.R.N.Z. 196.

contempt of court rules involved an unjustified fetter on freedom of expression—*Duff v. Communicado*.[46]

Privilege against self-incrimination—Section 25(d) NZBORA **7.54**
1990 (Article 6(1) ECHR).   Section 25(d) NZBORA 1990 grants to every-one who is charged with an offence certain minimum rights including the right not to be compelled to be a witness against himself or to confess guilt. The privilege against self-incrimination has been implied into Article 6(1) of the European Convention.

Right to a fair trial—Sections 25 and 27 NZBORA 1990 (Article 6 **7.55**
ECHR).   The right to a fair trial is conferred, in criminal proceedings, by section 25(a) of the Bill of Rights. In relation to civil proceedings, the closest provision to Article 6 is section 27, the "Right to Justice", which ensures that:

(1) principles of "natural justice" are adhered to in the "determina-tion of rights, obligations or interests protected or recognised by law";

(2) everyone whose rights, obligations or interests are affected by a public tribunal decision has the right to apply for judicial review; and

(3) everyone shall have the right to bring civil proceedings against the Crown in the same way as any other party.

Cases on the relationship between New Zealand law and international law.

One of the areas in which the New Zealand courts have been particularly **7.56**
vocal is the issue of the proper relationship between domestic and inter-national law, and the way in which international sources can and should be utilised in the interpretation of the domestic Bill of Rights. Perhaps the most famous case decided since the enactment of the New Zealand Bill is *Simpson v. A-G (Baigent's Case)*.[47] The case is famous for the actions of the Court of Appeal in implying the court's ability to grant remedies for breaches of the rights guaranteed in the Bill, no such ability being expressly granted within that Act itself. The discussion concerning the jurisprudence of Trinidad and Tobago, India, Ireland, the United States and Canada, and the importance of complying with the international obliga-tions imposed by the International Covenant on Civil and Political Rights may be of interest. This treaty was also discussed at some length in *Tavita v. Minister of Immigration*[48] (along with the Convention on the Rights of the

---

[46] 2 H.R.N.Z. 370.
[47] 1 H.R.N.Z. 42.
[48] 1 H.R.N.Z. 30.

Child),[49] *Re "Exposing the Aids scandal"*[50] (along with the Convention on the Elimination of All Forms of Racial Discrimination, European and Canadian case law), *Lawson v. Housing New Zealand*[51] (along with the Covenant on Economic, Social and Cultural Rights, and the Universal Declaration of Human Rights), *Tangiora v. Wellington District Legal Services Committee*,[52] Northern Regional Health Authority v. Human Rights Commission,[53] Nicholls v. Registrar of the Court of Appeal[54] (an interesting case on when grants of legal aid should be made in respect of appeals,[55] in which ECHR decisions were given "persuasive weight"), and *R. v. N. (No. 2)*[56] (in which it was argued that international obligations in the ICCPR required the Bill of Rights to apply to some purely private acts).

Canada

7.57   Canada has had a Bill of Rights since 1960. However, the 1960 Bill had the status only of a normal Act of Parliament, was of effect only in regard to federal laws, had no explicit provision authorising the courts to provide remedies, and as a consequence was not utilised as often or as robustly by the judiciary as some might have hoped—indeed in the 22 years between the enactment of the Bill and the introduction of the Charter there was only one case in which the Supreme Court of Canada held a statute to be inoperative for breach of the Bill.[57] This changed dramatically with the Constitution Act of 1982 which formally entrenched a new Charter of Rights within the Canadian Constitution[58] itself with an express direction that:

> "The Constitution of Canada is the supreme law of Canada, and any law that is inconsistent with the provisions of the Constitution is, to the extent of the inconsistency, of no force or effect." (section 52(1)).

There is however an "override" or "notwithstanding" provision in section 33(1), which dictates that:

> "Parliament or the legislature of a province may expressly declare in an Act of Parliament or the legislature . . . that the Act or provision thereof shall operate notwithstanding a provision included in section 2 or sections 7 to 15 of this Charter."

---

[49] See also *Rajan v. Minister of Immigration* 3 H.R.N.Z. 209.
[50] 1 H.R.N.Z. 170.
[51] 3 H.R.N.Z. 285.
[52] 5 H.R.N.Z. 201. See also the discussion at High Court level (3 H.R.N.Z. 267) and in the Court of Appeal (4 H.R.N.Z. 136).
[53] 4 H.R.N.Z. 37.
[54] 4 H.R.N.Z. 537.
[55] For another legal aid argument on similar lines, see *Bailey v. Whangarei District Court* 2 H.R.N.Z. 275.
[56] 5 H.R.N.Z. 72.
[57] *R. v. Drybones* [1970] S.C.R. 282.
[58] Although the Bill of Rights does retain limited utility in protecting some economic and property rights not covered by the Charter.

Parliamentary sovereignty is thus preserved, even if this section has been successfully invoked only twice.[59] Rights secured under the Charter are enforceable only "vertically"—relations between private individuals are not susceptible to constitutional challenge.

Limitations of rights—Section 1 Charter (Article 18 ECHR, referring to limitations included in many Articles of ECHR, e.g. Articles 8 and 10)

The Charter has given rise to a wealth of important decisions, particularly **7.58** *R. v. Oakes*,[60] in which Chief Justice Dickson laid down the criteria that must be established, if it is to be said that a limit to a Charter right is reasonable and justified in a free and democratic society.[61] His judgment has been construed as a four stage test,[62] made up of the following:

(1) Sufficiently important objective: the law must pursue an objective that is sufficiently important to justify limiting a Charter right.

(2) Rational connection: the law must be rationally connected to the objective.

(3) Least drastic means: the law must impair the right no more than is necessary to accomplish the objective.

(4) Proportionate effect: the law must not have a disproportionately severe effect on the persons to whom it applies.

Section 1 applies even to those sections which have their own qualifica- **7.59** tions in terms of reasonableness or regularity, and *Oakes* is accordingly the most frequently cited case in Canadian Charter jurisprudence. The various criteria have been analysed in depth in a procession of subsequent cases, especially those involving section 15 equality rights (upon which see further below) and the requirement that the objective of the law be stated with some high degree of specificity. A good example of this is *Andrews v. Law Society of British Columbia*,[63] a case also important for its limitation of the scope of section 15 itself (see below). Considerations of space preclude reference to any more of the vast corpus of decisions on all four parts of the *Oakes* requirement.

Freedom of expression—Section 2(b) Charter (Article 10 ECHR)

In *Irwin Toy v. Quebec*[64] the Supreme Court summarised the three rea- **7.60** sons for protecting freedom of expression in the following terms:

---

[59] The Government of Saskatchewan used s.33 to immunise its labour laws from s.2 of the Charter, and the Quebec Government used it to preserve its unique language laws.
[60] [1986] 1 S.C.R. 103.
[61] Above, at 138–139.
[62] See Part 35.8 of *Constitutional Law of Canada*, Looseleaf, Carswell. This is a good starting point in researching Canadian Charter jurisprudence.
[63] [1989] 1 S.C.R. 143.
[64] [1989] 1 S.C.R. 927.

"(1) seeking and attaining the truth is an inherently good activity; (2) participation in social and political decision making is to be fostered and encouraged; and (3) the diversity in forms of individual self-fulfilment and human flourishing ought to be cultivated . . . ".[65]

"Expression" was defined in the same case in these terms: "Activity is expressive if it attempts to convey meaning" and does not include that which is "purely physical and does not attempt to convey meaning".[66] Even threats of violence are protected by section 2(b)—see *R. v. Keegstra*[67] in which it was held that there were no content based restrictions on the section 2(b) right:

"The content of a statement cannot deprive it of the protection accorded by section 2(b) no matter how offensive it may be".[68]

This has been held to extend even to deliberate falsehoods, because by definition the truth or otherwise of a statement is a content based quality—see *R. v. Zundel*.[69] Pornography has been held to be a protected form of expression, but restrictions upon its dissemination are generally found to be sufficiently well justified, due to the harm to society that would be caused thereby.[70] Charter protection is not afforded to violent forms of expression,[71] and a person who is in a public place for the purpose of expressing himself must respect the functions of the place and cannot invoke freedom of expression so as to interfere with those functions.[72]

7.61   Freedom of expression also "necessarily entails the right to say nothing or not to say certain things". Thus in *RJR-MacDonald v. Canada*[73] a federal statute requiring cigarette manufacturers to display unattributed health warnings on cigarette packets was a breach of section 2(b) which could not be justified under section 1. The *RJR-MacDonald* decision demonstrates that the right to freedom of "commercial expression", so long controversially denied in the United States (see below), is protected under the Canadian Charter. Thus in another aspect of the *RJR-MacDonald* case the court were unable to accept that the government ban on all forms of tobacco advertising was the least drastic way of accomplishing the valid objective of reducing the harmful effects of smoking. Other important cases on advertising rights are *Irwin Toy v. Quebec*,[74] in which a prohibition on all commercial advertising directed at children under 13 years of

---

[65] *ibid.*, at 976.
[66] *ibid.*, at 968 and 969.
[67] [1990] 3 S.C.R. 697.
[68] *ibid.*, at 828.
[69] [1992] 2 S.C.R. 731 and confirmed in *R. v. Lucas* [1998] 1 S.C.R. 439; although falsehoods may of course be accorded less value in any balancing exercise that has to be carried out than other forms of expression—see *Hill v. Church of Scientology of Toronto* [1995] 2 S.C.R. 1130, for a discussion of the value of falsehoods compared to other forms of expression.
[70] See, *e.g. R. v. Butler* [1992] 1 S.C.R. 452.
[71] *Suresh v. Canada (Minister of Citizenship and Immigration)*, unreported, January 18, 2000, FCA 000/033/198.
[72] *MacMillan Bloedel Ltd v. Simpson* [1994] 113 D.L.R. (4th) 368.
[73] [1995] 3 S.C.R. 199.
[74] [1989] 1 S.C.R. 927.

age was found to be a contravention of section 2(b) but one which could be justified under section 1 by the valid objective of protecting a vulnerable group of people; and *Rocket v. Royal College of Dental Surgeons*,[75] in which a particularly onerous advertising restriction on the dental profession was held to be a violation of section 2(b) and one that was not justified in this case by the objective of maintaining high standards of professional conduct.[76]

Right to "Fundamental Justice"—Section 7 Charter (related to right to fair trial in Article 6 ECHR)

In section 7 it is made clear that the law can only deprive someone of life, liberty or security of the person if it conforms to the principles of "fundamental justice". "Liberty" has been held to mean more than mere freedom from physical constraint, including the right to personal autonomy and to make decisions that are of fundamental personal importance.[77] It was held in *Irwin Toy v. Quebec*[77A] that corporations were not entitled to the benefit of the section as they were not capable of possessing "life, liberty or security of the person". However, in *R. v. Wholesale Travel Group*,[78] it was held that a corporation could pray the section in aid in defending criminal proceedings. The court rejected the argument that a corporation could be convicted under an unconstitutional law, and accordingly there ought to be no disputing that the term "everyone" in Article 6 of the ECHR should always be interpreted as including corporations. **7.62**

Offences of absolute liability (*i.e.* no requirement of fault, either *mens rea* or negligence) have been held to be unconstitutional. In the main case on the area, *B.C. Motor Vehicle Reference*,[79] the court did not disguise the fact that the absence of a *mens rea* requirement was a substantive injustice, and thus made it clear that a section 7 review has a substantive as well as a procedural element.[80] **7.63**

Strict liability offences, on the other hand (*i.e.* those in which negligence will suffice for a conviction), have been found to be constitutionally sound. The *Wholesale Travel Group* case involved the offence of misleading advertising under the Competition Act, said by the court to be a "regulatory offence" rather than a "true crime", designed to establish standards of conduct for activity that could be harmful to others. "Fundamental justice" is satisfied if there is a defence of reasonable care. The offence also included a "reverse onus" clause which placed the burden of proof on the **7.64**

---

[75] [1990] 2 S.C.R. 232.
[76] Although note McLachlin J.'s comment that the commercial nature of the expression would be significant in the balancing exercise. Some commentators interpret this as a suggestion that restrictions on pursuit of economic profit may be easier to justify than restrictions on other forms of expression.
[77] *Blencoe v. British Columbia (Human Rights Commission)* [2000] 190 D.L.R. (4th) 513 (SCC).
[77A] [1989] 1 S.C.R. 927.
[78] [1991] 3 S.C.R. 154.
[79] [1985] 2 S.C.R. 486.
[80] Although there is an argument that s.7 only had effect in that case because the offence carried with it a minimum mandatory term of imprisonment and was accordingly a potential deprivation of liberty.

accused company to show that it had not been negligent. The constitutionality of this provision was also upheld, by a majority of five judges to four.

Right to equality and non-discrimination—Section 15 Charter (Article 14 ECHR)

7.65 Section 15(1) provides that:

> "Every individual is equal before and under the law and has the right to the equal protection and equal benefit of the law without discrimination and, in particular, without discrimination based on race, national or ethnic origin, colour, sex, age or mental or physical disability."

7.66 There has been much litigation on section 15. The Canadian development has characteristics which are "analogous" to those expressly listed in section 15 of the Charter and thus worthy of protection from discrimination under the section. These are particularly relevant as future cases in the United Kingdom could see the boundaries of Article 14 of the ECHR being challenged and extended. In a recent decision, *Corbiere v. Canada*[81] the Supreme Court summarised the case law and declared that an analogous ground could be defined as one based on "a personal characteristic that is immutable or changeable only at unacceptable cost to personal identity". It was held that once a ground was found to be analogous in one case it became so for all future cases, in effect taking on the properties of a ground expressly listed in section 15. Some of the grounds that have thus far been found to be analogous include marriage,[82] sexual orientation[83] and citizenship.[84] The pre-occupation with immutability, however consistent its application, can lead to some peremptory decisions which might strike some as strange or unjust—for example in *Worker's Compensation Reference*[85] the applicants argument that a law that denied an injured employee the right to sue his employer in tort was dismissed in only *one* paragraph—the status of a work related victim lacking the immutability to make it an analogous ground meant it was unnecessary to consider the matter further. It should be noted that in order to establish discrimination under section 15 it is necessary to show a particular disadvantage that is suffered by the individual or group (or arguably company) as a result of a distinction: "which has the effect of imposing burdens, obligations or disadvantages on such individual or group not imposed on others, or which withholds or limits access to opportunities, benefits or advantages available to other members of society."[86]

---

[81] [1999] 2 S.C.R. 203.
[82] *Miron v. Trudel* [1995] 2 S.C.R. 418.
[83] *Egan v. Canada* [1995] 2 S.C.R. 513.
[84] *Andrews v. Law Society of British Columbia* [1989] 1 S.C.R. 143.
[85] [1989] 1 S.C.R. 922.
[86] *Andrews v. Law Society of British Columbia* [1989] 1 S.C.R. 143 at 174, *per* McIntyre J. See also *Law v. Canada (Minister of Employment and Immigration)* [1999] 1 S.C.R. 497, in which the Supreme Court revisited the rationale of s.15, finding "human dignity" to be the key and guiding concept.

Right to privacy (Article 8 ECHR)

There is no Charter entitlement to privacy, although the concept has been **7.67** utilised as the driving force behind the section 8 right against unreasonable search and seizure.[87] The Federal Privacy Act protects some aspects of the right, but of more interest for present purposes are the Supreme Court decisions that have been generated by the right to privacy enshrined in section 5 of the Quebec Charter of Human Rights and Freedoms. Of particular note is *Aubry v. Les Editions Vice-Versa*,[88] in which it was held that even material (in this case a photograph) gathered in a public place was worthy of protection under the section.

Privilege against self-incrimination—Section 13 Charter (Article 6(1) ECHR)

Canada is almost unique in that section 13 of the Charter does *not* give a **7.68** witness the right not to answer a question on the ground that the answer might incriminate him. Such a right used to exist at common law but was abolished in 1893 by what is currently section 5(2) of the Canada Evidence Act 1985. Section 13 of the Charter provides that:

"A witness who testifies in any proceedings has the right not to have any incriminating evidence so given used to incriminate that witness in any other proceedings, except in a prosecution for perjury or for the giving of contradictory evidence."

The United States of America

The American Bill of Rights is to be found in the amendments to the **7.69** Constitution of the United States. The first 10 amendments were passed by Congress in September 1789 and ratified by the states in December 1791. The "due process" guarantee contained within the Fourteenth Amendment, and which has been the basis for so much of American Constitutional jurisprudence, was ratified in July 1868. Despite its antiquity, the Bill of Rights, interpreted and developed by so many renowned jurists, has proved adept at meeting the changing circumstances of the modern world. It remains a source of human rights law recognised and emulated globally. It would clearly be impossible to attempt to summarise over 200 years of law in just a page or two, and what follows is no more than the barest flavour of the rights jurisprudence that has developed and is developing still in the United States.

"Due process" and "equal protection of the laws"—Fourteenth Amendment (Articles 6 and 14 ECHR)

Section 1 of the Fourteenth Amendment states that: **7.70**

" . . . No state shall make or enforce any law which shall abridge the privileges and immunities of citizens of the United States; nor shall

---

[87] Worthy of note in this area is *R. v. Duarte* [1990] 1 S.C.R. 30, in which the Supreme Court held that electronic surveillance is caught by s.8 and is consequentially unlawful without the consent of *all* parties involved. Such surveillance is lawful only in situations where there is no reasonable expectation of privacy.
[88] [1998] 1 S.C.R. 591.

any state deprive any person of life, liberty, or property without due process of law; nor deny to any person within its jurisdiction the equal protection of the laws . . . "

7.71   As regards "equal protection", the Supreme Court has developed the doctrine of "reasonable classification" in reviewing those laws which impose burdens or confer benefits on specific groups within society. Where the differentiation between groups is a reasonable means of achieving a legitimate legislative purpose, the law will be constitutional, but such laws are reviewed on a two-tier scale. Where the legislation appears on its face to be within a specific "fundamental" prohibition of the Constitution, and is therefore "suspect", the standard of review will be "strict scrutiny"—nothing less than the justification of a "compelling state interest" will suffice to save the constitutionality of the law. Where the classification does not on the face of it involve "fundamental" rights, "minimal scrutiny" is employed. It is sufficient if there is a "rational basis" for the classification.[89]

7.72   The seminal case in which equal protection of the law was invoked is undoubtedly that of *Brown v. Board of Education*[90] in which the racial segregation of schools was declared unconstitutional. This was supported some years later by the decision in *Swann v. Board of Education*,[91] the case which determined the constitutionality of "bussing" schemes whereby black children were provided with free bus services in order to be able to attend (predominantly white) schools outside of their local area, and by *University of California Regents v. Bakke*[92] (constitutionality of minority "quotas" in university courses). In more recent times it has been held that even the preferential transfer of radio and television broadcast stations to minority owned firms is not a violation of equal protection principles—see *Metro Broadcasting Inc v. Federal Communications Commission*.[93]

7.73   Discrimination on grounds of sex used to be a "minimal scrutiny" differentiation, but the 1970s saw a change in attitude. An Idaho probate law giving preference to males was impugned, even under this less strict standard, in *Reed v. Reed*,[94] but sex was finally elevated to a "suspect" ground of discrimination in *Frontiero v. Richardson*[95] and *Craig v. Boren*,[96] the latter establishing an intermediate standard of review for gender issues, namely that classifications by gender must serve "important" government function and must be substantially related to achievement of those objectives. The test has been frequently followed in gender cases since then.

---

[89] On this topic, see in particular *United States v. Carolene Products Co.*, 304 U.S. 144 (1938), and see Tussman and Broeck, *"The Equal Protection of the Laws"* (1949) Calif. L. Rev. 341, on the doctrine. See also *Craig v. Boren* [reference below] in which the two tier doctrine was born.
[90] 347 U.S. 483 (1954).
[91] 402 U.S. 1 (1971).
[92] 438 U.S. 265 (1978).
[93] 497 U.S. 547 (1990).
[94] 404 U.S. 71 (1971).
[95] 411 U.S. 677 (1973).
[96] 429 U.S. 190 (1972).

The concept of "property rights" has been developed and extended by the **7.74** United States judiciary to include very many facets of everyday existence, leading to the uniquely procedural approach to justice in virtually all spheres of American life. As the court summarised in *Board of Regents v. Roth*[97]:

> "Certain attributes of property interests protected by procedural due process emerge from these decisions. To have a property interest in a benefit, a person clearly must have more than an abstract need or desire for it. He must have more than a unilateral expectation of it. He must, instead, have a legitimate claim of entitlement to it. It is a purpose of the ancient institute of, property to protect those claims upon which people rely on their daily lives, reliance that must not be arbitrarily undermined."

Property rights, welfare benefits,[98] education,[99] holding a driver's licence,[1] reputation[2] and privacy (see below) have all been recognised as a result of these principles.

Economic liberty and the attendant liberty of contract used to be recog- **7.75** nised as constitutionally protected in American law. In the seminal case of *Lochner v. New York*,[3] now best remembered for the dissenting judgment of Oliver Wendell Holmes, the Supreme Court held that freedom of contract could not be fettered by restrictions upon the amount of hours a person could be required to work, thus enforcing the laissez-faire economic policy of the government of the day. This doctrine has now long since passed away, and it is recognised that contracting parties can be constrained by laws legitimately protecting the interests of others. In determining whether or not the standards of due process of law have been met, the courts have often had regard to the test enunciated in the case of *Mathews v. Eldridge*,[4] namely the exercise of deciding whether there has been correct balancing between private interests, public interests, and the particular procedures used in depriving persons of property interests. *Mathews* was a case in which the question was whether the recipient of social security benefit was entitled to the opportunity for an evidentiary hearing before that benefit could be taken away, but the decision has been applied in many other spheres —for example in *Santosky v. Kramer*[5] it was held that a New York statute for terminating parental rights in a natural child was inconsistent with due process of law because only a "fair preponderance of the evidence" was required to find that the child had been "permanently neglected". Perhaps analogous "fair trial" arguments could be made in the United Kingdom as regards civil standards of proof

---

[97] 408 U.S. 564 (1972).
[98] *Goldberg v. Kelly,* 397 U.S. 254 (1970).
[99] *Goss v. Lopez,* 419 U.S. 565 (1975).
[1] *Bell v. Burson,* 402 U.S. 535 (1971).
[2] *Wisconsin v. Constantineau,* 400 U.S. 433 (1971).
[3] 198 U.S. 45 (1905).
[4] 424 U.S. 319 (1976).
[5] 455 U.S. 745 (1982).

in relation to certain allegations, for example fraud. The procedural propriety of certain legal presumptions has also been impugned.[6]

Privacy—derived from First, Fourth, Fifth and Fourteenth Amendments ABOR (Article 8 ECHR)

7.76   The right to privacy is not expressly mentioned in the American Constitution, and has instead been derived from various constitutional sources including (1) the rights to liberty and equal protection under the Fourteenth Amendment; (2) association, expression and thought under the First Amendment; (3) the right to maintain silence under the Fifth Amendment; and (4) the right to be free from search and seizure under the Fourth Amendment. Privacy as a constitutional doctrine was first suggested in *Boyd v. United States*,[7] developed in the dissenting judgment of Justice Brandeis in *Olmstead v. United States*[8] and finally adopted fully by the Supreme Court in *Katz v. United States*[9] in which it was held that the interception of any communication intended and expected to be private violates the Fourth Amendment.

7.77   Even if the courts have had difficulty articulating and in some cases agreeing upon what particular constitutional provision applies to a privacy claim, the general right to privacy has been extended to include: bodily integrity; the family and home (see for example *Stanley v. Georgia*[10] in which it was held that it could not be made unlawful to possess and view pornographic materials in the privacy of one's home); sexual choice and freedom: see *Griswold v. Connecticut*[11] (right to contraception established for married couples); *Eisenstadt v. Baird*[12] (same right secured for unmarried people); *Carey v. Population Services International*[13] (same right secured for people below the age of 16); and *Bowers v. Hardwick*[14] (laws prohibiting sodomy between homosexuals held unconstitutional)); and the right to have an abortion (see *Roe v. Wade*).[15]

Freedom of expression—First Amendment ABOR (Article 10 ECHR)

7.78   Freedom of expression is perhaps the most respected of all the constitutional freedoms in the U.S. Any limitations on speech or expression are extremely narrowly drawn. A content-neutral approach is adopted because there is "no such thing as a false idea. However pernicious an opinion may seem, we depend for its correction not on the conscience of

---

[6] *e.g.* presumption that gifts made shortly before death made in contemplation of death and therefore subject to inheritance tax *Schlesinger v. Wisconsin*, 270 U.S. 230 (1926) and *Heiner v. Donnan*, 285 U.S. 312 (1932)); and presumption that when unwed mother died state became ward of child as father unfit to have custody (*Stanley v. Illinois*, 405 U.S. 645 (1972)).
[7] 116 U.S. 616 (1886).
[8] 277 U.S. 438 (1928).
[9] 389 U.S. 347 (1967).
[10] 394 U.S. 557 (1969).
[11] 381 U.S. 479 (1965).
[12] 405 U.S. 438 (1972).
[13] 431 U.S. 678 (1977).
[14] 478 U.S. 186 (1986).
[15] 410 U.S. 113 (1973).

judges and juries but on the competition of other ideas".[16] This is the case even where violent acts are threatened. In *Brandenburg v. Ohio*[17] the applicant had made discriminatory remarks at a meeting of the Ku Klux Klan, at which he was a speaker, and had threatened the authorities with violent acts. It was unanimously held by the Supreme Court that his conviction was unconstitutional. Calls for the use of violence can, it was said, constitute legitimate criticism of the authorities and the structure of society. The authorities may only intervene where there is "incitement to imminent lawless action".

Neither is widespread public resentment and anger at the way in which **7.79** someone chooses to express himself a constitutionally sound reason for prevention of that expression. This has been clear for many decades and was reaffirmed in recent times during the trials of those who burned the American flag.[18]

Even the publication of classified government documents obtained without **7.80** authorisation will be permitted unless the government can show a compelling reason why not—see *New York Times Co. v. United States*[19] in which several of the judgments of the Supreme Court contain extremely strongly worded defences of the principle that a free and unfettered press is an indispensable prerequisite of a democratic society. This does not mean of course that all information is publishable—it is well established that secrecy in military and intelligence matters is vital to the running of the state and will be subject to constitutional protection. The state can also act against people who break an agreement with it not to publish unauthorised information. In a case similar to the recent United Kingdom case of *Attorney-General v. Blake*,[20] the U.S. courts held that the imposition of a constructive trust on the profits received from an unauthorised book written by a former CIA agent was a constitutionally sound method of dealing with the publication, even though no classified material was disclosed.[21]

Libel laws have also come under the scrutiny of the Supreme Court. In **7.81** *New York Times v. Sullivan*[22] it was held that, in order to ensure the freedom of political debate, where criticism is of a person in authority, inaccuracies and untruths in the criticism would not be enough to establish a libel. Actual *malice* is required.

Freedom of expression in America includes the right not to make state- **7.82** ments, and again, this can be to the detriment of politicians. In *Miami Herald Publishing Company v. Tornillo*[23] a Florida statute requiring any newspaper which had attacked "the personal character or official record" of an election candidate to publish his reply (of equal length and given comparable prominence) was held to be unconstitutional. A further example is *Columbia Broadcasting v. Democratic Committee*,[24] where a radio station's choice not to broadcast controversial advertisements was held to

---

[16] *Gertz v. Welch Inc.*, 418 U.S. 323 (1974).
[17] 395 U.S. 444 (1969).
[18] *Texas v. Johnson*, 491 U.S. 397 (1989) and *United States v. Eichmann*, 496 U.S. 310 (1990).
[19] 403 U.S. 713 (1971).
[20] [2000] 3 W.L.R. 625.
[21] *Snepp v. United States*, 444 U.S. 507 (1980).
[22] 376 U.S. 254 (1964).
[23] 418 U.S. 241 (1974).
[24] 412 U.S. 94 (1973).

be its constitutional right. The issue of whether the government grant of the radio licence made the applicant a governmental entity and thus subject to all the constitutional constraints imposed on the government was left undecided.

7.83 Despite decisions early last century in which "commercial speech" was excluded from the protection of the First Amendment, it was made clear in *Virginia Pharmacy Board v. Virginia Consumer Council*[25] that commercial speech was so protected. The court noted, however, that:

> "In concluding that commercial speech, like other varieties, is protected, we of course do not hold that it can never be regulated in any way. Some forms of commercial speech regulation are surely permissible. We mention a few only to make clear that they are not before us and therefore not foreclosed by this case".

The permissible forms of regulation mentioned were those relating to "mere time, place and manner restrictions", "false or misleading" advertisements, advertisements of illegal transactions, and the "special problems of the electronic broadcast media". Later the same year the Supreme Court listed a four part test for assessing the constitutionality of restrictions upon commercial speech. In *Central Hudson Gas & Electricity Corp. v. Public Service Commission*,[26] it was held that for such a restriction to be constitutional it had to be considered:

(1) whether the speech in issue concerns a lawful activity;

(2) whether the asserted government interest is substantial;

(3) whether the regulation directly advances the government interest asserted; and

(4) whether the regulation is more extensive than necessary to serve that interest.

Privilege against self-incrimination—Fifth Amendment ABOR (Article 6(1) ECHR)

7.84 The Fifth Amendment to the Constitution of the United States provides that no person shall be compelled in any criminal case to be a witness against himself.

Hong Kong

7.85 The Hong Kong Bill of Rights Ordinance entered into force on June 8, 1991. Part II of the Ordinance contains the Hong Kong Bill of Rights ("HKBOR"), consisting of 23 Articles that substantively mirror the rights provisions of the ICCPR. By virtue of a rather convoluted statutory scheme (see sections 3 and 4 of the Bill of Rights Ordinance), the ICCPR and not the Bill of Rights itself is effectively entrenched in Hong Kong law as applied to Hong Kong (*i.e.* including the reservations entered on behalf of Hong Kong). Despite the intention of the ICCPR that the rights contained therein should be guaranteed to all persons at all levels, the rights con-

---

[25] 425 U.S. 748 (1980).
[26] 447 U.S. 557 1980.

tained within the Hong Kong Bill have "vertical" effect only, that is to say they cannot be enforced in relationships between private individuals (*i.e.* no "horizontal" effect). This was confirmed in the case of *Tam Hing Yee v. Wu Tai-Wai.*[27]

After an enthusiastic start, in which the Hong Kong judiciary seemed prepared to embrace a new jurisprudential approach and derive assistance from international sources such as the bills of rights of Canada and the United States, as well as commonwealth jurisdictions and the work of the HRC,[28] the pendulum swung somewhat sharply in the opposite direction after the Privy Council decision of *Attorney General v. Lee Kwong-Kut*[29] in which the pre-eminent role of the legislature in formulating policy was stressed.[30] Nevertheless, despite this more cautious approach, there remain many decisions under the Hong Kong Bill of Rights of interest and relevance to those applying human rights standards elsewhere. The following constitutes a brief introduction to some of the more important cases. **7.86**

Right to fair trial/hearing—HKBOR Article 10 (Article 14 ICCPR; Article 6 ECHR)

In *Commissioner of Inland Revenue v. Lee Lai Ping*[31] the courts applied Article 10 of the HKBOR after comparing the French and English texts of the ICCPR. The judgment involves a consideration of the similarities between "rights and obligations in a suit at law" in ICCPR Article 14 and "civil rights and obligations" in Article 6 of the ECHR. **7.87**

Article 10 was also invoked in several cases concerning town planning board decisions, the facts of which were essentially similar: plans were drawn up by the town planning board in which certain land was "re-zoned" so as to substantively alter the use to which it could be put. Various property owners and developers who were affected by this re-zoning lodged objection to the plans which were heard by members of the board who made the original draft plan. When the draft plans were officially endorsed the developers went to the courts claiming that they had not received a fair hearing, on the basis that the planning board had effectively been a judge in its own cause. In the first of these cases, *R. v. Town Planning Board, ex p. Auburntown,*[32] it was held by Rhind J. that the ICCPR provision did apply to the town planning proceedings as "suit at law" was not necessarily restricted to a lawsuit, the phrase being a mere qualification of the nature of the rights and obligations. The judge held that the right to develop one's own land could conceivably be viewed as part of a wider right to engage in private commercial activity. This was said to be so even where no such right had formal existence in domestic law. The argument was heavily reliant upon various European decisions which supported such reasoning. The *Auburntown* decision was followed in *R. v.* **7.88**

---

[27] [1991] 1 H.K.P.L.R. 261.
[28] See *R. v. Sin Yau Ming* [1992] 1 H.K.C.L.R. 127.
[29] [1993] 3 H.K.P.L.R. 72.
[30] See generally *Chan, Hong Kong's Bill of Rights: Its reception of and contribution to international and comparative jurisprudence,* International and Comparative Law Quarterly, Vol. 47 (1998), 306.
[31] [1993] 3 H.K.P.L.R. 141.
[32] [1994] 4 H.K.P.L.R. 194.

Town Planning Board, ex p. Real Estate Developers Association[33] (in which Leonard J. conducts an interesting analysis of European law in the area). However, the approach in *Auburntown* was rejected by the Court of Appeal in *R. v. Town Planning Board, ex p. Kwan Kong Company Ltd,*[34] the court holding that "suit at law" could not be interpreted as extending to administrative proceedings such as those under the town planning board. It was however agreed that the meaning of the phrase was not restricted to "legal proceedings in a court of law". At first instance Waung J. had also rejected the argument that the right to a fair hearing before a competent, independent and impartial tribunal implied a right of access to a court.

Freedom of expression—HKBOR Article 16 (Article 19 ICCPR, Article 10 ECHR)

7.89 In *Hong Kong Polytechnic University v. Next Magazine*[35] the Court of Appeal rejected the magazine's argument that to allow a defamation suit to be brought against them on a matter of public interest was a breach of their right to freedom of expression. The court held that under Article 16 of the Bill of Rights freedom of speech could legitimately be limited if the limitation was "provided by law", and that there was nothing in the common law to prevent the university taking out a defamation suit. In this way the right under the Bill was side-stepped altogether. In *Attorney General v. Ming Pao Newspapers Ltd*[36] the defendants revealed the details of a bribery investigation, such revelation being contrary to a Prevention of Bribery Ordinance. They argued that the statutory provision was contrary to their right to freedom of speech. The Court of Appeal disagreed, holding that the statute was a justifiable restriction of the defendants' right. The Privy Council upheld the Court of Appeal decision. In *Cheung Ng Sheong v. Eastweek Publisher*[37] an appeal was made against a large award of damages by a jury in a libel trial (HK$2.4m.) on the grounds that the power to make such an award, in the largely unfettered discretion of the jury, was a violation of freedom of speech under Article 19. The Court of Appeal agreed, following the ECHR decision of *Tolstoy Miloslavsky v. United Kingdom*.[38]

No retrospective penalties—HKBOR Article 12 (Article 15.1 (?) ICCPR, Article 7 ECHR)

7.90 In *R. v. Chan Suen-Hay*[39] a disqualification order was made retrospectively under section 168E of the Companies Ordinance. It was argued that this constituted a retrospective penalty and was therefore contrary to Article 12. The court decided that a penalty had been imposed under the definition of Article 12, and that there had accordingly been a violation of the applicant's rights under the Bill. The concept of a "penalty" was said to be an autonomous one. In coming to this decision the court followed

---

[33] [1996] 6 H.K.P.L.R. 179.
[34] [1996] 6 H.K.P.L.R. 237.
[35] [1997] 7 H.K.P.L.R. 286.
[36] [1995] 5 H.K.P.L.R. 13, CA; [1996] 6 H.K.P.L.R. 103, PC.
[37] [1995] 5 H.K.P.L.R. 428.
[38] (1995) 20 E.H.R.R. 442.
[39] [1995] 5 H.K.P.L.R. 345.

Welch v. United Kingdom,[40] a decision on the same issue to the same effect.

Right of non-discrimination—HKBOR Article 1 (Articles 2.1 and 26 ICCPR, Article 14 ECHR)

R. v. Man Wai-Keung (No.2)[41] lays down the test of non-discrimination. It **7.91** is held that in certain circumstances a departure from the principle of literal equality would be justified, but that:

> "To justify such a departure it must be shown: one, that sensible and fair-minded people would recognise a genuine need for some difference of treatment; two, that the difference embodied in the particular departure selected to meet that need is itself rational; and, three, that such departure is proportionate to such need."

This test was in effect applied in *R. v. Secretary for the Civil Service and* **7.92** *the Attorney General,*[42] in which it was held that there should be equal access to the terms and conditions of service and the opportunities for promotion within the civil service.

Privilege against self-incrimination—HBOR Article 11(2)(g) (Article 14(2)(g) ICCPR; Article 6(1) ECHR)

In a section lifted verbatim from the ICCPR, the Hong Kong Bill of Rights **7.93** Act confers upon a defendant the right in criminal trials not to be compelled to testify or to confess guilt.

Conclusion

There are of course many other decisions of interest from the jurisdiction **7.94** of Hong Kong—there have been well over 300 decisions involving the various rights under the Bill—and the above is intended only as an inexhaustive list by way of example. The Hong Kong Public Law Reports should be consulted whenever a comparative exercise might be useful in interpreting the provisions of the ECHR and applying them to United Kingdom law.

South Africa

The (Final) Constitution of South Africa took effect on February 4, 1997. **7.95** The Bill of Rights is entrenched within the Constitution and a new Constitutional Court was established to have supremacy in the interpretation and protection of those rights, with exclusive jurisdiction over certain types of constitutional dispute. The court has, in prescribed circumstances, the power of prior control over parliamentary and provincial bills, and also has the power to postpone the application of a law that has already come into effect if it is in the interests of justice to do so and the applicants in the particular action have a reasonable prospect of successfully showing that

---

[40] (1995) 20 E.H.R.R. 247.
[41] [1972] 2 H.K.P.L.R. 164.
[42] [1995] 5 H.K.P.L.R. 490.

the law is contrary to the Constitution. The Constitution, not parliament, is sovereign. The rights mentioned in the Bill can be limited only in accordance with the general and specific limitation provisions in the Bill. The general limitation provision can be found in section 36, and it dictates that any limitation must be reasonable and justifiable in an open and democratic society based on human dignity, equality and freedom. The provision also lists several factors to be taken into account in this determination. These factors draw much from the Canadian decisions on the validity of limitations (see further in Canada section, above).

7.96 Section 9(4) of the Constitution makes it clear that all rights apply directly in private relationships, and a Human Rights Commission was established to monitor and assess the observance of human rights under the new Constitution. By virtue of section 39(1)(b) of that Constitution, "when interpreting the Bill of Rights, a court, tribunal or forum— . . . *must* consider international law." South African constitutional judgments are in themselves by necessity comparative exercises, and therefore make extremely worthwhile reading as assessments of international human rights norms.

7.97 As the new Constitution has only been in effect for a relatively short period, most of the early judgments have involved highly charged, non-civil matters such as the unconstitutionality of the death penalty,[43] of laws against sodomy between consenting adult males[44] and the general overhauling of virtually the entire criminal justice system. There have, however, been a few cases of interest for present purposes which are set out below.

Right to fair trial—Section 34 SABOR (Article 6 ECHR)

7.98 This right is widely drafted under the South African Bill. Section 34 in its entirety reads:

> "34 Access to courts
>
> Everyone has the right to have any dispute that can be resolved by the application of law decided in a fair public hearing before a court or, where appropriate, another independent and impartial tribunal or forum."

7.99 Cases which have so far touched upon this right have been *Ferriera v. Levin N.O.*[45] and *Bernstein v. Bester.*[46] A related case is *Besserglik v. Minister of Trade, Industry and Tourism*[47] (civil) in which it was unsuccessfully argued that the right to have a dispute resolved by the application of law included an unfettered right to appeal. On a similar topic, in *Mohlmomi v. Minister of Defence*[48] the court struck down a limitation period of effectively five months which applied to a civil action against the armed

---

[43] *S. v. Makwanyane*, 6 B.C.L.R., 1995, 665, C.C.
[44] *National Coalition for Gay and Lesbian Equality v. Minister of Justice*, 12 B.C.L.R., 1998, 11517, CC.
[45] 1996 (1) S.A. 984, CC.
[46] 1996 (2) S.A. 751, CC.
[47] 1996 (6) B.C.L.R. 745; however note that in *S. v. Rens* 1996 (1) S.A. 1218 it was held that there *was* a constitutional right to appeal in criminal cases.
[48] 1996 (12) B.C.L.R. 1559.

forces, on the ground that it represented an illegitimate restriction on access to the courts.[49] *Dabelstein v. Hildebrandt*[50] dealt with a challenge to the constitutionality of *Anton Piller* orders.

Privilege against self-incrimination—Section 35 SABOR (Article 6(1) ECHR)

The right of a suspect on arrest to remain silent and not to be compelled **7.100** to make any confession or admission that could be used in evidence against him is contained in section 35(1)(a), (c). A right to a fair trial, which includes the right to remain silent and not to testify during the proceedings and not to be compelled to give self-incriminating evidence, is included by virtue of section 35(3)(h)–(j).

Right to non-discrimination—Section 9 SABOR (Article 14 ECHR)

The emerging case law on discrimination is one of the areas of inter- **7.101** national human rights norms in which South Africa has already made a substantial contribution.[51] Section 9(3) of the Constitution declares that:

> "The State may not unfairly discriminate directly or indirectly against anyone on one or more grounds, including race, gender, sex, pregnancy, martial status, ethnic or social origin, colour, sexual orientation, age, disability, religion, conscience, belief, culture, language and birth."

In *Prinsloo v. Van der Linde*[52] the court held that section 9(3) covered two **7.102** forms of discrimination: differentiation on specified grounds, which is assumed to be discriminatory; and differentiation on a ground not specified in the statute, the discriminatory nature or otherwise of which must be examined by the court. What factors may go towards a differentiation being considered "unfair" is considered in the cases of *Harksen v. Lane NO*[53] and *President of the Republic of South Africa v. Hugo*.[54] Further examination of this fertile area is beyond the scope of this book, but practitioners are encouraged to seek assistance from the eloquent judgments of the South African Constitutional Court whenever a non-discrimination point arises.

India

The Indian Constitution was adopted on November 26, 1949, and came **7.103** into force on January 26, 1950. The "Fundamental Rights" in Part III of the Constitution pre-date but broadly correspond to the rights contained within

---

[49] Although this decision should be firmly viewed in the context of South Africa's uniquely underprivileged sections of society, for whom access to legal advice is particularly problematic.
[50] 1996 (3) S.A. 42(C).
[51] See generally *Disadvantage and Discrimination: The emerging jurisprudence of the South African Constitutional Court*, Grant and Small, Northern Ireland Legal Quarterly, Vol. 51, No. 2, p. 174.
[52] 1997 (3) S.A. 1012, CC.
[53] 1998 (1) S.A. 300, CC.
[54] 1997 (4) S.A. 1, CC.

the ICCPR. The following Articles are of particular interest to civil practitioners:

(1) Articles 14 to 16 cover various aspects of the right to equality and equal protection of law;

(2) Article 19 guarantees freedom of speech and expression (and which has been judicially interpreted as including a much wider range of rights and freedoms)[55];

(3) Article 20 ensures that there shall not be retrospective penalties or criminal law; and

(4) Article 21 prohibits the arbitrary deprivation of life or liberty.

7.104 Any law, whether made by the state legislature or the national government shall, by virtue of Article 13(2) of the Constitution, be void to the extent of any inconsistency with the fundamental rights secured by the Constitution. The same is true of any existing laws which so infringe these rights. The one exception to this principle is Article 31B. Introduced by the Ninth Schedule in 1951, Article 31B dictates that any law specified in the Ninth Schedule would be immune from challenge on the grounds that it violated any fundamental right. The exception has been utilised for close on 300 laws since 1951. Compensating in part for these deliberate government bypasses of the constitution has been the Indian judiciary, which several commentators have classified as the most activist in the world.[56] Particularly noteworthy in this regard is the line of decisions beginning with *People's Union for Democratic Rights v. Union of India*[57] in which the court held that where a legal remedy is sought for injury to a person or class of persons who "by reason of poverty, socially or economically disadvantaged position, or disability" are unable to approach the court themselves, any member of the public who is acting bona fide can maintain the action on their behalf. The Indian jurisprudence in the development of public interest litigation under the Constitution may be a useful source for anyone seeking to extend the ambit of standing in the United Kingdom in a borderline case under the HRA.[58]

7.105 The fundamental rights in the Indian Constitution are of "vertical" effect only—they apply solely to "state action". However, the judicial interpretation of this concept has extended to any private activities which operate with government encouragement or involvement. "State" has been held to cover statutory bodies and corporations, including insurance corporations, banks and financial institutions, airline corporations, electricity boards, and educational institutions whose administration is predominantly controlled by the state.

---

[55] Including freedom of the press; right of peaceful assembly; freedom to form association or unions; freedom of movement; and freedom to carry on any profession, trade or business.
[56] See, *e.g.* Baar, "Social Action Litigation in India: The Operation and Limitation of the World's Most Active Judiciary" (1990) 19 Pol.St.J. 140; and Cassels, "Judicial Activism and Public Interest Litigation in India" (1989) 37 Am. J. Comp. L. 495.
[57] *A.I.R.*, 1982 S.C. 1473. See also *S.P. Gupta v. U.O.I. A.I.R.*, 1982 S.C. 149.
[58] Although the European Convention approach to public interest challenges in the absence of a "victim" is clear: it is not permitted by Art. 41 of the Convention as interpreted by the European Court.

In 1993 the Protection of Human Rights Act provided for the constitution of **7.106** a National Human Rights Commission, States Human Rights Commissions, and specialist Human Rights Courts for the better protection of human rights and connected matters. Section 2 of the Act defines "human rights" as those rights relating to life, liberty, equality and dignity of the individual guaranteed by the Constitution or embodied in International Covenants and enforceable by Indian courts. "International Covenants" in this context means the ICCPR and the ICESCR (see above).

Right to equality and non-discrimination—Articles 14–16 IC (cf. Article 14 ECHR)

The cases on equality have been interesting in their development of the **7.107** principle that to treat all people exactly alike is to work its own form of injustice. The Indian jurisprudence has, in cases like *Moopil Nair v. State of Kerala,*[59] *State of Kerala v. Haji,*[60] Twyford Tea Company Ltd v. State of Kerala,[61] and *State of Kerala v. Thomas,*[62] been centred around establishing the proposition that discrimination may arise if persons manifestly unequal in resources, qualifications and attainments are treated similarly without regard to the relevant differences between them. The Indian jurisprudence on equality has also led to the development of the doctrine of the "absence of arbitrariness"—see *EP Royappa v. State of Tamil Nadu*[63] and the line of decisions following it in which any arbitrary act is without more a violation of Article 14.

Right to privacy (cf. Article 10 ECHR)

The right to privacy has been derived by the Indian courts as implicit[64] in **7.108** the constitutional guarantee of the right to life and personal liberty under Article 21, and it cannot be curtailed "except according to procedure established by law". This is established by a line of cases included *Kharak Singh v. State of UP,*[65] *Gobind v. State of MP*[66] and *Rajagopal v. State of TN.*[67] These cases were applied by the court in *People's Union for Civil Liberties v. Union of India*[68] in which telephone tapping, in the absence of government rules on the matter, was held to be unconstitutional on two grounds: first, that the right to privacy under Article 21 includes telephone calls in the privacy of one's own home or office, and secondly, because a person talking on the telephone is exercising his or her right to freedom of speech and expression under Article 19(1)(a). It was held that Article 17 of the ICCPR, which protects privacy, was not contrary to Indian law and that

---

[59] *A.I.R.* 1961 S.C. 552.
[60] *A.I.R.* 1969 S.C. 378.
[61] *A.I.R.* 1970 S.C. 1133.
[62] *A.I.R.* 1976 S.C. 490.
[63] *A.I.R.* 1974 S.C. 555.
[64] The Indian approach that some unarticulated rights are implicit in the express constitutional guarantees is of interest (see further on freedom of expression, below). Any practitioner seeking to induce such an approach from the U.K. judiciary under the European Convention might usefully consider the Indian jurisprudence.
[65] [1964] 1 S.C.R. 332.
[66] *A.I.R.* 1975 2 S.C. 1378.
[67] *A.I.R.* 1994 2 S.C. 1621.
[68] *A.I.R.* 1997 2 S.C. 1203.

accordingly, Article 21 had to be interpreted in conformity with the inter-national obligation.

Freedom of expression and freedom of the press—Article 19 IC (cf. Article 10 ECHR)

7.109 The Indian Supreme Court has ruled that freedom of the press is implicit in the right of freedom of speech under Article 19 of the Constitution—see *Brij Bhushan v. State of Delhi*[89] and *Indian Express Newspapers v. Union of India.*[70] This freedom has been interpreted as including restrictions in several novel areas. For example, in *Bennett Coleman & Co. v. UOI*[71] it was held that an Import and Export Control Act which purported to regulate the distribution of newsprint could not thereby control the growth and circulation of newspapers. Such control would be a fetter on the right to freedom of speech under Article 19. In *Ushodaya Publications Private Ltd v. Govt. of Andhra Pradesh*[72] the court ruled that the government could not use its discretion to place or not place adverts in a particular newspaper so as to punish those which criticise its policies and actions. To exercise the discretion in that way would constitute a breach of the newspaper's guarantee of freedom of speech. Such discretion had to be exercised for reasonable and proper purposes.

Privilege against self-incrimination—Article 20(3) IC (cf. Article 6(1) ECHR)

7.110 Article 20(3) of the Indian Constitution provides that no person accused of any offence shall be compelled to be a witness against himself.

Conclusion

7.111 Further miscellaneous cases of interest include:

(1) right to a livelihood—see *Tellis v. Bombay Corporation*[73];

(2) right against pollution—see *Rural Litigation and Entitlement Kendra v. Uttar Pradesh*[74];

(3) right against industrial hazards—see *MC Mehta v. India.*[75]

7.112 Again, this is an inexhaustive list and practitioners are advised to search the Indian reports, especially in relation to issues of equality, non-discrim-ination, freedom of speech or privacy.

Australia

7.113 Australia does not yet have a Bill of Rights or any constitutionally guaran-teed freedoms. It is, however, a party to several international human rights

---

[69] *A.I.R.* 1950 S.C. 129.
[70] *A.I.R.* 1986 S.C. 515.
[71] *A.I.R.* 1973 S.C. 106.
[72] *A.I.R.* 1981 A.P. 109.
[73] *A.I.R.* 1986 S.C. 180.
[74] *A.I.R.* 1985 S.C. 652.
[75] *A.I.R.* 1987 S.C. 965.

treaties and has implemented the Convention on the Elimination of All Forms of Racial Discrimination, and the Convention on Discrimination Against Women by means of domestic legislation. In 1986 the Human Rights and Equal Opportunities Commission was established in order to monitor Australia's compliance with the ICCPR. The Commission has no power to prescribe penalties for breaches of human rights and its main weapons are publicity and the mobilisation of public sentiment. It can however make submissions in court in cases in which it perceives human rights issues to be involved, and it would appear to have played a positive role in this respect. In 1991, Australia acceded to the Optional First Protocol of the ICCPR enabling citizens to make individual complaints to the HRC, and on Christmas Day 1991, the very day the power was brought into effect, Nicholas Toonen submitted a complaint to the HRC about Tasmania's criminalisation of male homosexuality, alleging that his rights to privacy and non-discrimination under Articles 17 and 26 of the ICCPR were thereby violated. The HRC's decision in *Toonen v. Australia*,[76] was that the Tasmanian law did violate Toonen's right to privacy under international law. No decision was made as to whether his right to non-discrimination was also violated.

Alongside the work of Australia's Human Rights and Equal Opportunities **7.114** Commission has been the recognition by the Australian judiciary that reference to international law can be made where the statutory or common law is unclear on the mater. It is recognised that Australian law should be developed in accordance with the relevant international human rights law, and it is also beginning to be questioned whether this ought to be so even where the common law *is* clear on a matter. As Justice Brennan said in *Mabo v. Queensland (No. 2)*,[77] "If a rule of common law seriously offends fundamental values of justice and human rights, it is appropriate to question whether that rule ought to be maintained". This is a clear indication that Australian law will have more reference to human rights and international sources in the future.

Table of Selected ECHR Rights and their Equivalents in the Human Rights Charters of the Jurisdictions Listed Above

7.115

ECHR Right	Hong Kong	India	South Africa	New Zealand	Canada	United States
Liberty and security of person—Art. 5	Art. 5	Art. 21	s.12	s.22	s.7	Fourth Amendment (no unreasonable search)
Fair trial/ determination of civil rights—Art. 6	Art. 10	–	ss.33, 34	s.27	s.7 ("fundamental justice")	Fifth and Fourteenth Amendments

---

[76] (1994) Communication No. 488/1992, U.N. Document CCPR/C/50/D/488/92.
[77] (1992) 175 C.L.R. 1.

ECHR Right	Hong Kong	India	South Africa	New Zealand	Canada	United States
Privilege against self-incrimination —Art. 6(1)	Art. 11(2)(g)	Art. 20(3)	s.35(1) (a),(c); s.35(3) (h)–(j)	s.25(d)	s.13 (but no privilege granted)	Fifth Amendment
No retrospective penalties—Art. 7	Art. 12	Art. 20	–	s.26	s.11 (criminal only)	–
Privacy and family life—Art. 8	Art. 14	–	s.14	Privacy Act 1993	–	–
Freedom of expression—Art. 10	Art. 16	Art. 19	ss.15, 16	s.14	s.2(b)	First Amendment
No discrimination —Art. 14	Arts. 1, 22	Arts. 14, 15	s.9	ss.19, 20	s.15	Fourteenth Amendment (equal protection)

PART II

Practice and Procedure

CHAPTER 8
Human Rights Litigation

1. INTRODUCTION

This chapter will consider some of the practical aspects of litigation involv- **8.01**
ing human rights arguments, including taking human rights points as a
free-standing or additional ground of "attack" under section 7(1)(a) of the
HRA and as a "defence" to an action by a public authority or a bolster to
an existing cause of action or defence under section 7(1)(b) of the HRA,
pleading human rights points in statements of case or notices of appeal,
advocacy, use of evidence, citation of authority and useful human rights
reference sources.

8.02 A person who can show that he or she has sufficient standing may claim that a public authority has acted or proposes to act in a way which is unlawful under section 6(1) of the HRA, either by:

(1) bringing proceedings against the public authority under the Act (section 7(1)(a) of the HRA); or

(2) relying on the Convention right in any legal proceedings (section 7(1)(b) of the HRA).

8.03 There is an exemption from liability for a public authority where it could not have acted differently as a result of one or more provisions of primary legislation or where it was acting to give effect to or enforce provisions of, or made under, incompatible primary legislation where the authority could not otherwise have acted in a way which was compatible (section 6(2)).

2. PROCEEDINGS UNDER SECTION 7(1)(a) OF THE HRA

Proceedings against a Public Authority

8.04 The cause of action created by section 7(1)(a) amounts to a new statutory right of action which can be relied upon, even where there is no pre-existing cause of action. Alternatively, a claim under section 7(1)(a) may be pleaded in the alternative to an existing cause of action.

8.05 Cases concerning HRA issues have not been centralised into any one court, though it is likely that many civil cases will be issued in the Administrative Court, given the public law element of these claims.[1] Proceedings based on the unlawful act of a court or tribunal may be brought only by exercising a right of appeal or on an application for judicial review.[1A]

Who Can Sue?

8.06 Article 34 of the Convention provides that only a "victim" can bring an application under the Convention. The HRA replicates the same test in domestic law in section 7(7). Accordingly, Strasbourg case-law is relevant in identifying whether a particular claimant is a "victim" of the act or omission complained of.

8.07 Generally, the alleged victim must be able to show that he has been directly affected by the alleged violation or is "at risk" of being affected, *i.e.* there must be a direct effect on the alleged victim with at least a *potential* personal effect on the alleged victim: *Klass v. Germany.*[1B]

---

[1] See para. 8.33 below.
[1A] See para. 2.28 above.
[1B] (1980) 2 E.H.R.R. 214. See also *Dudgeon v. United Kingdom* (1982) 4 E.H.R.R. 149; *Open Door Counselling v. Ireland* (1993) 15 E.H.R.R. 244; and *Campbell v. United Kingdom* (1982) 4 E.H.R.R. 293.

The violation alleged by the applicant must usually exist when the applica- **8.08** tion is made. However, the court has in some cases been prepared to rule that a future act would be a violation of the Convention where this is necessary to ensure that Convention rights are protected.[2] Where the violation is prospective, it must be reasonably likely that it will occur: *Hilton v. United Kingdom*.[3] Section 7(1) of the HRA has made it rather clearer that action can be taken in respect of a future violation through the words "proposes to act".

In some cases, an individual may be a victim where there has been a **8.09** violation of a Convention right affecting another person, for example, where a close relative of the victim can show some kind of prejudice as a result of the violation, or a personal interest in the cessation of the violation.[4] The parents of a minor whose human rights have been breached have standing to bring a claim under section 7 of the HRA.[4A]

Bodies with legal personality fall within Article 34.[4B] However, the court will **8.10** only "pierce the corporate veil" to allow actions by shareholders on behalf of a company to proceed where it is clear that it is impossible for the company to make an application itself, for example where the state has control over the company: *Agrotexim v. Greece*.[5] In *G.J. v. Luxembourg*,[6] a 90 per cent majority shareholder was a victim because he was in effect carrying out his business through the company and had, therefore, a direct personal interest in the subject-matter of the complaint. It was also relevant that the company itself could not bring proceedings because the complaints were targeted at its liquidators.[7] A voluntarily dissolved political party which remained in existence for the purposes of dissolution had standing to complain that its dissolution and the ban of its leaders from holding office in any other party violated Article 11.[7A] Governmental bodies may not bring proceedings.

An applicant cannot challenge a law in the abstract: *F v. Switzerland*.[8] The **8.11** European Court has consistently refused to recognise any form of *actio popularis* for the interpretation of the Convention.

Claims can be brought on behalf of victims who are unable to act on their **8.12** own behalf, provided that there is evidence of the representative's authority to do so. If possible, the victim must have consented to the application.[9] However, an action can be brought where the victim has died.[10] Further, an association, such as a trade union, can make an application on behalf

---

[2] *Soering v. United Kingdom* (1989) 11 E.H.R.R. 439.
[3] (1988) 57 D.R.108, Application No. 12015/86.
[4] See, *e.g. Kiliç v. Turkey*, Application No. 22492/93, March 28, 2000.
[4A] *R. (Holub) v. Secretary of State for the Home Department* [2001] 1 W.L.R. 1359, CA at 1364H.
[4B] See further Chapter 14.
[5] (1996) 21 E.H.R.R. 250.
[6] Application No. 21156/93, October 26, 2000. See also *Ankarcrona v. Sweden*, Application No. 35178/97, June 27, 2000 (applicant could claim to be a victim as sole shareholder of the company in question).
[7] *Ayuntamiento de M v. Spain* (1991) 68 D.R. 209, Application No. 15090/89.
[7A] *Özdep v. Turkey* (2001) 31 E.H.R.R. 674.
[8] (1988) 10 E.H.R.R. 411.
[9] *X v. Germany* (1956) 1 Yearbook 202.
[10] *X v. France* (1992) 14 E.H.R.R. 483.

of its members provided that it can identify those who are directly affected and prove that it has received specific instructions from each of them.[11]

8.13　An applicant is no longer a victim of a violation of the Convention within the meaning of Article 34 if he brings and settles civil proceedings for negligence based on the same complaint(s).[12] In accepting and receiving compensation, the applicant effectively renounces further use of those remedies. In *Powell (William and Anita) v. United Kingdom*,[13] the applicants settled a claim for clinical negligence arising out of the death of their child and in relation to the alleged falsification by certain doctors of medical records.[14] The European Court ruled their application inadmissible on the ground that the applicants could no longer claim to be victims in relation to the circumstances surrounding treatment of the deceased or the investigation into the death. In *R. v. Secretary of State for the Home Department, ex p. Bulger*,[15] the claimant, as father of the victim two convicted young people had abducted and killed, did not have standing to challenge by way of judicial review the tariff fixed by the Lord Chief Justice in respect of the minimum period of their sentences.

8.14　The victim test is narrower than the test for standing in judicial review proceedings in domestic law, which is whether a person has "a sufficient interest in the matter to which the application relates".[16] Unlike judicial review proceedings,[17] pressure groups and action groups do not have standing to make a claim under section 7(1) of the HRA, although they are permitted to support an individual who can show that he or she is a victim.[18] If a HRA point is raised in judicial review proceedings, the applicant will have to satisfy two different standing tests:

(1) the "sufficient interest" test for conventional judicial review grounds and

(2) the narrower "victim" test in relation to any human rights challenge.

It is therefore possible that an applicant who is granted permission for judicial review will not be permitted to argue a HRA point. There was recognition in Parliament that the tests were different.[19] However, this is a

---

[11] *Confédération des Syndicats Médicaux Français v. France* (1986) 47 D.R. 225.
[12] *Hay (Robert and Dinah-Anne) v. United Kingdom*, Application No. 41894/98, October 17, 2000 (the application concerned complaint against police under Arts 2, 16(1) and 13 of the Convention following a settlement which was expressly stated to be without prejudice to the right of those representing the estate to pursue proceedings under the Convention).
[13] Application No. 45305/99, May 4, 2000. See also *Caraher v. United Kingdom*, Application No. 24520/94, January 11, 2000.
[14] Such a settlement is held to have fulfilled the "just satisfaction" test outlined in para. 2.35. See also paras 9.21 *et seq.*
[15] (2001) 3 All E.R. 449; *The Times*, March 7, 2001, Div Ct.
[16] Supreme Court Act 1981, s.31(3); CPR, Sched. 1; R.S.C. Ord.53, r. 3(7).
[17] *R. v. Secretary of State for Foreign Affairs, ex p. World Development Movement Ltd* [1995] 1 W.L.R. 386.
[18] H.L. Deb., November 24, 1997, col. 831.
[19] In relation to standing, see H.L. Deb., November 24, 1997, cols 823–837 and February 5, 1998, cols 805–811 and H.C. Deb., June 24, 1998, cols 1058–1091.

reflection of the intention to allow domestic claimants to rely on Convention rights before domestic courts in exactly the same circumstances as they can rely on them in Strasbourg.[20]

Who Can be Sued?

Section 6(1) of the HRA states "It is unlawful for a *public authority* to act **8.15** in a way which is incompatible with a Convention right". A "public authority" includes courts and tribunals and "any person whose functions are of a public nature" (section 6(3)). This has created three classes of potential defendant: the obvious public authority, the hybrid public authority and the purely private body or individual. Beyond the limited guidance in section 6(3), the HRA deliberately does not define a public authority on the basis that it was thought better to have a principle rather than an exhaustive list.[21]

Obvious public authorities

An "obvious" public authority may be the subject of section 7(1)(a) pro- **8.16** ceedings in relation to any Convention-incompatible act or failure to act, whether public and private. The category would appear to include:

(1) central government departments (including executive agencies like the Benefits Agency of the Department of Social Security);

(2) local authorities;

(3) the police;

(4) prison officers;

(5) the Inland Revenue;

(6) the Commissioners for Customs and Excise;

(7) immigration officers;

(8) public prosecutors;

(9) non-departmental public bodies; and

(10) courts and tribunals.[22]

---

[20] For an expansive approach to a similar standing test for constitutional challenges, see the Canadian case law, in particular *Thorson v. Attorney General of Canada (No.2)* (1974) 43 D.L.R. (3d) 1, [1975] 1 S.C.R. 138; *Canada (Minister of Justice) v. Borowski* (1981) 130 D.L.R. 588, 64 C.C.C. (2d) 97; *Novia Scotia Board of Censors v. McNeil* 55 D.L.R. (3d) 588, [1976] 2 S.C.R. 607. The Canadian courts have also permitted a degree of extraterritorial application of the Charter despite s.32 of the Charter confining the application to the legislative bodies and governments of Canada and the provinces: *Schreiber v. Canada* [1998] 1 S.C.R. 841; *R. v. Cook* [1998] 2 S.C.R. 597. It is also possible under the Charter to bring challenges on another's behalf: *Morgentaler v. Prince Edward Island (Minister of Health and Social Services)* (1994) 112 D.L.R. (4th) 756 (courts granted discretionary public interest standing).

[21] Lord Chancellor, H.L. Deb., November 24, 1997, col. 796. For debates on the issue of what is a public authority, see H.L. Deb., November 24, 1997, cols 754–759, 787–802 and 809–816 and H.C. Deb., June 17, 1998, cols 399–434. See further paras 5.19 *et seq.* above.

[22] See White Paper, *Rights Brought Home* (Cm. 3782, 1997); H.L. Deb., November 24, 1997, col. 759 (Lord Williams of Mostyn); HRA, s.6(3).

The Court of Appeal has held that a parochial church council is an obvious public authority.[22A] The Court's reasons where that (a) it is an authority in the sense that it possesses powers which private individuals do not possess to determine how others should act (b) its notices to repair had statutory force; (c) it is created and empowered by law, (d) it forms part of the church by law established and (e) its functions include the enforcement through the courts of a common law liability to maintain its chancels resting upon persons who need not be members of the church. The Court stated that if this were incorrect, then the PCC would for the same reasons be a hybrid public authority, certain of whose functions, chancel repairs among them, are functions of a public nature.[22B]

It is possible that this category also includes nationalised industries. However, the position is not entirely clear because in *Young, James and Webster v. United Kingdom*,[23] the European Court assumed, though it did not decide, that British Rail was a non-governmental body.[24] Because an obvious public authority must comply with the Convention in relation to all of its acts, it will be potentially possible to challenge as incompatible with the Convention private functions such as contractual acts or employment practices.[25] Any challenge to courts or tribunals must be brought by way of appeal or judicial review and not by fresh proceedings (section 9(1)).

Hybrid bodies/individuals

8.17　Hybrid authorities will have to comply with the Convention only in relation to their *public functions*. Some examples of potential hybrid bodies include:

>　(1)　the privatised utility companies, for example British Telecom,[26] Railtrack,[27] etc., public broadcasters for example the BBC,[28] (and possibly Channel 4)[29];
>
>　(2)　the Broadcasting Standards Commission[30];

[22A] *Aston Cantlow and Wilmcote with Billesley Parochial Church Council v. Wallbank and another* [2001] 3 All E.R. 393, CA, para. 35.

[22B] *ibid.*

[23] (1982) 4 E.H.R.R. 38.

[24] *cf. Swedish Engine Drivers Union v. Sweden* (1979) 1 E.H.R.R. 617.

[25] In England and Wales, employment law has traditionally been regarded as private in nature (*e.g. R. v. British Broadcasting Corporation, ex p. Lavelle* [1983] I.C.R. 99). This contrasts with E.C. law and certain other European jurisdictions where employment disputes in relation to public authorities have generally been regarded as public in nature.

[26] H.C. Deb., June 17, 1998, cols 409–410.

[27] The Lord Chancellor, Lord Irvine, stated that Railtrack would be a public body in relation to its role as a safety regulator, but would be acting privately in its role as a property developer: H.L. Deb., November 24, 1997, col. 811.

[28] H.C. Deb., June 17, 1998, col.410. But *cf. Hilton v. United Kingdom,* Application No. 12105/86, 57 D.R. 108, where the European Commission left unresolved the question of whether the BBC was a public body. See also *BBC v. United Kingdom* (1996) 21 E.H.R.R. CD 97.

[29] Parliamentary Under-Secretary of State, Home Office, Lord Williams of Mostyn, H.L.Deb., November 3, 1997, cols 1309–1310. *Cf.* independent television companies which would probably not be public authorities (though it is for the courts to decide) or other branches of the media such as newspapers which are not intended to be public authorities.

[30] Already susceptible to judicial review: *e.g. R. v. Broadcasting Standards Corporation, ex p. British Broadcasting Corporation* [2001] 1 W.L.R. 550, HL [1999] E.M.L.R. 858, Forbes J.; *The Times,* April 12, 2000, CA.

(3) the British Board of Film Classification[31];

(4) the Advertising Standards Authority[32];

(6) the Press Complaints Commission[33];

(7) regulators such as the utility regulators (for example OFTEL, OFGEM, etc.) financial services regulators (for example the Financial Services Authority), competition regulators (for example the Competition Commission and the Office of Fair Trading);

(8) the regulating bodies of the professions in relation to their professional regulatory functions, for example the General Medical Council,[34] the Law Society,[34A] General Council of the Bar;

(9) the Jockey Club[35];

(10) the Royal National Lifeboat Institute in relation to charitable work[36];

(11) the City Take-Over and Mergers Panel[37];

(12) a private security company in relation to the management of a contracted-out prison (but not when guarding commercial premises)[38];

(13) doctors in general practice in relation to their National Health Service practice (but not their private practice).[39]

In *Popular Housing and Regeneration Community Association Ltd v. Donoghue*,[39A] the Court of Appeal has begun an attempt to define those bodies which will be held to be hybrid public authorities. It held that section 6 of the HRA required a generous interpretation of who was a public authority. It emphasised that the fact that a body performs an activity which otherwise a public body would be under a duty to perform cannot mean

---

[31] H.C. Deb., June 17, 1998, cols [407–413], Mr Jack Straw M.P.
[32] Already susceptible to judicial review: *e.g. R. v. The Advertising Standards Authority Ltd, ex p. The Insurance Service plc* [1990] C.O.D. 42, *The Times*, July 14, 1998, DC.
[33] Home Secretary, Mr Jack Straw M.P., H.C. Deb., June 17, 1998, col. 414. See also *R. v. Press Complaints Commission, ex p. Stewart-Brady, The Times*, November 18, 1996, CA.
[34] H.C. Deb., June 17, 1998, cols [407–413].
[34A] Simon Piner. Solicitors Disciplinary Tribunal, *sub nom. In the Matter of a Solicitor*, unreported, November 13, 2000 Div Ct (available on Lawtel). (Both the Law Society and the Solicitors Discplinary Tribunal were public authorities for the purposes of the HRA.)
[35] *cf. R. v. Disciplinary Committee of the Jockey Club, ex p. The Aga Khan* [1993] 1 W.L.R. 909, CA—Jockey Club not susceptible to judicial review as applicant had entered into a contract with the Club. It was thereby exercising private law functions. The Court left open the question of whether a person who had not contracted with the Club could ever obtain judicial review of one of its decisions.
[36] H.C. Deb., June 17, 1998, cols [407–413] Mr Jack Straw M.P.
[37] H.C. Deb., June 17, 1998, cols [407–413] Mr Jack Straw M.P.
[38] Lord Chancellor, Lord Irvine, H.L. Deb., November 24, 1997, col. 811.
[39] Lord Chancellor, Lord Irvine, H.L. Deb., November 24, 1997, col. 811. It seems logical that NHS Trusts would also be regarded as hybrid bodies exercising a public function in relation to the provision of health care. See also *Eldridge v. Attorney-General of British Columbia* (1997) 3 B.H.R.C. 137, Sup Ct Canada: hospitals held to be public bodies within the meaning of the Canadian Charter of Rights and Freedoms 1982, s.32.
[39A] [2001] EWCA Civ 595, April 27, 2001, CA.

that such performance is necessarily a public function.[39B] The purpose of section 6(3) of the HRA was not to make a body which does not have responsibilities to the public, a public body merely because it performs acts on behalf of a public body which would constitute public functions were such acts to be performed by the public body itself.[39C] The question is very much one of fact and degree.[39D] The fact that a body is a charity or is conducted not for profit means that it is likely to be motivated in performing its activities by what it perceives to be the public interest. However, this does not point to the body being a public authority.[39E] What can make an act, which would otherwise be private, public, is a feature or a combination of features which impose a public character or stamp on the act. Statutory authority for what is done can at least help to mark the act as being public. So can the extent of control over the function exercised by another body which is a public authority. The more closely the acts that could be of a private nature are enmeshed in the activities of a public body, the more likely they are to be public. However, the fact that the acts are supervised by a public regulatory body does not necessarily indicate that they are of a public nature.[39F] The Court held on the facts of *Poplar* that the role of the housing association in providing housing accommodation to those in need and in seeking possession was so closely assimilated to the local authority from which these functions were derived that it was performing public functions in respect of those activities.

8.18 It is not clear whether the courts will adopt the function test already in use in judicial review proceedings or some other test for the purpose of determining whether a person or body is exercising public functions within the meaning of section 6(3). In order to achieve consistency, it is likely that the courts will seek to adopt the same public function test as is currently applied in determining susceptibility to judicial review derived from the leading case of *R v. Take-Over Panel, ex p. Datafin plc*.[40] In *Poplar Housing and Regeneration Community Association Ltd v. Donoghue*,[40A] the Court of Appeal noted that the emphasis on public functions in section 6 of the HRA was inspired by and reflected the approach adopted in judicial review by the courts and textbooks since the *Datafin* decision.[40B] However, the test for judicial review is not entirely in line with the bodies predicted by the Government as likely to constitute hybrid bodies.[41] Further, the courts' approach to determining susceptibility for judicial review often focuses on the source of a body's powers and not solely on its functions.

[39B] At para. 58.
[39C] At para. 59.
[39D] At para. 66.
[39E] At para. 65(iv). See also *R. v. Leonard Cheshire Foundation & anr ex p. Heather and ors.*, unreported, June 15, 2001, Admin Ct. (charity running a nursing and residential care home was not exercising public functions within HRA, s.6(3)).
[39F] At para. 65(v).
[40] [1987] Q.B. 815, CA, where the Court held that the Take Over Panel was susceptible to judicial review, even though it had no authority derived from either statute or the exercise of the prerogative, and held that judicial review would lie against any persons or bodies who performed public duties or functions.
[40A] [2001] EWCA Civ 595, April 27, 2001, CA.
[40B] *ibid.* at para. 65.
[41] See, *e.g.* in relation to the Jockey Club, mentioned in para. 8.17, head (9) above.

An alternative source of assistance to the courts in determining what is a   **8.19**
public function may be the principles of European Community law in
relation to the direct effect of Directives where an individual may only rely
on the provisions of an unimplemented Directive against an emanation of
the state. In *Case C–188/89 Foster v. British Gas plc*,[42] the European
Court of Justice stated that the state included:

> "a body, whatever its legal form, which has been made responsible,
> pursuant to a measure adopted by the state, for providing a public
> service under the control of the state and has for that purpose special
> powers beyond those which result from the normal rules applicable in
> relations between individuals".[43]

Accordingly, a privatised utility was held to be an organ of the state. In
Case 152/84 *Marshall v. Southampton & South-West Hampshire Area
health authority*,[44] the European Court of Justice held that a health authority could be regarded as an organ of the state. On this analysis, it seems
likely that the courts will construe NHS Trusts to have "public functions" at
least in respect of the provision of healthcare. In Case 103/88 *Fratelli
Costanzo SpA v. Comune di Milano*,[45] the European Court of Justice
interpreted the state to include "all organs of the administration, including
decentralised authorities such as municipalities".[46] However, recourse to
E.C. law is somewhat limited by the fact that the ECJ has failed to provide
any authoritative definition of what amounts to an "emanation of the state"
or any indication of the criteria to be applied by national courts.[47]

It is probable that schools will be treated as hybrid bodies and that the   **8.20**
provision of education will constitute a public function. In *Costello-Roberts
v. United Kingdom*,[48] the European Court treated the responsibility of the
state as sufficiently engaged in relation to a private school.[49] It is also likely
that the Post Office will be held to exercise a public function in relation to
the distribution of mail. In New Zealand, the government-controlled postal
organisation was held to be a public body subject to the application of the
New Zealand Bill of Rights Act 1990 even though it was a private company.[50]

---

[42] [1990] E.C.R. I–3313; [1991] 1 Q.B. 405.
[43] *ibid.*, at 427.
[44] [1986] E.C.R. 723.
[45] [1989] E.C.R. 1839.
[46] See also Case 8/81 *Becker* [1982] E.C.R. 53 and Case 221/88 *ECSC v. Busseni* [1990]
E.C.R. I–495 (tax authorities) and Case 103/88 *Johnston v. Chief Constable of Royal Ulster
Constabulary* (police).
[47] *cf.* Advocate-General Van Gerven in Case 188/89 *Foster v. British Gas* [1990] E.C.R.
I–3313, [1991] 1 Q.B. 405, who suggested that the "state" may extend to a body which has
given itself powers which place it in a position to decisively influence the conduct of
persons—whatever their nature, public or private, or their sphere of activity—with regard to
the subject-matter of the Directive which has not been correctly implemented.
[48] (1995) 19 E.H.R.R. 112.
[49] *cf.* a Court of Appeal decision prior to the introduction of the HRA where the Court was
undecided whether a voluntary-aided school was an organ of the state as a matter of E.C.
law: *N.U.T. v. Governing Body of St Mary's Church of England (Aided) Junior School* [1997]
3 C.M.L.R. 360.
[50] *Federated Farmers of NZ Inc. v. New Zealand Post Ltd* (1990–92) N.Z.B.O.R.R. 331.

8.21 It is unclear whether and how far the conduct of litigation by a hybrid body will be considered to be a "public function" for the purposes of the HRA, so that a hybrid body will have to act compatibly with the Convention in relation to its role in any litigation. It seems likely that the answer will depend on the type of litigation in question. If litigation is entered into as a result of, or in pursuing, a regulatory or public function, the conduct of litigation will probably constitute a public function. By contrast, if the body is a party to litigation in relation to a private contract or property dispute, this is more likely to be considered a private function.

8.22 The position of the various Ombudsmen may depend on the source and nature of their regulatory powers.[50A] For example, the Pensions Ombudsman is already susceptible to judicial review. By contrast, in *R. v. Insurance Ombudsman Bureau, ex p. Aegon Life Insurance Ltd*,[51] it was held that judicial review did not lie against the Insurance Ombudsman Bureau because its jurisdiction was dependent on the contractual consent of its members and its decisions were of a private law arbitrative nature. The court stated that the Insurance Ombudsman Bureau would only be a public body susceptible to judicial review if it had been woven into the fabric of public regulation or into a system of government control or was integrated into a system of statutory regulation or, but for its existence, a governmental body would assume control.

8.23 Hybrid bodies do not have to act compatibly with the Convention in relation to purely private acts. It is likely in light of the approach traditionally taken by the domestic courts that their contractual relations and employment practices will continue to be regarded as private in nature.

Private bodies/individuals

8.24 Purely private bodies probably cannot be sued under the HRA for acting in breach of a Convention right, but the position is open to debate,[52] and the Convention might nonetheless be invoked to buttress an existing cause of action, even between purely private parties, under section 7(1)(b).

Parliament

8.25 The definition of "public authority" excludes both Houses of Parliament (section 6(3)) and the introduction or failure to introduce primary legislation is excluded from the operation of the Act (section 6(6)). Accordingly, Parliament remains free to legislate, fail to legislate or otherwise act incompatibly with the Convention and this will not be unlawful under section 6(1). Further, the failure to make a remedial order under section 10

[50A] A useful guide to Ombudsman schemes is *A-Z of Ombudsmen*, (National Consumer Council: 1997).

[51] *The Times*, January 7, 1994.

[52] See, *e.g.* Professor William Wade, "The United Kingdom's Bill of Rights", in J. Beatson, C. Forsyth and I. Hare (eds), *Constitutional Reform in the United Kingdom: Practice and Principles* (Oxford: Hart, 1998) and "Horizons of Horizontality" (2000) 116 L.Q.R. 217. *cf.* R. Buxton, "The Human Rights Act and Private Law" (2000) 116 L.Q.R. 48. Discussed further in Chap. 5, above at paras 5.000 *et seq*. See also *R. v. N.* [1999] 1 N.Z.L.R. 713, N.Z. CA. (private citizens attract the Bill of Rights under the New Zealand Bill of Rights Act 1990 s.3(b), if their acts are done in the performance of a public function, power or duty conferred or imposed on the citizen by or pursuant to law). See further para. 5.49 above.

of the HRA is not unlawful within section 6(1) (section 6(6)(b)). Section 6(3) also exempts "a person exercising functions in connection with proceedings in Parliament". This includes the Parliamentary Commissioner for Standards in Public Life: (*R v. Parliamentary Commissioner for Standards, ex p. Al Fayed*[53]) and will also cover disciplinary proceedings within Parliament.[54]

Ministers or other public officials responsible for incompatible subordinate legislation

One issue which appears to arise under the Act is whether a Minister or other public official acts unlawfully within the meaning of section 6(1) of the HRA and/or can be challenged by proceedings under section 7(1)(a) of the HRA for introducing incompatible subordinate legislation which is not required by the parent statute to be incompatible? Section 6(3) of the HRA is ambiguous—does the exemption from liability for "a person exercising functions *in connection with* proceedings in Parliament" include a Minister promulgating subordinate legislation? Section 6(6) provides that an "act" includes a failure to act but does not include a failure to (1) introduce in, or lay before, Parliament a proposal for legislation or (2) make any primary legislation or remedial order. **8.26**

Whilst it could be argued that a Minister is exempt from liability for promulgating subordinate legislation on a wide reading of section 6(3) and section 6(6)(a), it is very unlikely that the courts will uphold such a construction. It was implicit in the debates on the Human Rights Bill in Parliament that the promulgation of subordinate legislation which is incompatible following October 2, 2000 is an unlawful act within the meaning of section 6(1). The Opposition in the House of Commons tabled an amendment to the Bill proposing that subordinate legislation be treated in the same way as primary legislation so that neither could be held to be unlawful.[55] It was intended that the courts would have to confine themselves to making a declaration of incompatibility and would not be able to strike down incompatible subordinate legislation. The amendment was defeated. Further, during the Committee stage in the House of Commons, Mr Geoffrey Hoon M.P., Parliamentary Secretary at the Lord Chancellor's Department, stated in relation to section 3(2)(c): **8.27**

"it is perfectly reasonable to require that subordinate legislation be consistent both with the terms of its present statute and with the Human Rights Act. That is what the Bill provides. *It is inherent in the public authority provisions in [section] 6 that Ministers will be acting unlawfully if they make subordinate legislation that is incompatible with a Convention right, unless the parent statute requires the subordinate legislation to take that form* . . . If it is the will of Parliament that something should be done that is incompatible with a Convention right, Parliament must be prepared to say so in primary legislation . . . The nature of the primary legislation under which an order is made

---

[53] [1998] 1 W.L.R. 669, CA.
[54] See the position under the Convention: *Demicoli v. Malta* (1992) 14 E.H.R.R. 47.
[55] H.C. Deb., June 3, 1998, cols 433–434.

may be such that any subordinate legislation will necessarily be in conflict with Convention rights. If the courts were to have the power to strike down such subordinate legislation, it would, at least indirectly, amount to a challenge to the primary legislation itself. That would place the courts at odds with Parliament."[56]

8.28 It is therefore clear that there was no intention to equate the position of primary and subordinate legislation so that both are exempt from being treated as unlawful. Indeed, the rejection of the amendment suggests quite the contrary. The HRA is therefore intended to permit the striking down of all incompatible subordinate legislation save where primary legislation required secondary legislation to be made in a way that was incompatible with the Convention (where any attack on the lawfulness of the subordinate legislation would, in effect, amount to an indirect attack on the lawfulness of the primary legislation). Accordingly, a member of the executive making or instrumental in passing incompatible subordinate legislation must be intended to fall within the definition of a "public authority" within the meaning of section 6. Further, the structure of the HRA itself is to make the promulgation of subordinate legislation which is incompatible with a Convention right unlawful unless that legislation is required to be as it is by reason of irreconcilably incompatible primary legislation. Distinctions are made between primary and subordinate legislation in sections 3(2), 4(1) to (4) and 6(6).

8.29 A Minister or other public official who has introduced or made subordinate legislation after October 2, 2000 which was incompatible with the Convention and where this was not required by primary legislation has acted in a way which is unlawful within the meaning of section 6(1). Further, the unlawful act may be challenged under section 7(1)(a) by a person with standing.

8.30 In contrast, a Minister or other public official who has introduced or made subordinate legislation prior to October 2, 2000 which was incompatible with the Convention and, where this was not required by primary legislation, has not acted in a way which was unlawful within the meaning of section 6(1). The unlawful act cannot be the subject of a challenge under section 7(1)(a) by virtue of section 22(4) because the act took place prior to the coming into force of that subsection, though it may be relied upon by way of defence in proceedings brought by or at the instigation of a public authority.

8.31 By analogy, a Minister who has acted incompatibly with the Convention by failing to pass subordinate legislation (other than a section 10 remedial order), such failure occurring after the coming into force of the HRA on October 2, 2000, has arguably also acted unlawfully. This is because section 6(6)(b) only expressly exempts a failure to make primary legislation and section 10 remedial orders and not a failure to make subordinate legislation. However, the position is not without doubt as there is a discrepancy between section 6(6)(b) which refers only to primary legislation and section 6(6)(a) which exempts a "failure to introduce in or lay before Parliament a proposal for legislation". The subsection does not specify

---

[56] 313 H.C. Official Report (6 Series), col. 433 (June 3, 1998) [H.C. Deb.]

whether it is limited solely to a failure to introduce or lay before Parliament *primary* legislation. Not all subordinate legislation is required to be introduced or laid before Parliament and to hold that the legislation that is so introduced is not unlawful but subordinate legislation which is not so introduced is unlawful within section 6(1) would be to create a technical and unattractive distinction.[57] It is suggested that the most consistent approach would be for section 6(6)(a) to be read to relate to primary legislation only. Accordingly, a failure to introduce or make subordinate legislation where the omission is incompatible with Convention rights would be an unlawful act within section 6(1). A failure to introduce subordinate legislation prior to October 2, 2000 is without effect (save possibly in relation to the limited retrospective effect of the Act in proceedings by or at the instigation of public authorities under section 22(4)) because the duty to act compatibly with the Convention has only arisen as a matter of domestic law upon the coming into force of the HRA.

Exception

An obvious public authority or hybrid public authority will not act or fail to act unlawfully within the meaning of section 6(1) if: **8.32**

(1) as a result of one or more provisions of primary legislation, the authority could not have acted differently; or

(2) in the case of one or more provisions of, or made under, primary legislation which cannot be read or given effect in a way which is compatible with the Convention rights, the authority was acting so as to give effect to or enforce those provisions (section 6(2) of the HRA).

Section 6(2) gives protection to a public authority where it has no discretion but has to act in a particular way because of a provision (or combination of provisions) of primary legislation or subordinate legislation made pursuant to incompatible primary legislation which cannot be read or given effect to in a way which is compatible with the Convention.

Forum for Proceedings

Proceedings for breach of a Convention right at first instance may only be brought in the "appropriate court or tribunal" as determined by rules of court: section 7(2). CPR Rule 7.11 provides that a claim under section 7(1)(a) in respect of a judicial act may be brought only in the High Court[58] but any other claim under section 7(1)(a) may be brought in any court.[59] Accordingly, section 7(1)(a) claims may be brought by way of: **8.33**

---

[57] See the helpful analysis by D. Squires, "Challenging Subordinate Legislation Under the Human Rights Act" [2000] E.H.R.L.R. 116.
[58] CPR, 7.11(1) (inserted by the Civil Procedure (Amendment No. 4) Rules, S.I. 2000 No. 2092 (L.1) force October 2, 2000.
[59] CPR

(1) judicial review under existing procedures;

(2) in the county court or in the High Court where a claim for damages is made, by proceedings under Part 7 CPR by way of a claim or counterclaim (unless this is associated with a claim for judicial review). The normal jurisdictional limits apply. It should be noted, however, that county courts are not empowered to make declarations of incompatibility under section 4 of the HRA;

(3) in the county court or in the High Court following a finding of unlawfulness under section 7(1)(b) in some other court or tribunal which did not have the power to award damages or compensation, for example the magistrates' court or the Crown Court. In this situation, the party seeking a civil remedy may rely upon the finding of unlawfulness in the other court as prima facie evidence that the defendant acted unlawfully.[60] It is open to the defendant to refute the finding on factual or legal grounds pursuant to paragraph 4 of Schedule 1 to the Civil Procedure Act 1997.

Section 7(11) of the HRA enables the relevant Minister to make rules for individual tribunals to ensure that they can provide appropriate relief or remedies in relation to an act of a public authority, which is unlawful under section 6(1) of the HRA. High Court claims for a declaration of incompatibility or for damages for a judicial act may not be tried by a deputy High Court judge, master or district judge.[60A] In the county court, district judges and recorders do not have jurisdiction in claims for damages for judicial acts.

Appeals

8.34   A litigant can appeal on the ground that the court or tribunal has made an order which infringes a Convention right. It is irrelevant that the parties to the proceedings are private since it is the court which is the subject of the challenge. Alternatively, a litigant may seek judicial review of the court's decision as appropriate. On any appeal concerning a committal order, if the court ordering the release of the person concludes that his Convention rights have been infringed by the making of the order to which the appeal relates, the judgment or order should so state.[61] An appeal brought by an unsuccessful defendant is not to be treated as a proceeding brought or

---

[60] The previous finding of unlawfulness is treated in the same way as a conviction is treated in civil proceedings under the Civil Evidence Act 1968, s.11. The court hearing the claim may proceed on the basis of the finding of that other court or tribunal that there has been an infringement, but is not required to do so and may reach its own conclusion in light of that finding and of the evidence heard by that other court or tribunal: CPR, 33.9(2).
[60A] CPR Part 2 PD, para. 7A.
[61] CPR Part 40C PD, para.14.4. This procedure also relates to applications concerning a committal order.

instigated by a public authority. Accordingly, the retrospective operation of section 7(1)(b) did not apply to an appeal by an unsuccessful defendant against the decision of a Crown Court and he could not rely on section 6 of the HRA to challenge the judge's direction to the jury.[61A]

Notification to Crown

A court may not make a declaration of incompatibility under section 4 of the HRA unless 21 days notice (or such other period as the court may direct) is given to the Crown.[62] It is the court's duty to give formal notice to the Crown as required by the HRA and the CPR. However, the party seeking the declaration should give as much informal notice as possible to the Crown of the proceedings and the issues involved, sending a copy of this notice to the court.[62A] "The Crown" means a person named in a list under section 17 Crown Proceedings Act 1947 and "the court" means the court which will hear the proceedings in which the declaration is sought.[62B] Where a party makes a claim for a declaration of incompatibility, or an issue is raised which may lead the court to consider making such a declaration, the court can consider giving notice to the Crown at any time.[63] Where a question of incompatibility is an issue of general public importance likely to affect other trials and it was in the best interests of the parties that the issue should be heard in advance of the trial and without delay, permission should be granted to the Crown to join the proceedings prior to the commencement of the appeal where there was a possibility that a declaration of incompatibility might ultimately be made (even though the court had not yet been asked to consider the making of such a declaration).[63A] In *R. v. A*,[63B] the Crown was already a party to the appeal through the Director of Public Prosecutions. However, the DDP's role as prosecutor was different to that performed by ministers in the discharge of their executive duties. Section 5(2) of the HRA was intended to provide ministerial advice as to the purpose of the domestic legislation at issue. Accordingly, permission was given for the Secretary of State for the Home Department to intervene.[63C] Only the higher courts have power to make declarations of incompatibility, and provision has been made for the transfer of proceedings to the High Court where the question of making a

8.35

[61A] *R. v. Lambert* [2001] UKHL 37, July 5, 2001, HL (Lord Steyn dissenting, holding that the effect of section 6(1) of the HRA was that it was unlawful for the House of Lords to act in a way which was incompatible with a Convention right and that therefore the appellant could rely on his Convention rights on appeal from a trial which took place before the 1998 Act came into force).

[62] CPR 19.4A(1). See also para. 8.58 below.

[62A] *Poplar Housing and Regeneration Community Association Ltd v. Donoghue* [2001] EWCA Civ 595, April 27, 2001, CA.

[62B] *ibid.*

[63] CPR Part 19 PD, para. 6.1. See also CPR Part 54 PD, para. 8.2.

[63A] *R. v. A* [2001] 1 W.L.R. 789.

[63B] *ibid.*

[63C] In *Gunn v. Bowie*, March 21, 2001, I.H., Ct of Sess., Scot, it was held that where a personal injury action raised an issue about compatibility between provisions of the Court of Session Act 1988 and Article 6, it was appropriate to adjourn the proceedings so that the appropriate Scottish Ministers could apply to be joined as parties to address the court on the objects and purposes of the legislation.

declaration of incompatibility has arisen or may arise.[64] Where damages are being sought in respect of a judicial act, the Lord Chancellor must be notified (except where the appeal is to the Crown Court in which case the Lord Chancellor will only be notified if and when a breach is found).[65] The matter will probably usually be transferred to the Administrative Court.[66]

Time Limits

8.36   Proceedings under the HRA must be brought before the end of one year from the date of the act or omission complained of.[66A] However, this is subject to any stricter time limit for the particular proceedings in question: section 7(5). Accordingly, the three-month time limit for judicial review has been preserved and takes precedence over the one-year time limit under the HRA. The one-year time limit may be extended by the court if it considers it just and equitable to do so having regard to all the circumstances: section 7(5). The one-year limitation period under the HRA as opposed to the six-year general limitation period in tort seeks to achieve a balance between the interest of the individual bringing the case and those of the public authority alleged to have acted unlawfully, where a longer period would cause uncertainty and make effective administration very difficult. The limitation period does however have flexibility in the discretion to extend.[67]

8.37   A person can only rely on Convention rights provided that the act or omission complained of occurred *after* the coming into force of the relevant section of the HRA, save where the Act is used as a defence in proceedings brought against the complainant by a public authority under section 7(1)(b): section 22(4). A continuing failure to act in order to prevent or put an end to the infringement of a victim's Convention rights following the coming into force of the HRA may found a cause of action under section 7 of the HRA.[67A]

8.38   In *Biggin Hill Airport Ltd v. Bromley London Borough Council*,[68] Mr Nicholas Strauss Q.C. held that third parties, even if victims within the meaning of section 7(1) of the HRA, could not be joined to an existing action concerning the construction of a lease on the basis that the rights under the Convention would be infringed where the lease was entered into

---

[64] CPR, 30.3(2)(g) and Part 30 PD, para.7.
[65] CPR Part 19 PD, para. 6.6.
[66] CPR Part 30 PD, para. 7.
[66A] s.7(5).
[67] H.L. Deb., October 29, 1998, cols 2095–2102. In relation to the special limitation protection given by the HRA to public authorities, see *Zantsi v. Chairman of the Council of State* [1996] 1 C.H.R.D. 41, November 22, 1999, Sup Ct of S.A. (shorter limitation period for actions against state and officials not justifiable). In relation to the exercise of the discretion to extend, see *Mills v. The Commissioner of Police* [1996] 1 C.H.R.D. 37, May 4, 1995, High Ct, Trinidad and Tobago (a liberal interpretation must be given to any time limit under the Constitution especially where the delay could be reasonably explained).
[67A] *Marcic v. Thames Water Utilities Ltd*, unreported May 14, 2001, TCC (failure by defendant to take steps to remedy a drainage problem which had resulted in regular and serious flooding to the claimant's property by foul water from 1992 onwards. Under section 7(1)(a) of the HRA, the claimant established a breach of Article 8 and a partial expropriation under Article 1 of Protocol No. 1, the court recognising that the claimant had no cause of action under pre-existing domestic law).
[68] *The Times*, January 10, 2001, Mr Nicholas Strauss Q.C.

before October 2, 2000 and the Convention was no part of the factual background to the formation of the lease. The only recourse of the proposed claimants, as before October 2, 2000, was to the European Court of Human Rights. The Court of Appeal upheld the judge without substantive consideration of the Convention issue.[68A] In *R. v. Secretary of State for the Home Department, ex p. Mahmood (Amjad)*,[69] the Court of Appeal held that where after the coming into force of the HRA, a court reviewed an administrative decision made prior to that date but which would not take effect until after it, the court was not required to judge the decision by reference to its conformity with the affected individual's fundamental rights by treating them as incorporated into domestic law. The pre-HRA position applied and, where a fundamental right was engaged, the reviewing court required the decision maker to demonstrate either that his proposed action did not in truth interfere with the right, or if it did, that considerations which might reasonably be accepted as amounting to a substantial objective justification for the interference.[70] The test for review in *Mahmood* was refined by the House of Lords in *R. (Daly) v. Secretary of State for the Home Department*[70A] emphasising that the depth of review may be greater than the heightened *Wednesbury* test set out in *R. v. Ministry of Defence, ex p. Smith*[70B] through the Convention requirement to consider proportionality, but still short of a full merits review. This is discussed further in Chapter 4 at para. 4.30 above.

It is possible that a greater number of claims will be framed as actions for damages under Part 7 CPR rather than as applications for judicial review, with accompanying claims for damages, in order to take advantage of the more generous time limits available under the HRA. Such claims are likely to be struck out as an abuse of process if they are, in reality, public law challenges which should properly be brought by way of judicial review. Provided an individual is seeking to assert or defend private rights, an action will not be struck out as an abuse of process, even if it involves a challenge to the validity of a public law decision. **8.39**

3. PROCEEDINGS UNDER SECTION 7(1)(b) OF THE HRA

Reliance on the Convention in any Legal Proceedings

A Convention right can also be relied upon by a party who satisfies the "victim" test in any legal proceedings (section 7(1)(b) and section 7(6) of the HRA). The reference to legal proceedings includes, but is not limited to, proceedings brought by or at the instigation of a public authority and an appeal against the decision of a court or tribunal. An individual may raise **8.40**

[68A] Unreported, July 11, 2001, CA.
[69] [2001] 1 W.L.R. 840; *The Times*, January 9, 2001, CA.
[70] See further *R. v. Ministry of Defence, ex p. Smith* [1996] Q.B. 517 at 554; *R. v. Lord Saville of Newdigate, ex p. A* [2001] 1 W.L.R. 662, CA [1999] 4 All E.R. 860 at 872; and *R. v. Secretary of State for the Home Department, ex p. Launder* [1997] 1 W.L.R. 839 at 867.
[70A] [2001] 2 W.L.R. 1622.
[70B] [1996] Q.B. 517 at 554.

as a defence, to proceedings brought by a public authority, a claim that an act or proposed act of that authority is or would be unlawful by virtue of section 6(1). For example, it might be raised by way of defence to criminal charges that the police acted unlawfully. Judicial review proceedings are not "proceedings brought by or at the instigation of a public authority" within the meaning of section 7(1)(b) and section 22(4) of the HRA.[70C] The general scheme of sections 7 and 22(4), read together, was that a prior act could be relied upon by way of defence but could not be used offensively as a basis for advancing a claim. The presence of the Crown in judicial review proceedings was nominal, representing a contest between the applicant for judicial review and the authority against whom the proceedings were brought. The provisions of sections 7(1) and (3) clarified the position in that a person could only bring proceedings against a public authority if he was or would be a victim of an unlawful act. If judicial review proceedings were considered to be brought by the Crown, it would follow that no claim for a breach of the Convention could be advanced by way of judicial review unless the Crown was the victim. In judicial review proceedings, the applicant for judicial review was the person considered to bring the claim pursuant to section 7(1)(a) and so was precluded by section 22(4) from claiming damages retrospectively.[70D]

8.41 Unlike section 7(1)(a), such proceedings are not limited, on the face of the statute, to those to which a public authority is a party and may be raised in any proceedings between private parties where the lawfulness of an act of a public authority is relevant. An individual can therefore allege the unlawfulness of an act of a public authority in any proceedings in which it is relevant, even if all the parties to the litigation are private.

Using the HRA to Bolster an Existing Cause of Action or Defence

8.42 Where a party wishes to rely on the HRA as an additional argument in support of an existing cause of action, this will constitute proceedings under section 7(1)(b) and the limitation period in respect of the existing cause of action applies.[71] A party may wish to invoke the Convention in order to influence the court's approach to an existing cause of action, for example, by invoking the right to respect for private life in Article 8 in the context of an action for breach of confidence in order to establish greater protection for privacy.

8.43 The Convention may also be relevant to an existing domestic law defence. For example, the right to peaceful enjoyment of possessions under Article 1 of the First Protocol may be relevant to the scope of the restitutionary defence of change of position.[72]

[70C] *R. v. London Borough of Haringey ex p. Ben-Abdelaziz & anr* [2001] EWCA Civ 803, May 22, 2001, CA.

[70D] *ibid.*

[71] H.C. Deb., June 24, 1998, col. 1094 (Mr Mike O'Brien, Parliamentary Under-Secretary of State for the Home Department).

[72] The Convention is relevant to defences as well as causes of action: see, *e.g. Belvedere Alberghiera S.R.L. v. Italy*, Application No. 31524/96, Judgment May 30, 2000.

4. STATEMENTS OF CASE

Requirements for Pleading HRA Claims

CPR Part 16 PD, paragraph 16.1 prescribes certain pleading require-   **8.44**
ments in relation to claims against public authorities under section 7(1)(a)
of the HRA.[72A] A claimant must:

    (1) state the fact that he is bringing proceedings against a public
        authority under section 7(1)(a) of the HRA in the claim form;

    (2) in the claim form or in the particulars of claim (a) give details of
        the Convention right which it is alleged has been infringed and of
        the infringement, and (b) where the claim is founded on a finding
        of unlawfulness by another court or tribunal, give details of the
        finding.

Where an appellant is adding a claim against a public authority under   **8.45**
section 7(1)(a) of the HRA in an appeal, CPR Part 52 Practice Direction
paragraph 5.1A provides that the appeal notice must:

    state that fact; and

    give details of—(a) the Convention right which it is alleged has
    been infringed and of the infringement, and (b) the finding of the
    court or tribunal, where there is a finding of unlawfulness by
    another court or tribunal, or (c) the judicial act and the court or
    tribunal which made it, where it is the act or that court or tribunal
    which is complained of as provided by section 9 of the HRA.

Where a claim is made under the HRA for damages in respect of a judicial   **8.46**
act, that claim must be set out in the statement of case or the appeal
notice: CPR 19.4A(3).

The following are some suggested ingredients that a particulars of claim   **8.47**
will need to include:

    (1) the claimant or defendant respectively is a "victim" within section
        7(1) of the HRA;

    (2) the respondent is a public authority within the meaning of section
        6(1) (if he/she/it is an obvious public authority) or section 6(1)
        and section 6(3)(b) (if he/she/it is a body or individual exercising
        a public function);

    (3) the nature or content of the public authority's duty under the
        Convention;

    (4) particulars of breach of the Convention right (in practice, these
        are likely to be derived from the HRA, the text of the Convention
        right relied upon or the case-law of the European Court);

[72A] See also CPR Part 54 PD, para. 5.3.

(5) where vicarious liability for breach of Convention rights is in issue, identifying the body or individual for which the public authority is vicariously liable and the particulars of breach relied upon;

(6) the remedy sought;

(7) where damages are sought, the jurisdiction under which they are sought (*i.e.* section 8 of the HRA or an existing cause of action) and in the case of HRA damages, making clear whether they are pecuniary or non-pecuniary in nature;

(8) causation of loss (linking the loss to the violation complained of);

(9) interest on damages.

8.48 When pleading a defence, consideration should be given to whether a challenge will be made to:

(1) the standing of the claimant or applicant (is he/she/it "directly affected" by the act or omission within the meaning of Article 34 of the Convention?);

(2) the allegation that the defendant or respondent is a body with a duty to act compatibly with the Convention in relation to the act or omission of which complaint is made (ignoring the case of an obvious public authority which has to comply with the Convention in respect of all its acts, is it disputed that the act is in the exercise of a "public function"?);

(3) does the defendant or respondent have a defence under section 6(2) of the HRA, on the basis that it could not have acted differently as a result of one or more provisions of primary legislation (section 6(2)(a)) or it was acting so as to give effect to or enforce one or more provisions of, or made under, primary legislation which cannot be read or given effect in a way which is compatible with Convention rights?

(4) whether the cause of action properly falls within the field of a public law challenge or a private law action, and accordingly, whether the claim has been brought in the correct forum;

(5) in relation to the allegations of breach—(a) whether it is accepted that there was an interference with the right complained of; (b) if so, whether the interference was pursuant to a legitimate aim and is proportionate to that aim (for example Article 6(1)); alternatively, whether it was justified by an express justification in the Article at issue and is necessary in a democratic society (for example Articles 8–11)[73];

(6) causation of any loss (does it flow from the violation complained of?);

---

[73] The Articles and case law relating to the Convention right in issue will need to be read and considered carefully in this regard. See further paras 4.33 *et seq.*

(7) quantum of loss (was it actually, reasonably or necessarily incurred?);

(8) the claim for interest.

Limitation Points

A HRA limitation issue raised should be expressly pleaded in a defence. **8.49** There is a one-year time limit for bringing a section 7(1)(a) claim which runs from the date of the act complained of, subject to any stricter time limit for.the procedure in question, for example the three-month time limit for judicial review.

General points regarding statements of case

Where a Convention right is relied upon to buttress an existing cause of **8.50** action or defence in a private law action, it is highly desirable that this is pleaded in order to give the court and an opponent notice that a Convention issue is being raised. The statement of case should identify the specific Convention right(s) being relied upon and how they are alleged to enhance or otherwise affect the existing cause of action. This will enable questions of disclosure, evidence and case management to be considered in light of the pleaded case.

It is generally worth considering whether a similar right exists in European **8.51** Community law (for example protection of lawyer/client confidentiality), since it may be more advantageous to plead the case as a matter of E.C. law than under the Convention, given the supremacy of E.C. law over inconsistent domestic law (including primary legislation) by reason of section 2 of the European Communities Act 1972. The E.U.'s Charter of Fundamental Rights should also be considered since, in its draft form, it includes the rights already contained in the European Convention on Human Rights.[74]

5. ADVOCACY

Identifying whether HRA is relevant. The first and primary issue **8.52** for the advocate is in identifying the relevance of the HRA or the Convention to a case or legal problem. This will obviously apply whether an advocate is representing a claimant or a defendant. This requires a high level of familiarity with the nature, scope and effect of Convention rights. Whilst the Convention will continue to be primarily relevant to areas of law most heavily involving the state such as criminal or public law, the Convention is also likely to reach into general common law and equity. Accordingly, advocates and courts must take a fresh look at every area of law (including those traditionally regarded as well settled) from a Convention and human rights perspective. There is no substitute in this regard for a sound working knowledge of the HRA, the Convention and the jurisprudence of the European Court and the European Commission. An understanding of the scope of the Convention emerges from an appreciation of how the provisions have been construed or applied by the Strasbourg institutions, rather than the literal text. The Register of the European

---

[74] See further paras 6.159 *et seq.*

Court's Press Releases contain a list of forthcoming judgments together with a synopsis of areas covered and of actual judgments after they have been pronounced. They can be found on the Court's HUDOC database.[75] Further, a working knowledge of other human rights instruments and international case-law is also desirable.[76]

8.53 In *Daniels v. Walker: Practice Note*,[77] Lord Woolf issued a stern warning to advocates that following the HRA coming into force, they would need to show self-restraint if the Act was not to be discredited.[78] He further stated that it would be undesirable if the consideration of case management issues was made more complex by the injection into them of Article 6 style arguments[79] and that Article 6 did not have anything to add to the obligation of the court under the Civil Procedure Rules to deal with cases "justly".[80] Whilst the HRA clearly does have application to the Civil Procedure Rules because the content of the court's obligation to act "justly" will, through the Act, be informed by the Convention, the warning regarding the exercise of self-restraint if the HRA is not to become discredited is entirely apt and likely to be repeated if the Convention is raised unnecessarily. Advocates may wish to bear in mind the approach of the Judicial Studies Board training the judiciary on the HRA, which has been not to question whether the Convention applies (because there will be few cases where it does not) but what it adds to existing domestic law and practice.[81] On the other hand, advocates should not hesitate to take a point where it is clearly in their clients' interest that they do so and should also bear in mind the risk of a finding of express or implied waiver if they fail to take a Convention point that their client might wish to rely upon on a subsequent appeal or before the European Court.[82] It is worth noting that the court may take a Convention point of its own motion pursuant to section 6 of the HRA.[83]

8.54   **Remedies.** Advocates should be familiar with the remedies available for a breach of a Convention right, so that a suitable and effective remedy is pursued.[83A] If damages are sought, it should be noted that damages for breach of a Convention right under section 8 of the HRA are not automatic[84] and, subject to any changes brought about as a result of the recent report of the Law Commission on damages under the HRA,[85] awards are likely to be significantly less than damages awarded for a pre-existing cause of action. Most awards of non-pecuniary damages by the

---

[75] See Internet address under Human Rights Legal Reference Sources para. 8.79 below.
[76] See Chap. 7 International Sources of Human Rights Law.
[77] [2000] 1 W.L.R. 1382, CA.
[78] At 1387C.
[79] At 1387B-C.
[80] At 1386H.
[81] Sedley L.J. in *Counsel*, October 2000.
[82] See further Chap. 3 above, and Chap. 10 below.
[83] See *e.g. Wilson v. First County Trust* (2001) 2 W.L.R. 302, CA.
[83A] See further Chapter 9.
[84] In many cases, the European Court has found that the finding of a violation of itself constitutes just satisfaction and it declines to make any award of damages.
[85] Report Law Com. No. 266/Scot. Law Com. No. 180 entitled "Damages under the Human Rights Act 1998" (published October 2000)

European Court have not exceeded £15,000 and many have not exceeded £5,000.[85A]

Duty to have relevant Strasbourg case law available. Advocates **8.55** who do wish to rely on the provisions of the HRA are under a duty to have available any material in terms of decisions of the European Court (or Commission) on which they wish to rely or which might assist the court: *Barclays Bank v. Ellis.*[86] However, judgment should be used in citing authorities where there are a number of cases relating to the same principle or a case merely contains a statement which is extremely general in nature and therefore of limited practical assistance to the court. A selective approach should be adopted. In *Williams v. Cowell,*[86A] the Court of Appeal warned that advocates should resist the temptation to turn court hearings into international human rights seminars and should only put before the court that part of the researched material which is reasonably required for the resolution of the appeal. The *Practice Direction: Citation of Authorities*[86B] must be complied with in citing human rights cases, save that decisions and judgments of the European Court are not treated as "authorities decided in other jurisdictions" for the purpose of paragraph 9 of the Practice Direction.[86C] Accordingly, advocates must state in respect of each authority that they wish to cite the proposition of law that the authority demonstrates and the parts of the judgment that support the proposition. Reasons must be given for citing more than one authority in support of a given proposition.[86D] It might also be noted that in *Poplar Housing and Regeneration Community Association Ltd v. Donoghue*[86E] the Court of Appeal stated *obiter* that where a human rights argument was raised at a late stage, but it was nonetheless possible for the first instance judge to give a decision summarily without adjourning for further evidence, in a case where there was very likely to be an appeal, there could be substantial advantages in the judge adopting this course of action.

Access to materials. Advocates will need ready and accurate **8.56** access to the relevant international and comparative legal materials in order to determine the values underlying particular rights which will be relevant to a court considering the application of a right to a particular case, the interpretative principles adopted in approaching a particular provision as well as the nature, scope and effect of substantive rights. As outlined in Chapter 7, the following bodies all interpret similar rights: the Supreme Courts of Canada, the United States, Ireland, India, Mauritius and Zimbabwe; the New Zealand Court of Appeal; the Judicial Committee of the Privy Council; the U.N. Human Rights Committee and the Inter-

---

[85A] See further paras 9.33 *et seq.*
[86] *The Times*, October 24, 2000, CA. In this case, counsel for the defendant who was applying to set aside a judgment by default raised an infringement of Article 6 at the appeal hearing without advance notice but declined to develop the point or draw the court's attention to any case law. He naturally received very short shrift from the court.
[86A] [2001] 1 W.L.R. 187, CA at 198, 202.
[86B] [2001] 1 W.L.R. 1001.
[86C] Para. 9.3.
[86D] Para. 8.1. Reference should be made to the *Practice Direction* for the other requirements regarding citation.
[86E] [2001] E.W.C.A. Civ. 595, April 27, 2001, CA.

American Court of Human Rights.[87] Decisions of the European Court of Justice and Court of First Instance are also relevant and likely to become increasing so in the context of the Charter of Fundamental Rights of the European Union.[88] The principal reference sources for human rights law are set out in tabular form below. An advocate should always consider his or her tribunal and exercise some judgment as to what decisions to put before the court, since members of the judiciary may differ in their openness to, and willingness to apply, decisions of other jurisdictions in a domestic setting. Whilst domestic courts are under a duty pursuant to section 2 of the HRA to "take account of" relevant Strasbourg jurisprudence, there may be more hesitancy about considering international human rights jurisprudence unless it is clearly relevant. There appears also to be a discernable judicial desire in some quarters to seek to limit the scope and applicability of human rights arguments to their "proper" context.[89]

8.57   **Legislation.**   Where legislation is in issue, the starting point will be a consideration of whether it can be interpreted in a manner which is compatible with the Convention, in accordance with section 3(1) of the HRA. Unless it is impossible to do so, the court must give the legislation a meaning compatible with the Convention. It is important to check whether primary or secondary legislative provisions have been construed differently, cut down or declared incompatible with the Convention either by the European Court or by the domestic courts. For example, in *Stott, Procurator Fiscal (Dunfermline) v. Brown*, the Scottish High Court of Justiciary Appeal Court declared section 172 of the Road Traffic Act 1988 incompatible with Article 6(1) of the Convention.[90] The Privy Council subsequently reversed the decision on appeal and ruled it to be compatible.[91]

8.58   **Possible declaration of incompatibility.**   Where there is a possibility of a declaration of incompatibility being made, advocates should raise this with the court at an early stage, so that the Crown can be notified by the court, under section 5 of the HRA and CPR, 19.4A and Part 19 PD, paragraph 6, and joined as a party to the proceedings if it chooses to intervene. The notice must be given in all cases, including those where the Crown, a Minister or a governmental body is already a party to the proceedings. The Crown is allowed 21 days (or such other period as the court directs) to state whether it wishes to be joined as a party through an "appropriate person". If it does not apply to the court to be joined, the court may join the appropriate person as a party.[92]

---

[87] See Chap. 7, above.
[88] See paras 6.159 *et seq.*
[89] See, *e.g.* Lord Woolf M.R. in *Daniels v. Walker* [2000] 1 W.L.R. 1382, CA; L. Hoffmann, "Human Rights and the House of Lords" (1999) 62 M.L.R. 159; Lord Justice Buxton, "The Human Rights Act and Private Law" (2000) 116 L.Q.R. 48.
[90] [2001] 2 All E.R. 97; *The Times*, February 14, 2000, Appeal Court, High Court of Justiciary.
[91] [2001] 2 W.L.R. 817; The Times December 6, 2000. PC.
[92] CPR, 19.4A(4). See also para. 8.35 above.

6. CITATION OF AUTHORITY

Permitted reports. Citations of Strasbourg authorities are required **8.59** to be from an "authoritative and complete report".[93] Copies of the complete original texts issued by the European Court or Commission, either paper based or from the Court's HUDOC database on the internet, may be used.[94] Apart from these, no specific guidance is given as to authoritative sources, although the following reports which were listed in the draft rules (not incorporated into the final rules) may provide some assistance to the practitioner:

(1) judgments of the European Court of Human Rights, published by Carl Heymanns Verlag;

(2) reports, judgments and decisions of the European Court of Human Rights, published by Carl Heymanns Verlag;

(3) decisions of the European Commission of Human Rights, published by Carl Heymanns Verlag;

(4) decisions and reports of the European Commission of Human Rights, volumes 1 to 96, published by Carl Heymanns Verlag;

(5) European Human Rights Reports, published by Sweet & Maxwell;

(6) Human Rights Cases, published by Butterworths;

(7) Full texts taken from the following electronic databases: Case Law Service (Lawtel); Eurolaw (ILI); JUSTIS (Context Electronic Publishers); Lexis-Nexis; Westlaw UK.[94A]

Notice to other parties. Any party wishing to cite Strasbourg juris- **8.60** prudence is required to give the court and any other party a list of authorities and copies of the reports from which they are to be cited not less than three days before the hearing: CPR 39 PD paragraph 8.1(2).[95]

Status of Commission decisions. The function of the European **8.61** Commission, which is now defunct, was to filter cases by deciding their admissibility, and if admissible, to produce a report on the merits. No oral argument preceded the decisions or reports. Accordingly, the weight given to Commission decisions should arguably be less than that given to judgments of the European Court following oral argument.[96] Where the Court has given judgment, the judgment will usually take precedence over the Commissions' conclusions. However, where no Court judgment exists,

---

[93] CPR Part 39 PD, para. 8.1(1).
[94] CPR Part 29 PD, para. 8.1(3).
[94A] In relation to the operation of precedent in domestic law on human rights decisions, see para. 4.21 above. In relation to advocates' duties regarding citation, see para. 8.55 above.
[95] See further para. 8.55, above.
[96] This argument was put forward on behalf of the applicants in *R. v. Secretary of State for the Home Department, ex p. Anderson and Taylor, The Times*, February 27, 2001; [2001] EWHC ADMIN 181, paras 16, 20, DC.

the Commission's view remains a good, though necessarily limited, indication of the likely approach to be taken under the Convention.

7. EVIDENCE

8.62   **Evidence in support of HRA claim/defence.**   Where a Convention issue arises, a more creative approach to evidence may be needed. Whilst any dispute regarding the primary facts alleged to constitute an interference with a fundamental right will be determined in the same way as any other factual dispute, it will often be the case that the facts amounting to an interference are not in dispute and the real issue is the justification for the interference.

8.63   It will be necessary for the court to consider:

(1) in the case of implied rights (for example the right of access to a court under Article 6), whether the interference satisfies a legitimate aim;

(2) in the case of qualified rights (for example Articles 8 to 11), whether the interference falls within the limited categories of permitted interferences;

(3) where the defendant has to show that the interference is necessary in a democratic society (for example Articles 8 to 11), *i.e.* whether it answers a pressing social need and;

(4) whether the interference is proportionate to the aim to be achieved.

8.64   **Proportionality.**   The key issue in most cases will be proportionality. The court will have to arrive at its own view on the merits and not merely review the act or decision in question for irrationality. This will require the parties to provide evidence of a nature and to an extent that it can put the court in a position to conduct a substantive review and come to its own conclusions.

8.65   **Social and comparative evidence.**   It will often be necessary to gather and adduce cogent and relevant evidence about the actual consequences of an impugned act or legislative measure and the social and political context. It is likely to become commonplace in such cases for parliamentary debates, social statistics and evidence of comparative law and practice to be placed before the courts. The quality of the evidence required is similar to that needed to justify an interference with a European Community law right or freedom.[97]

8.66   **Legislative intent.**   Where an issue of construction of the HRA arises, evidence of legislative intention in the form of extracts from *Hansard* will be relevant. Where an issue of construction of the Convention

---

[97] See, *e.g*, in *R. v. Ministry for Agriculture, Fisheries and Food, ex p. First City Trading* [1997] 1 C.M.L.R. 250 at 279; *R. v. Chief Constable of Sussex, ex p. International Trader's Ferry* [1999] 1 All E.R. 129 at 145.

arises, it may be necessary for the court to consider the *travaux pré-paratoires*, although these are unlikely to be of great assistance in light of the evolving "living instrument" approach to interpretation under the Convention.

Burden of proof. The burden of justifying an interference with a **8.67**
Convention right is on the respondent public authority, which will be required to satisfy the court as to the reasons for the interference and that those reasons were relevant and sufficient. This represents a shift in the burden of proof since it contrasts with the Diceyan approach in domestic law pre-HRA, which presumed actions to be lawful if they had not been made unlawful. Accordingly, defendants or respondents will need to have the burden of proof issue firmly in mind when considering what evidence to adduce in relation to a particular action or application.[98]

Disclosure. The Convention's particular focus on the facts or merits **8.68**
of an individual case[99] will have implications for disclosure obligations in that litigants may require greater access to particular classes of documents. In addition, the court's decisions as to the admission and adducing of evidence in that a court may have to be prepared to allow a closer degree of consideration of the facts than pre-HRA.

***Amicus* and Brandeis briefs.** Where a Convention issue arises, **8.69**
interested parties, including public interest groups and human rights organisations, may wish to or be called upon to file *amicus* briefs or "Brandeis briefs". The "Brandeis brief" is a tool employed in the United States. It is named after Mr. Louis D. Brandeis who filed a written brief in the case of *Muller v. Oregon*,[1] in which he sought to defend the constitutionality of a state law limiting the hours worked by women in laundries. The copious brief included references to the legislation of states and foreign jurisdictions which imposed restrictions on the employment hours required of women, extracts from over 90 reports of committees, bureaus of statistics, commissioners of hygiene and inspectors of factories to show that long hours might constitute a health risk to women in certain circumstances and the general economic benefits of shorter hours. The American Supreme Court took judicial notice of the brief, without requiring strict proof of its contents. Henry L.J. in *R. v. Ministry of Defence, ex p. Smith*[2] anticipated that a domestic court, finding itself in a relatively novel constitutional position, might well ask for more material than the adversarial system normally provides, such as a Brandeis brief. A tool adopted by the European Court is the *amicus curiae* brief. This enables third parties to make written submissions, with permission of the President of the Court, on

---

[98] See further in relation to the standard of proof, paras 4.50 *et seq*, above.
[99] See *Osman v. United Kingdom* (2000) 29 E.H.R.R. 245; *cf. Z v. United Kingdom*, Application No. 29392/95, May 10, 2001; *The Times*, May 31, 2001. See also *T.P. and K.M. v. United Kingdom* Application No. 28945/95, May 10, 2001; *The Times*, May 31, 2001.
[1] 208 U.S. 412 (1908).
[2] [1996] Q.B. 517 at 564.

issues specified by the President.[3] The Lord Chancellor expressly antici-pated the filing of such briefs during debates on the Human Rights Bill.[4] Even before the coming into force of the HRA, the courts have increasingly been permitting third party intervention by human rights organisations. Recent examples include intervention in the House of Lords by Amnesty International,[5] Justice[6] and Liberty.[7] In a recent series of cases before the European Court concerning killings in Northern Ireland by officers of the Royal Ulster Constabulary or soldiers pursuant to an alleged "shoot to kill" policy, the Northern Ireland Human Rights Commission, acting as inter-venor, made submissions in relation to international standards concerning the right to life in this area, including the Inter-American Court's case law and findings of the U.N. Human Rights Committee.[8] By contrast, the Court of Appeal of Northern Ireland has held that the Northern Ireland Human Rights Commission did not have power to intervene as an interested party or to act as an *amicus curiae* in legal proceedings.[8A] The Court stated that the powers granted to the Commission to bring proceedings in its own name or to give assistance to individuals engaged in proceedings were quite adequate to ensure that it was able to make a substantial contribu-tion to the observance of human rights in Northern Ireland.

8. COSTS IN HUMAN RIGHTS CASES

8.70   **Will costs follow the event?** The presumption that costs follow the event may not always be followed in cases involving HRA issues. In Parliamentary debates on the Human Rights Bill, the Lord Chancellor was careful to refuse to answer the question of who would bear the Crown's costs following a claim under the HRA.[9] There is no clear rule requiring the Crown to bear its own costs. It might therefore be presumed that the general costs rule—that costs follow the event—should apply. However, in *Ahnee v. Director of Public Prosecutions*,[10] the Privy Council stated that where a challenge raises important questions affecting fundamental rights, an award of costs against an unsuccessful applicant may not be appropriate on the ground that resort to rights under the constitution which

---

[3] See, *e.g. Malone v. United Kingdom* (brief by Post Office Engineering Union on process of metering) and *Lingens v. Austria* (brief by International Press Institute containing survey of relevant law and practice of 10 Contracting States and the USA).

[4] H.L. Deb., November 24, 1997, cols 832–833 (". . . the natural position to take is to adopt the victim test as applied by Strasbourg when a complaint is made of a denial of Convention rights, recognising that our courts will be ready to permit *amicus* written briefs from non-governmental organisations, that is to say briefs, but not to treat them as full parties.").

[5] *R. v. Bow Street Metropolitan Stipendiary Magistrate, ex p. Pinochet Ugarte* [1998] 3 W.L.R. 1456, HL.

[6] *R. v. Secretary of State for the Home Department, ex p. Venables; R. v. Same, ex p. Thompson* [1998] A.C. 407, HL. A written submission was made by Justice with the leave of the Judicial Committee of the Privy Council in *Stott (Procurator Fiscal of Dunfermline) v. Brown* [2001] 2 W.L.R. 817; *The Times*, December 6, 2000.

[7] *R. v. Khan* [1997] A.C. 558, HL.

[8] See, *e.g. Jordan v. United Kingdom*, (2001) 31 E.H.R.R. 201 and *McKerr v. United Kingdom*, Application No. 28883/95, April 4, 2000.

[8A] *R. v. Greater Belfast Coroner, ex p. Northern Ireland Human Rights Commission, The Times*, May 11, 2001, NICA.

[9] H.L. Deb., November 17, 1997, cols 555–562.

[10] [1999] 2 A.C. 294, PC.

are made in good faith ought not to be discouraged.[11] This is similar to the approach in *Sanderson v. Attorney-General of the Eastern Cape*,[12] in which the Constitutional Court of South Africa held that it was necessary to be cautious in awarding costs against litigants who sought to enforce their constitutional rights against the state in order to avoid any inhibiting effect on other potential litigants in this category, but that approach should not be allowed to develop into an inflexible rule which might encourage frivolous litigants. On the facts, the court held that, notwithstanding the failure of the applicant's constitutional claim, it was a genuine complaint on a point of substance which, accordingly, did not merit the sanction of a costs order.[13]

Public interest challenges. An apparent analogy to proceedings **8.71** under the HRA might be the existing law relating to public interest challenges. However, the essential characteristics of a public interest challenge are that:

(1) it raises public law issues which are of general importance;

(2) the applicant has no private interest in the outcome.[13A]

Clearly, under the HRA "victim" test, a claimant will have a private interest in the outcome of the proceedings and any challenge will not be purely, or even mainly, in the public interest. Further, public interest groups do not have standing to bring a claim under the HRA, although they can support an applicant or claimant with standing. Accordingly, the courts will have to formulate their approach to the award of costs in human rights cases on the basis of a different rationale to costs in public interest challenges, though they may draw on similar principles.

Issue costs. The court has power to decide to make an order in **8.72** respect of "issue" costs in relation to a human rights issue in favour of or against the claimant in light of outcome of the argument and the reasonableness of bringing the human rights claim before the court pursuant to CPR, 44.3(4)(b) and 44.3(5)(b). The court's duty to take into account Strasbourg case law where a Convention issue arises, and the advocates' duty to bring that case law before the court should militate against too ready a use of the power to award issue costs against a party where the court does not decide the point on the ground of the Convention case law or does not find the Convention argument helpful.

Pre-emptive costs orders. It is unclear whether pre-emptive costs **8.73** orders will be made in order to give an applicant, raising a HRA challenge, protection from an adverse costs order following a proposed challenge if he is unsuccessful. The courts generally refuse to make such orders in the

---

[11] See also *Motsepe v. I.R.C.* (1997) 6 B.C.L.R. 692 at 705, Constitutional Court of South Africa.

[12] (1997) 3 B.H.R.C. 647.

[13] At 663f-h and 664c-d.

[13A] *R. v. Lord Chancellor, ex p. Child Poverty Action Group; R. v. Director of Public Prosecutions, ex p. Bull* [1999] 1 W.L.R. 347 at 353.

context of public interest challenges save in very exceptional circumstances.[14] In light of the availability of legal aid for human rights challenges, such applications should be rare.

9. REFERENCE SOURCES FOR HUMAN RIGHTS LAW

8.74 The primary sources of European and international human rights law are set out below in tabulated form together with some useful addresses for organisations which provide guidance on human rights matters to both lawyers and the public.

8.75 Treaties

Text	Publisher	Date
European Convention on Human Rights: Collected Texts	Council of Europe Press	1995
Yearbook of the European Convention on Human Rights	Martinus Nijhoff	1995 onwards
Collected Edition of the *Travaux Préparatoires*	Martinus Nijhoff	1975

8.76 Case-law

Text	Publisher	Date
Series A (includes the official report of every judgment of the European Court including the Commission's Report).	Carl Heymanns Verlag KG	Pre 1996
Series B (includes arguments and documents submitted by the parties).		
Reports of Judgments and Decision ("RJD")	Carl Heymanns Verlag KG	1996–date
European Human Rights Reports ("E.H.R.R.")	Sweet & Maxwell	1979–date

---

[14] See, *e.g. R. v. Lord Chancellor, ex p. Child Poverty Action Group; R. v. Director of Public Prosecutions, ex p. Bull* [1999] 1 W.L.R. 347. Dyson J. refused two such applications on the basis that the starting point was that costs were to follow the event, and pre-emptive orders for costs should only be made where the court was satisfied that the issues raised were truly ones of general public importance and that it had a sufficient appreciation of the merits of the claim to conclude that it was in the public interest to make the order. The court was more likely to make the order where the respondent clearly had superior capacity to bear the costs than the applicant and it was satisfied that the applicant would discontinue the proceedings if the order was not made.

Text	Publisher	Date
Human Rights Law Reports—U.K. Cases	Sweet & Maxwell	April 2000–date
Human Rights Case Digest	Sweet & Maxwell	Summaries of most European Court Decisions from 1996 onwards
The Times—Human Rights Section	*The Times*	
Current Law—Human Rights Section (also includes major case law from other European Contracting States)	Sweet & Maxwell	
Butterworths Human Rights Cases ("B.H.R.C.") (focus on human rights cases from international tribunals and other jurisdictions)	Butterworths	1997
Blackstones Human Rights Digest (includes the full text of all European Court of Human Rights judgments on CD)	Blackstones	2001
Human Rights Reports of New Zealand	Brookers, New Zealand (from U.K., through Sweet & Maxwell)	
New Zealand Bill of Rights Reports	Oxford University Press, Auckland	1990/92–date
International Human Rights Reports ("I.H.H.R.") (decisions of U.N. Human Rights Committee and the Inter-American Court of Human Rights)	Human Rights Law Centre, University of Nottingham	1994–date
Commonwealth Human Rights Caselaw Digest	Interights/Butterworths	1996–date
A Systematic Guide to the Case-Law of the European Court of Human Rights (a comprehensive compilation of extracts from cases of the European Court classified by Article)	Kluwer International	(Vols I & II 1960–1994; Vol. III 1995–1996)

Text	Publisher	Date
The Constitutional Library of South Africa (including the Constitution of the Republic of South Africa Act, full text of all South African constitutional cases and the South African Journal on Human Rights)	Jutastat UK Ltd CD Rom/Internet subscription	

8.77 Decisions and Reports of European Commission

Text	Publisher	Date
Collection of Decisions of the European Commission of Human Rights (CD)	Council of Europe Press (now out of print)	Pre-1975 only
Decisions and Reports of European Commission on Human Rights (DR)	Council of Europe Press	Post 1975 only
Commission Supplement to European Human Rights Reports (E.H.R.R. CD)	Sweet & Maxwell	1993–date

8.78 Decisions of the Committee of Ministers

Text	Publisher	Date
Yearbook of the European Convention on Human Rights	Martinus Nijhoff	1955–date

8.79 Internet.[15]

(a) European sites

Site	Address
European Court of Human Rights (Convention, protocols, press releases of Council of Europe, all Court decisions and all Commission cases reports in D&R series from 1986 onwards via HUDOC database)	http://www.echr.coe.int
Committee of Ministers (Committee of Ministers decisions from 1996 onwards—see also Court's web site and HUDOC database)	http://cm.coe.int

---

[15] The internet addresses listed are accurate at the date of submission for publication but may, of course, be subject to change. For a more comprehensive list of web-based sources of human rights legal resources, see J. Simor & B. Emmerson, *Human Rights Practice* (Sweet & Maxwell, 2000), App. D1.

Site	Address
Council of Europe	http://www.coe.fr
International Labour Organisation (Convention on Freedom of Association and Protection of the Right to Organise (No. 87); Right to Organise and Collective Bargaining (No. 98))	http://www.ilo.org
Court of Justice of the European Communities	http://www.europa.eu.int/cj/en/index.htm

(b) U.N. sites

Site	Address
U.N. Human Rights Sitemap	http://www.unhchr.ch/map.htm
U.N. Human Rights Committee	http://www.unhchr.ch/html/menu2/6/hrc.htm
U.N. Committee on Racial Discrimination	http://www.unhchr.ch/html/menu2/6/cerd.htm
U.N. Committee on the Elimination of Discrimination Against Women	http://www.unhchr.ch/html/menu2/6/cedw.htm
U.N. Committee Against Torture	http://www.unhchr.ch/html/menu2/6/cat.htm

(c) U.K. sites

Site	Address
Beagle human rights website (including the Judicial Studies Board summary of leading Strasbourg judgments)	http://www.beagle.org.uk/hra/newindex.htm
Lord Chancellor's Department Human Rights pages	http://www.lcd.gov.uk/humanrights/humanfr.htm
Hansard debates on Human Rights Bill	http://www.open.gov.uk/lcd/humanrights/parlfr.htm
Delia Venables	http://www.venables.co.uk (link to Human Rights section)
British and Irish Legal Information Institute (BAILII)	http://www.bailii.org/
Statewatch (technology and surveillance issues)	http://www.statewatch.org
Home Office (booklets—Putting Rights into Practice; Core Guidance for Public Authorities)	http://www.homeoffice.gov.uk http://www.homeoffice.gov.uk/hract/lawlist2.htm (archive on the Human Rights Bill by topic)
Law Commission (Report on Damages under HRA 1998, October 2000)	http://www.lawcom.gov.uk http://www.scotlawcom.gov.uk

(d) International sites

Site	Address
Interights Online Resources (summaries of many Commonwealth reported and unreported human rights cases starting from 1996 with some coverage of pre-1996 cases)	http://www.interights.org
Human Rights Web	http://www.hrweb.org/resource.html
University of Minnesota	http://www.umn.edu/humanrts
International Global Communications Human Rights Internet Resources Collection	http://www.igc.org/igc/issues/hr/or.html
Canadian Supreme Court	http://www.scc-csc.gc.ca/
United States Supreme & Federal Courts	http://www.findlaw.com/casecode/supreme.html
Australian case law	http://www.austlii.edu.au http://lawfoundation.net.au
Australian Journal of Human Rights	http://www.austlii.edu.au/cgi-bin/disp.pl/au/other/ahric/ajhr/V2NI/ajhr2102.html
New Zealand case law	http://www.austlii.edu.au/nz/cases http://lawfoundation.net.au
South African Constitutional Court	http://www.concourt.gov.za/

8.80 Journals

Text	Publisher	Date
European Human Rights Law Review (E.H.R.L.R.) —Emmerson (ed.)	Sweet & Maxwell	1996–date
Yearbook on European Law	Martinus Nijhoff, Council of Europe Press	1955–date
European Law Review—Human Rights Survey	Sweet & Maxwell	1976–date
British Yearbook of Interntional Law	Oxford University Press	1920/21 –date
Current Law—Human Rights Section	Sweet & Maxwell	1984–date
International and Comparative Law Quarterly) (I.C.L.Q.)	British Institute of International and Comparative Law	1947–date

Textbooks 8.81

Text	Publisher	Date
Human Rights Practice Looseleaf—Emmerson & Simor	Sweet & Maxwell	2000
Human Rights: The 1998 Act and the European Convention—Grosz, Beatson & Duffy	Sweet & Maxwell	2000
Human Rights Law & Practice—Lester & Pannick (eds.)	Butterworths	1999 (+2000 Supplement)
The Law of Human Rights—Clayton & Tomlinson	Oxford University Press	2000
European Human Rights Law—Starmer	Legal Action Group	1999
The Human Rights Act 1998—Coppel	Wiley	1999
Law of the European Convention on Human Rights—Harris, O'Boyle & Warbrick	Butterworths	1995
The Human Rights Bill. The Debate in Parliament—Cooper & Owers (eds.)	Hart Publishing	2000
The International Covenant on Civil and Political Rights and United Kingdom Law—Harris & Joseph (eds.)	Oxford University Press	1995
Rights and Freedoms—the New Zealand Bill of Rights Act 1990 and the Human Rights Act 1993—Huscroft & Rishworth	Wellington Press	1995

Useful Addresses 8.82

Body	Address
Human Rights Information Centre	The Council of Europe, 67006, Strasbourg Cedex France. Tel: 00–333–88–41–2024 Fax: 00–333–88–41–2704 Email: hricdoc@hric.doe.fr

Body	Address
Interights (The International Centre for the Legal Protection of Human Rights) (provides assistance to lawyers, courts and non-governmental organisations about international human rights law and procedures)	33 Islington High Street, London, N1 9LH, England Tel: +44 (0)20 7278 3230 Fax: +44 (0)20 7248 4334 Email: ir@interights.org.uk
Justice	59 Carter Lane, London, EC4V 5AQ, England Tel: +44 (0)20 7329 5100 Fax: +44 (0)20 7329 5055 Email: admin@justice.org.uk
Liberty (National Council for Civil Liberties)	21 Tabard Street, London, SE1 4LA, England Tel: +44 (0)20 7403 3888 Fax: +44 (0)20 7407 5354 Email: info@liberty-human-rights.org.uk
Liberty/The Public Law Project	Human Rights and Public Law Line Tel: 0808 808 4546 (Mon/Wed 2pm–5pm; Tue/Thurs 10am–1pm)

CHAPTER 9

Remedies

1. REMEDIES UNDER THE HRA 1998

The purpose of this chapter is to consider possible remedies for violations **9.01** of fundamental rights, including damages, declarations of incompatibility, injunctive and declaratory relief, restitution and remedies in criminal proceedings.

Section 8

Section 8 HRA enables a court or tribunal to grant an appropriate remedy **9.02** or remedies when it finds that a public authority has acted, proposes to act or has failed to act in a way which is incompatible with Convention rights and unlawful within the meaning of section 6(1).

9.03   The following new remedies have been created by the HRA:

> (1) a declaration of incompatibility (section 4);
>
> (2) a power to award damages in respect of an unlawful act within the meaning of section 6(1) of the HRA (section 8(2) to 8(4)[1]);
>
> (3) a general power to "grant such relief or remedy, or make such order, within its powers, as it considers just and appropriate" (section 8(1)).

9.04   Section 8(2) of the HRA provides that damages may only be awarded by a court which has power to award damages or to order the payment of compensation in civil proceedings. Accordingly, it does not create new types of remedy which were not previously within the powers of the court or tribunal, although where a tribunal's remedial powers are thought to be inadequate to provide an appropriate remedy in relation to an unlawful act (or proposed act) of a public authority, rules may be made to add to the relief or remedies which the tribunal may grant or the grounds on which it may grant any of them.[2]

9.05   Proceedings in respect of a judicial act may be brought only by exercising a right of appeal, applying for judicial review or "in such other forum as may be prescribed by rules",[3] and there is a limitation on awards of damages in respect of a judicial act done in good faith, in that damages may not be awarded other than to compensate a person in respect of unlawful arrest or detention to the extent required by Article 5(5) of the Convention.[4]

The Duty to Provide an Effective Remedy

9.06   Article 13 of the Convention, which confers on a person whose Convention rights have been violated the right to an effective remedy before a national authority, has not been incorporated into domestic law by the HRA. The exclusion of Article 13 would appear to have been at least partly prompted by the desire to avoid the judicial creation of any new remedies under the Act. Lord Irvine stated that if Article 13 were incorporated:

> "The courts would be bound to ask themselves what was intended beyond the existing scheme of remedies set out in the Bill. It might lead them to fashion remedies other than the Clause 8 remedies, which we regard as sufficient and clear."[5]

However, it would seem that the courts were intended to have regard to Article 13 in considering and interpreting the provisions of section 8(1),[6]

---

[1] HRA, s.9(3).
[2] HRA, s.7(11).
[3] HRA, s.7(1)(a), (2).
[4] HRA, s.9(3).
[5] H.L. Deb., November 18, 1997, col. 472.
[6] H.L. Deb., November 18, 1997, col. 475 (Lord Chancellor: " . . . the courts may have regard to art. 13. In particular, they may wish to do so when considering the very ample provisions of [section] 8(1).)"

and their duty under section 2(1) of the HRA to "take into account" the relevant Strasbourg case-law includes that relating to Article 13.[7]

2. DECLARATIONS OF INCOMPATIBILITY

Under the HRA, where a court finds that a piece of legislation is incompat- **9.07** ible with the Convention but has no power to strike it down, it may make a declaration that the legislation is incompatible with a Convention right.[8] Section 4 of the HRA provides that:

"(1) Subsection (2) applies in any proceedings in which a court determines whether a provision of primary legislation is compatible with a Convention right.

(2) If the court is satisfied that the provision is incompatible with a Convention right, it may make a declaration of that incompatibility.

(3) Subsection (4) applies in any proceedings in which a court determines whether a provision of subordinate legislation, made in the exercise of a power conferred by primary legislation, is compatible with a Convention right.

(4) If the court is satisfied—

(a) that the provision is incompatible with a Convention right, and

(b) that (disregarding any possibility of revocation) the primary legislation concerned prevents removal of the incompatibility,

it may make a declaration of that incompatibility."

Only the House of Lords, Privy Council, Court of Appeal, High Court and **9.08** the Courts-Martial Appeal Court have the power to make declarations of incompatibility.[9] This excludes county courts, coroners' courts, all criminal courts, all tribunals and several appellate bodies such as the Employment Appeal Tribunal or the VAT Tribunal that have no procedure to declare legislation incompatible with the Convention. Section 4(5) of the HRA does not appear to prevent lower courts and tribunals making a finding on compatibility. However, such a finding will not trigger the right of the government to use the fast track procedure to change the law which only applies if a "declaration" is made by a higher court.[10]

---

[7] *ibid.*

[8] HRA, s.4(2). The declaration of incompatibility procedure does not appear in the New Zealand Bill of Rights Act 1990 (on which the HRA model is based) or the Canadian Charter of Rights and Freedoms. Accordingly, its use and development is without any real precedent.

[9] HRA, s.4(5). In Scotland, the Court of Session and High Court of Justiciary (when not sitting as a trial court) and in Northern Ireland, the High Court and Court of Appeal may make declarations of incompatibility.

[10] See further John Wadham, "The Human Rights Act Mythology", N.L.J. 1482, October 13, 2000.

9.09 Where there is a possibility of a court making a declaration of incompatibility, the Crown has a right to intervene in the proceedings.[11] However, it is not clear who is to bear the Crown's costs of such intervention.[12] It is intended that a declaration of incompatibility is a course of last resort, the government having envisaged that a declaration of incompatibility will "almost certainly" lead to legislative change.[13] A court will seek to interpret legislation in such a way as to make it compatible with the litigant's Convention rights so far as it is possible to do so, and cannot make a declaration of incompatibility unless there is no alternative. In *Poplar Housing and Regeneration Community Association Ltd v. Donoghue*,[13A] the Court of Appeal stated that where despite the strong language of section 3(1) of the HRA, it is not possible to achieve a result which is compatible with the Convention, the court is not *required* to grant a declaration of incompatibility and presumably in exercising its discretion as to whether to grant a declaration or not it will be influenced by the usual considerations which apply to the grant of declarations.[13B]

9.10 Where a court makes a declaration of incompatibility, it does not affect the validity or continuing operation or enforcement of the provision in respect of which it was given. A Minister of the Crown has power to take remedial action to amend the legislation and remove the incompatibility using a "fast track" procedure created by section 10 of HRA 1998.[13C] Details of how remedial orders may be made are contained in Schedule 2 to the HRA 1998. Save in urgent cases (when an order may be made without approval of the draft),[14] the draft of the remedial order is laid before Parliament for 60 days after which it is approved by resolutions of both Houses.[15] Whilst a remedial order includes a power to amend or repeal primary legislation other than that which contains the incompatible provision, it is intended that the power to make incidental, supplementary and consequential changes to primary legislation should be limited to those which are deemed necessary to correct the incompatibility.[16] A remedial order may have retrospective effect.[17]

---

[11] HRA, s.5. See *e.g. Wilson v. First County Trust* [2001] 2 W.L.R. 302, CA, where the Court of Appeal held that it was arguable that the Consumer Credit Act 1974, s.127(3), which rendered a consumer credit agreement lacking a prescribed term unenforceable was a disproportionate restriction on the right of the lender, which existed in all other cases, to have the enforceability of his loan determined by the court. The Crown was given notice under the HRA, s.5, to the effect that the court was considering making a declaration of incompatibility.

[12] In the House of Lords Debates, Lord Irvine declined to say who would bear the Crown's costs: H.L. Deb., November 17, 1997, cols 555–562. See para. 8.70 above.

[13] White Paper, para. 2.2; H.L. Deb., November 3, 1997, col. 1231.

[13A] [2001] EWCA Civ 595, April 27, 2001, CA.

[13B] Para. 75.

[13C] See para. 2.46 above.

[14] HRA, Sched. 2, para. 2(b). Such an order is, however, subject to subsequent laying before Parliament. If as a result of representations, the Minister considers it appropriate to make changes to the original order, he may make a further remedial order replacing the original order and lay the replacement order before Parliament. If at the end of 120 days from the date the original order was made, a resolution has not been passed by each House approving the original or replacement order, the order ceases to have effect (but without affecting anything previously done under either order or the power to make a fresh remedial order): HRA, Sched. 2, para. 4 .

[15] HRA, Sched. 2, paras 2, 3.

[16] H.L. Deb., January 29, 1998, col. 402.

[17] HRA, Sched. 2, para. 1(b).

Section 6(6) of the HRA states that it is not unlawful under the Act to fail **9.11**
to introduce in or lay before Parliament a proposal for legislation[18] or to fail
to make any primary legislation or remedial order.[19] There is no sanction
in domestic law for failing to introduce remedial legislation, though there
will no doubt be strong political pressure on a government to do so.
Further, as Lord Cooke pointed out during the course of debates on the
Bill, where expeditious remedial steps do not follow, this will amount to a
plain invitation to take the matter to Strasbourg.[20] The Section 10 procedure is also applicable if it appears to a Minister that, having regard to a
finding of the European Court of Human Rights in proceedings against the
United Kingdom made after October 2, 2000, a provision of domestic
legislation is incompatible with an obligation of the United Kingdom arising
from the Convention.[21]

Section 4(6) of the HRA states that a declaration of incompatibility (1) does **9.12**
not affect the validity, continuing operation or enforcement of the provision
in respect of which it is given; and (2) is not binding on the parties to the
proceedings in which it is made. Accordingly, if a declaration of incompatibility is made, it seems unlikely that a court has power to grant injunctive
relief against primary legislation, pending remedial action by Parliament.

The Divisional Court made a declaration of incompatibility in *R. (Alconbury* **9.13**
*Developments Ltd) v. Secretary of State for Environment, Transport and
the Regions*,[22] relating to the procedure requiring the Secretary of State to
make decisions following referrals of planning applications or following
inquiries by planning inspectors on appeals from planning permission
refusals. The procedure was said to be incompatible with Article 6(1)
because the Secretary of State was not an independent and impartial
tribunal and review by the High Court was limited to legality and not the
merits. However, the legality of the procedure was provided for by primary
legislation and remained lawful, pursuant to the exception in section 6(2)
of the HRA. Subsequently, the House of Lords reversed the Divisional
Court and allowed an appeal holding that whilst the Secretary of State is
not an independent and impartial tribunal, the scope of judicial review
available was sufficient to comply with the standards of the Convention.[22A]
Accordingly, no declaration of incompatibility was needed. Further, in *R. v.
Mental Health Review Tribunal, North and East London Region*,[23] the
Court of Appeal made a declaration of incompatibility in relation to section
73 of the Mental Health Act 1983, which placed the burden of proof on a
restricted patient to show that he was no longer suffering from a mental
disorder warranting detention and was incompatible with Article 5.

Aside from the question of injunctive relief, it is not clear what course of **9.14**
action a court or tribunal should take in relation to proceedings where it
has made a declaration of incompatibility but it cannot be certain whether

---

[18] HRA, s.6(6)(a).
[19] HRA, s.6(6)(b).
[20] H.L. Deb., November 3, 1997, col. 1272.
[21] HRA, s.10(1)(b).
[22] Unreported, December 13, 2000, DC.
[22A] *R. (Alconbury Developments Ltd) v. Secretary of State for the Environment, Transport
and the Regions* [2001] 2 W.L.R. 1389, *The Times*, May 10, 2001; [2001] UKHL 23, HL.
[23] *The Times*, April 2, 2001 [2001] EWCA Civ 415, CA.

the legislation will be amended or if it is, whether it will have retrospective effect. As Lord Hobhouse stated in *R. v. Director of Public Prosecutions, ex p. Kebilene*,[24] "incompatibility does not found any right under the Act". It is unclear whether or not a court has any further jurisdiction following a declaration of incompatibility. Does the fact that a declaration will not affect the validity, continuing operation or enforcement mean that a court is compelled to determine the matter according to the incompatible primary legislation? Or does the domestic court, notwithstanding section 4(6), have jurisdiction to adjourn the proceedings *sine die* (indefinitely) or for a sufficient period of time in order to see whether retrospective legislation is introduced before making a final order determining the rights of the parties and assessing where the costs burden should fall? There is a divergence of views. Some suggest that a court has no further jurisdiction in the matter following a declaration of incompatibility.[25] Others suggest that it is possible to adjourn proceedings in order to see if the position is remedied.[26] On the latter approach, if retrospective remedial legislation is not introduced after an appropriate period of time, the court would then proceed to finally determine the proceedings and the applicant can take his case to the European Court of Human Rights, relying on the declaration of incompatibility. The practice of the Canadian courts and the Constitutional Court of South Africa is to adjourn proceedings to give the government and legislature an opportunity to remedy the problem, while retaining a continuing jurisdiction. It is likely that political pressure following a declaration of incompatibility, would mean that a similar approach would be effective in the United Kingdom.

3. PUBLIC LAW REMEDIES, INJUNCTIONS AND DECLARATIONS

9.15   **Declarations.**   A court which has the necessary jurisdiction[27] may, in an appropriate case, grant the remedies of declarations, injunctions or damages. Declaratory relief is generally an effective remedy because public authorities will usually act in accordance with the court's statement of the law. There is a discretion under section 8(1) of the HRA to refuse to

---

[24] [1999] 3 W.L.R. 175.
[25] See, *e.g.* Lord Lester of Herne Hill Q.C., "Challenges and Enigmas: The Human Rights Act 1998" [1999] J.R. 171 at 173.
[26] See, *e.g.* D. Feldman, "Remedies for Violations of Convention Rights under the Human Rights Act" [1998] E.H.R.L.R. 691 at 700, who suggests that to do any less would not offer an effective remedy for the violation of a right, as required by Art. 13, which, though excluded from the HRA, is still of persuasive force.
[27] The High Court has jurisdiction to grant mandatory, prohibitory and quashing orders pursuant to the Supreme Court Act 1981 s.29 (as amended by Access to Justice Act 1999, s.24 and Sched. 4, para. 23); declarations pursuant to the Supreme Court Act 1981, s.31 and injunctions pursuant to the Supreme Court Act 1981, ss.30, 31. County courts have all the same powers of the High Court but do not have power to order mandamus, certiorari and prohibition: County Courts Act 1984, s.38. They are also restricted in the grant of search orders and freezing injunctions: County Court Remedies Regulations 1991 (as amended by the County Court Remedies (Amendment) Regulations 1995).

grant a declaration, for example, if an adequate alternative remedy is available[28] or the question raised is an academic one.[29]

Prerogative orders. In judicial review proceedings, mandatory, **9.16** prohibitory and quashing orders are available. Indeed, these are likely to be the usual orders made following a challenge to the act of a public authority under section 7(1)(a) of the HRA.

Injunctions. The court will be able to order a final injunction where **9.17** the court is of the view that a public authority may continue in its unlawful action despite the decision of the court. The court has power to grant an injunction if it considers that would be just and convenient to do so.[30] The court will not usually grant an injunction if the damage complained of is minor or where it would be oppressive.

4. DAMAGES

Awards of Damages under the HRA.

Although "damages" are not specifically identified as a remedy in section **9.18** 8(1) of the HRA, it is clear from a construction of section 8 as a whole that damages are intended to be available as a potential remedy in respect of the unlawful act of a public authority in breach of Convention rights under the Act.[31]

"Damages" is defined to mean "damages for an unlawful act of a public **9.19** authority".[32] Damages may only be awarded by a court (or tribunal[33]) which has power to award damages, or to order the payment of compensation in civil proceedings.[34] Accordingly, criminal courts do not have power to award damages and an individual in such a case will have to pursue a claim for damages through the civil courts.The position of the Court of Appeal when exercising its criminal jurisdiction is unclear, since it is a court which, in civil proceedings, would have power to award damages. On the other hand, the structure of section 8 appears to be intended to limit claims for damages to civil proceedings. A claim for damages for breach of section 6(1) can be made in proceedings under Part 7 CPR or in judicial review proceedings.[35] It is possible for the powers of tribunals to award damages to be extended if it appears that they are inadequate.[36]

---

[28] *Grand Junction Waterworks Company v. Hampton Urban Council* [1898] 2 Ch.331, Stirling J.

[29] *Howard v. Pickford Tool Co. Ltd* [1951] 1 K.B. 417, CA.

[30] Supreme Court Act 1981, s.31(2).

[31] See s.8(3) (restricting the court's powers to award damages) and s.8(6) (referring to "damages for an unlawful act of a public authority").

[32] HRA 1998, s.8(6) .

[33] HRA, s.8(6).

[34] HRA, s.8(2).

[35] Supreme Court Act 1981, s.31(4), permits the High Court to award damages to the applicant if (1) he has joined with his application a claim for damages arising from any matter to which the application relates; and (2) the court is satisfied that, if the claim had been made in an action begun by the applicant at the time of making his application, he would have been awarded damages. See also CPR, Sched. 1, R.S.C., Ord. 53, r.7.

[36] HRA, s.7(11).

9.20   The section 8 power to award damages for an unlawful act is a limited one. By section 8(3), the court cannot make any award of damages unless, taking account of all the circumstances of the case, including (1) any other relief or remedy granted, or order made, in relation to the act by that or any other court; and (2) the consequences of any decision of that or any other court in respect of that act, the court is satisfied that the award "is necessary to afford just satisfaction to the person in whose favour it is made".

Just Satisfaction.

9.21   The "just satisfaction" test for making an award of damages is the same as that applied by the European Court of Human Rights in relation to an award of compensation under Article 41 of the Convention,[37] and a domestic court is obliged to "have regard to" the principles applied by the European Court of Human Rights under Article 41 in determining whether to award damages and in what sum.[38]

9.22   Article 41 of the Convention states:

> "If the Court finds that there has been a violation of the Convention or the Protocols thereto, and if the internal law of the High Contracting Party concerned allows only partial reparation to be made, the Court shall if necessary afford just satisfaction."

9.23   There are three pre-conditions to the recovery of damages before the European Court:

(1) the Court has found a violation of the Convention or its Protocols;

(2) the domestic law of the respondent State allows only "partial reparation"[39]; and

(3) the award is "necessary" to afford just satisfaction.

9.24   The European Court has not yet identified a clear and coherent set of principles which it applies in ascertaining when and what level of damages should be awarded. This weakness has been recognised by the European Court and there is a more detailed treatment of the issue of damages in some recent decisions.[40] The following principles can be derived from the existing case law but the Court's approach has varied considerably from case to case.

---

[37] As amended by Protocol No. 11 (formerly Art. 50).
[38] See s.8(4).
[39] In practice, this condition is rarely of significance and the Court has accepted jurisdiction to consider the question of just satisfaction in virtually all cases where it has found a violation. Further, the Court does not in practice require an applicant to return to the domestic courts to exhaust remedies after a finding of violation but will proceed to grant a remedy itself.
[40] See, e.g. Lustig-Prean and Beckett v. United Kingdom, (2001) 31 EHRR 601 Applications Nos 31417/96 and 32377/96, July 25, 2000 and Smith and Grady v. United Kingdom (2001) 31 EHRR 620 Application Nos 33985/96 and 33986/96, July 25. 2000.

Discretionary Award.

The European Court has interpreted the word "necessary" in Article 41 as **9.25** importing a discretion whether or not to award damages: *Guzzardi v. Italy.*[41] Accordingly, there is no right to compensation: it is discretionary. Compensation is only awarded if the Court considers it "necessary" to "afford just satisfaction" to the applicant. The European Court very frequently reaches the conclusion that the finding of a violation of Convention rights is sufficient reparation.[42] Damages tend to be awarded where a violation has caused serious injury, damage to property or clear financial loss. The Court does not tend to award damages for extradition and deportation cases[43] or to applicants with whom it is unsympathetic, for example terrorists[44] or convicted criminals.[45] Alternatively (though rarely), the Court may award only nominal damages[46] but in a number of cases has refused to make such an award.[47] The Court will not examine compensation of its own motion.[48]

Compensation may be awarded for both "pecuniary" loss consequent on **9.26** a breach of a Convention right and "non-pecuniary" loss, where an applicant has suffered, for example distress or anxiety as a result of the violation of a Convention right. In general, awards of damages made by the European Court are considerably lower than existing domestic awards of general or special damages. Where the Court finds one or more of the applicant's allegations of violation to be unfounded, it may reduce the costs awarded,[49] although it will not do so if a violation is found on the principal complaint.[50]

Pecuniary Loss.

The category of pecuniary loss encompasses a wide range of interests **9.27** including both financial loss and damage or depreciation of real property,[51] including loss of earnings,[52] loss of pension rights,[53] medical expenses,[54]

---

[41] (1981) 3 E.H.R.R. 333.
[42] See, *e.g. Saunders v. United Kingdom* (1997) 23 E.H.R.R. 313; *Minelli v. Switzerland* (1983) 5 E.H.R.R. 554; *Kopp v. Switzerland* (1999) 27 E.H.R.R. 91; *Hood v. United Kingdom* (2000) 29 E.H.R.R. 365.
[43] *Chahal v. United Kingdom* (1997) 23 E.H.R.R. 413; *Soering v. United Kingdom* (1989) 11 E.H.R.R. 439.
[44] See, *e.g. McCann v. United Kingdom* (1996) 21 E.H.R.R. 97 (no award to families of three suspected IRA terrorists killed in an SAS anti-terrorist operation in Gibraltar, having regard to the fact that the suspects had been intending to plant a bomb in Gibraltar).
[45] See, *e.g. Saunders v. United Kingdom* (1997) 23 E.H.R.R. 313; *Maxwell v. United Kingdom* (1995) 19 E.H.R.R. 97; *Bonner v. United Kingdom* (1995) 19 E.H.R.R. 246; *cf. Weeks v. United Kingdom* (1991) 13 E.H.R.R. 435.
[46] See, *e.g. Engel v. Netherlands* (1979) 1 E.H.R.R. 706, where a "token indemnity" of 100 Dutch guilders (£24) was awarded for breach of Art. 5(1).
[47] *Marckx v. Belgium* (1980) 2 E.H.R.R. 330.
[48] See, *e.g. Moore and Gordon v. United Kingdom* (2000) 29 E.H.R.R. 728, para. 28.
[49] See, *e.g. Le Compte, Van Leuven & de Meyere v. Belgium* (1982) 4 E.H.R.R. 1.
[50] See, *e.g. Soering v. United Kingdom* (1989) 11 E.H.R.R. 439.
[51] See, *e.g. Papamichalopoulos v. Greece* (1996) 21 E.H.R.R. 439; *Lopez Ostra v. Spain* (1995) 20 E.H.R.R. 277.
[52] *Lustig-Prean and Beckett v. United Kingdom* (2001) 31 EHRR 601, Applications Nos 31417/96 and 32377/96, July 25, 2000.
[53] *ibid.* In *Young, James and Webster v. United Kingdom* (1983) 5 E.H.R.R. 201, awards of £17,626, £45,215 and £8,706 were made to each application respectively for loss of earnings, loss of pension rights and loss of travel benefits.
[54] *Aksoy v. Turkey* (1997) 23 E.H.R.R. 553.

unlawfully expropriated property[55] and the reimbursement of fines.[56] In practice, the Court does not always separate out heads of loss but may award a global sum.[57]

9.28   On some occasions, the traditional "tortious" measure of loss has been adopted *i.e.* that the applicant should, as far as possible, be put into the position he or she would have been in had the Convention not been violated: for example *Pine Valley Developments Ltd v. Ireland.*[58] However, on other occasions, rather than engage in a complex assessment of damages, the European Court may choose to award damages on an "equitable basis": for example *Matos e Silva v. Portugal*[59] and *Tinnelly & Sons Ltd and McElduff v. United Kingdom.*[60] In *Lustig-Prean and Beckett v. United Kingdom,*[61] the Court recently stated the principles governing the grant of pecuniary damages as follows:

(1) the primary obligation is to restore the applicant so far as possible to the situation existing before the breach (in other words, *restitutio in integrum*): *Papamichalopoulos v. Greece*[62];

(2) however, the inherently uncertain character of damages flowing from a violation may prevent precise calculations: *Young, James & Webster v. United Kingdom*[63];

(3) in the result, the level may be just satisfaction, *i.e.* what is equitable: *Sunday Times v. United Kingdom.*[64]

9.29   Loss must actually have occurred,[65] and there must be a clear causal connection between the breach of Convention rights and the alleged losses, failing which the European Court will not engage in speculation, for example *Mauer v. Austria*[66]; *Saunders v. United Kingdom.*[67] However, the Court will award compensation when satisfied that the necessary causative link has been established.[68] In the case of violations under Article 6(1),

---

[55] *Papamichalopoulos v. Greece* (1996) 21 E.H.R.R. 439.
[56] *Baskaya and Okçuoglu v. Turkey,* Application Nos 23536/94 and 24408/94, July 8, 1999.
[57] See, *e.g. Bönisch v. Austria* (1991) 13 E.H.R.R. 409.
[58] (1992) 14 E.H.R.R. 319.
[59] (1997) 24 E.H.R.R. 573.
[60] (1999) 27 E.H.R.R. 249.
[61] (2001) 31 EHRR 601 Applications Nos 31417/96 and 32377/96, July 25, 2000.
[62] (1996) 21 E.H.R.R. 439.
[63] (1983) 5 E.H.R.R. 201.
[64] (1981) 3 E.H.R.R. 317, para. 15.
[65] See, *e.g. Oztürk v. Germany* (1984) 6 E.H.R.R. 409.
[66] (1998) 25 E.H.R.R. 91. See also *Tolstoy-Miloslavsky v. United Kingdom* (1995) 20 E.H.R.R. 442, para. 74; *Findlay v. United Kingdom* (1997) 24 E.H.R.R. 221, paras 84–85; and *Incal v. Turkey* (2000) 29 E.H.R.R. 449, para. 82 (insufficient proof of causal connection between Art. 10 violation and loss of professional and commercial income alleged).
[67] (1997) 23 E.H.R.R. 313. The Court held that no causal connection had been established between the pecuniary losses claimed by the applicant and the Court's finding of a violation of Art. 6(2), and the Court stated that it could not speculate as to whether the outcome of the criminal trial would have been different had the prosecution not made use of transcripts of interviews of the applicant by Department of Trade and Industry inspectors in exercise of their statutory powers of compulsion.
[68] See, *e.g. Bladet, Tromsø and Stensaas v. Norway* (2000) 29 E.H.R.R. 125; *Young, James & Webster v. United Kingdom* (1983) 5 E.H.R.R. 201; *Pine Valley Developments v. Ireland* (1993) 16 E.H.R.R. 379.

the European Court does not generally make an award of damages since it finds itself unable to speculate as to what would have occurred but for the violation. It will, however, make awards in relation to pecuniary loss attributable to unreasonable delay in proceedings.

Where the alleged loss is not readily quantifiable, the Court is also reluc- **9.30**
tant to award compensation. The Court has generally required claims for pecuniary damages to be supported by evidence[69] and rule 60(2) of the Rules of Court provides that:

> "Itemised particulars of all claims made, together with the relevant supporting documents or vouchers, shall be submitted, failing which the Chamber may reject the claim in whole or in part."

However, if the claim is unsupported by evidence but it is clear that pecuniary loss has occurred, the Court will sometimes make an assessment of an "equitable" sum.[70]

Unlike the domestic courts,[71] the Court has not formulated any clear **9.31**
measure of damages based on the loss of a chance of obtaining a financial benefit, though it does sometimes do so, for example in *Allenet de Ribemont v. France*,[72] compensation of 2,000,000 French francs [£243,000 at the date of the award] was awarded for a loss of business opportunities attributable to injury to his reputation after adverse comments by public officials; and in *Geouffre de la Pradelle v. France*,[73] where the Court stated that it could not speculate as to what conclusion the Conseil d'Etat might have reached if it had not dismissed the applicant's claim for review of the decision declaring his land an area of outstanding beauty as out of time but considered it reasonable to hold that on account of the breach, the claimant had suffered a loss of opportunities justifying an award of FRF 100,000.[74] On occasion, the Court has resorted to expert valuation evidence to assist it in determining damages[75]; on other occasions, it has assessed quantum without such evidence.[76]

Awards for pecuniary loss have tended to be highest in relation to Article **9.32**
1 of the First Protocol. For example in *Pine Valley Developments Ltd v. Ireland*,[77] IR£1.2M [£1,236,000 at the date of the award] was awarded to reflect the value that the property in question would have had, had the

---

[69] See, *e.g. Pressos Compania Naviera SA v. Belgium* (1996) 21 E.H.R.R. 301; *Ringeisen v. Austria (No. 2)* (1979) 1 E.H.R.R. 504; *Chassagnou v. France* (2000) 29 E.H.R.R. 615, para. 130. *cf. Open Door Counselling and Dublin Well Woman v. Ireland* (1993) 15 E.H.R.R. 244, where one applicant was awarded £25,000 for loss of income due to the discontinuance of abortion counselling services due to an injunction. Though it was not substantiated, the sum was awarded on the basis that the discontinuance "must have resulted in loss of income" (para. 87).
[70] See, *e.g. Open Door Counselling, ibid.* and *Probstmeier v. Germany*, Application No. 20950/92, July 1, 1997.
[71] See, *e.g. Allied Maples Group Ltd v. Simmons & Simmons* [1995] 1 W.L.R. 1602, CA.
[72] (1995) 20 E.H.R.R. 557.
[73] Application No. 12964/87, December 16, 1992.
[74] See also *Goddi v. Italy* (1984) 6 E.H.R.R. 457; *Colozza v. Italy* (1985) 7 E.H.R.R. 516; *Delta v. France* (1993) 16 E.H.R.R. 574.
[75] See, *e.g. Papamichalopoulos v. Greece* (1996) 21 E.H.R.R. 439.
[76] See, *e.g. Hentrich v. France* (1996) 21 E.H.R.R. 199.
[77] (1993) 16 E.H.R.R. 379.

applicant not been prevented from developing it in violation of the Convention.

Non-Pecuniary Loss

9.33   Damages may also be awarded for non-pecuniary loss. The Court has made awards for injury to feelings or distress, (for example *Halford v. United Kingdom*[78]); loss of reputation, (for example *Doustaly v. France*[79]); harassment, humiliation, stress, anxiety and deterioration in way of life and health of applicants and their families, (for example *Young, James and Webster v. United Kingdom*[80]); psychological harm, (for example *Aydin v. Turkey*[81]); feelings of helplessness and frustration, (for example *Papamichalopoulos v. Greece*[82]); "moral damage", (for example *Engel v. Netherlands*[83]); inconvenience[84] and feelings of injustice, (for example *Keegan v. Ireland*).[85]

9.34   The Court will award what it regards as "a just and equitable amount of compensation": see for example *Young, James and Webster v. United Kingdom*.[86] The Court does not make awards for non-pecuniary loss to legal persons.[87]

9.35   A causative link is again required so that it is shown that the damage of which complaint is made would not have occurred but for the violation of the Convention.[88] However, the Court has not to date required evidence in support, for example, medical reports evidencing distress and anxiety, and has, in effect, adopted the approach that such matters are incapable of substantive proof.[89]

9.36   The following table shows a sample of awards for non-pecuniary damage made by the European Court to give a general indication of the levels of award made in Strasbourg.[90] The awards set out below are as made with an approximate sterling value shown in square brackets as at the date of the award.[91] They have not been updated for inflation.

---

[78] (1997) 24 E.H.R.R. 523.
[79] Judgment April 23, 1998.
[80] (1983) 5 E.H.R.R. 201.
[81] (1998) 25 E.H.R.R. 251.
[82] (1996) 21 E.H.R.R. 439.
[83] (1979) 1 E.H.R.R. 706.
[84] *Olsson v. Sweden (No. 2)* (1994) 17 E.H.R.R. 134.
[85] (1994) 18 E.H.R.R. 342.
[86] (1983) 5 E.H.R.R. 201.
[87] See, *e.g. Comingersoll SA v. Portugal*, Application No. 35382/97, April 6, 2000, para. 35.
[88] See, *e.g. Goodwin v. United Kingdom* (1996) 22 E.H.R.R. 123, para. 50; *Bowman v. United Kingdom* (1998) 26 E.H.R.R. 1, para. 51.
[89] See, *e.g. Abdulaziz, Cabales and Balkandali v. United Kingdom* (1985) 7 E.H.R.R. 471, para. 96.
[90] For a comprehensive table of just satisfaction awards for both pecuniary and non-pecuniary loss, see Simon and Emmerson, *Human Rights Practice* (Sweet & Maxwell, 2000), App. A9. The table was originally compiled by Karen Reid, *A Practitioner's Guide to the European Convention on Human Rights* (Sweet & Maxwell, 1998) and has been updated by Simor and Emmerson. See also Law Commission, "Damages under the Human Rights Act 1998", Law Com. No. 266, Scot Law Com. No. 180, Cm. 4853 at Section B for an Article by Article analysis of the European Court's approach to and awards for just satisfaction.
[91] A useful foreign currency converter with exchange rates from 1990 to the present date is found on the internet at http://www.oanda.com.

Case	Date of Judgment	Award of Non-Pecuniary Damages
Article 3		
Aksoy v. Turkey (1997) 23 E.H.R.R. 553	December 18, 1996	4,283,450,000 Turkish lira [£24,300] for serious ill-treatment in custody.
Aydin v. Turkey (1998) 25 E.H.R.R. 251	September 15, 1997	£25,000 for alleged rape and ill-treatment of applicant whilst in custody.
Ribitsch v. Austria (1996) 21 E.H.R.R. 573		£6,287 awarded for personal injury contrary to Article 3 whilst in police custody.
Article 5		
Johnson v. United Kingdom (1999) 27 E.H.R.R. 296	October 24, 1997	£10,000 for continued detention following recovery from mental illness in breach of Article 5(1).
Weeks v. United Kingdom (1991) 13 E.H.R.R. 435	October 5, 1988	£8,000 for inability to challenge lawfulness of detention during currency of indeterminate life sentence contrary to Article 5(4) to reflect frustration and helplessness and possible loss of financial opportunity.
Article 6(1)		
ADT v. United Kingdom Application No. 35765/97	July 31, 2000	£20,929.05 for non-pecuniary and pecuniary loss where the applicant was convicted for gross indecency involving homosexual acts in private recorded on video where no evidence that video would be made public.
Aït-Mouhoub v. France (2000) 35 E.H.R.R. 382	October 28, 1998	30,000 French francs [£3,240] for violation of Article 6(1) by disproportionate order of security for costs.
Allenet de Ribemont v. France (1995) 20 E.H.R.R. 557	February 10, 1995	2,000,000 French francs [£243,000] for violations of Article 6(1) and Article 6(2) after failure to obtain compensation for damage to reputation caused by adverse comments by public officials.

Case	Date of Judgment	Award of Non-Pecuniary Damages
Article 6(1) continued		
Bock v. Germany (1990) 12 E.H.R.R. 247	March 29, 1989	10,000 DM [£3,800] for nine-year delay in divorce proceedings.
Delta v. France (1993) 16 E.H.R.R. 574	December 19, 1990	100,000 French francs [£10,250] for loss of opportunities where applicant deprived of opportunity to examine witnesses on the same conditions as witnesses against him.
H v. United Kingdom (1991) 13 E.H.R.R. 449	June 9, 1988	£12,000 for delay in proceedings concerning parental access to child in care.
Helmers v. Sweden (1993) 15 E.H.R.R. 285	October 29, 1991	25,000 Skr [£2,250] awarded for lack of opportunity to air claims in court.
Osman v. United Kingdom (2000) 29 E.H.R.R. 245	October 28, 1998	£10,000 to each applicant.
Philis v. Greece (1991) 13 E.H.R.R. 741	August 27, 1991	1,000,000 drachmas [£3,100] for frustration caused by inability to sue in person for fees.
X v. France (1992) 14 E.H.R.R. 483	March 23, 1991	150,000 French francs [£15,000] for length of compensation proceedings brought by haemophiliac infected with HIV following blood transfusions.
Article 8		
Funke v. France (1993) 16 E.H.R.R. 297	February 25, 1993	50,000 French francs [£6,325] awarded for search by customs officials contrary to Article 8 and infringement of Article 6(2).
Gaskin v. United Kingdom (1990) 12 E.H.R.R. 36	July 7, 1989	£5,000 awarded for absence of procedure to challenge refusal of local authority to disclose documents to applicant relating to his upbringing in care.
Gillow v. United Kingdom (1991) 13 E.H.R.R. 593	September 14, 1987	£10,000 for "considerable stress and anxiety" caused by refusal of authorities to grant a licence to occupy their home in Guernsey.

Case	Date of Judgment	Award of Non-Pecuniary Damages
Article 8 continued		
Govell v. United Kingdom, Application No. 27237/95, [1999] E.H.R.L.R. 121	January 14, 1998	£1,000 for installation of a secret listening device in applicant's home which was not in accordance with law contrary to Article 8(2).
Guerra v. Italy (1998) 26 E.H.R.R. 357	February 19, 1998	10,000,000 lire [£3,400] for failure to provide applicants with sufficient information about health risks of factory.
Guérin v. France (2000) 29 E.H.R.R. 210 at 237	July 29, 1998	20,000 French francs [£2,050] awarded for breach of Article 6(1) due to inability to submit arguments of law on appeal.
Halford v. United Kingdom (1997) 24 E.H.R.R. 523	June 25, 1997	£10,000 for interception of telephone calls for use against applicant in sex discrimination proceedings.
Lambert v. France [1999] E.H.R.L.R. 123	August 24, 1998	10,000 French francs [£1,000] for covert surveillance in breach of Article 8.
Lopez Ostra v. Spain (1995) 20 E.H.R.R. 277	December 9, 1994	4,000,000 pesetas [£19,400] awarded for distress caused by toxic fumes and anxiety about applicant's child's illness.
McMichael v. United Kingdom (1995) 20 E.H.R.R. 205	February 24, 1995	£8,000 for trauma, anxiety and feeling of injustice in connection with inability to see confidential documents and reports in care proceedings in breach of Article 8.
Smith & Grady v. United Kingdom, (2001) 31 EHRR 620	July 25, 2000	£19,000 for each of the applicants in respect of non-pecuniary damage.[92]
Tinnelly and McElduff v. United Kingdom (1999) E.H.R.R. 249	July 10, 1998	£15,000 and £10,000 to applicants respectively for denial of opportunity to obtain a ruling on the merits of their claims that they were victims of unlawful discrimination.

---

[92] In relation to pecuniary damage, Jeanette Smith received £59,000 comprising £30,000 for past loss of earnings, £15,000 for future loss of earnings and £14,000 for the loss of the benefit of a non-contributory pension scheme. Graeme Grady received £40,000 comprising £25,000 for future loss of earnings and £15,000 for loss of the benefit of a non-contributory pension scheme.

Case	Date of Judgment	Award of Non-Pecuniary Damages
Article 8 continued		
X and Y v. Netherlands (1986) 8 E.H.R.R. 235	March 26, 1985	3,000 Dutch guilders [£900] for deficiency of legislation giving rise to sexual abuse whilst in mental institution.
Z v. Finland (1998) 25 E.H.R.R. 371	February 25, 1997	100,000 MK [£12,250] for disclosure of applicant's HIV status in breach of Article 8.
Article 9		
Larissis v. Greece (1999) 27 E.H.R.R. 329	February 24, 1998	500,000 [£1,070] drachmas to each applicant.
Article 10		
Incal v. Turkey (2000) 29 E.H.R.R. 449	June 9, 1998	30,000 French francs [£3,100] for "a certain amount of distress".
Vogt v. Germany Application No. 17851/91; (1996) 21 E.H.R.R. 205 (merits judgment)	September 9, 1996 (just satisfaction)	117,639.55 DM (by agreement) [£52,000] for loss of salary and pension rights.
Article 11		
Young, James & Webster v. United Kingdom (1983) 5 E.H.R.R. 201	October 18, 1982	£2,000, £6,000 and £3,000 respectively to applicants for "harassment" "humiliation" and "stress and anxiety" in finding other work and deterioration in way of life and health of themselves and their families after dismissal in breach of Article 11.
Article 1, First Protocol		
Chassagnou v. France (2000) 29 E.H.R.R. 615	April 29, 1999	30,000 French francs [£3,000] to each applicant for breaches of Article 1, Protocol 1 and Article 11.
Papamichalopoulos v. Greece (1995) 21 E.H.R.R. 439	October 31, 1995	450,000 drachma [£1,230] to each applicant for occupation of their private property for six years without compensation.
Pine Valley Developments Ltd v. Ireland (1993) 16 E.H.R.R. 379	February 9, 1993	IR£50,000 [£51,500] to main shareholder for violation of Article 14 in conjunction with Article 1, First Protocol.

It can be seen that awards of damages for non-pecuniary loss have **9.37**
generally been less than £15,000 and in several cases, less than
£3,000.[93] As Alastair Mowbray has noted, one unsatisfactory aspect of the
Court's provision of this type of non-pecuniary damage has been its failure
to justify or explain the different levels of award.[94] This makes it quite
difficult for United Kingdom courts to assess levels of damages in accordance with Strasbourg "principles" as required by section 8 of the HRA.

It is clear that an award of damages under the HRA in the domestic courts **9.38**
will also be discretionary. As well as considering the principles under
Article 41, a domestic court considering whether to make an award of
damages, is expressly required by section 8(3)(a) to consider whether
other remedies (for example an order for a re-trial or a declaration of
violation) will suffice. Other remedies include any other award of damages
under a non-HRA cause of action. It is not entirely clear what is intended
by the requirement to take account of "the consequences of any decision
(by that or any other) court in respect of that act" in section 8(3)(b). It is
possible that the courts may have regard to resource and "floodgate"
considerations and limit an award of damages for breach of the Act in a
particular case pursuant to this subsection.

Exemplary Damages.

The principle behind awarding damages under Article 41 is compensatory **9.39**
(the affording of "just satisfaction") and not punitive. Further, the Court has
established that there must be a causative link between the violation and
the compensation. Accordingly, the European Court has never awarded
exemplary damages, even in the case of unlawful arrest or detention
under Article 5(5) of the Convention.[95] Whilst it is arguable that a domestic
court could award exemplary damages in an action brought against public
authorities under section 7(1)(a) of the HRA, it is unlikely that a domestic
court will depart from the European Court's approach to the award of
exemplary damages under section 8(3) of the HRA.[96-97] Nothing in the Act
interferes with the courts' existing powers in relation to another domestic
law cause of action to award aggravated or exemplary damages in an
appropriate case (section 11(b) of the HRA).

Aggravated Damages

The Court has not awarded aggravated damages, though it has taken **9.40**
account of distress and frustration or the seriousness of the violations[98] in
its awards for non-pecuniary loss as discussed above. In *Lustig-Prean v.*

---

[93] For comprehensive tables of awards of damages for pecuniary loss, non-pecuniary loss
and costs and expenses, see K. Reid, *A Practitioner's Guide to the European Convention on
Human Rights* (Sweet & Maxwell, 1998) pp. 399–425.
[94] A. Mowbray, "The European Court of Human Rights' Approach to Just Satisfaction" [1997]
P.L. 647 at 649.
[95] *Cumber v. United Kingdom* [1997] E.H.R.L.R. 191.
[96-97] See also the restrictive domestic approach adopted in relation to exemplary damages
in *A.B. v. South West Water Services Ltd* [1993] Q.B. 507, CA though there has been some
subsequent relaxation of the approach in *Kuddus v. Chief Constable of Leicestershire
Constabulary* [2001] 3 All E.R. 193, HL. See further M. Amos, "Damages for Breach of the
Human Rights Act 1998" [1999] E.H.R.L.R. 178 at 193.
[98] Especially in relation to violations of Art.3: see, *e.g. Aydin v. Turkey* (1998) 25 E.H.R.R.
251.

United Kingdom,[99] the applicants' claims for aggravated damages were dismissed.

Interest

9.41 The European Court recognises interest as a pecuniary loss which may be compensated under Article 41 on the ground that the adequacy of compensation would be diminished if it were to be paid without reference to the various circumstances liable to reduce its value, such as the time elapsed since the violation.[1] The Court appears to generally, though not always, take account of the rates of interest which would be awarded by a domestic court.[2] In some cases, a global sum is awarded which is expressed to include interest.[3] The Court does not always explain the calculation of interest.[4] The European Court has not awarded interest on non-pecuniary loss.[5]

9.42 In addition, the European Court has power to award simple interest on damages awards in default of payment.[6] Rule 75(3) of the Rules of Court provides that: "The Chamber may, when affording just satisfaction under Article 41 of the Convention, direct that if settlement is not made within a specified time, interest is to be payable on any sums awarded." The Court adopts the prevailing statutory rate of interest on judgments in the national jurisdiction at issue, and awards interest from the expiry of the date allowed for payment (three months after judgment) to the date of settlement at this rate.[7]

Costs and Expenses

9.43 The Court frequently awards costs and expenses under Article 41, assessed on an equitable basis. The Court must be satisfied that the sums were:

    (1) actually incurred

    (2) necessarily incurred and

    (3) reasonable in quantum.[8]

---

[99] (2001) 31 E.H.R.R. 601 Application Nos 31417/96 and 32377/96, July 25, 2000. See also *Cable. v. United Kingdom*, Application No. 24436/94, February 18, 1999.
[1] *Stran Greek Refineries v. Greece* (1995) 19 E.H.R.R. 293, para. 82.
[2] *Darby v. Sweden* (1991) 13 E.H.R.R. 774. *cf. Bergens Tidende v. Norway*, Application No. 26132/95, May 2, 2000.
[3] See, *e.g. Pine Valley Developments v. Ireland* (1993) 16 E.H.R.R. 379.
[4] *Schuler-Zgraggen v. Switzerland* (1996) 21 E.H.R.R. 404.
[5] See, *e.g. Smith and Grady v. United Kingdom*, (2001) 31 EHRR 620 Application Nos 33985/96 and 33986/96, July 25, 2000, where the Court rejected a claim by the applicants for interest on non-pecuniary loss noting that it did not consider an award of interest on this sum to be appropriate given the nature of the loss to which it related.
[6] See, *e.g. Bladet Tromsø and Stensaas v. Norway* (2000) 29 E.H.R.R. 125; *Stran Greek Refineries and Stratis Andreadis v. Greece* (1995) 19 E.H.R.R. 293; *Schuler-Zgraggen v. Switzerland* (1993) 16 E.H.R.R. 405.
[7] See, *e.g. Chassagnou v. France* (2000) 29 E.H.R.R. 615, para. 131.
[8] See, *e.g. Saunders v. United Kingdom* (1997) 23 E.H.R.R. 313, para. 93. The Court considers high litigation costs as a potential impediment to human rights protection and does not encourage these in its own costs awards: *Young, James and Webster v. United Kingdom* (1983) 5 E.H.R.R. 201.

Costs will only be "actually incurred" if there is a legal duty on the part of the applicant to pay them.[9] The Court will also allow recovery of domestic legal costs or expenses provided that they "were incurred to prevent or redress the breaches found by the Court".[10] However, only domestic costs incurred in the pursuit of Convention rights are recoverable. Any award of legal aid by the Council of Europe will be deducted from the award. The award will include any value added tax chargeable on costs. As in relation to damages, default interest may be awarded on the sum ordered in respect of costs and expenses from the expiry of the period given for payment until settlement.

Damages for Judicial Acts

Under the HRA, there is no entitlement to damages in respect of a judicial **9.44** act in good faith, save in relation to compensation to which a person is entitled under Article 5(5) of the Convention. A "judicial act" means a judicial act of a court and includes an act done on the instructions, or on behalf, of a judge.[11] A "judge" includes a member of a tribunal, a justice of the peace, and a clerk or other officer entitled to exercise the jurisdiction of the court.[12] Section 9 is not intended to affect any existing rule of law which prevents a court from being the subject of judicial review.[13]

Article 5(5) provides that any person who has been the victim of arrest or **9.45** detention in contravention of the provisions of Article 5 must have an enforceable right to compensation. This is irrespective of fault.[14] Any award of damages required by Article 5(5) in respect of a judicial act is to be made against the Crown,[15] and the appropriate person[16] is to be joined to the proceedings, if not already a party.[17] A claim for damages in respect of a judicial act must be set out in the statement of case or notice of appeal.[18] Decisions of unlawfulness in relation to Article 5(5) are most likely to be reached on appeal to the Court of Appeal or Divisional Court or an application for judicial review to the High Court. Aside from damages, proceedings under section 7(1)(a) in respect of a judicial act may only be brought by (1) exercising a right of appeal, (2) on an application for judicial review or (3) in such other forum as may be prescribed by the rules.[19]

Existing Damages Remedies

A right to damages pursuant to section 8 does not prejudice any existing **9.46** right to damages available to a litigant independently of the HRA.[20] However, the court will need to address the potential problem of double

---

[9] *Hokkanen v. Finland* (1995) 19 E.H.R.R. 139.
[10] *Oberschlick v. Austria* (1995) 19 E.H.R.R. 389.
[11] HRA, s.9(5).
[12] HRA, s.9(5).
[13] Crown Proceedings Act 1947, s.2(5), provides that: "no proceedings shall lie against the Crown . . . in respect of anything done or omitted to be done by any person while discharging . . . any responsibility of a judicial nature."
[14] *Benham v. United Kingdom* (1996) 22 E.H.R.R. 293; *Perks v. United Kingdom* (2000) 30 E.H.R.R. 33.
[15] HRA, s.9(4).
[16] The Minister responsible for the court concerned, or a person or government department nominated by him: HRA, s.9(5).
[17] HRA, s.9(4).
[18] CPR, 19.4A(3).
[19] HRA, s.9(1).
[20] HRA, s.11(b).

recovery if two separate awards of damages are made. By section 8(3)(a) the court must expressly take into account "any other relief or remedy granted, or order made, in relation to the act in question". This is in the past tense referring to remedies already granted, not possible future remedies. Accordingly, where no such relief has been granted, the mere possibility of such relief should not lead the court to deprive the applicant of a remedy under the HRA.

Development of Existing Remedies

9.47 It is unclear how far the courts will be creative in developing existing remedies in order to provide a remedy for breach of a fundamental right, for example by developing existing restitutionary remedies where a breach of Article 1 of the First Protocol is found. The development of a law of privacy grounded in the equitable doctrine of confidentiality in *Douglas v. Hello!*[20A] suggests that they may be minded to do so. Further, it is possible that the courts could develop a concept of state liability where domestic law fails to provide an effective remedy for breach of a Convention right, or in respect of non-judicial acts by an organ of the state, by analogy with the principle of state liability in E.C. law to make reparation in national law for the consequences of loss and damage caused by a breach of Community law for which a Member State can be held responsible.[21]

5. LAW COMMISSION RECOMMENDATIONS

9.48 **Introduction.** In its Report entitled "Damages under the Human Rights Act 1998",[22] the Law Commission has analysed the practice of the European Court governing the award of compensation and considered the implications for the award of damages by courts in the United Kingdom in relation to a claim brought under the HRA.

9.49 **Damages.** The Law Commission concludes that in most areas the approach of the European Court is not significantly different to the rules currently applied by courts in the United Kingdom to the award of damages. There are, however, some points at which the practice of the European Court does differ. For example, it does not award punitive damages and has awarded compensation for some forms of non-pecuniary loss—such as for loss of relationship between parent and child—which have not yet been recognised by courts in the United Kingdom. Following the practice of the European Court may require further development of the law by courts in this country. More generally, the courts will have to decide to what extent they will follow the European Court in

---

[20A] [2001] 2 W.L.R. 992.

[21] Cases C–6/90 and C–9/90 Francovich v. Italian Republic [1991] E.C.R. I–5357. See also *Brasserie du Pêcheur SA v. Germany; R. v. Secretary of State for Transport, ex p. Factortame* [1996] E.C.R. I–1029. See also para. 5.63 above. See, *e.g.* D. Feldman, "Remedies for Violations of Convention Rights under the Human Rights Act" [1998] E.H.R.L.R. 691 at 702; D. Oliver, *Common Values and the Public-Private Divide* (Butterworths, 1999) pp. 243–245. See also *Simpson v. Attorney-General (Baigent's Case)* [1994] 3 N.Z.L.R. 667, where an obligation was imposed on the state to pay damages, rather than the police who had conducted the unlawful search.

[22] Law Com. No. 266; Scot Law Com. No. 180, October 2000.

applying a general "equitable" discretion, which takes account of a range of factors including the character and the conduct of the parties, to an extent which is hitherto unknown to English law. In the majority of cases, section 8, read in light of the Strasbourg case law, will not require the courts awarding damages under the HRA to apply measures which are significantly different to those it would reach were the claim one in tort.[23]

The Law Commission notes that the European Court seeks to compensate applicants under the Convention fully for any loss which they can prove resulted from a violation of the Convention. It recommends that where courts in this country have established appropriate levels of compensation for particular types of loss in relation to claims in tort, it would seem appropriate for the same rules to be used in relation to a claim under the HRA.[24] The latter recommendation is controversial since it appears to suggest adopting the generally higher level domestic law awards of damages rather than the level adopted by the European Court for a claim under the HRA. This approach might be argued to be incompatible with the government's intention to equate the remedies in the United Kingdom for a breach of Convention rights with those which might be granted in Strasbourg. It is also inconsistent with Lord Woolf's suggested principles set out below.[25] However, if this recommendation is intended to be limited to situations where the award made in Strasbourg and by the domestic court in relation to an existing cause of action are similar, it will not be objectionable. Further, in the situation where a claim under the HRA is brought concurrently in tort (for example a claim for false imprisonment and a claim under Article 5(1) of the Convention), then it might be more convenient, and reach the same result, for the domestic law principles of damages to be applied to the HRA claim rather than say, for a lower sum to be awarded under the HRA and a further sum (representing the balance between that sum and the damages awardable at common law) in respect of the tort claim. However, this shortcut would seem inconsistent with the intention behind section 8 and will distort the levels of damages between those cases for a violation where there is a domestic law parallel and those for a violation where there is none. **9.50**

Interest. In relation to interest, the Law Commission suggests that the courts need only take into account the principle applied by the European Court, which is to award interest, and need not concern itself with the details of Strasbourg practice. It may either exercise its general power under section 8(1) to fashion a just and appropriate remedy to include interest in a global award or, which would seem simpler, exclude interest from the calculation of damages and exercise its statutory power to award interest under section 35A of the Supreme Court Act 1981 or section 69 of the County Courts Act 1984.[26] In relation to default interest, the normal statutory rules on interest on judgments will apply. **9.51**

---

[23] *ibid.*, at paras 4.92–4.97.
[24] Executive Summary.
[25] See para. 9.53, below.
[26] Law Commission Report, paras 4.89–4.91.

9.52 **Costs.** The Law Commission[27] suggests that the issue of costs will be dealt with by the domestic courts without regard to section 8, in accordance with normal rules which separate damages from costs.

9.53 **Lord Woolf's suggested approach to damages under the HRA.** The Law Commission relied on a paper given by Lord Woolf on "The Human Rights Act 1998 and Remedies"[28] as an important guide to the likely approach of the English courts to the grant of remedies under the Act. Lord Woolf emphasised the differences between the existing remedies for tort and those under the HRA, noting that in the case of a tort, there is a right to be paid such damages as will restore the claimant as far as possible to the position which would have existed if the tort had not been committed. He stated that the position is very different in the case of a breach of the Convention and, he suggested, under the Act.[29] He also noted that the principles should take account of the fact that damages would be paid out of public funds which are no longer regarded as having bottomless depths.[30] Lord Woolf suggested eight possible principles which the Law Commission suggested are likely to influence judicial thinking and it is for this reason that they are set out here (as summarised by the Law Commission):

(1) if there is any other remedy in addition to damages, that other remedy (for example an injunction or declaration) should usually be granted initially and damages should only be awarded in addition if necessary to afford just satisfaction;

(2) the court should not award exemplary or aggravated damages;

(3) an award should be "of no greater sum than that necessary to achieve just satisfaction". If it is necessary for a decision to be retaken, the court should wait and see what the outcome it;

(4) the quantum of the award should be "moderate" and "normally on the low side by comparison to tortious awards";

(5) the award should be restricted to compensating the victim for what has happened "so far as the unlawful conduct exceeds what could lawfully happen";

(6) failure by the claimant to take preventative or remedial action will reduce the amount of damages;

(7) there is no reason to distinguish between pecuniary and non-pecuniary loss. What matters is that the loss should be "real [and] clearly caused by the conduct contrary to the Act";

(8) domestic rules as to costs will probably cover any costs or expenses incurred by the complainant.

---

[27] *ibid.*, at para. 3.30.
[28] In M. Andenas and D. Fairgrieve (eds), *Judicial Review in International Perspective: II* (2000), pp. 429–436.
[29] *ibid.*, p. 432.
[30] *ibid.*, p. 433.

6. APPROACH OF OTHER JURISDICTIONS TO AWARDING DAMAGES

A number of other common law jurisdictions have considered whether to,   **9.54**
and on what principles to, award damages for breaches of fundamental
rights. Whilst the European Court has treated the concept of "just satisfaction" as an autonomous Convention concept and has not generally
referred to other international jurisprudence, it may nonetheless be valuable on occasion for a court to take into account the most important cases
on the issue of constitutional damages in other common law jurisdictions.
The enactment of constitutional rights has been held in some jurisdictions
to carry with it an entitlement to compensation.

New Zealand. In *Simpson v. Attorney-General* (generally known as   **9.55**
Baigent's Case),[31] the New Zealand Court of Appeal held that damages
could be awarded for a breach of the New Zealand Bill of Rights Act 1990,
even though the Bill made no specific reference to remedies. It was further
concerned with the prospect of double recovery of damages. The court
stated:

> "If damages are awarded on causes of action not based on the Bill of
> Rights, they must be allowed for in any award of compensation under
> the Bill of Rights so that there will be no double recovery. A legitimate
> alternative approach would be to make a global award under the Bill
> of Rights and nominal or concurrent awards on any other successful
> causes of action."

The Court did not consider that the remedy in every case would be an
action for damages or monetary compensation and stated that this would
depend on "the nature of the right and of the particular infringement and
the consequences of the infringement". The Court distinguished between
evidence obtained in violation of an individual's rights where the effective
remedy would be the prima facie exclusion of that evidence and breaches
which involved deprivation of liberty or invasion of privacy where damages
are likely to be the appropriate remedy.[32]

South Africa. In *Fose v. Minister of Safety and Security*,[33] the   **9.56**
Constitutional Court of South Africa held that the words "appropriate
relief", in section 7(4)(a) of the Interim Constitution, could include damages where this was "required to protect and enforce the Constitution". In
deciding appropriate relief, the interests of the complainant and society as
a whole, ought, as far as possible, to be served. Further, the Court held
that "appropriate relief" should not include exemplary damages because

---

[31] [1994] 3 N.Z.L.R. 667.
[32] The Court relied on the Privy Council judgment in *Maharaj v. Attorney-General of Trinidad & Tobago (No. 2)* [1979] A.C. 385. See also *Auckland Unemployed Workers Rights Centre Inc. v. Attorney-General* [1994] 3 N.Z.L.R. 720. In *Manga v. Attorney-General (No. 2)* [1999] N.Z.A.R. 507, (1999) 5 H.R.N.Z. 177, the High Court of New Zealand held that if other damages have been already awarded, a declaration of a Bill of Rights violation was the appropriate remedy.
[33] (1997) 2 B.H.R.C. 434.

these were the imposition of a penalty in civil law proceedings which would be paid by taxpayers and provide a windfall to the victim. In considering the issue of double recovery, the Court decided that an award of "constitutional damages" was not necessary as the applicant would be awarded substantial damages upon the future resolution of his claims for assault. The ability to take account of future remedies does not appear to be open to the domestic courts under the terms of section 8(3) of the HRA. However, unlike the *Fose* case where the Court was dealing with the issue of constitutional damages prior to the resolution of the other claims, it is unlikely that a domestic court will be resolving a claim for damages in respect of section 6(1) of the HRA independently of any additional non-HRA claims. The Court in *Fose* also rejected the concept of "punitive constitutional damages".[34]

9.57   **Canada.**   Section 24(1) of the Canadian Charter of Rights and Freedoms provides that anyone whose rights or freedoms have been infringed or denied may apply to a court to obtain "such remedy as the court considers appropriate and just in the circumstances". In *Saskatchewan Human Rights Commission v. Kodellas*,[35] the Saskatchewan Court of Appeal has interpreted "appropriateness" to mean "a remedy that, from the perspective of the person whose right was violated, will effectively redress the grievance brought about by the violation" and "justness" to mean "fair to all who are affected by [the remedy]".

9.58   **India.**   The Indian Constitution does not expressly provide for an award of damages for infringement of "constitutional rights" but, as with New Zealand, the courts have fashioned a damages remedy from Article 32 of the Constitution.

7. REMEDIES IN CRIMINAL (OR REGULATORY) PROCEEDINGS

Powers of Criminal Courts

9.59   In criminal proceedings under section 8 of the HRA, the courts have power to quash an indictment, to stay the proceedings as an abuse of process, to allow a submission of no case to answer, to exclude evidence[36] or to modify the sentence to reflect the breach.

Damages Generally

9.60   Damages may not be awarded by a criminal court since by section 8(2) of the HRA, they can only be awarded by courts with power to award damages. A criminal defendant wishing to make a claim for damages arising out of the criminal proceedings would have to bring a claim by way of separate proceedings in a civil court under section 7(1)(a) of the HRA

---

[34] At para. 70.
[35] (1989) 60 D.L.R. (4th) 143.
[36] See generally Chap. 11 (Evidence), below.

(for example, for a breach of Article 5) and/or under a domestic law cause of action (for example, the tort of false imprisonment).

Damages under Article 5(5)

Article 5(5) provides that: **9.61**

> "Everyone who has been the victim of arrest or detention in contravention of the provisions of [Article 5] shall have an enforceable right to compensation."

This provision has been interpreted as giving a right, where a breach of one or more of Article 5(1) to (4) have been established by a domestic court: "to bring before the Commission a breach of Article 5(5) after exhaustion of domestic remedies in this respect."[37] Thus where there has been a breach of the right:

(1) to be deprived of liberty in accordance with procedure prescribed by law (Article 5(1)); or

(2) to be informed of the reasons for the arrest in a language the detainee understands (Article 5(2)); or

(3) to a trial within a reasonable time (Article 5(3)); or

(4) to have the lawfulness of the detention determined speedily by a court (Article 5(4))

the detainee has a right to pursue any claim for compensation to the European Court if all domestic remedies have been exhausted. The principle of "compensation" within Article 5(5), as construed by the Court in *Wassink v. Netherlands*,[38] is sympathetic to the English common law position, namely that a domestic entitlement to "compensation" which requires the claimant to show some damage (whether pecuniary or nonpecuniary) in order to found his claim would not be in breach of Article 5(5).

In *Cumber v. United Kingdom*[39] the Court accepted in principle that a   **9.62**
compensation scheme which led to an award in domestic law so low as to be derisory might not qualify as an "enforceable" right of compensation. In that case it was held that an award of £350 for four and one-half hours unlawful imprisonment was not so low as to be negligible. Any breach of Article 5(1) to (4) causing damage will give rise to an entitlement to compensation under Article 5(5). There is no requirement that the breach of the Article in question be in bad faith: *Santa Cruz Ruiz v. United Kingdom*.[40] Article 5(5) applies only where there has been a breach of Article 5(1)–(4) and has no application to any other kind of violation in

---

[37] *Huber v. Austria* (1977) D.R. 6.
[38] (Wassink) Application No. 12535/86, September 27, 1990; (1990) Series A/185–A.
[39] [1997] E.H.R.L.R. 191.
[40] [1998] E.H.R.L.R. 208.

criminal cases. Such violations normally occur under Article 6 and the right to a fair trial. In these circumstances, there is no direct requirement within the Convention that compensation be available domestically. If the European Court finds that there has been a breach of the requirement of a fair trial, the award for the lost opportunity to advance a practical and effective case has tended to be fairly substantial. On the other hand, there are cases in which the European Court has held that its finding in relation to the breach of Article 6 represents of itself a fulfilment of "just satisfaction" for the claimant, and will decline to make a monetary award for non-pecuniary loss—see the recent case of *Rowe and Davis v. United Kingdom*.[41] Much depends upon the nature of the breach itself, but the European Court has been astute not to abuse its jurisdiction by speculating upon what the outcome of the trial might have been had the breach not occurred. It will not award damages where to do so would undermine the conviction of the domestic court: *Saunders v. United Kingdom*[42]; *Findlay v. United Kingdom*.[43]

Criminal Appeals

9.63 Section 2(1) of the Criminal Appeal Act 1968, as amended by the Criminal Appeal Act 1995, provides a single composite ground of appeal against a criminal conviction. The Court of Appeal "shall allow an appeal against conviction if it thinks that the conviction is unsafe". A conviction will not be liable to be quashed on account only of procedural irregularity, or abuse of process or a failure of justice to be seen to be done. In *R. v. Mullen*,[44] the Court of Appeal held that "unsafe" was to be given a broad meaning, favourable to defendants. The Court stated that the term was not limited to the safety of the conviction itself but encompassed the prior prosecution process. The Court should look at all the circumstances of the case, including questions of law, abuse of process and questions of evidence and procedure.

9.64 There is a distinction to be made between the "fairness" of the proceedings and the "safety" of a conviction under the Criminal Appeal Act 1968 as amended. In *Condron & Condron v. United Kingdom*,[45] the European Court distinguished the issue of the fairness of a conviction and the safety of that conviction. It stated that:

> "The Court must also have regard to the fact that the Court of Appeal was concerned with the safety of the applicants' conviction, not whether they had in the circumstances received a fair trial. In the Court's opinion, the question whether or not the rights of the defence guaranteed to an accused under Article 6 of the Convention were secured in any given case cannot be assimilated to a finding that his

---

[41] (2000) 30 E.H.R.R. 1.
[42] (1997) 23 E.H.R.R. 313.
[43] (1997) 24 E.H.R.R. 221.
[44] (1999) 2 Crim. App. Rep. 143, CA.
[45] Application No. 35718/97 reported at [2000] Crim.L.R. 679.

conviction was safe in the absence of any enquiry into the issue of fairness."[46]

In *R. v. Rowe, R. v. Davies, R. v. Johnson*,[47] the Court of Appeal held that **9.65** a finding by Strasbourg that a conviction was unfair[48] does not lead inexorably to the overturning of a conviction. However, in that case, the Court found that new matters had come to light that made the convictions unsafe.

Subsequently, in *Stott (Procurator-Fiscal, Dunfermline) v. Brown*,[49] Lord **9.66** Steyn in the Privy Council stated that where the conclusion is reached that the defendant has not had a fair trial, it means that the administration of justice has entirely failed, and subject to the possible exercise of a power to order a re-trial where appropriate, such a conviction can never be allowed to stand. However, where the trial is affected by irregularities not amounting to a denial of a fair trial, it is fair that a court of appeal should have the power, even when faced by the fact of irregularities in the trial procedure, to dismiss the appeal if, in the view of the court of appeal, the defendant's guilt is plain and beyond any doubt. The House of Lords also followed this stance in *R. v. Forbes*,[50] stating that if it is concluded that a defendant's right to a fair trial has been infringed, a conviction will be held to be unsafe within the meaning of section 2 of the Criminal Appeal Act 1968.[51] In *R. v. Kansal*,[51A] the Court of Appeal held that once the reference of a conviction had been made to it by the Criminal Cases Review Commission following trial, it was obliged to declare a conviction unsafe, however old the case, if that was the result of either the admission of evidence obtained in breach of Article 6 or of a change in the common law since trial. It stated that clarification was eagerly sought from Parliament or the House of Lords.

Accordingly, it would appear that where there has been a breach of the **9.67** right to a fair trial under Article 6, a conviction will be unsafe within the meaning of section 2 of the Criminal Appeal Act 1968 and the courts of criminal appeal should quash it. However, where a defect which rendered the trial unfair is capable of being cured by a fair and proper consideration by the Court of Appeal (for example by a review of evidence which was unavailable at trial),[52] there is no breach of Article 6.[53]

Delay

Where the periods of pre-trial and post-trial delay are inordinate and **9.68** unreasonable contrary to Article 6(1), the normal remedy is the quashing of the conviction.[54] Criminal proceedings should only be stayed as a result

---

[46] At para. 65.
[47] *The Times*, July 25, 2000, CA.
[48] See *Rowe & Davies v. United Kingdom* (2000) 30 E.H.R.R. 1.
[49] (2001) 2 W.L.R. 817, *The Times*, December 6, 2000, PC.
[50] [2001] 1 All E.R. 686.
[51] See also *R. v. A* [2001] 2 W.L.R. 1546; [2001] 3 All E.R. 1, HL at para. 38. See also *R. v. Togher, Doran and Parsons*, unreported, November 9, 2000, CA.
[51A] *The Times*, June 11, 2001; [2001] EWCA Crim 1260, CA.
[52] *R. v. Craven*, *The Times*, February 2, 2001, CA.
[53] See also *Edwards v. United Kingdom* (1993) 15 E.H.R.R. 417.
[54] *Darmalingum v. The State (Mauritius)*, [2000] 1 W.L.R. 2303; *The Times*, July 18, 2000, PC.

of the breach of the right to trial within a reasonable time (starting from the formal charge or summons) if the accused was prejudiced to an extent that interfered with his right to a fair trial.[54A]

Confiscation Orders

9.69   Confiscation orders made against a person convicted of drug trafficking are not incompatible with Article 6(2) of the Convention: *H.M. Advocate v. McIntosh*.[55] However, in making a confiscation order, the court had to act with scrupulous fairness in making its assessment to ensure that neither the accused nor any third person suffered any injustice. In *Phillips v. United Kingdom*,[55A] the European Court held that Article 6(2) was not applicable to confiscation orders because it considered that the confiscation procedure was analogous to the determination by a court of the amount of a fine or the length of a period of imprisonment to impose upon a properly convicted offender (see also *Welch v. United Kingdom*[55B]). Since Article 6(2) did not apply to sentencing, it was not applicable to the confiscation proceedings. The Court unanimously held that there was no violation of either Article 6(1) because the relevant provisions of the Drug Trafficking Act 1994 were confined within reasonable limits or of Article 1 of Protocol No. 1 because the interference with the applicant's right to peaceful enjoyment of his possessions was not disproportionate.

8. ORDERS FOR RESTITUTION

9.70   There is no express power in the Rules of Court for the European Court to make an order for restitution. Further, although it has power to award damages under Article 41, it does so on a compensatory basis and has not made any award of restitutionary damages. Unlike compensatory damages, which are measured by reference to the applicant's loss, restitutionary damages are measured by reference to the defendant's gain, or a proportion of it.[56] The rationale underlying restitutionary damages is the notion that a wrongdoer should not profit from his wrong. In English law, restitutionary damages have been awarded for many years for proprietary torts such as conversion, trespass to land, trespass to goods and nuisance. Other restitutionary remedies such as an account of profits in a partnership may also be awarded. Under the HRA, domestic courts may be able to award an account of profits or an award of restitutionary damages if that is the only way in which to afford a "just and appropriate" remedy under section 8(1) of the HRA, whether or not it falls within "just

---

[54A] *Attorney-General's Reference (No. 2 of 2001)*, The Times, July 12, 2001, CA.
[55] [2001] 3 W.L.R. 107, PC. See also *Taylor v. United Kingdom* [1998] E.H.R.L.R. 90. *cf. Welch v. United Kingdom* (1995) 20 E.H.R.R. 247 and *R. v. Malik*, The Times, May 30, 2000, CA.
[55A] Application No. 41087/98, July 5, 2001.
[55B] (1995) 20 E.H.R.R. 247.
[56] *Attorney-General v. Blake* [2000] 3 W.L.R. 625, HL.

satisfaction" under Article 41.[57] The principles on which orders for restitution are made may be broadened under the HRA in order to provide an effective remedy.[58]

9. RECOURSE TO THE EUROPEAN COURT OF HUMAN RIGHTS

Nothing in the HRA prevents an applicant bringing a complaint to the European Court. However, an applicant may only take a case to the European Court once domestic remedies have been exhausted (Article 35 of the Convention) and this now includes exhausting all remedies under the HRA. It is important to note that the limitation period for bringing a claim before the European Court is six months from the time of exhaustion of all domestic remedies, or if there are no remedies, from the alleged violation of Convention rights.[59] Situations where an applicant might wish to make an application to the European Court include: **9.71**

(1) a declaration of incompatibility is made but no action is taken to remedy the incompatibility;

(2) remedial action is taken following a declaration of incompatibility but it is not retrospective in its effect and does not benefit the applicant;

(3) where the domestic court applies Convention law wrongly;

(4) where the domestic court refuses to grant any relief.

The procedure involved in taking a case to the European Court is outside the scope of this book and the reader is referred to texts such as B. Emmerson and J. Simor, *Human Rights Practice*[60] or K. Starmer, *European Human Rights Law.*[61]

Stay of execution pending European Court proceedings. A stay of execution pending the outcome of proceedings before the European Court will not necessarily be granted.[62] **9.72**

---

[57] See Law Commission, "Damages under the Human Rights Act 1998" Law Com. No. 266, Scot Law Com. 180, para. 4.77.
[58] A more expansive approach was already being taken pre-HRA in relation to orders for restitution, *e.g.* in *Woolwich Equitable Building Society v. Inland Revenue Commissioners* [1993] A.C. 70, where the House of Lords held that the usual bar on recovery of money paid otherwise than under a mistake of fact was subject to the exception where a payment was made in response to a demand from a public authority under an *ultra vires* regulation. See D. Feldman, "Remedies for Violations of Convention Rights under the Human Rights Act" [1998] E.H.R.L.R. 691 at 706.
[59] Art. 35(1) of the Convention. See also *Keenan v. United Kingdom*, Application No. 27229/95, May 22, 1998 (where applicant had not made application within six months of alleged breach and no remedies had been exhausted, the European Commission held that the limitation period ran from the date applicant knew she had no effective remedy).
[60] (Sweet & Maxwell, 2000), Chap. 19.
[61] (Legal Action Group, 1999), Pt V.
[62] See, *e.g. Locabail (U.K.) Ltd v. Waldorf Investments (No. 4) Corp.*, [2000] H.R.L.R. 623 *The Times*, June 13, 2000, Ch Div.

CHAPTER 10
The Civil Procedure Rules

1. INTRODUCTION

The purpose of this chapter is to consider the manner in which the **10.01** Convention, through the HRA, is affecting civil procedure. Because of the procedural focus of Article 6 as well as its general concern with access to justice, civil procedure is a context in which human rights arguments are frequently raised.[1] The impact of the HRA on evidence is considered separately in Chapter 11.

The Civil Procedure Rules 1998 ("CPR") are a form of subordinate legisla- **10.02** tion made by statutory instrument and promulgated pursuant to powers given in the Civil Procedure Act 1997 to make rules of court " . . . governing the practice and procedure to be followed in—(a) the civil division of the Court of Appeal, (b) the High Court and (c) the county courts".[2] Since October 2, 2000, by section 3(1) of the HRA, the CPR is required to be construed in a manner which is compatible with Convention rights. Further, all exercises of discretion by the courts under the CPR and giving effect to the rules are required to be compatible with the HRA. Accordingly, the court must, in addition to determining that a rule is *intra vires* is outside the Rule Committee's powers conferred by the Civil Procedure Act, interpret it in a way which is compatible with Convention rights, so far as it is possible to do so. In some cases, it may not be "impossible" to construe a rule compatibly with the Convention. If a rule is *ultra vires* (*i.e.* is outside the rule-making powers of the parent Act) *and* additionally is incompatible with the Convention, it may be struck down on the basis of its lack of *vires*. However, where it is *intra vires* the powers of the parent Act, but is incompatible with the Convention, the position will probably depend on whether the rule is promulgated before or after October 2, 2000. If it is promulgated after the coming into force of the HRA, the Rule Committee will be regarded by virtue of the HRA as having had no law-making power to make rules which were incompatible with the Convention and the offending rule may be struck down as *ultra vires*. Where the rule was

---

[1] For an insightful article on the impact of the Convention on access to justice, see A. Le Sueur, "Access to Justice in the United Kingdom" [2000] E.H.R.L.R. 457.
[2] Civil Procedure Act 1997, (c.12), s. 1(1).

promulgated prior to the coming into force of the HRA, the position is unclear. Either the courts will:

(1) reformulate the traditional doctrine of *ultra vires* to add a new power to strike down incompatible subordinate legislation (which is not incompatible by reason of primary legislation) purely on the ground of its incompatibility with Convention rights; or

(2) the rule will continue to stand.[3]

A declaration of incompatibility would not seem to be available in this situation unless the rule is incompatible because it is required to be so by the Civil Procedure Act 1997. Given the generality of the rule making powers in the 1997 Act, it is unlikely that this will be the case. Professor Connor Gearty[4] and Dan Squires[5] argue for (1) above; *i.e.* that the impugned rule may be *ultra vires* the parent legislation (in this case the Civil Procedure Act 1997), with the rule-making power in that Act being interpreted narrowly under section 3(1) of the HRA so as to allow the promulgation only of Convention compatible rules.

10.03 The combined operation of sections 2 and 6 of the HRA obliges courts to seek to develop and apply the common law and equity consistently with Convention rights, not only when deciding disputes concerning the exercise of public law powers, but also when deciding disputes between private parties governed by the common law and equity. Accordingly, even where the domestic courts are concerned with the application of procedural or evidential rules derived from common law, the courts are required to examine compatibility with Convention rights.

10.04 The Articles of the Convention which have the most significant potential implications for civil procedure and evidence are Article 6 (the right to a fair trial incorporating the right of access to a court), Article 8 (the right to respect for private life), Article 10 (the right to freedom of expression) and Article 1 of Protocol No. 1 (the right to peaceful enjoyment of possessions). Reference should be made to Chapter 3 for an overview of these rights.

10.05 In relation to the general issue of the applicability of the Convention to the Civil Procedure Rules, advocates should note that the Court of Appeal gave a warning in the case of *Daniels v. Walker, Practice Note*[6] about the use of Convention arguments in the context of case management issues. Lord Woolf M. R. stated:

"Article 6 could not possibly have anything to add to the issue on this appeal . . . The provisions of the Civil Procedure Rules . . . make it clear that the obligation is on the court to deal with cases justly . . . It would be unfortunate if case management decisions in this jurisdiction involved the need to refer to the learning of the European Court of Human Rights in order for them to be resolved. In my judgment,

---

[3] See further paras 5.10 *et seq.*, above.
[4] C. Gearty, "The Human Rights Act and Civil Litigation" Civil Litigation Newsletter, Inside Track, Issue Eight, March 2000.
[5] D. Squires, "Challenging Subordinate Legislation under the Human Rights Act" [2000] E.H.R.L.R. 116.
[6] [2000] 1 W.L.R. 1382.

cases such as this do not require any consideration of human rights issues, certainly not issues under article 6. It would be highly undesirable if the consideration of case management issues was made more complex by the injection into them of article 6 style arguments. I hope that judges will be robust in resisting any attempt to introduce those arguments . . . When the Act of 1998 becomes law, counsel will need to show self-restraint if it is not to be discredited."[7]

Whilst a general warning against the use of irresponsible human rights arguments is appropriate, these remarks should not be interpreted to mean that the HRA has no implications for civil procedure, for there can be little doubt that it does. Whilst there is an obligation under the CPR to decide cases justly, Article 6 through the HRA informs that obligation and represents the minimum standard which a court must reach in order to act "justly". Domestic law may, however, go beyond the protection conferred by Article 6. As Lord Hope noted in *Stott (Procurator Fiscal, Dunfermline) v. Brown*,[8] the common law right to a fair trial has been reinforced by the right under Article 6(1) of the Convention to a fair trial and it is necessary to re-examine those principles, using the Article's more structured approach, when applying the overriding test of fairness to the facts. Further, in *Three Rivers District Council v. Bank of England*,[9] Lord Hope stated that whilst the difference between the tests applied in relation to the overriding objective in CPR 1.1 to deal with cases justly and the Article 6(1) right to a fair trial is elusive, in many cases, the practice effect will be the same. In more difficult and complex cases, attention to the overriding objective of dealing with the case justly is likely to be more important than a search for the precise meaning of the rule.[10] It should be noted that the test of proportionality under the CPR is not identical to the principle of proportionality under the Convention. The CPR principle of proportionality must also now be interpreted subject to the Convention requirement of a fair hearing, and a desire to save resources is generally not part of that test in Convention jurisprudence.[11] Whilst the HRA is already making its presence felt in relation to the Civil Procedure Rules and it is likely to continue to have an impact whilst individual procedural rules are measured against the benchmark of the Convention and where necessary adapted, in due course, recourse to the Convention should lessen, though it will no doubt still be raised in borderline or unusual cases or where a Convention point adds weight to an existing argument. The focus in this chapter is on decided cases which impact on civil procedure. There is undoubtedly room for further challenges affecting new areas. When deciding whether or not to raise a human rights point in relation to civil procedure, practitioners and litigants should bear in mind that not doing so at an early stage may amount to a waiver of at least some Article 6 rights. The principles of waiver are considered further in Chapter 3.[12]

---

[7] At 1386H—1387C.
[8] [2001] 2 W.L.R. 817, *The Times*, December 6, 2000, PC.
[9] [2001] 2 All E.R. 513, *The Times*, March 23, 2001, HL, [2001] UKHL/16, March 22, 2001.
[10] *ibid.*, para. 92.
[11] *Airey v. Ireland* (1980) 2 E.H.R.R. 305.
[12] See paras 3.152 *et seq.*, above.

2. BRINGING AND SERVING PROCEEDINGS

Restrictions on Bringing Proceedings

10.06 In domestic law, there are restrictions on certain categories of litigant commencing proceedings, for example, vexatious litigants[13] and bankrupts.[14] The right to institute civil proceedings is, of course, an aspect of the right of access to a court. It can be restricted, but only where the restriction pursues a legitimate aim and is proportionate to the aim to be achieved. The European Commission has stated that the requirement for judicial sanction of proceedings by a vexatious litigant is not inconsistent with Article 6(1) provided there is an objective evaluation of the merits of every application made.[15] Restrictions on access to the courts by minors,[16] prisoners[17] and bankrupts[18] have also been upheld. A complete absence of standing to sue will violate Article 6(1): *Canea Catholic Church v. Greece.*[19] Some of these restrictions on bringing proceedings are considered in more detail below.[19A]

10.07   **Vexatious litigants.** In *Ebert v. Venvil,*[20] the Court of Appeal considered the extent of the court's inherent jurisdiction to prevent initiation of civil proceedings likely to be vexatious. It held that the court's inherent jurisdiction to prevent further applications being made without the permission of the court extended, not merely to existing proceedings, but also to vexatious proceedings which were manifestly threatened but not yet initiated. Further, the inherent jurisdiction was additional to the statutory jurisdiction under section 42 of the Supreme Court Act 1981 and applied to anticipated county court proceedings as well as High Court proceedings. In the course of argument, reference was made to Article 6(1). The Court of Appeal stated that:

> "Article 6 does no more than reflect the approach of the common law indicated by Laws J in *R v. Lord Chancellor ex parte Witham* [1998] QB 575. As long as the inherent power is exercised only when it is appropriate for it to be exercised, no contravention of Article 6 or common law principle is involved."[21]

In *Johnson v. Valks,*[22] the Court of Appeal again recognised the general applicability of Article 6(1) to the question of whether a person, subject to

---

[13] Supreme Court Act 1981, s.42.
[14] Bankrupts only have limited rights of access to a court as a consequence of their property being vested in the trustee in bankruptcy. However, a bankrupt can claim for personal injury or for defamation affecting their personal reputation.
[15] *H v. United Kingdom* (1985) 45 D.R. 281, Application No. 11559/85 (review by senior judge of any case applicant wished to bring did not deny the essence of the right of access and was proportionate to the legitimate aim of the proper administration of justice). See also *Bahamas Entertainment Ltd v. Koll* [1996] 3 C.H.R.L.D. 359, Sup Ct, Bahamas.
[16] *Golder v. United Kingdom* (1979) 1 E.H.R.R. 524.
[17] *Campbell and Fell v. United Kingdom* (1985) 7 E.H.R.R. 165.
[18] *M v. United Kingdom* (1987) 52 D.R. 269, Application No. 12040/86.
[19] (1999) 27 E.H.R.R. 521.
[19A] See also stays of proceedings at para. 10.72 below.
[20] [1999] 3 WLR 670, CA, *sub nom. Ebert v. Birch.*
[21] *ibid.* at 680g.
[22] [2000] 1 W.L.R. 1502, CA.

a civil proceedings order as a vexatious litigant, required leave to appeal to the Court of Appeal against the final order of the first instance court. The Court held, as a matter of domestic law, that a substantive appeal to the Court of Appeal was either the institution of proceedings within section 42(1A)(a) of the Supreme Court Act 1981 or was an application in existing proceedings within section 42(1A)(c). Either way, the order permitting the claimant to institute a particular set of proceedings did not include within it permission for a substantive appeal to the Court of Appeal.[23]

In *Attorney-General v. Wheen*,[24] the Court of Appeal found that a conclu-   **10.08**
sion by the Employment Appeal Tribunal that a person had habitually and persistently instituted vexatious proceedings justified it exercising its discretion to make a restriction of proceedings order under section 33 of the Employment Tribunals Act 1996, notwithstanding the lapse of time since any new application to institute proceedings had been made by that person, did not infringe that person's Article 6(1) rights. This was because the order provided for access to the employment tribunal system by him so long as permission was obtained. Subsequently, in *Attorney-General v. Covey; Attorney-General v. Matthews*,[25] the Court of Appeal held that a vexatious litigant order under section 42 of the Supreme Court Act 1981 did not violate Article 6(1) even where it was made against a litigant who engaged in repeated litigation directed at a variety of defendants. Whilst the court in dealing with a section 42 application must ensure that Article 6 is complied with and the respondent must be given a fair opportunity to put his case, this does not involve giving him an unlimited and uncontrolled opportunity to address the court. The Court again noted that the ability of the court to give permission for the bringing of proceedings did not restrict or reduce the access left to the individual to an extent that the very essence of the right of access to justice was removed. In *Ebert v. Official Receiver*,[26] the Court of Appeal was categoric in stating that the HRA and the Convention had no effect on the general principles relating to the grant or refusal of leave to appeal to vexatious litigants under section 42 of the Supreme Court Act 1981.[26A]

Persons under mental disability. In relation to persons under   **10.09**
mental disability, in *Ashingdane v. United Kingdom*,[27] the European Court upheld a statutory limitation of liability in relation to the Secretary of State for Social Services, who had a duty to provide hospital accommodation to meet all reasonable requirements for the mentally ill, restricting any court

---

[23] In *R. v. Common Professional Examination Board, ex p. Mealing-McCleod* (May 19, 2000) unreported CA, Roch L.J. noted that if a defence fails, a vexatious litigant does require permission to institute appellate proceedings. He observed the possibility that a first instance judge, being convinced his decision was correct, not merely refused permission to appeal but also refused permission under s.42, leaving no ability for the Court of Appeal to consider the matter. He suggested that the change in the rules proposed by Sir Richard Scott, Vice-Chancellor, in *Johnson v. Valks* at 455G (to make clear that no further application under s.42 of the Supreme Court Act 1981 was needed once permission to institute proceedings had been granted) would remove a potential difficulty post-HRA.
[24] [2001] I.R.L.R. 91; *The Times*, January 23, 2001, CA.
[25] *The Times*, March 2, 2001, CA.
[26] [2001] EWCA Civ 340; *The Independent*, March 21, 2001, CA.
[26A] See also *HM Advocate v. Bell*, March 23, 2001 I.H. Ct. Sess. (reported on Lawtel, April 24, 2001) (A declaration that the respondent was a vexatious litigant did not violate Article 6).
[27] (1985) 7 E.H.R.R. 528.

action to acts done negligently or in bad faith. The limitation had the legitimate aim of reducing the risk of unfair harassment of those responsible for mental patients and did not transgress the principle of proportionality.[28]

10.10   **Refusal to hear contemnor.**   The historical approach of refusing to hear a contemnor[29] may violate Article 6(1).

10.11   **Multi-party litigation.**   A collective or multi-party system for dispute resolution may comply with Article 6(1) even if it excludes the right to bring private litigation. In *Lithgow v. United Kingdom*,[30] the applicants had certain of their interests nationalised under the Aircraft and Shipbuilding Industries Act 1977. The Act established a collective system for the settlement of disputes concerning compensation. Although individual shareholders were denied a direct right of access to the Arbitration Tribunal, their interests were represented and safeguarded, albeit indirectly. The limitation on the right of access pursued a legitimate aim (namely the desire to avoid, in the context of a large-scale nationalisation measure, a multiplicity of claims and proceedings brought by individual shareholders) and there was a proportionate relationship between the means employed and the aim. In *Taylor v. United Kingdom*,[31] the European Commission did not find a violation of Article 6(1) in relation to a procedure set up for multi-party litigation where an applicant had to withdraw from the litigation because of failure to meet the criteria for participation in the scheme. The withdrawal occurred in circumstances where the applicant had agreed to the criteria, which were themselves reasonable, and in any event, retained the ability to bring proceedings outside the scheme, albeit at much greater cost.

Limitation Periods

10.12   The existence of limitation periods *per se* does not infringe the right of access to a court in principle since they satisfy a legitimate aim of preventing stale claims and promoting legal certainty, provided that the periods prescribed do not deprive the right of effective access to a court of all substance and they are proportionate to the aim to be achieved.[32] In *Stubbings v. U.K.*,[33] the applicants, who all alleged that they had been sexually abused as children, complained that the House of Lords ruling in *Stubbings v. Webb*[34] imposing an inflexible six-year limitation period for

---

[28] *cf. Winterwerp v. Netherlands* (1980) 2 E.H.R.R. 387, where there was a breach of Art. 6(1) where a person under mental disability, who had been committed to a psychiatric hospital, automatically lost the capacity to administer his property without the opportunity to appear to be represented in the competent courts.

[29] *Re Jokai Tea Holdings Ltd* [1992] 1 W.L.R. 1996. In *X Ltd v. Morgan-Grampian* [1991] 1 A.C. 1, a trainee journalist was in contempt of a lower court order to reveal the source of confidential documents which had been leaked to him. The House of Lords had to address the question of whether a person in contempt should be heard at all and decided as a matter of discretion that he should.

[30] (1986) 8 E.H.R.R. 329.

[31] (1997) 23 E.H.R.R. C.D. 132.

[32] *Stubbings v. United Kingdom* (1997) 23 E.H.R.R. 213.

[33] (1997) 23 E.H.R.R. 213.

[34] [1993] A.C. 498.

assault and trespass to the person, including sexual abuse, was a disproportionate restriction on their right of access to a court. They argued
that the psychological damage suffered prevented them from appreciating
that they had a cause of action until after the limitation period had expired.
The Court held that the six-year limitation period did not violate Article 6(1)
stating that limitation periods

> "serve important purposes, namely to ensure legal certainty and
> finality, to protect potential defendants from stale claims which might
> be difficult to counter, and to prevent the injustice which might arise if
> courts were required to decide upon events which took place in the
> distant past on the basis of evidence which might have become
> unreliable or incomplete because of the passage of time".[35]

A three-year limitation period for paternity proceedings was held to be
reasonable.[36]

It may hypothetically be possible to challenge very short limitation periods **10.13**
such as the three-month time limits for applications for judicial review or
applications for unfair dismissal in employment cases. However, the existence of a discretion to extend time may save these provisions from
potential violation: see, for example, *Perez de Rada Cavanilles v. Spain*,[37]
in which the European Court held that the particularly strict application of
a time limit by the Spanish domestic courts deprived the applicant of the
right of access to a court. Though it did not arise for decision, the judgment
implied that had there been more flexibility in the manner of implementing
the time limit, even a three-day time limit for registering an application
might not violate Article 6(1). The European Commission has accepted a
final time limit which cannot be waived, even when new facts have arisen
after expiry of the limit: *X v. Sweden*.[38] In *Edificaciones March Gallego SA
v. Spain*,[39] the European Court upheld a time limit for applying to set aside
proceedings for payment of a bill of exchange, where the time limit was
mandatory and no extensions of time could be granted as within Article
6(1). It satisfied the legitimate purpose of speeding up payment of the
sums in issue and was proportionate. It was relevant that the proceedings
were designed solely to secure summary payment of a debt acknowledged by the debtors and not designed to determine the merits of the
claim and that the inadmissibility of the application was the result of an
avoidable mistake.

In *J.A. Pye (Oxford) Ltd v. Graham*,[40] the Court of Appeal upheld the **10.14**
limitation period of 12 years for bringing proceedings for recovery of land,
which was the subject of adverse possession, as compatible with Article 1
of Protocol No.1 since the provision did not deprive a person of his
possessions or interfere with his peaceful enjoyment of them, but merely
deprived a person of access to a court if he delayed proceedings for 12
years or more after being dispossessed of his land. Even if the Article did

---

[35] At para. 49. See also *Dobbie v. United Kingdom* [1997] E.H.R.L.R. 166.
[36] *X v. Sweden* (1982) 31 D.R. 223.
[37] (2000) 29 E.H.R.R. 109.
[38] (1982) 31 D.R. 223.
[39] Application No. 28028/95, Judgment February 19, 1998.
[40] [2001] 2 W.L.R. 1293, CA.

apply, the provisions were conditions provided by law in the public interest which were reasonably required and not disproportionate.[41] In *Cachia and others v. Faluyi*,[41A] assisted by a concession from the defendant, the Court of Appeal held that the requirement to construe statutes compatibly with the Convention meant that "action" in section 2(3) of the Fatal Accidents Act 1976 was to be interpreted as referred to "served process" so as to permit three dependent children to pursue a claim by writ for compensation for the death of their mother when a previous writ had been issued but never served. The Court relied upon its duty not to act in a way which was incompatible with the Convention under section 6(1) and its duty to construe legislation compatibly with Convention rights under section 3(1) in arriving at this construction.

Immunities

10.15 In *Osman v. United Kingdom*,[42] the European Court held that a line of English case law which operated to confer a blanket immunity on the police for acts or omissions relating to the investigation or suppression of crime was disproportionate. This followed *Fayed v. United Kingdom*[42A] which held that it would violate Article 6(1) if a state could without restraint of control by the Convention enforcement bodies, remove from the jurisdiction of the courts a whole range of civil claims or confer immunities from civil liability on large groups or categories of persons.[42B] This decision could possibly affect other immunities such as state immunity,[43] the extent of witness immunity[44] and the immunity of expert witnesses, recognised in *Stanton v Callaghan*.[45] It is notable that in the House of Lords case that abolished advocates' immunity for all types of proceedings *Arthur J.S. Hall v. Simons*,[46] Article 6 was fully argued (although the decision made it unnecessary for the Courts to consider whether or not a blanket immunity for advocates could be justified).[47]

---

[41] The claimant did not rely upon Art. 6(1). See the same result albeit via different reasoning in *Family Housing Association v. Donellan*, July 12, 2001, Ch.D. See further paras 16.94 *et seq.* below.

[41A] *The Times*, July 11, 2001, CA.

[42] (2000) 29 E.H.R.R. 245.

[42A] (1994) 18 E.H.R.R. 393.

[42B] At para. 65. See also *Z v. United Kingdom* Application No. 29392/95, May 10, 2001; *The Times*, May 31, 2001, at para. 98.

[43] The Court has declared admissible two applications based on the ground that as a consequence of the State Immunity Act 1978, the applicants were denied access to a court: see *Al-Adsani v. United Kingdom*, Application No. 35763/97, March 1, 2000 and *Fogarty v. United Kingdom*, Application No. 37112/97, March 1, 2000, *cf. Holland v. Lampen-Wolfe*, *The Times*, July 27, 2000, HL (held that sovereign immunity defeated a libel claim. Art. 6 did not confer on Contracting States adjudicative powers which they did not possess and state immunity was not a self-imposed restriction on the jurisdiction of its courts which the U.K. had chosen to adopt). The case of *Waite and Kennedy v. Germany* (2000) 30 E.H.R.R. 261 is also of some relevance in this context (European Court upheld a restriction on proceedings in a national court by employees of a supra-national agency arising out of the terms of their employment).

[44] *L v. Reading Borough Council*, unreported, March 12, 2001, CA.

[45] [1998] 4 All E.R. 961.

[46] [2000] 3 W.L.R. 543.

[47] Immunities are considered further in Chap. 17 (Professional Liability and Negligence) at paras. 17.41 *et seq.*, below.

Extensions to Validity of Claim Form

The right of access to a court pursuant to Article 6(1) is relevant to   **10.16**
applications for extensions to the validity of a claim form where it has not
been possible to effect service within the normal period. In *Barker v.
Casserly*,[48] it was unclear whether the claim form, issued under CPR Part
8 had been served and a district judge extended its validity in case it had
not. The defendant claimed that the power to extend the period of service
under CPR 7.6 was not expressly referred to in CPR Part 8. Johnson J.
held that it would be contrary to the claimant's right of access to a court
under the Convention for there to be no power to extend the period for
service.[49] This case and Article 6(1) arguments may assist those seeking
to challenge the rather harsh effect of CPR 7.6(3),[50] relating to extensions
of time for service of the claim form on an application made after the period
of validity has expired. It is possible that the problems created by CPR 7.6
may be alleviated by the court making an order dispensing with service
under CPR 6.9 in appropriate circumstances.[50A]

3. STRIKING OUT

General

The philosophy which underlies Article 6(1) is that of a fully presented and   **10.17**
argued hearing before an independent and impartial judge. Interlocutory
striking-out of a claim or a defence militates against this ideal and potentially infringes the right of access to a court. However, the right of access
to a court is qualified and restrictions on the right to take legal proceedings
are permitted, provided that they satisfy the three-fold test in *Stubbings v.
United Kingdom*,[51] namely that:

(1) they have a legitimate aim;

(2) they do not impair the very essence of the right; and

(3) they are proportionate.

The key test in practice is likely to be whether striking out a claim is
proportionate to the aim to be achieved.

The power to strike out the whole or part of a statement of case is set out   **10.18**
in Rule 3.4 of the Civil Procedure Rules which provides:

"(1) In this rule . . . , reference to a statement of case includes reference to part of a statement of case.
(2) The court may strike out a statement of case if it appears to the
court—

---

[48] Unreported, October 23, 2000, Fam Div (reported on Lawtel).
[49] At p. 7 of the transcript.
[50] As interpreted by the Court of Appeal in *Vinos v. Marks & Spencer plc*, unreported, June
8, 2000, and *Kaur v. CTP Coil Ltd*, unreported, July 10, 2000.
[50A] *Infantino v. Maclean, The Times*, July 20, 2001, Douglas Brown J.
[51] (1997) 23 E.H.R.R. 213.

> (a) that the statement of case discloses no reasonable grounds for bringing or defending the claim;
> (b) that the statement of case is an abuse of the court's process or is otherwise likely to obstruct the just disposal of the proceedings; or
> (c) that there has been a failure to comply with a rule, practice direction or court order.
>
> (3) When the court strikes out a statement of case it may make any consequential order it considers appropriate.
> (4) Where—
>
> (a) the court has struck out a claimant's statement of case;
> (b) the claimant has been ordered to pay costs to the defendant; and
> (c) before the claimant pays those costs, he starts another claim against the same defendant, arising out of facts which are the same or substantially the same as those relating to the claim in which the statement of claim was struck out,
>
> the court may, on the application of the defendant, stay the second claim until the costs of the first claim have been paid.
> (5) Paragraph (2) does not limit any other power of the court to strike out a statement of case."

10.19 Claims may be struck out either for disciplinary reasons or because they lack merit. Grounds 3.4(2)(a) and (b) include statements of case which are unreasonably vague, incoherent, vexatious, scurrilous or obviously ill-founded and other cases which do not amount to a legally recognisable claim or defence.[52] Ground 3.4(2)(c) covers cases where the abuse lies in the way the claim or defence has been conducted. In the case of non-compliance with a rule or practice direction, the court may instead order the non-complying party to pay a sum of money into court (CPR 3.1(5), (6)). In the case of non-compliance with a court order, the court may instead repeat its order, imposing conditions and/or specifying the conse-quences of failure to comply with the order or condition (CPR 3.1(3)).

Striking out for Disciplinary Reasons

Striking out for failure to follow court procedures and/or delay

10.20 It is clearly a legitimate aim that the courts should have power to regulate their operations to the extent that litigants who fail to follow court proce-dures may, in an appropriate case, have their actions struck out. The power to strike out for failure to comply with rules, practice directions or court orders is conferred by CPR 3.4(2)(c). The approach under the CPR to striking out for delay or non-compliance with court timetables has emerged in a series of Court of Appeal decisions beginning with *Biguzzi v. Rank*

---

[52] See *Crooks v. Haddow* [2000] G.W.D. 10–367, March 1, 2000, Second Division, Scotland (dismissal of claimant's case as a result of irrelevancy of pleadings, which were fully considered by the court, did not breach Art. 6(1)).

Leisure.[53] The court must consider the entire sliding scale of sanctions available to the court in the case of a litigant's delay and select a sanction which is proportionate to the conduct complained of. The court drew attention to several alternatives to a strike out under CPR 3.4 which might be appropriate to deal with non-compliance with time limits laid down by rules or orders, including awarding costs on an indemnity basis payable immediately, ordering a party to pay money into court and awarding interest at a higher or lower rate. This approach is considerably more flexible than the approach to dismissal for want of prosecution under the pre-existing rules[54] and aims to do justice in each individual case. The *Biguzzi* approach, provided the application of the proportionality test is reasonable in practice and the primary consideration is whether a fair trial is still possible, seems unlikely to offend Article 6(1). In *Annodeus Entertainment Ltd v. Gibson*,[55] Neuberger J., citing *Arrow Nominees v. Blackledge*,[56] a case relating to striking out for abuse of process,[57] stated that to strike out for delay would be both disproportionate and a breach of Article 6.

Striking out for abuse of process

The power to strike out a statement of case for abuse of the court's **10.21** process or because it is otherwise likely to obstruct the just disposal of the proceedings is set out in CPR 3.4(2)(b). In *Arrow Nominees v. Blackledge*,[58] Evans-Lombe J. stated that even contumacious conduct breaching a court order or contempt amounting to a fraud on the court is not of itself sufficient to justify striking out a case for abuse of process if it can be shown that, notwithstanding that conduct, there is no substantial risk that a fair trial of the action could not follow and to hold to the contrary would be likely to breach Article 6(1). Conversely, to strike out a contemnor's case, where the court takes the view that the acts constituting a contempt lead to a real risk that a fair trial cannot happen, would not constitute a breach of the Article.[59] He relied on the previous case of *Re Swaptronics Ltd*[60] in which Laddie J. had stated:

> " . . . it seems to me that were the courts to refuse to allow those in contempt access to the court simply on the grounds that they are in contempt they could well be acting in breach of the provisions of art 6.1 of the European Convention on Human Rights which entitles

---

[53] [1999] 1 W.L.R. 1926. See also, *e.g. Co-operative Retail Services v. Guardian Assurance*, unreported, July 28, 1999, CA; *Axa Insurance Co. Ltd v. Swire Fraser Ltd*, *The Times*, January 19, 2000, CA; *Purdy v. Cambran*, unreported December 17, 1999, CA; *Walsh v. Misseldine*, unreported, February 29, 2000, CA; *Hamblin v. Field*, *The Times*, April 5, 2000; and *Purefuture v. Simmons & Simmons*, unreported, May 25, 2000.

[54] See, *e.g. Birkett v. James* [1978] A.C. 297, HL; *Department of Transport v. Chris Smaller (Transport) Ltd* [1989] A.C. 1197, HL; and *Biss v. Lambeth, Southwark and Lewisham Health Authority (Teaching)* [1978] 1 W.L.R. 382 (strike out for inordinate and inexcusable delay where substantial risk that a fair trial would not be possible *or* prejudice to defendant, including prejudice other than that affecting the conduct of the trial such as prejudice to a defendant's business interests or possibly anxiety accompanying litigation).

[55] *The Times*, March 3, 2000, Ch Div.

[56] [2000] B.C.L.C. 709, *The Times*, December 8, 1999.

[57] See further below.

[58] [2000] B.C.L.C. 709, *The Times*, December 8, 1999.

[59] *ibid.*, at 724e-i.

[60] *The Times*, August 17, 1999.

everyone to the determination of his civil rights by means of a fair and public hearing before an independent and impartial tribunal. The 'everyone' in that article is not subject to an exception in respect of people who are guilty of serious offences or contempt of court."

If the *Arrow Nominees* approach is generally adopted by the courts, it is unlikely that striking out claims for abuse of process in appropriate cases will infringe Article 6(1). However, this approach does not yet appear to have been adopted by the superior courts. In *UCB Corporate Services v. Halifax (SW) Ltd*,[61] the Court of Appeal upheld an order striking out a case on the ground that the dilatory conduct of the claimant, with wholesale disregard of the rules and orders of the court, amounted to an abuse of process. This approach under the CPR was similar to that taken in the more recent authorities under the pre-existing Rules of the Supreme Court such as *Grovit v. Doctor*[62]; *Arbuthnott Latham Bank v. Trafalgar Holdings*[63] and *Choraria v. Sethia*[64] to the effect that wholesale disregard of the rules could amount to grounds for striking out, even in the absence of prejudice to the defendant or an inability to have a fair trial. No reliance was placed on Article 6(1) in the *UCB* case. The decision in *Habib Bank v. Jaffir*[65] was to the same effect. It is certainly arguable that the Court of Appeal's approach violates Article 6 and that the Evans-Lombe J. and Laddie J. line of reasoning is more compatible with the Convention.[66] Where an employment tribunal struck out a case of its own motion on the ground that the respondent's conduct of the proceedings was scandalous, it should have asked itself whether a fair trial was possible. The striking out arose out of the applicant's objection to the nature of instructions given to a doctor before whom the tribunal directed that she attend for a medical examination. The tribunal could have directed that another doctor be instructed. Such an examination did not breach Article 8. The respondent's defence (IT3) was therefore reinstated.[66A]

Striking out for re-litigation

10.22 The rule in *Henderson v. Henderson*[67] required the parties, when a matter became the subject of litigation between them in a court of competent jurisdiction, to bring their whole case before the court so that all aspects of it

---

[61] *The Times*, December 23, 1999.
[62] [1997] 1 W.L.R. 640, HL.
[63] *The Times*, December 29, 1997, CA.
[64] *The Times*, January 29, 1998, CA.
[65] *The Times*, April 26, 2000.
[66] See also *Abraham v. Commissioner of Police for the Metropolis*, unreported, December 8, 2000 (a case where the Court of Appeal allowed an appeal from an order striking out a civil claim against the police on the ground of abuse of process where the claimant had accepted a formal caution following her arrest. The Court recognised that the right to seek redress in the courts should not be lightly curtailed pursuant to both the common law and Articles 6(1) and 13).
[66A] *De Keyser Ltd v. L. Wilson*, March 20, 2001 (reported on Lawtel, May 17, 2001), EAT *cf.* *Terry v. Hoyer (UK) Ltd*, May 4, 2001 (reported on Lawtel May 4, 2001), CA (EAT justified in finding that the appellant had acted in a scandalous, vexatious or frivolous manner and was entitled to conclude that the originating summons should be struck out. The Court commented that there was no need for a radically different approach by reason of the HRA to the issues in that case [at para. 7].)
[67] (1843) 3 Hare. 100.

could be finally decided once and for all. In the absence of special circumstances, the parties could not return to the court to advance arguments, claims or defences which they could have put forward for decision on the first occasion but failed to raise. The rule was not based on the doctrine of *res judicata* in the narrow sense or even on a strict doctrine of issue or cause of action estoppel, but on a rule of public policy based on the desirability, in the general interest as well as that of the parties themselves, that litigation should not drag on for ever and that a defendant should not be oppressed by successive suits when one would do.[68] A strict application of the *Henderson v. Henderson* principle might potentially be contrary to Article 6(1) since it might be said to bar access to a court to a litigant who could have but did not bring his claim forward in previous proceedings: *Johnson v. Gore Wood & Co. (a firm)*.[69] In *Johnson*, Lord Millett stated that:

> "It is one thing to refuse to allow a party to relitigate a question which has already been decided; it is quite another to deny him the opportunity of litigating for the first time a question which has not previously been adjudicated upon. This latter (though not the former) is prima facie a denial of the citizen's right of access to the court conferred by the common law and guaranteed by Article 6 of the Convention . . ."

Against that, it might be argued that the litigant had his right of access to a court in the previous proceedings but failed to avail himself of it.

The issue may no longer have much importance since the modern **10.23** approach taken in *Bradford & Bingley Building Society v. Seddon Hancock*[70] and *Johnson v. Gore Wood* has made substantial changes to the law, which is now more likely to be compatible with Article 6(1). In *Bradford & Bingley*, the Court of Appeal held that mere "re"–litigation, in circumstances not giving rise to cause of action or issue estoppel, does not necessarily give rise to an abuse of process. Further, the maintenance of a second claim which could have been made as part of an earlier one, or which conflicts with an earlier one, should not of itself be regarded as an abuse of process justifying striking out. In the case of re-litigation falling short of *res judicata*, it was not necessary for the claimant to show special circumstances justifying litigating an issue that should have been litigated on an earlier occasion, but for the person alleging abuse of process to establish what it was that made the future litigation an abuse. Notably, Auld L.J. acknowledged that the court's jurisdiction had developed so as to be cautious before barring people from access to the courts.[71] In *Johnson*, the House of Lords held that just because a matter could have been raised in earlier proceedings, it did not mean that it should have been, and raising it in later proceedings was not necessarily abusive under the *Henderson v. Henderson* principle.

---

[68] See the explanation of the *Henderson, v. Henderson* principle in *Barrow v. Bankside Agency Ltd* [1996] 1 W.L.R. 257 at 260, *per* Sir Thomas Bingham M.R.
[69] [2001] 2 W.L.R. 72, *per* Lord Millett.
[70] [1999] 1 W.L.R. 1482, CA.
[71] *ibid.*, at 1494.

10.24 Accordingly, the courts presently appear to have retreated from an approach of barring claims which could have been previously litigated, save in circumstances where a cause of action or issue estoppel arises, giving rise to re-litigation of what is essentially the same cause of action or issue. This approach upholds the Article 6(1) right of access to a court where a claim has not previously been litigated on its merits. However, it is conceivable that a court may impose conditions or costs sanctions on a claimant whose claim should reasonably have been brought at the same time as earlier proceedings and where the failure to do so has resulted in duplication of preparation time or the increase in costs. Such a course may itself have Article 6(1) implications, particularly if the sanction were to be disproportionate or to have the practical effect of impeding the claimant's ability to bring his claim. However, such an approach arguably satisfies the legitimate aim of encouraging compliance with the general rule that all persons who are to be sued should, where such a course is reasonably practicable, be sued at the same time and in the same proceedings and, provided that the sanction imposed is proportionate and does not effectively disbar a claimant from bringing a claim, a violation of Article 6(1) is unlikely to be established.

10.25 The legal position is different where a first action is struck out as an abuse of process and a claimant wishes to bring a second action based on the same cause of action. In such cases, the burden is on the claimant to show some special reason for being allowed to proceed: *Securum Finance Ltd v. Ashton.*[72] The presumption against allowing a second action to proceed when a first has already been struck out for abuse of process, unless the claimant establishes special reasons for so doing, satisfies legitimate public policy aims. Provided that the test of showing special reasons is not applied so strictly as to amount to an absolute bar, the proportionality test is likely to be satisfied.

10.26 In *Securum Finance Ltd v. Ashton*, it was submitted that to refuse to strike out the claimant's claim in new proceedings, following an earlier set of proceedings having been struck out on grounds of delay, would infringe the *defendants'* right to a hearing within a reasonable time under Article 6(1) of the European Convention.[73] However, the Court of Appeal regarded Article 6(1) as providing no assistance to the defendants in that particular case, since the defendants had a claim of their own to pursue to trial and the reason for refusing to strike out the claimant's claim was because the primary issue which arose had to be decided in those proceedings in any event.

Striking out claims for content

10.27 There are two broad categories of claim which are likely to be struck out for content; those which are doomed to failure because they are misconceived or have no merit and those which are prevented from proceeding for reasons of public policy.

---

[72] [2001] 1 W.L.R. 538, HL *The Times*, July 5, 2000.
[73] See further paras. 10.98 *et seq.*, below.

Striking out claims with no merit

It is unlikely that a mechanism for striking out bad or misconceived claims at **10.28** an early stage would be found to contravene Article 6(1). It serves the obvious public purpose of avoiding expending the parties' and the courts' resources on hopeless claims. It is common for systems of justice to have a procedure for eliminating litigation which is bound to fail. Indeed, the European Court itself has power to filter out claims which are "manifestly ill-founded" pursuant to Article 35(3) of the Convention. It also has a power to strike out applications if further examination is not justified pursuant to Article 37. CPR 3.4(2)(a) gives a power to strike out the whole or part of a statement of case if it appears to the court "that the statement of case discloses no reasonable grounds for bringing or defending the claim." This encompasses the striking out of claims that are ill-founded, for example a negligence claim where there is no loss. The Court of Appeal has recently held that where a claim is clearly bound to fail there is no violation of Article 6(1) if such a claim is struck out: *Mowan v. London Borough of Wandsworth.*[74]

Striking out claims based on public policy exclusions

Historically, in domestic law, some claims that have been struck out as **10.29** disclosing no reasonable cause of action are in reality struck out on the basis of an exclusionary rule based on reasons of public policy. The applicability of Article 6 as formulated by the European Court in *Osman v. United Kingdom*[75] reshaped the approach of domestic courts to striking out cases where the basis was essentially one of public policy. The European Court resiled from this position in *Z v. United Kingdom*,[75A] conceding that the striking out of the cases where it was not fair, just and reasonable to impose a duty of care was a matter of substantive domestic law and did not violate Article 6(1). However, it notably did not overrule *Osman* and the question arises as to what, if anything, is left of *Osman* in relation to striking out. *Osman* and the chronological case history leading up to the judgment of the European Court in Z are considered below before turning to an analysis of Z and its implications. In *Osman*, the Court of Appeal had struck out a civil action in negligence against the police based on an alleged failure to protect the lives of the minor applicant, Ahmet Osman, and his father and to protect the family from harassment by a teacher at his school who eventually shot and injured Ahmet and shot and killed his father.[76] The Court decided that the action should be struck out on the ground that in light of the 1989 ruling of the House of Lords in *Hill v. Chief Constable of West Yorkshire*,[77] no action could lie for public policy reasons against the police for their negligence in the investigation and suppression of crime. Ahmet and his mother made an application in

---

[74] [2001] E.G.C.S. 4, (2001) E.H.L.R. Dig. 5, CA.
[75] (2000) 29 E.H.R.R. 245.
[75A] Application No. 29392/95, May 10, 2001; *The Times*, May 31, 2001. See also *T.P. and K.M. v. United Kingdom* Application No. 28945/95, May 10, 2001; *The Times*, May 31, 2001.
[76] *Osman v. Ferguson* [1993] 4 All E.R. 344, CA. For a full summary of the facts, see further Chap. 17 (Professional Liability), paras. 17.12 *et seq.*, below.
[77] [1989] A.C. 53.

Strasbourg, complaining of failures under Articles 2 and 8 of the Convention in relation to the failure to protect life and that they had been denied access to a court or to any other effective remedy in respect of that failure, contrary to Articles 6(1) and 13. The European Court held in a landmark judgment that there was no violation of Articles 2 and 8, but there was a violation of Article 6(1).

10.30 On the basis of a Government concession that the domestic approach to duty of care in this context did not automatically doom to failure a civil action from the outset but in principle allowed a domestic court to make a considered assessment on the basis of the arguments before it as to whether a particular case was or was not suitable for the application of the rule. On that understanding, the Court considered that the applicants must be taken to have had a right, derived from the law of negligence, to seek an adjudication on the admissibility and merits of an arguable claim that they were in a relationship of proximity to the police, that the harm caused was foreseeable and that in the circumstances it was fair, just and reasonable not to apply the exclusionary rule outlined in the *Hill* case. The assertion of that right was in itself sufficient to ensure the applicability of Article 6(1) of the Convention.

10.31 Since the applicants' claim never fully proceeded to trial, there was never any determination on its merits or of the facts on which the claim was based. The applicants' claim had been rejected by the Court of Appeal since it was found to fall squarely within the scope of the exclusionary rule formulated by the House of Lords in the *Hill* case. The Court held that the application of the rule in that manner, without further inquiry into the existence of competing public interest considerations, only served to confer a blanket immunity on the police for their acts and omissions during the investigation and suppression of crime and amounted to an unjustifiable restriction on an applicant's right to have a determination on the merits of his or her claim against the police in deserving cases. In the Court's view, it must be open to the domestic court to have regard to the presence of other public interest considerations which pull in the opposite direction to the application of the rule. Failing that, there would be no distinction made between degrees of negligence or of harm suffered or any consideration of the justice of a particular case.

10.32 In effect, the European Court held that, whilst the aim of the public interest immunity rule excluding the tortious liability of the police for policy and operational decisions might satisfy a legitimate aim, the automatic or mechanistic approach to the application of an exclusionary rule in striking out of proceedings was a disproportionate restriction on the claimants' right of access to a court since it left no room for adequate inquiry into the competing public policy considerations and the merits of the individual case.

10.33 The European Court attached particular weight to the facts that:

(1) that the applicants' claim involved an alleged failure to protect the life of a child;

(2) this resulted from a catalogue of acts and omissions which amounted to gross negligence as opposed to minor incompetence;

(3) in contrast to *Hill*, the Court of Appeal accepted that a sufficient degree of proximity had been established in the present case; and

(4) the degree of harm suffered was very grave.

It held that these were considerations which had to be examined on the merits and not excluded by the grant of immunity to the police.

The *Osman* decision threw up a number of difficulties. First, it is an **10.34** established principle that Article 6(1) is relevant to procedural and not substantive law, *i.e.* it does not control the content of a state's domestic law.[78] However, in *Osman* the Court appeared to recognise that the third constituent element of duty of care was a matter of substantive English law but nevertheless found that Article 6(1) applied. Secondly, it is not yet clear how the court is to examine the countervailing public interest considerations and what evidence is to be adduced relating to a particular public interest. Thirdly, it is not clear whether the claimant is always entitled to an examination on the merits and what amounts to a sufficient examination on the merits.

On one reading, *Osman* threatened to undermine the use of the strike-out **10.35** jurisdiction across a broad band of cases where domestic law is already well established, where as with public interest immunity on the part of the police, the third limb of the *Caparo Industries plc v. Dickman*[79] test, namely that it was not fair, just and reasonable to impose a duty of care, had been applied to exclude certain claims in negligence. Such situations included claims against auditors by prospective investors,[80] claims against local authorities arising out of their social services functions,[81] or special educational needs functions[82]; claims against highway authorities,[83] fire services[84] and building inspection authorities.[85] The general restrictive approach to recovery for economic loss is also grounded on considerations of fairness, justice and reasonableness. Lord Hoffmann expressed the view that:

"The whole English jurisprudence on the liability of public authorities for failure to deliver public services is open to attack on the grounds that it violates the right to a hearing before a tribunal".[86]

---

[78] See, *e.g. Powell and Rayner v. United Kingdom* (1990) 12 E..H.R.R. 355. However, it is not always easy to determine the divide between procedural and substantive restrictions under domestic law: *Fayed v. United Kingdom* (1994) 18 E.H.R.R. 393, para.65.

[79] [1990] 2 A.C. 605, HL. The House of Lords established a three limb test to determine the existence of a duty of care: (1) reasonable foreseeability of injury or damage; (2) a relationship of proximity between the claimant and defendant; and (3) it is fair, just and reasonable to impose a duty of care on the defendant.

[80] *Caparo Industries Plc v. Dickman* [1990] 2 A.C. 605, HL.

[81] *X v. Bedfordshire County Council* [1995] 2 A.C. 633, HL.

[82] *E (A minor) v. Dorset County Council*, reported with other cases *sub nom. X (Minors) v. Bedfordshire County Council* [1995] 2 A.C. 633, HL.

[83] *Stovin v. Wise* [1996] A.C. 923, HL.

[84] *Capital and Counties plc v. Hampshire County Council* [1997] 2 All E.R. 865.

[85] *Murphy v. Brentwood District Council* [1991] 1 A.C. 398, HL.

[86] Rt Hon Lord Hoffmann, "Human Rights and the House of Lords" (1999) 62 M.L.R. 159.

10.36   In *Barrett v. London Borough of Enfield*[87] Lord Browne-Wilkinson expressed the opinion that he found the *Osman* decision extremely difficult to understand. However, he reluctantly held that in view of the *Osman* decision and the fact that Article 6 was shortly to become part of English law, in such cases as those under appeal, it was difficult to say that it was a clear and obvious case calling for striking out.

10.37   In *Palmer v. Tees Health Authority & Hartlepool & East Durham NHS Trust*,[88] the allegation was of negligence on the part of the defendant public authorities in failing to take measures which would have prevented a child being murdered by a man with a psychopathic personality who was being treated by the defendants. The defendants applied to strike out the action, in part on the ground that it was not fair, just and reasonable to impose a duty of care. The claimant contended that in light of *Barrett*, it was no longer open to the court to strike out since proportionality demanded that the facts be determined by a trial judge before a decision in relation to the existence of a duty of care could be made. The Court of Appeal, rather grudgingly and assisted by a concession from the defendants, accepted that if the issue had been merely one of whether it was fair, just and reasonable to impose a duty of care, the matter would have to be decided once the facts were established. Stuart-Smith L.J. expressed the view that the situation was less than satisfactory since on a strike-out application the court is required to accept the facts as pleaded and it is therefore difficult to see how they can be any better from the claimant's point of view.[89] However, the action was struck out nonetheless on the ground that there was insufficient proximity. The Court of Appeal thus sought to confine the effect of *Osman* to striking out applications which involved only the third limb of *Caparo* and rejected the submission that the *Osman* decision affected striking out based on the absence of proximity.

10.38   In *Kinsella v. Chief Constable of Nottinghamshire*,[90] Tucker J. took a different view and held that it remained possible to strike out on the ground that it was not fair, just and reasonable to impose a duty of care, even prior to trial, if there was sufficient material evidence available on the pleadings to carry out the balancing exercise of weighing the general rule of immunity against any competing policy considerations. He noted that the *Hill* rule did not provide a blanket immunity in all cases, but that in each case a balancing exercise had to be carried out. In *Kent v. Griffiths*,[91] Lord Woolf adopted a similar approach, stating:

> " . . . it would be wrong for the *Osman* decision to be taken as a signal that, even when the legal position is clear and an investigation of the facts would provide no assistance, the Courts should be reluctant to dismiss cases which have no real prospect of success. Courts are

---

[87] [1999] 3 W.L.R. 79, HL (the claimant, who had been in the care of the defendant council for almost all of his childhood, brought a claim in negligence claiming damages for various psychological problems he claimed to be suffering as a result of the council's failure properly to safeguard his welfare).

[88] *The Times*, July 6, 1999, CA.

[89] *ibid.*, at para. 15.

[90] *The Times*, August 24, 1999.

[91] [2000] 2 W.L.R. 1158, CA.

now encouraged, where an issue or issues can be identified which will resolve or help to resolve litigation, to take that issue or those issues at an early stage of the proceedings so as to achieve expedition and save expense. There is no question of any contravention of Article 6 . . . in so doing."[92]

The refusal of the House of Lords to impose a duty of care by local authorities, psychiatrists and social workers in the exercise of their functions relating to child care in *X (Minors) v. Bedfordshire County Council*[93] was the subject of a complaint to Strasbourg and was examined by the European Commission in *Z v. United Kingdom*.[94] Applying the principles established by the European Court in *Osman*, the Commission held that the striking out of an action where negligence was asserted against local authorities by a child in its care, based on the exclusionary rule in *X*, was a disproportionate restriction on the claimant's right of access to a court under Article 6(1). The Court's judgment is discussed at paras 10.43 *et seq.* below. **10.39**

In *Bromiley v. United Kingdom*,[95] the European Court declared inadmissible a complaint following the striking out of proceedings against the Home Office for negligence in releasing a psychopath thereby giving him the opportunity to murder the applicant's daughter. The Court accepted that the striking out was based principally on the lack of foreseeability or proximity and that consequently no duty of care arose which those authorities could be found liable for breaching. The Commission in the above decisions held that a strike out on the ground of insufficient proximity was acceptable in Article 6(1) terms. This was interesting because it can be argued that "proximity" is as much as judicial construct based on policy considerations as the "fair, just and reasonable" ground. **10.40**

Subsequently, in *Jarvis v. Hampshire County Council*,[96] the claimant alleged that his local education authority had been both negligent in failing to provide him with appropriate education to meet his special educational needs and had committed acts or misfeasance in public office by placing him in inappropriate schools. The misfeasance allegation had been struck out but the judge refused to strike out the allegations of negligence. Both parties appealed and the Court of Appeal struck out both actions. The court had to consider whether the striking out of the misfeasance allegations was justified in light of Article 6(1). The claimant contended that the effect of *Osman* and *Barrett* was that no strike out could be ordered. However, the Court of Appeal held to the contrary, first, because the court was inclined to apply domestic law without regard to the Convention, the HRA 1998 not being in force, and secondly, the court pointed out that *Osman* was confined to the application of a blanket immunity or bar whereas the misfeasance allegations failed because they did not contain **10.41**

---

[92] *ibid.*, at para.38. This was further approved in *Outram v. Academy Plastics Ltd*, [2001] I.C.R. 367, CA.
[93] [1995] 2 A.C. 633, HL.
[94] (1999) 28 E.H.R.R. C.D. 65, E.C. Comm. See also *TP & KM v. United Kingdom*, Application No. 28945/95, (2000) 2 L.G.L.R. 181. E.C. Comm.
[95] (2000) 2 L.G.L.R. 181 Application No. 33747/96, Decision, November 23, 1999, ECHR (Third Section).
[96] *The Times*, November 23, 1999. CA.

the essential elements of the tort. It was clear and obvious that the claim was fatally flawed in law and ought to be struck out. In relation to the claim in negligence, the court struck this out too because no assumption of responsibility could be shown on the claimant's version of the facts. The judgment of the Court of Appeal in *Jarvis*, in relation to the negligence claim, was reversed on appeal by the House of Lords[97] which held that it would not be appropriate to strike out either the direct or vicarious liability claims against the local authorities at an interlocutory stage. Although Article 6(1) was invoked by the appellants, it became unnecessary for their lordships to consider the Convention, in light of their findings arrived at as a matter of domestic law.

10.42   In *L v. Reading Borough Council*,[98] a claim brought against the police and social services based on an allegedly negligent investigation into fictitious child abuse allegations, the Court of Appeal considered *Osman* and subsequent domestic cases. The judge had refused to strike out a claim by the child in question, L, but had struck out the claim by L's father, P. The Court of Appeal noted that the House of Lords had recognised in *Barrett* that "extreme care [has] to be taken in striking out claims in this confused and developing area of the law" and in allowing an appeal by L's father against the striking out of his claim against the defendants, held that:

> " . . . different policy considerations could arise in deciding whether it is fair just and reasonable to impose a duty to either [L], or [P], or both, when the officer conducting an interview with [L], or on a quite separate occasion, when reporting the contents of the interview to a superior officer."

The Court was also influenced by the fact that the claim raised issues as to whether the matters complained of constituted a violation of Article 8.

10.43   In *Z*, the failure by United Kingdom authorities to provide children with appropriate protection against serious, long-term neglect and abuse amounted to inhuman and degrading treatment in breach of Article 3. In relation to Article 6(1), the Court noted that the applicants were claiming damages on the basis of alleged negligence, a tort in English law which is largely developed through the case-law of the domestic courts. It was agreed between the parties that there was no previous court decision which indicated that liability existed in respect of damage caused negligently by a local authority in carrying out its child protection duties. It was in the applicants' case that the domestic courts were called on to rule whether this situation fell within one of the existing categories of negligence liability, or whether any of the categories should be extended to this situation. The Court was satisfied that at the outset of the proceedings there was a serious and genuine dispute about the existence of the right asserted by the applicants under the domestic law of negligence, as shown by the grant of legal aid to the applicants and the decision by the

---

[97] *The Times*, July 28, 2000, HL. Conjoined appeals of *Phelps v. London Borough of Hillingdon*; *Anderton v. Clwyd County Council*; *Jarvis v. Hampshire County Council* [2000] 3 W.L.R. 776.
[98] [2001] EWCA CIV 346, March 12, 2001, CA.

Court of Appeal that their claims merited leave to appeal to the House of Lords. Accordingly, Article 6(1) was applicable.[99]

In considering whether Article 6(1) was complied with, the Court reiterated that the right of access to a court is not absolute. Where the individual's access is limited either by operation of law or in fact, the Court will examine whether the limitation imposed impaired the essence of the right and in particular whether it pursued a legitimate aim and there was a reasonable relationship of proportionality between the means employed and the aim sought to be achieved.[1] The Court noted that the applicants were not prevented in any practical manner for bringing their claims before the domestic courts, right up to the House of Lords with legal aid provided for that purpose. The domestic courts were concerned with the pre-trial determination of whether, assuming the facts of the applicants' case as pleaded were true, there was a sustainable case in law. The Court stated that it was not persuaded that the House of Lords' decision as a matter of law that there was no duty of care in the applicants' case may be characterised as either an exclusionary rule or an immunity which deprived them of access to court. The House of Lords, after weighing in the balance the competing considerations of public policy, decided not to extend liability in negligence into a new area. In so doing, it circumscribed the range of liability under tort law. The Court stated that:

10.44

> "There is no reason to consider the striking out procedure which rules on the existence of sustainable causes of action as *per se* offending the principle of access to court. In such a procedure, the plaintiff is generally able to submit to the court the arguments supporting his or her claims on the law and the court will rule on those issues at the conclusion of an adversarial procedure."[2]

Because the decision concerned only one aspect of the exercise of local authorities' powers and duties, it cannot be regarded as an arbitrary removal of the courts' jurisdiction to determine a whole range of civil claims. The Court recalled that article 6 does not guarantee any particular content for civil rights and obligations in national law, save that the right to respect for family life in Article 8 and the right to property in Article 1 of Protocol No. 1 may do so. The Court held that:

> "It is not enough to bring Article 6(1) into play that the non-existence of a cause of action under domestic law may be described as having the same effect as an immunity, in the sense of not enabling the applicant to sue for a given category of harm.

Furthermore, it cannot be said that the House of Lords came to its conclusion without a careful balancing of the policy reasons for and against the imposition of liability on the local authority in the circumstances of the applicants' case."[3]

---

[99] At para. 89.
[1] At para. 93.
[2] At para. 97.
[3] At paras. 98–99.

10.45 The Court referred to *Osman*, stating that it now considered that its reasoning in *Osman* was based on an understanding of the law of negligence which has to be reviewed in light of the clarification subsequently made by the domestic courts and notably by the House of Lords. The Court is satisfied that the law of negligence as developed in the domestic courts since the case of *Caparo* and as recently analysed in *Barrett v. Enfield LBC* includes the fair, just and reasonable criterion as an intrinsic element of the duty of care and that the rule of law concerning that element in the Z case did not disclose the operation of an immunity. The inability to sue flowed from the applicable principles governing the substantive right of action in domestic law.

10.46 However, the Court having found that there was no violation of Article 6(1) nonetheless held that there was a violation of Article 13 (the right to an effective remedy for breach of a Convention right)[4] and awarded damages by way of just satisfaction for breach of the applicants' rights under Article 3 (the prohibition on torture, inhuman or degrading treatment). However, the acts and omissions on which the claims in *Z* were based pre-dated the introduction of the HRA. Whilst the Government pointed out that remedies such as the payment of compensation from the Criminal Injuries Compensation Board, the possibility of complaint to the Local Government Ombudsman and the complaints procedure under the Children Act 1989 went some way towards providing effective redress, it conceded that in the particular circumstances of *Z*, they were insufficient alone or cumulatively to satisfy the requirements of Article 13.[5] The government pointed out that from October 2000, there was a remedy for breach of a Convention rights through section 7(1)(a) of the HRA and the courts were empowered to award damages.[6]

Conclusion

10.47 *Osman* did not affect the striking out of claims because the claimant could not show reasonable foreseeability of harm or the necessary proximity or assumption of responsibility.

10.48 It seems that *Z* has now restored the important procedural mechanism of pre-trial striking out where the strike out is based on a rule of law that it is not fair, just and reasonable that a duty of care should exist. It is not altogether clear what is left of *Osman*. The court did not expressly overrule the decision. Does it survive in relation to public interest immunity on the part of the police? Is it simply confined to its facts? Or was the Court simply reluctant to admit that it had got it wrong in *Osman*? It is likely that courts will now simply treat *Osman* as impliedly overruled and will rely instead on the Court's approach *Z* in strike out applications based on public policy grounds.[6A]

10.49 However, if a strike out application is based on the existence of a true immunity[6B] or a more wide-ranging scope of exclusion of civil claims against a public authority, in light of the Court's approval of *Fayed v. United*

---

[4] Para. 111.
[5] Para. 107.
[6] *ibid.*
[6A] See further paras 17.30 *et seq.* and paras 17.37 *et seq.*
[6B] See para. 10.44 above and paras 17.41 *et seq.* below.

Kingdom,[6C] Article 6(1) may still present an obstacle to striking out without a full examination of the merits.

It is possible that the Court's finding of a violation of Article 13 may **10.50** indirectly lead to a reluctance to strike out claims where the lack of an adequate alternative remedy for claims based on acts or omissions occurring before October 2, 2000 which arguably amount to a breach of a Convention right will leave the claimant to a likely successful claim in Strasbourg based on Article 13, provided that he can establish an arguable claim that that Convention right has been breached.[6D]

4. SUMMARY JUDGMENT

The CPR introduced a new test for summary judgment in CPR 24.2 which **10.51** states:

> "The court may give summary judgment against a claimant or defendant on the whole of a claim or on a particular issue if—
>
> (a) it considers that—
>> (i) that claimant has no real prospect of succeeding on the claim or issue; or
>> (ii) that defendant has no real prospect of successfully defending the claim or issue; and
>
> (b) there is no other compelling reason why the case or issue should be disposed of at a trial."

The test under rule 24.2 is higher than the test under the previous rules which required the defendant to show merely that he had an "arguable" case. The new threshold requires litigants to prove that they do not merely have an arguable case, but one that they have a real prospect of winning. Further, by CPR 24.4, the court may give summary judgment on its own initiative as well as on application by a party. It would appear that by introducing the new test, the court is equating the principles on which summary judgment is given with the old test for setting aside regular default judgments espoused in *Alpine Bulk Transport Co. Inc. v. Saudi Eagle Shipping Co. Inc.*[7].

It had been suggested that the new test for summary judgment might **10.52** become a substitute for the trial stage, rather than acting as a filtering mechanism for ensuring that only meritorious cases reached the trial stage, since the court is required to form a provisional view of the probable outcome of the case at an early stage of the proceedings.[8] If the summary judgment procedure had been developed in such a way with a substantial

---

[6C] (1994) 18 E.H.R.R. 393.
[6D] In relation to Article 13, see para. 2.18 above.
[7] [1986] 2 Lloyd's Rep. 221.
[8] See D. O'Brien, "The New Summary Judgment: Raising the Threshold of Admission" (1999) 18 C.J.Q. 132.

blurring of the line between the standard of proof required at an interlocutory stage and the standard of proof imposed at trial, it is possible that the procedure would have infringed the rights subsumed in Article 6(1) including, in particular, the right to a fully argued adversarial hearing on the merits with the calling of all relevant evidence. However, whilst the respondent has to show some "real" prospect of success in order to defeat an application for summary judgment, the respondent is not required to show that, on the balance of probabilities, his case will succeed at trial. If there is a real prospect of success but it is improbable that a case will succeed, the court may make a conditional order: CPR 24.6.[9] The Court of Appeal in *Swain v. Hillman*[10] expressly stated that the hearing of an application for summary judgment does not involve the court conducting a mini-trial. The court should be wary of trying issues of fact on evidence where the facts are apparently credible and are to be set against the facts being advanced by the other side. Choosing between them is the function of the trial judge, not the judge on an interim application, unless there is some inherent improbability in what is being asserted or some extraneous evidence that would contradict it. If courts adopt this approach to summary judgment applications in practice, it seems unlikely that the procedure will infringe Article 6(1). If they do not, there is a higher possibility of a violation.[10A] The raising of the test for summary judgment will prevent the trial of some defences[11] which would have proceeded under the old lower test of "an arguable defence". Whilst it is arguable that in such cases, defendants have been deprived of a right of access to a court to which they were previously entitled, it seems likely that if challenged, the European Court would hold the modest change in the threshold for summary judgment to fall within the state's margin of appreciation. An application for summary judgment will not succeed unless the court is satisfied that (i) he had before it all substantial facts relevant to allegations of negligence which were reasonably capable of being before it; (ii) those facts were undisputed or there was no real prospect of successfully disputing them and (iii) there was no real prospect of oral evidence affecting the court's assessment of the facts. If the court concluded, upon those facts, that there was no real prospect of the claim in negligence succeeding and that there was no other reason why the case should be disposed of at a trial, it could give summary judgment and there would have been proper judicial scrutiny of the detailed facts of the particular case such as to constitute a fair hearing in accordance with Article 6(1): *S v. Gloucestershire County Council.*[11A]

---

[9] C.P.R. 24, Practice Direction, para. 4.

[10] [2001] 1 All E.R. 91; *The Times*, November 4, 1999.

[10A] See for example the approach taken by the first instance judge in *The Royal Brompton Hospital NHS Trust v. Hammond* who gave summary judgment to the defendant and struck out certain claims at the trial and on the basis of the witness statements but without hearing evidence, applying a balance of probabilities test. This was criticised by the Court of Appeal—[2001] Lloyd's Rep PN 526; *The Times*, May 11, 2001—and is probably also contrary to Article 6.

[11] Under R.S.C., Ord. 14, only claimants had *locus standi* to apply for summary judgment. The CPR now permits both claimants and defendants to apply for summary judgment: CPR 24.2.

[11A] [2000] 3 All E.R. 346 at 373.

5. Disclosure

Access to Documents

The principles of equality of arms and the principle of adversarial proceed- **10.53**
ings have implications for disclosure and inspection of documents under
Part 31 CPR. In *Vermeulen v. Belgium*,[12] the European Court held that the
parties (or at least their legal representatives[13]) must have the same
access to the records and documents in the case in circumstances where
the information is material to the court's opinion. In *Foucher v. France*,[14]
the Court held that the denial of access to the applicant's criminal file and
copies of the documents contained in it meant he had been unable to
prepare an adequate defence and had not been afforded equality of arms,
contrary to the requirements of Article 6(3) taken together with Article 6(1).
Article 6(1) can be relied upon to support a more general right to disclosure of relevant documents in civil proceedings. In *McMichael v. United
Kingdom*,[15] the Court invoked the principle of adversarial proceedings to
justify full disclosure of confidential documents such as social reports in
care proceedings. It ruled that the lack of disclosure was capable of
affecting the ability of participating parents not only to influence the outcome of the children's hearing but also to assess their prospects of making
an appeal.[16]

In *McGinley and Egan v. United Kingdom*,[17] the applicants, who had been **10.54**
stationed on or near Christmas Island during nuclear testing in 1958,
complained that the government had not disclosed documents which they
required for the purpose of proceedings before the Pensions Appeal
Tribunal to establish whether there was a link between their health problems and exposure to radiation. The European Court stated that if the
state had, without good cause, prevented the applicants from gaining
access to, or falsely denied the existence of, documents in its possession
which would have assisted them in establishing before the Tribunal that
they had been exposed to dangerous levels of radiation, this would have
violated Article 6(1).[18] There was no violation on the facts because some
of the documents had, without fault, been destroyed and the applicants
had not availed themselves of a procedure for seeking the remaining
documents in the Tribunal proceedings. In *Feldebrugge v. Netherlands*,[19]
the European Court found a violation of Article 6(1) where the applicant
was denied access to two experts' reports by a welfare benefits tribunal
with the result that she could neither comment on them or call for further
reports in circumstances where the reports were the sole basis for the
decision.[20]

---

[12] Application No. 58/1994/505/587, February 20, 1996, para. 33.
[13] *Kamasinski v. Austria* (1991) 13 E.H.R.R. 36, Application No. 9/1988/153/207, December 19, 1989.
[14] (1998) 25 E.H.R.R. 234.
[15] (1995) 20 E.H.R.R. 205.
[16] *ibid.*, at para.80.
[17] (1999) 27 E.H.R.R. 1.
[18] *ibid.*, at para. 86.
[19] (1986) 8 E.H.R.R. 425.
[20] *ibid.*, at paras, 42–47.

10.55 In *FAI General Insurance Co. Ltd v. Godfrey Merrett Robertson Ltd,*[21] the Court of Appeal referred to the general Article 6(1) right to public justice, but did not find that it could be applied to court rules on public access to documentary material brought before the court by way of evidence.

Private or Sensitive Documents

10.56 A right of access to documents may also arise under Article 8 if they relate to private or family life. In *McGinley and Egan,*[22] the European Court also found that Article 8 was applicable since the issue of access to information, which could either have allayed the applicants' fears or enabled them to assess the danger to which they had been exposed, was sufficiently closely linked to their private and family lives within the meaning of Article 8 and that there was a positive obligation to provide an effective and accessible procedure which enabled such persons to seek all relevant and appropriate information. The United Kingdom had fulfilled its positive obligation under Article 8 by providing the Tribunal procedure for disclosure of documents, which the applicants had not utilised. In *Gaskin v. United Kingdom,*[23] the applicant wanted unimpeded access to his medical file relating to his childhood in care in order to establish his medical condition. The European Court recognised that persons in the position of the applicant have a vital interest, protected by the Convention, in receiving the information necessary to know and to understand their childhood and early development. On the other hand, the confidentiality of public records was of importance for receiving objective and reliable information. A system which made access to records dependent on the consent of the contributor could in principle be considered to be compatible with the obligations under Article 8, taking into account the state's margin of appreciation. However, it would only comply with the principle of proportionality if there was an independent authority to decide whether access had to be granted if a contributor failed to answer or withheld consent. No such procedure was available with the result that Article 8 was breached. A further example is *Guerra v. Italy,*[24] where the European Court held that there was a positive obligation to provide information to occupants of a high risk area which might be subject to toxic emissions, so that they might make decisions to relocate. A failure to do so amounted to a breach of Article 8.[24A]

10.57 The disclosure of medical records in the context of proceedings may violate Article 8 where disclosure is not necessary in a democratic society.[25] A

---

[21] [1999] C.L.C. 566, CA.
[22] (1999) 27 E.H.R.R. 1.
[23] (1990) 12 E.H.R.R. 36.
[24] (1998) 26 E.H.R.R. 357.
[24A] See further paras 19.40 *et seq.*
[25] *Z v. Finland* (1998) 25 E.H.R.R. 371 (revelation by court of applicant's HIV status from confidential medical records ordered to be produced in proceedings against applicant's husband violation of Art. 8). *cf. MS v. Sweden* [1998] E.H.R.L.R.115 (disclosure of medical records by one institution to another in connection with applicants social security claim not a violation of Art. 8). In *R. v. Hertfordshire County Council, ex parte A,* March 22, 2001, the Court of Appeal held that a local authority had the power to communicate the conclusions of enquiries made under s. 47 Children Act 1989 where it reasonably believed it was necessary to do so to protect children from the risk of sexual abuse. Adequate controls existed through judicial review to ensure that the belief was not irrational and that the extent of disclosure was no more than required for the protection of children.

person's right to respect for private life would not be protected by Article 8 where the confidential matter in question did not relate to his private life, but rather to his employment, which was part of his public life.[25A]

Norwich Pharmacal Orders

A court order requiring a newspaper to disclose the name of its source **10.58** pursuant to the *Norwich Pharmacal* jurisdiction where this was necessary in the interests of justice did not infringe Article 10.[26]

Issue of Certificates to Prevent Disclosure

The issue of public interest immunity certificates may raise issues under **10.59** Article 6 of the Convention: *Edwards v. United Kingdom*[27]; *Jespers v. Belgium*.[28] However, there is no material difference between the English common law approach and that of the human rights jurisprudence: *R. v. Brushett*.[29] In each case, there is a recognition that legitimate restrictions have to be placed on the defendant's right to disclosure in the public interest.

Bench Memoranda

Non-disclosure of a bench memorandum prepared for a court by a judicial **10.60** assistant is not in breach of a litigant's right to a fair hearing, provided that if there is any question of a litigant being prejudiced by a bench memorandum, it would be disclosed by the members of the court on their own initiative.[30]

6. INTERIM REMEDIES

Search Orders

The practice for the grant of search orders and other interim remedies is **10.61** set out in Part 25 CPR.[31] It was established in *Niemietz v. Germany*[32] that the words "private life", "home" and "correspondence" in Article 8 of the Convention encompassed certain professional and business activities and thus that a search order made by a German court in respect of a lawyer's

---

[25A] *R. v. Law Society, ex p. Barry Francis Pamplin, The Independent*, July 9, 2001, QBD, Newman J.

[26] *Ashworth Security Hospital v. MGN Ltd*, [2001] 1 W.L.R. 515; *The Times*, January 10, 2001, CA.

[27] (1993) 15 E.H.R.R. 417. See also *Jasper v. United Kingdom* (2000) 30 E.H.R.R. 441; *Fitt v. United Kingdom* (2000) 30 E.H.R.R. 480; and *McKerr v. United Kingdom*, Application No. 28883/95, April 4, 2000 (during inquest, parts of some of the witness statements were deleted in the public interest for reasons of national security and public interest immunity certificates issued preventing disclosure of certain information. Court declared complaints under Arts. 2,13, and 14 admissible). See also *Shanaghan v. United Kingdom*, Application No. 37715/97, April 4, 2000.

[28] (1981) 27 D.R. 61.

[29] Unreported, December 21, 2000, CA.

[30] *Attorney-General v. Covey; Attorney-General v. Matthews, The Times*, March 2, 2001, CA, affirming the pre-HRA position stated in *Parker v. Law Society, The Times*, December 8, 1998.

[31] See CPR 25.1(1)(h) for search orders.

[32] (1993) 16 E.H.R.R. 97.

office was required to satisfy the requirements of necessity and proportionality. This view was confirmed in *Miailhe v. France*[33] in which customs officers seized some 15,000 documents from premises housing the head office of companies managed by the applicant. The Court, emphasising that exceptions to Article 8 were to be interpreted narrowly, found that the search was disproportionate to any legitimate aim pursued, having regard both to the absence of adequate legal safeguards and to the indiscriminate seizure of documents. Article 1 of Protocol No. 1 also has obvious implications in relation to search and seizure of property in that the subject of the order is deprived of his property (at least temporarily) or alternatively his property is subject to control of its use. In *Neimietz*, a search order in relation to a lawyer's office was required to satisfy necessity and proportionality. In *Miaihle*, the disproportionate, wholesale and indiscriminate seizure of documents where many of documents were irrelevant to the customs inquiry, was a breach of Article 1 of Protocol No. 1. In *Cremieux v. France*,[34] a house search by customs officers violated Article 8 because the relevant legislation and practice did not afford adequate safeguards against abuse.

10.62 The grant and execution of a domestic search order were upheld by the Court in *Chappell v. United Kingdom*[35] as necessary in a democratic society for the protection of the rights of others under Article 8(2) but not without serious restrictions on the manner of execution of the order. It is clear that the Act will require domestic courts to exercise close control over the breadth of any search order made and to ensure that there are adequate safeguards against over-enthusiastic implementation. The practice of conducting search orders has been considerably tightened in recent years and more particularly with the introduction of the CPR which includes various specific safeguards such as:

(1) the presence of a supervising solicitor experienced in the operation of search orders who is not an employee or member of the applicant's firm of solicitors;

(2) the search to be conducted only in the presence of the respondent or a responsible employee of the respondent;

(3) a provision that no material to be removed unless clearly covered by the terms of the order;

(4) the protection from disclosure of self-incriminating or privileged documents, etc.[36]

On occasion, there have been wholesale breaches of the safeguards provided by the Rules as in, for example, *Gadget Shop Ltd v. Bug.Com Ltd*,[37] where the search at issue did not include a partner from the applicant's solicitors, the level of experience of the supervising solicitors of search orders was minimal and material directly relevant to the execution

---

[33] (1993) 16 E.H.R.R. 332.
[34] (1993) 16 E.H.R.R. 357.
[35] (1990) 12 E.H.R.R. 1.
[36] Pt 25 PD, paras 7.4, 7.5.
[37] [2001] C.P. Rep. 13, Rimer J.

of the search had not been put in evidence before the court. Whilst Rimer J. properly set aside the search and seizure order, this is the type of situation where the circumstances involved in the making of the order may potentially have involved a breach of Article 8 or Article 1 of the First Protocol by either the court in granting the order (although it had been misled in this case), or by the party who obtained the order without complying with the Rules and Practice Direction and thereafter carried out the search and seizure, if that party was a public authority with the obligation to act compatibly under section 6. In *Birse v. Her Majesty's Advocate*,[38] a challenge to a Scottish search warrant issued under section 23 of the Misuse of Drugs Act 1971 as a breach of Article 8 was unsuccessful. The European Commission has held that proceedings relating to search orders are not required to be held publicly.[39]

Freezing Injunctions.

Freezing injunctions pursuant to CPR 25.1(1)(f) would fall under the second limb of Article 1 of the First Protocol relating to the control of property. Where freezing injunctions are issued, domestic courts will have to take particular care in relation to what the injunction is directed to. The European Court and European Commission have always said, in relation to Article 1 of the First Protocol, that it is a matter of proportionality and a fair balance must be preserved. The court must try to balance the interests of the individual to whom it is directed, so that an excessive burden is not imposed, and the interests of the applicant for the order. Article 8 is also likely to be engaged in relation to freezing injunctions by analogy with the case law relating to search orders above. In *Ewing v. United Kingdom*, Application No. 14720/89, May 6, 1989, an unsuccessful challenge was made to the non-public nature of proceedings relating to a freezing injunction.[40] In *St Merryn Meat Ltd v. Hawkings & ors*,[40A] Mr. G. Vos Q.C. sitting as a Deputy High Court Judge discharged freezing and search orders which had been obtained on application without notice without disclosure to the court that the evidence used to obtain the orders had been obtained by interception of the first defendant's telephone (which the judge held to have breached Article 8(1)).[41] **10.63**

Interim Injunctions

The impact of the Act on the grant of interim injunctions pursuant to CPR 25.1(1)(a) is likely to be primarily concerned with the area of freedom of **10.64**

---

[38] 2000 S.L.T. 869, Appeal Court, High Court of Justiciary.
[39] *Noviflora Sweden, Aktiebolag v. Sweden,* Application No. 14369/88, October 12, 1992.
[40] In *Murphy v. GM PB PC Ltd & GH* [1999] I.E.H.C. 5, the Irish High Court considered the constitutionality of a statute which provided for a freezing order to be made where the senior Garda officer attached to the Criminal Assets Bureau believed that a person was in possession or control of property that was directly or indirectly the proceeds of crime. Once certain criteria had been met, the provision provided for the burden of proof to shift to the respondent to prove the legitimacy of acquisition of the property. The constitutionality was challenged on the grounds of delay, the use of hearsay evidence and inequality of arms. The Court considered Strasbourg case law regarding Art. 6 but concluded that the statute did not violate Art. 6.
[40A] unreported, June 29, 2001, Ch.D.
[41] This is a surprising conclusion in light of the *vertical* effect of Article 8—see para. 3.96 above.

expression (Article 10). The *American Cyanamid v. Ethicon Ltd*[42] test for the grant of interim injunctions, namely:

(1) whether the claimant has an arguable case in law and if so;

(2) whether damages would be an adequate remedy if relief is refused but the claimant wins at trial; and if not

(3) the balance of convenience between the parties,

was considered in *Sunday Times v. United Kingdom*.[43] The reason given by the majority of the House of Lords for maintaining in force the injunctions against the newspaper, namely, the balance of convenience, was held to be a relevant but not sufficient reason to justify restraining publication of extracts from the book, which restraint became disproportionate once the book itself had been widely published outside the United Kingdom. The European Court noted that Article 10 did not in theory prohibit the imposition of prior restraints on publication, but stressed that the dangers inherent in such restraints (even those of a purely temporary nature) called for the most careful scrutiny. The balance of convenience test may therefore be modified where a litigant's fundamental rights are at stake.

10.65   Section 12 of the HRA specifically provides that a court considering whether to grant relief which might affect the exercise of Article 10 rights must not do so in the absence of the respondent or where there are compelling reasons why the respondent should not be notified (section 12(2) of the HRA). No interim relief can be granted to restrain publication before trial unless the court is satisfied that such relief would be granted at trial.

10.66   A court considering whether to grant interim relief must have "particular regard" to the importance of:

(1) the right to freedom of expression: section 12(4) of the HRA; and

(2) the right to freedom of thought, conscience and religion where the court's determination might affect the exercise by a religious organisation of that right: section 13 of the HRA.

10.67   Where proceedings relate to material which the respondent claims, or which appear to the court, to be journalistic, literary or artistic, the court must have "particular regard" to:

(1) the extent to which the material has, or is about to, become public;

(2) the public interest in publication; and

(3) any relevant privacy code: section 12(4).

---

[42] [1975] A.C. 396, HL.
[43] (1992) 14 E.H.R.R. 229.

In *Douglas v. Hello! Ltd*,[44] the Court of Appeal considered the principles **10.68** governing the grant of injunctive relief at an interlocutory stage where there were competing interests to privacy and freedom of expression. The claimants had granted exclusive rights to publish photographs of their wedding to OK! magazine. It came to the claimants' attention shortly after their wedding that Hello! a rival magazine had possession of some unauthorised photographs and was about to publish them. The Court of Appeal allowed an appeal against an injunction granted at first instance holding that when considering whether to grant any relief which might affect the exercise of the right to freedom of expression by restraining publication before trial, a court would take into account any rights under the Convention which were relevant. Article 10(2) qualified the right to freedom of expression in favour of the reputations and rights of others and the protection of information received in confidence. It was just as relevant as the right set out in Article 10(1). Neither element was a trump card. Each would be articulated by principles of legality and proportionality which, as always, constituted the mechanism on which the court reached its conclusion on countervailing or qualified rights. The Court further held that the claimants' right to privacy, which was now recognised in English law and was grounded in the equitable doctrine of breach of confidence, had been infringed but the consequences were such that in this case the claimants would be left to their remedy in damages. The balance of convenience was against an injunction. This case provides a good illustration of how the balance of convenience test operates where Convention rights are involved.

In *Imutran Ltd v. Uncaged Campaigns Ltd*,[45] the Vice-Chancellor held that **10.69** the test for interim injunctions had not been substantially altered by section 12 of the HRA. He stated that in relation to the *American Cyanamid* test, whilst "likelihood" was, as a matter of language, slightly higher in the scale of probability than "real prospect of success", the difference between the two was so small that it was unlikely that there would be many (if any) cases which would previously have succeeded but which would, following the Act, have a different outcome. In relation to section 12(4) of the HRA, the court had always emphasised the importance of free speech and the words "particular regard" merely contemplated a specific and separate consideration of that factor.[46] However, where the practical effect of an interim injunction would be to put an end to the matter and therefore seriously affect freedom of expression, the court should apply a slightly higher threshold under section 12(3) of the HRA.

Interim Relief before European Court

It is worth noting that a limited form of interim relief is available at the **10.70** European Court whose Rules of Court allow it, at the request of a party or of any person concerned or of its own motion, to "indicate to the parties any interim measure which it considers should be adopted in the interests

---

[44] [2001] 2 W.L.R. 992; *The Times*, January 16, 2001, CA.
[45] [2001] 2 All E.R. 385, Sir Andrew Morritt V.-C.
[46] See also *Ashdown v. Telegraph Group Ltd*, [2001] 2 W.L.R. 967; *The Times*, February 6, 2001, Sir Andrew Morritt V.-C.

of the parties or of the proper conduct of the proceedings before it".[47] Any such measure is, however, not binding on the parties: *Cruz Varas v. Sweden*.[48]

Orders Relating to Delivery up or Preservation of Property

10.71 Section 7 of the Civil Procedure Act 1997 provides a framework for the granting of orders to preserve evidence. There are express powers in CPR 25.1(1)(c) for the court to grant interim orders for the detention, custody or preservation of relevant property, inspection, taking a sample or carrying out of an experiment on or with relevant property, for its sale or for the payment of income from relevant property until a claim is decided. CPR 25.1(1)(e) gives the court power to make an order, under section 4 of the Torts (Interference with Goods) Act 1977, to deliver up goods. The granting of such orders will need to be made with Article 8 and Article 1 of No. 1 Protocol in mind. For example, on an application for a preservation order pending the outcome of court proceedings, the court will need to consider whether there is an interference with a person's private life (Article 8) or with the right to peaceful enjoyment of possessions (Article 1 of Protocol No. 1). The latter right applies to a company or other legal person, though Article 8 probably does not.[48A] The temporary deprivation of property probably does constitute an interference with both of those rights. It will then be necessary to consider whether under Article 8 the temporary deprivation of property pending the outcome of the claim falls within one of the permitted exceptions in Article 8(2), for example possibly, the protection of the rights and freedoms of others and answers a pressing social need (necessary in a democratic society) or under the second limb of Article 1 of Protocol No. 1, amounts to the control of property in the general public interest. In both cases, it is necessary to ensure that the interference is in accordance with the law (*i.e.* is the law sufficiently clear and accessible?) and is proportionate. The application of Convention rights is unlikely to change domestic procedure in most cases but the balancing exercise will need to be specifically considered to ensure that a fair balance is struck between the rights of the claimant and the rights of the defendant.

7. CASE MANAGEMENT AND INTERLOCUTORY HEARINGS

10.72 **Stay of proceedings.** A stay of proceedings other than by consent might potentially amount to an infringement of a litigant's right of access to a court under Article 6(1). In considering whether to grant a stay of proceedings in the United Kingdom on the basis that another jurisdiction was the more appropriate forum, the claimants' argument that lack of funding and legal representation in that other jurisdiction would breach their Article 6(1) rights to a fair trial and equality of arms did not add anything to the application of the *Spiliada Maritime Corp. v. Cansulex Ltd*[49]

---

[47] Rule 39.
[48] (1992) 14 E.H.R.R. 1.
[48A] See further para. 14.16 and para. 14.83 *et seq.*
[49] [1987] A.C. 460.

test, which already permitted consideration of whether or not a stay would lead to a denial of justice to a claimant.[50]

In *Stevens v. School of Oriental and African Studies*,[51] Pumfrey J. con- **10.73** sidered whether a stay of proceedings until the claimant had satisfied a costs order made against him in earlier proceedings, which had been struck out for want of prosecution violated Article 6. He held that the claim was in substance a re-litigation of the earlier proceedings and in those circumstances, the stay order was a reasonable and proportionate exercise of the court's jurisdiction and did not infringe Article 6.[51A] The lifting by the court of an automatic stay on libel proceedings imposed by CPR Practice Direction 51 (Transitional Arrangements), para. 19 was appropriate where to refuse to lift the stay (a fresh action being statute-barred) would arguably be inconsistent with the claimant's right of access to court under Article 6(1).[51B]

"Unless" orders. The principle behind making "unless" orders **10.74** (orders which provide that unless a litigant does a specified act by a specified time, his claim or defence will be struck out or subject to some other sanction) is not inconsistent with Article 6(1) since it is the litigant who deprives himself of the right of access to a court by deliberately refusing to comply with orders of the court in those proceedings: *Canada Trust v. Stolzenberg*.[52] The premise underlying this decision was that "unless" orders satisfy the legitimate aim of seeking to promote the efficient administration of justice. The issue has not yet been considered on appeal or by the European Court but it is unlikely that the use of "unless" orders in principle and in an appropriate case will violate Article 6(1). It is suggested however that striking out a claim (or a defence) for breach of an "unless" order may infringe Article 6 if its use or the sanction is disproportionate to the conduct of the party in breach. Accordingly, the courts will need to ensure when making unless orders that the time period for compliance does not make it impossible or unduly difficult for the party to whom it is directed to comply and that the sanction specified is both clear and proportionate to breach of the court order. Proportionality was the touchstone at first instance in *Federal Bank of the Middle East Ltd v. Hadkinson*[53] where Arden J. was considering whether to lift a stay imposed for breach of a freezing and disclosure order. She noted that

---

[50] *Lubbe v. Cape plc* (2000) 1 W.L.R. 1545, *The Times*, July 27, 2000, HL. See also *Reichhold Norway ASA v. Goldman Sachs International*, unreported, June 28, 1999, CA (bearing in mind Art. 6, stays were to be granted only in rare and compelling circumstances). See also *O.T. Africa Line Limited v. Fayed Hijazy & another* [2000] 1 Lloyd's Rep. 76 (anti-suit injunction did not violate Article 6(1) because Article 6 does not provide that a person has an unfettered choice of tribunal in which to pursue or defence his civil rights).
[51] *The Times*, February 2, 2001, Pumfrey J.
[51A] See also *Federal Bank of the Middle East Ltd. v. Hadkinson*, unreported, October 20, 1999, discussed at para. 10.74 below. See also para. 10.128 below.
[51B] *Dar v. Taylor*, unreported May 17, 2001, QBD (reported on Lawtel).
[52] Unreported, October 13, 1998, Rattee J. The judge derived support from the decision of the Court of Appeal in *Hytech Information Systems Ltd v. Coventy City Council* [1997] 1 W.L.R. 1666.
[53] [2000] 1 W.L.R. 1695, CA, Arden J. See also the Court of Appeal decision, *The Times*, December 7, 1999.

even where a court order has been disobeyed, the requirement of proportionality applies. Accordingly, she held that she must balance the clear public interest in ensuring that there was prompt and unquestioning observance of court orders with Mr Hadkinson's right under Article 6 to have his Part 20 claim proceed. Having concluded that there was a wide range of possible outcomes on the application, ultimately the judge concluded that the stay should be lifted on terms.

10.75   **Payment into court for default of court rules.** If a party has, without good reason, failed to comply with a rule or practice direction or relevant pre-action protocol, pursuant to CPR 3.1(5), the court has power to order him to pay a sum of money into court. The principles discussed in relation to security for costs below[54] have parallels for the case management powers of the court which have power to order a payment into court as a sanction for default of court rules. In particular, the court will need to take account of that party's means in order to avoid a disproportionate interference with his right of access to a court under Article 6(1).[55] In *Mealey Horgan plc v. Horgan*,[56] Buckley J. held that whilst the court had jurisdiction to order a party which had failed to serve its witness statements on time to make a payment into court, it should only do so where that party had repeatedly breached the rules or was not bona fide, and the other side needed to be protected. This is a balanced approach seeking to operate justly between litigants and is unlikely to have any Article 6(1) ramifications. However, if a disproportionate payment into court were to be ordered by way of a sanction for default in the timetable and this had the effect of barring a litigant from proceeding with his claim or defence, Article 6(1) may be violated.

10.76   **Extensions of time.** The right to a hearing within a reasonable time may have implications for court decisions regarding whether to grant applications for extensions of time.[57]

10.77   **Interlocutory hearings.** The European Court has generally taken the view that interlocutory hearings (save in relation to striking out or summary judgment)[58] are not determinative of civil rights and obligations within the meaning of Article 6(1). Accordingly, such proceedings are not required to be public: *APS v. Slovakia*.[59]

---

[54] See paras 10.126, 10.127, below.
[55] See, *e.g.*, *Tolstoy-Miloslavsky v. United Kingdom* (1995) 20 E.H.R.R. 442; *Federal Bank of the Middle East v. Hadkinson*, [2001] 1 W.L.R. 1695; *The Times*, December 7, 1999, CA; *Grepne v. United Kingdom*, Application No. 17070/90, October 1, 1990; *X v. Sweden*, Application No. 7973/77, February 28, 1979.
[56] *The Times*, July 6, 1999, Buckley J.
[57] See, *e.g.*, in the criminal context, *Warnes & Simpson v. Her Majesty's Advocate*, November 2, 2000, Appeal Court, High Court of Justiciary, Scotland (second extension by two months of time limit for prosecution was a breach of Art. 6). See further at paras 10.98 *et seq.* below particularly para. 10.100.
[58] See paras. 10.17 *et seq.*, above.
[59] Application No. 39754/98, January 13, 2000 (interim injunction). See also in relation to freezing orders or search orders, paras. 10.61 *et seq.* and 10.63 above.

8. TRIALS/HEARINGS

Onuses of Proof

The rule against self-incrimination in relation to criminal proceedings is set **10.78** out in Article 6(2) which provides that anyone charged with a criminal offence should be presumed innocent until proved guilty according to law. This principle is of particular relevance to investigations by regulatory bodies and to inquests or civil proceedings which precede a possible criminal trial. In *R. v. DPP, ex p. Kebilene*,[60] the Court of Appeal expressed the view that certain provisions of the Prevention of Terrorism Act 1989, which required a defendant to prove that (1) he did not know of the presence of particular items on his premises and (2) that the items were not possessed for a terrorist purpose or (3) that he had a reasonable excuse for the possession of information likely to be useful to terrorists, undermined the presumption of innocence enshrined in Article 6(2).[60A] However, in the criminal context, the European Commission and the European Court have accepted as compatible with Article 6(2) strict liability offences[61] and far-reaching statutory presumptions that a defendant is required to rebut.[62] Article 6(2) does not apply to civil proceedings and a civil presumption does not of itself violate the right to a fair trial, for example a statutory presumption that a company director is responsible for the company's debts does not violate the right to a fair trial: *G v. France*.[63] However, if the burden or standard of proof operate to unduly disadvantage one party against another in civil proceedings, the fairness of the hearing may be impugned under Article 6(1).[64]

Ability to Put One's Case

An essential requirement of the right to a fair trial is that a litigant has a real **10.79** opportunity to present the case sought to be made and that both parties have the right to be represented by counsel as well as the right to appear in person: *Dombo Beheer BV v. Netherlands*.[65] The litigant's right to a fair opportunity to put his case does not involve an unlimited and uncontrolled opportunity to address the court.[66] CPR 48.2 requires non-parties to be joined to the proceedings for the purpose of costs and be given a reasonable opportunity to attend a hearing. This represents a change from the

---

[60] *The Times*, March 31, 1999, CA. See also the judgment at [2000] 2 A.C. 326.
[60A] The House of Lords subsequently allowed an appeal against the Court of Appeal's decision—[2001] 2 A.C. 326—in part because the HRA was not yet in force and accordingly did not give rise to any legitimate expectation that prior to its coming into force the Director of Public Prosecutions would exercise his discretion to consent to a prosecution in accordance with Article 6(2). However, it held that it was open to the defendant to argue at trial or on appeal that the reverse onus provision should be construed as imposing only an evidential and not a legal burden. The majority observed that it was open to argument that Article 6(2) was not to be regarded as imposing an absolute prohibition on reverse onus provisions.
[61] *Bates v. United Kingdom* [1996] E.H.R.L.R. 312.
[62] *X v. United Kingdom* (1972) 42 C.D. 135. See further para. 3.82 *et seq.* above.
[63] (1988) 57 D.R. 100, Application No. 11941/86.
[64] *ibid.* See discussion of the principle of equality of arms in para. 10.81 *et seq.* below.
[65] (1994) 18 E.H.R.R. 213.
[66] *Attorney-General v. Covey; Attorney-General v. Matthews, The Times*, March 2, 2001, CA.

position pre-existing the Civil Procedure Rules and is more likely to accord with Article 6(1). Further, CPR 39.6 has removed the long-standing requirement in *Charles P. Kinnell & Co. Ltd v. Harding Wace & Co.*[67] that companies must appear by counsel or solicitor. The ability of a company to appear by an authorised employee is still restricted to circumstances where the court gives permission and this may possibly infringe the principle. However, this remaining restriction is likely to be justified provided that in each case, the discretion to grant permission is exercised generously and reasonably.

Presence of Litigant

10.80 In Strasbourg jurisprudence, a civil litigant has a right to be present at a hearing only where the conduct or personal character of that individual is at issue or his presence is indispensable for the fair disposal of the hearing: *Muyldermans v. Belgium.*[68] The right to be present may have implications for certain applications without notice under the CPR. In *Lamothe v. Commissioner of Police for the Metropolis,*[69] the claimants sued the defendant for damages arising out of an alleged unlawful entry by police officers. The defendant made a bare assertion of the lawfulness of the entry pursuant to section 17 of the Police and Criminal Evidence Act 1984 based on alleged reasonable grounds for a belief that there was a suspect at the premises whom the defendant's officers wished to arrest in connection with an arrestable offence. The claimants applied to strike out this part of the defence. Before the application was heard, a successful application was made by the defendant to the judge without notice and in the claimants' absence to a circuit judge for a ruling based on evidence never revealed to the claimants, that the defendant's officers had reasonable grounds for their alleged belief that there was a suspect on the premises entered by the police whom the defendant's officers wished to arrest in connection with an arrestable offence. The judge made an order debarring the claimants effectively from challenging the finding at trial and reserved the trial to himself. The judge treated the return date for the application to strike out as an application by the claimants to set aside his earlier order. The claimants were unsuccessful and appealed. Counsel for the claimants alleged that the procedure was plainly contrary to Article 6 and that the situation was not one which justified resort to such an extraordinary departure from the ordinary rules of procedure. The Court allowed the appeal as a matter of domestic law and did not expressly address the Article 6 argument. However, this is a situation where the submissions as to Article 6 were probably appropriate, though in the event unnecessary.

---

[67] [1918] 1 K.B. 405 at 413.
[68] (1993) 15 E.H.R.R. 204, para. 64. See also *X v. Sweden* (1959) 2 Y.B. 354; cf. *X v. Germany* (1963) 6 Y.B. 520. A person usually has a right to be present on determination of a criminal charge: see, *e.g.*, *Ludi v. Switzerland* (1993) 15 E.H.R.R. 173. See also *R. v. Hayward, Jones & Purvis*, unreported January 31, 2001, CA (principles established in relation to trial of absent defendant in English courts).
[69] Unreported, October 25, 1999, CA.

Equal Treatment of Parties in Relation to Conduct of Trial

The concept of "equality of arms" is an aspect of fairness which was **10.81**
implied into the Article 6(1) right to a fair trial in *Neumeister v. Austria*.[70] It
requires that:

> "each party must be afforded a reasonable opportunity to present his
> case—including his evidence—under conditions that do not place him
> at a substantial disadvantage vis-à-vis his opponent".[71]

A fair balance must therefore be maintained between parties involved in
litigation and each party must be given the same opportunity to call
witnesses. The principle of equality of arms applies equally to both criminal
and civil proceedings.[72] This is of course echoed in the overriding objective
set out in Part 1.1 of the CPR. The right to "equality of arms" applies equally
to both criminal and civil proceedings. The right also applies to litigation
between purely private parties: *Ankerl v. Switzerland*.[73]

What is essential is that the parties should be able to participate properly
in the proceedings before the court or tribunal. Accordingly, a litigant must
be allowed to oppose the arguments put forward by his opponent,[74] to
have knowledge of and comment effectively on all the evidence adduced
or observations filed with a view to influencing the court's decision (*Van
Orshoven v. Belgium*[75]) and to cross-examine opposing witnesses[76] and
to call witnesses.

Article 6(1) will be violated where these requirements are not met, irre- **10.82**
spective of whether the applicant can show identifiable prejudice or unfairness: *Bulut v Austria*.[77] Particular importance is attached in this context to
the appearance of the fair administration of justice. Accordingly, a legitimate doubt, objectively justified, of a lack of procedural equality is a
sufficient basis for a finding of a violation of Article 6(1).

Although discussion of the principle of equality of arms has been included **10.83**
here under the subject of trials or hearings, the principle of equality of arms
can play a role in every stage of the proceedings and with regard to many
subjects. The following are examples of the application of the principle
where a party is unable to call evidence in support of his/her claim or is not
in a position to effectively comment on or respond to the observations filed
or evidence adduced by the other party.

Inability to summon witnesses. In *Dombo Beheer BV v. Nether-* **10.84**
lands,[77A] the central question in the national proceedings was whether a

---

[70] (1979) 1 E.H.R.R. 91.
[71] *Dombo Beheer BV v. Netherlands* (1994) 18 E.H.R.R. 213 at para. 33. See also *Ankerl v. Switzerland*, Application No. 17748/91, Judgment, October 23, 1996; *Helle v. Finland* (1998) 26 E.H.R.R. 159; *Krcmár v. Czech Republic*, Application No. 35376/97, Judgment, March 3, 2000.
[72] *Dombo Beheer BV v. Netherlands* (1994) 18 E.H.R.R. 213 para. 33. See also *Ankerl v. Switzerland*, Application No. 17748/91, Judgment, October 23, 1996; *Feldbrugge v. Netherlands* (1986) 8 E.H.R.R. 425, para. 44.
[73] Application No. 11748/91, Judgment, October 23, 1996.
[74] *Feldbrugge v. Netherlands* (1986) 8 E.H.R.R. 425.
[75] (1998) 26 E.H.R.R. 55, paras 41–42.
[76] *X v. Austria* (1972) 42 C.D. 145, Application No. 5362/72.
[77] (1996) 24 E.H.R.R. 84, para. 49.
[77A] (1996) 18 E.H.R.R. 213.

certain agreement had been concluded between the applicant company and its bank. The person who represented the bank at the meeting where the alleged agreement was concluded, was allowed to testify before the court. The person who represented the applicant company, however, could not give evidence, because the national court identified him with the company itself. Thus, there was "a substantial disadvantage" of the company vis-à-vis the bank in violation of Article 6(1).

10.85   **Refusal to admit evidence of a party.**   In *De Haes & Gijsels v. Belgium*,[78] the European Court found a violation of the principle of equality of arms in defamation proceedings brought by a number of judges and Advocate-General against two journalists who had criticised their handling of a case. The applicants were not allowed to produce the opinions of three professors which had prompted the writing of their articles. They wished to do this to counter the statement made by the judges and Advocate-General that the criticism was not supported by the facts of the case. The Court concluded that: "coming as it did from the judges and Advocate-General who had handled the case, that statement had such credibility that it could hardly be seriously challenged in the courts if the defendants could not adduce at least some relevant documentary evidence or witness evidence to that end."[79]

10.86   **Failure to allow parties the same possibility to call evidence.**   In *Mantovanelli v. France*,[80] a violation of the principle of equality of arms was found where the applicants did not have a real opportunity to comment effectively on an expert medical report ordered to be prepared by the court, were prevented from cross-examining the individuals interviewed by the expert and only became aware of the documents taken into consideration by the expert once the report had been completed and transmitted. Accordingly, they were unable to comment effectively on a central piece of evidence pertaining to a technical field which was likely to have a major influence on the court's assessment of the facts.[81] In *Ankerl v. Switzerland*, the Court stated that: "a difference of treatment in respect to the hearing of the parties' witnesses may therefore be such as to infringe the principle in question."

10.87   **Inability of party to comment on all evidence adduced**   In *Krcmár v Czech Republic*,[82] a court requested material from a third party after a hearing and failed to either show it to the parties or give them the opportunity to comment on it. Although the parties were treated equally and there was no infringement of the principle of equality of arms, the right to adversarial proceedings was breached. The European Court stated that the parties must have the opportunity not only to make known any evidence

---

[78] (1998) 25 E.H.R.R. 1.
[79] *ibid.*, at para.54.
[80] (1997) 24 E.H.R.R. 370.
[81] See also *Bönisch v. Austria* (1987) 9 E.H.R.R. 191, where the Court found that the expert involved in the proceedings had to be considered as a witness for the prosecution rather than as an expert. Since the accused had not been given the same opportunity to call such an "expert", the principle of equality of arms was violated.
[82] Application No. 35376/97, Judgment, March 3, 2000.

needed for their claims to succeed, but also to have knowledge of, and to be able to comment on, all evidence adduced or observations filed. The ability to comment includes being able to make submissions about the existence, contents and authenticity of that evidence in an appropriate form and within an appropriate time.[82A] In *Evans v. Secretary of State for the Environment, Transport and the Regions*,[83] a finding of dishonesty was made in the absence of the victim and allegations of contributory negligence were made without notice to the victim.[84] Buckley J. doubted whether the procedure for assessing an award under the Motor Insurers' Bureau Untraced Drivers Agreement sufficiently complied with Article 6(1) because, amongst others things the victim does not see the initial report until after the MIB makes its award and has no opportunity to deal specifically with adverse points in it. There is no oral hearing or a formal exchange of cases or submissions, leaving the victim without an opportunity to deal with particular points which may impress the arbitrator. In *Kress v. France*,[85] the European Court did not find a violation of Article 6(1) where although submissions made by a party were not communicated to the applicant in advance of the hearing, neither were they communicated to any other party or to the judges. Since it was possible to file a memorandum in response after the hearing, a possibility of which the applicant had availed herself, neither was there any violation of the right to reply to those submissions.

**Party deprived of effective opportunity to counter case against   10.88
him/her.**   In *Hentrich v France*,[86] in proceedings to challenge the pre-emption of the applicant's purchase of property by the Inland Revenue, the applicant was not permitted by the tribunals of fact to challenge the Revenue's assessment by adducing evidence to show that she had acted in good faith and that the proper market value had been paid. In addition, the tribunals allowed the Revenue to confine its reasons for pre-emption such that they were too summary and general to enable the applicant to mount a reasoned challenge. The Court found a violation of Article 6(1).

Examination of Witnesses

Under CPR 32.1, a court has power to control the admission and giving of   10.89
evidence, including a power to limit cross-examination. In exercising those powers, the court will have to consider Article 6(1), not only in relation to the overall fairness of the proceedings,[87] but also in ensuring that cross-examination is under the same conditions for each party. In the case of *Bonisch v. Austria*,[88] Article 6 was infringed where the expert appointed by court was treated more favourably than the expert called by the defendant. In *Dombo Beheer BV v. The Netherlands*,[89] a violation of Article 6(1) was

---

[82A] Paras. 40 to 42.
[83] [2001] P.I.Q.R. 93.
[84] *ibid* at paras, 121–122.
[85] Application No. 39544/98, June 7, 2001.
[86] (1994) 18 E.H.R.R. 440.
[87] Matters of evidence are usually for the national court, subject to the supervision of the European Court in ensuring that the trial as a whole is fair pursuant to Article 6(1). See generally, paras 11.06 *et seq.*, below.
[88] (1987) 9 E.H.R.R. 191.
[89] (1994) 18 E.H.R.R. 213.

found where the only first-hand witness of disputed facts on behalf of the applicant was barred from giving evidence whereas the defendant bank's witness was allowed to be called, although both witnesses were equally well-qualified to testify. Where a court uses its case management powers to limit cross-examination or calling of oral evidence, it will have to be very careful to do this fairly as between each party. In *Delta v. France* (a criminal case),[90] the European Court found violations of Article 6(1) and Article 6(3)(d) where the applicant had been deprived of the right to examine witnesses and obtain the attendance and examination of witnesses on his own behalf under the same conditions as witnesses against him. In *Woolwich plc v. Daisystar Ltd & Raja*,[91] the Court of Appeal were considering *inter alia*, an application for an extension of time in which to renew orally an application rejected by Nourse L.J. on paper on December 19, 1995 for permission to appeal against the order of Robert Walker J. on June 6, 1995 refusing to adjourn the trial of the action which culminated in judgment against Mr Raja on June 14, 1995. Counsel for Mr Raja submitted that Mr Raja would potentially be entitled to rely on Article 6(1) of the Convention and the European Court's decisions on "equality of arms" in arguing that the trial at first instance was unfair because the refusal to adjourn prevented Mr Raja from defending the allegations of fraud against him in a complex case. It was suggested that:

(1) he was unable to deal with the lists of documents and the substantial trial bundles served at a time when he was without legal aid;

(2) he was placed at a disadvantage vis-à-vis the Woolwich who were represented by leading and junior counsel; and

(3) he was prevented by the debarring orders from giving evidence or challenging the evidence against him.

However, the Court of Appeal found that the trial was not unfair and did not involve any breach of Article 6(1). It stated that the complaints about an unfair trial must be viewed in the context of the long history of the litigation, during most of which Mr Raja had legal representation and a full opportunity to present his case and to challenge the case against him. His position at the trial was the result of his own failure to comply with orders of the court made with the object of ensuring that a fair trial would take place without yet further delay.

Adversarial Proceedings

10.90   The European Court has held that one of the elements of a fair hearing within the meaning of Article 6(1) is the right to adversarial proceedings.[92] This applies equally to civil as well as criminal proceedings.[93] Each party

---

[90] (1993) 16 E.H.R.R. 574.
[91] Unreported, March 16, 2000, CA.
[92] *Van Orshoven v. Belgium* (1998) 26 E.H.R.R. 55, para. 41; *JJ v. Netherlands* (1999) 28 E.H.R.R. 168, para. 43.
[93] *Szücs v. Austria* (1998) 26 E.H.R.R. 310 at 353, para. 66.

must in principle have the opportunity not only to make known any evidence needed for his claims to succeed, but also to have knowledge of, and comment on, all evidence adduced or submissions made with a view to influencing the court's decision.[94] What is essential is that the parties should be able to participate properly in the proceedings before the court or tribunal. Accordingly, a litigant must be allowed to oppose the arguments put forward by his opponent,[95] to have knowledge of and comment on the observations filed or evidence adduced by the other party[96] and to cross-examine opposing witnesses.[97] The ability to comment includes being able to make submissions about the existence, contents and authenticity of that evidence in an appropriate form and within an appropriate time (if need be, in a written form and in advance).[98] A court or tribunal should not make findings about issues on which it had prevented a party or his advocate from making submissions.[98A] The principle of adversarial proceedings has a degree of overlap with the principle of equality of arms.

Duty to Properly Examine the Merits

In *Kraska v. Switzerland*,[99] the European Court held that the right to a fair **10.91** hearing puts the court or tribunal:

"under a duty to conduct a proper examination of the submissions, arguments and evidence adduced by the parties, without prejudice to its assessments of whether they are relevant to its decision".

The fairness of proceedings is generally judged "in the round".

Reasons

Article 6(1) impliedly requires that a litigant is entitled to a reasoned **10.92** decision or judgment.[1] This is a departure from the common law approach, which is that there is no general duty to give reasons.[2] The requirement to give reasons has implications for tribunals and disciplinary proceedings where either no reasons or insufficiently full reasons are given. There is no prescription as to the form or content of any decision but a failure to

---

[94] *Lobo Machado v. Portugal* (1997) 23 E.H.R.R. 79, para. 31; *Nideröst-Huber v. Switzerland* (February 18, 1997), para. 24; *Mantovanelli v. France* (1997) 24 E.H.R.R. 370, para. 33.
[95] *Feldbrugge v. Netherlands* (1986) 8 E.H.R.R. 425.
[96] *Ruiz Mateos v. Spain* (1993) 16 E.H.R.R. 505; *McMichael v. United Kingdom* (1995) 20 E.H.R.R. 205, para. 80.
[97] *X v. Austria* (1972) 42 C.D. 145, Application No. 5362/72. See also *Mantovanelli v. France* (1997) 24 E.H.R.R. 370, paras, 34–36; and *Krcmár v. Czech Republic*, Application No. 35376/97, March 3, 2000, European Court. Note that the gathering of additional evidence by a court is not, in itself, incompatible with the requirements of a fair hearing (*ibid.*, para. 38).
[98] At paras. 40, 42.
[98A] *Katrinak v. Secretary of State for the Home Department, The Times*, June 12, 2001, CA.
[99] (1994) 18 E.H.R.R. 188, para. 30.
[1] See, *e.g. Hiro Balani v. Spain* (1995) 19 E.H.R.R. 566; *De Moor v. Belgium* (1994) 18 E.H.R.R. 372.
[2] See, *e.g. R. v. Secretary of State for the Home Department, ex p. Doody* [1994] 1 A.C. 531 at 561, 564–566; *Stefan v. General Medical Council* [1999] 1 W.L.R. 1293 at 1299.

address a key point which is decisive of the case may infringe the principle.[3] The requirement cannot be understood as requiring a detailed answer to every argument adduced by a litigant.[3A] The extent of the duty to give reasons may vary according to the nature of the decision at issue[4] and can only be determined in the light of the circumstances of the case.[5] Provided that a court addressed the essential issues which were submitted to its jurisdiction and did not merely endorse the findings reached by a lower court, the giving of sparse reasons upholding and incorporating the reasons of a lower court does not violate Article 6(1).[6] Where a supreme court refuses to accept a case on the basis that the legal grounds for such a case are not made out, very limited reasoning might satisfy the requirements of Article 6.[7] This principle extends to House of Lords' decisions on petitions for leave to appeal.[8]

Public Hearing

10.93   Article 6(1) expressly requires a public hearing, although it provides for circumstances where the press and public may be excluded from proceedings. These include situations where the interests of morals, public order or national security may be compromised; where the interests of juveniles or the protection of the private life of the parties requires or in situations where publicity could prejudice the interests of justice. The exclusion of the public is only permissible to the extent strictly necessary in the opinion of the court in special circumstances where publicity would prejudice the interests of justice.[9] The holding of court hearings in public is a "fundamental principle" enshrined in Article 6(1). The public character protects litigants against the administration of justice without public scrutiny and is also one of the means whereby people's confidence in the courts can be maintained: *Diennet v. France*.[10] Any restrictions on the right to a public

---

[3] *Hiro Balani v. Spain* (1995) 19 E.H.R.R. 566. See also *Stefan v. General Medical Council*, March 8, 1999, PC.

[3A] See *Gourlay v. HM Advocate*, unreported, May 15, 2001, H.C. Justiciary, Scot (reported on Lawtel).

[4] *Helle v. Finland* (1998) 26 E.H.R.R. 159.

[5] *Ruiz Torija v. Spain* (1995) 19 E.H.R.R. 553.

[6] *Helle v. Finland* (1998) 26 E.H.R.R. 159; *Garcia Ruiz v. Spain* (2001) 31 E.H.R.R. 589, para. 29.

[7] *Nerva v. United Kingdom*, Application No. 42295/98, July 11, 2000. See also *Plender v. Hyams*, [2001] 1 W.L.R. 32, CA, where the court stated that whilst a litigant has a right to a reasoned decision under Art. 6, on an application for permission to appeal, the judge dealing with the application can properly be brief in explaining his conclusion; per Peter Gibson L.J.

[8] *Nerva*, above (failure of House of Lords to give reasons for rejecting petition for leave to appeal did not violate Art. 6(1)). See also *Mphahlele v. First National Bank of South Africa Ltd* 1999 (3) B.C.L.R. 253 (CC), (1999) 6 B.H.R.C. 481, Constitutional Court of South Africa (reasons for refusing leave to appeal not required).

[9] *Scarth v. United Kingdom* (1999) 28 E.H.R.R. C.D. 47.

[10] (1996) 21 E.H.R.R. 554. See also *Gautrin v. France* (1999) 28 E.H.R.R. 196, para. 42. For international judicial statements of the right to a public hearing see *Boodram v. The Attorney-General* [1996] 1 C.H.R.D. 58, January 20, 1995, Court of Appeal, Trinidad & Tobago (an essential part of the notional of a fair trial was that it be conducted in public under the watchful eye of citizens, subject to a few exceptions) and *Canadian Broadcasting Corporation v. New Brunswick (Attorney General)* (1996) 139 DLR (4th) 385, [1996] 3 S.C.R. 481, (1996) 2 B.H.R.C. 210 (exclusion of public and media from court proceedings not justified).

hearing must be necessary and proportionate.[11] The right to a public hearing may be waived by a party.[12]

The impact of this principle can be seen in the changes brought about by CPR rule 39.2 which provides for all hearings to be in public subject to certain exceptions (for example involving matters of national security or confidential information, where the application is without notice and a public hearing would be unjust to the respondent or where a private hearing is necessary to protect the interests of a child or patient). Accordingly, small claims arbitrations in the county court are now heard in public[13] and members of the public have an automatic right to a transcript, subject to payment of the appropriate fee. Hearings in chambers are also public although there is no requirement for the court to make special arrangements for accommodating members of the public. In *Storer v. British Gas*,[14] an industrial tribunal conducted in the office of the regional chairman in a secure area protected by a coded locked door was not a "public" hearing. In *R. v. Bow County Court, ex p. Pelling*,[15] the Divisional Court held that the trying of small claims hearings in locked chambers to which the public only had access with the assistance of a member of staff did not infringe Article 6(1). On the facts, despite the locked door, the hearings were held in public. The Administrative Court could not make directions to courts regarding the holding of small claims hearings or direct uniformity of practice.

10.94

The right to a public hearing may also arise in the context of public inquiries. In *R. v. Secretary of State for Health, ex p. Wagstaff*,[16] the Divisional Court held that the decision by the Secretary of State for Health to hold a "public inquiry", whilst sitting in private, into the mass murder of patients by a general practitioner contravened Article 10 of the Convention in that it constituted an unjustified interference with the reception of information that others wished or might be willing to impart. Provided that there has been a public hearing at first instance, it may not be a violation of Article 6(1) for appeal proceedings to be in private where the appeal court is contemplating approving, as opposed to reversing, the judgment at first

10.95

---

[11] In *B. and P. v. United Kingdom* Application Nos. 36337/97 and 35974/97, April 24, 2001, *The Times*, May 15, 2001, the European Court held that the general presumption that proceedings involving children should be heard in chambers was not inconsistent with Article 6(1). The Court accepted that it may be necessary to limit the open and public nature of proceedings in the interests of safety or privacy or to promote the free exchange of information. Further, to pronounce judgment publicly would to a large extent frustrate the aim of protecting the privacy of the children and of the parties and to avoid prejudicing the interests of justice. In *Secretary of State for Defence v. Times Newspapers, The Independent*, May 14, 2001, QBD, Blofeld J. held that the principle of open justice had to be balanced against cosiderations of national security, the right to life and the right to protection against torture, inhuman or degrading treatment when considering whether proceedings against a former soldier in Northern Ireland should be held in open court.

[12] See para. 3.152 above.

[13] See the European Commission ruling in *Scarth v. United Kingdom* (1999) 28 E.H.R.R. C.D. 47 that the county court small claims procedure violated the right to a public hearing in Art. 6(1). This decision was subsequent to the introduction of the CPR but related to the pre-CPR position.

[14] [2000] 1 W.L.R. 1237, CA.

[15] [2001] U.K.H.R.R. 165, Admin Ct.

[16] [2001] 1 W.L.R. 292.

instance.[17] Proceedings before professional disciplinary bodies should also generally be held in public.[18] In *Diennet v. France*,[19] the Court held that the right of a public hearing extended to the disciplinary hearing of a doctor before the French Medical Association. By contrast, it is not a violation of Article 6(1) for certain other tribunal proceedings to be held in private.[20]

10.96 The requirement that judgment must be pronounced publicly does not require it to be read out in open court but it must be made publicly available.[21]

Oral Hearing

10.97 Under the CPR, in certain circumstances, the court may determine cases without an oral hearing: rules 1.4(2)(j) (power to deal with the case without the parties needing to attend at court) and 23.8 (applications). Rule 32.2 provides that whilst the general rule is that the evidence of witnesses is given orally, this is subject to any provision to the contrary in the rules or elsewhere or an order of the court. Article 6(1) confers the right to an oral hearing in proceedings before a court of first instance unless there are exceptional circumstances which justified dispensing with such a hearing: *Allan Jacobsson v. Sweden (No 2)*.[22] Where the issues are of a very limited nature and do not raise any issues of fact or law as to an applicant's individual interests, a tribunal may be exempted from the normal obligation to hold an oral hearing, even if there is no right of appeal.[23]

Length of Proceedings

10.98 A litigant has a right to a hearing within a reasonable time. In order to assess whether the hearing is within a reasonable time, it is necessary to identify the beginning and end of the relevant period, then assess the particular circumstances of the case with the help of the following criteria:

(1) the complexity of the case;

(2) the importance of the interest at stake;

(3) the conduct of the parties; and

---

[17] *Axen v. Germany* (1984) 6 E.H.R.R. 195 (appeal court sat in private to help reduce court's workload).

[18] *Gautrin v. France* (1999) 28 E.H.R.R. 196. See further para. 17.114 and Chapter 20.

[19] (1996) 21 E.H.R.R. 554.

[20] See, *e.g.*, *Mahon and Kent v. Rahn*, [2000] 1 W.L.R. 2150, CA (The Securities Association Authorisation Tribunal entitled to sit in private where there was a need to protect the reputation of the individual against whom the authorisation proceedings had been brought). See further on disciplinary proceedings, Chapter 20.

[21] *Pretto v. Italy* (1984) 6 E.H.R.R. 182. See also *Asan Rushiti v. Austria*, Application No. 28389/95, March 21, 2000, and *Szücs and Werner v. Austria*, Application No. 20602/92, November 24, 1997.

[22] Application No. 16970/90, Judgment, February 19, 1998 [1998] H.R.C.D. 270. See also *Fischer v. Austria* (1995) 20 E.H.R.R. 349.

[23] *Jacobsson (No. 2.) ibid.*

(4) the conduct of the judicial authorities dealing with the case.[24]

Only periods of delays imputable to the relevant judicial authorities are material but this includes all time taken to resolve the claim, including any appeal or application for judicial review[25] or costs determination.[26] A delay referable to a preliminary reference to the ECJ is not taken into account so as not adversely to affect the system instituted by Article 234 of the E.C. Treaty (formerly Article 177 of the EEC Treaty): *Pafitis v. Greece*[27] A dispute's complexity alone is not sufficient to justify lengthy delays and it is the conduct of the parties and the relevant judicial authorities which is most decisive.[28] Certain interests are given particular importance, for example claims involving the needs of children[29] or a person's employment status.[30] Where time is of greater importance due to a person's age[31] or deteriorating health,[32] there is a higher duty on the authorities to resolve proceedings expeditiously. There is a duty on the applicant to show diligence and to use any shortcuts available. To succeed in alleging unreasonable delay, it is not necessary to show prejudice.[33]

In *H v. United Kingdom*,[34] proceedings involving parental access to a child **10.99** which took two years and seven months were held to be unreasonably lengthy. In *Darnell v. United Kingdom*,[35] a nine-year period for proceedings relating to a claim for unfair dismissal infringed this right. In *Robins v. United Kingdom*,[36] a four year dispute over costs proceedings was not a reasonable time. In *X v. France*,[37] periods of over two years were unreasonable in compensation proceedings for applicants who had contracted HIV as a result of blood transfusions. In *Pafitis v. Greece*,[38] the applicants brought proceedings to challenge the legality of increases in the share capital of the Bank of Central Greece by a temporary administrator. The European Commission found that a period of over five years (including 12

---

[24] *Vernillo v. France* (1991) 13 E.H.R.R. 880, para. 30. See also *Howarth v. United Kingdom*, Application No. 38081/97, September 21, 2000 (whilst acknowledging a degree of complexity, the Court found that the total time of just over four years for proceedings involving various company law and financial services offences, could not be justified) and *Zielinski v. France* (2001) 31 E.H.R.R. 532 (proceedings lasting for five years and 10 months including a three-year delay in setting a date for the hearing of an appeal exceeded a "reasonable" time despite the undoubted complexity of the case).
[25] *Darnell v. United Kingdom* (1994) 18 E.H.R.R. 205.
[26] *Robins v. United Kingdom* (1998) 26 E.H.R.R. 527.
[27] (1999) 27 E.H.R.R. 566.
[28] *Pafitis*, above. See also *Zimmerman and Steiner v. Switzerland* (1984) 6 E.H.R.R. 17.
[29] *H v. U.K.* (1988) 10 E.H.R.R. 95.
[30] *Obermeier v. Austria* (1991) 13 E.H.R.R. 290; *Buchholz v. Germany* (1981) 3 E.H.R.R. 597.
[31] See, *e.g.* *Styranowski v. Poland*, Application No. 28616/95, Judgment October 30, 1998 (delay of four years in determining judge's pension complaint which was of "undeniable importance" in view of applicant's age violation of Art.6).
[32] See, *e.g.* *X v. France* (1992) 14 E.H.R.R. 483
[33] *Crummock (Scotland) Ltd v. Her Majesty's Advocate*, 2000 S.L.T. 677; *The Times*, May 9, 2000, CCA, Scot.
[34] (1988) 10 E.H.R.R. 95.
[35] (1994) 18 E.H.R.R. 205.
[36] (1998) 26 E.H.R.R. 527.
[37] (1992) 14 E.H.R.R. 483. See also *Vallée v. France* (1994) 18 E.H.R.R. 549.
[38] (1999) 27 E.H.R.R. 566.

adjournments) was unreasonable. In *Podbielski v. Poland*,[39] a delay of five years and five months with no final decision in a civil action for damages for breach of a building contract was unreasonable. The complexity of the proceedings did not justify their length. There is a positive obligation on a Contracting State to organise its legal systems in such a way as to deliver justice within a reasonable time: *Buchholz v. Germany*.[40]

10.100 The requirement to have a hearing within a reasonable time has implications for applications for striking out a claim on grounds of delay, case management (including the grant or refusal of extensions of time or adjournments)[41] and the time for judgments to be handed down following the conclusion of a hearing.

10.101 In the administrative context, a refusal to determine an application for planning permission may be declared *ultra vires* by the courts for offending against the applicant's legitimate expectation that the application would be determined within a reasonable time.[42] On a practical level, it is not clear how an individual who is a victim of unreasonable delay by the courts should challenge this situation under the HRA since he or she is effectively seeking to challenge a non-decision. There can be no appeal against a non-decision (though perhaps an order adjourning proceedings could be appealed)[43] and judicial review does not lie against the higher courts. It may be possible to view unreasonable delay as an "omission" covered by the HRA with the possibility of a claim for a declaration under section 7(1)(a) of the HRA.

10.102 Further, there can be no award of damages under the HRA for a judicial act, including delay caused by judicial action or inaction (except in bad faith) pursuant to section 9(3) of the HRA (although there would still be a remedy in Strasbourg).[43A] An award might possibly be made in relation to delay in proceedings attributable to public authorities other than the court (for example the Crown Prosecution Service).[44]

---

[39] Application No. 27916/95, Judgment, October 30, 1998.

[40] (1981) 3 E.H.R.R. 597. See also *Pafitis v. Greece* (1999) 27 E.H.R.R. 566, para. 100; *G.S. v. Austria* (2001) 31 E.H.R.R. 576, para. 35; and *Podbielski v. Poland*, Application No. 27916/95, Judgment, October 30, 1998, para. 38. In *Darmalingum v. The State (Mauritius)*, [2000] 1 W.L.R. 2303 the Privy Council quashed a conviction on the ground of excessive delay in sentence and determination of an appeal holding that the Mauritius Constitution reflected Art. 6 of the Convention and that Strasbourg case law should be followed.

[41] See by analogy, *Warnes & Simpson v. H.M. Advocate*, unreported, November 11, 2000, HCJ Appeal, (Scot.) (one extension of the 12-month time limit for prosecution under the Criminal Procedure (Scotland) Act 1995, s. 65(1), had been allowed). The Court held that a further extension of two months was a breach of Art. 6, as a backlog of cases/pressure of business was not a valid reason for an extension). Cf. *Alliance and Leicester plc v. Slayford*, [2001] 1 All E.R. (Comm.) 1, CA (Court granted appeal and extended time for serving notice of appeal which was only two days late. It held that there was no breach of the defendants' right under Art. 6 to have their rights and obligations determined within a reasonable time). The adjournment of a hearing for a litigant to obtain legal representation where the right of that litigant to a fair trial and the right of the other party to a trial within a reasonable time were carefully balanced will not infringe Article 6: *Nares v. Law Society*, unreported, June 13, 2001, QBD (reported on Lawtel).

[42] *Lafarge Redland Aggregates Ltd v. The Scottish Ministers*, 2001 S.C. 298, OHC of Sess (Scot.).

[43] See, *e.g. Turner Page Music Ltd v. Torres Design, The Times*, August 3, 1998, CA.

[43A] See further para. 9.44 above in relation to damages awards for judicial acts.

[44] See further R. Carnwath, "No pot of gold at the end of the court case", *The Times*, October 3, 2000.

Independent and Impartial Tribunal Established by Law

In order to comply with Article 6(1), a hearing must be by an independent **10.103**
and impartial tribunal established by law.

Tribunal established by law. This denotes "bodies which **10.104**
exhibit . . . common fundamental features" of which the most important
are independence and impartiality and "the guarantees of judicial procedure": *De Wilde, Ooms and Versyp v. Belgium.*[45] The tribunal must have
the power to make binding decisions. In *Van de Hurk v. Netherlands,*[46] the
right to a "tribunal" had been breached since the decisions of the Dutch
Industrial Appeals Board could be overruled by administrative authority,
although this had never in fact happened. A tribunal must be set up and
given jurisdiction by law and it will not cease to be "established by law" if
its rules are compiled by subordinate legislation provided that they are
susceptible to legal challenge: *Crociani v. Italy.*[47] Further, a tribunal does
not have to solely act in a judicial capacity and it may also carry out
administrative or other functions.[48]

Independence. A court or tribunal must be independent: *Campbell* **10.105**
& Fell v. United Kingdom.[49] "Independent" means independent of the
Executive, of the parties and of the legislature: *Bryan v. U.K.*[50] In *Findlay*
v. United Kingdom,[51] the European Court stated that:

> " . . . in order to establish whether a tribunal can be considered as
> 'independent', regard must be had, inter alia, to the manner of
> appointment of its members and their term of office, the existence of
> guarantees against outside pressures and the question whether the
> body presents an appearance of independence . . .
> As to the question of 'impartiality', there are two aspects to this
> requirement. First, the tribunal must be subjectively free of personal
> prejudice or bias. Secondly, it must also be impartial from an objective
> viewpoint, that is, it must offer sufficient guarantees to exclude any
> legitimate doubt in this respect . . . The concepts of independence
> and objective impartiality are closely linked . . . ".[51A]

Bias and impartiality. The right to an impartial tribunal under Article **10.106**
6(1) is a "fundamental principle" of the Convention: *De Cubber v. Belgium.*[52] In judging the impartiality of a tribunal, the test is both subjective
and objective. The test is whether a particular adjudicatory body has the

---

[45] (1979) 1 E.H.R.R. 373. See also *Benthem v. Netherlands* (1986) 8 E.H.R.R. 1, para. 43
(administrative body—the Crown—settled dispute).
[46] (1994) 18 E.H.R.R. 481.
[47] (1980) 22 D.R. 147, Application Nos. 8722/79, 8723/79, 8729/79.
[48] *Campbell and Fell v. United Kingdom* (1985) 7 E.H.R.R. 165 (Prison Board of Visitors).
[49] (1985) 7 E.H.R.R. 165. See also *Findlay v. United Kingdom* (1997) 24 E.H.R.R. 221 (in
relation to courts-martials) and *Coyne v. U.K.* [1998] E.H.R.L.R. 91.
[50] (1996) 21 E.H.R.R. 342, para. 37.
[51] (1997) 24 E.H.R.R. 221.
[51A] At para. 73.
[52] (1985) 7 E.H.R.R. 236.

required "appearance" of independence or the required "objective" impartiality.[53] Accordingly, the European Court considers not only actual impartiality but also the appearance of impartiality. The test is typically expressed in terms of "legitimate doubt" about the judge's impartiality. In *Piersack v. Belgium*,[54] the European Court stated:

> "Whilst impartiality normally denotes absence of prejudice or bias, its existence or otherwise can, notably under Article 6(1) of the Convention, be tested in various ways. A distinction can be drawn in this context between a subjective approach, that is endeavouring to ascertain the personal conviction of a judge in a given case, and an objective approach, that is determining whether he offered guarantees sufficient to exclude any legitimate doubt in this respect.
>
> As regards the first approach, the Court notes that the applicant is pleased to pay tribute to Mr. Van de Walle's personal impartiality; it does not itself have any cause for doubt on this score and indeed personal impartiality is to be presumed until there is proof to the contrary . . .
>
> However, it is not possible to confine oneself to a purely subjective test. In this area, even appearances may be of a certain importance . . . As the Belgian Court of Cassation observed in its judgment of 21 February 1979 . . . any judge of whom there is a legitimate reason to fear a lack of impartiality must withdraw. What is at stake is the confidence which the courts must inspire in the public in a democratic society."[55]

10.107 In *Langborger v. Sweden*,[56] a housing tribunal whose membership had the "possible appearance of lacking impartiality" violated Article 6(1). In *De Haan v. Netherlands*,[57] the judge who presided over an Appeals Tribunal was called upon to decide upon an objection for which he himself was responsible. Notwithstanding an absence of prejudice or bias on the part of the judge, the Court found that the applicant's fears as to the judge's participation were objectively justified. It was relevant to the Court that there had been no intervening decision by a higher body. The Court re-stated its case law that no violation of Article 6(1) could be found if the decision was subject to subsequent control by a judicial body that had full jurisdiction and did provide the guarantees of Article 6(1).[58] In *Oberschlick v. Austria (No. 1)*,[59] Article 6(1) was violated where the judge who had participated in the judgment at first instance also participated in the hearing of an appeal against the same judgment. In *Ferrantelli and Santangelo*

---

[53] *McGonnell v. United Kingdom*, Application No. 28488/95, February 8, 2000, European Court, para. 51.
[54] (1983) 5 E.H.R.R. 169.
[55] *ibid.*, para. 30. See also *Hauschildt v. Denmark* (1990) 12 E.H.R.R. 266.
[56] (1990) 12 E.H.R.R. 416.
[57] Application No. 84/1996/673/895 (26.8.97), paras 50–51.
[58] At para. 52. See also *Albert and Le Compte v. Belgium* (1983) 5 E.H.R.R. 533, European Court; *British-American Tobacco Company Ltd v. Netherlands* (1996) 21 E.H.R.R. 409.
[59] (1995) 19 E.H.R.R. 389.

v. Italy,[60] the European Court stated that the existence of impartiality for the purposes of Article 6(1) must be determined according to a subjective test, that is on the basis of the personal conviction and behaviour of a particular judge in a given case and also according to an objective test, that is ascertaining whether the judge offered guarantees sufficient to exclude any legitimate doubt in this respect.[61] In *Bulut v. Austria,*[62] the European Court held that the mere fact that the trial judge has also dealt with the case at a pre-trial stage cannot be held as in itself justifying fears as to his impartiality. In the instant case, the judge had merely questioned two witnesses and did not have to assess evidence or reach any kind of conclusion as to the applicant's involvement. Accordingly, the applicant's fear that the court lacked impartiality was not objectively justified.[63]

The European cases where a violation of the requirement of independ- **10.108** ence and impartiality has been found fall into six main groups[63A]:

(1) The involvement in a decision of a judge who had played a part in the preparatory stages of a case: for example *Belilos v. Switzerland*[64]; *Bulut v. Austria*[65]; *De Cubber v. Belgium*[66]; and *Piersack v. Belgium*[67] or had been involved in proceedings against the applicant: *Wettstein v. Switzerland.*[68]

(2) Where there is evidence of or a suspicion of actual prejudice or bias: for example *Pullar v. United Kingdom*[69] and *X v. Austria.*[70]

(3) Procedural irregularities: for example *Nideröst-Huber v. Switzerland*[71] and *Thorgierson v. Iceland.*[72]

(4) Cases concerning professional disciplinary bodies for example *Le Compte v. Belgium,*[73] and *Gautrin v. France.*[74]

(5) Cases concerning security of tenure: for example *Stieringer v. Germany.*[75]

---

[60] (1997) 23 E.H.R.R. 288.
[61] *ibid.,* at para. 56.
[62] (1997) 24 E.H.R.R. 84.
[63] *ibid.,* at paras 33—34.
[63A] R. Gordon Q.C., "Commercial Human Rights: Fact or Fantasy?" COMISAR Paper, March 28, 2000.
[64] (1988) 10 E.H.R.R. 466.
[65] (1997) 24 E.H.R.R. 84.
[66] (1985) 7 E.H.R.R. 236.
[67] (1983) 5 E.H.R.R. 169. See also *Castillo Algar v. Spain* (2000) 30 E.H.R.R. 827.
[68] Application No. 33958/96, December 21, 2000.
[69] (1996) 22 E.H.R.R. 391, *The Times,* June 24, 1996.
[70] (1960) Y.B. 288. See also *D.N. v. Switzerland* Application No. 27154/95, March 29, 2001 (judge rapporteur on appeal commission which determined whether psychiatric patient should be released was not impartial because prior to appointment he had interviewed the patient and expressed the view in an expert's report that she should not be released).
[71] [1997] E.H.R.L.R. 406.
[72] (1992) 14 E.H.R.R. 843.
[73] (1982) 4 E.H.R.R. 1.
[74] (1999) 28 E.H.R.R. 196.
[75] Application No. 28899/95 November 25, 1996.

(6) Cases concerning courts-martial: for example *Findlay v. United Kingdom*[76]; *Moore and Gordon v. United Kingdom*[77]; *Hood v. United Kingdom*[78]; and *Stephen Jordan v. United Kingdom*.[79]

10.109 In *McGonnell v. United Kingdom*,[80] the European Court found a violation of Article 6(1) when the Bailiff of Guernsey presided over a legislative assembly that promulgated certain planning legislation and subsequently sat in a judicial capacity on a planning appeal under the same legislation. There was no suggestion of subjective bias or prejudice. Nonetheless, the European Court held that

" . . . any direct involvement in the passage of legislation, or of executive rules, is likely to be sufficient to cast doubt on the judicial impartiality of a person subsequently called on to determine a dispute over whether reasons exist to permit a variation from the wording of the legislation or rules at issue . . .

. . . That doubt in itself, however slight its justification, is sufficient to vitiate the impartiality of the Royal Court . . . "[81]

Domestic Law

10.110 In the United Kingdom, the ability of the Lord Chancellor to sit in a judicial capacity, given his legislative and executive roles, is now open to question in light of the *McGonnell* judgment. The position of the Lord Chief Justice or members of the Appellate Committee of the House of Lords or the Judicial Committee of the Privy Council who have spoken on or voted on legislation which then forms the subject-matter of subsequent litigation must also be in doubt. Lord Bingham issued a statement in the House of Lords on June 22, 2000 to clarify the line between the Law Lords judicial functions and their role in the legislature. The Law Lords stated that they had the right, as peers, to participate in the business of the House but they would "bear in mind that they might render themselves ineligible to sit judicially if they were to express an opinion on a matter which might later be relevant to an appeal to the House".[82]

10.111 Domestic law on judicial impartiality prior to the coming into force of the HRA (though influenced by the Convention) is summarised in the leading cases of *R. v. Bow Street Metropolitan Stipendiary Magistrate, ex p. Pinochet Ugarte (No. 2)*[83] and *Locabail (U.K.) Ltd v. Bayfield Properties*.[84] In the *Pinochet (No. 2)* case, the legal representatives of General Pinochet applied to rescind the decision of the Appellate Committee of the House of

---

[76] (1997) 24 E.H.R.R. 221.
[77] (2000) 29 E.H.R.R. 728.
[78] (2000) 29 E.H.R.R. 365.
[79] Application No. 30280/96. See also *Wilkinson and Allen v. United Kingdom*, Application Nos. 31145/96 and 35580/97, February 6, 2001.
[80] Application No. 28488/95, February 8, 2000, European Court.
[81] *ibid*, at paras 55–57. See also *Procola v. Luxembourg* (1996) 22 E.H.R.R. 193, para. 45 (four of the five members of the Conseil d'Etat had carried out both advisory involvement in the preparation of a regulation and judicial functions in relation to the same).
[82] *Hansard*, H.L. Official Report, June 22, 2000; Vol 614, No. 109, p.419.
[83] [1999] 1 W.L.R. 272.
[84] [2000] 2 W.L.R. 870, CA.

Lords that the doctrine of sovereign immunity did not extend to his criminal acts as the former President of Chile.[85] The appellant submitted that Lord Hoffmann's position as a director of a charity closely allied to Amnesty International Charity Ltd, a party to the appeal, was such as to give a reasonable suspicion to a fair-minded and informed member of the public that he was biased. The House of Lords agreed to rescind the original decision and in so doing, extended the grounds for automatic disqualification to a limited class of non-financial interests. Lord Browne-Wilkinson stated that:

"if . . . the matter at issue . . . is concerned with the promotion of the cause, the rationale disqualifying a judge applies just as much if the judge's decision will lead to the promotion of a cause in which the judge is involved together with one of the parties."[86]

and

"Only in cases where a judge is taking an active role as trustee or director of a charity which is closely allied to and acting with a party to the litigation should a judge normally be concerned to recuse himself or disclose the position to the parties. However, there may well be other exceptional cases in which the judge would be well advised to disclose a possible interest."[87]

The House of Lords, in confirming that courts will assume that the possibility of bias exists, even when the decision maker has no financial or proprietary interest in the outcome, probably went further than the European Court has to date.

In *Locabail*, the Court of Appeal issued guidance in five conjoined appeals regarding disqualification of judges on grounds of actual or presumed bias, expressly taking into account Article 6(1) of the Convention, expressly acknowledging that in the determination of their rights and liabilities, civil and criminal, everyone is entitled to a fair hearing by an impartial tribunal, as guaranteed by Article 6 of the Convention. Where in any particular case the existence of partiality or prejudice deprives the litigant of this right, he has irresistible grounds for objecting to the trial of the case by that judge or for applying to set aside any judgment given. The proof of actual bias is very difficult and it is sufficient to show a real danger of bias.[88]   **10.112**

In *Smith v. Secretary of State for Trade and Industry*,[89] Morison J. stated that it was clear that there was a serious question about whether employment tribunals might properly and lawfully adjudicate on claims against the Secretary of State having regard to Article 6(1), since such tribunals were paid for, largely appointed and administered by the Secretary of State through a Department of Trade and Industry agency. In *Scanfuture U.K.*   **10.113**

---

[85] [1998] 4 All E.R. 897.
[86] *ibid.*, at 283.
[87] *ibid.*, at 284.
[88] See judgment for list of detailed factors a court should consider in assessing impartiality.
[89] [2000] I.R.L.R. 6, *The Times*, October 15, 1999, EAT.

Ltd v. Secretary of State for Trade and Industry,[90] Lindsay J. held that the employment tribunal in question was not Article 6(1) compliant because the Secretary of State was a party to the proceedings and had a large role in the appointment of two of the three members of the tribunal, in their length of appointment, possible re-appointment, removal and remuneration. However, he expressly considered the *current* employment tribunal procedure and stated that it did not fall foul of Article 6 because a number of changes to the rules had been made since July 1999 so that, although the Secretary of State still played a part in the appointment, there was no question of perceived bias in cases involving the Secretary of State.[90A] The position of temporary sheriffs in Scotland was called into question by the High Court of Justiciary (Appeal) in circumstances where a prosecution by the Procurator Fiscal in the sheriffs courts constituted an act of the Lord Advocate (a member of the Scottish Executive) for the purposes of section 57(2) of the Scotland Act 1988 and the Lord Advocate also played an important role in advising on the appointment of temporary sheriffs: *Starrs v. Procurator Fiscal.*[91] By contrast, in the subsequent case of *Clancy v. Caird,*[92] the Inner House of the Court of Session has found that it was not contrary to Article 6(1) for a civil claim for damages to be heard before a temporary judge appointed by the Crown to hold office for three years[93] with security of tenure during that appointment, where the Crown was not itself involved in the claim. It seems likely that a similar approach to the *Clancy* case would be taken if any challenge were made to the independence and impartiality of recorders in England and Wales. Recorders are appointed by The Queen on the recommendation of the Lord Chancellor who has power under the Courts Act 1971 to extend and re-extend an initial appointment. They sit judicially for between 20 and 50 days a year and initial appointments are normally made for a period of up to five years (with security of tenure during that time). Recorder appointments may be extended further by the Lord Chancellor for further terms of three years subject to a statutory retirement age of 70 and the fulfillment of the requirements that:

(1) the Lord Chancellor is satisfied that the recorder's performance fully meets the requirements of the office;

(2) the recorder has sat for the required number of days each year;

---

[90] (2001) I.R.L.R. 416, *The Times,* April 26, 2001. EAT.
[90A] In *R. v. Brent London Borough Council, ex p. S,* unreported, May 9, 2001, QBD (reported on Lawtel) Scott Baker J. held that a local education authority's involvement in the setting up of an independent appeal panel that heard cases involving the exclusion of pupils from school and received guidance on exclusion and reinstatement from the Secretary of State for Education did not breach the common law duty to ensure independence and impartiality.
[91] 2000 S.L.T. 42, *The Times,* November 11, 1999, HCJ (Appeal); *sub nom. Starrs v. Ruxton.* See also *Miller v. Dickson, The Times,* July 27, 2001, PC (the Lord Advocate acted incompatibly with a defendant's right to be tried before an independent and impartial tribunal under Article 6(1) by conducting a prosecution before a temporary sheriff unless the right was waived, which it had not been). In relation to waiver, see further para. 3.152 above.
[92] *The Times,* April 4, 2000, IH, C of Sess.
[93] In relation to the period of tenure, the Court relied on *Ringeisen v. Austria* (1979) 1 E.H.R.R. 455 and *Sramek v. Austria* (1985) 7 E.H.R.R. 351 (periods of appointment of five and three years respectively unobjectionable).

(3) he or she remains in active practice or holds a full-time judicial office; and

(4) there is a continuing operational need.

The position of assistant recorder was abolished in April 2000, shortly before the coming into force of the HRA, no doubt, in part, because of concerns over compliance with Article 6(1). This appointment was a temporary one which was used as a testing ground for subsequent appointment to recorder (thereby potentially putting pressure on the individual to avoid making decisions which might displease the Lord Chancellor) and the Lord Chancellor had power to withdraw authorisation to sit at any time if he considered this to be in the public interest. Accordingly, there was no security of tenure and it is likely that assistant recorders would have been found to be insufficiently independent within Article 6(1) if this particular judicial appointment had continued.

In *Hoekstra v. HM Advocate*,[94] the Appeal Court, High Court of Justiciary in Scotland, held that a senior member of the judiciary was not objectively impartial and should not continue to hear an appeal. This was because the judge in question, Lord McCluskey, had published a newspaper article in which he had reaffirmed his endorsement in 1986 of the words of a Canadian senator about the Canadian Charter of Rights and Freedoms being "a field day for crackpots, a pain in the neck for judges and legislators and a goldmine for lawyers", and his other comments about the incorporation of the Convention into Scottish law were overly negative, for example describing it as a "Trojan horse" which had brought an "avalanche" of claims with "devastating" results. In coming to its conclusion, the court stressed that it attached particular importance to the tone of the language and the impression which the author deliberately gave that his hostility to the operation of the Convention as part of domestic law was both long-standing and deep-seated. They expressly stated that the position would have been different if a judge had published an article drawing attention, in moderate language, to what he perceived to be the drawbacks of incorporating the Convention into domestic law.[95]   **10.114**

In *Hampshire County Council v. Gillingham*,[96] the Court of Appeal dismissed an appeal in which it was alleged that the judge's connection with a party to earlier proceedings involving the defendants (from which he had excused himself) disqualified him from deciding a subsequent case between the county council and the defendants. Sedley L.J. stated that the connection was not enough to engage the doctrine of apparent bias, whether one applied the "real danger" of bias test enunciated in *R. v. Gough* or one of the arguably lower threshold standards applied elsewhere in the United Kingdom and the Commonwealth and by the European Court of Human Rights. In *Khreino v. Khreino*,[97] the Court of Appeal   **10.115**

---

[94] [2000] 3 W.L.R. 1817, PC (HCJ Appeal), Scot.
[95] On appeal, the Privy Council declined jurisdiction to review this decision on the ground that it did not have power to review interlocutors of the High Court of Justiciary and no devolution issue was raised under the Scotland Act 1998, Sched. 6: *Hoekstra v H. M. Advocate*, [2001] 1 A.C. 216, *The Times*, October 31, 2000, PC.
[96] Unreported, April 5, 2000, CA.
[97] [2000] C.P. Rep. 29, CA.

held that where an application for permission to appeal was renewed orally after a refusal on paper, this was not an appeal from the consideration on paper and the tribunal was not improperly constituted by inclusion of the single Lord Justice who had refused permission on paper. Both the consideration on paper and the oral hearing complied with Article 6.[98]

10.116 The Court of Appeal in *Re Medicaments and Related Classes of Goods (No. 2)*[99] took the opportunity to review *R. v. Gough* to see whether the test it laid down was in conflict with European jurisprudence. They derived the following principles from the European Court:

(1) if a judge was shown to have been influenced by actual bias, his decision had to be set aside;

(2) where actual bias had not been established, the personal impartiality of the judge was to be presumed;

(3) the court then had to decide whether, on an objective appraisal, the material facts gave rise to a legitimate fear that the judge might not have been impartial. If they did, the judge's decision had to be set aside;

(4) the material facts were not limited to those which were apparent to the applicant. They were those which were ascertained upon investigation by the court;

(5) an important consideration in making an objective appraisal of the facts was the desirability that the public should remain confident in the administration of justice.

The Court noted that the only difference between the *Gough* approach and the European Court was that when the European Court considered whether the material circumstances gave rise to a reasonable apprehension of bias, it made plain that it was applying an objective test to the circumstances, not passing judgment on the likelihood that the particular tribunal under review was in fact biased. With that adjustment, the test in *Gough* was compatible with Article 6(1). Accordingly, in future, an objective test would be applied when considering whether material circumstances gave rise to a reasonable apprehension of bias.

10.117 Where a government law officer brought an application for a vexatious litigant order under section 42 of the Supreme Court Act 1981, the fact that the law officers had been consulted as to the appointment of judges to the High Court and were members of the government did not compromise the impartiality of those judges once appointed since they had taken the oath of office of judges and had security of tenure.[1]

---

[98] This would appear to have been decided as a preliminary issue on a renewed application for permission to appeal (see New Law Digest 200010101) and does not appear as part of the judgment on the application for permission.

[99] [2001] 1 W.L.R. 700; *The Times*, February 2, 2001, CA.

[1] *Attorney-General v. Covey; Attorney-General v. Matthews, The Times*, March 2, 2001, CA.

The Courts-Martial Appeal Court has held that courts-martial procedure is **10.118** now Convention compliant.[2]

Prejudicial publicity

The effect of prejudicial publicity may also influence the impartiality of a **10.119** tribunal, although it is probably sufficient if this issue can be raised on appeal.[3] In *Pullicino v. Malta*,[4] the European Court declared inadmissible a complaint about prejudicial publicity because the applicant had not made out a case that a media campaign was waged against him of such virulence as to sway the outcome of the jurors' deliberations. In *Montgomery v. H.M. Advocate*,[5] the Privy Council held that the test for whether a defendant's right to a fair trial under Article 6 would be infringed by prejudicial pre-trial publicity was similar to the common law test applied in Scotland when considering whether such publicity would support a plea of oppression, save that there was no place in the Article 6 test for a balancing exercise to be carried out between the Article 6 right and the public interest in the detection and suppression of crime. The only question to be addressed in terms of Article 6(1) was the right of the accused to a fair trial.[6]

Waiver

A party can lose the right to object to a particular tribunal under Article 6(1): **10.120** *Oberschlick v. Austria*[7]; *Hakansson and Sturrson v. Sweden*.[8] Litigants and their legal representatives should consider at an early stage whether to raise an objection to the independence or impartiality of the tribunal since a litigant may otherwise be held to have waived his right to challenge a court on this ground. However, a party will not be taken lightly to have waived this right. Any waiver must be clear and unequivocal and made with full knowledge of all the facts relevant to the decision whether to waive or not.[9] In *Times Newspapers Ltd v. Singh & Choudry*,[10] it was submitted on appeal that a judge who had made adverse preliminary findings should have excused himself from taxation of costs. The Court of Appeal held that if there were any reasons for asking the judge to recuse himself, he should have been asked straightaway and any objection had accordingly been waived. They derived support from *Bulut v. Austria*[11] in

---

[2] *R. v. Spear; R. v. Hastie; R. v. Boyd*, [2001] 2 W.L.R. 1692 (the appointment of permanent presidents or part-time judge advocates to courts-martial did not breach Art. 6(1) because there was no reason to doubt their independence and impartiality).
[3] *Adolf v. Austria* (1982) 4 E.H.R.R. 313.
[4] Application No. 45441/99, June 15, 2000.
[5] [2001] 2 W.L.R. 779; *The Times*, December 6, 2000, PC.
[6] See also *Boodram v. The Attorney-General* [1996] 1 C.H.R.D. 58, CA, Trinidad & Tobago (it was not sufficient to establish that the adverse publicity was likely to have a prejudicial effect on the minds of potential jurors. It had to be established that the prejudice was so widespread and indelibly impressed on the minds of potential jurors that it was unlikely that an impartial jury would be impannelled). *Boodrom v. State of Trinidad & Tobago, The Times*, May 15, 2001, PC.
[7] (1995) 19 E.H.R.R. 389.
[8] (1991) 13 E.H.R.R. 1. See also para. 3.152 above in relation to waiver.
[9] *Locabail (U.K.) Ltd v. Bayfield Properties Ltd* [2000] 1 2 W.L.R. 870, CA
[10] Unreported, December 17, 1999, CA.
[11] (1997) 24 E.H.R.R. 84. The European Court stated that it was not open to the applicant to complain that he had legitimate reasons to doubt the impartiality of the court which tried him, when he had the right to challenge its composition but refrained from doing so (para. 34).

coming to this conclusion. In *Clancy v. Caird*,[12] the Inner House held that even if (contrary to its ruling) a civil hearing not involving the Crown before a temporary judge appointed by the Crown to hold office was a breach of Article 6(1), the complaining litigant had not objected to the judge sitting at the time and had thereby waived his right to object later.

Cure of defects by appeal

10.121 A violation of Article 6(1) cannot be grounded on the alleged lack of independence or impartiality of a decision making tribunal or the breach of an essential procedural guarantee by that tribunal if the decision taken was subject to subsequent control by a judicial body that has full jurisdiction and ensures respect for the guarantees in Article 6(1): *British-American Tobacco Company Ltd v. Netherlands*.[13] Accordingly, a lack of independence and impartiality may be cured by an appeal or review by a court with all the Article 6 guarantees.

Restrictions on Reporting of Proceedings

10.122 CPR 39.2(4) provides that a court may order that the identity of any party or witness must not be disclosed if it considers non-disclosure necessary in order to protect the interests of that party or witness. Any restriction on reporting of the identity of parties or witnesses may raise issues under Article 8 (right to respect for private life) and Article 10 (freedom of expression). Where a party's livelihood or a risk to a person's property is in issue, Article 1 of Protocol No. 1 may also be relevant. Shortly before the coming into force of the HRA, in *British Broadcasting Corporation v. Kelly*,[14] the court held that an injunction restraining the BBC from broadcasting an interview with a ward of court would be set aside because the derogations from Articles 8 and 10 only overrode the rights guaranteed so far as it was "necessary" that they should do so, and publication of information about a ward by the media was not of itself a contempt of court and did not need the permission of the court. Post-HRA, in *Re X (A Child)*,[15] Bracewell J. held that the press had a right to publish information relating to a child in the absence of convincing evidence demonstrating the need to protect the child. She stated that decisions restricting the press needed to be reached in a manner compatible with Article 10. Subsequently, in considering whether to grant an injunction preventing the reporting of the identity and location of two infamous criminal defendants, Dame Butler-Sloss held that the provisions of Article 8 and the law of confidence could extend to prevent the identification of and whereabouts of individuals who were seriously at risk of injury or death if this information became known: *Venables and Thompson v. News Group Newspapers*.[16]

---

[12] 2000 S.L.T. 546, *The Times*, April 4, 2000, IH, Ct of Sess.

[13] November 20, 1995. See also *De Haan v. Netherlands*, Application No. 84/1996/673/895, August 26, 1997.

[14] *The Times*, August 9, 2000.

[15] Unreported, October 13, 2000, Bracewell J.

[16] [2001] 2 W.L.R. 1038. See also *Els v. Minister for Safety and Security* 1998 (4) B.C.L.R. 434, Sup C, Northern Cape Div. (disclosure of information relating to identity of police informers justifiably withheld on public policy grounds).

In *R v. Sherwood, ex p. Telegraph Group*[16A] the Court of Appeal formulated a three stage test on the approach to applications to restrict media coverage of court proceedings in light of Article 10:

(i) whether reporting would give rise to a "not insubstantial" risk of prejudice to the administration of justice in the relevant proceedings. If not, that would be an end to the matter;

(ii) if so, would a s.4(2) of the Contempt of Court Act 1981 order eliminate it? If not, there was no necessity for the ban. Even if it would, the judge would still have to consider whether the risk could satisfactorily be overcome by some less restrictive means;

(iii) the judge must then ask whether the degree of risk contemplated should be regarded as tolerable in the sense of being "the less of two evils". It is at this stage that value judgments might have to be made between competing public interests.

When proceedings were held in chambers (in the Family Division) but did not involve sensitive matters (children), there was nothing in the absence of a direction to the contrary, to prevent one of the parties making public disclosure of what had been determined at that hearing. The disclosing party's right to freedom of expression in Article 10 took precedence over the other party's right to private life under Article 8.[16B] In *H v. H; HM Attorney-General v. H*,[16C] guidance was given on dealing with the situation where a father had made his case into a public cause célèbre including fanatic and combative behaviour and the limits of the right to freedom of expression in the drafting, granting and limitations of *in personam* and *contra mundum*.

Final or Indefinite Injunctions

In *Ashworth Security Hospital v. MGN Ltd*,[17] the Court of Appeal considered an order by Rougier J. requiring the defendant publishers of a newspaper to disclose the identity of any employee who had been involved in acquiring hospital medical records relating to a convicted murderer held at the hospital in question. There had been an unauthorised leak of information from the hospital which had been passed to the newspaper through an intermediary. The court upheld the judge's decision, noting the various qualifications contained in Article 10(2), including the protection of health and the protection of the rights of others which included the prevention of disclosure of information received in confidence. In *Venables and Thompson v. News Group Newspapers*,[18] Dame Elizabeth Butler-Sloss granted an indefinite injunction against publication of the identity, whereabouts and appearance of two convicted young persons who had abducted and murdered a small child, on the ground that there was a genuine fear for the claimants' lives and safety which justified

10.123

[16A] *The Times*, June 12, 2001, CA.
[16B] *Clibbery v. Allan & anr. The Times*, July 2, 2001, Fam. Munby J.
[16C] unreported, June 6, 2001, Fam. Munby J. (reported on Lawtel).
[17] [2001] 1 W.L.R. 515; *The Times*, January 10, 2001, CA.
[18] [2001] 2 W.L.R. 1038.

such an exceptional order. The restriction on freedom of expression was justified by Article 10(2). In *Richmond upon Thames London Borough Council v. Holmes*,[19] an injunction restricting the publications of a local authority's alleged transracial fostering policy was too wide to be justified under Article 10(2) and was restricted accordingly.

Injunctions to Stop Proceedings Abroad

10.124 An injunction to stop a party continuing with actions abroad despite a contractual agreement that the claims would be determined in England did not violate Article 6, which did not provide a litigant with an unfettered choice of tribunal in which to pursue or defend his civil rights.[20]

9. COSTS

Liability to Pay Costs

10.125 It is not an infringement of Article 6(1) for an unsuccessful party to be ordered to pay costs to a successful party: *Grepne v. United Kingdom*.[21] This is so, even if the law is in a state of uncertainty.[22] Litigation costs are "contributions" within the meaning of Article 1, paragraph 2 of No. 1 Protocol and the principle that costs follow the event is reasonably regarded as "necessary" within the meaning of that paragraph.[23] In *Hamilton v. Al Fayed & Sir Robert McAlpine Ltd*,[23A] in considering an application for payment of costs under section 51 of the Supreme Court Act 1981 against a pure funder of a party to litigation Mr. Justice Morland noted obiter that any outlawing of funding of defamation actions by government would be incompatible with Article 6 as inhibiting access to justice. The rules and procedure for awarding costs must be fair and must not take an unreasonable length of time: *Robins v. United Kingdom*.[24] In relation to the award of costs under the HRA, see Chapter 8.[25]

Security for Costs

10.126 A court may order a litigant to provide security for the costs of a hearing or of an appeal pursuant to Part 25.13 of the CPR and section 726 of the Companies Act 1985. A provision requiring security for costs is not *per se* a violation of the right of access to a court provided that it is proportionate.[26] In *Tolstoy-Miloslavsky v. United Kingdom*,[27] Count Tolstoy was ordered to furnish almost £125,000 within 14 days as security for the costs of an appeal against a judgment against him in a libel action. He failed to pay the sum and his appeal was dismissed. He complained that the order

---

[19] [2001] 1 W.L.R. 515; *The Times*, October 20, 2000, Bracewell J.
[20] *OT Africa Line Ltd v. Hijazy (the Kribi)* [2001] 1 Lloyd's Rep 76. It was relevant that the parties could have a fair and public hearing in the English courts.
[21] (1990) 66 D.R. 268, Application No. 17070/90.
[22] *Antoniades v. United Kingdom* (1990) 64 D.R. 232, Application No. 15434/89.
[23] *ibid.*
[23A] *The Times*, July 25, 2001; Judgment July 13, 2001, QBD
[24] (1998) 26 E.H.R.R. 527.
[25] See paras 8.70 *et seq.*, above.
[26] *Tolstoy-Miloslavsky v. U.K.* (1995) 20 E.H.R.R. 442.
[27] *ibid.*

infringed his right of access to a court. The European Court declined to interfere with the order stating that its role was not to substitute itself for the competent British authorities in determining the most appropriate policy for regulating access to the Court of Appeal in libel cases. However, it noted that the applicant had a full hearing which had lasted 40 days in the High Court and in which he had every opportunity to adduce evidence, there were minimal prospects of success on an appeal, the amount ordered for security for costs was a reasonable estimate of his opponent's likely costs on the appeal and that there was no evidence that the applicant would have been able to meet the order for security for costs had he been given more time.[27A] Accordingly, it was not unreasonable that the applicant be required to provide security for costs and the restriction was held to be proportionate. Further, the security of costs order was held to clearly pursue a legitimate aim, namely to protect the plaintiff from being left with an irrecoverable bill for legal costs if the applicant were unsuccessful in the appeal.[28] Where an order to pay a sum of money does not actually prevent the applicant from having access to a court, there will be no violation of Article 6(1).[29] In *Grepne v. United Kingdom*,[30] the European Commission held that the requirement to pay security for costs on an appeal was not improper since it balanced the conflicting rights of the litigants over their legal costs at the appeal stage. By contrast, the European Court has held that an order for security for costs at first instance, which a legally-aided applicant cannot possibly afford to meet, is a disproportionate restriction on access to a court and will infringe Article 6(1): *Aït-Mouhoub v. France*.[31] In this case, the senior investigating judge had set security for costs at FRF 80,000, even though the applicant's income had been assessed for legal aid purposes at nil. The European Court held that the setting of such a large sum had been disproportionate considering the applicant had no financial resources, depriving him of his recourse before the investigating judge. In *Foecke v. University of Bristol*,[32] the Court of Appeal holding that striking the balance of justice between an appellant wishing to pursue an appeal and a respondent who may be required to shoulder all their costs of an unsuccessful appeal must depend on the particular circumstances of the case under consideration, stated that even if an order for security for costs on an appeal will stifle the appeal, this does not mean of itself that no order should be made any more than it means that an appellant is being deprived of his right of access to a court under Article 6(1). Article 14 may also be relevant in this context. In *Nasser v. United Bank of Kuwait*,[33] the claimant contended that

---

[27A] Whilst impecuniosity was a ground for ordering security in a domestic court, the Court of Appeal would consider whether to grant an application for an order would amount to a denial of justice to the defendant, in particular having regard to the merits of the appeal. The European Court held that the justification given by the Court of Appeal did not disclose any arbitrariness and was based on a full and thorough evaluation of the relevant factors.

[28] *Tolstoy*, para. 61.

[29] See, *e.g. P v. France* (1987) 52 D.R. 128, Application No. 10412/83 (order for payment of fine for having made an abusive appeal did not prevent the applicant's appeal and was contrasted with requirement for security for costs which could be a real hindrance to access to the courts).

[30] (1990) 66 D.R. 268, Application No. 17070/90.

[31] (2000) 30 E.H.R.R. 382.

[32] Unreported, July 30, 1996, CA.

[33] [2001] EWCA Civ 556, CA.

the grant of an order for security for costs violated the Article 6(1) right to a fair hearing and was discriminatory on the ground of nationality contrary to Article 14. The Court of Appeal allowed the application in part, holding that CPR 25.13 and 25.14 must be read in light of the Convention, that the new rules on security for costs potentially discriminated against those who were outside the Brussels/Lugano states, that the discretion to order security therefore had to be exercised on objectively justified grounds relating to obstacles to enforcement or the burden of enforcement in the context of a particular foreign claimant or country and impecuniosity was only relevant where its effect was likely to add to the burden of enforcement abroad.

10.127   In summary, a requirement for security for costs is not incompatible with Article 6(1) in principle. However, a defence to an application for security for costs based on the right of access to a court is more likely to succeed:

(1) where the security for costs is being sought in relation to a trial at first instance;

(2) the merits of the case are strong; and/or

(3) the sum required by way of security for costs is set at a figure which the litigant cannot afford and which effectively prevents him continuing with his claim or application.

Stay of Proceedings until Costs of Previous Proceedings Paid

10.128   It may be argued that the imposition of a stay of proceedings until the costs of previous proceedings have been paid amounts to a disproportionate restriction on the right of access to a court. The underlying purpose of such a stay order is to reflect the fact that there has been a needless duplication of proceedings directed to the determination of the same, or substantially the same, issues and there has thus been a misuse of the court's procedure which in many cases will fall short of an abuse of process such as might justify striking out.[34] A stay in these circumstances addresses a legitimate aim and is unlikely to offend the proportionality test in the absence of special circumstances that might be held to justify refusal of a stay in an individual case.[35] In *Stevens v. School of Oriental and African Studies*,[36] Pumfrey J. held that a stay in circumstances where the claim was in substance a relitigation of the earlier proceedings did not infringe Article 6.[36A]

Wasted Costs Orders

10.129   In a 1984 decision on the admissibility of an application under the Convention, *B v. United Kingdom*,[37] the European Commission stated that the

---

[34] *Society of Lloyd's v. Jaffray* [1999] 1 All E.R. (Comm) 354. The courts do not impose this sanction where the prosecution of the claim does not involve any element of needless procedural duplication.
[35] *ibid.*
[36] *The Times*, February 2, 2001, Pumfrey J.
[36A] See further para. 10.72 above.
[37] (1984) 38 D.R. 213, Application No. 10615/83.

making of a wasted costs order in that case against a solicitor who had failed to arrange legal representation in a criminal case did not involve the determination of "civil rights and obligations" but concerned the administration of justice and that Article 6(1) was not applicable. The issue has never come before the European Court of Human Rights and the soundness of that decision has not therefore been considered by the Court. Where considerations of impropriety are in issue, it is likely that Article 6(1) is engaged in light of the settled view of the European Court that professional disciplinary proceedings regulating the right to practice a profession concern the determination of civil rights and must conform to Article 6(1): *Le Compte v. Belgium*.[38] The formulation by the European Court of the "identification of a pecuniary right or interest" test for deciding whether a procedure is determinative of civil rights or obligations in *Editions Périscope v. France*[39] (which post-dates *B v. United Kingdom*), might now also be argued to encompass a wasted costs application.

In *Arthur J.S. Hall v. Simons*,[40] Lord Hope warned that wasted costs orders   **10.130**
might infringe the HRA where they were ordered for wasting time by raising unnecessary arguments.

Wasted costs orders do not, in principle, violate the right to peaceful   **10.131**
enjoyment of property.[41]

10. ENFORCEMENT

Failure to Enforce Judgment

Failure by the domestic legal system to take the necessary steps to ensure   **10.132**
that a final binding judicial decision is enforced may violate Article 6(1). In *Hornsby v. Greece*,[42] the European Court held that the right of access to a court would be illusory if a Contracting State's domestic legal system allowed a final binding judicial decision to remain inoperative to the detriment of one party.

> "Execution of a judgment given by any court must therefore be regarded as an integral part of the "trial" for the purposes of Article 6".[43]

In *Ignaccollo-Zenide v. Romania*,[44] the European Court upheld a complaint   **10.133**
by the applicant that the failure of the Romanian authorities to enforce an injunction ordering her children to be returned to her infringed her right to respect for family life set forth in Article 8 of the Convention. In *Pialopoulos*

---

[38] (1982) 4 E.H.R.R. 1. See more recently *Gautrin v. France* (1999) 28 E.H.R.R. 196. *cf. App. No. 10331/83 v. United Kingdom* (1984) 6 E.H.R.R. C.D. 583 (a purely disciplinary matter of professional misconduct for which a barrister was not disbarred or suspended but only reprimanded did not amount to a determination of his civil rights and obligations within Article 6(1)). See further para. 20.08 below.
[39] (1992) 14 E.H.R.R. 597.
[40] [2000] 2 W.L.R. 543 at 588–589.
[41] *X v. Germany* (1978) 14 D.R. 60, Application No. 7544/76. In relation to wasted costs and legal professional privilege, see further para. 11.69.
[42] (1997) 24 E.H.R.R. 250.
[43] *ibid.*, at para. 40. See also *Di Pede v. Italy* and *Zappia v. Italy*, September 26, 1996, European Court, paras, 20–24 and 16–20 respectively.
[44] Application No. 31679/96. January 25, 2000, European Court.

v. Greece,[45] the Court found that a state's failure to comply with a court decision in the applicants' favour constituted a violation of Article 6(1).

Enforcement and Article 8

10.134   In *Haig v. Aitken*,[46] Jonathan Aitken was successful in challenging an attempt by his trustee in bankruptcy to sell nine boxes of private correspondence to the press for publication for the sum of £100,000. Rattee J. held that the sale of Mr Aitken's private correspondence would be an infringement of his right to privacy under Article 8 of the Convention. In *St. Brice v. Southwark London Borough Council*,[46A] the Court of Appeal held that the administrative act of issuing a warrant for possession did not infringe a tenant's rights under Article 8. Whilst the possession proceedings undoubtedly interfered with the tenant's right to respect for a home, they were clearly in accordance with the law and were a legitimate and proportionate response to the tenant's non-payment of rent.

Contempt and Committal Proceedings

10.135   Civil contempt proceedings are classified as criminal proceedings for the purposes of the Convention[47] and attract the provisions of Article 6(3), including the right of the respondent to be informed promptly and in detail of the nature and cause of the accusation against him,[48] and the right to have adequate time and facilities for the preparation of his defence[49]: *Newman v. Modern Bookbinders Ltd.*[50] The *Newman* case involved an application to commit for contempt under section 92(1) of the County Courts Act 1984, a respondent who had removed levied goods. The Court of Appeal, anticipating the coming into force of the HRA, considered the effect of Article 6 on applications to commit. Sedley L.J. emphasised the requirements for clarity of procedure and that a respondent should understand in detail the true nature and case of the accusation against him.[51] Article 6(3)(c) also provides a right to free legal assistance if the respondent does not have the means to pay for this and the interests of justice so require. Echoing this, Sedley L.J. stated that it was a denial of justice not to give the respondent an opportunity to apply for legal aid as soon as the possibility of imprisonment became apparent.[52]

---

[45] Application No. 37095/97, February 15, 2001, European Court.
[46] [2000] 3 All E.R. 80, [2000] B.P.I.R. 462, Ch Div. See further Chap. 15 (Insolvency), paras. 15.72, below.
[46A] July 17, 2001, CA.
[47] *Benham v. United Kingdom* (1996) 22 E.H.R.R. 293. Though they are not re-categorised as a matter of domestic law: *Director of Public Prosecution v. Tweddle* [2001] EWHC ADMIN 188, unreported, March 1, 2001, DC (a sanction for breach of a civil law did not preclude punishment for breach of a criminal law even if the two actions arose out of the same set of facts).
[48] Art. 6(3)(a) of the Convention.
[49] Art. 6(3)(b) of the Convention.
[50] [2000] 1 W.L.R. 2559, CA—see judgment of Sedley L.J. in particular. See also *Benham v. United Kingdom* (1996) 22 E.H.R.R. 293.
[51] [2000] 1 W.L.R. 2559 at 2566, para. 22.
[52] *ibid.*, at 2567, paras 23, 24. See also the Legal Aid Act 1988, s.29, regarding availability of legal aid which remedied the violation found in *Benham v. United Kingdom* (1996) 22 E.H.R.R. 293.

As a result of the *Newman* judgment, the CPR Practice Direction entitled **10.136**
"Committal Applications" was re-issued to ensure that civil committal
proceedings were made compliant with the Convention.[53] Paragraph 1.4
of the Practice Direction states that in all cases the Convention rights of
those involved should particularly be borne in mind and the burden of
proof, having regard to the possibility that a person may be sent to prison,
is that the allegation be beyond reasonable doubt (the criminal standard).

CPR Schedule 1, R.S.C. Ord.45, rule 1(1) states that generally, in a case **10.137**
to which rule 5 of the Order applies, a judgment or order for the payment
of money may be enforced by an order for committal. Rule 5(1) states that,
where a person required by a judgment or order to do an act within a
specified time refuses or neglects to do it, then the judgment or order may
be enforced by various means, including (subject to the Debtors Acts 1869
and 1878) an order for committal. Subject to certain exceptions (for
example an order for maintenance in family proceedings) an order for
committal may not be made for disobedience to an order for payment of
money. Where the Debtors Act does apply, section 5 requires that the
jurisdiction to commit should not be exercised unless the respondent has
the means to pay. The judgment summons procedure, pursuant to section
5 of the Debtors Act 1869, has been classified as a criminal proceeding for
the purposes of the Convention *(Mubarak v. Mubarak)*[54] and the Practice
Direction regarding general committals should be read to apply to the
judgment summons procedure.[55] In *Cuff v. Quinn*,[56] the Court of Appeal
allowed an appeal against a suspended committal order, holding that the
Practice Direction applied to family proceedings as well as to civil proceedings and applications under the Debtors Act 1896 and the procedure set
out in the Practice Direction must be followed if applications to commit are
not to fall foul of the HRA 1998. The husband's wilful refusal to pay was not
established to the criminal standard and the judgment summons was
remitted to the county court.

11. APPEALS

The European Court has held that there is no guarantee of right to appeal **10.138**
but if a route of appeal is provided, it must comply with due process.[57] A
failure to communicate the fact of an appeal to a party and the consequent
lack of opportunity by that party to make representations will violate Article
6(1).[58] Restrictions on a right of appeal, such as a requirement for permission and prohibitions on new evidence or new legal argument being raised

---

[53] White Book, scpd52–001; ccpd29–001.
[54] [2001] F.L.R.1, CA
[55] *ibid.*
[56] Unreported, January 15, 2001, CA.
[57] *Delcourt v. Belgium* (1979) 1 E.H.R.R. 355, paras 25–26. See also *Brualla Gómez de la Torre v. Spain*, Application No. 26737/95, December 19, 1997 (applicant's claims had been heard by both first instance and appellate court—no violation of Art. 6(1) where no appeal to Supreme Court). See also *S v. Twala* (2000) (1) B.C.L.R. 106, Const C. of South Africa (provisions qualifying right of appeal fair and reasonable).
[58] *Beer v. Austria*, Application No. 30428/96, February 6, 2001.

on the hearing of the appeal, may be permitted, provided they are proportionate. The conditions of admissibility of an appeal on points of law may
be stricter than for an ordinary appeal.[59]

10.139   The European Court's approach to Article 6(1) has been to hold that the
Article 6(1) guarantees are not breached where a court, tribunal or administrative decision maker is subject to subsequent and adequate control by
a judicial body which has full jurisdiction, encompassing issues of fact as
well as law, and itself provides the Article 6(1) guarantees. Accordingly, an
appeal can "cure" breaches by the court, tribunal or decision maker
below: *Bryan v. United Kingdom.*[60] This has implications for appeal procedures where there is no hearing on the merits in the adjudicating body
below and limitations on the extent of review are inherent in the appeal
process, for example, on an application for judicial review from an administrative decision.[61] Conversely, where an Article 6(1) compliant hearing
has taken place at first instance, requirements such as the right to be
present or the right to a public hearing may not need to be so strictly
applied on appeal.[62]

10.140   Courts considering whether to grant permission to appeal will have to take
account of an individual's right to an effective remedy under Article 13
where the subject-matter of the appeal concerns an "arguable" claim of
violation of a Convention right.[63]

12. JUDICIAL REVIEW

10.141   There are three traditional grounds of judicial review: illegality, irrationality
and procedural impropriety. "Illegality" means that the decision maker has
not correctly understood the law regulating his decision-making power or
given effect to it. Accordingly, if a decision maker has acted *ultra vires* or
beyond his legal powers, judicial review will provide a remedy.[64]

10.142   "Irrationality" or what is commonly referred to as "*Wednesbury* unreasonableness",[65] applies to a decision which is so illogical or out of accord
with accepted moral standards that no reasonable or sensible person, who
had applied his mind to the question to be decided, could have come to it.
This is a circumscribed ground of judicial review, both because of the high
threshold of the irrationality test and the court's inability to review a
decision on the facts. Where the existence or non-existence of a fact is left
to the judgment or discretion of a public body, it is generally the duty of the

---

[59] *Levages Prestations Services v. France*, Application No. 21920/93, October 23, 1996,
paras 44–45; *Brualla Gómez de la Torre v. Spain*, Application No. 26737/95, December 19,
1997, para.37.
[60] (1996) 21 E.H.R.R. 342, para. 40. See also *Albert and Le Compte v. Belgium* (1983) 5
E.H.R.R. 533, para. 29, and *Edwards v. United Kingdom* (1993) 15 E.H.R.R. 417.
[61] See also *Kingsley v. United Kingdom, The Times*, January 9, 2001,.Application No.
35605/97, November 17, 2000.
[62] See, *e.g. Axen v. Germany* (1984) 6 E.H.R.R. 195.
[63] The obligation to afford an effective remedy is only in respect of an "arguable" claim of
violation of a Convention right: *Boyle & Rice v. United Kingdom* (1988) 10 E.H.R.R. 425;
Silver v. United Kingdom (1983) 5 E.H.R.R. 347. See also *Z. v. United Kingdom*, Application
No. 29392/95, May 10, 2001; *The Times*, May 31, 2001.
[64] *Associated Provincial Picture Houses v. Wednesbury Corporation* [1948] 1 K.B. 223,
CA.
[65] *ibid.*

court to leave the decision of fact to the public body to whom Parliament has entrusted the decision-making power, save in a case where it is obvious that the public body, consciously or unconsciously, is acting perversely.[66] Judicial review will provide a remedy if a decision maker:

(1) has reached conclusions which there were no facts to support;

(2) took into account irrelevant considerations;

(3) failed to take account of relevant considerations;

(4) reached conclusions which no reasonable person in his position could have reached[67]; or

(5) if his findings have not been properly based on material which has probative value.[68]

However, a mistake of fact cannot form the basis of a challenge to an administrative decision unless the fact was a condition precedent to an exercise of jurisdiction, or the fact was the only evidential basis for a decision or the fact was to a matter which expressly or impliedly had to be taken into account.[69] Even pre-the HRA, the English courts had already begun to modify the irrationality test in the human rights context. In *R. v. Ministry of Defence, ex p. Smith*,[70] Sir Thomas Bingham M.R. held that:

"The more substantial the interference with human rights, the more the court will require by way of justification before it is satisfied that the decision is reasonable in the sense outlined above."

"Procedural impropriety" covers failure to observe basic rules of natural **10.143** justice or failure to act with procedural fairness towards the person who will be affected by the decision, as well as failure to observe procedural rules that are expressly laid down, even where such failure does not involve any denial of natural justice. The grounds on which judicial review will provide a remedy include prejudice or bias on the part of the decision maker,[71] dishonesty or bad faith of the decision maker,[72] and where the decision maker has acted unfairly[73] or contrary to the rules of natural justice[74] or against the legitimate expectations of those concerned.[75]

---

[66] *R. v. Hillingdon LBC, ex p. Puhlhofer* [1986] A.C. 484 at 528, HL, *per* Lord. Brightman.
[67] *Associated Provincial Picture Houses v. Wednesbury Corporation* [1948] 1 K.B. 223, CA.
[68] *Mahon v. Air New Zealand* [1985] A.C. 808, PC.
[69] *R. v. London Residuary Body, ex p. Inner London Education Authority, The Times*, July 24, 1987, DC. See also *R. v. Criminal Injuries Compensation Board, ex p. A* [1999] 2 W.L.R. 974, HL. *per* Lord Slynn; Marie Demetriou and Stephen Houseman, "Review for Error of Fact—A Brief Guide" [1997] J.R. 27 and Michael Kent Q.C., "Widening the Scope of Review for Error of Fact" [1999] J.R. 239.
[70] [1996] Q.B. 517 at 554.
[71] *Franklin v. Minister of Town and Country Planning* [1948] A.C. 87, HL.
[72] *Associated Provincial Picture Houses v. Wednesbury Corporation* [1948] 1 K.B. 223, CA.
[73] *Re Pergamon Press Ltd* [1971] 1 Ch. 388, CA; *Maxwell v. Department of Trade* [1974] 1 Q.B. 523, CA; *R. v. Panel on Takeovers and Mergers, ex p. Guinness Plc* [1990] 1 Q.B. 146, CA.
[74] *Wiseman v. Borneman* [1971] A.C. 297, HL.
[75] *Council of Civil Service Unions v. Minister for the Civil Service* [1985] A.C. 375, HL.

10.144   The European Court is very familiar with the domestic law principles of judicial review[76] but has in the past generally declined to consider the adequacy of the judicial review procedure in the abstract.[77] Nonetheless, the judicial review procedure did attract some criticism. In *Weeks v. United Kingdom*,[78] the European Court held that the scope of judicial review of a decision of the parole board in relation to a prisoner was insufficient to allow a determination whether "it was consistent with and thereby justified by the objectives of the indeterminate sentence imposed on him" by looking at the underlying facts of his individual case. In *Kingsley v. United Kingdom*,[79] the European Court found that, in the circumstances of that case, judicial review proceedings were insufficient to satisfy the requirements of Article 6(1) where there was a complaint concerning the lack of impartiality of the decision-making body itself because of the limited powers of the High Court in that situation.

Test for review

10.145   The adequacy of judicial review is now coming under increasing attack by reference to the HRA and/or Article 6(1) of the Convention (and indirectly through section 2 of the HRA, by reference to the excluded Article 13 of the Convention), at least where the original decision maker did not comply with the Article 6(1) guarantees of fairness, publicity and independence and impartiality. Any limitations on judicial review, including the limits on review of the facts, or the high threshold of *Wednesbury* unreasonableness, the requirement to obtain permission to make an application for judicial review or the limitation period for judicial review[80] are potentially susceptible to challenge.

10.146   If the decision sought to be reviewed was Article 6(1) compliant, it is unlikely that any challenge to a limited power of review will be successful. Where the decision was not Article 6(1) compliant, it is arguable that the inherent limitations on judicial review prevent the complainant having an Article 6(1) compliant hearing at any stage of the legal process. Accordingly, it will be necessary to examine carefully whether the procedural guarantees provided by the first instance decision maker or tribunal were Article 6 compliant. An adjudicating tribunal does not fail to achieve independence and impartiality solely because of the presence of civil servants.[81] Accordingly a hearing before the General and Special Commissioners of Income Tax may not violate Article 6(1) solely because of the presence of civil servants appointed from the staff of the Inland Revenue, although the private nature of a hearing may be held to do so. Courts-martial have been held to infringe the independence and impartiality requirement in *Findlay v. United Kingdom*.[82] The Criminal Injuries Compensation Board (which has been replaced by the Criminal Injuries

---

[76] See, *e.g. Fayed v. United Kingdom* (1994) 18 E.H.R.R. 393, paras 44–45.
[77] *Air Canada v. United Kingdom* (1995) 20 E.H.R.R. 150.
[78] (1988) 10 E.H.R.R. 293.
[79] *The Times*, January 9, 2001, Application No. 35605/97, November 17, 2000.
[80] See para. 10.13, above.
[81] See *ETTL v. Austria* (1988) 10 E.H.R.R. 255.
[82] (1997) 24 E.H.R.R. 221.

Compensation Authority) decided awards of compensation to victims of criminal injuries under the 1993 Criminal Injuries Compensation Scheme (and its predecessors). The Board held its proceedings in private and was probably not therefore Article 6(1) compliant. The determinations of the various ombudsmen may not comply with Article 6(1). For example, the Pensions Ombudsman[83] may investigate and determine complaints alleging "injustice in consequence of maladministration" by pension scheme trustees. He may also investigate and determine any dispute of fact or law relating to an occupational pension scheme.[84] There is no clear definition of "maladministration" in the statutory provisions or any guidance as to how it should be interpreted. The Pensions Ombudsman has conducted investigations of complaints with an extremely high financial value without exercising his power to hold hearings and receive oral evidence. In *Seifert v. Pensions Ombudsman*,[85] the Pensions Ombudsman was criticised on appeal for making a finding of breach of trust against trustees on the basis of written material which the trustees were not shown and were given no chance to comment on.

Even if the decision or proceedings under review were not Article 6(1) **10.147** compliant, the court may still consider a limited power of review to be sufficient. Sufficiency of review must be assessed having regard to the subject-matter of the decision appealed against, the manner in which the decision was arrived at, the content of the dispute and the desired and actual grounds of appeal or review.[86] The court will particularly need to address whether a full power to review on appeal is either practical or reasonable.

In *Bryan v. United Kingdom*,[87] the European Court found that in enforce- **10.148** ment proceedings for breach of town and country planning controls, only a limited power of review by the High Court could reasonably be expected. The Court relied upon the specialised and technical field character of the subject matter of the proceedings, the respective roles of the Executive and the judiciary in making discretionary judgments in planning regulation and the fact that the prior planning inquiry was run on fair and adversarial lines in coming to its conclusion.[88] Further, in *Chapman v. United Kingdom*,[89] a challenge to a planning decision brought by a gypsy, the Court found that the scope of review by the High Court which was available to the applicant after a public procedure before a planning inspector, was sufficient to comply with the requirement under Article 6(1) of access to an

---

[83] An office first instituted by the Social Security Act 1990.
[84] See the Pensions Schemes Act 1993, 146 *et seq.*
[85] [1997] 1 All E.R. 214, Lightman J.; [1997] 4 All E.R. 947, CA. See also *Edge v. Pensions Ombudsman* [1998] 3 W.L.R. 466 (Scott V.-C.).
[86] See, *e.g. Albert v. Belgium* (1983) 5 E.H.R.R. 533, para. 36; *Wickramsinghe v. United Kingdom* [1998] E.H.R.L.R. 338; *W v. United Kingdom* (1988) 10 E.H.R.R. 29, para. 82; *Obermeier v. Austria* (1991) 13 E.H.R.R. 290, para. 70; and *Schmautzer v. Austria* (1996) 21 E.H.R.R. 511, para. 36.
[87] (1996) 21 E.H.R.R. 342.
[88] Note that in *Bryan* it would appear that some grounds of factual appeal were dropped by the applicant before the judicial review hearing. See also *Ma Wan Farming Ltd v. Chief Executive in Council* (1998) 4 B.H.R.C. 295, [1998] 1 H.K.L.R.D. 514, Hong Kong CA (courts' full jurisdiction not required when reviewing executive decisions)
[89] Application No. 27238/95, January 18, 2001. See also *Jane Smith v. United Kingdom*, Application No. 25154/94, January 18, 2001.

independent tribunal and provided adequate judicial control of the administrative decisions in issue.

Consideration of Merits

In *Air Canada v. United Kingdom*,[90] the European Court found no breach of Article 6(1) in the conduct of judicial review proceedings concerning statutory construction but declined to give a view as to whether in the abstract judicial review proceedings would comply with Article 6(1). By contrast, in *R. v. Secretary of State of the Environment Transport and the Regions, ex p. Alconbury Developments Ltd, Holding & Barnes plc*,[91] the Administrative Court held that a public planning inquiry, where the decision was that of an inspector appointed by the Secretary of State and the court had only restricted powers of review, was incompatible with Article 6(1). The acts of the Secretary of State were not, however, unlawful because the relevant legislation required him to act as he did within the exception in section 6(2) of the HRA.[92] The House of Lords subsequently reversed the Divisional Court and allowed an appeal holding that whilst the Secretary of State is not an independent and impartial tribunal, the scope of judicial review available was sufficient to comply with the standards of the Convention.[92A]

10.149   In relation to consideration of the facts the European Court of Justice has recently been called on to consider whether the English system of judicial review provided adequate protection of European Community rights in the context of the licensing of medicines. In Case C–120/97 *Upjohn Ltd v. Licensing Authority Established under the Medicines Act 1968*,[93] the ECJ held that a directly effective provision in the Medicines Directive 65/665 did not require the existence of a judicial review of the decisions of a Member State's medicines licensing authority which extended to "empowering the national court to substitute their assessment of the facts, and in particular, of the scientific evidence relied on in support of the revocation decision . . . ."[94]

10.150   By contrast, in *W v. United Kingdom*,[95] the European Court of Human Rights held that in childcare cases where parents sought access or custody of their children who were in local authority care, Article 6(1) required that local authority decisions be reviewed by a court having jurisdiction to examine the factual merits of the case.

---

[90] (1995) 20 E.H.R.R. 150.
[91] [2001] 2 W.L.R. 1389, HL.
[92] See also *County Properties Ltd v. Scottish Ministers, The Times*, September 19, 2000, OH, Ct of Sess (the tribunal considering a planning decision was not independent and impartial because the respondents would be adjudicating on an issue between the petitioner and the respondents' executive agency, that compliance with Art. 6(1) could be secured by the availability of a right of appeal to a court with full jurisdiction but that no such right of appeal was available).
[92A] *R (Alconbury Developments Ltd) v. Secretary of State for the Environment, Transport and the Regions* [2001] 2 W.L.R. 1389, *The Times*, May 10, 2001; [2001] UKHL 23, HL.
[93] [1999] 1 W.L.R. 927, ECJ.
[94] *ibid.* at p. 946. Note that the ECJ were influenced by the fact that the licensing authority could be approached for the grant of a fresh licence on the basis of relevant scientific material coming to light after the decision.
[95] (1988) 10 E.H.R.R. 29.

Impact of Article 13

Although it has not been incorporated into domestic law by the HRA, **10.151** Article 13 (the right to an effective remedy) of the Convention is also relevant in this context. In *Soering v. United Kingdom*,[96] the European Court considered judicial review to be an effective remedy in that it was satisfied that the English courts could review the "reasonableness" of an extradition decision in the light of the kind of factors relied on by the applicant before the Convention institutions in the context of Article 3 of the Convention. Similarly, in *Vilvarajah v. United Kingdom*,[97] the European Court was persuaded that the English judicial review procedure complied with the Convention's requirements under Article 13 in the circumstances of the case by providing an effective degree of control over the decisions of administrative authorities in asylum cases. However, in *W v. United Kingdom*,[98] a case concerning parental access to a child taken into local authority care, the European Court noted that on an application for judicial review, the courts will not review the merits of the decision but will confine themselves to ensuring, in brief, that the authority did not act illegally, unreasonably or unfairly. The scope of the review effected in the context of wardship proceedings is similarly confined. The Court held the lack of a review on the merits violated Article 6(1) and that, in light of this violation, no separate issue arose under Article 13. It stated that:

"In a case of the present kind, however, there will in the Court's opinion be no possibility of a 'determination' in accordance with the requirements of Article 6(1) of the parent's right in regard to access . . . unless he or she can have the local authority's decision reviewed by a tribunal having jurisdiction to examine the merits of the matter. And it does not appear from the material supplied by the Government or otherwise available to the Court that the powers of the English courts were of sufficient scope to satisfy fully this requirement during the currency of the parental rights resolution."[99]

Significantly, in *Grady and Smith v. United Kingdom*,[1] the European Court **10.152** found that the judicial review procedure failed to provide an effective remedy for breach of the applicants' fundamental rights before a national court and thereby violated Article 13 of the Convention because the threshold for a successful review, namely *Wednesbury* unreasonableness or irrationality, was set too high. The test effectively excluded any consideration by the domestic courts of the question of whether the interference with the applicants' rights answered a pressing social need or was proportionate to the national security and public order aims pursued, principles which lie at the heart of the Court's analysis of complaints under Article 8 of the Convention. The Court expressly contrasted the cases of *Soering* and *Vilvarajah* above, stating that in those cases the Court found that the tests applied by the domestic courts in applications for judicial

[96] (1989) 11 E.H.R.R. 439.
[97] (1992) 14 E.H.R.R. 248 (a refugee case).
[98] Application No. 4/1986/102/150, Judgment July 8, 1987.
[99] At para. 82.
[1] (2000) 29 E.H.R.R. 493.

review coincided with the Court's own approach under Article 3 of the Convention.[2] Following *Smith and Grady*, the traditional ground of *Wednesbury* review has been substantially modified. In *Mahmood*, Lord Phillips M.R. stated:

> "When anxiously scrutinizing an executive decision that interferes with human rights, the court will ask the question, applying an objective test, whether the decision-maker could reasonably have concluded that the interference was necessary to achieve one or more of the legitimate aims recognised by the Convention. When considering the test of necessity in the relevant context, the court must take into account the European jurisprudence in accordance with section 2 of the 1998 Act."[3]

Mahmood was followed by the Court of Appeal in *R. (Isiko) v. Secretary of State for the Home Department*[4] and by Thomas J in *R (Samaroo) v. Secretary of State for the Home Department*.[5] The test adopted by Lord Phillips M.R. in *Mahmood* were further considered and refined by the House of Lords in *R. (Daly) v. Secretary of State for the Home Department*.[6] Lord Steyn noted that the observations were couched in language reminiscent of the *Wednesbury*[7] ground of review and in particular the heightened scrutiny test formulated in *R. v. Ministry of Defence, ex p. Smith*.[8] Lord Steyn noted that there is a material difference between the *Wednesbury* and *Smith* grounds of review and the approach of proportionality applicable in respect of review when Convention rights are at stake. He stated that:

> "The starting point is that there is an overlap between the traditional grounds of review and the approach of proportionality. Most cases would be decided in the same way whichever approach is adopted. But the intensity of review is somewhat greater under the proportionality approach . . . First, the doctrine of proportionality may require the reviewing court to assess the balance which the decision maker has struck, not merely whether it is within the range of rational or reasonable decisions. Secondly, the proportionality test may go further than the traditional grounds of review inasmuch as it may require attention to be directed to the relative weight accorded to interests and considerations. Thirdly, even the heightened scrutiny test developed in *R. v. Ministry of Defence, ex p. Smith* [1996] QB 517, 554 is not necessarily appropriate to the protection of human rights . . . In other words, the intensity of review, in similar cases, is guaranteed by the twin requirements that the limitation of the right was necessary in a democratic society, in the sense of meeting a pressing social need, and the question whether the interference was really proportionate to the legitimate aim being pursued."[9]

---

[2] *ibid.*, paras 133–139.
[3] At para. 40.
[4] *The Times*, February 20, 2001, CA.
[5] Unreported, December 20, 2000.
[6] [2001] 2 W.L.R. 1622.
[7] *Associated Provincial Picture Houses Ltd v. Wednesbury Corpn* [1948] 1 K.B. 223.
[8] [1996] Q.B. 517 at 554.
[9] At 1635–1636, para. 27.

Lord Steyn stated that the differences between the traditional grounds of review and the proportionality approach may sometimes yield different results and it is therefore important that cases involving Convention rights are analysed in the correct way. He emphasised that this approach did not mean that there had been a shift to merits review. The respective roles of judges and administrators remain distinct. To this extent the general tenor of the observations in *Mahmood* are correct. Accordingly, the court does not substitute its own decision for that of the administrative decision-maker. However, the degree of scrutiny is greater than a heightened *Wednesbury* test and the requirements of proportionality must be expressly considered. As Laws L.J. emphasised in *Mahmood*, the intensity of review will depend on the subject matter at hand.[10]

Restrictions on standing for judicial review

Applications for judicial review which can only be brought by third parties **10.153** may also violate the right of access to a court in Article 6(1) or fail to provide an effective remedy in Article 13. In *Philis v. Greece*,[11] the applicant was a consultant engineer of Greek nationality. Greek law denied the right to seek direct redress through the courts for non-payment of fees for design projects: only the Technical Chamber of Greece could do so on his behalf. The European Court found a violation of Article 6(1) because the applicant was not able to institute proceedings, directly and independently, to obtain payment from his clients of fees which were owed to him.[12]

Permission

Applicants for judicial review must first obtain the permission of the court.[13] It **10.154** is unlikely that this will be held to violate Article 6(1) provided the discretion is exercised in a reasonable way and permission is given in properly arguable cases. However, where the proposed application concerns violation of an "arguable" Convention right, pursuant to section 2 of the HRA, the court will have to take account of the jurisprudence relating to Article 13, which requires the state to afford an individual an effective remedy before a national authority in considering whether to grant permission.[14]

13. CONTRIBUTION PROCEEDINGS

In *Skrine & Co. v. Euromoney Publications Plc.*,[15] Marland J. held that the **10.155** making of a contribution order in respect of the settlement of a defamation claim was a breach of Article 10(1), and in deciding the appropriate amount of contribution to award, the court would have to have particular regard to Article 10, pursuant to sections 6 and 12 of the HRA, and would limit it to an amount which was necessary in a democratic society and proportionate.

---

[10] [2001] 1 W.L.R. 840 at 847, para. 18 approved by Lord Steyn in *Daly* at page 1636, para. 28.
[11] (1991) 13 E.H.R.R. 741.
[12] *ibid.*, para. 65.
[13] Supreme Court Act 1981, s.31(3); CPR, Sched. 1; CPR 54.4.
[14] *Boyle & Rice v. United Kingdom* (1988) 10 E.H.R.R. 425; *Silver v. United Kingdom* (1983) 5 E.H.R.R. 347.
[15] [2001] E.M.L.R. 16; *The Times*, November 10, 2000, QBD.

CHAPTER 11
Evidence

1. Introduction

The purpose of this chapter is to consider the impact of the Convention on **11.01** the rules of evidence. Whilst the primary focus is intended to be on civil evidence, most of the Strasbourg case law has been generated in the context of criminal evidence. Although the principles applying to criminal and civil evidence in light of the HRA will often be similar, it is nevertheless likely that (as under pre-HRA domestic law) greater leeway will be given in relation to the admission or assessment of evidence in civil proceedings in light of the fact that the adverse consequences of decisions relating to admissibility and assessment of evidence to a party in a civil action are usually less than to an accused in a criminal prosecution.

2. Domestic Courts' Powers to Control Evidence

Civil Proceedings

In civil proceedings, a court has various powers to control the admission **11.02** of evidence, for example:

(1) CPR 3.1(2)(k) (power to exclude an issue from consideration);

(2) CPR 32.1 (power to control evidence);

(3) CPR 35.1 (duty to restrict expert evidence to that reasonably required to resolve the proceedings); and

(4) CPR 35.4 (court's power to restrict number of experts and issues on which expert evidence may be given).

The general power to control evidence is a far-reaching one and allows a **11.03** court to direct that it requires evidence only on certain issues, and not on others, and to stipulate the type of evidence that may be given and the way in which it is to be placed before the court. In all of its decisions, including those relating to evidence, the court must further consider the overriding objective (CPR 1.1), which includes deciding cases justly. Prior to the CPR, the extent to which a judge in civil proceedings had discretion to exclude relevant and admissible evidence was not clear. There existed no general power to exclude relevant and admissible evidence. However, CPR 32.1(2) provides that the court may use its power under that rule to exclude evidence that is otherwise admissible. The power must be exercised in accordance with the overriding objective of dealing with cases justly: *Grobbelaar v. Sun Newspapers Ltd.*[1] It is evident from the case of

---

[1] *The Times*, August 12, 1999.

General Mediterranean Holdings v. Patel[2] that domestic courts will take the Convention in account in an appropriate case when considering the validity of rules of evidence prescribed by the Civil Procedure Rules.

Criminal Proceedings

11.04 In criminal proceedings, section 78 of the Police and Criminal Evidence Act 1984 states that:

> "(1) In any proceedings the court may refuse to allow evidence on which the prosecution proposes to rely to be given if it appears to the court that, having regard to all the circumstances, including the circumstances in which the evidence was obtained, the evidence would have such an adverse effect on the fairness of the proceedings that the court ought not to admit it.
> (2) Nothing in this section shall prejudice any rule of law requiring a court to exclude evidence."

11.05 Accordingly, a court must have regard to all the circumstances in concluding whether or not the admission of evidence would have such an adverse effect on the fairness of the proceedings that the court ought, in its discretion, to exclude it.

3. GENERAL APPROACH UNDER THE CONVENTION

Absence of Specific Rules of Evidence

11.06 Article 6(1) does not specify any particular rules of evidence in civil proceedings. Issues of admissibility and the probative value to be attached to the evidence are in principle a matter for the domestic courts. Nonetheless, the European Court is concerned about the extent to which rules of evidence may affect the right to a fair trial as a whole and whether the rights of the parties were adequately respected: *Miailhe v. France (No. 2)*[3] Accordingly, any evidential unfairness will be looked at in light of the fairness of the proceedings taken in the round. The way in which both oral and written evidence is admitted or excluded may prejudice the fairness of the hearing, particularly in relation to the ability of a litigant to participate effectively in the proceedings.

11.07 It is important to note that the restraint exercised to date by the European Court in relation to reviewing the admissibility and assessment of evidence by domestic courts is primarily a product of its more distant supervisory role as an international body.[4] The Court takes the view that the assessment of evidence is a matter for the domestic courts and it will not substitute its own view of the facts for an assessment which has been fairly reached by an independent and impartial tribunal. The admissibility of evidence is, therefore, primarily for regulation through national law. This

---

[2] [1999] 3 All E.R. 673.
[3] (1997) 23 E.H.R.R. 491, para. 43.
[4] See, *e.g.* approach taken in *Edwards v. United Kingdom* (1993) 15 E.H.R.R. 417, para.34 and *Miailhe v. France* (1997) 23 E.H.R.R. 491, para.43. See further, K. Reid, *A Practitioner's Guide to the European Convention of Human Rights* (Sweet & Maxwell: 1998), p. 84.

rationale does not, of course, apply to domestic courts. Accordingly, courts are in principle free to develop specific rules regarding the admissibility and assessment of evidence in light of the HRA if the fact that they can more closely assess such matters materially affects the approach that would otherwise be taken by following the European Court.

Admissibility of Evidence

In *Schenk v. Switzerland*,[5] the Court stated: **11.08**

> "While Article 6 of the Convention guarantees the right to a fair trial, it does not lay down any rules on the admissibility of evidence as such, which is therefore primarily a matter for regulation under national law.
> The Court therefore cannot exclude as a matter of principle and in the abstract that unlawfully obtained evidence of the present kind may be admissible. It has only to ascertain whether Mr. Schenk's trial as a whole was fair."[6]

The admissibility of evidence is a matter for the court or tribunal in **11.09** question, and if the European Court's approach is adopted, the touchstone of admissibility is the impact on the fairness of the proceedings as a whole. In *Khan v. United Kingdom*,[7] the European Court emphasised that:

> "It is not the role of the Court to determine, as a matter of principle, whether particular types of evidence—may be admissible or, indeed, whether the applicant was guilty or not. The question which must be answered is whether the proceedings as a whole, including the way in which the evidence was obtained, were fair. This involves an examination of the 'unlawfulness' in question and, where violation of another Convention right is concerned, the nature of the violation found."

The nature of the alleged illegality, and where this amounts to a violation **11.10** of a Convention right, the nature of the violation, will therefore be relevant to the assessment of the fairness of the admission or exclusion of the evidence on the proceedings.

Assessment of evidence. It is for the national court to determine **11.11** the weight to be given to any evidence: *Bernard v. France*.[8] If, however, the national court has drawn arbitrary or unfair conclusions from the evidence before it, the European Court is prepared to interfere: *Edwards v. United Kingdom*.[9]

---

[5] (1991) 13 E.H.R.R. 242. See also *Teixeira de Castro v. Portugal* (1999) 28 E.H.R.R. 101, para.34 and *Khan v. United Kingdom* [2000] 8 B.H.R.C. 310, para. 34.
[6] At para.46.
[7] [2000] 8 B.H.R.C. 310, para. 34.
[8] (2000) 30 E.H.R.R. 808. See also *Alberti v. Italy* (1989) 59 D.R. 100.
[9] (1993) 15 E.H.R.R. 417, para. 34. See also *Van Mechelen v. Netherlands* (1998) 25 E.H.R.R. 647, para. 50; and *Schuler-Zgraggen v. Switzerland* (1993) 16 E.H.R.R. 405 (failure to probe validity of a discriminatory assumption by weighing arguments to the contrary violated Art. 14 taken together with Art. 6(1)).

11.12 **Non-disclosure of evidence.** Non-disclosure of relevant evidence contrary to a duty to disclose can form the basis of a challenge under Article 6(1): *Edwards v United Kingdom*.[10] In *Jespers v. Belgium*,[11] the Commission held that this duty extended to investigating authorities as well as the prosecution and included an obligation to disclose any material to which they could gain access, even if it was not in their possession.

11.13 **Waiver of right to object to evidence.** A party can potentially waive his ability to claim that admission of evidence has violated his right to a fair trial in Article 6(1) if he fails to object to its admission. Accordingly, failure by a litigant to object to the admission or exclusion of evidence is an important, but not necessarily decisive, factor in assessing whether there has been a violation: *X v. United Kingdom*.[12]

11.14 **Ability of appeal to cure evidential defect.** The extent of any subsequent review by a judge or appeal court is important because it may cure any evidential defects at the trial: *Edwards v United Kingdom*.[13] However, the review of undisclosed evidence on appeal will not always remedy the unfairness caused at trial.[14]

4. EVIDENCE OBTAINED BY SELF-INCRIMINATION

Confessions

11.15 Confessions may generally be admitted into evidence provided the domestic courts investigate any allegations of coercion: *Ferrantelli & Santangelo v. Italy*.[15] In *G v. United Kingdom*,[16] the Commission suggested that a confession obtained whilst the accused was kept incommunicado would require careful scrutiny. In *Barbera, Messegue and Jabardo v. Spain*,[17] the Court also expressed reservations about the use of such confessions, especially where the authorities could not clearly demonstrate that the accused had waived his right to the assistance of a lawyer. The admission of evidence obtained as a result of torture or ill-treatment

---

[10] (1993) 15 E.H.R.R. 417 (violation of Art. 6(1) where prosecution failed to disclose evidence to the defendant which might have been used to attack the veracity of the police testimony and conviction was based mainly on the police evidence). See further *Disclosure* in Chap. 10 at paras 10.53 *et seq.*, above.
[11] (1981) 27 D.R. 61.
[12] Application No. 7306/75 (1976) 7 D.R. 115 (counsel and jury were fully aware of the circumstances under which the evidence of an accomplice granted immunity from prosecution was obtained and, whilst this might put in question the fairness of a hearing under Art. 6(1), the applicant's counsel did not object to the accomplice giving evidence—application declared inadmissible); see also *X v. Belgium*, Application No. 8901/80, (1980) 23 D.R. 237.
[13] (1993) 15 E.H.R.R. 417. See also *Jespers v. Belgium* (1981) 27 D.R. 61; *Rowe & Davis v United Kingdom* (2000) 30 E.H.R.R. 1.
[14] *Rowe and Davis v. United Kingdom* (2000) 30 E.H.R.R. 1.
[15] (1997) 23 E.H.R.R.288.
[16] Application No. 9370/81, (1984) 35 D.R. 75.
[17] (1989) 11 E.H.R.R. 360.

with the object of extracting a confession will unquestionably violate Article 6: *Austria v. Italy.*[18]

Evidence Obtained under Compulsory Powers

The admission of evidence obtained by powers of compulsory questioning **11.16** in criminal proceedings may infringe the privilege against self-incrimination implied into Article 6(1). Since the right against self-incrimination does not apply to civil proceedings, the use of evidence which has been compulsorily obtained in the civil context will not infringe Article 6(1). The European Court held in *Saunders v. United Kingdom,*[19] that the provisions of the Companies Act 1985 which allowed evidence given by a defendant to the inspectors to be used against him in a criminal trial breached Article 6. The Court considered that the right not to incriminate oneself together with the right to silence presupposed that the prosecution must prove its case without resorting to evidence obtained through methods of coercion and oppression of the accused.[20] However, in *Staines v. United Kingdom,*[21] the Court declared inadmissible an application based on Article 6(1) and 6(2) where the applicant who was prosecuted under the Company Securities (Insider Dealing) Act 1985 had been compelled to answer Department of Trade and Industry inspectors' questions on oath. The case was different to *Saunders* since the applicant had already provided unsolicited statements to the inspectors, she did not object to the prosecution's use of the statements and the prosecution did not rely on the statements given by the applicant under oath in order to incriminate her.

In *R. v. Morrissey and Staines,*[22] the Court of Appeal considered whether **11.17** a judge should have excluded evidence which the defendants, who had been convicted of insider dealing, had been obliged to give to Department of Trade and Industry inspectors. It held, despite the *Saunders* decision, that the Financial Services Act 1986 expressly authorised the use of such evidence and that this amounted to a statutory rebuttable presumption that the evidence was fair. This decision was overruled in *R. v. Faryab,*[23] which held that section 433 of the Insolvency Act 1986 answers could not be used in a trial for handling stolen goods. In *Official Receiver v. Stern,*[24] the Court of Appeal held that whilst material obtained under compulsion would often be inadmissible, there was no absolute rule to that effect and the issue of a fair trial must be considered in the round. Relevant factors included:

(1) in relation to the hearing:

---

[18] (1963) 6 Y.B. 740. In relation to confessions, see also *R. v. Swaffield, Pavic v. R.* (1998) 151 A.L.R. 98, H C of Australia (confession elicited by an undercover officer breaches the right to silence). *cf. R. v. Liew* [1999] 2 S.C.R. 227; (1999) 7 B.H.R.C. 708, Sup. Ct of Canada (voluntary statements obtained by undercover police officer admissible).

[19] (1997) 23 E.H.R.R. 313.

[20] See also *IJL, GMR and AKP v. United Kingdom,* Application Nos. 29522/95, 30056/96 and 30574/96, September 19, 2000, and *Heaney and McGuinness v. Ireland,* Application No. 34720/97, December 21, 2000. See further para. 14.76.

[21] Application No. 41552/98, May 16, 2000.

[22] *The Times,* May 1, 1997.

[23] [2000] Crim L.R. 180.

[24] [2000] 1 W.L.R. 2230, CA; [2000] U.K.H.R.R. 322.

(a) the nature of the proceedings;

(b) the nature of the allegations; and

(c) the potential stigma involved;

(2) in relation to the gathering of evidence:

(a) the degree of coercion involved in the available investigative procedures;

(b) the degree of prejudice likely to result from the admission of statements obtained by such procedures.

The Court also observed that issues of fairness were generally best left for decision by the trial judge. In *R. v. Hertfordshire County Council, ex p. Green Environmental Industries*,[25] the House of Lords accepted that the protection against self-incrimination was relevant where the prosecution sought to introduce evidence obtained under powers of compulsory questioning in the course of a criminal trial, and that under the HRA it would be incumbent on a judge to consider whether Article 6(1) required the exclusion of such evidence in the exercise of his discretion under section 78 of the Police and Criminal Evidence Act 1984.[26]

11.18 In *Stott (Procurator Fiscal, Dunfermline) v. Brown*,[27] the Privy Council allowed an appeal from the Appeal Court, High Court of Justiciary in Scotland[28] holding that the admission in evidence of replies obtained pursuant to the statutory requirement in section 172 of the Road Traffic Act 1988 on the keeper of the vehicle to identify the driver of the vehicle when required to do so by the police was not incompatible with the privilege against self-incrimination and would not violate Article 6(1). The Judicial Committee stated that the answer under section 172 could not of itself incriminate the suspect, since it was not of itself an offence to drive a car. There was no prolonged questioning, the penalty for declining to answer was moderate and non-custodial and there was no suggestion of improper coercion or oppression such as might give rise to unreliable admissions or contribute to miscarriages of justice. Further, those who owned or drove motor cars knew that by so doing they subjected themselves to a regulatory regime which did not apply to members of the public who did neither, and section 172 represented a proportionate response to the problem of maintaining road safety and of balancing the interests of the community at large and the interests of the individual in a manner which was not unduly prejudicial to the individual.[29]

11.19 The use of evidence obtained pursuant to compulsory powers of questioning will not therefore be automatically excluded from criminal proceedings on the basis of the right against self-incrimination which, as the Privy Council held in *Stott*, is not an absolute right. However, its admission will be judged against the benchmark of a fair trial as a whole. The nature of

---

[25] [2000] 1 All E.R. 773, HL.

[26] *ibid.*, At 781D, *per* Lord Hoffman. Art. 6 did not, however, prohibit the use of compulsory questioning powers during the investigative stage of an inquiry.

[27] [2001] 2 W.L.R. 817; *The Times*, December 6, 2000, PC.

[28] [2000] S.C.C.R. 314.

[29] *Per* Lord Bingham. See also *Director of Public Prosecutions v. Wilson, The Times*, March 21, 2001, Div. Ct. following *Stott*.

the proceedings in question, the circumstances in which the evidence came to be obtained, the consequences of failure to provide answers and the general public interest will be relevant to the decision in each case.[30]

Production of Documents

The European Court of Justice has distinguished between factual informa- **11.20** tion that is accessible from elsewhere (for example public records) or is pre-existing and information which does not pre-exist and might be treated as a confession, regarding the latter as self-incriminating: Case 374/87 *Orkem SA v. Commission*.[31] The European Court of Human Rights has adopted a similar approach to real evidence such as intimate samples.[32] Since the right against self-incrimination is a "testimonial immunity" which protects a person against being forced to speak, it would not seem necessarily to apply to the obtaining of documents, which do not require a person to speak and where the evidence obtained is already in existence.[33] However, in *Funke v. France*,[34] the European Court appears to have regarded the obligation to compel production of incriminating documents as contrary to the right against self-incrimination. The Court held that by attempting to compel the applicant to produce incriminating evidence, namely bank statements relevant to investigations into customs offences that might have been committed by him, the applicant's right to silence and right not to incriminate himself had been infringed. It is unclear whether *Saunders* has overruled *Funke* in relation to the use of documents, production of which is made under compulsory powers, and the right against self-incrimination. In *Saunders*, the Court considered that the privilege against self-incrimination was primarily concerned with the right to remain silent and not with the use of compulsory evidence. It stated that the right did not extend to the use in criminal proceedings of material which may be obtained from the accused through the use of compulsory powers but which had an existence independent of the will of the suspect such as documents acquired pursuant to a warrant or blood, urine and bodily tissue samples.[34A] In *Attorney-General's Reference (No. 7 of 2000)*,[34B] the Court of Appeal upheld the distinction drawn in *Saunders* in preference to the approach in *Funke*.[34C] However, in *J.B. v. Switzerland*,[34D] the European Court adopted an approach which was more analogous to *Funke*, drawing a distinction between material which had an existence independent of the persona concerned and that, including documents, which was obtained by means of coercion. The Court held that the imposition of a fine

---

[30] See further Chap. 14 (Companies and Financial Services), paras 14.66 *et seq.*, below, and Chap. 15 (Insolvency) paras 15.61 *et seq.*, below. See also *R. v. White* (1999) 7 B.H.R.C. 120, Sup, Ct of Canada (statements required by statute unusable in subsequent criminal proceedings).
[31] [1989] E.C.R. 3283, [1991] 4 C.M.L.R. 502, ECJ.
[32] See below.
[33] *Procurator Fiscal, Dunfermline v. Brown* 2000 S.L.T. 379 at 390–391, HCJ Appeal.
[34] (1993) 16 E.H.R.R. 297.
[34A] (1997) 23 E.H.R.R. 313, at para. 69.
[34B] *The Times*, April 12, 2001.
[34C] See also *L v. United Kingdom* [2000] F.L.R. 322 where the European Court endorsed the approach taken by the majority in *Saunders*.
[34D] Application No. 31827/96, May 3, 2001.

in proceedings for tax evasion following the accused's failure to comply with a request to submit certain documents amounted to a violation of his right against self-incrimination.[34E] The case-law seems inconsistent. Whilst there are arguments based on *Funke* and *J.B.* that the admission into evidence of documents (as opposed to bodily samples) obtained pursuant to compulsory powers will violate the right against self-incrimination, *Saunders, L v. United Kingdom*[34F] and *Attorney-General's Reference (No. 7 of 2000)* suggest that their admission will not violate the right.[34G] Where admission of such evidence would render the trial as a whole unfair, there is likely to be a breach of the general right to a fair trial in Article 6 in any event.[35]

11.21   A production order may be made under section 9 of and Schedule 1 to the Police and Criminal Evidence Act 1984 even where it infringes a person's right against self-incrimination: *R. v. Central Criminal Court, ex p. The Guardian, The Observer and Martin Bright.*[36]

Intimate or Physical Samples

11.22   The use in evidence in criminal proceedings of fingerprints, intimate and non-intimate samples does not, of itself, infringe the right against self-incrimination. In *Saunders v. United Kingdom*,[37] the Court stated that the right:

> ". . . does not extend to the use in criminal proceedings of material which may be obtained from the accused through the use of compulsory powers but which has an existence independent of the will of the suspect such as, inter alia, documents acquired pursuant to a warrant, breath, blood and urine samples and bodily tissues for the purpose of DNA testing."[38]

The Commission has held that compulsory urine testing administered in prison does not violate Article 8.[39] Whilst the taking of samples does not of itself violate Article 6, the means by which such samples are obtained may nevertheless involve a breach of the Convention, *e.g.* under Article 8.[39A] In *Attorney-General's Reference No.3 of 1999*,[40] the House of Lords held that it was not a violation of either Article 6 or Article 8 to admit in evidence in respect of a criminal charge a sample of DNA previously and lawfully taken from an accused in respect of another criminal charge of which he was subsequently acquitted.

[34E] See also para. 14.77.
[34F] [2000] F.L.R. 322.
[34G] See the potential areas for challenge outlined in para. 14.78.
[35] See further Chap 14 (Companies and Financial Services), paras 14.74 *et seq.*, below, and Chap. 15 (Insolvency), paras 15.61 *et seq.*, below.
[36] [2001] 1 W.L.R. 662; *The Times*, July 26, 2000 (production order made in relation to journalistic material—two important factors were that Parliament had created safeguards in the form of a series of access conditions, fulfilment of which had to be proved to a court, and a judicial discretion had to be exercised before a production order could be made).
[37] (1997) 23 E.H.R.R. 313.
[38] *ibid.*, at para. 69.
[39] *Peters v. Netherlands* (1999) 27 E.H.R.R. C.D. 241.
[39A] Keir Starmer, *European Human Rights Law* (Legal Action Group, 1999) p. 309.
[40] [2000] 3 W.L.R. 1164, HL.

Entrapment

Evidence obtained by entrapment may infringe Article 6. In *Teixeira de* **11.23**
Castro v. Portugal,[41] two undercover police officers approached a suspected petty drug trafficker and asked if he could obtain some cannabis for
them. He agreed to do so but was unable to locate a supplier. The police
officers then returned to his home and asked if he could obtain some
heroin for them. He took them to another person and they jointly introduced the officers to the applicant, who agreed to supply them with heroin.
On providing the officers with a quantity of heroin, he was arrested and
was subsequently convicted. The European Court held that there had
been a breach of Article 6(1). It stated that the Convention does not
preclude the reliance at the investigative stage on sources such as anonymous informants. However, it emphasised that their use to found a conviction was a different matter and that the use of undercover agents should
be restricted and safeguards put in place. It noted that the Portugese
Government did not argue that the officers' actions were part of a judicially
supervised anti-drugs operation, and they had no good reason to suspect
that the applicant was a drug trafficker since he had no criminal record and
was not known to the police. Further, he did not personally possess drugs
and there was no evidence suggesting that he was predisposed to commit
offences. The Court therefore concluded that the actions of the officers
went beyond those of passive investigation of criminal activity as undercover agents in that they instigated the offence and there was nothing to
suggest that without their intervention it would have been committed.[42]
Accordingly, even the public interest does not justify the use of evidence
obtained as a result of police incitement.

By contrast, where an undercover agent who was placed in a prison **11.24**
eavesdropped on conversations involving the accused, this did not breach
Article 6.[43] In *Lüdi v. Switzerland*,[44] the Court held that by engaging in
criminal activities such as drug dealing, the applicant must have voluntarily
assumed the risk of interference with his private life since he must have
known that he might encounter undercover agents. Accordingly, there was
no breach of Article 8. However, where the agent was not called to give
evidence at trial in order to avoid revealing his identity with the result that
the applicant who wished to clarify the extent to which he had been
influenced by the agent was unable to examine him, this did amount to a
breach of Article 6(1).[44A]

There are now domestic statutory guidelines on the use of informers or **11.25**
undercover officers in the Regulation of Investigatory Powers Act 2000.[45]
In *Attorney-General's Reference (No. 3 of 2000)*[45A] the Court of Appeal
stated that when there was an application to exclude police evidence on

---

[41] (1999) 28 E.H.R.R. 101. See Professor Andrew Ashworth's commentary on this case in
[1998] Crim.L.R. 751 and "Article 6 and the Fairness of Trials" [1999] Crim.L.R.261.
[42] At para.39. *Cf.* the approach taken by the Division Court in *Nottingham City Council v.
Amin* (2000) 1 Cr. App. Rep. 426, *per* Lord. Bingham C.J. See further J. Chalmers, "Test
Purchasing, entrapment and human rights" N.L.J., October 6, 2000, p. 1444.
[43] *X v. Germany* (1989) 11 E.H.R.R. 84.
[44] (1993) 15 E.H.R.R. 173.
[44A] *ibid.*
[45] For guidelines preceding the Act, see *R v. Smurthwaite* [1994] 1 All E.R. 898.
[45A] *The Times*, June 27, 2001, CA.

the ground that an accused had been incited to commit an offence that he would not otherwise have committed, the question to be asked was whether the undercover officers had done more than give the accused an opportunity to break the law which the accused had freely taken.[45B]

Adverse Inferences

11.26 The drawing of adverse inferences from an accused's silence under police questioning where there are insufficient safeguards against unfairness may also infringe Article 6(1).[46]

5. HEARSAY EVIDENCE

Admission of Hearsay Evidence

11.27 The use of peripheral written statements without oral evidence does not automatically make a trial unfair. In *Blastland v. United Kingdom*,[47] a criminal case, the European Commission upheld the English hearsay rule, although it was influenced by the fact that the defendant had had the opportunity to call the maker of the statement.[48] However, where a criminal conviction is based wholly or primarily on hearsay evidence from witnesses whom the applicant did not have the opportunity to examine, the trial may be unfair: *Unterpertinger v. Austria*.[49] The relevant factors which the Court will take into account are:

(1) whether there was an opportunity to challenge a witness whose written evidence is used against the applicant;

(2) the efforts made to find or bring to court an absent witness[50];

(3) whether the hearsay evidence is central to the case or merely peripheral;

(4) whether the outcome is based solely or primarily on the hearsay evidence.

In *Lucà v. Italy*[50A] the European Court held that it could prove necessary in certain circumstances to refer to depositions made at the investigative stage (*e.g.* where a witness refused to give evidence because of intimidation) and their admission into evidence would not in itself contravene

---

[45B] The point of law has been referred to the Appellate Committee of the House of Lords. In relation to entrapment, see also *R. v. Elwell & Derby*, unreported, May 18, 2001, CA (reported on Lawtel) and *R. v. Wright & Livingstone McGregor*, unreported, June 14, 2001, CA.

[46] See *Condron v. United Kingdom* [2000] Crim.L.R. 679; and more generally on the drawing of adverse inferences from the accused's silence at interview or trial, *Murray v. United Kingdom* (1996) 22 E.H.R.R. 29.

[47] (1988) 10 E.H.R.R. 528.

[48] See also *Alberti v. Italy* (1989) 59 D.R. 100 (Art. 6(1) does not exclude the use of indirect evidence which is sufficient in the eyes of the law to establish the guilt of the accused and is produced in the presence of the accused at a public hearing with a view to adversarial argument.

[49] (1991) 13 E.H.R.R. 175; *cf. X v. Germany* (1983) 39 D.R. 43.

[50] *K v. Netherlands* (1993) 74 D.R. 241.

[50A] Application No. 33354/96, February 27, 2001.

Article 6(1) or Article 69(3)(d). However, if the conviction was based solely on the basis of such evidence and the accused or his lawyer did not have the opportunity of challenging the witness at any stage in the proceedings, this could render the trial unfair.

Where a witness cannot attend for examination by reason of serious **11.28** illness or death, reliance on hearsay evidence will not ordinarily violate Article 6, provided that the rights of the accused are protected.[51] If there is an alternative that can avoid recourse to hearsay evidence, for example, by conducting the examination of the witness at his home in the case of illness, this will be a relevant factor.[52] Where a judge exercised his discretion in a criminal case to allow witness statements to be read in evidence because the witnesses were in fear of attending court, he was correct to do so and did not breach the Convention.[53] Evidence from a child witness by television link where a criminal defendant had a full opportunity to cross-examined was not unfair to the defendant.[54]

It is probable that the requirements of Article 6 are more relaxed regarding **11.29** the admission of hearsay evidence in civil, rather than criminal proceedings. In *Clingham v. Kensington & Chelsea London Borough Council*,[55] the Divisional Court held that on an application for a civil anti-social order under section 1 Crime and Disorder Act 1998, the admission of hearsay evidence consisting of statements made by a person who could not be cross-examined did not prevent a fair trial as required by Article 6. It noted that even in a criminal case, there was no automatic exclusion of hearsay evidence.

Article 6(3)(d)

In criminal proceedings, Article 6(3)(d) provides a specific guarantee to an **11.30** accused to "examine or have examined witnesses against him". In *Barbera, Messegue and Jabaro v. Spain*,[56] the European Court stated that this required that:

(1) all the evidence is produced in the presence of the accused;

(2) the examination of witnesses is adversarial.

Further, the accused should have an adequate and proper opportunity to challenge and question a witness against him, either at the time the witness made the statement or subsequently in the proceedings.[57] Article 6(3)(d) does not prevent a court from admitting hearsay evidence, but where this occurs the rights of the accused must be preserved.[58] Relevant factors include the opportunities afforded to the accused to challenge the evidence prior to trial, whether the accused requested the attendance of

---

[51] *Ferrantelli and Santangelo v. Italy* (1997) 23 E.H.R.R. 288. See also *Trivedi v. United Kingdom* [1997] E.H.R.L.R. 521; and *MK v. Austria* (1997) 24 E.H.R.R. C.D. 59.
[52] *Bricmont v. Belgium* (1990) 12 E.H.R.R. 217.
[53] *R. v. Denton The Times*, November 22, 2000, CA.
[54] *R. v. Redbridge Youth Court, ex p. Director of Public Prosecutions*, unreported, March 22, 2001, D. C.
[55] *The Times*, February 20, 2001, D. C.
[56] (1989) 11 E.H.R.R. 360.
[57] *Kostovski v. Netherlands* (1990) 12 E.H.R.R. 434.
[58] *ibid.*

the witness and the overall impact of the evidence on the fairness of the trial. Where witnesses abscond, the admission of hearsay evidence may breach Article 6(3)(d) if that evidence is crucial to the case.[59] Further, whilst the use of anonymous witnesses is not specifically prohibited by Article 6(3)(d), the measures restricting the rights of the accused must be the least restrictive possible,[60] and where a conviction is based solely or primarily on evidence from anonymous witnesses, this is likely to infringe the Article.[61]

Exclusion of Hearsay Evidence

11.31 The exclusion of hearsay evidence is not contrary to Article 6(1) where its purpose is partly to ensure that the best evidence is before the court and partly to avoid undue weight being given to evidence which cannot be tested by cross-examination.[62]

6. UNLAWFULLY OBTAINED EVIDENCE

Unlawfully Obtained Evidence

11.32 Under the case law developed by the European Court in criminal cases, evidence obtained unlawfully or illegally is not excluded automatically, although its admission may be unfair on the facts of a particular case. The Court's position was stated in *Mantovanelli v France*:

> " . . . the Convention does not lay down rules on evidence as such. The Court therefore cannot exclude as a matter of principle and in the abstract that evidence obtained in breach of provisions of domestic law may be admitted. It is for the national courts to assess the evidence they have obtained and the relevance of any evidence that a party wishes to have produced. The Court has nevertheless to ascertain whether the proceedings considered as a whole, including the way in which the evidence was taken, were fair as required by Article 6(1)."[63]

11.33 In considering illegally obtained evidence, the court must assess whether the proceedings as a whole were fair, taking into account:

(1) the manner in which the evidence has been obtained;

(2) the role it has played in the trial or hearing; and

(3) the opportunity afforded to the litigant to challenge it.

---

[59] *Delta v. France* (1993) 16 E.H.R.R. 574; *cf. Doorson v. Netherlands* (1996) 22 E.H.R.R. 330 (witness absconded but domestic court could have regard to his statement since it was corroborated by other evidence).
[60] *Van Mechelen v. Netherlands* (1998) 25 E.H.R.R. 647.
[61] *Doorson v. Netherlands* (1996) 22 E.H.R.R. 330.
[62] *Blastland v. United Kingdom* (1988) 10 E.H.R.R. 528, (1987) 52 D.R. 273.
[63] (1997) 24 E.H.R.R. 370, para. 34. See also *Schenk v. Switzerland* (1991) 13 E.H.R.R. 242, paras 46–48; *X v. Germany* (1989) 11 E.H.R.R. 84.

In *Miailhe v. France (No. 2)*,[64] a prosecution based partly on documents **11.34** that had been unlawfully obtained was not unfair. In *Schenk v Switzerland*,[65] the use in evidence of a recording, which was not ordered by the investigative judge, did not render the trial automatically unfair or of itself found a violation.

Evidence Obtained in Breach of a Fundamental Right

One of the key issues which arises in relation to evidence is whether a **11.35** court has power to exclude evidence obtained in breach of a Convention right, for example, by illicit telephone tapping, intrusive surveillance or unlawful access to bank account information. The issue of admissibility of evidence obtained through breach of a fundamental or constitutional right is a narrower issue than the admission of unlawfully obtained evidence discussed above.

In *Schenk v Switzerland*,[66] the allegation against the accused was that he **11.36** hired a man to kill his wife. Part of the evidence against him was a tape recording of a telephone conversation between the accused and the man he had hired, made by the latter. The Swiss courts admitted the evidence. The applicant argued that the evidence had been obtained unlawfully and its admission made his trial unfair in breach of Article 6. The Swiss Government did not dispute that the recording had been obtained unlawfully. The Court found that the admission of the evidence, which had been obtained in breach of Article 8, did not itself violate the requirements of Article 6. The Court relied upon the fact that the rights of the defence were not disregarded, the applicant was not unaware that the recording complained of was unlawful and he had the opportunity (which he took) of challenging its authenticity and opposing its use, having initially agreed that it should be heard. That his attempts were unsuccessful made no difference. The fact that the man allegedly hired was a witness to give evidence of what the applicant had said during the telephone conversation was also emphasised by the Court.

In the leading case of *Khan v.United Kingdom*,[67] evidence was obtained **11.37** for use in criminal proceedings by use of a secret bugging device. It was submitted on behalf of the defendant first, that there had been a violation of Article 8, secondly, that a conviction obtained solely on the basis of such evidence was incompatible with Article 6, and thirdly, that section 78 of the Police and Criminal Evidence Act 1984 was not capable of affording an effective remedy under Article 13. This raised the question of whether a criminal court, in considering its power under section 78, was required or permitted to have regard to the jurisprudence of the Convention and if so, whether a violation of the Convention was to be regarded by itself as a ground for excluding otherwise admissible evidence. The judge allowed the evidence to be admitted at the trial. The Court of Appeal held that the Convention was irrelevant because no ambiguity in the legislation existed.

---

[64] (1993) 16 E.H.R.R. 332.
[65] (1991) 13 E.H.R.R. 242.
[66] (1991) 13 E.H.R.R. 242.
[67] The European Court judgment is reported at (2000) 8 B.H.R.C. 310; [2000] Crim.L.R. 684.

The House of Lords[68] dismissed the appeal and held that Convention case law under Article 6 did not establish the admission into evidence of material obtained in breach of a right of respect to private life will necessarily render a criminal trial unfair. The European Court held that the installation of the listening device was not in accordance with the law,[69] since the Home Office Guidelines of 1984, which regulated covert surveillance at the relevant time, were neither legally binding nor sufficiently publicly accessible and were therefore inadequate to meet the requirements of Article 8. Accordingly, the Court found a violation of Article 8 in relation to the obtaining of the covert surveillance evidence. In relation to Article 6, the Court stated that where unlawfully obtained evidence was relied upon to secure a conviction, the compatibility of the proceedings with Article 6 would depend on an examination of the nature of the unlawful activity alleged and if it involved a violation of another Convention right, the nature of the violation found. In examining the nature of the unlawful activity, the Court noted that, since no legally enforceable right to privacy then existed in English law, the use of the listening device was not unlawful under domestic law at the relevant time. In addition, the police had acted compatibly with the Home Office Guidelines and the incriminatory statements were made voluntarily and without incitement. The "unlawfulness" therefore related solely to the absence of a statutory basis for the surveillance. Where the unlawfully obtained evidence was very strong, the need for supporting evidence became correspondingly weaker. The applicant had had the opportunity of challenging both the authenticity and use of the tape and as soon as the evidence was ruled admissible, he changed his plea to guilty. Further, the discretion under section 78 of the Police and Criminal Evidence Act 1984 had been decided on the question of the impact of admission of the evidence on the fairness of the trial at all levels up to the House of Lords. Accordingly, there was no violation of Article 6.[70]

Admission of Unlawfully Obtained Evidence and Article 8

11.38　　In *Schenk v. Switzerland*,[71] the European Court rejected an argument that the use made of the evidence obtained in breach of Article 8 at the applicant's trial was also contrary to Article 8, holding that the question was subsumed within the complaint under Article 6.

---

[68] *The Times*, July 5, 1996, CA.

[69] Citing *Govell v United Kingdom* [1999] E.H.R.L.R. 121. The Police Act 1997 and the Regulation of Investigatory Powers Act 2000 now regulate the use of covert surveillance devices by the police. See also *A v. France* (1994) 17 E.H.R.R. 462; *Choudhary v. United Kingdom,* Application No. 40084/98, May 4, 1999.

[70] The European Court did, however, find a violation of Art. 13 by reason of the failure of the U.K. to provide any adequate remedy for the violation of Art. 8 (the discretion to exclude the evidence under the Police and Criminal Evidence Act 1984, s.78, being an insufficient remedy). The Court also rejected the Government's submission that it was open to the applicant to lodge a complaint with the Police Complaints Authority. It noted the role played by the Secretary of State in appointing and dismissing members of this body, and considered that the system failed to meet the required standard of independence to ensure protection against abuse of authority. See also *Govell v. United Kingdom* [1999] E.H.R.L.R. 121.

[71] (1991) 13 E.H.R.R. 242, paras 52–53.

Domestic Courts' Approach

It is unclear whether domestic courts will exercise their broad discretion in **11.39** relation to the control of evidence in order to exclude evidence obtained in violation of a Convention right, even where the admission of that evidence would *not* prejudice a fair trial. However, at least in the criminal law context, the courts would not seem to be adopting any principle of automatic or prima facie exclusion.

Prior to the entry into force of the HRA, in *Morgans v. Director of Public* **11.40** *Prosecutions*,[72] the House of Lords held that information recorded by an unwarranted telephone call logging device attached to a suspected computer hacker's telephone line should neither be used in evidence nor disclosed to the defence on the basis that the prohibitions were inconsistent with the defendant's right to a fair trial.[73] However, neither Article 6 nor Article 8 was expressly considered. Subsequently, in *R. v. X, Y & Z*,[74] the Court of Appeal held that domestic courts should attach "considerable importance" to any breach of Article 8 in determining an application under section 78 to exclude evidence but that it was still necessary to review and balance all the circumstances of the case. The House of Lords considered the issue following the entry into force of the HRA in *R. v. P*.[75] The case concerned the prosecution of a number of British defendants under section 20 of the Misuse of Drugs Act 1971 in connection with the alleged commission of drugs offences in two other European Union countries. The authorities in one of those countries had lawfully obtained an order authorising the interception of telephone calls between one of their nationals and the British defendants, which resulted in recordings of various such conversations. The question of admissibility of those recordings arose. It was not disputed that the use made of an intercept could amount to a breach of Article 8. However, since the relevant information had been lawfully obtained pursuant to statutory authority and judicial supervision, there was no breach of Article 8. In relation to Article 6, their Lordships noted that the critical question was the fairness of the trial and that the fair use of intercept evidence meant that the trial did not breach Article 6, even if that evidence was unlawfully obtained. However, Article 6 entitled the accused to the opportunity to challenge its use and admission in evidence and to a judicial assessment of its admission upon the fairness of the trial. This was provided by section 78 of the Police and Criminal Evidence Act 1984 and the direct operation of Articles 6 and 8 did not invalidate the role of section 78 as the means by which questions of the use of evidence obtained in breach of Article 8 were to be resolved at a criminal trial. The same criterion of fairness applied under Article 6 and section 78. In *R. v. Baily, Brewin & Gangji*[75A] the Court of Appeal applied *R. v. P* in holding that the fairness of a trial required that the best evidence of what was said should be admissible. Accordingly, there was no reason why the principle by which a witness was permitted to refresh his memory should be confined to reading a piece of paper. If modern technology such as tape recordings

---

[72] February 17, 2000.
[73] Citing *R. v. Preston* [1994] 2 A.C. 130.
[74] *The Times*, May 23, 2000, CA.
[75] [2001] 2 W.L.R. 463, HL.
[75A] March 19, 2001, CA.

provided a better or different means for the same purpose, it should be available in court. The criteria concerning fairness under Article 6 and an application for exclusion of evidence under section 78 were the same. On the facts, the evidence was not obtained in violation of Article 8 and its admission would not violate Article 6. In *R. v. Bailey,*[76] the Court of Appeal upheld the judge's decision to admit into evidence covert tape recorded conversations, holding that there was no violation of Article 6 in so doing.[77] In *R. v. Loveridge, Lee & Loveridge*[77A] the Court of Appeal upheld the appellants' convictions as safe despite the police having unlawfully video-taped them at court and adduced the evidence of a facial mapping expert to compare that video with CCTV footage. The breach of Article 8 did not violate the appellants' right to a fair hearing and the evidence was admissible under section 78 Police and Criminal Evidence Act 1984 because it did not prevent a fair trial. In *R. v. Wright & Livingstone McGregor,*[77B] the Court of Appeal stated that there was no rule of public policy in English law that telephone intercept and video surveillance evidence should not be used at criminal trials. The critical question was the fairness of the trial.

11.41 The relevant principles for the domestic courts may perhaps be summarised as follows.

(1) evidence obtained in breach of a Convention right may be excluded by domestic courts, although there is no express obligation to do so unless it will render the proceedings as a whole unfair and in violation of Article 6(1);

(2) where admission of evidence would render the proceedings as a whole unfair, a court is under a duty pursuant to section 6(1) of the HRA to exclude the evidence;

(3) however, a court is not obliged to exclude evidence in either criminal or civil proceedings merely on the ground that it was obtained in violation of a Convention right.

7. OTHER JURISDICTIONS

11.42 In considering whether to exercise the discretion to exclude evidence obtained in breach of a Convention right that is otherwise admissible, it may be instructive to consider the approaches of other common law jurisdictions.[78] Few jurisdictions have formulated an absolute rule of exclusion of evidence obtained through breach of a fundamental right. Even

---

[76] [2001] EWCA Crim. 733.

[77] The Court expressly did not decide whether there were breaches of the relevant statutory principles or of Art. 8 but stated that even if it had, the members of the court remained wholly unconvinced that anything the police officers did caused any unfair prejudice to the appellants (para.34).

[77A] *The Times,* May 3, 2001, CA.

[77B] unreported, June 14, 2001, CA.

[78] See generally the Joint Written Comments by Justice and Liberty to the European Court in the case of *Khan v. United Kingdom,* dated September 17, 1999, by Andrew Ashworth Q.C. (available from Justice's offices—see para. 8.82 above, for contact details).

where this has occurred, (*e.g.* the United States) exceptions have subsequently been allowed. In some jurisdictions, (*e.g.* Canada) the question of whether the violation was in good faith is material. The approaches vary according to whether the rationale for exclusion of evidence is to uphold the administration of justice, (*e.g.* Canada) to protect constitutional rights, (*e.g.* Trinidad and Tobago) or to deter police misconduct, (*e.g.* the United States).

New Zealand. The New Zealand Bill of Rights Act 1990 does not **11.43** expressly provide for the exclusion of evidence obtained through violation of a fundamental right. However, in *Simpson v. Attorney-General (Baigent's Case)*,[79] the New Zealand Court of Appeal adopted a principle of prima facie exclusion of evidence obtained in violation of the 1990 Act. Hardie Boys J. noted that the principle was justifiable to emphasise the importance of those rights, to preserve the integrity of the administration of justice and to secure general recognition by law enforcement authorities of the rights affirmed by the relevant sections of the Act.[80] Some of the more recent New Zealand decisions have indicated a willingness to consider the restriction of rights in the wider public interest provided the circumstances do not bring the law into disrepute, *e.g. R. v. Grayson and Taylor*.[81]

Canada. Section 24(2) of the Charter of Rights and Freedoms **11.44** states that evidence obtained in breach of a Charter right must be excluded if: "having regard to all the circumstances, the admission of it in proceedings would bring the administration of justice into disrepute." The standard of "disrepute" is an objective test by reference to the standard of the reasonable citizen. In *R v. Collins*,[82] the Supreme Court held that the courts, when applying section. 24 (2), should take into account:

(1) whether the admission of the evidence would affect the fairness of the trial;

(2) whether the violation of the Charter was serious, or in good faith, inadvertent, technical or motivated by urgency; and

(3) whether the effect of excluding the evidence might itself bring the administration of justice into disrepute, particularly if a serious charge would be jeopardised by a non-serious breach of the Charter, although the seriousness of the offence should not otherwise be a reason for admitting the evidence.

Where the material exists independently of the Charter violation, (*e.g.* real evidence; *cf.* self-incriminatory evidence), this will be an important factor.[83]

---

[79] [1994] 3 N.Z.L.R. 667.
[80] See also *R. v. Kirifi* [1992] 2 N.Z.L.R. 8 (exclusion of admissions by accused questioned without being informed of his right to a lawyer) and *R. v. Te Kira* [1993] 3 N.Z.L.R. 257.
[81] [1997] 1 N.Z.L.R. 399 at 411.
[82] [1987] 1 S.C.R. 265.
[83] *R. v. Plant* [1993] 3 S.C.R. 281.

11.45	**United States.** The Fourth Amendment to the U.S. Constitution declares a right not to be subjected to unlawful search and seizure. In *Mapp v. Ohio*,[84] the U.S. Supreme Court held that evidence obtained in breach of this right should be excluded automatically from trial in the State courts. However, in subsequent decisions, the exclusionary rule has been modified, for example, it does not apply if the law enforcement officers acted in good faith in relying on a warrant that was legally defective: *United States v. Leon*.[85]

11.46	**South Africa.** Section 35 of the Constitution Act 1996 provides that evidence obtained through the breach of a constitutional right must be excluded if its admission "would render the trial unfair or otherwise be detrimental to the administration of justice". In *State v. Motloutsi*,[86] the court stated that a strict exclusionary approach would be appropriate in a case where there had been a conscious and deliberate breach of a constitutionally protected right unless "extraordinary excusing circumstances" existed, but that a principle of discretionary exclusion should apply to unfairly obtained evidence generally.[87]

11.47	**Trinidad and Tobago.** The Judicial Committee of the Privy Council held in *Mohammed v. The State*,[88] in relation to an appeal from Trinidad and Tobago, that the fact of a breach of a constitutional right would be a cogent factor in favour of exclusion of evidence in order to respect the constitutional character of the infringed right and accord it a high value.[89]

8. EVIDENCE OBTAINED BY COVERT SURVEILLANCE FOR PURPOSE OF CIVIL LITIGATION

11.48	The right to respect for private life in Article 8 (and depending on the nature of the intrusion, possibly also the right to peaceful enjoyment of possessions in Article 1 of the First Protocol) may have implications for evidence obtained by covert video surveillance or by inquiry agents for use in litigation, at least where the party carrying out the surveillance is a public body.[90]

---

[84] 367 U.S. 643n (1960). See also *Weeks v. United States* 232 U.S. 383 (1913), and *McNabb v. United States* 318 U.S. 332 (1942).
[85] 468 U.S. 897 (1984) *cf. Commonwealth v. Edmunds* 586 A.2d 887 (1991). See also evidence obtained in violation of the Fifth Amendment right to counsel: *Miranda v. Arizona* 384 U.S. 436 (1965) *cf. New York v. Quarles* 467 U.S. 649 (1984).
[86] [1996] 1 S.A.C.R. 78C.
[87] See also *State v. Melani* [1995] 2 S.A.C.R. 141E, relying on an Irish decision in *The People (Attorney-General) v. O'Brien* [1965] I.R. 142, where the Supreme Court of Ireland held that where evidence has been obtained by breach of a constitutional right, there is a much stronger presumption that the evidence should be excluded than where there has merely been some other unlawful act during the investigation.
[88] [1999] 2 W.L.R. 552, PC; [1999] 2 A.C. 111.
[89] At See 562–563.
[90] See, *e.g. R v. Broadcasting Standards Commission, ex p. British Broadcasting Corporation* [2000] 3 W.L.R. 1327, CA.

Strasbourg Approach

Article 8 is vertical in its effect, in that it is intended to restrain arbitrary **11.49**
interferences with individual privacy by *public authorities*, although the
European Court has engineered a certain degree of horizontal effect
through the doctrine of positive obligations.[91] There is very limited Strasbourg authority on the use of covert surveillance evidence in civil proceedings. In *J.S. v. United Kingdom*,[92] the European Commission treated the
surveillance of one private individual by another (an insurance company)
in connection with a claim as falling outside the ambit of Article 8, because
there was no indication that the activities of the insurance company were
conducted in a way which could give rise to positive obligations on the part
of the State and declared the application inadmissible. In arriving at its
conclusion, the Commission did not appear unduly concerned about the
fact of the surveillance, noting that:

> " . . . the insurance company's activities were directed to protecting its
> position in litigation which had taken place between the applicant's
> husband as plaintiff and the company, and . . . there is no reason to
> suppose that the insurance company was conducting any kind of
> 'vendetta' against the applicant or her husband."

However, in *Klass v. Germany*,[93] the European Court summarised its **11.50**
misgivings about the growth of covert State surveillance:

> " . . . powers of secret surveillance of citizens, characterising as they
> do the police state, are tolerable under the Convention only insofar as
> strictly necessary for safeguarding the democratic institutions"[94]

This reasoning potentially also applies to surveillance for the purpose of **11.51**
obtaining evidence in litigation. In *Arnott v. United Kingdom*,[95] the applicants complained of being the subject of surveillance in error by a detective agency hired by an insurance company on about twenty-five
occasions over three years. The insurance company were attempting to
prove fraud by a claimant, who was unconnected to the applicants in
ongoing proceedings, but the detective agency erroneously kept under
surveillance the applicants and not the relevant claimant. The Court struck
the application out of its list following a friendly settlement by the Government in the sum of £1,000 including legal costs. Whilst the case concerns
surveillance for the purpose of litigation, the complaint was directed to the
lack of a domestic remedy in relation to the surveillance and, following the
friendly settlement, was not considered on its merits. The forthcoming
European Court decision in *Peck v. United Kingdom*,[95A] which concerns
CCTV in public areas and the extent to which this infringes the right to

---

[91] See paras 5.28 *et seq.*, above.
[92] Application No. 19173/91, January 8, 1993. See also the Commission decision in *Bausson
v. France*, Application No. 21120/93, December 1, 1993 (French text only).
[93] (1980) 2 E.H.R.R. 214.
[94] See para. 42.
[95] Application No. 44866/98, October 3, 2000.
[95A] Application No. 44647/98.

privacy, will no doubt provide some guidance for courts on the Court's approach to the issue.[95B]

Likely Approach of Courts Post-HRA to Surveillance Evidence

11.52 Although the Regulation of Investigatory Powers Act 2000 regulates covert and intrusive surveillance by the police, intelligence services and other public authorities,[96] it does not authorise or address surveillance for the purpose of use in evidence in civil proceedings. A domestic civil court faced with an application to exclude surveillance evidence from use in evidence on the ground that it has been obtained in violation of the right to respect for privacy will have to start from basic principles.[96A] To decide whether the evidence has been obtained in breach of Article 8, the court will have to ask itself:

> (1) Whether the surveillance engages Article 8(1)? This will involve considering:
>
>> (a) whether the party who has instructed or carried out the surveillance is a true public authority? If so, Article 8(1) is engaged because section 6 of the HRA requires such an authority to comply with the Convention in relation to all of its acts;
>>
>> (b) If a hybrid body carries out the surveillance, does the act of surveillance constitute carrying out a "public function"? It is suggested that it is unlikely in most cases to do so;
>>
>> (c) If the surveillance is carried out by a private individual or a hybrid body in the exercise of a private function, then, subject to arguments about the court's own duties to protect private individuals from surveillance by other private individuals under section 6 of the HRA,[97] Article 8 is not engaged.
>
> (2) If Article 8 is not engaged, then the surveillance evidence was not obtained in violation of a Convention right.
>
> (3) If Article 8 is engaged, the court will then need to address:
>
>> (a) whether the surveillance is justified within the categories set out in Article 8(2)—the most relevant justification will be "the protection of the rights and freedoms of others" and the party who obtained the surveillance evidence will no doubt argue that it was obtained in order to protect his right to a fair trial under Article 6(1) or at common law[98];

[95B] See further paras 19.52 *et seq.* on surveillance generally.

[96] C.23. See generally Pt II, and particularly ss 26–29, and Sched. 1.

[96A] This section considers the application of the Convention. It is beyond its scope to consider the Data Protection Act 1998, though this will also be relevant to surveillance.

[97] See further para. 11.55, below.

[98] If the subject of the surveillance may be committing a fraud, the category relating to "the prevention of crime" may also be relevant.

(b) whether the surveillance is in accordance with law? Unlike state agencies who now operate under a statutory regime,[99] there is no statutory code expressly authorising public authorities to carry out covert surveillance of private individuals for the purpose of furthering their own defence to a claim made by that person in litigation. Surveillance is not of itself a criminal offence. Neither has it amounted to a tort to date,[1] although this may well be because a freestanding right to privacy was not recognised in England and Wales prior to the case of *Douglas v. Hello!*,[2] there was no recognition by the English courts of a right of privacy *per se*.[3] Nonetheless, the European Court has required interferences with an individual's privacy to be positively authorised by either domestic or international law, and to be sufficiently clear and publicly accessible in order to satisfy with the Article 8(2) requirement to "be in accordance with law".[3A] This is the hurdle at which most state agencies have fallen, in challenges to secret surveillance before the European Court, and it will be necessary for a court to consider whether any surveillance by a private individual for the purpose of court proceedings is "in accordance with law" by reason of the courts' historic acceptance of the practice of obtaining surveillance evidence for the purpose of court proceedings[4];

(c) whether the surveillance is necessary in a democratic society, *i.e.* whether it answers a pressing social need and is proportionate. The need to avoid fraudulent claims by litigants is likely to constitute a "pressing social need" and the primary issue will be proportionality. This will turn on the degree of intrusion into private life and the extent to which the surveillance assists the party who has carried it out or the court in assessing a claim brought by the subject of the surveillance. For example, surveillance in a public place of an activity that is not inherently private in nature is more likely to be proportionate than entry into a person's house under false pretences or filming from outside into a person's private living room.

In summary, in the case of a private individual and (probably also) a hybrid body, the covert surveillance of another private individual for the purpose   **11.53**

---

[99] See the Police Act 1997 and the Regulation of Investigatory Powers Act 2000.
[1] See *Kaye v. Robertson, The Times,* March 21, 1990, where the courts could not provide a remedy to a television actor who was subjected to a reporter taking photographs of him without his consent when he was seriously injured in hospital following an accident.
[2] [2001] 2 W.L.R. 992; *The Times,* January 16, 2001, CA.
[3] In the case of surveillance for litigation, there is no equitable duty of confidence owed by the party carrying out the surveillance to the subject of the surveillance.
[3A] See paras 4.43 *et seq.*, above.
[4] The courts, if not Parliament, would do well to take the opportunity to lay down clear legal guidelines regarding the legitimate use of inquiry agents and practice of obtaining covert video surveillance evidence, so that there is a clear and accessible legal code for the obtaining of such evidence for the purpose of court proceedings.

of obtaining evidence for court proceedings, Article 8 is not engaged and any evidence is not obtained in violation of Article 8. Accordingly, no issue of evidence obtained in breach of a Convention right arises. In the case of a true public authority (or in the unusual event that surveillance by a hybrid body for the purpose of court proceedings constitutes a public function), Article 8 is engaged and the surveillance may have been obtained in violation of Article 8 unless it can be shown that it was carried out "in accordance with law" and that the interference with private life was proportionate.

Article 1 of Protocol No. 1

11.54 If the surveillance took place on property owned by the claimant, there might also be an argument that this infringes the claimant's right to peaceful enjoyment of his possessions under Article 1 of the First Protocol.

Court's Duty under Section 6 of the HRA

11.55 Even if the court finds that evidence was obtained in violation of Article 8, it is not under any duty to automatically exclude it. If the surveillance does violate Article 8, the court will not act incompatibly with the Convention pursuant to section 6 of the HRA in relation to the admission or exclusion of the evidence provided that the trial as a whole is fair. If the surveillance does not engage or violate Article 8 because it is commissioned by an insurance company indemnifying a private individual, in the absence of the type of full horizontal effect envisaged by Professor Wade,[5] the court will not be acting in breach of the Convention in admitting evidence which is not itself obtained in breach of any Convention right. However, where the admission of evidence under ordinary principles of evidence makes the trial unfair pursuant to Article 6(1), the court will be acting unlawfully within the meaning of section 6 of the HRA.

Domestic Case Law

11.56 Pre-CPR, the position was that evidence taken out of court in the form of video recordings was admissible in domestic courts.[5A] A surveillance video taken of the claimant in order to show that he was a malingerer had to be disclosed in advance of the trial.[5B] Post-HRA, in *Rall v. Hume*,[5C] the Court of Appeal gave guidance on the practice to be followed where a defendant wishes to deploy video evidence at the trial of a personal injuries claim in order to cast doubt upon the claim made by the claimant. The claimant suffered injury to her neck, shoulder and lower back as a result of an accident. In seeking to establish whether the claimant was indeed unable to perform the activities she had alleged she could not

---

[5] See para. 5.49, above.
[5A] *J. Barber & Sons v. Lloyd's Underwriters* [1987] Q.B. 103, Evans J. (taking of evidence by videotape from abroad); *Taylor v. Chief Constable of Cheshire* [1986] 1 W.L.R. 1479, DC (evidence of a witness to an alleged crime about what was seen on an erased video tape admissible).
[5B] *Khan v. Armaguard Ltd* [1994] 1 W.L.R. 1204, CA.
[5C] [2001] 3 All E.R. 248, CA.

perform, the defendant secretly filmed the claimant on two occasions. The two video films were alleged to show the Claimant going about her tasks without much difficulty. They included footage filmed through the windows of the claimant's house showing her movements within the home and also inside a nursery with her child. The defendant wished to rely on the video evidence but because it had not been disclosed in the usual way, the court considered at a case management conference whether permission should be given to introduce it. The judge indicated that in principle, he was prepared to allow the evidence to be admitted except for the footage showing the claimant inside her own home and the nursery. However, the judge refused to admit the evidence because the defendant had failed to disclose the evidence in sufficient time and it would mean that the time allowed for trial of four hours would be insufficient. An appeal against the decision was made but was subsequently dismissed. A further appeal was then made to the Court of Appeal who agreed to hear the appeal because it felt that the case raised an issue of public importance, because neither the CPR nor the Practice Directions contained any rule or particular direction as to the use of video evidence for the purpose of cross-examination and casting doubt upon the claim. The Court allowed the appeal and decided that the video evidence was admissible as a document within the extended meaning contained in CPR 31.4. If disclosure is made in accordance with CPR Part 31, the claimant will be deemed to admit the authenticity of the film unless notice is served that the claimant wishes the document to be proved at trial. If the claimant does so, the defendant must serve a witness statement by the person who took the film in order to prove its authenticity. If the claimant does not do so, the film is, in the absence of any ruling to the contrary, available to the defendant for the purpose of cross-examination of the claimant or the claimant's medical experts. The court observed that if video evidence existed which portrayed an overall level and freedom of activity which was inconsistent with the picture presented in the medical reports and statement of the claimant, justice to the defendant requires an opportunity to cross-examine on the content of the videos.[5D] The court left open the question of whether the footage alleged to amount to an intrusion into the claimant's privacy was admissible because the defendant was content to abandon reliance upon the footage complained of.[5E] *Rall* has provided an express legal basis for admission into evidence of video evidence through CPR 31.4, though the absence of a legal basis for surveillance interfering with Article 8(1) rights remains. It is unfortunate that the Court did not have occasion to substantively address the issue of privacy or indeed to consider the implications of Article 8. The lower court appears to have assumed that it was under an obligation to exclude evidence that might be said to infringe privacy although it is only necessary to do so if it infringes Article 6(1). It might also be questioned whether filming in a child's nursery, as opposed to the claimant's home, would infringe the right to respect for private life within the meaning of Article 8(1). In relation to the wider issue of covert surveillance other than for court proceedings, some guidance as to the courts' likely approach may be found in *R. v. Broadcasting Standards*

[5D] At para. 22.
[5E] *ibid.*

Commission, ex p. British Broadcasting Corporation.[6] The BBC had made a secret film in 1997 of transactions involving staff at Dixons' stores for a consumer programme which concerned the selling of second-hand goods as new. Dixons were told that there had been secret filming of 12 purchases in Dixons' stores and they were asked to respond to allegations that they sold second-hand goods as though they were new. The secret filming did not in fact reveal evidence of misselling and the secret filming was not used in the programme. The British Standards Commission ("BSC") concluded that the programme makers did not have sufficient evidence to warrant the decision to film secretly in Dixons' stores and found that the infringement of Dixons' privacy was unwarranted. Forbes J. accepted that Article 8 was not designed or intended to protect companies and held that the Broadcasting Act 1996 should be construed in conformity with the Convention and restricted to human individuals. He held that the approach of the BSC that secret filming alone was an infringement of privacy even when the event was being filmed in public, was wrong in law.[7] At the Court of Appeal stage, Liberty as intervener submitted that the case-law derived from the European Convention of Human Rights and the Canadian Charter of Rights and Freedom supported a contention that to film a person without his consent was in itself a breach of the right to privacy because it interfered with the idea of personal autonomy or control every person has over his own identity.[8] The Court of Appeal, however, decided the matter on the basis of domestic law, holding that the Broadcasting Act 1996 did extend to the privacy of a company and that to so hold did not conflict with the Convention. The Court stated that it would not use Article 8 case-law to cut down the protection which the statute otherwise afforded and upheld the Broadcasting Standards Commission's decision that there was an infringement of privacy because there was no justification for the secret filming. The Court attached importance to the fact that the filming was secret and rejected a submission on behalf of the BBC that this was immaterial. The Court of Appeal's approach suggests that domestic courts are likely to generally seek to safeguard the privacy of individuals from covert surveillance.

11.57 However, past practice and current indications suggest that it is unlikely that the domestic courts will seek to exclude all surveillance evidence obtained for the purpose of litigation. In *The Law Debenture Trust Group v The Pensions Ombudsman*,[9] Alliott J. disagreed with the Pensions Ombudsman, who had considered that the covert surveillance of the complainant was an unwarranted intrusion into his private and family life amounting to maladministration by the trustees of a pension scheme and the independent trustee. His lordship regarded such surveillance as "not unlawful" and "a legitimate course to pursue on appropriate occasions in the investigation of claims". He was however swayed by his observation that in personal injury work, covert surveillance of claimants suspected of malingering is not uncommon and is not challenged as inadmissible or unlawful. This view may have to be revisited in the context of a challenge

---

[6] [2000] 3 W.L.R. 1327, CA.
[7] *The Times,* September 14, 1999, [1999] E.M.L.R. 858.
[8] Reliance was placed upon *Les Editions Vice-Versa v. Aubrey* [1998] 5 B.H.R.C. 437.
[9] [1999] O.P.L.R. 167, Alliott J.

to the admissibility or lawfulness of such evidence under the HRA, especially in light of the recent recognition of a freestanding right to privacy.[10] Further challenges to the admissibility of evidence obtained by inquiry agents are likely to be made using the HRA and the place, manner and methods of surveillance will be subjected to increasing scrutiny.

9. EXPERT EVIDENCE

Assessors or Court-Appointed Experts

Part 35.15 gives the Court the power to appoint assessors and confers a **11.58** wide discretion in respect of the use that is made of them. Although the parties can object to the identity of an assessor at the stage his or her appointment is made, the practice direction specifically provides that thereafter no cross examination or questioning of the assessor will be permitted. Although it appears that this provision has in fact been little used in practice, such provisions may come into conflict with the HRA. The use of court appointed experts has implications for the right to adversarial proceedings or the principle of equality of arms under Article 6(1). In *Mantavanelli v. France*,[11] the applicants complained that they were denied a fair hearing, relying on Article 6(1), since an expert medical report ordered by an administrative court was not prepared in accordance with the adversarial principle. The Court by a majority found a violation of Article 6(1) because the expert evidence was likely to have had a preponderant influence on the court's assessment of the facts and the applicants had been prevented from being able to comment effectively on it. However, the Court warned that the right to adversarial proceedings did not mean a general abstract principle should be inferred from this provision that where an expert has been appointed by a court, the party must in all instances be able to attend the interviews held by the expert or be shown the documents the expert has taken into account.[12]

In *Bönisch v. Austria*,[13] the expert whose report was relied upon to institute **11.59** a prosecution was given preferential treatment by the court compared to the defence expert. The former was able to attend throughout, ask questions of the accused and make comments. The Court held that he should have been treated as a prosecution expert since his evidence was adverse to the accused and the preferential treatment of him breached the principle of equality of arms. The failure by a court-appointed expert to produce a report within a reasonable time is incompatible with Article 6(1).[14] Where a court-appointed expert was a member of the same institute as the expert whose report was relied upon to institute a prosecution, this was of itself insufficient to give rise to a legitimate doubt about that expert's neutrality.[15]

---

[10] *Douglas v. Hello!* [2001] 2 W.L.R. 992; *The Times*, January 16, 2001, CA.
[11] (1997) 24 E.H.R.R. 370.
[12] *ibid.*, para. 33.
[13] (1987) 9 E.H.R.R. 191.
[14] *Ruiz Torija v. Spain* (1995) 19 E.H.R.R. 553, para.30.
[15] *Brandsetter v. Austria* (1993) 15 E.H.R.R. 378.

11.60   In *JJ v. Netherlands*,[16] the applicant complained that Article 6 had been
violated during the conduct of a tax appeal to the Netherlands Supreme
Court because a report had been received from the Advocate-General of
the Supreme Court which the applicant had not had the opportunity to
comment on or to challenge. The Court found that such a procedure
infringed the applicant's right to adversarial proceedings. Such a right
meant that the parties should have an opportunity to have knowledge of
and comment on all evidence adduced or observations filed, even by an
independent member of the national legal service.

Single Joint Experts

11.61   The court's power to appoint a single joint expert also raises similar
issues. In *H v. France*,[17] the Court found that on the facts there had not
been a breach of Article 6 by reason of the court's refusal to allow a party
to call an medical expert. It was held to be reasonable in circumstances
where the applicant had failed to make out a prima facie case in relation
to the existence of a causal link between the treatment he received and
the alleged damage. However, the potential for conflict in other factual
scenarios remains. It seems an arguable point that a party should be
entitled to instruct his own expert where there is sufficient evidence to
enable him to proceed with a claim.

11.62   In *Daniels v. Walker*,[18] the claimant was left brain-damaged and in need of
future care following a road traffic accident. Liability was conceded and the
parties jointly instructed an occupational therapist to ascertain the claimant's care needs. The expert recommended full time residential care and
the defendant, who wished to challenge this evidence, sought permission
from the court to obtain and rely on its own expert occupational therapist.
The judge refused. The Court of Appeal allowed the appeal stating that
where a party sensibly agreed to a joint expert report, that party was not
prevented from obtaining further evidence and, if necessary, relying on
that evidence to challenge the joint expert report in circumstances where
the reasons for doing so were not fanciful and it was in accord with the
overriding objective, having regard to the sums involved. The defendant
made reference to Article 6(1) and the case of *Mantovanelli v. France* in
support of the appeal. Whilst Lord Woolf M.R. robustly stated that Article
6 had no possibly application to the case, had there been a different
outcome to the case, the European Court would have been unlikely to take
the same view. Further, it is possible that the decision reached as a matter
of domestic law, which was itself a little surprising in light of previous
indications as to the use of separate experts in addition to joint experts,
was at least partly influenced by the Convention arguments. Following
Daniels v. Walker, in *Cosgrove v. Pattison*,[19] Neuberger J. allowed the
defendant's appeal from the judge's refusal of permission to call his own
expert witness following the appointment of a single joint expert but
outlined factors likely to be relevant for the determination of such an
application including, *inter alia*, the nature of the dispute and amount of

---

[16] (1999) 28 E.H.R.R. 168.
[17] (1990) 12 E.H.R.R. 74.
[18] [2000] 1 W.L.R. 1382, CA.
[19] *The Times*, February 13, 2001, Neuberger J.

money at stake, the reasons for needing another expert report, the effect on the conduct of the trial (including consideration of the delay calling a further expert would cause) and the overall justice to the parties in the context of the litigation. This general approach, focusing on the fairness of the proceedings as a whole, is likely to be compatible with Article 6(1).

Admission of Expert Evidence

Article 6 entitles a party to submit expert evidence where this is relevant to his claim and is necessary in order to provide him with a fair hearing.[20] Where the expert evidence that a party sought to adduce could not reasonably have assisted the case, there is no violation of Article 6(1) if the court does not permit such evidence to be called: *Asch v. Austria*.[21] In *H v. France*,[22] the Court found that there was no violation of Article 6(1) where the national court had refused to commission an expert report because the party applying for it had failed to establish a prima facie link between the injuries and the medical treatment which was the subject of the complaint.

11.63

10. LEGAL CONFIDENTIALITY AND PRIVILEGE

Lawyer/Client Confidentiality and the Convention

The European Court has recognised under Article 8 the principle of the right to respect for communications between a person and his lawyer (this being important for the furtherance of a person's rights under Article 6): *Silver v. United Kingdom*.[23] The issue has principally arisen in the context of control over prisoners' correspondence by prison authorities. In *Campbell v. United Kingdom*,[24] the Court stated:

11.64

> "It is clearly in the general interest that any person who wishes to consult a lawyer should be free to do so under conditions which favour full and uninhibited discussion. It is for this reason that the lawyer-client relationship is, in principle, privileged . . .
> . . . the Court sees no reason to distinguish between the different categories of correspondence with lawyers which, whatever their purpose, concern matters of a private and confidential character. In principle, such letters are privileged under Article 8. This means that the prison authorities may open a letter from a lawyer to a prisoner when they have reasonable cause to believe that it contains an illicit enclosure which the normal means of detection have failed to disclose. The letter should, however, only be opened and should not be read. Suitable guarantees preventing the reading of the letter should be provided e.g., opening the letter in the presence of the prisoner.

---

[20] *H v. France* (1990) 12 E.H.R.R. 74.
[21] (1993) 15 E.H.R.R. 597.
[22] (1990) 12 E.H.R.R. 74.
[23] (1983) 5 E.H.R.R. 347.
[24] (1993) 15 E.H.R.R. 137.

The reading of a prisoner's mail to and from a lawyer, on the other hand, should only be permitted in exceptional circumstances when the authorities have reasonable cause to believe that the privilege is being abused in that the contents of the letter endanger prison security or the safety of others or are otherwise of a criminal nature."[24A]

11.65 In *Niemietz v. Germany*,[25] police searched a lawyer's offices looking for information to reveal the identity and possible whereabouts of a person who was the subject of a criminal investigation. The European Court held that the search violated Article 8, recognising that activities of a professional character could fall within the concept of private life and correspondence in Article 8. It also recognised that where a lawyer was involved, an encroachment on professional secrecy might have repercussions on the proper administration of justice and the rights guaranteed by Article 6. In *Foxley v. United Kingdom*,[26] the European Court found a violation of Article 8 when the applicant's trustee in bankruptcy, to whom the applicant's post was being redirected by order under section 371 of the Insolvency Act 1986, had opened and made copies of correspondence addressed to the applicant from his legal advisers.

Lawyer/Client Confidentiality and E.C. Law

11.66 In *Case 155/79 A.M.&S. Europe Ltd v. Commission of the European Communities*,[27] the European Court of Justice held that the protection of legal confidence was a principle of Community law, stating:

"18 . . . Community law, which derives from not only the economic but also the legal interpenetration of the member states, must take into account the principles and concepts common to the laws of those states concerning the observance of confidentiality, in particular, as regards certain communications between lawyer and client. That confidentiality serves the requirement, the importance of which is recognised in all of the member states, that any person must be able, without constraint, to consult a lawyer whose profession entails the giving of independent legal advice to all those who need of it . . .
25. Having regard to the principles of the Treaty concerning freedom of establishment and the freedom to provide services the protection thus afforded by Community law . . . to written communications

---

[24A] At para. 46. See also *Demirtepe v. France* (2001) 31 E.H.R.R. 708 (the opening of a prisoner's correspondence by prison authorities was an unquestionable and unjustified interference with the right to respect for correspondence) and *R. (Daly) v. Secretary of State for the Home Department* [2001] 2 W.L.R. 1622, HL (blanket prison policy of searching cells including prisoner's correspondence following exclusion of prisoner infringed the common law right to legal professional privilege. The same result would have been achieved by reliance on Article 8(1)).
[25] (1993) 16 E.H.R.R. 97.
[26] (2001) 31 E.H.R.R. 637, Application No. 33274/96, June 20, 2000., *The Times*, July 4, 2000.
[27] [1983] Q.B. 878.

between lawyer and client must apply without distinction to any lawyer entitled to practice his profession in one of the member states, regardless of the member state in which the client lives."[28]

The ECJ recognised that the principle of lawyer/client confidentiality was **11.67** subject to two general conditions; first, that the communications were made for the purposes and in the interests of the client's rights of defence, and secondly, that the lawyers were independent and not in the client's employment.[29]

Domestic Law

In the United Kingdom, the common law recognises the right to legal **11.68** confidentiality which arises between a person and their legal adviser as a matter of substantive law, not just procedure (except where the client is trying to use the relationship to commit a crime or for some unlawful purpose). Legal confidentiality is regarded as a right of great constitutional importance because it is seen as a necessary bulwark of a person's right of access to justice whether as a claimant or as a defendant: *R. v. Derby Magistrates' Court, ex p. B.*[30] The general protection given to legal confidentiality in English law, through both the common law doctrine of legal professional privilege and the equitable doctrine of confidence, is likely to satisfy, and arguably go beyond, the requirements of Article 8.[31] The protection of legal professional privilege in domestic law is so strong that it will not be abrogated even where it may be relevant to the defence of a defendant charged with murder in a criminal trial.[32] However, the interrelationship between legal confidentiality and the right to a fair trial may need to be further scrutinised in light of the Convention, especially since Article 8(2) permits an interference with Article 8(1) rights in the interests of "the protection of the rights and freedoms of others" including the right to a fair trial under Article 6.[33] The protection given to legal professional privilege under Article 8 may also yield to the interests of the economic well-being of the country.[34]

---

[28] *ibid.*, at 949–951.
[29] *ibid.*, at 950.
[30] [1996] A.C. 487, HL.
[31] See, *e.g. R. v. Special Commissioners, ex p. Morgan Grenfell & Co.*, November 8, 2000, Admin Ct.
[32] *R. v. Derby Magistrates' Court, ex p. B* [1996] A.C. 487, HL. Further, domestic courts have been quick to strike down legislation or rules which abrogated legal professional privilege. To take a pre-HRA example, in *R. v. Secretary of State for the Home Department, ex p. Leech* [1994] Q.B. 198, CA, the provision of the prison rules which provided that the governor had a right to read letters between prisoners and legal advisers was held *ultra vires* the regulation-making power under the Prison Act 1952. This decision was clearly influenced by fundamental rights considerations.
[33] See further, in relation to wasted costs orders below. The absolutist approach of the House of Lords in *ex p. B* contrasts with the more qualified approach taken by the Canadian courts in *L.C. et al v. Mills*, Application No. 8901/80 2000) 180 D.L.R. (4th) 1; *Jones v. Smith* [1999] 1 S.C.R. 455; and *R. v. Murray* (2000) 48 O.R. (3d) 437; and the H C of Australia in *Carter v. Northmore Hale Davy and Leake* 183 C.L.R. 121, *per* Toohey J.
[34] *R. v. Special Commissioner, ex p. Morgan Grenfell & Co. Ltd* [2001] S.T.C. 497; [2001] EWCA CIV 329, March 2, 2001, CA, unreported, November 8, 2000, Admin Ct.

Wasted Costs Orders[34A]

11.69 Toulson J. considered the proposed abrogation of legal professional privilege by the Civil Procedure Rules in *General Mediterranean Holdings v. Patel*.[35] He held that CPR Rule 48.7(3) (subsequently revoked), which permitted the court to order disclosure of privileged documents to the court and/or to the other party in the context of a wasted costs application against solicitors, was *ultra vires* to the extent that it cut down the substantive right to legal confidentiality. He had regard to the "high value which the [Strasbourg] court accorded to legal confidentiality" in coming to his decision. Because the issue concerned the right of solicitors to defend themselves against applications for costs made by a party other than their client, the interrelationship between Article 6 and Article 8 arose for consideration. Toulson J. stated:

> "Article 6 gives every person a right to a fair trial, but I do not accept that it follows as a general proposition that this gives a right to interfere with another person's right to legal confidentiality. If that were generally so, the right to legal confidentiality recognised by the court would be useless, since its very purpose is to enable a person to communicate with his lawyer secure in the knowledge that such communications cannot be used without his consent to further another person's cause. In the absence of a general right under article 6 to make use of another person's confidential communications with his lawyer, I do not see how solicitors have a particular right to do so under that article for the purpose of defending a wasted costs application."[36]

11.70 He did not accept that the approach of the House of Lords in *ex p. B*[36A] in rejecting any qualification of the right to legal confidentiality in the interests of ensuring that a third party[37] had a fair trial was a violation of Article 6 or that the Convention required a balancing exercise in individual cases of the kind which the House of Lords considered and rejected as a matter of English law. He stated that even if he were wrong about this, he had considerable doubt whether a general discretion to order the disclosure of privileged material on an application for a wasted costs order was necessary and proportionate for the purpose of doing justice to the legal profession, bearing in mind that the courts have been used to making allowances for the lawyer's inability to disclose privileged information without the clients consent.[38] The prescribed procedure of making full allowance for the inability of a lawyer to disclose privileged information (and not making wasted costs orders unless full allowance can be made),

---

[34A] See paras 10.129 *et seq.*, above.
[35] [2001] 1 W.L.R. 272.
[36] *ibid.*, at pp. 295–296.
[36A] [1996] A.C. 487.
[37] In an action or application brought by a client against his own lawyer, privilege is treated as impliedly waived and the issue of legal confidentiality preventing a fair trial does not arise. It is, however, a serious problem, where an application for wasted costs is made against a lawyer by the opposing party or raised by the court of its own motion and where privileged information is relevant to the lawyer's defence.
[38] *ibid.*, p. 296.

as a mechanism for reconciling any conflict between legal confidentiality under Article 8 and the right to a fair trial under Article 6, may be coming under greater scrutiny in relation to whether it constitutes a sufficient safeguard of the fairness of wasted costs proceedings.[39]

Disclosure of Privileged Documents to Inspector of Taxes

In *R. v. A Special Commissioner, ex p. Morgan Grenfell & Co.,*[40] the Court   **11.71**
of Appeal, upholding a ruling of the Administrative Court, held that neither the rules relating to legal professional privilege nor Article 8 prohibited delivery of privileged documents to an inspector of taxes relating to potential tax liabilities and their quantification. This was because the Inland Revenue was charged with the public duty of collecting revenue and the facts of the particular case fully justified the investigative step.[41]

Disclosure of Privileged Information by Expert

CPR 35.10(3) provides that an expert's report must state the substance of   **11.72**
all material instructions, whether written or oral, on the basis of which the report was written. CPR 35.10(4) provides that these instructions "shall not be privileged against disclosure". The court will not, however, order disclosure of specific documents or cross-examination of the expert in relation to his instructions, unless it is satisfied that there are reasonable grounds to consider the statement of instructions to be inaccurate of incomplete. The purpose of the provision is to avoid pressure being put on an expert to come to or change a specific opinion leading to suppression of material opinions or material which is adverse to the party instructing that expert. It is intended that this provision will bolster the independence of the expert, who might otherwise be inclined to modify his opinion in order to assist the party who is actually paying him. This is clearly a legitimate reason for the rule that increases the fairness to the other parties to the litigation and does not affect lawyer-client confidentiality, though it does narrow the scope of litigation privilege to some extent. Provided that CPR 35.10(4) is interpreted narrowly and privilege is only

---

[39] See, *e.g. Drums and Packaging Limited v. Martin Freeman*, unreported, August 6, 1999, Mr George Laurence Q.C. sitting as a Deputy High Court Judge (privilege had been waived at the eleventh hour and the application for a wasted costs order was not granted—however, the Deputy Judge expressly doubted whether he would have made full allowance for the inability to disclose privileged information, had the waiver not been made—at para.43). See also *Medcalf v. Mardell* [2000] Lloyd's Rep P.N. 146, *The Times*, January 2, 2001, CA (order for wasted costs made against two barristers who argued that their inability to reveal privileged information prejudiced their ability to have a fair hearing and that the making of an order would violate Art. 6) and *cf. Harley v. McDonald* [2001] 2 W.L.R. 1749, PC (fairness to a legal practitioner defending wasted costs proceedings required that notice be given of allegations of breach of duty against him and an opportunity given to challenge those allegations, if so advised, by cross-examining witnesses and leading evidence [at 1769]. The Judicial Committee allowed an appeal against an order for wasted costs in part because the trial judge had unfairly exceeded the limits of his inquiry by taking into account matters of fact on which the respondent had not had an opportunity to address him or given evidence. The New Zealand Court of Appeal acted similarly by simply endorsing the judge's conclusion [at 1773]).
[40] [2001] S.T.C. 497; *The Times*, April 17, 2001; *The Independent*, March 15, 2001, [2001] EWCA CIV 329, CA; unreported, November 8, 2000, Admin Ct.
[41] See also *Guyer v. Walton (HMIT)*, March 19, 2001, Special Commissioners (reported on Lawtel at May 1, 2001).

overridden where there are clearly reasonable grounds to suppose that the statement of instructions is inaccurate or incomplete, it is unlikely that the rule will violate the Convention. Any attempt to further erode privilege may have implications for the instructing party's right to a fair trial under Article 6.[42] The application of Article 8 to this situation, which unlike the cases that have to date come before the European Court, does not involve a communication between a client and his lawyer, but between a client or his lawyer and an expert, is uncertain.

---

[42] See by analogy *Re L* [1997] A.C. 16, HL, where the House of Lords held that litigation privilege did not arise in family proceedings because the proceedings were not adversarial in nature. Lord Nicholls suggested that such a result might deny to a parent a fair hearing under Art. 6(1), read in conjunction with Art. 8, of the Convention (at p. 32).

CHAPTER 12

Access to the Courts: Arbitration, ADR, Legal Aid, Court Fees

1. INTRODUCTION

The Right of Access to a Court

Article 6 of the Convention contains no express right of access to a court **12.01** but there are implied into Article 6 two rights of access to courts:

>   (1) the right to institute proceedings and

>   (2) the right to pursue proceedings through to a hearing.

The rationale for this is that without access to a court, an individual's right to a fair trial is devoid of substance. In *Golder v. United Kingdom*,[1] the European Court held that it would be "inconceivable" that Article 6 should describe in detail the procedural guarantees afforded to parties in a pending law suit and should not protect that which alone makes it possible

---

[1] (1979) 1 E.H.R.R. 524

to benefit from such guarantees, *i.e.* a right of access to a court.[2] The Court observed:

> "The principle whereby a civil claim must be capable of being submitted to a judge ranks as one of the universally recognised fundamental principles of law; the same is true of the principle of international law which forbids the denial of justice. Article 6(1) must be read in light of these principles."[3]

12.02 Until about 1980, it was not possible for inmates in United Kingdom prisons to obtain legal advice about civil claims without the Home Secretary's permission. Further, it was permissible for prison governors to intercept and read correspondence between an inmate and his solicitor. In *Golder*, the Court found this was in breach of Article 6(1), and, not only must a right of access to court exist, it must be effective. By refusing the applicant permission to contact a solicitor, the Home Secretary hindered his right of access to the courts. Hindrance in fact was capable of contravening the Convention just like a legal impediment.[4] The Court had to decide whether Article 6(1) was limited to guaranteeing the right to a fair trial in pending legal proceedings or whether it extended to securing a right of access to court for actions concerning civil rights and obligations. It found the wider approach appropriate, reasoning that otherwise Contracting States would be free to remove jurisdiction over whole classes of action.[5]

12.03 The right of access to a court is qualified since by its very nature, it calls for regulation by the state.[6] The European Court in *Golder* stated:

> "As this is a right which the Convention sets forth without, in the narrower sense of the term, defining, there is room, apart from the bounds delimiting the very content of any right, for limitations permitted by implication."[7]

12.04 The state may vary the access in time and in place according to the needs and resources of the community and individuals. However, such regulation must never injure the substance of the right by restricting or reducing the access available, nor must it conflict with other rights in the Convention.[8] Any limitation must have a legitimate aim and be reasonably proportionate to the aim sought to be compatible with Article 6(1).[9] In *Tinnelly & Sons Ltd and McElduff v. United Kingdom*, the European Court observed:

> " . . . the final decision as to the observance of the Convention's requirements rests with the Court. It must be satisfied that the limitations applied do not restrict or reduce the access left to the individual

---

[2] *ibid.*, at para. 35.
[3] Para. 35.
[4] Para. 26
[5] K.Reid, *A Practitioners Guide to the European Convention of Human Rights* (London: Sweet & Maxwell: 1998) at p. 63.
[6] *Golder v. United Kingdom* (1979) 1 E.H.R.R. 524, para. 38
[7] *ibid.*, para. 38. See also *Fayed v. United Kingdom* (1994) 18 E.H.R.R. 393, para. 65; *Tinnelly & Sons Ltd and McElduff v. United Kingdom* (1999) 27 E.H.R.R. 249, para. 72.
[8] *ibid.*
[9] *Ashingdane v. United Kingdom* (1985) 7 E.H.R.R. 528, paras 56–59

in such a way or to such an extent that the very essence of the right is impaired. Furthermore, a limitation will not be compatible with Article 6(1) if it does not pursue a legitimate aim and if there is not a reasonable relationship of proportionality between the means employed and the aim sought to be achieved."[10]

Article 6(1) is only applicable to the determination of "civil rights and obligations". The right of access to a court will not therefore arise in relation to certain classes of proceedings that are not concerned with the determination of civil rights or obligations such as proceedings concerned with public rights.[11]   **12.05**

This chapter considers the implications of the right of access to a court for arbitration and other forms of alternative dispute resolution, the provision and choice of publicly funded legal advice and assistance and prescribed court fees.   **12.06**

Alternative Dispute Resolution

Article 6(1) is also concerned to ensure that disputes about civil rights and obligations should be dealt with in adversarial proceedings before an independent and impartial tribunal and where the parties are allowed to make a fully-argued case. That the tribunal should ideally be composed of an independent judge or judges is implicit in Article 6(1). For example, in *Klass v. Germany*,[12] the European Court stated that: **12.07**

"The rule of law implies, inter alia, that an interference by the executive authorities with an individual's rights should be subject to an effective control which should normally be assured by the judiciary, at least in the last resort, judicial control offering the best guarantee of independence, impartiality and a proper procedure."[13]

The European Court has tended to reject forms of dispute resolution which fall short of the Article 6 ideal as insufficient, including public inquiries, ombudsmen investigations and criminal injury compensation schemes.[14] Accordingly, and perhaps somewhat ironically when the English and Welsh legal system is moving away from litigation towards alternative methods of dispute resolution with less formality and expense, the HRA will act as a force in the opposite direction.   **12.08**

Complaints concerning the use of alternative dispute resolution procedures will usually concern the Article 6(1) guarantees provided that the determination of civil rights and obligations is at issue. The issues arising include: **12.09**

(1) whether the procedure infringes the right of access to a court

---

[10] (1999) 27 E.H.R.R. 249, para. 72. See also *National & Provincial Building Society v. United Kingdom* (1998) 25 E.H.R.R. 127, para. 105.
[11] See further paras 3.56 *et seq.*, above.
[12] (1980) 2 E.H.R.R. 214.
[13] *ibid.*, para. 56.
[14] See, *e.g. Osman v. United Kingdom* (2000) 29 E.H.R.R. 245; *Z v. United Kingdom* (1999) 28 E.H.R.R. C.D. 65; Application No. 29392/95, May 10, 2001; *The Times* May 31, 2001. See further paras 17.09 *et seq.*

    (2) whether it prevents the applicant having a public hearing

    (3) whether the hearing is before an independent and impartial tribunal

    (4) whether there is a review of the case on its facts

    (5) whether an appeal to an Article 6(1) compliant court or tribunal is available[15]

12.10 Article 6 guarantees that any waiver of rights must be established in an unequivocal manner and be accompanied by sufficient safeguards against abuse.[16] If there is no waiver, then if a dispute resolution procedure is to survive challenge, either the adjudicating body will have to provide the requisite Article 6(1) procedural safeguards of a public hearing, independent and impartial tribunal, etc., or a right of appeal to an Article 6(1) compliant court or tribunal must exist.

12.11 The European Court has accepted that in certain circumstances, such as family proceedings, there may be good reasons for opting for an adjudicatory body that does not have the composition or procedures of a court of law of the classic kind: *e.g. X v. United Kingdom*[17]; *McMichael v. United Kingdom.*[18]

2. ARBITRATION

General

12.12 An arbitration usually involves the resolution of a dispute by a mechanism which is very different to that envisaged by Article 6. There will usually be no public hearing or judgment and whilst arbitrators are under a duty under section 33(1) of the Arbitration Act 1996 to "act fairly and impartially as between the parties, giving each party a reasonable opportunity of putting his case and dealing with that of his opponent", only rarely will arbitrations satisfy the full requirements of Article 6(1). Provided that the determination of civil rights and obligations within the meaning of Article 6(1) is in issue,[19] Article 6(1) is applicable to arbitration proceedings since they potentially deprive a party of the right of access to litigation in court.

Voluntary Arbitration

12.13 Arbitration proceedings agreed to by contract or other voluntary manner are generally compatible with Article 6(1) on the basis that the parties have

---

[15] The approach in (5) has been reflected in Scottish case law: see, *e.g. County Properties Limited v. The Scottish Ministers*, unreported, July 25, 2000 [reference] (court looked at the process as a whole, not tier by tier).

[16] *Pfeifer and Plankl v. Austria* (1992) 14 E.H.R.R. 692, para. 37 (waiver of procedural rights requires minimum guarantees commensurate to its importance); *Bramelid & Malmström v. Sweden* (1982) 5 E.H.R.R. 249; *Suovaniemi v. Finland,* Application No. 31737/96, February 23, 1999, European Court.

[17] (1982) 4 E.H.R.R. 188, para. 53.

[18] (1995) 20 E.H.R.R. 205, para. 80.

[19] See paras 3.55 *et seq.*, above.

expressly or tacitly renounced or waived their right of access to an ordinary court: *Suovaniemi v. Finland.*[20] However, any waiver should be subjected to "particularly careful review" to ensure that the applicant is not subject to constraint: *Deweer v. Belgium.*[21] In *Deweer,* the applicant, a Belgian butcher, was alleged to have committed an offence of selling meat at an illegal profit. The public prosecutor ordered the closure of his shop either until judgment was given in an intended criminal prosecution or until he paid an agreed fine by way of settlement. Under protest, the applicant paid the fine. He brought a complaint invoking Article 6(1), complaining in substance of the imposition of a fine by way of settlement under constraint of provisional closure of his shop. The European Court found a violation of Article 6(1). It held that Article 6(1) is not in principle infringed by an individual waiving his right to a court. The Court identified that in Contracting States' legal systems, a waiver is frequently encountered both in civil matters, notably in the shape of arbitration clauses in contracts, and in criminal matters in the shape of fines paid by way of compensation. The waiver, which has undeniable advantages for the individual concerned as well as for the administration of justice, does not in principle offend against the Convention. However, the *"ordre public"* character of Article 6(1) requires any measure or decision alleged to be in breach of Article 6(1) to be subjected to "particularly careful review". Absence of constraint is one of the conditions to be satisfied.[22] Settlements which have barred criminal proceedings must be shown to have been free from constraint. Mr. Deweer's waiver of a fair trial was tainted by constraint, resulting in a breach of Article 6(1).[23] Where consent is given under duress, the waiver will not be unequivocal.[24]

There is no violation of Article 6(1) where a voluntary waiver of court **12.14** proceedings in favour of arbitration exists.[25] In *Nordström-Janzon & Nordström-Lehtinen v. Netherlands,*[26] two Finnish companies entered into a joint-venture agreement with a Dutch company, which provided for arbitration according to the rules of the Netherlands Arbitration Institute. The applicants requested the Institute to arbitrate in various disputes which had arisen from the agreement. Three arbitrators were appointed by the Institute, who rejected all the applicants' claims following a hearing. The applicants appealed to the Regional Court which rejected the claim. The applicants appealed, alleging *inter alia* that one of the arbitrators was not independent or impartial, invoking Article 6. The Court of Appeal dismissed the appeal holding that there were no objectively justified reasons for questioning the independence and impartiality of the arbitrator in question. The Supreme Court rejected a further appeal. The applicants complained to the European Commission that their right to a fair trial was violated since the national courts had upheld an arbitral award which had been

---

[20] Application No. 31737/96, February 23, 1999.
[21] (1980) 2 E.H.R.R. 439. See also *Jon Axelsson v. Sweden,* Application No. 11960/86, July 13, 1990.
[22] Deweer, *ibid.,* para. 49.
[23] *ibid.,* para. 54.
[24] *Nordström-Janzon & Nordström-Lehtinen v. Netherlands* (1996) 87 D.R. 112, Application No. 28101/95, November 27, 1996.
[25] *Suovaniemi v. Finland,* Application No. 31737/96, February 23, 1999.
[26] (1996) 87 D.R. 112, Application No. 28101/95, November 27, 1996.

given by three arbitrators, one of whom allegedly lacked independence and impartiality. The European Commission noted that the arbitration was based on a voluntary agreement according to which disputes between the parties should be settled not by the ordinary courts but under a special arbitration system. Consequently, there was a renunciation of a procedure before the ordinary courts satisfying all the guarantees of Article 6. It had not been alleged that the arbitration agreement was concluded under duress. Further, there was no requirement for national courts to ensure that arbitral proceedings conformed to Article 6(1). It was not unreasonable for Dutch law to require strong reasons for quashing an already rendered award since quashing would often mean a long and costly arbitral procedure would become useless and considerable expense must be invested in new proceedings. Accordingly, no violation of Article 6(1) was found.

12.15 In *Jon Axelsson v. Sweden*,[27] the applicants were taxi owners who were members of a taxi economic association (the MTEA). It was economically essential for the applicants to join the MTEA, which was the only taxi association for their particular zone at the relevant time. There was a clause in the membership agreement providing that disputes between the association and a member must be submitted to settlement according to the current Swedish law on arbitration. Three of the taxi drivers left the MTEA after having been excluded from use of a taxi dispatch exchange, which provided about 70 per cent of a taxi's business, for a lengthy period. They brought proceedings for damages against the MTEA. The MTEA argued that the court had no jurisdiction because of the arbitration clause. The Court of Appeal agreed, holding that the arbitration clause was applicable. The applicants therefore brought a complaint before the European Commission, alleging, *inter alia*, a breach of the right of access to a court in respect of their dispute with the MTEA. The European Commission held that the right to access to the Court is not absolute. It is "restricted or subject to special conditions in respect of . . . persons who are bound by an arbitration agreement". In principle, such regulation is not contrary to Article 6 "where the aim pursued is legitimate and the means employed to achieve the aim is proportionate". The Commission noted that in so far as arbitration is based on agreements between the parties to the dispute, it is a natural consequence of their right to regulate their mutual relations as they see fit. From a more general perspective, arbitration procedures can also be said to pursue the legitimate aim of encouraging non-judicial settlements and of relieving the courts of an excessive burden of cases. The Commission found no indication that the dispute involved any issues of public interest which would have made an arbitration inappropriate or unreasonable. Further, it found that the applicants must be regarded as having themselves renounced court procedures. Accordingly, it found no violation of Article 6(1). One might question the actual decision in *Axelsson* on the basis that when the taxi drivers joined the association, it was economically essential to do so and there was no other association in their zone. Consequently, it would not seem that they really had much choice about the membership agreement into which they

---

[27] Application No. 11960/86, July 13, 1990.

had entered. However, the Commission held that the arbitration clause was agreed to by the claimants in those circumstances.

The possibility is raised in *Axelsson* that where a dispute involves issues **12.16** of public interest, this may make an arbitration procedure inappropriate or unreasonable.[28] Further, it may be possible to argue that there is no unequivocal waiver of the right of access to a court where an arbitration agreement is only included in a contract by reference.[29]

Non-Voluntary Arbitration

Where an arbitration procedure is imposed by law or the agreement has **12.17** been subject to compulsion, the Article 6(1) guarantees must be met. Alternatively, there must be a right of appeal to an Article 6(1) compliant court or tribunal. In *Bramelid & Malsmtröm v. Sweden*,[30] the applicants owned shares in a limited company. Under Swedish company law, any company which held more than 90 per cent of the shares of another company was entitled to purchase the remaining shares from the minority shareholders. Any dispute concerning the right to purchase the shares or the price payable for them had to be referred to three arbitrators. Appeal against the arbitration award was limited. The arbitrators ruled that the majority shareholder was entitled to purchase the outstanding shares owned by the applicants at a particular purchase price. The applicants complained that the arbitrators did not constitute a "tribunal" within the meaning of Article 6(1). They alleged that the arbitrators were not independent and impartial. It was not in dispute that the purpose of the arbitration proceedings was to determine the applicants' private rights and obligations. Accordingly, the applicants were entitled to a hearing before a tribunal within the meaning of Article 6(1). However, the European Commission drew a distinction between voluntary arbitration and compulsory arbitration. It stated that "normally Article 6 poses no problem where arbitration is entered into voluntarily". If, on the other hand, arbitration is compulsory in the sense of being required by law, the parties have no option but to refer their dispute to arbitration and the procedure must offer the guarantees set forth in Article 6(1). Since in the case at issue, recourse to arbitration was compulsory, the Commission had to consider whether the Article 6(1) guarantees were respected in those proceedings. The Commission held that the ability of one party (the majority shareholder) to influence the composition of the arbitration panel in a way which was not open to the minority shareholders meant that the independence and impartiality required by Article 6(1) was not fulfilled. Further, there was no public hearing as required by Article 6(1). (Subsequent to the case, the Swedish Parliament amended the legislation giving a party who was not satisfied with a decision of the arbitrators a right to start proceedings before an ordinary court.)

---

[28] See also *Jakob Boss Söhne KG v. Germany,* Application No. 18749/91, December 2, 1991; *Firma Heinz Schiebler KG v. Germany,* Application No. 18805/91, December 2, 1991.

[29] See, *e.g. Birse v. St, David* [2000] B.L.R. 57; *Lobb v Aintree* [2000] B.L.R. 65; *Aughton v. M.F. Kent Services Ltd* (1991) 57 B.L.R. 1.

[30] (1982) 5 E.H.R.R.249.

Duties on Courts with Control over Arbitration

12.18   Where the courts exercise judicial control over arbitration proceedings or possess an executory function in relation to an arbitral award, State responsibility does attach to such judicial proceedings, which must be fair and comply with the Article 6(1) guarantees.[31] Section 6(1) of the HRA means that when a court decides an appeal on a point of law under section 69 of the Arbitration Act 1996 or on the basis of an allegation of "serious irregularity" which has caused substantial injustice to the applicant under section 68 of the 1996 Act or is asked to enforce an arbitral award, it must act compatibly with the Convention. Further, pursuant to section 3(1) of the HRA, the court is required to interpret the Arbitration Act 1996 in accordance with Convention rights. An issue may arise where the court is asked to enforce an award that has been made following an arbitrator's failure to act fairly and impartially under section 33 of the 1996 Act. Whilst the protection of the Convention applying to the administration of justice in the Contracting States who are parties to it does not vary according to the nationality of the persons affected,[32] it is not yet clear how the HRA and the Arbitration Act 1996 will interrelate where the arbitration took place abroad.[33]

Arbitration Procedure

12.19   A waiver does not necessarily amount to a waiver of *all* the rights under Article 6. An unequivocal waiver is valid only in so far as such waiver is "permissible". Waiver may be permissible with regard to some rights but not with regard to others. However, the case law is not yet fully developed in relation to which rights may or may not be waived. It is clear that the right to a public hearing can be validly waived, even in court proceedings.[34] This applies *a fortiori* to arbitration proceedings, one of the very purposes of which is often to avoid publicity.[35] The fundamental right to an independent and impartial tribunal can also be waived in relation to arbitration proceedings, at least where an applicant has approved the choice of arbitrator despite being aware of grounds for challenging him: *Suovaniemi v. Finland*.[36] Impartiality is unlikely to generate substantial complaint under the HRA since the domestic courts have held that the same test is to be applied in determining whether an arbitral award should be set aside for bias or apparent bias as would be used at common law in relation to any other court or tribunal—see, for example. *Rustal v. Gill & Duffus*[37]; *Laker Airways v. FLS Aerospace Ltd.*[38] Arbitrators' immunity is discussed at para. 17.54 below.

---

[31] *Jakob Boss Söhne KG v. Germany,* Application No. 18479/91, December 2, 1991.
[32] *General Mediterranean Holdings SA v. Patel* [2000] 1 W.L.R. 272 at 295, Toulson J.
[33] See further, C. Newmark & D. Green, "Human Rights, Arbitration and ADR" Sol. Jo. December 1, 2000, at 1094–1095.
[34] *Håkansson and Sturesson v. Sweden* (1991) 13 E.H.R.R. 1. See further paras 3.152 and 10.93 above.
[35] *Suovaniemi v. Finland* Application No. 31737/96, February 23, 1999.
[36] Application No. 31737/96, February 23, 1999.
[37] [2000] 1 Lloyds' L.R. 14 at 18.
[38] [1999] 2 Lloyds' Rep. 45 at 48.

Conclusion

In many commercial contexts, the parties will usually be taken to have **12.20** consented to the manner and the method by which arbitrations are conducted, thereby ousting the application of Article 6(1). Further, the courts do retain ultimate power to intervene in relation to the conduct of a reference.[39] It is therefore unlikely that it will be possible to invoke the Human Rights Act successfully in relation to the procedure being followed at an arbitration, given that defects can generally be remedied by a court.[40] It may, however, be appropriate for the court to be reminded of the provisions of Article 6 if only to seek to achieve a judgment that it is appropriate to set aside an arbitration pursuant to statute or at common law, on the basis that the domestic law should fully accord with the Human Rights Act. Where an arbitration procedure does not entail a fair hearing, it may be open to a party to argue that it has not unequivocally waived this particular right by submitting to arbitration and that there is a violation of Article 6(1) if the defect is not remedied by the courts.

3. MEDIATION

Mediation is fast becoming a popular method of alternative dispute resolu- **12.21** tion, which enables parties to negotiate in the presence of a neutral mediator in a private, informal procedure. It is unlikely that the HRA will have any implications for mediation because the procedure does not involve the determination of civil rights and obligations by a tribunal or prevent a party from continuing with litigation if mediation does not result in a settlement. It is a consensual process and accordingly, there is no deprivation of the right of access to a court.

By contrast, if mediation were to be compulsorily imposed and not purely **12.22** consensual as at present, the requirement delaying the parties their right of access to a court might have potential HRA implications. However, even in this situation, the ability to mediate without prejudice to the ability of the participants to begin or continue with litigation if the mediation is unsuccessful would probably avoid any incompatibility with the right of access to a court in Article 6(1). Any significant overall delay caused by compulsory mediation would also need to be considered in light of the right of the parties to a hearing within a reasonable time under Article 6(1).

4. ADJUDICATION AND CONCILIATION IN CONSTRUCTION CASES

Adjudication

The Housing Grants, Construction and Regeneration Act 1996 introduced **12.23** a statutory scheme for speedy interim adjudications in construction cases

---

[39] See, *e.g.* Arbitration Act 1996, s.24, which permits the removal of an arbitrator on the grounds that he has failed properly to conduct the proceedings or has not used all reasonable despatch in conducting the proceedings or making an award. See also *Andrews v. Bradshaw* [2000] B.L.R. 60.
[40] See *County Properties Limited v. The Scottish Ministers, The Times*, September 19, 2000, OH Ct of Sess.

based on limited evidence, which are binding on the parties until final judgment or award.[41] The procedure is intended to introduce a quick interim remedy for the benefit of underpaid contractors and subcontractors but its summary and binding nature may operate unfairly in some cases. An adjudicator is not a "public authority" within the meaning of section 6 of the HRA and an adjudication is not a final "determination" of civil rights and obligations: *Elanay Contracts Limited v. The Vestry.*[42] In *Austin Hall Building Ltd v. Buckland Securities Ltd,*[42A] the Technology & Construction Court repeated that an adjudicator was not a "public authority" within the meaning of section 6 of the HRA and that the adjudicator was further protected by section 6(2)(4) in that he could not have conducted the hearing in public because he was bound by statute. It further held that the claimant was not a "victim" under section 7 of the HRA because it had not requested a public hearing from the adjudicator. The court expressed the *obiter* view that in any event the whole process including the court proceedings necessary for the enforcement of an adjudicator's award was Article 6(1) compliant in relation to the 28 day period for the complaint.

12.24   The suggestion that the whole process including court enforcement complies with Article 6(1) is open to some question in light of the pre-HRA approach to enforcement irrespective of the existence of defects in procedure or fairness. However, in *Discain Project Services Ltd v. Opecprime Development Ltd,*[42B] HHJ Peter Bowsher Q.C. stated that the court should not enforce a decision reached after substantial breach of the rules of natural justice. He declined to enforce the award of an adjudicator who had received submissions by telephone from one party and not reported them to the other party, giving rise to a risk of apparent bias. A court is clearly a public authority under section 6 of the HRA. Prior to the HRA, adjudications were rigorously enforced by the courts, even where the adjudicator acts in breach of natural justice or makes a mistake. For example,

(1) in *Macob,*[43] Dyson J. held that, as a matter of law, it was not open to him to investigate the validity of the objection which had been taken on the grounds of natural justice against the decision of the adjudicator;

(2) in *How Engineering Services Ltd v. Lindner,*[44] HHJ Seymour, Q.C. held, *obiter*, that a decision supported by no evidence at all amounted only to a mistake of fact rather than law;

(3) in *Bouygues (UK) Ltd v Dahl-Jensen (UK) Ltd (in liquidation),*[45] the Court of Appeal held that an adjudicator's interim award ought to be enforced by proceedings for summary judgment

---

[41] See the 1996 Act, s.108.
[42] Unreported, August 30, 2000, TCC. The court stated that the application of Art. 6(1) to the procedure would "drive a coach and horses" through it.
[42A] (2001) B.L.R. 90, (2001) C.I.L.L. 1734; (2001) E.G.C.S. 155, QBD [TCC].
[42B] Unreported, April 4, 2001, QBD [TCC].
[43] [1999] B.L.R. 93, Dyson J.
[44] (2001) B.L.R. 90, QBD (TCC).
[45] *The Times*, August 17, 2000, [2000] B.L.R. 50, CA Dyson J.

> unless the adjudicator had exceeded his jurisdiction. Accordingly, although an error was manifest within an adjudicator's decision, it would nonetheless not be corrected and the decision would be binding.

This approach has been criticised by a number of commentators who find it surprising that a decision arrived at in serious breach of a principle of natural justice must as a matter of law be enforced for the lengthy period before final judgment or award, where the consequence may be to precipitate the insolvency of the party affected.[46]

However, the adjudication itself is interim and the question arises whether   **12.25** its enforcement amounts to a "determination" of civil rights and obligations. Whilst the adjudication is interim, pending final judgment in litigation or a final award in arbitration, if it operates in practice as a final determination of the dispute, perhaps due to the insolvency of one party which has been ordered to pay money to another, that party is arguably deprived of its right of access to a court complying with Article 6(1) safeguards in the determination of the dispute. Since the adjudication procedure is implied into every contract by law and cannot be contracted out of, there is no question of the voluntary waiver of access to a court or of the Article 6(1) guarantees.

Conciliation

Conciliation is a similar interim procedure provided for in certain I.C.E.   **12.26** contracts. Like adjudication, it is interim, pending litigation or arbitration following completion of the construction contract. However, unlike adjudication but like arbitration, it is voluntarily agreed to by contract. Accordingly, it is unlikely that conciliation will fall foul of Article 6(1) since the parties will probably be held to have voluntarily waived their Article 6(1) rights by consenting to the procedure, knowing that it might, in practice, finally determine the dispute if the conciliator's interim rulings cannot be overturned on appeal.

5. PROVISION OF LEGAL AID

Criminal Legal Aid

Article 6(3)(c) guarantees the right to free legal aid in the defence of a   **12.27** criminal charge provided that:

(1) the accused does not have "sufficient means" to pay for legal assistance and

(2) when the "interests of justice so require".

The interests of justice will require provision of free legal representation where the case is complex or the accused is unable to effectively present

---

[46] See, *e.g.* Ian Duncan Wallace Q.C., "HGCRA Adjudicators' Errors and Enforcement" (2000) 16 Con. L.J. 104.

the case without such assistance: *Benham v. United Kingdom.*[47] The seriousness of any potential sanction is also important and where deprivation of a person's liberty is at stake, this is a situation which will usually require provision of legal representation.[48] The legal representation provided is required to be practical and effective: *Artico v. Italy.*[49] It is not necessary to prove actual prejudice, since such a requirement would in large measure deprive Article 6(3)(c) of its substance.[50]

12.28 The right to investigation and preparation of a defence under Article 6(3)(b) may also have implications for provision of legal aid in criminal cases. In *Procurator Fiscal, Fort William v. McLean,*[51] an appeal was allowed against a sheriff's decision to dismiss prosecutions against the respondents, on the ground that the Scottish criminal legal aid regulations, which limit the amount payable to a solicitor in summary proceedings to a fixed fee of £550 without provision for payment of increased costs where those were reasonable and necessary, produced an inequality of arms as between an accused person and the Crown and violated the right to a fair trial under Article 6 and the right to the investigation and preparation of a defence under Article 6(3)(b). The appeal court held that whilst there might be situations involving clear present disadvantage to an accused, although falling short of identifiable past or future detriment, where Article 6(3) might be said to have been breached. However, the respondents had not shown such disadvantage. The Privy Council held that limitations on remuneration did not breach Article 6 in light of the fact that the solicitors would continue to act despite the levels of remuneration.[51A] The position if lawyers were not prepared to continue to act remains unclear. In *Steven Gayne v. Vannet,*[52] it was held that setting limits on legal aid fees does not necessarily breach Article 6 unless the result is to deny the defendant effective legal representation. Judgment is awaited in relation to a challenge brought by two prisoners under Article 6(3) against the inability to have legal representation and the lack of free legal aid in disciplinary proceedings before a prison governor in *Ezeh and Connors v. United Kingdom.*[53]

12.29 **Representation of choice in criminal proceedings.** Article 6(3)(c) also confers the right on an accused to defend himself in person or through legal assistance of his own choosing.[54] However, where free legal representation is provided, of necessity there is no absolute right to counsel of the accused's own choice: *Croissant v. Germany.*[55] Similarly,

---

[47] (1996) 22 E.H.R.R. 293. See also *Granger v. United Kingdom;* (1990) 12 E.H.R.R. 469; *Hoang v. France* (1993) 16 E.H.R.R. 53.
[48] *Benham,* above. See also *Perks v. United Kingdom* (2000) 30 E.H.R.R. 33 (charge of failure to pay community charge which carried penalty of imprisonment, required provision of free legal representation before the magistrates' court because of severity of penalty and complexity of the law).
[49] (1981) 3 E.H.R.R. 1. See also *Kamasinski v. Austria* (1991) 13 E.H.R.R. 36.
[50] *Artico,* (above), para. 35.
[51] *The Times,* August 11, 2000, HCJ, Scot.
[51A] May 24, 2001, PC.
[52] [1999] S.L.T. 1292.
[53] Referred to in a Registrar's Press Notice. The hearing took place on January 30, 2001.
[54] See also *Stroek v. Belgium,* Application Nos. 36449/97 and 36467/97, March 20, 2001.
[55] (1993) 16 E.H.R.R. 135. See also *X v. United Kingdom* (1984) 6 E.H.R.R. 345, E.C. Comm.

the right to defend in person is qualified and a requirement for an accused to be legally represented in particular proceedings will not necessarily violate the Convention.[56]

Adjournment of trial to arrange legal representation. In *Bullock* **12.30** *v. Her Majesty's Advocate*,[57] the Scottish Appeal Court held that where an accused in a criminal trial who was representing himself requested an adjournment during the trial in order to obtain legal representation, the refusal by the judge to adjourn rendered the trial unfair. The court was influenced by the fact that the prosecution took advantage of the fact that the accused was unrepresented when bringing their case and the judge's conduct of the trial contributed to its unfairness. Accordingly, it is not necessarily the case that a refusal to adjourn proceedings to arrange legal representation will be unfair in every case.

Civil Legal Aid

In *Airey v. Ireland*,[58] the Court held that right of access to a court was a **12.31** right of *effective* access to court and that this might include a right to civil legal aid. Mrs, Airey wished to petition for judicial separation in the Irish High Court in what would be an emotional and legally complex dispute. She could not afford to pay for legal representation and she could not obtain legal aid for civil proceedings. The European Court held that the guarantee of real and effective access to a court and the concept of "equality of arms" did require a lawyer to be provided free of charge to Mrs, Airey by the Irish State. The European Court referred to the right to criminal legal aid in Article 6(3)(c) and stated:

" . . . despite the absence of a similar clause for civil litigation, Article 6(1) may sometimes compel the State to provide for the assistance of a lawyer when such assistance proves indispensable for an effective access to court either because legal representation is rendered compulsory as is done by the domestic law of certain Contracting States for various types of litigation, or by reason of the complexity of the procedure or of the case."

There are four factors derived from *Airey* to be taken into account in **12.32** assessing whether there is an Article 6(1) right to civil legal aid:

(1) the complexity of the procedure;

(2) the complexity of the law;

(3) the possible need to cross-examine expert witnesses;

(4) the difficulty of presenting a case in which the litigant is emotionally involved.

---

[56] *Croissant, ibid.*
[57] 1999 at S.L.T. 1319, AC, Scot.
[58] (1980) 2 E.H.R.R. 305.

12.33   A fifth factor, derived from *Faulkner v. United Kingdom*,[59] is where legal representation is compulsory under the procedure in question. In *Faulkner*, a man detained in Guernsey wanted to bring civil proceedings against the Guernsey authorities for false imprisonment, assault and battery. There existed no system of legal aid and the case did raise arguable claims. The Commission upheld as admissible the applicant's complaint that the absence of civil legal aid violated Article 6(1). The proceedings before the European Court were compromised by a "friendly settlement" reached between the parties on terms that the United Kingdom Government would introduce a civil legal aid scheme that would enable Guernsey to comply with the provisions of the Convention and would pay Mr Faulkner compensation and costs. The Court declined to continue its examination of the case, stating that the decisions of *Airey v. Ireland*,[60] *Tolstoy-Miloslavsky v. United Kingdom*,[61] and *Aït-Mouhoub v. France*[62] specified the nature and extent of the Contracting States' obligation under the Convention in relation to access to court.[63]

12.34   **Civil legal aid not automatic.**   There is no automatic right to civil legal aid and the circumstances in which lack of legal representation can deny an applicant effective access to court are still being worked out. It is clear that any entitlement to civil legal aid as a requirement of Article 6(1) is subject to a number of qualifications.

12.35   **Straightforward cases.**   In a simple case, it is not essential that legal aid be provided: *Stewart-Brady v. United Kingdom*[64] where the Commission held that there is only a violation of Article 6(1) for a failure to provide legal aid where legal representation is essential to the success of the case and cannot be obtained without legal aid (for example, the mentally ill who are required by law to be represented). In *Webb v. United Kingdom*,[65] the Commission held that Article 6(1) was not infringed where the applicant could defend himself in person and the judge ensured the fairness and proper conduct of the proceedings.

12.36   **Selection based on merits.**   A system which selects only meritorious cases is justified. In *Stewart-Brady v. United Kingdom*,[66] the applicant complained about a failure to provide legal aid on an appeal against the striking out of a civil action. Legal aid was refused because there were no reasonable prospects of success and because the costs were disproportionate to any likely damages to be awarded. The Commission did not consider the refusal of legal aid to be arbitrary and, as such, it could not be criticised as constituting a denial of access to court.[67] In *Winer v. United*

---

[59] [1999] E.H.R.L.R. 519; Application No. 30308/96, May 21, 1998, E.C. Comm; November 30, 1999, European Court.
[60] (1980) 2 E.H.R.R. 305.
[61] (1995) 20 E.H.R.R. 442. See para. 10.126 above.
[62] [1999] E.H.R.L.R. 215. See para. 10.126 above.
[63] *ibid.*, para. 30.
[64] (1997) 24 E.H.R.R. C.D. 38.
[65] Application No. 9353/81; (1983) 33 D.R. 133.
[66] (1997) 24 E.H.R.R. C.D. 38.
[67] There may be a need in some cases for the court to be the arbitrator of the prospects of success: *Aerts v. Belgium* (2000) 29 E.H.R.R. 50, (1998) 5 B.H.R.C. 382. Refusal of legal aid must not be arbitrary.

Kingdom,[68] the European Commission held that certain categories of legal proceedings may be excluded from legal aid either by reference to financial criteria or the prospects of success of the proceedings or because of limited financial resources of civil legal aid schemes, provided that this is not arbitrary.

Importance of interest at stake. The obligation to provide civil legal aid depends on the importance of the interest at stake. It is more likely to be established where a case involves personal or family relationships than in relation to cases of a more general nature. In *S v. Principal Reporter & Lord Advocate*,[68A] the Court of Session adjourned proceedings pending notification to the Crown that it was considering making a declaration of incompatibility that legislative provisions dealing with legal aid for proceedings before children's hearings under the Criminal Procedure (Scotland) Act 1995 that were held to be civil in nature, were incompatible with Article 6(1). In *Munro v. United Kingdom*,[69] the European Commission upheld the absence of legal aid in defamation cases, distinguishing the position in *Airey*, which involved intimate family relationships with potential serious consequences for children of the family. It also noted that claims for defamation were inherently risky and were open to abuse. **12.37**

Requirement for financial contribution. The requirement for a financial contribution to be made by assisted persons is not, in itself, incompatible with Article 6(1): *X v. United Kingdom*.[70] Further, it is relevant if a person is able to institute court proceedings by other means, either by bringing the claim himself or by seeking assistance elsewhere.[71] **12.38**

Late withdrawal of legal aid. A failure to adjourn a hearing following the very late withdrawal of legal aid might be vulnerable to assault under Article 6(1): *Lloyd's Bank plc. v. Dix*.[72] **12.39**

Margin of appreciation. A margin of appreciation is granted to the state in terms of the method it adopts for ensuring effective access to a court. Whilst Article 6(1) guarantees an effective right of access to the courts for the determination of their "civil rights and obligations", it leaves to the State a free choice of the means to be used towards this end. The European Court does not regard it as its function to indicate, let alone dictate, what measures should be taken.[73] Accordingly, Article 6(1) does not necessarily require the provision of civil legal aid. In *Andronicou and Constantinou v. Cyprus*,[74] the offer of *ex gratia* financial assistance by the Attorney-General was a sufficient solution to help overcome the applicants' lack of resources and there was no violation of Article 6(1). Alternatively, informal or simple procedures which enable a litigant to represent **12.40**

---

[68] (1986) 48 D.R. 154, Application No. 10871/84.
[68A] March 30, 2001, I.H. Ct. Sess, Scot.
[69] (1987) 52 D.R. 158, Application No. 10594/83.
[70] (1980) 21 D.R. 95, Application No. 8158/78.
[71] *ibid.*, para. 17.
[72] Unreported, October 26, 2000, CA.
[73] *Airey v. Ireland* (1980) 2 E.H.R.R. 305, para. 26. See also *Andronicou and Constantinou v. Cyprus* (1998) 25 E.H.R.R. 491.
[74] (1998) 25 E.H.R.R. 491.

themselves may be sufficient.[75] If pro bono representation is available to a litigant, there may be no breach even in the absence of a grant of civil legal aid.[76]

12.41   **Complaints pre-HRA.**   In *R v. Secretary of State for the Environment, Transport and the Regions, ex p. Challenger*,[77] an application for judicial review in relation to the lack of legal representation at a public inquiry based on the principle of equality of arms and Article 6(1), failed as premature, the HRA not yet being in force.

12.42   **Access to Justice Act 1999.**   There may be potential for challenge to the Access to Justice Act 1999 using the HRA in relation to:

> (1) the removal of legal aid from various classes of civil action (at least where no other form of legal representation is obtainable)
>
> (2) the structure and capping of legal aid funding whereby civil funding may be exhausted by prior calls on the fund in criminal proceedings; and
>
> (3) the exclusion of funded representation in relation to most tribunals[78] and the European Court of Justice.

The Access to Justice Act engages human rights standards including the right of effective access to a court and the principle of equality of arms under Article 6, the right to an effective remedy under Article 13, and freedom from discrimination under Article 14.[79]

12.43   **Legal aid for human rights cases.**   Applications for funding to the Legal Services Commission bring special criteria into play when judicial review or a damages claim against a public authority is proposed. Provided that the case raises significant human rights issues, it can be funded even if the prospects of success are only in the borderline category. The Legal Services Commission also has a wider discretion on the cost versus benefit test. The applicant will have to show that the Convention points sought to be raised have reasonable prospects of success and are material to the case.[79A]

12.44   **Representation of choice in civil proceedings.**   Where civil legal aid is provided, there is no absolute right to legal representation of choice.

---

[75] *Airey v. Ireland* (1980) 2 E.H.R.R. 305, para. 26.
[76] *McTear v. United Kingdom*, Application No. 40291/98, Decision, September 7, 1999.
[77] *The Times*, July 11, 2000, Harrison J.
[78] Not including the Employment Appeal Tribunal and the Mental Health Review Tribunal.
[79] See Opinion of Philip Havers Q.C. and Tim Eicke performing a human rights impact assessment on behalf of Justice; and the Justice Briefing and Human Rights Audit to the House of Commons Committee Stage, April 1999, available from the Justice offices. See also, G.Mansfield Q.C., "Costs, Conditional Fees and Legal Aid" in *An Introduction to Human Rights & the Common Law*, (R.English & P.Havers Q.C. (eds), Oxford: Hart: 2000).
[79A] See Direction by Lord Chancellor, section 6(8) Access to Justice Act 1999 and Legal Services Commission Manual, Volume 3, The Funding Code at paras 3.3.4 and 6.6.

In *R. v. Legal Aid Board, ex p. Duncan and Mackintosh*,[80] the Divisional Court held that although a fundamental right to choose one's legal representative existed at common law,[81] the right is not absolute and may be limited by circumstances, including the client's ability to pay, the availability of the representative or the possession of legal aid. In the latter case, the legal aid authority may not be prepared to fund a legally aided party's particular selection of legal representative. The legal aid schemes were designed to help those who could not obtain legal services by their own means. However, they did not exist to provide an unlimited choice of lawyers.[82] The court left open the possibility of a successful challenge by a person who could not find an adviser competent enough to protect his interests adequately. The courts will not interfere with a person's right to choose his legal representative if that person can afford to pay the legal representative he wishes to retain,[83] although no party has the right to expect a hearing date to be fixed on the basis of the availability of his or her choice of solicitor or advocate.[84]

Right to an effective lawyer. Where a legal aid lawyer is **12.45** appointed, there is a right to an effective lawyer. In *Artico v. Italy*,[85] the applicant complained about the appointment of a legal aid lawyer who refused to act for the applicant. The European Court held that mere appointment of a lawyer was not enough since it did not ensure effective assistance. However, the state cannot be held responsible for every shortcoming on the part of a legal aid lawyer.[86] Where an applicant's legal advisers were incompetent at trial, the overriding consideration on an appeal is whether there has been a fair trial.[87] The Court of Appeal has held that the mere fact that an appellant's solicitors may have failed to carry out their duties to the appellant in a proper manner in the preparation of the case did not of itself mean that his conviction was unsafe.[87A] However, in a criminal context, where it had been demonstrated that

---

[80] Unreported, February 16, 2000, DC t.
[81] The Court noted that the position in the law of England and Wales is in line with the European Convention. A right to legal representation in criminal and civil matters was upheld by the South African High Court in *Bangindawo v. Head of the Nyanda Regional Authority; Hlantlalala v. Head of the Western Tembuland Regional Authority* 1998 (3) B.C.L.R. 314 (Tk), which struck out a statutory prohibition against legal representation before regional authority courts as unconstitutional. In *R. v. Secretary of State for the Home Department and The Lord Chancellor, ex p. Shafiq ur Rehman*, unreported, June 17, 1999, a pre-HRA case, the Court of Appeal held that where the Immigration Advisory Service had agreed to represent an applicant on his appeal against a notice of intention to deport him, but the applicant was seeking representation by a counsel of his choice, the Lord Chancellor was not acting unreasonably in refusing to extend legal aid for that purpose. The court stated that there was no evidence that the IAS or its barristers were incapable of dealing with the applicants' case and any errors on the law made could be corrected by the Court of Appeal. It is unlikely that the outcome of this decision would be different post-HRA.
[82] See also *Maltez v. Lewis, The Times*, May 4, 1999, Neuberger J., cited with approval by the Divisional Court.
[83] *R v. Legal Aid Board, ex p. Duncan and Mackintosh*, unreported, February 16, 2000, para. 460.
[84] *Maltez v. Lewis, The Times*, May 4, 1999, Neuberger J.
[85] (1981) 3 E.H.R.R. 1.
[86] *ibid.*, paras, 36, 37.
[87] *R. v. Nangle, The Times*, January 9, 2001, CA.
[87A] *R. v. Joshil Thakrar*, unreported, May 9, 2001, CA (reported on Lawtel).

counsel's incompetence or failure to perform his duties were of a fundamental nature, an appellate court should proceed with great care before
concluding that even if the incompetence or failures had not occurred the
verdict would have been the same: *Boodram v. State of Trinidad &
Tobago.*[87B]

12.46   **Article 5.**   A right to civil legal aid may also arise in the case of
unlawful detention contrary to Article 5. In the Canadian case of *New
Brunswick (Minister of Health and Community Services) v. G (J)*,[88] it was
held that the provision of legal aid was essential where proceedings
impacted on a person's liberty and security of the person. The right to a fair
hearing required representation by counsel because of the seriousness of
the interests at stake, the complexity of the proceedings and the party's
capacity. Proposed budgetary savings to the legal aid bill did not amount
to justification in such a case.

6. COURT FEES

Requirement to Pay Court Fees

12.47   In order to issue a civil claim, payment of the appropriate fee to the court
concerned is generally required. The requirement to pay court fees is not
in itself a violation of the right of access to a court. However, if a person
without means is deprived of access to the courts by reason of the inability
to pay prescribed court fees, this may constitute a violation of Article 6(1)
or, alternatively, the common law right of access to a court. In *R. v. Lord
Chancellor, ex p. Witham*, the Divisional Court held invalid so much of the
Supreme Court (Amendment) Order 1996 as withdrew the exemption from
court fees for those on income support and withdrew the discretion to
reduce or remit fees in exceptional cases of hardship. Laws J. based his
decision on the common law constitutional right of access to a court which
he held attracted no less protection in domestic law than might be vindicated in Strasbourg.

12.48   Subsequently, in *R. v. Lord Chancellor, ex p. Lightfoot*,[89] the Court of
Appeal dismissed an appeal from the decision of Laws J. who declined to
apply the principle of the right of access to a court to the presentation of
a debtor's bankruptcy petition which requires a deposit of £250.00. Laws
J. held that the presentation of a bankruptcy petition was a benign administrative process for the relief of debtors and was not concerned with the
adjudication of general disputes. The Court of Appeal agreed that the
deposit was security for a fee to be paid to the official receiver for the
performance of his services for the benefit of the petitioning creditor on the
making of the bankruptcy order and was not for access to the court.

International Cases

12.49   In *Harvest Sheen Ltd v. Collector of Stamp Revenue*,[90] the Hong Kong
High Court held that a statutory requirement to pay stamp duty as a

---

[87B] *The Times*, May 15, 2001, PC.
[88] [1999] 3 S.C.R. 46, (1999) 7 B.H.R.C. 615.
[89] [2000] 2 W.L.R. 318, CA. See also *Kreuz v. Poland* [1998] 25 E.H.R.R. CD 80.
[90] [1997] 2 H.K.C. 380, (1997) 2 C.H.R.L.D. 246.

condition of an appeal from an assessment of the Collector of Stamp Revenue contravened the constitutional guarantee under the Bill of Rights Ordinance to a fair hearing since a would-be appellant who simply could not pay the duty would be effectively denied access to the court. The court stated that it would not be difficult to introduce provisions for the giving of security rather than the payment of duty or for the court to defer payment or dispense with security in an appropriate case.[91]

In *MLB v. SLJ*,[92] the U.S. Supreme Court held, in relation to fee require-   **12.50** ments in civil cases, that the state was not obliged to adjust its tolls to account for disparity in material circumstances. However, in a narrow category of civil cases, including cases involving state controls or intrusions on family relationships, the interests of the parties were so fundamental that the state had to provide access to its judicial processes without regard to a party's ability to pay court fees pursuant to the Fourteenth Amendment.

Current Arrangements

The current arrangements for payment of court fees seem unlikely to   **12.51** violate Article 6(1). The Supreme Court Fees Order 1999[93] provides that no fee prescribed by the Order shall be payable by a party who, at the time when a fee becomes payable, is (1) in receipt of any qualifying social security benefit and (2) is not in receipt of legal aid.[94] Further, where it appears to the Lord Chancellor that the payment of any fee prescribed by the Order would, owing to the exceptional circumstances of the particular case, involve undue financial hardship, he may reduce or remit the fee in that case.[95] The requirement for payment of a deposit on payment of a bankruptcy or insolvency petition under the Insolvency Fees Order 1986[96] has been unsuccessfully challenged.[97]

---

[91] cf. *Bahamas Entertainment Ltd v. Koll*, [1996] 3 C.H.R.L.D. 359, Sup Ct Bahamas (the requirement to pay stamp duty on filing of court documents did not infringe right of access to court since the rate of duty was not manifestly excessive and indigent persons could seek an exemption.)

[92] (1996) 3 B.H.R.C. 47, U.S. SC.

[93] S.I. 1999 No. 687. Promulgated by the Lord Chancellor pursuant to powers conferred by the Supreme Court Act 1981, s.130, the Insolvency Act 1986, ss. 414, 415 and the Finance Act 1990, s.128.

[94] s.5. See also the County Courts Fees Order 1999, S.I. 1999 No. 689, art. 5 in like terms.

[95] s.6. See also the County Court Fees Order 1999 S.I. 1999 No. 689, art. 6 in like terms.

[96] S.I. 1986 No. 2030, art. 7.

[97] *R. v. Lord Chancellor, ex p. Lightfoot* [1999] 2 W.L.R. 1126; [2000] 2 W.L.R. 318, CA, above.

PART III

Applications for Civil Practice

Chapter 13
Employment

1. INTRODUCTION

13.01   **General.** The European Convention on Human Rights ("the Convention") was devised at a time when Europe was struggling to come to terms, not only with the devastation wrought by the Second World War, but also with the new geopolitical order suggested by the Cold War.[1] Little wonder then that the primary focus of the text of the Convention is on enshrining individuals' civil and political rights rather than protecting their social and economic rights as workers.[2] The Convention's preoccupation with civil and political rights, which finds expression in the Convention not least in the guarantees of the right to life and the right to freedom from torture, has led some commentators to conclude that incorporation of the Convention into domestic law, which was achieved through the enactment of the Human Rights Act 1998 ("HRA"), is unlikely to have anything other than a very limited impact in the employment field.[3] The view taken here is that, whilst in many cases placing reliance on HRA and, by extension, the Convention, is unlikely to avail either employee or employer, incorporation of the Convention is nonetheless going to alter the legal constitution of employment relations in a number of important respects and, for this reason, cannot simply be ignored by those working in the employment law field.[4] The purpose of this chapter is to examine the principal ways in which the incorporated Convention is likely to impact in the sphere of employment relations.

13.02   **Structure and scope of this chapter.** The chapter begins by considering the distinction which the HRA draws between *vertical* employment relations, which is to say relations which obtain in the context of employment by "public authorities",[5] and *horizontal* employment relations, which is to say relations which obtain between employees and employers in the purely private sector. This distinction, which it must be said is not always an easy one to draw, has great practical significance not least

---

[1] The Convention was signed by representatives of the Member States on November 4, 1950.

[2] *cf.* the Social Charter which was signed by representatives of the Member States of the Council of Europe in 1961. That Charter, which was ratified by the United Kingdom in 1962, is far more obviously a vehicle for protecting the fundamental rights of workers. For example, it enshrines rights including the right to work (Art. 1(2)); the right to receive fair remuneration (Art. 4) and, further, the right of workers to organise (Art. 5). It is beyond the scope of this chapter to consider the implications of this particular international treaty for workers in the United Kingdom. However, it is worth noting that this Charter, along with other treaties such as the various Conventions of the International Labour Organisation, have tended to be woefully neglected by human rights lawyers with the result that those seeking to identify and protect their fundamental rights in the employment field have been obliged to fall back on the relatively scant protection afforded by the European Convention on Human Rights (see further K. D. Ewing, "Social Rights and Human Rights: Britain and the Social Charter—the Conservative Legacy" [2000] E.H.R.L.R. 91. See also John Hendy ᴏ.ᴄ.'s article, "The Human Rights Act, Article 11 and the Right to Strike" [1998] E.H.R.L.R. 582).

[3] See especially K. D. Ewing "The Human Rights Act and Labour Law" (1998) 27 I.L.J. 275.

[4] See further Sir Gavin Lightman and J. Bowers, "Incorporation of the ECHR and its Impact on Employment Law" [1998] E.H.R.L.R 560. These authors consider that the Convention contains several rights which are likely to have a major effect on the employment relationship.

[5] The term "public authority" has a very particular meaning in the context of the HRA. This particular meaning is discussed further below. See also paras 8.15 *et seq.*, above.

because the structure of the HRA is such that those who are employed by public authorities will tend to have substantially enhanced rights as against their employers when compared with those working in the private sector. Consideration is then given to the following specific matters:

(1) the impact of incorporation on the contract of employment. Particular issues which fall to be considered here are:

    (a) whether particular contractual provisions such as the implied term as to trust and confidence are likely to be recast by the domestic courts as a result of incorporation; and

    (b) whether the contract of employment can be used as a vehicle for contracting out of Convention rights;

(2) the impact of incorporation on the construction and application of the employment protection legislation;

(3) the degree to which trade union rights are likely to be affected by incorporation of the Convention;

(4) the extent to which rights guaranteed under specific Convention Articles are likely to inform employment relations post-incorporation. Particular consideration is given here to the rights guaranteed by Articles 8–10 of the Convention; and

(5) the conduct of tribunal proceedings post-incorporation of Convention rights into domestic law.

2. THE PUBLIC/PRIVATE DIVIDE

Introduction

It is ironic that, in an era when the principles of equal treatment have come to be regarded as the keystone of good industrial relations practice, the HRA should institute a set of legal principles which ensure that employees doing similar types of work are treated differently simply because they are doing work for public as opposed to private bodies, yet that is exactly the situation which the HRA has brought into being.[6]   **13.03**

The source of this particular difference in treatment can be located above all in sections 6 and 7 of the Act. Section 6 establishes that, so far as the Act is concerned, a body which acts in a way which is incompatible with a Convention right[7] will only be acting "unlawfully" if that body is a "public authority" for the purposes of section 6. In practice, what this means is that, rather than seeking to impugn the incompatible acts of all bodies,   **13.04**

---

[6] Note, whilst this inequality of treatment may appear to be ironic in the circumstances, it is in no sense surprising. The principal purpose of the Act was always to "bring rights home" (see *Rights Brought Home: the Human Rights Bill*, Cm. 3792, 1997) in the sense of enabling those whose Convention rights had been violated by the state to bring an action against the state in the domestic courts. Had the Act purported to go further and to give individuals rights against bodies which were not emanations of the state it would have gone much further than the Convention itself, which is concerned only with violations of Convention rights by the High Contracting Parties to the Convention (see further Art. 34).

[7] See further HRA, s.1 which identifies which of the Convention rights have been incorporated by the Act, also discussed at paras 2.12 *et seq.*

irrespective of whether those bodies are private or public in nature, the Act only purports to impugn the incompatible acts of those bodies which are:

(1) obvious public authorities for the purposes of section 6(1) (examples of such authorities would include local authorities, the police, government departments, and prisons)[7A]; or

(2) public authorities by virtue of section 6(3)(a) (section 6(3)(a) provides that courts and tribunals are also public authorities for the purposes of the Act)[7B]; or

(3) hybrid public authorities by virtue of section 6(3)(b) (section 6(3)(b), read in conjunction with section 6(5), provides that hybrid bodies which have mixed private and public functions will be "public authorities" but only where the act which is being impugned is public rather than private in nature).[7C]

13.05 Hybrid bodies which are "public authorities" for the purposes of section 6(3)(b) might include, for example, organisations such as Railtrack, the NSPCC, private security companies managing contracted out prisons and doctors in general NHS practice. It is important to note that, in contrast with hybrid public authorities, *each and every act* of an obvious public authority (*i.e.* a section 6(1) public authority) may be challenged by victims on the ground that those acts are incompatible with the Convention, even if in general those acts are apparently done in a private law context. Therefore, actions taken by a section 6(1) public authority in respect of their employees will be acts which can be subject to a section 6 challenge, even though ordinarily those actions appear to be done in a private law context.[8]

Challenging Unlawful Acts

13.06 Section 7 establishes that an individual, who is or would be "a victim"[9] of an act which section 6(1) deems to be unlawful, may use section 6 either as a sword or a shield. Thus, under section 7(1)(a), individuals may use

---

[7A] See also para. 8.16.
[7B] *ibid.*
[7C] See also para. 8.17.
[8] See further J. Coppel, *The Human Rights Act 1998: Enforcing the European Convention in Domestic Courts* (Wiley, 1999) para. 2.19; the Lord Chancellor's discussion of "public authorities" in the Committee Stage in the Lords, H.L. Debs, November 24, 1997, cols 810–811; and also the case of *Swedish Engine Driver's Union v. Sweden* A/20 (1979) 1 E.H.R.R. 617 at 626–627 (European Court held that an individual could rely on the Convention as against the state even where the individual's relationship with the state would ordinarily be characterised as a private law relationship, for example, by reason that it was founded upon a common law contract). Although *cf.* G. Morris, "The Human Rights Act and the Public/Private Divide" (1998) 27 I.L.J. 293 at 297–8J
[9] S.7(7) provides that person will be a "victim" for the purposes of s.7(1) if he or she would be a victim for the purposes of Art. 34 of the Convention. In general, a person will be a victim for the purposes of Art. 34 if he or she is a person who is or might potentially become directly affected by the act or omission in issue (see, *e.g.*, *Corigliano v. Italy* (1983) 5 E.H.R.R. 334 and *Campbell and Cosans v. United Kingdom* (1982) 4 E.H.R.R. 293). See further paras 8.06 *et seq.*, above.

section 6 as a sword to bring proceedings in an appropriate court of tribunal against the responsible authority on the basis that the authority has committed a statutory tort under section 6(1).[9A] In the alternative, under section 7(1)(b), individuals may rely on section 6(1) as a shield in legal proceedings which have been brought against them by or at the instigation of a public authority or, alternatively, when those proceedings amount to an appeal against the decision of a court or tribunal (section 7(1)(b)).[9B]

Implications for Employment Law

The principal practical implications of these provisions in the employment law context are as follows:

13.07

    (1) Employees who are employed by obvious public authorities will very probably be able to challenge *any act* of their employers which is incompatible with their Convention rights on the ground that those actions amount to a statutory tort for the purposes of section 6(1).[10] Such challenges can be made in the context of proceedings brought against the employer (section 7(1)(a) proceedings) or in the context of proceedings brought by or at the instigation of the employer (section 7(1)(b) proceedings). If the employee's section 6(1) complaint is successful, he or she may be awarded damages and/or such other remedy as is within the court's powers (section 8). However, the court will only award damages under section 8 in circumstances where such an award is necessary to afford "just satisfaction" to the employee, taking into account, in particular: (a) other relief or remedy already granted by the courts (or tribunals) in respect of the employee's complaint; and (b) the consequences of any decision made by the courts or tribunals in respect of the employer's act (see section 8(3)).

    (2) Employees of hybrid public authorities will likewise be able to challenge the incompatible acts of their employers but only where the act in question is done *in pursuance of a public law function*. Again, if the employee's challenge is successful he or she may be awarded damages and/or such other remedy as is within the court's powers pursuant to section 8 of the Act.

    (3) However, employees will not have recourse to section 6 in circumstances where either they are employed by a purely private employer or they are employed by a hybrid, mixed function

---

[9A] See further paras 8.04 *et seq.*
[9B] See further paras 8.40 *et seq.*
[10] See further *Swedish Engine Drivers Union v. Sweden* (No. 2) A/20 (1979) 1 E.H.R.R. 617: employment decisions of state authorities are not exempt from scrutiny. See also G. Morris "The Human Rights Act and the Public/Private Divide in Employment Law" [1998] 27 I.L.J. 293.

public authority but the act which the employee is seeking to impugn is itself a "private act". Importantly, employees who fall into either one of these categories will be able to obtain protection of their Convention rights only *indirectly*, for example:

(a) by placing reliance on section 3 of the HRA[11] and section 6 of the HRA[12] to enhance their rights under various provisions in the employment protection legislation; or, alternatively,

(b) by arguing that the court will be in breach of its own section 6 obligation to act compatibly with the Convention if it fails to develop common law principles relating to the contract of employment so as to be in a way that is consistent with the employees' Convention rights.[13]

Resisting Section 6 Challenges

13.08 Of course, even if the employee can show that a particular act of a public authority employer is, prima facie, amenable to a section 6 challenge, this does not automatically mean that that employee will succeed if and when he does challenge that act in the courts.[13A] There are three principal reasons why this is so.[14]

(1) Despite appearances, the act in question may not in fact interfere with any recognisable Convention right belonging to the employee. For example, the act may itself amount only to a breach of the individual's contractual rights rather than to a breach of his or her fundamental rights under the Convention.

(2) Again, despite the appearance of a breach, there may be no actual breach of the individual's Convention rights because, even if the act itself does amount to an interference with the individual's Convention rights, that act may be one that can be justified under the Convention (see further, for example, the express justifications contained in Article 10(2): an interference with an individual's right to freedom of expression will be justified where it is (a) necessary in a democratic society to fulfil one of the legitimate aims identified in Article 10(2) (*i.e.* there is a

---

[11] S.3 obliges the courts to construe legislation, so far as possible, so as to make it compatible with the Convention, see further paras 2.39 and 5.02.

[12] S.6 obliges courts and tribunals to act compatibly with the Convention save where they are prohibited from doing so by incompatible primary legislation

[13] See further G. Morris, "The Human Rights Act and the Public/Private Divide in Employment Law" (1998) 27 I.L.J. 293.

[13A] See also para. 8.48 in relation to defences to HRA claims.

[14] Note, it may be that in addition to the three reasons set out in this paragraph, public authority employers may also be able to resist s.6 challenges on the basis that the employee has contracted out of the Convention right in question by entering into the contract of employment. This is a controversial proposition which is considered further below at para. 13.33.

pressing social need for the interference); (b) it is prescribed by law; and (c) it is proportionate to the achievement of the particular legitimate aim).[15] Where applicable, such justifications have the effect of ensuring that the act in question is not regarded as giving rise to an actual violation of the individual's Convention rights.[16]

(3) Even if the act cannot be justified within the eyes of the Convention, the act may yet fall short of being "unlawful" for the purposes of section 6(1) because it may be an act which was effectively *authorised or required by primary legislation* which cannot be read down or given effect to in a way that is compatible with the Convention (see further section 6(2) of the HRA which has the effect of preserving the lawfulness of those acts of a public authority which, rather than being acts which flowed from the exercise of the authority's discretionary powers, were effectively foisted onto the authority by incompatible primary legislation.)[17]

13.09 Moreover, if the employee is an employee of a hybrid public authority, then the employer may in any event be able to avoid having its actions subject to a section 6 challenge on the basis that the act in question was private rather than public in nature. This raises the important question of when, if ever, acts done by a hybrid authority in its capacity as employer can be said to be "public" rather than "private" in nature.

Identifying "Public Acts"

13.10 Currently, no authoritative answer can be given to the question of when an act done by a public authority will be public rather than private in nature. This is so, first, because the HRA itself does not purport to set out when an act of a hybrid body will be public rather than private and, secondly, because there is as yet no judicial authority which establishes when a hybrid employer's acts will be treated as being a public as opposed to a private act for the purposes of HRA. That being said, it is suggested here that the courts are likely to adopt an approach to this particular question which mirrors the approach already taken to the "public/private divide" in traditional judicial review proceedings.[18]

---

[15] The nature and operation of the justification contained in the Convention are discussed at paras 4.33 *et seq.* above.

[16] That an individual's rights under the Convention are not absolute but are subject to restrictions which are either express or implied is an uncontroversial principle. See further Chap. 3, above, and J. Coppel, *The Human Rights Act 1998: Enforcing the European Convention in Domestic Courts* (Wiley, 1999), paras 6.31–6.32.

[17] In effect, the authority is immunised against a s.6(1) claim in these circumstances because it is deemed to be the "innocent agent" of primary legislation which Parliament intended should be incompatible with the Convention. See further the discussion of s.6(2) in J. Coppel, *The Human Rights Act 1998: Enforcing the European Convention in Domestic Courts* (Wiley, 1999), paras 2.86–2.87.

[18] See further Dawn Oliver, *Common Values and the Public-Private Divide* (Butterworths, 1999).

13.11 That approach provides that, where relations between the parties are rooted in a common law contract, the presumption will be that the act done by the defendant will be private rather than public in nature; that presumption can only be rebutted where there is a clear public law element governing the relationship, for example, the relationship has a self-evident statutory underpinning and/or is subject to rigorous state controls.[19] Applying this approach to the example of a private security company which is responsible for providing security services both in Her Majesty's prisons and in private commercial premises produces the following results.

(1) Acts taken by the company in respect of employees guarding commercial premises will be presumed to be private in nature since the relationship between employer and employee is purely contractual and is not subject to any public law element.

(2) Acts taken in respect of those company employees who work in the prisons will be presumed to be private since the relationship between the company and the employee is governed principally by a contract of employment. However, that presumption can be rebutted in circumstances where the relationship is nonetheless shot through with a public law element because, for example, provision of services at the prison is broadly underpinned by statutory rules and/or the employment of prison workers is subject to a regime of close governmental control.[20] It is suggested that this is likely to be the preferred approach of the courts not least because of its consonance with traditional judicial approaches to the private/public divide.

Some Practical Examples

13.12 It is useful at this point to illustrate the principles identified above by way of certain concrete examples. Consider then the position of Miss A. Miss A is a local authority employee who is dismissed for expressing political views which run contrary to the views espoused by the majority political party. In addition to any claim for unfair dismissal, which she might bring under section 98 of the Employment Rights Act 1996 (ERA 1996), Miss A will have a free-standing section 6(1) claim against the authority for breach of her Article 10(1) right to freedom of expression. That claim, which may be brought in the county court or the High Court, depending on the value of the claim, will be bound to succeed unless Miss A's dismissal can be justified by the authority under Article 10(2)[21] or, alternatively, unless the

---

[19] *R v. East Berkshire Health Authority, ex p. Walsh* [1985] Q.B. 152; *R v. Secretary of State for the Home Department, ex p. Benwell* [1985] Q.B. 554; *McClaren v. Home Office* [1990] I.C.R. 824; *R. v. Lord Chancellor, ex p. Hibbert and Saunders* [1993] C.O.D. 326; *R. v. Crown Prosecution Service, ex p. Hogg* [1994] 6 Admin. L.R. 778; *R. v. Independent Broadcasting Authority, ex p. Rank Organisation, The Times,* March 14 1996.

[20] See generally, G Morris, "The Human Rights Act and the Public/Private Divides in Employment Law" (1998) 27 I.L.J. 293.

[21] See further *Vögt v. Germany* (1996) 21 E.H.R.R. 205 (schoolteacher's Art. 10 rights were breached when she was dismissed because of her membership of the Communist Party).

dismissal was effectively required or authorised by primary legislation.[22] Further, if the claim does succeed, then Miss A may be granted damages under section 8 of the Act provided that, having taken into account any other relief or remedy granted to Miss A and, further, the consequences of any decision taken by the courts in respect of Miss A's dismissal, the court (or tribunal) considers that damages are necessary to award Miss A "just satisfaction" (section 8(3)).

13.13 Compare the position of Mr B who is hired to clean commercial premises by a mixed function cleaning company (the company also carries out street-cleansing functions pursuant to a contracting-out arrangements entered into with the local authority) and who is dismissed for expressing political views which the chairman of the company finds distasteful. Unlike Miss A, Mr B cannot rely on section 6 to bring a claim against the company for breach of his Article 10(1) rights because, so far as the Act is concerned, the company is not a "public authority" for the purposes of section 6 and, as such, is not liable to a section 6(1) claim.[23]

13.14 Compare also the position of Mr C who is employed by the company which employs Mr B but who is hired to carry out duties as a street cleaner. Assuming that the courts adopt the approach to the private/public divide identified above and, assuming further the provision of street-cleansing services by private companies is not subject to stringent statutory or governmental controls, section 6(1) will also probably not assist Mr C in circumstances where he is dismissed for expressing views similar to the views expressed by Mr B. Section 6(1) will probably not assist Mr C in these circumstances since the court will probably conclude: (1) that the relationship between Mr C and the company is governed by a contract of employment; (2) that, since the provision of street-cleansing services by the company is not subject to significant statutory or governmental controls, there is no sufficient public law element to warrant rebutting the presumption that the act in question is private rather than public; and (3) that in the circumstances section 6 of the HRA simply does not apply to the company's act of dismissing Mr C.

13.15 In light of the fact that section 6 of the HRA affords direct benefits only to a fairly limited class of employees, it is important to consider whether the HRA offers employees any other indirect means for enhancing the protection of their Convention rights in the workplace.

---

[22] Note, in September 1998, the European Court held that restrictions on participation in political activities imposed on certain local government workers by the Local Government and Housing Act 1989 and regulations made thereunder (included restrictions on speaking to the public on party political matters) did not violate Art. 10(1) of the Convention because the legislative provisions could be justified under Art. 10(2) (see *Ahmed v. United Kingdom* [1999] I.R.L.R. 188). Given the domestic courts' obligations to take into account Strasbourg jurisprudence when deciding s.6 claims (see further HRA, s.2), it is highly unlikely that a senior local authority officer who was dismissed for acting contrary to his obligations under these provisions would be able to mount a successful s.6 claim against his employer. See further G. Morris, 'The political activities of local government workers and the European Convention on Human Rights' [1999] P.L. Summer 211.

[23] However, that is not to say that the dismissal will be lawful for the purposes of fair dismissal provisions in the ERA 1996. The impact of the HRA on the provisions of ERA 1996 is discussed further below.

Indirect Reliance on Convention Rights

13.16 It is suggested here that there are potentially two methods by which employees will indirectly be able to avail themselves of the Convention. The first method involves developing the contract of employment so that it becomes essentially Convention compliant. The second method involves requiring the courts to construe provisions contained in the employment protection legislation so as to reaffirm the primacy of Convention rights in the workplace. This latter method entails placing reliance in particular on the interpretative provisions contained in section 3 of the Act, as to which see further paras 5.02 *et seq.*). These two methods are now considered in turn.

3. THE CONTRACT OF EMPLOYMENT

Introduction

13.17 This section is concerned with exploring the potential of the HRA to effect changes in the courts' attitude to the contract of employment. The section begins with an analysis of the ways in which the courts' own section 6(1) obligations are likely to impact on the courts' approach to certain terms implied into the contract of employment. It concludes with an examination of the issue of contracting out of Convention rights.

Developing the Common Law

13.18 As has been affirmed in earlier chapters, the question of the extent to which the courts will, post-incorporation, seek to develop common law principles so as to make them compatible with Convention rights is a question which cannot be answered with any great certainty at the present time. This is so, not least, because the Act itself gives no indication as to how incorporation of the Convention is to influence the development of common law principles.[24]

13.19 In chapter 5, three possible outcomes were identified:

(1) the courts would desist from developing common law principles so as to be compatible with the Convention and they would do so on the basis that the statutory provisions of the HRA were never designed to encroach on such principles;

(2) whilst recognising that they had no authority to use HRA to create new common law causes of action, the courts would still develop existing common law causes of action so as to be compatible with the Convention and they would do so because that was what was effectively required by section 6(1); and, finally,

(3) the courts would construe their section 6(1) obligations as requiring them to develop the common law not only by adapting

---

[24] See further the discussion of the impact of the HRA on the development of the common law in paras 5.15 *et seq.*, above.

existing causes of action so as to be compatible with the Convention but also by creating new Convention driven causes of action, for example, a new Article 8 right to privacy.

The ensuing analysis proceeds on the assumption that, of these three **13.20** possibilities, the second is the most likely to become an actuality. This assumption is made on the basis that the courts are likely to want to avoid the first approach because it is so inherently conservative and may well result in the courts being made the subject of section 6 challenges, and are likely to want to avoid the third approach because it risks creating the impression that the judiciary is seeking to use the common law as a means of usurping Parliament's legislative function.[25] If the courts were to adopt the second approach, then they would be mirroring the approach which has been taken by the courts, for example, in Canada.[26] It should be noted however that, in the event that the courts consider that section 6 of the HRA does not oblige them to develop the common law so as to be consonant with Convention principles, the ensuing analysis will have no realm of application: the contract of employment will not be developed so as to render it broadly Convention compliant and, consequently, employees operating in the purely private sphere, *i.e.* in horizontal relationships, will not be able to use the contract of employment as a vehicle for factoring Convention rights into their relationship with their employer.

Developing the Contract of Employment

If one assumes that, post-incorporation, the courts will tend to develop **13.21** common law principles so as to be compatible with the Convention, whilst stopping short of creating new causes of action, then this has the following important implication for the construction of contracts of employment by the courts[27]:

(1) the courts may well develop the existing obligations which are currently implied into all contracts of employment so as to render those obligations consonant with the employee's Convention rights;

(2) this may entail developing the employer's implied obligation to maintain trust and confidence so as to incorporate an obligation on the part of the employer not to act incompatibly with the

---

[25] The decision of the Court of Appeal in *Douglas v. Hello!* ([2001] 2 W.L.R. 992) would appear to provide some support for the proposition that, of the three approaches identified, the second approach will be the one that the courts will ultimately favour. See further the Lord Chancellor's claim that, in the context of s.6: "the courts may not act as legislators and grant new remedies for infringement of Convention rights unless the common law itself enables them to develop new rights or remedies.": H.L. Debs., November 24, 1997, col. 785.

[26] See further, in the employment law field, the case of *Re Canadian Pacific Ltd v. United Transportation Union* (1987) 31 L.A.C. 179.

[27] Note, for the purposes of this section all references to "courts" should be construed as references to both the employment tribunals and the ordinary courts.

employee's rights under the Convention, save, that is, where that action can be justified by the employer [28];

(3) The question why the courts might be likely to develop implied obligations contained in the contract of employment in this way can be answered in the following terms. Under the Convention, the state has a limited positive obligation to regulate relations between its citizens so as to protect an individual's Convention rights from interference by other individuals. That positive obligation includes an obligation, which is subject to the state's margin of appreciation,[29] to ensure that individuals who suffer interference with their Convention rights at the hands of other individuals have a remedy for that interference.[30] It may be that this positive Convention obligation requires the courts to provide a remedy to private sector employees whose Convention rights have been unjustifiably interfered with by their employers.[31] If such a positive obligation can be said to exist, then the courts may themselves be acting in breach of their section 6(1) obligation to act compatibly with the Convention, such that they can be rendered liable to have their decisions subject to review in the appellate courts or in the European Court on the ground that they have acted in breach of their section 6(1) obligations, if they do not provide a remedy to employees who have suffered an unjustified interference with their Convention rights at the hands of their employer. If the courts do seek to develop implied obligations contained in the contract of employment so as to render those obligations Convention compatible, then they may go some considerable way towards immunising themselves against a section 7 challenge mounted by a private sector employee who has suffered an interference with his Convention rights.

13.22 The question then arises as to how the courts will set about recrafting obligations implied into the contract of employment so as to render those obligations Convention consonant. Some tentative responses to this question are set out below.

---

[28] See further B. Hepple, "Human Rights and Employment Law", *Amicus Curiae* (June 8, 1998), pp. 19–23; J. Craig and H. Oliver, "The Rights to Privacy in the Public Workplace: Should the Private Sector be Concerned?" [1998] I.L.J. 49 at 54–55; and S. Palmer, "Human Rights: Implications for Labour Law" [2000] C.L.J. 168 at 181. See also the American case of *Luck v. Southern Pacific Transportation Co.*, 267 Cal. Reptr. 618 (CA 1st Dist, 1990) where the Californian Court of Appeal held that the implied covenant of good faith and fair dealing contained in the contract of employment imposed an obligation on employers to abide by human rights principles when dealing with their employees: at 624–628.
[29] As to which see further paras 4.22 *et seq.*, above.
[30] See further the cases of *Rommelfanger v. Germany* (1989) 62 D.R. 151; *Plattform "Ärzte für das Leben" v. Austria* (1991) 13 E.H.R.R. 204; *Lopes Ostra v. Spain* (1995) 20 E.H.R.R. 277; *Stubbings v. U.K.* (1997) 23 E.H.R.R. 213; *A v U.K.* [1998] 2 F.L.R. 959; *Spencer v. U.K.* (1998) 25 E.H.R.R. C.D. 105; *Otto-Preminger-Institut v. Austria* (1994) 19 E.C.H.R.R. 34; and *Douglas v. Hello!* ([2001] 2 W.L.R. 992, CA). See further the discussion of the doctrine of positive obligation in Chap. 5, above.
[31] Such a possibility was seemingly recognised by the European Court in the case of *Rommelfanger v. Germany* (1989) 62 D.R. 151.

Developing "Trust and Confidence" Obligations

There is a term implied into every contract of employment that the **13.23** employer shall not:

> "without reasonable and proper cause, conduct itself in a manner calculated [or] likely to destroy or seriously damage the relationship of trust and confidence between employer and employee."[32]

Over time, this particular implied term has been substantially expanded by the courts so as to try to maximise employees' protection against unacceptable treatment suffered at the hands of their employers. Thus, for example, whereas in the past, the term was concerned only with prohibiting forms of behaviour by the employer which would render the working for that employer intolerable,[33] today it also encapsulates the principle that, beyond ensuring that its employee finds his working conditions tolerable, the employer must also ensure that it does not, during the life of the employment contract, act in a way that results in its employees being stigmatised in the job market once the contract has terminated.[34]

Whilst there are, of course, limits on the extent to which the implied **13.24** obligation to maintain trust and confidence,[35] it is suggested here that, if the courts do consider they are bound under the HRA to develop the common law so as to make it consonant with the Convention, then the courts may well conclude that this particular implied obligation constitutes the ideal vehicle for factoring Convention rights into the contractual relationship between employer and employee.

If, the courts do decide that the implied obligation to maintain trust and **13.25** confidence is the ideal vehicle for factoring Convention rights into the employment relationship, then, at least in the context of private sector employment relations, it is suggested that this is likely to have the implications set out below.

> (1) The obligation to maintain trust and confidence will incorporate a duty on the part of the employer not to do anything which is calculated, or likely to interfere with the employee's Convention rights, save where the act in question can be justified by the employer.

---

[32] *Woods v. WM Car Services (Peterborough) Ltd* [1981] I.R.L.R. 347, para. 17; [1981] I.C.R. 666, EAT, *affd.* [1982] I.R.L.R. 413, [1982] I.C.R. 693, CA. See also *Lewis v. Motorworld Garages* [1986] I.C.R. 157, and *Imperial Group Pension Trust Limited v. Imperial Tobacco Limited* [1991] 1 W.L.R. 589.

[33] See, *e.g.*, *Woods v. WM Car Services (Peterborough) Ltd* [1981] I.R.L.R. 347.

[34] See further the case of *Malik v. Bank of Credit and Commerce International SA* [1997] I.C.R. 606, and also *TSB plc v. Harris* [2000] I.R.L.R. 197, EAT (breach of trust and confidence to send prospective employer a reference which stated that a number of complaints had been made against the employee some of which had been upheld in circumstances where the employer had failed to inform the employee of the complaints or given her an opportunity to make representations about them). See also *Macari v. Celtic Football and Athletic Co* [1999] I.R.L.R. 787 (Ct of Sess) (giving instruction in bad faith and then dismissing the employee for failing to obey the instruction was a breach of trust and confidence).

[35] See further, in particular, *Johnson v. Unisys* [2001] 2 W.L.R. 1076, HL (stigma damages cannot be recovered for breaches of the implied obligation as to trust and confidence which related to the manner of the employee's dismissal).

(2) An employer will be able to justify the impugned act in circumstances where he can show that the act: (a) was done in furtherance of a legitimate business aim and, further, (b) was reasonably proportionate to the achievement of that legitimate aim.

13.26 Clearly, the form of "justification" outlined above bears more resemblance to the form of justification which has been accepted by the courts in restrictive covenant cases[36] than it does to the forms of justification which are to be found in the Convention Articles themselves.[37] It is suggested here that, in the context of private sector employment relations, the courts would probably choose to adopt the former restrictive covenant-style justification rather than the justifications already present in the Convention for three reasons.

(1) The Convention justifications were evidently designed to be applicable only to emanations of the state and cannot therefore appropriately be applied to private businesses operating in the commercial sector.

(2) The restrictive covenant-style justification appears to strike "a fair balance" between the rights of employees not to suffer interferences with their Convention rights and the rights of the employers to take reasonable steps to promote their legitimate business interests.[38]

(3) The justification successfully incorporates the principle of proportionality, a principle which is in many ways the touchstone of Convention justifications,[39] whilst at the same time avoiding the highly technical approach required by the Convention justifications.

So far as public authority employers are concerned, it remains to be seen what would amount to a justification in the context of alleged breaches of the common law contractual obligation to maintain trust and confidence. On one view, an act which potentially breaches trust and confidence should only be regarded as justified where it accords with the strict technical justifications contained in the Convention because only then will the common law be rendered truly consonant with Convention principles. On another view, however, such technical justifications should be dispensed with in favour of the looser restrictive covenant type of justification outlined above. In support of this latter viewpoint, it could be argued that such a looser justification is more appropriate given the contractual, non-

---

[36] As to which, see further Brearley & Bloch, *Employment Convenants and Confidential Information* (Butterworths, 1999), Chap. 9, pp. 142–152.

[37] See further paras 4.33 *et seq.* above, on the subject of Convention justifications.

[38] As to the importance of "striking a fair balance" between competing rights in Convention jurisprudence, see further especially *Sporrong and Lönnroth v. Sweden* (1983) 5 E.H.R.R. 35.

[39] See further the Opinion of Advocate-General Van Gerven in the leading ECJ case of *SPUC v. Grogan* [1991] E.C.R. 1–4685 at 4719–4720; *Dudgeon v. United Kingdom* (1982) 4 E.H.R.R. 149 at 167; and Eissen, "The Principle of Proportionality in the Case-Law of the European Court of Human Rights" in MacDonald, Matscher and Petzold (eds), *The European System for the Protection of Human Rights* (Martinus Nijhoff, 1993).

statutory nature of the issue which falls to be determined by the tribunal.

Some Practical Examples

The approach to the trust and confidence term outlined above will now be considered in the context of two concrete examples.   **13.27**

(1) Mr X has worked for his employer in the United Kingdom for a number of years. The employer subsequently decides that Mr X should be posted to India for five years. Mr X's contract of employment contains a mobility clause which permits such a posting. Mr X resists the decision on the basis that it will interfere with his right to family life under Article 8, not least because it is entirely impractical for his family to remove itself to India for five years. The employer nonetheless insists that Mr X take up his post in India notwithstanding that: the work which Mr X is to do in India could quite easily have been done by another of the employer's employees already situated in India; that there was work available for the employee to do in the United Kingdom; and that it is quite obvious that it would be entirely impractical for Mr X's family to uproot itself and move abroad. The employee resigns claiming constructive unfair dismissal on the basis that the employer breached the implied term as to trust and confidence. In such a case, the tribunal may well arrive at the following conclusions:

    (a) Mr X had acted incompatibly with the employee's Article 8(1) right to family life by refusing the employee's request;

    (b) the employer had no justification for that incompatible act because, even if Mr X's request was refused in order to further a legitimate business aim of the employer, the refusal itself was evidently not reasonably necessary to achieve that aim, *i.e.* its effects were disproprortionate;

    (c) in the circumstances, it is clear that the employer had so damaged the relationship of trust and confidence between employer and employee that the contract of employment was repudiated, thereby entitling Mr X to resign claiming constructive dismissal;

    (d) finally, the dismissal was clearly unfair in all the circumstances.

(2) An employer discovers that that one of its employees is stealing goods from its storeroom as a result of going through its stock records. The employer does not have any idea who the thief is. Moreover, so many of the employer's employees have access to its storeroom that in practice it is very difficult for the employer to identify the thief. The employer secretly installs video surveillance cameras in the storeroom for the purpose of discovering the thief. Subsequently, the cameras show one particular employee hiding goods in her pockets. The employee can offer no explanation for her conduct and is dismissed. A fellow

employee, Mrs Y, subsequently discovers that she has been subject to secret video surveillance and resigns claiming constructive dismissal on the basis that her employer has breached the implied obligation to maintain trust and confidence by acting incompatibly with her Article 8(1) right to privacy. In a case such as this, it is suggested that the court will be likely to come to the following conclusions:

(a) whilst prima facie the employer may have been interfering in the Mrs Y's private life, the employer's actions do not amount to a breach of the implied obligation to maintain trust and confidence because the employer has a justification for his actions;

(b) in particular, the employer has a justification in that the surveillance system was set up solely for the purpose of furthering the employer's legitimate business aim of rooting out a criminal member of staff and was, in the circumstances, proportionate to the achievement of that legitimate aim since the surveillance was limited to the storeroom area and did not extend to areas where employees might be expected to engage in private acts;

(c) in light of the fact that the employer had a justification for its acts, it cannot be said that those acts amounted to a breach of the employee's Article 8(1) rights;

(d) in the circumstances, there is no breach of the implied term as to trust and confidence and, hence, Mrs Y's resignation was just that: a resignation.[40]

"Trust and Confidence" and Reasonableness

13.28   It is worth noting at this point that, if, post-incorporation, the tribunal were to adopt an approach to the trust and confidence term which focused on whether the employer had, without justification, acted incompatibly with its employee's Convention rights, it would inevitably be moving away from the traditional approach to trust and confidence. The reason for this is that such an approach, in effect, requires that the tribunal consider whether the employer has acted "reasonably" in the circumstances and, as is clear from a number of pre-incorporation authorities, traditionally considerations relating to the reasonableness of the employer's conduct have been regarded as being largely irrelevant to the issue of whether or not the employer has acted in breach of its obligations to maintain trust and confidence (see further *Western Excavating v. Sharp* [41] and also the case

---

[40] See further Craig and Oliver, "The Rights to Privacy in the Public Workplace: Should the Private Sector be Concerned?" [1998] I.L.J. 49 at 55 and Westin, "Privacy in the Workplace: How Well Does American Law Reflect American Values" 72 Chi-Kent L.R. 271 (1996). In the context of the monitoring of business calls, Westin has argued that employee privacy is not threatened by legitimate employer monitoring of work and "it simply offends reason and common sense to assert an immunity from supervision—as a 'privacy right'—for business calls": at 281. *Cf.* the Canadian case of *Re Canadian Pacific Ltd v. United Transportation Union* (1987) 31 L.A.C. 179, Canadian arbitrator rejected the employer's submission that it was within its management prerogative to implement a policy of random drug testing. In relation to surveillance generally see further paras 19.52 *et seq.*
[41] [1978] Q.B. 761, [1978] 1 All E.R.713.

of *White v. Reflecting Road Studs* [42]: an employer was not acting in breach of its obligations as to trust and confidence merely because it exercised its rights under a mobility clause contained in the employee's contract of employment unreasonably, although, the employer would be acting in breach of those obligations in the context of the mobility clause if it exercised the clause in a way that was capricious or arbitrary; although *cf. Woods v. WM Car Services* [43] where the EAT went some way towards rehabilitating the notion that the reasonableness of the employer's conduct was central to the determination of whether there had been a breach of the term as to trust and confidence).

It is suggested here that the mere fact that the post-incorporation **13.29** approach to the construction of the trust and confidence obligations outlined above signals a move towards a more reasonableness-centred approach is unlikely in itself to be sufficient to rule out the adoption of that approach by the courts and tribunals. The reasons for this include the fact that, as cases such as *Woods v. WM Car Services* [44] illustrate, it would appear that the EAT has never been wholly reconciled to an approach to the trust and confidence term which rules out consideration of the reasonableness of the employer's conduct. [45] In the circumstances, it is unlikely that the new approach will be rejected simply on the grounds that it implicitly imports considerations relating to the reasonableness of the employer's conduct. Even if this were not the case, it may well be that courts and tribunals will consider that they are compelled to embrace an approach which factors in the reasonableness of the employer's conduct because such an approach is the necessary product of any attempt to construe the trust and confidence term so as to be compatible with the employee's Convention rights. [46]

It is clear that, if and in so far as the courts and tribunals do adapt the **13.30** implied term as to trust and confidence in this way, then any number of employment matters are likely to be affected including the exercise of management discretion in respect of non-fraternisation policies, dress codes, and the treatment of whistle-blowers. [47]

---

[42] [1991] I.R.L.R. 331, [1991] I.C.R. 773, EAT.

[43] [1981] I.R.L.R. 347, [1981] I.C.R. 666, EAT; *affd.* [1982] I.R.L.R. 413, [1982] I.C.R. 693, CA

[44] [1981] I.R.L.R. 347, para. 17, [1988] I.C.R. 666, EAT; *affd.* [1982] I.R.L.R. 413, [1982] I.C.R. 693, CA.

[45] See further *Harvey on Industrial Relations and Employment Law* (Butterworths) para. A[448].

[46] It should be noted that this particular approach is broadly consistent with the approach taken to the processing of employee data under the European Directive on Data Protection, Directive 95/46. Art. 1(1) of the Directive obliges Member States to "protect the right to privacy with respect to the processing of personal data". Art. 7 of that Directive stipulates that data processing must be "legitimate". The test of legitimacy may be satisfied where the employee has "unambiguously given his consent" to data processing (Art. 7(a)) or where the employer is able to advance a legitimate interest furthered by the data processing which is capable of overriding the privacy interests of those employees subject to the processing (Art. 7(f)). See further Chap. 19, below.

[47] See further Craig and Oliver, "The Rights to Privacy in the Public Workplace: Should the Private Sector be Concerned?" [1998] I.L.J. 49 at 54; Bowers and Lewis, "Whistleblowing, Freedom of Expression in the Workplace" [1996] E.H.R.L.R. 637 (Note, due to the timing of its publication, this art. does not address the issue of whether the Public Interest Disclosure Act 1998 will suffice to protect whistleblowers in the workplace); and Clayton and Pitt, "Dress Codes and Freedom of Expression" [1997] E.H.R.L.R. 54.

Summary

13.31   To summarise, if the courts decide that they are compelled, as a result of
section 6(1) of the HRA, to develop common law causes of action so that
they are compatible with the Convention, then this is likely to impact on the
courts' approach to the construction of the trust and confidence term in
employment contracts. In particular, it is likely to result in the courts
expanding that term so as to incorporate the concept that an employer
may be acting in breach of trust and confidence if, without justification, it
acts incompatibly with its employee's Convention rights. It has been suggested here that the courts are likely to conclude that there will be a
justification for the incompatible act in circumstances where the act in
question is done in furtherance of a legitimate aim on the part of the
employer and is proportionate to the achievement of that aim.

Contracting Out

13.32   It is important at this point to bear in mind that, in individual cases, the
construction of contractual terms does not take place in a vacuum. Indeed,
when construing the implied term as to trust and confidence in the context
of a particular contract of employment, the courts and tribunals are bound
to have regard to other aspects of the employment relationship, most
notably whether the employee has consented to the acts in question. The
question whether an employee's consent can operate to vitiate any Convention right which the employee might enjoy in the workplace is considered below.

4. CONTRACTING OUT OF CONVENTION RIGHTS

Introduction

13.33   It is clear on the pre-incorporation authorities that, where an employee
does consent to particular acts being done by his employer, that employee
cannot then turn around and say that, by performing those acts, the
employer has acted in breach of its implied obligations to maintain trust
and confidence. However, the employee may succeed in his claim if the
acts are done in a manner which was not consented to by the employee
and which objectively undermines the employee's trust and confidence in
his employer.[48]

13.34   The question now is whether, post-incorporation, the fact that an
employee has consented to a particular form of conduct which is incompatible with that employee's Convention rights can likewise operate so as
to negate any claim brought by the employee that the employer has
breached its obligations as to trust and confidence by engaging in that

---

[48] See especially *United Bank v. Akhtar* [1989] I.R.L.R. 507, EAT (employee consented to the
inclusion of a mobility clause in his contract of employment; mere fact that employer sought
to rely on that consent so as to move its employee from one location to another did not
amount to a breach of trust and confidence; however, manner in which the employer
exercised its discretion under the mobility clause was not consented to by the employee and
did, in the circumstances, amount to a breach of trust and confidence).

conduct. Put another way: can the contract of employment be used as a vehicle for contracting out of Convention rights and obligations?[48A]

The Conservative Response

The conservative response[49] to the question set out above is that it is entirely appropriate to use the contract of employment as a vehicle for contracting out of Convention rights and it is entirely appropriate for the three reasons: **13.35**

(1) It would create excessive uncertainty in the sphere of employment relations if a contractual consent, which would ordinarily operate to vitiate the unlawfulness of the employer's conduct, could not operate in this way where the employee's Convention rights were in issue.

(2) To decide that, in the case of prima facie violations of the Convention rights of employees, the trust and confidence term should not be hewn back by reference to whether the employee has consented to the violation would be to ignore the fact that the implied obligations as to trust and confidence are essentially contractual obligations which ought invariably to remain subject to the terms which have been freely agreed by employer and employee.

(3) Such Strasbourg jurisprudence as there is on the issue of contracting out of Convention rights tends to affirm the principle that, at least in the sphere of horizontal relations, it is possible for employees to contract out of their Convention rights.

No doubt, those who would wish to subscribe to the conservative approach to the issue of contracting out would rely on the following Strasbourg decisions to support their approach: **13.36**

— the case of *Vereinging Rechtswinkel Utrecht v. The Netherlands*.[50] An association concerned with prisoners' rights agreed with the governor of a particular prison that, in return for being granted certain rights of access to prisoners, it would not publish information relating to occurrences at the prison. The association subsequently, and in breach of the agreement, published a press release relating to the suicide of a particular prison inmate. The association's rights of access were subsequently withdrawn by the prison governor. The association claimed that the withdrawal of rights of access amounted to a breach of its Article 10 right to freedom of expression. The Commission concluded that there was

---

[48A] See further paras 3.152 *et seq.*
[49] The term "conservative response" is used here to refer to that response which aims at minimising the impact of the Convention so far as is possible within the terms of the HRA. This response is contrasted with the more "liberal" response which aims to ensure that the incorporation of the Convention ensures that individuals are, so far as possible within the terms of the HRA, endowed with rights which are both practical and effective.
[50] (1986) 46 D.R. 200 at 203.

no breach of Article 10 since the withdrawal of the right of access:

> "did not restrict the applicant's right to impart information any further than the applicant accepted when entering into the agreement. The decision taken by the authorities not to grant the applicant further permission to operate in prison thus cannot be considered to constitute an interference with the applicant's rights"[51];

— the case of *Rommelfanger v. Federal Republic of Germany.*[52] The applicant was a doctor who was employed by a Catholic foundation under a contract of employment which stipulated that he owed a duty of loyalty to the Catholic Church. The applicant was dismissed for expressing publicly views on abortion contrary to the Catholic Church's doctrines. The applicant brought a claim before the Commission that he had suffered a breach of his Article 10 right to freedom of expression. The Commission concluded: (1) that "in principle" the Convention permits contractual obligations as between private parties which limit freedom of expression "if they are freely entered into by the person concerned"; (2) consequently, the state would not be acting in breach of its obligations under the Convention if it enforced the contractual restriction contained in the applicant's contract of employment, provided that those restrictions were freely agreed to by the applicant. (Although, note, the Commission also concluded, relying in part on the decision of *Young, James and Webster v. United Kingdom,*[53] that any positive obligation on the part of the state to secure the effective protection of Convention rights of individuals within its jurisdiction could not be narrowed by reference to contractual restrictions which were themselves inherently unreasonable, *i.e.* the domestic law must be sufficient to protect the employee from unreasonable restrictions imposed by the employer);

— the case of *Ahmad v. United Kingdom.*[54] The applicant was a Muslim schoolteacher who wished to attend at his mosque on Friday afternoons whilst remaining on a full-time contract. The applicant alleged that the requirement that he remain at work on Friday afternoons constituted an infringement of his Article 9 right to freedom of religion. The Commission concluded that the case was not admissible because Mr Ahmad had voluntarily accepted his job and, hence, the restrictions on his religious freedoms which that job imposed. The Commission further concluded that, in the circumstances of the case, if Mr Ahmad wanted to enjoy his religious freedoms, then he need only resign his position[55];

---

[51] *ibid.*, at 203.
[52] (1989) 62 D.R. 151
[53] (1982) 4 E.H.R.R. 38.
[54] (1982) 4 E.H.R.R 125.
[55] [1982] 4 E.H.R.R. 126. Note, in the English Court of Appeal, Scarman L.J. in a dissenting judgment expressed the strong view that Mr Ahmad's rights had been infringed. [1978] Q.B. 36.

— the case of *Kottinen v. Finland*.[56] The applicant was a Seventh-Day Adventist who had begun to take unauthorised leaves of absence from his work for the purposes of observing his Church's Sabbath. The applicant was dismissed when, despite warnings from his superiors, he continued to keep the Sabbath in accordance with his convictions. The Commission held that he was not dismissed because of his religious convictions but, rather, for having refused to respect his contractual working hours, a refusal which, even if motivated by his religious convictions, was not as such protected by Article 9. As the Commission put it, the "ultimate guarantee" of his right to freedom of religion was his freedom to "relinquish his post".

— the case of *Stedman v. United Kingdom*.[57] The applicant's complaint that her Article 9 rights were being infringed because her new contract of employment obliged her to work on Sundays, a religious day for that employee, was held not to be admissible by the Commission since the applicant could eliminate the restrictions imposed on her religious freedoms by getting a different job. (See also *X v. Denmark*[58] and *Knudsen v. Norway*[59] where the same form of reasoning was applied).

Clearly, this case law does much to assist those who subscribe to the conservative approach to contracting out. Indeed, it may be that this case law would be sufficient to persuade the English courts that they should adopt a similarly conservative approach. **13.37**

However, it is suggested here that alternative, more liberal approaches to the issue of contracting out still need to be considered. In particular, it is suggested that they need to be considered because there is an argument, which the English judges may in fact be prepared to accept, that these decisions are inherently flawed by reason that they are rooted in the self-evident misconception that individual employees truly have the freedom to change jobs whenever it becomes apparent that the conditions of their employment cannot accommodate their Convention rights.[60] This particular argument would have to be advanced on the basis that, because of the inherent inequality of the bargaining relationship between employers and employees and, further, because of the inevitable economic and market constraints on individual employees, it cannot be readily assumed that an employee has in fact *freely* consented to the particular restraints on his Convention rights which are to be found in his contract of employment. This has the result that it cannot be automatically assumed that the employer's obligations as to trust and confidence can be hewn back by reference to those restraints. It should be added at this point that, in any **13.38**

---

[56] Application No. 24949/94, (1996) 87 D.R. 68.
[57] (1997) 23 E.H.R.R. C.D. 168.
[58] (1976) 5 D.R. 157.
[59] (1985) 42 D.R. 247.
[60] These arguments have already been advanced in a number of articles. See, *e.g.* G. Morris, "The European Convention on Human Rights and Employment: To Which Acts Does it Apply" [1999] 5 E.H.R.L.R. 496 at 506 and Sir Patrick Elias and Jason Coppel, "Freedom of Expression and Freedom of Religion: Some Thoughts on the Glenn Hoddle Case" in *Freedom of Expression and Freedom of Information: Essays in Honour of Sir David Williams*, eds Jack Beatson and Yvonne Cripps (OUP, 2000).

event, the decisions referred to above may be found wanting by the domestic courts on the basis that they do little to ensure that employees are afforded Convention rights which are "practical and effective".[61]

The Liberal Response

13.39   It is suggested here that, if the courts do accept the argument outlined above, then they may well choose to develop an approach to contractual restraints on an employee's Convention rights which is more liberal than the conservative approach outlined above. In particular, they may decide to develop an approach which mimics the approach already taken by the courts in respect of traditional post-termination restrictive covenants. Such an approach would be likely to be founded upon the following rules:

> (1) the contractual restraint on the individual's Convention rights will prima facie be void for illegality since it runs contrary to the public policy requirement that employees should be free to enjoy their Convention rights in the workplace;
>
> (2) the restraint can only be deemed to be lawful and, hence, enforceable in circumstances where it can be justified on the basis that it is reasonably necessary in order to protect the employer's legitimate business aims.[62]

A Practical Example

13.40   This approach is now illustrated in the context of the following concrete example. An individual is employed as a printer in a printing company. The employee's contract of employment contains a provision that he may not speak out in favour of animal testing notwithstanding that the business of the company has no connection with animal testing. The employee is disciplined for speaking out in favour of animal testing. The employee resigns claiming constructive dismissal on the basis that the company has violated his Convention rights and has, consequently, acted in breach of the implied term as to trust and confidence. In this case, there is every chance that the tribunal will consider that the term which purports to limit the employee's right to speak out about animal testing is not a term which protects any legitimate interest on the part of the company in that it is a term which does not touch on any aspect of the company's business. If the tribunal does come to this conclusion, then it will not narrow down the scope of the company's obligations as to trust and confidence by reference to this term, since the term will be held to be void for illegality. The tribunal will then be left with the question of whether the decision to discipline the employee did amount to a breach of the implied obligation to

---

[61] The importance of the Convention principle that the courts should take steps to ensure that individuals are afforded Convention rights which are "practical and effective" is illustrated, *e.g.* by the case of *Loizidou v. Turkey (Preliminary Objections)* (1995) 20 E.H.R.R. 99, see especially para. 72. See further para. 4.09.
[62] See further the leading restrictive covenants cases of *Herbert Morris v. Saxelby* [1916] A.C. 688, *Stenhouse Australia Ltd v. Phillips* [1974] 1 All E.R. 117; and *Office Angels v. Rainer-Thomas* [1991] I.R.L.R. 214. See also Brearley and Bloch, *Employment Covenants and Confidential Information* (Butterworths, 1999), para. 9.4, p. 143.

maintain trust and confidence. It is suggested here that the tribunal would be likely to find, on the facts of this case:

(1) that there had been a breach of trust and confidence since:

(a) the act of disciplining the employee for expressing views about animal testing would inevitably amount to an inter-ference with the employee's Article 10 right to freedom of expression; and

(b) the act of disciplining the employee did not serve any legit-imate business interest on the part of the employer;

(2) that, in the circumstances the employee was constructively dis-missed; and,

(3) that the dismissal was clearly unfair in the circumstances.

The advantage of this particular approach is that it both recognises the **13.41** inequality of bargaining power which tends to exist as between employer and employee and affirms the primacy of Convention rights in the work-place. Further, it is not an approach which Strasbourg would of necessity reject. Consider, not least, the *Rommelfanger* case where the Commission readily expressed the view that the state's positive obligations may be such that they would preclude the courts from enforcing "unreasonable" contractual restraints in a contract of employment between private parties. The most substantial disadvantage of this approach is that it is likely to produce a significant degree of commercial uncertainty as the courts will have to become engaged in the complex task of assessing the reason-ableness and proportionality of the employer's actions not just in respect of the narrow right of the ex-employee to trade freely once his employment has terminated (the traditional restrictive covenant approach) but in respect of all rights guaranteed to the individual under the Convention, including rights to privacy, family life, freedom of thought and religion and freedom of expression. This disadvantage may in itself be sufficient to throw the courts back upon the more conservative approach to contractual restraints.

Summary

In summary, with respect to the issue of "contracting out of Convention **13.42** rights", it is suggested here that:

(1) it is presently unclear whether the domestic courts will mirror the very conservative approach to the issue of contracting out of Convention rights adopted by the Commission or will, instead, adopt a more liberal approach;

(2) if the courts choose to adopt the former conservative approach, then, in the absence of duress, an express consent to a partic-ular restraint on the employee's Convention rights will invariably operate so as to preclude the employee relying on those rights to establish a breach of trust and confidence;

(3) if, however, the courts choose to adopt a more liberal approach, then this may signal a move towards a restraint of trade style analysis of contractual provisions which purport to restrict an employee's Convention freedoms. Thus, the restraint will be deemed to be void and, hence, of no relevance to the construction of the employer's obligations to maintain trust and confidence, if:

(a) it does not protect a legitimate interest on the part of the employer; and

(b) it is not reasonably proportionate to the achievement of that aim.

5. THE EMPLOYMENT PROTECTION LEGISLATION

Introduction

13.43   In this section, consideration is given to the question whether the employee might be able reaffirm the primacy of Convention rights in the workplace by relying on sections 3 and 6 of the HRA to effect changes in the scope and application of certain provisions of the employment legislation. Under section 3 of the HRA, the judiciary is compelled to construe all legislation so that it is, so far as possible, compatible with the Convention. It would appear that this particular provision has the effect of enabling courts to rewrite particular incompatible statutory provisions so as to render them Convention compatible, save where it is clear that such a rewriting is prohibited by the statute itself.[63] Under section 6 of the HRA, courts and tribunals will be acting unlawfully if they act incompatibly with the Convention, save where they are compelled to do so by primary legislation which cannot be read down or given effect so as to render it compatible with the Convention.

13.44   The section focuses in particular on the unfair dismissal provisions contained in the Employment Rights Act 1996 ("ERA 1996") and the anti-discrimination provisions contained in the Sex Discrimination Act 1975 ("SDA 1975") and the Race Relations Act 1976 ("RRA 1976"). The reason for this particular focus is that these are the provisions which are, it is suggested, the most likely to be "rewritten" as a result of the enactment of sections 3 and 6 of the HRA.

Unfair Dismissal

13.45   Under section 94 of ERA 1996, an employee has a statutory right not to be unfairly dismissed by his employer. Section 98 of the ERA 1996 describes the circumstances in which a dismissal will be unfair for the purposes of section 94. In essence, there are two ways in which an employee can argue that her dismissal was unfair for the purposes of section 98. First,

---

[63] See further the Court of Session's decision in *The Secretary of State for Defence v. MacDonald* [2001] I.R.L.R. 431 and also J. Coppel, *The Human Rights Act 1998: Enforcing the European Convention in Domestic Courts* (Wiley, 1999), paras 2.45–2.47. See also F. Bennion "What Interpretation is 'Possible' Under Section 3(1) of the Human Rights Act 1998?" [2000] P.L. 77.

she can argue that the procedures adopted by the employer for the purposes of determining whether or not she should be dismissed were unfair. Secondly, she can argue that the dismissal was substantively unfair either because she was dismissed for an unfair reason or because the employer acted unreasonably in treating the reason given as a sufficient reason for the dismissal. The issue of how these arguments might evolve post-incorporation of the Convention is considered below.

Procedural unfairness

There are, it is suggested, two ways in which Convention principles could, **13.46** via the combined effect of sections 3 and 6 of the HRA, affect the tribunal's approach to the issue of procedural unfairness. First, the tribunal might conclude that the dismissal was unfair if the employer did not comply with the procedural requirements of Article 6(1) before dismissing the employee. Article 6(1) provides that an individual has a right to "a fair and public hearing within a reasonable time by an independent and impartial tribunal established by law" wherever his or her civil rights are determined. Secondly, the tribunal might conclude that procedures culminating in dismissal may be unfair in circumstances where they had the effect of themselves causing specific breaches of the employee's Convention rights, for example:

(1) the procedures were inhuman and degrading such that they amounted to a breach of the employee's Article 3 right not to suffer degrading or inhuman treatment;

(2) the procedures amounted to a breach of the employee's Article 10 right to freedom of expression by reason that they imposed a prohibition on the employee's right to talk to the press during a period of suspension;

(3) the procedures breached Article 8 because they entailed over-intrusive investigations into the employee's private life or unnecessarily invasive surveillance.[64]

With regard to the first of these issues, namely whether procedures **13.47** culminating in dismissal will be unfair if they do not comply with the provisions of Article 6(1), it is suggested that this will not generally be the case for the reasons set out below:

(1) It would appear that, in the majority of cases, internal disciplinary hearings do not need to be Article 6(1) compliant, not least because generally speaking those hearings do not finally "determine" the employee's civil rights since there is generally the right of appeal or review to an Article 6(1) compliant tribunal (see further *Albert and Le Compte v. Belgium*,[65] para. 29: internal disciplinary hearings do not need to be Article 6(1) compliant in

---

[64] See further Supperstone, Goudie and Coppel (eds.) *Local Authorities and the Human Rights Act 1998* (Butterworths, 1999), pp. 36–7. See also *Smith and Grady v. United Kingdom* (2000) 29 E.H.R.R. 493.
[65] (1983) 5 E.H.R.R. 533.

circumstances where there is a right of appeal or review to an
Article 6(1) compliant court or tribunal).[66]

(2) In the circumstances, whilst it will be procedurally unfair to fail to
accord with the requirements of natural justice when determining
whether or not to dismiss the employee,[67] it will generally not be
unfair to fail to accord with all the requirements of Article 6(1).
Thus, for example, the dismissal will not generally be unfair on
procedural grounds simply if a hearing into the matter is not held
in public.[67A] (Note, in practice, even if internal disciplinary hearings needed to be Article 6(1) compliant in order to avoid a
finding that a dismissal was procedurally unfair, this would be
unlikely to result in a dramatic shift in the tribunals' approach.
The reason for this is that the current EAT guidance on fair
procedures in disciplinary hearings in any event already imposes
many of the requirements imposed by Article 6(1)).[68]

13.48   With regard to the second issue, namely whether procedures which themselves constitute a breach of the employee's substantive Convention
rights could be held to be unfair by virtue of that breach, the view taken
here is that there seems to be no reason in principle why procedures
which breached an employee's substantive Convention rights should not
render a dismissal unfair, even if the decision taken by the employer to
dismiss was not itself unfair *per se* (see further the House of Lords
decision in *Polkey v. AE Dayton Services Ltd*[69]: in deciding whether the
dismissal was unfair, the question for the tribunal is not whether the
employee would still have been dismissed if fair procedures had been
adopted but rather whether, in adopting the procedures he did, the
employer acted reasonably at the time).

Substantive unfairness

13.49   When assessing the fairness of a decision to dismiss, the tribunal is
required to take into account the reasonableness or unreasonableness of
the employer's decision in all the circumstances of the case (section
98(4)(a)). It is clear that, post-incorporation of the Convention, one particularly important "circumstance" will be whether the employer's decision
involved a violation of the employee's Convention rights.

13.50   It is suggested here that the approach the tribunals will take to decisions
involving violations of the employee's Convention rights is likely to be as
set out below.

---

[66] See further "Article 6 and the Right to a Fair Hearing" in Supperstone, Goudie and Coppel
(eds), *Local Authorities and the Human Rights Act 1998*, pp. 45–48, on the reasons why
generally internal disciplinary hearings will probably not need to be Art. 6(1).
[67] See further, *e.g. Clark v. Civil Aviation Authority* [1991] I.R.L.R. 412, EAT.
[67A] Although *cf.* situations where the individual is subject to an adjudication by an internal
disciplinary body which has the effect of denying him or her the right to practice in his or her
chosen profession: see further *Casado Coca v. Spain* (1994) 18 E.H.R.R. 1 and *Tehrani v.
UK Central Council for Nursing, Midwifery and Health Visiting* [2001] I.R.L.R. 208.
[68] See *ibid.*
[69] [1988] A.C. 344.

(1) Where the employee is employed by a public authority (either an obvious section 6(1) public authority or a hybrid public authority under section 6(3)(b)), unless the violation in question can be justified by the authority in accordance with the provisions of the Convention, the dismissal will be held to be unfair. The position would be the same if the employee were employed by a hybrid employer and the act in question was deemed to be a "public act" for the purposes of section 6(3) of the HRA.[70]

(2) Where the employee is employed by a purely private employer, unless the violation can be justified by the employer as falling within the band of reasonable employer responses, the dismissal will be held to be unfair.[71]

If tribunals do adopt the approach outlined above then, absent a justification, a tribunal would be likely to find that the dismissals were unfair in the following examples: **13.51**

(1) the employee is dismissed because he sought to take a religious holiday during the working week (breach of Article 9 right to freedom of religion)[72];

(2) the employee is dismissed for reasons relating to his sexuality or sexual orientation (breach of Article 8 right to privacy)[73];

(3) the employee is dismissed for expressing political views outside the employment context which were distasteful to senior management (breach of Article 10 right to freedom of expression)[74];

(4) the employee is dismissed for her refusal to remove a nose-stud (breach of Article 10 right to freedom of expression);

(5) the employee is dismissed for refusing to submit to random drugs testing or alternatively, to an HIV test (breach of Article 8 right to privacy).

It should be noted that, in practice, an employee would probably not need to rely upon his or her Convention rights in the cases cited above in order to obtain a finding that the dismissals were unfair since, in the absence of any rational justification, the dismissals would probably be held to be unreasonable in any event. This is significant because it illustrates the practical point that placing reliance upon human rights arguments in the context of unfair dismissal proceedings may well, in the majority of cases, **13.52**

---

[70] Note, if the tribunal were to hold otherwise, it would itself be acting in breach of its own section 6 obligations to act compatibly with the Convention.

[71] See further *Foley v. Post Office and HSBC Bank v. Madden* [2000] I.C.R. 1283.

[72] *cf.* the indirect discrimination case of *JH Walker Ltd v. Hussain* [1996] I.R.L.R. 11.

[73] Lightman and Bowers [1998] E.H.R.L.R. 560 at 576–8).

[74] *cf.* the case of *Ahmed v. United Kingdom* [1999] I.R.L.R. 188, statutory restrictions on a local authority officer's right to express political opinions did not breach Art. 10 since they could be justified under Art. 10(2).

do little more than put a gloss on the employee's claim.[74A] Put another way, it will only rarely be the case that placing reliance upon human rights arguments will enable an otherwise doomed unfair dismissal claim to succeed.

Jurisdictional limits

13.53 It is important to bear in mind that, under current statutory provisions, the tribunal's jurisdiction to hear claims for unfair dismissal is limited in a number of ways including the following:

(1) the employee must have one year's continuity of service with the respondent employer (section 108(1) of the ERA 1996);

(2) the employee must bring his claim for unfair dismissal: (a) within three months of the effective date of termination of the contract of employment or (b) within such other time as the tribunal considers reasonable in a case where it is satisfied that it was not reasonably practicable for the employee to bring the claim within three month of the effective date of termination (section 111(2) of the ERA 1996).

13.54 As to the question whether these particular jurisdictional limits could be challenged in section 7(1) proceedings on the basis that they breach the employee's right to a fair hearing under Article 6(1), the view taken here is that such challenges would be unlikely to succeed for the following reasons. First, any challenge mounted against the one year's continuity of service requirement would be almost certain to fail since the Commission has already held that a qualifying period of two years was not contrary to the Convention (see further *Stedman v. United Kingdom*[75]). Secondly, any challenge to the current limitation period contained in section 111(2) of the ERA 1996 would be likely to fail by reason that the European Court has recognised that imposing reasonable time limits for bringing proceedings does not run contrary to the requirements of Article 6(1)[76] and the section 111(2) time limit does appear to be reasonable in all the circumstances. However, it may be the case that the tribunal will, post-incorporation of HRA, have to be more careful about refusing to extend time where the employee has argued that it was not reasonably practical to bring his claim within time. In particular, it may be the case that refusing to extend time in circumstances where the employee had been misadvised by representatives or, alternatively, was simply ignorant of his legal rights could be challenged on the basis that such a refusal was unreasonable and, hence, was itself an unjustified interference with the employee's Article 6(1) rights.

[74A] See further the case of *Liddiard v. Post Office* [2001] EWCA Civ 940, where the Court of Appeal concluded that the HRA added nothing to the applicant's claim for unfair dismissal.

[75] (1997) 23 E.H.R.R. C.D. 168.

[76] See *Stubbings v. United Kingdom* (1997) 23 E.H.R.R. 213.

Remedies

The maximum compensatory award for unfair dismissal is currently **13.55**
£51,700 (see section 124(1) of the ERA and the Employment Rights
(Increase of Limits) Order 2001 (S.I. 2001 No. 21)). It may be argued
before the tribunals that this limit upon a successful applicant's award
prevents the tribunal from providing a "just and appropriate" remedy
where the dismissal was unfair because it involved a breach of a Convention right. Under section 8 of the HRA, the tribunal is obliged to provide a
just and appropriate remedy where it makes a finding of unlawfulness
within the meaning of section 6(1) of the HRA. It is suggested here that
such an argument would be likely to fail for two cumulative reasons. First,
the tribunal would not be making an award on the basis that the employer
has acted unlawfully contrary to section 6(1) of the HRA but rather on the
basis that the employer had dismissed its employee contrary to the provisions of ERA 1996. This would seem prima facie to rule out the application
of section 8 of the HRA. Secondly, the finding of unfair dismissal and an
award of compensation made by the tribunal would not preclude the
employee of a public authority from seeking further compensation from his
employer in the county court or the High Court on the basis that his
employer had committed a section 6(1) statutory tort. In the circumstances, the £51,700 limit for unfair dismissal would not seem to prevent
the employee from obtaining "just satisfaction" for the Convention
breaches which he or she had suffered.[77]

It has been suggested, however, that an employee may be able to chal- **13.56**
lenge the principle currently applied in the tribunals that no award for injury
to feeling can be made where the tribunal makes a finding of unfair
dismissal.[78] This argument may be put on the basis that, if a tribunal fails
to make an award for distress suffered by the employee as a result of her
Convention rights being violated, it may be failing to comply with its section
6 obligation to act compatibly with the Convention. Not least, it may be
failing to comply with its section 6 obligation because there is nothing in
the ERA which would preclude an award for injury to feeling, the tribunal
must simply "have regard" to the employee's losses. Clearly, if the tribunal
were to conclude that it should make an award for injury to feeling where
the unfair dismissal involved a distressful violation of the employee's
Convention rights, it would have to take into account the European Court's
jurisprudence on what constitutes "just satisfaction" for a violation of
rights: see section 8(3) and (4) of the HRA.[79]

---

[77] Note, it is suggested that the abolition on the limit on compensation for sex discrimination
following the decision of the ECJ in *Marshall v. Southampton and South West Hampshire
Health Authority (No. 2)* [1993] I.C.R. 893, would be unlikely to enable the employee to take
his argument on this point much further. Note also that Art. 13 of the Convention, which
requires an effective remedy for any violations of Convention rights, has not been incorporated by the HRA: see further HRA, s.1.
[78] See further "Unfair Dismissal" in Supperstone, Goudie and Coppel (eds), *Local Authorities
and the Human Rights Act 1998* (Butterworths, 1999), pp. 38–39
[79] Following the decision of the House of Lords in *Johnson v. Unisys*, [2001] 2 W.L.R. 1076,
it may in any event be the case that an employee can now claim for injury to feeling in
circumstances where he or she is unfairly dismissed. See also Chapter 9 on HRA remedies
and just satisfaction at para. 9.21.

Anti-Discrimination Legislation

13.57 When considering the approach which the Convention itself takes to discriminatory conduct, it should be observed from the outset that that approach is decidedly limited. In particular, the Convention's approach is limited because, whilst the Convention does prohibit discrimination in the securing of the rights and freedoms guaranteed by the Convention (see further Article 14), it does not endow individuals with any free-standing right not to be discriminated against.[80]

13.58 However, that is not to say that the Convention cannot potentially be used as a vehicle for impugning discriminatory practices or policies which in turn give rise to an unjustified interference with the individual's Convention rights. Indeed, it may well be that the Convention can be used for impugning such practices and policies precisely where E.U. law would give them safe harbour. Compare, for example, the following cases: *Grant v. South-West Trains* [81] (discrimination on the grounds of sexuality was not prohibited by the Equal Treatment Directive), and *Smith and Grady v. United Kingdom* [82] (practices and policies which were adopted in respect of members of the armed forces and which were discriminatory on the grounds of sexuality amounted to an unjustified interference with the applicants' Article 8 right to privacy and their Article 14 right to enjoy their Convention rights free from discrimination).

13.59 The question which falls to be answered now is whether and how those who suffer discrimination at work, on grounds not currently recognised by the domestic legislation, might yet be able to impugn such discriminatory treatment by availing themselves of the Convention (such grounds might include discrimination on the grounds of sexuality and discrimination on the grounds of religion and discrimination on the grounds of language).

Private and public employers

13.60 It is important to distinguish here between employees of public authorities on the one hand and private sector employees on the other. The reason for this is that, even if prima facie the Convention has the effect of condemning conduct on the grounds of sexuality or religion, it is only public authority employees who can use that condemnation directly, in the context of an action for breach of section 6 of the HRA 1998, to attack the discriminatory conduct of their employers. Thus, whereas a public authority employee would be able to impugn such discriminatory conduct directly under section 6(1) of the HRA on the grounds that that conduct was incompatible with the employees' Convention rights, private sector employees would have to look for alternative indirect means of impugning their employer's discriminatory conduct. In particular, such private sector employees would have to argue that the effect of incorporation of the Convention is such that the courts and tribunals have an obligation to develop common law or, alternatively, statutory causes of action so as to

---

[80] *cf.* the right not to be discriminated against on the grounds of sex contained in the European Union's Equal Treatment Directive 76/207. *Cf.* further Protocol 12 of the Convention.
[81] [1998] I.C.R. 449, ECJ.
[82] (2000) 29 E.H.R.R. 493.

afford private sector employees the right not to suffer, for example, discrimination on the grounds of sexuality, or religion, or political opinion. Each of these types of employment will now be considered in turn.

Public authority employees

There seems to be little doubt, following in particular the decision of *Smith* **13.61** *and Grady v. United Kingdom*,[83] that if a public authority breaches its employees' Convention rights, for example their Convention rights to privacy, and, moreover, it does so in a discriminatory manner (for example, it only invades the privacy of those employees who are homosexual) then, absent any Convention justification, that authority:

(1) will have breached both the specific right (for example the right to privacy under Article 8) and the right not suffer discrimination under Article 14; and

(2) will be ordered to provide "just satisfaction" to that employee (see section 8(3) of the HRA), probably in the form of a compensatory award.

Examples of conduct by a public authority amounting to a breach of Article **13.62** 14 could include the following:

(1) the employer intercepts the private telephone calls of its female employees (breach of Article 8) but not of its male employees (breach of Article 14: discrimination on the grounds of sex)[84];

(2) the employer dismisses employees who seek to celebrate Eid (a muslim festival) outside working hours (breach of Article 9 freedom of religion; breach of Article 14: discrimination on the grounds of religion);

(3) the employer requires all its homosexual male employees to submit to random drug testing during the course of their employment (breach of Article 8 right to privacy and also breach of Article 14: discrimination on the grounds of sexuality);

(4) the employer repeatedly and publicly mocks and insults a Hindustani employee on the basis that he does not speak English properly (possible breach of Article 3 right not to suffer degrading and inhuman treatment and also breach of Article 14: discrimination on the grounds of religion and language). However, see further *Smith and Grady v. U.K.*: Ministry carried out extremely intrusive and distressing investigations in respect of certain homosexual army recruits and then dismissed the recruits on the grounds of their homosexuality; conduct did not amount to breach of the applicants' Article 3 right not to suffer degrading and inhuman treatment, even though it caused the recruits to suffer distress and humiliation and was of a grave nature; the

---

[83] (2000) 29 E.H.R.R. 493.
[84] See further *Halford v. United Kingdom* (1997) 24 E.H.R.R. 523.

treatment of the recruits was not such that it reached "the minimum level of severity" which would bring it within the scope of Article 3.[85] It is also worth noting that, so far as the Court was concerned, to say that the discriminatory treatment of the applicants was contrary to the applicants' Article 14 right not to suffer discrimination in the securing of their Convention rights, was simply to consider the same complaint "from a difficult angle" and "accordingly the applicants complaint under Article 14 in conjunction with Article 8 did not give rise to any separate issue".[86]

Private sector employees

13.63 The question whether private sector employees will be able to rely likewise on the anti-discrimination provisions contained in the Convention is not an easy question to answer. The reason for this is that private sector employees would only be able to rely on such provisions if, by placing reliance on sections 3(1) and 6(1) of the HRA, they were able to require the courts to insinuate such provisions into the fabric of the existing domestic anti-discrimination legislation, and it is presently not clear the extent to which this may be possible.

13.64 Importantly, a recent decision by the Scottish Court of Session in the case of *The Secretary of State for Defence v. MacDonald*[87] suggests that, in fact, the opportunities for relying upon the interpretive obligations contained in section 3(1) of the HRA to forge new Convention-compliant interpretations of existing provisions in the employment protection legislation may be considerably more limited than some had originally imagined. The case itself was concerned with the legality of the Ministry of Defence's decision to require Mr MacDonald to leave the armed forces on the grounds of his homosexuality and hinged essentially on the interpretation of the word "sex" in the SDA 1975. The particular issue which taxed the Court of Session in this case was whether the word should now, post-incorporation, be construed as referring not only to gender but also to sexuality or sexual orientation.

13.65 In its rather perplexing judgment, the Scottish EAT had come to the following conclusions on this particular issue: the word "sex" in the SDA 1975 was ambiguous since it potentially referred both to gender and sexuality; the Tribunal was compelled to resolve that ambiguity by having regard to Strasbourg jurisprudence, in particular it was compelled to have regard to that jurisprudence because there was a common law presumption that Parliament intended to legislate in conformity with international commitments including the Convention; having had regard to that jurisprudence and, in particular, to the cases of *Smith and Grady v. UK*[88] and *Salgueiro da Silva Mouta v. Portugal*,[89] it was clear that the ambiguity

---

[85] See paras 120–123.
[86] *ibid.*, paras 115–116. See further Lightman and Bowers, "Incorporation of the ECHR and its Impact on Employment Law", [1998] 5 E.H.R.L.R. 560 at 576.
[87] [2001] I.R.L.R. 431. It should be noted that Lord Prosser dissented from the decisions of Lord Caplan and Lord Kirkwood but not on human rights related issues.
[88] (2000) 29 E.H.R.R. 493.
[89] [2001] 1 F.C.R. 653.

present in the SDA 1975 should be resolved in favour of expanding the meaning of the word "sex", as that word appears in the SDA 1975, so that it included the concept of sexuality; in the circumstances, the Ministry of Defence did act contrary to the provisions of the SDA 1975 when it discriminated against Mr MacDonald on the grounds of his sexual orientation.[90]

13.66 The Scottish EAT's decision, which was taken prior to the coming into force of the HRA, is certainly perplexing, not least because it manages to discern an ambiguity in the legislation which both the domestic courts and the ECJ have repeatedly concluded does not exist, see further *Grant v. South West Trains Ltd,*[91] [1998] ICR 449; *R. v. Secretary of State for Defence, ex parte Perkins (No. 2)*[92]; and *Pearce v. Governing Body of Mayfield Secondary School*[93] (in each of these cases, the view was taken that the word "sex" was not ambiguous and was clearly meant to refer only to gender and not sexual orientation). Having said that, it is quite clear why the Scottish EAT decided both to reject the settled approach to this particular issue and, further, to strive to insinuate Convention principles into the fabric of the seemingly unambiguous provisions of the SDA 1975: the EAT was anticipating the coming into force of the HRA; in particular, it was anticipating the creation of an interpretive obligation which would force courts and tribunals to recognise the hegemony of Convention principles in the context of statutory construction.[93A]

13.67 The key question which the Court of Session had to determine on appeal was whether the EAT had understood correctly the nature and scope of the interpretive obligations which the HRA would being into being as and when it came into force. In a decision which was unanimous on this particular issue, their Lordships came to the view that, in fact, the interpretive obligations created under section 3(1) of the HRA were not such that they enabled the word "sex" in the SDA 1975 to be construed expansively so that they included the concept of sexuality. Indeed having regard to their Lordships' Opinion, it is clear that their view was that the word "sex" could not be construed because the statutory context in which that word was to be found simply prohibited such an expansive reading of that word: so far as their Lordships were concerned that statutory context was such that there was patently no ambiguity in the word "sex" as it appeared in the SDA 1975; the word referred to gender only and could not be stretched so as to lend itself to alternative constructions.[93B] In reaching this particular conclusion, the Court of Session was clearly reiterating a view which had been adopted time and time again by both the domestic courts and the ECJ and it is suggested here that it is the conclusion which

---

[90] *MacDonald v. Ministry of Defence* [2000] I.R.L.R. 748, EAT.
[91] [1998] I.R.L.R. 206, ECJ.
[92] [1998] I.R.L.R. 508, HC.
[93] [2000] I.R.L.R. 548 [2000] I.C.R. 920, EAT.
[93A] See further the paragraph 8 of Lord Prosser's Opinion in the Court of Session decision.
[93B] See further paragraph 28 of Lord Prosser's Opinion; paragraph 7 of Lord Kirkwood's Opinion and paragraph 10 of Lord Caplan's Opinion. Rather bizarrely not one of their Lordships referred to the decision of the ECJ in *Grant v. South West Trains* notwithstanding that this is the leading (binding) authority on the interpretation of the word "sex" in the SDA 1975.

in fact logically flows from the application of the provisions of the HRA to the provisions of the SDA 1975.

13.68 The lessons which one draws from this particular decision are, it is suggested, as follows: the courts will be prepared to recognise, in the context of employment protection legislation, that the interpretive obligations imposed by section 3(1) of the HRA are very far reaching indeed in that they can enable and indeed require a court "to impose upon legislation meanings which were clearly never intended by Parliament when it chose the words which it used"[93C]; however, the judiciary's obligation to endow that legislation with new Convention-compliant meanings is clearly not limitless since that obligation will effectively be excluded where the legislation itself is intractable in the sense that it is structured in such a way that it simply will not admit of new Convention-compliant constructions; whilst it is clear that the SDA 1975 is intractable in the sense that its structure prohibits the inclusion of sexuality discrimination, it remains to be seen whether other provisions within the corpus of employment protection legislation will be construed as being more welcoming to Convention principles.

6. TRADE UNIONS

Introduction

13.69 Under English law, there is no positive right to freedom of association, although sections 136 to 137 of the Trade Union and Labour Relations (Consolidation) Act 1992 accord limited protection to trade unionists who are discriminated against by their employers. Currently, these protections may be claimed only by employees or prospective employees (although the Employment Relations Act 1999 empowers the Secretary of State to extend their application). In contrast, under Article 11(1) of the Convention, everyone has the right "to form and join trade unions for the protection of his interests".

13.70 It might be thought that enshrining such a right would produce a noticeable shift in the structure of employment relations. However, such thoughts would not be warranted, not least because this particular right has been construed so restrictively in Strasbourg with the result that historically it has had very little practical impact in the sphere of industrial relations.

Limits on Article 11 Rights

13.71 The restrictive approach which the European Court has adopted in respect of the Article 11 right to form and join trade unions is demonstrated in particular by the fact that the European Court has decided that the freedom to join trade unions does not guarantee any particular treatment of unions or their members. Thus, for example, according to the European Court, Article 11 does not guarantee:

> (1) the right to strike. (See in particular *Schmidt and Dahlstrom v. Sweden*.[94] Although note, following *Schmidt* it would appear that

---

[93C] *Per* Lord Prosser, paragraph 28.
[94] (1979) 1 E.H.R.R. 632, para. 36.

an absolute ban on strike action would violate Article 11. *Cf.* the position adopted by the International Labour Organisation in the International Labour Office, *Freedom of Association: Digest of decisions and principles of the Freedom of Association Committee of the Governing Body of the ILO.*[95] See also the European Social Charter of 1961, which specifically includes the rights to bargain collectively and to strike. This may be regarded as persuasive by the United Kingdom courts in determining the scope of Convention rights, not least because it was referred to by the Court in *Schmidt.* It should be noted that the particular issue of whether Article 11 does or does not guarantee a right to strike is to be revisited by the European Court when it hears the case of *Wilson and Palmer v. United Kingdom*[96];

(2) the right to conclude a collective agreement. (See in particular *Swedish Engine Drivers' Union v. Sweden*[97]: Article 11 "does not secure any particular treatment of trade unions, or their members, by the State, such as the right that the State should conclude any given collective agreement with them", paragraph 39. See also *Gustafsson v. Sweden*[98]: decides that the state will be given a very broad margin of appreciation when it comes to state action taken in respect of trade unions, paragraph 45);

(3) the right to be consulted. (See further *National Union of Belgian Police v. Belgium*[99]: Article 11 does not incorporate a right to consultation although it does incorporate a right for trade union members to have their trade unions heard. Importantly, in this case, the European Court concluded that Article 11 left each state "a free choice of the means to be used" to achieve the ends envisaged by Article 11, paragraph 39. See also, the case of *NATFHE v. United Kingdom*[1]: obligation under TULCRA 1992 to disclose names of trade union members to an employer before strike action was taken, was not a "significant limitation on the right to take collective action", note 77 at 126. Although, note, the position might be different if an anti-union employer used the information to put undue pressure on employees not to participate in the ballot); or

(4) the right to join a trade union, irrespective of the union's rules. (See in particular, the Commission decision in the case of *Cheall*

---

[95] (4th ed., 1996).
[96] Applications 30668/96, 30671/96, 30678/96. See further the European Court of Justice case of *Maurissen and European Public Service Union v. Court of Auditors* [1990] E.C.R. I–95: representational rights seen as integral to trade union activity in the context of adjudication on an internal staffing matter. See also J. Hendy q.c. "The Human Rights Act, Art. 11 and the Right to Strike" [1998] E.H.R.L.R. 582. Note, the Supreme Court of Canada has concluded that the right to freedom of association, which is guaranteed under the Canadian Charter of Rights, does not guarantee the right to bargain collectively or the right to strike: see the leading case of *Reference Re Public Service Employee Relations Act* [1987] 1 S.C.R. 313 ("The Alberta Reference"). See also *Dunmore v. Attorney-General of Ontario* (1997) 155 D.L.R. (4th) 193, Ont Ct, Gen Div.
[97] (1979) 1 E.H.R.R. 617.
[98] (1996) 22 E.H.R.R. 409.
[99] (1979) 1 E.H.R.R. 578.
[1] (1998) 25 E.H.R.R. C.D. 122.

v. United Kingdom.[2] In that case, the Commission made it clear that the right to join a trade union did not confer "a general right to join the union of one's choice irrespective of the rules of the union" and, further, that "unions must remain free to decide, in accordance with union rules, questions concerning admission to and expulsion from the union".[3] However, notwithstanding the absence of any general right, the state must take steps to protect the individual against any abuse of a dominant position by a trade union. Thus, for example, it might be a breach of Article 11 for the state to fail to intervene in the following circumstances: where the union sought to exclude or expel a member in a manner contrary to the union's rules; where the union adopted unreasonable or arbitrary rules; where the employee suffered exceptional hardship as a consequence of the exclusion or expulsion resulted in the employee suffering exceptional hardship, for example he lost his job because of a closed shop agreement: see further *Cheall* at 186).

13.72 Moreover, this jurisprudence, which is so restrictive in its effects, is in addition to the restrictions already contained in Article 11(2). In Article 11(2) "lawful restrictions" include restrictions on the right to freedom of association by "members of the armed forces, or the police or of the administration of the state".[4]

Rights Afforded by Article 11

13.73 That being said, Article 11 has been held to afford an individual certain rights which might otherwise not have been enjoyed. Consider, in particular, the following cases:

— *Young, James and Webster v. United Kingdom* [5]: individual has a right under Article 11 not to join a union and closed shop agreements may be difficult to justify under Article 11(2); in particular, compulsion to join a trade union will be likely to amount to a breach of Article 11 where the compulsion is based on "the threat of dismissal involving loss of livelihood" and the employee was working for the employer "before the introduction of any obligation to join a particular trade union".[6] (See also *Sigurjonsson v. Iceland* [7]; *cf.* the case of *Sibson v. United Kingdom* [8]: no breach of Article 11 where employee was not threatened with dismissal but was, instead, requested to join a particular union or move to a different depot owned and operated by the employer);

[2] (1985) 42 D.R. 178.
[3] *ibid.*, at 185.
[4] Note, it would appear that "members . . . of the administration of the state" does not include local government workers: *Council of Civil Service Unions v. United Kingdom* (1988) 10 E.H.R.R. 269.
[5] (1982) 4 E.H.R.R. 38.
[6] *ibid.*, at para. 55.
[7] (1993) 16 E.H.R.R. 462, para. 35.
[8] (1994) 17 E.H.R.R. 193.

— *X v. Ireland* [9]: Commission considered that threats of dismissal or other actions intended to make an employee relinquish the office of a shop steward could, in certain circumstances, seriously restrict or impede the lawful exercise of Article 11 rights;

— *National Union of Belgian Police v. Belgium* [10]: trade union members have the right to have their occupational interests protected by trade union action and, as a consequence, members have a right "that trade union should be heard". [11] (Note, the recognition procedures contained in the Employment Relations Act 1999 will not necessarily result in this rule being disapplied in cases where the union in question is not "recognised" in accordance with the Act: the employer should still provide a channel for the views of members of non-recognised unions to be heard, see further *Swedish Engine Drivers' Union v. Sweden* [12]).

It should be noted that the Commission has declared admissible an **13.74** application by United Kingdom trade unionists that their employer's act of making a pay rise conditional on a transfer from collectively-agreed terms and conditions of employment to "personal contracts" amounted to a breach of their Article 11 rights and, further, to the Article 14 right not to suffer discrimination in the enjoyment of this right (see further *Associated Newspapers Ltd v. Wilson; Associated British Ports v. Palmer* [13] (House of Lords held that the employer's act did not constitute action short of dismissal against those trade unionists who did not agree to transfer) and *Wilson, Palmer and Doolan v. United Kingdom* [14]).

It remains to be seen how far the domestic courts will seek to go beyond **13.75** the fairly restrictive approach adopted by the European Court in respect of Article 11. What is certain, however, is that much will depend on the extent to which the domestic courts seek to interpret the right guaranteed by Article 11 by reference to other international legal instruments, for example, the Social Charter of 1961 of the Council of Europe and, further, on the extent to which they consider that the development and extension of trade union rights remains above all the provenance of Parliament.

7. SPECIFIC CONVENTION RIGHTS

Introduction

The impact of specific Convention rights in the workplace has already **13.76** been touched upon at various points in this chapter. The purpose of this section is to provide a number of illustrations of the ways in which certain rights guaranteed under the Convention might in practice impact on the employment relationship.

---

[9] Application 4125/69 (1971).
[10] (1979) 1 E.H.R.R. 578.
[11] *ibid.*, para. 39.
[12] (1976) 1 E.H.R.R. 617.
[13] [1995] I.R.L.R. 258; [1995] I.C.R. 406.
[14] Applications Nos 30668/96, 30671/96, 30678/96.

Article 3

13.77 Article 3 of the Convention provides individuals with absolute right not to suffer inhuman or degrading treatment or punishment.[14A] As the case of *Smith and Grady v. United Kingdom*[15] powerfully illustrates, it will in practice be very difficult for an employee to show that her employer's conduct has breached the right guaranteed by Article 3. Consider the case of *Smith and Grady*. There, the Ministry of Defence carried out excessively intrusive investigations into the lives of certain homosexual army recruits and then went on to dismiss those recruits on the grounds of their sexuality. The European Court concluded that these actions amounted to grave breaches of the recruits' Article 8 and Article 14 rights. It also concluded that the Ministry's conduct caused the recruits to suffer substantial distress and humiliation. However, the European Court nonetheless refused to find that the Ministry had acted in breach of the recruits' rights not to suffer inhuman and degrading treatment under Article 3. It is clear from this judgment that the European Court takes a very conservative approach to Article 3 and will only find a breach in the most serious of circumstances.

13.78 However, it is suggested that breaches of Article 3 may yet be found, for example:

(1) where the employee, who is in the process of being disciplined, is subjected to an extremely lengthy suspension;

(2) where the employee is publicly and repeatedly mocked by his employer because of some aspect of his character; physical appearance or disability and the employer's acts of mocking cause the employee to suffer substantial distress and humiliation;

(3) where the employee is forced to work in extremely unsanitary conditions.

Article 8

13.79 Under Article 8, an individual has a right to respect for his or her private and family life, home and correspondence.[15A] This particular right is perhaps the one which is most likely to be invoked in the employment context since it has a potentially wide range of application.

13.80 Examples of the application of this particular right include those set out below.

(1) The right to privacy may be breached in circumstances where: (a) the employer seeks to intercept its employee's telephone calls, e-mail or other correspondence and (b) there is no justification for the interception in question. See especially *Halford v.*

[14A] See further paras 3.23 *et seq.*
[15] (2000) 29 E.H.R.R. 493.
[15A] See further paras 3.94 *et seq.*

United Kingdom[16]: applicant had brought claim of sex discrimination against Merseyside police; in order to ascertain the applicant's strategy in respect of her claim for sex discrimination, the applicant's superiors installed a "private telephone line" for the applicant to use at work and then proceeded to intercept calls she made on that line; the European Court held, first, that the interceptions did amount to an interference with the applicant's Article 8(1) right and, secondly, that in the circumstances of the case the interceptions could not be justified.[17] However, it may be that there will be no breach of Article 8 in circumstances where the employee has freely consented to being monitored at work.[18]

(2) The right to privacy may be breached in circumstances where the employer carries out health checks on its employee without the informed consent of the employee in question (see *X v. Commission*).[19]

(3) The right to privacy may be breached in circumstances where the employer seeks to impose a particular dress code on its employees. See, for example, *Kara v. United Kingdom*[20]: bisexual male transvestite who wore female clothes to express his identity established that restrictions placed on his form of dress breached the right to private life; however, the Commission took the view that the interference was legitimate and proportionate in that case. *Cf.* the decision of the EAT in *Smith v. Safeway plc*[21]: dismissal of male assistant, who worked on a delicatessen counter, because he had a pony-tail did not contravene the SDA 1975.[22]

(4) Absent a justification, the right to privacy will probably be breached in circumstances where the employer carries out investigations into the employee's private life. See further *Smith*

---

[16] (1997) 24 E.H.R.R. 523.

[17] It is suggested that the fact that the applicant in this case was not an employee (she was a police officer) will not prevent this case being applied in the ordinary employment context.

[18] Although, see further the section on "contracting out" above: the consent may not operate to render the monitoring lawful in circumstances where the monitoring is not reasonably necessary to protect the employer's legitimate business interests. It should be noted that the Regulation of Investigatory Powers Act 2000 and the Telecommunications (Lawful Business Practice)(Interception of Communication) Regulations 2000 creates a new statutory regime to control the interception of communications, *inter alia*, made and received by employees. There is currently concern that this legislation substantially cuts back an employee's Art. 8 right not to suffer interference with his correspondence. If it is incompatible with the Convention, it remains to be seen whether this piece of legislation can and will be "read down" by the courts so as to render it compatible with the Convention.

[19] [1995] I.R.L.R. 320. See further B. Wyatt, "The Legal Protection of HIV and Health Care Workers and the Human Rights Jurisprudence of the European Court of Justice" [1998] E.H.R.L.R. 301.

[20] (1998) 27 E.H.R.R. C.D. 272.

[21] [1996] I.R.L.R. 132.

[22] There has been considerable litigation in the United States on the question as to whether the control of dress or grooming is unconstitutional: see L. Tribe, *American Constitutional Law* (2nd ed.) (Foundation Press 1998), para. 15–15. See also G. Clayton and G. Pitt, "Dress Codes and Freedom of Expression" [1997] E.H.R.L.R. 54.

> *and Grady v. United Kingdom.*[23] Consider, also the case of *Leander v. Sweden*[24]: storing information about the applicant in a secret police register and releasing it to his prospective employers during the course of security vetting amounted to an interference with the applicant's Article 8 rights; although, in the circumstance of the case, the interference was justified. See also *Hilton v. United Kingdom.*[25]
>
> (5) The right to family life may be breached in circumstances where the employer exercises a mobility clause in a way that prevent the employee from living with or, alternatively, in the near vicinity of his or her family.
>
> (6) The right to family life may also be breached where the employer requires its employees to work very long hours.[26]

Article 9

13.81　Article 9 of the Convention guarantees a right to freedom of thought, conscience and religion.[26A] Thus far, the jurisprudence of the European Court has ensured that this particular right has only a very limited realm of application in the context of employment relations. Thus, for example, the European Court has shown no compunction in holding that there will be no breach of the Article 9 right to freedom of religion in circumstances where the contract of employment entitles the employer to require the employee to perform duties which conflict with the employee's religious obligations and the employer requires the employee to perform those duties (see especially the cases of *Ahmad v. United Kingdom*[27]; *Kottinen v. Finland*[28]; *Stedman v. United Kingdom*[29]; *X v. Denmark*[30] and *Knudsen v. Norway*[31], discussed at paragraph 13.36, above).

13.82　In essence, the European Court's approach to the issue appears to be this: where an employer requires an employee to perform duties under a contract of employment, even if the performance of those duties conflicts with the employee's religious obligations, there will be no breach of Article 9. This is because, in order to experience his freedom of religion, the employee simply has to leave his job. See further the case of *Stedman v. United Kingdom*[31A]: employee who was dismissed for refusing to work on Sundays, a day which was a religious day for the employee, did not suffer a breach of her Article 9 rights since she was dismissed "for failing to agree to work certain hours rather than for her religious beliefs as such".

---

[23] [2000] 29 E.H.R.R. 493.
[24] (1987) 9 E.H.R.R. 433. See also paras 19.27 *et seq.*
[25] (1988) 57 D.R. 108.
[26] An employer which requires its employees to work more than 48 hours a week will in any event be breaching the provisions of the Working Time Regulations 1998 in circumstances where the employee has not consented to the longer hours via an opt-out agreement under regs 4, 5.
[26A] See further paras 3.103 *et seq.*
[27] (1981) 4 E.H.R.R 126.
[28] Application No. 24949/94, (1996) 87 D.R. 68.
[29] (1997) 23 E.H.R.R. C.D. 128.
[30] (1976) 5 D.R. 157.
[31] (1985) 42 D.R. 247.
[31A] (1997) 23 E.H.R.R. C.D. 128.

Cf. the case of *Vogt v. Germany* [32]: German teacher who was dismissed because of her active membership of the Communist party was dismissed in breach of her Article 9 right since she was dismissed because of her political alliances. See also *Knusden v. Norway* [33] where the Commission indicated that there might be a breach of Article 9 where an employee faced dismissal for refusing to change his religious beliefs.

It is suggested here that this very harsh approach to Article 9 rights in the workplace is flawed by reason that it does not recognise the inequality of bargaining power which tends to be inherent in the employment relationship and, further, by reason that it does not afford to employees rights which are "practical and effective" (see *Loizidou v. Turkey (Preliminary Objections)*[34]). It is also suggested here that the domestic courts may, in practice, be reluctant to adopt the European Court's approach, preferring instead to adopt a more flexible approach which recognises the lack of parity in bargaining power as between employer and employee. **13.83**

It should be noted that, in any event, the European Court has emphasised that Article 9 does not protect every act motivated or inspired by a religious belief (*Kalac. v. Turkey* [35]) and it remains to be seen whether an employer who penalises non-conformity with discretionary rules, for example rules relating to dress codes, which run contrary to religious practices will be regarded by the domestic courts as "interfering" with the exercise of the right. **13.84**

Article 10

Under Article 10 of the Convention, an individual has right to freedom of expression.[35A] This right would appear to extend, in certain circumstances, to include an employee's right to express opinions which run contrary to views adopted by the employer (see, for example, *Vögt v. Germany* [36]) and also an employee's right not to be subjected to certain dress code rules (see, for example, *Stevens v. United Kingdom* [37]). Having said that, an employer may be able to lawfully restrict the expression of opinion where that expression conflicts with a duty of loyalty expressed in the employees contract of employment (*Rommelfanger v. Germany* [38]) or, alternatively, the restriction is reasonably necessary in the interests of national security. (Note, the question of whether restrictions on freedom of expression imposed upon employees who work for the secret services in virtue of the Official Secrets Act 1989 could be justified under Article 10(2) was touched upon in argument before the House of Lords in the case of *Attorney General v. Blake*,[39] however, no decision was made by their Lordships on this point). **13.85**

---

[32] (1996) 21 E.H.R.R. 205.
[33] (1985) 42 D.R. 247.
[34] (1995) 20 E.H.R.R. 99, para. 72.
[35] (1999) 27 E.H.R.R. 552.
[35A] See further paras 3.110 *et seq.*
[36] (1996) 21 E.H.R.R. 205.
[37] (1986) 46 D.R. 245.
[38] (1989) 62 D.R. 151.
[39] [2001] 1 A.C. 268.

13.86 In the case of *Vögt v. Germany*,[40] the European Court held that dismissing a teacher because of her active involvement with the German Communist Party was a breach of Article 10. This decision can be compared with the decisions in the cases of *Glasenapp v. Germany*[41] and *Kosiek v. Germany*.[42] In *Glasenapp*, the applicant was a teacher who had her appointment revoked because she was a member of the Communist Party. The European Court held that it was not a breach of the applicant's Article 10 right to require the applicant to make it a condition of recruitment that the applicant uphold the free democratic constitutional system in German (a similar result was followed in *Koziek*). In the case of *Vogt*, the European Court concluded that the earlier cases of *Glasenapp* and *Koziek* could be distinguished on the basis that there the Court was assessing a refusal to grant access to the civil service on the basis that the applicant did not possess one of the necessary qualifications, whereas in the instant case the applicant had been working in her capacity as teacher for seven years before she was dismissed.

13.87 Apart from pointing out the important distinction between applicants who are in employment and those who are seeking access to employment, the *Vogt* decision is significant because it illustrates how difficult it will be for public sector employers to justify restrictions on their employees' Article 10 rights under Article 10(2). In the *Vogt* case, the European Court found that a dismissal of a civil servant for refusing to be loyal to the constitutional principles upon which the state was founded could be "necessary in a democratic society". However, it also found that on the facts of that case the dismissal was a disproportionate measure by reason that the teacher had not been criticised for attempting to exert improper influence on her pupils; *i.e.* the dismissal was not justified in the circumstances.[43]

13.88 Notwithstanding the decision in *Vogt*, it would seem, following in particular the Commission decision in *Morissens v. Belgium*,[44] that the European Court would be prepared to accept the principle that certain types of public sector employment necessarily involve a degree of restriction on free speech. Thus, for example, the European Court would be likely to hold that those who work for the secret services, the police or local education authorities necessarily accepted a limitation on their Article 10 rights when they commenced their employment. To take just one example, a teacher who was an active member of a group which was trying to advance the rights of convicted paedophiles in society would probably find it difficult to found a claim that her dismissal for membership of this particular group constituted a breach of her Article 10 rights.

13.89 As the case of *Morrisens* illustrates, attacking the reputation of one's employers in a highly public manner, for example on television, may justify disciplinary action being taken by the employer with the result that the employee is not able to complain of any breach of Article 10. See further

---

[40] (1996) 21 E.H.R.R. 205.
[41] (1987) 9 E.H.R.R. 25.
[42] (1986) 9 E.H.R.R. 328.
[43] *cf.* the case of *Van der Heijden v. Netherlands*, where the Commission decided that dismissal of an employee who worked at an immigration foundation but who belonged to a political party which was hostile to immigrant workers was justified in the circumstances).
[44] (1988) 56 D.R.127.

the case of *Tucht v. Germany* [45]: specialist in mental and lung diseases in the German regional health service dismissed for criticising aspects of the organisation in letters sent to his superiors, the regional parliament, trade unions, professional associations, colleagues and political parties; dismissal was not an unjustified breach of the specialist's Article 10 rights. See also the Commission decisions in *B v. United Kingdom* [46] and *Haseldine v. United Kingdom.* [47] It should be noted, at this point, that constraints placed on employees in respect of their right to express views critical of their employer are in any event subject to the Public Interest Disclosure Act 1998 ("PIDA 1998"). It may well be that in practice disciplinary action taken in respect of "whistleblowing" disclosures which are not "protected" under PIDA 1998 will be easy to justify under the Convention.

Finally, it is important to note that freedom of speech may be legitimately **13.90** restricted by reference to particular statutory instruments. Consider the case of *Ahmed v. United Kingdom* [48]: restrictions placed on senior local government officers limiting their ability to participate in certain types of political activity, such as standing for election as a local councillor, not a violation of Article 10; in particular, not a violation because, having regard to the state's margin of appreciation, the statutory restrictions were aimed at a legitimate objective and were not disproportionate to the achievement of that objective.

8. TRIBUNAL PROCEEDINGS

Introduction

It is clear that employment tribunals must comply with the requirements of **13.91** Article 6(1) as and when they are determining "civil rights". In practice, what this means is that, in the majority of cases which come before the tribunal, the tribunal must ensure at the very least:

(1) that the panel is independent and impartial[48A];

(2) that the hearing is held within a reasonable time of the applicant's complaint being lodged[48B]; and

(3) that the hearing is fair and held in public[48C] unless there is a justification for holding it in private. Note, challenges made against acts and decisions of an employment tribunal by parties to the proceedings should be made by way of an appeal to the EAT (HRA, s.9(1)(a)). By way of contrast, non-parties who wish to challenge tribunal acts and decisions ought probably to have recourse to judicial review proceedings (HRA, s.9(1)(b)—see

---

[45] Application No. 9336/81 (1982) (unreported).
[46] (1985) 45 D.R. 41.
[47] Application No. 18957/91, 73 D.R. 225.
[48] (2000) 29 E.H.R.R. 1.
[48A] See also para. 10.103 *et seq.*
[48B] See also para. 10.98 *et seq.*
[48C] See also para. 10.93 *et seq.*

further the pre-incorporation case of *R. v. London (North) Industrial Tribunal, ex p. Associated Newspapers*[48D]: Applicant succeeded in application to review judicially a decision of the employment tribunal to grant a restricted reporting order). Note further, pursuant to HRA, section 9(2), such challenges could be ruled out in circumstances where there was a rule of law prohibiting the making of such challenges.

Specific Issues

13.92 Issues which fall to be considered in respect of these procedural requirements include, in particular, the following:

— *Handling evidence:* The coming into force of the HRA does raise a number of difficult issues when it comes to the tribunal's handling of evidence. Not least, tribunals may risk acting in breach of individuals' Article 8(1) right to privacy in circumstances where they allow certain types of evidence to be brought into the "public" arena of the tribunal hearing. Most obviously, tribunals may risk breaching their Convention obligations:

(a) where the tribunal panel watches video tape evidence which records individuals engaging in private acts (for example, acts undertaken in private settings such as in the individual's home or in staff changing rooms or toilets) or alternatively causes that evidence to be seen by others in the course of tribunal proceedings; and, further,

(b) where the tribunal panel itself peruses e-mail or other correspondence which was clearly intended to be private or alternatively allows such correspondence to be considered in the course of tribunal proceedings.

However, that is not to say that a tribunal will in fact be breaching its section 6 obligations as and when it considers such evidence or, alternatively, allows such evidence to be adduced in the course of proceedings. The reason for this is that very frequently the tribunal will be able to justify such prima facie interferences with the individual's private life under Article 8(2). Thus, the interference by the tribunal will very often be justified as "in accordance with law" and "necessary in a democratic society for . . . the protection of the rights and freedoms of others" (Note, the interference will clearly not be justified where the material to be adduced is manifestly not relevant to the issues before the tribunal). Moreover, it should be remembered that the tribunal will often wish to avail itself of such a justification so as to avoid any Article 6 challenge brought against the tribunal by the party who is endeavouring to adduce the contested evidence.[48E]

[48D] [1998] I.C.R. 1212.
[48E] See further in relation to confidential information, Chapter 19.

— *Adjournments:* It is clear that excessive delay in hearing the applicant's claim will amount to a violation of Article 6(1) (see *Darnell v. United Kingdom* [49]) and, no doubt, this is a point which those who are seeking to resist a lengthy adjournment or other delaying tactics will frequently seek to raise before the tribunal.

— *Reading witness statements:* It may also be the case that the fairly common practice of tribunals reading witness statements in private and taking the evidence as read may be held to be a breach of the obligations to hold the hearing in "public" since those attending the hearing, other than the parties, will not have access to the material contained in witness statements which are read in private. However, it should be noted that parties who freely waive their Convention rights, for example, by consenting to having the witness statements read in private, cannot subsequently complain as and when the tribunal does decide to read the statements in private (see further *Hakansson v. Sweden*[49A]: the parties may legitimately waive their Convention rights provided that the waiver is clear and unequivocal).

— *Hearings in private:* The tribunal's power, under rule 8(3) of the Employment Tribunal Rules,[50] to order that a hearing be held in private where, for example, hearing evidence would cause substantial injury to an undertaking belonging to one of the parties, may be contrary to the requirements of Article 6(1), since it does not seem to fit into the express justification contained in Article 6(1) (Article 6(1) states that the public or press may be excluded from all or part of the trial "in the interests of morals, public order or national security in a democratic society"[50A]). In any event, it may be that, in particular cases, a decision to hold the hearing in private will amount to a breach of the applicant's Article 6(1) rights if, for example, the discretion was exercised unreasonably or arbitrarily.

— *Confidentiality clauses in settlement agreements:* It may be that a confidentiality clause contained in a settlement agreement entered into between the parties would be unenforceable by the courts on the basis that it breached the parties' right to freedom of expression under Article 10. However, this will depend on the extent to which the courts will conclude that the parties have effectively waived this particular right by entering into the settlement agreement. A further point to note is that the media may seek in any event to challenge particular confidentiality clauses on the basis that they deny the media access to information which may be of public interest. Prima facie, such a claim might be permitted by Article 10 by reason that that Article creates a right not only to freedom of expression but also to receive information in certain

---

[49] (1994) 18 E.H.R.R. 205. See also paras 10.98 *et seq.*
[49A] (1990) 13 E.H.R.R. 1.
[50] See further the Employment Tribunals (Constitution, etc.) Regulations 1993, Sched. 1.
[50A] See further paras 10.93 *et seq.*

circumstances (see *Autronic v. Switzerland*[51]; but *cf. Gaskin v. United Kingdom*[52]). However, the view taken here is that the tribunal would consider that it lacked the power to disapply the provisions of the contract so that confidential information could be disclosed to the press.

— *Compromise agreements:* As for settlement agreements which purport to preclude an employee from bringing a claim before the tribunal in future, these agreements are already subject to stringent restrictions on enforceability (see further section 203 of the ERA and also the recent House of Lords decision of the case of *BCCI v. Ali* (2001) UKHL/8, March 1, 2001). However, it may be that the pre-existing judicial tendency to limit enforcement of such agreements will be further reinforced as a result of the incorporation of Article 6.[53]

— *Independence/impartiality of tribunal:* Employment tribunals are paid for, and largely appointed and administered, by the employment tribunal service, a Department of Trade and Industry agency. The lay members do not have any security of tenure. In the circumstances, it is arguable that employment tribunals are not "independent" for the purposes of Article 6(1). However, see in particular *Scanfuture UK Ltd v. Secretary of State for Department of Trade and Industry*.[54] In that case, the EAT decided: (1) that in the absence of actual bias, the test for whether a tribunal was "independent" for the purposes of Article 6 was whether a "fair-minded and informed observer" would on objective grounds perceive that there was a possibility or a real danger that the tribunal was biased; and (2) that changes in the rules governing employment tribunals, which came into effect in July 1999, resulted in a situation where there will be no question of perceived bias in cases where the Secretary of State is a party to the action.[55]

— *Restricted reporting orders (RROs):* Tribunals have powers to impose RROs in cases involving allegations of sexual misconduct or alternatively claims brought under section 8 of the Disability Discrimination Act 1995. It may be that a party would object to such an order on the basis that it interferes with his or her Article 6 right to a fair hearing in public. However, such objections are rarely likely to found a successful section 6 challenge to any particular RRO. The reason for this is that Article 6 implicitly endows the tribunal with a power to make such orders: (a) where they are "in the interests of morals, public order"; (b) where they are required for "the protection of the private life of the parties";

---

[51] (1990) 12 E.H.R.R. 585.
[52] (1990) 12 E.H.R.R. 36. See also paras 3.113 and 19.40.
[53] See further, 'Unfair Dismissal' in Supperstone, Goudie and Coppel, *Local Authorities and the Human Rights Act 1998* (Butterworths, 1999), p. 39.
[54] [2001] EWCA CIV 405, EAT.
[55] *cf. Smith v. Secretary of State for Industry* [2000] I.C.R. 69, EAT: it was a serious questions about whether a tribunal might properly and lawfully adjudicate on claims brought against the Secretary of State. See further para. 10.103 on independence and impartiality.

and (c) where the tribunal itself considers that an RRO is necessary since "publicity would prejudice the interests of justice" (see further paragraph 2 of Article 6). Hence, provided that the RRO was proportionate to the achievement of one of these legitimate aims, the order could not be impugned on the basis that it breached Article 6 since Article 6 itself permits the making of the order.

— *Restriction of proceedings order:* It is probably not a breach of an applicant's Article 6(1) rights for the Employment Appeal Tribunal to grant a "restriction of proceedings" order under section 33 of the Employment Tribunals Act 1996 in respect of a vexatious litigant. (See further *Attorney-General v. Wheen* [56]: the order does not amount to a breach of the litigant's Article 6(1) rights by reason that the right guaranteed under Article 6(1) is not absolute and the order can be justified as being reasonably necessary to protect the administration of justice; in any event, the order does not breach Article 6(1) since it does not automatically prevent the litigant from bringing claims before the tribunal but only requires that the litigant obtain the permission of the Employment Appeal Tribunal before proceeding with his claim).[56A]

— *Giving reasons for decisions:* Tribunals have historically been subject to an obligation to give reasons for their decisions (see further the leading pre-incorporation case of *Meek v. City of Birmingham District Council* [56B]). This obligation has already begun to be recast by the courts as a result of incorporation so that now tribunals are subject to more rigorous requirements when it comes to drafting the reasons for their decision. Consider, in particular, the recent case of *Dr Anya v. University of Oxford.*[56C] In that case, the Court of Appeal concluded: (a) that it was not adequate, so far as the tribunal's obligations under Article 6 were concerned, for the tribunal to merely state that they believed one witness rather than another; and, further, (b) that Article 6 required tribunals to justify their beliefs by referring to specific inconsistencies in the witnesses' evidence and by explaining why it considers that those inconsistencies require the witness in question to be treated as not credible. It remains to be seen whether the tribunals' obligation to give reasons will be developed even further so that, for example "mere infelicitous language" will no longer be so readily forgiven by the courts (*cf.* the case of *Meek* where the Court of Appeal refused to conclude that infelicitous language was itself sufficient to flaw a tribunal's reasoned decision).

Arbitration under ER(DR)A 1998. It is worth noting that the arbitration scheme introduced under the Employment Rights (Dispute Resolution) Act 1998 may be subject to challenges on the basis that it is not **13.93**

---

[56] [2001] I.R.L.R. 91.
[56A] See further the discussion of vexatious litigants at paras 10.07 *et seq.*
[56B] [1987] I.R.L.R. 250.
[56C] [2001] I.R.L.R. 377.

section 6(1) compliant, for example, if arbitrations are held in private. The view taken here is that, if arbitrators wish to avoid being challenged on the ground that they have not conducted the arbitration in a way that complies with the requirements of Article 6(1), they should require the parties to sign a document in which they agree to waive their Article 6(1) rights. Having said that it may be that, since the scheme can only be used where the parties have consented to arbitration under the scheme, any challenges made against particular arbitrators would in any event founder on the basis that the parties had agreed to certain limitations on their Article 6(1) rights as and when they agreed to submit to arbitration.[56D]

13.94   **Legal aid.** It is also worth noting that whilst currently legal aid is not available in the tribunal, this situation may not continue for very much longer. The reason for this is that there is an argument that the refusal of the Legal Services Committee to provide legal aid for the purposes of conducting legal proceedings in the employment tribunals itself amounts to a breach of the parties' Article 6(1) rights.[56E] Such an argument was run before the courts in Scotland and has since resulted in the Scottish Executive taking a decision to introduce legal aid in the Scottish employment tribunals.

[56D] See further para. 12.12 *et seq.*
[56E] In relation to the Convention requirements for the provision of legal aid, see further para. 12.31 *et seq.*

CHAPTER 14
Companies and Financial Services

1. INTRODUCTION

Application of the Convention

14.01 The primary aim of the Human Rights Act 1998 is to protect the rights of individuals. This underlying policy is reflected not only in the title of the HRA but also in the fact that many of the rights, for example the prohibition of slavery and forced labour, prohibition of torture and the right to marry can only be relied upon by individual persons. However, the European Court of Human Rights has long recognised that as regards other rights, a company may be a "person" for the purposes of the Convention and may have rights capable of protection and may, therefore, be considered as a "victim" of a violation of a Convention right. A company may also be obliged to act compatibly with Convention rights so as to protect an individual from suffering an infringement of the rights to which he is entitled.

The HRA will have direct application against companies which are con- **14.02** sidered to be "public authorities".[1] These companies will have a duty to act compatibly with the Convention rights when they are carrying out their public functions. The meaning of "public authority" for the purposes of the HRA is wide and includes "any person certain of whose functions are of a public nature".[1A]

In the area of financial services the HRA will have particular application **14.03** with regard to the regulatory powers of the Financial Services Authority which is likely to be regarded as a public authority for the purposes of the HRA at least when it is carrying out functions of a public nature. The Financial Services and Markets Tribunal will certainly be regarded as a public authority for the purposes of the HRA as it is a "court".

Strictly speaking, only persons considered to be carrying out public func- **14.04** tions are under an obligation to act compatibly with the Convention.[2] However, other persons will also find themselves effectively having to comply with rights contained in the Convention. This is because courts and tribunals are considered as public authorities for the purposes of the HRA,[3] and therefore have a duty to act compatibly with the Convention when making decisions. Overall, how far this horizontal effect of the Convention will affect parties to litigation is the subject of much academic and practitioner debate and is discussed further above in Chapter 5.[3A] The question of horizontal effect is likely to be of great significance in civil and commercial law where the majority of claims involve two private par- ties.[3B]

Areas Affected by Convention Rights

The Convention and the HRA has already had a substantial impact on **14.05** companies and the financial services regime. This has been both as a result of direct challenges made to the European Court in Strasbourg and also as a result of the amendment of existing legislation and the vetting of new legislation to ensure compatibility with the HRA.

Since the introduction of the HRA, companies have been active in invoking **14.06** Articles of the Convention. There have been many decisions in relation to access to the courts under Article 6—unreasonable delays in proceedings, the right to a fair trial by an independent and impartial tribunal and blanket immunities.

The HRA has also been invoked in respect of directors' disqualification **14.07** proceedings. Such proceedings which have serious consequences for the individual have given rise to a number of human rights points, such as the

---

[1] See further paras 8.15 *et seq.*
[1A] HRA, s.6(3)(b). See also paras 8.17 *et seq.*
[2] HRA, s.6(5), qualifies s. 6(3)(b) by stating that a person is not a public authority if the nature of the act is private. See also para. 8.24.
[3] HRA, s.3(a).
[3A] At paras 5.15 *et seq.*
[3B] See for further discussion as to the impact of the HRA on companies, Michael Smyth, *Business and the Human Rights Act 1998* (Jordans, 2000); Alan Dignam and David Allen, *Company Law and the Human Rights Act* (Butterworths, 2000).

unavailability of legal aid for such proceedings and the considerable delays all too often associated with them.

14.08 The subsequent use in criminal proceedings of evidence obtained under compulsory powers, such as those contained in the Companies Act 1985 or the Insolvency Act 1986, is another area in which Convention rights have had particular impact. In this area, the arrival of the HRA has already provoked a change in some domestic legislation.[4] While the European Court of Human Rights has not directly criticised the use of compulsory powers to obtain information and has not sought to undermine the basis of the powers in domestic law, it has held on a number of occasions that evidence obtained under those powers may not be used against a defendant in the course of criminal proceedings.[5]

Applicable Principles of European Law

14.09 The HRA requires the courts to take account of the European Court's case law when determining Convention rights, although this case law is not binding on domestic courts. Common law judges and lawyers will develop a different approach when considering cases as, unlike English decisions which may be based on rigorous analysis of legal precedent, most Strasbourg cases are decided on their particular facts. The common law doctrine of precedent has no application at the European Court.[5A]

14.10 Further, there are two specific principles which are applied by the European Court in deciding cases. First, the Court will apply the principle of proportionality, balancing the rights of the individual against the "general interests of the community".[5B] A domestic court when dealing with a Convention point will have to consider this doctrine and look at the merits of administrative action. This is different from the narrower concept of *Wednesbury* unreasonableness in public law.[6] Secondly, the European Court will invoke the margin of appreciation when deciding cases. This is an international law concept aimed at maintaining a respect for the Contracting States' social, economic, cultural and political traditions. The effect of the doctrine is that the Court will not disturb the actions of a Member State unless they fall outside a general measure of discretion. However, it does not apply at the domestic level where the courts should principally be concerned with the doctrine of proportionality, although some deference may be shown to the legislature or the Executive in appropriate cases.[7]

14.11 To take one example of how these principles may work in practice, the loss of legal aid to certain categories of litigant may mean that their chances of defending a case are reduced or that there is an inequality of arms. However, the decision to draw the line somewhere as regards legal aid may be justified by its underlying policy. The European Court will be

---

[4] See, *e.g.* Insolvency Act 2000, s.11; Youth Justice and Criminal Evidence Act 1999, s.59.
[5] See *Saunders v. United Kingdom* (1997) 23 E.H.R.R. 313 and paras 14.58 *et seq.* below.
[5A] See further para. 4.17.
[5B] See paras 4.38 *et seq.*
[6] See further paras 4.14 *et seq.* and 4.28 *et seq.*, above.
[7] See further paras 4.22 *et seq.*, above.

reluctant to interfere if, having regard to both the doctrine of proportionality and the margin of appreciation, the decision can be justified.

2. RELEVANT ARTICLES OF THE CONVENTION

Introduction

The Articles of the Convention most relevant to companies and financial **14.12** services are Article 6 (right to a fair trial), Article 8 (right to respect for private life), Article 10 (freedom of expression) and Article 1 of Protocol No. 1 (protection of property).

Save for the right to a fair trial conferred by Article 6, none of the Conven- **14.13** tion rights is absolute. Some are subject to express qualification such as Article 10, which recognises that the freedom of expression may be subject to restraints imposed by law and necessary in a democratic society.[8] Similarly, in relation to Article 8, an interference may be legitimate if it is in accordance with the law and necessary in a democratic society.[9] Article 1 of Protocol No. 1 is heavily qualified and does not impair the right of a state to enforce laws to control the use of property in accordance with the general interest.[9A]

Right to a Fair Trial—Article 6(1)

Article 6(1) of the Convention confers a right to a fair hearing by an **14.14** independent and impartial tribunal established by law in the determination of "civil rights and obligations" and any "criminal charge".[9B]

Article 6 does not confine itself to trials. It is concerned with any serious **14.15** and genuine dispute as to a civil right or obligation that is arguably recognised under domestic law and where the proceedings are determinative of that right or obligation. This extends its scope beyond trial purposes to disciplinary and regulatory tribunal hearings. As mentioned above, Article 6 is by far the most frequently invoked of the Convention rights. Article 6(1) requires as a minimum:

(1) a fair and public hearing;

(2) an independent and impartial tribunal;

(3) trial within a reasonable period;

(4) public judgment.

In addition to the minimum requirements which are set out in Article 6(1) there are certain other rights which have been incorporated within the meaning of Article 6(1) by implication. These include most importantly:

(1) the right of access to a court;

---

[8] Art. 10(2). See further paras 3.110 *et seq.*
[9] Art. 8(2). See further, paras 3.94 *et seq.* and paras 16.03 *et seq.*
[9A] See further paras 3.131 *et seq.* and paras 16.43 *et seq.*
[9B] See further paras 3.53 *et seq.*

(2) equality of arms; and

(3) the right to participate effectively in proceedings.[10]

Right to Respect for Private and Family Life—Article 8

14.16 This article encompasses protection of four separate interests:

(1) private life;

(2) family life;

(3) the home; and

(4) correspondence.[11]

The extent to which a company can rely on Article 8 is not entirely clear.[11A] In a commercial context, it has so far been mainly invoked by individuals who have complained about the invasion of their home and work place as a result of investigatory powers exercised by public authorities. The question of whether a company has a right to privacy of its office-space has not as yet been tested by the European Court.

14.17 In *Douglas v. Hello!*[12] the Court of Appeal expressly recognised the right to personal privacy in English law. Sedley L.J. said at 1021:

> "The courts have done what they can, using such legal tools as were to hand to stop the more outrageous invasions of individuals' privacy; but they have felt unable to articulate their measures as a discrete principle of law. Nevertheless, we have reached a point at which it can be said with confidence that the law recognizes and will appropriately protect a right of personal privacy.
> The reasons are twofold. First, equity and the common law are today in a position to respond to an increasingly invasive social environment by affirming that everybody has a right to some private space. Secondly, and in any event, the Human Rights Act 1998 requires the courts of this country to give appropriate effect to the right to respect for private and family life set out in article 8 of the European Convention for the Protection of Human Rights and Fundamental Freedoms."

It is anticipated that the operation of Article 8 generally will assist the development of the common law of privacy in the domestic courts.[13]

---

[10] Keir Starmer, *European Human Rights Law*, (Legal Action Group: 1999), p.120. See also, for a discussion on Art. 6: Robert Walker L.J., "Opinion: The Impact of European Standards on the Right to a Fair Trial in Civil Proceedings in United Kingdom Domestic Law" [1999] E.H.R.L.R. 4.

[11] See further paras 16.20 *et seq.*

[11A] See *R. v. Broadcasting Standards Commission, ex p. British Broadcasting Corporation* [2000] 3 W.L.R. 1327.

[12] [2001] 2 W.L.R. 992.

[13] See also Singh, "Privacy and the Media after the Human Rights Act" [1998] E.H.R.L.R. (6) 712; *Hellewell v. Chief Constable of Derbyshire* [1995] 1 W.L.R. 804.

Qualified right.   Proportionality will play an important role in decid-   **14.18**
ing cases under Article 8. Many investigations which are authorised by
statute and approved by the courts will be considered as necessary and in
the public interest. This is given effect to in Article 8(2). Therefore, in
assessing whether there has been an infringement of Article 8 the court
should have regard to:

(1) whether the investigation is justified by reference to Article
    8(2)[13A];

(2) whether it is in accordance with the law[13B]; and

(3) whether it is necessary in a democratic society.[13C]

These three factors inevitably allow Member States considerable room to
decide what is necessary in the context of a particular society. Where the
privacy in question is commercial in nature the degree of protection
accorded under Article 8 is generally of a lesser character than the
protection afforded to individuals.[14]

Right to Freedom of Expression—Article 10

Article 10 grants the right to freedom of expression. It is considered by the   **14.19**
European Court as one of the essential foundations of a democratic
society and one of the basic conditions for its progress.[15] The Court has
held that Article 10 may be invoked by both natural and legal persons.[16]
The term "expression" has been widely construed and includes words,   **14.20**
pictures, images and acts which convey information. Freedom of expression also includes the right to hold opinions, and to receive and impart
information and ideas. The means of expression include print, radio,
television broadcasting, artistic creations, film. Advertising also comes
within the scope of the provision.[16A]
The right has been used both in traditional freedom of the press cases and   **14.21**
also in cases concerning state broadcasting monopolies and broadcasting
licences.[17]

Qualified right.   Like all the rights contained in the HRA, freedom of   **14.22**
expression is subject to the doctrine of proportionality.[17A] It would always
be open to the authority in question to argue that any restrictions imposed
were proportionate to the legitimate aim pursued by the state. In addition,
Article 10 is also subject to similar qualifications as contained in Article 8.
However, there are two key differences:

[13A] See para. 4.33.
[13B] See paras 4.43 et seq.
[13C] See paras 4.34 et seq.
[14] See further detailed analysis of Art. 8 at paras 16.03 et seq., below.
[15] Handyside v. United Kingdom (1979) 1 E.H.R.R. 737; Lingens v. Austria (1986) 8 E.H.R.R.
407; Jersild v. Denmark (1995) 19 E.H.R.R. 1.
[16] Autronic AG v. Switzerland (1990) 12 E.H.R.R. 485.
[16A] See further paras 19.98 et seq.
[17] See, e.g. Radio ABC v. Austria (1998) 25 E.H.R.R. 185, where the applicant was successful in complaining about the state's refusal to grant it a licence to operate a private radio
station. See further paras 19.110 et seq., below.
[17A] See paras 4.38 et seq.

(1) the special function of freedom of expression under the Convention has led to heightened scrutiny by the European Court of any restrictions on it; and

(2) the list of permitted restrictions under Article 10(2) is longer and more specific that those contained in Article 8(2).[18] For this reason the European Court has been prepared to allow a greater degree of autonomy in certain areas by invoking the doctrine of margin of appreciation.

Right to Protection of Property—Article 1 of Protocol No. 1

14.23   Article 1 of Protocol No. 1 confers a right to the peaceful enjoyment of possessions. This right is subject to heavy qualification as the needs of a society inevitably entail situations where a person may be deprived of their property or where their property is subject to control.

14.24   **Possessions.**   Article 1 of Protocol No. 1 refers to "possessions" rather than "property". The term possessions has been given a broad definition by the European Court and the Commission. It includes moveable and immoveable property, economic interest including shares,[19] patents,[20] the ownership of a debt,[21] contractual rights and legal claims.[22]

14.25   **Deprivation or control of property.**   Article 1 of Protocol No. 1 draws a distinction between deprivation and control of property. If there is a deprivation of property it must be in the public interest and in accordance with general principles of international law. Control of property is permitted in a wider range of circumstances and reflects the underlying policy in a democratic society that some form of control over property is necessary. The principles to be applied to both are similar, although those in relation to control will be applied less strictly. The restriction on the property must be:

(1) for a legitimate purpose;

(2) the achievement of that purpose must strike a fair balance between the demands of the general interest of the community and the need to protect individual rights.[23]

Article 1 of Protocol No. 1 also protects interference with possessions where the interference does not amount to deprivation or control.[24]

---

[18] Keir Starmer, *European Human Rights Law*, (Legal Action Group: 1999), p. 137.
[19] *Bramelid and Malmström v. Sweden* (1982) 29 D.R. 64.
[20] *Smith Kline and French Laboratories v. Netherlands* (1990) 66 D.R. 70.
[21] *Agneessens v. Belgium* (1988) 58 D.R. 63.
[22] Note that the French text uses the word "*biens*" which is far wider than the concept of possessions.
[23] Keir Starmer, *European Human Rights Law*, (Legal Action Group: 1999), pp. 148–149. See further analysis of Art. 1 of Protocol No. 1 at paras 16.43 *et seq.* below.
[24] See *Spörrong and Lonnroth v. Sweden* (1983) 5 E.H.R.R. 35.

3. PARTIES

Introduction

Only public authorities or organisations undertaking public functions have **14.26** a duty to comply with the Convention. As mentioned above, the HRA does not make Convention rights directly enforceable against private companies or bodies which are not considered to be carrying out public functions or deemed a public authority, although the Convention will inevitably have some horizontal effect.[25] There have, for example, already been a number of decisions where the English courts have construed domestic law in accordance with the Convention in actions between private parties.[26]

Courts and Tribunals as Public Authorities

Section 6(3) of the HRA includes courts and tribunals within the meaning **14.27** of "public authority". A court or tribunal, therefore, has a duty to act compatibly with the HRA when making decisions. It must therefore give effect to Convention rights and may be required to consider decisions relating to Convention rights even where the matter is between two private companies pursuant to HRA, ss.2 and 6. In so doing the court will not be deciding a claim based solely on a violation of a Convention right, but will rather be giving effect to existing common law or statutory rights in a manner compatible with the Convention.[27] It should be noted that where a domestic statute is incompatible with the HRA the court can only give effect to the statute as enacted.[28]

Companies as Public Authorities

An organisation may fall into one of three categories for the purposes of **14.28** the HRA. It may be considered an "obvious" public authority all of whose functions are public.[28A] It may be considered a quasi-public authority with both public and private functions.[28B] Or it may be an organisation which carries out no public functions and is not a public authority at all. A company may be considered a public authority or quasi-public authority if it carries out functions of a public nature. The categorisation will be relevant to the question of whether the company has a direct obligation to comply with Convention rights.

Test for determining whether a public authority. The test for **14.29** determining whether a company will be considered a public authority in respect of any particular act is two-tier. The questions to be answered are:

---

[25] See paras 5.15 *et seq.*
[26] See, *e.g. Rantzen v. Mirror Group Newspapers* [1993] 4 All E.R. 975; *Middlebrook Mushrooms v. TGWU* [1993] I.C.R. 612; *Douglas v. Hello!* [2001] 2 W.L.R. 992, CA.
[27] H.L. Debs, November 24, 1997, cols 781, 783.
[28] HRA, s.3(2)(b). However, it may make a declaration of incompatibility under HRA, s.4. See further paras 2.41, 2.44 and 9.07.
[28A] See para. 8.16.
[28B] See para. 8.17.

(1) does the company carry out functions of a public nature; and

(2) is the particular act in question a public function.[29]

Note that section 6(5) of the HRA specifically provides that "in relation to a particular act, a person is not a public authority by virtue only of subsection (3)(b) if the nature of the act is private".

14.30 Obvious examples of companies which will be caught by this definition are the privatised utility companies and privatised transport companies such as Railtrack plc when these companies are carrying out public functions. The Government White Paper for the draft Human Rights Bill referred to companies being considered as public authorities as follows:

> "to the extent that they are exercising public functions, companies responsible for areas of activity which were previously within the public sector, such as the privatized utilities".[30]

14.31 **Dividing line between public and private functions.** Under the HRA, it is envisaged that a company may be treated as a public authority as regards certain, but not all, of its acts. For the purposes of deciding whether a company has a direct obligation to comply with the Convention, it is necessary to determine where the dividing line should be drawn between acts of a public nature and private acts. This dividing line may not always be easy to determine; for example, Railtrack plc where it is operating as a property developer. In this operation it is not acting entirely privately as it has certain planning privileges which only state bodies possess. It also receives a subsidy from the Government to maintain its operation as a property developer. These two factors, and the receipt of a subsidy in particular, arguably qualify Railtrack plc as exercising a "public function" for the purposes of the HRA despite the apparent intention of the Government that its roles should be distinct.

Bodies Subject to Judicial Review

14.32 A body which is already subject to judicial review proceedings in relation to all or part of its activities will almost certainly be considered a public authority for the purposes of the HRA as regards similar activities. However, it would appear that the HRA embraces bodies which fall outside the scope of judicial review. Sporting bodies such as the Jockey Club and the Football Association have so far been considered, by the English courts at least, as falling outside the ambit of bodies which are judicially reviewable.[31] However, as regards the HRA it is contemplated by the Government that they may be caught.[32] In the Commons debates the Home

---

[29] See Chap. 8 for a discussion on the definition of public functions.
[30] Rights Brought Home, The Human Rights Bill (Cm. 3782).
[31] *R v. Disciplinary Committee of the Jockey Club, ex p. Aga Khan* [1993] 1 W.L.R. 909; but note that in Scotland the Scottish Football Association was subject to judicial review in *St Johnston FC v. Scottish Football Association*, 1965 S.L.T. 171.
[32] In the debate in Parliament on the definition of a "public authority" the government considered the Jockey Club would be a "public authority". See H.C. Debs, May 20, 1998, col. 1018. See further *Aston Cantlow PCC v. Wallbank* [2001] 3 All E.R. 393, CA, at para. 34 (amenability of bodies to judicial review relevant but not necessarily determinative of whether a body is a public authority under the HRA).

Secretary referred to Clause 6 of the Convention as adopting a "non-exhaustive definition of a public authority".[33]

The narrower scope of judicial review proceedings lies in the test applied **14.33** to bodies which may be susceptible to judicial review.[34] In particular, judicial review does not apply where the body concerned is exercising a power derived solely from contract or from the consensual submission to its jurisdiction.[35] Additionally, a body will generally only be susceptible to judicial review if there is not only a public, but also a governmental interest, in the decision making power.[36]

Regulatory Bodies

Regulatory bodies are not inevitably characterised as public authorities **14.34** and not all of their functions are functions of a public nature.[37] Regulatory bodies such as the Department of Trade and Industry (DTI) and the Financial Services Authority (FSA) which undertake public functions will be considered public authorities. Other bodies with regulatory functions, such as the Panel on Takeovers and Mergers which sets and enforces standards for takeovers and mergers and the Stock Exchange, will also fall within the definition of a public authority or may be considered a quasi-public authority where only certain of their functions are public in nature. These bodies will therefore have to act compatibly with the Convention in carrying out their functions which are public in nature. They will also have to ensure that the regulatory regime they operate gives effect to their positive obligation to protect Convention rights from violation by private parties. One of the key areas which will fall under the scrutiny of the HRA is where these bodies hold regulatory or disciplinary hearings. In so far as these hearings are determinative of civil rights and obligations they must be compatible with the Article 6 right to a fair hearing before an independent and impartial tribunal.

Similarly, other bodies which set and enforce professional standards **14.35** within a particular profession such as the Law Society,[38] and Lloyd's of London are likely to fall within the definition of public authority in the HRA.

For many of the regulatory bodies, it has yet to be decided whether they **14.36** will be treated as carrying out entirely public functions or whether they will be treated as quasi-public authorities carrying out some public and some private functions. It will ultimately depend upon the functions of the body in question. This distinction will be of importance as the body will only be under a direct obligation to act compatibly with Convention rights where it is carrying out its public function.

---

[33] H.C. Debs, February 16, 1998, col. 776.

[34] See para. 8.18.

[35] *R. v. Panel on Takeovers and Mergers, ex p. Datafin Plc* [1987] 1 Q.B. 815; *R. v. Disciplinary Committee of the Jockey Club, ex p. Aga Kahn* [1993] 1 W.L.R. 909.

[36] *R. v. Chief Rabbi of the United Hebrew Congregations of Great Britain and the Commonwealth, ex p. Wachmann* [1992] 1 W.L.R. 1036; *Law v. National Greyhound Racing Club Ltd* [1983] 1 W.L.R. 1302.

[37] See, for a discussion, Jack Beatson Q.C., "Which Regulatory Bodies are Subject to the Human Rights Act?" *The Human Rights Act and the Criminal Justice and Regulatory Process* (Oxford, 1999).

[38] Both the Law Society and the Solicitors Disciplinary Tribunal were considered public authorities in *Re A Solicitor* (unreported) November 13, 2000 (DC).

Effect of Being a Public Authority on Victim Status

14.37   The European Court has held that a public authority may not claim victim status under the Convention.[39–40] However, it is arguable that a quasi-public authority may be a victim when it is carrying out its non-public functions.

Companies as Victims

14.38   The categories of eligible applicants for the purposes of complaining of Convention rights violations is found in Article 34 of the Convention. It provides that complaints of a violation of a Convention right may be made by "any person, non-governmental organisation or group of individuals". It is well established by the European Court that a company may be a "person" for the purposes of the Convention and therefore able to rely on Convention rights.[41]

Shareholders as Victims

14.39   The question of whether shareholders of a company are entitled to bring a claim for violation of a Convention right is more complex and may depend in part on what right is being claimed. It appears that shareholders (minority and majority) may enjoy the protection of Article 6[42] while claims based on Article 1 of Protocol No. 1 may be brought by shareholders only in exceptional circumstances, for example where it is shown that the company itself in unable to claim.[43] The distinction may be explained by a shareholder trying to assert his own rights as a shareholder (Article 6 cases) and a shareholder trying to assert the company's rights (Article 1 of Protocol No. 1 cases).[44]

Decisions of the European Court—Article 1 of Protocol No. 1

14.40   In asserting property rights based on Article 1 of Protocol No. 1, the European Court has in certain circumstances allowed applications by shareholders where it has been impossible for the company itself to bring a claim.[45] Conversely, in an earlier case, the Commission held that where a company has the right to claim then a shareholder may not.[46] This approach has an obvious attraction as regards allowing an individual a

---

[39–40] *Ayuntamiento de M v. Spain* (1990) 68 D.R. 209. See generally para. 8.06 *et seq.* on standing.

[41] *The Sunday Times v. United Kingdom* (1980) 2 E.H.R.R. 245; *Autronic v. Switzerland* (1990) 12 E.H.R.R. 48, in which the Court held that "neither Autronic AG's legal status as a limited company nor the fact that its activities were commercial nor the intrinsic nature of freedom of expression each deprive Autronic AG of the protection of Article 10. The Article applies to 'everyone', whether natural or legal persons. The Court has, moreover, already held on three occasions that it is applicable to profit-making corporate bodies". See also *Kaplan v. United Kingdom* (1982) 4 E.H.R.R. 64.

[42] *Ruiz-Mateos v. Spain* (1993) 16 E.H.R.R. 505; *Neves e Silva v. Portugal* (1991) 13 E.H.R.R. 535.

[43] *Agrotexim v. Greece* (1996) 21 E.H.R.R. 250.

[44] See also Michael Smyth: "The United Kingdom's Incorporation of the European Convention and Its Implications for Business" [1998] E.H.R.L.R. 273.

[45] *Pine Valley Developments v. Ireland* (1993) 16 E.H.R.R. 250. See also *Agrotexim Hellas SA v. Greece* (1996) 21 E.H.R.R. 250.

[46] *Yarrow v. United Kingdom* (1983) 30 D.R. 155.

remedy in circumstances where he would otherwise be prevented from seeking redress. On the other hand it creates some tension with decisions of the English courts which reveal a reluctance to ignore the long-standing principle contained in *Salomon v Salomon*.[47]

In *Yarrow v. United Kingdom*[48] the Commission drew a distinction between **14.41** a claim made by minority shareholders and a claim by majority shareholders. It considered that minority shareholders would not normally fulfill the requirements of victim status, as the acts complained of were directed against the company and not against the shareholders' personal interests, whereas the majority shareholders could fulfill victim status as their direct personal interest had been affected by an act directed at the company. On the facts of the case, however, the shareholders could not claim victim status as the company itself had a right to claim.[49]

In *Pine Valley Developments Ltd v. Ireland*, the Court adopted a broader **14.42** approach on the question of whether shareholders could be victims.[50] In that case applications were brought by related companies and an individual shareholder relating to the purchase of land for development. The first applicant was a company struck off the Register of Companies and the original owner of the land, the second applicant was a company (in receivership) to whom the land had been sold and the third applicant was the individual sole beneficial shareholder of the second applicant. The Court held that all three were capable of being victims and therefore entitled to bring a claim. It said in relation to the first applicant that neither its sale of the land nor it being subsequently struck off the register altered the fact that it had been the owner for a certain period of time, which enabled it to claim a violation. In relation to the second and third applicants, the Court held that insolvency of the company did not preclude either the insolvent company or its shareholders from being victims.[51]

More recently, the European Court has taken a stricter line on the issue of **14.43** whether shareholders may claim as victims. In *Agrotexim v. Greece*,[52] the applicant companies were minority shareholders in a brewery company. The company itself did not make a claim. The brewery had been prevented from property development by measures adopted by the Athens Council. The applicants argued that their financial interests had been damaged because of a fall in the value of shares which had followed the decision. The European Court in refusing their application expressed concern about reducing the risks and difficulties which would be entailed by piercing the "corporate veil" or disregarding a company's legal personality. Such action would "be justified only in exceptional circumstances, in

---

[47] [1897] A.C. 22.
[48] (1983) 30 D.R. 155.
[49] See, however, *Neves e Silva v. Portugal* (1991) 13 E.H.R.R. 535, where the European Court rejected the state's submission that Mr Neves failed to qualify as a victim because he was a minority shareholder.
[50] (1993) 16 E.H.R.R. 250.
[51] Note that a similar approach was taken in *Groppera Radio AG v. Switzerland* (1990) 12 E.H.R.R. 321. The Court held, in the context of an Article 10 claim, that all the applicants (the company, its sole shareholder and statutory representative) had a direct interest in the continued transmission of the radio programmes and were, therefore, victims.
[52] (1996) 21 E.H.R.R. 250.

particular where it is clearly established that it is impossible for the Company to apply to the Convention institutions through the organs set up under its articles of incorporation or—in the event of liquidation—through its liquidators". Not even the fact that the brewery company was under the control of the state and therefore practically was prevented from acting was a sufficient reason for permitting the application. This decision appears to be at odds with some of the earlier European decisions.

14.44 *Agrotexim* was followed by the Commission in *Penton v. Turkey*.[53] In that case a shareholder in a Cypriot company claimed victim status on the basis of an interference with his property resulting from the Turkish invasion and occupation of Northern Cyprus. The Commission followed the Court in *Agrotexim* in holding that the shareholder did not qualify for victim status.

Decisions of the European Court—Article 6

14.45 In asserting Article 6 rights, the Court has taken the view that shareholders may have standing as victims. In *GJ v. Luxembourg*[54] the Court appeared to place some importance on the fact that the shareholder in question had a 90 per cent holding. The company was in liquidation and the 90 per cent majority shareholder was claiming under Article 6(1) that the liquidation had not concluded within a reasonable time. The liquidation had taken six years during which time the applicant was debarred from being a director, shareholder or employee of the company for a period of two years and his freedom of movement was restricted. The applicant also claimed under Article 8 that the proceedings interfered with his right to respect for family life. The Commission held, distinguishing *Agrotexim*, that he was entitled to claim as a victim as he held a substantial majority shareholding of 90 per cent in the company, had a direct personal interest in the subject-matter of the complaint and because the complaint related to the actions of the liquidator.

14.46 Overall, although the European decisions are not always entirely consistent, a general trend can be discerned drawing a distinction between cases where shareholders are asserting their rights and those where they are asserting the rights of the company.[55]

Domestic decisions

14.47 The English courts have so far been far more conservative in their treatment of shareholders as victims and have tended to view the company as an entity entirely separate from its members in accordance with the principles in *Salomon v. Salomon*. The courts have been reluctant to look behind the separate personality of the company to its members.

---

[53] Application No. 24463/94 (1998). See also *Credit and Industrial Bank and Moravec v. Czech Republic*, Application No. 29010/95 (1998).
[54] [2000] B.P.I.R. 1009. See also *Patifis v. Greece* (1999) 27 E.H.R.R. 566, where the European Court allowed minority shareholders to fulfill victim status in relation to a claim of an Art. 6 violation; *Wojnowicz v. Poland*, Application No. 33082/96, September 21, 2000.
[55] See also *Wasa Liv Omsesidigt, Forsakringbolaget Varlands Pensionsstiftelse v. Sweden* (1988) 58 D.R. 163, where policyholders in an insurance company were held not to be victims on grounds that they did not have any legal claim to direct ownership of the insurance company's assets.

Judicial conservatism in this area has also been influenced by the long-standing rule in *Foss v. Harbottle*[56] that the company is the proper plaintiff in proceedings concerning its rights. This rule has been followed consistently by the courts when dealing with minority shareholder rights. Ultimately the decisions of the courts reflect the underlying rationale of company law which generally allows companies to decide their own policies and settle their own disputes by majority decision.[57] **14.48**

There have been some exceptions to the general rule in *Foss v. Harbottle*.[58] However, in practice most minority actions are taken by shareholders relying on the statutory remedy afforded to them by section 459 of the Companies Act 1985 to challenge unfairly prejudicial conduct. **14.49**

4. Procedure

Introduction

Article 6 is the most frequently invoked of all the Convention rights and is designed to ensure that the safeguards of a fair hearing are protected. This is applicable to litigation to which companies are parties as well as where the parties are individuals. Some areas where Article 6 has been applied in relation to cases where a company has been a party are referred to below. **14.50**

Fair and Public Hearing

Article 6 guarantees the right to a fair and public hearing. Where a litigant was guilty of conduct that put the fairness of any trial in jeopardy, or which was such as to render further proceedings unsatisfactory and to prevent the court from doing justice, the court was bound to refuse to allow that litigant to take any further part in the proceedings and (where appropriate) to determine the proceedings against him. A litigant who demonstrates that he is determined to pursue proceedings with the object of preventing a fair trial may forfeit his right to take part in a trial.[59] **14.51**

Independent and Impartial Tribunal

Article 6(1) requires that civil rights and obligations be determined by an "independent and impartial" tribunal. The European Court held in *Belilos v. Switzerland*[60] that a tribunal must satisfy a number of requirements: **14.52**

> "independence, in particular of the executive; impartiality; duration of its members terms of office; guarantees afforded by its procedure".

---

[56] (1843) 2 Hare. 461.
[57] See also *Adams v. Cape Industries plc* [1990] Ch. 433, where the court held that claims against a parent company for the actions of its subsidiaries should fail; *Yukong Line Ltd of Korea v. Rendsburg Investments Corp of Liberia, The Rialto (No. 2)* [1998] 4 All E.R. 82, [1998] 1 W.L.R. 294, [1998] 1 Lloyd's Rep 322.
[58] See, *e.g.* *Edwards v. Halliwell* [1950] 2 All E.R. 1064; *Prudential Assurance Co. Ltd v. Newman Industries (No. 2)* [1982] Ch. 204.
[59] *Arrow Nominees v. Blackledge* [2000] 1 B.C.L.C. 709. On the right of a litigant to be present at a hearing, see para. 10.80.
[60] (1988) 10 E.H.R.R. 466.

In deciding whether the requirement of independence is fulfilled it is necessary to have regard to the manner of appointment of a tribunal's members and their term of office, the existence of guarantees against outside pressure and whether there is an appearance of independence. Impartiality means both subjective impartiality and objective impartiality.

14.53 In *Kingsley v. United Kingdom*,[61] the applicant was the managing director of a company which owned and controlled six licensed casinos in London. The company's premises were subject to police raids and a large number of documents were seized. The Gaming Board of Great Britain lodged objections to the company's annual application for renewal of its casino licences with the Licensing Magistrates. The result of the proceedings was to prevent the applicant from holding any management position in that industry and therefore determined his civil rights and obligations. As a result, it had to be determined whether the Board was an independent impartial tribunal within the meaning of Article 6(1).

14.54 Relevant factors included how members of the Board were appointed, the existence of guarantees against external pressure, and whether the body presented an appearance of fairness. The three panel members who decided to revoke the applicant's certificate were amongst those who had prejudged him publicly and thus the panel hearing did not have the appearance of impartiality necessary to constitute a tribunal within the meaning of Article 6(1). This appearance of bias could have been corrected if there had been available to the applicant a review by a judicial body which had full jurisdiction and which provided the guarantees of Article 6(1). Although judicial review of the Board's decision was available, the domestic courts were not able to quash the decision and remit it for a first decision by an independent and impartial tribunal. This ability was considered to be the essence of a fair hearing. The domestic courts reviewed rather than reheard the Board's decision and so could not themselves fulfil the requirements enshrined by Article 6.

Trial within a Reasonable Period

14.55 One of the aspects of procedural fairness most frequently relied upon is the Article 6 guarantee of the right to a hearing within a reasonable time.[61A] In assessing reasonableness, all the circumstances of the particular case will be considered. For example, in *Wojnowicz v. Poland*[62] the European Court held, in relation to a winding up of a company, that the reasonableness of the length of proceedings had to be assessed in light of the circumstances of the case, its complexity and both the applicant's and the judicial authorities' conduct in contributing to the delay.[63]

14.56 Complex cases where there may be numerous interconnected companies and which require lengthy investigation will not necessarily violate Article

---

[61] Application No. 35605/97, November 7, 2000.

[61A] See further paras 10.98 *et seq.*

[62] Application No. 33082/96, September 21, 2000. See also *GJ v. Luxembourg* [2000] B.P.I.R. 1009.

[63] See also *Comingersoll SA v. Portugal*, Application No. 35382/97, April 6, 2000, where damages were awarded by the Court where proceedings had dragged on for over 17 years before a final decision was given.

6 when the proceedings take a considerable time. It depends upon what is appropriate in the circumstances.[64]

Judgment

The judgment should be available publicly.[64A] Certain tribunals are already **14.57** required to give reasoned decisions.[65] Those who presently do not may find it necessary to do so in order to avoid a breach of Article 6. Lord Clyde in *Stefan v. General Medical Council*[66] suggested that the reasons:

> "need not be elaborate nor lengthy. But they should be such as to tell the parties in broad terms why the decision was reached. In many cases a very few sentences should suffice to give such explanation as was appropriate to the particular situation".

5. COMPANY INVESTIGATIONS

Introduction

The wide ranging powers contained in various statutes requiring individ- **14.58** uals and company officers to answer questions, hand over documentation and submit to oral examinations have been the subject of a considerable amount of litigation involving Convention Articles. This is largely due to the subsequent use of compulsorily obtained evidence in criminal proceed- ings rather than the scope of the investigation itself.

Statutory Powers to Compel Evidence

The statutory powers conferred upon the DTI and officeholders, which **14.59** compel an individual to answer potentially incriminating questions or hand over potentially incriminating documentation, are far reaching.[67] The power to investigate and compel answers may not, as a general rule, give rise to a challenge under Article 6 of the HRA because it is not considered determinative of civil rights and obligations.[68] However, the subsequent use at a criminal trial of evidence obtained under compulsion may be challenged under Article 6 where the use of that evidence will either render the trial unfair or infringe the privilege against self-incrimination.[69]

---

[64] *Hozee v. The Netherlands*, Application No. 21961/93, May 22, 1998.
[64A] See para. 10.96.
[65] See the Tribunals and Inquiries Act 1992, s.10. See also para. 10.92.
[66] [1999] 1 W.L.R. 1293. See also *Hiro Balani v. Spain* (1995) 19 E.H.R.R. 566.
[67] See Insurance Companies Act 1982, s.43(1); Companies Act 1985, s.436; Insolvency Act 1986, ss.218, 236 and 237, 433; Financial Services Act 1986, ss.94, 105, 177 and 178; Criminal Justice Act 1987, s.2; Banking Act 1987, ss.39, 41, 42; and Companies Act 1989, ss.82 and 83.
[68] See *Fayed v. United Kingdom* (1994) 18 E.H.R.R. 393, where the investigation process was examined in the light of Art. 6 and the court drew a distinction between the process of investigation and the trial.
[69] See paras 11.16 *et seq.*, above.

Challenges to the Investigation Itself

14.60 There is some scope for challenging the investigation itself where the powers are being used in a disproportionate, oppressive or indiscriminatory way.[70] The Court has previously exercised its discretion not to allow investigations where they may be unnecessary, oppressive or disproportionate without recourse to the HRA.

14.61 Before the HRA came into force, a DTI investigation was successfully challenged by Kevin Maxwell. The inspectors sought to question him, after his acquittal, on 131 topics. He refused to answer questions on the basis among others that the vast amount of material sent to him was an unlawful demand by the inspectors to "perform forced or compulsory labour" under Article 4(2) of the Convention. In proceedings brought by the inspectors against Maxwell for failure to co-operate, the Vice-Chancellor held that the inspectors could not place demands upon witnesses that were unreasonable as to time or expense.[71]

14.62 In *Fayed v. United Kingdom*,[72] the applicants argued that the investigation process itself amounted to a "determination of a civil right" and that therefore was subject to Article 6. The Court found that the function of the inspectors was to investigate and not to adjudicate and therefore did not amount to a determination of a civil right. The ability of independent inspectors to investigate fearlessly was an important aim of the regulatory regime. The Court drew a distinction between the process of investigation and the trial process and said:

> " . . . the Court is satisfied that the functions performed by the Inspectors were, in practice as well as in theory, essentially investigative. The Inspectors did not adjudicate, either in form or in substance. They themselves said in their report that their findings would not be dispositive of anything. They did not make a legal determination as to criminal or civil liability concerning the Fayed brothers, and in particular concerning the latter's civil right to honour and reputation. The purpose of their inquiry was to ascertain and record facts which might subsequently be used as the basis for action by other competent authorities—prosecuting, regulatory, disciplinary or even legislative . . . In short, it cannot be said that the Inspectors' inquiry 'determined' the applicants' civil right to a good reputation, for the purposes of Article 6(1), or that its result was directly decisive for that right."

Classification of Proceedings as Civil or Criminal

14.63 The classification of proceedings as criminal or civil is crucial to the issue of whether compulsory evidence may be used in the course of those proceedings. The European Court has made it clear that classification by

---

[70] See, *e.g. Cloverbay Ltd v. Bank of Credit and Commerce International SA* [1991] 1 All E.R. 894; *Re JN Taylor Finance Pty Ltd* [1999] B.C.L.C. 256; *Re Atlantic Computers, The Times,* April 25, 1997.
[71] *Re An Inquiry Into Mirror Group Newspapers plc* [1999] 2 All E.R. 641.
[72] (1994) 18 E.H.R.R. 393.

the Member States themselves will not necessarily be decisive, particularly when the state classifies a proceeding as civil.[73] The European Court has given "civil" and "criminal" an autonomous meaning.[73A]

If proceedings are defined as a matter of domestic law as "criminal" then **14.64** that is likely to be sufficient for the court to determine that the proceedings are also criminal for the purposes of Article 6. Where domestic law classifies proceedings as civil the court will need to consider the following further factors:

(1) the nature of the offence in question; and

(2) the severity of the maximum permissible penalty.

The maximum penalty which may be imposed is a key factor in determining whether proceedings are criminal or civil. If imprisonment is a possibility, the proceedings will almost certainly be classified as criminal. This may also be the case even if the initial sanction is a low level fine and imprisonment could only follow the non-payment of that fine.[74] Search and seizure orders, however, are not likely to be classified as criminal proceedings even though they may allow the imposition of fines.[75] Similarly, where a company is subject to a statutory seizure order executed by a government body, the proceedings are unlikely to be regarded as criminal.[76]

Regulatory offences which can result only in disqualification are unlikely to **14.65** be regarded as criminal. In *X v. United Kingdom*,[77] the Secretary of State objected to the applicant's appointment as chief executive of an insurance company on the ground that he was not a "fit and proper person", as required by the Insurance Companies Act 1982. The Commission in that case assumed that the proceedings were civil in nature.[77A]

Evidence in Criminal Proceedings—Privilege against Self-Incrimination

This principle means that a person cannot be compelled to give evidence **14.66** in response to questions which is subsequently used against him in criminal proceedings. It is a common law privilege which applies in criminal proceedings.[78]

The privilege against self-incrimination only exists as regards evidence in **14.67** criminal proceedings. It does not apply to civil proceedings although it may

---

[73] See *Engel v. Netherlands (No. 2)* (1979) 1 E.H.R.R. 706.

[73A] See paras 3.76 *et seq.*

[74] *Umlauft v. Austria* (1996) 22 E.H.R.R. 76.

[75] *Krone-Verlag GmbH and Mediaprint Anzeigen GmbH and Co. KG v. Austria* (1997) 23 E.H.R.R. 152.

[76] *AGOSI v. United Kingdom* (1987) 9 E.H.R.R. 1; *Air Canada v. United Kingdom* (1995) 20 E.H.R.R. 150.

[77] Application No. 28530/95, January 18, 1998. See also *APB v. United Kingdom*, Application No. 30552/96, January 15, 1998.

[77A] See paras 14.108 *et seq.* for a discussion of directors disqualification proceedings.

[78] See also the International Covenant on Civil and Political Rights, Art. 14(2)(g), which expressly provides that an accused person has the right "not to be compelled to testify against himself or to confess guilt". Relevant rules of international law applicable between the parties will be taken into account in the interpretation of the Convention. The history of the privilege in English law lies in a response to the horrors of the medieval Star Chamber and a protection for the people against the exercise of arbitrary power by the Crown.

be considered in determining whether there has been a fair hearing. However, as mentioned above, the definition of proceedings as criminal or civil by a Member State is not necessarily determinative. Further, there is a tension in the current law on criminal evidence under section 78 of the Police and Criminal Evidence Act 1984, which gives the court a discretion to exclude evidence but does not compel the court to do so, and the guidelines on prosecutorial practice which are currently in force but which are not binding.[79]

Section 78 of the Police and Criminal Evidence Act 1984

14.68 The present state of the law relating to criminal evidence explains some of the inconsistency in decisions of the English courts. Section 78 of the Police and Criminal Evidence Act 1984 provides:

> "(1) In any proceedings the court may refuse to allow evidence on which the prosecution proposes to rely to be given if it appears to the court that, having regard to all the circumstances, including the circumstances in which the evidence was obtained, the admission of the evidence would have such an adverse effect on the fairness of the proceedings that the court ought not to admit it.
>
> (2) Nothing in this section shall prejudice any rule of law requiring a court to exclude evidence."

It does not, therefore necessarily follow that because evidence is obtained under compulsion that the court when having regard to section 78 will exclude it. It is a matter of the court's discretion taking into account all the circumstances.

14.69 With the advent of the HRA in mind, the Attorney-General issued a Guidance Note on the use of compelled evidence at criminal trials.[80] But the guidance does not constitute an absolute ban and contains a discretion to use evidence obtained under compulsion which is introduced by the defendant, is based on the silence of the defendant or where the answers to questions are untrue. The incompatibility between section 78 of the Police and Criminal Evidence Act 1984 and Article 6 of the Convention may need to be dealt with if anomalies in decisions on criminal evidence are to be avoided.[81]

Decisions of the European Court

14.70 The application of Article 6 was examined by the European Court in the context of a regulatory investigation in *Saunders v. United Kingdom*.[82] Saunders was charged with false accounting and conspiracy arising out of an illegal share support scheme operated during the Guinness' contested takeover bid. Before and after he was charged Saunders was interviewed by DTI inspectors to investigate the circumstances of the bid. His answers

---

[79] See also paras 11.15 *et seq.*, above.
[80] Attorney-General Guidance Note, February 3, 1998.
[81] See also *Nottingham City Council v. Amin* [2000] 2 All E.R. 946.
[82] (1997) 23 E.H.R.R. 313.

given before he was charged were put before the jury. The European Court held that there had been a violation of Article 6 and said:

> "The right not to incriminate oneself, in particular, presupposes that the prosecution in a criminal case must prove their case without resort to evidence obtained through methods of coercion or oppression in defiance of the will of the accused."[83]

The Court in *Saunders* made it clear that its decision related only to the subsequent use of the statements at Saunders' trial and was not concerned with a general condemnation of compelled evidence or specifically the use of compulsion under section 432 of the Companies Act 1985 to obtain testimony for the purposes of a regulatory investigation.[84]

The analysis of this issue in earlier decisions of the European Court in   **14.71**
Funke v. France[85] and the European Court of Justice in *Orkem v. Commission*[86] are not wholly consistent with the decision in *Saunders*.

Domestic Decisions

In the light of the HRA and European case law, a decision of the Court of   **14.72**
Appeal, in which the Court refused to interfere with criminal convictions for insider trading based on compelled evidence, has been challenged.[87] Other decisions of the courts have held in line with the European authorities that the subsequent use of evidence obtained under compulsory powers at a criminal trial is a breach of Article 6. In *R. v. Faryab*[88] the Court of Appeal held that evidence obtained under section 433 of the Insolvency Act 1986 could not be used in relation to a prosecution for handling stolen goods. In *R. v. Hertfordshire County Council, ex p. Green Environmental Industries*,[89] the House of Lords accepted that the privilege against self-incrimination was relevant where the prosecution sought to introduce evidence obtained under compulsory powers in criminal proceedings and that the court must consider whether Article 6 required the exclusion of such evidence.

However, where evidence contained under compulsion does not tend to   **14.73**
incriminate that person then subject to any statutory bar, it would appear that it may be used in subsequent criminal proceedings.[90] But the court will have to scrutinise the evidence in relation to Article 6 and examine whether such evidence in any way will prevent the applicant from having a fair trial.

---

[83] (1997) 23 E.H.R.R. 313.
[84] See also *IJL, GMR and AKP v. United Kingdom, The Times,* October 13, 2000, [2001] Crim. L.R. 133; *R v. Hertfordshire County Council, ex p. Green Environment Industries Ltd* [2000] 1 A.C. 412, HL.
[85] (1993) 16 E.H.R.R. 297.
[86] [1989] E.C.R. 3283.
[87] *R. v. Staines; R. v. Morrisey* (1997) 2 Cr. App. Rep. 426. See *Staines v. United Kingdom,* Application No. 41552/98, June 8, 1999. See for a recent case *R. v. Kensal, The Times,* June 11, 2001.
[88] [1999] B.P.I.R. 569.
[89] [2000] 1 All E.R. 773, HL.
[90] See *Stott (Procurator Fiscal, Dunfermline) v. Brown,* [2001] 2 W.L.R. 817, PC.

Documents

14.74 In many company investigations, it is the ability to compel the production of documents which may ultimately cause the greatest harm to the individual at a subsequent criminal trial. However the authorities are not consistent on whether there is a distinction to be drawn between the compulsion as regards the production of documents and compulsion as regards answering questions.[91]

14.75 In *Funke v. France*[92] the European Court held that a conviction for failure to produce documents was a violation of Article 6. This decision, which did not draw a distinction between documents and answering questions, was not followed in *Saunders v. United Kingdom*[93] where the Court considered that the privilege against self-incrimination was primarily concerned with the right to remain silent and not with the use of compulsory evidence. In *Saunders* the Court stated that the right:

> " . . . does not extend to the use in criminal proceedings of material which may be obtained from the accused through the use of compulsory powers but which has an existence independent of the will of the suspect such as, inter alia, documents acquired pursuant to a warrant, breath, blood and urine samples and bodily tissues for the purpose of DNA testing."[94]

14.76 The Court of Appeal, however, upheld the distinction drawn in *Saunders* in preference to the approach in *Funke v. France* in the recent case of the *Attorney-General's Reference (No 7 of 2000)*.[95] In that case the Court of Appeal held, in the context of criminal proceedings against a bankrupt for an offence under the Insolvency Act 1986, the use by the Crown of documents which were delivered to the Official Receiver under compulsion but which did not contain statements made by the bankrupt under compulsion did not violate the bankrupt's right to a fair trial. The Court said:

> "It seemed to their Lordships that the distinction made in paragraphs 68 and 69 of the judgment of the European Court of Human Rights in *Saunders v United Kingdom* . . . between a statement made and other material independent of the making of the statement, was jurisprudentially sound . . . article 6 of the Convention, the right to silence and the right not to incriminate oneself, are generally recognized international standards while at the heart of the notion of a fair procedure under article 6. Their rationale lies, inter alia, in the protection of the accused against improper compulsion by the authorities thereby contributing to the avoidance of miscarriages of justice and to the fulfillment of the aims of Article 6. The right not to incriminate

---

[91] See *Funke v. France* (1993) 16 E.H.R.R. 297; *Saunders v. United Kingdom* (1997) 23 E.H.R.R. 313; *Attorney-General's Reference (No. 7 of 2000)*, *The Times* April 12, 2001, CA. See further paras 11.16 *et seq.* and particularly para. 11.20.

[92] (1993) 16 E.H.R.R. 297.

[93] (1997) 23 E.H.R.R. 313.

[94] At para. 69.

[95] *The Times*, April 12, 2001; see also *L v. United Kingdom* [2000] F.L.R. 322 where the ECHR endorsed the approach taken by the majority in *Saunders*.

oneself, in particular, presupposes that the prosecution in a criminal case seek to prove their case against the accused without resort to evidence obtained through methods of coercion or oppression in defiance of the will of the accused. In this sense, the right is closely linked to the presumption of innocence contained in article 6.2 of the Convention."

A further decision of the European Court in *J.B. v. Switzerland*[96] has been published which is closer to the approach of the Court in *Funke v. France* than to *L v. United Kingdom*. The case involved proceedings for tax evasion during which the defendant was requested to submit all the documents he had concerning certain companies and to explain the source of income which he had invested. He did not comply with these requests and was duly fined. He filed an administrative law appeal complaining that under Article 6 he was not required to incriminate himself. The European Court held that the proceedings imposing the fine determined a criminal charge and were therefore criminal proceedings. The Court however drew a distinction between material which had an existence independent of the person concerned and that which was obtained by means of coercion and against the will of that person. It held that there had been a violation of the right under Article 6 not to incriminate oneself. **14.77**

Another area of difficulty arises under section 2(2) of the Criminal Justice Act 1987 which deals with investigations initiated by the Director of the Serious Fraud Office (SFO) into suspected offences involving serious fraud. By virtue of section 2(2) of the 1987 Act a person may be required to answer questions or furnish information. There is a procedural safeguard in section 2(8) whereby a statement may only be used in evidence against someone for knowingly or recklessly making a false or misleading statement to the SFO or for some other offence where he gives evidence inconsistent with his statement. However, section 2(8) does not limit the use which can be made of documents produced under section 2(3) since it applies only to statements. The Criminal Justice Act 1987, therefore, allows the SFO to circumvent the protection under section 2(8) by obtaining transcripts from investigatory authorities.[97] There is a discretionary bar imposed by the United Kingdom Government against the transfer of documents from investigatory authorities to the SFO but there is no legal prohibition.

The distinction between the compulsion to provide answers to questions and the compulsion to disclose documents would appear to relate to the right to remain silent according to the decision in *Saunders*. However, the decision of the European Court in *J.B. v. Switzerland* suggests that further consideration will have to be given to the meaning of "material having an existence independent of the person concerned". It also leaves a number of issues unresolved. For example, is there a distinction between material which could have been obtained from third parties but which was obtained instead under compulsion from the defendant? Is there a distinction between material of which the defendant is the author and material which **14.78**

---

[96] Application No. 31827/96, May 3, 2001.
[97] See *Re Arrows Ltd (No. 4)* [1993] Ch. 452; *Re British and Commonwealth Holdings Plc (Nos 1 and 2)* [1993] A.C. 426.

does not owe its existence to the defendant? For example, cash books prepared by the defendant as against bank statements. The current state of authorities leave much room for future challenges.

Evidence in Civil Proceedings

14.79 The privilege against self-incrimination is a principle enshrined in the criminal context.[98] In relation to civil proceedings, Article 6 requires a general standard of fairness and generally the courts have allowed evidence to be used even though it was obtained under compulsion. For example, in *Official Receiver v. Stern*,[99] the Court of Appeal held that compulsory evidence obtained under section 235 of the Insolvency Act 1986 could be used, at the discretion of the court in director's disqualification proceedings because they were civil and not criminal in character. In that case, Henry LJ referred to the existing protection afforded by the courts to the improper use of information obtained by the exercise of the extraordinary powers of investigation:

> "There is already a large body of authority as to the circumstances in which an order for examination under s. 236 may be refused, as being oppressive, because of the likelihood of future civil proceedings against a company officer; see for instance *Soden v Burns, R v Secretary of State for Trade & Industry, ex parte Soden . . .* which refers to many of the most important recent cases in this area. These cases show that in the field of corporate insolvency, as in other fields, the human rights implications of compelled evidence are not a new or alien importation, but are already a familiar use for judges whose duty it is to safeguard a fair trial".[1]

Evidence at Disciplinary Hearings

14.80 The issue of use of compulsory testimony has also arisen in the course of disciplinary proceedings. In a case involving the Institute of Chartered Accountants of England and Wales, Sedley J. held that answers given under compulsion to a professional body might expose an individual to loss of livelihood, thus determining his civil rights and obligations.[2] However, it was held in that case that Mr Nawaz had waived his privilege against self-incrimination when he agreed to become a member of the Institute. The Court of Appeal upheld the judgment and noted that when individuals participate in the activities of an organisation in a way which expressly renders them subject to that organisation's rules, they waive any privilege which they might otherwise have asserted.[3]

---

[98] See *British & Commonwealth Holdings plc v. Barclays de Zoete Wedd Ltd* [1999] 1 B.C.L.C. 74, where Neuberger J. notes the distinction between civil and criminal proceedings.

[99] [2000] 1 W.L.R. 2230.

[1] See also *DC, HS and AD v. United Kingdom*, Application No. 39031/97, September 14, 1999; *EDC v. United Kingdom* [1998] B.C.C. 370; *Bhimji v. Chatwani* [1992] 1 W.L.R. 1158.

[2] *R. v. Institute of Chartered Accountants of England and Wales, ex p. Taher Nawaz* [1997] P.N.L.R. 433.

[3] (unreported) April 25, 1997, CA. See also *R. v. Herefordshire County Council, ex p. Green Environmental Industries Ltd* [2000] 1 All E.R. 773. See generally Chapter 20, Disciplinary Proceedings.

Reform in Domestic Law

The decision of the European Court in *Saunders* has produced reform in   **14.81**
some statutes in order to clarify the positions as regards the use of
compulsory evidence at criminal trials. To this end, section 59 of the Youth
Justice and Criminal Evidence Act 1999 was introduced which amends
various statutory provisions[4] by restricting the use that may be made in
criminal trials of evidence obtained under compulsory powers. The
amendments qualify those provisions by providing that the answer may be
used by the prosecution at trial where:

(1) the defendant himself introduces them; or

(2) where the defendant is being prosecuted for his failure or refusal
to answer a question, or his failure to disclose a material fact, or
his having given an untruthful answer.

In addition section 11 of the Insolvency Act 2000 amends section 219 of
the Insolvency Act 1986 so that, except in limited circumstances, answers
given by an individual under the powers contained in section 218 of the
Insolvency Act 1986 cannot be used in subsequent criminal proceedings.

6. COMPANIES AND PROPERTY RIGHTS

Introduction

The protection of property rights will be affected by both Article 8 of the   **14.82**
Convention and Article 1 of Protocol No. 1. Both these rights are subject
to qualification and overall it is a matter of performing a balancing exercise
between the competing interests of the person and the general interests of
a democratic society.[4A]

Search of Business Premises

The case law suggests that an individual will have protection under Article   **14.83**
8 which may extend beyond his home to his work place. It is much less
clear to what extent a company itself has a right to privacy.[4B]

In *Niemietz v. Germany*[5] a lawyer's office was searched as part of an   **14.84**
ongoing criminal investigation. The applicant complained that respect for
his home and correspondence had been infringed and that the business
goodwill and reputation of his firm had been damaged. The European
Court held that Article 8 had been breached and that the private life of an

---

[4] S.59 amends *inter alia* Insurance Companies Act 1982, s. 43A; Companies Act 1985,
s.434; Insolvency Act 1986, s.433; Companies and Directors Disqualification Act 1986, s.20;
Financial Services Act 1986, ss.105 and 177; Banking Act 1987, ss.39, 41 and 42; Companies Act 1989, s.83; and Criminal Justice Act 1987, s.2.
[4A] See further Chapter 16.
[4B] See *R. v. Broadcasting Standards Commission, ex p. British Broadcasting Commission*
[2000] 3 W.L.R. 1327.
[5] (1993) 16 E.H.R.R. 97.

individual is not confined to the home and could extend to the office space in which an individual worked. It stated that there was:

" . . . no reason of principle why this understanding of the notion of 'private life' should be taken to exclude activities of a professional or business nature since it is . . . in the course of their working lives that the majority of people have a significant, if not the greatest, opportunity of developing relationships with the outside world."[6]

However, despite the fact that Article 8 operated in the workplace, the European Court in *Niemietz* also considered that the state would retain the entitlement to interfere and that entitlement "might well be more far-reaching where professional or business activities or premises were involved than would otherwise be the case". In *Miaihle v. France*[7] the European Court held that Article 8 had been breached where French customs officials behaved disproportionately in indiscriminately seizing around 15,000 documents from the applicant's head office.

14.85 Decisions of the European Court of Justice in the context of searches of business premises have on the whole tended to uphold the right of the state to interfere in the workplace. In *National Panasonic v. Commission*,[8] the European Court of Justice examined Article 8 in relation to a search carried out by officials from Brussels without a warrant and without any representatives from the company present. It held that the search did not breach Article 8 as the use of the search power contributed:

"to the maintenance of the system of competition intended by the Treaty [of Rome] . . . ".

It is likely that the courts will uphold searches as being necessary as long as the action is not disproportionate and in accordance with the law. An *Anton Piller* order was upheld by the European Court in the case of *Chappell v. United Kingdom*.[9] *Chappell* will also have to be considered in the context of local courts' powers to order search and seizure under Part 25 of the CPR 1998.[10]

14.86 Decisions from the European Court such as *Niemietz* suggest that Article 8 is fundamentally a personal right and it is the individual who may rely on it. As yet the question of whether a company can rely on Article 8 in connection with a search of its premises has not been tested by the European Court.

Surveillance

14.87 This subject is considered in more detail in Chapter 19.[10A] However, it is worth considering one particular case in detail in this section. In *R v.*

---

[6] Note that the French text of the Convention uses the word "*domicile*" which has a wider connotation than the word "home" and can extend to a professional's office.
[7] (1993) 16 E.H.R.R. 332.
[8] [1980] E.C.R. 2057.
[9] (1990) 12 E.H.R.R. 1.
[10] See *Adams Phones v. Goldschmidt, The Times*, August 17, 1999. See further paras 10.61 *et seq.*, above.
[10A] At paras 19.52 *et seq.*

Broadcasting Standards Commission, ex p. BBC[11] the Court of Appeal had to consider whether secret filming of a company's premises amounted to an infringement on its right to privacy. The BBC secretly filmed Dixons' stores, for the purposes of an investigation into misselling of goods for a consumer programme. Dixons were told that there had been a secret filming of some of their stores and were asked to respond to allegations about selling secondhand goods as new. The secret filming was not used in the programme. Dixons complained to the Broadcasting Standards Commission on the basis that the secret filming was an unwarranted infringement of its privacy. The Court of Appeal held that a company did have a right to privacy within the meaning of the Broadcasting Act 1996. Lord Woolf M.R. stated:

"[w]hile the intrusions into the privacy of an individual which are possible are no doubt more extensive than the infringements of privacy which are possible in the case of a company, a company does have activities of a private nature which need protection from unwarranted intrusion."

Hale L.J. stated

"There are many things which companies may (legitimately or illegitimately) wish to keep private, including their property, their meetings, and their correspondence. There are still more about which they may (legitimately or illegitimately) wish to avoid publicity."

The case is not determinative of whether a company enjoys a right to respect for private life under Article 8.[11A]

Compulsory Purchase of Land

The European Court has upheld national laws which permit the compulsory purchase of land where compensation has been provided to those affected. It would appear that the compensation granted need not be at full market rate in order to satisfy Article 1 of Protocol No. 1. In *Lithgow v. United Kingdom*,[12] the Government compulsorily took possession of securities belonging to companies as part of a nationalisation scheme empowered by the Aircraft and Shipbuilding Industries Act 1977. The applicants companies complained about the low level of compensation which was based upon a hypothetical assessment of the individual share value of the companies immediately prior to the decision to nationalise was announced. The Court rejected their claim stating that "[l]egitimate objectives of public interest may justify reimbursement at less than the full market value".[13]   **14.88**

Compulsory Purchase of Shares

The Companies Acts contain provisions which enable companies or other   **14.89**
shareholders to deprive shareholders of their shares. These provisions

---

[11] [2000] 3 W.L.R. 1327, CA.
[11A] At para. 17 of the judgment of Lord Woolf M.R.
[12] (1986) 8 E.H.R.R. 329. See also *James v. United Kingdom* (1986) 8 E.H.R.R. 123.
[13] See further paras 16.99 *et seq.*, below.

are sections 428 to 430F of the Companies Act 1985. For example, under these provisions a shareholder may be required to sell his shares to a take-over bidder who has obtained a 90 per cent or higher shareholding in a company. These provisions need to be tested by reference to the HRA.[14]

14.90   The compulsory purchase mechanism operates by a company making a take-over offer for all the shares or a class of shares. If the offer is accepted within four months of its being made by the holders of 90 per cent or more in the value of shares to which the offer relates, the offeror may within two months serve a notice to acquire the remaining shares. The recipients of the notice have six weeks in which to apply to the court, which may allow or disallow the final acquisition on such terms as it sees fit.

14.91   However, the fact that the effect of the provisions is to deprive individuals of their private property against their will does not of itself mean that they may be challenged under the HRA. The European Commission considered similar provisions in *Bramelid and Malmström v. Sweden*[15] and found that they did not breach Article 1 of Protocol No. 1. The Commission stated in that case that the compulsory transfer of property between individuals was a feature of the law in all Member States and referred to the balancing exercise between the rights of the individual and the interests of a majority shareholder in a company.

Fair Balance Test

14.92   The test which has so far been applied by the courts was whether the offer was fair to the shareholders as a body rather than to the individual applicants. If shareholders wish to object to the compulsory acquisition of shares, the onus is on them to convince the court that such acquisition would be unfair.[16] The fact that one individual might have been forced to act against their will is not relevant. Whether there is a fair balance in the legislation depends upon various considerations and in particular, upon the provisions for the compensation of the minority shareholders.[17] If the offer results in the minority receiving compensation at market rate it is highly unlikely that Article 1 of Protocol No. 1 will be violated.

14.93   The policy behind the United Kingdom domestic provisions was to resolve the conflict of interest between the owners or contingent owners of a newly acquired majority shareholding in a company and the minority shareholders in the same company.[18] In this sense it is likely that, overall, the provisions will be upheld as justified by reference to their policy in the

---

[14] See for further discussion of compulsory purchase of shares and share allotment: Alan Dignam and David Allen, *Company Law and the Human Rights Act 1998* (Butterworths 2000).

[15] (1982) 29 D.R. 64.

[16] See *Re Lifecare International plc.* [1990] B.C.L.C. 222.

[17] Peter Duffy, "The Protection of Commercial Interests Under the European Convention of Human Rights in Making Commercial Law" in Essays in Honour of Roy Goode (R. Cranston ed.) (1997).

[18] Prior to the Companies Act 1929 the rights of the individual minority shareholder were protected absolutely, so that the majority shareholder had no right to acquire minority shares compulsorily.

interests of promoting commerce. However, the introduction of the HRA may mean a change in emphasis in two particular areas:

(1) the court will give greater consideration to the rights of the individual minority shareholder as opposed to considering the rights of the body of shareholders as a whole; and

(2) if the offer of compensation is significantly less than the market value this is likely to have to be justified rationally.

Compulsory Purchase of Shares under the Articles of Association

A second way in which shares may be compulsorily acquired is under **14.94** provisions in the articles of association of a company. These provisions may exist from the incorporation of the company or may by special resolution be included in the articles of association by amendment. While a future shareholder has a choice not to purchase shares in a company where the articles of association provide for compulsory expropriation of shares, an existing shareholder may find himself forced to sell his shares in the company if the articles are subsequently amended to include such a provision.

Where articles are subsequently amended to allow for compulsory expro- **14.95** priation, it would of course be open for the shareholder to sell his shares in the company if he did not wish to be subjected to such expropriation.

Share Allotment

The Companies Act 1985 allows the board of directors to allot and issue **14.96** shares of the company to the potential detriment of some or all of the shareholders.[19] There is some protection afforded to shareholders under the Companies Act 1985 whereby authorisation by the shareholder or by the company's articles is required and rights of pre-emption are to be given to existing shareholders. But in practice, such protection is little more than notional as such authority is easily given and the pre-emption rights easily disapplied. This leaves shareholders at risk of the directors using their power to allot shares to whomsoever they decide, resist take-overs, entrench their own internal voting position at the general meeting, or to engage in share watering and vote watering with the consequential detrimental effect on the shareholder's property.[20]

The directors' abuse of their power to allot shares has already been the **14.97** subject of successful minority shareholder actions, where the directors have used their powers not for the purpose of capital raising but to gain voting control for themselves at the general meeting,[21] or to deprive others of their control,[22] or to defeat a take-over bid.

---

[19] Companies Act 1985, ss.80–116.
[20] See further Alan Dignam and David Allen, *Company Law and the Human Rights Act 1998* (Butterworths 2000).
[21] *Re Jermyn St Turkish Baths Ltd* [1970] 3 All E.R. 57; [1970] 1 W.L.R. 1194.
[22] *Howard Smith Ltd v. Ampol Petroleum Ltd* [1974] A.C. 821.

Unfair Prejudice

14.98 Most challenges by shareholders are brought by way of claim under section 459 of the Companies Act 1985. Section 459 provides that a shareholder may apply to the court on the ground that the company's affairs are or have been conducted in a manner which is unfairly prejudicial to the interests of the members generally or some members. Section 459 contains the concept of "unfairly prejudicial conduct" and allows the court a wide range of discretion from regulating the conduct of the company's affairs to providing for the purchase of the shares of any members by other members or by the company itself. Section 459 therefore gives the court the power to interfere with the property rights of shareholders and of the company. It is therefore necessary to examine whether the powers under section 459 might be affected by the HRA.

14.99 Historically, the courts have interpreted section 459 broadly to cover not just strict legal rights but also expectations. In some instances the courts have allowed shareholders to bring an action, even where the property in issue is company property. In that sense the section may in fact give a wider remedy than might be accorded under the HRA.[23]

14.100 More recently, in the wake of a number of successful section 459 applications, the House of Lords in *O'Neill v. Phillipps*[24] expressed the view that the courts might in future take a more restrictive approach. Lord Hoffmann indicated in that case that the courts would attempt to restrict the concept of unfairness to breach of the articles or using the articles in a manner which equity would regard as contrary to good faith. He said:

> "[I]n my view, a balance has to be struck between breadth of the discretion given to the court and the principle of legal certainty. Petitions under s. 459 are often lengthy and expensive. It is highly desirable that lawyers should be able to advise their clients whether or not a petition is likely to succeed."

The courts have already held in the context of section 459 that strict legal rights contained in the articles and the Companies Act can be restricted by equitable considerations.[25] For the reasons given above, while the HRA may implement a different approach in analysis of a claim of this type, it is unlikely that it will have any significant effect of the decision.

Offers to Purchase Shares

14.101 In *O'Neill v. Phillips*[26] the House of Lords considered whether a strike out application should succeed where a reasonable offer to purchase shares is made but is not accepted. Lord Hoffmann in his judgment stated that a reasonable offer will contain the following elements:

> (1) an offer to purchase the shares at a fair value—this ordinarily requires the offer to represent an equivalent proportion of the

---

[23] See section on shareholders as victims, paras 14.39 *et seq.*, above.
[24] [1999] 2 B.C.L.C. 1.
[25] *Ebrahimi v. Westbourne Galleries Ltd* [1973] A.C. 360.
[26] [1999] B.C.C. 600, HL.

total issued share capital, without any discount for its being a minority holding;

(2) the value if not agreed should be determined by a competent expert—an accountant to be agreed by the parties or in default nominated by the President of the Institute of Chartered Accountants;

(3) the offer should be to have the value determined by the expert as an expert—the objective should be economy and expedition so he should not be required to comply with the full machinery for arbitration not to give full reasons for his decision;

(4) the offer should provide for equality of arms between the parties—both should have the same right of access to information about the company which relates to the value of the shares and both should have the right to make submissions to the expert;

(5) the respondent should be given a reasonable time to make the offer before the offer needs to include an offer to pay costs—the mere fact that the petitioner has presented a petition before the offer does not mean that the respondent must offer to pay the costs if he was not given a reasonable time.

The HRA was not considered in *O'Neill v. Phillips*. It is questionable **14.102** whether these requirements satisfy Article 6. In particular, where the value is determined without giving reasons and where the expert is free to determine the weight, if any, to give to the parties submissions and there may be no right to an oral hearing for the parties, the process may not comply. By striking out the petition the court is effectively imposing the offer on the offeree. However, unless the offer is entered into voluntarily it will not comply with Article 6. The position is analogous to arbitration agreements which must satisfy Article 6 if they are compulsory as opposed to voluntary agreements.[27]

7. COMMERCIAL EXPRESSION

Introduction

The protection afforded by Article 10 falls into two categories. The first **14.103** relates to the freedom of the press and its importance as a fundamental basis of a democratic society. This form of commercial expression is given a high degree of protection.[28] A more detailed analysis of this may be found in sources relating to the media and defamation law.[29]

The second form of commercial expression is that which falls outside **14.104** freedom of the press. This includes expression which is aimed at protecting or advancing the business interests of a commercial enterprise either

---

[27] *Deweer v. Belgium* (1979) 2 E.H.R.R. 439; *Axelsson v. Sweden* (1983) 38 D.R. 18.
[28] See *Goodwin v. United Kingdom* (1996) 22 E.H.R.R. 123.
[29] See, *e.g.* Michael Smyth, *Business Law and the Human Rights Act* (Jordans, 1999).

through advertising or any form of consumer communication. The European Court has been much less concerned to protect this form of expression which is considered further below. The lesser protection afforded to this form of expression is shown by the tendency of the European Court in this area to decide cases allowing for a wide margin of appreciation to be granted to national authorities in restricting freedom of expression.[29A]

Protecting or Advancing Business Interests

14.105 The European Court considered whether there had been a breach of Article 10 in *Markt Intern Verlag and Klaus Beerman v. Germany.*[30] In that case a publishing company and its editor continuously reported on the status of dissatisfied clients of mail-order firms in their information bulletin. This caused a number of companies which suffered from the adverse criticism to institute proceedings against the company for infringement of the German Unfair Competition Act 1909. The Court stated that the national authorities had a large margin of appreciation with regard to such commercial matters as they were in a better position to determine the right balance between the various interests concerned. In that case the qualification in Article 10(2), regarding the rights of others, justified the restriction imposed and no violation of the freedom of expression was found by the Court.

14.106 The European Court also accorded national authorities a wide margin of appreciation in *Groppera Radio AG v. Switzerland.*[31] The applicant was a company broadcasting music and advertising from a base in Italy for reception in Switzerland. In Switzerland the broadcasts were either received directly or redistributed by Swiss cable companies. The Swiss authorities banned any broadcasts by cable operators which did not comply with international standards. Groppera challenged the ban in Switzerland and then in Europe. The European Court found that the expression in question—the music and advertising—although commercial in nature, came within the scope of Article 10. The Court also found that the Swiss authorities had a wide margin of appreciation with regard to such matters. It emphasised the fact that the act of the Swiss authorities was not aimed at censorship of the broadcasting content but at ensuring proper recognised international standards of broadcasting within the Swiss jurisdiction.[32]

14.107 In *Benjamin v. Minister of Information & Broadcasting*[33] the Privy Council considered whether the suspension of a phone-in radio programme on a Government sponsored radio station was a breach of section 11(1) of the Constitution of Anguilla, which protected freedom of expression, where the suspension was an arbitrary or capricious withdrawal of a platform that had previously been made available by the Government. The Court held that circumstances might exist where freedom of speech might be hindered, within the meaning of section 11(1), where there was no contractual

---

[29A] See also paras 19.93 *et seq.*
[30] (1990) 12 E.H.R.R. 161.
[31] (1990) 12 E.H.R.R. 321.
[32] See also *Autronic AG v. Switzerland* (1990) 12 E.H.R.R. 485; *Tele 1 Privatferngesellschaft MBH v. Austria*, Application No. 32240/96, September 21, 2000.
[33] [2001] 1 W.L.R. 1040, PC.

and no absolute generalised right to speak in the way in which the individual wished to express his views. The circumstances of each case had to be looked at and in this particular case the motive of the Government in suspending the programme was a relevant factor in the Court holding that section 11(1) of the Constitution of Anguilla had been infringed.[34]

8. DIRECTORS DISQUALIFICATION

Introduction

Disqualification proceedings are brought by or at the direction of the **14.108** Secretary of State for Trade and Industry in the public interest. The effects of disqualification are far reaching for the individual. Disqualification orders are widely publicised and a register of disqualified persons kept at Companies House. They may therefore, have a substantial impact on an individual's future employment. For this reason, the HRA has been frequently invoked in the course of such proceedings.

Classification as Criminal or Civil Proceedings

Directors disqualification proceedings have been classified as civil pro- **14.109** ceedings. It was held in *Official Receiver v. Stern*[35] that directors disqualification proceedings are civil proceedings for the purposes of the HRA. The Commission in *Wilson v. United Kingdom*[36] said:

"[T]he disqualification of directors is a matter which is regulatory rather than criminal, and the penalty is neither a fine nor a prison sentence, but rather a prohibition on acting as a company director without the leave of the court. None of these criteria indicates that the applicant was charged with a 'criminal offence".

However, in other respects disqualification proceedings do contain ele- **14.110** ments of a criminal proceeding. [37] In *Re Barings plc*.[38] Sir Richard Scott V.-C. said in the context of an application for discovery:

"Disqualification proceedings, although properly classified as civil proceedings, do not involve litigation about private rights. They involve public law. Proceedings are brought for the protection of the public and, if the case is proved, the directors must suffer disqualification for the protection of the public. The proceedings have, in many respects, much more in common with criminal proceedings than with civil litigation about private rights. There is no doubt, in my opinion, but that in criminal proceedings the report would, if relevant, have had to be disclosed. I do not understand why in these proceedings, and in

---

[34] See further paras 19.110 *et seq.*, below.
[35] [2000] 1 W.L.R. 2230, CA.
[36] (1998) 26 E.H.R.R. C.D. 195.
[37] *Secretary of State v. Hickling* [1996] B.C.C. 678; *Re Barings plc.* [1998] Ch. 356; *Re Astra Holdings plc.* [1998] 2 B.C.L.C. 44.
[38] [1998] Ch. 356.

the absence of any ground justifying a claim to public interest immunity, the Secretary of State has been resisting disclosure. I would have thought it would be her wish that the conduct of the proceedings should be as fair to the respondent directors as a proper prosecution of the case permitted. Be that as it may, I hold that the report is not covered by legal professional privilege and must be produced for inspection."

Consequences of Classification

14.111 The classification of disqualification proceedings as civil has an important impact on the use which can be made of compulsorily obtained evidence in the course of these proceedings.[39]

Although statements obtained under compulsory powers will not be excluded from the proceedings under the rule in *Saunders v. United Kingdom* as would be the case for criminal proceedings, the court should nevertheless consider whether a decision not to exclude such statements may violate a defendant's right to a fair hearing. Each case will depend upon its facts.

14.112 In *Official Receiver v. Stern*,[40] Henry L.J. cited as a relevant factor the degree of coercion involved in the investigative procedures which may be reflected in the degree of prejudice involved in the admission of the statements obtained by such procedures at a hearing. The Court also referred to the serious consequences of the proceedings as regards the individual. It held:

> "(i) that disqualification proceedings are not criminal proceedings, and are primarily for the protection of the public, but do nevertheless often involve serious allegations and almost always carry a degree of stigma for anyone who is disqualified; (ii) that there are degrees of coercion involved in different investigative procedures available in corporate insolvency, and these differences may be reflected in different degrees of prejudice involved in the admission, in disqualification proceedings, of statements obtained by such procedures; and (iii) that in this field as in most other fields, it is generally best for issues of fairness or unfairness to be decided by the trial judge, either at a pre-trial review or in the course of the trial."[41]

Legal Aid

14.113 There has been much discussion as to whether a defendant can have a fair hearing in directors disqualification proceedings if he cannot afford legal representation. Such proceedings have a very significant effect on an individual's ability to earn a living and their future employment. The subject-matter of a particular case may well be complex and as the proceedings brought against the director are funded by the DTI there is

---

[39] Note the amendment to the Companies and Directors Disqualification Act 1986, s.20, contained in of the Youth and Criminal Evidence Act 1999, s.59, which prevents the use of statements in directors disqualification proceedings from being adduced in subsequent criminal proceedings unless evidence is adduced by the defendant himself.
[40] [2000] 1 W.L.R. 2230, CA.
[41] See also *R. v. Secretary of State, ex p. McCormick* [1998] B.C.C. 379.

likely to be a real inequality of arms if the director is not able to afford legal representation. The lack of available funds to pay for legal representation has the effect that many directors will choose to compromise the proceedings admitting liability through the *Carecraft*[42] procedure rather than risk an adverse costs order in the event of an unsuccessful defence to the proceedings.[43]

Burton J. considered the question of legal aid for such proceedings in *R. v. Legal Services Commission, ex parte Jarrett*.[44] The respondent in that case was Turkish and did not have a good grasp of English nor or commercial affairs. Burton J. referred to the decision of the European Court in *X v. United Kingdom*,[45] in which it was said: **14.114**

> "only in exceptional circumstances, namely where withholding of legal aid would make the assertion of a civil claim practically impossible, or where it would lead to an obvious unfairness of the proceedings, can such a right be invoked by virtue of Article 6(1) of the Convention."

The Legal Services Commission had not attempted to ask or answer any of the questions set out in *X v. United Kingdom*. Consideration needed to be given to those factors and the court held that it was premature to consider the matter before this had taken place.[46]

Delay

Serious delay in proceedings will have an obvious adverse effect on respondents in directors disqualifications. Where there is more than one defendant and the delay is not connected to all the defendants, then the court may order a split trial on the application of a co-defendant to avoid delay against him. However, in practice, split trials may add to costs and where there are criminal proceedings pending against one or more directors, the disqualification proceedings will invariably be stayed pending the outcome of those proceedings. This means that there may be justified reasons for delays and that it may only be in exceptional circumstances that a respondent is able to rely on Article 6 to bring a claim.   **14.115**

In *Secretary of State for Trade & Industry v. Crane*,[46A] Ferris J. considered whether a stay of the civil proceedings should be granted where criminal proceedings had been threatened but not yet brought. In that case a police officer attended at the disqualification proceedings with the intention of gaining assistance in order to start criminal proceedings. As such, his presence did not have any bearing on the civil trial, but could only relate to fairness of the criminal trial. It was held that no stay of the civil proceedings should be granted in that case as it was not necessary to prevent unfairness to the respondent and that a stay would conflict with

---

[42] *Re Carecraft Construction* [1994] 1 W.L.R. 172.
[43] See in this context *Official Receiver v. Stern* [2000] 1 W.L.R. 2230. See also Roger Birch, "Human Rights, directors and legal aid—Part 1" (2001) 151 N.L.J. 162; Part 2 (2001) 151 N.L.J. 277.
[44] [2001] EWHC Admin 389 (May 22, 2001).
[45] (1984) 6 E.H.R.R. 136.
[46] See paras 12.27 *et seq.*, above, for a general discussion as to legal aid.
[46A] *The Times*, June 4, 2001.

the public interest in the due prosecution of proceedings by the Secretary of State. It was noted that section 20(2) of the Companies and Directors Disqualification Act 1986 as amended by section 59 of the Youth Justice and Criminal Evidence Act 1999 would prevent statements made in the civil proceedings being admitted in evidence in subsequent criminal proceedings.

14.116 A five year delay in proceedings was considered not to infringe Article 6 in *Re Abermeadow Ltd.*[47] The inordinate delay in that case was as a result of the court acceding to the second and third defendants' applications to stay the trial of the proceedings pending their criminal proceedings, and the Secretary of State had not been responsible for unreasonable delay thereafter. As against the first defendant, neither the lapse of time nor the death of the Secretary's of State's chief witness prevented a fair trial being possible since it required little more than his own admissions in his evidence that he never had any real knowledge of the company's affairs and not the lapse of time which had deprived him of recollection of them. Furthermore, the delay had not caused the first defendant any serious prejudice since throughout he had been able to continue his livelihood as a director of another company.[48]

Pleadings

14.116A As a result of disqualification proceedings not being treated as criminal proceedings, it follows that the allegations regarding the respondent director need not be pleaded with the degree of particularity expected in a criminal case.[48A] In addition, the practice of pleading every possible allegation against defendants should be approached with care. In appropriate cases the court may order that charges should be reduced or amended, which will also have an effect on the amount of preparation for the hearing and the hearing date.

Carecraft Procedure and Undertakings

14.117 Where a respondent to disqualification proceedings accepts all or part of the case against him and accepts that he is unfit to be concerned in the management of a company, he may adopt one of three courses:

(1) he may enter no opposition to the proceedings;

(2) he may enter into a *Carecraft*[48B] agreement with the claimant;

(3) he may offer an undertaking as provided for by section 1A of the CDDA.[48C]

---

[47] [2000] 2 B.C.L.C. 824.
[48] In the context of delay, see also *EDC v. United Kingdom* [1998] B.C.C. 370; *Secretary of State for Trade & Industry v. Staton,* (unreported) April 28, 2000; *Secretary of State for Trade & Industry v. Eastaway,* (unreported), February 15, 2001 (ChD) (there was no breach of Art. 6 even though proceedings had been on foot for over eight years).
[48A] *Re Continental Assurance Co of London plc.* [1997] 1 B.C.L.C. 48.
[48B] [1994] 1 W.L.R. 172.
[48C] As inserted by s.6 of the Insolvency Act 2000.

The route of no opposition will save the costs of negotiating a *Carecraft* agreement, although it contains the obvious disadvantage that the respondent will not be able to challenge any of the allegations made against him and will likely find that they are all proved.

In adopting the *Carecraft* procedure the parties will attempt to agree a schedule of facts to present to the court. In practice, the respondent has little say in the drafting of this statement. This is of particular concern where directors in disqualification proceedings are effectively coerced into adopting this route because they do not have sufficient funds to meet the Secretary of State's costs in a fully contested hearing. A similar criticism may be made of the undertaking pursuant to section 1A of the CDDA.

Under the new procedure for the giving of undertakings, the Secretary of State requires the director to admit the main allegations against him. The admission is in the form of wording to the effect that:

> "For the purposes solely of the CDDA and for any other purposes consequential to the giving of a disqualification undertaking, I do not dispute the following matters . . . "

However, the body of the document containing matters relating to unfitness may contain wording which is closer to an admission of facts, which the director is not in a position to be able to challenge. The question then arises as to what use can be made of this statement in subsequent proceedings. As the statement is a public document there is nothing to prevent the liquidator from seeking to adduce it in evidence in proceedings brought by him. Although the admission in evidence of such a statement may not preclude a director in other proceedings from adducing evidence to show that the facts are wrong, the statement may be prejudicial and may place the director in a difficult position in subsequent proceedings. The court must under Article 6 ensure that in such circumstances his fair hearing rights are not violated.

9. FINANCIAL SERVICES

Introduction

A new regime for regulation of the financial services industry was introduced by the Financial Services Act 1986 (the 1986 Act), which regulated for the first time the carrying on of most forms of investment business. In the 12 years during which this system of regulation has been operating, there have been a number of cases where the system was viewed as having failed. This led to a movement to reform the existing regulatory regime which culminated in the introduction of the Financial Services and Markets Act 2000 (FSMA 2000). The new regime introduces a unified system of regulation for the industry.[49]   **14.118**

The 1986 Act created a two-tier system of regulation. The Securities and Investment Board ("SIB") was the principal body responsible for regulation of the financial services industry. It changed its name in 1997 to the   **14.119**

---

[49] See George Staple Q.C.: "Financial Services and the Human Rights Act", in *The Human Rights Act and the Criminal Justice and Regulatory Process*, (Oxford, 1999).

Financial Services Authority ("FSA"). The SIB was responsible for authorising and recognising the second-tier authorities, typically, self-regulating organisations ("SROs"). The 1986 Act also introduced a set of Principles, Rules and Codes of Practice and Ethics. Breach of these, or misconduct in general, could lead to the bringing of disciplinary proceedings. It also established the Financial Services Tribunal with powers to investigate and report on matters referred to it by the SIB and the FSA.

14.120   The FSMA 2000 provides for the regulation of "authorised persons" by a single regulator, the FSA. The FSA assumes the regulatory functions of the existing self-regulating bodies and also assumes responsibility for banking supervision previously carried out by the Bank of England. In addition, the FSA will have the responsibility for prosecuting financial crime and enforcing a new civil regime in relation to "market abuse".

14.121   The FSMA 2000 introduces two sets of Principles and a set of Rules which govern various aspects of the conduct of financial services activities. It provides for disciplinary procedures and sanctions, including potentially unlimited fines for breach of the Rules or Principles. A Financial Services and Markets Tribunal (the Tribunal) has been established with the power to remit a matter to the Financial Services Authority (FSA), impose, revoke or vary the amount of a fine, make recommendations as to the FSA's regulating provisions or procedures or make any other decision which the FSA could have made.[49A]

14.122   Because of the wide ranging powers of enforcement of the regulator, the Financial Services and Markets Bill was vetted by various committees to ensure it was HRA compliant before it was finally enacted. Some, although not all, of the recommendations of amendment made by those committees were adopted. It should not, therefore, be assumed that the FSMA 2000 safeguards all the Convention rights and the particular provisions should be examined closely in the light of the HRA.[50]

Public Authorities

14.123   The 1986 Act allowed self regulation in the financial services industry provided that the houses were a member of at least one of the four SROs—LAUTRO, FIMBRA, IMRO, SFA—or they accepted direct regulation by the SIB. These SROs have been held subject to judicial review.[51]

14.124   The FSA and the Tribunal are similarly susceptible to judicial review and will be "public authorities" within the meaning of the Convention and will therefore be under a duty to act compatibly with the HRA when carrying out their functions.

14.125   It is questionable as to whether the entirety of the Ombudsman Scheme established under Part XVI of the FSMA 2000 is subject to judicial review. There are two methods of dealing with complaints under that Scheme—a

---

[49A] FSMA 2000, s.133.
[50] See Lord Lester and Javan Herberg and Lord Lester and Monica Carrs-Frisk: "Counsels' Opinions on the Impact of the ECHR on the Draft Financial Services and Markets Bill", reproduced in *The Human Rights Act and the Criminal Justice and Regulatory Process* (Oxford, 1999).
[51] *R. v. Lautro, ex p. Ross* [1993] Q.B. 17.

compulsory jurisdiction[52] and a voluntary jurisdiction.[53] While the compulsory jurisdiction would appear to fall within the scope of judicial review it is arguable that the voluntary jurisdiction will fall outside, given that the Ombudsman's power to make an award depends upon the parties' consensual submission to the jurisdiction. However, as regards the HRA, it is likely that the entire scheme will fall within the meaning of public authority.

Classification of Proceedings

As mentioned above at paras 14.63 *et seq.*, the classification of an offence **14.126** under domestic law is not necessarily determinative of its classification for the purposes of the European Court. The nature of the offence (whether it applies to the population as a whole or only to a specific class) and the nature and severity of the penalty will also be taken into account.

In general regulatory proceedings which relate to those engaged in a **14.127** particular market or profession will be regarded as civil.[54] Where the imposition of a financial penalty related to a regulatory or disciplinary matter which could only affect a limited class, the Court has rejected the submission that it involved a criminal charge.[55] In *Bendenoun v. France* there was a risk of imprisonment for contempt of court for non-payment of the fine.[55A] However, in a couple of cases the European Court considered that substantial financial penalties although classified as civil were criminal for the purposes of the Convention.[56] In general it would appear that regulatory offences will be regarded as civil where the sanction is a fine. In *R. v. The Securities and Futures Authority, ex p. Fleurose*,[56A] the decision of the Disciplinary Appeal Tribunal established by the Securities and Futures Authority (SFA) was judicially reviewed on the grounds that the proceedings violated the HRA. It was submitted by the applicant that the disciplinary proceedings were criminal for the purposes of the HRA. Morrison J. held:

> "In Convention jurisprudence the disciplinary proceedings are to be classified as civil rather than criminal. They are categorised under domestic law as civil . . . I do not think that the penalty which can be imposed, namely an unlimited fine, leads to a different conclusion when carrying out the balancing exercise. In the field of financial regulation, the size of a fine can, I think, fairly remain open . . . In my view it would be illogical to say that the size of the fine determined the classification. The essential feature of a financial penalty imposed through the SFA disciplinary process is that it is recoverable only as

---

[52] FSMA 2000, s.226.
[53] FSMA 2000, s.227.
[54] See, *e.g. APB v. IMRO*, Application No. 30552/96, January 15, 1998; see *R. v.The Securities and Futures Authority, ex p. Fleurose, Daily Telegraph*, May 1, 2001, QBD.
[55] *Ravensborg v. Sweden* (1994) 18 E.H.R.R. 38; *Air Canada v. United Kingdom* (1995) 20 E.H.R.R. 150; *Irving-Brown v. United Kingdom*, Application No. 38644/97, November 24, 1998.
[55A] See paras 14.129 *et seq.* below.
[56] See *Ozturk v. Germany* (1984) 6 E.H.R.R. 409; *Bendenoun v. France* (1994) 18 E.H.R.R. 54.
[56A] *The Daily Telegraph*, May 1, 2001, QBD.

a civil debt, without the possibility of recourse to the sanction of imprisonment for default or for contempt of court. This distinguishes the case from *Brown* where there was ultimately a risk of imprisonment for contempt of court, and from *Bendenoun.* The purpose of the fine is plainly both punitive and a deterrent; but that does not tip the scales in favour of a 'criminal' categorisation."

14.128 In the discussions relating to the Financial Services and Markets Bill, one of the key areas of debate was whether the FSA's exercise of its disciplinary powers would amount to a criminal proceeding for the purposes of the HRA. It was suggested to the Joint Committee that the procedures of the Tribunal should comply with the Article 6 safeguards applicable to criminal proceedings, including the presumption of innocence, the right to legal assistance, the principle of certainty in the definition of the offence and the right against self-incrimination. Although the Government made certain concessions in relation to particular offences, namely "market abuse", ultimately it did not accept that the FSA's regulatory powers would amount to criminal proceedings.

Market Abuse

14.129 The provisions for "market abuse" contained in the FSMA 2000 were the subject of much debate and concern that proceedings for market abuse would be classified as criminal by virtue of the FSA's power to impose unlimited fines for this offence.

14.130 Part VIII of the FSMA 2000 gives the FSA the power to impose unlimited fines on persons engaging in market abuse or inducing others to do so by taking or refraining from any action. Market abuse is defined as behaviour of a particular kind occurring in relation to investments, including investments whose subject-matter is a prescribed investment, on markets which are likely to affect the confidence of informed market participants that the market is a true and fair one. The scope of the regime is therefore very wide and applies to all market participants. It is therefore not limited to people who are regulated under the general FSA regime.

14.131 The Government accepted in a Treasury memorandum[57] that the arguments that the market abuse regime would be classified as criminal were at least serious enough to pose a real risk that the provisions for fines for market abuse in the FSMA would be classified as criminal for European Convention purposes.[58] In addition, there is some overlap in conduct which qualifies as market abuse and existing criminal offences such as insider dealing[59] and misleading statements and practices.[60] In this respect, it is difficult to see why different procedures should apply depending on whether the conduct is dealt with as market abuse or an insider dealing case.

14.132 To that end, the Government proposed in relation to market abuse proceedings that some of the safeguards for criminal proceedings should be

---

[57] H.M. Treasury Memorandum of May 14, 1999 to the Joint Committee on Financial Services and Markets.
[58] FSMA 2000, s.174.
[59] Criminal Justice Act 1993, s.52.
[60] FSA 1986, s.47, now re-enacted as FSMA 2000, s.397.

adopted. In particular, a statement made by a person in compliance with the compulsory powers contained in sections 171 to 173 of the FSMA 2000 is not admissible in evidence in market abuse proceedings. Legal aid is also available in appropriate market abuse cases.[61] However, despite these concessions, the Government has continued to maintain throughout that the proceedings ultimately should be classified as civil.[62]

If these proceedings were held to be criminal by a court decision a number of other important consequences will follow under the Convention. For example, the burden of proof will be on the prosecution to prove their case beyond a reasonable doubt.[63] Most importantly, evidence obtained under any compulsory powers would not be admissible in market abuse proceedings in accordance with the principles in *Saunders v. United Kingdom*.[64]   **14.133**

Financial Services Investigations

The FSA has all the investigatory powers previously enjoyed by the SIB. In addition, the FSA can also enter and search premises of both authorised persons or appointed representatives, or those of people outside the regulatory system, under warrant.[65]   **14.134**

Under sections 171 to 173 of the FSMA 2000, any person may be required to answer questions under oath, provide information, produce documents and give the investigator all the assistance he requires. Under section 177 of the 1986 Act in an investigation into insider dealing, a person may be required to produce any document, attend before investigators and give all assistance which he is able to give. Under section 178 of the 1986 Act, where a person refuses to answer any question put to him without reasonable excuse, a court may punish him as if he had been guilty of criminal contempt.   **14.135**

Statements made under the compulsory powers contained in the 1986 Act and the FSMA 2000 should not be admissible in criminal proceedings against that individual following the decision of the European Court in *Saunders v. United Kingdom*.[66]   **14.136**

The Tribunal

As stated above, the European Court held in *Belilos v. Switzerland*[67] that a tribunal must satisfy a number of requirements: **14.137**

"independence, in particular of the executive; impartiality; duration of its members terms of office; guarantees afforded by its procedure".

In satisfying the independence requirement, there must be a degree of separation between the tribunal and the organisation.[68] This need not be

[61] FSMA 2000, s.134.
[62] See also Michael Blair Q.C., "Human Rights and Market Abuse" in *The Human Rights Act and the Criminal Justice and Regulatory Process* (Oxford, 1999).
[63] *Barbera, Messegue and Jabardo v. Spain* (1989) 11 E.H.R.R. 360.
[64] (1997) 23 E.H.R.R. 313.
[65] FSMA 2000, s.176.
[66] See paras 14.58 *et seq.*, above. See also amendment to the FSA 1986, ss.105 and 177, made by virtue of the Youth and Criminal Evidence Act 1999, s.59.
[67] (1988) 10 E.H.R.R. 466.
[68] *Re S (a Barrister)* [1981] 2 All ER 952.

total separation. However, it is important that the members of the Tribunal are appointed by someone other than the prosecutor and do not have close links with that official so as to lead to a perception of bias.

14.138 The FSMA 2000 envisages first that decisions about the registration of persons and all aspects of their regulation will be taken by the FSA. The FSA is to establish a Regulatory Decisions Committee which will take regulatory decisions. The Committee members are to be appointed and are to be independent of the executive of the FSA.[69] Decisions taken by the FSA in relation to such applications may be referred to the Tribunal.

14.139 The powers of the Tribunal are wide—it has the power to remit a matter to the FSA, impose, revoke or vary the amount of a fine, make recommendations as to the FSA's regulating provisions or make any other decision which the FSA could have made. It may look at evidence available to the FSA both at the time and after the issuance of a decision of notice of appeal. It may hear arguments not raised at the time the FSA made the decision, as well as the grounds on which the FSA made its decision and any action taken by the FSA in relation to it.

Compliance with Article 6

14.140 One of the important safeguards of Article 6 is for a fair and public hearing by an independent and impartial tribunal. The Tribunal established under the FSMA 2000 is under the control of the Lord Chancellor's Department which has the power to make any rules necessary for the expedient conduct of proceedings before the Tribunal.[70] While the FSA will effectively make decisions which may not be Article 6 compliant, it is necessary that the Tribunal is an independent and impartial tribunal and has the power to hold a full re-hearing which does satisfy Article 6.

14.141 It would appear that the Tribunal effectively has the power to hold a full re-hearing of the matter which would satisfy Article 6 as it is able to consider any evidence relating to the subject matter of the reference, including material which was not available to the FSA at the time.[71] However, it will be necessary in practice to examine closely the procedures of the Tribunal in order to test whether they in fact comply with the HRA.

14.142 It is also important that the Tribunal which hears the case is independent of the executive which makes the decision relating to the individual. A court will have regard to the manner and terms of appointment, the existence of guarantees of freedom from pressure and the appearance of independence. In this sense the perception of independence is as important as the objective existence of independence.

14.143 It would appear that the Tribunal is fully independent of the FSA, being under the control of the Lord Chancellor's Department. The Lord Chancellor is to appoint a panel of persons for the purposes of sitting as chairmen of the Tribunal in order to hear cases and designate one of the

---

[69] FSMA 2000, s.395; provides that the procedure for giving of supervisory, warning and decision notices must ensure that the decision which gives rise to the issue of such notice is taken by a person not directly involved in establishing the evidence on which that decision is based.
[70] FSMA 2000, s.132.
[71] FSMA 2000, s.133(3).

chairmen to preside over the Tribunal. These chairmen must have certain legal qualifications and experiences.[72] He must also appoint another panel of persons who need not have legal qualifications who may also sit and hear references to the Tribunal. Any reference to the Tribunal must be heard by a panel consisting of at least one chairman.[73] The Lord Chancellor is responsible for fixing the level of salary and paying members of the Tribunal and also for appointing other staff for the Tribunal as he may deem necessary. An appeal on a point of law from a decision of the Tribunal lies with permission to the Court of Appeal.[74]

Immunity from Suit

A rule which precludes a particular category of defendant from suit must be examined under Article 6. A blanket immunity of a particular class may be disproportionate and so may constitute a breach of Article 6. In *Osman v. United Kingdom*[75] the Court held that an absolute rule which took no account of the fundamental rights of the applicant and the degree of harm suffered was a disproportionate restriction on that applicant's right of access to court. In *Z v. United Kingdom*,[75A] the European Court expressly did not follow *Osman* in relation to its finding that the striking out of a claim on the basis that it was not fair, just and reasonable to impose a duty of care was a disproportionate restriction on the applicant's right of access to a court. Nevertheless, the principle underlying the objection to immunities or disproportionate restrictions on access to a court remains intact.[76]   **14.144**

The FSA has statutory immunity from suit for damages under the FSMA 2000.[77] Although this is not a blanket immunity and does not apply so as to prevent an award of damages made in respect of an act or omission, on the ground that the act or omission was unlawful as a result of Article 6(1), it may still be open to challenge on the basis that it is disproportionate to the legitimate needs of society.   **14.145**

---

[72] FSMA 2000, ss.2, 3, Sched. 13, Pt II.
[73] FSMA 2000, s.7, Sched. 13, Pt III.
[74] FSMA 2000, s.137.
[75] [1999] 1 F.L.R. 193; (2000) 29 E.H.R.R. 245.
[75A] Application No. 29392/95 [2001] 2 F.C.R. 246.
[76] See also *Fayed v. United Kingdom* (1994) 18 E.H.R.R. 393. See further paras 10.15 *et seq.*, above, and paras 17.41 *et seq.*, below.
[77] Sched. 1, para. 19. See also s. 102.

CHAPTER 15

Insolvency

1. INTRODUCTION

Application of the Convention

The insolvency regime inevitably deprives companies and individuals of 15.01
their rights over their property and their freedom to carry on business.
Whether those infringements and restrictions are compatible with the HRA
will have to be tested by reference to the Articles of the Convention and
the justification of the policy behind the provisions.

The history of the bankruptcy and insolvency regime in England and the 15.02
policy reasons for introducing a "harmonised and integrated" system with
"less formal procedures as alternatives to bankruptcy and company winding up" was considered in the Cork Report[1] which preceded the introduction of the Insolvency Act 1986 (IA 1986) bringing with it wide scale reform
in this area. One of the purposes of the new regime implemented by the
IA 1986 was to remove some of the stigma associated with bankruptcy
and ensure that it operated fairly in a democratic society with a need for
measures to control the abuse of credit, yet without those controls being
excessive.

The HRA may have a direct effect on many aspects of both corporate and 15.03
personal insolvency in that officeholders, such as liquidators and trustees
in bankruptcy, may be treated as carrying out public functions so that they
have a duty to act compatibly with the Articles of the Convention. Another
area which may be affected by the introduction of the HRA is in administrative decision-making powers of officeholders. To be compatible with
the Convention rights, in so far as these administrative decisions determine civil rights and obligations, they must be subject to a full review which
complies with Article 6.

However, despite the fact that the insolvency regime gives rise to many 15.04
issues which will have a direct bearing on Convention rights, the effect of
the HRA on decision making is likely to be heavily tempered by the amount
of judicial discretion already invoked in this area long before the enactment of the HRA.[2]

Areas Affected by Convention Rights

The right to a fair trial is one of the most frequently relied upon of the 15.05
Convention rights. To give just one example, because of the fundamental
importance of insolvency proceedings both on the individual and a company, the length of time which these proceedings can take has led to
challenges under Article 6 in the European Court.

---

[1] Insolvency Law and Practice, Report of the Review Committee, Sir Kenneth Cork, 1982,
Cmnd. 8558.
[2] See for other discussions on insolvency and the HRA generally, Conor Gearty and Stephen
Davies Q.C., "Insolvency Practice and the Human Rights Act 1998" A Special Bulletin,
November 2000; Marion Simmons Q.C. and Tom Smith, "The Human Rights Act 1998: the
practical impact on insolvency" [2000] 16 I.L.&P. 165; William Trower, "Human Rights: Article
6 The Reality and the Myth, seminar paper given at the ILA Conference 10 March 2001".

15.06 The subsequent use in criminal proceedings of evidence obtained under compulsory powers such as those contained in IA 1986 is another area in which Convention rights have had particular impact. In this area, the arrival of the HRA has already provoked a change in some domestic legislation.[3] While the European Court has not directly criticised the use of compulsory powers to obtain information and has not sought to undermine their basis in domestic law, it has held on a number of occasions that evidence obtained under those powers may not be used against a defendant in the course of criminal proceedings.[4]

15.07 Another key area which is affected by the HRA is the interference with property rights which the insolvency regime imposes. In particular, challenges have been made by bankrupts against the interference with certain personal property items by trustees in bankruptcy.

Applicable Principles of European Law

15.08 The HRA requires the courts to take account of the European Court's case law when determining Convention rights, although this case law is not binding on domestic courts.[4A] Common law judges and lawyers will develop a different approach when considering cases as, unlike English decisions which may be based on rigorous analysis of legal precedent, most Strasbourg cases are decided on their particular facts. The common law doctrine of precedent has no application at the European Court.[4B]

15.09 Further, there are two specific principles which are applied by the European Court in deciding cases. First, the Court will apply the principle of proportionality, balancing the rights of the individual against the "general interests of the community".[4C] A domestic court when dealing with a Convention point will have to consider this doctrine and look at the merits of administrative action. This is different to the narrower concept of *Wednesbury* unreasonableness in public law.[5]

15.10 Secondly, the European Court will invoke the margin of appreciation when deciding cases. This is an international law concept aimed at maintaining a respect for the Contracting States' social, economic, cultural and political traditions. The effect of the doctrine is that the Court will not disturb the actions of a Member State unless they fall outside a general measure of discretion. However, it does not apply at the domestic level where the courts should principally be concerned with the doctrine of proportionality, although some deference may be shown to the legislature or Executive in appropriate cases.[6]

15.11 To take one example of how these principles may work in practice, the loss of the right to bring proceedings without leave of the court because of the imposition of a *Grepe v. Loam*[7] order on a vexatious litigant will be an infringement of his civil rights. However, the decision to make the order may be justified in appropriate cases because of the need to curb frivolous

---

[3] See the Insolvency Act 2000, s.11 amending IA 1986, s.219.
[4] See *Saunders v. United Kingdom* (1997) 23 E.H.R.R. 313.
[4A] See paras 2.49 *et seq.*
[4B] See para. 4.17.
[4C] See paras 4.38 *et seq.*
[5] See further paras 4.14 *et seq.* and 4.26 *et seq.*, above.
[6] See further paras 4.22 *et seq.*, above.
[7] (1887) 37 Ch.D. 168. See paras 15.47 *et seq.*, below.

and unmeritorious applications to the court which affect the efficient working of the legal system and escalate costs unnecessarily. So a decision of
an English court to declare that a litigant is vexatious is one with which the
European Court would be reluctant to interfere unless it infringed the
doctrine of proportionality or was outside the margin of appreciation which
is permitted to the national court.

2. Relevant Articles of the Convention

Introduction

As is the case for companies, the right to a fair hearing guaranteed by   **15.12**
Article 6 is likely to be one of the most frequently invoked Convention
rights in the area of insolvency. Other than Article 6, the most frequently
invoked rights in relation to insolvency proceedings are Article 8[7A] and
Article 1 of Protocol No. 1[7B] given the effect of such proceedings on
property and private life. Article 10 is less likely to be of importance.[7C]

Right to a Fair Trial—Article 6(1)

Article 6(1) of the Convention confers a right to a fair hearing by an   **15.13**
independent and impartial tribunal established by law in the determination
of "civil rights and obligations" and any "criminal charge".[8]

Article 6 does not confine itself to trials. It is concerned with any serious **15.14**
and genuine dispute as to civil rights or obligations that is arguably
recognised under domestic law and where the proceedings are determinative of that right or obligation. This extends its scope beyond trial
purposes to the determination of civil rights and obligations which includes
disciplinary and regulatory tribunal hearings. As mentioned above, Article
6 is by far the most frequently invoked of the Convention rights. Article 6(1)
requires as a minimum:

    (1) a fair and public hearing;

    (2) an independent and impartial tribunal;

    (3) trial within a reasonable period;

    (4) public judgment.

In addition to the express requirements which are set out in Article 6(1)   **15.15**
there are certain other rights which have been held to be embraced within
the meaning of Article 6(1). These include most importantly:

    (1) the right of access to a court;

    (2) equality of arms; and

[7A] See paras 3.94 *et seq.* and paras 16.03 *et seq.*
[7B] See paras 3.131 *et seq.* and paras 16.43 *et seq.*
[7C] See paras 3.110 *et seq.* for a discussion of Article 10.
[8] See further paras 3.53 *et seq.*

(3) the right to participate effectively in proceedings.[9]

15.16 The hearing of a winding up or bankruptcy petition will certainly concern the determination of civil rights and obligations of the company or individual concerned. This will mean that the procedures used in the hearing of these petitions will have to satisfy the rights protected by Article 6. This issue is considered further below in paragraphs 15.35 *et seq.*

Right to Respect for Private and Family Life—Article 8

15.17 This Article encompasses protection of four separate interests:

(1) private life;

(2) family life;

(3) the home; and

(4) correspondence.[9A]

15.18 **Qualified Right.** This area is one where proportionality will play an important role. Many investigations which are authorised by statute and approved by the courts will be considered as necessary and in the public interest. This is given effect to in Article 8(2). Therefore, in assessing whether there has been an infringement of Article 8 the court should have regard to:

(1) whether the investigation is justified by reference to Article 8(2)[9B];

(2) whether it is in accordance with the law[9C]; and

(3) whether it is necessary in a democratic society.[9D]

These three questions inevitably allow Member States considerable room in deciding what is necessary in the context of a particular society. Where the privacy in question is commercial in nature the degree of protection accorded under Article 8 is generally of a lesser character that the protection afforded to individuals.

15.19 Article 8 has already been relied upon in a number of cases involving insolvency proceedings where an individual's property rights have been infringed. For example, in *M v. United Kingdom*,[10] the applicant complained that inquiries made by the Official Receiver into the contents of his mother's will were a violation of Article 8. M did not demonstrate that he was compelled to answer questions relating to his mother's will or that he

---

[9] Keir Starmer, *European Human Rights Law*, (Legal Action Group, 1999), pp. 120–121. See also for a discussion on Art. 6: Robert Walker L.J.: "Opinion: The Impact of European Standards on the Right to a Fair Trial in Civil Proceedings in United Kingdom Domestic Law" [1999] E.H.R.L.R. 4.
[9A] See further paras 16.20 *et seq.*
[9B] See para. 4.33.
[9C] See paras 4.43 *et seq.*
[9D] See paras 4.34 *et seq.*
[10] (1988) 10 E.H.R.R. 527.

would have been subjected to any penalty if he had failed to do so and the Court held that his claims were inadmissible.

Article 8 may be relied upon in future proceedings in relation to applica- **15.20** tions to repossess the family home and where private and family life is infringed, for example by the issue of a warrant of arrest of a debtor against whom a bankruptcy petition has been presented,[11] by the use of a warrant to enter premises,[12] or by the issue of a warrant for the arrest of a bankrupt or other person who has been summoned to appear before the court.[13–14] All these measures will have to be tested by reference to the HRA to ensure that they are compatible.

The Cork Report referred to the importance of rehabilitation of the bank- **15.21** rupt.[15] The Insolvency Act 1986 abolished some of the most draconian of measures, including abolishing mandatory public examinations and the automatic vesting of after-acquired property. In a consultation paper, "Bankruptcy—A Fresh Start", the Government has recently outlined possible reforms of our bankruptcy law which would include a shortening of the period for certain types of bankruptcies and the relaxation of certain statutory provisions attached to the status of a bankrupt.[16] Both Article 8 and Article 4 (the right not to be held in servitude) may apply to the principle of rehabilitation.

Right to Freedom of Expression—Article 10

Article 10 grants the right to freedom of expression. It is considered by the **15.22** European Court as one of the essential foundations of a democratic society and one of the basic conditions for its progress.[17] The Court has held that Article 10 may be invoked by both individuals and corporate entities.[18]

The definition of "expression" has been widely construed and includes **15.23** words, pictures, images and acts which convey information. Freedom of expression also includes the right to hold opinions, to receive and impart information and ideas. The means of expression include print, radio, television broadcasting, artistic creations, film. Advertising also comes within the scope of the provision.[19]

The right is qualified by reference to Article 10(2) and so far has not had **15.24** any great impact on insolvency proceedings. It was, however, cited in *M v. United Kingdom*[20] where the applicant argued that he was denied the right to freedom of expression at the first creditors' meeting as he was unable to attend. It was held in that case that Article 10 did not confer a right of

---

[11] IA 1986, s.364.
[12] IA 1986, s.365. See also *Chappell v. United Kingdom* (1989) 12 E.H.R.R. 1.
[13–14] S. 366.
[15] Insolvency Law and Practice, Report of the Review Committee, Sir Kenneth Cork, 1982, Cmnd. 8558, paras, 192–3, 198(c).
[16] Bankruptcy A Fresh Start, A Consultation on Possible Reform to the Law relating to Personal Insolvency in England and Wales (The Insolvency Service, April 6, 2001).
[17] *Handyside v. United Kingdom* (1979) 1 E.H.R.R. 737; *Lingens v. Austria* (1986) 8 E.H.R.R. 407; *Jersild v. Denmark* (1995) 19 E.H.R.R. 1.
[18] *Autronic AG v. Switzerland* (1990) 12 E.H.R.R. 485.
[19] See further Chap. 19 (Consumer Protection and Advertising), paras 19.98 *et seq.,* below.
[20] (1988) 10 E.H.R.R. 527.
[20A] See analysis at paras 16.43 *et seq.*

access to all meetings and accordingly there was no violation of the Convention.

Right to Protection of Property—Article 1 of Protocol No. 1

15.25 Article 1 of Protocol No. 1 confers a right to the peaceful enjoyment of possessions. This right is subject to heavy qualification as the needs of society inevitably entail situations where a person may be deprived of their property or where their property is subject to control. Both bankruptcy and liquidation will deprive or interfere with the rights of the individual or the company to their property. These property rights will have to be tested against the provisos contained in Article 1 of Protocol No. 1.[20A]

15.26 **Possessions.** Article 1 of Protocol No. 1 refers to "possessions" rather than "property". The term possessions has been given a broad definition by the European Court and the Commission. It includes moveable and immoveable property, economic interest including shares,[21] patents,[22] the ownership of a debt,[23] contractual rights, and legal claims.[24]

15.27 **Deprivation or control of property.** Article 1 of Protocol No. 1 draws a distinction between deprivation and control of property. If there is a deprivation of property it must be in the public interest and in accordance with general principles of international law. Control of property is permitted in a wider range of circumstances and reflects the underlying policy in a democratic society that some form of control over property is necessary. The principles to be applied to both are similar although those in relation to control will be applied less strictly. The restriction on the property must be:

(1) for a legitimate purpose;

(2) the achievement of that purpose must strike a fair balance between the demands of the general interest of the community and the need to protect individual rights.[25]

Article 1 of Protocol No. 1 also protects interference with possession where a measure cannot be defined as deprivation or control.[26] This Article, coupled with Article 8, will have some effect on insolvency proceedings.

3. PARTIES

Introduction

15.28 Only public authorities or organisations undertaking public functions have a duty to comply with the Convention. As mentioned above, the HRA does

---

[20A] See analysis at paras 16.43 *et seq.*
[21] *Bramelid and Malmström v. Sweden* (1982) 29 D.R. 64.
[22] *Smith Kline and French Laboratories v. Netherlands* (1990) 66 D.R. 70.
[23] *Agneessens v. Belgium* (1988) 58 D.R. 63.
[24] Note that the French text uses the word *"biens"* which is far wider than the concept of possessions.
[25] Keir Starmer, *European Human Rights Law*, (Legal Action Group, 1999), p. 148–149.
[26] See *Sporrong and Lonnroth v. Sweden* (1983) 5 E.H.R.R. 35.

not make Convention rights directly enforceable against private companies or bodies which are not considered to be carrying out public
functions or deemed a public authority, although the Convention will inevitably have some horizontal effect.[27]

Courts and Tribunals as Public Authorities

Section 6(3) of the HRA includes courts and tribunals within the meaning **15.29**
of "public authority". A court or tribunal, including the Insolvency Practitioners Tribunal, therefore, has a duty to act compatibly with the HRA when
making decisions. On this basis it must give effect to Convention rights
and consider decisions relating to Convention rights even where the
matter is between two private companies pursuant to sections 2 and 6 of
the HRA. In so doing the court will not be deciding a claim based solely on
a violation of a Convention right, but rather on the basis that existing
common law or statutory rights must be given effect to in a manner
compatible with the Convention.[28]

Companies as Public Authorities

Consideration of this area is given in Chapter 14: Companies and Finan- **15.30**
cial Services.

Officeholders as Public Authorities

The IA 1986 provides for various court functions to be delegated to **15.31**
persons such as the liquidator of a company in compulsory liquidation or
a trustee in bankruptcy. In these instances, the court appointed liquidator
or trustee acts as an officer of the court and undertakes public functions on
behalf of the court and for the benefit of society as a whole and the
creditors. They will therefore be considered as a public authority for the
purposes of the HRA.

It is clear that a court appointed liquidator, the Official Receiver and a **15.32**
trustee in bankruptcy appointed by the Secretary of State will be considered as exercising public functions. What about other officeholders
such as a liquidator in a voluntary liquidation who is not appointed by the
court? Given the courts are likely to define "public authority" and "functions of a public nature" broadly, it seems likely that many of the decisions
taken by officeholders of all types (whether court appointed or not) will fall
within the ambit of Article 6. For example, the liquidator in a voluntary
liquidation still undertakes certain functions of a public nature and therefore is likely to be considered a "public authority" in respect of these
functions. Similarly, it is likely that an administrator will be considered to be
engaged in functions of a public nature.[29]

---

[27] See paras 5.15 *et seq.*,
[28] H.L. Debs., November 24, 1997, cols 781, 783.
[29] See IA 1986, ss.38, 41, 46, 48, and the Companies and Directors Disqualification Act
1986, s.7(3).

15.33   The position is less clear as regards administrative receivers, supervisors of voluntary arrangements and officerholders generally when not undertaking "public functions".

Victims for the Purposes of the Insolvency Act

15.34   Companies, both solvent and insolvent, will be capable of being victims of violations of Conventions rights. The question of whether shareholders of insolvent companies may be victims is dealt with more fully in Chapter 14: Companies and Financial Services.[30] In general the case law suggests that shareholders will be able to claim as victims where they are claiming in their personal capacity, for example where they personally rely on Article 6 rights. Where they are basing their claim on what is properly a claim of the company, they may only claim in exceptional circumstances such as where the company itself is subject to insolvency procedures and may be unable to bring a claim.[31]

4. PROCEDURE

Introduction

15.35   As mentioned above the right to a fair trial enshrined in Article 6 is the most frequently invoked right generally. This remains true for insolvency litigation and many of the insolvency procedures have already been the subject of a HRA challenge. Unreasonable delay in the course of proceedings, the loss of the right to litigate once adjudged bankrupt and civil procedure orders preventing litigants from bringing further applications without leave of the court are some examples of how the Convention rights have been applied in this context.

Fair and Public Hearing

15.36   A court will not make a winding up or bankruptcy order where the petition debt is bona fide disputed on genuine grounds. Where the company or individual asserts a cross-claim which cannot be set off against the petition debt, the court may hear the winding up or bankruptcy petition. The question then arises as to whether there is a fair hearing of the cross-claim. The approach taken by the court is to determine whether the cross-claim is genuine and serious and whether the respondent has been unable to litigate it. A potential infringement of Article 6 may occur where the court makes a winding up or bankruptcy order on the basis that the cross-claim is not genuine or serious. Arguably Article 6 will have been infringed because the court will have determined the cross-claim without full consideration of it such as would take place at a trial of the cross-claim. Once the order has been made in practice it may not be possible to litigate the cross-claim.[32]

15.37   Another area where Article 6 may be invoked is in relation to private hearings in bankruptcy hearings. Unlike winding up petitions, bankruptcy

---

[30] See paras 14.39 *et seq.*,
[31] See, *e.g. Pine Valley Developments Ltd v. Ireland* (1993) 16 E.H.R.R. 250.
[32] See *Re Bayoil SA, Seawind Tankers Corp v. Bayoil SA* [1999] 1 B.C.L.C. 62.

petitions are not advertised and the hearings are in private. Although CPR dictates that as a general rule hearings should be in public (CPR 39.2) a hearing or part of it may be in private if: "it involves confidential information (including information relating to personal financial matters) and publicity would damage that confidentiality."

In most cases a bankrupt will not want their case heard in public. However, **15.38** where they do it is arguable that the refusal to have a hearing in open court would amount to an infringement of Article 6. This point was successfully argued in *Scarth v. United Kingdom*.[33]

The practice of presenting administration petitions on the same day as **15.39** seeking the administration order under sections 9 to 11 of the IA 1986 is a further area where Article 6 may be relevant. Most applications are made without notice and often confidential information is given to the judge which it is expected will not be available to creditors, whatever the extent of their interests. Consideration should be given to the appropriateness of applying without notice and protecting information from inspection. While it may be justifiable to apply without notice and withhold information from creditors, the reasons for doing so should be analysed with care.

Independent and Impartial Tribunal

Article 6(1) requires that civil rights and obligations be determined by an **15.40** "independent and impartial" tribunal.[33A] The Insolvency Practitioners Tribunal[34] will be subject to the provisions of the HRA and its procedures will have to comply with the Convention rights. In addition the insolvency regime provides that many judicial or quasi-judicial decisions are taken by officeholders in the course of carrying out their functions under the IA 1986. These decisions too will have to comply with the Article 6 safeguards.

Trial within a Reasonable Period

One of the aspects of procedural fairness most frequently relied upon is **15.41** the Article 6 guarantee of the right to a hearing within a reasonable time.[34A] Delays are all too frequent in liquidations and in bankruptcies and practically are difficult for a creditor to do anything about.

If the delays are unreasonable in the light of all the circumstances, they **15.42** may be challenged. In *GJ v. Luxembourg*,[35] the applicant was a shareholder of an insolvent company. He claimed a breach of Article 6(1) on the basis that the administration of the insolvency had lasted six years. The European Court held that the reasonableness of the length of proceedings had to be assessed in light of the circumstances of the case. Despite the submission of 49 creditors' claims in liquidation proceedings, it was not

---

[33] (1999) 28 E.H.R.R. C.D. 47. See also paras 10.98 *et seq.*
[33A] See further paras 10.103 *et seq.*
[34] It is not clear that the Tribunal meets the standards required by Art. 6. See Sealy and Milman, *Annotated Guide to the Insolvency Legislation*, (5th ed. CCH Editions, 1999), p. 500. See also the Scottish decision in *Starrs and Chalmers v. Procurator Fiscal*, 2000 S.L.T. 42; *Clancy v. Caird*, 2000 S.L.T. 546; and the English decision relating to the independence of employment tribunals in *Smith v. Secretary of State for Trade and Industry* [2000] I.C.R. 69.
[34A] See also paras 10.98 *et seq.*
[35] [2000] B.P.I.R. 1009.

found that the case was unduly complex and G's conduct did not contribute to the length of the case. The "reasonable time" requirement had not been satisfied and there had been a violation of Article 6(1) of the Convention.

15.43 In *Wojnowicz v Poland*,[36] the applicant complained, in the context of the winding up of a company he had owned with two others, that proceeding which had continued for seven years and four months amounted to unreasonable delay. The Court did not consider the case to be complex enough to justify the length of proceedings and the conduct of the judicial authorities, as opposed to the applicant's behaviour, did contribute to the length of proceedings. Accordingly, it held that there had been a violation of Article 6(1) of the Convention in light of the circumstances of the case, its complexity and both the applicant's and the judicial authorities' conduct in contributing to the delay.[37]

15.44 There are, however, alternatives open to a creditor if he feels the cause of delay lies with the officeholder. It may be possible to remove the officeholder by a democratic vote of the creditors' committee, or a creditor can apply to the court for an order that the liquidator or trustee in bankruptcy be removed and replaced by an alternative person.[38] Where a creditor is aggrieved by an act or decision of the liquidator or trustee in bankruptcy he may apply to the court for an order to reverse or modify the act or decision complained of.[39]

Access to Court

15.45 Article 6 guarantees the right of access to a court as well as that of a fair trial. This may be particularly important in the context of insolvency proceedings and their consequences on the individual. Individuals who are adjudicated bankrupt only have limited rights of access to a court, by virtue of the fact that their property has vested in their trustee in bankruptcy. The bankrupt therefore has no right to a fair trial as regards his property rights as he has no cause of action.[39A]

15.46 When a company has gone into administration it is necessary, by virtue of section 11 of the IA 1986, to get leave to commence proceedings against the company. The threshold for obtaining leave is a high one—the claim must be seriously arguable on the merits.[40]

15.47 **Vexatious Litigants.** In the context of bankruptcy proceedings in particular, the courts are on occasion faced with multiple proceedings brought by vexatious litigants. In an appropriate case the court has an inherent jurisdiction to make an order requiring the litigant to obtain permission from the court before bringing further applications in existing

---

[36] Application No. 33082/96, September 21, 2000.
[37] See also *Comingersoll SA v. Portugal*, Application No. 35382/97, April 6, 2000 where damages were awarded by the Court where proceedings had dragged on for over 17 years before a final decision was given.
[38] IA 1986, ss.171–172.
[39] IA 1986, ss.168 and 303.
[39A] See further para. 15.65 below.
[40] *Re Polly Peck International plc (in administration) (No. 4)* [1998] 2 B.C.L.C. 185.

proceedings.[41] The court may also make a civil proceedings order pursuant to section 42 of the Supreme Court Act 1981 to prevent all civil and all criminal proceedings being intiated without permission of the court. Such an order is wider that the conventional *Grepe v. Loam* order and must be made by the Attorney-General and heard in a Administrative Court.[42] Provided that such an order is a proportionate response in the circumstances aimed at ensuring the proper administration of justice, it is likely that it will be compatible with Article 6.[43]

The Divisional Court (since renamed the Administrative Court) on the eve   **15.48** of the HRA coming into force had regard to the Convention in the light of its jurisdiction to make such an order.[44] The Court held in the context of numerous applications arising out of bankruptcy proceedings that, although a civil proceedings order was a very draconian measure, it was in the public interest in the circumstances to make an order so that the court process itself might be protected and a proper service provided to bona fide litigants. In that case, it was not controversial that the litigant had habitually and persistently instituted civil proceedings without reasonable grounds, misled the court and sought to re-litigate matters decided against him time and time again.

The Court of Appeal held in *Ebert v. Venvil*[45] that the court also has   **15.49** jurisdiction to prevent fresh proceedings being commenced without permission of the court. This was compatible with Article 6(1) of the Convention as long as the power was exercised in appropriate circumstances. The Court said:

> "Article 6 does no more than reflect the approach of the common law indicated by Laws J. in *Reg. v. Lord Chancellor, Ex parte Witham* [1998] Q.B. 575. As long as the inherent power is exercised only when it is appropriate for it to be exercised, no contravention of article 6 or common law principle is involved."

Court Fees.   The Divisional Court has held that the access to courts   **15.50** must not be made practically impossible by the imposition of court fees.[46] But it was held in *R. v. Lord Chancellor, ex p. Lightfoot*[47] that the court fee of £250 required before a bankruptcy petition can be presented was not a violation of the Article 6 right to access to the courts. The court held in that case that the deposit was not for access to the court but for the cost of administrative services provided by others for the benefit of the petitioning creditor or debtor. A petition brought by a debtor for her own bankruptcy did not involve the determination of civil rights and obligations and therefore the principle of access to justice was not infringed. The court also held in that case that even if Article 6 were applicable, the requirement to pay

---

[41] *Grepe v. Loam* (1887) 37 Ch.D. 168.
[42] See further paras 10.07 *et seq.*, above.
[43] *H v. United Kingdom* (1985) 45 D.R. 281.
[44] *Attorney-General v. Bishop* (unreported) July 5, 2000, D.C.
[45] [2000] Ch. 484, [1999] 3 W.L.R. 670. See also *Ebert v. Official Receiver* [2001] EWCA Civ 340; *The Independent* March 21, 2001; *Johnson v. Valks* [2000] 1 W.L.R. 1502, CA. See further para. 10.08.
[46] *R. v. Lord Chancellor, ex p. Witham* [1998] 2 W.L.R. 849. See also *Kreuz v. Poland* [1998] 25 E.H.R.R. C.D. 80. See also paras 12.47 *et seq.*
[47] [2000] Q.B. 597, [1998] 4 All E.R. 764.

a deposit was compatible with its requirements.[48] Simon Brown L.J. said:

> "I would distinguish this case from *Ex parte Witham* [1998] Q.B. 575 on the ground that the mandatory deposit is not for access to the court but rather towards the costs of services being provided by others for the petitioner's benefit. No doubt the position (and the distinction from *Ex parte Witham*) would be the plainer if, instead of imposing the requirement as a precondition of filing the petition, it was made a precondition of the court actually making the bankruptcy order which sets the administrative process in train".

Immunity from Suit

15.51 A rule which removes a particular category of defendant from suit must be examined under Article 6. A blanket immunity of a particular class may be disproportionate and so may constitute a breach of Article 6 even if its aim is legitimate. In *Osman v. United Kingdom*[49] the Court held that an absolute rule which took no account of the fundamental rights of the applicant and the degree of harm suffered was a disproportionate restriction on that applicant's right of access to court.[50] In *Z v. United Kingdom*,[50A] the European Court expressly did not follow *Osman* in relation to its finding that the striking out of a claim on the basis that it was not fair, just and reasonable to impose a duty of care was a disproportionate restriction on the applicant's right of access to a court. Nevertheless, the principle underlying the objection to immunities or disproportionate restrictions on access to a court remains intact.

15.52 The Official Receiver has wide-ranging immunity in respect of statements made by him in the course of bankruptcy proceedings. This immunity was recently upheld by the Court of Appeal in *Mond v. Hyde*.[51] It has also been held that the court has no power to direct the Official Receiver as to the performance of his public law duties.[52] These decisions would appear to be inconsistent with the reasoning in *Osman v. United Kingdom* and may be subject to challenge in the future.[53]

15.53 The IA 1986 also confers other immunities which may give rise to challenge under Article 6. For example, an administrator may be released by the court. Such release has the effect of discharging the administrator from all liability both in respect of acts or omissions of his in the administration and otherwise in relation to his conduct as an administrator.[54] In every

---

[48] See also *M v. United Kingdom*, Application No. 12040/86, May 4, 1987; commentary on *Lightfoot* in M.C. Elliott, "Lightfoot: Tracing the Perimeter of Constitutional Rights" [1998] J.R. 217.

[49] (2000) 29 E.H.R.R. 245.

[50] See also *Fayed v. United Kingdom* (1994) 18 E.H.R.R. 393. See further para. 10.15 above and paras 17.41 *et seq.* below.

[50A] Application No. 29392/95 [2001] 2 F.C.R. 246.

[51] *Mond v. Hyde* [1998] 2 B.C.L.C. 340.

[52] *Hardy v. Focus Insurance Co. Ltd* [1997] B.P.I.R. 77.

[53] See Marion Simmons Q.C. and Tom Smith, "The Human Rights Act 1998: the practical impact on insolvency" (2000) 16 I.L.&P. 165.

[54] IA 1986, s.20. See also IA 1986, s.234, which provides that where an officeholder is getting in company's property he is not liable to any person in respect of loss or damage except where it results from his own negligence; cf. s. 304 IA 1986 for the corresponding provision in bankruptcy.

case where there is a blanket immunity, it will be necessary to scrutinise the policy underlying the immunity.

Waiver of Access to Courts. This may well be important in the context of the insolvency regime and it has been recognised by the European Court that access to court may be waived by the parties in appropriate circumstances and where there are appropriate safe-guards.[55] **15.54**

In *Re Hawk Insurance Company Ltd*[56] it was held that a creditors' scheme of arrangement which denied access to the courts could be upheld by invoking the principle of waiver and by pointing out that there had been no dissenting creditors. The court was satisfied that the adjudication provision involved no infringement of a creditor's Convention rights under Article 6 which could not be waived. The role of the adjudicator was intended to be limited to issues of valuation arising out of scheme claims, and was not intended to empower the adjudicator to deal with issues of construction or other matters of law. **15.55**

5. INSOLVENCY INVESTIGATIONS

Introduction

The wide-ranging powers afforded to officeholders under sections 235 to 236 of the IA 1986 to investigate the affairs of companies and their directors and members have been likened to the draconian powers of the medieval Star Chamber. Similarly there are powers (albeit less far reaching) under section 333 of the IA 1986 in relation to investigating the affairs of bankrupts. The subject of company investigations has already been considered in Chapter 14 above on Companies and Financial Services. Reference should therefore be made to that section as regards companies and generally in relation to the subsequent use of compulsorily obtained information. **15.56**

Statutory powers to compel evidence—individuals

Every bankruptcy is under the general control of the court and the court has full power to decide all questions arising out of the bankruptcy.[57] As regards investigation into the affairs of a bankrupt, the court has considerable powers of enforcement and in particular may issue warrants for arrest,[58] seizure,[59] and inquiry.[60] In so far as it can be shown that these powers are being exercised for a legitimate purpose and that their use is proportionate to the aim in question then it is unlikely that the Convention rights will be violated. **15.57**

---

[55] See in relation to waiver generally paras 3.152 *et seq.*, and in relation to waiver in the context of arbitration para. 12.14 above.
[56] (unreported) January 24, 2000, ChD.
[57] IA 1986, s.363.
[58] IA 1986, s.364; the power to arrest might be challenged under Art. 5 but in practice could be justified on the basis of the qualifications to Art. 5.
[59] IA 1986, s.365.
[60] IA 1986, ss.366, 367.

Statutory powers to compel evidence—companies

15.58   Sections 235 to 236 of the IA 1986 give an officeholder various powers to inquire into the dealings of a company. The officers and directors of the company are under a duty to co-operate with the officeholder and the officeholder may apply for an order for their examination.[61]

15.59   **Challenges to the investigation itself.**   As the powers are investigative in nature rather than adjudicative (or determinative of a civil right or obligation) they are not subject to Article 6; but the manner in which the powers are exercised may give rise to a challenge if the other Convention rights are not respected, particularly Article 8. However, given that the courts already impose limits on these powers in the exercise of their discretion as to whether to make an order, it is likely that the Convention rights will simply reinforce existing limits rather than create new restrictions.[62]

15.60   It should be noted that the courts have a discretion whether to make an order for examination under section 236 and will not do so where it would be unreasonable, unnecessary or oppressive. In practice, a court may refuse to make an order where the officeholder has commenced proceedings. The courts can also control access to the information received as a result of the section 236 examination.[63]

15.61   **Use of evidence in civil and criminal proceedings.**   For a full discussion on this see Chapter 14 Companies and Financial Services.[64] As mentioned above[65] section 219 of the Insolvency Act 1986 has been amended by section 11 of the Insolvency Act 2000. This makes it clear that compelled evidence obtained under section 218 of the Insolvency Act 1986 may not be used in subsequent criminal proceedings against a person.

6. PROPERTY RIGHTS

Introduction

15.62   Both bankruptcy and liquidation have the effect of depriving an individual or a company of their property. Although challenge to the making of a bankruptcy or winding-up order is unlikely where those orders are made within the provisions of the law, it may be possible in certain circumstances to challenge the extent to which the orders interfere with property rights.

Priority of Debts in Insolvency Proceedings

15.63   Under the insolvency regime, certain preferential creditors are entitled to have their debts paid in priority to the general body of unsecured creditors.[66] The question then arises as to whether this is an infringement on

---

[61] See Campbell, "Investigations by Insolvency Practitioners: powers and restraints—Part. 1" (2000) 16 I.L.&P. 182; Part 2 (2000) 16 I.L.&P. 211.
[62] See, *e.g. Cloverbay Ltd v. Bank of Credit and Commerce International SA* [1991] 1 All E.R. 894, and a recent case *Re Pantmaenog Ltd, The Times,* November 23, 2000.
[63] Insolvency Rules 1986, r. 9.5.
[64] At paras 14.63 *et seq.,* above.
[65] See paras 14.81 *et seq.,* above.
[66] See IA 1986, ss.175, 328, Sched. 6.

the rights to property of the other unsecured creditors. There are two points to note in relation to this which suggest that a challenge may not be successful:

(1) an unsecured creditor has no right as such to any property of the creditor prior to liquidation or bankruptcy, but only to a cause of action against the debtor. On liquidation or bankruptcy the unsecured creditor is entitled to prove based on the scheme laid out in the IA 1986;

(2) the payment of certain preferential debts may be justified by policy reasons.

Set off in insolvency

Set off in insolvency proceedings is a complex subject which is dealt with at length in various practitioner texts.[67] One of its features is that a creditor of an insolvent person may in certain circumstances have a right to set-off a debt owed to the insolvent against debts which the debtor owes the creditor. This effectively places that creditor in a much better position as regards other creditors who may not have rights of set-off.[68] Arguably, this right of set-off infringes the rights of other unsecured creditors who might be better off if the creditor with the right of set-off were to have to pay the full extent of their debt to the debtor and then share *pari passu* in the proceeds of the pool of assets. However, for similar reasons to those cited above in relation to preferential debts, it may be difficult to mount a challenge based on Article 6.

15.64

Bankrupts—Loss of Right to Litigate

A bankrupt's estate, including any causes in action, vests in the Official Receiver or the trustee in bankruptcy on their appointment pursuant to section 306 of the IA 1986. This may mean that a decision is taken not to pursue pending litigation for the benefit of the bankrupt's estate. In *M. v. United Kingdom* it was argued that where the Official Receiver decided to stay proceedings which had been issued by the bankrupt prior to a bankruptcy order being made on the grounds that the costs were likely to exceed recoverable damages there was a breach of Article 6, the Commission held in that case that there was no such breach. This followed from the fact that the bankrupt himself had no right to a trial at all, the cause of action having been vested in the Official Receiver.[69]

15.65

Similarly, after a bankruptcy order has been made, a bankrupt has no standing to appeal against a judgment entered against him or her—even if the judgment was wrongly entered and itself formed the basis of the bankruptcy petition.[70]

15.66

---

[67] See Rory Derham, *Set-Off*, (2nd ed.) (Clarendon Press 1998); Philip Wood, *English and International Set-Off* (Sweet & Maxwell, 1989).
[68] The position relating to set off is different in many civil law jurisdictions which do not recognise set off in the context of insolvents.
[69] *M v. United Kingdom* (1987) 52 D.R. 266.
[70] *Heath v. Tang* [1993] 1 W.L.R. 1421.

15.67 However, in a few cases, even before the HRA came into force, the courts recognised certain rights of a bankrupt in his capacity as litigant. This was particularly the case where questions of possession of the family home were concerned. These rights have been described as "procedural" or "basic" rights and have been distinguished from substantive rights. In *Heath v. Tang*[71] the Court of Appeal held that there were certain causes of action personal to the bankrupt which do not vest in his trustee, including cases in which "the damages are to be estimated by immediate reference to pain felt by the bankrupt in respect of his body, mind or character, and without immediate reference to his rights of property". They included actions in defamation and for assault.[72]

Matrimonial Home

15.68 As regards the matrimonial home, it is arguable that the spouse or children of the bankrupt have a right to peaceful enjoyment of the family home protected by Article 1 of Protocol No. 1, even if they have no strict legal entitlement to the property itself. Equally the family might rely on Article 8 of the Convention. However, arguably such rights are adequately protected by section 336 of the IA 1986 which requires the interests of the spouse and children to be taken into account by the court on any application for possession of the matrimonial home.[73] It is as yet unclear to what extent the HRA will have any significant effect on the court in this area. More recent cases reveal the extent to which the court will consider Article 8 carefully in coming to a decision, even if they do not necessarily need to base their decision on Article 8.[74]

15.69 One area where Article 8 may have impact is as regards co-habitees who arguably are not currently protected by section 366 of the IA 1986 which applies to the interests of the spouse and children.

Personal Possessions

15.70 Section 283 of the IA 1986 excludes from the estate in bankruptcy all clothing, bedding, furniture, household equipment and provisions which are necessary for satisfying the basic domestic needs of the bankrupt and his family. It is arguable that the protection in Article 1 of Protocol No. 1 is wider than that which is protected by the basic domestic needs of the bankrupt and his family. Arguably, the right to property includes a right to those possessions which are necessary in order to lead a fulfilling life in the community.[75]

---

[71] [1993] 1 W.L.R. 1421.

[72] See also *Seven Eight Six Properties Ltd v. Ghafoor* [1997] B.P.I.R. 519; *Nationwide Building Society v. Purvis* [1998] B.P.I.R. 625; *In Re Rae* [1995] B.C.C. 102.

[73] See *Re Bremner* [1999] B.P.I.R. 185, where the needs of a bankrupt's wife to care for him because he was both elderly and terminally ill created exceptional circumstances which outweighed the interests of creditors to justify an order delaying the sale of the bankrupt's house. See also *Claughton v. Charalambous* [1998] B.P.I.R. 558; *Re Raval* [1998] 2 F.L.R. 718, where a six month suspension for sale of a property was extended to one year.

[74] See Pines-Richman, "*Using the Human Rights Act to save the family home*" (2000) 150 N.L.J. 1102; *Mortgage Corporation v. Shaire* [2000] B.P.I.R. 483.

[75] See Marion Simmons Q.C. and Tom Smith, "The Human Rights Act 1998: the practical impact on insolvency" (2000) 16 I.L.&P. 165.

Correspondence

In *Foxley v. United Kingdom*[76] the European Court held that a trustee in **15.71** bankruptcy to whom a bankrupt's mail had been directed pursuant to an order under section 371 of the IA 1986 was not entitled, even during the currency of the order, to open and read correspondence to the bankrupt from his legal advisers, and should not have continued to open and read correspondence of any kind after the time period prescribed by the order had lapsed. The Court accepted that section 371 of the IA 1986 pursued a legitimate aim, namely the tracing of the bankrupt's assets for the benefit of his creditors. However, the interception of letters from his legal advisers could not be said to be "necessary in a democratic society", within the meaning of Article 8(2). The lawyer-client relationship was, in principle, privileged. Further, once the three month re-direction order had expired the trustee's continued opening and reading of any of Foxley's correspondence was a violation of Article 8.[77]

In *Haig v. Aitken*[78] the trustee in bankruptcy of Jonathan Aitken claimed **15.72** that all personal correspondence fell within the definition of "property" under the IA 1986 which vested in the trustee on his appointment taking effect. Rattee J referring to Article 8 held that Jonathan Aitken's trustee in bankruptcy should not be able to sell Aitken's personal papers. This was the case even where the bankrupt was famous and his correspondence might be of particular value to the media. Rattee J. said:

> " . . . it is inconceivable that Parliament envisaged, by passing the Act, that the effect of bankruptcy should be that a bankrupt's personal correspondence should be available for publication to the world at large at the behest of the trustee in bankruptcy. In my opinion, the concept of such a gross invasion of privacy is repugnant . . . [T]he effect of the Act is that a bankrupt's estate does not include the bankrupt's personal correspondence which, like a right of action for damages for libel, is of a nature peculiarly personal to him and his life as a human being."

Pensions

Since the decision in *Re Landau (A Bankrupt)*,[79] it has been clear that **15.73** pension policies are considered as part of the bankrupt's estate and therefore vest in the trustee in bankruptcy on his appointment. The effect of this decision is reversed by section 11 of the Welfare Reform and Pensions Act 1999, although its provisions do not apply retrospectively. Therefore bankruptcy orders made before the coming into force of the new legislation will be governed by the principles in *Re Landau*.

---

[76] *The Times*, July 4, 2000.
[77] Prior to the decision in *Foxley*, the legality of the IA 1986, s.371, in the light of the Convention and also the Interception of Communications Act 1985 had been questioned; see *Jaconelli* [1994] Conv. 370; *Singh v. Official Receiver* [1997] B.P.I.R. 530, where the court expressed reservations about the manner of obtaining such orders.
[78] [2000] 3 All E.R. 80.
[79] [1998] Ch. 223.

15.74　In *Krasner v. Dennison*,[80] it was argued *inter alia* that the vesting of the entire pension policy including the income arising from those pensions, in the trustee constituted a breach of Article 1 of Protocol No. 1. The Court of Appeal examined in particular whether the vesting in the trustee in bankruptcy of the bankrupt's rights under retirement annuity contracts and personal pension schemes, in circumstances which excluded the power of the court to make an income payment order under section 310 of the IA 1986, was in the public interest.

15.75　The Court said it was relevant: "to have in mind that national authority is, in principle, better placed than the international judge to appreciate what is in the 'public interest', and so must be allowed a certain margin of appreciation". In forming its decision that there was no violation of the Convention, the Court had regard to the activism of Parliament in the area of pensions law against the background of judicial decisions which reflected the public interest element that a bankrupt's property should be available to meet the claims of his creditors and the fact that Parliament has already legislated to exclude certain pension rights from the full operation of bankruptcy law.[81]

Right to Income

15.76　In *Ord v. Upton*[82] the Court of Appeal held that a trustee in bankruptcy should receive the benefit of damages for loss of future earnings suffered by a bankrupt in respect of pre-bankruptcy personal injury. In coming to their decision the Court of Appeal relied on a decision of the British Columbia Supreme Court in *Re Bell*[83] which held that the bankrupt's "capacity to earn" was a property right, the damage to which was not personal but of such a nature that any compensation should be applied for the benefit of his creditors "subject to retention for maintenance". This decision does not square easily with the principle of rehabilitation and where compensation is for his future inability to make a living.[84]

15.77　It is worth noting in this context that a bankrupt is entitled to work during the course of his bankruptcy and earn a living without having to account to his trustee. It is open of course to the trustee to apply for an income payments order in so far as the income is greater than that required for his reasonable domestic needs.[85] Once a bankrupt is discharged (usually three years from the making of the bankruptcy order) his income is insulated and free from the claims of his creditors.

15.78　The conclusion that the capacity of a human being to earn a living is a "capital asset" and "property right", the value of which is realisable for the

---

[80] *Krasner v. Dennison* [2001] Ch. 76. But see now Welfare Reform and Pensions Act 1999, s. 11.

[81] See also Deacock and Martin, "The Rights of a Trustee in Bankruptcy to the Bankrupt's Pension: Pension Industry v. Insolvency Practitioners—A score draw?" (2000) 16 I.L.&P. 127.

[82] [2000] B.P.I.R. 104.

[83] [1998] B.P.I.R. 26.

[84] See Conor Gearty and Stephen Davies Q.C., "Insolvency Practice and the Human Rights Act 1998" A Special Bulletin, November 2000, p. 44; see also *Haig v. Aitken* [2001] Ch. 110.

[85] See *Re Rayatt* [1998] B.P.I.R. 495, where it was held that reasonable domestic needs could include educating children privately.

benefit of his creditors, may well be the subject of a challenge based on the Convention in the future.

Companies—Loss of Ability to Trade

Once a petition has been presented for the winding up of a company, any **15.79** subsequent disposition of the company's property is, unless the court otherwise orders, automatically void.[86] As a result of the operation of section 127 of the IA 1986, a company's bank will invariably freeze its bank accounts following advertisement of the petition to prevent themselves from suffering loss.[87] This may well prevent the company from trading which may in itself lead to insolvency regardless of whether the petition is based upon a genuinely undisputed debt.

It is arguable that section 127 of the IA 1986 is incompatible with at least **15.80** two of the Convention rights, namely the right to property and that there has in effect been a determination of the civil rights of the company without a fair hearing. In relation to the right to a fair hearing, the effect of section 127 of the IA 1986 is to interfere with the civil rights of the company. However, it can be argued that the interference is only temporary and does not constitute a "determination" of the company's rights since it only lasts until the date of the hearing of the petition and the company can always apply to the court for a validation order.[88] Similar arguments to those justifying *ex parte* injunctions may also be relied upon.[89]

With regard to property rights, measures designed to control the use of **15.81** property may be legitimate if that measure has a legitimate aim and the measure is proportionate to that aim.[90] However, it is questionable whether section 127 of the IA 1986, which may mean that the company effectively ceases trading, is a proportionate measure to protect the position of the company's creditors pending the hearing of a petition which might in fact be dismissed.[90A] Other provisions of the IA 1986 could be invoked in order to protect creditors if necessary.[91] It is, of course, always open to the company to seek an injunction restraining advertisement of the petition in circumstances where the procedure is clearly incorrect.

Leave of Court to Repossess Assets

Where a company has gone into insolvency proceedings (whether it is in **15.82** liquidation or administration), it is necessary for an owner of property to seek the leave of the court before repossessing his or her asset from the insolvent or the officeholder.[92]

---

[86] IA 1986, s.127.

[87] *Hollicourt (Contracts) Ltd v. Bank of Ireland* [2000] 1 W.L.R. 906. See also *Coutts & Co v. Stock* [2000] 1 W.L.R. 895.

[88] See Marion Simmons Q.C. and Tom Smith, "The Human Rights Act 1998: the practical impact on insolvency" (2000) 16 I.L.&P. 165.

[89] For a discussion on interim remedies generally, see paras 10.61 *et seq.*, above and particularly para. 10.70.

[90] *Wasa Liv Omsesidigt, Forsakringsbolaget valands Pensionsstiftelse v. Sweden* (1988) D.R. 163.

[90A] *cf.* para 12.25 in relation to adjudication under the Housing Grants, Construction and Regeneration Act 1996.

[91] See, *e.g.* IA 1986, ss.238, 239, 423.

[92] See, *e.g.* IA 1986, ss.10, 11, 130(2), 285(3).

15.83 This would appear to conflict with Article 1 of Protocol No. 1, which states that no one shall be deprived of his possessions except in the public interest. It is necessary to consider in this context the qualification contained in the Article recognising the right of a state to enforce laws to control the use of property in accordance with the general interest.

15.84 The policy behind the requirement of seeking the leave of the court before repossessing assets has been considered at length by the courts in a number of decisions. In *Re Atlantic Computer Systems plc*[93] for example the Court of Appeal held that it was in the public interest to allow the administrators a period of time in which to make proposals to creditors. The guidelines set down by the Court of Appeal in their decision referred to the need to carry out a balancing exercise between the observance of the proprietary rights of the owner on the one hand, and the effect on the administration if leave were granted on the other. The Court said:

> "Indeed, Parliament must have intended that when exercising its discretion the court should have due regard to the property rights of those concerned. But Parliament must also have intended that the court should have regard to all the other circumstances, such as the consequences which the grant or refusal of leave would have, the financial position of the company, the period for which the administration order is expected to remain in force, the end result sought to be achieved, and the prospects of that result being achieved."

15.85 It would appear, therefore, that if the European Court were to consider an application regarding the interference with property rights in the context of an administration, that it would have regard to the policy behind the legislation and decide the case in line with the principle of margin of appreciation and not interfere with a domestic decision.

Schemes of Arrangement

15.86 The Court of Appeal criticised the standard method of sanctioning schemes of arrangement in *Re Hawk Insurance Co. Ltd.*[94] The issue on appeal was whether the judge was right to take the view that she had no jurisdiction to sanction the scheme of arrangement because she was not satisfied that the scheme creditors constituted a single class for the purposes of the statutory requirement that the scheme be approved by the requisite majority at a meeting of the creditors or class (or classes) of creditors with whom the compromise or arrangement proposed by the scheme was to be made.[95]

15.87 It was necessary to ensure not only that those whose rights really were so dissimilar that they could not consult together with a view to a common interest should be treated as parties to distinct arrangements, so that they should have their own meetings, but also that those whose rights were

---

[93] [1992] Ch. 505.
[94] [2001] EWCA Civ. 241.
[95] The test to determine whether separate class meetings were required was set out by Bowen J. in *Sovereign Life Assurance Co. v. Dodd* (1892) 2 Q.B. 573: a class must be confined to those persons whose rights were not so dissimilar as to make it impossible for them to consult together with a view to their common interest.

sufficiently similar to the rights of others that they could properly consult together should be required to do so; lest by ordering separate meetings the court gave veto to a minority group. The question of whether separate class meetings were required in *Hawk Insurance Co. Ltd* depended upon an analysis of:

(1) the rights which were to be released or varied under the scheme; and

(2) the new rights (if any) that the scheme gave, by way of compromise or arrangement, to those whose rights were to be released or varied.

In a statutory scheme of arrangement where a scheme adjudicator is appointed to determine disputed claims the adjudication process should not violate Article 6. If the adjudicator's decision is to be final then Article 6 safeguards should be in place. If there is to be a right to review that review should satisfy Article 6 if the decision making process which led to the initial decision did not satisfy Article 6.[95A]

In the light of the criticism of the Court of Appeal in *Hawk* about the current practice in relation to the convening of scheme meetings, new proposals for procedure are likely to be introduced such that the court will have to satisfy itself that the classes of creditors have been correctly identified at the first stage where the court directs a creditors meeting to be convened.

7. REVIEW OF DECISION-MAKING POWERS OF OFFICEHOLDERS

Introduction

One important respect in which the HRA will have an impact on insolvency **15.88** proceedings is in relation to the decision making processes of public authorities. As referred to above, many if not all, officeholders will be deemed public authorities within the meaning of the HRA when carrying out their decision making functions. Where these decisions can be said to be determinative of civil rights and obligations they must satisfy the requirements of Article 6.

Decision Making by Officeholders

There are two types of decision making powers exercised by office- **15.89** holders:

(1) administrative powers, for example to realise assets and to value assets; and

(2) quasi-judicial powers affecting the substantive rights of creditors, such as decisions as to the status or their rights, for example by deciding whether to admit or reject a proof of debt.

[95A] See *Re Hawk Insurance Company Ltd* (unreported) January 24, 2001, Ch.D.

15.90   Both administrative decisions and quasi-judicial decisions made by office-holders in insolvency proceedings may affect individual civil rights and obligations. Specific examples of decisions by officeholders which may determine a person's civil rights and obligations include a decision on a proof of debt, a decision to disclaim onerous property, and a decision not to pursue a debtor's cause of action. Administrative decisions because they are administrative rather than judicial may be made by bodies that do not provide all the guarantees of Article 6, provided there is a right of review or appeal which does provide the safeguards enshrined in Article 6. It is necessary to test whether a review which is compliant with Article 6 requirements exists in relation to these administrative decisions.

Requirement of a Full Review

15.91   Article 6 requires that in determining civil rights and obligations there be a fair hearing by an independent tribunal. This has been interpreted by the European Court as a full right of hearing by a court as to the determination of the civil rights and obligations.[96]

15.92   In order for a decision to be properly reviewable, the court must have full jurisdiction to review the decision and the review of the decision must be adequate.[97] This question is determined by reference to all the circumstances including the subject matter of the decision appealed against, the circumstances in which the decision was originally made and the nature of the dispute.[98] It will, therefore, not always be necessary for the appeal to provide for a complete rehearing of matters of fact and law.

15.93   For example, the position of a liquidator in the case of a compulsory winding up is that the decisions of that liquidator may be reviewed by the court under section 167 of the IA 1986. Section 168 of the IA 1986 provides that a person aggrieved by an act or decision of the liquidator may apply to the court and the court may confirm, reverse or modify the act or decision and make such order in the case as it thinks just. In practice, however, the threshold required to challenge an act or decision of the liquidator is that it must be so unreasonable that no reasonable man could have made it.[99]

15.94   This test is similar to the classic test for reviewing the reasonableness of decisions as set out in *Associated Provincial Picture Houses v. Wednesbury*.[1] It is questionable that a review along the *Wednesbury* principles is an adequate review to satisfy Article 6.[2] In many instances it will not be possible to review the decision of the liquidator as the decision will not be so unreasonable as to satisfy the threshold.

---

[96] *Le Compte, Van Leuven and De Meyer v. Belgium* (1981) 4 E.H.R.R. 1. See further paras 12.07 *et seq.*
[97] *Fisher v. Austria* (1995) 29 E.H.R.R. 340.
[98] *Bryan v. United Kingdom* (1995) 21 E.H.R.R. 342.
[99] *Re Edennote Ltd, Tottenham Hotspur Plc. v. Ryman* [1996] B.C.C. 718. See also *Leon v. York-O-Matic Ltd* [1966] 1 W.L.R. 1450.
[1] [1948] 1 KB 223.
[2] See *Smith and Grady v. U.K.* [2000] E.H.R.R. 493, where the court indicated that the *Wednesbury* test may not be appropriate since it requires so high a threshold of unreasonableness as to exclude consideration of proportionality and legitimate expectation. See also paras 10.141 *et seq.*

However, Robert Walker LJ drew a distinction in *Mitchell v. Buckingham* **15.95**
International Plc[3] between liquidators exercising their administrative powers and where they exercise quasi-judicial powers. Where they exercise
administrative powers the court should be slow to interfere with their
decision making. The situation is different where for example they take
decisions relating to the balancing of different creditors' claims.[4]

Following the decision in *R. v. Secretary of State for the Home Depart-* **15.96**
ment, ex parte Daly,[5] the position as to the applicable test for scrutinising
decisions where Convention rights are at stake has been clarified. The
correct approach is to subject the review or hearing to the test of proportionality rather than using *Wednesbury* reasonableness. Lord Steyn
explained the differences in the two types of review:

> "The starting point is that there is an overlap between the traditional
> grounds of review and the approach of proportionality. Most cases
> would be decided in the same way whichever approach is adopted.
> But the intensity of review is somewhat greater under the proportion-
> ality approach. Making due allowance for important structural differ-
> ences between various convention rights, which I do not propose to
> discuss, a few generalizations are perhaps permissible. I would men-
> tion three concrete differences without suggesting that my statement
> is exhaustive. First, the doctrine of proportionality may require the
> reviewing court to assess the balance which the decision maker has
> struck, not merely whether it is within the range of rational or reason-
> able decisions. Secondly, the proportionality test may go further than
> the traditional grounds of review inasmuch as it may require attention
> to be directed to the relative weight accorded to interests and con-
> siderations. Thirdly, even the heightened scrutiny test developed in *R
> v Ministry of Defence, Ex p Smith* [1996] QB 517, 554 is not neces-
> sarily appropriate to the protection of human rights."

In future the courts will have to take a more robust approach to consideration of the exercise of office-holders powers and ensure that their decisions satisfy the doctrine of proportionality.

---

[3] [1998] 2 B.C.L.C. 369.
[4] See also for the distinction between the two roles *Re Minotaur Data Systems Ltd* [1999] 1
W.L.R. 1129, [1999] B.P.I.R. 560; and *Mond v. Hyde* [1999] 2 W.L.R. 499. See further *Mitchell
v. Buckingham International plc.* [1998] 2 B.C.L.C. 369; *Re Greenhaven Motors Ltd* [1999] 1
B.C.L.C. 635.
[5] [2001] 2 W.L.R. 1622, HL.

CHAPTER 16
Property, Planning and Environment

1. INTRODUCTION

16.01   The aim of this chapter is to analyse the effect of the HRA in the property
sphere. It focuses primarily on the two Articles of the Convention which
impact most in this area: Article 8 (the right to respect for private and family
life); and Article 1 of Protocol No. 1 (the right to peaceful enjoyment of
possessions), with more peripheral consideration of Article 6 (the right to
a fair trial). Due to the broad scope of the rights protected by Article 8 and
Article 1 of Protocol No. 1, and in particular the key protected elements of
"respect" and "peaceful enjoyment", the result of this focus is to widen the
scope of this chapter beyond an analysis of the effect of the HRA on
"pure" or "real" property rights. The chapter accordingly incorporates
consideration of areas related to the ownership, use and enjoyment of
property such as privacy, planning and environmental law, expropriation of
property, intellectual property and nuisance. However, because Article 8 in
particular has considerable impact in areas far outside the property sphere
this chapter is not intended to be an exhaustive analysis of either Article of
the Convention for which reference should be made either to other parts
of this work or to more general texts.

The chapter is divided into two main sections: the first considers each of **16.02** the two Articles and their interpretation in so far as that may be relevant to the property sphere; the second addresses specific areas of impact in the broad property context. The chapter goes into some detail with regard to the general application of the two Articles considered, in particular Article 1 of Protocol No. 1. Although a general outline of the Articles is provided in Chapter 3,[1] it is not possible to understand the application of the Articles to a particular case without first having examined their general effect in some detail. Further, Article 1 of Protocol No. 1 has not been subjected to so extensive a scrutiny by the Court as have more frequently cited Articles such as Article 6. The number of cases in which examples of violation can be found is limited, and accordingly a sound foundation in general principles is necessary if Article 1 of Protocol No. 1 arguments are to be developed and used in the courts.

2. RELEVANT ARTICLES

Article 8—the Right to Respect for Private and Family Life

General

Rights of privacy before the HRA. Prior to the introduction of the **16.03** HRA there was no express or widely recognised right to privacy in English law.[2] However, the concept and protection of privacy had been taken into account in a number of cases.[3] There was also some indirect protection of privacy in specific areas such as the tort of trespass, and the laws relating to breach of confidence, data protection and police surveillance.[4] Specific attempts in the latter half of the twentieth century to consider or to introduce a statutory right to privacy foundered either at a preliminary phase or in the course of Parliamentary consideration.[5]

Vertical effect. Article 8 is intended primarily to be of vertical effect: **16.04** its primary object is to protect individuals from arbitrary infringement of their rights by a public authority.[6] It has no direct application between two

---

[1] See paras 3.94 *et seq.*, for consideration of Article 8, and paras 3.131 *et seq.* for consideration of Article 1 of Protocol No. 1.
[2] *e.g. Re X (A Minor)* [1975] Fam. 47 at 58; *Malone v. Metropolitan Police Comissioner* [1979] Ch. 344 at 372; *Kaye v. Robertson* [1991] F.S.R. 62; *R. v. Khan* [1997] A.C. 558 (particularly Lord Nolan at 570, *c.f.* Lord Browne-Wilkinson and Lord Slynn at 571 and Lord Nicholls at 582–583); *R. v. Brentwood Borough Council, ex p. Peck, The Times,* December 18, 1997.
[3] *e.g. Derby v. Weldon (No. 2), The Times,* October 20, 1998; *Haig v. Aitken* [2000] 3 All E.R. 80.
[4] For more detailed consideration of these and other areas of pre-existing indirect privacy protection see R. Clayton and H. Tomlinson, *The Law of Human Rights* (Oxford University Press, 2000), vol. 1, pp. 781–810, paras 12.09–12.80. In relation to data protection and surveillance see further paras 19.18 *et seq.,* below.
[5] *e.g.* in 1972 the Younger Committee on Privacy (established following a 1969 private members bill) voted by majority against the establishment of a general right to privacy; in the 1988–89 session of Parliament the Protection of Privacy Bill failed to reach its Third Reading.
[6] *Belgian Linguistic (No. 2)* (1979–80) 1 E.H.R.R. 252, para. 7; *Marckx v. Begium* (1979–80) 2 E.H.R.R. 330; *X and Y v. Netherlands* (1986) 8 E.H.R.R. 235; *Abdulaziz, Cabales and Balkandali v. United Kingdom* (1985) 7 E.H.R.R. 471; *Rees v, United Kingdom* (1987) 9 E.H.R.R. 56; *Keegan v. Ireland* (1994) 18 E.H.R.R. 342; *Hokkanen v. Finland* (1995) 19 E.H.R.R. 139; *Kroon v. Netherlands* (1995) 19 E.H.R.R. 263.

private individuals. However, the Court has made it clear that the Article is not limited to imposing only a negative obligation on public authorities not to interfere with individuals' rights. It also imposes positive obligations. As the Court stated in *Marckx v. Belgium*:

> "The object of the Article is essentially that of protecting the individual against arbitrary interference by public authorities. Nevertheless, it does not merely compel the State to abstain from interference: in addition to this primarily negative undertaking, there may be positive obligations inherent in an effective 'respect' for family life."[7]

Accordingly, in addition to requiring the state actively to respect the protected rights, the Article may also impose on public authorities an obligation to take positive action in appropriate circumstances to ensure that the protected rights of individuals are not affected by the actions of other individuals.[8] As the Court stated in *Botta v. Italy*:

> "These obligations may involve the adoption of measures designed to secure respect for private life even in the sphere of the relations of individuals between themselves."[9]

16.05   **The impact of Article 8 on the common law.**   Accordingly, whilst Article 8 does not introduce a specific and absolute right to privacy *per se*, it is considered to be an appropriate base from which such a right might be developed. In the course of the debates on the Human Rights Bill, the Lord Chancellor, Lord Irvine, stated:

> "I believe that the true view is that the courts will be able to adapt and develop the common law by relying on existing domestic principles in the laws of trespass, nuisance, copyright, confidence and the like to fashion a common law right to privacy"[10]

16.06   To a large extent this approach was adopted in *Douglas v. Hello! Ltd*,[11] the first case since the HRA came into force in which the right to privacy has been considered by the Court of Appeal. Two celebrities, Michael Douglas and Catherine Zeta Jones, having entered into an exclusive agreement with *OK!* magazine with regard to the publication of photographs from their wedding, sought an injunction to prevent *Hello!* magazine from publishing a series of unauthorised photographs taken at the wedding. At first instance Douglas, Zeta Jones and *OK!* magazine obtained an injunction to prevent publication. Although the Court of Appeal allowed the appeal by *Hello!* magazine and discharged the injunction, their Lordships made a number of comments regarding the right to privacy.

---

[7] (1979–80) 2 E.H.R.R. 330, para. 31. See also *X and Y v. Netherlands* (1986) 8 E.H.R.R. 235, para. 23.
[8] In addition see paras 16.119 *et seq.*, below.
[9] (1998) 26 E.H.R.R. 241, para 33; see also *X and Y v. Netherlands* (1986) 8 E.H.R.R. 235, para. 23; *Stjerna v. Finland* (1997) 24 E.H.R.R. 195, para. 38.
[10] *Hansard*, H.L. November 24, 1997, col. 785.
[11] [2001] 2 W.L.R. 992, *The Times*, 16 January, 2001, CA.

Brooke L.J. stated that it was well established that equity could intervene **16.07**
to prevent the publication of photographs taken in breach of confidence
and that such a confidence could arise on private occasions where it was
made clear either expressly or impliedly that no photographs were to be
taken or published. However, English law had to date been reluctant to
recognise an obligation of confidence where these conditions did not exist.
Under section 12(4) of the HRA, the court was obliged to take into account
"any relevant privacy code" which included the *Code of Practice* of the
Press Complaints Commission,[12] clause 3 of which concerned privacy. A
newspaper flouting clause 3 was likely to have its claim to an entitlement
to freedom of expression trumped by considerations of privacy under
Article 10(2) of the Convention. He was accordingly satisfied that the
claimants would be likely to be able to establish at trial that publication of
the photographs should not be allowed on confidentiality grounds, but felt
that the balance of convenience with regard to the continuation of the
injunction favoured *Hello!* magazine.

Sedley L.J. held that a point had been reached at which it could be said **16.08**
with confidence that the law recognised a right of personal privacy for two
reasons. First, equity and the common law were now in a position to affirm
that everybody had a right to some private space. The legal landscape had
altered since the 1991 decision of the Court of Appeal in *Kaye v. Robertson*,[13] when it had largely been accepted that English law recognised no
right of privacy. The right of privacy was grounded in the equitable doctrine
of breach of confidence and was not unqualified. However, a concept of
privacy accorded recognition to the fact that the law had to protect, not
only those people whose trust had been abused, but those who simply
found themselves subjected to an unwanted intrusion into their personal
lives. Secondly, the HRA required the courts to give appropriate effect to
the rights protected by Article 8.

Keene L.J. stated that it seemed unlikely that *Kaye v. Robertson*,[14] which **16.09**
held that there was no actionable right of privacy in English law, would be
decided the same way on that aspect today. Convention jurisprudence
acknowledged different degrees of privacy. In *Dudgeon v. United Kingdom*,[15] the Court ruled that the more intimate the aspect of private life
being interfered with, the more serious must be the reasons for interference. As Douglas and Zeta Jones had lessened the degree of privacy
by allowing widespread publicity of their wedding in *OK!* magazine the
balance between their rights and other considerations would be
affected.

It is therefore apparent that the legal landscape has altered since 1991, so
that a right of privacy arising out of the general law of breach of confidence
is now recognised. Article 8 may be considered one factor that has
influenced the change in the legal landscape, however it is clear that the
Court of Appeal prefer to develop any laws of privacy by the incremental

[12] November, 1997.
[13] [1991] F.S.R. 62.
[14] [1991] F.S.R. 62.
[15] (1982) 4 E.H.R.R. 149.

development of the common law and equity rather than through the wholesale adoption of an unlimited right to privacy.[15A]

Interpretation

16.10　　**Article 8.**　Article 8 of the Convention provides:

> "1. Everyone has the right to respect for his private and family life, his home and his correspondence.
>
> 2. There shall be no interference by a public authority with the exercise of this right except such as is in accordance with the law and is necessary in a democratic society in the interest of national security, public safety or the economic well-being of the country, for the prevention of disorder or crime, for the protection of health or morals, or for the protection of the rights and freedoms of others."

16.11　　**General.**　Article 8(1) sets out the absolute right protected by the Article. It is of key importance to note that the Article does not guarantee privacy, only "respect" for private and family life, the home and correspondence. Article 8(2) sets out the circumstances in which interference by a public authority with the absolute right is permissible. A potential infringement of Article 8 may arise either from a failure actively to ensure "respect" for private life or from a direct act of infringement by a public authority. In the latter case, the infringement may be justified only if it is carried out in accordance with the law and is "necessary in a democratic society" in pursuit of one of the legitimate aims named in Article 8(2).

(a) Article 8(1)

16.12　　**"Everyone".**　Unlike Article 1 of Protocol No. 1, Article 8 does not apply to "every natural or legal person", and therefore would not immediately appear to apply to any legal entities other than human victims of rights violations. It falls into the same category of rights as Article 2 (the right to life), Article 3 (the prohibition of torture), Article 4 (the prohibition of slavery and forced labour) and Article 5 (right to liberty and security) in using the term "everyone" (or "no one" as in Articles 3 and 4) to describe the potential "victim" for the purposes of the Convention. A company cannot be a victim of a violation of the right to life, of torture, or of a loss of liberty. However, the position of a company or corporation with regard to Article 8 rights of privacy is less clear cut. In *R. v. Broadcasting Standards Commission, ex p. BBC*,[16] Forbes J. at first instance concluded that "privacy", as referred to in section 107(1) of the Broadcasting Act 1996, when construed in accordance with Article 8 was a right available to natural persons only and not to companies or corporations. On appeal,

---

[15A] See also *Venables v. News Group Newspapers Ltd* [2001] 2 W.L.R. 1038; and the decision of Laurence Collins J. in *Heather Mills v. News Group Newspapers Ltd* (judgment handed down June 4, 2001, transcript from Casetrade).
[16] [2000] 3 W.L.R. 1327, CA.

overturning Forbes J., Lord Woolf stated that privacy under the Convention was not the same concept as that referred to in the Broadcasting Act 1996, and went on:

> "While the intrusions into the privacy of an individual which are possible are no doubt more extensive than the infringements of privacy which are possible in the case of a company, a company does have activities of a private nature which need protection from unwarranted intrusion. It would be a departure from proper standards if, for example, the BBC without any justification attempted to listen clandestinely to the activities of a board meeting. The same would be true of secret filming of the board meeting. The individual members of the board would no doubt have grounds for complaint, but so would the board and thus the company as a whole. The company has correspondence which it could justifiably regard as private and the broadcasting of the contents of that correspondence would be an intrusion on its privacy. It could not possibly be said that to hold such actions an intrusion of privacy conflicts with the ECHR."[17]

16.13 Although he also allowed the appeal, Lord Mustill expressed the view that an infringement of privacy was an intrusion into personal space or an affront to the personality, and that whilst a company or corporation might be entitled under breach of confidence provisions to protect its secrets, he saw that as "different from the esentially human and personal concept of privacy".[18] Whilst there can be no doubt that every natural person is accorded the protection of the Article, the debate with regard to companies and corporations remains open. The correct view is perhaps found in the middle ground hinted at by Lord Woolf, recognising that whilst companies and corporations may have rights of privacy in certain circumstances, by virtue of the distinctions of personality between a company and a human individual, the rights enjoyed by a company or corporation are not so absolute or extensive as those enjoyed by natural persons.

16.14 **"Respect".** Article 8 does not provide for the absolute protection of family and home life, the home and correspondence, only a guarantee of "respect" for them. As noted in paragraph 15.03 above, this imposes a dual burden on public authorities: to ensure that their own actions do not arbitrarily infringe the protected rights, and to take action to ensure the protection of those rights from interference by other parties.[19]

16.15 Public authorities will not be placed under a positive obligation to take steps to prevent or punish every infringement of the rights protected by Article 8. Whether such an obligation exists is likely to depend on many factors including the extent to which it would impose a burden on the state or public authority,[20] the importance of the rights requiring protection (for example whether they represent aspects "fundamental" or "essential" to

---

[17] [2000] 8 E.M.L.R. 587, at 599–600, para. 33.
[18] [2000] E.M.L.R. 587, at 605, para, 49.
[19] See, *e.g. Lopez-Ostra v. Spain* (1995) 20 E.H.R.R. 277, para. 51, where the Court stated that there was a positive duty to take reasonable and appropriate measures to secure Art. 8 rights.
[20] *Rees v. United Kingdom* (1987) 9 E.H.R.R. 56, paras 43–44.

private life),[21] whether there is any general consensus of approach to the issue in other Contracting States (although this aspect may have less significance when the Article is relied upon in domestic courts, see discussion of the margin of appreciation below),[22] the general practice of the particular state or public authority in relation to similar matters,[23] whether the obligation sought is narrowly defined or too broad to impose,[24] and the potential impact of such an obligation on other Convention rights.[25]

16.16   Examples of accepted positive obligations are the obligation to take steps to prevent crime,[26] to provide legal aid,[27] to provide a legal framework for the development of family ties and the integration of children into the family,[28] to provide actionable remedies for interference by the press,[29] and to provide protection from environmental harm.[30]

16.17   For understandable reasons, it has been said that the concept of "respect" is "not clear cut"[31] and that it belongs "more to the world of manners rather than the law".[32] The use of such a loose term, and the existence of widely varying social standards in the Contracting States, has resulted in the Court viewing the requirement of "respect" differently both from state to state and from case to case.[33] As the Court stated in *Botta v. Italy*:

> " . . . the concept of respect is not precisely defined. In order to determine whether such obligations exist, regard must be had to the fair balance that has to be struck between the general interest and the interests of the individual, while the state has, in any event, a margin of appreciation."[34]

16.18   This "margin of appreciation" is an essential element to the workings of an international tribunal such as the Court, and reflects an accepted understanding that the government of a particular state is often better placed than the Court to determine how best to implement the provisions of the Convention within the boundaries of that state.[35] Without the application of

---

[21] *Gaskin v. United Kingdom* (1990) 12 E.H.R.R. 36, para. 49; *X & Y v Netherlands* (1985) 8 E.H.R.R. 235.

[22] *B v. France* (1992) 16 E.H.R.R. 1, para. 48; *X, Y and Z v. United Kingdom* (1997) 24 E.H.R.R. 143, para. 52.

[23] *Rees v. United Kingdom* (1987) 9 E.H.R.R. 56, para. 42.

[24] *Botta v. Italy* (1998) 26 E.H.R.R. 241.

[25] *Winer v. United Kingdom*, Application No. 10871/84, (1986) 48 D.R. 154, in which the conflict between the right to privacy under Art. 8 with the right to freedom of expression under Art. 10 was considered.

[26] See, *e.g. X and Y v. Netherlands* (1985) 8 E.H.R.R. 235.

[27] In appropriate circumstances, see *Airey v. Ireland* (1979–80) 2 E.H.R.R. 305; *cf. Stewart-Brady v. United Kingdom* (1997) 24 E.H.R.R. C.D. 38.

[28] See, *e.g. Kroon v. Netherlands* (1994) 19 E.H.R.R. 263; *Marckx v. Belgium* (1979–80) 2 E.H.R.R. 330.

[29] *Earl and Countess Spencer v. United Kingdom* (1998) 25 E.H.R.R. C.D. 105 at 112.

[30] See, *e.g. Lopez Ostra v. Spain* (1995) 20 E.H.R.R. 277, para. 51. Positive obligations in the property sphere are discussed below. For a more detailed analysis of positive obligations generally and specifically those outside the property sphere, see B. Emmersson and J. Simor *Human Rights Practice* (Sweet & Maxwell, 2000) paras 8.040–8.051.

[31] *Abdulaziz, Cabales and Balkandali v. United Kingdom* (1985) 7 E.H.R.R. 471, para. 67.

[32] J.E.S. Fawcett, *The Application of the European Convention on Human Rights* (2nd ed., 1987), p. 211.

[33] *Abdulaziz, Cabales and Balkandali v. United Kingdom* (1985) 7 E.H.R.R. 471, para. 67.

[34] (1998) 26 E.H.R.R. 241, para. 33.

[35] For a more extensive detailed analysis of the margin of appreciation, see para. 4.22, above.

the margin of appreciation the Court might often be accused of imposing upon Contracting States the cultural and moral standards of the members of the Court without fully understanding or giving proper appreciation to the differences between Contracting States. The doctrine was summarised by the Court in a property context in *James v. United Kingdom*,[36] as follows:

> "Because of the their direct knowledge of their society and its needs, the national authorities are in principle better placed than the international judge to appreciate what is 'in the public interest' . . . The Court, finding it natural that the margin of appreciation available to the legislature in implementing social and economic policies should be a wide one, will respect the legislature's judgment as to what is 'in the public interest' unless that judgment be manifestly without reasonable foundation."[37]

The margin of appreciation is accordingly a necessary symptom of an **16.19** international tribunal which seeks to adjudicate a standard set of principles in widely varying social, cultural, economic, and religious contexts. Its place in the domestic context is less obvious. The courts of England and Wales, for example, exist within the same social, cultural, economic, and religious context as the Government of England and Wales. Certainly, their obligation to consider Strasbourg jurisprudence will require them to apply a form of "margin of appreciation" when considering judgments of the Court with regard to other Contracting States and their application to the domestic context. When considering the actions of the state or of a public authority within England and Wales in terms of potential infringement of Convention rights, however, the margin of appreciation cannot be applied as such.[38] Lord Hope recently explained in *R. v. D.P.P., ex p. Kebilene* that: "the technique is not available to national courts when they are considering Convention issues within their own countries".[39] The spirit of the doctrine, in allowing the Executive some lee-way in decision making, is likely to be followed,[40] however, in the application by the domestic courts of the principle of "proportionality".[41] As Lord Hope went on to explain in *Kebilene*:

> "The questions which the courts will have to decide . . . will involve questions of balance between competing interests and issues of proportionality . . . In some circumstances it will be appropriate for the courts to recognise that there is an area of judgment within which the judiciary will defer, on democratic grounds, to the considered opinion

---

[36] (1986) 8 E.H.R.R. 123.
[37] *ibid.*, at 142, para. 46.
[38] For discussion on this point see D.R. Jean Howell, 'Land and Human Rights', The Conveyancer [1999] 287 at 289–291.
[39] [1999] 3 W.L.R. 972 at 993.
[40] See, *e.g. R. v. Secretary of State for the Home Department, ex p. Brind* [1991] 1 A.C. 696 at 151, *per* Lord Templeman.
[41] Namely, that there be a reasonable relationship between the particular objective to be achieved and the means employed to achieve that objective. This principle is considered in greater detail at paras 4.38 *et seq.*, above.

of the elected body or person whose act or decision is said to be incompatible with the Convention."[42]

16.20   **"Private and family life".**   "Private life" is broadly defined to protect the moral, physical and psychological integrity of the individual. It is intended to ensure the development of the personality of each individual both privately and in his relations with other human beings without outside interference or unwanted publicity or attention.[43] In *Niemetz v. Germany* the Court stated:

> "The Court does not consider it possible or necessary to attempt an exhaustive definition of the notion of 'private life'. However, it would be too restrictive to limit the notion to an 'inner circle' in which an individual may choose to live his personal life as he chooses and to exclude entirely the outside world not encompassed within that circle. Respect for private life must also comprise to a certain degree the right to establish and develop relationships with other human beings.
>
> There appears furthermore, to be no reason in principle why this understanding of the notion of 'private life' should be taken to exclude the activities of a professional or business nature since it is, after all, in the course of their working lives that the majority of people have a significant, if not the greatest opportunity of developing relationships with the outside world."[44]

16.21   The scope of an individual's "private life" is not without limits: it does not extend to his entire immediate surroundings and does not necessarily encompass every aspect of his life that he might wish to keep private.[45] The right to respect for an individual's private life will be narrower when it is either brought into contact with public life or in conflict with other protected interests.[46] From a property perspective, the right to private life is not generally considered to be limited only to those areas in which an individual has exclusive rights of occupancy,[47] but extends to those areas in which he has a reasonable expectation of privacy.[48]

16.22   Accordingly "private life" can be taken to include an individual's moral and physical integrity, his personal identity and sexuality, his personal information, and most importantly for the purposes of this chapter, his personal and private space.

16.23   The right to respect for "family life" protects family relationships and matters essential to those relationships. Although the Court has stated that "family life" does not include only social, moral or cultural relations

---

[42] [1999] 3 W.L.R. 972 at 994.

[43] See *X v. Iceland* (1976) 5 D.R. 86; *Bruggeman and Scheuten v. Germany,* Application No. 6959/75 (1977) 10 D.R. 100; *DeKlerck v. Belgium,* Application No. 8307/78 (1980) 21 D.R. 116; *X and Y v. Netherlands* (1986) 8 E.H.R.R. 235, paras 22–27; *Botta v. Italy* (1998) 26 E.H.R.R. 241.

[44] (1993) 16 E.H.R.R. 97, para. 29.

[45] *X v. Iceland* (1976) 5 D.R. 86.

[46] *Bruggeman and Scheuten v. Germany* (1981) 3 E.H.R.R. 244, paras 55–58.

[47] Although on this point, see *Friedl v. Austria* (1996) 21 E.H.R.R. 83, paras 48–51, and *Murray v. United Kingdom* (1995) 19 E.H.R.R. 193.

[48] *Halford v. United Kingdom* (1997) 24 E.H.R.R. 523.

and may include interests of a material kind if they are an essential element of family life,[49] it is otherwise of limited relevance to this chapter.

"Home". The term "home" has been given a wide interpretation. **16.24** Although generally the "home" is understood to mean the place where an individual lives on a settled basis,[50] that is not its absolute limitation and it can be applied to a wide variety of properties and forms of occupation. An individual is not limited to one "home" and whether a property can be considered to be an individual's "home" for the purposes of Article 8 will depend on the nature and extent of the ties between the individual and the property concerned.[51] It can include a holiday home.[52] An individual can establish a "home" in a property in which he or she has no proprietary right or interest.[53] Conversely, the mere fact that an individual has a proprietary interest in land or property does not necessarily make it his or her "home".[54] A "home" does not have to have been lawfully established to attract the protection of Article 8.[55] However, the fact that an individual has no legal entitlement to occupy a property may mean that it is not his or her "home".[56] The fact that a residential property is also used for business purposes does not preclude it from being a "home". However, whilst some business premises may also fall within the definition (for example a professional person's office), a property used solely for work purposes is not likely to attract Article 8 protection as a "home".[57]

In *Loizidou v. Turkey*,[58] the applicant sought to assert that he had a **16.25** "home" for the purposes of Article 8 on land where he planned to build a house, in an area in which his family had its roots but where he no longer lived. The Court held that the fact that the applicant intended to build a property on the land was not sufficient to make it his "home", nor was it his "home" by virtue of the fact that his family had its origins in the area.[59]

In *Gillow v. United Kingdom*,[60] the applicants sought to assert that a **16.26** property owned by them on Guernsey was their "home" despite the fact that they had not lived there for almost 19 years. The Court held that the fact that the couple had kept the property furnished, that they had sold their other property in England, and that they had always intended to

---

[49] *Marckx v. Belgium* (1979–80) 2 E.H.R.R. 330, paras 51–53. See also *Stoutt v. Ireland*, Application No. 10978/84 (1986) 49 D.R. 144 at 155–156.
[50] *Murray v. United Kingdom* (1995) 19 E.H.R.R. 193, paras 84–96.
[51] *Gillow v. United Kingdom* (1989) 11 E.H.R.R. 335; *Mabey v. United Kingdom*, Application No. 28370/95 (1996) 22 E.H.R.R. C.D. 123.
[52] *Kanthak v. Germany* (1988) 58 D.R. 94, Eur Comm HR.
[53] *Cyprus v. Turkey*, Application Nos 6780/74 and 6950/75 (1982) 4 E.H.R.R. 482; *Akdivar v. Turkey* (1997) 23 E.H.R.R. 143.
[54] *Loizidou v. Turkey* (1997) 23 E.H.R.R. 513.
[55] *Buckley v. United Kingdom* (1997) 23 E.H.R.R. 101.
[56] *S v. United Kingdom*, Application No. 11716/85 (1986) 47 D.R. 274.
[57] *Niemietz v. Germany* (1993) 16 E.H.R.R. 97. See also *R v. Austria*, Application No. 12592/86 (1989) 60 D.R. 201; *Botka and Paya v. Austria*, Application No. 15882/89 (1993) 74 D.R. 48; *Cremieux v. France* (1993) 16 E.H.R.R. 357; *Funke v. France* (1993) 16 E.H.R.R. 297; *Miaihe v. France* (1993) 16 E.H.R.R. 332; *Kopp v. Switzerland* (1999) 27 E.H.R.R. 91.
[58] (1997) 23 E.H.R.R. 513.
[59] *Loizidou v. Turkey* (1997) 23 E.H.R.R. 513, para. 66.
[60] (1989) 11 E.H.R.R. 335.

return to the property to live there permanently demonstrated sufficient ties to the property to enjoy respect of it as their "home".[61]

16.27   In *Buckley v. United Kingdom*,[62] a gypsy occupied a mobile home sited on her own land. The mobile home required planning permission but the applicant had neither sought nor obtained the requisite permission. Accordingly the mobile home was not a lawful residence. However, the Court held that as the applicant had lived there continuously for five years, intended to remain there and had no residence elsewhere, the mobile home satisfied the definition of a "home" for the purposes of Article 8.[63]

16.28   In *S v. United Kingdom*,[64] the applicant continued to occupy a local authority property after the death of her partner to whom the property had actually been rented. As she had no legal entitlement to do so the Commission held that the property was not her "home".

16.29   In *Niemietz v. Germany*,[65] the Court considered whether business premises could be a "home" for the purposes of Article 8 and stated that:

> "As regards the word 'home' appearing in the English text of Article 8, the Court observes that in certain contracting states, notably Germany . . . it has been accepted as extending to business premises. Such an interpretation is, moreover, fully consonant with the French text, since the word 'domicile' has a broader connotation than the word 'home' and may extend, for example, to a professional person's office."[66]

16.30   In *Pentidis v. Greece*,[67] the Court considered whether public places could be within the definition of a "home". The premises in question were a meeting room which had been hired out for weddings and meetings. The Court concluded that the meeting room was not a "home". Premises that are freely accessible to the public and used for purposes of a not purely private nature may accordingly fall outside the definition of a "home" for the purposes of Article 8.

16.31   Article 8 only creates a right to respect for the home and not an absolute right to a home or to be provided with a home[68]: whether a state provides funds to enable everyone to have a home is a matter for political not

---

[61] See also *Wiggins v. United Kingdom*, Application No. 7456/76 (1978) 13 D.R. 40; *Z.A. I.M.A. v. Austria*, Application No. 11332/85.

[62] (1996) 23 E.H.R.R. 101.

[63] *Buckley v. United Kingdom* (1997) 23 E.H.R.R. 101, para. 54. That a caravan occupied in breach of planning requirements can be a "home" for the purposes of Art. 8 appears to have been accepted without question in a series of gypsy cases, *e.g. Beard v. United Kingdom*, Application No. 24882/94 (1998) 25 E.H.R.R. C.D. 28; *Chapman v. United Kingdom*, Application No. 27238/95 (1998) 25 E.H.R.R. C.D. 64; *Coster v. United Kingdom*, Application No. 24876/94 (1998) 25 E.H.R.R. C.D. 24; *Lee v. United Kingdom*, Application No. 25289/94 (1998) 25 E.H.R.R. C.D. 46; *Jane Smith v. United Kingdom*, Application No. 25154/94 (1998) 25 E.H.R.R. C.D. 42 (the judgment of the Court in relation to this group of cases is reported in *The Times*, 30 January, 2001).

[64] Application No. 11716/85 (1986) 47 D.R. 274.

[65] (1993) 16 E.H.R.R. 97.

[66] *Niemietz v. Germany* (1993) 16 E.H.R.R. 97, para. 30.

[67] (1997) 24 E.H.R.R. C.D. 1.

[68] *X v. Germany* (1956) 1 Y.B. 202

judicial decision.[69] In *X v. Germany*,[70] the Court held that failure to provide a refugee with a decent home did not constitute a breach of Article 8. There is no positive obligation on the state to provide alternative accommodation of an applicant's choosing.[71] Thus, the Court has refused to accept that, where statistically the number of gypsies is greater than the number of places available in authorised gypsy sites, decisions not to allow the applicants to occupy land where they wished to install their caravans constituted a violation of Article 8. Further, the Court has not accepted that Article 8 imposes a positive obligation to make available to the gypsy community an adequate number of suitably equipped sites.[72]

Respect for the home goes further than the mere integrity of home life, **16.32** what is intended to be covered is the physical security of a person's living quarters and possessions.[73] This includes the ability to live freely in the home and to enjoy it,[74] and accordingly goes beyond the mere right to possess it.[75]

"Correspondence". The term "correspondence" incorporates all **16.33** forms of private communication including by letter,[76] telephone,[77] and private radio transmitters.[78] The right to respect for correspondence protects the basic right to communicate, the right to communicate without interference, and the confidentiality of communications. Unsurprisingly the most common areas in which allegations of interference with correspondence arise are prisoner correspondence, telephone tapping, and searches and seizures.

Preventing a prisoner from contacting a solicitor is an infringement of **16.34** Article 8 even though there is no interference with any specific commu-

---

[69] This is a well established principle but for a recent decision in which it was repeated see the decision of the Court in the group of gypsy cases against the United Kingdom of *Beard, Chapman, Coster, Lee, and Jane Smith* reported in *The Times*, January 30, 2001.

[70] (1956) 1 Y.B. 202

[71] *Burton v. United Kingdom*, Application No. 31600/96 (1996) 22 E.H.R.R. C.D. 134; *Buckley v. United Kingdom* (1997) 23 E.H.R.R. 101.

[72] See *Beard v. United Kingdom*, Application No. 24882/94 (1998) 25 E.H.R.R. C.D. 28; *Chapman v. United Kingdom*, Application No. 27238/95 (1998) 25 E.H.R.R. C.D. 64; *Coster v. United Kingdom*, Application No. 24876/94, (1998) 25 E.H.R.R. C.D. 24; *Lee v. United Kingdom*, Application No. 25289/94 (1998) 25 E.H.R.R. C.D. 46; *Jane Smith v. United Kingdom*, Application No. 25154/94 (1998) 25 E.H.R.R. C.D. 42 ; particularly the judgment of the Court in relation to this group of cases as reported in *The Times*, 30 January, 2001.

[73] *Gillow v. United Kingdom* (1989) 11 E.H.R.R. 335; *Selcuk and Asker v. Turkey* (1998) 26 E.H.R.R. 477.

[74] *Lopez Ostra v. Spain* (1995) 20 E.H.R.R. 277; *Guerra v. Italy* (1998) 26 E.H.R.R. 357.

[75] *Howard v. United Kingdom* (1987) 52 D.R. 198.

[76] *Silver v. United Kingdom* (1983) 5 E.H.R.R. 347.

[77] *Klass v. Germany* (1979–80) 2 E.H.R.R. 214. See also *Margareta and Roger Andersson v. Sweden* (1992) 14 E.H.R.R. 615; *Lüdi v. Switzerland* (1993) 15 E.H.R.R. 173; *Halford v. United Kingdom* (1997) 24 E.H.R.R. 523; *Kopp v. Switzerland* (1999) 27 E.H.R.R. 91.

[78] *X and Y v. Belgium*, Application No. 8962/80 (1982) 28 D.R. 112.

nication.[79] Stopping,[80] supervising,[81] screening or scrutinising,[82] censoring[83] and failing to forward[84] prisoners' letters have all been found to be interferences with the Article 8 protection.

16.35 House searches and seizures of documents raise Article 8 issues. With regard to seizure of documents, the protection of Article 8 is not limited to certain types of "correspondence", nor does the correspondence in question have to be "personal" to attract protection. In *Niemietz v. Germany*,[85] Article 8 was applied to professional documents seized from a lawyer's offices.

16.36 Legislation permitting telephone surveillance[86] or the establishment of a system for the secret surveillance of telephone communications[87] in themselves constitute infringements of Article 8 rights whether or not the applicant can demonstrate a particular infringement. In *Halford v. United Kingdom*,[88] the Court held that personal telephone calls made on a private line at work were "correspondence" attracting the protection of Article 8.

16.37 Article 8 does not impose a positive obligation on the state to provide a faultless postal delivery system.[89]

(b) Article 8(2)

16.38 **General.** Article 8(2) sets up the possibility of justifiable interference by a public authority with the rights protected by Article 8(1). In order to be justifiable the interference must be carried out in accordance with the law and it must be necessary in a democratic society in pursuit of one of the specified legitimate aims: national security; public safety; the economic well-being of the country; the prevention of disorder of crime; the protection of health or morals; the protection of the rights and freedoms of others. Article 8(2) is to be narrowly interpreted,[90] and the reasons for any interference must be convincingly established.[91]

16.39 **"In accordance with the law".** This gives rise to a number of requirements.[92] The interference being challenged must have a basis in

---

[79] *Golder v. United Kingdom* (1979–80) 1 E.H.R.R. 524, paras 41–45.
[80] *Silver v. United Kingdom* (1983) 5 E.H.R.R. 347; *McCallum v. United Kingdom* (1991) 13 E.H.R.R. 597.
[81] *De Wilde, Ooms and Versyp v. Belgium (No 1)* (1979–80) 1 E.H.R.R. 373.
[82] *Campbell v. United Kingdom* (1993) 15 E.H.R.R. 137; *Herczegfalvy v. Austria* (1993) 15 E.H.R.R. 437.
[83] *Pfeifer and Plankl v. Austria* (1992) 14 E.H.R.R. 692; *Niedbala v. Poland*, Application No. 27915/95 (Comm. Rep 1.3.99).
[84] *Schönenberger and Durmaz v. Switzerland* (1989) 11 E.H.R.R. 202, para. 23; *Messina v. Italy* Series A No. 257–H (1993).
[85] (1993) 16 E.H.R.R. 97.
[86] *Klass v. Germany* (1979–80) 2 E.H.R.R. 214.
[87] *Malone v. United Kingdom* (1984) 7 E.H.R.R. 14.
[88] (1997) 24 E.H.R.R. 523, paras 53–58.
[89] *X v. Germany*, Application No. 8383/78 (1979) 17 D.R. 227.
[90] *Klass v. Germany* (1979–80) 2 E.H.R.R. 214.
[91] *Funke v. France* (1993) 16 E.H.R.R. 297, para. 55. See also *Silver v. United Kingdom* (1983) 5 E.H.R.R. 347; *Olsson v. Sweden* (1989) 11 E.H.R.R. 259; *Dudgeon v. United Kingdom* (1982) 4 E.H.R.R. 149.
[92] For a more detailed consideration of this issue, see paras 4.43 *et seq.*, above.

domestic law.[93] It is not necessary for the law to be statutory,[94] it can be based in the common law whether written or unwritten.[95] However, the mere existence of a domestic law is not sufficient, as the "quality" of the law itself must be subjected to scrutiny. There must be adequate and effective safeguards in the law to protect against arbitrary interferences by public authorities with the rights guaranteed by the Article.[96] The law must be accessible to the persons concerned, and formulated with sufficient precision to enable an individual to foresee, to a reasonable degree, the consequences which a given action may entail.[97] The mere fact that a law entails the exercise of a discretion does not, of itself, make it incompatible with the requirement of foreseeability provided that the scope of the discretion and the manner of its exercise are indicated with sufficient clarity to provide adequate protection against arbitrary interference.[98]

"Necessary in a democratic society". "Necessary" does not **16.40** mean "indispensable" but equally is not so flexible as to mean "admissible", "ordinary", "useful", "reasonable" or "desirable".[99] It requires the public authority to demonstrate that the interference responds to a "pressing social need", that it pursues a legitimate aim and that the interference is proportionate to the legitimate aim pursued.[1] The principle of proportionality requires that there be a reasonable relationship between a particular objective to be achieved and the means used to achieve that objective.[2] The extent to which the interference restricts the right is important, and an interference that impairs the very essence of the right should be regarded as being disproportionate.[3]

The reasons put forward to justify any interference must be relevant and **16.41** sufficiently persuasive.[4] Such reasons must therefore accord with what is understood to be meant by the concept of a democratic society. The Court has held that the hallmarks of a "democratic society" are tolerance,

---

[93] *Leander v. Sweden* (1987) 9 E.H.R.R. 433, para. 50; *Margareta and Roger Andersson v. Sweden* (1992) 14 E.H.R.R. 615; *A v. France* (1993) 17 E.H.R.R. 462; *Murray v. United Kingdom* (1995) 19 E.H.R.R. 193, para. 88.

[94] Although statutory laws (*Norris v. Ireland* (1988) 13 E.H.R.R. 186) and non-statutory enactments (*Golder v. United Kingdom* (1979–80) 1 E.H.R.R. 524) are clearly covered.

[95] See, *e.g. Dudgeon v. United Kingdom* (1982) 4 E.H.R.R. 149, para. 44; *Malone v. United Kingdom* (1985) 7 E.H.R.R. 14; *Chappell v. United Kingdom* (1990) 12 E.H.R.R. 1, para. 56; *Huvig v. France* (1990) 12 E.H.R.R. 528, para. 28; *Kruslin v. France* (1990) 12 E.H.R.R. 547, para. 29.

[96] See, *e.g. Malone v. United Kingdom* (1985) 7 E.H.R.R. 14; *Chappell v. United Kingdom* (1990) 12 E.H.R.R. 1.

[97] *Olsson v. Sweden (No. 1)* (1989) 11 E.H.R.R. 259. See also *Sunday Times v. United Kingdom* (1979–80) 2 E.H.R.R. 245, para. 49, where this point was considered in the context of Art. 10(2).

[98] *Malone v. United Kingdom* (1985) 7 E.H.R.R. 14, paras 68 and 79; *Silver v. United Kingdom* (1983) 5 E.H.R.R. 347, para. 88.

[99] *Handyside v. United Kingdom* (1979–80) 1 E.H.R.R. 737, para. 48.

[1] *Handyside v. United Kingdom* (1979–80) 1 E.H.R.R. 737, paras 48–50; *Dudgeon v. United Kingdom* (1982) 4 E.H.R.R. 149, paras 50–53; *Silver v. United Kingdom* (1983) 5 E.H.R.R. 347, para. 97; *Gillow v. United Kingdom* (1989) 11 E.H.R.R. 335, para. 55; *Leander v. Sweden* (1987) 9 E.H.R.R. 433, para. 58; *Olsson v. Sweden (No. 1)* (1989) 11 E.H.R.R. 259; *Schönenberger and Durmaz v. Switzerland* (1989) 11 E.H.R.R. 202, para. 27; *Campbell v. United Kingdom* (1993) 15 E.H.R.R. 137.

[2] For a detailed consideration of the requirement of "proportionality", see paras 4.38 *et seq.*, above.

[3] *Belgian Linguistic Case* (1979–80) 1 E.H.R.R. 252 at 281, para. 5.

[4] *Olsson v. Sweden* (1989) 11 E.H.R.R. 259, para. 68; *Dudgeon v. United Kingdom* (1982) 4 E.H.R.R. 149, para. 54.

pluralism and broadmindedness.[5] The more intimate the area of private life interfered with the stronger will need to be the reasons required to justify it.[6]

16.42   The issue of what is "necessary in a democratic society" is discussed in more detail elsewhere in this work,[7] as are the majority of the legitimate aims set out in Article 8(2).[8] Except for the ground of "the economic well-being of the country", the remaining legitimate aims are repeated in at least two of Articles 9 to 11 of the Convention. The ground of "the economic well-being of the country" is only found in Article 8(2) and has been relied upon to justify, amongst other things: the operation of an international airport[9]; the control by the authorities on Guernsey of the number of inhabitants on the island[10]; and the disclosure of medical records for the purposes of assessing a social security claim.[11]

Article 1 of Protocol No. 1—the Right to the Peaceful Enjoyment of Possessions

General

16.43   **Rights of property prior to the HRA.**   Unlike the right of privacy, rights to ownership of property and rights of enjoyment of possessions have always formed a fundamental part of the common law.[12]

16.44   **The primary area of impact of Article 1 of Protocol No. 1.**   The Court has explained that the Article guarantees the right of property:

> "By recognising that everyone has the right to the peaceful enjoyment of his possessions, Article 1 is in substance guaranteeing the right of property. This is the clear impression left by the words 'possessions' and 'use of property' (in French: *biens, propriété, usage des biens*); the drafters continually spoke of 'right of property' or 'right to property' to describe the subject matter of the successive drafts which were the forerunners to the present Article 1. Indeed, the right to dispose of one's property constitutes a traditional and fundamental aspect of the right of property."[13]

16.45   This right of property encapsulates both the right of disposal of property and the owner's right to use his property as he wishes. The Article is,

---

[5] *Handyside v. United Kingdom* (1979–80) 1 E.H.R.R. 737, para. 49 ; *Dudgeon v. United Kingdom* (1982) 4 E.H.R.R. 149, para. 53; *Young, James and Webster v. United Kingdom* (1982) 4 E.H.R.R. 38, para. 63.
[6] See, *e.g. Dudgeon v. United Kingdom* (1982) 4 E.H.R.R. 149 (concerning the maintenance of criminal punishment for homosexual acts in Northern Ireland after their abolition in the rest of the U.K.); *Lustig-Prean and Beckett v. United Kingdom* (1999) 7 B.H.R.C. 65; *Smith and Grady v. United Kingdom* (2000) 29 E.H.R.R. 493 (both of which concern investigations into homosexuality in the armed forces).
[7] See paras 4.34 *et seq.*, above.
[8] See paras 3.101 *et seq.*, above.
[9] *Powell & Rayner v. United Kingdom* (1990) 12 E.H.R.R. 355.
[10] *Gillow v. United Kingdom* (1989) 11 E.H.R.R. 335.
[11] *M S v. Sweden* (1999) 28 E.H.R.R. 313.
[12] For a detailed analysis of the right in English law before the HRA, see R. Clayton and H. Tomlinson, *The Law of Human Rights* (Oxford University Press, 2000), vol. 1, pp. 1293–1301, paras 18.04–18.25.
[13] *Marckx v. Belgium* (1979–80) 2 E.H.R.R. 330, para. 63.

however, concerned primarily to protect an individual's property against arbitrary interference by the state or, under the HRA, public authorities. In *Bramelid and Malmström v. Sweden*,[14] the Commission stated as follows when commenting on that part of the Article concerned with deprivation of possessions:

> "Even though the word 'expropriated' does not appear in the text, the terms of this provision, in particular the words 'deprived of his possessions . . . in the public interest' as well as the reference to 'the general principles of international law' show clearly that it relates to expropriation, whether formal or *de facto*, that is to say the act by which the state seizes—or gives another the right to seize—a specific asset to be used for realisation of a goal in the public interest."[15]

Accordingly, responsibility arises where the state interferes with property **16.46** rights or provides for another party to be able to do so.[16] The Article is not concerned with relationships between private individuals of a purely contractual nature.[17] Nor will the state generally be held responsible for the regulation of private law matters and rights unless it has used its authority in some way to interfere with them.[18] The fact that a court has judicially determined the outcome of a private dispute does not necessarily constitute an interference by the state.[19]

Interpretation

Article 1 of Protocol No. 1. Article 1 of Protocol No. 1 provides: **16.47**

> "Every natural or legal person is entitled to the peaceful enjoyment of his possessions. No one shall be deprived of his possessions except in the public interest and subject to the conditions provided for by law and by the general principles of international law.
> The preceding provisions shall not, however, in any way impair the right of a State to enforce such laws as it deems necessary to control the use of property in accordance with the general interest or to secure the payment of taxes or other contributions or penalties."

General. The Article has been interpreted as encapsulating three **16.48** distinct rules. In *Sporrong and Lönnroth v. Sweden*,[20] the Court explained the rules as follows:

> "The first rule, which is of a general nature, enounces the principle of peaceful enjoyment of property; it is set out in the first sentence of the first paragraph. The second rule covers deprivation of possessions

---

[14] (1983) 5 E.H.R.R. 249.
[15] *Bramelid and Malmström v. Sweden* (1983) 5 E.H.R.R. 249 at 255.
[16] See, *e.g. S v. United Kingdom*, Application No. 10741/84 (1984) 41 D.R. 226; *James v. United Kingdom* (1986) 8 E.H.R.R. 123.
[17] *Gustaffson v. Sweden* (1996) 22 E.H.R.R. 409, para. 60.
[18] *H v. United Kingdom*, Application No. 10000/82 (1983) 33 D.R. 247; *Bramelid and Malmström v. Sweden* (1983) 5 E.H.R.R. 249.
[19] *Ruiz Mateos v. United Kingdom*, Application No. 13021/87 (1988) 57 D.R. 268.
[20] (1983) 5 E.H.R.R. 35.

and subjects it to certain conditions; it appears in the second sentence of the same paragraph. The third rule recognises that the states are entitled, amongst other things, to control the use of property in accordance with the general interest, by enforcing such laws as they deem necessary for the purpose; it is contained in the second paragraph. The Court must determine, before considering whether the first rule was complied with, whether the last two are applicable."[21]

16.49 The three rules are not "distinct" in the sense of being unconnected. The Court has stated, in *James v. United Kingdom*,[22] that the second and third rules are "concerned with particular instances of interference with the right to peaceful enjoyment of possessions" and must be construed in the light of the first rule.[23]

16.50   **"Every natural and legal person".** As noted above Article 1 of Protocol No. 1 uses this phrase in place of the "everyone" found in Article 8. It is the only Article of the Convention to make reference to legal persons. In the case of Article 1 of Protocol No. 1 it is clear, therefore, that companies and corporations can be victims of infringements of the rights protected by the Article. The crucial questions are whether the individual or company concerned has a right to the property in question,[24] and whether the individual or company concerned is the true "victim" of the infringement. To satisfy this latter question (the "victim" test), it is not sufficient for the individual concerned simply to allege that the mere existence of a law violates his rights. He must demonstrate that he is "directly affected" by the relevant act or omission in the absence of any specific measure of implementation.[25] It is not necessary, however, where his rights have been breached, for the individual to demonstrate that he has suffered a detriment or been prejudiced,[26] although that fact might obviously impact on the availability and extent of any compensation.[27]

16.51 In *Agrotexim v. Greece*, the Commission had come to the view that a fall in the value of a company's shares, caused by an interference with the company's property rights, constituted an infringement of the shareholders' rights. In the light of the potentially differing and competing interests between groups of shareholders and the board of directors, the Court,[28] in rejecting this view, felt that such an approach would run the risk of creating difficulties in determining who was actually entitled to bring any action based on the alleged infringement. The Court indicated that it would not normally pierce the corporate veil to permit shareholders to bring applications alleging infringement of Article 1 of Protocol No. 1 rights as the company was the true "victim" not the shareholders:

---

[21] *Sporrong and Lönnroth v. Sweden* (1983) 5 E.H.R.R. 35, para. 61.
[22] (1986) 8 E.H.R.R. 123, para. 37.
[23] See also *AGOSI v. United Kingdom* (1987) 9 E.H.R.R. 1, para. 48; *Iatridis v. Greece* (1999) 30 E.H.R.R. 97, para. 55.
[24] *X, Y and Z v. Germany*, Application No. 8387/78 (1980) 19 D.R. 233; *Pentidis v. Greece* (1997) 24 E.H.R.R. C.D. 1.
[25] *Klass v. Germany* (1979–80) 2 E.H.R.R. 214.
[26] See, *e.g. Campbell and Cosans v. United Kingdom* (1982) 4 E.H.R.R. 293; *Eckle v. Germany* (1983) 5 E.H.R.R. 1; *Bowman v. United Kingdom* (1998) 26 E.H.R.R. 1.
[27] See, *e.g. Eckle v. Germany* (1983) 5 E.H.R.R. 1, para. 66; *Adolf v. Austria* (1982) 4 E.H.R.R. 313, para. 37; *Amuur v. France* (1996) 22 E.H.R.R. 533, para. 36.
[28] Decision reported at (1996) 21 E.H.R.R. 250.

"The piercing of the 'corporate veil' . . . will be justified only in exceptional circumstances, in particular where it is clearly established that it is impossible for the company to apply to the Convention institutions through the organs set up under its Articles of incorporation or—in the event of liquidation—through its liquidators."[29]

An association may bring a claim whether it is incorporated or unin- **16.52** corporated.[30] It may bring a claim either on its own behalf or on behalf of its members. When it does so on behalf of its members it must be able to identify the members it represents and demonstrate that each member represented has given specific instructions to the association to act on his or her behalf.[31]

Its wide wording also affords children the protection of Article 1 of Protocol **16.53** No. 1.[32]

"Possessions". This is an autonomous term and therefore will not **16.54** necessarily be limited to domestic concepts of what constitutes a possession.[33] In the French language version of the Convention the term used; "*biens*", is a very much wider concept incorporating all property rights and interests susceptible to appropriation. The term is not synonymous with ownership,[34] and property may be an individual's possession even where the ownership of it is in dispute.[35]

In order to demonstrate that something is his "possession" for the pur- **16.55** poses of the Article, an individual must demonstrate the existence of a property right and his entitlement to enjoy it.[36] The property right must be of real economic value, but its actual value need not have been ascertained. The term includes only "existing possessions".[37] Mere expectations are insufficient. It therefore does not include any right to acquire[38] or inherit[39] property at some unknown point in the future. Nor does it include a right to future revenue or income[40] unless it has already been earned or

---

[29] *Agrotexim v. Greece* (1996) 21 E.H.R.R. 250, para. 66.

[30] *Könkämä and 38 other Saami Villages v. Sweden*, Application No. 27033/95 (1996) 87–A D.R. 78.

[31] *Zentralrat Deutscher Sinti und Roma and Rose v. Germany* (1997) 23 E.H.R.R. C.D. 209.

[32] *Inze v. Austria* (1988) 10 E.H.R.R. 394.

[33] *Gasus Dösier-und-Fördertechnik GmbH v. Netherlands* (1995) 20 E.H.R.R. 403, para. 53; *Holy Monasteries v. Greece* (1995) 20 E.H.R.R. 1, paras 69–71; *Matos e Silva, Lda. v. Portugal* (1997) 24 E.H.R.R. 573, para. 75; *Beyeler v. Italy*, Application No. 33202/96 (Judgment January 5, 2000), para. 100.

[34] *Matos e Silva, Lda. v. Portugal* (1997) 24 E.H.R.R. 573, para. 75.

[35] *Inze v. Austria*, Application No. 8695/79 (1986) 8 E.H.R.R. 498, (1988) 10 E.H.R.R. 394.

[36] *S v. United Kingdom* (1986) 47 D.R. 274 at 279; *Agneessens v. Belgium* (1988) 58 D.R. 63.

[37] *Marckx v. Belgium* (1979–80) 2 E.H.R.R. 330, para. 50; *Van der Mussele v. Belgium* (1983) 6 E.H.R.R. 163, para. 48.

[38] *British American Tobacco Company Ltd v. Netherlands* (1996) 21 E.H.R.R. 409, paras 72–74; *Batelaan and Huiges v. Netherlands* (1984) 41 D.R. 170.

[39] *Marckx v. Belgium* (1979–80) 2 E.H.R.R. 330, para. 50.

[40] *Batelaan and Huiges v. Netherlands* (1984) 41 D.R. 170. See also *Ian Edgar (Liverpool) Limited v. United Kingdom* Application No. 37683/97, January 25, 2000 (a complaint brought by a firearms distributor about the statutory ban on hand-guns introduced following the Dunblane massacre was considered inadmissible on the grounds that the applicant had no legitimate expectation that it would be able to continue to deal in a particular type of firearm and had in any event received statutory compensation at market value).

where an enforceable claim to it already exists.[41] It may, however, include rights contingent upon the satisfaction of certain conditions (provided those conditions are fulfilled and have not lapsed),[42] property where there is a legitimate expectation that an entitlement will arise,[43] or rights which are in existence but yet to be enforced.[44] Although the term is autonomous, and not necessarily dependent on recognition of a particular right in domestic law, the starting point is the establishment of an entitlement in domestic law,[45] unless the effect of the law determining the entitlement is itself contrary to the object and purposes of Article 1 of Protocol No. 1.[46]

16.56   Where a retrospective change in the law results in the extinguishment of an existing claim before the domestic courts, this will only constitute an infringement of Article 1 of Protocol No. 1 rights where it can be shown that there was a legitimate expectation that the claim would be determined on the basis of the domestic law as it stood at the relevant time. Thus, in *Stran Greek Refineries v. Greece*,[47] the applicants claimed for losses under a contract with the Greek military junta to build an oil refinery which had been terminated by the democratic administration on its restoration to power. The applicants succeeded in their claim in arbitration proceedings and successfully withstood two legal challenges by the government, each of which confirmed that the arbitration award was due in the amount determined at arbitration. Restrospective legislation without any provision for compensation was then introduced depriving the applicants of their rights. The Court found a violation of Article 1 of Protocol No. 1 on the basis that the arbitration award conferred a right to the sums awarded, and that, although the right was revocable as the award could still be annulled, the Greek courts had twice held that there was no ground for such an annullment. The right to receive the arbitration award was accordingly a "possession" which had been unjustifiably interfered with.

16.57   Similarly, in *Pressos Compania Naviera S.A. v. Belgium*,[48] a claim for compensation under rules of tort, the Court found that, on the basis of the judgments of the Court of Cassation, the applicants could argue that they had such an expectation. However, in *National & Provincial Building Society, Leeds Permanent Building Society and Yorkshire Building Society v. United Kingdom*,[49] the Court found that there was no such legitimate

---

[41] *Størksen v. Norway* (1994) 78–A D.R. 88; *Gialouris and Christopoulos v. Greece* (1995) 81–A D.R. 123.

[42] *De Napoles Pacheco v. Belgium* (1978) 15 D.R. 143; *Agneessens v. Belgium* (1988) 58 D.R. 63.

[43] *Stran Greek Refineries and Stratis Andreadis v. Greece* (1995) 19 E.H.R.R. 293, para. 59; *Pressos Compania Naviera S.A. v. Belgium* (1996) 21 E.H.R.R. 301, paras 31–32; *National & Provincial Building Society, Leeds Permanent Building Society and Yorkshire Building Society v. United Kingdom* (1998) 25 E.H.R.R. 127, para. 69.

[44] *Inze v. Austria*, Application No. 8695/79 (1986) 8 E.H.R.R. 498; (1988) 10 E.H.R.R. 394.

[45] *A, B and Company A.S. v. Germany* (1978) 14 D.R. 146; *Agneessens v. Belgium* (1988) 58 D.R. 63.

[46] *Pressos Compania Naviera S.A. v. Belgium* (1996) 21 E.H.R.R. 301, paras 31–32. See also *Van Marle v. The Netherlands* (1986) 8 E.H.R.R. 483 (where the Court found that clientele could constitute an asset and possession for the purposes of Article 1 of Protocol No. 1 despite the fact that Dutch law did not recognise an right of goodwill)

[47] (1995) 19 E.H.R.R. 293.

[48] (1996) 21 E.H.R.R. 301.

[49] (1998) 25 E.H.R.R. 127.

expectation. The case concerned tax regulations regarding interest paid by building societies which had been subject to earlier challenge in the courts by the Woolwich Building Society. As Parliament had shown an intention retrospectively to validate the tax regulations, and as the House of Lords had yet to determine the Woolwich Building Society's entitlement to restitution, the Court found that the basis upon which the various building societies sought to assert a right amounting to a possession was "at best . . . precarious".[50]

The Court of Appeal considered retrospective effect and legitimate expec- **16.58** tation in the case of *Heil v. Rankin*,[51] as a result of which certain levels of award in personal injury cases were revised upwards. The defendants and their insurers sought to argue that any changes operating retrospectively amounted to a deprivation of property under Article 1 of Protocol No. 1 and a breach of process under Article 6. The Court of Appeal dismissed these arguments on the basis that any interference was in the public interest in providing fair compensation for victims of personal injury, that the Convention did not inhibit the incremental development of the common law, and that there was no legitimate expectation as to the level of personal injury awards preventing a court order from having retrospective effect.

The term "possessions" can cover movable and immovable property and **16.59** corporeal and incorporeal interests. For example, it has been found to include the value and goodwill of a business,[52] shares,[53] securities,[54] intellectual property,[55] contractual rights[56] including leases and other contractual rights over property,[57] licences[58] including a liquor licence,[59] fishing rights,[60] crystallised debts,[61] judgment debts,[62] welfare benefits,[63] rights to receive benefits under a contributory state pension scheme,[64] a

---

[50] *National & Provincial Building Society, Leeds Permanent Building Society and Yorkshire Building Society v. United Kingdom* (1998) 25 E.H.R.R. 127, para. 69.
[51] [2000] 2 W.L.R. 1173.
[52] *Van Marle v. Netherlands* (1986) 8 E.H.R.R. 483, para. 41; *Tre Traktörer Aktiebolag v. Sweden* (1991) 13 E.H.R.R. 309, para. 53.
[53] *Bramelid and Malmström v. Sweden* (1982) 29 D.R. 64 at 81, (1983) 5 E.H.R.R. 249 at 255; *Lithgow v. United Kingdom* (1986) 8 E.H.R.R. 329; *S Co. and T. v. Sweden* (1986) 50 D.R. 121 at 139, (1988) 10 E.H.R.R. 132 at 140.
[54] *Jasinskij v. Lithuania* (1994) 94–A D.R. 147, para. 149.
[55] *Smith Kline and French Laboratories Ltd v. Netherlands* (1990) 66 D.R. 70 at 79; *British American Tobacco Company Ltd v. Netherlands* (1996) 21 E.H.R.R. 409, paras 72–74; *Lenzing AG v. United Kingdom* [1999] E.H.R.L.R. 132, para. 146.
[56] *A, B and Company A.S. v. Germany* (1978) 14 D.R. 146 at 168; *Association of General Practitioners v. Denmark* (1989) 62 D.R. 226 at 234.
[57] *Mellacher v. Austria* (1990) 12 E.H.R.R. 391, para. 43; *Lundquist v. Sweden* (1986) 48 D.R. 191 at 195, (1987) 9 E.H.R.R. 531 at 532; *D.P. v. United Kingdom* (1988) 10 E.H.R.R. 149 at 155; *cf. Pentidis v. Greece* (1997) 24 E.H.R.R. C.D. 1 at 7. See also *Gasus Dösier-under-Fördertechnik GmbH v. Netherlands* (1995) 20 E.H.R.R. 403 (where property subject to a retention of title clause was considered to be a "possession" for the purposes of the Article).
[58] *Pudas v. Sweden* (1988) 10 E.H.R.R. 380.
[59] *Tre Traktörer Aktiebolag v. Sweden* (1991) 13 E.H.R.R. 309.
[60] *Bauer v. Sweden* (1989) 60 D.R. 128
[61] *Agneesens v. Belgium* (1988) 58 D.R. 63.
[62] *Stran Greek Refineries and Stratis Andreadis v. Greece* (1995) 19 E.H.R.R. 293.
[63] *Gaygusz v. Austria* (1997) 23 E.H.R.R. 364.
[64] *Müller v. Austria* (1975) 3 D.R. 25 at 31; *National Federation of Self-Employed v. United Kingdom* Application No. 7995/77 (1978) 15 D.R. 198 at 200; *C v. France* (1988) 56 D.R. 20 at 34; *Szraber and Clarke v. United Kingdom* [1998] E.H.R.L.R. 230.

claim for damages in negligence,[65] and the interests connected with owning property covered by outline planning permission.[66]

16.60   **Interference generally.**   Whether any interference with the right can be justified under the Article depends on the nature and extent of that interference. The Article is considered to give rise to four potential categories of interference: an interference in peaceful enjoyment of property not amounting to deprivation or control; deprivation; control of use in accordance with the general interest; and, control of use to secure the payment of taxes or other contributions or penalties. Each category of interference gives rise to different considerations and, in theory at least, their justification is subject to different provisions.[67] The Court has tended to give far greater latitude to states in relation to measures amounting only to control of use rather than deprivation. However, when formulating an appropriate test for considering whether any interference is justified, the Court and Commission have tended to draw little distinction between the categories of interference and have generally applied a single "fair balance" test: any interference must not place a disproportionate burden on the individual owner or result in discriminatory treatment.[68]

16.61   It is important to note that, unlike Article 8, Article 1 of Protocol No. 1 is concerned only with interferences affecting the economic or market value of property and not those which simply affect the owner's aesthetic or environmental enjoyment of it. It does not, in principle, guarantee the right to the peaceful enjoyment of possessions in a pleasant environment.[69] Further, interferences of minor economic effect may not be covered.[70] Judicial determinations of private property rights may engage Article 6, but absent horizontal application of the HRA between private individuals,[71] are unlikely to engage Article 1 of Protocol No. 1.[72]

16.62   **"Peaceful enjoyment".**   The first sentence (or first rule) of the Article essentially enounces the general right of property,[73] and, as noted above, it is possible in some circumstances for there to be an interference with the peaceful enjoyment of property without it necessarily amounting

---

[65] *Pressos Compania Naviera S.A. v. Belgium* (1996) 21 E.H.R.R. 301, para. 31.

[66] *Pine Valley Developments Ltd v. Ireland* (1992) 14 E.H.R.R. 319.

[67] See paras 16.62 *et seq.*, below.

[68] See, *e.g.* D.J. Harris, M. O'Boyle and C. Warbrick *The European Convention on Human Rights* (Butterworths, 1995) p. 525. The "fair balance" test is further considered in paras 16.91 *et seq.*, below.

[69] See, *e.g. S v. France* (1990) 65 D.R. 250 at 261 (a case concerning noise pollution caused by the construction of a nuclear power plant where the Commission only considered the effect of the pollution on the value of the property rather than its effect in terms of loss of amenity). See also *Powell and Rayner v. United Kingdom* (1990) 12 E.H.R.R. 355 (a case concerning aircraft noise, the fact that the noise made the enjoyment of the land concerned "less pleasant" was not sufficient to engage Article 1 of Protocol No. 1 although *cf.* the Commission's earlier view in *Rayner v. United Kingdom* (1987) 9 E.H.R.R. 375 that "aircraft noise nuisance of considerable importance both as to level and frequency may seriously affect the value of real property or even render it unsaleable and thus amount to a partial taking of property").

[70] See, *e.g. Langborger v. Sweden* (1990) 12 E.H.R.R. 416 (a case concerning a disputed 0.3 per cent commission).

[71] The possibility and extent of which has yet to be clarified by the courts following the introduction of the HRA.

[72] See *Di Palma v. United Kingdom* (1988) 10 E.H.R.R. 149.

[73] *Sporrong and Lönroth v. Sweden* (1982) 5 E.H.R.R. 35, para. 61.

to "deprivation" or "control of use" within the second or third rules.[74] The Court has used this "catch-all" category on a number of occasions, and it is of particular relevance where the interference occurs over a long period.[75]

In *Sporrong and Lönroth v. Sweden*,[76] the existence of expropriation **16.63** permits over the applicants' land placed it under threat of expropriation by proceedings at some unknown point in the future. Although the existence of the permits did not deprive the applicants of their land or control their use of it, the Court found that there was an interference with their peaceful enjoyment of their possessions within the first rule.

In *Loizidou v. Turkey*,[77] the applicant was a Greek Cypriot who had been **16.64** prevented from gaining access to her property following the occupation of northern Cyprus by Turkish troops and the declaration of the Turkish Republic of northern Cyprus. Although there were dissenting opinions, the Court was of the view that, by reason of the fact that the legitimacy of the Turkish Republic of northern Cyprus was not recognised by the international community, the administration could not deprive and had not deprived the applicant of legal title to her property. Accordingly, as the applicant remained the legal owner of the property, she had not been deprived of her possessions. The Court also found that the applicant's use of the property was not being controlled. However, the Court held that there was a violation of her rights under Article 1 of Protocol No. 1 on the basis that: "as a consequence of the fact that the applicant has been refused access to the land . . . she has effectively lost all control as well as all possibilities to use and enjoy her property".[78]

In *Iatridis v. Greece*,[79] the applicant held a licence to operate a cinema in **16.65** premises from which he was evicted by the state. The domestic court quashed the eviction order. The state refused to reinstate the applicant. The Court held that, as the applicant held no proprietary interest in the premises, his eviction and the subsequent failure of the state to reinstate him, despite the domestic court's order, constituted both a fundamental breach of domestic Greek law and an interference with the peaceful enjoyment of the applicant's licence rather than a deprivation of his possessions.

Other situations in which the Court has found that there has been an **16.66** interference with peaceful enjoyment but no deprivation or control of use, include land consolidation proceedings,[80] the adoption of a land-use plan,[81] and the grant of planning permission over property adjacent to the applicant's land.[82]

Any interference with the peaceful enjoyment of possessions in this catch- **16.67** all category under the first rule (*i.e.* not amounting to either deprivation or

---

[74] See, *e.g. Stran Greek Refineries and Stratis Andreadis v. Greece* (1995) 19 E.H.R.R. 293.
[75] As in *Sporrong and Lönroth v. Sweden* (1983) 5 E.H.R.R. 35.
[76] (1983) 5 E.H.R.R. 35.
[77] (1997) 23 E.H.R.R. 513.
[78] *Loizidou v. Turkey* (1997) 23 E.H.R.R. 513, para. 63.
[79] (1999) 30 E.H.R.R. 97.
[80] *Erkner and Hofauer v. Austria* (1987) 9 E.H.R.R. 464; *Poiss v. Austria* (1988) 10 E.H.R.R. 231; *Wiesinger v. Austria* (1993) 16 E.H.R.R. 258.
[81] *Katte Klitsche de la Grange v. Italy* (1995) 19 E.H.R.R. 368.
[82] *M v. Italy* Application No. 14563/89 (1991) 72 D.R. 129.

control of use) cannot be justified unless it is in accordance with the law, in the general interest and proportionate to the aim pursued. These concepts are discussed in greater detail below.[83]

16.68 **"No one shall be deprived of his possessions".** The starting point in establishing deprivation is the extinction of all of the owner's legal rights either by operation of law or through the exercise of a legal power.[84] The Court has generally been reluctant to find that "deprivation" has occurred. The Commission has stated that the second rule is directed at those cases where the state seizes, or gives another the right to seize, a specific asset to be used for the realisation of a goal in the public interest.[85] The most frequent example of deprivation is therefore that of the expropriation of land by the state by compulsory purchase orders,[86] compulsory transfer orders,[87] or other means such as nationalisation.[88] A less obvious example of deprivation can be found in the case of *Bullock v. United Kingdom*,[89] where the seizure and destruction of a dog pursuant to the Dangerous Dogs Act 1991 was considered to be a deprivation of possessions for the purposes of Article 1 of Protocol No. 1.

16.69 In *Holy Monasteries v. Greece*,[90] the Greek Government had introduced legislation establishing a statutory presumption that certain monastery land belonged to the state. Although the presumption was rebuttable, the monasteries' own title to the land was founded upon ancient adverse possession and therefore the evidence necessary to rebut the presumption did not exist. The Court rejected the Greek Government's argument that the presumption was merely a procedural device to enable the settlement of disputes, and despite the fact that no steps to implement the transfer of title had taken place found that the presumption itself effectively transferred title as the monasteries were not in a position to challenge it. In the circumstances, there had been an expropriation of land by the state and the monasteries had been deprived of their property.

16.70 In *James v. United Kingdom*,[91] the challenge brought on behalf of the Duke of Westminster to tenants' rights of enfranchisement under the Leasehold Reform Act 1967, the Court found that since landlords were unable to refuse to sell the property to the tenants in the event that the statutory conditions were satisfied and since the price of the sale was set by statute, the legislation did deprive the landlords of their possessions.[92]

16.71 The Court has recognised that deprivation may occur even in circumstances falling short of formal expropriation, in stating that:

---

[83] See paras 16.86 *et seq.*
[84] *Lithgow v. United Kingdom* (1986) 8 E.H.R.R. 329, para. 107.
[85] *Bramelid and Malmström v. Sweden* (1983) 5 E.H.R.R. 249 at 255. See also *D.P. v. United Kingdom*, Application No. 11949/86 (1988) 10 E.H.R.R. 149 at 154.
[86] See, *e.g. Howard v. United Kingdom* (1987) 52 D.R. 198, 9 E.H.R.R. 116; *Grech v. Malta* (1995) 20 E.H.R.R. C.D. 95.
[87] See, *e.g. X v. Sweden* (1986) 8 E.H.R.R. 106.
[88] *Lithgow v. United Kingdom* (1986) 8 E.H.R.R. 329, para. 105.
[89] (1996) 21 E.H.R.R. C.D. 85.
[90] (1995) 20 E.H.R.R. 1.
[91] (1986) 8 E.H.R.R. 123.
[92] The legislation survived the challenge only on the basis that it was in the public interest.

"In the absence of a formal expropriation, that is to say a transfer of ownership, the Court considers that it must look behind the appearance and investigate the realities of the situation complained of. Since the Convention is intended to guarantee rights that are 'practical and effective', it has to be determined whether the situation amounted to a *de facto* expropriation . . . "[93]

A *de facto* expropriation of this kind can only occur where there has been **16.72** so substantial an interference with the ownership and use of the possession concerned that it effectively equates to the total extinction of ownership notwithstanding the fact that the owner retains legal title. Deprivation may thus occur if the owner is deprived of all meaningful use of his property.[94] However, any form of provisional or temporary loss of rights is very unlikely to constitute deprivation.[95] Equally, interferences which do not affect the value of the possession at all,[96] or which affect its value to a severe degree but not so as to render it worthless,[97] are also unlikely to be considered deprivations. A finding of *de facto* expropriation is accordingly, and is likely to remain, extremely rare.

In *Papamichalopoulos v. Greece*,[98] the applicant's land had been trans- **16.73** ferred to the Greek navy without compensation. Due to the extent of the physical occupation of the land, the length of time for which it was to be occupied, and the remoteness of any potential dealings with the land by the applicant, the Court found that a *de facto* expropriation had occurred without expressly referring either to the second rule or to deprivation.

In *Vasilescu v. Romania*,[99] the applicant was the owner of a number of **16.74** gold coins confiscated and retained by the Romanian authorities. A decision ordering the return of the coins was quashed by the Supreme Court. The fact that the applicant lost all ability to sell the coins and the failure of the authorities to remedy the situation was held to amount to a sufficiently serious interference to constitute *de facto* deprivation.

Deprivation has been unsuccessfully argued in a number of cases. In a **16.75** case similar to the *Vasilescu* case,[1] *Allegemeine Gold-und Silberscheideanstalt (AGOSI) v. United Kingdom*,[2] the applicants had sold Krugerrands to buyers who, having defaulted on payment, tried to smuggle the coins into the United Kingdom where they were seized, declared forfeit and retained by H.M. Customs and Excise. The applicants obtained a court order in Germany declaring the original transaction void but the coins were not returned. The Court found, on the basis that the seizure was

---

[93] *Sporrong and Lönroth v. Sweden* (1983) 5 E.H.R.R. 35, para. 63.
[94] *Fredin v. Sweden (No. 1)* (1991) 13 E.H.R.R. 784, para. 42.
[95] See, *e.g. Handyside v. United Kingdom* (1979–80) 1 E.H.R.R. 737, para. 62; *Erkner and Hofauer v. Austria* (1987) 9 E.H.R.R. 464, para. 74; *Poiss v. Austria* (1988) 10 E.H.R.R. 231, para. 64; *Wiesinger v. Austria* (1993) 16 E.H.R.R. 258, para. 72; *Sporrong and Lönroth v. Sweden* (1983) 5 E.H.R.R. 35, para. 63.
[96] *S v. United Kingdom*, Application No. 10741/84 (1984) 41 D.R. 226.
[97] *Pine Valley Developments Ltd v. Ireland* (1992) 14 E.H.R.R. 319, para. 56.
[98] (1993) 16 E.H.R.R. 440.
[99] (1999) 28 E.H.R.R. 241.
[1] *Vasilescu v. Romania* (1998) 28 E.H.R.R. 241.
[2] (1987) 9 E.H.R.R. 1.

intended to enforce an import prohibition, that the seizure amounted to a control of use rather than a deprivation.

16.76 In *Sporrong and Lönroth v. Sweden*,[3] the applicants sought to argue that the fact that their property had been subject to building restrictions and expropriation permits for an extended period, thus restricting their ability to sell the land, amounted to an interference sufficient to constitute deprivation within the second rule. The Court found that although the existence of the permits and restrictions had made the land more difficult to sell, it had not made sale impossible. That fact, and the fact that the applicants were still able to use the land, resulted in the Court finding that there was no deprivation.[4]

16.77 In *Matos e Silva, Lda. v. Portugal*,[5] the first applicant worked land in the Algarve for the extraction of salt and the breeding of fish. His right to do so, at least in part, arose under a royal decree originally granted in 1884. The Court held that this right was a "possession" for the purposes of Article 1 of Protocol No. 1. The Portuguese Government withdrew the concession and put in place provisions intended to limit building on the land or any change of use with the intention of creating a nature reserve. The Court held, distinguishing the case from that of *Papamichalopoulos v. Greece*,[6] that although the applicants' rights had been substantially reduced, they had not disappeared and the situation was not irreversible. Accordingly, there was no deprivation.[7]

16.78 Any deprivation of possessions under the second rule cannot be justified unless it is in the public interest, and subject to the conditions provided for by law and by the general principles of international law. The measure must also be proportionate to the aim pursued. These concepts are discussed in greater detail below.[8]

16.79 The Court has confirmed that the unequivocal and genuine consent of the property owner to any deprivation will preclude him from making any later claim under Article 1 of Protocol No. 1.[9]

16.80 Compensation is a crucial element to the justification of any deprivation of possessions, even where the public interest pursued is particularly strong.[10] In the absence of compensation a deprivation of possessions will only be justifiable in exceptional circumstances.[11] The Court has rarely interfered with the levels of compensation paid, affording the state a wide margin of appreciation, and would only do so if, on its assessment, the value of the property taken and the compensation paid for it is "manifestly

---

[3] (1983) 5 E.H.R.R. 35.
[4] *Sporrong and Lönroth v. Sweden* (1983) 5 E.H.R.R. 35, para. 63.
[5] (1997) 24 E.H.R.R. 573.
[6] (1993) 16 E.H.R.R. 440. See paras 16.73 *et seq.*, above.
[7] But there was interference with the enjoyment of possessions and, no fair balance having been struck, accordingly a violation of Article 1 of Protocol No. 1.
[8] See paras 16.86 *et seq.*
[9] *Holy Monasteries v. Greece* (1995) 20 E.H.R.R. 1, paras 76–78. See also the earlier decision of the Commission in *Di Palma v. United Kingdom* (1988) 10 E.H.R.R. 149 at 155.
[10] *Stran Greek Refneries and Stratis Andreadis v. Greece* (1995) 19 E.H.R.R. 293, paras 70–72.
[11] *Lithgow v. United Kingdom* (1986) 8 E.H.R.R. 329, para. 120; *James v. United* Kingdom (1986) 8 E.H.R.R. 123, para. 54; *Pressos Compania Naviera S.A. v. Belgium* (1996) 21 E.H.R.R. 301, para. 38; *Holy Monasteries v. Greece* (1996) 20 E.H.R.R. 1, para. 71.

disproportionate".[12] Article 1 of Protocol No. 1 does not guarantee full compensation in all circumstances. The Court has stated: "legitimate objectives of 'public interest', such as pursued in measures of economic reform or measures designed to achieve greater social justice, may call for less than reimbursement of the full market value".[13] The system used to calculate the compensation should, however, be flexible enough to cope with different situations and not be manifestly without reasonable foundation.[14]

"Laws . . . to control the use of property". It is important to note   **16.81** that the third rule of Article 1 of Protocol No. 1 entitles the state to enforce "such laws" as it deems necessary to control the use of property. The rule accordingly only bites in relation to legislative rather than purely administrative measures.

The category is both wide and self-defining, incorporating all legislative   **16.82** measures engaged in controlling the use of property. A legislative measure which falls short of being a sufficiently serious interference to amount to deprivation will, in many cases, fall into the category of "control of use" under the third rule. This has, on occasion lead to decisions which at first glance appear confusing, where, for example the Court has considered the wholesale seizure of property to be a control of use rather than a deprivation where the aim pursued is considered to fall within the justifications set out in the third rule.[15] In *Allegemeine Gold-und Silberscheideanstalt (AGOSI) v. United Kingdom*,[16] the applicants had sold Krugerrands to buyers who, having defaulted on payment, tried to smuggle the coins into the United Kingdom where they were seized, declared forfeit and retained by H.M. Customs and Excise. The applicants obtained a court order in Germany declaring the original transaction void but the coins were not returned. The Court found, on the basis that the seizure was intended to enforce an import prohibition (an aim in the general interest), that the seizure amounted to a control of use rather than a deprivation. In *Air Canada v. United Kingdom*,[17] H.M. Customs and Excise impounded an Air Canada aircraft on which they had found a large cannabis consignment, refusing to release it until Air Canada paid a £50,000 fine. The Court felt that the impounding of the aircraft pending the payment of a fine was a measure controlling its use rather than a deprivation on the basis that there was no attempt to transfer ownership of the aircraft. The Court held the action taken by H.M. Customs and Excise to be a proportionate control of use in light of the legitimate aim pursued (combating the smuggling of drugs) and previous warnings issued to Air Canada about security measures.

---

[12] *Scotts of Greenock (Est'd 1711) Ltd and Lithgows Ltd v. United Kingdom* (1990) 12 E.H.R.R. 147, para. 90.
[13] *Lithgow v. United Kingdom* (1986) 8 E.H.R.R. 329, para. 121.
[14] For a broader discussion of compensation under Art. 1 of Protocol No. 1 see D. Anderson, "Compensation for Interference with Property" [1999] E.H.R.L.R. 543.
[15] See, *e.g. Handyside v. United Kingdom* (1979–80) 1 E.H.R.R. 737 (where copies of obscene materials were seized and destroyed).
[16] (1987) 9 E.H.R.R. 1.
[17] (1995) 20 E.H.R.R. 150.

16.83   Examples of control of use include: rent controls[18]; planning controls[19] including building[20] and use[21] restrictions; environmental orders[22]; inheritance laws governing the distribution of estates[23]; powers to suspend eviction from residential property[24]; agricultural production quota allocation[25]; the extension of public fishing rights[26]; the compulsory transfer of hunting rights to land owned by individuals opposed to hunting on ethical grounds[27]; the revocation of a licence for the commercial exploitation of land[28]; forfeiture provisions relating to the use or possession of property[29]; seizure of property for legal proceedings[30]; the seizure and/or confiscation of illicit property in criminal or other proceedings.[31]

16.84   An interference constituting a control of use of property cannot be justified unless it is in accordance with the law for the general interest or to secure the payment of taxes or other contributions or penalties. It must also be proportionate to the aim pursued. These concepts are discussed in greater detail below.[32]

16.85   Unlike the position with regard to property deprivation, where compensation is payable save in exceptional circumstances, there is no requirement for the payment of compensation for an interference constituting a control of use. Thus, no compensation was payable to the Duke of Westminster's trustees for the reduction in value of his property holdings following the introduction of the Leasehold Reform Act 1967.[33] However, it should be noted that the payment of compensation may well result in a finding that a fair balance has been struck between the interests of the property owner and the general interest.[34]

16.86   **"Public interest" and "general interest".**   No distinction has been made by the Court between the two terms "public interest" used in the second rule, and "general interest" used in the third rule of Article 1 of

---

[18] *E.g. Kilbourn v. United Kingdom* (1985) 8 E.H.R.R. 81; *Mellacher v. Austria* (1990) 12 E.H.R.R. 391.

[19] *E.g. Jacobsson v. Sweden* (1990) 12 E.H.R.R. 56; *Pine Valley Developments Ltd v. Ireland* (1992) 14 E.H.R.R. 319.

[20] *E.g. Lundquist v. Sweden* (1987) 9 E.H.R.R. 531.

[21] *E.g. Chater v. United Kingdom* (1988) 10 E.H.R.R. 534; *Ryder v. United Kingdom* (1989) 11 E.H.R.R. 80; *ISKCON v. United Kingdom* (1994) 18 E.H.R.R. C.D. 133.

[22] *E.g. Denev v. Sweden* (1989) 59 D.R. 127; *Fredin v. Sweden (No. 1)* (1991) 13 E.H.R.R. 784; *Oerlemans v. Netherlands* (1993) 15 E.H.R.R. 561.

[23] *E.g. Inze v. Austria* (1986) 8 E.H.R.R. 498; (1988) 10 E.H.R.R. 394.

[24] *E.g. Spadea and Scalabrino v. Italy* (1996) 21 E.H.R.R. 482; *Scollo v. Italy* (1996) 22 E.H.R.R. 514.

[25] *Procola v. Luxembourg* (1996) 22 E.H.R.R. 193.

[26] *Baner v. Sweden* (1989) 60 D.R. 128.

[27] *Chassagnou v. France* (2000) 29 E.H.R.R. 615 (although this could be interpreted as a control of use case).

[28] *Fredin v. Sweden (No. 1)* (1991) 13 E.H.R.R. 784.

[29] *E.g. Handyside v. United Kingdom* (1979–80) 1 E.H.R.R. 737; *Allegemeine Gold-und Silberscheideanstalt (AGOSI) v. United Kingdom* (1987) 9 E.H.R.R. 1; *Air Canada v. United Kingdom* (1995) 20 E.H.R.R. 150.

[30] *E.g G, S and M v. Austria* (1983) 34 D.R. 119.

[31] *E.g. X v. Sweden* (1983) 5 E.H.R.R. 510; *Raimondo v. Italy* (1994) 18 E.H.R.R. 237; *Venditelli v. Italy* (1995) 19 E.H.R.R. 464.

[32] See paras 16.86 *et seq.*

[33] *James v. United Kingdom* (1986) 8 E.H.R.R. 123.

[34] See, *e.g. Baner v. Sweden* (1989) 60 D.R. 128.

Protocol No. 1. Although the margin of appreciation may be of questionable relevance in application of the HRA in the domestic courts,[35] the Court and Commission have afforded states a very wide margin of appreciation as to what they consider to be in the "public" or "general" interest. The Court has yet to reject an argument of public interest put forward by a state. Measures to secure payment of taxes are generally presumed to be in the general interest.[36] Other examples of measures in the "public" or "general" interest include: social welfare measures such as rent controls,[37] or measures intended to resolve housing shortages[38]; public works measures such as the expropriation of land to build roads,[39] or provide services[40]; planning, and other measures intended to control the use of land to improve or protect agriculture,[41] or the environment[42]; and measures intended to protect public health such as the control of the sale of alcohol[43] or drugs.[44]

16.87 It is not necessary for the public in general to benefit from an interference, as the pursuance of a policy calculated to enhance social justice within the community (such as leasehold enfranchisement under the Leasehold Reform Act 1967) can properly be described as "being in the public interest".[45] The fairness of laws governing property rights between private parties is a matter of public concern and legislation intended to bring about such fairness can be in the public interest even where it involves the compulsory transfer of property between two individuals without payment of compensation.[46]

16.88 **In accordance with the law.** Both the second rule, in expressing that deprivations must be subject to the conditions provided for by law, and the third rule, in allowing the state to enact such laws as it deems necessary to control the use of property, are subject therefore to the requirement that any interference with the Article 1 of Protocol No. 1 right must be in accordance with the law. This gives rise to a number of requirements.[47] The interference being challenged must have a basis in domestic law.[48] It is not necessary for the law to be statutory,[49] it can be

---

[35] See paras 16.18 *et seq.* above.
[36] See, *e.g. Hentrich v. France* (1994) 18 E.H.R.R. 440, para. 39.
[37] See, *e.g. Mellacher v. Austria* (1990) 12 E.H.R.R. 391.
[38] See, *e.g. Spadea and Scalabrino v. Italy* (1996) 21 E.H.R.R. 482; *Immobiliare Saffi v. Italy* (2000) 30 E.H.R.R. 756.
[39] See, *e.g. Andersson v. Sweden* (1992) 15 E.H.R.R. C.D. 64; *Papachelas v. Greece* (1999) 30 E.H.R.R. 923.
[40] See, *e.g. X v. Austria* (1986) 8 E.H.R.R. 226.
[41] See, *e.g. Denev v. Sweden* (1989) 59 D.R. 127; *Hakansson and Sturesson v. Sweden* (1991) 13 E.H.R.R. 1; *Procola v. Luxembourg* (1996) 22 E.H.R.R. 193.
[42] See, *e.g. N. v. Austria* (1986) 9 E.H.R.R. 389; *Jacobsson v. Sweden* (1989) 12 E.H.R.R. 56; *ISKCON v. United Kingdom* (1994) 18 E.H.R.R. C.D. 133.
[43] *Tre Traktörer Aktiebolag v. Sweden* (1991) 13 E.H.R.R. 309.
[44] *X. v. Sweden* (1983) 5 E.H.R.R. 510.
[45] *James v. United Kingdom* (1986) 8 E.H.R.R. 123, para. 41.
[46] *James v. United Kingdom* (1986) 8 E.H.R.R. 123, para. 41.
[47] For a more detailed consideration of this issue, see paras 4.43 *et seq.* above.
[48] *Leander v. Sweden* (1987) 9 E.H.R.R. 433, para. 50; *Margareta and Roger Andersson v. Sweden* (1992) 14 E.H.R.R. 615; *A v. France* (1993) 17 E.H.R.R. 462; *Murray v. United Kingdom* (1995) 19 E.H.R.R. 193, para. 88.
[49] Although statutory laws (*Norris v. Ireland* (1991) 13 E.H.R.R. 186) and non-statutory enactments (*Golder v. United Kingdom* (1979–80) 1 E.H.R.R. 524) are clearly covered.

based in the common law whether written or unwritten.[50] However, the mere existence of a domestic law is not sufficient, as the "quality" of the law itself must be subjected to scrutiny. There must be adequate and effective safeguards in the law to protect against arbitrary interferences by public authorities with the rights guaranteed by the Article.[51] The law must be accessible to the persons concerned, and formulated with sufficient precision to enable an individual to foresee, to a reasonable degree, the consequences which a given action may entail.[52] The mere fact that a law entails the exercise of a discretion does not, of itself, make it incompatible with the requirement of foreseeability provided that the scope of the discretion and the manner of its exercise are indicated with sufficient clarity to provide adequate protection against arbitrary interference.[53]

16.89   **"The general principles of international law".** The second rule requires that any deprivation be subject to the conditions provided for by the general principles of international law. In essence the general principles of international law referred to protect against arbitrary expropriation and provide for compensation in the event of nationalisation. Although it has been an area of some debate,[54] it is clear that the general principles referred to do not apply when a state takes properties from its own nationals, only from non-nationals.[55]

16.90   **"Laws . . . to secure the payment of taxes or other contributions or penalties".** The Court has afforded states a very wide margin of appreciation in relation to laws controlling the use of property to secure the payment of taxes or other contributions or penalties. Provided taxation legislation does not amount to an abitrary confiscation[56] and is not devoid of reasonable foundation[57] it is likely to be justified. This chapter is not otherwise concerned to deal with the aspects of Article 1 of Protocol No. 1 dealing with taxation.[58]

16.91   **The "fair balance" test.** In order to justify any interference with the right under Article 1 of Protocol No. 1 it is necessary to determine:

---

[50] See, *e.g. Dudgeon v. United Kingdom* (1982) 4 E.H.R.R. 149, para. 44; *Malone v. United Kingdom* (1985) 7 E.H.R.R. 14; *Chappell v. United Kingdom* (1990) 12 E.H.R.R. 1, para. 56; *Huvig v. France* (1990) 12 E.H.R.R. 528, para. 28; *Kruslin v. France* (1990) 12 E.H.R.R. 547, para. 29.
[51] *Hentrich v. France* (1994) 18 E.H.R.R. 440, para. 42.
[52] *Lithgow v. United Kingdom* (1986) 8 E.H.R.R. 329, para. 110; *Olsson v. Sweden (No 1)* (1989) 11 E.H.R.R. 259; *Ollila v. Finland* (1992) 15 E.H.R.R. C.D. 101 at 104. See also *Sunday Times v. United Kingdom* (1979–80) 2 E.H.R.R. 245, para. 49, where this point was considered in the context of Art. 10(2).
[53] *Malone v. United Kingdom* (1985) 7 E.H.R.R. 14, paras 68 and 79; *Silver v. United Kingdom* (1983) 5 E.H.R.R. 347, para. 88; *Fredin v. Sweden* (1991) 13 E.H.R.R. 784, para. 50; *Hentrich v. France* (1994) 18 E.H.R.R. 440, para. 42.
[54] See, *e.g.* R. Clayton and H. Tomlinson, *The Law of Human Rights* (1st ed., 2000), vol. 1, pp. 1316–1317, paras 18.70–18.72.
[55] See, *e.g. Lithgow v. United Kingdom* (1986) 8 E.H.R.R. 329; *Gasus Dosier-und Fördertechnik Gmbh v. Netherlands* (1995) 20 E.H.R.R. 403; *Gudmunsson v. Iceland* (1996) 21 E.H.R.R. C.D. 89.
[56] *Gasus Dosier-und Fördertechnik Gmbh v. Netherlands* (1995) 20 E.H.R.R. 403, para. 59.
[57] *National & Provincial Building Society, Leeds Permanent Building Society and Yorkshire Building Society v. United Kingdom* (1998) 25 E.H.R.R. 127, para. 72.
[58] Reference should instead be made to Chap. 18, which deals exclusively with taxation issues and the HRA.

" . . . whether a fair balance was struck between the demands of the general interest of the community and the requirements of the protection of the individual's fundamental rights. The search for this balance is inherent in the whole of the Convention and is also reflected in the structure of Article 1."[59]

This fair balance requires the interference in question to be in pursuit of a legitimate aim, and there must be a reasonable relationship of proportionality between the means employed and the aim pursued.[60] There is no fair balance if the owner of the property has had to bear "an individual and excessive burden".[61] The availability of alternative solutions and different means of achieving the relevant aim does not, of itself, render the contested legislation or act unjustified, as it is not for the Court to determine whether the relevant interference represented the best solution.[62] **16.92**

Factors which may be relevant in considering whether a fair balance has been achieved include: the availability of compensation[63]; the existence of procedural safeguards[64] and/or a procedure for challenging the interference[65]; whether the applicant has taken advantage of all remedies reasonably available to him to challenge the interference[66]; the duration of the interference[67] and any procedural delays (for example in the granting of compensation)[68]; and, whether the applicant was aware of the interference or of the risk of interference prior to purchasing the property.[69]

3. SPECIFIC AREAS OF IMPACT

Introduction

The purpose of this section of the chapter is to cover those areas of the law affecting property and those rights connected with property in which the Convention already has impacted, or almost inevitably will impact. Both prior to and since the introduction of the HRA into law there has been widespread speculation about its likely effects. Debate as to the degree to **16.93**

---

[59] *Sporrong and Lönroth v. Sweden* (1983) 5 E.H.R.R. 35, para. 69. See also *Stran Greek Refineries and Stratis Anreadis v. Greece* (1995) 19 E.H.R.R. 293, para. 69.
[60] See, *e.g. Chassagnou v. France* (2000) 29 E.H.R.R. 615, para. 75. For a more detailed discussion of the concept of proportionality, see paras 4.38 *et seq.*, above.
[61] *Lithgow v. United Kingdom* (1986) 8 E.H.R.R. 329, para. 120; *Tre Traktörer Aktiebolag v. Sweden* (1991) 13 E.H.R.R. 309, para. 62.
[62] *Mellacher v. Austria* (1990) 12 E.H.R.R. 391, para. 53; *Panikian v. Bulgaria* (1997) 24 E.H.R.R. C.D. 63 at 67.
[63] *Sporrong and Lönroth v. Sweden* (1983) 5 E.H.R.R. 35, para. 73; *Panikian v. Bulgaria* (1997) 24 E.H.R.R. C.D. 63 at 68.
[64] *Immobiliare Saffi v. Italy* (1999) 30 E.H.R.R. 756, para. 54.
[65] *Sporrong and Lönroth v. Sweden* (1983) 5 E.H.R.R. 35.
[66] *Katte Klitsche de la Grange v. Italy* (1995) 19 E.H.R.R. 368, para. 46; *Air Canada v. United Kingdom* (1995) 20 E.H.R.R. 150, para. 44.
[67] *Poiss v. Austria* (1988) 10 E.H.R.R. 231.
[68] *Sporrong and Lönroth v. Sweden* (1983) 5 E.H.R.R. 35, para. 73; *Erkner and Hofauer v. Austria* (1987) 9 E.H.R.R. 464, para. 76; *Agrotexim v. Greece* (1996) 21 E.H.R.R. 250, paras 76 and 78; *Matos e Silva, Lda. v. Portugal* (1997) 24 E.H.R.R. 573, para. 92.
[69] *Jacobsson v. Sweden* (1990) 12 E.H.R.R. 56, para. 61; *Fredin v. Sweden* (1991) 13 E.H.R.R. 784, para.54.

which the courts will use the Convention to interpret and develop the law has been extensive, particularly in relation to the vexed question, as yet not fully answered by the courts,[70] as to whether Convention rights can or should be applied between private individuals. This section of the chapter does not seek to enter into extensive speculation as to the future, and accordingly the subject areas covered do not reach far into uncharted waters. If developments occur in the manner predicted by many commentators then future editions of this work will record and reflect upon those developments. In so far as any part of this section is not based upon existing case law or established principle it is intended not as a prediction but simply as a guide to possible areas of future challenge. The section contains a broad spectrum of subject-matter, and a number of the areas covered, such as planning and environmental law must be considered specialist areas. In all areas covered, the specialist areas in particular, this section is not intended to be an exhaustive guide to the area of law concerned, but instead to provide a useful guide to the general human rights principles applicable and an insight into the impact of the Convention in that area. For any more detailed analysis reference should be made to specialist texts.

Adverse Possession

The Limitation Act 1980

16.94 There has been some speculation[71] that the acquisition of land by adverse possession may violate Article 1 of Protocol No. 1. The justifying principle behind adverse possession is that of providing certainty of ownership and security of occupation for those occupying land of which they are not the legal owner without challenge for an extended period of time. Thus, although the legal title is not extinguished by adverse possession, the Limitation Act 1980 bars any action by the legal owner for the recovery of land so occupied 12 years after the right of action accrues, thus effectively extinguishing his title to it. Limitation periods on bringing proceedings are not in principle incompatible with the Convention.[72] However, the effect of the Act is to deprive the legal owner of his possession, namely the freehold title to the land, without any payment of compensation. As noted above,[73] compensation is a crucial element to the justification of any deprivation of possessions, even where the public interest pursued is particularly

---

[70] Although the Lord Chancellor, Lord Irvine made his (and accordingly the Government's) view plain in the course of the debate on the Human Rights Bill in stating that there was no intention to provide for the Convention rights to be directly justiciable in actions between private individuals (*Hansard* H.L. Deb., February 5, 1998, col. 840) but that it was right as a matter of principle for the courts to have the duty of acting compatibly with the Convention not only in cases involving other public authorities, but also in developing the common law in deciding cases between individuals (*Hansard* H.L. Deb., November 24, 1997, col 783). See paras 5.15 *et seq.*, above.

[71] See, *e.g.* D.R. Jean Howell, "Land and Human Rights", The Conveyancer [1999] 287 at 305–306.

[72] *Stubbings v. United Kingdom* (1997) 23 E.H.R.R. 213. See further paras 10.12 *et seq.*, above.

[73] See paras 10.12 *et seq.*

strong,[74] and in the absence of compensation a deprivation of possessions will only be justifiable in exceptional circumstances.[75] The principle
of adverse possession might therefore be considered a violation of Article
1 of Protocol No. 1.

Only one domestic case since the coming into force of the HRA has   **16.95**
considered this point at appeal level,[76] and then it was neither fully argued
nor the issue determinative of the appeal. In *J.A. Pye (Oxford) Ltd v.
Graham Ltd*,[77] a licensee remained in occupation of farm land for more
than 12 years after the determination of his grazing licence and sought to
claim title to the land by adverse possession under the provisions of
section 15 of the Limitation Act 1980. The Court of Appeal held that there
was no evidence that Mr Graham ever changed his intention regarding the
use of the land, namely for the limited purpose of grazing it, and that
simply continuing a limited use of the land after the expiration of a personal
limited licence did not necessarily justify the inference of the requisite
intention to possess. In the absence of such an intention there could be no
adverse possession. Success on that point rendered any consideration of
the HRA and its impact on adverse possession unnecessary for the
purposes of that appeal. The Court of Appeal did, however ask itself
whether section 3 of the HRA and Article 1 of Protocol No. 1 would have
had any impact on the outcome of the appeal, and came to the conclusion
that they would not. The reasoning of Mummery L.J., who gave the lead
judgment, is worth considering in full[77A]:

> "The only Convention right relied on (The Protection of Property in
> Article 1 of Protocol No. 1) does not impinge on the relevant provi-
> sions of the 1980 Act. Those provisions do not deprive a person of his
> possession or interfere with his peaceful enjoyment of them. They
> deprive a person of his right of access to the courts for the purpose of
> recovering property, if he has delayed the institution of his legal
> proceeding for 12 years or more after he has been dispossessed of
> his land by another person, who has been in adverse possession of
> it for at least that period. The extinction of title of the claimant in those
> circumstances is not a deprivation of possessions or a confiscatory
> measure for which the payment of compensation would be appro-
> priate: it is simply a logical and pragmatic consequence of the barring
> of his right to bring an action after the expiration of the limitation
> period.
>
> Even if, contrary to my view, the Convention right potentially impinges
> on the relevant provisions of the 1980 Act, those provisions are
> conditions provided for by law and are "in the public interest" within
> the meaning of Article 1. Such conditions are reasonably required to

---

[74] *Stran Greek Refneries and Stratis Andreadis v. Greece* (1995) 19 E.H.R.R. 293, paras
70–72.
[75] *Lithgow v. United Kingdom* (1986) 8 E.H.R.R. 329, para. 120; *James v. United* Kingdom
(1986) 8 E.H.R.R. 123, para. 54; *Pressos Compania Naviera S.A. v. Belgium* (1996) 21
E.H.R.R. 301, para. 38; *Holy Monasteries v. Greece* (1995) 20 E.H.R.R. 1, para. 71.
[76] The United Kingdom doctrine of adverse possession has not been challenged in the Court
or Commission.
[77] [2001] 2 W.L.R. 1293, CA.
[77A] [2001] 2 W.L.R. 1293, at 1309 A-E.

avoid the real risk of injustice in the adjudication of stale claims; to ensure certainty of title; and to promote social stability by the protection of the established and peaceable possession of property from the resurrection of old claims. The conditions provided in the 1980 Act are not disproportionate; the period allowed for the bringing of proceedings is reasonable; the conditions are not discriminatory; and they are not impossible, or so excessively difficult, to comply with as to render ineffective the exercise of the legal right of a person, who is entitled to the peaceful enjoyment of his possessions, to recover them from another person, who is alleged to have wrongfully deprived him of them."

16.96   Keene L.J. and Sir Martin Nourse concurred with this view. Keene L.J. added his own views on the impact of the Convention on adverse possession. He noted, relying upon the Court authority of *Stubbings v. United Kingdom*,[78] that limitation periods are not, in principle, incompatible with the Convention.[78A] The effect of a limitation period in some circumstances is to deprive "persons of property rights, whether real or personal, or damages".[78B] He noted that damages are themselves capable of constituting a "possession".[79] Accordingly, he felt that there was nothing inherently incompatible as between the Limitation Act 1980 and Article 1 of Protocol No. 1.

Conclusion

16.97   The *Pye* case[80] is likely to put an end to any argument below Court of Appeal level that adverse possession is incompatible with Article 1 of Protocol No. 1.[80A] Nevertheless, Mummery L.J.'s view that adverse possession by means of the Limitation Act 1980 does not deprive a person of his possessions or interfere with his peaceful enjoyment of them, only of his right of access to the courts to recover those possessions, may be open to challenge as being too literal an interpretation. Although there is no formal expropriation of the property by means of a transfer of ownership, the effect of the limitation period is to extinguish the owner's rights to the property. The court is entitled to look at the reality of the situation:

---

[78] (1997) 23 E.H.R.R. 213.
[78A] [2001] 2 W.L.R. 1293, at 1309 G-H.
[78B] *ibid.*, at 1310A.
[79] In reliance upon *Pressos Compania Naviera SA v. Belgium* (1995) 21 E.H.R.R. 301.
[80] *J.A. Pye (Oxford) Ltd v. Graham Ltd*, [2001] 2 W.L.R. 1293, CA; *The Times*, February 13, 2001; New Law Online Case 201022501 (Judgment handed down on February 6, 2001).
[80A] Indeed it was relied upon at first instance in the Chancery Division before Park J. in the as yet unreported case of *Family Housing Association v. Donellan* (the transcript should soon be available on NewLaw Online or Casetrack). Judgment was handed down on July 12, 2001. The claimant sought to amend its particulars of claim to allege that adverse possession was contrary to Article 1 of Protocol No. 1. Park J. refused the amendment and rejected the argument. He reached this view not on the basis of Mummery L.J.'s reasoning in *Pye* (although he was referred to the case) but rather on the basis that the non-deprivation provision of Article 1 of Protocol No. 1 was directed only against expropriations by the state, or authorised by the state, for public purposes. It was not directed against matters which were essentially ones of private law. Without seeing the full transcript (not yet available) it is difficult to be certain but for the reasons set out above the case may be wrongly decided.

"In the absence of formal expropriation, that is to say a transfer of ownership, the Court considers that it must look behind the appearance and investigate the realities of the situation complained of. Since the Convention is intended to guarantee rights that are 'practical and effective', it has to be ascertained whether that situation amounted to a *de facto* expropriation . . . ".[81]

It could readily be argued that, although it is of course correct that the limitation period simply bars access to the courts to recover the property in question rather than effecting a transfer of title, the reality of the situation is that the owner is thereby deprived of his possession. Certainly, the owner has effectively lost all control as well as all possibility to use and enjoy his property.[82] Although Mummery L.J. goes on to set out compelling secondary reasoning as to public interest and the accessibility of the relevant law, he avoids the crucial issue of compensation. Compensation is an essential element in the justification of any deprivation of possessions, even where the public interest pursued is particularly strong.[83] In the absence of compensation, a deprivation of possessions will only be justifiable in exceptional circumstances.[84] It would seem probable that a challenge will at some point be made as to whether Mummery L.J. identified sufficiently exceptional circumstances in his defence of the doctrine of adverse possession so as to justify the fact that no compensation is available. The means to justify the fact that compensation is not available may lie in Keene L.J.'s approach (agreed with by Mummery L.J. and Sir Martin Nourse), relying on the unquestionable facts that limitation periods are widely accepted in Convention states (and have existed since 1540) and by the Court itself (without compensation), and must inevitably result in deprivation, therefore they should be regarded as one of the rare situations where deprivation can be justified in the general interest without compensation.

16.98

Compulsory Purchase and Acquisition, Expropriation of Property

The Statutory basis for compulsory purchase

In common with most Convention states, the United Kingdom has put in place a statutory framework to provide for the acquisition by the state and local authorities of property necessary for the development of public services and infrastructure, and for the payment of compensation to property owners subject to such compulsory acquisition. This framework can be found in the Land Compensation Act 1961, the Compulsory Purchase Act 1965, the Land Compensation Act 1973, the Acquisition of Land Act 1981 and in Part IX of the Town and Country Planning Act 1990.

16.99

---

[81] *Sporrong and Lönroth v. Sweden* (1983) 5 E.H.R.R., para. 63.
[82] Thus constituting an interference with the peaceful of enjoyment of that property at least, see *Loizidou v. Turkey* (1997) 23 E.H.R.R. 513, para. 63.
[83] *Stran Greek Refneries and Stratis Andreadis v. Greece* (1995) 19 E.H.R.R. 293, paras 70–72.
[84] *Lithgow v. United Kingdom* (1986) 8 E.H.R.R. 329, para. 120; *James v. United Kingdom* (1986) 8 E.H.R.R. 123, para. 54; *Pressos Compania Naviera S.A. v. Belgium* (1996) 21 E.H.R.R. 301, para. 38; *Holy Monasteries v. Greece* (1995) 20 E.H.R.R. 1, para. 71.

The effect of compulsory purchase

16.100 It is obvious that the compulsory acquisition of an individual's property by the state or any public authority is a significant infringement of that individual's property rights. That it should not occur except when expressly authorised by Parliament for purposes in the public interest was an established principle of domestic law long prior to the introduction of the HRA.[85]

16.101 From the point of view of the Convention, the compulsory acquisition of property is a "deprivation of . . . possessions" within the second rule of Article 1 of Protocol No. 1 as enunciated in *Sporrong and Lönroth v. Sweden*.[86] Accordingly, in order to be justified under Article 1 of Protocol No. 1, the relevant compulsory acquisition of property must be in the public interest, and subject to the conditions provided for by law and by the general principles of international law.[87] Where there is non-compliance with domestic law and procedure that constitutes a violation of Article 1 of Protocol No. 1.[88] Where a compulsory purchase order is challenged on the basis of an infringement of Article 1 of Protocol No. 1 the court will ask whether a "fair balance" has been struck between the public interest and the interest of the owner of the property in question.[89] This fair balance requires the interference in question to be in pursuit of a legitimate aim, and there must be a reasonable relationship of proportionality[90] between the means employed and the aim pursued.[91] There is no fair balance if the owner of the property has had to bear "an individual and excessive burden".[92]

16.102 In addition to an interference with his Article 1 of Protocol No. 1 rights, where the compulsory purchase is of a home, it will also constitute an interference with the owner's right to respect for his home under Article 8.[93] To be justified under Article 8 the compulsory purchase of a home must be in accordance with the law[94] and necessary in a democratic society[95] for the pursuit of one of the legitimate aims set out in the second paragraph of the Article.[96] Again, the interference must be proportionate to the aim pursued.[97]

16.103 The Commission and Court appear to accept almost without question that compulsory purchase orders can be in the public interest, and in most cases have accepted, on explanation by the state concerned, that the

---

[85] See, *e.g. Prest v. Secretary of State for Wales* (1983) 266 E.G. 527.

[86] (1983) 5 E.H.R.R. 35. See paras 16.48, 16.49 and 16.86 *et seq.*, above.

[87] For discussion of these concepts, see paras 16.86 *et seq.*, above.

[88] See, *e.g. Guillemin v. France* (1998) 25 E.H.R.R. 435.

[89] *Sporrong and Lönroth v. Sweden* (1983) 5 E.H.R.R. 35, para. 69. See also *Stran Greek Refineries and Stratis Anreadis v. Greece* (1995) 19 E.H.R.R. 293, para. 69.

[90] For a discussion of proportionality, see para. 16.92, above, and Chap. 4, paras 4.48 *et seq.*, above.

[91] See, *e.g. Chassagnou v. France* (2000) 29 E.H.R.R. 615, para. 75. For a more detailed discussion of the concept of proportionality, see paras 4.48 *et seq.*, above.

[92] *Lithgow v. United Kingdom* (1986) 8 E.H.R.R. 329, para. 120; *Tre Traktörer Aktiebolag v. Sweden* (1991) 13 E.H.R.R. 309, para. 62.

[93] *Howard v. United Kingdom* (1987) 9 E.H.R.R. C.D. 91, 116.

[94] See para. 16.39, above.

[95] See para. 16.40, above.

[96] See para. 16.38, above.

[97] *Dudgeon v. United Kingdom* (1982) 4 E.H.R.R. 149, paras 50–53; *Silver v. United Kingdom* (1983) 5 E.H.R.R. 347, para. 97.

orders concerned are in fact in the public interest.[98] The real question in most cases is therefore whether a fair balance has been struck between the public interest and that of the individual owner. Since the owner's rights are extinguished by the implementation of the order, the main issue is normally the availability and adequacy of any compensation paid.

Expropriation of property by other means

16.104 The same principles apply to other forms of expropriation. Examples of state expropriation by other means that might be encountered in the United Kingdom include nationalisation,[99] and possibly seizure in time of war.[1] An example of expropriation elsewhere in Europe, but unlikely to be repeated in the United Kingdom (at least in modern times), can be found in *Holy Monasteries v. Greece*,[2] where the Greek Government had introduced legislation establishing a statutory presumption that certain monastery land belonged to the state. Although the presumption was rebuttable, the monasteries' own title to the land was founded upon ancient adverse possession and therefore the evidence necessary to rebut the presumption did not exist. The Court rejected the Greek Government's argument that the presumption was merely a procedural device to enable the settlement of disputes, and despite the fact that no steps to implement the transfer of title had taken place found that the presumption itself effectively transferred title as the monasteries were not in a position to challenge it. In the circumstances, there had been an expropriation of land by the state and the monasteries had been deprived of their property.

Achieving a fair balance: the availability of compensation

16.105 The taking of property in the public interest without payment of compensation is justifiable only in exceptional circumstances.[3] The Court has rarely interfered with the levels of compensation paid, affording the state a wide margin of appreciation. Such interference should only occur if the value of the property taken and the compensation paid for it is "manifestly disprportionate".[4] Article 1 of Protocol No. 1 does not guarantee full compensation in all circumstances. The Court has stated that legitimate objectives of "public interest" may call for less than reimbursement of the full market value of the property expropriated.[5] However, the taking of property without payment of an amount reasonably related to its value will normally

---

[98] See, *e.g. Howard v. United Kingdom* (1987) 52 D.R. 198, 9 E.H.R.R. 116; *Grech v. Malta* (1995) 20 E.H.R.R. C.D. 95; *Akkus v. Turkey* (1997) 30 E.H.R.R. 365; *Papechelas v. Greece* (1999) 30 E.H.R.R. 923. This accords with the general approach of the Court in respecting the legislature's judgment as to what is in the public interest unless that judgment is "manifestly without reasonable foundation": see *James v. United Kingdom* (1986) 8 E.H.R.R. 123, para. 46.
[99] See, *e.g. Lithgow v. United Kingdom* (1986) 8 E.H.R.R. 329.
[1] Under the War Damages Act 1965.
[2] (1995) 20 E.H.R.R. 1.
[3] *Lithgow v. United Kingdom* (1986) 8 E.H.R.R. 329. An example of such an exceptional circumstance might be seizure of property in the national interest in times of war under the War Damages Act 1965 where no compensation is payable.
[4] *Scotts of Greenock (Est'd 1711) Ltd and Lithgows Ltd v. United Kingdom* (1990) 12 E.H.R.R. 147, para. 90.
[5] *Lithgow v. United Kingdom* (1986) 8 E.H.R.R. 329, para. 121.

constitute a disproportionate interference that cannot be justified.[6] The system used to calculate the compensation should accordingly be flexible enough to cope with different situations[7] and not be manifestly without reasonable foundation.[8] Compensation for the loss sustained by the interference can only constitute adequate reparation where it takes into account the damage arising from the length of the deprivation. It must moreover be paid within a reasonable time.[9]

16.106 In *Lithgow v. United Kingdom*,[10] the applicants challenged the level of compensation paid under the Aircraft and Shipbuilding Industries Act 1977 following the nationalisation of certain industries. Under the compensation scheme, companies were generally valued according to an average of the market value of their shares over a period selected by the government. Naturally, the actual market value of shares in non-listed companies could not easily be determined and accordingly they were allocated a hypothetical market value in the relevant period. The applicants, as non-listed companies, claimed that the system of valuation was contrary to Article 1 of Protocol No. 1. The Court found that the system was not in principle inconsistent with the Article and that, despite substantial disparities between the companies' own assessment of their share values and the compensation received, the effects of the scheme on individual companies was not such as to render it unlawful.

16.107 In *Guillemin v. France*,[11] the applicant was the owner of land made subject to a public interest declaration in 1982 which required the acquisition of the land by compulsory purchase in order to develop a residential area. An expropriation order was made and the level of compensation set. The applicant successfully applied for an increase in the compensation, the setting aside of the public interest declaration on the grounds that it was *ultra vires*, and the setting aside of the relevant expropriation orders. These actions were concluded in 1990 at which point the applicant sought compensation which was not forthcoming. Taking into account the unlawful expropriation of the land, the failure to pay compensation and the length of the proceedings instituted by the applicant the Court found a violation of Article 1 of Protocol No. 1.

16.108 In *Akkus v. Turkey*,[12] the applicant complained of a violation of her right to the peaceful enjoyment of her possessions on account of the National Water Board's delay in paying her additional compensation for expropriation. In reference to its earlier decision of *Stran Greek Refineries and Stratis Anreadis v. Greece*,[13] the Court held that:

> "the adequacy of compensation would be diminished if it were to be paid without reference to various circumstances liable to reduce its value such as unreasonable delay. Abnormally lengthy delays in the payment of compensation for expropriation lead to increased financial

[6] *Papachelas v. Greece* (1999) 30 E.H.R.R. 923, para. 48.
[7] *Papachelas v. Greece* (1999) 30 E.H.R.R. 923, para. 53.
[8] For a broader discussion of compensation under Art. 1 of Protocol No. 1, see D. Anderson, "Compensation for Interference with Property" [1999] E.H.R.L.R. 543.
[9] *Guillemin v. France* (1998) 25 E.H.R.R. 435.
[10] (1986) 8 E.H.R.R. 329.
[11] (1998) 25 E.H.R.R. 435.
[12] (1997) 30 E.H.R.R. 365.
[13] (1995) 19 E.H.R.R. 293, para. 82.

loss for the person whose land has been expropriated putting him in a position of uncertainty especially when the monetary depreciation which occurs in certain States is taken into account."[14]

The difference between the compensation as determined and its value when actually paid caused the applicant loss. The deferring of payment rendered the compensation inadequate and was therefore a violation of Article 1 of Protocol No. 1.[15]

Conclusion

Compulsory purchase is and for some time has been a necessary part of modern society, and most Convention States have some form of legislative provision regarding the compulsory acquisition of property by the state. On their face the relevant Articles of the Convention recognise the need for such legislative measures, for example under Article 1 of Protocol No. 1, in permitting the deprivation of possessions by the state in the public interest. Accordingly, compulsory purchase legislation itself has largely been left untouched by the Commission and the Court on the basis that individual states are afforded a wide margin of appreciation in determining what is in the public interest within their own boundaries.[16]   **16.109**

The relevant statutory framework in the United Kingdom is certain, accessible and the results of its invocation reasonably foreseeable. There is provision made for compensation. Accordingly, it is unlikely that the compulsory purchase legislation itself will be subject to successful challenge in the domestic courts[17] on the basis that it constitutes an infringement of the Convention rights. However, this does not preclude the application of the relevant principles under Article 1 of Protocol No. 1 and Article 8 to individual cases, where challenges might well be made to the application of the statutory framework by the state or local authority on the basis that it constitutes a specific interference with the rights concerned. Examples might include the use of compulsory purchase powers by a local authority for purposes arguably not in the public interest,[18] excessive delay by a local authority in determining or implementing its plans,[19] or failures to pay any or any adequate compensation[20] either at all or within a reasonable period.[21]   **16.110**

Environmental

The application of the Articles of the Convention in an environmental context

The Convention makes no specific reference to the environment in its list of rights and freedoms. In 1976 an application brought by members of an   **16.111**

---

[14] *Akkus v. Turkey* (2000) 30 E.H.R.R. 365, para. 29.
[15] *Akkus v. Turkey* (2000) 30 E.H.R.R. 365, paras 30–31.
[16] See, *e.g. James v. United Kingdom* (1986) 8 E.H.R.R. 123, para. 46.
[17] As indeed it has not been subject to any successful challenge in the Commission or the Court.
[18] See, *e.g. Guillemin v. France* (1998) 25 E.H.R.R. 435 (where the public interest declaration was set aside as being *ultra vires*); see para. 16.107, above.
[19] See, *e.g. Zubani v. Italy* (1999) 28 E.H.R.R. C.D. 62.
[20] See, *e.g. Akkus v. Turkey* (2000) 30 E.H.R.R. 365; see para. 16.108, above.
[21] See, *e.g. Guillemin v. France* (1998) 25 E.H.R.R. 435; see para. 16.107, above.

environmental group concerned about the use of marshland was rejected by the Court on the basis that the concerns raised did not constitute an alleged violation of one of the Convention rights.[22] As more positive attitudes to the environment have developed so the Court has sought to find protection for the environment within the Articles of the Convention, most particularly in Article 8. In *Fredin v. Sweden*,[23] the Court stated that it recognised: "that in today's society the protection of the environment is an increasingly important consideration". Despite this change of approach, however, it is important to remember that there is no specific protection for the environment *per se* in the Convention.

16.112   Respect for the home under Article 8 goes further than the mere integrity of home life, what is intended to be covered is the physical security of a person's living quarters and possessions.[24] This includes the ability to live freely in the home and to enjoy it,[25] and accordingly goes beyond the mere right to possess it.[26] Thus, Article 8 affords protection to any environmental and aesthetic qualities of the home enjoyed by its owners.[27]

16.113   Unlike Article 8, Article 1 of Protocol No. 1 is concerned only with interferences affecting the economic or market value of property and not those which simply affect the owner's aesthetic or environmental enjoyment of it. It does not, in principle, guarantee the right to the peaceful enjoyment of possessions in a pleasant environment.[28] Interferences of an environmental nature will therefore only be actionable under Article 1 of Protocol No. 1 if they actually impact on the economic value of the possession affected. Further, interferences of minor economic effect may not be covered.[29]

16.114   In very extreme cases of environmental interference it is possible that Article 2 (the right to life) might be infringed if a sufficient causative link could be demonstrated between the environmental damage and the threat to life.[30] It would be necessary to establish a real risk of being subjected

---

[22] *X and Y v. Federal Republic of Germany* (1976) 5 Eur. Com. H.R. Dec. & Rep.

[23] (1990) 13 E.H.R.R. 784.

[24] *Gillow v. United Kingdom* (1989) 11 E.H.R.R. 335; *Selcuk and Asker v. Turkey* (1998) 26 E.H.R.R. 477.

[25] *Lopez Ostra v. Spain* (1995) 20 E.H.R.R. 277; *Guerra v. Italy* (1998) 26 E.H.R.R. 357.

[26] *Howard v. United Kingdom* (1987) 52 D.R. 198, Eur Comm HR, 9 E.H.R.R. 91, 116.

[27] *Powell and Rayner v. United Kingdom* (1990) 12 E.H.R.R. 355.

[28] See, *e.g. S v. France* (1990) 65 D.R. 250 at 261 (a case concerning noise pollution where the Commission only considered the effect of the pollution on the value of the property rather than its effect in terms of loss of amenity); also *Powell and Rayner v. United Kingdom* (1990) 12 E.H.R.R. 355 (the fact that aircraft noise from Heathrow airport made the enjoyment of the land concerned "less pleasant" was not sufficient to engage Article 1 of Protocol No. 1 although *cf.* the Commission's earlier view in *Rayner v. United Kingdom* (1986) 9 E.H.R.R. 375, that "aircraft noise nuisance of considerable importance both as to level and frequency may seriously affect the value of real property or even render it unsaleable and thus amount to a partial taking of property"). See also earlier applications *Arondelle v. United Kingdom*, Application No. 7889/77 (1982) 19 D.R. 186 (where the land's proximity to the M23 motorway and Gatwick airport meant that the intolerable levels of noise made it virtually impossible to sell. The U.K. Government settled for £7,000) and *Baggs v. United Kingdom*, Application No. 9310/81 (1985) 44 D.R. 13 (where the U.K. Government settled for £24,000); see also *Pine Valley Developments Ltd v. Ireland* (1992) 14 E.H.R.R. 319.

[29] See, *e.g. Langborger v. Sweden* (1990) 12 E.H.R.R. 416 (a case concerning a disputed 0.3 per cent commission).

[30] In *LCB v. United Kingdom* (1999) 27 E.H.R.R. 212, the applicant claimed that her leukaemia had been caused by her father's exposure to radiation. The Court was not satisfied that a causal link between her disease and his exposure had been established.

to circumstances endangering health and physical integrity thereby putting at serious risk the right to life.[31]

In *Lopez Ostra v. Spain*,[32] although a violation of Article 3 (prohibition of **16.115** torture and inhuman or degrading treatment) was not made out on the facts, the Court accepted in principle that it could be applied to circumstances of environmental interference. The applicant complained that a waste treatment plant had been built just 12 metres from her home, subjecting her to noxious fumes which caused health problems amongst local residents. Although the Court accepted that she had lived in "difficult conditions" it did not feel that the high threshold under Article 3 had been met, finding instead a violation under Article 8.

The procedural aspects of decisions made by the state, local authorities **16.116** and the courts which have environmental impact may also engage Article 6 (the right to a fair trial).

As with all aspects of Convention rights, there is always the potential for **16.117** allegations of discrimination under Article 14 to be made in conjunction with any allegation of infringement of the relevant environmental rights.

Parties capable of being held responsible for environmental interference

Clearly, the primary impact of the Convention in this area is to impose **16.118** negative obligations on public authorities not to cause environmental damage themselves. Thus, central and local government and local authorities, as "obvious" public authorities,[33] can be held directly responsible for any relevant infringement of the "environmental" Convention rights set out above. In addition, "hybrid" authorities[34] (such as British Nuclear Fuels and the privatised utility companies supplying gas, electricity, transport, water and waste services) will be subject to similar responsibilities in relation to their public functions.[34A] As public authorities under section 6(3)(a) of the HRA, courts and tribunals will also have to ensure that their decisions do not directly infringe the relevant Convention rights. The position between private individuals remains open to debate, however, the courts' own obligations under section 6 of the HRA may at least lead to some application of the principles of the Convention to disputes between private individuals.

In addition to their responsibility for their own actions, public authorities **16.119** may, in certain circumstances, be under positive obligations to take action to protect individuals from interference with their environmental rights by other private individuals. As a matter of general principle, public authorities will not be placed under a positive obligation to take steps to prevent or punish every infringement of the rights protected by the relevant Articles. Whether such an obligation exists is likely to depend on many factors, including the extent to which it would impose a burden on the state or

---

[31] See opinions of Judges Jambrek and Walsh in *Guerra v. Italy* (1998) 26 E.H.R.R. 357.
[32] (1995) 20 E.H.R.R. 277.
[33] See paras 2.25 and 8.16 *et seq.*, above.
[34] Under the HRA, s.6(3)(b): "any person certain of whose functions are functions of a public nature". See paras 2.25 and 8.17 *et seq.*, above.
[34A] See *e.g. Marcic v. Thames Water Utilities Ltd*, May 14, 2001, decision of H.H.J. Richard Havery Q.C. in the Technology and Construction Court, reported on Newlaw Online as judgment no. 2010712703.

public authority,[35] the importance of the rights requiring protection (for example whether they represent aspects "vital", "fundamental" or "essential" to private life),[36] whether there is any general consensus of approach to the issue in other Contracting States,[37] the general practice of the particular state or public authority in relation to similar matters,[38] whether the obligation sought is narrowly defined or too broad to impose,[39] and the potential impact of such an obligation on other Convention rights.[40]

16.120   Applying these general principles the Court has accepted that there is a positive obligation on public authorities to take action to safeguard individuals' environmental rights under Article 8 by regulating the activities of other private individuals or companies.[41] Further, it has accepted that public authorities are under a positive obligation to provide individuals with information necessary to enable them to assess the environmental risk to which they were or are being subjected, even where that environmental risk is posed by a private individual or company.[42]

No requirement that health be endangered

16.121   An individual's rights regarding his quality of life may be infringed by an environmental interference even if his health is not endangered.[43]

Relevant case law: achieving a "fair balance"

16.122   A number of cases have been brought against the United Kingdom regarding noise pollution.[44] The most significant of these is *Powell and Rayner v. United Kingdom*,[45] which concerned the noise levels suffered in properties close to Heathrow airport. The applicants sought to argue that the United Kingdom's Government's measures for reducing the nuisance caused by aircraft taking off and landing were inadequate. The Court accepted that the allegations could be considered under Article 8 because: "the quality of the applicant's private life and the scope for enjoying the amenities of his home had been adversely affected by the noise generated by aircraft using Heathrow airport". It did not matter whether the Government's obligations under Article 8 were considered in positive or negative terms. In considering whether a fair balance between the rights of the applicants and the needs of society had been achieved the Court considered the significant strategic and economic importance of

[35] *Rees v. United Kingdom* (1987) 9 E.H.R.R. 56, paras 43–44.
[36] *Gaskin v. United Kingdom* (1990) 12 E.H.R.R. 36, para. 49; *X & Y v. Netherlands* (1986) 8 E.H.R.R. 235, para. 27.
[37] *B v. France* (1993) 16 E.H.R.R. 1, para. 48; *X, Y and Z v. United Kingdom* (1997) 24 E.H.R.R. 143, para. 52.
[38] *Rees v. United Kingdom* (1987) 9 E.H.R.R. 56, para. 42.
[39] *Botta v. Italy* (1998) 26 E.H.R.R. 241.
[40] *Winer v. United Kingdom*, Application No. 10871/84, 48 D.R. 154 in which the conflict between the right to privacy under Art. 8 with the right to freedom of expression under Art. 10 was considered.
[41] See, *e.g. Powell and Rayner v. United Kingdom* (1990) 12 E.H.R.R. 355; *Lopez Ostra v. Spain* (1995) 20 E.H.R.R. 277.
[42] *Guerra v. Italy* (1998) 26 E.H.R.R. 357.
[43] *Lopez Ostra v. Spain* (1995) 20 E.H.R.R. 277.
[44] See, *e.g. Arondelle v. United Kingdom* Application No. 7889/77 (1982) 19 D.R. 186 (settled for £7,000); *Baggs v. United Kingdom* Application No. 9310/81 (1985) 44 D.R. 13 (settled for £24,000).
[45] (1990) 12 E.H.R.R. 355.

a major international airport to the country as a whole and the steps taken by the Government to control, abate and compensate for aircraft noise. The Court found, ultimately, that the airport pursued a legitimate social aim and that the fair balance between the competing interests of the individual and the community as a whole had not been upset.

In *S v. France*,[46] the applicant complained of noise and the general **16.123** disruption of her previously peaceful rural surroundings on the banks of the River Loire following the construction of a large nuclear power station some 300 metres from her home. She alleged that the level of compensation awarded to her by the *Conseil d'État* was inadequate and claimed violations of both Article 8 and Article 1 of Protocol No. 1. Whilst the Commission accepted that the construction of the power station interfered with her ability to enjoy the amenity of her home, it found that a complaint was not established. With regard to the issues to be considered in determining whether a fair balance had been struck and when seeking to justify an interference, the Commission stated:

> "It is not in dispute that the nuclear power station was lawfully built and brought into service by Électricité de France. Nor can there be any doubt that the construction of a nuclear power station serves the interest of the economic well-being of the country. In order to determine whether the interference in this case can be regarded as 'necessary in a democratic society', it must first be decided whether it was proportionate in relation to the legitimate interest the works were intended to serve. When a State is authorised to restrict rights or freedoms guaranteed by the Convention, the proportionality rule may well require it to ensure that these restrictions do not oblige the person concerned to bear an unreasonable burden."

In *Lopez Ostra v. Spain*,[47] the applicant lived in Lorca, Spain, where there **16.124** was already a heavy concentration of environmentally insensitive factories connected with the leather industry. A waste plant for the treatment of liquid and solid waste from that industry was constructed by a private company some 12 metres from the applicant's home, and commenced processing waste without a licence. The plant was intended to reduce pollution in the area but, in fact, released noxious fumes and smells that caused a nuisance to and health problems amongst the local residents, including the applicant and her family. The Court said that although the Spanish authorities were theoretically not directly responsible for the emissions in question the town had allowed the plants to be built on its land and the state had subsidised the plant's construction. The Court unanimously found that there had been a violation of Article 8 on the basis that: " . . . despite the margin of appreciation left to the respondent state, the court considers that the state did not succeed in striking a fair balance between the interests of the town's economic well-being—that of having a waste treatment plant—and the applicant's effective enjoyment of her right to respect for her home and her private and family life".[48] In reaching that

---

[46] Application No. 13728/88 (1990) 65 D.R. 250.
[47] (1995) 20 E.H.R.R. 277.
[48] *ibid.*, para. 58.

conclusion, the Court considered the failure of the local authorities to take sufficient measures to protect the applicant's rights. Despite a temporary shutdown of the plant and the rehousing of affected residents, the authorities had stood by whilst pollution continued and challenged two national courts' orders that the plant be closed termporarily. Although the applicant's daughter was made seriously ill by the noxious fumes, the Court emphasised that an environmental interference could violate Article 8 without endangering health: "Severe environmental pollution may affect individuals' well-being and prevent them from enjoying their homes in such a way as to affect their private and family life adversely, without, however, seriously endangering their health".[49]

16.125   From these cases it can be seen that to a large extent the question as to whether a fair balance has been achieved between the rights of the individual on the one hand and the general interest of the community on the other turns on the facts of each individual case. However, some obvious general hypotheses might be drawn from these decisions. First, that the extent to which the interference is necessary in the general interest of the community is likely to determine whether the interference can in fact be justified. Thus, where the general interest of the community in the interference in question is very significant, for example in the national interest (such as an airport[50] or power station[51]), an interference of even very substantial proportions (such as with the large number of people affected by noise from Heathrow airport[52]) is likely to be justified, even where measures taken to reduce the interference are of limited impact. Conversely, where an interference is of lesser general benefit (such as a waste disposal plant in one town intended to reduce local pollution and that in fact increases it[53]), the interference is less easily justified. Secondly, and looking at the same concept from the other side, that the severity of the interference with the rights of the individual determines whether it can in fact be justified irrespective of the general interest. Thus, where the severity of the interference is particularly severe (such as a very proximate pollution of the environment seriously affecting health and requiring the individual to move)[54] this readily prevents justification on public interest grounds. Whereas, where the only impact of it is really a purely aesthetic one (such as the loss of a pleasant rural environment)[55] the interference is more easily justified. These two hypotheses really do no more than restate and demonstrate the goal of achieving a fair balance between the interests of the community as a whole and the rights of the individual. The real point of significance is to note that, perhaps unsurprisingly, the only two cases in which a violation has been found to have occurred[56] have been those in which the impact on the individual is particularly severe.

---

[49] *ibid.*, para. 51.
[50] *Powell and Rayner v. United Kingdom* (1990) 12 E.H.R.R. 355.
[51] *S v. France*, Application No. 13728/88 (1990) 65 D.R. 250.
[52] *Powell and Rayner v. United Kingdom* (1990) 12 E.H.R.R. 355.
[53] *Lopez Ostra v. Spain* (1995) 20 E.H.R.R. 277.
[54] *ibid.*
[55] *S v. France*, Application No. 13728/88 (1990) 65 D.R. 250.
[56] *Lopez Ostra v. Spain* (1995) 20 E.H.R.R. 277; *Guerra v. Italy* (1998) 26 E.H.R.R. 357.

Provision of information about environmental threats

Public authorities must provide an accessible and effective procedure by **16.126** which individuals under environmental threat may gain access to the information necessary to enable them to assess the environmental risk to which they are being subjected.[57] If a public authority fails to meet this obligation it will have violated Article 8. Further, a public authority may be under such an obligation even where the environmental pollution is caused by a private company with which it has no connection.[58]

In *Guerra v. Italy,*[59] there were 40 applicants, all of whom lived in Man- **16.127** fredonia near a privately owned chemical factory. Following an accident resulting in the poisoning and admission to hospital of 150 people in 1976 the factory had been classified by the Italian Government as being high-risk. A technical report in 1988 criticised safety standards at the factory. The applicants waited until 1994, when production of fertilisers ceased at the factory, for essential information that would have enabled them to assess the risks they might run if they continued to live near the factory. The applicants relied upon Article 8 and Article 2 in claiming that the local authority's inaction over many years and failure to take steps to limit the risk of pollution constituted a breach of their rights. They also relied on Article 10 in claiming that the failure to inform the public about the risk and to advise them as to what action to take in the event of an accident was a breach of their right to receive information. The Court held that both Article 10 and Article 2 were inapplicable. The Court did, however, hold that there was a violation of Article 8 on the basis that the national authorities failed to take the necessary steps to ensure effective protection of the applicants' right to respect for their private and family life.

In *McGinley and Egan v. United Kingdom,*[60] the applicants were British **16.128** servicemen stationed on Christmas Island in the Pacific during 1957 and 1958 when the United Kingdom carried out six atmospheric nuclear explosion tests. The applicants later suffered health problems and sought to claim, when applying for a government pension, that they had been exposed to dangerous levels of radiation. Their application was rejected on the basis that they had not been exposed to dangerous levels of radiation. Documents setting out the radiation levels on the island at the relevant time were available to the applicants under a rule of procedure. The Court accordingly held that there was no violation of Article 8, but stated:

> "Where a Government engages in hazardous activities, such as those in issue in the present case, which might have hidden conse-quences on the health of those involved in such activities, respect for private and family life under Article 8 requires that an effective and accessible procedure be established which enables such persons to seek all relevant and appropriate information."

[57] *McGinley and Egan v. United Kingdom* (1999) 27 E.H.R.R. 1.
[58] *Guerra v. Italy* (1998) 26 E.H.R.R. 357.
[59] (1998) 26 E.H.R.R. 357.
[60] (1999) 27 E.H.R.R. 1.

16.129   The effect of these two cases is to place a considerable burden on public authorities, not only to ensure that they do not cause unjustifiable environmental harm themselves, but also to ensure that others do not do so. In addition, they must make available a procedure by which information about their own hazardous activities is accessible to those likely to be affected, and must monitor and provide a similar procedure for the provision of and access to information about the hazardous activities of private parties.

Standing and procedural issues

16.130   In order to bring a claim of interference with one of the environmental rights identified above, an individual would have to satisfy the "victim" test. It is not sufficient for the individual concerned simply to allege that the mere existence of a law violates his rights. He must demonstrate that he is "directly affected" by the relevant act or omission in the absence of any specific measure of implementation.[61] It is not necessary, however, where his rights have been breached, for the individual to demonstrate that he has suffered a detriment or been prejudiced,[62] although that fact might obviously impact on the availability and extent of any compensation.[63] These principles mean that it is not possible for an individual or an organisation simply to bring a claim for violation of Convention rights on behalf of the environment generally or to protect an environment in which he or it is not directly engaged. In other words, third parties will generally have difficulties in seeking to rely on Convention rights. In *Balmer Schaforth v. Switzerland*,[64] the applicants complained that they had been denied access to a tribunal considering the extension of the operating licence of a nuclear power station close to their homes. The Court held that Article 6 did not apply because the applicants had not shown that the power station exposed them personally to a danger that " . . . was not only serious but also specific and, above all imminent".[65] In some ways this is distinct from the approach in domestic law which has permitted interested or concerned parties to bring applications for the protection of a particular environment,[66] and it remains to be seen whether domestic courts will adopt or extend these restrictive views of the Court about third party involvement in environmental claims under the Convention.

16.131   Article 6 may also have impact on the decision making process and on decisions taken by public authorities in relation to environmental matters (such as the granting of licences) where they can be said to amount to a determination of civil rights and obligations.[67] Article 6 may give rise to challenges both to the independence and impartiality of those making relevant decisions and as to the fairness of any relevant procedures. In

---

[61] *Klass v. Germany* (1979–80) 2 E.H.R.R. 214.
[62] See, *e.g. Campbell and Cosans v. United Kingdom* (1982) 4 E.H.R.R. 293; *Eckle v. Germany* (1983) 5 E.H.R.R. 1; *Bowman v. United Kingdom* (1998) 26 E.H.R.R. 1.
[63] See, *e.g. Eckle v. Germany* (1983) 5 E.H.R.R. 1, para. 66; *Adolf v. Austria* (1982) 4 E.H.R.R. 313, para. 37; *Amuur v. France* (1996) 22 E.H.R.R. 533, para. 36.
[64] (1998) 25 E.H.R.R. 598.
[65] *Balmer-Shaforth v. Switzerland* (1998) 25 E.H.R.R. 598, para. 40.
[66] See, *e.g. R. v. Somerset County Council and ARC Southern Ltd, ex p. Dixon* [1997] J.P.L. 1030.
[67] See *Bryan v. United Kingdom* (1996) 21 E.H.R.R. 342.

Fredin v. Sweden,[68] the applicant, who was the owner of a gravel pit, successfully established a violation of Article 6 where he was unable to appeal or secure the review of decisions: first, to revoke his licence to extract gravel after he had made a considerable investment; and, secondly, to force him to secure the cost of making the site good himself. The Article may also provide a basis for challenging procedures adopted, for example in the investigation and prosecution of breaches of environmental legislation, where answers given might prove self-incriminatory.[69] Article 6 will not, however, provide such protection where the questions asked, for example under the Environmental Protection Act 1990, are simply requests for factual information and do not invite any admission of wrongdoing.[70]

Housing

No general right to housing

There is no general right to a home under the Convention. Article 8 only   **16.132** creates a right to respect for the home and not an absolute right to a home or to be provided with a home[71]: whether a state provides funds to enable everyone to have a home is a matter for political not judicial decision.[72] In *X v. Germany*,[73] the Court held that failure to provide a refugee with a decent home did not constitute a breach of Article 8. In *Burton v. United Kingdom*,[74] the applicant suffered from cancer and claimed that her local authority's failure to provide accommodation in a caravan for her to live her remaining days in the traditional lifestyle of a Romany gypsy constituted a breach of her Article 8 rights. The Commission rejected her claim on the basis that there is no positive obligation on the state to provide alternative accommodation of an applicant's choosing.[75] Thus, the Court has also refused to accept that, where statistically the number of gypsies is greater than the number of places available in authorised gypsy sites, decisions not to allow the applicants to occupy land where they wished to install their caravans constitute a violation of Article 8. Further, the Court has not accepted that Article 8 imposes a positive obligation to make available to the gypsy community an adequate number of suitably equipped sites.[76]

---

[68] (1991) 13 E.H.R.R. 784.
[69] By analogy with the similar situation regarding the investigation of the conduct of a company's affairs by the DTI, see *Saunders v. United Kingdom* (1997) 23 E.H.R.R. 313.
[70] See *R. v. Hertfordshire County Council, ex p. Green Environmental Industries* [1998] Env. L.R. 153; *The Times*, October 9, 1997.
[71] *X v. Germany* (1956) 1 Y.B. 202.
[72] This is a well established principle but for a recent decision in which it was repeated, see the decision of the Court in the group of gypsy cases against the United Kingdom of *Beard*, *Chapman*, *Coster*, *Lee*, and *Jane Smith* reported in *The Times*, January, 30, 2001.
[73] (1956) 1 Y.B. 202.
[74] (1996) 22 E.H.R.R. C.D. 134.
[75] *Burton v. United Kingdom* (1996) 22 E.H.R.R. C.D. 134; *Buckley v. United Kingdom* (1997) 23 E.H.R.R. 101.
[76] See *Beard v. United Kingdom*, Application No. 24882/94 (1998) 25 E.H.R.R. C.D. 28; *Chapman v. United Kingdom*, Application No. 27238/95 (1998) 25 E.H.R.R. C.D. 64; *Coster v. United Kingdom*, Application No. 24876/94 (1998) 25 E.H.R.R. C.D. 24; *Lee v. United Kingdom*, Application No. 25289/94 (1998) 25 E.H.R.R. C.D. 46; *Jane Smith v. United Kingdom*, Application No. 25154/94 (1998) 25 E.H.R.R. C.D. 42; particularly the judgment of the Court in relation to this group of cases as reported in *The Times*, January 30, 2001.

Public authorities

16.133   Local authorities are clearly public authorities for the purposes of the HRA and accordingly must act compatibly with the Convention in the exercise of all their functions. Much of the responsibilty for social housing has now been passed to registered social landlords under the Housing Act 1996. At the very least these registered social landlords (formerly the housing associations) must be "hybrid" public authorities,[77] obliged to act compatibly with the Convention in the exercise of their public functions. This issue was considered by the Court of Appeal in *Poplar Housing and Regeneration Community Association Ltd v. Donoghue.*[77A] The Court of Appeal emphasised that the fact that a body performs an activity which otherwise a public body would be under a duty to perform cannot mean that such performance is necessarily a public function.[77B] The purpose of section 6(3) of the HRA was not to make a body, which does not have responsibilities to the public, a public body merely because it performs acts on behalf of a public body which would constitute public functions were such acts to be performed by the public body itself.[77C] Nevertheless, the question was one of fact and degree and that while the activities of housing associations need not involve the performance of public functions in all circumstances, the provision of accommodation and seeking of possession was so closely assimilated to the role of the local authority that the relevant housing association was therefore a functional or "hybrid" public authority in that regard.

General impact of the Convention on housing

16.134   The effect of the HRA on public sector landlords is likely to be significant, affecting housing policy, the monitoring of public sector housing, the extent to which landlords are required to repair and improve public sector housing, and the degree to which landlords may be required to seek to resolve disputes amongst their tenants. In the main these are issues of public law outside the scope of this text, however some consideration is appropriate.

Positive obligations

16.135   Public sector landlords may find themselves under positive obligations under Article 8 to protect their tenants from nuisance. However, as a matter of general principle, public authorities will not be placed under a positive obligation to take steps to prevent every infringement of the rights protected by the relevant Articles. Whether such an obligation exists is likely to depend on many factors including the extent to which it would impose a burden on the state or public authority,[78] the importance of the rights requiring protection (for example whether they represent aspects

---

[77] Under the HRA, s.6(3)(b): "any person certain of whose functions are functions of a public nature". See Chap. 2, para. 2.25 & Chapter 8, para. 8.17, above.
[77A] [2001] 3 W.L.R. 183, judgment of the Court of Appeal Civil Division of April 27, 2001, transcript of judgment available from Newlaw Online as decision 201047901.
[77B] Judgment paragraph 58.
[77C] Judgment paragraph 59.
[78] *Rees v. United Kingdom* (1987) 9 E.H.R.R. 56, para. 42.

"vital", "fundamental" or "essential" to private life),[79] whether there is any general consensus of approach to the issue in other Contracting States,[80] the general practice of the particular state or public authority in relation to similar matters,[81] whether the obligation sought is narrowly defined or too broad to impose,[82] and the potential impact of such an obligation on other Convention rights.[83] It is possible that public sector landlords will be placed under positive obligations regarding the improvement of unfit housing in both the public and private sector, and in providing protection from "pollution" in its loosest sense (to include the qualitative and aesthetic aspects of enjoyment of the "home"), from noise, and from anti-social neighbours. How far this will extend is a matter for debate. It may be the case, for example, that in a reversal of the House of Lords' decision in *Southwark London Borough Council v. Mills; Baxter v. London Borough of Camden*,[84] public sector landlords might find themselves under a positive obligation to provide soundproofing in their flats to protect their tenants from noise from their neighbours. In *Southwark v. Mills*,[85] the House of Lords found that noise levels had to be excessive to constitute a breach of the covenant of quiet enjoyment, that the lack of soundproofing was an inherent structural condition for which the landlord assumed no responsibility, it predated the occupation of the premises by the tenants and the soundproofing had not been reduced since their occupation, and that the covenant of quiet enjoyment could not impose an obligation to improve the premises. The normal use of a residential flat by neighbours could not constitute a nuisance and if, as appeared to be the case, the noise complained of resulted from the normal use of neighbouring flats no nuisance was committed and the landlords could not be held liable. Further, although Parliament had dealt extensively with problems of substandard housing it had declined to impose any obligation of soundproofing and the courts should not attempt to fill that gap. Factors most likely to determine whether an obligation of soundproofing could be imposed by reliance upon Convention rights are the extent to which that would place an excessive burden on public sector landlords (at the time of the decision in *Southwark v. Mills* it was widely recognised that the burden would be enormous), the extent to which the noise pollution impacts on the tenants' quality of life, and the extent to which soundproofing had been carried out by other public sector landlords. Overall, it might be anticipated that the enormous expense required to carry out such soundproofing, far beyond the means of most public sector landlords, might tend to push the courts

---

[79] *Gaskin v. United Kingdom* (1990) 12 E.H.R.R. 36, para. 49; *X & Y v. Netherlands* (1985) 8 E.H.R.R. 235.
[80] *B v. France* (1992) 16 E.H.R.R. 1, para. 48; *X, Y and Z v. United Kingdom* (1997) 24 E.H.R.R. 143, para. 52.
[81] *Rees v. United Kingdom* (1987) 9 E.H.R.R. 56, para. 42.
[82] *Botta v. Italy* (1998) 26 E.H.R.R. 241.
[83] *Winer v. United Kingdom*, Application No. 10871/84, 48 D.R. 154, in which the conflict between the right to privacy under Art. 8 with the right to freedom of expression under Art. 10 was considered.
[84] [1999] 3 W.L.R. 939.
[85] *Southwark London Borough Council v. Mills; Baxter v. London Borough of Camden* [1999] 3 W.L.R. 939.

in the direction of finding that the imposition of such an obligation on public sector landlords was not justifiable.

The Housing Act 1996: Eviction for anti-social behaviour

16.136 One housing legislative provision that will almost certainly be scrutinised closely is the Housing Act 1996, which permits the eviction by a landlord of a secure[86] or assured tenant[87] on the basis of certain specified anti-social behaviour. The required anti-social behaviour may be one or more of: conduct amounting to or likely to amount to a nuisance to anyone residing, visiting or engaging in lawful activity in the locality; being convicted of using the premises in question or allowing them to be used for immoral or unlawful purposes; or, being convicted of an arrestable offence committed in the locality. Eviction under the 1996 Act in those circumstances would amount to a deprivation of possessions within the second rule of Article 1 of Protocol No. 1 as enunciated in *Sporrong v. Lönroth v. Sweden*.[88] It also might possibly engage Article 8. It is extremely unlikely that the legislation itself would be declared incompatible with the Convention in its entirety. It pursues a legitimate aim in seeking to prevent, discourage, and limit the impact of anti-social behaviour on other tenants. Whether a "fair balance" has been achieved is debatable, particularly in the absence of compensation for eviction and due to the severity of the remedy available in cases where there may be limited impact of the behaviour concerned on other residents. The provisions of the 1996 Act are certainly open to abuse by unscrupulous landlords using it to rid themselves of undesirable tenants guilty of no more than minor infractions. More likely than a successful attack on the legislation itself, however, is the scrutiny of the use of its powers by public landlords. Thus arguments might well be run, in challenging a particular decision to seek to evict under the 1996 Act, on the basis that the particular behaviour was not of a particularly anti-social nature, or that the likelihood of it causing a nuisance was minimal, or that there had in fact been no negative impact of the behaviour on other tenants.

Intellectual Property

Intellectual property rights and the Convention

16.137 Intellectual property rights, such as patents, are capable of being regarded as "possessions" for the purposes of Article 1 of Protocol No. 1.[89] As such, the same principles will apply to intellectual property rights as apply generally to property in relation to the protection afforded by Article 1 of Protocol No. 1. Thus, any deprivation, control of use or general interference with the peaceful enjoyment of an individual's intellectual property

---

[86] Housing Act 1996, s.144.
[87] *ibid.*, s.148.
[88] (1983) 5 E.H.R.R. 35. See paras 16.48–16.49, paras 16.68 *et seq.*, above.
[89] *Smith Kline and French Laboratories Ltd v. Netherlands* (1996) 66 D.R. 70 at 79; *British American Tobacco Company Ltd v. Netherlands* (1995) 21 E.H.R.R. 409, paras 72–74; *Lenzing AG v. United Kingdom* [1999] E.H.R.L.R. 132, para. 146.

rights by the state or any public authority will need to be justified in accordance with established principles.[90]

No extension by Convention of statutory defences in copyright

In *Ashdown v. Telegraph Group Ltd*,[91] the Defendant sought to argue that   **16.138** Article 10 of the Convention (the right to freedom of expression) extended the statutory defences available to an alleged infringement of copyright under the Copyright, Designs and Patents Act 1988. The claim was brought by "Paddy" Ashdown, a Member of Parliament and the former leader of the Liberal Democrat Party. In October 1998 he had made a minute of a meeting he had attended with the Prime Minister, a copy of which was disclosed to the defendant, and portions of which were subsequently published in a number of articles. The claimant sought injunctions and damages or an account of profits for breach of confidence and infringement of copyright. The defendant primarily relied on the statutory defences contained in section 30 (fair dealing) and section 17(3) (preventing or restricting the enforcement of copyright on the ground of public interest) of the Copyright, Designs and Patents Act 1988. Sir Andrew Morritt, V.-C., rejected both these defences. In addition, the defendant relied on Article 10 in order to influence either the interpretation or the application of the 1988 Act as required by section 3(1) of the HRA. The defendant submitted that the provisions of the 1988 Act did not satisfy the requirement of Article 10(2) that any restriction on the exercise of the right of freedom of expression be limited to that which was necessary in a democratic society. Accordingly, all the individual facts had to be considered in every case to ascertain whether the restriction on the right to freedom of expression imposed by the 1988 Act was necessary in a democratic society. Sir Andrew Morritt, V.-C., rejected that argument. Although intellectual property rights in general and copyright in particular constituted restrictions on the right to freedom of expression, it did not follow that the facts of each case had to be considered to determine whether the restriction went beyond what was necessary in a democratic society. The provisions of the 1988 Act were required to satisfy that test, and in his judgment they did so. The needs of a democratic society included the recognition and protection of private property, which included copyright. He saw no reason why the court should travel outside the provisions of the 1988 Act and recognise on the facts of particular cases further or other exceptions to the restrictions on the exercise of the right to freedom of expression constituted by the 1988 Act. None of the decisions of the Court relied upon by the defendant suggested otherwise. Accordingly, Article 10 did not extend the defences available with regard to an infringement of copyright.[91A]

---

[90] See paras 16.60 *et seq.* above.

[91] [2001] 2 W.L.R. 967, *The Times*, February 6, 2001.

[91A] The Vice Chancellor reiterated this view in the case of *Imutran Limited v. Uncaged Companions Limited & Daniel Louis Lyons* the judgment which he handed down immediately after the *Ashdown* case on January 11, 2001 (transcript available from Casetrack). The public interest defences to a claim in copyright are not affected by the Convention, and do not run any wider than determined by the Court of Appeal in *Hyde Park Residence Ltd v. Yelland* [2000] 3 W.L.R. 215.

Landlord and Tenant

Generally

16.139 Aside from public sector property,[92] almost all other property occupied on a landlord and tenant basis is occupied under the terms of a private law contract. As such, absent the widespread adoption by the courts of horizontal application of the Convention, the Convention implications for such private landlord and tenant relationships is generally limited to challenges to any governing legislative framework (such as the Rent Acts), to the common law, or to procedure (for example with regards to possession[93]). The fact that the state, either through legislation or through the courts, may regulate or determine private law disputes does not render it responsible for the consequences.[94]

Regulatory legislation

16.140 In *James v. United Kingdom*,[95] the Court considered the Convention implications on the leasehold enfranchisement legislation contained in the Leasehold Reform Act 1967. Subject to the satisfaction of a number of conditions, the Act (and later legislation of similar effect) permits tenants to force their landlord to sell to them the freehold of their properties. The legislation was challenged on behalf of the Duke of Westminster, a landowner with vast and valuable property holdings in the centre of London, on the basis that it unjustifiably deprived him of his possessions. The Court found, and indeed it was not disputed, that since landlords were unable to refuse to sell the property to the tenants in the event that the statutory conditions were satisfied and since the price of the sale was set by statute, the legislation did deprive the landlords of their possessions. The real issue in the case was whether such deprivation could be justified as being in the "public interest". The Duke's trustees argued that the transfer of property from one individual to another did not benefit the public in general. The Court was not prepared to accept so narrow a definition of public interest, stating that the taking of property in pursuance of a policy calculated to enhance social justice within the community can properly be described as being "in the public interest" and went on:

> "In particular, the fairness of a system of law governing the contractual or property rights of private parties is a matter of public concern and therefore legislative measures intended to bring about such fairness are capable of being in the 'public interest', even if they involve the compulsory transfer of property from one individual to another."[96]

Further stating:

---

[92] Considered in a residential context in the "Housing" section, paras 16.132 *et seq.*, above.
[93] As to which see paras 16.164 *et seq.*, below.
[94] See, *e.g. X v. Belgium* (1977) D.R. 8; *Di Palma v. United Kingdom* (1988) 10 E.H.R.R. 149.
[95] (1986) 8 E.H.R.R. 123.
[96] *James v. United Kingdom* (1986) 8 E.H.R.R. 123, para. 41.

" . . . a taking of property effected in pursuance of legitimate social, economic or other policies may be 'in the public interest', even if the community at large has no direct use or enjoyment of the property taken."[97]

The Court found that the Leasehold Reform Act 1967 pursued such a **16.141** legitimate policy in preventing the unjust enrichment of landlords on the reversion of the property following the end of the lease.[98] Accordingly, and notwithstanding the deprivation of possessions resulting from its enactment, such interference was found to be justified by the Court.

A number of legislative provisions interfere with rent levels and the rights **16.142** of landlords to recover possession of the property. The Rent Acts do both and thus clearly engage the "control of use" provisions of Article 1 of Protocol No. 1. In *Kilbourn v. United Kingdom*,[99] the Commission considered the compatibility of rent control legislation with Convention rights. It concluded that rent controls pursued a legitimate aim of social policy and that the Rent Acts were an appropriate means of achieving that aim. In *R. v. Secretary of State for Transport, Environment and the Regions, ex p. Spath Holmes Ltd*,[1] landlords challenged an order of the Secretary of State capping rent levels for regulated tenancies. The Court of Appeal accepted that the right to receive a fair rent was a "possession" within Article 1 of Protocol No. 1. The court determined that the balancing of landlords' and tenants' interests and the decision as to whether the burden should be borne by the landlords or the taxpayer was a political issue. Having consulted with landlords the Government had chosen not to accept their objections and the decision reached regarding rent levels was not irrational.

In *Antoniades v. United Kingdom*,[2] the applicant had let rooms in a house **16.143** owned by him under licences intended to avoid the effect of the Rent Acts. Some months later the House of Lords in *Street v. Mountford*,[3] held that the true legal nature of a transaction is not to be altered by the description the parties choose to give it and that the Court should be astute to detect and frustrate "sham devices and artificial transactions whose only object is to disguise the grant of a tenancy and to evade the Rent Acts". In the county court the judge followed *Street v. Mountford* and held that the occupants were tenants not licensees. This decision was overturned by the Court of Appeal who held that the intention of the parties was not to create a tenancy and that the agreements were not a "sham". The House of Lords overturned the Court of Appeal and reinstated the decision of the first instance judge holding that as it was the intention that the occupants should have joint and exclusive possession of the flat they thus became tenants, not licensees. Following that decision the occupants applied to the Rent Office for a "fair rent". The applicant then sought to allege violation of Article 1 of Protocol No. 1 on the basis that the rent he was then

---

[97] *ibid.*, para. 45.
[98] *ibid.*, para. 56.
[99] (1985) 8 E.H.R.R. 81.
[1] [2000] 1 All E.R. 884.
[2] Application No. 15434/89, declared inadmissible by the Commission on February 15, 1990.
[3] [1985] A.C. 809.

able to receive bore no relation to the market value of the property or to the capital investment involved; further, he had incurred enormous expense in the domestic proceedings due to the uncertainty of the law. The Commission found that the clarification of the legal status of the occupation of the applicant's flat did not constitute a deprivation of possession. It could not be said that the rights of the applicant as stipulated in the agreements (principally to repossess the flat but also to the licence fee) constituted individual rights enjoying, in their own right, the protection awarded to possessions. The effect of the House of Lords' finding in the applicant's case was the devices such as those employed by him were, and should always have been seen as, invalid attempts to avoid the Rent Acts. There was no question of an interference with his property rights, as the courts merely declared the true meaning of the agreements entered into. In any event, the application was ill-founded as the legislation pursued the legitimate aim of seeking to protect the interests of tenants in a situation of a shortage of housing. The interference was proportionate to that aim in that the reduction in rent was not that striking and that had the applicant taken appropriate advice, he might well have been told about the uncertainty of the law, and therefore should be regarded as having accepted a certain risk when entering into the agreements.

16.144 In *Fitzpatrick v. Sterling Housing Association Ltd,*[4] the House of Lords considered whether a homosexual partner could succeed to a 1977 Rent Act statutory tenancy (as amended by the Housing Act 1988). In order to succeed to the tenancy the partner had to demonstrate either that he was living with the original tenant as "his or her wife or husband" within the meaning of paragraph 2(2) of Schedule 1 to the Rent Act 1977 (as amended by the Housing Act 1988), or that he was "a member of the original tenant's family" within the meaning of paragraph 3(1) of Schedule 1 to the Rent Act 1977 (as amended). The first requirement could not be satisfied because a person could only live with a man as his wife when that person was a woman, or with another person as a husband when that other person was a woman. However, in extending the protection for those deriving rights from tenants to include members of the tenant's family,[5] the underlying intention of the legislation was to provide a secure home for those who shared their lives together with the original tenant in the manner which characterised the family unit. This purpose would be at risk if the courts were not able to take into account changing social attitudes to the concept of a family and accordingly a same-sex partner of a deceased tenant could, on appropriate facts, establish the necessary familial link. The House of Lords recognised that in reaching this decision, they went beyond the established position of the Court that same-sex partners do not qualify for "family" rights under Article 8.[6]

---

[4] [1999] 3 W.L.R. 1113.
[5] Under the Increase of Rent and Mortgage Interest (Restrictions) Act 1920, ss.5(1), 12(1).
[6] See, *e.g.* *S v. United Kingdom*, Application No. 11716/85 (1986) 47 D.R. 274 (where the applicant had lived with her partner, a local authority tenant, in a homosexual relationship for a number of years. Since they were in a homosexual relationship the tenancy did not vest in her on her partner's death under the Housing Act 1980. The Commission failed to recognise any property right or view the property as the applicant's "home").

In *Bareto v. Portugal*,[7] the applicants had sought the eviction of tenants **16.145**
from their property in order that they could live there themselves.[8] The
domestic courts refused to evict the tenants. The applicants sought to
allege violation of their Article 1 of Protocol No. 1 and Article 8 rights, but
their claim was rejected by the Court on the basis that the legislation on
which the domestic courts had relied in reaching their decision not to evict
the tenants pursued the legitimate aim of protecting tenants and was
justified under both Articles.

Forfeiture

The right of a private landlord to forfeit a lease in accordance with its terms **16.146**
does not constitute deprivation of possessions or interference with the
right to respect for the home by a public authority in violation of either
Article 1 of Protocol No. 1 or Article 8. Nor can the state be held responsible for such forfeiture where it occurs by order of the court, either under
Article 1 of Protocol No. 1 or under Article 8. Under Article 1 of Protocol No.
1, such a court order merely enforces a private law contract, freely entered
into between landlord and tenant and thus does not constitute a deprivation of possessions by a public authority. Under Article 8 the interference
with the right of respect for the home is justified under Article 8(2) in pursuit
of the legitimate aim of protecting the rights of others, namely the landlord.
These points can in the main be gleaned from *Di Palma v. United Kingdom*,[9] where the Commission noted that forfeiture provisions were "a
common feature of tenancy agreements under the legal systems of all the
member states of the Council of Europe". The applicant argued that she
had been deprived of her possessions (the lease) in violation of Article 1
of Protocol No. 1. The landlord forfeited the lease for non-payment of
service charges and took possession of the applicant's flat by way of
county court proceedings. The county court did not have the power to
grant relief from forfeiture. The Commission rejected the complaint, stating:

> " . . . the relations between the applicant and the landlord were regu-
> lated by a private contract (the lease) which set out the mutual
> obligations of the parties. The terms of the lease were neither directly
> prescribed nor amended by legislation . . . In view of the exclusively
> private law relationship between the parties to the lease the Commis-
> sion considers that the respondent Government cannot be responsi-
> ble by the mere fact that the landlord by its agents, who were private
> individuals, brought the applicant's lease to an end in accordance with
> the terms of that lease, which set out the agreement between the
> applicant and the company. The question arises whether any other
> aspect of the applicant's complaint under Prot. No. 1 Art. 1 would give
> rise to a breach of the State's responsibility under the Convention. It
> is true that the landlord issued proceedings in the domestic courts in
> order to forfeit the applicant's lease. This fact alone is not however

---

[7] [1996] E.H.R.L.R. 212.
[8] Similar grounds for possession exist in U.K. legislation, *e.g.* Schedule 15 Case 9 of the
Rent Act 1977; Schedule 2 Part I Ground 1 of the Housing Act 1988.
[9] (1988) 10 E.H.R.R. 149.

sufficient to engage State responsibility in respect of the applicant's right to property, since the public authority in the shape of the County Court merely provided a forum for the determination of the civil right in dispute between the parties. In contending that State responsibility for an interference with rights protected by the Convention arises in respect of this complaint, the applicant seeks to demand that a State be subject to a positive obligation to protect the property rights of an individual in the context of his dispute with another private individual. It is not necessary for the purposes of the present decision to attempt an exhaustive description of the circumstances in which such an obligation may arise. In the present case the applicant and the landlord had entered into contractual arrangements set out in the lease which expressly provided for the applicant's tenancy to terminate if rent remained unpaid once demanded."[10]

Distress

16.147 There has been widespread speculation as to whether the landlord's remedy of distress for rent can be regarded as incompatible with Convention rights.[11] The right has its origins in the common law where the landlord was entitled to seize and retain the tenant's goods until rent was paid, and since 1689 this common law right has been regulated by statute in the form of the Distress for Rent Act 1689, which permits the sale of goods seized. There are various bases upon which it is suggested that distress might be challenged. As distress is a remedy conducted without legal process it might be possible to argue a violation of the right to a fair hearing under Article 6. Further, as a landlord is entitled to seize any goods found on the premises, no matter to whom they belong, this might constitute an unjustifiable interference with the peaceful enjoyment of possessions under Article 1 of Protocol No. 1. In circumstances where the distress is levied at the tenant's home, there may be an infringement of Article 8. However, consideration needs to be given as to how and against whom this alleged violation would be pursued. Clearly, the potential for raising these arguments against a public authority landlord is far greater than against a private landlord, who is not subject to any requirement to act compatibly with the Convention rights. As a common law remedy, distress itself cannot be subject to a "declaration of incompatibility" under the HRA, although the power of sale under the Distress for Rent Act 1689 perhaps could be. The state could not be pursued for permitting the existence of a common law remedy, and it is unlikely that any positive obligation to reform the law could be imposed. However, if the courts were to be given an opportunity to adjudicate a dispute regarding the levying of distress, it is possible that they might, in accordance with their duty to develop the common law in a manner compatible with the Convention, review the law of distress. In those circumstances, it would be possible for the landlord concerned to argue that any interference with Article 1 of Protocol No. 1 or Article 8 caused by the law of distress was in any event

---

[10] *Di Palma v. United Kingdom* (1988) 10 E.H.R.R. 149, 154–155.
[11] See, *e.g.* Jonathan Karas and James Maurici "The human rights factor" (1999) 17 E.G. 126; Charles Harpum "Property Law-the human rights dimension (Part 2)" (2000) 4 L. & T. Rev. 29 at 30.

justifiable in the public interest to protect the rights of landlords.[12] Whether this would be successful remains to be seen, and in the meantime it is perhaps worth noting that the Law Commission has in any event recommended the abolition of distress and thus this speculation may well become academic. The most that has occurred to date is that Lightman, J. has issued a warning to private landlords regarding the levying of distress. In the case of *Fuller v. Happyshopper*,[12A] he was required to consider whether the levying of distress by a landlord had been unlawful in circumstances where, notwithstanding certain admitted arrears of rent at the date distress was levied, a later sum was due to the tenant which he alleged should be offset against and cancel out the arrears of rent. Although Lightman, J. held that a claim for damages for breach of a settlement agreement was to be ignored when taking accounts to ascertain what if any rent was due, he held that any overpayments of rent could and should be taken into account, for they were immediately repayable and were the subject of a right of equitable set off against the arrears of rent. He went on to issue the following warning[12B]:

> "This means that a landlord is bound to take the greatest care before levying distress that there are no claims on the part of the tenant which may be available by way of equitable set off to be offset against and satisfy the rent outstanding. In any ordinary case he would be well advised to give notice of his intention and invite the tenant to agree what is owing and to inform him whether there are any cross-claims and (if so) to identify them. The ancient (and perhaps anachronistic) self help remedy of distress involves a serious interference with the right of the tenant under Article 8 of the European Convention on Human Rights to respect for his privacy and home and under Article 1 of the First Protocol to the peaceful enjoyment of his possessions. The human rights implications of levying distress must be in the forefront of the mind of the landlord before he takes this step and he must fully satisfy himself that taking this action is in accordance with the law."

Nuisance

Public nuisance

This topic is discussed in detail in the Environmental section of this chapter at paragraphs 16.111, above.

16.148

Private nuisance

As in many other areas where considering the implication of the Convention between private individuals, absent the horizontal application of the

16.149

---

[12] For further potential lines of argument on both sides, see Jonathan Karas "Feudal Rights in the 21st Century—Can the Law of Distress for Rent survive the Convention" in Wilberforce Chambers' *The Essential Human Rights Act 1998* (1st ed., 2000), Chap. 9, pp. 115–121.
[12A] Decision handed down on February 14, 2001 in the Chancery Division, the transcript of the approved judgment is available on Casetrack but is otherwise as yet unreported.
[12B] At para. 27 of his judgment.

Convention, it is likely to have limited effect. However, the court's responsibility, under section 6(3) of the HRA, to develop the common law through decisions compatible with the Convention may lead to change in some areas. In *Hunter v. Canary Wharf Ltd*,[13] a residential occupier living close to the Canary Wharf development in East London brought an action in private nuisance against the developer for interference with television reception caused by the extremely large buildings. The House of Lords rejected the claim on the basis that such a claim could not be made in private nuisance by a mere occupier or licensee. It was not possible to make a claim in the absence of an exclusive interest in the property concerned, such as ownership of the freehold, a tenancy in possession, or a licence conferring exclusive rights of occupation. It might now be argued that such a legal position is incompatible with Article 8 on the basis that even an unlawfully established residence can be a "home" for which its occupiers are entitled to respect.[14] The finding in *Hunter* is essentially too restrictive of the category of persons entitled to respect for their home, and accordingly in the future the courts may need to widen the category of persons capable of bringing an action in private nuisance.[15]

Planning

Generally

16.150　As restrictions on the freedom of property owners to use and develop their property in any manner that they might see fit, planning regulations clearly have the potential to engage a number of Convention rights, of which the most significant are Article 6, Article 8 and Article 1 of Protocol No. 1. Most planning regulation or enforcement will be an interference with one or more of these rights, the question in each case will be whether that interference is justifiable. Although planning controls generally are likely to be regarded as being in the public interest,[16] arguments will tend to focus on whether a fair balance has been achieved between the public and individual interest in the particular case, or whether the restriction imposed is proportionate to the legitimate aim sought to be achieved.

Article 1 of Protocol No. 1: Deprivation or control of use

16.151　Planning controls[17] including building[18] and use[19] restrictions will generally constitute "controls of use" or general "interferences with peaceful enjoyment" but not "deprivations" for the purposes of Article 1 of Protocol No. 1, and thus fall to be considered within either the first or the third rule

---

[13] [1997] A.C. 655.

[14] *Buckley v. United Kingdom* (1997) 23 E.H.R.R. 101.

[15] For a broader discussion of the development of the private law of nuisance, see Tiffany Scott "Extending the Scope of Private Nuisance", in Wilberforce Chambers' *The Essential Human Rights Act 1998* (1st ed., 2000), Chap. 10, pp. 122–127.

[16] *N. v. Austria* (1986) 9 E.H.R.R. 389; *Fredin v. Sweden* (1991) 13 E.H.R.R. 784; *Pine Valley Developments Ltd v. Ireland* (1992) 14 E.H.R.R. 319.; *Herrick v. United Kingdom* (1986) 8 E.H.R.R. 66.

[17] *E.g. Jacobsson v. Sweden* (1990) 12 E.H.R.R. 56; *Pine Valley Developments Ltd v. Ireland* (1992) 14 E.H.R.R. 319.

[18] *E.g. Lundquist v. Sweden* (1986) 9 E.H.R.R. 531.

[19] *E.g. Chater v. United Kingdom* (1988) 10 E.H.R.R. 534; *Ryder v. United Kingdom* (1989) 11 E.H.R.R. 80; *ISKCON v. United Kingdom* (1994) 18 E.H.R.R. C.D. 133.

rather than the second rule as enunciated in *Sporrong and Lönroth v. Sweden.*[20]

In *Sporrong and Lönroth v. Sweden*,[21] the applicants sought to argue that **16.152** the fact that their property had been subject to building restrictions and expropriation permits for an extended period, thus restricting their ability to sell the land, amounted to an interference sufficient to constitute deprivation within the second rule. The Court found that although the existence of the permits and restrictions had made the land more difficult to sell, it had not made sale impossible. That fact, and the fact that the applicants were still able to use the land, resulted in the Court finding that there was no deprivation. Although, the expropriation permits clearly were a control of use, they were the first step in a procedure leading to deprivation, and thus fell to be considered within the first rule.[22]

In *Matos e Silva, Lda. v. Portugal*,[23] the first applicant worked land in the **16.153** Algarve for the extraction of salt and the breeding of fish. His right to do so, at least in part, arose under a royal decree originally granted in 1884. The Court held that this right was a "possession" for the purposes of Article 1 of Protocol No. 1. The Portuguese Government withdrew the concession and put in place provisions intended to limit building on the land or any change of use with the intention of creating a nature reserve. The Court held, distinguishing the case from that of *Papamichalopoulos v. Greece*,[24] that although the applicants' rights had been substantially reduced, they had not disappeared and the situation was not irreversible. Accordingly, there was no deprivation.[25]

Article 8

Planning controls and their enforcement are obviously capable of inter- **16.154** fering with an individual's right to respect for the home under Article 8. In *Buckley v. United Kingdom*,[26] a gypsy occupied a mobile home sited on her own land. The mobile home required planning permission but the applicant had neither sought nor obtained the requisite permission. Accordingly the mobile home was not a lawful residence. However, the Court held that as the applicant had lived there continuously for five years, intended to remain there and had no residence elsewhere, the mobile home satisfied the definition of a "home", and she was entitled to respect for it under Article 8.[27]

---

[20] (1983) 5 E.H.R.R. 35.

[21] (1983) 5 E.H.R.R. 35.

[22] *Sporrong and Lönroth v. Sweden* (1983) 5 E.H.R.R. 35, para. 63.

[23] (1997) 24 E.H.R.R. 573.

[24] (1993) 16 E.H.R.R. 440. See para. 16.73, above.

[25] But there was interference with the enjoyment of possessions and, no fair balance having been struck, accordingly a violation of Art. 1 of Protocol No. 1.

[26] (1997) 23 E.H.R.R. 101.

[27] *Buckley v. United Kingdom* (1997) 23 E.H.R.R. 101, para. 54. That a caravan occupied in breach of planning requirements can be a "home" for the purposes of Art. 8 appears to have been accepted without question in a series of gypsy cases, *e.g. Beard v. United Kingdom*, Application No. 24882/94 (1998) 25 E.H.R.R. C.D. 28; *Chapman v. United Kingdom*, Application No. 27238/95 (1998) 25 E.H.R.R. C.D. 64; *Coster v. United Kingdom*, Application No. 24876/94 (1998) 25 E.H.R.R. C.D. 24; *Lee v. United Kingdom*, Application No. 25289/94 (1998) 25 E.H.R.R. C.D. 46; *Jane Smith v. United Kingdom*, Application No. 25154/94 (1998) 25 E.H.R.R. C.D. 42 (the judgment of the Court in relation to this group of cases is reported in *The Times*, January, 30, 2001).

Development plans and planning policy

16.155   The established practice of local authorities adopting a particular development plan or a particular planning policy in relation to a scheme of
development may engage Convention rights. Thus, in *Katte Klitshe de la
Grange v. Italy*,[28] a land-use plan adopted by the local authority prevented
the applicant from developing his land. Although this was acknowledged to
be an interference with Article 1 of Protocol No. 1 rights[29] it was held that
a fair balance had been achieved between the general interest and those
of the applicant. The decision to adopt a particular planning policy could
constitute the determination of a civil right within the meaning of Article
6(1), and accordingly an affected individual would be entitled to rely on the
procedural protection afforded to him by the Article.[30]

Planning permission: consideration of personal circumstances

16.156   As domestic law stands, the personal circumstances of an applicant for
planning permission are only to be taken into account in exceptional
circumstances.[31] This contrasts starkly with the general approach of the
Convention, where personal circumstances are put first,[32] and where any
interference with individual rights cannot be justified unless public interest
reasons are put forward which are of sufficient importance. Current planning policy guidance suggests that personal circumstances will seldom
outweigh more general planning considerations[33] and it has been suggested,[34] rightly, that policy may have to change to recognise Convention
rights implications.

Compensation

16.157   As noted above,[35] planning controls will generally be regarded either as a
general interference with the peaceful enjoyment of possessions or as a
control of use. As such, and unlike in cases of deprivation of possession
such as compulsory purchase,[36] where exceptional circumstances would
be required to justify the absence of any compensation even if the public
interest were particularly strong,[37] there is no general requirement that
compensation should be payable to justify any planning interference.
However, it should be noted that the payment of compensation may well
result in a finding that a fair balance has been struck between the interests
of the property owner and the general interest.[38]

---

[28] (1995) 19 E.H.R.R. 368.
[29] See also *Matos e Silva, Lda. v. Portugal* (1997) 24 E.H.R.R. 573.
[30] See generally, paras 3.53 *et seq.*
[31] *Great Portland Estates v. City of Westminster Council* [1985] A.C. 661.
[32] See, *e.g. Britton v. Secretary of State for the Environment* [1997] J.P.L. 617.
[33] See the Government's Planning Policy Guidance, para. 39.
[34] *E.g.* by T. Corner, in "Planning, Environment and the European Convention on Human
Rights" [1998] J.P.L. 301.
[35] See paras 16.151 *et seq.*, above.
[36] See paras 16.99 *et seq.*, above.
[37] *Lithgow v. United Kingdom* (1986) 8 E.H.R.R. 329, para. 120; *James v. United* Kingdom
(1986) 8 E.H.R.R. 123, para. 54; *Pressos Compania Naviera S.A. v. Belgium* (1996) 21
E.H.R.R. 301, para. 38; *Holy Monasteries v. Greece* (1995) 20 E.H.R.R. 1, para. 71; *Stran
Greek Refneries and Stratis Andreadis v. Greece* (1993) 19 E.H.R.R. 293, paras 81–88.
[38] See, *e.g. Baner v. Sweden* (1989) 60 D.R. 128.

Where compensation is payable, the Court has rarely interfered with the   **16.158**
levels of compensation paid, affording the state a wide margin of appreciation, and would only do so if, on its assessment, the value of the property
taken and the compensation paid for it is "manifestly disproportionate".[39]
Article 1 of Protocol No. 1 does not guarantee full compensation in all
circumstances. The Court has stated: "legitimate objectives of 'public
interest', such as pursued in measures of economic reform or measures
designed to achieve greater social justice, may call for less than reimbursement of the full market value".[40] The system used to calculate the
compensation should, however, be flexible enough to cope with different
situations and not be manifestly without reasonable foundation.[41]

Procedural considerations

A key area in which planning regulation may engage Convention rights is   **16.159**
that of procedural considerations and the impact of Article 6, particularly in
relation to the availability and sufficiency of any right of appeal.

The grant of planning permission over neighbouring land may amount to   **16.160**
an interference with the peaceful enjoyment of possession and thus a
violation of Article 1 of Protocol No. 1.[42] In addition, such a grant may
engage Article 6 rights. In *Ortenburg v. Austria*,[43] the applicant sought to
claim Article 6 protection in relation to the grant of planning permission
over land neighbouring her property on the basis that it constituted a
determination of her civil rights. The Austrian Government argued that the
right of a neighbour to object to planning permission was a public law right
on the basis of their seeking to protect the environment, and thus was not
a civil right which could engage Article 6(1). This argument was rejected by
the Court on the basis that the applicant was complaining about the
infringement of her pecuniary rights, in that the proposed work on the
neighbouring land would diminish both the value of her land and her
enjoyment of it. Accordingly, although there had been no breach in the
particular case, the applicant was entitled to the protection of Article
6(1).

In *Bryan v. United Kingdom*,[44] the Court considered whether the right of   **16.161**
appeal of enforcement notices under the Town and Country Planning Act
1990 satisfied the requirement of "a fair and public hearing . . . by an
independent and impartial tribunal established by law" under Article 6. The
applicant complained that the appeal to an inspector did not satisfy Article
6 because at all times it was possible that the Secretary of State for the
Environment, Transport and the Regions would recover the appeal from
the inspector and determine the matter for himself. The inspector was thus
not sufficiently independent from the Executive that had appointed him.
The Court found that the Article 6 rights were adequately protected by the
availability of the statutory appeal from the inspector to the High Court

---

[39] *Scotts of Greenock (Est'd 1711) Ltd and Lithgows Ltd v. United Kingdom* (1990) 12
E.H.R.R. 147, para. 90.
[40] *Lithgow v. United Kingdom* (1986) 8 E.H.R.R. 329, para. 121.
[41] For a broader discussion of compensation under Art. 1 of Protocol No. 1, see D. Anderson,
"Compensation for Interference with Property" [1999] E.H.R.L.R. 543.
[42] *M v. Italy*, Application No. 14563/89 (1991) 72 D.R. 129.
[43] (1995) 19 E.H.R.R. 524.
[44] (1996) 21 E.H.R.R. 342.

under section 289 of the Town and Country Planning Act, even though that appeal was akin only to a judicial review in that the High Court was neither capable of reviewing the inspector's findings of fact, or of substituting its own decision for that of the inspector.

16.162   The finding in *Bryan*, and the topic of the separation of the Executive from planning appeals, has recently been revisited in a domestic context, since the HRA came into force, and with surprising results. At first instance in *R. v. Secretary of State for the Environment, Transport and the Regions, ex p. Holding & Barnes Plc.*,[45] the Divisional Court heard four cases concerning the various powers vested in the Secretary of State that enable him to enforce planning policy on local authority decision makers. The first of the four cases (*Alconbury Developments*) concerned development proposals at Alconbury Airfield, which is owned by the Ministry of Defence, and the right of the Secretary of State to "recover" the appellate jurisdiction from the inspector and thus take over the decision-making role.[46] Two of the cases (*Holding & Barnes* itself and the case of *Premier Leisure U.K. Ltd*) concerned the call-in by the Secretary of State of planning applications.[47] In the fourth case (*Legal and General Assurance Society*), the Secretary of State was the applicant, and it concerned the power of the Secretary of State to make orders under the Highways Act 1980 and the Acquisition of Land Act 1981 for the purposes of a scheme of road development.[48] In each case, the fundamental question was whether the dual role of policy maker and decision taker was compatible with Article 6. At first instance the court held that it was not and made declarations of incompatibility in relation to the legislation in issue. In reaching its decision, the court referred to *Bryan v. United Kingdom*,[49] and the Scottish case of *County Properties Ltd v. Scottish Ministers*,[50] which distinguished *Bryan* and held that a call-in mechanism triggered by objections from a Government agency would be incompatible with Article 6. The court distinguished the four cases being considered from *Bryan* on the basis that there was: "such a lack of independence and impartiality in the processes involved in the instant cases that the limited scope of review by the High Court is insufficient for compliance with Article 6". In explaining the decision the court commented in relation to the role of the Secretary of State:

> "What is objectionable in terms of Article 6 is that he should be the judge in his own cause where his policy is in play. In other words he cannot be both policy maker and decision taker. In the Alconbury case there is the added factor of the financial interest of the Government. In the [Legal and General] case, as we think in any case where the [Secretary of State] through the Highways Agency promotes [Highways Act] and [compulsory purchase] orders, it cannot possibly be said that as a decision maker the [Secretary of State] is objectively

[45] Judgment of Tuckey L.J. and Harrision J. in the Queen's Bench Division, December 13, 2000. Currently reported only in [2001] 05 E.G. 170.
[46] Under the Town and Country Planning Act 1990, s.78, Sched. 6, para. 3.
[47] Under the Town and Country Planning Act 1990, s.77.
[48] In this case the provision of a dual carriageway for the A34 through traffic under the M4 about 100 metres to the west of Junction 13.
[49] (1996) 21 E.H.R.R. 342. See para. 16.161, above.
[50] 2000 S.L.T. 965.

impartial. He is a party to the cause in which he is also the judge. Where the Highways Agency is simply a party at the inquiry as in the Alconbury case the same may also be said."[51]

The four cases were taken straight to the House of Lords by means of a **16.163** "leap-frog" appeal instigated by the Secretary of State and heard at the end of February 2001. The Secretary of State indicated that he intended to continue making use of the relevant powers pending the outcome of the appeal. The House of Lords allowed the appeal and overturned the decision of the Divisional Court.[51A] Their Lordships held that the disputes concerned involved the determination of "civil rights" within the meaning of Article 6(1) of the Convention; that, although the Secretary of State was not himself an independent and impartial tribunal, decisions taken by him were not incompatible with Article 6(1) provided they were subject to review by an independent and impartial tribunal which had full jurisdiction to deal with the case as the nature of the decision required; that when the decision at issue was one of administrative policy the reviewing body was not required to have full power to re-determine the merits of the decision and any review by a court of the merits of such a policy decision taken by a minister answerable to Parliament and ultimately to the electorate would be profoundly undemocratic; that the power of the High Court in judicial review proceedings to review the legality of the decision and the procedures followed was sufficient to ensure compatibility with Article 6(1); and that, accordingly, the impugned powers of the Secretary of State were not incompatible with Article 6(1). Lord Hoffmann emphasised the distinction between decisions of policy and expediency (*e.g.* decisions regarding the grant or refusal of planning permissions) and findings of fact (*e.g.* a finding that planning permission had been breached) and found that the Divisional Court had erred in seeing no distinction. In deciding questions of primary fact or fact and degree the existence of various accepted safeguards was relevant, as in such a quasi-judicial capacity the planning inspector was "no mere bureaucrat. He was an expert tribunal acting in a quasi-judicial manner and therefore sufficiently independent to make it unnecessary that the High Court should have a broad jurisdiction to review his decisions on questions of fact".[51B] In relation to decisions of policy and expediency Lord Hoffmann relied upon the leading authority of *Zumtobel v. Austria*,[51C] in finding that it is not necessary for the purposes of Article 6 for there to be a means to fully review the merits of a policy decision:

"If, therefore, the question is one of policy or expediency, the 'safeguards' are irrelevant. No one expects the inspector to be independent or impartial in applying the Secretary of State's policy and this was the reason why the court said that he was not for all purposes an independent and impartial tribunal. In this respect his position is no

---

[51] Extract taken from summary by Denzil Millichap in Current Law Week Focus, March 2, 2001 (Sweet & Maxwell) vol. 9, issue 8/2001.
[51A] *R (Alconbury Developments Ltd and others) v. Secretary of State for the Environment, Transport and the Regions* [2001] 2 W.L.R. 1389.
[51B] *R (Alconbury Developments Ltd and others) v. Secretary of State for the Environment, Transport and the Regions* [2001] 2 W.L.R. 1389, *per* Lord Hoffmann at 1422G-H.
[51C] (1993) 17 E.H.R.R. 116.

different from that of the Secretary of State himself. The reason why judicial review is sufficient in both cases to satisfy article 6 has nothing to do with 'safeguards' but depends upon the *Zumtobel* principle of respect for the decision of an administrative authority on questions of expediency. It is only when one comes to findings of fact, or the evaluation of facts, such as arise on the question of whether there has been a breach of planning control, that the safeguards are essential for the acceptance of a limited review of fact by the appellate tribunal."[51D]

Clearly the impact of this decision is widespread, and runs beyond the planning sphere. It is likely to hinder the success of any human rights arguments in those cases where it might have been thought that the limited scope of judicial review would mean that a number of policy decisions (as opposed to quasi-judicial decisions) were open to challenge on the basis of failure to comply with Article 6 due to the lack of impartiality or independence of the relevant decision taker.

Possession Proceedings

Generally

16.164   Where a court conducts private possession proceedings, in either a landlord and tenant or a mortgage context, where it has no discretion to do otherwise it cannot be held responsible under the Convention for granting a possession order in accordance either with the terms of the lease or with the terms of the mortgage in question. No violation by the court could be made out, either as having deprived an individual of their possessions in violation of Article 1 of Protocol No. 1 or as having interfered with the individual's right to respect for his home in violation of Article 8. A possession order is not a violation of these Convention rights by a public authority as the court simply provides a forum for the determination of the civil right in question between the parties, and gives effect to the contractual terms agreed between them.[52] In essence, where the making of the possession order is mandatory, either because mandatory grounds for possession are made out in a landlord and tenant context or because the proceedings are mortgage possession proceedings, there is no "decision" of the court to be considered incompatible with the Convention rights. However, where the court is entitled to exercise its discretion, either as to the making of the possession order itself, or as to its subsequent enforcement, the court will be required to ensure that its decision is compatible with Convention rights. Equally, where possession proceedings are brought by an obvious public authority its conduct in bringing and conducting those proceedings should of itself be compatible with the Convention rights.[53] The position of

---

[51D] *R (Alconbury Developments Ltd and others) v. Secretary of State for the Environment, Transport and the Regions* [2001] 2 W.L.R. 1389, *per* Lord Hoffman at 1424B-D.
[52] *Di Palma v. United Kingdom* (1988) 10 E.H.R.R. 149.
[53] For further consideration of the impact of the HRA on possession proceedings generally, see Jon Luba q.c. "Possession day in the county court" (2000) N.L.J. October 6, 1456–1457; Andrew Henderson "Possession proceedings and the HRA" Solicitors Journal, October 6, 2000, 906–907.

hybrid public authorities in bringing possession proceedings is likely to vary, and not every hybrid public authority is likely to be required to act compatibly with the Convention in bringing possession proceedings. Thus, if the hybrid authority is a registered social landlord, the bringing of possession proceedings falls within its general public function of providing housing, whereas if the hybrid authority is, for example, a utility provider, the recovery by possession proceedings of privately occupied premises owned by the utility provider is unlikely to fall within any of its public functions. These issues were considered by the Court of Appeal in the recent case of *St Brice & anr v. London Borough of Southwark*,[53A] in which a tenant sought to complain that the procedure for issue of a warrant for possession some two and a half years after the making of the order for possession contravened the tenant's Convention rights under Article 6, Article 8, and Article 14. It was common ground that the eviction of a tenant from his home under order of the court constituted interference by a public authority with the right conferred by Article 8(1) where the order was sought and obtained by a local authority. Also, as possession proceedings are determinative of civil rights and obligations they accordingly attract the protection of Article 6. The Court of Appeal considered that Convention issues are weighed at the time of the original possession hearing and of the making of the possession order. At that time the court, in considering whether it is "reasonable to make the order" (under section 84(1) and (2) of the Housing Act 1985) is in fact considering the Convention issues as to whether the order is sought in accordance with the law, is necessary in a democratic society, and is proportionate. Provided there is compliance with the procedure prescribed by law and a fair hearing is held, the making of the order is necessary and proportionate in that it pursues the legitimate aim of eviction for non-payment of rent (and it might be said, by analogy, for non-payment of mortgage instalments) and there will therefore be no breach of either Article 8 or Article 6. Procedure provides for the issue of a warrant of possession without permission in certain circumstances. The Court of Appeal held that such a procedure was a purely administrative act that did not attract the protection of Article 6 and that given there was no complaint as to the fairness of the original possession hearing there was no breach of the Convention under Article 6 or Article 8. There was and could be no requirement that there needed to be a further Court hearing prior to the warrant being issued. Section 85(2) of the Housing Act 1985 permits the tenant to secure a further hearing in order to seek the stay or suspension of the order. The fact that that section threw the burden back onto the tenant to make an application did not constitute a breach of Article 6. Nor was there any discrimination against the tenant under Article 14 because proceedings were issued in the county court rather than the High Court where notice of an application for a warrant for possession was required. The landlord's choice of forum was not based on any personal characteristic of the tenant and could be objectively justified. From this judgment it is possible to observe that provided proper procedures are followed and a fair hearing held then there is unlikely to be any real prospect of successfully arguing breach of Convention rights with regard

---

[53A] [2001] EWCA Civ 1138, unreported at time of going to press except on Newlaw Online as judgment No. 2010713203.

to possession proceedings, even where the person seeking possession is a public authority.

Mortgages generally

16.165　Contrary to the perception of many mortgagors, commercial high street lender mortgagees are neither obvious nor hybrid public authorities for the purposes of the HRA, as they do not perform a public function. The only circumstances in which a mortgagee might be considered a hybrid public authority would be if there were some direct connection of the lender in question to the state, or some involvement by it in a social housing scheme subsidised by the local authority or government. Neither proposition is likely to be encountered with any frequency, if indeed at all, within the United Kingdom, and in those circumstances such a mortgagee would only be obliged to act compatibly with the Convention in the exercise of its public functions. The impact of the Convention in mortgage possession proceedings is therefore likely to be limited as there is no obligation on the part of mortgagees to act compatibly with the Convention. A mortgagee's decision to seek to enforce its right to possession, which right arises "before the ink is dry on the mortgage",[54] cannot therefore be challenged either as an interference with the peaceful enjoyment of the mortgagor's possessions under Article 1 of Protocol No. 1 or as a violation of the mortgagor's right to respect for his home under Article 8.[55] Orders for possession made following a failure on the part of the mortgagor to make mortgage repayments have been held to be justified as necessary for the protection of the rights and freedoms of others.[56]

16.166　In *Locabail (UK) Ltd v. Waldorf Investments Corp.*,[57] the second defendant had sought to argue that the deputy judge who had ordered possession of the property in question was biased. She failed in this argument before the Court of Appeal and sought a stay of execution of the warrant of possession pending determination of her complaint to the ECHR under Article 6 on the basis that she had been denied "a fair trial by an independent and impartial tribunal". The second defendant sought the stay on the basis that if she were successful in her complaint the judgment would be declared unlawful, and that accordingly the execution of the warrant in the meantime would itself constitute a violation of her Article 8 and Article 1 of Protocol No. 1 rights. This argument was rejected by Evans-Lombe J., who held that if she were successful in her application that would not render the decision of the deputy judge unlawful as the proceedings before the ECHR would not determine her property rights but whether the United Kingdom had failed to provide her with a court to decide her case which conformed to her rights as defined by Article 6(1) of the Convention. Her rights with regard to the property had been finally determined by the Court of Appeal, and would not be affected by any decision of the ECHR

---

[54] *Four Maids Ltd v. Dudley Marshall (Properties) Ltd* [1957] Ch. 317 at 320.
[55] However, see *Albany Home Loands Ltd v. Massey* [1997] 2 All E.R. 609, *per* Schiemann L.J. (where prior to the introduction of the HRA the court appeared to consider that Art. 8 might be relevant to the considerations applicable to the making of a possession order).
[56] *Wood v. United Kingdom* (1997) 24 E.H.R.R. C.D. 69.
[57] Judgment of Evans-Lombe J. in the Chancery Division (May 25, 2000), New Law Online Case 200059401.

which could only result in the "just satisfaction" of compensation in damages. There was therefore no restraint on execution of the warrant.

Mortgages: physical re-possession

The Court of Appeal has recently reiterated the right of mortgagees, **16.167** subject to the limited protection of section 6 of the Criminal Law Act 1977 (where the mortgagor is physically present in premise when entry is attempted), to exercise their right to possession by physical re-entry rather than by legal process.[58] This right is equally unaffected by the Convention as, absent the horizontal application of the HRA and the Convention, there can be no requirement that a private mortgagee comply with Article 6.

A court adjudicating mortgage possession proceedings will rarely have **16.168** any discretion as to whether a possession order is in fact made, given the mortgagee's absolute entitlement to call in its security, even where there is a set-off or counterclaim brought by the mortgagor admitted by the mortgagee to exceed the amount outstanding under the mortgage.[59] However, the court does have powers, under section 36 of the Administration of Justice Act 1970 and section 8 of the Administration of Justice Act 1973, to adjourn, stay or suspend possession in circumstances where it considers it likely that the mortgagor will be able within a reasonable period to pay any arrears or remedy any default under the mortgage. It is rare for these powers not to be used in circumstances where the mortgagor seeks and has good reason to seek the delay of the enforcement of the possession order. In exercising its discretion the court will have to ensure that its decision is compatible with the Convention. Accordingly, it may wish to consider the deprivation of the mortgagor's possessions under Article 1 of Protocol No. 1 and issues concerning respect for the home under Article 8. Against this, of course, needs to be balanced the mortgagee's own Convention rights, particularly its right to the peaceful enjoyment of its possessions, namely its right to enforce its security.[60] It is unlikely that these rights considerations will impact greatly on the process carried out by the court prior to the introduction of the HRA in which the interests of both parties were invariably placed in the balance in any event.

Mortgage security and the Housing Grants, Construction and Regeneration Act 1996

The Housing Grants, Construction and Regeneration Act 1996 may in **16.169** some circumstances have the effect of wiping out the value of a mortgagee's security. Although yet to be subjected to scrutiny in this regard, the Act provides for the recovery by the local authority, on the occurrence of certain specified circumstances, most notably sale, of the value of renovation grants made.[61] It is not desirable to scrutinise the complex provisions of the Act here, however the key point is that recovery may be

---

[58] *Ropaigeleach v. Barclays Bank Plc.* [1999] 4 All E.R. 235.
[59] *Ashley Guarantee Plc. v. Zacaria* [1993] 1 W.L.R. 62; *National Westminster Bank Plc. v. Skelton* [1993] 1 W.L.R. 72.
[60] Held to be a justifiable interference with the rights of the mortgagor in *Wood v. United Kingdom* (1997) 24 E.H.R.R. C.D. 69.
[61] See s.45 of the Act.

made on sale even by subsequent owners, defined as the person entitled to receive rent on the property at the relevant time.[62] The definition appears to capture mortgagees in possession. Thus a mortgagee may discover, on bringing possession proceedings and conducting a local land charges search, that the mortgagor obtained the benefit of a renovations grant under the Act subsequent to the mortgage and without the knowledge of the mortgagee. The provisions of the Act would then appear to require the mortgagee to pay back the grant on sale, despite the fact that it had no knowledge of the grant and even where the value of the property is less than that of the grant. The mortgagee's security would accordingly be worthless or at least significantly diminished in value. This would seem to amount either to a deprivation of property within the second rule, or a control of use within the third rule, of Article 1 of Protocol No. 1 as enunciated in *Sporrong and Lönroth v. Sweden*.[63] The Act certainly pursues a legitimate purpose, and the provisions in question are intended to avoid the unjust enrichment of individuals using the renovations grants to improve property for profit, or to avoid the unjust enrichment of subsequent owners. However, given the lack of compensation for mortgagees for the loss of their security, the Act will almost inevitably be challenged, in cases where the renovation has not in fact increased the value of the property, for failing to secure a fair balance between the general interest and that of mortgagees.

Peaceable right to re-entry in the landlord and tenant context

16.170　As with mortgages, the right of a private landlord to make use of the existing right of peaceable re-entry where appropriate is unlikely to be affected by the Convention, absent the horizontal application of the rights between private individuals. However, questions have been raised as to the continuation of the doctrine, imposing as it does a significant interference with the tenant's Article 6, Article 8 and Article 1 of Protocol No. 1 rights.[64] By reason of the Court's decision in *Di Palma*,[65] it would seem likely that there is limited scope for challenging the doctrine, except perhaps against public sector landlords. Even there the right of peaceable re-entry could probably be justified on the basis that it pursued the legitimate aim of ensuring that property was available for letting in the event of default by the tenant, and that purpose did not impose an excessive burden on the individual tenant as it was one to which he lent his hand when entering into the lease.[66]

Extended suspension of possession

16.171　A system of delaying and staggering possession orders may, if inflexible and prolonged for an extended period of time, constitute a violation of

---

[62] See s.99 of the Act.
[63] (1983) 5 E.H.R.R. 35. See paras 16.48–16.49, above.
[64] See, *e.g.* Andrew Bruce "Barring peaceable re-entry" N.L.J. Practitioner, March 31, 2000, pp. 462–463.
[65] (1988) 10 E.H.R.R. 149.
[66] Andrew Bruce "Barring peaceable re-entry" N.L.J. Practitioner, March 31, 2000, pp. 462–463 at 463.

Article 1 of Protocol No. 1.[67] In *Immobiliare Saffi v. Italy*,[68] in order to deal with chronic housing shortage, the Italian Government adopted a series of emergency measures designed to control rent increases and to extend the validity of existing leases. In 1982 and 1983, when the last statutory extension expired, the Italian state considered it necessary to resort to emergency provisions to suspend the enforcement of non-urgent orders for possession. The Court had previously held such measures to be appropriate to achieve the legitimate aim pursue, regard being had to the need to strike a fair balance between the interest of the community and the right of landlords. The Court held that in principle, a system of temporary suspension for staggering the enforcement of court orders followed by the reinstatement of the landlord was not of itself open to criticism, but that such a system runs the risk of imposing an excessive burden on landlords in terms of their ability to deal with their property. Accordingly the system should provide procedural safeguards to ensure that its operation was neither arbitrary nor unforeseeable. The Italian system was inflexible, giving automatic priority to urgent requests where the landlord required the property for himself and his family. The result of this was that, despite obtaining a possession order in 1983 the applicant's order was passed over by more urgent requests until 1990 when they were promised police assistance to remove the tenant by no later than the end of 1993. After further delays, this deadline was extended finally to April 26, 1996 but the applicants regained possession on the death of the tenant two weeks beforehand. The Court found a violation of Article 1 of Protocol No. 1 in that the uncertainty of the system and the lack of compensation for the delay imposed an excessive burden on the applicant, upset the balance between the protection of the right of property and the general interest. This case should be contrasted with that of *Spadea & Scalabrino v. Italy*,[69] where a landlord's complaint about the repeated suspension of eviction orders was rejected by the Court on the basis that the suspension met the reasonable aim of seeking to prevent a large number of people becoming homeless at the same time.

Registration

Generally

The registration or non-registration of title to land and of interests in land may give rise to Article 1 of Protocol No. 1 issues. Title to land is clearly a possession for the purposes of Article 1 of Protocol No. 1. Other interests in or rights over property can be possessions for the purposes of Article 1 of Protocol No. 1 provided the individual concerned can demonstrate the existence of a property right and his entitlement to enjoy it.[70] The property right must be of real economic value, but its actual value need not have been ascertained. It may, however, be a right contingent upon the satisfaction of certain conditions (provided those conditions are fulfilled and have

16.172

[67] *Immobiliare Saffi v. Italy* (2000) 30 E.H.R.R. 756.
[68] (2000) 30 E.H.R.R. 756.
[69] (1995) 21 E.H.R.R. 482.
[70] *S v. United Kingdom* (1986) 47 D.R. 274 at 279 Eur Comm HR; *Agneessens v. Belgium* (1988) 58 D.R. 63, Eur Comm HR.

not lapsed),[71] property right where there is a legitimate expectation that an entitlement will arise,[72] or a right which is in existence but yet to be enforced.[73] It can readily be seen that this definition will broadly cover most, if not all, registerable interests in land.

Deprivation through non-registration

16.173 Various provisions of land registration can give rise to the permanent or temporary loss of an interest through non-registration. The Land Registration Act 1925 provides that, on transfer of the legal title, the new owner must register his title within an allotted period. Where the land has not previously been registered, failure to register the land within the allotted time results in the loss of the legal estate. The owner does, however, retain equitable title. Where the land has previously been registered, the transfer does not take effect in law until the new owner is registered. Similarly, a legal charge over property must be registered to have effect in law. In either case, until registration occurs both the transfer and charge take effect only in equity. Failure to register minor interests (including the aforementioned equitable interests) results in their loss as against a later bona fide purchaser for value without notice of their existence. The Law Commission has considered the reduction of the status of overriding interests to minor interests, but rejected the proposals on the grounds that to do so might result in the loss of some interests through non-registration equating to a deprivation without compensation and thus a violation of Article 1 of Protocol No. 1.[74] It is suggested by some commentators,[75] that if the Law Commission's general concern in that regard is correct then "any loss caused by failure to register could be a violation of Article 1: in none of the cases is any compensation paid".[76] The argument is certainly easily seen, the provisions regarding registration are statutory in origin, accordingly in so far as they can result in the deprivation of possessions they possibly violate Article 1 of Protocol No. 1. Nevertheless, the purpose behind the registration of land is a strong legitimate aim to the benefit of society as a whole, that of providing certainty of ownership and interest in property, enabling free transaction in land without unnecessary fear of future discovery of overriding interests. The system of registration is accessible and effective, and any deprivation that might occur essentially results from the failure of the individual owner to register his rights. Whether these points would be sufficiently strong to justify deprivation in the absence of compensation is a matter of some debate, and even the Law Commission was fearful that the proposal to reduce the status of

---

[71] *De Napoles Pacheco v. Belgium* (1978) 15 D.R. 143; *Agneessens v. Belgium* (1988) 58 D.R. 63, Eur Comm HR.
[72] *Stran Greek Refineries and Stratis Andreadis v. Greece* (1995) 19 E.H.R.R. 293, para. 59; *Pressos Compania Naviera S.A. v. Belgium* (1996) 21 E.H.R.R. 301, paras 31–32; *National & Provincial Building Society, Leeds Permanent Building Society and Yorkshire Building Society v. United Kingdom* (1998) 25 E.H.R.R. 127, para. 69.
[73] *Inze v. Austria*, Application No. 8695/79 (1986) 8 E.H.R.R. 498, Commission; (1988) 10 E.H.R.R. 394, Court.
[74] Law Commission, *Land Registration for the Twenty-First Century. A Consultative Document* (1998) Law Com. No. 254.
[75] D.R. Jean Howell "Land and Human Rights" [1999] 63 Conv. 287 at 303–305.
[76] *ibid.* at 305.

overriding interests to minor interests gave an unacceptable risk of violation of Article 1 of Protocol No. 1 in the absence of the availability of
compensation.[77]

Rights over Property

General

There are a number of ways in which the Convention can and does impact   **16.174**
on rights over property, such as licences or permits to use property for a
particular purpose. The cases can be divided into two categories: those in
which an established or permitted use is revoked or overridden, and those
in which land owners have obligations or the rights of others imposed upon
them.

Revocation or limitation of use

The economic benefit derived from a licence to use land in a particular way   **16.175**
can be a "possession" within the meaning of Article 1 of Protocol No. 1.[78]
In order to demonstrate that the benefit is "existing" the user must establish a reasonable and legitimate expectation that he will be able to continue the activity and demonstrate that any conditions or laws regulating its
use have been met.[79]

In *Fredin v. Sweden*,[80] the applicant, who was the owner of a gravel pit,   **16.176**
successfully established a violation of Article 6 where he was unable to
appeal or secure the review of decisions: first, to revoke his licence to
extract gravel after he had made a considerable investment; and, secondly, to force him to secure the cost of making the site good himself. The
applicant also established a violation of Article 1 of Protocol No. 1 on a
"control of use" basis, but in the view of the Court was not entitled to any
compensation as a result.

In *Matos e Silva, Lda. v. Portugal*,[81] the first applicant worked land in the   **16.177**
Algarve for the extraction of salt and the breeding of fish. His right to do so,
at least in part, arose under a royal decree originally granted in 1884. The
Court held that the right to the income derived from these activities was a
"possession" for the purposes of Article 1 of Protocol No. 1. The Portuguese Government withdrew the concession and put in place provisions
intended to limit building on the land or any change of use with the
intention of creating a nature reserve. The applicant was subjected to a
long period of uncertainty both about the future of the land and the issue
of compensation for the lost rights. The Court held, distinguishing the case
from that of *Papamichalopoulos v. Greece*,[82] that although the applicants'
rights had been substantially reduced, they had not disappeared and the
situation was not irreversible. Accordingly, there was no deprivation and

---

[77] Law Commission, *Land Registration for the Twenty-First Century. A Consultative Document* (1998) Law Com. No. 254.
[78] *Tre Traktörer Aktiebolag v. Sweden* (1991) 13 E.H.R.R. 309, para. 53 (the case concerned
a licence to serve alcohol).
[79] *Batelaan and Huiges v. Netherlands* (1984) 41 D.R. 170 at 173; *Pudas v. Sweden* (1988)
10 E.H.R.R. 380; *Størksen v. Norway* (1994) 78–A D.R. 88.
[80] (1991) 13 E.H.R.R. 784.
[81] (1997) 24 E.H.R.R. 573.
[82] (1993) 16 E.H.R.R. 440.

the case did not fit within the second rule of *Sporrong and Lönnroth v. Sweden*.[83] Nevertheless, there had been an interference with the peaceful enjoyment of possessions, and although there was a public interest in environmental protection, a fair balance between the public interest and the interests of the applicant had not been achieved, and accordingly there had been a violation of Article 1 of Protocol No. 1.

16.178 *Iatridis v. Greece*,[84] concerned the operation of an open-air cinema on a site in Illioupolis in Greece. The cinema had been built in 1950 following the obtaining of the necessary permit from the local authorities showing the lessors of the cinema as the owners of the land in question. However, ownership of the cinema site became a matter of dispute between the lessors of the cinema and the state in 1953 when the Minister of Agriculture determined that the site on which the cinema was operated was in fact public forest owned by the state. Over the ensuing decades proceedings to determine ownership continued but failed finally to resolve the issue. This did not stop the state from levying inheritance tax from the lessors of the cinema on the death of the then claimed owner. The applicant had leased the cinema from the lessors in 1978 and completely restored it. He then operated the open-air cinema for some 11 years and built up a clientèle of local residents. In 1989, however, an eviction order was made by the Lands Department of the Attica Prefecture and a month later the applicant was evicted. The applicant challenged the eviction order in the Athens District Court which found for the state. The Athens Court of First Instance heard the applicant's appeal and quashed the eviction order on the basis that the Lands Department could issue an eviction order only if the property in question belonged to the state, if the state's title to the property was not in dispute, and if the property was being unjustifiably occupied by a third party. Given the dispute over ownership and the applicant's occupation of the site for 11 years under a formally valid lease, these conditions were not satisfied. Although the applicant then applied to the State Lands Authority to have the cinema returned to him, the state failed to return it and continued to operate the cinema on the site. The state argued[85] before the Court that a lessee's right to use a leased property is limited in scope and in duration (since the lease can be terminated at any time by either party) and is relative (since it cannot be relied on against a third party with an overriding right over the leased property, such as a property right *in rem*) therefore the lease had never given the applicant a sufficiently well-founded property right enforceable against the state. The Court reiterated that the concept of "possessions" in Article 1 of Protocol No. 1 has an autonomous meaning which is certainly not limited to ownership of physical goods: certain other rights and interests constituting assets can also be regarded as "property rights", and thus as "possessions" for the purposes of Article 1 of Protocol No. 1.[86] On the point made by the state, given the unresolved dispute as to ownership of the land in question, the Court confined itself to observing that before the applicant was evicted, he had operated the cinema for 11

---

[83] (1983) 5 E.H.R.R. 35.
[84] (2000) 30 E.H.R.R. 97
[85] See *Iatridis v. Greece* (2000) 30 E.H.R.R. 97, para. 53.
[86] *Iatridis v. Greece* (2000) 30 E.H.R.R. 97, para. 54.

years under a formally valid lease without any interference by the authorities, as a result of which he had built up a clientèle that constituted an
asset; in that connection, the Court took into account the role played in
local cultural life by open-air cinemas in Greece and to the fact that the
clientèle of such a cinema is made up mainly of local residents. The Court
held that the refusal to revoke the assignment of the land to the council
constituted an interference with the applicant's property rights. Since he
held only a lease of his business premises, this interference amounted
neither to an expropriation nor was it an instance of controlling the use of
property but came under the first sentence of the first paragraph of Article
1 of Protocol No. 1.[87] From the time the eviction order had been quashed
by the Athens Court of First Instance (from which there was no appeal) the
applicant's eviction ceased to have any legal basis and the Council
became an unlawful occupier and should have returned the cinema to the
applicant. The interference with the applicant's possessions was manifestly in breach of Greek law and accordingly a violation of Article 1 of
Protocol No. 1. Given the unlawfulness of the eviction there was no need
to consider whether a fair balance had been struck between the demands
of the general interest of the community and the requirements of the
protection of the individual's fundamental rights.[88]

Imposition of use by third parties and obligations of ownership

In some cases the imposition or extension of the rights of third parties over
an individual's land can be an interference with Article 8 and/or Article 1 of
Protocol No. 1.[89] **16.179**

In *Chassagnou v. France*,[90] the applicants complained that, in violation of
their rights under Article 1 of Protocol No. 1 and despite their opposition to
hunting on ethical grounds, under the *Loi Verdeille* of 1964 they had been
obliged to transfer hunting rights over their land to approved municipal
hunters' associations, had been made automatic members of those associations, and could not prevent hunting on their property. The applicants
also claimed violation of Article 14 in conjunction with Article 1 of Protocol
No. 1 and Article 11 on the basis that they had been discriminated against,
as only landlowners with land exceeding a minimum area could avoid the
provisions regarding hunting rights. The Court found the second paragraph of Article 1 of Protocol No. 1 to be applicable on the basis that,
although there was no deprivation of property, the compulsory transfer of
hunting rights prevented the applicants from using the right to hunt as they
saw fit, which in this case amounted to not wishing to use it at all and
objecting to the use of it by others.[91] The Court accepted that the law in
question pursued a legitimate purpose in seeking to avoid unregulated
hunting and encourage the rational management of game stocks.[92] However, the compensation available, that of being entitled to hunting rights **16.180**

---

[87] *Iatridis v. Greece* (2000) 30 E.H.R.R. 97, para. 55.
[88] *Iatridis v. Greece* (2000) 30 E.H.R.R. 97, paras 61–62.
[89] See further in this regard the discussion of trespass in paras 16.181 *et seq.* below. See
also *Baner v. Sweden* (1989) 60 D.R. 128 (a case concerning the extension of public fishing
rights).
[90] (2000) 29 E.H.R.R. 615.
[91] *Chassagnou v. France* (2000) 29 E.H.R.R. 615 at para. 74.
[92] *ibid.* at para. 79.

over the entirety of the municipality's territory under association control, and that for the loss of profits suffered through the loss of the ability, for example to rent out the hunting rights, was inadequate to compensate the applicants, who neither wanted to hunt nor wanted to rent out their land for hunting.[93] The Court concluded that the fair balance had been upset:

> "Compelling small landowners to transfer hunting rights over their land so that others can make use of them in a way which is totally incompatible with their beliefs imposes a disproportionate burden which is not justified under the second paragraph of Article 1 of Protocol No. 1. There has therefore been a violation of that provision."[94]

16.181　As to the question of obligations that may be imposed upon the owners of land, the domestic courts have made interesting use of human rights arguments in an unusual (and for many, unfamiliar) area of the law, namely that of chancel repairs. Whilst the area may be unfamiliar, and to some anachronistic, the case concerned has very widespread implications.

16.182　As an historical legacy of the common law, the lay owners of the whole or part of rectorial property were, in the absence of any custom to the contrary, liable to repair the chancel of the parish church. Although a common law duty and obligation, the method by which a particular Church Council might require a lay proprietor of rectorial property to repair or pay for the repair of the chancel is determined by the Chancel Repairs Act 1932. In *Wallbank v. The Parochial Church Council of the Parishes of Aston Cantlow and Wilmcote with Billesley*, the obligations of chancel repairs have been swept away by the Court of Appeal. The Parochial Church Council ("PCC") had served notice under the 1932 Act informing the owners of glebe land that the chancel of the parish church at Aston Cantlow was in disrepair and calling upon them to put it into proper repair. Proceedings were commenced under section 2(2) of the 1932 Act claiming the amount required to carry out the repair. At first instance,[94A] Ferris J. was required to determine a preliminary issue on the interaction of the law of chancel repairs with the Convention. At the time of his decision the HRA was enacted but not in force. It was accepted that accordingly Ferris J. was not able to rule that the obligation to carry out chancel repairs was unenforceable rather that were he to find the law uncertain he should declare and develop it in a manner consistent with the Convention. Ferris J. held that the law was not uncertain and that, even if that were not the case, there was no infringement of other rights under Article 1 of Protocol No. 1 (peaceful enjoyment of possessions), Article 9 (freedom of religion), or Article 14 (freedom from discrimination). Regarding Article 1 of Protocol No. 1 Ferris J. found that to be no deprivation of possessions nor any entrenchment upon the owner's enjoyment of their possessions. He found the liability to repair the chancel to be one of the incidents of ownership of the land in question. He went on[94B]:

---

[93] *ibid.* at para. 82.
[94] *ibid.* at para. 85.
[94A] March 28, 2000, Chancery Division reported as Newlaw Online judgment 100055501.
[94B] Paragraph 23 of his judgment.

"It is, of course, an unusual incident because it does not amount to a charge on the land, is not limited to the value of the land and imposes a personal liability on the owner of the land. But in principle I do not find it possible to distinguish it from the liability which would attach to the owner of land which is purchased subject to a mortgage, restrictive covenant, or other incumbrance created by a predecessor in title. In such a case the enforcement of the mortgage, restrictive covenant or other incumbrance involves no deprivation of possessions because the possessions in question were always liable to such enforcement. The case is quite different from that in which an outright owner of property finds that his ownership is entrenched upon by some outside intervention in the form of taxation, compulsory purchase or control over the way in which the property can be used".

By the time of the appeal,[94C] the HRA was in force and the shape of the **16.183** argument before the Court of Appeal altered accordingly to consider two questions: first, whether the PCC was a public authority within section 6 of the HRA; second, whether its action in serving the relevant notice was unlawful by reason of Article 1 of Protocol No. 1, read either alone or with Article 14 of the Convention. The Court of Appeal held that it was "inescapable" that the PCC was a public authority for the purposes of the HRA:

"It is an authority in the sense that it possesses powers which private individuals do not possess to determine how others should act. Thus, in particular, its notice to repair has statutory force. It is public in the sense that it is created and empowered by law; that it forms part of the church by law established; and that its functions include the enforcement through the courts of a common law liability to maintain its chancels resting upon persons who need not be members of the church. If this were to be incorrect, the PCC would nevertheless, and for the same reasons, be a legal person certain of whose functions, chancel repairs among them, are functions of a public nature."[94D]

This conclusion is open to question. First, it assumes the basic premise that the Church of England, being created by statute and holding a number of statutory powers is by definition a public authority. This is not a premise which is widely recognised or easily accepted, as it could be argued that the statutory position of the Church of England constitutes no more than a recognition of its special and historical status as the primary faith of England as defined by its monarch. The Church of England is a private organisation, with private landholdings, and the Statutory provisions regarding its administration and the exercise of its powers can be regarded as being no different from those associations (such as a number of public schools) established by Royal Charter that require a private Act of Parliament to alter their basic administration. The simple fact that an organisation is created or recognised by law should not necessarily result in it being considered a public authority for the purposes of the HRA.

[94C] [2001] 3 All E.R. 393 (CA).
[94D] Paragraph 35 of the judgment, [2001] 3 All E.R. 393 (CA) at 402g-j.

Second, it is certainly debatable whether the function of securing chancel repairs should be regarded as a public function. Churches are not "public" buildings in the same sense that a Town Hall or Local Authority building might be considered a public building. The mere fact of public access does not make a building one the maintenance of which is a public function. Churches are privately owned and their maintenance is a private obligation of the Church (or of lay rectors) for which, generally speaking, no public funding is available. The reliance of the Court of Appeal on the concept that because the repair of churches was in the public "interest" it constituted a public function is readily challenged. The public interest in the repair of churches arises for church-goers in a desire to make use of those churches, and for others for aesthetic reasons and in seeing the preservation of historical buildings and the heritage of the nation. The latter point might be made in respect of the preservation and repair of a privately owned listed building. Nevertheless, no suggestion could be made that in repairing a privately owned listed building its owner was performing a public function, even in circumstances where that owner was prepared to allow members of a particular select group to use that property for the purposes of assembly or to allow access to the public generally. The obligation to repair the chancel is a private obligation upon the owners of rectorial land, and it might be argued that the actions of any church in seeking to enforce such obligations through the courts are no different to those of a tenant seeking to enforce the statutory repair obligations of his or her landlord. That a particular act is or may be in the public interest does not mean that the person carrying it out is necessarily carrying out a public function. Notwithstanding these questions for the time being the case establishes Court of Appeal authority for the proposition that the Church of England, and its subsidiary organisations such as Parochial Church Councils, are public authorities for the purposes of the HRA. It should be noted that the logic adopted by the Court of Appeal, if relied upon elsewhere, may result in other surprising additions to the category of public authority.

16.184 As to the issues of infringement of human rights, the Court of Appeal held that the obligation and liability for chancel repairs is an arbitrary tax that does not satisfy the basic standard set by Article 1 of Protocol No. 1 and that the manner in which it singles out particular owners is arbitrary, unjustifiably discriminatory and thus contrary to Article 14. Accordingly, the PCC could not lawfully recover the cost of chancel repairs. This decision essentially puts an end to chancel repairs in the common law. The Court of Appeal found that the "possession" interfered with for the purposes of Article 1 of Protocol No. 1 was not the property itself, as the ownership of that property, whilst being the source of the liability, was not disturbed by what was essentially a levy on the owners' private funds. Although rejected by the Court of Appeal, it could certainly be argued (as it was by Counsel for the PCC) that there was in fact no interference, either with the enjoyment of the property itself, or with the owners' private funds or wealth. The obligation to pay chancel repairs pre-existed the owners' purchase of the property, in purchasing the property they became subject to that obligation, or put another way, they acquired a possession limited by the existence of that obligation. They could not acquire the property free of it. This viewpoint concurs with that of Ferris J. at first instance. Accordingly, the purchase itself was of no more than the property as affected by the obligation, and therefore in choosing to make the purchase in knowledge of the potential obligation the subsequent owners were knowingly affecting their possession of funds or wealth. The subsequent demand with regard to chancel repairs was therefore not of itself an interference with the owners' possessions as they had already been affected by their own actions. A failure to view the chancel repair obligation in this way, namely as in incidence of ownership of the property concerned, may well widen the scope of challenge on human rights grounds to other incidences of ownership such as restrictive covenants and charges.

Trespass

Generally

Trespass potentially brings into conflict the right of property owners to **16.185** exclude strangers from their property and the rights of those strangers, for example, to freedom of movement, assembly and expression.

Exclusion of strangers

These concepts and the conflict of rights between land owner and **16.186** stranger were addressed in the Court of Appeal in *CIN Properties Ltd v. Rawlins*,[95] whose decision was later challenged by application to the Commission in *Mark Rawlins v. United Kingdom*.[96] The case concerned a shopping centre covering some 12 acres in Wellingborough, occupied by CIN Properties Ltd on a long lease from the local authority. In the 1990s the shopping centre came to be frequented by a group of local youths, most of whom were black and/or unemployed. The centre was policed by private security firms who referred to the group as "chimpanzees" and sought to have them arrested for trifling offences such as whistling in public. In 1991, 10 of the youths were charged with public order offences and CIN Properties Ltd sought, by solicitor's letter, to threaten injunctive proceedings and to ban them for life from entering the centre for any purpose whatsoever. After the criminal trials collapsed CIN Properties Ltd sought the injunctive relief they had threatened, resulting in undertakings being obtained from the youths, and later committal proceedings. The injunction application was heard by Mr Recorder Philip Cox, Q.C. who held that members of the public in their use of pedestrian ways or "Malls" of the shopping centre which had replaced the former street pattern of Wellingborough were not to be considered bare licensees whose rights could be revoked at will, and that subject to their "reasonable conduct" were entitled to an equitable or irrevocable right to enter and use the shopping centre during its normal opening hours. His decision was reversed by the Court of Appeal,[97] who, in the approved judgment of Balcombe L.J. rejected this idea of an equitable or irrevocable right and refused to accept

[95] [1995] 2 E.G.L.R. 130.
[96] Application No. 33689/96, [1998] E.H.R.L.R. 218.
[97] [1995] 2 E.G.L.R. 130.

that a landowner's power of exclusion was limited to circumstances in which he is able to show good cause for that exclusion. This decision itself was subject to an unsuccessful challenge to the Commission.[98] The United Kingdom has not ratified the guarantee to liberty of movement in Article 2 of Protocol No. 4 of the Convention,[99] and accordingly the applicants were unable to make use of any arguments as to the violation of that right. Instead, they sought to rely on Article 11, the right to freedom of assembly and association. The Commission rejected the complaint on the basis that freedom of assembly did not, in Convention law, "guarantee a right to pass and re-pass in public places, or to assemble for purely social purposes anywhere one wishes". Nor did the right to freedom of association assist. The applicants had no history of using the centre for any form of organised assembly or association. Accordingly, the common law right to exclude strangers would appear to survive Convention scrutiny, at least on the basis of those Articles currently ratified by the United Kingdom.[1] The Court of Appeal recognised that this position might change and that the law might have to adapt to "new social facts" but declined at that time to construct an appropriate legal framework.[2]

The "Right to Roam"

16.187 The "right to roam" contained in the Countryside and Right of Way Act 2000 may be one example of changing attitudes and adaptation to "new social facts" as anticipated by the Court of Appeal. Under section 2 of the Act any person is entitled on foot to enter and remain on any "access land" for the purposes of open-air recreation, provided he does so without breaking or damaging any wall, fence, hedge stile or gate and observes the restrictions imposed by the Act. If the person exercising the right steps outside the scope of section 2 or fails to observe the relevant restrictions he becomes a trespasser, and he cannot re-enter that land or any land under the same ownership for a period of 72 hours. "Access land" is defined by section 1 of the Act and, in addition to common and dedicated land, includes land shown as "open country" on the conclusive form map of open country to be prepared by the appropriate countryside body, and any land situated more than 600 metres above sea level in any area for which no such map relating to open country has been issued. "Open country" means land which "appears to the appropriate countryside body to consist wholly or predominantly of mountain, moor, heath or down", and is not registered common land. Although land can be excepted under section 1 and schedule 1, section 2 of the Act therefore represents a significant interference with the right discussed in the preceding paragraph of private landowners to exclude strangers, and accordingly may be considered a "control of use" within the third rule of Article 1 of Protocol No. 1 as defined by *Sporrong and Lönnroth v. Sweden*.[3] Although the Act

---

[98] Application No. 33689/96 [1998] E.H.R.L.R. 218.
[99] Nor is it one of the rights that can be relied upon under the HRA.
[1] For a very detailed analysis of *Rawlins* and trespass both in the human rights context and in relation to "quasi-public" space, see Kevin Gray and Susan Francis Gray, "Civil Rights, Civil Wrongs and Quasi-Public Space" [1999] E.H.R.L.R. Issue 1, 46.
[2] [1995] 2 E.G.L.R. 130 at 134H-J.
[3] (1983) 5 E.H.R.R. 35.

received royal assent on November 30, 2000, and some of its provisions are now in force, as at the date of press section 2 and many of its related provisions are not yet in force. The main delay in giving life to the "right to roam" will be the preparation of the conclusive "open country" maps, which it is anticipated will take a number of years, although it is hoped that certain types of land will be subject to a "fast-track" procedure in order to open up access to the public as soon as possible. For the time being, therefore, the human rights implications of the "right to roam" are unlikely to be significant. Once the right becomes exercisable, however, it is quite likely that private landowners will wish to challenge the compatibility of the right with their own rights under Article 1 of Protocol No. 1, and possibly Article 8. Except in relation to damage caused by access by persons authorised to do so for defined purposes by specified public bodies, no compensation is made available to landowners for the access conferred by the Act. This is despite the fact that there are substantial restrictions imposed on those owning or having rights over "access land", in that, for example, if an owner or person interested in the land wishes to exclude or restrict public access they may do so only on giving appropriate notice to the relevant authority. Further, such exclusion or restriction of access must not exceed 28 days per calendar year and there are additional restrictions as to public holidays and on the number of weekends on which such notices can operate.[4] The concerns of landowners and the human rights implications of the Act were one of the reasons that the progress of the Bill through Parliament was slow. Although some changes were made to the Bill to take these concerns into account, and there are significant restrictions on those making use of the "right to roam", there would still appear to be scope for challenge to the Act on human rights grounds. The Act can certainly be said to pursue a legitimate aim in the general interest, whether a fair balance has in fact been struck between the interests of the public and the interests of landowners remains open to question.

Tresspass: no general defence of acting in the public interest

Recent public reaction to the growth of genetically modified crops has lead to the scrutiny by the Court of Appeal of a possible defence of trespass in the public interest. Although Convention issues were not directly relied upon, the case of *Monsanto v. Tilly*,[5] gives useful guidance in the event that similar arguments are raised under the HRA. Monsanto was a company licensed by the Department of the Environment to conduct trials of genetically modified plants and crops at a number of sites. The defendants belonged to a political group, GenetiX Snowball, active in campaigning against GM crops and plants, and were involved in a publicity protest in which they entered a Monsanto site and pulled up a number of GM plants. Monsanto issued proceedings for injunctive relief, basing their claim in trespass to land or goods, and sought summary judgment. The defendants obtained unconditional leave to defend on the grounds *inter alia* of an arguable defence to trespass of justification in the public interest in that

16.188

---

[4] In this regard see para. 16.174 *et seq.* above concerning rights over land.
[5] Court of Appeal (Civil Division) (Judgment November 25, 1999) New Law Online judgment no. 1991112403.

their acts were "necessary to protect third parties and their property and/or were in the public interest". Monsanto appealed the grant of unconditional leave. The Court of Appeal considered carefully the pre-existing defence to trespass of necessity in response to an immediate and obvious danger such that a reasonable person would conclude that there was no alternative to trespass. This defence was extremely prescribed. The court allowed the appeal on the basis that the object of the defendant's campaign was to change government policy, and that in a democratic society that had to be effected by lawful and not unlawful means. No amount of argument or expert evidence would alter the fact that the matters relied upon by the defendants were not capable of affording a defence in law.

Chapter 17
Professional Liability and Negligence

1. INTRODUCTION

17.01   **Application of Human Rights Act to claims against professionals.** This chapter considers the impact of the Human Rights Act 1998 ("the HRA") on professional liability and negligence. A claim by a client against a professional usually arises in both contract and tort. Human rights law generally respects freedom of parties to contract as they wish and its application to contract law is therefore very limited. The primary impact of the Convention is seen in relation to tort and general procedure. The developments in relation to Article 6 and the duty of care are of key importance to professional negligence cases. Contrasted with the other areas of civil practice identified in this book, there is, as yet, a relative paucity of European case law directly relating to the professional liability field (save in the field of medical law), and the effect of the HRA in domestic law is, where appropriate, considered in relation to analogous subject areas.

17.02   **Structure and scope of this chapter.** The structure of the chapter is as follows. First, those Articles of primary relevance to professional liability are briefly summarised. Secondly, the duty of care in negligence and the implications of the landmark decisions of *Osman v. United Kingdom* and *Z. v. United Kingdom* are considered. Thirdly, the professional immunities of advocates, experts and arbitrators are discussed. Fourthly, the field of clinical negligence and medical law which has been the subject of the majority of the Strasbourg case law is discussed. Fifthly, the application of the HRA to professional duties of client confidentiality is noted. Finally, proceedings involving professionals are considered, including inquests and professional disciplinary proceedings both in the medical and general professional context.[1] Procedural issues of generic relevance to professionals and applications for wasted costs orders, which are of relevance in the context of lawyers' liabilities,[2] are discussed in Chapter 10 on Civil Procedure. Issues of legal professional privilege are considered in Chapter 11 on Evidence.[2A] No doubt the HRA itself will raise new issues in the lawyers' liability context, where lawyers have failed to consider or raise HRA points or where wasted costs orders are sought for the raising

---

[1] See also Chap. 20 Civil Disciplinary Proceedings.
[2] Chap. 10, paras 10.129 *et seq.*, above.
[2A] At paras 11.64 *et seq.*

of what a judge regards as unnecessary arguments,[2B] possibly including unnecessary human rights arguments.[2C]

2. RELEVANT ARTICLES

The Articles of the Convention that are, in general terms, of most rele- **17.03** vance to professional liability are Article 6 (the right to a fair trial) and Article 8 (the right to respect for private and family life, home and correspondence).

The right of access to a court, which has been implied into Article 6,[3] is of **17.04** general importance in relation to any potential or actual limitations on the liability of professionals. This right is not absolute but is qualified. However, any restriction must be justified in that:

(1) it must have a legitimate aim;

(2) it must not impair the very essence of the right; and

(3) the restriction must be proportionate to the aim to be achieved.[4]

Article 6 is applicable to all proceedings including actions between private **17.05** parties and is therefore of particular relevance to the professional liability context, which will often involve purely private parties.

Article 8 provides a right to respect for private and family life, home and **17.06** correspondence. The right to private life provided by this section is a qualified right and is subject to restrictions justified by reference to Article 8(2). It is also important that Article 8 has *vertical* effect in that it restrains infringements of privacy by a public authority. It does not, prima facie, apply between individuals. The extent to which the HRA has horizontal effect is still developing. However, since the court is a public body, it can be argued that it should ensure that there are no unwarranted interferences with the interests protected by Article 8, even by private bodies.[5]

In relation to clinical negligence and medical law, Article 2 (the right to life) **17.07** is of fundamental importance and other rights including Article 3 (the right to freedom from inhuman and degrading treatment) and Article 12 (the right to marry and found a family) are also relevant. These rights are discussed further at paragraphs 17.55 *et seq.,* below.

It should be borne in mind in professional and clinical negligence proceed- **17.08** ings (as in other proceedings) that any compromise of those proceedings may prevent applicants from being "victims" within the meaning of Article 34 of the Convention should they wish to make an application to the

---

[2B] *Arthur J. S. Hall v. Simons* [2000] 3 W.L.R. 543, HL at 589B-C *per* Lord Hope (the power of the judge to make a wasted costs order in a criminal case in regard to advancing what the judge may regard as unnecessary arguments may breach the HRA).
[2C] See *e.g., Daniels v. Walker, Practice Note* [2000] 1 W.L.R. 1382 at 1386H–1387C.
[3] See *Golder v. United Kingdom* (1979) 1 E.H.R.R. 524.
[4] *Stubbings v. United Kingdom* (1997) 23 E.H.R.R. 213.
[5] See Chap. 5, paras 5.29, 5.31 and 5.40 *et seq.,* above.

European Court based on the same complaints.[6] In accepting and receiving compensation, the applicant effectively renounces further use of those remedies. In *Powell (William and Anita) v. United Kingdom*,[7] the applicants settled a claim for clinical negligence arising out of the death of their child and in relation to the alleged falsification by certain doctors of medical records.[8] The European Court ruled their application based on Article 2 to be inadmissible on the ground that the applicants could no longer claim to be victims in relation to the circumstances surrounding treatment of the deceased or the investigation into the death.

3. NEGLIGENCE & DUTY OF CARE

17.09   The European Court has considered the interrelation between the duty of care in negligence and the right of access to a court protected by Article 6(1). The three-limb test laid down by *Caparo Industries plc v. Dickman*,[9] an auditors' negligence case, for the existence of a duty of care may be summarised as follows. There must be:

(1) reasonable foreseeability of loss or damage;

(2) proximity between the claimant and defendant; and

(3) it must be fair, just and reasonable to impose a duty of care in negligence.

17.10   Where it is clear that a claimant has no real prospect of success in relation to establishing one or more of the elements which give rise to a duty of care, the courts are willing to strike out a claim at an interlocutory stage. It is rare that reasonable foreseeability of loss or damage is in issue. However, in a new or developing area, there is often great contention over the issue of proximity and the "public policy" ground, namely whether it is fair, just and reasonable to impose a duty of care in negligence. The courts have, at times, striven by one or other or both of these mechanisms to restrict the liability of professionals to avoid, in the words of Cardozo C.J., "liability in an indeterminate amount, for an indeterminate time, to an indeterminate class".[10]

17.11   The applicability of Article 6 as formulated by the European Court in *Osman v. United Kingdom*[11] reshaped the approach of domestic courts to striking out cases where the basis was essentially one of public policy. For a couple of years this undoubtedly hindered the use of striking out, a very

---

[6] *Hay (Robert and Dinah-Anne) v. United Kingdom*, Application No. 41894/98, October 17, 2000 (the application concerned complaint against police under Arts 2, 16(1) and 13 of the Convention following a settlement which was expressly stated to be without prejudice to the right of those representing the estate to pursue proceedings under the Convention).

[7] Application No. 45305/99, May 4, 2000. See also *Caraher v. United Kingdom*, Application No. 24520/94, January 11, 2000.

[8] Such a settlement is held to have fulfilled the "just satisfaction" test outlined in Chap. 2, para. 2.35. See also Chap. 9, para. 9.21, above.

[9] [1990] 2 AC 605, HL.

[10] *Ultramares Corporation v. Touche* (1931) 174 N.E. 441, 255 N.Y. 170.

[11] (2000) 29 E.H.R.R. 245.

important tactical weapon in professional negligence cases. The European Court subsequently resiled from this position in *Z v. United Kingdom*[12] and *T.P. & K.M. v. United Kingdom*[12A] (both complaints to Strasbourg arising out of *X (Minors) v. Bedfordshire County Council*[12B]) conceding that the striking out of the cases where it was not fair, just and reasonable to impose a duty of care was a matter of substantive domestic law and did not violate Article 6(1). This appears to have restored the utility of interlocutory striking out where no duty of care is established. The current position in relation to Article 6(1) and striking out is discussed at para. 10.29 *et seq.* above. However, in *Z* and *T.P.*, the Court notably did not overrule *Osman* leaving its residual impact uncertain and importantly, it has switched the focus from Article 6(1) to Article 13 (which provides the right to an "effective remedy before a national authority" to everyone who claims that his rights and freedoms under the Convention have been violated). Even if *Osman's* effect has now been circumscribed, the Court's approach in *Z* and *T.P.* will itself have very significant implications for professional negligence cases in developing areas of tort law. The judgments in *Osman*, *Z* and *T.P.* are summarised below prior to turning to consider the actual and potential implications of these developments for the liability of professionals.

The *Osman* Case

The facts of *Osman* were as follows. In 1987, Ahmet Osman, then aged 14, became the subject of the obsessive attention of Mr Paul Paget-Lewis, a teacher at his school. The police visited the school but took no further action. The teacher's disturbing behaviour continued. Amongst other things, Mr Paget-Lewis changed his name to "Osman", he drove his car into a van containing a former school friend of Ahmet of whom he was jealous and he informed officers from the education authority that he was thinking of "doing a Hungerford" (an indiscriminate mass killing carried out in the town of Hungerford). The police investigated periodically but took no significant action to protect Ahmet or his family. In March 1988, Mr Paget-Lewis shot and killed Mr Ali Osman (Ahmet's father) and shot and injured Ahmet. In October 1988, he was convicted of two charges of manslaughter, having pleaded guilty on the ground of diminished responsibility. He was sentenced to be detained in a secure mental hospital. In September 1989, Ahmet Osman and Mrs Mulkiye Osman (Ahmet's mother) commenced a civil action in negligence against the Commissioner of the Metropolitan Police. In August 1991, the police applied to strike out the action. In October 1992, the Court of Appeal[13] decided that the action should be struck out on the ground that in light of the 1989 ruling of the House of Lords in *Hill v. Chief Constable of West Yorkshire*,[14] no action could lie for public policy reasons against the police for their negligence in the investigation and suppression of crime. In their application to the European Commission of Human Rights, lodged on November 10, 1993,

17.12

---

[12] Application No. 29392/95, May 10, 2001; *The Times*, May 31, 2001.
[12A] Application No. 28945/95, May 10, 2001; *The Times*, May 31, 2001.
[12B] [1995] 2 A.C. 633, HL.
[13] *Osman v. Ferguson* [1993] 4 All E.R. 344, CA.
[14] [1989] A.C. 53.

the applicants complained that there had been a failure to protect the lives of Ali and Ahmet Osman and to protect the family from harassment, contrary to Articles 2 and 8 of the Convention, and that they had been denied access to a court or to any other effective remedy in respect of that failure, contrary to Articles 6(1) and 13. The Commission adopted a report on July 1, 1997 expressing the opinion that there had been no violation of Articles 2 and 8, that there had been a violation of Article 6(1) and that no separate issue arose under Article 13. On October 28, 1998, the European Court of Human Rights upheld the Commission's findings as to non-violation of Articles 2 and 8, the violation of Article 6(1) and the lack of necessity for consideration of Article 13. The reasoning in relation to Article 6(1) was as follows.

Applicability of Article 6(1)

17.13   The Court had to consider whether the dispute involved the determination of a "civil right or obligation" to bring it within Article 6(1). The Court did not accept the Government's argument that the applicants could not rely on Article 6 given that the Court of Appeal had dismissed their case as showing no cause of action. It observed that the common law had long accorded a claimant the right to submit to a court a claim in negligence against a defendant and to request that court to find that the facts of the case disclosed a breach of a duty of care owed by the defendant to the claimant which had caused harm to the latter. The Court accepted the Government's concession that the rule did not automatically doom to failure a civil action from the outset but in principle allowed a domestic court to make a considered assessment on the basis of the arguments before it as to whether a particular case was or was not suitable for the application of the rule. On that understanding, the Court considered that the applicants must be taken to have had a right, derived from the law of negligence, to seek an adjudication on the admissibility and merits of an arguable claim that they were in a relationship of proximity to the police, that the harm caused was foreseeable and that in the circumstances it was fair, just and reasonable not to apply the exclusionary rule outlined in the *Hill* case. The assertion of that right was in itself sufficient to ensure the applicability of Article 6(1) of the Convention.

Compliance with Article 6(1)

17.14   The Court noted that the applicants' claim never fully proceeded to trial in that there was never any determination on its merits or of the facts on which the claim was based. The applicants' claim had been rejected by the Court of Appeal since it was found to fall squarely within the scope of the exclusionary rule formulated by the House of Lords in the *Hill* case. Whilst observing that the aim of such a rule might be accepted as legitimate, being directed to the maintenance of the effectiveness of the police service and hence to the prevention of disorder or crime, the Court stressed that, in turning to the issue of proportionality, it must have particular regard to the rule's scope and especially its application in the case at issue. It appeared to the Court that the application of the rule in that manner, without further inquiry into the existence of competing public interest considerations, only served to confer a blanket immunity on the police for their acts and omissions during the investigation and suppression of crime and amounted to an unjustifiable restriction on an applicant's right to have a determination on the merits of his or her claim against the police in deserving cases. In the Court's view, it had to be open to the domestic court to have regard to the presence of other public interest considerations which pulled in the opposite direction to the application of the rule. Failing that, there would be no distinction made between degrees of negligence or of harm suffered or any consideration of the justice of a particular case. In effect, the European Court held that, whilst the aim of the public interest immunity rule excluding the tortious liability of the police for policy and operational decisions might satisfy a legitimate aim, the automatic or mechanistic approach to the application of an exclusionary rule in striking out of proceedings was a disproportionate restriction on the claimants' right of access to a court since it left no room for adequate inquiry into the competing public policy considerations and the merits of the individual case. The European Court held that the facts:

(1) that the applicants' claim involved an alleged failure to protect the life of a child;

(2) that this resulted from a catalogue of acts and omissions which amounted to gross negligence as opposed to minor incompetence;

(3) that in contrast to *Hill*, the Court of Appeal accepted that a sufficient degree of proximity had been established in the present case; and

(4) that the degree of harm suffered was very grave,

were considerations which had to be examined on the merits and not excluded by the grant of immunity to the police.[15]

Problems of the decision

The *Osman* decision threw up a number of difficulties. Firstly, it is an **17.15** established principle that Article 6(1) is relevant to procedural and not substantive law, *i.e.* it does not control the content of a state's domestic law.[16] However, in *Osman* the Court appeared to recognise that the third constituent element of duty of care was a matter of substantive English law but nevertheless found that Article 6(1) applied. Secondly, it was not yet clear how the Court was to examine the countervailing public interest considerations and what evidence was to be adduced relating to a particular public interest. Thirdly, it was not clear whether the claimant was *always* entitled to an examination on the merits and indeed what amounted to a sufficient examination on the merits.

---

[15] *ibid.*, paras 151–154.
[16] See, *e.g.*, *Powell and Rayner v. United Kingdom* (1990) 12 E.H.R.R. 355. However, as the European Court itself acknowledges, it is not always easy to determine the divide between procedural and substantive restrictions under domestic law: *Fayed v. United Kingdom* (1994) 18 E.H.R.R. 393, para.65.

Domestic reaction

17.16 Domestic judicial reaction took the form of general consternation and there
was much extra-judicial and judicial criticism of *Osman*. On one reading,
Osman threatened to undermine the use of the strike-out jurisdiction
across a broad band of cases where domestic law was already well
established, that is in those areas where, as with public interest immunity
on the part of the police, the third limb of the *Caparo Industries plc v.
Dickman*[17] test (that it was not fair, just and reasonable to impose a duty
of care) had been applied to exclude certain claims in negligence. Such
situations included claims against auditors by prospective investors,[18]
claims against psychiatrists or their employing local authorities arising out
of social services work,[19] claims against educational psychologists or their
employing local education authorities arising out of their diagnosis and
management of school childrens' special educational needs[20] and claims
against construction industry professionals where the loss claimed by third
parties was often economic in nature.[21] Lord Hoffmann expressed the
view that the effect of *Osman* was that:

> "The whole English jurisprudence on the liability of public authorities
> for failure to deliver public services is open to attack on the grounds
> that it violates the right to a hearing before a tribunal".[22]

17.17 The House of Lords accepted that *Osman* had diminished the ability to
strike out claims at the interlocutory stage in *Barrett v. London Borough of
Enfield*.[23] Lord Browne-Wilkinson expressed the opinion that he found the
Osman decision extremely difficult to understand and commented on the
difficulties of application of the principles in that decision. In particular, he
noted that the issue of whether it was fair, just and reasonable to impose
liability in negligence was a prerequisite to there being any liability in
negligence at all. This is decided in English law as a question of law. In his
Lordship's view, Article 6(1) presupposed the existence of a primary right
(right A) as a matter of substantive domestic law. Article 6(1) then created
a secondary right (right B) of access to the courts to assert the primary
right, which he regarded as separate and free-standing. He queried
whether the rejection by the domestic courts of the claim in *Osman* could
properly have amounted to a breach of Article 6(1) and wondered how any
generally applicable principles of law which were based on public policy

---

[17] [1990] 2 A.C. 605, HL. The House of Lords established a three limbed test to determine the
existence of a duty of care: (1) reasonable foreseeability of injury or damage; (2) a relationship of proximity between the claimant and defendant and (3) it is fair, just and reasonable
to impose a duty of care on the defendant.
[18] *Caparo Industries Plc v. Dickman* [1990] 2 A.C. 605, HL.
[19] *X v. Bedfordshire County Council* [1995] 2 A.C. 633, HL.
[20] *E (A minor) v. Dorset County Council*, reported with other cases *sub nom.* X (Minors) v.
Bedfordshire County Council [1995] 2 A.C. 633, HL.
[21] *D&F Estates v. Church Commissioners of England* [1989] A.C. 177; *Murphy v. Brentwood
District Council* [1991] 1 A.C. 398, HL.
[22] Rt. Hon. Lord Hoffmann, "Human Rights and the House of Lords" (1999) 62 M.L.R.
159.
[23] [1999] 3 W.L.R. 79, HL (the claimant, who had been in the care of the defendant council
for almost all of his childhood, brought a claim in negligence claiming damages for various
psychological problems he claimed to be suffering as a result of the council's failure properly
to safeguard his welfare).

could survive. He further stated that once that decision was taken as a matter of law, it applied to all future cases of the same kind and the decision did not depend on weighing the balance between the extent of the damage to the claimant and the damage to the public in each particular case.[24] Lord Browne-Wilkinson reluctantly held that in view of the *Osman* decision and the fact that Article 6 was shortly to become part of English law, in such cases as those under appeal, it was difficult to say that it was a clear and obvious case calling for striking out.

The pattern in relation to the Court of Appeal was quite mixed. The Court of Appeal cases addressing the *Osman* issue are set out at paras 10.35 *et seq.* above. **17.18**

The X v. Bedfordshire County Council cases

The refusal of the House of Lords to impose a duty of care by local authorities, psychiatrists and social workers in the exercise of their functions relating to child care in *X (Minors) v. Bedfordshire County Council*[25] was the subject of an application by one group of claimants to Strasbourg and their case was given the new title of *Z v. United Kingdom.*[26] The applicants in *Z* were four siblings. In October 1987, the applicants' family was referred to the social services by its health visitor because of concerns about the children, including reports that *Z* was stealing food. Over the next four and a half years, the social services monitored the family and provided various forms of support to the parents. During that period, problems continued. In October 1989, when investigating a burglary, the police found the children's rooms to be filthy and the mattresses to be soaked in urine. In March 1990, it was reported that *Z* and another sibling were stealing food from bins in school. In September 1990, two of the siblings were reported as having bruises on their faces. On a number of occasions, it was reported that the children were locked in their rooms and were smearing excrement on the windows. Finally in June 1992, the children were placed in emergency foster care on the demand of their mother who said she would batter them if they were not removed. The consultant psychologist who examined the children found that the older three were showing signs of serious psychological disturbance and noted that it was the worst case of neglect and emotional abuse that she had seen. The Official Solicitor commenced proceedings on behalf of the applicants against the local authority, claiming damages for negligence on the basis that the authority, through its child protection staff including psychiatrists and social workers, failed to have proper regard for the children's welfare and to take effective steps to protect them. Following proceedings which terminated in the House of Lords, the applicants' claims were struck out. Lord Browne-Wilkinson held, amongst other things, that public policy considerations were such that local authorities **17.19**

---

[24] This view echoes the arguments put forward on behalf of the U.K. Government and rejected by the European Court in *Osman*: see paras 133–140.

[25] [1995] 2 A.C. 633, HL.

[26] Application No. 29392/95, May 10, 2001; *The Times*, May 31, 2001, European Court; (1999) 28 E.H.R.R. C.D. 65, European Commission. See also *TP & KM v. United Kingdom*, Application No. 28945/95, May 10, 2001; *The Times*, May 31, 2001, European Court; European Commission.

should not be held liable in negligence in respect of the exercise of their statutory duties safeguarding the welfare of children under the Children Act 1989. In *Z*, the Government, before both the European Commission and the Court, challenged the decision in *Osman* on two principal grounds:

(1) that the judgment was *per incuriam* because it was based on a mistaken concession by the United Kingdom Government in the case; and

(2) because it was illogical for the European Court to accept that a case could acceptably be struck on the ground that there was insufficient proximity (the second limb of *Caparo*) but not where the court decided that it was not fair, just and reasonable to impose a duty of care (the third limb of *Caparo*), when "proximity" was just as much a question of judicial policy as the fair, just and reasonable ground.[27]

When the case came before the European Commission, applying the principles established by the European Court in *Osman*, it held in its Report that the striking out of an action where negligence was asserted against local authorities by a child in its care based on the exclusionary rule formulated in *X* was a disproportionate restriction on the claimant's right of access to a court under Article 6(1). It is relevant to note that reasonable foreseeability of damage and the existence of sufficient proximity had been conceded by the defendant local authority in the *Z* case. Using similar reasoning to *Osman*, the Commission decided that although the preservation of the efficiency of child care services was a legitimate public aim, the exclusionary rule that it was not fair, just and reasonable that a duty of care should exist was disproportionate because it failed to allow for differing circumstances and, in particular, gave no consideration to the seriousness or otherwise of the damage or the nature or degree of the negligence alleged or the fundamental rights of the applicants which were involved. The Commission found that:

"the courts in the applicants' case imposed a restriction on their access to court by the application of a bar to their claims operating to protect a particular defendant from negligence actions for damage caused in a particular sphere of their competence."[28]

17.20 The Commission rejected the Government's argument that the applicants' claims failed for *substantive law* reasons, namely on the basis that even if their allegations were true, they disclosed no substantive cause of action and not because of any procedural bar. The Commission saw no basis on which to reach a different conclusion from *Osman*, noting that in *X* Lord Browne-Wilkinson had referred to the exclusionary rule applied to the police as furnishing the nearest of analogies. It noted that until the present case, there was no precedent which established that the applicants could

---

[27] See *e.g. Stovin v. Wise* [1996] A.C. 923 at 932 *per* Lord Nicholls.
[28] para. 113.

not make claims against the local authority for damage resulting from their negligence and the matter was considered sufficiently arguable in domestic law terms to warrant the provision of legal aid and for the Court of Appeal to grant permission to appeal to the House of Lords. The Commission found that the applicants' claims against the local authorities were arguably based on an existing right in domestic law, making Article 6(1) applicable.[29] The Government further argued that the principles applied by the domestic courts did not disclose a blanket immunity but a balancing exercise by which competing policy considerations could be assessed. However, the Commission dismissed this argument, finding that the House of Lords rejected the applicants' claims on the basis that actions against the social services for decisions taken in relation to their child protection functions were to be excluded. The fact that in other situations, not involving the child protection aspect of local authority responsibility, liability was not so excluded did not alter the fact that an exclusionary rule had been applied in the present case.[30] The Commission also found that the failure to provide the children with appropriate protection against serious long-term neglect and abuse amounted to inhuman and degrading treatment in violation of Article 3 (the prohibition on torture, inhuman and degrading treatment).[31] Although the applicants had alleged a breach of Article 13, the Commission found that in light of its finding of violation under Article 6(1), it was not necessary to separately examine the applicants' complaints under Article 13[32] as "its requirements are less strict than, and are here absorbed by, those of Article 6(1)".[33]

When Z came before the European Court, the Government (having con-   **17.21**
tested these before the Commission) conceded a violation of both Article 3 and of Article 13 but continued to contest the finding of a violation of Article 6(1).

Article 3

In its judgment,[34] the Court upheld the violation of Article 3, agreeing with   **17.22**
the Commission that the failure to provide the applicants with appropriate protection against serious, long-term neglect and abuse breached the prohibition on inhuman and degrading treatment.[35]

Article 6(1)

In relation to Article 6(1), the Court noted that the applicants were claiming   **17.23**
damages on the basis of alleged negligence, a tort in English law which is largely developed through the case-law of the domestic courts. It was agreed between the parties that there was no previous court decision

---

[29] paras 109—111.
[30] para. 113. See also *T.P. & K.M. v. United Kingdom*, Application No. 28945/95, unreported, September 10, 1999, European Commission.
[31] At para. 98.
[32] At para. 121.
[33] See *e.g. R. v. United Kingdom* (1988) 10 E.H.R.R. 74, para. 90.
[34] Application No. 29392/95, May 10, 2001; *The Times*, May 31, 2001.
[35] At para. 75.

which indicated that liability existed in respect of damage caused negligently by a local authority in carrying out its child protection duties. It was in the applicants' case that the domestic courts were called on to rule whether this situation fell within one of the existing categories of negligence liability, or whether any of the categories should be extended to this situation. The Court was satisfied that at the outset of the proceedings there was a serious and genuine dispute about the existence of the right asserted by the applicants under the domestic law of negligence, as shown by the grant of legal aid to the applicants and the decision by the Court of Appeal that their claims merited leave to appeal to the House of Lords. Accordingly, Article 6(1) was applicable.[36]

17.24 In considering whether Article 6(1) was complied with, the Court reiterated that the right of access to a court is not absolute. Where the individual's access is limited either by operation of law or in fact, the Court will examine whether the limitation imposed impaired the essence of the right and in particular whether it pursued a legitimate aim and there was a reasonable relationship of proportionality between the means employed and the aim sought to be achieved.[37] The Court noted that the applicants were not prevented in any practical manner from bringing their claims before the domestic courts, right up to the House of Lords with legal aid provided for that purpose. The domestic courts were concerned with the pre-trial determination of whether, assuming the facts of the applicants' case as pleaded were true, there was a sustainable case in law. The Court stated that it was not persuaded that the House of Lords' decision as a matter of law that there was no duty of care in the applicants' case may be characterised as either an exclusionary rule or an immunity which deprived them of access to court. The House of Lords, after weighing in the balance the competing considerations of public policy, decided not to extend liability in negligence into a new area. In so doing, it circumscribed the range of liability under tort law. Because the decision concerned only one aspect of the exercise of local authorities' powers and duties, it could not be regarded as an arbitrary removal of the courts' jurisdiction to determine a whole range of civil claims. The Court recalled that Article 6 does not guarantee any particular content for civil rights and obligations in national law, save that the right to respect for family life in Article 8 and the right to property in Article 1 of Protocol No. 1 may do so. The Court held that:

> "It is not enough to bring Article 6(1) into play that the non-existence of a cause of action under domestic law may be described as having the same effect as an immunity, in the sense of not enabling the applicant to sue for a given category of harm.
>
> Furthermore, it cannot be said that the House of Lords came to its conclusion without a careful balancing of the policy reasons for and

---

[36] At para. 89.
[37] At para. 93.

against the imposition of liability on the local authority in the circumstances of the applicants' case."[38]

Retreat from Osman

The Court expressly resiled from *Osman*, stating that: **17.25**

"The Court considers that its reasoning in the *Osman* judgment was based on an understanding of the law of negligence (see in particular paragraphs 138 and 139 of the *Osman* judgment) which has to be reviewed in the light of the clarifications subsequently made by the domestic courts and notably by the House of Lords. The Court is satisfied that the law of negligence as developed in the domestic courts since the case of *Caparo* . . . and as recently analysed in the case of *Barrett v. Enfield LBC* . . . includes the fair, just and reasonable criterion as a intrinsic element of the duty of care and that the ruling of law concerning that element in this case does not disclose the operation of an immunity. In the present case, the Court is led to the conclusion that the inability of the applicants to sue the local authority flowed not from an immunity but from the applicable principles governing the substantive right of action in domestic law. There was no restriction on access to court of the kind contemplated in the *Ashingdane*[39] judgment."[40]

Accordingly, the Court appears to have effectively accepted that *Osman* was decided *per incuriam* although it has not expressly overruled the decision. Nonetheless, the Court found in *Z* that the inability to sue flowed from the applicable principles governing the substantive right of action in domestic law. Since Article 6(1) does not create substantive law rights in domestic law,[41] there was therefore no violation of Article 6(1).

Article 13

However, the Court having found that there was no violation of Article 6(1)   **17.26**
went on to hold that there was a violation of Article 13 (the right to an effective remedy for breach of a Convention right)[42] and awarded damages by way of just satisfaction for breach of the applicants' rights under Article 3. Since the acts and omissions on which the claims in *Z* were based pre-dated the introduction of the HRA and the right to bring proceedings for breach of a Convention right under section 7 of the Act,[43] the Government conceded that there existed no effective remedy for the violation of the applicants' Article 3 rights, though it highlighted that remedies such as the payment of compensation from the Criminal Injuries Compensation Board, the possibility of complaint to the Local Government Ombudsman and the complaints procedure under the Children Act 1989 went some way towards providing effective redress. It was however, not in

---

[38] At paras 98–99.
[39] *Ashingdane v. United Kingdom* (1985) 7 E.H.R.R. 528, paras 56–59.
[40] Application No. 29392/95, May 10, 2001; *The Times*, May 31, 2001, para. 100.
[41] See para. 17.15 above.
[42] Para. 111.
[43] Para. 107.

dispute that, in the circumstances of the case, these remedies were sufficient alone or cumulatively to satisfy the requirements of Article 13.[44]

T.P. & K.M. v. United Kingdom

17.27 In *T.P. & K.M. v. United Kingdom*,[45] an application was brought by a mother, TP and her daughter, KM. Between 1984 and 1987, the local authority, the London Borough of Newham, suspected that KM was being sexually abused. Following a case conference in July 1987, KM was placed on the child protection register under the category of emotional abuse. On November 13, 1987, KM who was then four years old, was interviewed by a consultant child psychiatrist. A social worker was also present during the interview which was video taped. In the course of the interview, KM disclosed that she had been abused by someone named X. TP's boyfriend XY, who lived with the applicants shared the same first name as the abuser. However, KM indicated that XY was not the abuser and stated that X had been thrown out of the house. TP was informed that KM had stated that she had been sexually abused by XY. When she became angry, the psychiatrist and social worker concluded that TP would be unable to protect KM from abuse and that she was attempting to persuade KM to retract the allegation. They removed KM from her mother's care. Shortly after, the local authority applied for a place of safety order. TP, having excluded all men from her home, applied for KM to be made a ward of court. The local authority was given care and control of KM and TP was granted limited access. Almost a year later, in October 1988, TP's representatives applied for access to the video of the disclosure interview. The health authority and the psychiatrist lodged an objection to disclosure of the video to TP. On an unspecified date at about that time, TP's solicitors obtained sight of the transcript which showed that KM had said that XY had not abused her and that she had identified that her abuser had been thrown out of the house by TP. After a further hearing, KM was restored to TP and remained with her thereafter. In November 1990, the applicants issued proceedings claiming negligence and breach of statutory duty against the local authority, alleging that the social worker and psychiatrist had failed to investigate the facts with proper care. The applicants claimed that as a result of their enforced separation, they had each suffered psychiatric damage. Following proceedings which terminated in the House of Lords, the applicants' claims were struck out: *X (Minors) v. Bedfordshire County Council*.[46] The European Court found that the failure by the local authority to submit promptly the question of disclosure of a video interview and its transcript for determination in care proceedings deprived the applicants of an adequate involvement in the decision-making process and violated the right to respect for family life in Article 8 of the Convention.[47] It also found a violation of Article 13 because the applicants did not have the possibility of obtaining an enforceable

---

[44] Para. 107.
[45] Application No. 28945/95, May 10, 2001; *The Times*, May 31, 2001.
[46] [1995] 2 A.C. 633.
[47] At para. 82.

award of compensation for the damage suffered due to breach of Article 8.[48] The Court stated:

> "Article 13 of the Convention guarantees the availability at the national level of a remedy to enforce the substance of Convention rights and freedoms in whatever form they might happen to be secured in the domestic legal order. Article 13 thus requires the provision of a domestic remedy to deal with the substance of an 'arguable complaint' under the Convention and to grant appropriate relief, although the Contracting States are afforded some discretion as to the manner in which they conform to the Convention obligations in this provision. The scope of the obligation under Article 13 must be 'effective' in practice as well as in law . . . The Court considers that, where an arguable breach of one or more of the rights under the Convention is in issue, there should be available to the victim a mechanism for establishing any liability of State officials or bodies for that breach. Furthermore, in appropriate cases, compensation for the pecuniary and non-pecuniary damage flowing from the breach should in principle be available as part of the range of redress."[49]

The Court did not find a violation of Article 6(1) for similar reasons to *Z* above.[50]

Implications

Of all the decisions of the European Court of Human Rights affecting civil **17.28** litigation, *Osman v. United Kingdom* is the probably the one which provoked the most violent reaction. Though its application extended to many areas of civil law, looked at solely from the professional negligence perspective, it had very significant implications. Firstly, it seriously hampered the highly important tactical weapon of striking out a claim for no reasonable cause of action under CPR 3.4 for failure to establish a duty of care. Secondly, it arguably indirectly contributed to the recent, expansionist approach to the tortious liability of advocates (*Arthur J.S. Hall v. Simons*[51]) and educational psychologists (*Phelps v. Hillingdon LBC*[52]) where in both cases, Article 6 and the case of *Osman* were invoked by the appellants in support of their appeals before the House of Lords.

The following issues arise as a result of the Court's judgment in *Z*: **17.29**

(a) What is left of *Osman*, if anything, in relation to striking out?

(b) What is the effect of the switch of focus by the European Court from Article 6(1) to Article 13?

(c) Will claims in new or developing areas of tort law in future proceed instead, or in addition, as claims under section 7(1)(a) of the

---

[48] At para. 110.
[49] At para. 107.
[50] See paras 100–103.
[51] [2000] 3 W.L.R. 543, HL.
[52] [2000] 3 W.L.R. 776, HL.

HRA? If so, what are the key differences between such claims and a traditional claim framed in negligence?

(d) In the case of claims arising out of acts and omissions which took place prior to October 2, 2000, where no section 7(1)(a) HRA claim lies, what will the courts now do in respect of the tortious claims that come before them?

Striking out—what is left of Osman?

17.30 In light of Z, there is almost certainly now no restraint on domestic courts imposed by Article 6(1) in relation to striking out claims based on a failure to establish a duty of care because of application of the third limb in Caparo. The European Court has accepted that this constitutes a matter of substantive domestic law and that Article 6(1) is not violated in principle.

17.31 However, in Z, the Court did not expressly overrule Osman. Accordingly, it is not wholly clear whether Osman survives but is now confined to its own facts (and therefore continues to apply in relation to public interest immunity on the part of the police arising from the decision of Hill v. Chief Constable of West Yorkshire[53]) or whether Osman has been impliedly overruled. It is suggested that the domestic courts will probably treat the case as decided per incuriam and Osman's residual effect in relation to striking out for public policy reasons will in practice be minimal. However, it should be noted that the Court has left open the possibility that where a decision concerns more than one aspect of the exercise of local authorities' powers and duties such that it can be said to amount to an arbitrary removal of the courts' jurisdiction to determine a whole range of civil claims,[54] a violation of Article 6(1) may nevertheless be found.[55]

Effect of switch from Article 6(1) to Article 13

17.32 Article 13 guarantees an "effective remedy before a national authority" to everyone who claims that his rights and freedoms under the Convention have been violated,[56] so long as that claim is arguable in terms of the Convention.[57] Unlike Article 6(1) which applies to protect the right of access to a court in relation to any civil right or obligation which is merely arguable in domestic law, the right to an effective remedy under Article 13 is limited to providing an effective remedy for an arguable breach of another Convention right. Accordingly, Article 13 is parasitic upon establishing the arguability of another Convention right. It is therefore weaker in protection given to a complainant than Article 6 (which applies to merely an arguable civil right). Article 13 case-law requires that there be only an arguable, not necessarily an actual breach of another Convention right. The test of arguability may be a difficult one to satisfy, since even a substantive claim which is declared admissible by the Commission will not

---

[53] [1989] A.C. 53, HL.
[54] (1994) 18 E.H.R.R. 393. See further para. 17.42 below.
[55] Z v. United Kingdom Application No. 29392/95, May 10, 2001; The Times, May 31, 2001, para. 98.
[56] Klass v. Germany (1980) 2 E.H.R.R. 214, para. 64.
[57] Boyle and Rice v. United Kingdom (1988) 10 E.H.R.R. 425, para. 52.

necessarily be "arguable" for the purposes of Article 13.[58] Article 13 requires that where an individual considers himself to have been prejudiced by a measure allegedly in breach of the Convention, he should have a remedy before a national authority in order both to have the claim decided and, if appropriate, to obtain redress.[59] The authority referred to in Article 13 does not need to be a judicial authority[60] and Article 13 does not require any particular remedy[61] and not necessarily a remedy in damages. The aggregate of the possible channels of redress in the national legal system may be taken into account.[62]

The implications of the switch to Article 13 in relation to the domestic **17.33** courts' own duties under section 6 of the HRA should be considered. Article 6(1) is incorporated into domestic law through the HRA. Article 13 is not. Accordingly, on the face of it, the courts will not be in breach of their obligation under section 6 of the HRA to act compatibly with Convention rights if they fail to provide an effective remedy pursuant to Article 13. However, the reason given by the Lord Chancellor for the omission was that it was not to avoid conferring the protection of Article 13 but because it was thought by the Government that the remedies in the HRA in section 8 were sufficient to comply with the United Kingdom's obligations under Article 13.[63] Before the European Court, the State (in the "person" of the UK Government) can be liable for its collective failure (including by its courts) to provide an effective remedy before a national authority for an individual to argue that his Convention rights have been violated. Since courts do have a duty under section 2 to take into account Strasbourg case-law, including that relating to Article 13,[64] this may influence courts in favour of allowing a claim to proceed to a full hearing on the merits as a matter of existing domestic law in order to avoid the State subsequently being found by the European Court to be in breach of Article 13 for having struck out the claim.

The Court recognised in *Z* that a claimant who wishes to complain of a **17.34** breach of his Convention rights now has an effective remedy for Article 13 purposes through the claim mechanism in section 7(1) of the HRA. However, the operation of section 22(4) of the HRA means that a claim can only be brought under section 7(1)(a) if the act or omission occurs on or after the date of the HRA coming into force *i.e.* October 2, 2000.[65] This gives rise to a potential inconsistency in treatment between claims based on acts or omissions which occurred prior to October 2, 2000 where no HRA claim will lie, and those based on acts or omissions following that date, where a claimant can bring a claim under the HRA based on the same set of facts and circumstances. This inconsistency may also influence the willingness of the courts to countenance claims in tort to avoid divergence of treatment in similar cases.

---

[58] *Friedl v. Austria* (A/305–B) (1996) 21 E.H.R.R. 83, (Opinion of Commission, para. 71).
[59] *Klass v. Germany* (1980) 2 E.H.R.R. 214, para. 64; *Leander v. Sweden* (1987) 9 E.H.R.R. 433, para. 77(a).
[60] *Leander v. Sweden* (1987) 9 E.H.R.R. 433, para. 77(b).
[61] *Vilvarajah v. United Kingdom* (1992) 14 E.H.R.R. 248, para. 122.
[62] *Silver v. United Kingdom* (1983) 5 E.H.R.R. 347, paras 113(c), 118; *Leander v. Sweden* (1987) 9 E.H.R.R. 433, para. 77(c).
[63] See further para. 2.19 above.
[64] *ibid.*
[65] See para. 2.31 above.

Tort or Convention?

17.35   The case of *Z* is probably less advantageous to claimants seeking a full hearing on the merits than the case of *Osman* because it will only be in those cases where claim can be framed as an arguable breach of a substantive *Convention* right that they will be able to argue for a full hearing on the merits by reference to Article 13 (which is not binding on the courts), whereas previously this argument could be made in relation to any arguable *civil* right to which Article 6(1) (which is binding on the courts) was applicable.[66]

17.36   One likely result of *Z* is that in circumstances where a cause of action in tort is not clearly established as a matter of domestic law, claims are now more likely to be framed as claims under section 7(1)(a) of the HRA either independently of or, more probably in addition to, a tortious claim. Examples include the following:

(a) actions against the police arising out of death or serious injury— Article 2 (right to life);

(b) clinical negligence—Article 2 (right to life);

(c) claims based on failures in child protection against psychiatrists, social workers and local authorities—Article 3 (prohibition on torture inhuman or degrading treatment), or if less serious, Article 8 (right to respect for private life);

(d) claims against educational psychologists based on failure to diagnose dyslexia or other special needs—Article 8 (right to respect for private life) or Article 2 of Protocol No. 1 (right to education).

Framing a claim under the HRA instead of or in addition to a claim in tort has the following implications:

(a) a one year limitation period applies rather than the usual six year limitation period in tort (three years where the claim includes a claim for damages for personal injuries)[67];

(b) there may be a potential difference in level of damages awarded.[68] Domestic courts are obligated by section 8 HRA to award damages on same principles as the European Court, whose awards have generally been low. This is subject to the courts adopting the Law Commission's invitation to apply domestic law principles where a Convention and domestic cause of action are closely related[69];

(c) under certain Convention Articles (*e.g.* Articles 8 and 10), once an interference is established by the claimant or admitted by the defendant, the burden of proof is then on the defendant to justify

---

[66] See paras 3.56 *et seq.* above.
[67] See para. 2.29 above.
[68] See paras 9.18 *et seq.* above.
[69] See paras 9.48 *et seq.* above.

his conduct. This amounts to an effective reversal of the traditional burden of proof in civil claims[70];

(d) the legal principles in relation to assessing whether there is a
violation of Convention rights are not necessarily the same as
under the common law. For example, under Article 2, the European Court takes less account of the defendant's resources in
determining whether there has been a violation of the duty to take
adequate steps to protect life than is the case in relation to
establishing a duty of care in tort;

(e) the evidential requirements in a Convention claim may be different. Evidence of social statistics, government policy and the
existence of other remedies may be required, in contrast to common law claims.[71]

Claims not governed by HRA

In the case of claims arising out of acts and omissions which took place **17.37**
prior to October 2, 2000, where no section 7(1)(a) HRA claim lies, the
issue arises as to what the courts will now do in relation to applications to
strike out tortious claims that come before them which also raise arguable
violations of Convention rights.

It is possible that there will be an indirect effect arising from the Court's **17.38**
finding in *Z* of a violation of Article 13. If a claim based on an act or
omission which pre-dates the coming into force of the HRA can be:

(i) framed as an arguable breach of a substantive Convention right;
and

(ii) there is no adequate alternative extra-judicial remedy

this may lead to a reluctance on the part of domestic courts to strike out a
claim brought in tort because this will encourage the claimant who has
been shut out to take his case immediately to Strasbourg. Such a claimant
is likely to succeed in Strasbourg in showing a violation of Article 13 if he
can make out an arguable[72] breach of a substantive Convention right and
show that he has been denied an effective remedy before a national
authority. In those circumstances, it is in fact the Government that will be
obliged to pay any damages awarded by way of just satisfaction under
Article 41, rather than the "true" defendant *e.g.*, a local authority (who will
have separate financing arrangements to central government). From the
claimant's point of view, this may be less satisfactory both because of the
time involved in obtaining a judgment from the European Court and
because the non-pecuniary damages may be lower than in relation to a
claim in tort.[73] Whilst there is no HRA obligation on the part of the domestic

---

[70] See paras 4.50 and 8.67 above.
[71] See paras 8.62 *et seq.* above.
[72] See further para. 17.33 above.
[73] See para. 9.37 above, but note that in *Z*, Lady Justice Arden who concurred with the
judgment dissented as to the sum of non-pecuniary damages awarded, suggesting that a
lower award would have been made in the domestic courts. She would have awarded them
£6,000 each rather than the £10,000 awarded by the Court. In arriving at its award, the Court
stated that awards made in comparable domestic cases was a relevant, though not decisive
consideration (para. 131).

court to comply with Article 13 in providing an effective remedy because it is not incorporated, the courts' duty under section 2 HRA to take account of Strasbourg case-law including that in relation to Article 13 may reduce the domestic courts' willingness to strike out a case where no other adequate extra-judicial remedy exists. If courts tend towards a more inclusive approach to the duty of care in tort in order to encompass cases which would be brought under the HRA but for the fact that the acts or omissions complained of pre-date October 2, 2000, the ultimate result will be that domestic courts are still less likely to strike out than was the position prior to the advent of *Osman*. It is perhaps also of note that before the House of Lords, *X* had comprised conjoined appeals by one class of claimants who had suffered sexual abuse as children and wished to sue their local authorities for failing to prevent this happening and by another class of claimants whose special educational needs had gone undiag-nosed and who wished to sue their local education authorities for failing to meet their educational needs. Because of a chink in the law left open by the House of Lords in the case of the educational psychologist appeals, these two classes of action have followed different courses. *Z* and *T.P. & K.M.* in the child protection cases took their complaint to Strasbourg and succeeded in establishing damages under Article 13. Further domestic claims in tort were brought in a series of cases relating to special educa-tional needs, culminating in the conjoined appeals of *Phelps v. Hillingdon London Borough Council*[74] in which it was held that the claimants were owed a duty of care in negligence and their claims should not have been struck out on this ground. Accordingly, despite the adverse House of Lords judgment in *X*, a similar result was arrived at in respect of both classes of claim via very different routes.

Conclusion

17.39 Some possible implications of *Z* for claims against professionals and public authorities have been suggested above. *Osman* undoubtedly enhanced the prospects of a claim surviving a strike out application and arguably influenced a more expansionist approach to substantive liability in tort (*e.g.* in relation to advocates' immunity or claims against educational psychologists). The influence of *Z* and the hitherto less well-known Article 13 may mean that, despite the fact that *Osman*, read in the light of *Z*, no longer outlaws the striking out of cases for failure to establish a duty of care on public policy grounds because it is contrary to Article 6(1), there are still Convention constraints on the striking out of claims and the expansionist trend to tortious liability in novel areas of the law may never-theless continue. It is likely that *Z* will provide an impetus for the future development of claims under HRA and in tort in *parallel* with each other. There is perhaps an analogy here with the developments in judicial review as a result of the HRA, where the modified test for review in cases affecting Convention rights is leading to a widening of the scope for successful judicial review where previously an application would have failed because it was not irrational.[75]

---

[74] [2000] 3 W.L.R. 776.
[75] See further para. 10.152 above.

Breach of Statutory Duty

In cases where a professional's (or his employing public authority's) duties **17.40** are subject to statutory underpinning, it may be open to a claimant to argue that one or the other has committed the tort of breach of statutory duty. It would appear from the decision of the European Commission in *Z v. United Kingdom*,[76] that the common law test for establishing a breach of statutory duty, namely that it must be shown to have been the intention of Parliament to create a private law cause of action, is not incompatible with the right of access to a court in Article 6. The applicants in *Z* did not submit that the House of Lords' judgment (namely, that there was no cause of action for breach of statutory duty) imposed an immunity from suit in respect of actions for breach of statutory duty. The Commission noted that the reasoning of the courts concerning the claims of breach of statutory duty appeared to apply general principles of statutory interpretation and it did not consider it necessary to examine this aspect any further. This aspect was not considered by the Court in *Z*.

4. PROFESSIONAL IMMUNITIES

Strasbourg Case-Law on Immunities

The right of access to a court is also central to the issue of immunities. In **17.41** *Dyer v. United Kingdom*,[77] the applicant challenged the former immunity from liability in tort which was formerly accorded to the Crown and to members of the armed forces under section 10(1)(b) of the Crown Proceedings Act 1947. He failed before the European Commission on the facts of the case. However, the Commission held, for the first time, that the right to compensation for damages caused by negligence was a civil right for the purpose of Article 6(1). This laid the foundation for the development of subsequent case law relating to the right of access to a court.

In *Fayed v. United Kingdom*,[78] the European Court, in a strong statement, **17.42** held that it would not be consistent with the rule of law or the basic principle underlying Article 6(1) if a state could:

> "without restraint or control by the Convention enforcement bodies, remove from the jurisdiction of the courts a whole range of civil claims or confer immunities from civil liability on large groups or categories of persons."[79]

In *Osman v. United Kingdom*,[80] the European Court held that a line of **17.43** English case law which operated to confer a blanket immunity on the police for acts or omissions relating to the investigation or suppression of crime was disproportionate. *Osman* must be read in light of *Z v. United*

---

[76] (1999) 28 E.H.R.R. C.D. 65. See also *TP & KM v. United Kingdom*, Application No. 28945/95, unreported, September 10, 1999, European Commission.
[77] Application No. 10475/83 (1984) 39 D.R. 246.
[78] (1994) 18 E.H.R.R. 393.
[79] *ibid.*, para.65.
[80] (2000) 29 E.H.R.R. 245.

Kingdom[81] as discussed above.[82] In *Z*, the Court referred with approval to the principle established in *Fayed* quoted above[83] but found on the facts that no immunity was disclosed in fact or practical effect due to its allegedly sweeping or blanket nature. The Court stated that the decision of the House of Lords in *X (Minors) v. Bedfordshire County Council*[84] (the case was re-titled in Strasbourg)

> "concerned only one aspect of the exercise of local authorities powers and duties and cannot be regarded as an arbitrary removal of the courts' jurisdiction to determine a whole range of civil claims."[85]

The Court clarified that it was not enough to bring Article 6(1) into play that the non-existence of a cause of action under domestic law may be described as having the same effect as an immunity, in the sense of not enabling the applicant to sue for a given category of harm.[86] Accordingly, the prohibition in *Fayed* would appear now to be limited to *true* immunities, *i.e.* where in the absence of the immunity, there would exist a cause of action as a matter of substantive domestic law.[87] An example is the former immunity of advocates. Although an advocate clearly owed a duty of care to his client (*e.g.* in relation to advisory work), a judicial immunity from suit was developed in relation to the conduct of court proceedings. State immunity is another example. The European Court has declared admissible two applications based on the ground that as a consequence of the State Immunity Act 1978, the applicants were denied access to a court: see *Al-Adsani v. United Kingdom*[88] and *Fogarty v. United Kingdom*.[89] In *Waite and Kennedy v. Germany*[90] the European Court upheld the immunity from national jurisdiction granted to the European Space Agency, an international organisation. However, the court was heavily influenced by the fact that the applicants had available to them reasonable alternative means to protect their rights under the Convention, through a procedure provided for settlement of private law disputes in relation to staff matters and other litigation through the independent ESA Appeals Board. The Court stated that bearing in mind the legitimate aim of immunities of international organisations, the test of proportionality cannot be applied in such a way as to compel an international organisation to submit itself to national litigation in relation to employment conditions prescribed under national labour law. To construe Article 6(1) in this way would thwart the proper functioning of international organisations and run counter to the current trend towards extending and strengthening international

---

[81] Application No. 29392/95, May 10, 2001; *The Times*, May 31, 2001 (European Court). See also *T.P. & K.M. v. United Kingdom* Application No. 28945/95, May 10, 2001; *The Times*, May 31, 2001.
[82] At paras 17.09 *et seq.*
[83] At para. 98.
[84] [1995] 2 A.C. 633, HL.
[85] *ibid.*
[86] *ibid.*
[87] See *Arthur J.S. Hall v. Simons* [2000] 3 W.L.R. 543 at 607D, *per* Lord Hobhouse.
[88] Application No. 35763/97, March 1, 2000.
[89] Application No. 37112/97, March 1, 2000.
[90] (2000) 30 E.H.R.R. 261.

co-operation.[91] In *Holland v. Lampen-Wolfe*[92] the House of Lords held that Article 6(1) did not confer on Contracting States adjudicative powers which they did not possess and state immunity was not a self-imposed restriction on the jurisdiction of its courts which the United Kingdom had chosen to adopt. It remains to be seen whether the Court will agree when it comes to substantively consider state immunity.

The European Court's general approach to immunities is to examine them **17.44** for the legitimacy of their aim, their proportionality and the extent to which the right of access to a court is impaired. As demonstrated by *Waite and Kennedy* the existence of alternative avenues of recourse is highly relevant. With this in mind, some of the immunities which arise in the professional context are now considered.

Advocates' Immunity

Barristers and solicitors formerly enjoyed the unusually privileged position **17.45** of being immune against any claim for liability in negligence if the claim arose from acts or omissions arising out of the conduct of court proceedings. The immunity had existed since the seventeenth century and was thought to arise from the absence of a contractual relationship between counsel and their clients. The *quid pro quo* to barristers for being unable to sue for unpaid fees was that they were not subject to liability in negligence. The more recent justifications for the immunity were three considerations of public policy[93]:

(1) The risk of a possible action for negligence is a source of pressure on the practitioner, which is liable to interfere with the performance of the paramount duty owed to the court.

(2) That the risk of liability would unnecessarily increase the tension of proceedings in court.

(3) It was thought undesirable to allow re-litigation of a dispute against different parties if the process is likely to involve discrediting an earlier judgment or verdict (*i.e.* collateral attack). In *Hunter v. Chief Constable of the West Midlands Police*,[94] the court held that it was not possible to proceed if the action amounted to a collateral attack on the decision of the court in the original case.

In the conjoined appeals of *Arthur J.S. Hall v. Simons*,[95] (three appeals **17.46** concerning allegations of negligence by solicitors) this position and the so-called "advocates' immunity from suit" has been abrogated in its entirety for both barristers and solicitors. The Bar Counsel's intervention

---

[91] At para. 72.
[92] *The Times*, July 27, 2000, HL.
[93] *Rondel v. Worsley* [1969] 1 A.C. 191, at 227–231, *per* Lord Reid, at 247–254, *per* Lord Morris, at 267–277, *per* Lord Pearce, at 281–284, *per* Lord Upjohn, and at 293e, *per* Lord Pearson's agreement with the other four speeches; *Saif Ali v. Sidney Mitchell & Co* [1980] A.C. 198 at 212–215, *per* Lord Wilberforce, at 219–223, *per* Lord Diplock, and at 227–230, *per* Lord Salmon.
[94] [1982] A.C. 529, HL.
[95] [2000] 3 W.L.R. 543, HL.

and the broad argument before their Lordships' House meant that the decision affected the immunity of barristers as well as solicitors. It is notable that in the House of Lords case that abolished advocates' immunity for all types of proceeding, *Arthur J.S. Hall v. Simons*, Article 6 was fully argued, although the decision arrived at as a matter of existing domestic law made it unnecessary for their Lordships to consider whether or not a blanket immunity for advocates could be justified. Advocates' immunity was probably a *true* immunity and not simply a state of affairs in which there was no relevant substantive right.[96] It operated as a limitation on a right of access to the court which would otherwise have existed and permitted cases to be struck out at an interlocutory stage where they fell within the scope of the immunity. However, when the immunity operated as a complete or "blanket" defence to a claim, it was difficult to see how the "essence of the right" was not being effectively impaired unless the requirements of Article 6 were met. It is likely that Article 6 did have at least some impact on the ultimate decision to abolish advocates' immunity.

17.47 In his Opinion, Lord Hope did specifically consider the HRA and Convention jurisprudence.[97] He anticipated the effect of HRA 1998, which was shortly to come into force, and took account of this in his decision. He noted the common law and Convention principle that immunity from suit is a derogation from the fundamental right of access to the court, the presumption that a wrong should not be without a remedy, and a derogation from the normal accountability for wrong doing, which has to be justified. Interestingly, unlike the majority, he found that there was sufficient justification for retention of the immunity in criminal cases, by reason of the public interest in the administration of justice. He was of the view that this limited immunity would be proportionate as there were unlikely to be a large number of unsatisfied claims in the criminal justice system. Further, he based his view on the experience in Scotland after the removal of advocates immunity,[98] which has meant that each appeal has included an allegation of negligence, necessitating a change of representation and the obtaining of evidence from those formerly instructed. This prolongs appeals and removes those originally instructed from acting on the appeal. He stated that the *Hunter* principle was not a sufficient basis for discarding the immunity in criminal cases because, although collateral challenge cases would be covered, protection for events in court was needed. Further, if a conviction was set aside on appeal, the client's right of action for damages remained. He stated that if *Hunter* is applied to cases where an advocate's client is raising a claim for damages, it might offend the fundamental right to a trial under the Convention. In his view, advocates' immunity was justified on firmer public policy principles than the *Hunter* principle in these cases. By contrast, he found the immunity in civil cases to be disproportionate since it derogated from the principle of access to the courts and was no longer justified on public policy grounds. Lord Hutton also took the view that immunity for criminal cases should be retained and that it would not breach Article 6(1) because it had a legitimate aim

---

[96] See at 607D, *per* Lord Hobhouse.
[97] At 589.
[98] Following *Anderson v. Her Majesty's Advocate*, 1996 S.C.29.

(advancing administration of justice and protecting from harassment those under a public duty), and was proportionate.

The Hunter principle

The principle of collateral attack set out in *Hunter v. Chief Constable of the* **17.48** *West Midlands Police*,[99] that it is an abuse of process for a person to bring a civil action by way of a collateral attack on a final decision of the court remains extant, despite *Arthur J.S. Hall v. Simons*, although its future use is uncertain where the collateral attack is on an earlier decision of a *civil*, as opposed to a criminal, court. This principle could arguably be regarded as a separate ground of immunity. As Lord Hoffmann noted, the limits of *Hunter* become more important in absence of advocates' immunity. There remains the potential for an Article 6(1) argument since the basis of the *Hunter* principle is that it is applied to bar access to the courts to bring a civil claim where this would amount to a collateral attack on a judgment of a criminal (and possibly, another civil) court. Since the application of the principle requires a collateral attack on an existing judgment of the court, this should mean the claimant will already have had an Article 6(1) compliant hearing relating to the essential subject-matter of the complaint and that no infringement of the right of access to a court will arise if a subsequent claim is struck out. However, the way in which *Hunter* will be applied following the abolition of advocates' immunity remains to be worked out in practice and if extended beyond narrow limits, may give scope for further Article 6(1) argument.

Retrospective or prospective effect

Further, in *Arthur J.S. Hall v. Simons*, the House of Lords left unclear the **17.49** question whether its judgment was to have retrospective or prospective effect and if the former, from which date. Lord Hope stated that he considered the change in law should take effect only from the date of judgment.[1] None of the other members made the position clear although the decision to abolish the immunity was taken on the basis that public policy had changed over time.[2] It is not even clear whether their Lordships have power to make a prospective only ruling (if that was their intention).[3] If the removal of advocates' immunity is of only *prospective* effect, a person who wishes to litigate a claim against an advocate based on alleged negligence which preceded the date on which the judgment has effect might argue that such an approach, preserving the immunity prior to the specified date, infringes his right of access to a court under Article 6(1). It would then have to be shown that the restriction of the ruling to prospective only effect fulfils a legitimate aim and is proportionate to the aim to be achieved. If the judgment is of *retrospective* effect, potential defendants might argue that this infringes their legitimate expectations under Article 1 of Protocol No.1 (the right to peaceful enjoyment of possessions).

---

[99] [1982] A.C. 529, HL.
[1] [2000] 3 W.L.R. 343, HL, at 597.
[2] See, *e.g.*, at 554, *per* Lord Steyn, and at 576, *per* Lord Hoffmann.
[3] See the operation of the doctrine of precedent as discussed in *Kleinwort-Benson Ltd v. Lincoln City Council* [1998] 4 All E.R. 513. See further S.Carr (ed.), *Jackson & Powell, Professional Liability Precedents* (Sweet & Maxwell, 2000).

It could probably be argued that Article 1 of Protocol No. 1 is applicable because the judgment interferes with both the pecuniary position of defendants and the existence of a defence to a claim in tort.[4] Unlike the response to this argument by defendants and their insurers in *Heil v. Rankin*,[5] a change in the law of this nature is not a mere change in a tariff of damages which can be dismissed as not constituting a change in the law.[6] Further, such a change in the common law may (arguably) infringe the rule of law underlying Article 1 of Protocol No. 1, which requires such a change to be reasonably foreseeable.[7]

17.50   It can be seen that advocates' negligence claims may yet have Convention implications despite the abolition of the "core immunity".

Immunity of Witnesses and Expert Witnesses

17.51   The same three public policy considerations outlined in para. 17.45 above in relation to advocates also underlie the immunity of witnesses. However, the most compelling reason for witness immunity is to encourage witnesses to come forward and tell the truth. If they are to be so encouraged they must be protected, and accordingly, witnesses (and judges and court staff) cannot be sued for libel, malicious falsehood or conspiring to give false evidence: *Marrinan v. Vibart*.[8] They have an absolute immunity. The avoidance of re-litigation, or multiplicity of actions is also an underlying reason for witness immunity.[9] The policy is intended to protect freedom of expression in court proceedings in the interests of justice, and to encourage witnesses to come forward and tell the truth. Whilst the judge and witnesses owe no duty of care to the parties in a court case, they owe a public duty to respectively administer justice and tell the truth. In *Arthur J.S. Hall v. Simons*,[10] the House of Lords appeared to accept the policy underlying witness immunity as legitimate and proportionate.[11] However, in *Darker v. Chief Constable of the West Midlands*,[12] the House of Lords allowed an appeal against the striking out of a claim brought against the police on the ground of witness immunity. Following their acquittal of conspiracy to import prohibited drugs, the claimants brought an action for conspiracy to injure and misfeasance in public office alleging that the police officers had fabricated evidence, wrongly instructed officers to act as *agents provocateurs* and manipulated a police informer. The House of

---

[4] See paras 3.139 *et seq.*, above.
[5] [2000] 2 W.L.R. 1173.
[6] See further para. 3.139, above.
[7] See further paras 4.43 *et seq.*, above.
[8] [1963] 1 Q.B. 528.
[9] *Per* Lord Wilberforce in *Roy v. Prior* [1971] A.C. 470 at 480.
[10] [2000] 3 W.L.R. 543, HL.
[11] See, *e.g.* Lord Steyn who accepted the policy underlying witness immunity noting that it rests on the public policy of encouraging freedom of speech in court so that the court is fully informed on issues in the case and that this had little to do with any policy that requires immunity from actions for negligent acts (at 551). Lord Hoffman noted that all parties in court are absolutely immune from libel suit, malicious falsehood or conspiring to give false evidence because this encourages freedom of expression and, in particular, encourages witnesses to come forward and tell the truth (at 568). Lord Hobhouse noted that court officials, judges, juries and expert witnesses have civil immunity, in the public interest (at 611).
[12] [2000] 3 W.L.R. 747, HL.

Lords held that public policy required in principle that those who suffered a wrong should have a right to a remedy and that witness immunity did not extend to things done by the police during the investigative process which could not fairly be said to form part of their participation in the judicial process as witnesses (and in particular, to the fabrication of false evidence).

Further, in *L v. Reading Borough Council*,[13] the Court of Appeal sum-   **17.52** marised the position in relation to witness immunity stating that witnesses have immunity both in relation to evidence given in court and work on the evidence which is preliminary to its presentation in court.[14] The immunity is recognised and justified on the ground that it is necessary for the administration of justice. It noted that witness immunity is not a total bar to proceedings since it does not preclude actions founded on an abuse of process, such as malicious prosecution.[15] In *L*, the Court of Appeal expressly recognised the implications of Article 6 in this area and held, on the facts, that witness immunity should not be used to shield police from suit whilst acting as law enforcers or investigators and, if decided to the contrary, the immunity might be disproportionate to the public interest both under the common law and under the jurisprudence arising out of the Convention.

Expert witness immunity rests on the same public policy as factual witness   **17.53** immunity, namely, to ensure that the court is truthfully informed on the expert or technical issues that are part of the court proceedings. There is an essential distinction between an expert acting *qua* expert witness, and an expert acting *qua* adviser to a party instructing him. The former owes an overriding duty to tell the truth in court, and is therefore accorded immunity when giving evidence in court, the latter has contractual obligations to his client (for example, to be careful in relation to the advice he gives), but his overriding duty is to his client, and he is not immune from suit in negligence. Accordingly, where an expert witness is paid to advise, if the does so negligently, he is liable. But once he "becomes engaged on providing expert evidence for use in court"[16]—see CPR 35.2—his duty to the court becomes paramount, and civil immunity is attributable to that function. In *Stanton v. Callaghan*,[17] the expert witness in a building dispute was sued for agreeing to a joint statement in which he changed his mind about the remedial works required to correct a subsidence problem after an experts' meeting, causing the clients to settle for a much smaller sum than he had previously advised would be needed to effect repairs. The clients sued the expert for negligence. The Court of Appeal stated that the law recognised witness immunity from suit in relation to certain things done in preparing for, or taking part in, a trial on the basis of a supervening public interest of ensuring the orderly management and conduct of the

---

[13] [2001] EWCA CIV 346; March 12, 2001, CA.
[14] See *Evans v. London Hospital Medical College* [1981] 1 All E.R. 715 at 721B; *Silcott v. Commissioner of Police for the Metropolis* [1996] 8 Admin L.R. 633 and *Taylor v. Director of the Serious Fraud Office* [1999] 2 A.C. 177.
[15] *Taylor v. Director, Serious Fraud Office* [1999] 2 A.C. 177 at 215C-D and 219G-H.
[16] *Arthur J.S. Hall v. Simons* [2000] 3 W.L.R. 593, at 611, 612, *per* Lord Hobhouse.
[17] [2000] 1 Q.B. 75.

trial, and that the public interest required expert witnesses before trial to be free to make proper concessions without fear that any departure from previous advice given to those retaining them could be taken as evidence of negligence. Accordingly, the immunity extended to claims made against an expert witness by the party retaining him in respect of his conduct in preparing a joint statement.[18] This immunity was largely based on a public policy ground, namely that full and frank discussion between experts should be encouraged at such meetings and extended to work done before he commenced actually giving evidence in court. Will that immunity be at risk as a result of the impact of Article 6(1)? The issue is one of proportionality of the restriction on bringing a civil claim. Provided that witness immunity is based squarely, and narrowly, on the public interest in witnesses speaking the truth when giving their evidence without constraint or fear of a negligence action, it is very unlikely to infringe Article 6(1). In so far as the immunity strays from matters intimately connected with the giving of evidence in court, it may be susceptible to challenge.

Immunity of judges and arbitrators

17.54 In *Arthur J.S. Hall v. Simons*,[19] Lord Hoffman noted that the basis for judicial immunity was founded on the public duty to administer justice and a judge owed no duty to either of the parties.[20] Lord Hutton stated that judicial immunity would not breach Article 6.[21] Arbitrators are in a slightly different position since they often act as a cross between an expert and a judge.[22] However, if the current judicial and witness immunities do not themselves violate Article 6, the current immunity of arbitrators in their "judicial" role[23] is unlikely to be contrary to Article 6. Beyond this narrow limit, any immunity granted to arbitrators may raise Article 6(1) implications. An analogy arises in arbitration contracts, where the engineer has a "quasi-arbitrator/adjudicator" role to play in contracts that have a two-tier process for complaints. The complainant must first notify the claim and the other side's response or rejection of the claim to the engineer who was contracted into the project, for the engineer to make a decision. Only when the engineer has done this and his decision is not accepted can the complainant ask for a reference to arbitration. Clause 67 FIDIC and clause 66 ICE contracts require such an adjudication by the engineer employed on the contract. In *Sutcliffe v. Thackrah*,[24] the House of Lords held that the engineer was *not* immune as a matter of domestic law when performing this role as this would deprive the engineer's client of a right to claim compensation for negligence. The same result would be likely applying Article 6(1).

---

[18] At 88, 101–103, 108 and 109–110.
[19] [2000] 3 W.L.R. 543.
[20] At 570.
[21] At 605.
[22] See paras 12.12 *et seq.* above for general consideration of arbitration and Art. 6(1).
[23] See, *e.g. Arenson v. Casson* [1975] 3 W.L.R. 815, HL; *Sutcliffe v. Thackrah* [1974] A.C. 727.
[24] [1974] A.C. 727.

5. CLINICAL NEGLIGENCE AND MEDICAL LAW

Introduction

Cases involving medical issues are attracting increasing publicity. Patients **17.55** have become increasingly aware of their "rights" in relation to those who treat them and the days of healthcare professionals being viewed with great deference appear long gone. Expectations of medical care and treatment have increased. As advances in science have brought benefits, there are also increasing legal and moral difficulties as to how such technology should be applied. To date, the courts have remained relatively dispassionate in their treatment of such issues, despite their complexity and emotive nature. The extent of the impact the HRA will have in this area of the law an interesting question.

A distinction in the Act's application may need to be drawn between the **17.56** public and the private sectors. National Health Service ("NHS") patients being treated by general practitioners, health authorities and trusts can expect them as public authorities to act compatibility with Convention rights in relation to the provision of health care services. Individual rights of action under the HRA will also lie against the Department of Health in appropriate circumstances. However, the position of private patients is less clear. Whilst it would appear that Parliamentary intention was that those who treated patients privately would not be "public authorities" for the purpose of the HRA,[25] the position is less clear where, for example, NHS Trusts contract the treatment of patients out to private clinics. It would seem undesirable for a two-tier health care system to develop depending on the capacity in which a patient was being treated. It may well be that the courts will use their ability to interpret rights and duties in a manner which is compatible with Convention rights in such a way as to prevent such a situation arising. It seems unlikely that individual healthcare professionals, as opposed to their employing organisations, are regarded as falling within the definition of "public authority".

Relevant Articles in Relation to Medical Law

Medical issues encompass a fairly wide range of Convention articles, **17.57** namely:

    (1) Article 2:   the right to life;

    (2) Article 3:   the right not to be subject to inhuman and degrading treatment;

    (3) Article 6:   the right to a fair trial, including proceedings before the General Medical Council and the General Dental Council[26];

    (4) Article 8:   the right to respect for private and family life;

---

[25] H.L. Deb., November 24, 1997, col. 811 (Lord Chancellor stated that doctors would be public authorities within the meaning of the HRA, s.6, in relation to their NHS practice but not their private practice). See further paras 8.04 *et seq.*, above.
[26] See paras 17.106 *et seq.* below.

(5) Article 9:   the right to respect to freedom of thought, conscience and religion;

(6) Article 12: the right to marry and found a family;

(7) Article 14: the prohibition of discrimination in relation to Convention rights.

Article 2

17.58   Article 2 concerns the protection by law of human life. The right is absolute and, with one limited exception,[27] cannot be subject to derogation. The Article imposes two duties on the state (and through section 6 of the HRA, on health authorities, NHS Trusts and the Department of Health):

(1) not to take a person's life save in the limited circumstances set out in Article 2(2)[28];

(2) to take reasonable measures to protect life.

17.59   The Article imposes both a negative obligation to refrain from depriving someone of their life and a positive duty to take reasonable measures to protect life: *X v. United Kingdom*.[29] It also includes a duty on the state to take preventative operational measures to protect an individual whose life is at risk from the criminal acts of another individual: *Osman v. United Kingdom*.[30]

17.60   Recognised as one of the most fundamental of all human rights, this Article is likely to play a significant role in medical law issues. Despite the reference to "life", Article 2 is not restricted to cases where actual loss of life occurs. It is sufficient if loss of life is one possible consequence of the conduct complained of.[31]

Article 3

17.61   The right not to be subjected to inhuman or degrading treatment may be invoked in relation to issues of forced treatment or the maintenance of life by artificial support. It will often conflict with the right to life, but may nonetheless be relied upon as a basis for complaint. Whilst Article 3 has been extensively invoked in relation to the treatment of prisoners and mental patients, an examination of these issues is outside the scope of this book.

---

[27] The only derogation permitted by Art. 15 is in respect of deaths resulting from lawful acts of war.

[28] Art. 2 expressly provides that deprivation of life shall not be regarded as inflicted in contravention of the Article when it results from the use of force which is no more than absolutely necessary: (1) in defence of any person from unlawful violence; (2) in order to effect a lawful arrest or to prevent the escape of a person lawfully detained; or (3) in action lawfully taken for the purpose of quelling a riot or insurrection.

[29] (1978) 14 D.R. 31.

[30] (2000) 29 E.H.R.R. 245.

[31] Reaffirmed by the European Court of Human Rights in *William and Anita Powell v. United Kingdom* [2000] E.H.R.L.R. 650–654, Application No. 45305/99, May 4, 2000.

Article 6

Article 6 is perhaps the most important Article as far as clinical negligence **17.62** generally and tribunal procedure is concerned. The implications of the HRA for civil procedure and evidence are discussed in Chapters 10 and 11. It will also be possible for healthcare professionals to invoke Article 6 to protect their rights in disciplinary proceedings before their regulatory bodies. Even prior to the coming into force of the HRA, regulatory bodies were changing certain procedures in order to ensure compatibility with the Convention.

Article 8

The right to respect for private and family life affects a wider range of **17.63** issues than might at first be thought including, for example, consent to treatment, the confidentiality of medical records, a patient's right of access to medical records or disclosure of the fact that a person has HIV or AIDS.

Article 9

The right to freedom of thought, conscience and belief may be invoked in **17.64** relation to issues of refusal of treatment. It may also be relevant where a healthcare professional holds a conscientious objection to abortion and the extent to which they may lawfully object to having any association whatsoever with an abortion procedure.[32]

Article 12

The right to marry and found a family may be relevant to issues of who is **17.65** entitled to receive fertility treatment on the NHS.[33]

Clinical Negligence and the *Bolam* Test

It is suggested by some practitioners that Article 2 may provide a means **17.66** for challenging the long-established *Bolam* test and the court's adherence to the "respectable body of medical opinion" approach.[34] The argument put forward is that the *Bolam* test is inconsistent with the right to life unless the domestic courts construe the requirement to take reasonable care as equivalent to the requirement to make adequate provision for medical care. If the care provided is negligent then, by definition, it will not have been adequate. However, the converse may not apply and care that is inadequate is not necessarily negligent. It is suggested that Article 2 may do away with the need to establish negligence at all if a health authority fails to show that it has made adequate provision for medical care in circumstances where the life of the patient was at risk.

---

[32] See further Leonard Hammer, "Abortion Objection in the United Kingdom Within the Framework of the European Convention on Human Rights and Fundamental Freedoms" [1999] E.H.R.L.R. 564–575, who argues that the Abortion Act 1967, s.4, does not provide sufficient protection for abortion objectors.
[33] See, *e.g. R. v. Human Fertilisation and Embryology Authority, ex p. Blood* [1999] Fam.151, [1997] 2 All E.R. 687.
[34] See further Philip Havers Q.c. in Powers & Harris, *Medical Law* (Butterworths, 1999).

17.67 It is also suggested that Article 2 might be used to argue in the context of clinical negligence claims that death or injury could have been avoided if a more senior doctor had been made available to carry out the operation or provide the necessary care or treatment.[35] This could raise the *Bolam* standard from the "reasonably competent doctor" to, for example, the "reasonably competent consultant". The willingness of the courts to accept such changes to the principles for establishing liability in clinical negligence cases remains to be seen. In the light of the decision in *Powell v. United Kingdom*,[36] defendants to clinical negligence claims are likely to argue that once the healthcare system itself is found to be adequate, the behaviour of individual professionals within that system does not fall within the jurisdiction of Article 2. Support for this proposition may also be derived from the European Commission's decision in *Buckley v. United Kingdom*,[37] where the administration of drugs in circumstances leading to a patient's death did not disclose grounds for negligence in domestic law, thereby resulting in the Commission finding that the complaint under Article 2 was "manifestly ill-founded". However, in the *Powell* case,[38] the Court did state that the procedural obligation under Article 2:

> "extends to the need for an effective independent system for establishing the cause of death of an individual under the care and responsibility of health professionals and any liability on the part of the latter"

17.68 Whilst it is uncertain whether the HRA will cause the traditional principles of negligence in the medical context to be modified, Article 2 will undoubtedly provoke a re-evaluation of the policy considerations underlying the courts' review of professional judgments. Further, the ability to bring a direct action against a public authority for breach of Article 2 under section 7 of the HRA potentially creates a new and additional cause of action against health authorities or NHS Trusts which may develop on the basis of different principles to the tort of negligence.

Abortion

17.69 Prior to the HRA, the position in English law was that an unborn child had no existence separate from its mother and could be aborted under the terms of the Abortion Act 1967.[39] The impact, if any, which the Act will have on this controversial area is uncertain. The European Court and Commission have tended to tread cautiously on this subject, no doubt aware of the moral and political passions such subjects arouse and the wide variety of national laws in this area. Unfortunately, the result has been that the jurisprudence of the Convention is not particularly clear. In *Paton v. United Kingdom*,[40] an estranged husband sought to prevent his wife from having

---

[35] *ibid.*
[36] [2000] 12 E.H.R.R. 355.
[37] (1997) 23 E.H.R.R. 101.
[38] [2000] 12 E.H.R.R. 355.
[39] *Re F (in utero)* [1988] Fam. 122, CA; *St George's Healthcare N.H.S. Trust v. S* [1998] 3 W.L.R. 936 at 957A.
[40] (1980) 3 E.H.R.R. 408.

an abortion. The Commission held that a foetus had no absolute right to life as the term "everyone" in Article 2 generally only applied post-natally. Accordingly, the termination of a foetus that was less than 10 weeks old and had no viable life outside of its mother did not violate Article 2. However, it left open the question whether the foetus did have some right to life, for example, if it was able to live independently of its mother. Further, it did not determine the validity of any potential limitations on the exercise of such a right to life, including, for example, adverse implications for the health of the mother.

In *H v. Norway*,[41] the Commission held that the abortion of a foetus for social reasons was not contrary to Article 2 where there was "a difficult situation of life" in relation to the mother. It stated that this was a "delicate area" in which states should be allowed a wide margin of appreciation. In *Open Door Counselling and Dublin Well Woman v. Ireland*,[42] the Commission recognised the possibility that Article 2 might in certain circumstances offer protection to the unborn child but the Court offered no further guidance on the issue. **17.70**

These decisions, which allow a wide margin of appreciation in relation to the right to life, were relied on by one member of the Court of Appeal in the case of the conjoined twins in *Re A (Minors) (Conjoined Twins: Separation)*.[43] Ward L.J. stated that Article 2 was subject to an implied limitation that justified the balancing approach taken by the court in allowing the twins to be separated despite the fact that this would cause certain death to one of the twins. However, Walker L.J. and Brooke L.J. preferred to base their decision on the fact that the doctor's purpose in performing the operation was to save life, even if the extinction of another life was a virtual certainty and therefore this was not intentional killing. The word "intentionally" in Article 2 was said to apply only where the purpose of the prohibited action was death (consistent with existing domestic law on this subject). The court's consideration of the human rights aspects of the appeal is extremely brief. Whilst it might be arguable that the right to respect for private life in Article 8 supports an entitlement to abortion, this issue has yet to be ruled upon by the court. **17.71**

In *Greenfield v. Irwin & Ors*,[44] the Court of Appeal held that it was not open to a woman who had had an unwanted child due to the failure of a medical practice nurse to diagnose a pregnancy, to claim damages for loss of employment on the grounds that, had she known she was pregnant, she would have terminated the pregnancy. The Appellant alleged that her Article 8 rights would be infringed if she was not entitled to claim damages of loss of employment. This aspect of the appeal had not been argued before the judge at first instance (the HRA not being in force at the time of the original judgment) and was therefore found to be technically inadmissible. However, Lord Justice Buxton indicated that the Appellant was highly unlikely to be able to rely on Article 8 so as to require the regime of damages contended for by her in any event. Such a claim was a financial privilege and nothing to do with just compensation. The Court further

---

[41] (1992) 73 D.R. 155.
[42] (1993) 15 E.H.R.R. 244.
[43] [2001] 2 W.L.R. 480; [2000] Lloyd's Rep. Med. 425, CA.
[44] [2001] 1 W.L.R. 1279.

pointed out that states were allowed a wide margin of appreciation in relation to Article 8.

Euthanasia

17.72 Article 2 confers a right to life but not a right to die. Neither the Commission nor the Court has given a substantive ruling on the issue of euthanasia and again a wide margin of appreciation would seem applicable. To date, the approach of the domestic courts to the withdrawal of treatment has been cautious and the HRA seems unlikely to provide scope for sanctioning active, as opposed to passive, euthanasia. The court's duty to respect the sanctity of human life and the refusal to sanction a course of conduct aimed at terminating life or accelerating death was recently affirmed at first instance in *A National Health Service Trust v. D.*[45]

Right to Treatment

17.73 There is scope for arguing under the HRA that health authorities and NHS Trusts are obliged to make adequate provision for medical care in all cases where the right to life of the patient in question would otherwise be endangered. The question was raised in *X. v. Ireland*,[46] but the Commission held that it was unnecessary to determine this issue because the applicant had in fact received treatment and her life had not been endangered. In *Association X v. United Kingdom*,[47] it was held that the state must take adequate and appropriate steps to protect life and that this might raise issues with respect to the adequacy of medical care. The case concerned the steps taken by the state to reduce the risks to life by introducing a vaccination programme for children. On the facts before it, the Commission found no evidence to suggest that the vaccinations had been administered poorly or that proper steps had not been taken to minimise any risks.[48]

17.74 The European Court has allowed states an almost unfettered discretion in relation to the allocation of resources pursuant to the doctrine of the margin of appreciation.[49] Prior to the implementation of the HRA, domestic courts also showed a marked reluctance to become involved in decisions in this area. For example, in *R. v. Cambridge Health Authority, ex p. B*,[50] the Health Authority decided not to give a particular treatment to a young female patient suffering from leukaemia on the basis that it might only have a 20 per cent chance of success and therefore it was not in her best interests and scarce resources should not be allocated to it. The Court of Appeal upheld the Health Authority's decision stating that this was an area in which the court could not make a judgment as to how a limited budget

---

[45] [2000] 2 F.L.R. 677, [2000] Lloyd's Rep. Med. 411; *The Times*, July 19, 2000, Cazalet J.
[46] (1974) 7 D.R. 78.
[47] (1978) 14 D.R. 31.
[48] See also *Paschim Banga Khet Mazdoor Samity v. State of West Bengal* (1996) 4 S.C.C. 37; (1996) 3 S.C.J.25, Sup Ct India (right to life breached and compensation awarded for failure to provide adequate services for emergency patient).
[49] See further paras 4.22 *et seq.*, above.
[50] [1995] 1 W.L.R. 898.

was best allocated to the maximum advantage of the maximum number of patients.[51]

It might at first appear that such an approach would not longer be con- **17.75** sistent with the Convention. The right to life is an absolute right to which, in theory, lack of financial resources to provide the care in question provides no defence. However, the European Court has recently stated in *Osman v. United Kingdom*,[52] albeit in the context of the obligations on the police to take positive steps to protect life, that the Article 2 obligation must be interpreted in a way which "does not impose an impossible or disproportionate burden on the authorities".[53] Further, in *Powell v. United Kingdom*,[54] the Court stated that whilst Article 2 required the state to take appropriate steps to safeguard the lives of those within its jurisdiction, where the state made adequate provision for securing high professional standards among health professionals and the protection of patients' lives, matters such as errors of judgment or negligent co-ordination among health professionals were insufficient to call a Contracting State to account from the standpoint of its obligations under Article 2.[55] The HRA, however, allows courts to look at both the decision making process and the merits of the decision. Thus, resource allocation decisions will have to become more transparent.[56]

NHS Funding of Treatment

Blanket bans on treatment may be challenged as being incompatible with **17.76** the Convention. For example, a blanket ban on the basis of age may arguably contravene Articles 3, 8 and 14. If the ban related to resuscitation, it might also breach Article 2. A decision not to fund fertility treatment could potentially violate Articles 8 and 12.

Hospital waiting lists may also be challenged if the facts merit it. In **17.77** *Passannante v. Italy*,[57] the Commission held that excessive delay by a public authority in providing a medical service to which a patient is entitled, and the fact that such delay has (or is likely to have) a serious impact on the patient's health could amount to an interference with the right to respect for private life under Article 8(1). In *R. v. North and East Devon Health Authority, ex p. Coughlan*,[58] the Court of Appeal held that the decision of the health authority to close an NHS home in which the applicant was a resident constituted a breach of Article 8. Although Article 8(2) permits justification for an interference with the right to respect for

---

[51] At 906, *per* Sir Thomas Bingham M.R. See also James and Longley, "Judicial Review and Tragic Choices" [1995] P.L. 367, and O'Sullivan, "The Allocation of Scarce Resources and the right to life under the ECHR" [1998] P.L. 389
[52] (2000) 29 E.H.R.R. 245.
[53] *ibid.*, para. 116.
[54] (1990) 12 E.H.R.R. 355.
[55] See also the decision of the Constitutional Court of South Africa in *Soobramoney v. Minister of Health* 1997 (12) B.C.L.R. 1696, (1997) 4 B.H.R.C. 308, Const Ct of South Africa (refusal to afford treatment to a terminally-ill patient because of resource shortages constitutional).
[56] See Lord Irvine of Lairg, "The Development of Human Rights in Britain under an Incorporated Convention on Human Rights" [1998] P.L. 221 at 224.
[57] (1998) 26 E.H.R.R. C.D. 153.
[58] [2000] 2 W.L.R. 622, [1999] C.O.D. 340, CA.

private life on the ground of resources, such derogation would have to be applied without discrimination "on any ground" pursuant to Article 14.

Patient's Refusal of Treatment

17.78 At present, in English law, the capability of an individual to take decisions for him or herself in relation to treatment may override the right to life. In *St George's Healthcare N.H.S. Trust v. S*,[59] a pregnant woman who refused to consent to a Caesarean section was admitted, also without her consent, to a hospital for assessment on an application under section 2 of the Mental Health Act, and was then transferred to another hospital where a Caesarean was carried out. The Court of Appeal held that the woman's detention in both hospitals was unlawful and the Caesarean amounted to trespass to her person. It was stated that an individual has a right to refuse medical treatment, even if it seems unreasonable to do so, and the right to self-determination can only be overridden when the carefully prescribed circumstances set out in the mental health legislation are met. Such principles would appear to find support in Article 3 and also Article 9. However, they do conflict with the foetus' potential right to life. The latter is an area that merits further exploration in English jurisprudence, the Court and the Commission having thus far failed to provide clear guidance on the issue. In the context of Article 3, the courts will have to grapple with whether the patient's definition of inhuman or degrading treatment, or that of the medical profession, should prevail.

17.79 A particularly difficult problem may arise where a child wishes to refuse to consent to treatment. It has been held by the English courts that even where a child is competent to give a legally valid consent (including children over 16 years of age), the child's right to refuse treatment can be overridden by the child's parent or the court.[60] This may be challenged in the light of Article 3. It will also have to be balanced against Article 2 if the refusal of treatment may result in the child's death.

Withdrawal of Treatment

17.80 As stated above, Article 2 provides for a right to live. It does not state that there is a duty to live. Equally, there is no right to die. This area is further complicated by the potential incapacity of patients to make clear their own wishes by reason of their medical condition. In *D v. United Kingdom*,[61] the European Court emphasised the importance of dying with dignity, although it declined to rule on the Article 2 contentions. Prior to the HRA, the courts tended to rely heavily on medical opinion in respect of deciding what decisions should be taken in this area. In the landmark case of *Airedale National Health Service Trust v. Bland*,[62] the House of Lords applied the *Bolam* principle in concluding that the patient's existence in a permanent vegetative state was no use to him and therefore artificial nutrition and hydration and medical treatment should cease. Interestingly,

---

[59] [1998] 3 W.L.R. 936, CA.
[60] *Re C (a Minor)(Medical treatment: Court's jurisdiction)*, The Times, March 21, 1997. See also *Re W (a Minor) (Medical treatment: Court's jurisdiction)* [1993] Fam. 64.
[61] (1997) 24 E.H.R.R. 423.
[62] [1993] A.C. 789.

in *Bland*, it was argued that the court ought to preserve the dignity and moral integrity of the patient in accordance with Article 8 of the Convention by executing his or her previously expressed wish to be allowed to die. Whilst the House of Lords did not directly address Article 8, it did emphasise that the "right to life" as provided for in the Convention was not to be considered in terms of a biological existence only. Thus, the right to life was not to be interpreted simply as the right to continue a futile existence.

The case of *A National Health Service Trust v. D,*[63] indicates that a similar **17.81** approach is likely to continue to be applied. The case involved a 19-month old child who suffered from a severe, chronic and worsening lung disease which meant that his life expectancy was very short. The paediatricians involved in his care were firmly of the opinion that it would not be in the child's best interest to be readmitted to intensive care to undergo further resuscitation involving artificial ventilation. His parents were totally opposed to any such inaction but the paediatrician they instructed for the purpose of the hearing expressed the same opinion as the doctors in charge of their child's care. Cazalet J. agreed with the expressed medical opinion as to what was in the child's best interests in granting a declaration that treatment to prolong the child's life would not be required. Such a declaration was held not to infringe Article 2 because the decision was in the child's best interests. Article 3 was relied upon to support the principle that a person had a right to die with dignity. The judge set out four general principles to be used as a framework in such cases:

(1) the court's paramount consideration is the best interests of the child and this involves a careful consideration of the views of the parents. However, those views cannot override the court's views of the child's best interests;

(2) the court's respect for the sanctity of human life imposes a strong obligation to take all steps capable of preserving life, save in exceptional circumstances;

(3) there is no question of approving a course of action aimed at terminating life or accelerating death;

(4) it is well established that a court will not direct a doctor to provide treatment which he or she is unwilling to give and which is against clinical judgment.

In *NHS Trust A v. M; NHS Trust B v. H,*[64] Dame Elizabeth Butler-Sloss held **17.82** that a decision to cease treatment in a patient's best interests was not an intentional deprivation of life contrary to Article 2, which imported a deliberate act, not an omission. In relation to the state's positive obligation under Article 2 to take adequate and appropriate steps to safeguard life, where a responsible clinical decision was made to withhold treatment that was

[63] [2000] 2 F.L.R. 677, [2000] Lloyd's Rep. Med. 411, *The Times*, July 19, 2000, Cazalet J.
[64] [2001] 2 W.L.R. 942; [2001] 1 All E.R. 801, (2001) Lloyd's Rep. Med. 28, *The Times*, November 29, 2000, Dame Elizabeth Butler-Sloss, P.

not in the patient's best interests, and that accorded with a respectable body of medical opinion, the state's positive obligation was discharged.

Experimental Treatment

17.83 The European Commission has held that experimental medical treatment may amount to inhuman treatment, if not torture, in the absence of consent: X v. Denmark.[65] The definition given to the term "experimental" in this context is significant because it will determine the width of application of this principle. Taken to an extreme, "experimental" treatment might be argued to include any treatment whose effects have not been fully or properly established. Further, it could be argued that any apparent consent to a particular treatment is invalidated in the event that a patient has not been fully informed of any experimental aspects of such a procedure. Under the HRA, it will not be necessary to prove actual "damage" as in negligence claims, provided that the claimant satisfies the "victim" test in section 7.[66] It is enough to show that there is a breach of Article 3.

Consent to Treatment

17.84 When the courts are asked to consider the issue of the extent of a doctor's duty to warn the patient of the risks and complications of a procedure, this Article may be sought to be relied upon in support of a doctrine of "informed consent" based on a patient's right to know, in place of the doctor-based duty which is currently favoured by the English courts. Consent can however be overridden in certain circumstances. For example, in Acmanne v. Belgium,[67] the applicant's challenge to compulsory tuberculosis screening failed. It was held that although there was interference with private life, it was justified in order to protect health.[68]

Right to Information on Life-Threatening Risks

17.85 Article 2 has been applied in the health and environmental contexts to life-threatening hazards in so far as these hazards may be attributed to the state. In LCB v. United Kingdom,[69] a woman who had been diagnosed with leukaemia brought a claim against the Government under Article 2, on the basis that the disease had been caused by her father's exposure to radiation whilst serving with the Royal Air Force during nuclear tests conducted on Christmas Island in the late 1950s. She could not challenge the actual exposure to radiation because this occurred prior to the United Kingdom granting the right of individual petition. Instead, she alleged that the United Kingdom owed a duty to warn and advise her parents of the dangers involved in the nuclear testing and to monitor her health prior to the diagnosis of leukaemia, and that this duty had been breached. The

---

[65] Application No. 9974/82, (1983) 32 D.R. 282.
[66] See further paras 8.06 et seq., above.
[67] (1983) 40 D.R. 251.
[68] See also Grare v. France (1993) 15 E.H.R.R. C.D. 100 (even if treatment regime of a voluntary patient in a psychiatric hospital which had unpleasant side effects could be said to be an invasion of the applicant's private life, it was justified by need).
[69] (1999) 27 E.H.R.R. 212.

European Court dismissed the claim on the basis that there was insufficient evidence of causation between the father's exposure to radiation and his daughter's leukaemia. It stated that the test to be applied was whether, given the circumstances of the case, the state did all that could have been required of it to prevent a life from being avoidably put at risk. The Court accepted that the state might have been required by Article 2 to take steps to warn and advise if it appeared likely at the relevant time that the father's exposure to radiation might endanger the health of any future children.

The right to respect for private and family life under Article 8 of the **17.86** Convention is also relevant in this context. In Guerra v. Italy,[70] the applicants lived within a mile of a chemical factory, which was classified as a high risk in terms of hazards to the environment and to the local population. The European Court held that Article 8 had been breached by reason of the state's failure to provide the applicants with information about the risks to them or to provide instructions as to the action which ought to be taken in the event of an accident.

Analogous principles may be argued to apply in the context of medical law. **17.87** The HRA ought to be considered by public authorities when deciding how to deal with potential life-threatening health risks and particularly in relation to the provision of advice or information relating to those risks. Whilst it is likely that a reasonably wide discretion will be granted to the state in deciding what steps to take to regulate a potential danger in the light of known risks, a new potential liability exists through the medium of Articles 2 and 8.

AIDS

HIV and AIDS cases raise difficult questions regarding disclosure of a **17.88** patient's condition and the apparent conflict between the duty of confidence owed by the doctor to the patient and the doctor's obligation to protect that individual's partner, those caring for him and others who may be at risk of infection. The Guidance issued by the General Medical Council on this issue advises that each patient should receive counselling to explain the need for disclosure. If the patient is still unwilling to disclose the information, the only circumstance in which the doctor should make an unauthorised disclosure is where there would otherwise be a "serious risk" of infection to the patient's sexual partner or those treating him. The European Court has been willing to accept justifications for breaches of Article 8 on similar grounds. For example, in Z v. Finland,[71] the Court found that the prima facie breaches of Article 8, which arose when a woman's HIV status was revealed during the course of criminal proceedings against her husband, who was charged with deliberately attempting to infect others with the virus, was justified as being in the pursuit of the prevention of crime.[72] Where a local authority applied for an order that a baby be subjected to an HIV test despite the vehement opposition of her parents, the Article 8 right of the parents and baby to have their family life

---

[70] (1998) 26 E.H.R.R. 357.
[71] (1998) 25 E.H.R.R. 371.
[72] In a rather different context, it was not a breach of Art. 2 or Art. 3 to refuse a foreign national who was HIV positive exceptional leave to enter the U.K.: *R. v. Chief Immigration Officer, ex p. R, The Times*, November 29, 2000.

respected supported the formulation of a rebuttable presumption that the united view of the parents was correct in identifying where the welfare of the baby lay.[73]

Fertility Treatment

17.89   The right to marry and found a family may be relevant to issues of who is entitled to receive fertility treatment on the National Health Service,[74] and, in conjunction with Articles 8 and 14, might be used to challenge the so-called "postcode rationing" of treatment. The considerable doubts surrounding the safety and efficacy of many treatments may mean that the courts will be slow to interfere with professional judgments.[75] However, as such treatments become more established, it may be difficult for the state to justify withholding them from certain sections of the population.

17.90   Interesting questions may arise in relation to the current domestic rules governing in vitro fertilisation ("IVF") treatment. Pursuant to section 13(5) of the Human Fertilisation and Embryology Act 1990, a woman may not be provided with treatment:

> "unless account has been taken of the welfare of any child who may be born as a result of the treatment (including the need of that child for a father) and of any other child who may be affected by the birth".

This provision permits a doctor treating a woman to refuse treatment on grounds other than her own best interests. However, in doing so, he may be compromising her Article 12 rights. In this regard, the provisions of Article 14, which prohibit discrimination on the basis of membership of any social group, may also be relevant. If single mothers were to be refused treatment, it is arguable that a breach of the Article would be disclosed.

6. CLIENT CONFIDENTIALITY

Right to Access to Confidential Information

17.91   In principle, Article 8 may confer a right of access by a person to personal or confidential information.[76] For example, in Gaskin v. United Kingdom,[77] the Strasbourg Court upheld G's argument that his rights under Article 8 had been breached by the refusal of the local authority to disclose documents relating to his upbringing in care. This has implications for the domestic common law position that a former patient had no right of access

---

[73] Re C (A Child) (HIV test), The Times, September 14, 1999, Wilson J.
[74] See R. v. Human Fertilisation and Embryology Authority, ex p. Blood [1999] Fam.151, [1997] 2 All E.R. 687.
[75] See Briody v. St Helens and Knowsley Area Health Authority [2001] 2 F.C.R. 481; The Independent, July 3, 2001: following the Health Authority's negligence the claimant was deprived of a womb, but it was held that a claim for the costs of surrogacy was not recoverable. Expenditure on surrogacy was said not to be reasonable such that it should be funded by the Defendant. Article 12 rights should not be arbitrarily restricted, but could not be used to create a right to be supplied with a child.
[76] See further paras 19.29 et seq. below for a further description of the European case-law on confidentiality of personal records.
[77] (1990) 12 E.H.R.R. 36.

to records at common law in *R. v. Mid-Glamorgan Family Health Services, ex p. Martin*.[78]

Disclosure of Confidential Information

Equally, the disclosure of confidential information may breach Article 8. In **17.92** *Z v. Finland*,[79] a reference in a published judgment to an applicant's full name which led to the disclosure of her HIV status breached her right to a private life. These cases may have relevance to disclosure of documents and the duties of confidentiality owed by professionals.

Disclosure of Medical Records and Confidentiality

The European Court of Human Rights has confirmed that a patient's **17.93** medical records are included in Article 8. In *MS v. Sweden*[80] the applicant claimed she had suffered a back injury as a result of a fall at work with the consequence that she was unable to return to work. She therefore made a claim against the Social Insurance Office. However, she was a long-term sufferer from spondylolisthesis, which can cause chronic back pain. Without her consent, the Social Insurance Office obtained her medical records from the clinic that had treated her back injury and rejected her claim for compensation on the basis that they showed her injuries had not been caused at work. The records revealed that the applicant had had an abortion after the alleged injury at work, but the abortion records related the abortion to serious back problems suffered during an earlier pregnancy and not a work-related injury. Importantly, the Court held that the applicant had not waived her rights by commencing the action and that:

> "The protection of personal data not least medical data is of fundamental importance to a person's enjoyment of his or her right to respect for private and family life . . . ".

However, on the facts, it was held that whilst there was an interference **17.94** with the applicant's rights, Article 8(2) was satisfied because there was a proportionate and legitimate aim in the information being sought, namely the protection of the economic well-being of the country by reason of the allocation of public funds. It may be harder to impose a duty of confidentiality on a large Health Trust where files are passed from one department to another and viewed by doctors, nurses, secretaries and administrators alike.[81] In *A Health Authority v. X & ors*[82] Munby J. applied the principles set out in *Z. v. Finland*[83] and *MS v. Sweden*[84] in holding that there was a compelling public interest requiring the disclosure of medical records to a health authority investigating allegations that medical practitioners had

---

[78] (1995) 1 W.L.R. 110; (1995) 1 All E.R. 356, CA.
[79] (1998) 25 E.H.R.R. 371.
[80] (1999) 28 E.H.R.R. 313. See also *Z v. Finland* (1998) 25 EHRR 371
[81] In relation to disclosure of medical reports, see also *R. v. Secretary of State for the Home Department, ex p. Amnesty International*, unreported, February 15, 2000, DC (fairness required that medical reports on Senator Pinochet should be disclosed to the four states which had requested sight of them).
[82] Unreported, May 10, 2001, Munby J.
[83] (1997) 25 E.H.R.R. 371.
[84] (1997) 28 E.H.R.R. 313.

breached their terms of service. However, he also emphasised that such disclosure was an interference with a patient's rights under Article 8 and could only be justified where there were effective and adequate safeguards against abuse. The following safeguards were said to be typically required:

(i) the maintenance of the confidentiality of the documents themselves;

(ii) the minimum public disclosure of any information derived from the documents; and

(iii) the protection of the patient's anonymity.

It was also emphasised that it was the duty of every public body, including the court, to ensure that that confidentiality was preserved and that there were effective and adequate safeguards against abuse before authorising the transfer of medical records from one doctor to a public body or from one public body to another.

Patients' Complaints Procedures

17.95 On applications for disclosure of documents created pursuant to patients' complaints procedures, Article 8 may have to be considered, both in relation to the rights of the patient and the rights of those being investigated.

7. INQUESTS

General

17.96 Inquests are inquisitorial proceedings to which the Convention has relevance under Article 2 (the right to life) and where it is not possible for litigation to follow an inquest, Article 13 (the right to an effective remedy). They are particularly relevant to proceedings arising from a death in medical care, whose conduct has implications for any subsequent clinical negligence proceedings in the High Court or county courts.

Coroners' Inquests

17.97 The coroner is an independent judicial officer charged with inquiring into deaths of various categories. Following certain deaths and regardless of the cause, an inquest into the death must be held.[85] Certain deaths (for example of prisoners in custody) must be held with a jury.[86] The coroner's duties have been judicially defined:

"It is the duty of the coroner as the public official responsible for the conduct of inquests, whether he is sitting with a jury or without, to ensure that the relevant facts are fully, fairly and fearlessly investigated. He is bound to recognise the acute public concern rightly

---

[85] Coroners Act 1988, s.8(1).
[86] Coroners Act 1988, s.8(3).

aroused where deaths occur in custody. He must ensure that the relevant facts are exposed to public scrutiny, particularly if there is evidence of foul play, abuse or inhumanity."[87]

Rule 20 of the Coroners' Rules 1984 allows, amongst others, parents, spouses, personal representatives or other "interested persons" to examine witnesses at an inquest either in person or by counsel or a solicitor. There is, however, no legal aid for representation at inquests. Historically, there was no right to disclosure of documents, although rule 57(1) of the Coroners' Rules 1984 now provides that a properly interested party can apply on payment of the prescribed fee, if any, for a copy of any post mortem or special examination report, or of any notes of evidence or of any document put in evidence at an inquest. Alternatively, such a party can inspect such report, notes of evidence or document without charge: rule 57(2). **17.98**

Pursuant to section 11(5)(b) of the Coroners Act 1988 and rule 36 of the Coroners' Rules 1984, proceedings and evidence at an inquest must be directed solely to ascertaining: (1) who the deceased was; (2) where the deceased came by his death; (3) when the deceased came by his death and; (4) how the deceased came by his death. No verdict may be framed in such a way as to appear to determine any questions of the criminal liability of a named person or civil liability pursuant to rule 42 of the Coroners' Rules. The scope of an inquest has been described as follows: **17.99**

" . . . It is noteworthy that the task is not to ascertain how the deceased died, which might raise general and far-reaching issues, but 'how . . . the deceased came by his death', a far more limited question directed to the means by which the deceased came by his death . . . ".[88]

"The cases established that although the word 'how' is to be widely interpreted, it means 'by what means' rather than in what broad circumstances . . . In short, the inquiry must focus on matters directly causative of death and must, indeed, be confined to those matters alone . . . ".[89]

" . . . it should not be forgotten that an inquest is a fact finding exercise and not a method of apportioning guilt. The procedure and rules of evidence which are suitable for one are unsuitable for the other. In an inquest it should never be forgotten that there are no parties, no indictment, there is no prosecution, there is no defence, there is no trial, simply an attempt to establish the facts. It is an inquisitorial process, a process of investigation quite unlike a trial. . . ".[90]

---

[87] *R. v. North Humberside Coroner, ex p. Jamieson* [1995] Q.B. 1 at 26C, CA.
[88] *ibid.*, *per* Sir Thomas Bingham M.R.
[89] *R. v. Coroner for Western District of East Sussex, ex p. Homberg*, (1994) 158 J.P. 357, *per* Simon Brown L.J.
[90] *R. v. South London Coroner, ex p. Thompson* (1982) 126 S.J. 625, *per* Lord Lane C.J.

Section 6 of the HRA

17.100 A coroner's court is a court or tribunal for the purposes of section 6(3) of the HRA. A coroner is therefore under a duty pursuant to section 6(1) of the HRA to act compatibly with the Convention.

Obligation to Conduct Effective Investigation into Deaths Involving the State

17.101 Under Article 2, the state is under a positive obligation to carry out an effective investigation into deaths arising out of circumstances involving state authorities such as security forces: *McCann v. United Kingdom.*[91]

17.102 Where access to documents and information by interested parties is circumscribed, it seems doubtful that such a limited inquiry provides an effective investigation into deaths. The courts may, however, be reluctant to question such fundamental matters of procedure. In *Taylor v. United Kingdom,*[92] the applicants failed in their complaint that there was a violation of Article 2 by reason of the state's failure to set up a public inquiry into deaths alleged to have been caused by a hospital nurse. In *Jordan v. United Kingdom,*[93] the Court held that the failure to conduct a proper investigation into the circumstances of the deaths of persons killed in the fight against terrorism in Northern Ireland violated Article 2.

17.103 In *R. v. H.M. Coroner for Inner London North, ex p. Peter Francis Touche,*[94] the Court of Appeal held, with reference to Article 2, that although a coroner's original decision not to hold an inquest could not be impugned, information on neglect that subsequently came to light should have forced the conclusion that an inquest had to be held. In *R. v. Home Office, ex p. Wright & Bennett,*[95] an order for an independent official investigation into the death of an inmate was permitted where it was held that his treatment has arguably been contrary to Articles 2 and 3 of the Convention.[96]

17.104 Further, the Court has stated that given the fundamental importance of the right to the protection of life, Article 13 requires, in addition to the payment of compensation where appropriate, a thorough and effective investigation capable of leading to the identification and punishment of those responsible for the deprivation of life, including effective access for the complainant to the investigation procedure: *Kaya v. Turkey.*[97] Where the parent of a mentally-ill prisoner, who had died by hanging whilst in prison in circumstances where the deficiencies in medical care constituted a violation of Article 3, was unable to bring civil proceedings in relation to her son's

---

[91] (1996) 21 E.H.R.R. 27. See also *Kaya v. Turkey* (1999) 28 E.H.R.R. 1 and *Çokici v. Turkey* (2001) 31 E.H.R.R. 133.
[92] Application No 23412/94; (1994) 79A D.R. 127. cf. *Wright v. Secretary of State for the Home Department, Daily Telegraph,* June 26, 2001; June 20, 2001, Jackson J.
[93] (2001) 31 E.H.R.R. 6.
[94] [2001] 3 W.L.R. 148, CA (available on Lawtel).
[95] Unreported, June 6, 2001.
[96] See also *Orange v. Chief Constable of West Yorkshire Police* [2001] EWCA Civ 611, CA at para. 47 where the Court stated (*obiter*) that the decision in *Keenan v. United Kingdom* Application No. 27229/95, April 3, 2001 confirmed its view that the special and unusual duty to take reasonable care to prevent a prisoner taking his own life is one which is only owed where the authorities know or ought to know of a suicide risk in an individual prisoner's case.
[97] (1999) 28 E.H.R.R. 1, para.107. See also *Keenan v. United Kingdom,* Application No. 27229/95, April 3, 2001, para.122.

death, either on her own behalf or as the representative of her son's estate, an inquest did not provide a remedy for determining the liability of the authorities for any alleged mistreatment, or for providing compensation and there was a breach of Article 13.[98] The European Court has recently declared admissible two applications alleging violations of the Convention based on the denial of the provision of witness statements to representatives of the family of the deceased.[99]

It is arguable that Article 6 applies to inquests, not merely in relation to the deceased's family, but also in relation to the healthcare professionals who are called to give evidence to the court and their employers, in so far as the procedure can be characterised as the determination of a civil right or obligation as opposed to a merely investigatory procedure.[1] Issues may therefore arise as to the fairness of such hearings given the rather limited nature of the inquiry being undertaken. It is debatable whether the procedure followed at inquests can be said to comply with this obligation, because at present, in light of the relevant rules, the scope of the inquiry is substantially limited, particularly in relation to findings of fault.[2] However, where there exists the avenue of a civil negligence claim in a fully Article 6(1) compliant court, any deficiencies in the inquest procedure are unlikely to be material for the purpose of Article 6 which considers the proceedings as a whole.[3]

17.105

8. PROFESSIONAL DISCIPLINARY PROCEEDINGS

Professional disciplinary proceedings will amount to the determination of civil rights and obligations for the purpose of Article 6(1) if the private right of the professional to practice his profession is actually or potentially interfered with.[4] In *Gautrin v. France*,[5] the European Court confirmed that Article 6(1) applies to hearings before medical and dental disciplinary bodies where these affect the professional's right to continue to practise his profession. This confirmed the position set out in several earlier cases including *Diennet v. France*,[6] in which it was held that the French Medical Disciplinary Council fell within the article.[7] The European Court has left

17.106

---

[98] *Keenan v. United Kingdom*, Application No. 27229/95, April 3, 2001, paras 127–132, (the Court concluded that the applicant should have been able to apply for compensation for her own non-pecuniary damage, *i.e.* her stress, anxiety and frustration, and for that suffered by her son before his death. Under Art. 41, it awarded £7,000 to her son's estate and £3,000 to the applicant in her personal capacity.

[99] *Kelly v. United Kingdom*, Application No. 30054/96, April 4, 2000 (during inquest, families' representatives were not permitted to see various witness statements. Violation of Arts 2,6,13 and 14 alleged); *McKerr v. United Kingdom*, Application No. 28883/95, April 4, 2000 (during the inquest some of the witness statements were deleted in the public interest for reasons of national security under public interest immunity certificates. Violation of Arts 2, 13 and 14 alleged).

[1] See, *e.g. Fayed v. United Kingdom* (1994) 18 E.H.R.R. 393, and *R. v. Lord Chancellor, ex p. Lightfoot* [2000] 2 W.L.R. 318, CA; [1999] 2 W.L.R. 1126, Laws J. See further paras 3.60 *et seq.*, above.

[2] *R. v North Humberside Coroner ex p. Jamieson* [1994] 3 All E.R. 972.

[3] *Edwards v. United Kingdom* (1993) 15 E.H.R.R. 417.

[4] *Le Compte, Van Leuven and De Meyere v. Belgium* (1982) 4 E.H.R.R. 1, paras 47–49.

[5] (1999) 23 E.H.R.R. 196.

[6] (1996) 21 E.H.R.R. 554.

[7] See also *König v. Germany* (1980) 2 E.H.R.R. 170, and *Albert and Le Compte v. Belgium* (1983) 5 E.H.R.R. 533.

open the question whether professional disciplinary proceedings amount to the determination of a criminal charge, an issue which became superfluous following the finding that there was a determination of civil rights and obligations.[8]

17.107   It follows that any disciplinary tribunal which can interfere with a practitioner's ability to practice will have to itself comply with the requirements of Article 6 or there must be a full appeal to, or review by, an Article 6 compliant court or tribunal with jurisdiction to rectify factual errors or to examine whether the sanction is proportionate to the fault or which can remedy any incompatibility below.[9] In the legal context, this includes the respective disciplinary tribunals of the Law Society and the Bar Council. In the accountancy context, it includes the disciplinary tribunal of the Institute of Chartered Accountants. In the medical context, this includes the Professional Conduct Committee and Health Committee of the General Medical Council and the General Dental Council and the equivalent bodies for other medical practitioners such as nurses, midwives, health visitors and physiotherapists.[10]

Independence and Impartiality of Tribunal Members

17.108   In *Gautrin*, proceedings were brought against medical practitioners who were all members of an organisation known as "SOS Médicins", whose object was to provide emergency services on call to patients. The National Union of Duty Doctors and the French Federation of Paris General Practitioners brought a complaint against SOS Médicins. It was alleged that by displaying "SOS Médicins" on their vehicles, they were breaching the code of professional conduct on advertising. Both the lower and appeal tribunal upheld the complaint. However, the European Court held that there had been a violation of Article 6 because the disciplinary tribunal had not been held in public and the tribunal had not been seen to be impartial. The Court set out two tests to be applied in determining whether or not a tribunal was impartial:

> (1) the personal convictions of a particular judge;

---

[8] *Le Compte, Van Leuven and De Meyere v. Belgium* (1982) 4 E.H.R.R. 1, para.53. But see *In the Matter of a Solicitor* (2001), unreported, January 11, 2001, DC. (held that proceedings in issue before the Solicitors Tribunal for failing to maintain proper accounts and permitting misleading information to be delivered to the Law Society not the determination of a criminal charge and no requirement for legal representation).

[9] *Le Compte, Van Leuven and De Meyere v. Belgium* (1982) 4 E.H.R.R. 1, para. 51; *Gautrin v. France* (1999) 28 E.H.R.R. 196, para.57. In *R v. United Kingdom Central Council for Nursing, Midwifery & Health Visiting, ex p. Tehrani* (2001) I.R.L.R. 208, the Outer House of the Court of Session held that it was not necessary that the respondent's professional conduct committee should itself meet all the requirements of an independent and impartial tribunal, within the meaning of Art. 6(1), given that an automatic right of appeal to the Court of Session lay from any order striking the name of one of its members from the register. See also *Dr Purabi Ghosh v. General Medical Council* (2001) unreported, June 18, 2001, PC, in which it was held that, whilst proceedings against a general practitioner attracted the protection of Art. 6, the Privy Council was not concerned with whether the committee fulfilled the Convention requirements of independence and impartiality because the court's appellate jurisdiction was sufficient to remedy any deficiency in those respects.

[10] On the European Court's analysis, it seems unlikely that internal proceedings such as HC–90(9) inquiries which do not have direct power to interfere with a practitioner's right to practise will be subject to Art. 6: see *Fayed v. United Kingdom* (1994) 18 E.H.R.R. 393.

(2) whether the judge offered sufficient guarantees to exclude legitimate concerns in this regard.

On the facts of the case, the doctors sitting on the tribunal were members **17.109** of the same unions and competing organisations that had brought the complaint. Therefore, they had a common interest with the complainants. The Court has therefore shown itself willing to uphold complaints based not on actual bias but on the mere appearance of lack of independence. Thus, there is a heightened need for the members of professional conduct committees, whether professional or lay, to ensure that they are not in fact embarrassed by sitting in judgment on a particular practitioner and, further, that any interests or associations that each may have cannot be said to conflict with the need for impartiality and independence.

In the case of *In the Matter of a Solicitor* (2001),[11] the Divisional Court held **17.110** that the Solicitors Disciplinary Tribunal was an independent and impartial tribunal in relation to a hearing that took place before the coming into force of the HRA 1998. The court held that both the Law Society and the tribunal were public authorities for the purpose of the HRA. The Tribunal was independent of the Law Society and there was no indication that the Law Society could influence its decisions, except by making submissions to the Tribunal as a party.

Equality of Arms

The right to a fair hearing means that all parties must have a reasonable **17.111** opportunity of presenting their respective cases under conditions that do not place them at a substantial disadvantage *vis-à-vis* their opponents.[12] This principle applies both to preliminary and final proceedings.

Disclosure of Documents

In *R. v. General Medical Council, ex p. Toth*,[13] Lightman J. referred to the **17.112** new form of practice adopted by the General Medical Council in the light of the coming into force of the HRA. In relation to all complaints received by the General Medical Council after July 1, 2000, any material submitted by the doctor under investigation to the Council screener is copied to the complainant, unless the screener considers there are "exceptional circumstances" which ought to preclude this. A specific example of an exceptional circumstance is given, namely where disclosure could cause "substantial harm" to the doctor or a third party by the disclosure of confidential medical material. In such circumstances, the screener can permit disclosure on terms such a requiring a cross-undertaking not to disclose the information or by allowing partial or edited disclosure. In the *Toth* case, the court was asked to decide whether certain documentation put before the screener in relation to the ill health of the doctor under investigation ought to be provided to the complainant. Lightman J. held that the complainant could only see the documentation in question provided he gave an undertaking of confidentiality. He further held that if the

---

[11] Unreported, November 13, 2000, DC.
[12] See *Dombo Beheer v. Netherlands* (1994) 18 E.H.R.R. 213.
[13] [2000] 1 W.L.R. 2209.

General Medical Council decided that such material ought to be disclosed in the interests of fairness, it was entitled to impose conditions which likewise accorded with the principles of fairness. To do otherwise would be calculated to discourage practitioners from submitting relevant but confidential material to the Council for consideration by the screener. The judge therefore carried out a balancing exercise between the rights of both the complainant and the health professional.

Ability to Comment upon Advice of Legal Advisers and Assessors

17.113   Analogous principles will apply in respect of information and advice supplied to the tribunal at the final hearing. Most disciplinary tribunals are assisted by a legal adviser or assessor. In *Nwabuaze v. General Medical Council*,[14] the Privy Council stated that:

> "the principle which lies behind the requirement that the parties should be informed of the assessor's advice to the committee is that of fairness, and that fairness requires that the parties should be afforded an opportunity to comment on that advice and that the committee should have an opportunity to consider their comments before announcing their determination."

In that case, the legal assessor decided to intervene twice in the deliberations of the Committee to give them advice. The content of that advice was not disclosed to the parties until immediately before the Committee gave its decision. The Privy Council stated its view that consideration should be given to changing the practice so that parties are aware that they are entitled to comment upon, or criticise, the advice which has been given by the legal adviser. Further, this should be done so that the assessor may consider, in the presence of the parties, whether his advice to the Committee ought to be changed.

Duties in Relation to Sanction to be Imposed

17.114   The need for the professional's appearing before the disciplinary tribunal to be explicitly warned that the question of immediate suspension is a possible sanction under consideration has recently been emphasised in *Gupta v. The General Medical Council*.[15] The Court stated that fairness demanded that the Doctor in question should be given the opportunity to make representations on this distinct issue, and if necessary call witnesses. Further, in *Sudesh Madan v. The General Medical Council*[16] the Divisional Court held that there must be a sufficient balancing of the public interest and the impact of the suspension order upon the doctor in question. The court commented that the right to practise should be elevated to the status of a civil right requiring any interference to be proportional given

---

[14] [2000] 1 W.L.R. 1760.
[15] Unreported, July 25, 2001.
[16] [2001] EWHC Admin 577.

that suspension was capable of giving rise to serious and grave consequences for the future professional career of a doctor.

Public Hearing

Article 6(1) requires that professional disciplinary proceedings are held in **17.115** public, unless the limited exceptions set out in the Article apply.[17] Where matters of professional secrecy or protection of the private life of a professional or his patient or client is concerned, this may justify sitting *in camera*.[18] Where the professional waives his right to a public hearing expressly or tacitly, the conduct of disciplinary proceedings in private does not contravene the Convention.[19]

Reasons

An Article 6 compliant disciplinary tribunal also has to give reasons for its **17.116** decision.[20] The extent to which reasons need to be given is as yet unclear. In *Selvanathan v. General Medical Council*,[21] the House of Lords referred to the new obligation on the General Medical Council to give reasons and Lord Hope indicated that a general explanation would be required identifying:

(1) the reasons for the finding made; and

(2) the reasons for the imposition, or non-imposition of a penalty.

In *Madan v. General Medical Council*,[22] the Divisional Court held that the reasons given would only be adequate if they informed the recipient of the basis for the decision. In particular, the professional was entitled to know why a submission on his behalf had been rejected.

Privilege against Self-Incrimination

In *R. v. Institute of Chartered Accountants of England and Wales, ex p.* **17.117** *Taher Nawaz*,[23] Sedley J. upheld as a matter of public law the waiver of the privilege against self-incrimination in disciplinary investigations by the taking up of membership of a professional body.[24] Unless professional disciplinary proceedings are held to be the determination of a criminal charge, it is unlikely that such a membership rule would be contrary to the right against self-incrimination in Article 6(1).

Lawyers' Freedom of Expression and Article 10

Whilst Article 10, which protects freedom of expression, permits lawyers to **17.118** comment in public on the administration of justice, such criticism has to be

---

[17] *Gautrin v. France* (1999) 28 E.H.R.R. 196, para.42.
[18] *Le Compte, Van Leuven & De Meyere v. Belgium* (1982) 4 E.H.R.R. 1, para.59.
[19] *ibid.*
[20] See *Ruiz Torija v. Spain* (1995) 19 E.H.R.R. 553; *Georgiadis v. Greece* (1997) 24 E.H.R.R. 606; *Helle v. Finland* (1998) 26 E.H.R.R. 159.
[21] *The Times*, October 26 2000.
[22] [2001] EWHC Admin 577.
[23] [1997] P.N.L.R. 433, *The Times*, November 7, 1996, Sedley J.
[24] Upheld on appeal, unreported, April 25, 1997, CA.

tempered by the need to achieve the right balance between the interests involved, including the public's right to receive information about questions arising from judicial decisions, the requirements of the proper administration of justice and the dignity of the legal profession. Accordingly, the disciplining of a lawyer for criticisms of the judiciary did not violate Article 10 because his statement at a press conference was incompatible with the contribution expected of lawyers towards maintaining public confidence in the judicial authorities: *Schöpfer v. Switzerland.*[25]

Disciplinary Proceedings Based on Convictions

17.119 In *Dr Kailash Shanker Trivedi v. General Medical Council,*[26] the Privy Council held that the suspension of a medical practitioner from practice for a criminal conviction could not be affected by any decision of the Convention.

---

[25] (1998) 4 B.H.R.C. 623 at 631–632, European Court. It is, however, relevant that the European Court relied on the doctrine of margin of appreciation in coming to its decision. This doctrine does not, of itself, apply in domestic courts (see further Chap. 4, above) and so, there is scope for a different decision at the domestic level.
[26] Unreported, November 18, 1996, PC.

CHAPTER 18

Taxation

1. INTRODUCTION

There have been around 240 cases relating to tax before both the Euro- **18.01**
pean Commission on Human Rights ("the Commission") and the European Court of Human Rights ("the European Court") since the Treaty
entered into force on September 3, 1953. Of these cases, around 56 can
be said to have succeeded, which is a surprisingly high success rate of
about 23 per cent.[1] The number of successful cases includes cases where
the European Commission has found a complaint admissible and the
action has been compromised or the matter is proceeding to the European
Court. The European Court has found a breach of the Convention in 23 of
these successful cases (a success rate of around 9 per cent).

Whilst the figures suggest that it will be unusual for a tax case to succeed **18.02**
before the European Court, it is evident that issues relating to tax fall

---

[1] See the invaluable article by Philip Baker "Taxation and the European Convention on
Human Rights" [2000] British Tax Review, which includes a comprehensive survey of the
European Court and European Commission jurisprudence relating to tax.

foursquare within the ambit of the Convention. The scope for relying on Convention rights in disputes with the tax authorities is therefore significant.

18.03   It follows that the HRA has considerable significance for tax law. As tax concerns the state's own money and is a core activity of government, the tax system has a number of features not found in other areas of civil practice, which have the cumulative effect of tipping the balance in favour of the state. For example, the burden of proof in most tax proceedings is on the citizen disputing his tax liability not on the state; the tax authorities are given wide-ranging powers to obtain information and to seize property; retrospective legislation is frequently used to plug a gap in previous legislation or practice to prevent tax leakage. In these areas, and others, there is scope for challenges based on Convention rights.

18.04   It is likely that in the early years of the HRA, tax tribunals will be faced with a raft of challenges based on Convention rights, many unmeritorious. Until the higher courts have established guidelines in the tax field, there will be a period of uncertainty. One of the aims of this chapter is to seek to identify those challenges which have some merit from those which are hopeless.

18.05   In this chapter the relevant Convention Articles for tax purposes will be identified; the effect of the HRA, in relation to the tax authorities and the tax tribunals will be explained and the procedural and substantive effects of the HRA will be examined.

2. THE RELEVANT CONVENTION ARTICLES FOR TAX PURPOSES

The Three Principal Convention Articles Relevant to Tax

18.06   The three principal Articles are: Article 1 of the First Protocol (right to peaceful enjoyment of possessions); Article 14 (freedom from discrimination in the enjoyment of Convention rights) and Article 6 (right to a fair hearing).

18.07   There are also a number of other Convention Articles on which tax challenges have been based with varying degrees of success and ingenuity.

Article 1 of the First Protocol

18.08   This Article consists of three parts. The first part provides that:

> "Every natural or legal person is entitled to the peaceful enjoyment of his possessions."

18.09   It is significant in the field of tax that the right extends not only to individuals, but to legal persons, such as companies.

18.10   There then follow what amount to two permitted interferences with this primary right. The first is that:

> "No one shall be deprived of his possessions except in the public interest and subject to the conditions provided for by law and by the general principles of international law."

The reference to the general principles of international law can be ignored **18.11** for all practical purposes as, somewhat surprisingly, the European Court has held that it has no application between a state and its own nationals.[2] It follows that a state may deprive its nationals of their property in the public interest and subject to the conditions provided for by law.

The second permitted interference is set out in the last paragraph of the **18.12** Article and provides that:

> "The preceding provisions shall not, however, in any way impair the right of a State to enforce such laws as it deems necessary to control the use of property in accordance with the general interest or to secure the payment of taxes or other contributions or penalties".

Accordingly, a state may control the property of a citizen if it deems it **18.13** necessary for the general interest or to secure the payment of taxes or the like. It was argued that "secure" referred only to the collection of tax, not its levying. However, there is no doubt that "secure" includes both the levying and collection of tax.[3]

The European Court has held that these three rules must be read together **18.14** and in particular that the two permitted interferences must be construed in the light of the primary right.[4]

Taxation is within the scope of Article 1 of the First Protocol. The European **18.15** Commission has stated that taxation is in principle an interference with the right guaranteed by the first paragraph of Article 1, but that such interference is justified by the succeeding paragraph.[5]

It follows that a state may impose taxation only if the conditions of the **18.16** permitted interferences with the primary right to enjoyment of possessions are met.

The European Court has held that a state has an extremely wide measure **18.17** of discretion in the levying and collection of tax. The decisions of the state in this area will normally be respected unless there is no reasonable foundation for the state's action.[6] The European Court has observed that the intention of the framers of the Article was to allow states to pass whatever fiscal laws they considered desirable provided that measures in this field did not amount to arbitrary confiscation.[7] Decisions in the area of tax involve economic, political and social questions with which the European Court will not wish to interfere.[8]

In assessing whether a state has infringed the right to enjoyment of **18.18** possessions the European Court will examine the state's actions in the light of the principle of proportionality. In a tax context, the principle requires a fair balance between the protection of the right to enjoyment of

---

[2] *James v. United Kingdom* (1986) 8 E.H.R.R. 123, paras 58–66; and *Lithgow v. United Kingdom* (1986) 8 E.H.R.R., 329, paras 111–119.
[3] *The Building Societies Case* (1998) 25 E.H.R.R. 127
[4] *Lithgow v. United Kingdom* (1986) 8 E.H.R.R. 329, para. 106; and *Tre Traktorer Aktiebolag v. Sweden* (1991) 13 E.H.R.R. 309, para.54.
[5] *D.G. and D.W. Lindsay v. United Kingdom* 49 D.R. 181 at 189.
[6] *Gasus Dosier und Fordertechnik GMBH v. Netherlands* (1995) 20 E.H.R.R. 403, para. 60.
[7] *ibid.*, para. 59.
[8] *Kaira v. Finland,* Application No. 27109/95.

possessions and the public interest in levying and collecting tax.[9] In deciding whether a measure is proportionate, the principal factors are whether the measure in question is "manifestly without reasonable foundation" and to whether it imposes on a citizen an "individual and excessive burden".[10]

18.19 There have been around 65 tax cases based on Article 1 of the First Protocol. Only two have succeeded. Both of these cases were against France. The first, *Lemoine v. France,* Application No. 26242/95, involved the tax authorities taking a charge on nine properties worth around Fr.1 million to guarantee a payment of taxes of around Fr.80,000. Whilst the decision is not fully reported, it is thought that the breach was a lack of proportionality reflected in the disparity between the value of the properties charged and the amount of tax in issue and a lack of adequate judicial supervision. The second, *Hentrich v. France,*[11] concerned a discretionary power which the French tax authorities had to exercise a right of preemption to buy property where a property was sold at less than market value. The European Court held there was a breach of Article 1 of the First Protocol owing to the arbitrary nature of the power and the lack of an adequate procedure to protect the citizen's rights.

Article 14 of the Convention

18.20 Article 14 provides that:

> "The enjoyment of the rights and freedoms set forth in this Convention shall be secured without discrimination on any ground such as sex, race, colour, language, religion, political or other opinion, national or social origin, association with a national minority, property, birth or other status."

18.21 Article 14 is not a free-standing right to non-discrimination. The right only arises where there is discrimination in the "enjoyment of the rights and freedoms set forth in this Convention". Where there is a complaint of discrimination in relation to tax, the Convention right which is being infringed will normally be the right to the peaceful enjoyment of possessions in Article 1 of the First Protocol. Furthermore, the European Court has held that a measure which is otherwise in conformity with the Convention, say with Article 1 of the First Protocol, may nonetheless infringe Article 14 if it is of a discriminatory nature.[12] It follows that there can be a breach of Article 14 in the absence of a breach of any other Convention right.

18.22 The European Court has held that Article 14 applies to the duties imposed on citizens of Contracting States to pay tax and has held a national tax to be discriminatory in its effects and contrary to Article 14.[13]

---

[9] *e.g. Travers v Italy,* 80–B D.R. 5
[10] *ibid.*
[11] (1994) 18 E.H.R.R. 440.
[12] *Belgian Linguistics Case No.2* (1979) 1 E.H.R.R. 252.
[13] *e.g., Darby v. Sweden* (1991) 13 E.H.R.R. 774.

To succeed under Article 14, it is not enough to show that one taxpayer **18.23** rather than another has been taxed, but it must be shown that the provision in question operates to distinguish between *similar* taxpayers on discriminatory grounds.

Further it is not every distinction in treatment which will amount to discrim- **18.24** ination, but only those differences which have no reasonable and objective justification, which is to say that the measure in question does not pursue a legitimate aim and there is no reasonable relationship of proportionality between the means and aim.[14]

In summary: a taxpayer must show that he is in a materially identical **18.25** position to another taxpayer; that he has not been treated in the same manner as another taxpayer in the enjoyment of a Convention right. If he succeeds in that, the burden shifts to the public authority to show that: there is an objective and reasonable justification for the difference in treatment; and, that, any such difference is not disproportionate, in other words that the difference in treatment strikes a fair balance between the protection of the interests of the community and the enjoyment of Convention rights.

Around 49 tax cases have been based on discrimination. Six were suc- **18.26** cessful. In five of those the discrimination was on grounds of gender and one was on grounds of residence.[15] This may give an unfair impression as Article 14 is normally included by applicants as an alternative to another Convention challenge.

Article 6 of the Convention

Article 6(1) provides: **18.27**

> "In the determination of his civil rights and obligations or of any criminal charge against him, everyone is entitled to a fair and public hearing within a reasonable time by an independent and impartial tribunal established by law. Judgment shall be pronounced publicly but the press and public may be excluded from all or part of the trial in the interest of morals, public order or national security in a democratic society, where the interests of juveniles or the protection of the private life of the parties so require, or to the extent strictly necessary in the opinion of the court in special circumstances where publicity would prejudice the interests of justice."

Article 6.2 states that everyone *charged with a criminal offence* shall be **18.28** presumed innocent until proved guilty according to law and Article 6(3) sets out five *minimum* rights which everyone *charged with a criminal offence* shall have.

In considering the application of Article 6, it is necessary to consider **18.29** whether a determination of a person's civil rights and obligations are

---

[14] *ibid.*, para. 31.
[15] The cases are *Darby, above* (residence); *Schmidt v. Germany* (1994) 18 E.H.R.R. 513 (sex discrimination against men); *Van Raalte v. The Netherlands* (1997) 24 E.H.R.R. 503 (sex-men); *Crossland v. United Kingdom,* Application No. 36120/97 (sex-men); *Fielding v. United Kingdom,* Application No. 36940/97 (sex-men); and *MacGregor v. United Kingdom,* Application No. 30548/96 (sex-women).

involved, and further or alternatively whether the determination of a criminal charge is in issue. If a criminal charge is in issue, it is necessary to also consider Article 6(2) and 6(3).

18.30   **Determination of civil rights and obligations.**   There are at least 34 decisions of the European Commission which hold that the concept of civil rights and obligations does not include ordinary tax proceedings[16] and at least two statements from the European Court.[17] Ordinary tax proceedings would include a statutory appeal to the General or Special Commissioners or the VAT and Duties Tribunal against an assessment to tax under the normal statutory appeal rules.

18.31   The ground for the exclusion of ordinary tax proceedings is that tax disputes are in form and substance disputes between the citizen and the state (and hence akin to public law matters) and thus not civil rights and obligations. The sharp distinction between public and private law which exists in many continental European countries (some of which have separate court systems for each type of right) is not mirrored in English law. Accordingly doubts have been raised as to whether this categorisation of rights can or should be followed in English law.

18.32   Furthermore, doubts have been raised on the basis of the background to the drafting of Article 6(1), in particular the *travaux preparatoires*, as to whether it was intended to exclude tax matters.[18] The exclusion of tax matters from the scope of the protection for civil matters given under Article 6 is difficult to justify.

18.33   A tax claim which is not an ordinary tax proceeding should be treated as a determination of civil right and obligation for the purposes of Article 6(1). A claim against the tax authorities for damages or restitution should be treated as a civil claim on the ground that the subject-matter of the claim is pecuniary in nature and is founded on an infringement of pecuniary rights.[19] An application for judicial review of the Revenue will probably be treated as a civil claim as a consequence of succeeding will very probably be the recovery of money.

18.34   The case law of the European Court suggest that tax cases which involve a claim for damages,[20] recovery of overpaid taxes,[21] seizure of property[22] and an action to annul a tax assessment[23] should be treated as the determination of civil rights and obligations. The United Kingdom VAT and Duties Tribunal has held that proceedings resulting from the imposition of a tax penalty involved a determination of the civil rights of a person who had imported hand rolling tobacco for his own use as it affected his right to bring his property into the country.[24]

---

[16] *e.g. X v. France* (1983) 32 D.R. 266. For a full list see Philip Baker, *op. cit.,* Table 3(1).
[17] *Editions Periscope* (1992) 14 E.H.R.R. 597, and *Vidacar SA and Opergroup SL v. Spain,* Application Nos. 41601/98 and 41775/98.
[18] See the discussion in Philip Baker *op. cit.*
[19] *Editions Periscope v. France* (1992) 14 E.H.R.R. 597.
[20] *ibid.*
[21] *DC v. Italy,* Application No. 13120/87; *National and Provincial Building Societies* (1998) 25 E.H.R.R. 127.
[22] *K v. Sweden,* 71 DR 105; *S v. Austria,* Application No. 18778/91; *Basic v. Austria* (1999) 28 E.H.R.R. 118; *Klavedianos v. Greece,* Application No. 38841/97; *Air Canada v. United Kingdom* (1995) 20 E.H.R.R. 150.
[23] *Filippello v. Italy,* Application No. 25564/94.
[24] *Hodgson v. HMCE* (1996) V. & D.R. 200.

Although this distinction between private and public law rights is some-   **18.35**
what confusing, what does seem clear is that whilst a pure tax claim (such
as appealing against a tax assessment) may not be within Article 6(1), a
claim that the Revenue has infringed other rights, such as acting in breach
of statutory duty, acting *ultra vires* or making unlawful demands for money,
will be rights within Article 6(1).

A right to a fair hearing involves access to a court, procedural equality,   **18.36**
judicial process (impartiality and the absence of bias), normally a publicly
declared reasoned decision and determination within a reasonable time.
Whilst there are other aspects of this right, these form the core concepts
of a fair trial. An interference in a person's civil rights will be a breach of
Article 6(1) unless the state can show that the measure complained of is
within its "margin of appreciation", is not disproportionate and is not discriminatory.

The meaning of criminal charge.   Criminal charge has an autono-   **18.37**
mous Convention meaning. Whilst a matter which is treated as criminal for
domestic law purposes will be treated as criminal for the purposes of
Convention law, a matter which is classified as civil by domestic law may
be treated as criminal for Convention purposes.

There are three criteria to be taken into account in determining whether a   **18.38**
penalty is to be categorised as criminal for the purposes of Convention
law[25]:

> (1). The classification of the offence under domestic law—this is only
>   likely to be determinative where the matter is classified as crimi-
>   nal under domestic law;
>
> (2). The nature of the offence. Offences which arise from fraudulent
>   conduct or wilful negligence may well be treated as criminal;
>
> (3). Degree and severity of the penalty which the person committing
>   the offence risked. An offence which gives rise to a risk of
>   imprisonment, or results in an entry in a criminal record is likely
>   to be treated as criminal. A financial penalty which is meant to
>   punish rather than compensate for a loss of tax revenue or
>   interest and which is "tax geared" (where the penalty is a per-
>   centage of the amount of tax avoided or evaded) may well be
>   treated as criminal. The decisions of the European Court and
>   European Commission suggest that a tax geared penalty of 25
>   per cent or more will fall to be treated as criminal.[26] The relevant
>   factor is not the amount of the penalty imposed, but the amount
>   of the penalty risked.

If proceedings do involve the determination of a criminal charge, the   **18.39**
additional guarantees in Article 6(2) and 6(3) apply.

---

[25] *e.g. AP MP and TP v. Switzerland,* Application No. 19958/92.
[26] In *Kovexin SA v. France,* Application No. 32509/96, it was assumed that a 25 per cent
penalty was a criminal charge; 50 per cent penalties were treated as criminal in *Benendoun
v. France* (1994) 18 E.H.R.R. 54 and see the comprehensive survey of the case law in Philip
Baker, *op.cit.*

18.40 Article 6 has been raised in around 160 cases before the European Court and the European Commission and the applicant has succeeded in around 47 (or 30 per cent) of those cases.

Other Convention Articles Raised in Tax Proceedings

18.41 Article 8 right to respect for private and family life Article 8(1) states that:

> "Everyone has the right to respect for his private and family life, his home and his correspondence"

Article 8(2) allows interference with this right if such interference is:

> " . . . in accordance with the law and is necessary in a democratic society in the interests of national security, public safety or the economic well-being of the country, for the prevention of disorder or crime, for the protection of health or morals, or for the protection of the rights and freedoms of others".

18.42 This Article is primarily relevant to tax in respect of the exercise of investigatory powers by the revenue authorities and the obligations on taxpayers to provide information to determine their fiscal liability.

18.43 Article 8 has been raised in 26 cases, and the applicant has succeeded in two. The breach in both cases was a lack of adequate judicial supervision of the powers in issue.[27]

Article 2 right to life; Article 3 prohibition of torture; Article 4 prohibition of slavery and forced labour

18.44 Articles 2 to 4 have no obvious relevance to tax and whilst a small number of cases have relied on them, in none of them has the applicant been successful. Articles 3 and 4 have been raised in connection with obligations to make returns and operate tax withholding systems.[28] Article 2 was raised in a case where it was alleged that an applicant's wife had died consequent upon a visit by the tax authorities.[29]

Article 9 freedom of thought, conscience and religion; Article 12 right to marry

18.45 Article 9 has been raised unsuccessfully in 14 cases. Most of the challenges have involved church taxes or taxpayers objecting to paying a proportion of their income tax on the ground that such proportion is to be used for military expenditure to which they are opposed on grounds of religion and conscience.[30] Article 12 has been relied on unsuccessfully in two cases to challenge national tax provisions which lead to an overall

---

[27] *Funke v. France* (1993) 16 E.H.R.R. 297, and *Huvig v. France* (1990) 12 E.H.R.R. 528.
[28] See, *e.g. W X Y and Z v. Austria*, 7 D.R. 148.
[29] *Józef Lewandowski v. Poland*, Application No. 43457/98.
[30] See, *e.g. C v. United Kingdom*, 37 D.R. 142.

higher burden of tax on married couples than on unmarried couples living together.[31]

3. APPLICATION OF THE HRA TO THE REVENUE AUTHORITIES AND TAX TRIBUNALS

The application of the HRA to the Inland Revenue, Her Majesty's Commissioners of Customs and Excise (referred to together as the "revenue authorities"), and to the General and Special Commissioners and the VAT and Duties Tribunal (referred to together as the "tax tribunals") is examined here.   **18.46**

The Obligation to Interpret

Both the revenue authorities and the tax tribunals are bound by the obligation in section 3(1) of the HRA to interpret all primary and subordinate legislation in a way which is compatible with Convention rights. This applies in respect of all legislation whenever enacted: section 3(2)(a) of the HRA. The approach to interpretation, which the courts were enjoined to adopt during the course of the passage of the HRA through parliament, is to find a possible meaning of the provision which conforms with Convention rights, as opposed to the true meaning of the statute, even if this means doing some violence to the statute.   **18.47**

If the provision in question cannot be interpreted so as to conform with Convention rights, the validity, operation and continued enforcement of primary legislation is not affected: section 3(2)(b) of the HRA. In the case of incompatible subordinate legislation, its validity, operation and continued enforcement is not affected if primary legislation prevents removal of the incompatibility: section 3(2)(c) of the HRA. Incompatible subordinate legislation will be unlawful under section 6(1) of the HRA (as it will have been created in the exercise of an unlawful discretion by a public authority) unless because of the terms of the enabling primary legislation the public authority was constrained to frame the subordinate legislation in a manner incompatible with Convention rights, section 6(2) of the HRA.   **18.48**

Section 2(1)of the HRA sets out the materials which the tax tribunals must take into account in determining a question relating to Convention rights. It is understood that the Lord Chancellor's Department will be issuing guidance notes to tax tribunals and applicants as to the manner in which evidence of Convention law should be given: section 2(3) HRA.   **18.49**

Obligation to Act in a Manner Compatible with Convention Rights

Section 6(1) of the HRA makes it unlawful for a public authority to act in a manner incompatible with a Convention right. The revenue authorities are public authorities within section 6(1) of the HRA. The tax tribunals are included as public authorities as section 6(3) of the HRA states that public authority includes "any court or tribunal".   **18.50**

---

[31] *Hubaux v. Belgium,* Application No. 11088/84; *Lindsay v. United Kingdom,* 49 D.R. 181.

18.51 It follows that the exercise of discretionary powers by the revenue authorities and the tax tribunals must conform with Convention rights.

Remedies which the Tax Tribunals Can Grant for Breach of a Convention Right

18.52 Section 8(1) of the HRA provides that where a court (which includes a tribunal, section 8(6)) finds that an act of a public authority was unlawful by reason of the HRA, the court may:

> "Grant such relief or remedy, or make such order, within its powers as it considers just and appropriate."

Tax tribunals are statutory tribunals and not courts of original jurisdiction. Accordingly they have only the powers granted to them by statute. The role of tax tribunals is in general limited to adjudicating upon assessments. Accordingly they have no power to award damages, restitution or to grant judicial review remedies in respect of a breach of Convention rights or an unlawful act of a public authority.[32]

18.53 The General and Special Commissioners, when determining an appeal in relation to a self-assessment or other assessment, have power to reduce or increase the assessment.[33] It is understood that in a case before the Special Commissioners, the appellant contested an assessment on the ground, *inter alia*, of unreasonable delay on the part of the Inland Revenue contrary to Article 6(1) of the Convention.[34] The problem was to what, if any, remedy the Special Commissioners could grant if they were persuaded that there had been such a breach as such a breach does not affect the *amount* of the tax in issue. The appellant, however, argued that there was an appropriate remedy which they had power to grant. The appellant invited the Special Commissioners to remedy the breach by using their power to vary the assessment by reducing it to nil, notwithstanding that the correct amount of tax was greater than nil. It is understood that the final decision of the Special Commissioners is awaited.

Declaration of Incompatibility

18.54 Tax tribunals have no power to make a declaration of incompatibility pursuant to section 4(2) of the HRA as they fall outside the definition of "court" for these purposes : section 4(5) of the HRA.

Damages for Breach of Convention Rights

18.55 A claim for damages for breach of a Convention right may be made against both the revenue authorities and the tax tribunals. As no damages may be awarded in respect of a judicial act done in good faith,[35] there are unlikely to be many successful claims against the tax tribunals.

---

[32] See also HRA, s.8(2).
[33] Taxes Management Act 1970, s.50(6).
[34] This is on the assumption that Art. 6(1) applies to appeals against tax assessments.
[35] HRA, s.9(3). This limitation does not apply in respect of a claim for compensation for unlawful arrest or detention arising from the Convention, Art. 5(5).

4. APPLICATION OF THE HRA TO DIRECT TAX MATTERS

In this section the areas of direct tax (being income tax, capital gains tax, corporation tax, inheritance tax) where the HRA is likely to be relevant are identified. Where the case law of the European Court and European Commission suggests that a particular type of challenge to a national tax system is likely to fail, the equivalent United Kingdom provision is referred to in order to identify what are likely to be hopeless challenges. The approach adopted is to examine first the procedural aspects of the direct tax system, being the mechanics of assessment, disclosure obligations, and appeals where it may be alleged that there is a conflict with Convention rights; and secondly, to examine a number of substantive areas of direct tax which may be incompatible with Convention rights.

18.56

Direct Tax—Procedure

Obligation to make a return

Fundamental to the operation of the United Kingdom tax system both for individuals and companies is the obligation to make a return of income and gains in order to determine tax liability. Linked to this obligation is the requirement to hold and retain records which substantiate the return. These obligations are particularly central given that both companies and individuals now self-assess their tax liability. For individuals, partnerships, trustees and companies outside the charge to corporation tax the relevant statutory provisions are in sections 7 to 12B of the Taxes Management Act 1970, and for companies within the charge to corporation tax in Schedule 18 of the Finance Act 1998.

18.57

The European Court has recognised that a state is entitled to oblige a person to supply the information necessary to determine that person's tax liability and to investigate that person's tax affairs.[36] Whilst this may amount to an interference with a person's right to private life under Article 8, it will normally be excused by Article 8(2) provided the interference is in accordance with law and necessary in the public interest.

18.58

Accordingly, there is no basis for challenging the obligation to make a return of income and profits on the basis of Article 8.

18.59

It is conceivable that a taxpayer might rely on Article 4 (prohibition of slavery and forced labour) to challenge the obligation to make a return. Any such challenge would fail on the ground that the obligation to make a return does not fall within the definition of "forced or compulsory labour", or even if it does is removed from the definition on the ground that the obligation falls within Article 4(3)(d) as being "any work or service which forms part of normal civic obligations".

18.60

Support for this conclusion may be drawn from the decision of the European Commission in *Companies W, X, Y and Z v. Austria*[37] where the applicants alleged that obligations imposed on them to account for tax on their employees' wages breached Article 4. Their applications were found

18.61

---

[36] See, *e.g. Funke, Mailhe and Crémieux v. France* (1993) 16 E.H.R.R. 297.
[37] 7 DR 148

to be inadmissible as, whether or not the obligation amounted to "forced or compulsory labour", the obligations were within Article 4(3)(d).[38]

18.62 In the light of this decision, the obligations imposed on United Kingdom. employers to account for their employees' tax and national insurance by deduction at source[39] will not breach Article 4.

Information powers

18.63 The Revenue's powers to gather documents and information are, as one would expect, wide ranging. The broadest and most controversial powers are those in section 20 to section 20D of theTaxes Management Act 1970 ("TMA 1970"). Aspects of these powers have been challenged on the ground of Convention rights even before HRA came into force.[40]

18.64 Section 20 of the TMA 1970 contains three distinct powers:

(1) Section 20(1) confers power on an inspector to issue a notice requiring a person to deliver documents which, in the inspector's reasonable opinion, contain or may contain information relevant to any tax liability to which the person is subject or the amount any such tax liability. The inspector must obtain the consent of a General or Special Commissioner to issue such a notice: section 20(7) of the TMA 1970. The person concerned must have been given a reasonable opportunity to provide the documents or information in question and the inspector must give the taxpayer concerned a written summary of his reasons for applying for the notice: section 20(8E) and section 20B(1) This does not apply to documents held by the recipient relating to the conduct of any pending appeal by him : section 20B(2).

(2) Section 20(2) confers power on the Board of Inland Revenue to issue a notice requiring a person to deliver documents or furnish information relevant to his tax liability or to the amount of it. The Board does not require the consent of a General or Special Commissioner to issue such a notice, but must have reasonable grounds for believing the person has failed to comply with tax law and that such failure has led or is likely to lead to serious prejudice to the proper assessment or collection of tax.[41]

(3) Section 20(3) is perhaps the most controversial power. It confers power on an inspector inquiring into the tax liability of any person ("the taxpayer"), power to issue a notice to another person to deliver such documents as may contain information relevant to any tax liability (or amount of any such liability) to which the taxpayer is or may have been subject.[42] The inspector requires the consent of a General or Special Commissioner to issue such

---

[38] See also *Borghini v. Italy,* Application No. 21568/93.

[39] Under the Income and Corporation Taxes Act 1988, ss 203 *et seq.*

[40] See *Applicant v. Inspector of Taxes* [1999] S.T.C., (SCD) 128.

[41] TMA 1970, s.20(7A).

[42] See *R. v. IRC, ex p. Banque Internationale a Luxembourg SA* [2000] S.T.I. 919, where the exercise of this power was unsuccessfully challenged under Art. 8 as the exercise was justified as being in pursuit of a legitimate aim and necessary in a democratic society for protecting the taxation system and revenue.

a notice, should give the recipient written reasons, and should normally identify the taxpayer (unless various conditions are met). The recipient of such a notice is entitled to object on the ground that it would be onerous to comply with the notice, in which case the matter is to be resolved by the Special Commissioners (section 20(8B)). This does not apply to documents relating to the conduct of a pending appeal by the taxpayer: section 20B(2).

Save for the right to object on the ground that compliance with a section   **18.65**
20(3) TMA 1970 notice would be onerous, there is no right of appeal from the decision of an inspector to issue, or from the decision of a Special or General Commissioner to consent to the issue, of a notice under section 20(1). Judicial review would in principle be available in respect of such decisions, but to succeed the taxpayer would have to establish that the decision in question was "wholly unreasonable" or otherwise perverse in public law terms and there would not be a review of the decision on the merits. Where a penalty is imposed for failure to comply with a section 20(1) notice, there is a right of appeal and it is accepted that on any such appeal the validity of the notice issued may be called in question.[43]

Whilst a taxpayer will normally know that a section 20 application is to be   **18.66**
made by an inspector, he has no right to attend the hearing at which the inspector seeks the consent of a General or Special Commissioner to the issue of a notice.[44]

The other material feature of section 20(1) to (3) notices, is that there is no   **18.67**
exception from disclosure of material which would ordinarily qualify for legal professional privilege save where the privileged documents are held by a barrister, advocate or solicitor (there is also some protection for documents held by auditors or tax advisers), section 20B(8) to (9). It follows that there is no exception to disclosure of what would in ordinary civil litigation be legally privileged documents, such as notes of advice or Counsel's Opinion as to the tax analysis of a transaction and its vulnerability to challenge, where those documents are held by a taxpayer and not that taxpayer's legal advisers or accountants.[45] Whilst it is arguable that documents containing a lawyer's opinion as to the tax effects of a particular transaction cannot be information relevant to the determination of a tax liability within section 20(1) to (3), the Revenue have pressed for disclosure of such documents, *inter alia*, on the basis that the application of many anti-avoidance provisions turns on a taxpayer's purpose in entering into a transaction and such documents may evidence that purpose.

Sections 20BA (introduced by the Finance Act 2000) allows the Revenue,   **18.68**
with the approval of a Circuit judge, to issue an order for the delivery of documents and is designed for use in cases where serious fraud is involved. A proposed subject of the notice is entitled to notice of and to attend the consent hearing. There is a saving for any item to which legal professional privilege attaches. Section 20C provides for the obtaining of

---

[43] See *Taxpayer v. Inspector of Taxes* (1996) S.T.C. (SCD) 2261 at 264, para.9.
[44] *Taxpayer v. Inspector of Taxes* (1996) S.T.C. (SCD) 2261; and *Applicant v. Inspector of Taxes* (1999) S.T.C. (SCD) 128.
[45] See *Applicant v. Inspector of Taxes* (1999) S.T.C. (SCD) 128.

search and seizure warrants by the Revenue. Only the section 20(1) to (3) information powers are examined in detail here.

18.69   There are a number of issues as to the compatibility of the section 20 TMA 1970 powers and Convention rights.

Should the consent hearing under section 20(1) and (3) be with both parties present?

18.70   If the issue of a section 20 notice and the application for the consent of a General or Special Commissioner to its issue amounts to the determination of a civil right of obligation within Article 6(1), then the right to a fair hearing would normally require that the taxpayer be entitled to be present. The cases[46] in which it has been argued unsuccessfully that the hearing should be in the presence of both parties all predate the implementation of the HRA and can no longer be regarded as good authority.

18.71   The normal objection that Article 6(1) does not apply to tax proceedings is not a definitive answer as the section 20 powers are normally exercised outside the context of an appeal against an assessment. In so far as the issue of a notice imposes an obligation on a person to deliver documents and furnish information and results in a liability to a penalty if not complied with, it would seem to involve the imposition of a civil obligation.

18.72   Whilst many administrative decisions impose civil obligations on persons, the right to a fair trial is normally satisfied not by a right to be present at the making of a decision, but by the person having an effective right of appeal against the decision. The question is then whether the consent hearing before the General or Special Commissioners is characterised as merely a part of the administrative machinery by which the decision to issue a notice is made (in which case the emphasis would be on whether the taxpayer had an effective right of appeal) or as a judicial hearing (in which case one would expect the taxpayer to have the right to be present).[47]

18.73   United Kingdom authority suggests that the role of the General or Special Commissioners is more akin to that of a monitor of an administrative decision making process than a judicial one. In this context the General or Special Commissioners act as part of the administrative machinery rather than as a judicial body adjudicating on its lawfulness.[48] This limited administrative role may be a residue of the formerly far more extensive administrative functions of the General Commissioners who once formed part of the Revenue. If this analysis is correct, then a satisfaction of a taxpayer's Article 6(1) right would be in a right to an adequate review or appeal of the decision to issue a notice rather than a right to be present at the consent hearing. This analysis may however not be followed for the purposes of Convention law. The General and Special Commissioners are a judicial body, fully integrated into the judicial structure and do not form part of the administration.[49] Their role in section 20 proceedings can only be to

---

[46] Being *Taxpayer v. Inspector of Taxes* [1996] S.T.C. (SCD) 2261, and *Applicant v. Inspector of Taxes* [1999] S.T.C.(SCD) 128.

[47] See *Albert Le Compte v. Belgium* (1983) 5 E.H.R.R. 533, and *Bryan v. United Kingdom* (1996) E.H.R.R. 342.

[48] See *R. v. I.R.C., ex p. Coombs* (1991) S.T.C. 97 at 110, per Lord Lowry cited with approval in *Taxpayer v. Inspector of Taxes* (1996) S.T.C. 261 at 264.

[49] *cf. De Cubber v. Belgium* (1984) 7 E.H.R.R. 236.

protect the interests of the taxpayer where an Inspector wishes to issue a section 20 notice. Given that, as discussed below, there is no formal appeal procedure against the issue of a notice and hence little scope for challenge, the hearing before the General or Special Commissioner is particularly important for the protection of the taxpayer and this consideration suggests that it should be characterised as judicial and not administrative. Notwithstanding these considerations, the Court of Appeal has held that the HRA does not give rise to any right to an oral hearing.[49A]

As the Board of the Inland Revenue may issue as section 20(2) notice **18.74** without the consent of a General or Special Commissioner, the question of a right to an *inter partes* hearing does not arise. As an administrative process, Article 6(1) should be satisfied if there is an adequate right of appeal from the decision.

Is there an adequate right of appeal or review of a decision to issue a section 20(1) to (3) notice?

There is no right of appeal against the issue of a section 20(1) to (3) notice. **18.75** Whilst it may be suggested that there is in effect a right of appeal in that the validity of the notice may be questioned in an appeal against a penalty imposed for non-compliance, this is unlikely to be regarded as an adequate remedy given that a person has to expose himself to a risk of penalties by non-compliance with the notice to exercise it.

There is a right to judicial review of a decision to issue a section 20 notice. **18.76** However, there must be serious doubts as to whether a right to take lengthy and expensive judicial review proceedings is an adequate remedy, particularly given that such proceedings will not involve any decision on the merits, but will merely examine the procedural regularity of the decision, not whether it is the right decision on the facts. In *Hodgson v. H.M. Customs and Excise*[50] the Tribunal did not consider that a right to challenge a penalty, in respect of an importation of hand-rolling tobacco, by way of judicial review was an adequate remedy for Article 6(1) purposes.

If there is a breach of Article 6(1), can it be justified? Whilst procedural **18.77** restrictions on the right of access to a court are allowed (and indeed are a fundamental part of any legal system), the restrictions must not be such as to destroy entirely the right protected by Article 6.[51] This raises difficult questions where there is no right of appeal on the merits, but a right to judicial review. The United Kingdom. would need to put forward some principled justification for the restriction on the right to a fair hearing.

If the absence of a right to be present at a section 20(1) and (3) consent **18.78** hearing, the absence of any consent requirement for a section 20(2) notice, and the absence of an effective appeal mechanism amount to an unjustifiable breach of Article 6(1), what are the consequences?

So far as section 20(1) and section 20(3) hearings are concerned, it may **18.79** be contended that the General or Special Commissioner has an inherent jurisdiction to order his own conduct and should, in accordance with the

---

[49A] *Morgan Grenfell & Co's Application* [2001] S.T.C. 497.
[50] [1996] V.&.D.R. 200.
[51] See *Stubbings v. United Kingdom* (1997) 23 E.H.R.R. 213.

duty imposed by section 6(1) of the HRA on public authorities to act in accord with Convention rights, allow a taxpayer to be present at the consent hearing.

18.80 The position is more difficult as regards section 20(2) notices issued by the Board which do not require consent. A taxpayer might contend in penalty proceedings for failure to comply that the absence of a right to a fair trial in respect of the issue of a section 20(2) notice, means that no penalty should be upheld by the General or Special Commissioners as this is the only way in which his Convention rights can be protected. Further, or alternatively, a decision to issue a notice by the Board in circumstances where there is a breach of Article 6(1) by reason of no adequate appeal or review, may mean that any such decision is unlawful given the duty on public authorities under section 6(1) to act in a manner compatible with Convention rights. The procedural remedy would be by way of judicial review and/or perhaps by raising the unlawfulness of the issue of the notice in penalty proceedings for non-compliance.

Absence of protection for legal professional privilege

18.81 There is a serious anomaly between the section 20 powers and the section 20BA power to demand the delivery of documents and the section 20CC power (as amended by the Finance Act 2000) to obtain a search warrant, in that under the latter two sections there is an express saving for documents benefiting from legal professional privilege in any person's hands, whereas under section 20 there is a saving only in respect of such documents held by the lawyer and not by the client. The question is why is protection of disclosure of legally privileged documents given in the case of section 20BA and section 20CC cases and not in the case of section 20 notices?

18.82 The assertion, confirmed by the Special Commissioners,[52] that under section 20 of the TMA 1970 the Revenue are entitled to require disclosure of confidential communications relating to legal advice between lawyer and client is extraordinary. It has, however, post the enactment of the HRA been upheld by the Court of Appeal which considered that it was Parliament's manifest intent that legal privilege should yield to the statutory disclosure scheme.[52A] There may, however, for the reasons discussed below, be scope for further argument on the point but any such argument would now have to be conducted in the House of Lords or the ECtHR.

18.83 It is well established as a matter of Convention law that equality of arms is a central and inherent element of a fair trial. Each party must be:

"... afforded a reasonable opportunity to present his case—including his evidence—under conditions that do not place him at a substantial disadvantage vis-à-vis his opponent"[53]

18.84 A requirement to disclose legally privileged material even where the obligation to disclose may arise well before an actual trial in which that

---

[52] See *Applicant v. Inspector of Taxes* (1999) S.T.C. (SCD) 128.
[52A] *Morgan Grenfell & Co's Application* [2001] S.T.C. 497.
[53] *Dombo Beheer B.V. v. Netherlands* (1994) 18 E.H.R.R. 213, para. 33; and see also Keir Starmer "*European Human Rights Law*" Legal Action Group 1999, para. 13.54.

material is used, puts the disclosing party at a severe disadvantage to the other party. The other party is enabled to look over his shoulder and to benefit from the advice which the disclosing party has obtained (and paid for).

There is however doubt as to whether Article 6(1) would apply as the material is being sought to determine a tax liability, which, much of the case law suggests, is not a civil right or obligation.[54] **18.85**

Even if Article 6.1 is not engaged, Article 8 should afford protection from an obligation to disclose privileged material. Article 8 provides a right to respect for private and family life, home and correspondence. It covers business and professional activities.[55] Whilst there is no case directly on the point, the European Court has given considerable importance to the right to confidential communications between lawyer and client in rejecting attempts by states to justify an interference under Article 8(2), thus prisoners are allowed confidential communications with their legal advisers.[56] **18.86**

If the absence of a right to non-disclosure of privileged material under section 20 TMA 1970 notices is a breach of Article 8(1), it will be particularly difficult for the United Kingdom to justify the interference given that such protection is given under section 20BA and section 20CC of the TMA 1970.[57] **18.87**

Where a disclosure of documents may reveal evidence of a criminal offence

Whilst there is a debate about whether Article 6(1) applies to civil tax proceedings, there is no doubt that if the proceedings involve the determination of a criminal charge, Article 6 applies with full force. **18.88**

It may often be the case that documents or information required to be disclosed pursuant to section 20 of the TMA 1970 notices may evidence the commission of a criminal offence by the taxpayer or liability to a penalty which is criminal for the purposes of Convention law. In such circumstances may a taxpayer refuse to disclose documents or information on the ground that it may incriminate him (the right against self-incrimination being an Article 6 guarantee in a criminal context)? **18.89**

The answer appears to be "No" in the case of ordinary tax investigations, but "Yes" if the purpose of the requirement is primarily to force a taxpayer to incriminate himself by producing incriminating documents. **18.90**

In *Abas v. The Netherlands*,[58] the European Commission rejected as inadmissible a claim by a taxpayer that the use in a subsequent criminal prosecution of a statement obtained from him by a tax inspector where the taxpayer was legally obliged to provide the information breach his right against self-incrimination. The European Commission said it was necessary to look at the entirety of the domestic proceedings. It found that the functions performed by the inspector were essentially investigative in **18.91**

---

[54] See paras 18.30–18.32, above.
[55] *Silver v. U.K.* (1983) 5 E.H.R.R. 347; *Campbell v. U.K.* (1992) E.H.R.R. 137; *Niemitz v. Germany* (1993) 16 E.H.R.R. 97
[56] See *Golder v. United Kingdom* (1975) 1 E.H.R.R. 524, and Lester & Pannick "*Human Rights Law and Practice*" (Butterworths) paras 4.8.43f.
[57] cf. *General Mediterranean Holdings v. Patel* [2000] 1 W.L.R. 272.
[58] 88-B D.R. 120.

nature. His purpose was to ascertain and record facts for fiscal purposes and not in order to determine the taxpayer's criminal liability, even though the results of his investigation might be used in criminal proceedings. The European Commission went on to say that a requirement that a tax inspector should, in the course of an ordinary tax investigation, be subject to the guarantees of a judicial procedure would:

" . . . unduly hamper the effective functioning in the public interest of the activities of fiscal authorities . . . ".

18.92   On the other hand in *Funke v. France*,[59] French Customs officers searched the taxpayer's house, seized documents and required the taxpayer to produce copies of his overseas bank statements, he refused and was fined and convicted for failing to do so. The European Court upheld the taxpayer's complaint and stated that Customs had secured the taxpayer's conviction in order to obtain documents which they believed must exist, although they were not certain. They could have sought the documents by other means, but instead attempted to compel the taxpayer to produce evidence of offences he had allegedly committed. This amounted to an infringement of his right to remain silent and his right against self-incrimination.

18.93   In *Abas* and *Funke*, an important factor in the European Court's reasoning appears to have been when it could be said that criminal proceedings against the taxpayer had begun for the purposes of Article 6. In *Abas*, the information in question had been disclosed in the course of an investigation into fiscal liability without there necessarily being any question of criminal proceedings and before the taxpayer had been "substantially affected" by any criminal proceedings. In *Funke* the European Court was of the view that the information was being sought to facilitate a criminal conviction.

Appeals to the General and Special Commissioners

Does Article 6(1) apply to hearings before the General and Special Commissioners?

18.94   It is necessary to consider the various types of hearings with which the General and Special Commissioners deal.

Appeals in respect of assessments to income, capital gains and corporation tax

18.95   As discussed at paragraphs [18.03–18.32] above, there is a substantial body of decisions of the European Commission and a few decisions of the European Court which hold that ordinary tax proceedings are not civil rights and obligations. In the United Kingdom. the phrase "ordinary tax proceedings" would almost certainly cover appeals against assessments. As discussed at paragraph [18.32] above, there are some grounds for challenging this proposition and this will be one of the early points for decision by the higher courts.

---

[59] (1993) 16 E.H.R.R. 297

Appeals in respect of social security

Since April 1, 1999 the General and Special Commissioners have had **18.96** jurisdiction over appeals against decisions of the Board of Inland Revenue in respect of various social security matters including liability to national insurance contributions.[60]

There is a substantial body of case law which suggests that entitlement to **18.97** welfare payments is a civil right or obligation within Article 6(1),[61] the basis for this conclusion being that such payments are intimately related to the means of subsistence of the individual. As regards the payment of national insurance contributions, the issue is not so clear. The payment of contributions under a compulsory social insurance scheme administered by the state, where there may be no clear link between payments into the scheme and entitlement to a particular benefit or amount of benefit has a number of "public" features. However in *Schouten and Meldrum v. Netherlands*,[62] the applicant complained of unreasonable delay in the determination of his liability to pay Dutch social security contributions. The European Court approached the question by seeking to identify the public and private law aspects of the scheme and then balancing them against each other. On balance the European Court decided that the determination of civil rights and obligations was in issue.

Whilst it remains a matter for decision, it is highly likely that the United **18.98** Kingdom system of compulsory social insurance will be characterised as involving the determination of civil rights and obligations. If so, then Article 6(1) will apply in appeals involving national insurance contributions.

The result would be an indefensible distinction between national insur- **18.99** ance and tax appeals before the General and Special Commissioners, in the former there would be right to a fair trial under Article 6(1), but not in the latter.

Appeal against interest

An appeal against an interest determination should follow the treatment of **18.100** the underlying matter on which it is assessed, so that if it is imposed for late payment of tax, it will probably be treated as outside the scope of Article 6(1). Interest on late payment of tax at commercial rates or at a reasonable rate above should not be characterised as criminal for Article 6 purposes.[63]

Appeals against penalties

In so far as an appeal against a penalty is imposed in relation to the **18.101** determination of a person's tax liability, its characterisation for Article 6(1) purposes should follow that of the underlying tax proceeding to which it relates. If, however, a tax penalty can be characterised as imposed for

---

[60] See Social Security (Transfer of Functions, etc.) Act 1999 and Social Security (Transfer of Functions, etc.) Act 1999 (Commencement No. 1 and Transitional Provisions) Order 1999, S.I. 1999 No. 527.
[61] See, *e.g. Feldbrugge v. Netherlands* (1986) 8 E.H.R.R. 425, and *Schuler-Zgaggen v. Switzerland* (1993) 16 E.H.R.R. 405.
[62] (1994) 19 E.H.R.R. 432.
[63] *Riener v. Bulgaria*, Application No. 28411/95.

something other than a matter relating to the determination of a person's liability to tax, which can be described as a civil obligation, then an appeal against such a penalty may be within Article 6(1). An example of this is *Hodgson* [64] where a penalty imposed on a person for importing tobacco was held to relate to a person's right to bring his goods into the country and hence fell within Article 6(1).

18.102   The more significant question with regard to penalties is whether they involve a criminal charge and so merit the full protection of Article 6. The meaning of criminal for Convention law purposes has been discussed above at paragraph [18.38]. The conclusion reached there was that tax-geared penalties (where the amount of the penalty is a percentage of the underlying tax involved) which might exceed 25 per cent would almost certainly be classified as criminal for Convention law purposes.

18.103   Under the United Kingdom direct tax system, there are two principal types of penalty. Fixed penalties of a relatively modest amount normally imposed automatically for breach of a procedural requirement, such as late submission of a tax return[65]; and tax-geared penalties in which the penalty may be up to 100 per cent of the underlying tax involved.

18.104   All tax-geared penalties are discretionary and the Revenue has an over-riding power to mitigate any penalty.[66] It is not the amount of the actual penalty imposed, but the maximum amount of the penalty which could have been imposed, which is determinative of civil/criminal character-isation for Convention purposes. For this reason, all of the United King-dom's tax-geared penalties are criminal for the purposes of Article 6.[66A]

18.105   There is thus a further disparity in the application of Article 6 to proceed-ings before the General or Special Commissioners. Article 6 does not apply at all to ordinary tax appeals; Article 6(1) will probably apply to national insurance appeals and to penalties which can be characterised as relating to another protected Convention right; and Article 6 will apply in its entirety to appeals against tax-geared penalties.

Appeal against assessment and tax-geared penalty heard together

18.106   It is frequently the case that an appeal against an assessment to tax and against a penalty determination in respect of non-disclosure of matters relating to the determination of that liability or in respect of non-payment of the tax, will be heard together. This give rise to practical problems if Article 6 is inapplicable to the appeal in so far as it relates to the assessment, but applicable in its full rigour to the appeal against the penalty as a criminal charge. Normally the determination of the underlying assessment will be a precondition of deciding on the appeal against the penalty.

18.107   If the two appeals are heard together, then Article 6 should apply to the entire proceedings, as the determination of the penalty appeal will overlap

---

[64] (1996) V. & D.R. 200.
[65] See, *e.g.* TMA 1970, s.93.
[66] TMA 1970, s.102. The basis on which the Revenue will mitigate penalties is set out in the leaflet IR 73.
[66A] See *King v. Walden* [2001] S.T.C. 822 and compare *Han & Yau and Others v. Commis-sioners of Customs and Excise*, Court of Appeal, July 3, 2001 (on appeal from the VAT and Duties Tribunal [2000] V & DR 312) as to VAT civil evasion penalties.

on many factual issues with the assessment appeal. If the two appeals are heard separately, even if by different panels, it is unsatisfactory to assert that Article 6 will not apply in the appeal against the assessment, but will apply in the appeal against the penalty as the appeal against the assessment will in many respects be determinative of the penalty appeal. If, for example, as a result of the application of Article 6 certain types of evidence are not admissible in then penalty appeal, should such evidence be admissible in the appeal against the assessment, in so far as the determination of the assessment may determine issues which are fundamental to the penalty determination? The answer would seem to be that Article 6 will apply to the appeal against the assessment in so far as issues determined in such appeal affect the appeal against the penalty.[66B]

Practical Consequences for Hearings before the General and Special Commissioners if Article 6(1) or Article 6 in its Entirety Applies[67]

Unreasonable delay

Article 6 guarantees the right to a fair hearing within a reasonable time. There have been around 43 cases where a taxpayer has alleged a breach of Article 6 on this ground and 28 have been successful. In determining what period of time amounts to unreasonable delay, the European Court considers the complexity of the case, the conduct of the parties and the importance of the matter to the applicant. As a rule of thumb, five years is the watershed, periods of delay less than five years are likely to be acceptable and periods in excess are more likely to constitute a breach. The period of time runs in a civil case from the initiation of court proceedings to the final resolution of the dispute (including appeals); and, in a criminal case, from the time at which a person is charged or substantially affected by criminal proceedings. **18.108**

In most tax cases, court proceedings will be initiated by the taxpayer entering a notice of appeal, which is normally required to be given in writing within 30 days of the issue of the assessment or self-assessment amendment.[68] What frequently follows is a period of correspondence and negotiation. If the Revenue fails to respond or to take any steps towards listing the matter for hearing within a reasonable period, this may constitute a relevant delay. If this delay continues for around five years, the taxpayer may be able to argue that there has been a breach of Article 6 and that the Revenue should not take any further steps or that the Special or General Commissioners should simply allow the appeal without a hearing in order to protect the taxpayer's Article 6 rights. There is a suggestion in the case law that where a period of delay is reflected in a reduction, for example, of a penalty, there will be no Article 6 breach. A taxpayer may therefore argue that where there has been unreasonable **18.109**

[66B] *Georgiou and Another (trading as Marios Chippery) v. United Kingdom* Application No. 40042/98 [2001] S.T.C. 80.
[67] For a detailed treatment of Art. 6, see Lester & Pannick, Keir Starmer, *op. cit.*, and for a survey of the case law in so far as it relates to tax, see Philip Baker, *op cit.*
[68] Taxes Management Act 1970, s. 31.

delay, the Tax Commissioners should reduce the amount of the assessment or penalty concerned to reflect the delay.

18.110   However, given that a taxpayer, in most appeal proceedings before the General and Special Commissioners, can serve a notice on the clerk that he wishes a date for a hearing to be fixed,[69] it may be difficult for a taxpayer to show that he does not also share responsibility for the delay.

Public hearing

18.111   Article 6 guarantees the right to a public hearing. Hearings before the General Commissioners are in private and those before the Special Commissioners are normally in public, although an application can be made for the hearing to be in private.[70] If Article 6 applies to an appeal or other hearing before the General Commissioners, an applicant should be able to insist that the hearing is held in public. The General Commissioners (Jurisdiction and Procedure) Regulations 1994 (S.I. 1994 No. 1812) which stipulate that the proceedings should be held in private, are secondary legislation and in so far as they conflict with Convention rights are *ultra vires* as there is no requirement in the enabling legislation that such hearing should be in private.[71]

Legal aid

18.112   In the determination of a criminal charge, Article 6(3)(c) guarantees the right to a person to defend himself in person, or through legal assistance of his own choosing or "if he has not sufficient means to pay for legal assistance, to be given it free when the interests of justice so require". It follows that in tax proceedings where a "criminal" charge is involved, such as appeals against tax-geared penalties, the taxpayer has a *prima facie* right to legal aid subject to his financial circumstances. There is at present no right to legal aid in proceedings before tax tribunals, although it is understood that this is a matter which the Lord Chancellor's Department is considering.

Quality of evidence and burden of proof

18.113   Strict rules of evidence do not apply in proceedings before the Tax Commissioners. The Tax Commissioners may hear any evidence and in assessing its truth and weight may take account of its nature and source.[72] In practice this frequently means that all and any evidence is admitted including statements from anonymous informants, not present for cross-examination. Whilst the European Court has not laid down any specific

---

[69] Para. 3(1) of the General Commissioners (Jurisdiction and Procedure) Regulations 1994, S.I. 1994 No. 1812 and of the Special Commissioners (Jurisdiction and Procedure) Regulations 1994, S.I. 1994 No. 1811.

[70] General Commissioners (Jurisdiction and Procedure) Regulations 1994, S.I. 1994 No. 1812, para. 13(1); Special Commissioners (Jurisdiction and Procedure) Regulations 1994, S.I. 1994 No. 1811, para.15.

[71] The enabling legislation is Taxes Management Act 1970, s.46A and s.56B; and see HRA, s.6.

[72] See the Special Commissioners Regulations, *op. cit*, para. 15, and the Special Commissioners Regulations, *op. cit.*, para. 17.

requirements for the standard of evidence where Article 6 applies, in view of the general requirement of a fair trial it is thought that the taxpayer should have the opportunity to challenge any evidence put forward by the Revenue. In practical terms that would mean the opportunity to cross-examine any witness of fact led by the Revenue. Where, as in an appeal against a tax-geared penalty, Article 6 applies on the ground that the appeal involves the determination of a criminal matter under Convention law, the issue has arisen as to whether domestic criminal rules of evidence apply. There has been no definitive decision on this issue as yet although one member of the Court of Appeal has stated that:

> "It by no means follows from a conclusion that Article 6 applies that civil penalty proceedings are, for other domestic purposes, to be regarded as criminal and, therefore subject to those provision [sic] of PACE [the Police and Criminal Evidence Act 1984] and/or the Codes produced thereunder, which relate to the investigation of crime and the conduct of criminal proceedings as *defined by English law*".[72A]

The burden of proof in most tax appeals lies on the appellant. It is not thought that there is necessarily incompatible with Article 6 provided the burden is not treated in practice by the Tax Commissioners as insuperable. **18.114**

The role of the clerk to the General Commissioners

Unlike the Special Commissioners, a panel of General Commissioners will not normally include a qualified lawyer. For legal assistance the General Commissioners in practice rely heavily on their clerk, who is normally a solicitor. Normally once the parties have concluded their submissions, the General Commissioners will retire with their clerk. The clerk may offer his opinion on legal matters to the General Commissioners in the absence of the parties, who do not know what the Clerk has said about the law and who have no opportunity to comment on his views on the law. Whilst many appeals raise pure questions of fact, clerks may give advice to Commissioners as to how they should determine whether the taxpayer has discharged the legal burden of proof which lies on the taxpayer to discharge the assessment. **18.115**

A underlying principle of Article 6 is equality of arms, each party should have an equal opportunity to present its case and comment on the other party's submissions. A particular feature of this principle is the right to an adversarial hearing. In substance this means the right to know of and to comment upon the evidence adduced by and the legal submissions made by others. This principle appears to extend beyond the acts of the parties **18.116**

[72A] *Han & Yau v. Commissioners of Customs and Excise*, Court of Appeal, July 3, 2001 (on appeal from the VAT and Duties Tribunal [2000] V & DR 312) Potter L.J. at para. 84, but compare the decision of the VAT and Duties Tribunal in *John Lucas Murrell v. Commissioners of Customs and Excise* LON/99/121, where interviews were excluded where no sufficient caution was given. Compare also the decision of the VAT and Duties Tribunal in *Wing Lee Carry Out v. Commissioners of Customs and Excise* [2001] S.T.I. 840 where the position as to admissibility of evidence was said to be different under Scottish law.

and to include submissions made by others which may influence the tribunal's decision.[73]

18.117   It follows that the parties should know of any advice which the clerk gives which could be said to in fact or be capable of influencing the tribunal's decision and should have the opportunity to comment upon it or in complex cases to have advance knowledge of it.

Reasons

18.118   Article 6 requires that the court or tribunal concerned gives reasons for its decision.[74] At the end of a hearing, the General Commissioners normally simply confirm or amend the assessment, and will not give detailed reasons unless the appellant requests a case to be stated for the opinion of the High Court.[75] The party requesting the case must pay a fee of £25 on requesting a case.[76] If Article 6 applies, the General Commissioners would be obliged to provide reasons whether or not a case is requested.

Direct Tax—Substance

18.119   This section considers the substantive areas of direct tax where there may be a conflict with Convention rights. The areas are organised under the principal Convention right under which a challenge is likely to arise (although it should be borne in mind that any challenge will normally rely on multiple Convention rights).

Discrimination—Article 14

18.120   **Gender.** Discrimination on grounds of gender is obviously contrary to Article 14, and whilst such discrimination is subject to a justification defence, a very clear objective justification and demonstration of proportionality would be required.[77]

18.121   There are a small number of provisions of direct tax law in the United Kingdom which are overtly discriminatory on grounds of gender, although most have been amended or are transitional provisions which are effectively being phased out with the passage of time. These provisions are those which use a particular definition of "dependant relative", where a dependant relative means:

> "in relation to any person, a relative of his, or of his spouse, who is incapacitated by old age or infirmity from maintaining himself, or the mother of that person, or of his spouse, if the mother is widowed or living apart from her husband, or, in consequence of dissolution or annulment of marriage, a single woman"

---

[73] See Keir Starmer, paras. 13.55–58; see also *Ruiz - Mateos v. Spain* (1993) 16 E.H.R.R. 505, at para. 63; *Lombo Machado v. Portugal* (1997) 23 E.H.R.R. 79, para. 31; *Van Orshoven v. Belgium* (1998) 26 E.H.R.R. 55.

[74] See, *e.g. Ruiz Torija v. Spain* (1994) E.H.R.R. 553.

[75] General Commissioners Regulations, *op. cit.,* para. 20.

[76] Taxes Management Act 1970, s.56(2).

[77] See *Van Raalte v. Netherlands* (1997) 24 E.H.R.R. 503.

but does not include a widowed, separated or divorced father unless incapacitated.

This definition of dependent relative was used in section 367 of the **18.122** Income and Corporation Taxes Act (interest relief—repealed) and is used in section 226 of the Taxation of Chargeable Gains Act 1992 (private residence relief in respect of residence occupied by dependant relative before April 6, 1988—transitional provision) and section 11(3) of the Inheritance Tax Act 1984 (dispositions for maintenance of family—current).

In *McGregor (Helen) v. United Kingdom*,[78] the European Commission **18.123** found a complaint of sex discrimination relating to section 259 of the Income and Corporation Taxes Act 1988 to be admissible. Section 259 provides tax relief in the form of an extra tax allowance to a man married to and living with a totally incapacitated wife with a dependant child, but not to a woman in the same situation. It is understood that the United Kingdom did not oppose the application and section 259 was amended by the Finance Act 1998 so as to remove the discrimination.

In *Crossland v. United Kingdom*[79] and *Fielding v. United Kingdom*[80] the **18.124** European Commission found a complaint that the widow's bereavement allowance was only given to a woman and not to a widower whose wife had been the breadwinner (under section 262 of the Income and Corporation Taxes Act 1988) to be admissible.

Sexual orientation. For a same sex couple, the main fiscal disad- **18.125** vantages, as compared to heterosexual couples, are those which stem from the inability to marry. Under English law a marriage between two persons of the same sex is void. The principal tax disadvantage which results from this inability to marry is the absence of the inheritance tax spouse exemption by virtue of which property passes between spouses free of inheritance tax both on *inter vivos* transfers and death.

The European Court has held that states are entitled to deny the right to **18.126** marry to persons of the same sex.[81] However, this depends to some extent on the prevailing views of society and may change, particularly in the light of the changes in some signatory states whereby formal unions between same sex couples have been given legal recognition and protection. Subject to such developments, there seems little prospect in the immediate future of any discrimination claim on these grounds succeeding.

Married and unmarried heterosexual couples. Challenges based **18.127** on the different treatment in the tax system of married and unmarried couples are likely to fail in the light of the current case law, but this is an area where societal changes may eventually make a difference.[82]

Employed and self-employed. In many respects the self- **18.128** employed enjoy advantages over the employed in tax terms, for example

---

[78] Application No. 305448/96.
[79] Application No. 336120/97.
[80] Application No. 36940/97.
[81] See, *e.g. Rees v. United Kingdom* (1987) 9 E.H.R.R. 56, and *Cossey v. United Kingdom* (1991) 13 E.H.R.R. 622.
[82] See, *e.g. D.G. and W.D. Lindsay v. United Kingdom* (1986) 49 D.R. 181.

in the rules for allowable deductions. The decisions of the European Commission to date suggest that differences in treatment between the employed and self-employed will normally be justified so that there will not be a breach of Article 14.[83]

18.129 **Selective policy of prosecution.** The Revenue operate a selective policy of prosecution. A selective policy of prosecution is one where two taxpayers may be suspected to be guilty of equally serious offences, yet only one will be prosecuted. The policy reason for this is that the Revenue's principal task is to collect revenue not prosecute, and whilst it is a prosecuting authority this is ancillary to its main role. Prosecutions serve a useful deterrent purpose.

18.130 It is inherent in such a policy that there may be inconsistency and unfairness as between one taxpayer and another. Notwithstanding this inherent unfairness (which is acknowledged by the Revenue), the policy was upheld as valid in terms of English public law in *R. v. I.R.C., ex p. Mead and Cook*.[84]

18.131 In the light of the Convention right to non-discrimination, this decision can no longer be regarded as good authority. Given the inherent discriminatory nature of the policy, the burden will be on the Revenue to demonstrate an objective and reasonable basis for the policy and that it is not disproportionate on a case by case basis. The method of challenge under United Kingdom domestic law will be by way of judicial review of a decision to prosecute on the grounds of a breach of the obligation imposed on public authorities in exercising their discretion to abide by Convention rights under section 6(1) of the HRA.

18.132 **Revenue's managerial discretion in the collection of tax.** It has been held[85] that the Revenue has a broad managerial discretion in the collection of tax and may make special arrangements with particular groups of taxpayers, which may involve a more favourable treatment being extended to one particular group of taxpayers as opposed to another. Such arrangements may now be subject to challenge under Article 14 with the Revenue being obliged to justify such differences in treatment on a case-by-case basis.

Article 6—as it applies in criminal matters

18.133 **Penalties imposed on a deceased's executors.** Section 100A of the Taxes Management Act 1970 permits the imposition of a penalty incurred by the actions of the deceased on the deceased's executors. If the penalty sought to be imposed is tax-geared, then, as discussed above, the penalty should be classified as of a criminal nature for Convention purposes.

---

[83] See, *e.g. National Federation of Self-Employed v. United Kingdom* (1978) 15 D.R. 198 and see also *R. (on the application of Professional Contractors Group Ltd and Others v. Inland Revenue Commissioners* [2001] S.T.C. 629.
[84] (1992) S.T.C. 482.
[85] *R. v. I.R.C., ex p. National Federation of the Self-Employed* (1981) S.T.C 260, the "Fleet Street Casuals" case.

The consequence of this appears to be that as the imposition of this **18.134**
penalty would infringe the presumption of innocence (as the "defendant"
is not in a position to answer the charge), no such penalty may be
imposed.

In *AP MP and TP v. Switzerland* [86] a penalty for tax evasion was imposed **18.135**
on the deceased's heirs (who under Swiss law inherited the estate directly,
there being no concept of personal representatives as in English law) in
respect of the conduct of the deceased. The penalty was tax geared and
was held to be criminal in nature. The European Court observed that the
penalty depended on the "guilt" of the deceased in that it assumed the
deceased had engaged in tax evasion.

The European Court held that it is a fundamental rule of criminal law that **18.136**
criminal liability does not survive the person who committed the criminal
act and that this rule is required by the presumption of innocence. The
Court, for these reasons, held the penalty sought to be imposed to be
contrary to Article 6.[87]

Article 1 of the First Protocol

Windfall taxes. The Finance Act 1997 imposed a windfall tax on the **18.137**
privatised industries. Such taxes raise many issues of fairness. Is it fair to,
in effect, tax the present shareholders in privatised companies in respect
of benefits enjoyed in many cases by previous shareholders? Is it discriminatory to tax a privatised company where it may have competitors who
are not subject to tax, for example in the case of utilities the competitor
may be the off-shoot of another state's utility company not subject to the
windfall tax?

Whilst such taxes may be challenged on the grounds of expropriation of **18.138**
property under Article 1 of the First Protocol or Article 14 discrimination, it
is likely that where the state can give some good reason for raising the tax,
such as pressing budgetary reasons, and where the reasons are not party
political or political dogma, such taxes will be held to be within the margin
of appreciation allowed to states in raising tax.

In *Wasa Liv v. Omsesidigt*,[88] a Swedish mutual life assurance company **18.139**
mounted a challenge under Article 1 of the First Protocol to a one-off
windfall tax on certain types of financial institutions raised to curb a
growing budget deficit. The European Commission held that the levying of
such a tax was within the state's margin of appreciation as it was introduced with a specific public purpose in mind and was considered to be in
the public interest. A complaint of discrimination was also rejected, the
European Commission observing that any national tax system inevitably
differentiates between different groups of taxpayers and that the implementation of any tax system inevitably creates marginal situations.

Prospective and retrospective legislation. Both prospective and **18.140**
retrospective legislation affects legal certainty and hence the rule of law,

---

[86] Application No. 20919/92.
[87] See also *EL, RL, JOL v. Switzerland,* Application No. 20919/92.
[88] (1998) 58 D.R. 163.

so that it is impossible for a citizen to know what the legal consequences of his actions are.

18.141 Prospective legislation occurs virtually every year in the Budget, when Budget changes are announced to have effect from Budget Day (normally in March) when the legislation will not be available until July or August. Hence a taxpayer who relies on the terms of a press announcement may find that the actual legislation may well have a different effect than the press release suggested. Such a taxpayer might rely on Article 1 of the First Protocol on the ground that his property had been expropriated on an arbitrary or unfair basis.

18.142 Retrospective legislation is used not infrequently to staunch a loss of revenue resulting from defective drafting or the emergence of a particularly successful tax avoidance scheme.

18.143 In terms of Article 1 of the First Protocol retrospective legislation may deprive a person of a vested right, for example a right to repayment of overpaid tax, or may interfere with a legal claim being made by a taxpayer, which may amount to a denial of the right to a fair trial within Article 6(1).

18.144 Not surprisingly, in the field of tax the European Court and European Commission have shown a considerable degree of respect for the margin of appreciation of states where retrospective legislation is in issue.

18.145 In *A B C D v. United Kingdom*,[89] the Commission found that retrospective legislation in the Finance Act 1978 designed to combat a particular avoidance scheme was justified in the circumstances to combat an artificial avoidance scheme which otherwise had no commercial purpose.

18.146 Most recently in *National & Provincial Leeds Permanent and Yorkshire Building Societies v. United Kingdom*,[90] a number of building societies challenged a retrospective provision of United Kingdom law which took away the right to a repayment of tax made under an invalid statutory instrument. In broad terms the Court found that the United Kingdom's actions did not unduly affect the balance between the building societies' rights and the collection of taxes. One aspect of the case which appears to have weighed heavily with the European Court was that the invalidity arose from a technical argument of which the taxpayers sought to take advantage, and given the various government announcements that had been made, the taxpayers should not have been surprised that retrospective legislation was introduced to cure the error.

18.147 Whilst in the tax field, it appears that the United Kingdom has a wide margin of appreciation with regard to retrospective legislation, it will be necessary for such legislation to be objectively justified and to be shown to be proportionate.

Overpayment of tax

18.148 Where a taxpayer pays a sum by way of income or corporation tax under an assessment which is not due, there is a statutory right to repayment,[91] but such right is subject to a number of restrictions on recovery in the form

---

[89] (1981) 23 D.R. 203.
[90] (1998) 25 E.H.R.R. 127.
[91] TMA 1970, s.33.

of a time limit, and the so-called "prevailing practice defence", whereby no relief is given if the return was made in accord with a generally prevailing practice. Furthermore the Revenue is only obliged to give such relief as is "reasonable and just".

Whilst there is a restitutionary right to recovery of overpaid tax paid by **18.149** mistake, there are a number of common law defences available to the state against such claims such as change of position and passing on.

A right to recovery of overpaid tax is capable of constituting property within **18.150** Article 1 of the First Protocol,[92] so that any such restrictions on recovery are capable of challenge as an infringement of that Article.

5. INDIRECT TAX

While there is, as will be seen, no difference in principle between the **18.151** impact the HRA will have on the direct tax field as opposed to that of indirect tax, it is convenient to consider the two areas separately. Thus in this part we consider the indirect taxes (*i.e.* value added tax ("VAT"), stamp duty, insurance premium tax ("IPT"), landfill tax ("LFT"), air passenger duty ("APD") and customs and excise duties), concentrating in the main on VAT. What should be stated at the outset, however, is that the consideration above of the impact of the new regime on procedural matters before the General and Special Commissioners will be replicated in proceedings before the VAT and Duties Tribunal save that reference should be made to the appropriate Tribunal Rules.[93] This allows a more focused approach to particular issues which may (indeed, will) arise in practice.

Indirect Tax—Procedure

Application of Article 6

The most immediate issue in the procedural field before the VAT and **18.152** Duties Tribunal is the extent to which Article 6 (the "right to a fair trial") will apply to such hearings. As we have attempted to set out above (see paragraphs [18.30–18.36]), above there are two discernible approaches in the Convention jurisprudence: the "traditional" view that Article 6 is concerned with "civil rights and obligations" which do not extend to tax matters; and the more "modern" view that Article 6 can apply, notwithstanding a tax framework, where there are other rights in play (usually a right to property). The indirect tax field has examples of both.

The cases which stand as authority for the traditional view are discussed **18.153** at paragraph [18.30] above.

In contrast, in *Air Canada v. United Kingdom*[94] the seizure of an airliner as **18.154** a result of unlawful importation of drugs and the demand that the owner should pay a penalty before it could be returned was accepted by the European Court to involve the owner's civil rights within Article 6. There

---

[92] See *The Building Societies Case* (1998) 25 E.H.R.R. 127.
[93] See the VAT Tribunal Rules 1986, S.I. 1986 No. 590.
[94] (1995) 20 E.H.R.R. 150.

was, in the language of the Convention, an underlying right to property.[95]

18.155 Likewise in *Hodgson*[96] the VAT and Duties Tribunal decided that the imposition of a particular type of excise duty penalty involved the determination of the civil rights of a person who had imported his own hand rolling tobacco for his personal use. This constituted a breach of Article 6 since Mr Hodgson had no substantive right of appeal; his theoretical entitlement to seek judicial review was not a sufficient remedy.[97]

18.156 In *Ellinas v. H.M. Customs*[98] the application of Article 6 to a VAT penalty appeal was assumed by the VAT Tribunal, apparently without Customs' objection. The case concerned a claim to public interest immunity by Customs, and the conflict with the appellant's rights to a fair hearing.

18.157 In *Coleman et al*,[99] the VAT Tribunal considered the requirements imposed on traders to pay VAT and make returns before an appeal is entertained (see section 84(2), (3) of the Value Added Tax Act 1994 ("VATA 1994") and sections 60(3), (4) of the FA 1994 (IPT) and sections 55(2), (3) of the FA 1996 (LFT)). The requirements to pay the tax in dispute and make the return for the disputed period(s) were upheld as being compatible with E.C. law; the requirement to make all returns was declared to be incompatible with E.C. law.[1] The position under Convention law was not considered by the Tribunal.

18.158 In light of the above, the prudent course is to proceed on the basis that Article 6 is capable of applying to indirect tax disputes; indeed, as a matter of principle it is difficult to see why this should not be the case. If a person has rights guaranteed by Article 6 in relation to disputes concerning employment matters, family law matters or social security, why should this not also be the case in relation to tax matters, whether direct or indirect? The importance of a fair trial is no greater or lesser in one rather than another.

A "proper" hearing

18.159 Consequently there are a number of areas where consideration must be given to the application of Article 6. For example, some (if not most) of the matters which can be brought to the VAT and Duties Tribunal under section 83 of the VATA 1994 can be expressed in terms of underlying rights which would allow reliance to be placed on Article 6. The significance of this is that in some areas (see particularly appeals against certain directions made by Customs and Excise—see section 84(4) to (4D), (7)) the Tribunal cannot—under the terms of the VATA 1994—entertain a full appeal on the merits but is limited to reviewing, or supervising, decisions already made by officers of H.M. Customs and Excise. To the extent that such a limited review can be portrayed as a fetter on the right to a proper hearing before an independent and impartial tribunal then there would be a breach of Article 6. The question then is whether such a

---

[95] cf. *Editions Periscope* and the *Building Societies* case considered above.
[96] [1996] V.&D.R. 200.
[97] cf. *Smith and Grady v. United Kingdom* [2000] EHRR 493.
[98] Case 15346, 11/02/98.
[99] Case No. 5/7/1999.
[1] cf. *Garage Molenheide v. Belgium* (1998) S.T.C. 126.

supervisory jurisdiction of the tribunals—akin in many respects to the judicial review jurisdiction in the High Court—is a sufficient remedy.

Again here there are two approaches which can be identified as the **18.160** "traditional" and the "modern" approach. According to the former the English remedy of judicial review is a sufficient legal avenue for the resolution of disputes; by extension the same would apply to the supervisory jurisdiction of the VAT and Duties Tribunal—see the decisions of the European Court in *Air Canada*[2] *(discussed above) and the other case involving Customs and Excise, AGOSI v. United Kingdom*[3] where the "taxpayer's" right to seek judicial review of the seizure of allegedly smuggled gold coins was regarded as an adequate remedy. However, in more recent times the European Court has questioned such a conclusion by indicating that there are certain matters which cannot be dealt with merely by a review of the "reasonableness" or otherwise of the original decision but must be considered at a full appeal on the merits: see *Smith and Grady v. United Kingdom.*[4]

Barriers to a hearing

Access to a tribunal can, by statute, either be barred or made conditional **18.161** upon the satisfaction of certain requirements. An example of the former is the rule that a document cannot be relied upon in court unless it has been validly stamped in accordance with the Stamp Act 1891 or the Finance Act 1999. This is, at least on its face, a breach of Article 6; such a conclusion has been reached (in parallel contexts) in both Ireland and the Bahamas: see *O'Connell v. Ireland*[5] and *Bahamas Entertainment Ltd v. Koll*[6] (this latter authority being of particular interest since the relevant provision in the Bahamian constitution is similar to Article 6). Examples of the latter are, first, the requirement to pay the tax in dispute before an appeal hearing (see the discussion of *Coleman*[7] above) and, secondly, the ability of Customs and Excise to apply to strike out an appeal for want of prosecution of the appeal (rule 18(2) of the VAT Tribunal Rules 1986).

Criminal charges and tax penalties

In light of the matters discussed above (see paragraph 18.38), in relation **18.162** to direct tax penalties, it can equally be contended that penalties for failure to comply with, say, provisions of the VAT system are to be treated as falling within Article 6(2). Thus, any penalty which is "tax-geared" (*i.e.* fixed by reference to the amount of tax in issue) and is at least 25 per cent or 30 per cent of the tax sum can—indeed should—be regarded as a criminal charge, whether or not the penalty can be mitigated by Customs and Excise. There is a further issue with regard to VAT civil evasion penalties which are imposed under section 60(1) of the VATA 1994 (which are

---

[2] (1995) 20 E.H.R.R 150.
[3] (1986) 7 E.H.R.R. 251.
[4] (2000) 29 E.H.R.R. 493.
[5] (1998) (unreported).
[6] (1996) 2 L.R.C. 45.
[7] Case No. 5/7/99 and para. [18.157], above.

undoubtedly criminal for Article 6 purposes—see the *Han* case[7A]) and rely on the concept of dishonesty as a constituent element of the offence. "Dishonesty" for these purposes follows the criminal law definition known as the *Ghosh*[8] test, which turns on whether the defendant realised that what he was doing was dishonest according to the standards of reasonable and honest people. The Law Commission in considering whether a general offence of dishonesty should be introduced considered that this concept of dishonesty might well fail the European Court's "quality of law test", *i.e.* was not sufficiently certain so as to allow citizens to know the consequences of their actions.[9] Customs' power in section 77(4) of the VATA 1994 to issue out of time assessments also turns in part on whether a person has acted dishonestly.

Application of Article 1 of the First Protocol

18.163 Although it will be necessary to consider right to property issues in more detail in relation to substantive rather than procedural disputes, it is possible that Article 1 of the First Protocol will be relevant in relation to procedural matters as well. As we have summarised in paragraphs 18.18 *et seq.*, above, a person is given—by the Convention—a right to peaceful enjoyment of his "possessions" subject (in broad terms) to a "public interest" defence and a "tax raising" defence. Where the revenue authorities (here Customs and Excise) attempt to interfere—consciously or unwittingly—in the preparation of disputes for hearing before a tribunal or Court or take steps as part of an investigation into a taxpayer's affairs there will, in many cases, be a "deprivation" of possessions or, at best, an interference in the peaceful enjoyment of those possessions. The issue will then arise as to whether such deprivation or interference can be justified in the public interest or under the state's "margin of appreciation" for the levying and collecting of taxes. This will not be the case if the action taken by the state is discriminatory, arbitrary or disproportionate or (to put these tests in another way) if there is no "fair balance" between the interest of the state (representing the public interest) in collecting taxes and the interest of a particular individual.

Penalties

18.164 In the case of tax penalties (for example for failure to comply with the VAT accounting system) it is arguable that any particular penalty is so disproportionate as to amount to arbitrary confiscation of a person's possessions (see *AP, MP and TP v. Switzerland*[10] and, in a United Kingdom

---

[7A] *Han & Yau v. Commissioners of Customs and Excise*, Court of Appeal, July 3, 2001 (on appeal from the VAT and Duties Tribunal [2000] V & DR 312) and the decision of the VAT and Duties Tribunal in *John Lucas Murrell v. Commissioners of Customs and Excise* LON/99/121 and *Wing Lee Carry Out v. Commissioners of Customs and Excise* [2001] S.T.I. 840.
[8] [1982] Crim. L.R. 608, applied for VAT purposes in *Gandi Tandoori Restaurant* [1987] V.A.T.T.R. 39.
[9] Law Commission Consultation Paper No. 155 "Fraud and Deception" (1999) and see also *Hashman and Harrup v. United Kingdom,* Application, No. 25594/94, summarised at [2000] Crim. L. R. 185.
[10] (1997) 26 E.H.R.R. 541.

context, the proportionality argument wrongly rejected by the courts in *P.& O. v. H.M. Customs and Excise*,[11] point not considered on appeal.[12]).

Seizure of documents

Equally it will be open to a taxpayer to rely on the terms of Article 1 of the   **18.165**
First Protocol (in addition to contentions which may be made under Articles 6 and 8) where Customs take steps to seize documents (or indeed other items such as computers or computer records) as part of an investigation into the trader's affairs (see *Air Canada v. United Kingdom*[13] and *Agosi v. United Kingdom*[14]). As is the case in the direct tax field, the question to be determined by the VAT and Duties Tribunal (and ultimately the courts) is whether such a seizure can be justified as being in the public interest, particularly where, in a procedural context, such a seizure may hamper the trader's ability to deal with the investigations and the proceedings which may follow. In *Popely and Harris v. Customs and Excise*[15] an unsuccessful challenge was brought to a raid by Customs on the office of a solicitor where—at least in part—legally privileged material was seized. While the case turned on specific United Kingdom statutory provisions (the Court holding that it was proper for seized material to be bagged up for review by an independent counsel as to any privilege which attached to it; and see *Re An Applicant*[16] considered above) it would be possible to make similar arguments by reference to the provisions of Article 1 of Protocol 1. As with many other areas of overlap with the Convention however, it is doubtful whether—had the "right to property" been raised—a different answer would have been reached.

Similar issues will arise where Customs seek documents from—for   **18.166**
example—a bank where the documents concerned relate to third parties. To the extent that such records belong to the bank (rather than their customer) it is conceivable that a bank could also rely on Article 1 of the First Protocol on the basis that the public interest in the investigation of tax avoidance or tax evasion cannot justify onerous, wide ranging, requests for detailed information, perhaps going back many years. Article 8 would also be in point, although it may not be immediately apparent as to who's privacy—the bank or their customer—is capable of being protected by the terms of Article 8. An Article 8 challenge on this basis was rejected in *R. v. I.R.C., ex p. Banque Internationale a Luxembourg SA*[17] on the basis that there was ample justification for the notices. Whether such justification exists must, however, be assessed on a case-by-case basis.

Article 14 and the right of non-discrimination

Although it is possible that Article 14 will be relied upon in a procedural   **18.167**
context—why are documents sought from one taxpayer and not another? Why is an extended time for appealing granted in one case and not in

---

[11] [1992] S.T.C. 809.
[12] [1994] S.T.C. 259.
[13] (1995) 20 E.H.R.R. 150.
[14] (1986) 7 E.H.R.R. 251.
[15] [1999] S.T.C. 1016.
[16] [1999] S.T.C. (SCD) 128, and para. 18.82, above.
[17] [2000] S.T.I. 919.

another?—there are no specific issues which have yet arisen or which can be foreseen in the indirect tax field. As and when such issues arise, it will be necessary to test the applicability of Article 14 by reference to the three key stages: whether the taxpayer is in a materially identical position to another taxpayer; whether he has been treated differently to that taxpayer in the enjoyment of a right protected by the Convention; and whether, if this is the case, there is any objective and reasonable justification for such treatment.

Indirect Tax—Substance

The more relevant articles

18.168 In this part we propose to concentrate on those provisions of the Convention which are most likely to arise in a substantive rather than procedural context. This means—in effect—considering Article 1 of the First Protocol and Article 14; much of the material set out above relating to direct tax matters is of equal relevance here.

Article 1 of the First Protocol

18.169 The present position is that there have been few challenges to the substance of a tax itself where the Convention was, or could realistically have been, argued. One such case was the challenge to the increase in beer duty announced by the Chancellor on Budget Day (see *R v. H.M. Treasury, ex p. Shepherd Neame*[18]); the then proposed increase so irritated Kent brewers, who were (and are) particularly badly hit by "beer running" (illicit smuggling of cheap foreign, duty paid, beer into the United Kingdom under the guise of importation for personal use) that judicial review proceedings were brought contending that the increase contravened European Community law which—at the level of directives—regulates all intra-E.C. excise duties. The challenge was unsuccessful (for reasons concerned with E.C. law) but was one which could have been framed in terms of a breach of Article 1 of the First Protocol (and, very possibly, in terms of Article 14 as well) on the basis that the duty constituted a deprivation of the brewer's possessions, the increase was "arbitrary" and disproportionate since it went further—given the differences in the rates of duty in E.C. Member States—than could be said to be necessary in pursuit of any legitimate policy aim. While such a full frontal assault on a tax (or an increase in tax) is, perhaps, unlikely to succeed (see the Swedish windfall tax case of *Wasa Liv v. Sweden*[19]) the contention remains an open one in suitable cases.

18.170 Other areas of potential application of the right to property argument are: the seizure of goods by Customs and Excise (for example for failure to pay any or the proper amount of duty); the seizure of property concerned in illicit importation of dutiable goods (for example the seizure of ships, aircraft or—more commonly—white vans); the withdrawal of approval for

---

[18] January 21, 1998 (unreported).
[19] See para. 18.139, above.

"bonded" warehouses, since the approval itself which allows a person to trade is a form of property—see section 18A of the VATA 1994 and *Tre Traktorer Aktiebolag v. Sweden*[20] (a case concerning the withdrawal of a licence to sell alcohol).

Discrimination and Article 14

Arguments based on the principles of Article 14 have been raised in a **18.171** number of cases. In the main test case where the Convention was raised in relation to the application of the three-year cap on the recovery of sums of overpaid tax[21] the High Court (Moses J.) and later the Court of Appeal found no difficulty in rejecting the contention that one group of traders (those who paid a net sum each period to Customs and Excise—"payment traders") were not in a materially identical position to another group of traders (those who received a net sum each period from Customs and Excise—"repayment traders")—see *Marks & Spencer plc v. H.M. Customs and Excise.* [22] Conversely, in a case in which the Convention was not specifically raised (the argument turning on matters of E.C. law) it would have been open to the taxpayer to contend that differential rates of IPT, which depended on who were the contracting parties to the insurance policy contravened Article 14 just as much as other principles of E.C. law—see *Lunn Poly.*[23]

The areas of potential application of Article 14 are many since (to state the **18.172** obvious) wherever one person is subject to a tax (or excluded from a relief or exemption) and another person is not, there is the possibility of a claim of discrimination. Arguments already being considered include differential treatment accorded to married persons as opposed to the unmarried in the application of the market value rules for VAT in Schedule 6 paragraphs 1 and 2 of Schedule 6, of the VATA 1994; the limitations placed on the special VAT treatment for goods and services provided for the chronically sick and disabled (Group 12, note 3 of Schedule 8 of the VATA 1994) whereby distinctions are drawn on the basis of degrees or types of disability (*cf. The Dyslexia Institute Ltd*[24]*);* the special zero rating for approved alterations to, *inter alia*, "ecclesiastical buildings" (Group 6, note 6(a) of Schedule 8) which may amount to discrimination against non-Christian religions (*cf. Bedfordshire C.C. v. Howard United Reform Church*,[25] and *Church of Scientology v. HMCE*[26]).

Other Articles of the Convention

Although it may have no greater success than in the direct tax field (see **18.173** paragraph 18.44, above) it is highly likely that a VAT registered trader will

---

[20] (1991) 13 E.H.R.R. 309.
[21] VATA 1994, s.80.
[22] [1999] S.T.C. 205; [2000] S.T.C. 16.
[23] [1999] S.T.C. 350.
[24] Case 12654, 1994.
[25] [1976] A.C. 363.
[26] [1981] S.T.C. 65.

soon contend that the requirement imposed by the statute upon him to be an unpaid "tax collector" for the Government is a breach of Article 4 since it amounts to "forced labour"; on the authority of *Four Companies v. Austria*[27] this is not a contention that will find much (if any) judicial support.

---

[27] 7 D.R. 148 and para.[18.61], above.

CHAPTER 19

Consumer Protection and Advertising

1. INTRODUCTION

19.01 This first part of this chapter will address several of the implications of the HRA on areas of domestic law which affect private individuals and consumers, including data protection, surveillance, product liability and consumer credit. The second part of the chapter will discuss the HRA's impact on commercial expression and advertising. Where the construction or application of a European Directive is under consideration, in, for example, the product liability or data protection contexts, the rights set out in the E.U. Charter of Fundamental Rights, which is of declaratory effect and is used by the European Court of Justice as an aid to interpretation of Community law, should also be considered.[1]

2. THE RELEVANT CONVENTION RIGHTS

19.02 The Convention rights that are the most generally relevant to consumer protection and advertising are Article 8 (the right to respect for private and family life, home and correspondence), Article 10 (the right to freedom of expression) and to a lesser extent, Article 1 of Protocol No. 1 (the right to peaceful enjoyment of possessions). Article 6 (the right to a fair hearing) is applicable to court or tribunal proceedings. In relation to product liability issues, Article 2 (the right to life) is also relevant.

Article 2

19.03 Article 2 provides that everyone's right to life shall be protected by law.[2] Article 2 concerns the protection by law of human life. The right is absolute and, with one limited exception,[3] cannot be subject to derogation. The Article imposes two duties on the state (and through section 6 of the HRA, on public authorities):

    (1) not to take a person's life save in the limited circumstances set out in Article 2(2)[4];

---

[1] See the discussion of the Charter at paras 6.159 *et seq.*
[2] See paras 3.14 *et seq.* for the text of Art. 2 and a brief overview.
[3] The only derogation permitted by Art. 15 is in respect of deaths resulting from lawful acts of war.
[4] Art. 2 expressly provides that deprivation of life shall not be regarded as inflicted in contravention of the Article when it results from the use of force which is no more than absolutely necessary: (1) in defence of any person from unlawful violence; (2) in order to effect a lawful arrest or to prevent the escape of a person lawfully detained; or (3) in action lawfully taken for the purpose of quelling a riot or insurrection.

(2) to take reasonable measures to protect life.

The Article imposes both a negative obligation to refrain from depriving **19.04** someone of their life and a positive duty to take appropriate measures to protect life: *X v. United Kingdom*.[5] It also includes a duty on the state to take preventative operational measures to protect an individual whose life is at risk from the criminal acts of another individual: *Osman v. United Kingdom*.[6] Despite the reference to "life", Article 2 is not restricted to cases where actual loss of life occurs. It is sufficient if loss of life is one possible consequence of the conduct complained of.[7] Importantly for the product liability context, Article 2 has been applied to require the state to provide warning and advice about any life-threatening risks, so far as these may be attributed to the state: *LCB v. United Kingdom*.[8]

Article 8

Article 8 is a qualified right. Article 8(1) provides that everyone has the **19.05** right to respect for his private and family life, his home and his correspondence. The obligation to comply with Article 8 is imposed on the state, and through the medium of the HRA, on "public authorities".[9] It contains both a negative obligation to refrain from interferences in individual privacy and a positive obligation to take reasonable and appropriate measures to protect an individual's private life, etc. An interference with the rights contained in Article 8(1) is permitted if it is:

(1) authorised by law;

(2) imposed for a reason listed in Article 8(2); and

(3) is "necessary in a democratic society" (*i.e.* (a) it corresponds to a pressing social need and (b) it is proportionate to the aim to be achieved).

Article 8(2) provides for certain interferences with the right which fall within **19.06** the broad categories of justification set out (national security, public safety, the economic well-being of the country, the prevention of disorder or crime, the protection of health or morals, the protection of the rights and freedoms of others).

Article 8 is primarily vertical in its effect, in that it is concerned with **19.07** interferences by a "public authority" with the right. However, the European Court has developed a doctrine of positive obligations, whereby it has placed an obligation in certain circumstances on state authorities to prevent interferences with the right to respect for private life by private bodies or individuals.[10] The extent to which Article 8 will have a degree of

---

[5] (1978) 14 D.R. 31.
[6] (2000) 29 E.H.R.R. 245.
[7] Reaffirmed by the European Court in *William and Anita Powell v. United Kingdom* [2000] E.H.R.L.R. 650–654, Application No. 45305/99, May 4, 2000.
[8] (1999) 27 E.H.R.R. 212. See further at para. 19.73 below.
[9] See further para. 3.94 for the text of Article 8 and a brief overview and para. 16.03 *et seq.* for an in-depth analysis of the European Court's approach to Art. 8.
[10] See further para. 5.28 *et seq.*

horizontal effect in the domestic courts remains to be worked out in practice.[11]

19.08   The right to respect for correspondence is relevant to areas such as data protection or interception of telecommunications. The right is a right to uninterrupted and uncensored communication with other people and covers all forms of communication.[12]

19.09   It was widely debated both in Parliament and in the media whether the incorporation of Article 8 into domestic law would create a new law of privacy. The courts have now recognised a right to privacy, grounded in the equitable doctrine of confidence in *Douglas v. Hello! Ltd.*[13] This raises the possibility that members of the public can sue public authorities in relation to unauthorised CCTV surveillance and that employees of public authorities will be able to sue their employers for breach of confidence or privacy should their personal emails be intercepted without clear guidelines that would allow an employee to predict when this might happen.

19.10   To date, only individuals and not corporate bodies have been recognised as having a right to respect for private life under Convention case law. In *R. v. Broadcasting Standards Commission, ex p. BBC*,[14] a case involving secret filming by the BBC of sales transactions in branches of Dixons' electrical stores for an investigatory documentary, Forbes J. at first instance had held that "privacy" as referred to in section 107(1) of the Broadcasting Act 1996, when construed in accordance with Article 8 was a right available to natural persons only. However, allowing the appeal, the Court of Appeal stated that privacy under the Convention was not the same concept as that referred to in the Broadcasting Act 1996 and that Dixons' corporate privacy was given protection under the 1996 Act. A company could make a complaint under section 111 of the 1996 Act and there was nothing in the Act which prevented it complaining of unfairness or an infringement of privacy. Lord Woolf M.R. indicated that certain corporate activities might well be construed as "private" in nature.

> "While the intrusions into the privacy of an individual which are possible are no doubt more extensive than the infringements of privacy which are possible in the case of a company, a company does have activities of a private nature which need protection from unwarranted intrusion. It would be a departure from proper standards if, for example, the BBC without any justification attempted to listen clandestinely to the activities of a board meeting. The same would be true of secret filming of the board meeting. The individual members of the board would no doubt have grounds for complaint, but so would the board and thus the company as a whole. The company has correspondence which it could justifiably regard as private and the broadcasting of the contents of that correspondence would be an intrusion of its privacy. It could not possibly be said that to hold such actions an intrusion of privacy conflicts with the ECHR"[15]

---

[11] See generally paras. 5.22 *et seq.*
[12] *A v. France* (1994) 18 E.H.R.R. 462.
[13] [2001] 2 W.L.R. 992; *The Times*, January 16, 2001, CA.
[14] [2000] 3 W.L.R. 1327, CA; [1999] E.M.L.R. 858 Forbes J.; [2001] 1 W.L.R. 550, HL (petition for leave to appeal dismissed).
[15] At para. 33.

The Court of Appeal held that their finding that a corporation could complain of infringement of privacy did not conflict with the Convention. On the facts, the court found an infringement of Dixons' privacy. The Broadcasting Standards Commission had found that secret filming required justification and that Dixons could reasonably complain about its staff being secretly filmed without good cause. The court declined to interfere with the BSC's decision, which was within the BSC's discretion, although it noted that the degree of infringement of privacy was small and that any justification required by the BBC would be correspondingly small.

Although a corporate right to respect for its private life has not yet been **19.11** recognised by the court under Article 8, it is clear that an individual's right to respect for private life can extend to the workplace and certain professional activities.[16] In *Niemietz v. Germany*,[17] the Court held that a search of a lawyer's office violated Article 8 by implementing on lawyer/client confidentiality and by reason of the absence of procedural safeguards. The interference was disproportionate to the legitimate aims of preventing crime and protecting the rights and freedoms of others under Article 8(2). The court stated:

> " . . . it would be too restrictive to limit the notion [of private life] to an 'inner circle' in which the individual may live his own personal life as he chooses and to exclude therefrom entirely the outside world not encompassed within that circle. Respect for private life must also comprise to a certain degree the right to establish and develop relationships with other human beings.
>
> There appears, furthermore, to be no reason of principle why this understanding of the notion of 'private life' should be taken to exclude activities of a professional or business nature since it is, after all, in the course of their working lives that the majority of people have a significant, if not the greatest, opportunity of developing relationships with the outside world".[18]

Accordingly, the court has concluded that there was an interference with **19.12** private life when telephone tapping covered both business and private calls[19] and where a search was directed solely against business activities.[20] The Court also interprets the word "home" in Article 8 as possibly extending to a person's office, based on the word in the French text—"domicile"—which has broader connotation than the English word.[21] A narrow interpretation of "private life" or "home" would risk inequality of treatment because activities which are related to a profession or business may well be conducted from a person's private residence and activities which are not so related may be carried on in an office or commercial premises.[22]

---

[16] *Niemietz v. Germany* (1993) 16 E.H.R.R. 97; *Halford v. United Kingdom* (1997) 24 E.H.R.R. 523. See further paras 16.20 *et seq.*
[17] (1993) 16 E.H.R.R. 97.
[18] At para. 29.
[19] *Huvig v. France* (1990) 12 E.H.R.R. 528, paras 8 and 25. See also *Halford v. United Kingdom* (1997) 24 E.H.R.R. 523.
[20] *Chappell v. United Kingdom* (1990) 12 E.H.R.R. 1, paras 26 and 51.
[21] *Niemietz v. Germany* (1993) 16 E.H.R.R. 97, para. 30.
[22] *ibid.*

19.13   Article 8 may also entail a positive obligation on the state to provide information on environmental and health hazards to those affected by them: *Guerra v. Italy*.[23]

Article 10

19.14   Like Article 8, Article 10 is a qualified right. Article 10(1) provides a right to freedom of expression, which includes the freedom to hold opinions and to receive and impart information and ideas without interference by a public authority and regardless of frontiers.[24] A corporate body has a right to freedom of expression. The word "everyone" in Article 10 means that both legal and natural persons are entitled to the right to freedom of expression. In *Autronic AG v. Switzerland*,[25] the court stated that:

> " . . . neither Autronic AG's legal status as a limited company nor the fact that its activities were commercial nor the intrinsic nature of freedom of expression can deprive Autronic AG of the protection of Article 10. The Article applies to 'everyone', whether natural or legal persons."[26]

19.15   However, Article 10(1) does not prevent states from requiring the licensing of broadcasting, television or cinema enterprises.

19.16   Further, Article 10(2) provides that the right to freedom of expression, since it carries with it duties and responsibilities, may be subject to such formalities, conditions, restrictions or penalties as are prescribed by law and are necessary in a democratic society, in the interests of:

> (1) national security;
>
> (2) territorial integrity or public safety;
>
> (3) for the prevention of disorder or crime;
>
> (4) for the protection of health or morals;
>
> (5) for the protection of the reputation or rights of others;
>
> (6) for preventing the disclosure of information received in confidence; or
>
> (7) for maintaining the authority and impartiality of the judiciary.

An interference with the right to freedom of expression will only be necessary in a democratic society if it: (i) answers a pressing social need and (ii) is proportionate to the aim to be achieved.[27] As with Article 8, the requirement for a legal basis for any interference is important.[28]

---

[23] (1998) 26 E.H.R.R. 357. See para. 19.75 below.
[24] See para. 3.110 for the text of the article and a brief overview.
[25] (1990) 12 E.H.R.R. 485.
[26] At para. 47.
[27] See further paras 4.34 *et seq.*
[28] See further paras 4.43 *et seq.*

There is clearly scope for conflict between the right to freedom of expression under Article 10 and the right to respect for private life in Article 8.

Article 1 of Protocol No. 1

Article 1 of Protocol No. 1 confers the right to every natural or legal person **19.17** to peaceful enjoyment of his possessions. No one shall be deprived of his possessions except in the public interest and subject to the conditions provided for by law and by the general principles of international law. The State is, however, entitled to enforce such laws as it deems necessary to control the use of property in accordance with the general interest.[29]

3. DATA COLLECTION AND DATA PROTECTION

Data Protection and Fundamental Rights

The E.U. Directive on the Protection of Individuals with regard to the **19.18** Processing of Personal Data and on the Free Movement of such Data[30] (the parent Directive for the Data Protection Act 1998) states in its preamble that:

> "the object of national laws in the processing of personal data is to protect fundamental rights and freedoms, notably the right to privacy, which is recognised both in Article 8 of the European Convention . . . and in the general principles of Community law . . . "

It is therefore clear that the Data Protection Act 1998[31] is grounded in the fundamental right to respect for private life in the Convention and in Community law. The HRA incorporates into domestic law the right to respect for private life, family, home and correspondence set out in Article 8, which like the Data Protection Act 1998, embraces core data protection principles.[32] The HRA requires that the Data Protection Act itself be interpreted in accordance with Convention rights.[33] This section focuses on aspects of data collection and processing which have HRA implications[34] but does not consider pure data protection issues that solely arise from the Data Protection Act which are beyond the scope of this book.

---

[29] See paras 3.131 *et seq.* for a broader overview of Art. 1 of Protocol No. 1 and paras 16.43 *et seq.* for a more detailed analysis of the Article.

[30] Directive 95/46. See also Directive 97/66 concerning the processing of personal data and the protection of privacy in the telecommunications sector.

[31] The Data Protection Act 1998 is to be amended by the Freedom of Information Act 2000, in particular to extend the definition of "data" to cover, as far as public authorities are concerned, all personal information held, including structured and unstructured manual records. See further discussion of the Freedom of Information Act 2000 at para. 19.43 below.

[32] See also Art. 17 International Covenant of Civil and Political Rights and U.N. General Comment 16 (issued March 23, 1988) paras 7 & 10 regarding the legal implementation of data protection guarantees.

[33] See *e.g.*, R. Jay, "UK Data Protection Act 1998—the Human Rights Context", (2000) I.R.L.C.&T. Vol. 14, No. 3 at 385–395 who suggests that the interpretation of the right of subject access and the definitions of a "relevant filing system", "substantial distress" and "unwarranted" distress, may all have to be determined with the Convention in mind.

[34] See also L. Bygrave, "Data Protection Pursuant to the Right to Privacy in Human Rights Treaties", (1998) I.J.L.I.T. Vol. 6, No. 3 at 247–284; J. Wilson, "Data Protection and Fundamental Freedoms", Computers and Law, Aug/Sep 1997 at 24–26; R. Jay, "UK Data Protection Act 1998—the Human Rights Context", (2000) I.R.L.C.&T. Vol. 14, No. 3 at 385–395.

Who Has a Duty to Comply with Article 8?

19.19   Pursuant to section 6 of the HRA, all "public authorities" have a duty to comply with Article 8. Accordingly, any obvious public authority or hybrid public authority must comply with Article 8, amongst other things, in relation to all employment and data protection issues. The Information Commissioner (formerly the Data Protection Commissioner) is also a public authority for the purposes of section 6.[35] It is possible that a private employer may also have to comply with Article 8 because of the court's own positive duty under section 6 HRA to protect individual Convention rights in legal cases that come before it.[36]

Who May Bring Proceedings under Section 7 HRA?

19.20   If a public authority does act in violation of Article 8, an individual who can show that he is directly and actually affected by the act or omission of which he complains can bring an action for breach of his Convention rights or rely on breach of the right concerned in any legal proceedings. In general, in order to have standing to bring a claim based on a breach of Article 8 under section 7 HRA, an individual would have to prove that there was a "reasonable likelihood" that the actions allegedly constituting interference had occurred. On the basis of existing Strasbourg case-law, it is not necessary to show that the information in question has been used to the *detriment* of the individual concerned.[37]

19.21   Article 8 clearly encompasses certain data protection issues. As Simor and Emmerson state,[38] there are three aspects to personal data under Article 8. There are:

   (1) the collection and retention of personal data relating to an individual by public authorities;

   (2) the disclosure of personal data by public authorities without the individual's consent;

   (3) the refusal by public authorities to grant the individual access to personal data.

19.22   Whether or not the collection, processing or retention of personal data will amount to an interference within the meaning of Article 8(1) is likely to depend on:

   (1) the extent to which the data relating to an individual is private or sensitive;

   (2) whether the consent of the data subject is obtained (although even consent may not be sufficient to avoid the processing of data being an interference) or the data subject has a reasonable expectation that the interference will take place;

---

[35] See further at para. 19.51 below.
[36] See further paras 5.22 *et seq.* for a detailed analysis of the issue of horizontal effect and the Convention.
[37] See *e.g., Klass v. Germany* (1980) 2 E.H.R.R. 214.
[38] *Human Rights Practice*, (Sweet & Maxwell: 2000) at para. 8.094.

(3) the circumstances surrounding the processing of the data (including whether the maintenance or use of the data has negative or adverse consequences for the individual in question).

Unlike the Data Protection Act 1998, Article 8 does not distinguish between manual or automatically processed data. The collection, processing and storage of personal data about a data subject under either system is likely to constitute an "interference" with the right to respect for private life under Article 8(1). **19.23**

If an interference does take place, the data processing will usually fall within one of the legitimate aims in Article 8(2). However, it will also be necessary to show that the interference is "in accordance with the law" and that it is necessary in a democratic society *i.e.*, that it answers a pressing social need and is proportionate to the aim.[39] The more sensitive the data, the more necessary and proportionate the interference must be. **19.24**

Article 8 may go further than the Data Protection Act 1998 by providing some protection for a person's interest in access to non-personal information affecting him that is held by others. This aspect will be governed domestically by the Freedom of Information Act 2000 as it comes into effect.[40] **19.25**

CCTV and Stored Images

Images captured by closed circuit television or on camera constitute personal data for the purposes of the Data Protection Act 1998.[41] The application of human rights principles is discussed in relation to surveillance below.[42] Similar principles will apply to photographs,[43] or video-recordings of employees. **19.26**

Information on Potential Employees

Security or other clearances of potential employees involving the surreptitious registration and communication of information about their private lives raises issues under Article 8. In *Leander v. Sweden*,[44] a Swedish carpenter was prevented from gaining employment at a naval museum because police records (to which he was refused access) contained information on his past allegedly showing him to be a security risk. The European Court held that storing information about the complainant in a secret police register and releasing it to his prospective employers (for posts of importance for national security) during the course of security vetting amounted to interference within the meaning of Article 8(1). On the facts of the case, the Court held that the interference was necessary in a **19.27**

---

[39] See further paras 4.34 *et seq.* and 4.38 *et seq.*
[40] See further below at paras 19.43 *et seq.*
[41] The Information Commissioner has issued a CCTV Code of Practice for users of CCTV and similar surveillance systems, available on the Information Commissioner's website at http://www.dpu.gov.uk.
[42] At para. 19.52.
[43] *Murray v. United Kingdom* (1996) 22 E.H.R.R. 29.
[44] (1987) 9 E.H.R.R. 433.

democratic society for reasons of national security. However, where a potential position of employment did not affect national security, it would be much more difficult to justify vetting candidates in this manner.

19.28   In *Hilton v. United Kingdom*,[45] the applicant applied for a job with the BBC and challenged the legitimacy of cover security checks by the Security Services which delayed the BBC's communication to her of the success of her application. The Commission held that a security check *per se* did not constitute an interference with the right to respect for private life and that an interference only occurs when security checks are based on information about a person's private affairs. It is however, not necessary that the person actually show that such information has been used to his or her detriment. On the facts of the case, because the applicant had accepted alternative employment prior to the date of the security check, the Commission dismissed the application as manifestly ill-founded.

Health Records

19.29   In the context of health records, the Data Protection Act 1998, which provides a right of subject access to health records, must be read together with Article 8 and the Access to Medical Records Act 1988.[46] A "health record" is defined in the 1998 Act as being any record which consists of information relating to the physical or mental health or condition of an individual, and has been made by or on behalf of a health professional in connection with the care of that individual.[47] There is no right of access to medical records at common law.[48]

19.30   It is clear that Article 8 requires domestic legal systems to afford appropriate safeguards to prevent any communication or disclosure of personal health data that may be inconsistent with the Article 8 guarantees.[49] In *Z v. Finland*,[50] the applicant and her estranged husband were both HIV positive. Her husband was convicted of crimes involving deliberately subjecting others to a risk of infection from HIV through unprotected sex. In order to establish when the applicant's husband knew or had reason to suspect his infection with HIV, the court ordered the applicant's medical advisers to give evidence in the criminal proceedings against her husband. The prosecution took possession of the applicant's medical records and included them in its investigation file. The European Court concluded that such steps involved an interference with the right to respect for private life under Article 8 but held that such actions were justified in the Article 8(2) aims of preventing crime and protecting the rights and freedoms of others and were proportionate to those aims, having regard to the fact that

---

[45] (1988) 57 D.R. 108.

[46] Most of the Access to Health Records Act 1990 has been repealed by the Data Protection Act 1998 except for the sections dealing with requests for access to records relating to the deceased. Requests for access to health records relating to living individuals, whether manual records (which the Access to Health Records Act gave access to) or automated, now fall within the scope of the 1998 Act's subject access provisions.

[47] Section 68(2)(b) of the Data Protection Act 1998.

[48] *R v. Mid-Glamorgan Family Health Services, ex parte Martin* [1995] 1 W.L.R. 110; [1995] 1 All E.R. 356, CA.

[49] See further Chap. 17 (Professional Liability and Negligence) at paras 17.91 *et seq.* in relation to access to medical records, disclosure of confidential information and unauthorised disclosure of medical records.

[50] (1998) 25 E.H.R.R. 371.

there were safeguards against abuse and the fact that the evidence was heard in private. However, the Court did find a violation of Article 8 on the basis that the material in the medical records was to be made publicly accessible after the expiry of the ten year limitation on the confidentiality order. The Court emphasised the importance of safeguarding the confidentiality of medical data, stating that:

" . . . the Court will take into account that the protection of personal data, not least medical data, is of fundamental importance to a person's enjoyment of his or her right to respect for private and family life as guaranteed by Article 8 of the Convention. Respecting the confidentiality of health data is a vital principle in the legal systems of all the Contracting Parties to the Convention. It is crucial not only to respect the sense of privacy of a patient but also to preserve his or her confidence in the medical profession and in the health services in general.

Without such protection, those in need of medical assistance may be deterred from revealing such information of a personal and intimate nature as may be necessary in order to receive appropriate treatment and, even, from seeking such assistance, thereby endangering their own health and, in the case of transmissible diseases, that of the community.

The domestic law must therefore afford appropriate safeguards to prevent any such communication or disclosures of personal health data as may be inconsistent with the guarantees in Article 8 of the Convention."[51]

In *MS v. Sweden*,[52] a clinic which had treated the applicant for long term **19.31** spondylolisthesis of the spine communicated medical records to the Social Insurance Office to enable the latter to consider a compensation claim by the applicant for an alleged injury at work. The release of the records was made without the applicant's consent. The records showed that the applicant's injuries had not been caused at work as the applicant had had an abortion after the alleged injury at work stating the reason for the abortion to be serious back problems suffered in an earlier pregnancy. The European Court held that the applicant's medical history and medical records were part of her private life and that Article 8 was engaged. It again reiterated the importance of the protection of personal data, particularly medical data as part of the Article 8 guarantee.[53] This confirmed the view of the Commission in *Chave, née Jullien v. France*,[54] concerning the need for confidentiality in the storage of hospital records.

However, on the facts of the case, and bearing in mind the margin of **19.32** appreciation enjoyed by the state, the court considered under Article 8(2) that there were relevant and sufficient reasons for the communication of the applicant's medical records by the clinic to the Social Insurance Office, namely, the protection of the economic well-being of the country since the

---

[51] At para. 95.
[52] (1999) 28 E.H.R.R. 313.
[53] At para. 41. See also *Z v. Finland* (1998) 25 E.H.R.R. 371, para. 95.
[54] (1991) 71 D.R. 141.

communication of the records was potentially decisive for the allocation of public funds to deserving claimants.[55] The communication was in accordance with the law[56] and the measure was not disproportionate to the legitimate aim pursued in circumstances where:

(1) there was limited disclosure of the data by one public institution to another;

(2) it remained confidential whilst in the possession of the Office[57]; and

(3) the disclosure took place in the context of an assessment of whether the applicant satisfied the legal conditions for obtaining a benefit requested by her.

The Office had a legitimate need to check information received from the applicant against data in the possession of the clinic. In the absence of objective information from an independent source, it would have been difficult for the Office to determine whether the claim was well-founded.[58] Accordingly, there was no violation of Article 8.[59] Importantly, the Court held that the applicant had not waived her right to confidentiality in the medical data simply by applying to the Social Insurance Office for compensation.[60]

19.33 The European Court has leant against applicants seeking to prevent disclosure of medical information in order to facilitate the running of contradictory claims in simultaneous proceedings. In *Vernon v. United Kingdom*,[61] the Court rejected a complaint by an applicant who had been required to produce psychiatric reports from custody proceedings in the context of a civil claim for damages for personal injury in circumstances where the psychiatric reports appeared to contradict the expert evidence as to the applicant's mental condition in the personal injury action.

19.34 Pre-HRA, in *X v. Y and others*,[62] the High Court granted a permanent injunction to a health authority to prevent the publication in a national newspaper of information from hospital records which identified two doctors as having AIDS. The information had been passed to the newspaper by health workers. The court held that the public interest in preserving the confidentiality of hospital records identifying AIDS sufferers outweighed the public interest in the freedom of the press to provide such information, because victims of the disease should not be deterred by fear of discovery from attending hospital for treatment. This case emphasised the importance in the confidentiality of medical data.

19.35 Post-HRA, in *A Health Authority v. X*,[63] Munby J. held that disclosure of medical records to a public body was an interference with a patient's rights

---

[55] At para. 38.
[56] At para. 36.
[57] At para. 39.
[58] At para. 42.
[59] At paras 42–44.
[60] At para. 35.
[61] Application No. 38753/97, September 7, 1999.
[62] [1998] 2 All E.R. 648.
[63] *The Independent*, June 25, 2001, Munby J.

under Article 8 and could only be justified where there existed effective and adequate safeguards against abuse. Such safeguards included:

(1) the maintenance of confidentiality in the records;

(2) the minimum public disclosure of any information derived from the documents;

(3) the protection of the patient's anonymity.

The judge further held that it was the duty of every public body, including the court, to ensure that confidentiality was preserved and that there were effective and adequate safeguards against abuse before authorising the transfer of records from a doctor to a public body or from one public body to another.

The existence of safeguards for respecting the confidentiality of health **19.36** data is therefore assuming greater importance through the impact of Article 8 and the Data Protection Act 1998.[64] Nevertheless, under Article 8, the duty to keep medical data confidential is not absolute and can be overridden in certain circumstances by public interest considerations, for example in order to investigate or prosecute a crime: *Z v. Finland*.[65]

Confidentiality of Other Personal Data

The need for confidentiality extends beyond health records to other types **19.37** of data, for example, data compiled for the purpose of a compulsory public census: *X v. United Kingdom*.[66] The registration and holding of information relating to criminal investigations after they have been concluded may also violate Article 8. In *Murray v. United Kingdom*,[67] military authorities had taken photographs of a woman who had been arrested for alleged involvement in terrorist activities but was released shortly afterwards. They registered and stored information about her without her consent. The Court found that the recording and retention of the information and photographs interfered with the applicant's right to respect for private life under Article 8(1).[68] However, it found the interference to be justified in the interests of national security under Article 8(2).

Use of Data Acquired without Consent in Civil or Criminal Proceedings

The use of information or data acquired by data collection or processing **19.38** under statutory powers in civil or criminal proceedings might infringe the

---

[64] See also the General Medical Council's updated pamphlet, "Confidentiality: Protecting and Providing Information" (2000) which is intended to be Data Protection Act 1998 compliant. This focuses on permissible disclosure where the patient consents (*e.g.* to disclosure of health information to a potential employer) or mandatory disclosure without consent (*e.g.* where failure to do so may expose the patient or others to risk of death or serious harm). In the case of risk to third parties, the GMC encourages doctors to seek consent to disclosure where practicable. If it is not practicable, the information is to be disclosed promptly to an appropriate person or authority and the doctor should generally inform the patient before disclosure. See further B. Mahendra, "Medical disclosure and confidentiality", NLJ January 12, 2001, 10–11.
[65] (1998) 25 E.H.R.R. 371.
[66] (1982) 30 D.R. 239.
[67] (1995) 19 E.H.R.R. 193.
[68] *Cf. X v. United Kingdom* Application No. 5877/72, 16 Yearbook 328.

right against self-incrimination in Article 6(1) if it is obtained without warning to an individual that it might be used for these purposes.[69]

Data Matching

19.39 Data matching (the automated exchange of data between different official bodies) is not specifically regulated by the Data Protection Act 1998 and raises Article 8 concerns because of the analysis of information about large numbers of people without cause for suspicion.[70] A report from the Public Audit Forum in 2000 expressed concern that plans to set up data matching between different government agencies could be contrary to Article 8, although there was an obvious public interest in preventing crime and ensuring that citizens received all benefits to which they were entitled.[71]

Access to Personal Information

19.40 Article 8(1) may also protect a person's interest in gaining access to certain types of information about himself, particularly where the information is important for that person's private or family life. This, again, is in line with data protection principles as set out in the Data Protection Act 1998. In *Gaskin v. United Kingdom*,[72] the complainant was able to obtain access to social services records detailing his childhood in care by invoking Article 8, where the information was important for the psychological well-being and identity of the applicant. The particular circumstances in *Gaskin* and the position adopted by the Court does not mean that an individual can claim an unrestricted right of access to information or documents in the possession of a public authority. Much will depend on the type of information at issue and the reasons for it being compiled. In *Leander v. Sweden*,[73] the court held that a refusal to allow the applicant access to information held in a secret police register for the purpose of assessing suitability for employment in a position which was of importance for national security, though amounting to an interference within Article 8(1), was justified under Article 8(2) in the interests of national security.[74] The duty to provide access to information may also encompass non-personal information which relates to the health situation of individuals and which is not necessarily dependent on a request for such information.[75]

19.41 In order to establish that a refusal to grant access to information engages Article 8, the applicant must show that there was a positive duty on the

---

[69] See further paras 11.16 *et seq.* regarding evidence used in criminal proceedings which has been obtained under compulsory powers.

[70] See *e.g.* Justice Briefing for the second reading of the Data Protection Bill in the House of Lords, Monday February 5, 1998, available from Justice (whose contact details appear in the table at para. 8.82).

[71] See further R. Norton-Taylor, "Matching Personal Data Risk to Privacy", Guar, August 10, 2000, 9.

[72] (1990) 12 E.H.R.R. 36.

[73] (1987) 9 E.H.R.R. 433.

[74] See also *Willsher v. United Kingdom* (1997) 23 E.H.R.R. C.D. 188 (Commission rejected complaint relating to refusal of access to a personal file).

[75] *Guerra v. Italy* (1998) 26 E.H.R.R. 357.

public authority to provide such access.[76] In *Guerra v. Italy*,[77] the European Court found a violation of Article 8 on the basis of the failure by public authorities to inform residents about serious environmental hazards which might affect their well-being and prevent them enjoying their homes in such a way as to adversely affect their private and family life.

In *McGinley & Egan v. United Kingdom*,[78] the Court held that national **19.42** authorities who had carried out nuclear testing were under a positive duty to establish an effective and accessible procedure which enabled individuals who were involved in such activity to seek all relevant and appropriate information.

Freedom of Information Act 2000

The Freedom of Information Act 2000, which concerns access to informa- **19.43** tion other than that relating to the applicant, was passed on November 30, 2000. The 2000 Act must be brought fully into force by November 30, 2005, although this may take place sooner. Implementation will be gradual, with different groups of public authorities coming within the scope of the Act in stages. Individuals' rights of access to information is also being phased in. The Act gives a general right of access to all types of "recorded" information held by public authorities and those providing services for them, sets out a number of exemptions from that right and places a number of obligations on public authorities. Only public authorities are covered by the Act. These include, amongst others, central government departments, local authorities, NHS bodies (including hospitals, doctors, dentists, pharmacists and opticians), schools, colleges, universities, the police, the Houses of Parliament, the Northern Ireland Assembly and the National Assembly for Wales. The 2000 Act extends the "subject access rights" of individuals to access information about them held on computer and in some manually processed files under the Data Protection Act 1998 to allow access to all types of information held by the public authorities specified, whether personal or non-personal. The individual has two related rights:

(1) the right to be told whether the information exists;

(2) the right to receive the information (and where possible, in the manner requested, *i.e.* in the form of a copy or summary or by personal inspection).

The rights relate to information recorded both before and after the Act was **19.44** passed. As soon as a public authority is brought within the scope of the Act, applicants will be able to exercise their rights of access of the information held.

There are twenty-three exemptions in the Act from the obligation to **19.45** release information. Exemptions have to be considered in two stages.

---

[76] *McGinley & Egan v. United Kingdom* (1999) 27 E.H.R.R. 1 at para. 98. See Simor & Emmerson, *Human Rights Practice* (Sweet & Maxwell: 2000) at para. 8.097.
[77] (1998) 26 E.H.R.R. 357 discussed at para. 19.76 below. See also *LCB v. United Kingdom* (1999) 27 E.H.R.R. 212 (duty to provide information regarding risks to health) discussed at para. 19.71 below.
[78] (1998) 27 E.H.R.R. 1 at para. 101.

First, the public authority must decide whether the exemption applies to all or part of the information requested. Second, if it does apply, the authority will then have to decide whether it must disclose in the public interest, irrespective of the exemption (except in a few cases).

19.46 Some exemptions apply to a whole class of documents and are always exempt. Examples include:

    (1) information relating to investigations and proceedings conducted by public authorities (s.30);

    (2) court records (s.32);

    (3) trade secrets (s.43);

    (4) formulation of government policy (s.35).

Other exemptions are subject to a "prejudice" test and in such cases, the information only becomes exempt if disclosing it would or would be likely to prejudice the interest or activity described in the exemption. Examples include where disclosure would, or would be likely to, prejudice:

    (1) law enforcement (s.31);

    (2) the interests of the United Kingdom abroad (s.27).

19.47 In most cases where information is exempt, the public authority must then consider the "public interest" in providing the information. This involves considering the circumstances of each particular case and the exemption that covers the information. The information may only be withheld if the public interest in withholding it is greater than the public interest in releasing it. However, there are some absolute exemptions where, if the exemption applies, it is not necessary to go on to consider disclosure in the public interest. These include:

    (1) information accessible to the applicant by other means (s.21);

    (2) information supplied by, or relating to, bodies dealing with security matters (s.23)[79];

    (3) court records (s.32);

    (4) personal information (s.40).[80]

19.48 In general, a public authority must respond to a request for information under the Act within 20 working days. Every public authority must adopt and maintain a publication scheme setting out how it intends to publish the different classes of information it holds, and whether there is a charge for the information.

---

[79] A certificate signed by a Minister of the Crown is conclusive proof that the exemption is justified. There is a separate appeals mechanism against such certificates.
[80] An individual has a right of subject access to information about himself under the Data Protection Act 1998.

The 2000 Act is to be enforced by the Information Commissioner, combin- **19.49** ing the roles of data protection and freedom of information.[81] The Commissioner will have power to issue decisions or enforcement notices requiring disclosure of information in the public interest, subject to an "executive override" by the public authority obtaining a signed certificate from a Cabinet Minister overriding the Commissioner's notice. There is no right of appeal against a Ministerial certificate. All decision notices may be appealed by either the complainant or the public authority to an independent Information Tribunal, which may uphold, overturn or vary the notice. A public authority may appeal to the Information Tribunal against an information or enforcement notice. Appeals to the High Court against decisions of the Tribunal may be made by any party to the appeal. Two codes of practice issued under the Act will provide guidance to public authorities

(1) about responding to requests for information and associated matters[82];

(2) on records management.[83]

Concerns were raised at the Bill stage about the compatibility of the **19.50** Freedom of Information Act with human rights principles.[84] These related principally to the breadth of exemptions from the duty to release information and to certain weaknesses in supervision over discretionary disclosure. Some modifications were made prior to enactment to meet such concerns and the 2000 Act has been ministerially certified as compatible with the HRA.[85] Due to the timing of its implementation, challenges to the 2000 Act are as yet in the future.

Regulation of Data Protection

From January 30, 2001, the Office of the Data Protection Commissioner **19.51** has been known as the Office of the Information Commissioner,[86] having as it does responsibility for both data protection and freedom of information. The Office of the Information Commissioner is an independent supervisory authority. The Commissioner can deal with complaints informally, but if this is not possible, the Commissioner can take enforcement action against the data controller. The data controller may appeal to an independent Data Protection Tribunal. The Tribunal deals with appeals against decisions of the Commissioner to issue enforcement, information and special information notices. As a tribunal, it is under a duty pursuant to section 2 of the HRA to take into account Strasbourg jurisprudence and through this route (and the duty to interpret the Data Protection Act in a way that is compatible with the Convention under section 3 of the HRA),

---

[81] An Introduction to the Freedom of Information Act 2000 is available from the Information Commissioner's website at www.dataprotection.gov.uk.
[82] See draft available at www.homeoffice.gov.uk/foi.
[83] See draft available at www.pro.gov.uk/recordsmanagement.
[84] See e.g., "Freedom of Information—Response by Justice to the government's consultation paper on draft Freedom of Information Legislation", July 1999, available from Justice (whose contact details appear in table at para. 8.82).
[85] See para. 2.21.
[86] For further information, visit the Data Protection web-site at www.dataprotection.gov.uk.

Article 8 is likely to feed back into the original enforcement decision process.[87] If the Tribunal agrees with the Commissioner's enforcement action, the data controller's continuing breach of the principles of data protection may result in the commission of a criminal offence. Individuals can claim compensation through the ordinary courts if damage is caused as a result of a data controller not meeting the requirements of the Data Protection Act 1998. The Information Commissioner is at least a hybrid (and probably, an obvious) public authority within the meaning of section 6 of the HRA with a duty to act compatibly with the Convention in the exercise of her functions under the Data Protection Acts.[88]

4. SURVEILLANCE

19.52   This section considers some aspects of the surveillance of private individuals and its interrelationship with Article 8 including the use of CCTV and interception of telephone and email communications. The obtaining of video evidence by enquiry agents for use in civil proceedings is discussed in relation to evidence in Chapter 11.[89] Surveillance in the workplace is discussed further in Chapter 13 Employment Law.[90] A brief overview of the statutory framework for investigatory surveillance in criminal proceedings is included here by way of background only.

The Victim Requirement

19.53   The European Court has taken a broad approach to the question of whether an applicant who complains about state surveillance can claim to be a "victim" of a violation within the meaning of Article 34 of the Convention. In *Klass v. Germany*,[91] although the applicants could not prove that any surveillance measure had been taken against them, the Court found that because the contested legislation permitted the monitoring of post and telecommunications from any citizen, the applicants were potentially affected and could claim the status of "victims". In *Malone v. United Kingdom*,[92] the Court stated that the mere existence of laws and practices establishing the system of secret surveillance of communications amounted in itself to an interference with the applicant's right guaranteed under Article 8, "apart from any measures actually taken against him". In the absence of such laws and practices, the applicant must prove that there is a "reasonable likelihood" that the actions alleged to constitute interference have occurred.[93]

Surveillance Must Be "in Accordance with the Law"

19.54   In relation to the requirement that an interference with the right to respect for private life be "in accordance with the law", the European Court has

---

[87] R. Jay, "UK Data Protection Act 1998—the Human Rights Context", (2000) 14 I.R.L.C.T. 3, 385–395 at 390.
[88] See further paras 8.15 *et seq*.
[89] At paras 11.48 *et seq*.
[90] At paras 13.80 *et seq*.
[91] (1980) 2 E.H.R.R. 214.
[92] (1985) 7 E.H.R.R. 14 at para. 64.
[93] *Halford v. United Kingdom* (1997) 24 E.H.R.R. 523, paras 47 and 57. See also *Hilton v. United Kingdom* (1988) 57 D.R. 108.

vigorously applied the requirement of "foreseeability" and has required the relevant domestic law to be formulated with sufficient certainty and precision. It considers:

> "whether the essential elements of the power to intercept communications are laid down with reasonable precision in accessible legal rules that sufficiently indicated the scope and manner of exercise of the discretion conferred on the relevant authorities".[94]

The "precision" test requires that there be "adequate safeguards against **19.55** various possible abuses" to be prescribed in law.[95] National law must define the scope and conditions for the exercise of the discretion of the executive authorities.

Proportionality

In assessing proportionality, the Court looks closely at the seriousness of **19.56** the interference and allows a narrower margin of appreciation in this context.[96] Where considerations of national security or protection against organised crime are in issue, the Court will allow a wider margin of appreciation but even here, it requires the State to prescribe in law "adequate and effective safeguards against abuse".[97] There must be a sufficient degree of democratic control (usually judicial control) over the exercise of discretion enjoyed by executive authorities.

CCTV and Stored Images

Surreptitious interception by the state authorities of an individual's com- **19.57** munications constitutes an interference with that person's rights under Article 8(1) which falls to be justified under Article 8(2).[98] The lack of regulation over the use of closed circuit television recordings ("CCTV") in public places was challenged domestically in *R. v. Brentwood Borough Council, ex p. Peck*.[99] Mr Peck had tried to commit suicide by cutting his wrists with a knife. Unknown to him, his actions were video recorded. He was released by the police without charge. Subsequently, the local authority distributed copies of the incident to the media. The footage showed the applicant walking along a street with a knife but did not show him cutting his wrists. He was recognised by friends and neighbours when it was

---

[94] *Malone v. United Kingdom* (1985) 7 E.H.R.R. 14 at para. 70; *Halford v. United Kingdom* (1997) 24 E.H.R.R. 523. See further paras 4.43 *et seq.*
[95] *Kruslin v. France* (1990) 12 E.H.R.R. 547; *Huvig v. France* (1990) 12 E.H.R.R. 528. See further para. 4.45.
[96] In *Leander v. Sweden* (1987) 9 E.H.R.R. 433, the Court stated: "However, the Court recognises that the national authorities enjoy a margin of appreciation, the scope of which will depend not only on the nature of the legitimate aim pursued but also on the particular nature of the interference involved. In the instant case, the interest of the respondent State in protecting its national security must be balanced against the seriousness of the interference with the applicant's right to respect for his private life". (at para. 59). See further paras 4.22 *et seq.*
[97] *Klass v. Germany* (1980) 2 E.H.R.R. 214, para. 50. See also *Leander v. Sweden* (1987) 9 E.H.R.R. 433, para. 60.
[98] See *e.g.*, *Klass v. Germany* (1980) 2 E.H.R.R. 214; *Malone v. United Kingdom* (1985) 7 E.H.R.R. 14.
[99] [1998] E.M.L.R. 697, CA; [1997] T.L.R. 676, Harrison J.

shown on television and depicted in a local paper. Harrison J. held that the local authority did not act unlawfully in giving to the media copies of the CCTV recording made in a public place. The Claimant's appeal to the Court of Appeal was dismissed. This case is now the subject of an application to the European Court in *Peck v. United Kingdom*[1] and the European Court's forthcoming judgment should provide some valuable guidance on the issue of CCTV.

19.58 There is an issue over whether there can be any remaining right to respect for private life in relation to the recording of images in public places.[2] However, the approach taken by the Court of Appeal in *R. v. Broadcasting Standards Commission, ex p. BBC*,[3] showed that privacy is not lost solely because filming takes place in a public place at least as a matter of domestic law.[3A]

19.59 Internal surveillance of staff by employers involving the use of CCTV may violate Article 8 unless an employer can bring himself within Article 8(2) and show that the surveillance went no further than was necessary in a democratic society for the Article 8(2) aim sought to be achieved. It may be possible to imply a waiver of Article 8 rights (or consent to processing of data by CCTV pursuant to the Data Protection Act 1998) if employees or individuals are notified in advance that CCTV cameras will be recording them. Against that, it might be argued that the mere knowledge that an individual is undergoing surveillance hampers their ability to lead a private life and nevertheless contravenes Article 8.[4]

"Eavesdropping" or Interception of Telecommunications

19.60 Telephone tapping and the surveillance or interception of email also raises Article 8 issues. In *Malone v. United Kingdom*,[5] the European Court of Human Rights found that the regulation of telephone-tapping by administrative practice violated Article 8 because of the lack of a clear and accessible legal regulatory framework. The lack of a proper legal basis has been the principal reason for a finding of violation of Article 8 in a series of telephone-tapping cases.[6] As a result of this decision, the United Kingdom enacted the Interception of Communications Act 1985. The current law is principally contained in the Police Act 1997, the Regulation of Investigatory Powers Act 2000 and the Telecommunications (Lawful Business Practice) (Interception of Communications) Regulations 2000.

19.61 The case of *Halford v. United Kingdom*[7] is of importance in the civil context because it did not relate to surveillance of possible criminals but to surveillance of an employee's telephone lines at work. Alison Halford, who

---

[1] Application No. 44647/98.
[2] See J. Wadham, "Remedies for unlawful CCTV surveillance—Part 2", NLJ, August 11, 2000, at 1236.
[3] [2000] 3 W.L.R. 1327, CA; [1999] E.M.L.R. 858 Forbes J; [2001] 1 W.L.R. 550, HL (petition for leave to appeal dismissed).
[3A] See further paras 11.56 and 14.87.
[4] See further para. 13.80.
[5] (1985) 7 E.H.R.R. 14.
[6] See *e.g.*, *Govell v. United Kingdom* [1999] E.H.R.L.R. 121; *Khan v. United Kingdom* [2000] 8 B.H.R.C. 310; *The Times*, May 23, 2000.
[7] (1997) 24 E.H.R.R. 523.

was Assistant Chief Constable of Merseyside, complained that private calls from her office telephone were intercepted to obtain information to use against her in her sex discrimination claim against the police. The European Court held that telephone calls from business premises as well as from home may be covered by the notion of "private life" and "correspondence" within Article 8(1). Since Ms Halford had not been warned that calls on the internal telecommunications system might be intercepted, she had a "reasonable expectation" of privacy. Emphasis was placed on the fact that she was not given any warning about the possibility of tapping and had been provided with a second telephone designated for her private use. Since the telephone system fell outside the ambit of the Interception of Communications Act 1985, the interception was not in accordance with law and a violation of Article 8 was established.

One significant issue in this context relates to the fact that Article 8 is **19.62** primarily vertical in its effect. Accordingly, public authorities will have to comply with the Convention. However, the horizontal effect of the Act in the context of a private employer and private employee or private body and private individual is yet unclear.[8] It is likely that the courts will endeavour, where this issue arises in the context of other private law claims, to ensure consistency of approach with the public employment context.

It may be possible to justify interception of telephone calls (for example, for **19.63** the maintenance of quality standards in a call centre) or of employees' email (for example, carrying out ad hoc checks where private use is regulated) as falling within one or more of the justifications in Article 8(2) such as the prevention of crime or the interests of the economic well-being of the country. For example, in *R. (on the application of N) v. Ashworth Special Hospital Authority and Secretary of State for Health*,[9] Newman J. held that although the random monitoring of telephone calls of patients in high security hospitals was an interference with patients' right to respect for private life under Article 8, it went no further than strictly necessary to achieve the permitted aim.[9A] The judge relied particularly on the fact that there was cogent and compelling evidence to justify the conclusion that patients in high security hospitals were likely, unless prevented, to abuse the use of telephone calls in a manner which would give rise to security risks to themselves, other patients, staff and members of the public. It is essential that that there are adequate safeguards against abuse and that any interference with the right to respect for private life is both necessary in a democratic society and proportionate. Where practical, the provision of clear warnings or guidelines, so that the individual or employee can reasonably anticipate the circumstances in which surveillance will or might place, will be of considerable importance.

On the subject of email, the failure of an authority or employer to arrange **19.64** secure encryption of confidential information identifying or relating to individuals might arguably constitute a failure to protect individual rights to privacy under Article 8.

---

[8] See the discussion of Vertical and Horizontal Effect in paras 5.15 *et seq.*
[9] *The Times*, June 26, 2001, QBD.
[9A] Calls protected by legal professional privilege were not subject to monitoring.

19.65 The opening of personal correspondence may also potentially constitute a breach of Article 8: *Campbell v. United Kingdom*.[10] The interference need not be surreptitious in order to amount to a violation of Article 8(1): *Silver v. United Kingdom*.[11]

The Regulation of Investigatory Powers Act 2000

19.66 Following a number of cases in which the European Court held that the legal basis for surveillance and use of undercover agents by state bodies was insufficiently clear and accessible to comply with the rule of law,[12] the law in this area was increasingly tightened up[13] and culminated in the passing of the Regulation of Investigatory Powers Act 2000 which deals with surveillance in Part II (sections 21 to 48).[14] Part II statutorily regulates "directed surveillance", "covert human intelligence" and "intrusive surveillance" in section 26. Accordingly, the use of informants, undercover agents and telephone tapping or other interception of communications for the purposes of investigation are all now regulated by the 2000 Act. The Act was passed in order to ensure that surveillance techniques are probably regulated by law and externally supervised.[15] Surveillance is regulated by a number of agencies for example, the Secretary of State in relation to the security services and senior police officers in the case of the police, subject to external supervision by the Surveillance Commissioners. Considerations of necessity and proportionality are expressly built into the grant of authorisation for surveillance.[16] Where the persons making and receiving the communications have consented to the interception, it is not prohibited by the 2000 Act.[17]

The Telecommunications (Lawful Business Practice) (Interception of Communications) Regulations 2000

19.67 The 2000 Regulations came into force on October 24, 2000.[18] They authorise certain interceptions of telecommunication communications which would otherwise be prohibited by section 1 of the Regulation of

---

[10] (1993) 15 E.H.R.R. 137.

[11] (1983) 5 E.H.R.R. 347.

[12] See *e.g.* the cases on telephone tapping including *Malone v. United Kingdom* (1985) 7 E.H.R.R. 14, which led to the passing of the Interception of Communications Act 1985, *Govell v. United Kingdom* [1999] E.H.R.L.R. 121 *cf. Esbester v. United Kingdom* (1994) 18 E.H.R.R. C.D. 72.

[13] See the Home Office Circular 97/1969 on the use of informants and undercover officers, the 1984 Home Office Guidelines on the use of equipment in police surveillance operations, the Interception of Communications Act 1985 (telephone tapping), the Police Act 1997 (intrusive surveillance), the ACPO guidelines for the police and Customs & Excise produced in May 1999 (which also deal with test purchasing). See further A. Jennings & D. Friedman, "The Future of Covert Policing: will it rest in peace?" Part 1, Archbold News, Issue 8, October 26, 2000 and Part 2, Archbold News, Issue 9, November 29, 2000.

[14] This came into force on September 25, 2000: Regulation of Investigatory Powers Act 2000 (Commencement No 1 and Transitional Provisions) Order 2000, S.I. 2000 No. 2543.

[15] H.C. Deb., March 6, 2000, col. 677.

[16] See section 28 of the 2000 Act.

[17] For a discussion of the human rights concerns raised by the 2000 Act whilst it was proceeding through Parliament, see *e.g.* Justice Human Rights Audit for the second reading of the Bill in the House of Lords, May 2000 available from Justice (whose contact details appear in the table at para. 8.82).

[18] S.I. 2000 No. 2699.

Investigatory Powers Act 2000.[19] The interception has to be by or with the consent of a person carrying on business[20] for purposes relevant to that person's business and using that business's own telecommunications system. Interceptions are authorised for the purposes of:

(1) monitoring or recording communications;

    (a) to establish the existence of facts, to ascertain compliance with regulatory or self-regulatory practices or procedures or for quality control and training;

    (b) in the interests of national security (but only certain specified public officials may make the interception);

    (c) to prevent or detect crime;

    (d) to investigate or detect unauthorised use of telecommunication systems; or

    (e) to secure, or as an inherent part of, effective system operation.

(2) monitoring received communications to determine whether they are business or personal communications;

(3) monitoring communications made to anonymous telephone helplines.[21]

19.68 Importantly, interceptions are authorised only if the controller of the telecommunication system on which they are effected has made all reasonable efforts to inform potential users that interceptions may be made.[22] This is intended to be compatible with the rule of law and the proportionality test under Article 8.[22A]

Regulators of State Surveillance

19.69 A Chief Surveillance Commissioner and ordinary Surveillance Commissioners were established under sections 57 to 64 Regulation of Investigatory Powers Act 2000, the former being appointed in July 1998, the latter in November 1998. Under section 38 of the 2000 Act, any senior authorising officer can appeal to the Chief Surveillance Commissioner against the refusal of an ordinary Surveillance Commissioner to approve authorisation for the carrying out of surveillance. There is a seven-day time limit for the lodging of an appeal from the date that approval was refused. If the Chief Surveillance Commissioner dismisses the appeal, he reports to the person applying for the appeal and the Prime Minister. There is no opportunity for making oral representations and the Chief Surveillance Commissioner does not have to give reasons for his decisions on

---

[19] To the extent that the interceptions are also prohibited by Art. 5.1 of Directive 97/66 of the European Parliament and of the Council dated December 15, 1997 concerning the processing of personal data and the protection of privacy in the telecommunications sector, the authorisation does not exceed that permitted by Arts 5.2 and 14.1 of the Directive: reg. 3(3).

[20] This includes the activities of government departments, public authorities and others exercising statutory functions.

[21] See reg. 2(2).

[22] See reg. 2(2)(c).

[22A] See further para. 13.80.

appeals lodged under section 38. The Surveillance Commissioners are at least hybrid public authorities (and possibly, obvious public authorities) within the meaning of section 6 of the HRA and have a duty to act compatibly with the Convention in relation to their statutory functions.[22B] Section 65 of the 2000 Act has created a special tribunal to deal with complaints in relation to the use of surveillance techniques. However, there is no power of appeal or review from a decision of the tribunal to a court of law. Further, it is immune from civil liability, which may in itself contravene the approach taken by the European Court to the right of access to a court and to immunities generally.[23]

5. PRODUCT LIABILITY

19.70 The HRA is likely to have an impact in domestic law claims involving product, medicine or food safety through the application of Articles 2 and 8 of the Convention.

Article 2

19.71 An important case which is relevant to product liability under Article 2 is *LCB v. United Kingdom*.[24] In this case, a woman who had been diagnosed with leukaemia brought a claim against the Government under Article 2, on the basis that the disease had been caused by her father's exposure to radiation whilst serving with the Royal Air Force during nuclear tests conducted on Christmas Island in the late 1950s. She could not challenge the actual exposure to radiation because this occurred prior to the United Kingdom granting the right of individual petition. Instead, she alleged that the United Kingdom owed a duty to warn and advise her parents of the dangers involved in the nuclear testing and to monitor her health prior to the diagnosis of leukaemia, and that this duty had been breached. The European Court dismissed the claim primarily because it had no jurisdiction to consider the complaint, the events of which complaint was made having taken place prior to the United Kingdom's grant of the right of individual petition. However, it went on to consider the complaint under Article 2 on its merits and found there was no violation because there was insufficient evidence of causation between the father's exposure to radiation and his daughter's leukaemia at the relevant time, or even subsequently. The Court concluded that:

> " . . . it [did] not find it established that, given the information available to the State at the relevant time concerning the likelihood of the applicant's father having been exposed to dangerous levels of radiation and of this having created a risk to her health, it could have been expected to act of its own motion to notify her parents of these matters or to take any other special action in relation to her."[25]

[22B] See further paras 8.15 *et seq.*
[23] See further Chap. 17 (Professional Liability & Negligence) where immunities are discussed at paras 17.41 *et seq.*
[24] (1999) 27 E.H.R.R. 212.
[25] At para. 41.

However, importantly, the Court stated that the test to be applied was **19.72**
whether, given the circumstances of the case, the state did all that could
have been required of it to prevent a life from being avoidably put at risk.
It stated:

> "The applicant complained . . . that the respondent State's failure to
> warn and advise her parents to monitor her health prior to her diag-
> nosis with leukaemia in October 1970 had given rise to a violation of
> Article 2 of the Convention.
>
> In this connection, the Court considers that the first sentence of
> Article 2(1) enjoins the State not only to refrain from the intentional
> and unlawful taking of life, but also to take appropriate steps to
> safeguard the lives of those within its jurisdiction. It has not been
> suggested that the respondent State intentionally sought to deprive
> the applicant of her life. *The Court's task is, therefore, to determine
> whether, given the circumstances of the case, the State did all that
> could have been required of it to prevent the applicant's life from
> being avoidably put at risk.*" (emphasis added)[26]

The Court accepted that the State might have been required to take steps **19.73**
to warn and advise if it appeared likely at the relevant time that the father's
exposure to radiation might endanger the health of any future children.
However, it seems that the State was only required to take such steps in
relation to the applicant if:

> "it had appeared *likely* at that time that any such exposure of her
> father to radiation might have engendered *a real risk to her health.*"
> (emphasis added)[27]

The duty to establish that a real risk to health appeared to be likely at the
time in question appears to be a fairly significant hurdle to a claimant
seeking to allege that the state should have warned him about a risk to
health that was only "theoretical" or merely "possible" at the time in
question.

The right to life has also been utilised to extend constitutional protection **19.74**
for human health and a cleaner environment in other jurisdictions, particularly on the Indian sub-continent. In India, the constitutional right to life
set out in Article 21 of the Indian Constitution has been held to extend to
the right to pollution free air and to a decent environment.[28] Accordingly,
smoking in public places was declared unconstitutional and the state of
Kerala was ordered to take affirmative action to promulgate instructions for
the prosecution of all persons found guilty of smoking in public places as
a "public nuisance" within section 268 of the Indian Penal Code.[29] In a
case challenging the construction of high voltage transmission lines on the
ground that the electromagnetic field would pose a serious health hazard
to the residents such as to infringe their constitutional right to life, the

---

[26] At para. 36.
[27] At para. 38.
[28] *Ramakrishnan v. State of Kerala*, 1999 (2) KLT 725, High Court, Kerala.
[29] Above.

Pakistan Supreme Court has held that where there is a state of uncertainty, the authorities should observe "the rules of prudence and precaution" by considering first the welfare and safety of human beings and the environment and adopting a policy suitable to obviate the possible danger or, alternatively, by taking such precautionary measures as might ensure safety.[30] The court stated that any action taken which may create hazards of life would be encroaching upon the citizen's right to life. A person was entitled to protection of law from being exposed to hazards of electromagnetic fields or any other such hazards which might be due to the installation and construction of any grid station, factory, power station or similar installation. However, a balance needed to be struck between the rights of citizens on the one hand and plans executed by the power authorities for the welfare, economic progress and prosperity of the country on the other. The above international cases do, however, appear to go beyond the more limited purview of the state's duty in relation to Article 2 set out in *LCB* to which domestic courts must have regard under section 2 of the HRA and are mainly of interest in relation to possible contexts in which Article 2 might in future be invoked.

Article 8

19.75 Further, the right to respect for private and family life under Article 8 of the Convention may also be relevant in the product liability context. In *Guerra v. Italy*,[31] the applicants lived within a mile of a chemical factory which produced fertilisers and captolactam and was classified as a high risk in terms of hazards to the environment and to the local population. In the course of production, the factory released large quantities of inflammable gas and other toxic substances, including arsenic trioxide. On a previous occasion, following the explosion of part of the factory, several tonnes of toxic substances escaped and 150 people had to be hospitalised because of acute arsenic poisoning. The European Court held that the direct effect of the toxic emissions on the applicants' right to respect for their private and family life meant that Article 8 was applicable.[32] The complaint was in relation to not an act of the state but a failure to act. The court held that there may be positive obligations on the state inherent in effective respect for private and family life.[33] The test in the present case was whether the national authorities took the necessary steps to ensure effective protection of the applicant's right to respect for private and family life.[34] The court found a violation of Article 8 because the applicants had to wait several years for essential information that would have enabled them to assess the risks they and their families might run if they continued to live in the vicinity of the factory, a place particularly exposed to danger in the event of a further accident at the factory, or as to the action which ought to be

---

[30] *Shehla Zia & ors v. Wapda*, February 12, 1994, Sup. Ct., Pakistan, digested in [1996] 1 CHRD 83 (The court ordered that in light of the highly technical science, a Commissioner be appointed to further examine and report on the scheme and on the likelihood of any hazard).
[31] (1998) 26 E.H.R.R. 357.
[32] At para. 57.
[33] See further in relation to positive obligations at paras 5.28 *et seq.*
[34] At para. 58.

taken in the event of such an accident.[35] The duty to provide information as to severe environmental hazards which carry a risk to health under Article 8 echoes the approach taken in *LCB* above in relation to Article 2.

In *McGinley & Egan v. United Kingdom*,[36] a case which, like *LCB* related **19.76** to nuclear testing at Christmas Island during the 1950s, the applicants who were then stationed on the island complained that their rights to a fair hearing under Article 6 before the Pensions Appeal Tribunal and to respect for their private and family lives under Article 8 had been violated by the withholding of documents which would have helped them to ascertain whether there was a link between their health problems and exposure to radiation. The court ruled that there had been no violation of the Convention in this case. However, it stated that Article 8 was applicable because in the absence of individual monitoring, the applicants, who had been ordered to take part in a line-up procedure in the open during each explosion, were left in doubt as to whether or not they had been exposed to radiation levels engendering risk to their health. The issue of access to information which could either have allayed their fears or enabled them to assess the danger to which they had been exposed was sufficiently closely linked to their private and family lives within the meaning of Article 8 as to raise an issue under that provision. The court held that given the applicants' interest in obtaining information relating to radiation levels on Christmas Island following the tests, and the apparent absence of any countervailing public interest in retaining it, a positive obligation on the national authorities to establish an effective and accessible procedure which enabled persons such as the applicants to seek all relevant and appropriate information arose. The court stated that:

> "Where a Government engages in hazardous activities, such as those in issue in the present case, which might have hidden adverse consequences on the health of those involved in such activities, respect for private and family life under Article 8 requires that an effective and accessible procedure be established which enables such persons to seek all relevant and appropriate information".[37]

Despite this finding of a positive obligation, the court ruled that there had **19.77** been no violation of Article 8 on the facts because a procedure existed in the Pension Appeals Tribunal by which the applicants could have obtained disclosure of the relevant documents. Neither of the applicants had availed themselves of this procedure or requested from the competent authorities at any other time the production of the documents in question.[38]

In *López Ostra v. Spain*,[39] a case concerning the release of nauseating **19.78** smells, noxious fumes and persistent noise from a waste treatment plant close to the applicant's home, the court held that the municipality, which

---

[35] At paras 59–60.
[36] (1997) 27 E.H.R.R. 1.
[37] At para. 101.
[38] At paras 102–104.
[39] (1995) 20 E.H.R.R. 277.

had a supervisory jurisdiction over the waste treatment plant had failed to take the measures necessary for protecting the applicant's right to respect for her home and for her private and family life under Article 8. The court held that:

> " . . . severe environmental pollution may affect individuals' well-being and prevent them from enjoying their homes in such a way as to affect their private and family life adversely, without, however, seriously endangering their health".[40]

19.79 The court did not find it necessary to categorise the state's duty under Article 8 as a positive obligation stating that the real test was whether a fair balance had been struck between the competing interests of the individual and the community as a whole, in relation to which the state enjoys a certain margin of appreciation:

> "Whether the question is analysed in terms of positive duty on the State—to take reasonable and appropriate measures to secure the applicant's rights under paragraph 1 of Article 8—, as the applicant wishes in her case, or in terms of an 'interference by a public authority' to be justified in accordance with paragraph 2, the applicable principles are broadly similar. In both contexts regard must be had to the fair balance that has to be struck between the competing interests of the individual and of the community as a whole, and in any case the State enjoys a certain margin of appreciation. Furthermore, even in relation to the positive obligations flowing from the first paragraph of Article 8, in striking the required balance the aims mentioned in the second paragraph may be of a certain relevance".

This "fair balance" approach to Article 8 in the context of severe environmental nuisances echoes that taken by the court to interferences with the right to peaceful enjoyment of possessions under Article 1 of Protocol No. 1. On the facts of *López Ostra*, despite the margin of appreciation afforded by the Court to the State, the Court held that, the State did not succeed in striking a fair balance between the interest of the town's economic well-being in having a waste treatment plant—and the applicant's effect enjoyment of her right to respect for her home and her private and family life. Accordingly, it found a violation of Article 8.

19.80 It is relevant that in *López Ostra*, the plant had caused health problems to many local people.[41] Further, the applicant had been forced to move from her home in part because her daughter's paediatrician had recommended that they do so following her daughter's presentation with nausea, vomiting, allergic reactions and anorexia which the paediatrician was of the view could only be explained by the fact that she was living in a highly polluted area.[42]

19.81 In the absence of a serious risk to health, the Court has generally been less receptive towards complaints of environmental nuisance based on

---

[40] At para. 51.
[41] See paras 7, 8 and 52.
[42] See paras 16, 17, 19 and 57.

Article 8 more generally. In *Powell & Rayner v. United Kingdom*,[43] owners of property situated near Heathrow Airport brought a complaint against the United Kingdom government about failing to take sufficient action to regulate excessive noise levels arising from the operation of the airport. Whilst the court found that aircraft noise may constitute an environmental nuisance in that the quality of the applicants' private lives and the scope for enjoying the amenities of their homes was adversely affected by the noise, albeit to differing degrees,[44] it did not find a violation of Article 8. The court held that irrespective of the nature of the obligations imposed on the respondent government under Article 8, a fair balance had to be struck between the competing interests of the individual and of the community as a whole. In its regulation of aircraft noise, the respondent government had not exceeded the margin of appreciation or upset the fair balance required to be struck.[45]

Similarly, in *Khatun and 180 others v. United Kingdom*,[46] the Commission **19.82** rejected as manifestly unfounded and inadmissible a complaint brought by residents of the Docklands about high levels of dust contamination caused by the construction of the Limehouse Link Road giving access to the Docklands Area from Central London. The House of Lords had held that residents who did not have a proprietary right to the land could not bring an action in private nuisance and in the case of those that did, their only damage was not for discomfort to the person but for the loss of amenity or diminution in value of the land.[47] The Commission considered that Article 8(1) applied to all the applicants in the case, whether they were owners or merely occupiers living on the property. However, having regard to the fair balance that had to be struck between the competing interests of the individual and the community as a whole, and in any case, bearing in mind the state's margin of appreciation, the Commission considered that in light of the general community interest in regeneration of the Docklands, to which the construction of the road was essential, and the limits on the extent to which the applicants suffered from the dust caused, it could not find that a fair balance had not been achieved.[47A]

Applicability of Article 10?

In *Guerra v. Italy*,[48] the court expressly rejected the applicability of Article **19.83** 10 in this context, holding that the freedom to receive information referred to in Article 10(2) "basically prohibits a government from restricting a person from receiving information that others wish or may be willing to impart to him".[49] That freedom could not be construed as imposing on a state in circumstances such as the *Guerra* case, positive obligations to collect and disseminate information of its own motion.

---

[43] (1990) 12 E.H.R.R. 355.
[44] At para. 40.
[45] At paras 42–46.
[46] (1998) 26 E.H.R.R. C.D. 212.
[47] *Hunter and others v. Canary Wharf Ltd; Hunter and others v. London Docklands Development Corp.* [1997] 2 All E.R. 426, HL.
[47A] See further in relation to environmental nuisance, paras 16.111 *et seq.*
[48] (1998) 26 E.H.R.R. 357.
[49] *Leander v. Sweden* (1987) 9 E.H.R.R. 433, para. 74. See also *Gaskin v. United Kingdom* (1990) 12 E.H.R.R. 36, para. 52.

Duty on Public Authorities in Response to Health Risks

19.84   It is clear from the European Court's case-law that the HRA must now be borne in mind by public authorities when deciding how to respond to and regulate potentially life-threatening health risks and more particularly, in relation to the provision of advice or information relating to those risks to those who are or might potentially be affected. Further, arguments invoking the HRA will almost certainly be raised in proceedings involving public authorities where the subject matter is concerned with the response to and regulation of actual or potential risks to life, health and safety, including that of severe environmental pollution with potentially adverse implications for human health. A new potential domestic law liability exists through the medium of Articles 2 and 8, although section 22(4) of the HRA prevents any free-standing section 7(1)(a) claim against a public authority for breach of a Convention right based on any act or omission occurring prior to October 2, 2000.[50] It may also be possible to buttress an existing cause of action in negligence concerning the duty to warn of potential health risks under section 7(1)(b) of the HRA by reference to approach taken under the Convention.[51]

19.85   It is likely, however, that a reasonably wide discretion will be granted to the public authority in question in deciding what steps to take to regulate a potential danger in the light of known risks in the same way that the European Court grants a fairly wide margin of appreciation to the State in this context. In the case of environmental nuisances where there is no potential health risk, consideration of whether a fair balance has been struck between the general community interest and the interest of the individual is central to the issue.[51A]

The Food Standards Agency as Regulator

19.86   The Food Standards Agency was established by the Food Standards Act 1999 and came into being on April 1, 2000. The Food Standards Agency was created to:

> "protect public health from risks which may arise on connection with the consumption of food, and otherwise to protect the interests of consumers in relation to food".[52]

19.87   The Food Standards Agency does not hold proceedings *per se*, but indicates that it will consult widely before taking action and making recommendations, unless urgent action is essential. The Agency occupies a unique legal position in that it has the power to publish the advice it gives to the Government. It is almost certainly a public authority within the meaning of section 6 of the HRA.[52A] However, the fact that it does not hold proceedings will limit the scope for challenges based on Article 6.

---

[50] See further paras 8.36 *et seq.*
[51] See further paras 8.42 *et seq.*
[51A] See further paras 16.111 *et seq.*, particularly para. 16.122.
[52] See the Food Standards Agency web-site at www.foodstandards.gov.uk
[52A] See paras 8.16 *et seq.*

Other Regulators Concerned with Product Safety

There are a great variety of bodies concerned with the safety of products, **19.88** both on the European Community level and domestic level. These include the European Commission, central government departments such as the Ministry of Agriculture, Fisheries and Food and the Department of Health. In relation to medicines, the Medicines Commission, the Committee on the Safety of Medicines and the Licensing Authority are the relevant bodies. At the local level, the environmental health departments of local authorities have regulatory responsibilities. All of these bodies are likely to constitute public authorities for the purposes of section 6 of the HRA and must comply with the Convention in the exercise of their functions.[52B] The primary mechanism for the determination of product liability issues is through litigation in the ordinary courts which are themselves under a duty pursuant to section 6 of the HRA to comply with Article 6(1).

6. CONSUMER CREDIT

The Consumer Credit Act 1974

Following the coming into force of the HRA, the Court of Appeal raised a **19.89** novel HRA point of its own motion, in the context of a dispute over a consumer credit transaction which culminated in the Court of Appeal making a declaration that section 127(3) of the Consumer Credit Act 1974, which makes a loan agreement unenforceable where there has been a failure to comply with certain prescribed requirements, was incompatible with the rights of the creditor under Article 6(1) and Article 1 of Protocol No. 1 to the Convention. The case of *Wilson v. First County Trust*,[53] arose out of a loan agreement in which First County Trust, a pawnbroker, agreed to lend to the claimant the sum of £5,000 for six months on the security of her BMW convertible. It also charged a £250 document fee which it was agreed could be added to the amount of the loan. The agreement, which was regulated by the Consumer Credit Act 1974 stated the amount of the loan to be £5,250. The claimant did not repay the loan on the due date and First County sought payment of the full amount due, in default of which it intended to enforce its security against the BMW. The claimant brought proceedings in the country court, claiming that the agreement was unenforceable under the Consumer Credit Act because the prescribed term incorrectly stated the amount of credit. The claimant did not succeed before H.H.J. Hull Q.C. at first instance but was granted permission to appeal. The claimant appealed against the decision, alleging that the loan agreement was unenforceable for failure to contain the terms prescribed by section 61 Consumer Credit Act 1974 and Schedule 6 to the Consumer Credit (Agreements) Regulations 1983 and that the court was therefore precluded by section 127(3) of the 1974 Act from enforcing the agreement. The court adjourned the appeal holding that it was unclear whether section 127(3) of the 1974 Act was compatible with the Convention, and with

---

[52B] See further paras 8.15 *et seq.*
[53] *(No. 1)* (2001) 2 W.L.R. 302, CA; *(No. 2)*, [2001] 3 W.L.R. 42, [2001] EWCA Civ 633, CA.

Article 6(1) and Article 1 of Protocol No. 1 in particular, because it arguably deprived the lender of his right to be repaid the loan made to the claimant.[54] Notice was given to the Crown under section 5 of the HRA because the court was considering making a declaration of incompatibility. The issue was heard over two days of argument and on May 2, 2001, the Court of Appeal gave judgment in *Wilson v. First County Trust (No. 2).*[55] In relation to its jurisdiction to apply the Convention to the subject matter of the case before it, the court held that section 6(1) of the HRA, in conjunction with section 6(3)(a) of the HRA, required the court to refrain from acting in a way which was incompatible with a Convention right. The court held that it had to ask itself in any case coming before it after October 2, 2000 whether the order it was about to make was compatible with Convention rights. The relevant event was the making of the order on the appeal and not the making of the original agreement.[56] The court then went on to hold that the inflexible prohibition in section 127(3) of the Consumer Credit Act 1974 against the making of an enforcement order in a case where a loan agreement signed by the debtor did not include the prescribed terms, infringed both Article 6 and Article 1 of Protocol No. 1 to an extent which was disproportionate.

19.90 The Court of Appeal rejected an argument on behalf of the Secretary of State for Trade and Industry that the creditor had no relevant possessions to the peaceful enjoyment of which it was entitled, or of which it was deprived, in relation to Article 1 of Protocol No. 1, on the basis that where there was no document signed by the debtor, or where the document signed by the debtor did not contain all the prescribed terms of the agreement, neither the agreement nor the delivery of the pawn conferred any enforceable rights on the creditor. The court held that nothing in the 1974 Act prevented an improperly executed regulated agreement from giving rise to contractual rights.[57] The correct analysis was that the agreement, and delivery of the pawn, did confer rights on the creditor, but those rights were subject to restrictions on enforcement. Those restrictions attracted the operation of Article 6(1) by reason of the exclusion of a judicial remedy.[58] Further, the effect of sections 65(1) and 127(3) of the 1974 Act was to deprive the pawnbroker of its ability to enjoy benefit from the contractual rights arising from the agreement or the rights arising from delivery of the pawn, attracting the applicability of Article 1 of Protocol No. 1.[59] Article 1 of Protocol No. 1 required a fair balance to be struck between the rights of the individual to enjoy possessions and the general interest.[60] Whilst the policy aim of section 127(3), namely to ensure that particular attention was paid to the inclusion in the document to be signed by the debtor of certain terms prescribed by the Secretary of State, was a legitimate one, the effect of an inflexible statutory prohibition against the

---

[54] (2001) 2 W.L.R. 302, CA.
[55] [2001] 3 W.L.R. 42, CA; [2001] EWCA Civ 633.
[56] At para. 17.
[57] At para. 24.
[58] At para. 28.
[59] At para. 32.
[60] The Court cited *Sporrong and Lonnroth v. Sweden* (1983) 5 E.H.R.R. 35, paras 69–70; *James v. United Kingdom* (1986) 8 E.H.R.R. 123, para. 50 and *Allgemeine Gold-und Silberscheideanstalt v. United Kingdom* (1987) 9 E.H.R.R. 1, paras 52–55.

making of an enforcement order in a case where the document signed by the debtor did not include the prescribed terms was neither necessary nor proportionate. No reason had been advanced or identified as to why an inflexible prohibition was necessary in order to achieve the legitimate aim. There was no reason why that aim could not be achieved through judicial control, by empowering the court to do what is just in the circumstances of a particular case.[61] Since it was not possible to read and give effect to the relevant provisions of the 1974 Act in a way that was compatible with Convention rights,[62] the court made a declaration of incompatibility under section 4 of the HRA.[63] Such a declaration does not affect the validity, continuing operation or enforcement of the provision in respect of which it was given.[64] It is yet to be seen whether the Government will now take remedial action under section 10 of the HRA.[65]

The decision is an example of the perhaps unexpected operation of the HRA in a commercial context and raises the possibility of other claims where a remedy is barred by non-compliance with mechanistic legal requirements.[66] It is relevant that the court noted:

19.91

"[Section 127(3) of the Consumer Credit Act 1974] excludes all consideration of the circumstances of the particular case in favour of a mechanistic approach: does the document contain all the prescribed terms?"

The court's hostility to a mechanistic bar on a judicial remedy and desire for the flexible application of the law to the facts of a particular case is notably similar to that taken by the European Court in relation to the mechanistic striking out of negligence claims based on a strict exclusionary rule in *Osman v. United Kingdom*[67] which was held to violate Article 6.[68]

---

[61] At para. 39.
[62] At para. 45.
[63] At para. 47.
[64] HRA, s.4(6).
[65] See further para. 2.46 and paras 9.14 *et seq.* See by contrast to the *Wilson* approach, the case of *Al-Kishtaini v. Shanshal* [2001] EWCA CIV 264, February 23, 2001, CA (unenforceability of claim on ground of illegality not breach of Art. 1 of Protocol No. 1. Even if the unenforceability of a claim on grounds of illegality was a deprivation of possessions under Art. 1 of Protocol No. 1, the case clearly fell within the public interest exception to the right).
[66] See further, N. Underhill Q.C., "A hard act to follow", The Lawyer, May 21, 2001, p. 43, where he suggests that possible areas for challenge include Employment Rights Act 1996, s.25(4) (where unlawful deduction by employer from employee's wages, employer prevented from recovering the debt by other means), Statute of Frauds Act 1677, s.4 (no recovery under a guarantee where no written and signed memorandum), Law of Property (Miscellaneous Provisions) Act 1989, s.2 (dispositions of interest in land rendered unenforceable by non-compliance with statutory requirements) and Employment Rights Act 1996, s.203 (unenforceability of certain compromise agreements).
[67] (2000) 28 E.H.R.R. 245. See also *Z v. United Kingdom* (1999) 28 E.H.R.R. C.D. 65; Application No. 29392/95, May 10, 2001 (Judgment).
[68] The *Osman* case was cited by the Court of Appeal in the *Wilson (No. 2)* judgment. See further discussion of *Osman* at paras 10.29 *et seq.* and in Chap. 17 (Profesional Liability) at paras 17.11 *et seq.*

Implications of *Wilson* for Lawyers' Liability

19.92   The decision in *Wilson v. First County Trust (No. 2)* has considerable implications for the liabilities of solicitors or barristers who have given advice on the enforceability of consumer credit agreements and the extent of any loss resulting from such advice in the context of professional negligence actions by clients.

7. COMMERCIAL FREE EXPRESSION AND ADVERTISING

Commercial Free Expression

19.93   The fundamental nature of freedom of expression in Article 10 is such that the European Court has interpreted it broadly. However, despite the Court's disavowel of the theoretical basis for differences in the degree of protection afforded to different types of expression,[69] of the three principal forms of expression identified by the Court, namely political expression, artistic expression and commercial expression, it is evident that commercial expression has the least protection.

19.94   Successive governments have attempted to argue that commercial expression does not fall within the scope of Article 10, but this argument has been staunchly rejected. The Court has specifically stated that information of a commercial nature cannot be generally excluded from the scope of Article 10.[70] In *Casado Coca v. Spain*,[71] the Court held that:

> "The guarantee in Article 10 extends to everyone regardless of whether their aim is commercial or not. It protects information of a commercial nature . . . ".

19.95   However, not all information of a commercial nature benefits from the protection afforded by Article 10. In *Jacubowski v. Germany*,[72] a news agency issued a press release questioning the abilities of a former editor. The former editor who was in the course of establishing his own news agency then sent newspaper articles critical of his former employer to a number of journalists. An injunction was issued preventing the former editor from continuing with the mailings. The European Court held that there had been no breach of Article 10, and part of its reasoning was that restriction on publication was justified on the basis of the "essentially competitive purpose of the exercise". It appears therefore that commercial expression which intentionally denigrates a competitor is excluded from the ambit of Article 10.

19.96   It is apparent from Strasbourg case-law that the mode of communication of commercial information is largely irrelevant, although the degree of impact the medium has will be taken into account. In common with the approach of "inclusivity" usually followed in the interpretation of Article 10, the Court has steadfastly refused to give a definition of "information and

---

[69] *Thorgeirson v. Iceland* (1992) 14 E.H.R.R. 843.
[70] *Markt Intern Verlag GmbH & Klaus Beermann v. Germany* (1990) 12 E.H.R.R. 161.
[71] (1994) 18 E.H.R.R. 1.
[72] (1995) 19 E.H.R.R. 64.

ideas" for the purpose of Article 10.[73] This has led to the application of Article 10 to a number of different media. It has already been held to apply to the audio-visual media,[74] satellite broadcasts[75] and newspapers.[76] It will presumably also cover the internet and communications using wireless application protocol ("WAP") mobile telephones, text messages and electronic mail.[77] More recently, Article 10 has been held to apply in the context of a contractual commercial relationship between private persons, where the subject matter of the restriction related to a matter of national debate.[78]

Whilst Article 10 has been held to apply to most forms of commercial information, the court has nevertheless not found a breach of the Article in the majority of cases concerning freedom of expression in the commercial context. In the main, this is because the cases concern whether a restriction can be justified under Article 10(2) and in so deciding, the court has afforded the Member State in question a very significant margin of appreciation[79] in relation to the restrictions placed upon commercial information.[80] The extent of the margin of appreciation is also governed by the degree of commercial information in the publication in question. For example, where a publication contributes to a discussion of a matter of genuine public interest, there will be a narrower margin of appreciation than if the publication's sole effect is to promote a particular project.[81] Accordingly, whilst Article 10 will apply to most types of commercial information, the way in which the margin of appreciation translates into the domestic context will influence the degree of protection afforded to such information by the HRA.[82] Present indications suggest that in practice, whilst the doctrine of "margin of appreciation" will not itself apply, due judicial deference will be shown to legislative or administrative decision makers where this is appropriate. It seems unlikely that there will be any necessity for general deference in relation to commercial free expression, save perhaps where this is concerned with legislative acts. This may therefore be an area in which domestic law is likely to develop in advance of the European Court. **19.97**

---

[73] *Groppera Radio AG v. Switzerland* (1990) 12 E.H.R.R. 321.
[74] *Jersild v. Denmark* (1995) 19 E.H.R.R. 1.
[75] *Autronic AG v. Switzerland* (1990) 12 E.H.R.R. 485.
[76] *Sunday Times v. United Kingdom* (1992) 14 E.H.R.R. 229.
[77] But see also *Brook v. United Kingdom* Application No. 38218/97, July 11, 2000 (admissibility decision) in which it was held to be proportionate to exclude short wave frequencies from the licensing regime.
[78] *Fuentes Bobo v. Spain*, Application No. 39293/98, February 29, 2000.
[79] See for example, *Handyside v. United Kingdom* (1979) 1 E.H.R.R. 737 where it was held that state authorities were better placed than an international court to assess the necessity for a restriction designed to protect morals. See further paras. 4.22 *et seq.*
[80] *Markt Intern Verlag GmbH & Klaus Beermann v. Germany* (1990) 12 E.H.R.R. 161. See also the decision of the European Commission on Human Rights in *Colman v. United Kingdom* (1994) 18 E.H.R.R. 119, in which the restrictions placed upon medical practitioners by the General Medical Council were held to be within the state's margin of appreciation.
[81] *Barthold v. Germany* (1985) 7 E.H.R.R. 383. See also *Casado Coca v. Spain* (1994) 18 E.H.R.R. 1 in which the primary purpose of the publication was publicity, but the secondary effect was the provision of information to persons requiring legal assistance and *Hertel v. Switzerland* (1999) 28 E.H.R.R. 534 where the Court took a more restrictive approach to the margin of appreciation where the submission of a research paper to a scientific journal brought about a criminal conviction.
[82] See further para. 4.22.

Advertising

19.98   According to the Advertising Standards Authority,[83] over 170 statutes directly affect advertising. The Human Rights Act 1998 is but one of those statutes and its potential impact is considered here. Article 10, which protects the right to freedom of expression, is likely to be the most influential of all of the Convention Articles, but there are also potential implications for advertising implicit in Article 14 which prohibits discrimination in the enjoyment of Convention rights and freedoms.

19.99   It is perhaps surprising that the right to advertise a product or service for sale in a particular way falls within the ambit of Article 10. Strictly speaking, such a right is a private commercial right as distinct from a civil or political right of the kind protected by an international human rights instrument. However, the European Court has shown little tolerance for such a distinction, other than affording Contracting States a broader margin of appreciation in respect of restrictions on commercial expression in general, than on other forms of expression, for example political or artistic expression as discussed above. The approach towards advertising has, in common with much other jurisprudence emanating from Strasbourg, nevertheless been incremental.

European Court's Approach to Advertising

19.100   In *Markt Internal Verlag GmbH & Klaus Beermann v. Germany*,[84] the court gave its first indication that commercial information in the form of an information bulletin could, in certain circumstances, benefit from the protection of Article 10. In that case, a publishing company included in their information bulletin an account of a customer who was dissatisfied with the service of a mail order firm. The publishing company was restrained from repeating the account, and subsequently alleged a violation of Article 10. The German Government contended that there was no violation of Article 10 on the ground that the aim of the account included in the information bulletin fell

> " . . . within the scope of the freedom to conduct business and engage in competition, which is not protected by the Convention".

Although the European Court did not find a breach of Article 10 on the facts of the case, it nevertheless made clear that the protection afforded by Article 10 was not restricted to certain types of information or ideas or forms of expression. The court explicitly stated that information of a commercial nature, which by its very definition includes advertisements, could not be excluded from the scope of Article 10. It is relevant that the

---

[83] The Advertising Standards Authority (ASA) is independent of both the Government and the advertising industry. It was established in 1962 to provide independent scrutiny of the self-regulating system set up by the advertising industry. According to paragraph 68.11 of the Advertising Code, the chief tasks of the ASA are "to promote and enforce high standards in adverts, to investigate complaints, to identify and resolve problems through its own research, to ensure that the system operates in the public interest and to act as channels for communications with those who have an interest in advertising standards". It is implicit in this that part of the ASA's remit will extend to the implications for advertising raised by the Convention and HRA.

[84] (1990) 12 E.H.R.R. 161.

court was not compelled to make such a statement since the information bulletin in question was circulated only to a limited number of people in the relevant industry and did not directly concern the public. The court could therefore have quite easily refrained from comment on whether commercial information fell within the scope of Article 10 more generally by distinguishing the material in *Markt Intern* from material that was widely available to the public. It chose not to do so. The judgment in *Markt Intern* thus paved the way for explicit acknowledgement that advertising could fall within the scope of Article 10.

The opportunity for such an acknowledgment arose in *Barthold v. Germany.*[85] In this case, proceedings for a breach of the rules of professional conduct were brought against a veterinary surgeon, who had been critical in a newspaper interview of the lack of late night emergency services in his locality. The applicant had been held to be in breach of Germany's Unfair Competition Act 1909 because the interview had praised his own services and indicated that he was the only veterinary surgeon in the region to provide such a service. The European Commission found a violation of Article 10 and held that whilst the interview in question did not itself involve commercial advertising, commercial advertising did not fall outside the scope of Article 10. The European Court was not quite as bold. Whilst the court reached the same conclusion that:

19.101

> "The presentation of opinions and information in a manner affording publicity cannot be dissociated from the substance of the right to freedom of expression."

because the court considered that the primary object of the newspaper interview was to inform the public about a "genuine problem", it left open the question of whether "pure" advertising fell within the scope of Article 10. Cases such as *Barthold* illustrate the difficulties that may arise in distinguishing between the exchange of ideas and economic activity. There may be difficulties, for example, in relation to articles in consumer magazines in which similar products manufactured by different companies are evaluated. There is no demarcation between an article written by a journalist praising a product or service, and an advertisement. Despite having before it the opportunity to clarify the situation, the court failed to do so, much to the chagrin of Judge Pettiti, who, whilst concurring with the majority opinion, nevertheless made it clear that a valuable opportunity had been wasted:

> "I nonetheless believe that the decision of our Court could have been more explicit with regard to freedom of expression in as much as the approach to the question of commercial advertising was also evoked by the applicant . . . The great issues of freedom of information, of a free market in broadcasting, of the use of communication satellites cannot be resolved without taking account of the phenomenon of advertising; for a total prohibition of advertising [which could presumably result if Article 10 were held not to apply] would amount to a

---

[85] (1985) 7 E.H.R.R. 383.

prohibition of private broadcasting, by depriving the latter of its financial backing."

19.102 Notwithstanding the decision of the court to leave open the question of whether advertising could be protected by Article 10, Judge Pettiti was convinced that there was a move towards freedom of expression and that such a move was applicable in the context of broadcasting and communications.[86]

19.103 However, in *Casado Coca v. Spain*,[87] the European Court made explicit that Article 10 extended to commercial advertising. The applicant was a lawyer who had placed notices giving details of his legal practice in a local newspaper and who had received a written warning from the Barcelona Bar Council enjoining him from so doing in the future. Although the European Court found no violation of Article 10 and its general approach was that, in the absence of a common European standard, the regulation of advertising by lawyers did not fall outside the state's margin of appreciation, it held that:

> "The guarantee in Article 10 extends to everyone regardless of whether their aim is commercial or not. It protects information of a commercial nature and in the instant case commercial advertising . . . "[88]

The court was at pains to note that any distinction between commercial and other information could potentially fall foul of Article 14, the prohibition on discrimination. It should be noted however that the applicability of Article 10 was decided in part upon the basis that the advertisement in question also provided persons requiring legal assistance with information that could facilitate their access to justice. So, whilst as in *Casado Coca*, organisations "helping" claimants to pursue personal injury claims may seek the protection of Article 10 in respect of their commercial advertising, it remains to be seen how the courts will react to advertisements that are solely commercial in nature. The courts are perhaps more likely to encounter advertising campaigns dressed up as serving a public need, for example, campaigns emphasising the health benefits of a particular food product, or the safety aspects of a particular car, in order to invoke the protection of Article 10. Given that these are currently popular advertising strategies, it is likely that advertising agencies would face little difficulty in persuading the court that their advertisements also had a public benefit of the type that would bring the advertisement within the scope of Article 10. The European Court did however make it clear that rights under Article 10 can be curtailed in order to:

(1) prevent unfair competition;

(2) prevent untruthful or misleading advertising;

---

[86] Such a move was also evident in *Jersild v. Denmark* (1994) 19 E.H.R.R. 1, in which the protection of the Convention was extended from printed media to audio-visual media.
[87] (1994) 18 E.H.R.R. 1.
[88] The applicability of Art. 10 both to limited companies and to commercial activities was also upheld in *Autronic AG v. Switzerland* (1990) 12 E.H.R.R. 485.

(3) ensure respect for the rights of others or owing to the special circumstances of particular business activities and professions.[89]

Domestic Cases

In the domestic context, since the HRA came fully into force on October 2, 2000, there has been little activity in the courts in relation to advertising. The most notable case in this area is that of *R v. Advertising Standards Authority Limited, ex p. Matthias Rath BV.*[90] In this case, the applicant published leaflets making a number of claims in relation to the health benefits of a number of its vitamin-based supplements. The Advertising Standards Authority contacted the applicant, stating that they would be publishing an adjudication which was adverse to him. The applicant requested a review of the adjudication which was granted, but the Independent Reviewer upheld the original findings of the ASA. The applicant, through his solicitors, wrote to the ASA, stating that he was going to apply for judicial review and that publication of the ASA adjudication, before the application had been made, would be inappropriate. The applicant contended in the judicial review proceedings that the publication of the adjudication would constitute a breach of Article 10. However, the Administrative Court held that the British Code of Advertising and Sales Promotion, under which the Advertising Standards Authority operated, complied with the requirements of Article 10(2) and that publication of adjudications served the public interest. Accordingly, there had been no breach of Article 10. The Advertising Standards Authority ("ASA") stated in response to this decision:

19.104

> "As far as we know, this judgment is the first judicial ruling on advertising regulation since the Human Rights Act 1998 came fully into force, and the first attempt to challenge directly a decision by the Independent Reviewer. The judgment shows that the ASA's procedures are fair and that its decisions are a matter of public interest. This judgment is excellent news for the self-regulatory system of non-broadcast advertising. The ASA will vigorously resist attempts by some advertisers to place unjustified legal road blocks in its path".[91]

Subsequently, in *Smithkline Beecham plc v. Advertising Standards Authority,*[92] the claimant argued that the ASA should have recognised a range of claims which could reasonably be made and asked whether the advertising claim in question was within that margin. It was said that this was especially important as it impacts on the exercise of commercial free speech where a requirement of justification or pressing need arises in relation to any interference.[93] Hunt J. held that the code under which the

---

[89] *ibid.*, para. 51.
[90] [2001] E.M.L.R. 22.
[91] "ASA welcomes High Court Decision", ASA press release, December 6, 2000.
[92] [2001] E.M.L.R. 23, Hunt J.
[93] Reference was made to *R. v. Secretary of State for the Home Department, ex parte Simms* [2000] 2 A.C. 115 and *R v. Advertising Standards Authority, ex p. Robertson* [2000] E.M.L.R. 463.

ASA acted, which was a restriction on advertising but one designed to prevent misleading claims, was consistent with Article 10. He stated that:

> "Article 10 of the European Convention for the Protection of Human Rights is no different from English law on the subject. I find that the Code under which the ASA acts, which is indeed a restriction on advertising but one designed to restrict misleading claims, is entirely consistent with Article 10 to which the ASA does have regard. It is not a blanket ban. The advertiser can advertise his product within the Code which is designed for the protection of the public. Under the Code requirements for substantiation the more stark, categorical or absolute the claim the greater the degree of substantiation required. With an absolute claim there can be no margin. Following the test in *Casado Coca v. Spain* 18 EHRR 1 at page 24 I ask myself whether the measures taken at national level are justifiable in principle and proportionate. I find they are and that the interference in question is properly limited. I find that the ASA approached the claim appropriately within the application of their Code and asked themselves whether the absolute claim being made was substantiated. When they found that it was not there was no room for any margin of reasonable claims argument."

19.105 If the Hunt J. approach is followed, it is unlikely that Article 10 will add a great deal to domestic law in this area, subject to further challenge before the European Court. In *O'Shea v. MGN Ltd and Free4Internet.Net Ltd,*[93A] Morland J. refused to extend the strict liability principle in defamation to the situation where a photograph of one person in a compromising situation (in this case, an advertisement) was a lookalike of someone else. He held that to do so would be an unjustifiable interference with the right to freedom of expression disproportionate to the legitimate aim of protecting the reputations of look-alikes and would be contrary to Article 10. He noted that Article 10 applied to commercial advertising, citing *Casado Coca v. Spain,* but held that whilst the advertisement at issue would be regarded by many as squalid and degrading to women, it was not unlawful and was a form of expression protected by Article 10.

19.106 The most topical example of restriction of the freedom of expression in the advertising context perhaps arises in relation to the promotion of tobacco. In *R v. Secretary of State for Health and Others, ex p. Imperial Tobacco Ltd,*[94] the Court of Appeal held that freedom of expression is an important, though not unqualified, right but that human rights arguments could not be advanced to challenge the validity of regulations restricting the advertising of tobacco, if the European Directive under which the relevant regulations were made, was found to be valid. Since the European Court of Justice subsequently held that the Directive was adopted on an incorrect legal basis,[95] the human rights dimension was not considered further when the

---

[93A] *The Independent*, June 18, 2001, QBD.
[94] [2001] 1 W.L.R. 127; *The Times*, December 17, 1999, CA.
[95] *The Times*, October 10, 2000, ECJ.

issue returned to the domestic courts.[96] In a domestic context however, provided that there is a valid legal basis for any restriction, it would no doubt be argued that restrictions on freedom to advertise or promote tobacco are justified under Article 10(2) on grounds of the protection of health, answer a pressing social need and are proportionate.

In summary, the European Court has, in the past, avoided having to **19.107** decide whether advertising falls within the scope of Article 10, either by finding that the matter complained of was within the Contracting State's margin of appreciation, or that the publicity element of the publication was secondary to the purpose of public information. The European Court has not, so far, had to consider whether "pure" advertising falls within the scope of Article 10, but given the fine line between the distribution of commercial information and advertising (and the fact that a communication can quite easily be a combination of the two), it is likely that the domestic courts will be unable to resist the argument that advertising should be afforded the protection guaranteed by Article 10. Given also that the doctrine of the margin of appreciation does not strictly apply in the domestic context,[97] it is likely that the issue will fall to be decided in the United Kingdom, rather than in Europe.

Regulation of Advertising

Non-broadcast advertising is regulated by the Advertising Standards **19.108** Authority Limited ("ASA").[98] The general procedure adopted by the ASA is as follows. Complaints regarding advertisements are considered by the 12-strong ASA at its monthly meetings. The advertiser in question is told the outcome of the Council's rulings and whether the advertisement should be amended or withdrawn completely. The ruling is then published in the ASA's monthly report. Publishers and media owners or any other agent involved in producing, placing or publishing advertisements accept rulings of the ASA Council as binding. In exceptional circumstances, the Council can be asked to review their decision, but only on two grounds:

(1) where additional evidence has come to light; or

(2) where a substantial flaw in the Council's adjudication can be demonstrated.

A request for a review is forwarded to an Independent Reviewer and two **19.109** Assessors. The Council's adjudication on reconsidered cases is final, subject to judicial review. It is unlikely that the ASA's own procedures are compliant with Article 6(1), which provides for a fair hearing before an independent and impartial tribunal in the determination of an individual's civil rights and obligations. Certainly, Article 6 would appear to be applicable. Restrictions on commercial advertising may in principle affect an individual's ability to earn a living, and thus to constitute a right of a pecuniary nature of the sort envisaged by the court to benefit from the

---

[96] *The Times*, December 20, 2000, HL.
[97] See further paras 4.22 *et seq*.
[98] For further information, see the British Codes of Advertising and Sales Promotion on the ASA's web-site at www.asa.org.uk.

protection of Article 6 in respect of civil rights.[99] In addition, the rulings of the ASA Council certainly appear to go beyond the investigative or administrative stage,[1] and hence involve a *determination* of a civil right. The remaining question is whether the publisher receives, at any stage of the process, a fair hearing before an independent and impartial tribunal. Certainly, the ASA proceedings, up to the point of an application for judicial review, do not appear to comply fully with Article 6(1). The advertiser in question is not given the opportunity to make representations, written or otherwise, aside from requesting a review of the initial decision which would appear to be granted on very limited grounds. Decisions are taken during the Council's monthly meetings, which are in private and not notified to the advertiser. The fact that the ASA's procedure does not provide an Article 6(1) compliant hearing will not matter if there is a full right of appeal to an Article 6(1) compliant court. However, given the current criticisms being made by the European Court of domestic judicial review procedures, based on the lack of a full review of the merits and their inability to provide an adequate remedy as required by Article 13,[2] it is questionable whether the availability of judicial review is sufficient to remedy the incompatibilities of the ASA proceedings. In a challenge to an adjudication of the ASA Council based on alleged bias, Hunt J held that a fair-minded and informed observer would not conclude that there was a real danger of bias where an expert advising the ASA had expressed an adverse opinion about a product before his engagement because he was only an adviser or consultee and not a decision-maker.[3] The resolution of the more general issue awaits a challenge by either the advertising industry or a commercial organisation to the procedures of the ASA based upon Article 6(1).[4]

Broadcasting

19.110   Non-broadcast advertising has been considered above. There are a considerable number of cases relating to broadcasting. A full discussion of these is outside the scope of this book which does not consider media law more generally.[5] However, a few cases are mentioned here to illustrate the limits of the protection given by Article 10 to commercial freedom of expression. Article 10(1) permits states to require licences for broadcasting, television and cinema. In *Groppera Radio AG v. Switzerland*,[6] the European Court stated:

> "[T]he purpose of the third sentence of Article 10 para. 1 of the Convention is to make clear that states are permitted to control by a

---

[99] *Editions Périscope v. France* (1992) 14 E.H.R.R. 597. See further paras 3.56 *et seq.*
[1] See for example *Fayed v. United Kingdom* (1994) 18 E.H.R.R. 393 and *R v. Lord Chancellor, ex p. Lightfoot* [2000] 2 W.L.R. 318, CA, [1999] 2 W.L.R. 1126, Laws J. See further paras 3.60 *et seq.*
[2] See further paras. 10.141 *et seq.*
[3] *Smithkline Beecham plc v. Advertising Standards Authority* [2001] E.M.L.R. 23.
[4] An unsuccessful challenge has already been mounted under Art. 10—see *R v. Advertising Standards Authority Limited and anr, ex parte Matthias Rath BV* [2001] E.M.L.R. 22.
[5] A detailed analysis of the impact of the HRA on media law and defamation can be found in M. Smyth, *Business Law and the Human Rights Act*, (Jordans: 1999).
[6] (1990) 12 E.H.R.R. 321.

licensing system the way in which broadcasting is organised within their territories, particularly in its technical aspects."[7]

However, even if an interference is legitimate under Article 10(1), the requirements of Article 10(2) must also be satisfied.[8] Accordingly, the interference must fall within one of the express justifications, must be necessary in a democratic society and in accordance with the law.[9] **19.111**

The European Court has not shown itself in this context overly willing to empower those who wish to broadcast through the medium of Article 10. For example, in *Tele 1 Privatfernsehgesellschaft MBH v. Austria*,[10] a company applied for a licence to set up and operate a television transmitter in and around Vienna. The application was dismissed on the ground that Austrian constitutional law provided for the independence of broadcasting and legislation had only been enacted in respect of the Austrian Broadcasting Corporation. The European Court held that there had been a violation of Article 10 for the period 1993 to 1996 when there was no legal basis whereby a licence to set up and operate a television transmitter could be granted to any station other than the Austrian Broadcasting Corporation. However, there was no violation for the period 1996 to 1997 when private broadcasters were free to create and transmit their own programmes via cable net. **19.112**

Further, in *Brook v. United Kingdom*,[11] the applicant applied to the Foreign and Commonwealth Office in 1986 for a short wave radio licence to broadcast scientific, technological and media news. Over the following 10 years, the authorities acknowledged the applicant's request but did not give a definitive response. The European Court declared that application based on Article 10 inadmissible because it was proportionate to exclude short wave radio frequencies from the licensing regime.[12] **19.113**

Provided that the state refuses an application for a licence with reasonable justification and care and there does not exist a state broadcasting monopoly,[13] the applicant is unlikely to secure such a licence by invoking Article 10. The approach illustrates the relatively weak level of protection given by the Convention to commercial free expression generally. **19.114**

The right to receive information attracts stronger protection than the right to broadcast information. In *Autronic AG v. Switzerland*,[14] the court held that the refusal by the Swiss government to grant permission to the applicant to receive uncoded television programmes from a Soviet telecommunications satellite violated Article 10.[15] **19.115**

---

[7] At para. 62.
[8] *ibid.*
[9] See further paras 3.110 *et seq.* and paras 4.33 *et seq.*
[10] Application No. 32240/96, September 21, 2000.
[11] Application No. 38218/97, July 11, 2000.
[12] See further, Simor and Emmerson, *Human Rights Practice*, (Sweet & Maxwell: 2000) at 10.103 *et seq.*
[13] *Informationsverein Lentia v. Austria* (1994) 17 E.H.R.R. 93 (state broadcasting monopoly contrary to Article 10).
[14] (1990) 12 E.H.R.R. 485.
[15] See also *Benjamin v. Honourable Minister of Information & Broadcasting* [2001] 1 W.L.R. 1040, PC (suspension of phone-in radio programme on government sponsored radio station breach of constitutional right to freedom of expression) discussed in Chap. 14 (Companies & Financial Services) at para. 14.107.

CHAPTER 20

Disciplinary Proceedings

1. INTRODUCTION

20.01   Disciplinary proceedings involve a wide range of different bodies and tribunals. Some disciplinary bodies are established or are recognised by statute.[1] Others are the creation of professional bodies or voluntary associations, membership of which usually involves submission to the jurisdiction of such bodies: examples are the various professional conduct bodies, self-regulating commercial organisations, sports bodies and trade unions. In addition, many employers use internal disciplinary hearings to resolve issues of misconduct. In what follows we have tried to analyse how the Convention and the HRA will affect proceedings before such bodies, focusing above all on the requirements of Article 6. Similar considerations apply to licensing decisions. We have not considered disciplinary proceedings involving prisoners or in the education field, both of which give rise to issues which are rather specific to the institutions concerned.

20.02   Nor do we explore the distinction between those bodies which are and are not susceptible to judicial review as a matter of English law. It is probably true that most disciplinary bodies are not subject to challenge by way of judicial review because their decisions are not viewed by the courts as public functions.[2] In practice the procedural question is of decreasing importance with the courts (at least outside the sphere of the typical

---

[1] *e.g.* the police under the Police (Conduct) Regulations 1999, S.I. 1999 No. 730, and the Solicitors' Disciplinary Tribunal (see Solicitors Act 1974, s.46).

[2] See especially *R. v. Disciplinary Committee of the Jockey Club, ex p. Agha Khan* [1993] 1 W.L.R. 909 and the recent case of *R. v. Association of British Travel Agents, ex p. Sunspell Ltd* [2001] A.C.D. 16. Where the disciplinary process is laid down by statute, rather than by voluntary submission to contractual rules, it is more likely that judicial review is available: see Michael Fordham, *Judicial Review Handbook* (Wiley, 1999) at para. 15.53.

employment relationship[3]) requiring a disciplinary body to act in accordance with duties of fairness whether it is subject to public or private law. As a result the legal principles of supervision are similar (though not identical) in each case, as the courts have on occasions recognised.[4]

The question whether disciplinary bodies are or are not "public authorities" within the meaning of section 6 of the HRA is not explored here.[5] Many disciplinary functions are likely to be viewed as "private acts" so that section 6 will not apply to what are termed "mixed function" or "hybrid" bodies.[6] **20.03**

2. ARTICLE 6

The Article of principal relevance to disciplinary proceedings and the one under which most challenges are likely to be brought is Article 6 of the Convention. It states: **20.04**

"In the determination of his civil rights and obligations or of any criminal charge against him, everyone is entitled to a fair and public hearing within a reasonable time by an independent and impartial tribunal established by law. Judgment shall be pronounced publicly but the press and public may be excluded from all or part of the trial in the interests of morals, public order or national security in a democratic society, where the interests of juveniles or the protection of private life so require, or to the extent strictly necessary in the opinion of the court in special circumstances where publicity would prejudice the interests of justice."

In what follows we consider first when Article 6 applies to disciplinary proceedings—that is, in what circumstances such proceedings can determine civil rights or obligations or a criminal charge—before considering, secondly, the effect of Article 6 on such proceedings.

The Right to Practise a Profession or Engage in a Business

As mentioned in Chapter 3 above, the phrase "civil rights and obligations" has an autonomous meaning though it only includes rights which arguably exist under national law. It includes the right to practise a profession, which is recognised in English law as part of a general background freedom.[7] In **20.05**

---

[3] See paras 20.10 and 20.11, below.
[4] See the comments of Lord Woolf in *Modahl v. British Athletic Federation Limited* [1997] C.L.Y. 778 subsequently appealed to the House of Lords (*The Times*, July 23, 1999). Some procedural differences remain: in a private action oral evidence is more likely, for example.
[5] See paras 8.15 *et seq.*, above.
[6] See paras 8.17 *et seq.*, above, and HRA 1998, s.6(3)(b), (5). In *RSPCA v. H.M. Attorney General* [2001] EWHC Admin 470, January 26, 2001, Lightman J. considered that a question relating to the regulation of membership was a private act within the meaning of HRA 1998, s.6(5).
[7] In other words, domestic law permits such practice in the absence of a law prohibiting it. English law has not thus far recognised a positive right to work however; but *cf. Nagle v. Feilden* [1966] 2 Q.B. 633.

Konig v. Germany,[8] Article 6 was engaged when Dr Konig's authorisation to engage in medical practice was withdrawn by the state at the request of the regional medical society following allegations about his incompetence. The Court held that his right to practise was a civil right despite the fact that the regulation of the medical profession was largely driven by the public interest. In other cases the Court has held that the right to practise a trade or profession is a civil right.[9] The rights to engage in forms of commercial activity similarly engage Article 6.[10] Disciplinary proceedings which result in barring a person from a profession or business, therefore, will usually engage Article 6.[10A]

20.06 Whether the right to pursue a particular sport also attracts Article 6(1) protection has never been addressed by the Court or Commission. Although recent admissibility decisions suggest that the right to pursue a sporting activity as a hobby is not protected under Article 8 or Article 1 of Protocol No. 1,[11] it does not follow that a disciplinary decision which interferes with the right of professional sportsmen and women to pursue their careers does not determine civil rights and obligations within the meaning of Article 6(1).

20.07 The right to practise is determined by a disciplinary decision even if the exclusion is not permanent or even particularly lengthy. In *Le Compte v. Belgium* doctors were suspended from medical practice by the Belgian *Ordre des médicins* for three months in one case and 15 days in two others but the Court held nonetheless that this was "a direct and material interference with the right to continue to exercise the medical profession. The fact that the suspension was temporary did not prevent its impairing that right".[12]

Other Disciplinary Sanctions

20.08 Disciplinary decisions which do not affect the right to practise or engage in a business probably fall outside Article 6 (although to the extent they involve a breach of contract an individual can bring a claim in the courts at which point the court procedure must comply with Article 6). In *Le Compte*, the Court's starting point was that "disciplinary proceedings do not normally lead to a contestation" (dispute) over "civil rights and obligations".[13]

---

[8] (1979–80) 2 E.H.R.R. 170. In relation to the autonomous meaning of civil rights and obligations the Court stated that "Whether or not a right is to be regarded as civil . . . must be determined by reference to the substantive contents and effects of the right—and not its legal classification—under the domestic law of the state concerned".

[9] See, *e.g. H. v. Belgium* (1988) 10 E.H.R.R. 339, and *Ginikawa v. United Kingdom* (1988) 55 D.R. 251 (practice as a barrister); *Guchez v. Belgium* (1984) 40 D.R. 100 (practice as an architect), and *Diennet v. France* (1996) 21 E.H.R.R. 554 (disqualification from medical practice).

[10] See similarly *Purdas v. Sweden* (1988) 10 E.H.R.R. 380 (withdrawal of licence to run taxi business), *Benthem v. Netherlands* (1986) 8 E.H.R.R. 1 (withdrawal of licence to run petrol garage).

[10A] See *R. v. Securities and Futures Authority ex p. Fleurose, Daily Telegraph,* June 19, 2001.

[11] See *RC, AWA and 1566 others v. U.K.* (July 1, 1997) and *Green and others* (May 9, 2000).

[12] (1981) 4 E.H.R.R. 1, para. 49.

[13] *ibid.,* para. 42, citing from *Engel v. Netherlands (No. 1)* (1979) 1 E.H.R.R. 647. See para. 3.76 above.

It contrasted a sanction which prevented the doctors practising with other sanctions, such as a warning, censure or reprimand, which would not.[14] The implication is that disciplinary proceedings which lead to sanctions of this kind do not attract the protection of Article 6. This distinction has been adopted or referred to in other cases, even in a case when an applicant was fined.[15]

It is important to bear in mind, however, that the Convention is intended to **20.09** give rise to effective practical protection against the infringement of rights, so that the practical rather than legal effect of a disciplinary decision on the right to practise a trade is no doubt relevant. In *Tehrani v. United Kingdom Central Council for Nursing, Midwifery and Health Visiting*[16] the Court of Session, in holding that Article 6 potentially applied to disciplinary proceedings which might result in a person's name being removed from the register of nurses, focused on the practical effect of exclusion.[17] Removal from the register would prevent the petitioner as a matter of law performing only those duties which are expressly reserved by statute to registered nurses; legally she was not barred from working as a nurse in other areas. In practice, however, many other forms of employment as a nurse would be effectively barred to her because prospective employers in fact required registration as a qualification for employment. In those circumstances for "all practical purposes, removal of the petitioner's name from the register would prevent her from pursuing, at least within the United Kingdom, [her] career as a nurse".[18]

Other Relevant Rights

Claims by an employee that a decision following a disciplinary hearing **20.10** amounted to wrongful dismissal or unfair dismissal[19] are likely to involve the determination of civil rights within the meaning of Article 6[20]; the same applies to other breach of contract actions based on disciplinary rule books. The civil rights in question are the relevant contractual rights and the statutory right not to be unfairly dismissed. But the rights in these circumstances are determined in the court or employment tribunal so that compliance of the disciplinary proceedings with Article 6 is of little relevance.

A civil right is also potentially engaged when a person is offered a specific **20.11** position. In *X v. United Kingdom*[21] the applicant was prevented from taking up an offer of the post of chief executive of an insurance company

---

[14] At 18, para. 49.
[15] See, *e.g. App. No. 10331/93* (1984) 6 E.H.R.R. 583: disciplinary proceedings against barrister not within art. 6 when applicant only reprimanded. *HAR v. Austria* (1999) 27 E.H.R.R. C.D. 330 (fine on barrister by Disciplinary Appeals Board) in which the Commission noted, without deciding the issue, that all the cases within Art. 6 had involved temporary suspension or permanent prohibition from exercising a profession.
[16] [2001] I.R.L.R. 208.
[17] See paras 38–42.
[18] See para. 44.
[19] See Employment Rights Act 1996, Pt X.
[20] See Chap. 3, para. 3.58, above.
[21] (1998) 25 E.H.R.R. C.D. 88.

because of a letter from the Secretary of State, issued following a hearing in accordance with a statutory procedure, to the effect that he was not a fit and proper person to occupy such a position.[22] In those circumstances the Commission held that the applicant's civil rights—presumably his contractual right to accept the offer—were affected by the decision of the Secretary of State "irrespective of whether the decision had wider ramifications for the employment prospects of the applicant".

Excluded Service

20.12   Following a series of Commission decisions, the Court has held that decisions concerning the recruitment, careers and termination of service of civil servants fall outside Article 6.[23] The rationale for this difference in treatment is hard to grasp, particularly in a state like the United Kingdom where civil servants, if theoretically subject to dismissal at will, probably have contracts of employment and in most other respects are in an identical position to other employees.[24] Recently, in *Pellegrin v. France*,[25] the Court restricted the category of excluded worker to those whose "duties typify the specific activities of the public service in so far as the latter is acting as the depositary of public authority responsible for protecting the general interests of the State or other public authorities", giving the police and armed forces as examples. Public sector employees with ordinary contracts of employment outside of this category clearly can potentially benefit from Article 6.[26]

This exclusion probably has limited practical consequences in the United Kingdom for public servants. A civil servant employed under a contract can challenge dismissal following disciplinary proceedings in an action for wrongful dismissal or unfair dismissal.[27] To that extent his or her civil rights are determined by an independent and impartial body—the court or employment tribunal—in accordance with Article 6. The police are in a different position.[28] They cannot bring proceedings for unfair dismissal

---

[22] The letter was issued under the Insurance Companies Act 1982, s.60, which sets out a statutory procedure for regulating the appointment of chief executives.

[23] See para. 3.58, above; *Neigel v. France* [1997] E.H.R.L.R. 424; *Huber v. France* (1998) 26 E.H.R.L.R. 457 at para. 47; *Balfour v. U.K.* noted [1997] E.H.R.L.R. 665; and *Argento v. Italy* (1999) 28 E.H.R.R. 719. The same conclusion was reached in relation to police officers in the U.K., who do not have contracts of employment: *X v. U.K.* (1980) 21 D.R. 168. *Cf. Vogt v. Germany* (1995) 21 E.H.R.R. 205 at 231, 232, paras 43–44, in which the Court considered that the restriction should be confined to the *recruitment* of civil servants, a right which was deliberately omitted from the Convention (see similarly *Kosiek v. Germany* (1986) 9 E.H.R.R. 328, and *Glasenapp v. Germany* (1987) 9 E.H.R.R. 25).

[24] See *R. v. Lord Chancellor's Department, ex p. Nangle* [1991] I.C.R. 743, in which the court thought it probable that civil servants did have contracts of employment. *Cf. R. v. Civil Service Appeal Board, ex p. Bruce* [1988] I.C.R. 649.

[25] *Pellegrin v. France* (2001) 31 E.H.R.R. 26.

[26] See, *e.g. Darnell v. U.K.* (1991) 69 D.R. 306, in which the Commission held that Art. 6 applied to the dismissal of a director of public laboratory and consultant microbiologist to a regional health authority, who was not a civil servant. *Cf. Balfour v. U.K.* [1997] E.H.R.L.R. (Commission): dismissal of vice-consul outside Art. 6.

[27] See Employment Rights Act 1996, s.191. Note the power to exclude certain categories in the interests of national security: see s.193.

[28] Note that the Employment Rights Act 1996, s.192 (not yet in force), brings the armed forces within the unfair dismissal jurisdiction.

before an employment tribunal and are not engaged under contracts of employment.[29] Instead there exist statutory disciplinary procedures with extensive procedural safeguards, including the right to legal representation in some circumstances and rights of appeal to a police appeals tribunal.[30] Unless, therefore, their disciplinary proceedings are deemed to determine a "criminal charge" (see below) it appears that Article 6 is inapplicable. It is possible, however, that these anomalous exclusions from Article 6 will be ignored by domestic courts.

A Determination of Civil Rights

For Article 6 to apply there must be a "determination" of civil rights. In **20.13** *Kaplan v. United Kingdom*[30A] the Commission drew a distinction between a body which resolves a dispute, on the one hand, and the acts of an administrative or other body exercising a legal power on the other. Article 6 only applied to the former, so that a decision of the Secretary of State imposing restrictions on the business of an insurance company under the (then) Insurance Companies Act 1974 affected the applicants' civil rights but did not determine them. But in *Alconbury* Lord Clyde pointed out that the distinction drawn in *Kaplan* has not been taken up by the court and reflected an earlier stage in the development of Article 6.[30B] It is likely, then, that the elusive distinction between exercising and determining rights will not appeal to the English courts. On Lord Clyde's reasoning it should follow that if, for example, a ruling body of an association decides to dismiss a member it will be held to have determined his or her civil rights rather than to have exercised any contractual power vested in it by the rules.

Criminal Charges

Article 6 applies both to the determination of civil rights and of "any **20.14** criminal charge". The concept "criminal charge" also has an autonomous meaning under the Convention and is not resolved by the label attached to the proceedings or sanction.[31] The Court will have regard to how the national legal system defines the relevant matter, the nature of the offence

---

[29] See Employment Rights Act 1996, s.200, and *Fisher v. Oldham Corporation* [1930] 2 K.B. 364. The armed forces are similarly excluded from the unfair dismissal jurisdiction: see n. 28, above, and the Employment Relations (Consolidation) Act 1978, s.138(3), retained in force in the Employment Rights Act 1996, Sched. 2.

[30] See the Police (Conduct) Regulations 1999, S.I. 1999 No. 730 and the Police (Conduct) Senior Officers Regulations 1999, S.I. 1999 No. 731.

[30A] (1982) 4 E.H.R.R. 64 at para. 154. *cf. X v. United Kingdom* (1998) 25 E.H.R.R. CD88 in which the Commission held that there was a determination of an applicant's civil rights when the Secretary of State indicated that he was considering issuing a notice that a person was not a fit and proper person to be chief executive of an insurance company.

[30B] *R. (on the application of Alconbury) v. Secretary of State for the Environment, Transport and the Regions* [2001] 2 All E.R. 929, HL at 1000. Lord Clyde cited *X v. United Kingdom* (1982) 28 DR 177 in support.

[31] See para. 3.76, above, *R. v. Securities and Futures Authority ex p. Fleurose, Daily Telegraph,* May 1, 2001, and for discussion see C. Kidd, "Disciplinary Proceedings and the Right to a Fair Criminal Trial under the European Convention on Human Rights" (1987) 36 *International and Comparative Law Quarterly* 856.

and the severity of the penalty.[32] The practice in other states is relevant—for example whether they classify a particular kind of offence as criminal.

20.15 But it is only in exceptional cases that disciplinary proceedings are likely to concern a criminal charge. In *Engel v. Netherlands*[33] the Court held, in the context of military disciplinary proceedings, that if the sanction involved deprivation of liberty for more than a short period the proceedings might be characterised as "criminal". On the facts it found that three applicants, charged with disciplinary offences which were also criminal offences under the Netherlands Military Penal Code and who were at risk of a maximum penalty of between three to six months in a disciplinary unit, were the subject of criminal charges. But an applicant who risked a penalty of only three days arrest, albeit with some deprivation of liberty, was not "charged with a criminal offence" for Article 6 purposes.[34] Applying *Engel*, the Commission has held that a police officer who was required to resign after disciplinary proceedings and an army officer who was given a compulsory transfer by a disciplinary tribunal were not charged with criminal offences.[35] Directors disqualification proceedings probably do not determine a criminal charge[36] and nor did a decision barring a person from practising as a doctor.[37]

20.16 In *Findlay v. United Kingdom*[38] the government conceded that the court-martial proceedings involved the determination of a criminal charge: the applicant pleaded guilty to three charges of common assault and the court-martial sentenced him to two years' imprisonment. If a court-martial were not determining a criminal charge, however, it would fall outside Article 6 because of the exclusion of the armed forces from the civil limb of the Article (see above).

Investigations; Self-Incrimination

20.17 An investigation, perhaps as a precursory to disciplinary proceedings, does not engage Article 6 because at that stage no rights or obligations (or

---

[32] See *Engel v. The Netherlands* (1979) 1 E.H.R.R. 64; *Campbell and Fell v. United Kingdom* (1985) 7 E.H.R.R. 165; and *Shmautzer v. Austria* (1996) 21 E.H.R.R. 511, para. 27. According to Kidd (n. 31, above), if the national law defines a charge as criminal that is decisive; if it does not, then the central issue is whether other Member States define the particular offence as criminal (see *Ozturk v. Germany* (1984) 6 E.H.R.R. 409).

[33] (1979–80) 1 E.H.R.R. 647.

[34] The same applied to an applicant who faced four days "light arrest" not involving deprivation of liberty.

[35] See *X v. United Kingdom* (1980) 21 D.R. 168, and *Saraiva de Carualho v. Portugal* (1980) 26 D.R. 26 (in both cases the applicants sought to rely upon the criminal charge provision because the nature of their posts meant that they were excluded from the civil rights provisions—see above). See too *Kaplan v. United Kingdom* (1980) 4 E.H.R.R. 64: trading restrictions were not a criminal penalty.

[36] See *DC, HS and AD v. United Kingdom* (September 14, 1999, Application No. 39031/97) followed by the High Court *Re Westminster Property Management Ltd*, [2001] 1 W.L.R. 2230, CA. These were "unfitness" proceedings; other directors disqualification proceedings may lead to different results: see A. Mithani, *Directors Disqualification Proceedings*, Part VIII.

[37] See *Wickramsinghe v. United Kingdom* [1998] E.H.R.L.R. 338. See also *Brown v. United Kingdom* Application No. 38644/97 (fine by Solicitors Complaints Tribunal not criminal charge).

[38] (1997) 24 E.H.R.R. 221. See too *Moore v. United Kingdom* (2000) 29 E.H.R.R. 728 and *Coyne v. United Kingdom*, September 24, 1997.

criminal charges) are determined.[39] (An investigation may, however, engage Article 8.)

Article 6 prevents the use of compulsorily compelled oral testimony or documents in criminal proceedings, which will include disciplinary proceedings deemed to be determining a "criminal charge".[40] In some instances statute expressly provides that compulsorily compelled questions or documents may be used in civil proceedings, including disciplinary proceedings.[41] The courts have recognised that the common law privilege against self-incrimination can extend to questions posed by a disciplinary body, although membership of the relevant professional body is likely to amount to waiver of the privilege.[42] **20.18**

But it is doubtful if the principle derived from Article 6, based as it is on the right of an accused not to incriminate himself, goes any further or even extends to disciplinary proceedings.[43] The use of compulsorily obtained evidence in proceedings for the disqualification of directors was not said to lead to unfairness or, as a result, a breach of Article 6 in *DC, HS and AD v. United Kingdom*,[44] a decision consistent with existing Court of Appeal authority.[45] Although the general principle of fairness in Article 6 might prevent one party to civil proceedings making use of evidence obtained through compulsory questioning to obtain an unfair advantage over the other party, many forms of disciplinary proceedings are likely to be viewed as quasi-regulatory proceedings rather than normal civil litigation.[46] **20.19**

A Sufficient Appeal

The primary focus of Article 6 is on court procedure. A public and impartial trial is seen as a fundamental element of the rule of law[47]; but the translation of its requirements into disciplinary proceedings is not straightforward. Take the requirement of independence and impartiality, which the Court has interpreted in strict terms as requiring independence (and the **20.20**

---

[39] See *Fayed v. United Kingdom* (1994) 18 E.H.R.R. 393; *Saunders v. United Kingdom* (1997) 23 E.H.R.R. 313.

[40] See *Saunders* (n. 39, above (compelled answers to DTI inspectors) and *Funke v. France* (1993) 16 E.H.R.R. 297. But see *J.B. v. Switzerland*, Application No. 31827/96, May 3, 2001, on the important distinction between self-incrimination and documents said to have an independent existence.

[41] See, *e.g.* Companies Act 1985 ss.449, 451A, which expressly refers to the use of information obtained by inspectors for disciplinary proceedings against, among others, solicitors, auditors and accountants.

[42] See *R. v. Institute of Chartered Accountants of England and Wales, ex p. Nawaz*, CA, April 15, 1997 (unreported).

[43] For general discussion, see P. Davies, "Self-Incrimination, Fair Trials, and the Pursuit of Corporate and Financial Wrongdoing" in B. Markesinis (ed.), *The Impact of the Human Rights Bill on English Law* (Clarendon Press: 1998).

[44] September 14, 1999, Application No. 39031/97. See Company Directors Disqualification Act 1996.

[45] See *R. v. Secretary of State for Trade and Industry, ex p. McCormick* [1998] B.C.C. 379, CA, in which the Court of Appeal upheld a first instance ruling that Art. 6 did not prevent the use of compelled testimony in directors' disqualification proceedings. See also *Official Receiver v. Stern* [2000] 1 W.L.R. 2230, CA and *R. v. Securities and Futures Authority ex p. Fleurose, The Daily Telegraph*, May 1, 2001.

[46] In *R. v. Secretary of State for Trade and Industry, ex p. McCormick* at first instance Rimer J. considered that disqualification proceedings were not ordinary civil proceedings but were brought in the public interest: see Davies (n. 43, above), pp 55–58.

[47] See *Delcourt v. Belgium* (1979) 1 E.H.R.R. 1; *Diennet v. France* (1996) 21 E.H.R.R. 554, para. 33.

appearance of independence) from the parties and the Executive and freedom from outside pressure.[48] It is plain that many disciplinary bodies may have difficulty meeting this standard. In some cases, where the composition of the body is laid down by statute, it may be legally impossible for the tribunal to exhibit the necessary degree of independence; in others it is impracticable for a disciplinary body to be sufficiently independent of the prosecution function. Similar considerations may apply to a requirement of a hearing in public.

20.21 In those (rare) cases in which a criminal charge is determined in disciplinary proceedings, the first instance disciplinary body must comply in full with the requirements of Article 6, subject to an exception for minor offences.[49] Further, decisions taken by "courts of the classic kind", defined as courts and tribunals "integrated within the standard judicial machinery of the country",[50] must comply with Article 6 at each stage. What follows is concerned only with civil rights and obligations where the initial determination is made by a disciplinary body.

20.22 Recognising that to require that every stage of the determination of civil rights comply with Article 6 would run counter to efficient and flexible administration and decision-making, the Court has repeatedly held that Article 6 is met provided that there is a sufficient appeal to a body, such as a court, which itself meets the requirements of Article 6. In *Albert and le Compte v. Belgium* the Court said[51]:

> "In many member States of the Council of Europe, the duty of adjudicating on disciplinary offences is conferred on jurisdictional organs of professional associations. Even in instances where Article 6(1) is applicable, conferring powers in this manner does not in itself infringe the Convention . . . Nonetheless, in such circumstances the Convention calls at least for one of the two following systems: either the jurisdictional organs themselves comply with the requirements of Article 6(1), or they do not so comply but are subject to subsequent control by a judicial body that has full jurisdiction and does provide the guarantee of Article 6(1)."

Applying the approach set out in *Albert and Le Compte*, in *Tehrani v. United Kingdom Central Council for Nursing, Midwifery and Health Visiting*, the Court of Session rejected an argument that each stage of the disciplinary proceedings relating to nurses must comply with the requirements of Article 6. The existence of a statutory right of appeal to the Court of Session from a decision of the professional conduct committee to remove a person's name from the register of nurses was sufficient.[52]

---

[48] See *Ringeisen v. Austria* (1979) 1 E.H.R.R. 455, para. 95 and *Langborger v. Sweden* (1990) 12 E.H.R.R. 416 at 425 and paras 10.103 *et seq.*, above.

[49] See *Findlay v. United Kingdom* (1997) 24 E.H.R.R. 221, para. 7; and, on the minor offences exception, *Schmautzer v. Austria* (1996) 21 E.H.R.R. 511 (which held that in such cases any appeal to a court must be open to all points, on both facts and law).

[50] See *De Cubber v. Belgium* (1985) 7 E.H.R.R. 236.

[51] (1983) 5 E.H.R.R. 533, para. 29. Applied and cited in *Bryan v. United Kingdom* (1996) 21 E.H.R.R. 342.

[52] See paras 55–61. The statutory right of appeal arose under the Nurses, Midwives and Health Visitors Act 1997, s.12. See too *Everest v. United Kingdom* [1997] 4 E.H.R.L.R. 410: appeal to Visitors from Professional Conduct Committee of the Bar was sufficient appeal.

The key question in relation to disciplinary proceedings is: what is an **20.23** appeal of sufficient jurisdiction? The Convention has laid down some guidance on this matter. In *Bryan v. United Kingdom*[53] the applicant challenged the issue of a planning enforcement notice. The court held that the proceedings before the planning inspector did not comply with Article 6 because he was insufficiently independent of the Secretary of State. As to whether an appeal to the High Court restricted to errors of law was sufficient, the Court said that relevant factors were "the subject-matter of the decision appealed against, the manner in which the decision was arrived at, the content of the dispute, including the desired and actual grounds of appeal".[54] Noting that the applicant did not challenge primary facts or the factual inferences drawn by the Inspector, the Court went on to endorse a review jurisdiction restricted to examining whether facts or inferences were perverse or irrational in "specialised areas of law like the one at issue, particularly where the facts have already been established in the course of a quasi-judicial procedure governed by many of the safe-guards required by Article 6(1)".[55] Mr Bratza Q.C., then a member of the Commission, went furthest in *Bryan* in his concurring opinion that:

> "It appears to me that the requirement that a court or tribunal should have "full jurisdiction" cannot mechanically be applied with the result that in all circumstances and whatever the subject matter of the dispute, the court or tribunal must have full power to substitute its own findings of fact and its own inferences from those facts, for that of the administrative authority concerned."[56]

Bryan should be contrasted with other authorities. In *W v. U.K.*,[57] in the **20.24** context of disputed rights of access to children following local authority decisions, the Court ruled that while judicial review provided "valuable safeguards" it was not sufficient for the purposes of Article 6; what was needed was "a tribunal having jurisdiction to examine the merits of the matter".[58] The same result was reached in *Albert and Le Compte v. Belgium*[59]: the lack of a public hearing before a professional disciplinary body—the Appeals Council—was not remedied by a public hearing before the Court of Cassation because that court would not examine the merits of a case.[60] Because the *Conseil d'Etat* had no power to assess the pro-portionality of a penalty on appeal from a private disciplinary hearing there was a breach of Article 6 in *Diennet v. France*.[61] The absence of a merits hearing before a court led to a breach in *Obermeier v. Austria*, although

---

[53] (1996) 21 E.H.R.R. 342.
[54] At para. 45. See also *R. (on the application of Alconbury Developments Ltd) v. Secretary of State for the Environment, Transport and the Regions* [2001] 2 W.L.R. 1389, HL.
[55] See para. 47.
[56] See at 354.
[57] (1988) 10 E.H.R.R. 29.
[58] At para. 82.
[59] (1983) 5 E.H.R.R. 533.
[60] At para. 36.
[61] (1996) 21 E.H.R.R. 554.

that decision should probably be read in the light of the rather peculiar facts.[62]

20.25 The distinctions between these authorities are not explained by the Court and are far from clear. It is notable that in *W v. U.K.* the decision-making process of the local authority did not include any of the "quasi-judicial" safeguards which operated before the inspector in *Bryan* and it is possible, too, that the Court in *W v. U.K.* was particularly anxious that there should be full procedural safeguards because of the importance it accorded to the substantive rights at stake. *Albert and Le Compte* and *Diennet* can perhaps be reconciled with *Bryan* because of the nature of the complaint: the right to a public hearing is, presumably, intended to embody a hearing (or at least effective review) of all the facts and evidence and all elements of the decision, including sentence (see below under "Public Hearing").

20.26 *Bryan* was applied by the Court to quasi-disciplinary proceedings in *Kingsley v. United Kingdom*.[63] Following a hearing before the Gaming Board, the applicant's certification to practise in the gaming industry was withdrawn. Rejecting an argument that a judicial review confined to points of law was an insufficient appeal because it could not examine the merits, the Court stated that the case was concerned with the regulation of the gaming industry, "a classic exercise of administrative discretion", drawing comfort for its conclusion from the quasi-judicial nature of the hearing before the Gaming Board Panel.[64] (The challenge succeeded on other grounds: see below). A decision that a person was not fit to be a chief executive in an insurance company under insurance legislation was equally held by the Commission to be a classic exercise of administrative discretion in *X v. United Kingdom*.[65] A hearing which led to expulsion of a company from membership of IMRO, a self-regulatory board to which public functions were delegated under financial services legislation, was treated as a decision subject to "specialised rules" in *APB Ltd, APP and EAB v. United Kingdom* so that a restricted scope of judicial review was justified.[66]

20.27 The Commission has reached the same conclusion even in relation to disciplinary decisions which are with difficulty categorised as illustrations of "classic" administrative discretions. In the admissibility decision of *Kenneth Wickramsinghe v. U.K.*[67] W challenged a decision of the Professional Conduct Committee of the General Medical Council removing

---

[62] (1991) 13 E.H.R.R. 290. In brief the applicant sought to challenge, *inter alia*, the validity of his suspension by his employers (the relevant civil right for the purpose of Art. 6: see para. 66). His claim was rejected following a successful plea by his employer that in the meantime he had been dismissed and so he had no legal interest in challenging the validity of the suspension. The decision to dismiss the applicant was confirmed by an administrative body (the Disabled Persons Board and then the Provincial Governor) whose decision could only be challenged before the Administrative Court on the ground that it acted outside the scope of its discretion (para. 70). In those circumstances the absence of a merits hearing to challenge the dismissal effectively barred the way to claiming the suspension was invalid. If the Court had treated the applicant's civil right to challenge his suspension as circumscribed by the dismissal provisions, it seems no claim could have been brought.
[63] Application No. 35605/97, November 7, 2000.
[64] At paras 53–54.
[65] (1998) 25 E.H.R.R. C.D. 88 at 97.
[66] (1998) 25 E.H.R.R. C.D. 140 at 150.
[67] [1998] E.H.R.L.R. 338.

his name from the medical register. He appealed to the Privy Council under statute[68] whose powers in practice are restricted to overturning findings which are perverse or unsupported by any evidence.[69] Though the Commission considered that the Professional Conduct Committee was not independent and impartial as required by Article 6,[70] it held that the restricted appeal to the Privy Council was sufficient. It drew attention to the important procedural guarantees before the Professional Conduct Committee and noted that it was able to consider each of the applicant's complaints raised before it, which were essentially based on errors of law.[71] In a further admissibility decision concerning the GMC's disciplinary function, *Stefan v. United Kingdom,*[72] the applicant mounted a "comprehensive challenge" to the decision of the Health Committee before the Privy Council, including to the Committee's factual findings. Despite what appears to have been an absence of careful reasons from the Committee, the Commission again pointed to the important procedural safeguards before that Committee and held that, in the light of those factors, "the fact that the Privy Council did not redetermine the facts of the case cannot be seen to conflict with the requirements of [Article 6]".[73] It is not clear how this decision is to be reconciled with those authorities which require a hearing on the merits (see above).

How do these principles apply to disciplinary proceedings under domestic **20.28** law? As a general rule the courts in the United Kingdom exercise a relatively restrained supervisory jurisdiction with regard to disciplinary tribunals, close in approach to examining whether the body erred in law.[74] The exception to this is an appeal to a court from a disciplinary hearing under a "normal" contract of employment. Such contracts do not have the principles of natural justice implied into them,[75] although those workers categorised as "office-holders" are entitled to disciplinary hearings in accordance with those principles and it seems that the category, whose

---

[68] See Medical Act 1983, s.40.

[69] See *Libman v. GMC* [1972] A.C. 217, PC, *per* Lord Hailsham at 221G–222A. This is largely a consequence of the Privy Council not hearing witness evidence. *cf. Ghosh v. General Medical Council, The Times,* June 18, 2001, in which the Privy Council stated that it had wide powers on appeal although because of the nature of the questions before it, such as whether matters amount to serious professional misconduct, it would defer to the judgement of the GMC.

[70] See below under "Independence and Impartiality".

[71] The applicant appealed on the grounds that he did not receive a fair hearing because of delay, non-disclosure of evidence and poor legal representation and that the penalty was excessive.

[72] Application No. 29419/95 (1998) 25 E.H.R.R. C.D. 130.

[73] Earlier it noted that "it is in the nature of a review jurisdiction of a disciplinary body that the reviewing authority reviews the preceding proceedings rather than taking factual decisions". See also *Ghosh v. GMC*, note 69 above.

[74] It is probably inaccurate simply to talk of appeals on the merits, on the one hand, or appeals restricted to points of law on the other. In truth there is a spectrum of supervision by higher courts, ranging from proceedings in which the court hears all the evidence, makes its own findings of fact and substitutes its own views on the merits to those in which the court merely examines whether there was some evidence which permitted a body to reach a conclusion, that the body did not misdirect itself and that its decision was not perverse. The spectrum reflects different legal approaches, according more or less autonomy to the body under review.

[75] See *Post Office v. Crouch* [1995] I.R.L.R. 159.

conceptual boundaries were always somewhat hazy, is expanding.[76] It follows that in a claim for wrongful dismissal brought by an employee after an internal disciplinary hearing, a court will hear live evidence, make its own findings of fact and rule whether those facts were sufficient to amount to a breach of contract. Provided the court (or employment tribunal) itself satisfies the requirements of Article 6, the appeal to it will amount to compliance with that Article. The point is reinforced when an employee can challenge the fairness of dismissal under the statutory jurisdiction on unfair dismissal.[77]

20.29 But outside the employment sphere, the courts tend to accord a much greater degree of autonomy to disciplinary tribunals. The court's role is, in general terms, only to examine whether the body made an error of law, whether by breaching the duty of fairness or otherwise. Disciplinary bodies are required to act in accordance with principles of fairness; but no doubt as a consequence courts exercise a supervisory rather than an original jurisdiction over the findings of such bodies. Whether the challenge is by way of private law or judicial review a court will not, for example, overturn a finding of fact unless there was no evidence to support it, the finding was perverse or was based on an inference which amounted to a misdirection in law. Reflecting the same deference to the autonomy of the disciplinary body, a court will not substitute its own view for a penalty unless it is outside the range of reasonable sanctions which a rational disciplinary body acting within its rules might impose.[78] The paradoxical result is that challenges based on Article 6 are less likely to arise in relation to disciplinary bodies which are not under a legal duty to act in accordance with the principles of fairness than in relation to those which are under such a duty and whose factual findings are, as a consequence, subject to less scrutiny.

20.30 But it is clear from the approach of the Court in *Bryan* and *Kingsley* and of the Commission in *Stefan* and *Wickramsinghe* that the more disciplinary proceedings themselves embody the procedural protections required by Article 6 (and other procedural safeguards) the more likely it is that a review jurisdiction in general terms restricted to points of law is sufficient. Likewise, if a decision is classified as the exercise of a classic administrative discretion or as a specialist function, an appeal restricted to a review jurisdiction is more likely to be sufficient. The second relevant consideration in *Bryan*, the manner of the decision, permits an examination of the whole procedure, from disciplinary proceedings to court. Probably anxious to preserve their supervisory role, the domestic courts may well seek to impose primary duties on disciplinary bodies to comply with some aspects of Article 6 and to embody other forms of procedural safeguards, rather

---

[76] See *Ridge v. Baldwin* [1964] A.C. 40; *Malloch v. Aberdeen Corporation* [1971] 1 W.L.R. 1578; *R. v. BBC, ex p. Lavelle* [1983] I.C.R. 101. In *ex p. Lavelle* Woolf J. (as he then was) thought that as a result of the statutory right not to be unfairly dismissed "even the ordinary contract of master and servant now has many of the attributes of an office, and the distinction which previously existed between pure cases of master and servant and cases where a person holds an office are no longer clear" (at 111H–112A). As early as *Malloch*, the distinction between those workers who have been held to benefit from the principles of natural justice and those who do not was described as looking "illogical and even bizarre" by Lord Wilberforce (at 1595).

[77] See the Employment Rights Act 1996, Pt. X.

[78] See M. Beloff, T. Kerr, M. Demetriou, *Sports Law* (Hart: 1999), pp. 206–210.

than to expand their own jurisdiction.[79] But so far there has been limited examination of this issue.

One means in particular by which the courts might reduce the likelihood of **20.31** challenges based on a restricted supervisory jurisdiction is through imposing greater duties on the supervised bodies to give adequate reasons. There are already hints that domestic courts might adopt such an approach. In *Stefan v. General Medical Council*[80] the Privy Council referred to Article 6 and *Wickramsinghe* and referred a duty on the GMC to give reasons for the suspension of a doctor in part from the fact that reasons would assist in determining any appeal[81]:

> "The appeal was on a ground of law but, as has already been mentioned, the existence of such a provision points to the view that as a matter of fairness in deciding whether there are grounds for appeal, and as a matter of assistance in the presentation and determination of any appeal, the reasons for the decision should be given."

Such an approach has much in its favour. If a disciplinary body has given reasons, has made careful factual findings and has provided transcripts of the evidence, in practice a supervisory jurisdiction can be more exacting than if a court only has the barest materials upon which to decide whether a particular conclusion was justified. Article 6 may therefore accelerate the common law's gradual trend towards a duty to give reasons.

Adequate Remedies

A particular problem may arise if there is an appeal to a court but that court **20.32** is unable to cure the very defect in the disciplinary procedure about which complaint is made. In those circumstances the appeal to the court may be insufficient. In *Kingsley v. United Kingdom*[82] the applicant's challenge by way of judicial review to a decision of a Panel of the Gaming Board on ground of bias failed, first, because while there was an appearance of bias as a result of an earlier decision, there was insufficient evidence that it gave rise to a "real danger of injustice" having occurred; and secondly, because under the "doctrine of necessity" the Panel had a non-delegable statutory duty to perform so that the decision could not be taken by an independent body.[83] After rejecting a claim by the applicant that he should have been given a full merits hearing before a court, the Court nevertheless held that:

> "The Court considers it generally inherent in the notion of judicial review that, if a ground of challenge is upheld, the reviewing court has

---

[79] See the High Court in *Alconbury Developments v. SSETR* [2001] H.R.L.R. 2 which declined to expand the judicial review jurisdiction to allow a hearing on the facts and merits (at 52). *Alconbury* subsequently went to the House of Lords which overturned the Divisional Court's declaration of incompatibility: see [2001] 2 W.L.R. 1389, note 54 above.
[80] [1999] 1 W.L.R. 1293. See also *R. v. Ministry of Defence ex p. Murray* [1998] C.O.D. 134.
[81] At 1301G–H. See too at 1300 C–D.
[82] *The Times*, January 9, 2001.
[83] See the summary of the decision of Jowett J. at paras 22–24 and of the Court of Appeal refusing permission to appeal at para. 26.

power to quash the impugned decision, and that either the decision will be taken by the review court, or the case will be remitted for a fresh hearing before the same or a different body. Thus where, as here, complaint is made of a lack of impartiality on the part of the decision-making body, the concept of "full jurisdiction" involves that the reviewing court not only considers the complaint but has the ability to quash the impugned decision and to remit the case for a new decision by an impartial body.

In the present case the domestic courts were unable to remit the case for a first decision by the Board or by another independent tribunal. The Court thus finds that, in the particular circumstances of the case, the High Court and the Court of Appeal did not have "full jurisdiction" within the meaning of the case-law on Article 6 when they reviewed the Panel's decision."

A similar issue arose in *Gautrin v. France* although based on Article 26.[84]

20.33 Similar problems are likely to arise in the future under English law. A court may agree with an argument that a statutorily constituted disciplinary body is not objectively impartial or failed to hold a public hearing in breach of Article 6 but, faced with clear statutory wording, have no power to remit the matter to an impartial body for a public hearing and no jurisdiction to hear the matter itself.[85] If the decision was remitted to the same body, the court would have failed to provide an effective remedy. In those circumstances the only option may be a declaration of incompatibility under section 4 of the HRA 1998.

Procedural Rights in Article 6: General

20.34 As we have set out above, the requirements of Article 6—the rights of access to a court, to a fair hearing in public, to a hearing within a reasonable time, to an independent and impartial tribunal and to a rea-soned decision—will remain relevant to disciplinary hearings despite the existence of an appeal to a court. So will other procedural safeguards, such as rights to be informed of charges promptly and fully, to have adequate time to prepare, to call evidence and question witnesses, to legal representation, to the disclosure of documents and to the provision of transcripts of evidence.[86] These fair trial factors should be considered having regard to all the circumstances.[86A] It is therefore important to

---

[84] (1999) 28 E.H.R.R. 196. In *Gautrin* the *Conseil d'Etat* could only allow an appeal on the ground of the bias of individual members of the Council and not on the ground of the "objective" bias of the Councils—which was precisely the applicants' complaint. In those circumstances the Court held that the applicants had not failed to exhaust domestic remedies for the purpose of Art. 26 of the Convention by declining to appeal to the *Conseil d'Etat*. As a matter of logic the same conclusion ought to have followed if the French Government argued that the hearing before the *Conseil d'Etat* was a sufficient appeal for the purposes of Art. 6.

[85] In *Alconbury Developments v. SSETR* [2001] H.R.L.R. 2, the Divisional Court faced such a problem. It declined to expand its judicial review jurisdiction to deal with the matter.

[86] See, especially, *Wickramsinghe v. United Kingdom* [1998] E.H.R.L.R. 338, discussed above in para. 20.27, above and *R. v. Securities and Futures Authority ex p. Fleurose*, *Daily Telegraph* May 1, 2001.

[86A] See *Official Receiver v. Stern* [2001] 1 W.L.R. 2230, CA and *ex p. Fleurose* (note 86 above).

examine the extent to which a particular disciplinary body, only subject to a supervisory jurisdiction, meets or goes beyond the procedural safeguards in Article 6. In addition, a body may be under primary duties to comply with the requirements of the Article. An obvious candidate is the right to a hearing within a reasonable time. Delay by a disciplinary body in hearing a matter is likely to result in court challenges based on Article 6. These general requirements are discussed in Chapter 10 above[86B]; below we only consider two of particular relevance to disciplinary proceedings: the right to an independent and impartial tribunal and the right to a public hearing.

Independence and impartiality

It is likely that many challenges to disciplinary proceedings will be based **20.35** on an argument that the relevant bodies are not independent and impartial. Provided there is a sufficient appeal to a court and it can grant an effective remedy, no breach of Article 6 will arise (see above); but the absence of impartiality will provide the starting point for a challenge.
The test was summarised in *Findlay v. United Kingdom*[87]: **20.36**

> "The Court recalls that in order to establish whether a tribunal can be considered as "independent", regard must be had inter alia to the manner of appointment of its members and their terms of office, the existence of guarantees against outside pressure and the question whether the body presents an appearance of independence.
> As to the question of impartiality, there are two aspects to this requirement. First, the tribunal must be subjectively free of personal prejudice or bias. Secondly, it must also be impartial from an objective viewpoint, that is, it must offer sufficient guarantees to exclude any legitimate doubts in this respect.

In practice, as the Court recognised, the concepts of independence and impartiality overlap conceptually and tend to be considered together. On the facts of *Findlay* the court-martial gave an appearance of insufficient objective independence. First, the convening officer played a central part in the prosecution and was closely linked to the prosecution authorities. Secondly, the other members of the court-martial were insufficiently independent of that officer: they were, for example, subordinate in rank to him.
Assuming that there is no personal link between members of a disciplinary **20.37** body and any of the parties before them, the mere fact that the body is constituted by members of a particular profession is not sufficient in itself to lead to a lack of independence.[88] In *HAR v. Austria* half the members of a disciplinary appeal board were barristers from the Bar Chamber of which the applicant was a member, but for the Commission the presence of

---

[86B] At paras 10.98 *et seq.*
[87] (1997) 24 E.H.R.R. 22. See especially *Lanborger v. Sweden* (1990) 12 E.H.R.R. 416, para. 32.
[88] See *H v. Belgium* (1988) 10 E.H.R.R. 339 and *Gautrin v. France* (1999) 28 E.H.R.R. 221, discussed above. The principle was recently affirmed in *Stefan v. United Kingdom* (1997) 25 E.H.R.R. C.D. 130.

impartial judges constituting the other half, which included the Chair, proved an assurance of impartiality.[89] Questions of subjective or objective[90] bias under Article 6 are similar to the existing tests under domestic law; but *Kingsley v. United Kingdom* illustrates that an effective remedy may be needed once bias is shown without the need to go on and show a real risk of injustice.[91]

20.38 The requirement of independence remains an exacting one. In *Wickramsinghe* and *Stefan*, the Commission held that the Conduct and Health Committee respectively of the GMC lacked a sufficient appearance of independence. The Commission relied upon the facts that the relevant committee members did not determine cases independently of the GMC's general policies; that members served for a limited term of one year or (in the case of the Health Committee) were appointed on an *ad hoc* basis; that the President played a role in the investigation of complaints prior to the hearing; and that the sole legal advisor took no part in the deliberations.[92]

20.39 The Solicitors Disciplinary Tribunal, which is independent of the Law Society, was held by the High Court to comply with Article 6.[93] So was the recently reformed court-martial system, in which a court administration officer independent of the prosecution selects members and in which permanent presidents are outside the ordinary claim of military command.[94]

Established by law

20.40 In *APB v. United Kingdom* the Commission raised as a question whether an Appeals Tribunal constituted under the rules of IMRO was "established by law".[95] It is notable that rules of a voluntary association are capable, depending on the context of amounting to law for the purposes of "prescribed by law" in Article 10[96] and an internal policy is capable of amounting to law within the meaning of Article 8[97]: what matters is whether the applicable rules are accessible to those affected by them.[98] Although the case law is sparse, a similar approach might be adopted in relation to Article 6. However, it is at least arguable that the requirement that a court or tribunal be "established by law" indicates that the focus for Article 6(1) purposes is on the adequacy of review by a court with "full jurisdiction", rather than the procedural fairness of first-instance decision makers.

---

[89] (1999) 27 E.H.R.R. C.D. 330.
[90] On the test for objective bias, see *Hasuchildt v. Denmark* (1990) 12 E.H.R.R. 266. See also paras 10.106 *et seq.*
[91] See para. 20.32, above.
[92] See too *Bryan v. United Kingdom* (1996) 21 E.H.R.R. 342, in which the mere possibility that the Secretary of State might revoke the power of a planning inspector to decide an appeal undermined the inspector's appearance of independence (para. 38).
[93] See *In the Matter of a Solicitor and In the Matter of the Solicitors Act 1974* (HC, November, 13, 2000).
[94] See *R. v. Spear* [2001] 2 W.L.R. 1692.
[95] (1998) 25 E.H.R.R. C.D. 141 at 149.
[96] See *Barthold v. Germany* (1985) 7 E.H.R.R. 383.
[97] See *Smith v. United Kingdom* (2000) 29 E.H.R.R. 493.
[98] See *Spacek v. Czech Republic* (November 9, 1999).

A hearing in public

If a disciplinary body has a discretion to hear proceedings in public but **20.41** declines to do so without exercising that discretion in accordance with the criteria of Article 6, there may be a breach even if there exists a right on appeal to a hearing in public before a court. In holding that a restricted review jurisdiction was insufficient in *Albert and le Compte v. Belgium* the Court stated that[99]:

> "The public character of [the Court of Cassation] proceedings does not suffice to remedy the defect found to exist at the stage of the disciplinary proceedings. The Court of Cassation does not take cognisance of the merits of the case which means that many aspects of 'contestations' (disputes) concerning 'civil rights and obligations' including review of the facts and assessment of the proportionality between the fault and sanction, fall outside its jurisdiction."

One justification underlying this typically opaque reasoning is that the very purpose of a hearing in public is to hear all the facts and evidence, to protect against secrecy and to ensure proper public scrutiny,[1] so that an appeal restricted to somewhat arid legal arguments is insufficient. It may be that the same jealous regard for public hearings influenced the Court in *Diennet v. France*, in which an appeal unable to examine the proportionality of sentence was insufficient.[2] However, the extent of any review by the Court of Cassation in *Albert and le Compte v. Belgium* is far from clear and it is difficult to see why the requirement of a public hearing should be strictly enforced in relation to private bodies when the requirements of independence and impartiality are not.

A person may waive his right to a public hearing. As the Commission **20.42** pointed out in *Ginikawana v. United Kingdom*,[3] it is often in the interests of a person the subject of disciplinary proceedings to have hearings in private to limit the damage to his or her reputation. Because the applicant had the opportunity to apply for a public hearing there was no breach of Article 6. Equally, it is arguable that an individual who joins a voluntary association agrees to be bound by its rules, which may include a rule that internal proceedings are conducted in private.

3. OTHER ARTICLES

The other Articles of the Convention are of less importance to disciplinary **20.43** proceedings. They are only dealt with briefly below.

Article 10. In *Barthold v. Germany* proceedings under competition **20.44** law were brought against the applicant, a veterinary surgeon, because he had breached a professional rule against advertising.[4] On the issue of

---

[99] (1983) 5 E.H.R.R. 533, para. 36.
[1] On this point in the context of disciplinary proceedings, see *Diennet v. France* (1996) 21 E.H.R.R. 554, para. 33.
[2] (1996) 21 E.H.R.R. 554.
[3] (1988) 55 D.R. 251 at 260.
[4] (1985) 7 E.H.R.R. 383.

whether the interference with his freedom of expression was "prescribed by law" the Court held that the rules of professional conduct, which emanated from the Veterinary Surgeons' Council rather than Parliament were nonetheless to be regarded as "law".[5] It follows that disciplinary proceedings brought on the basis of a breach of such rules will be potentially "prescribed by law", though in each case the proportionality test must be applied to the particular facts.

20.45   **Article 8.**   This Article is dealt with in Chapter 3, above. It may have consequences for disciplinary decisions brought by sports bodies as a result of drug tests. In principle drug tests engage Article 8, particularly if they are intrusive (for example blood testing) or require nudity, as in the case of some sports' urine testing (to detect hidden urine samples).[6] Most cases will turn, therefore, on the issue of proportionality. Disclosure of the results of drug tests or other health information and powers to demand other forms of private information will also potentially engage the Article.[7] The Data Protection Act 1998 will often apply affording protection equivalent to Article 8.[7A]

20.46   **Article 11.**   The right to freedom of association is inapplicable to membership of bodies which are, in Convention terms, public law institutions. In *Le Compte v. Belgium* the Court held that membership of the *Ordre des médicins* fell outside the umbrella of Article 11 because the Ordre was set up by the state, was integrated within state institutions and was intended to exercise public control over the practice of medicine.[8] Hence a disciplinary decision of that body did not engage Article 11, although the Court noted the position would be different if the body in question prevented practitioners from forming other voluntary professional associations.[9] By contrast, a car organisation which exercised the public function of issuing taxi licences fell within Article 11 because of its predominantly private aspects: it was established under private law and aimed above all to promote the interests of its members and not the wider public.[10]

20.47   But an organisation within Article 11 remains free to decide on the rules of membership and, therefore, to discipline those who it honestly believes are in breach of the rules or who are damaging to the organisation, unless the rules are wholly unreasonable or the sanctions lead to exceptional hardship (for example if membership of an organisation is essential to obtain a particular kind of work).[11]

---

[5] At para. 46. On the facts the interference was disproportionate.
[6] See *Peters v. The Netherlands* (1994) 77–A D.R. 75 (compulsory urine sample from prisoner); *X v. Austria* (1979) 18 D.R. 154 (blood test pursuant to court order).
[7] Some cycling federations, such as the French federation (the FFC) engage in repeated monitoring of riders health, in part to detect anomalies caused by drugs such as EPO.
[7A] Se further paras 19.18 *et seq.* on data collection and data protection.
[8] (1981) 4 E.H.R.R. 1, para. 64.
[9] At para. 65.
[10] *Sigurdur A. Sigurjonsson v. Iceland* (1993) 16 E.H.R.R. 462.
[11] See *Cheall v. United Kingdom* (1985) 42 D.R. 178, followed by Lightman J. in *Royal Society for the Prevention of Cruelty to Animals v. H.M. Attorney General* [2001] EWHC Admin 470).

Article 14. The prohibition on discrimination in Article 14 can be **20.48** invoked in conjunction with the right to a fair and public hearing in the determination of civil rights and obligations, but is not free-standing.[12] What must be shown is discrimination between individuals who are in the same or similar position.[13] However, not every difference in treatment is discriminatory. The essential question is whether a "reasonable and objective justification" can be shown for the difference in question,[14] and whether the measure in issue is proportionate.

---

[12] See *Rasmussen v. Denmark* (1985) 7 E.H.R.R. 371.
[13] See *Van der Mussele v. Belgium* (1984) 6 E.H.R.R. 163.
[14] See *Belgian Linguistics Case* (1979) 1 E.H.R.R. 241.

APPENDICES

APPENDICES

APPENDIX A

The Human Rights Act 1998

Human Rights Act 1998

1998 CHAPTER 42

ARRANGEMENTS OF SECTIONS

Introduction

Legislation

Public authorities

Remedial action

Other rights and proceedings

Derogations and reservations

Judges of the European Court of Human Rights

Parliamentary procedure

Supplemental

22. Short title, commencement, application and extent.

Schedules

An Act to give further effect to rights and freedoms guaranteed under the European Convention on Human Rights; to make provision with respect to holders of certain judicial offices who become judges of the European Court of Human Rights; and for connected purposes.

[9TH NOVEMBER 1998]

BE IT ENACTED by the Queen's most Excellent Majesty, by and with the advice and consent of the Lords Spiritual and Temporal, and Commons, in this present Parliament assembled, and by the authority of the same, as follows:—

Introduction

The Convention Rights

1.—(1) In this Act "the Convention rights" means the rights and fundamental freedoms set out in—

(a) Articles 2 to 12 and 14 of the Convention,

(b) Articles 1 to 3 of the First Protocol, and

(c) Articles 1 and 2 of the Sixth Protocol,

as read with Articles 16 to 18 of the Convention.

(2) Those Articles are to have effect for the purposes of this Act subject to any designated derogation or reservation (as to which see sections 14 and 15).

(3) The Articles are set out in Schedule 1.

(4) The Secretary of State may by order make such amendments to this Act as he considers appropriate to reflect the effect, in relation to the United Kingdom, of a protocol.

(5) In subsection (4) "protocol" means a protocol to the Convention—

(a) which the United Kingdom has ratified; or

(b) which the United Kingdom has signed with a view to ratification.

(6) No amendment may be made by an order under subjection (4) so as to come into force before the protocol concerned is in force in relation to the United Kingdom.

Interpretation of Convention rights

2.—(1) A court or tribunal determining a question which has arisen in connection with a Convention right must take into account any—

(a) judgment, decision, declaration or advisory opinion of the European Court of Human Rights,

    (b) opinion of the Commission given in a report adopted under Article 31 of the Convention,

    (c) decision of the Commission in connection with Article 26 or 27(2) of the Convention, or

    (d) decision of the Committee of Ministers taken under Article 46 of the Convention,

whenever made or given, so far as, in the opinion of the court or tribunal, it is relevant to the proceedings in which that question has arisen.

    (2) Evidence of any judgment, decision, declaration or opinion of which account may have to be taken under this section is to be given in proceedings before any court or tribunal in such manner as may be provided by rules.

    (3) In this section "rules" means rules of court or, in the case of proceedings before a tribunal, rules made for the purposes of this section—

    (a) by the Lord Chancellor or the Secretary of State, in relation to any proceedings outside Scotland;

    (b) by the Secretary of State, in relation to proceedings in Scotland; or

    (c) by a Northern Ireland department, in relation to proceedings before a tribunal in Northern Ireland—

        (i) which deals with transferred matters; and
        (ii) for which no rules made under paragraph (a) are in force.

Legislation

Interpretation of legislation

    3.—(1) So far as it is possible to do so, primary legislation and subordinate legislation must be read and given effect in a way which is compatible with the Convention rights.

    (2) This section—

    (a) applies to primary legislation and subordinate legislation whenever enacted;

    (b) does not affect the validity, continuing operation or enforcement of any incompatible primary legislation; and

    (c) does not affect the validity, continuing operation or enforcement of any incompatible subordinate legislation if (disregarding any possibility of revocation) primary legislation prevents removal of the incompatibility.

Declaration of incompatibility

    4.—(1) Subsection (2) applies in any proceedings in which a court determines whether a provision of primary legislation is compatible with a Convention right.

    (2) If the court is satisfied that the provision is incompatible with a Convention right, it may make a declaration of that incompatibility.

    (3) Subsection (4) applies in any proceedings in which a court determines whether a provision of subordinate legislation, made in the exercise of a power conferred by primary legislation, is compatible with a Convention right.

    (4) If the court is satisfied—

    (a) that the provision is incompatible with a Convention right, and

    (b) that (disregarding any possibility of revocation) the primary legislation concerned prevents removal of the incompatibility,

it may make a declaration of that incompatibility.

(5) In this section "court" means—

(a) the House of Lords;

(b) the Judicial Committee of the Privy Council;

(c) the Courts-Martial Appeal Court;

(d) in Scotland, the High Court of Justiciary sitting otherwise than as a trial court or the Court of Session;

(e) in England and Wales or Northern Ireland, the High Court or the Court of Appeal.

(6) A declaration under this section ("a declaration of incompatibility")—

(a) does not affect the validity, continuing operation or enforcement of the provision in respect of which it is given; and

(b) is not binding on the parties to the proceedings in which it is made.

Right of Crown to intervene

5.—(1) Where a court is considering whether to make a declaration of incompatibility, the Crown is entitled to notice in accordance with rules of court.

(2) In any case to which subsection (1) applies—

(a) a Minister of the Crown (or a person nominated by him),

(b) a member of the Scottish Executive,

(c) a Northern Ireland Minister,

(d) a Northern Ireland department,

is entitled, on giving notice in accordance with rules of court, to be joined as a party to the proceedings.

(3) Notice under subsection (2) may be given at any time during the proceedings.

(4) A person who has been made a party to criminal proceedings (other than in Scotland) as the result of a notice under subsection (2) may, with leave, appeal to the House of Lords against any declaration of incompatibility made in the proceedings.

(5) In subsection (4)—

"criminal proceedings" includes all proceedings before the Courts-Martial Appeal Court; and

"leave" means leave granted by the court making the declaration of incompatibility or by the House of Lords.

Public authorities

Acts of public authorities

6.—(1) It is unlawful for a public authority to act in a way which is incompatible with a Convention right.

(2) Subsection (1) does not apply to an act if—

(a) as the result of one or more provisions of primary legislation, the authority could not have acted differently; or

(b) in the case of one or more provisions of, or made under, primary legislation which cannot be read or given effect in a way which is compatible with the Convention rights, the authority was acting so as to give effect to or enforce those provisions.

(3) In this section "public authority" includes—

(a) a court or tribunal, and

(b) any person certain of whose functions are functions of a public nature,

but does not include either House of Parliament or a person exercising functions in connection with proceedings in Parliament.

(4) In subsection (3) "Parliament" does not include the House of Lords in its judicial capacity.

(5) In relation to a particular act, a person is not a public authority by virtue only of subsection (3)(b) if the nature of the act is private.

(6) "An act" includes a failure to act but does not include a failure to—

(a) introduce in, or lay before, Parliament a proposal for legislation; or

(b) make any primary legislation or remedial order.

Proceedings

7.—(1) A person who claims that a public authority has acted (or proposes to act) in a way which is made unlawful by section 6(1) may—

(a) bring proceedings against the authority under this Act in the appropriate court or tribunal, or

(b) rely on the Convention right or rights concerned in any legal proceedings,

but only if he is (or would be) a victim of the unlawful act.

(2) In subsection (1)(a) "appropriate court or tribunal" means such court or tribunal as may be determined in accordance with rules; and proceedings against an authority include a counterclaim or similar proceeding.

(3) If the proceedings are brought on an application for judicial review, the applicant is to be taken to have a sufficient interest in relation to the unlawful act only if he is, or would be, a victim of that act.

(4) If the proceedings are made by way of a petition for judicial review in Scotland, the applicant shall be taken to have title and interest to sue in relation to the unlawful act only if he is, or would be, a victim of that act.

(5) Proceedings under subsection (1)(a) must be brought before the end of—

(a) the period of one year beginning with the date on which the act complained of took place; or

(b) such longer period as the court or tribunal considers equitable having regard to all the circumstances,

but that is subject to any rule imposing a stricter time limit in relation to the procedure in question.

(6) In subsection (1)(b) "legal proceedings" includes—

(a) proceedings brought by or at the instigation of a public authority; and

(b) an appeal against the decision of a court or tribunal.

(7) For the purposes of this section, a person is a victim of an unlawful act only if he would be a victim for the purposes of Article 34 of the Convention if proceedings were brought in the European Court of Human Rights in respect of that act.

(8) Nothing in this Act creates a criminal offence.

(9) In this section "rules" means—

(a) in relation to proceedings before a court or tribunal outside Scotland, rules made by the Lord Chancellor or the Secretary of State for the purposes of this section or rules of court,

(b) in relation to proceedings before a court or tribunal in Scotland, rules made by the Secretary of State for those purposes,

(c) in relation to proceedings before a tribunal in Northern Ireland—

(i) which deals with transferred matters; and
(ii) for which no rules made under paragraph (a) are in force,

rules made by a Northern Ireland department for those purposes,

and includes provision made by order under section 1 of the Courts and Legal Services Act 1990.

(10) In making rules, regard must be had to section 9.

(11) The Minister who has power to make rules in relation to a particular tribunal may, to the extent he considers it necessary to ensure that the tribunal can provide an appropriate remedy in relation to an act (or proposed act) of a public authority which is (or would be) unlawful as a result of section 6(1), by order add to—

(a) the relief or remedies which the tribunal may grant; or

(b) the grounds on which it may grant any of them.

(12) An order made under subsection (11) may contain such incidental, supplemental, consequential or transitional provision as the Minister making it considers appropriate.

(13) "The Minister" includes the Northern Ireland department concerned.

Judicial remedies

8.—(1) In relation to any act (or proposed act) of a public authority which the court finds is (or would be) unlawful, it may grant such relief or remedy, or make such order, within its powers as it considers just and appropriate.

(2) But damages may be awarded only by a court which has power to award damages, or to order the payment of compensation, in civil proceedings.

(3) No award of damages is to be made unless, taking account of all the circumstances of the case, including—

(a) any other relief or remedy granted, or order made, in relation to the act in question (by that or any other court), and

(b) the consequences of any decision (of that or any other court) in respect of that act,

the court is satisfied that the award is necessary to afford just satisfaction to the person in whose favour it is made.

(4) In determining—

(a) whether to award damages, or

(b) the amount of an award,

the court must take into account the principles applied by the European Court of Human Rights in relation to the award of compensation under Article 41 of the Convention.

(5) A public authority against which damages are awarded is to be treated—

(a) in Scotland, for the purposes of section 3 of the Law Reform (Miscellaneous Provisions) (Scotland) Act 1940 as if the award were made in an action of damages in which the authority has been found liable in respect of loss or damage to the person to whom the award is made;

(b) for the purposes of the Civil Liability (Contribution) Act 1978 as liable in respect of damage suffered by the person to whom the award is made.

(6) In this section—

"court" includes a tribunal;
"damages" means damages for an unlawful act of a public authority; and
"unlawful" means unlawful under section 6(1).

Judicial acts

9.—(1) Proceedings under section 7(1)(a) in respect of a judicial act may be brought only—

(a) by exercising a right of appeal;

(b) on an application (in Scotland a petition) for judicial review; or

(c) in such other forum as may be prescribed by rules.

(2) That does not affect any rule of law which prevents a court from being the subject of judicial review.

(3) In proceedings under this Act in respect of a judicial act done in good faith, damages may not be awarded otherwise than to compensate a person to the extent required by Article 5(5) of the Convention.

(4) An award of damages permitted by subsection (3) is to be made against the Crown; but no award may be made unless the appropriate person, if not a party to the proceedings, is joined.

(5) In this section—

"appropriate person" means the Minister responsible for the court concerned, or a person or government department nominated by him;
"court" includes a tribunal;
"judge" includes a member of a tribunal, a justice of the peace and a clerk or other officer entitled to exercise the jurisdiction of a court;
"judicial act" means a judicial act of a court and includes an act done on the instructions, or on behalf, of a judge; and
"rules" has the same meaning as in section 7(9).

Remedial action

Power to take remedial action

10.—(1) This section applies if—

(a) a provision of legislation has been declared under section 4 to be incompatible with a Convention right and, if an appeal lies—

(i) all persons who may appeal have stated in writing that they do not intend to do so;

(ii) the time for bringing an appeal has expired and no appeal has been brought within that time; or

(iii) an appeal brought within that time has been determined or abandoned; or

(b) it appears to a Minister of the Crown or Her Majesty in Council that, having regard to a finding of the European Court of Human Rights made after the coming into force of this section in proceedings against the United Kingdom, a provision of legislation is incompatible with an obligation of the United Kingdom arising from the Convention.

(2) If a Minister of the Crown considers that there are compelling reasons for proceeding under this section, he may by order make such amendments to the legislation as he considers necessary to remove the incompatibility.

(3) If, in the case of subordinate legislation, a Minister of the Crown considers—

(a) that it is necessary to amend the primary legislation under which the subordinate legislation in question was made, in order to enable the incompatibility to be removed, and

(b) that there are compelling reasons for proceeding under this section,

he may by order make such amendments to the primary legislation as he considers necessary.

(4) This section also applies where the provision in question is in subordinate legislation and has been quashed, or declared invalid, by reason of incompatibility with a Convention right and the Minister proposes to proceed under paragraph 2(b) of Schedule 2.

(5) If the legislation is an Order in Council, the power conferred by subsection (2) or (3) is exercisable by Her Majesty in Council.

(6) In this section "legislation" does not include a Measure of the Church Assembly or of the General Synod of the Church of England.

(7) Schedule 2 makes further provision about remedial orders.

Other rights and proceedings

Safeguard for existing human rights

11. A person's reliance on a Convention right does not restrict—

(a) any other right or freedom conferred on him by or under any law having effect in any part of the United Kingdom; or

(b) his right to make any claim or bring any proceedings which he could make or bring apart from sections 7 to 9.

Freedom of expression

12.—(1) This section applies if a court is considering whether to grant any relief which, if granted, might affect the exercise of the Convention right to freedom of expression.

(2) If the person against whom the application for relief is made ("the respondent") is neither present nor represented, no such relief is to be granted unless the court is satisfied—

(a) that the applicant has taken all practicable steps to notify the respondent; or

(b) that there are compelling reasons why the respondent should not be notified.

(3) No such relief is to be granted so as to restrain publication before trial unless the court is satisfied that the applicant is likely to establish that publication should not be allowed.

(4) The court must have particular regard to the importance of the Convention right to freedom of expression and, where the proceedings relate to material which the respondent claims, or which appears to the court, to be journalistic, literary or artistic material (or to conduct connected with such material), to—

(a) the extent to which—

(i) the material has, or is about to, become available to the public; or
(ii) it is, or would be, in the public interest for the material to be published;

(b) any relevant privacy code.

(5) In this section—

"court" includes a tribunal; and

"relief" includes any remedy or order (other than in criminal proceedings).

Freedom of thought, conscience and religion

13.—(1) If a court's determination of any question arising under this Act might affect the exercise by a religious organisation (itself or its members collectively) of the Convention right to freedom of thought, conscience and religion, it must have particular regard to the importance of that right.

(2) In this section "court" includes a tribunal.

Derogations and reservations

Derogations

14.—(1) In this Act "designated derogation" means—

(a) the United Kingdom's derogation from Article 5(3) of the Convention; and

(b) any derogation by the United Kingdom from an Article of the Convention, or of any protocol to the Convention, which is designated for the purposes of this Act in an order made by the Secretary of State.

(2) The derogation referred to in subsection (1)(a) is set out in Part I of Schedule 3.

(3) If a designated derogation is amended or replaced it ceases to be a designated derogation.

(4) But subsection (3) does not prevent the Secretary of State from exercising his power under subsection (1)(b) to make a fresh designation order in respect of the Article concerned.

(5) The Secretary of State must by order make such amendments to Schedule 3 as he considers appropriate to reflect—

(a) any designation order; or

(b) the effect of subsection (2).

(6) A designation order may be made in anticipation of the making by the United Kingdom of a proposed derogation.

Reservations

15.—(1) In this Act "designated reservation" means—

(a) the United Kingdom's reservation to Article 2 of the First Protocol to the Convention; and

(b) any other reservation by the United Kingdom to an Article of the Convention, or of any protocol to the Convention, which is designated for the purposes of this Act in an order made by the Secretary of State.

(2) The text of the reservation referred to in subsection (1)(a) is set out in Part II of Schedule 3.

(3) If a designated reservation is withdrawn wholly or in part it ceases to be a designed reservation.

(4) But subsection (3) does not prevent the Secretary of State from exercising his power under subsection (1)(b) to make a fresh designation order in respect of the Article concerned.

(5) The Secretary of State must by order make such amendments to this Act as he considers appropriate to reflect—

(a) any designation order; or

(b) the effect of subsection (3).

Period for which designated derogations have effect

16.—(1) If it has not already been withdrawn by the United Kingdom, a designated derogation ceases to have effect for the purposes of this Act—

(a) in the case of the derogation referred to in section 14(1)(a), at the end of the period of five years beginning with the date on which section 1(2) came into force;

(b) in the case of any other derogation, at the end of the period of five years beginning with the date on which the order designating it was made.

(2) At any time before the period—

(a) fixed by subsection (1)(a) or (b), or

(b) extended by an order under this subsection,

comes to an end, the Secretary of State may by order extend it by a further period of five years.

(3) An order under section 14(1)(b) ceases to have effect at the end of the period for consideration, unless a resolution has been passed by each House approving the order.

(4) Subsection (3) does not affect—

(a) anything done in reliance on the order; or

(b) the power to make a fresh order under section 14(1)(b).

(5) In subsection (3) "period for consideration" means the period of forty days beginning with the day on which the order was made.

(6) In calculating the period for consideration, no account is to be taken of any time during which—

(a) Parliament is dissolved or prorogued; or

(b) both Houses are adjourned for more than four days.

(7) If a designated derogation is withdrawn by the United Kingdom, the Secretary of State must by order make such amendments to this Act as he considers are required to reflect that withdrawal.

Periodic review of designated reservations

17.—(1) The appropriate Minister must review the designated reservation referred to in section 15(1)(a)—

(a) before the end of the period of five years beginning with the date on which section 1(2) came into force; and

(b) if that designation is still in force, before the end of the period of five years beginning with the date on which the last report relating to it was laid under subsection (3).

(2) The appropriate Minister must review each of the other designated reservations (if any)—

(a) before the end of the period of five years beginning with the date on which the order designating the reservation first came into force; and

(b) if the designation is still in force, before the end of the period of five years beginning with the date on which the last report relating to it was laid under subsection (3).

(3) The Minister conducting a review under this section must prepare a report on the result of the review and lay a copy of it before each House of Parliament.

Judges of the European Court of Human Rights

Appointment to European Court of Human Rights

18.—(1) In this section "judicial office" means the office of—

(a) Lord Justice of Appeal, Justice of the High Court or Circuit Judge, in England and Wales;

(b) judge of the Court of Session or sheriff, in Scotland;

(c) Lord Justice of Appeal, judge of the High Court or county court judge, in Northern Ireland.

(2) The holder of a judicial office may become a judge of the European Court of Human Rights ("the Court") without being required to relinquish his office.

(3) But he is not required to perform the duties of his judicial office while he is a judge of the Court.

(4) In respect of any period during which he is a judge of the Court—

(a) a Lord Justice of Appeal or Justice of the High Court is not to count as a judge of the relevant court for the purposes of section 2(1) or 4(1) of the Supreme Court Act 1981 (maximum number of judges) nor as a judge of the Supreme Court for the purposes of section 12(1) to (6) of that Act (salaries etc.);

(b) a judge of the Court of Session is not to count as a judge of that court for the purposes of section 1(1) of the Court of Session Act 1988 (maximum number of judges) or of section 9(1)(c) of the Administration of Justice Act 1973 ("the 1973 Act") (salaries etc.);

(c) a Lord Justice of Appeal or judge of the High Court in Northern Ireland is not to count as a judge of the relevant court for the purposes of section 2(1) or 3(1) of the Judicature (Northern Ireland) Act 1978 (maximum number of judges) nor as a judge of the Supreme Court of Northern Ireland for the purposes of section 9(1)(d) of the 1973 Act (salaries etc.);

(d) a Circuit judge is not to count as such for the purposes of section 18 of the Courts Act 1971 (salaries etc.);

(e) a sheriff is not to count as such for the purposes of section 14 of the Sheriff Courts (Scotland) Act 1907 (salaries etc.);

(f) a county court judge of Northern Ireland is not to count as such for the purposes of section 106 of the County Courts Act Northern Ireland) 1959 (salaries etc.).

(5) If a sheriff principal is appointed a judge of the Court, section 11(1) of the Sheriff Courts (Scotland) Act 1971 (temporary appointment of sheriff principal) applies, while he holds that appointment, as if his office is vacant.

(6) Schedule 4 makes provision about judicial pensions in relation to the holder of a judicial office who serves as a judge of the Court.

(7) The Lord Chancellor or the Secretary of State may by order make such transitional provision (including, in particular, provision for a temporary increase in the maximum number of judges) as he considers appropriate in relation to any holder of a judicial office who has completed his service as a judge of the Court.

Parliamentary procedure

Statements of compatibility

19.—(1) A Minister of the Crown in charge of a Bill in either House of Parliament must, before Second Reading of the Bill—

    (a) make a statement to the effect that in his view the provisions of the Bill are compatible with the Convention rights ("a statement of compatibility"); or

    (b) make a statement to the effect that although he is unable to make a statement of compatibility the government nevertheless wishes the House to proceed with the Bill.

(2) The statement must be in writing and be published in such manner as the Minister making it considers appropriate.

Supplemental

Orders, etc. under this Act

20.—(1) Any power of a Minister of the Crown to make an order under this Act is exercisable by statutory instrument.

(2) The power of the Lord Chancellor or the Secretary of State to make rules (other than rules of court) under section 2(3) or 7(9) is exercisable by statutory instrument.

(3) Any statutory instrument under section 14, 15 or 16(7) must be laid before Parliament.

(4) No order may be made by the Lord Chancellor or the Secretary of State under section 1(4), 7(11) or 16(2) unless a draft of the order has been laid before, and approved by, each House of Parliament.

(5) Any statutory instrument made under section 18(7) or Schedule 4, or to which subsection (2) applies, shall be subject to annulment in pursuance of a resolution of either House of Parliament.

(6) The power of a Northern Ireland department to make—

    (a) rules under section 2(3)(c) or 7(9)(c), or

    (b) an order under section 7(11),

is exercisable by statutory rule for the purposes of the Statutory Rules (Northern Ireland) Order 1979.

(7) Any rules made under section 2(3)(c) or 7(9)(c) shall be subject to negative resolution; and section 41(6) of the Interpretation Act Northern Ireland) 1954 (meaning of "subject to negative resolution") shall apply as if the power to make the rules were conferred by an Act of the Northern Ireland Assembly.

(8) No order may be made by a Northern Ireland department under section 7(11) unless a draft of the order has been laid before, and approved by, the Northern Ireland Assembly.

Interpretation, etc.

21.—(1) In this Act—

    "amend" includes repeal and apply (with or without modifications);

    "the appropriate Minister" means the Minister of the Crown having charge of the appropriate authorised government department (within the meaning of the Crown Proceedings Act 1947);

    "the Commission" means the European Commission of Human Rights";

"the Convention" means the Convention for the Protection of Human Rights and Fundamental Freedoms, agreed by the Council of Europe at Rome on 4th November 1950 as it has effect for the time being in relation to the United Kingdom;

"declaration of incompatibility" means a declaration under section 4;

"Minister of the Crown" has the same meaning as in the Ministers of the Crown Act 1975;

"Northern Ireland Minister" includes the First Minister and the deputy First Minister in Northern Ireland;

"primary legislation" means any—

    (a) public general Act;

    (b) local and personal Act;

    (c) private Act;

    (d) Measure of the Church Assembly;

    (e) Measure of the General Synod of the Church of England;

    (f) Order in Council—

        (i) made in exercise of Her Majesty's Royal Prerogative;

        (ii) made under section 38(1)(a) of the Northern Ireland Constitution Act 1973 or the corresponding provision of the Northern Ireland Act 1998; or

        (iii) amending an Act of a kind mentioned in paragraph (a), (b) or (c);

and includes an order or other instrument made under primary legislation (otherwise than by the National Assembly for Wales, a member of the Scottish Executive, a Northern Ireland Minister or a Northern Ireland department) to the extent to which it operates to bring one or more provisions of that legislation into force or amends any primary legislation;

"the First Protocol" means the protocol to the Convention agreed at Paris on 20th March 1952;

"the Sixth Protocol" means the protocol to the Convention agreed at Strasbourg on 28th April 1983;

"the Eleventh Protocol" means the protocol to the Convention (restructuring the control machinery established by the Convention) agreed at Strasbourg on 11th May 1994;

"remedial order" means an order under section 10;

"subordinate legislation" means any—

    (a) Order in Council other than one—

        (i) made in exercise of Her Majesty's Royal Prerogative;

        (ii) made under section 38(1)(a) of the Northern Ireland Constitution Act 1973 or the corresponding provision of the Northern Ireland Act 1998; or

        (iii) amending an Act of a kind mentioned in the definition of primary legislation;

    (b) Act of the Scottish Parliament;

    (c) Act of the Parliament of Northern Ireland;

    (d) Measure of the Assembly established under section 1 of the Northern Ireland Assembly Act 1973;

    (e) Act of the Northern Ireland Assembly;

    (f) Order, rules, regulations, scheme, warrant, byelaw or other instrument made under primary legislation (except to the extent to which it operates to bring one or more provisions of that legislation into force or amends any primary legislation);

    (g) Order, rules, regulations, scheme, warrant, byelaw or other instrument made under legislation mentioned in paragraph (b), (c), (d) or (e) or made under an Order in Council applying only to Northern Ireland;

    (h) Order, rules, regulations, scheme, warrant, byelaw or other instrument made by a member of the Scottish Executive, a Northern Ireland Minister or a Northern Ireland department in exercise of prerogative or other executive functions of Her Majesty which are exercisable by such a person on behalf of Her Majesty;

"transferred matters" has the same meaning as in the Northern Ireland Act 1998; and

"tribunal" means any tribunal in which legal proceedings may be brought.

(2) The references in paragraphs (b) and (c) of section 2(1) to Articles are to Articles of the Convention as they had effect immediately before the coming into force of the Eleventh Protocol.

(3) The reference in paragraph (d) of section 2(1) to Article 46 includes a reference to Articles 32 and 54 of the Convention as they had effect immediately before the coming into force of the Eleventh Protocol.

(4) The references in section 2(1) to a report or decision of the Commission or a decision of the Committee of Ministers include references to a report or decision made as provided by paragraphs 3, 5 and 6 of Article 5 of the Eleventh Protocol (transitional provisions).

(5) Any liability under the Army Act 1955, the Air Force Act 1955 or the Naval Discipline Act 1957 to suffer death for an offence is replaced by a liability to imprisonment for life or any less punishment authorised by those Acts; and those Acts shall accordingly have effect with the necessary modifications.

Short title, commencement, application and extent

22.—(1) This Act may be cited as the Human Rights Act 1998.

(2) Sections 18, 20 and 21(5) and this section come into force on the passing of this Act.

(3) The other provisions of this Act come into force on such day as the Secretary of State may by order appoint; and different days may be appointed for different purposes.

(4) Paragraph (b) of subsection (1) of section applies to proceedings brought by or at the instigation of a public authority whenever the act in question took place; but otherwise that subsection does not apply to an act taking place before the coming into force of that section.

(5) This Act binds the Crown.

(6) This Act extends to Northern Ireland.

(7) Section 21(5), so far as it relates to any provision contained in the Army Act 1955, the Air Force Act 1955 or the Naval Discipline Act 1957, extends to any place to which that provision extends.

SCHEDULES

SCHEDULE 1

THE ARTICLES

PART I

THE CONVENTION

RIGHTS AND FREEDOMS

ARTICLE 2

RIGHT TO LIFE

1. Everyone's right to life shall be protected by law. No one shall be deprived of his life intentionally save in the execution of a sentence of a court following his conviction of a crime for which this penalty is provided by law.

2. Deprivation of life shall not be regarded as inflicted in contravention of this Article when it results from the use of force which is no more than absolutely necessary:

(a) in defence of any person from unlawful violence;

(b) in order to effect a lawful arrest or to prevent the escape of a person lawfully detained;

(c) in action lawfully taken for the purpose of quelling a riot or insurrection.

ARTICLE 3

PROHIBITION OF TORTURE

No one shall be subjected to torture or to inhuman or degrading treatment or punishment.

ARTICLE 4

PROHIBITION OF SLAVERY AND FORCED LABOUR

1. No one shall be held in slavery or servitude.

2. No one shall be required to perform forced or compulsory labour.

3. For the purpose of this Article the term "forced or compulsory labour" shall not include:

(a) any work required to be done in the ordinary course of detention imposed according to the provisions of Article 5 of this Convention or during conditional release from such detention;

(b) any service of a military character or, in case of conscientious objectors in countries where they are recognised, service exacted instead of compulsory military service;

(c) any service exacted in case of an emergency or calamity threatening the life or well-being of the community;

(d) any work or service which forms part of normal civic obligations.

ARTICLE 5

RIGHT TO LIBERTY AND SECURITY

1. Everyone has the right to liberty and security of person. No one shall be deprived of his liberty save in the following cases and in accordance with a procedure prescribed by law:

(a) the lawful detention of a person after conviction by a competent court;

(b) the lawful arrest or detention of a person for non-compliance with the lawful order of a court or in order to secure the fulfilment of any obligation prescribed by law;

(c) the lawful arrest or detention of a person effected for the purpose of bringing him before the competent legal authority on reasonable suspicion of having committed an offence or when it is reasonably considered necessary to prevent his committing an offence or fleeing after having done so;

(d) the detention of a minor by lawful order for the purpose of educational supervision or his lawful detention for the purpose of bringing him before the competent legal authority;

(e) the lawful detention of persons for the prevention of the spreading of infectious diseases, of persons of unsound mind, alcoholics or drug addicts or vagrants;

(f) the lawful arrest or detention of a person to prevent his effecting an unauthorised entry into the country or of a person against whom action is being taken with a view to deportation or extradition.

2. Everyone who is arrested shall be informed promptly, in a language which he understands, of the reasons for his arrest and of any charge against him.

3. Everyone arrested or detained in accordance with the provisions of paragraph 1(c) of this Article shall be brought promptly before a judge or other officer authorised by law to exercise judicial power and shall be entitled to trial within a reasonable time or to release pending trial. Release may be conditioned by guarantees to appear for trial.

4. Everyone who is deprived of his liberty by arrest or detention shall be entitled to take proceedings by which the lawfulness of his detention shall be decided speedily by a court and his release ordered if the detention is not lawful.

5. Everyone who has been the victim of arrest or detention in contravention of the provisions of this Article shall have an enforceable right to compensation.

ARTICLE 6

RIGHT TO A FAIR TRIAL

1. In the determination of his civil rights and obligations or of any criminal charge against him, everyone is entitled to a fair and public hearing within a reasonable time by an independent and impartial tribunal established by law. Judgment shall be pronounced publicly but the press and public may be excluded from all or part of the trial in the interest of morals, public order or national security in a democratic society, where the interests of juveniles or the protection of the private life of the parties so require, or to the extent strictly necessary in the opinion of the court in special circumstances where publicity would prejudice the interests of justice.

2. Everyone charged with a criminal offence shall be presumed innocent until proved guilty according to law.

3. Everyone charged with a criminal offence has the following minimum rights:

(a) to be informed promptly, in a language which he understands and in detail, of the nature and cause of the accusation against him;

(b) to have adequate time and facilities for the preparation of his defence;

(c) to defend himself in person or through legal assistance of his own choosing or, if he has not sufficient means to pay for legal assistance, to be given it free when the interests of justice so require;

(d) to examine or have examined witnesses against him and to obtain the attendance and examination of witnesses on his behalf under the same conditions as witnesses against him;

(e) to have the free assistance of an interpreter if he cannot understand or speak the language used in court.

ARTICLE 7

NO PUNISHMENT WITHOUT LAW

1. No one shall be held guilty of any criminal offence on account of any act or omission which did not constitute a criminal offence under national or international law at the time when it was committed. Nor shall a heavier penalty be imposed than the one that was applicable at the time the criminal offence was committed.

2. This Article shall not prejudice the trial and punishment of any person for any act or omission which, at the time when it was committed, was criminal according to the general principles of law recognised by civilised nations.

ARTICLE 8

RIGHT TO RESPECT FOR PRIVATE & FAMILY LIFE

1. Everyone has the right to respect for his private and family life, his home and his correspondence.

2. There shall be no interference by a public authority with the exercise of this right except such as is in accordance with the law and is necessary in a democratic society in the interests of national security, public safety or the economic well-being of the country, for the prevention of disorder or crime, for the protection of health or morals, or for the protection of the rights and freedoms of others.

ARTICLE 9

FREEDOM OF THOUGHT, CONSCIENCE AND RELIGION

1. Everyone has the right to freedom of thought, conscience and religion; this right includes freedom to change his religion or belief and freedom, either alone or in community with others and in public or private, to manifest his religion or belief, in worship, teaching, practice and observance.

2. Freedom to manifest one's religion or beliefs shall be subject only to such limitations as are prescribed by law and are necessary in a democratic society in the interests of public safety, for the protection of public order, health or morals, or for the protection of the rights and freedoms of others.

ARTICLE 10

FREEDOM OF EXPRESSION

1. Everyone has the right to freedom of expression. This right shall include freedom to hold opinions and to receive and impart information and ideas without interference by public authority and regardless of frontiers. This Article shall not prevent States from requiring the licensing of broadcasting, television or cinema enterprises.

2. The exercise of these freedoms, since it carries with it duties and responsibilities, may be subject to such formalities, conditions, restrictions or penalties as are prescribed by law and are necessary in a democratic society, in the interests of national security, territorial integrity or public safety, for the prevention of disorder or crime, for the protection of health or morals, for the protection of the reputation or rights of others, for preventing the disclosure of information received in confidence, or for maintaining the authority and impartiality of the judiciary.

ARTICLE 11

FREEDOM OF ASSEMBLY AND ASSOCIATION

1. Everyone has the right to freedom of peaceful assembly and to freedom of association with others, including the right to form and to join trade unions for the protection of his interests.

2. No restrictions shall be placed on the exercise of these rights other than such as are prescribed by law and are necessary in a democratic society in the interests of national security or public safety, for the prevention of disorder or crime, for the protection of health or morals or for the protection of the rights and freedoms of others. This Article shall not prevent the imposition of lawful restrictions on the exercise of these rights by members of the armed forces, of the police or of the administration of the State.

ARTICLE 12

RIGHT TO MARRY

Men and women of marriageable age have the right to marry and to found a family, according to the national laws governing the exercise of this right.

ARTICLE 14

PROHIBITION OF DISCRIMINATION

The enjoyment of the rights and freedoms set forth in this Convention shall be secured without discrimination on any ground such as sex, race, colour, language, religion, political or other opinion, national or social origin, association with a national minority, property, birth or other status.

ARTICLE 16

RESTRICTIONS ON POLITICAL ACTIVITY OF ALIENS

Nothing in Articles 10, 11 and 14 shall be regarded as preventing the High Contracting Parties from imposing restrictions on the political activity of aliens.

ARTICLE 17

PROHIBITION OF ABUSE OF RIGHTS

Nothing in this Convention may be interpreted as implying for any State, group or person any right to engage in any activity or perform any act aimed at the destruction of any of the rights and freedoms set forth herein or at their limitation to a greater extent than is provided for in the Convention.

ARTICLE 18

LIMITATION ON USE OF RESTRICTIONS ON RIGHTS

The restrictions permitted under this Convention to the said rights and freedoms shall not be applied for any purpose other than those for which they have been prescribed.

Part II

The First Protocol

ARTICLE 1

PROTECTION OF PROPERTY

Every natural or legal person is entitled to the peaceful enjoyment of his possessions. No one shall be deprived of his possessions except in the public interest and subject to the conditions provided for by law and by the general principles of international law.

The preceding provisions shall not, however, in any way impair the right of a State to enforce such laws as it deems necessary to control the use of property in accordance with the general interest or to secure the payment of taxes or other contributions or penalties.

ARTICLE 2

RIGHT TO EDUCATION

No person shall be denied the right to education. In the exercise of any functions which it assumes in relation to education and to teaching, the State shall respect the right of parents to ensure such education and teaching in conformity with their own religious and philosophical convictions.

ARTICLE 3

RIGHT TO FREE ELECTIONS

The High Contracting Parties undertake to hold free elections at reasonable intervals by secret ballot, under conditions which will ensure the free expression of the opinion of the people in the choice of the legislature.

Part III

The Sixth Protocol

ARTICLE 1

ABOLITION OF THE DEATH PENALTY

The death penalty shall be abolished. No one shall be condemned to such penalty or executed.

ARTICLE 2

DEATH PENALTY IN TIME OF WAR

A State may make provision in its law for the death penalty in respect of acts committed in time of war or of imminent threat of war; such penalty shall be applied only in the instances laid down in the law and in accordance with its provisions. The State shall communicate to the Secretary General of the Council of Europe the relevant provisions of that law.

SCHEDULE 2

REMEDIAL ORDERS

Orders

1.—(1) A remedial order may—

(a) contain such incidental, supplemental, consequential or transitional provision as the person making it considers appropriate;

(b) be made so as to have effect from a date earlier than that on which it is made;

(c) make provision for the delegation of specific functions;

(d) make different provision for different cases.

(2) The power conferred by sub-paragraph (1)(a) includes—

(a) power to amend primary legislation (including primary legislation other than that which contains the incompatible provision); and

(b) power to amend or revoke subordinate legislation (including subordinate legislation other than that which contains the incompatible provision).

(3) A remedial order may be made so as to have the same extent as the legislation which it affects.

(4) No person is to be guilty of an offence solely as a result of the retrospective effect of a remedial order.

Procedure

2. No remedial order may be made unless—

(a) a draft of the order has been approved by a resolution of each House of Parliament made after the end of the period of 60 days beginning with the day on which the draft was laid; or

(b) it is declared in the order that it appears to the person making it that, because of the urgency of the matter, it is necessary to make the order without a draft being so approved.

Orders laid in draft

3.—(1) No draft may be laid under paragraph 2(a) unless—

(a) the person proposing to make the order has laid before Parliament a document which contains a draft of the proposed order and the required information; and

(b) the period of 60 days, beginning with the day on which the document required by this sub-paragraph was laid, has ended.

(2) If representations have been made during that period, the draft laid under paragraph 2(a) must be accompanied by a statement containing—

(a) a summary of the representations; and

(b) if, as a result of the representations, the proposed order has been changed, details of the changes.

Urgent cases

4.—(1) If a remedial order ("the original order") is made without being approved in draft, the person making it must lay it before Parliament, accompanied by the required information, after it is made.

(2) If representations have been made during the period of 60 days beginning with the day on which the original order was made, the person making it must (after the end of that period) lay before Parliament a statement containing—

(a) a summary of the representations; and

(b) if, as a result of the representations, he considers it appropriate to make changes to the original order, details of the changes.

(3) If sub-paragraph (2)(b) applies, the person making the statement must—

(a) make a further remedial order replacing the original order; and

(b) lay the replacement order before Parliament.

(4) If, at the end of the period of 120 days beginning with the day on which the original order was made, a resolution has not been passed by each House approving the original or replacement order, the order ceases to have effect (but without that affecting anything previously done under either order or the power to make a fresh remedial order).

Definitions

5. In this Schedule—

"representations" means representations about a remedial order (or proposed remedial order) made to the person making (or proposing to make) it and includes any relevant Parliamentary report or resolution; and
"required information" means—
(a) an explanation of the incompatibility which the order (or proposed order) seeks to remove, including particulars of the relevant declaration, finding or order;
(b) a statement of the reasons for proceeding under section 10 and for making an order in those terms.

Calculating periods

6. In calculating any period for the purposes of this Schedule, no account is to be taken of any time during which—

(a) Parliament is dissolved or prorogued; and

(b) both Houses are adjourned for more than four days.

SCHEDULE 3

DEROGATION AND RESERVATION

PART I

DEROGATION

The 1988 notification

The United Kingdom Permanent Representative to the Council of Europe presents his compliments to the Secretary General of the Council, and has the honour to convey the following information in order to ensure compliance with the obligations of Her Majesty's Government in the United Kingdom under Article 15(3) of the Convention for the Protection of Human Rights and Fundamental Freedoms signed at Rome on 4 November 1950.

There have been in the United Kingdom in recent years campaigns of organised terrorism connected with the affairs of Northern Ireland which have manifested themselves in activities which have included repeated murder, attempted murder, maiming, intimidation and violent civil disturbance and in bombing and fire raising which have resulted in death, injury and widespread destruction of property. As a result, a public emergency within the meaning of Article 15(1) of the Convention exists in the United Kingdom.

The Government found it necessary in 1974 to introduce and since then, in cases concerning persons reasonably suspected of involvement in terrorism connected with the affairs of Northern Ireland, or of certain offences under the legislation, who have been detained for 48 hours, to exercise powers enabling further detention without charge, for periods of up to five days, on the authority of the Secretary of State. These powers are at present to be found in Section 12 of the Prevention of Terrorism (Temporary Provisions) Act 1984, Article 9 of the Prevention of Terrorism (Supplemental Temporary Provisions) Order 1984 and Article 10 of the Prevention of Terrorism (Supplemental Temporary Provisions) (Northern Ireland) Order 1984.

Section 12 of the Prevention of Terrorism (Temporary Provisions) Act 1984 provides for a person whom a constable has arrested on reasonable grounds of suspecting him to be guilty of an offence under Section 1, 9 or 10 of the Act, or to be or to have been involved in terrorism connected with the affairs of Northern Ireland, to be detained in right of the arrest for up to 48 hours and thereafter, where the Secretary of State extends the detention period, for up to a further five days. Section 12 substantially re-enacted Section 12 of the Prevention of Terrorism (Temporary Provisions) Act 1976 which, in turn, substantially re-enacted Section 7 of the Prevention of Terrorism (Temporary Provisions) Act 1974.

Article 10 of the Prevention of Terrorism (Supplemental Temporary Provisions) (Northern Ireland) Order 1984 (SI 1984/417) and Article 9 of the Prevention of Terrorism (Supplemental Temporary Provisions) Order 1984 (SI 1984/418) were both made under Sections 13 and 14 of and Schedule 3 to the 1984 Act and substantially re-enacted powers of detention in Orders made under the 1974 and 1976 Acts. A person who is being examined under Article 4 of either Order on his arrival in, or on seeking to leave, Northern Ireland or Great Britain for the purpose of determining whether he is or has been involved in terrorism connected with the affairs of Northern Ireland, or whether there are grounds for suspecting that he has committed an offence under Section 9 of the 1984 Act, may be detained under Article 9 or 10, as appropriate, pending the conclusion of his examination. The period of this examination may exceed 12 hours if an examining officer has reasonable grounds for suspecting him to be or to have been involved in acts of terrorism connected with the affairs of Northern Ireland.

Where such a person is detained under the said Article 9 or 10 he may be detained for up to 48 hours on the authority of an examining officer and thereafter, where the Secretary of State extends the detention period, for up to a further five days.

In its judgment of 29 November 1988 in the Case of *Brogan and Others*, the European Court of Human Rights held that there had been a violation of Article 5(3) in respect of each of the applicants, all of whom had been detained under Section 12 of the 1984 Act. The Court held that even the shortest of the four periods of detention concerned, namely four days and six hours, fell outside the constraints as to time permitted by the first part of Article 5(3). In addition, the Court held that there had been a violation of Article 5(5) in the case of each applicant.

Following this judgment, the Secretary of State for the Home Department informed Parliament on 6 December 1988 that, against the background of the terrorist campaign, and the over-riding need to bring terrorists to justice, the Government did not believe that the maximum period of detention should be reduced. He informed Parliament that the Government were examining the matter with a view to responding to the judgment. On 22 December 1988, the Secretary of State further informed Parliament that it remained the Government's wish, if it could be achieved, to find a judicial process under which extended detention might be reviewed and where appropriate authorised by a judge or other judicial officer. But a further period of reflection and consultation was necessary before the Government could bring forward a firm and final view.

Since the judgment of 29 November 1988 as well as previously, the Government have found it necessary to continue to exercise, in relation to terrorism connected with the affairs of Northern Ireland, the powers described above enabling further detention without charge for periods of up to 5 days, on the authority of the Secretary of State, to the extent strictly required by the exigencies of the situation to enable necessary enquiries and investigations properly to be completed in order to decide whether criminal proceedings should be instituted. To the extent that the exercise of these powers may be inconsistent with the obligations imposed by the Convention the Government has availed itself of the right of derogation conferred by Article 15(1) of the Convention and will continue to do so until further notice.

Dated 23 December 1988.

The 1989 notification

The United Kingdom Permanent Representative to the Council of Europe presents his compliments to the Secretary General of the Council, and has the honour to convey the following information.

In his communication to the Secretary General of 23 December 1988, reference was made to the introduction and exercise of certain powers under section 12 of the Prevention of Terrorism (Temporary Provisions) Act 1984, Article 9 of the Prevention of Terrorism (Supplemental Temporary Provisions) Order 1984 and Article 10 of the Prevention of Terrorism (Supplemental Temporary Provisions) (Northern Ireland) Order 1984.

These provisions have been replaced by section 14 and paragraph 6 of Schedule 5 to the Prevention of Terrorism (Temporary Provisions) Act 1989, which make comparable provision. They came into force on 22 March 1989. A copy of these provisions is enclosed.

The United Kingdom Permanent Representative avails himself of this opportunity to renew to the Secretary General the assurance of his highest consideration.

23 March 1989.

PART II

RESERVATION

At the time of signing the present (First) Protocol, I declare that, in view of certain provisions of the Education Acts in the United Kingdom, the principle affirmed in the second sentence of Article 2 is accepted by the United Kingdom only so far as it is compatible with the provision of efficient instruction and training, and the avoidance of unreasonable public expenditure.

Dated 20 March 1952.

Made by the United Kingdom Permanent Representative to the Council of Europe.

SCHEDULE 4

JUDICIAL PENSIONS

Duty to make orders about pensions

1.—(1) The appropriate Minister must by order make provision with respect to pensions payable to or in respect of any holder of a judicial office who serves as an ECHR judge.

(2) A pensions order must include such provision as the Minister making it considers is necessary to secure that—

> (a) an ECHR judge who was, immediately before his appointment as an ECHR judge, a member of a judicial pension scheme is entitled to remain as a member of that scheme;
>
> (b) the terms on which he remains a member of the scheme are those which would have been applicable had he not been appointed as an ECHR judge; and
>
> (c) entitlement to benefits payable in accordance with the scheme continues to be determined as if, while serving as an ECHR judge, his salary was that which would (but for section 18(4)) have been payable to him in respect of his continuing service as the holder of his judicial office.

Contributions

2. A pensions order may, in particular, make provision—

> (a) for any contributions which are payable by a person who remains a member of a scheme as a result of the order, and which would otherwise be payable by deduction from his salary, to be made otherwise than by deduction from his salary as an ECHR judge; and
>
> (b) for such contributions to be collected in such manner as may be determined by the administrators of the scheme.

Amendments of other enactments

3. A pensions order may amend any provision of, or made under, a pensions Act in such manner and to such extent as the Minister making the order considers necessary or expedient to ensure the proper administration of any scheme to which it relates.

Definitions

4. In this Schedule—

> "appropriate Minister" means—
> > (a) in relation to any judicial office whose jurisdiction is exercisable exclusively in relation to Scotland, the Secretary of State; and
> > (b) otherwise, the Lord Chancellor;
>
> "ECHR judge" means the holder of a judicial office who is serving as a judge of the Court;

"judicial pension scheme" means a scheme established by and in accordance with a
    pensions Act;
"pensions Act" means—
    (a) the County Courts Act Northern Ireland) 1959;
    (b) the Sheriffs' Pension (Scotland) Act 1961;
    (c) the Judicial Pensions Act 1981; or
    (d) the Judicial Pensions and Retirement Act 1993; and
"pensions order" means an order made under paragraph 1.

APPENDIX B

COUNCIL OF EUROPE
EUROPEAN TREATIES
ETS No. 5

Convention for the Protection of Human Rights and Fundamental Freedoms as amended by Protocol No. 11

ROME, 4.XI.1950

The text of the Convention had been amended according to the provisions of Protocol No. 3 (ETS No. 45), which entered into force on 21 September 1970, of Protocol No. 5 (ETS No. 55), which entered into force on 20 December 1971 and of Protocol No. 8 (ETS No. 118), which entered into force on 1 January 1990, and comprised also the text of Protocol No. 2 (ETS No. 44) which, in accordance with Article 5, paragraph 3 thereof, had been an integral part of the Convention since its entry into force on 21 September 1970. All provisions which had been amended or added by these Protocols are replaced by Protocol No. 11 (ETS No. 155), as from the date of its entry into force on 1 November 1998. As from that date, Protocol No. 9 (ETS No. 140), which entered into force on 1 October 1994, is repealed and Protocol No. 10 (ETS No. 146) has lost its purpose.

The governments signatory hereto, being members of the Council of Europe,

Considering the Universal Declaration of Human Rights proclaimed by the General Assembly of the United Nations on 10th December 1948;

Considering that this Declaration aims at securing the universal and effective recognition and observance of the Rights therein declared;

Considering that the aim of the Council of Europe is the achievement of greater unity between its members and that one of the methods by which that aim is to be pursued is the maintenance and further realisation of human rights and fundamental freedoms;

Reaffirming their profound belief in those fundamental freedoms which are like-minded and have a common heritage of political traditions, ideals, freedom and the rule of law, to take the first steps for the collective enforcement of certain of the rights stated in the Universal Declaration,

Have agreed as follows:

Article 1—Obligation to respect human rights

The High Contracting Parties shall secure to everyone within their jurisdiction the rights and freedoms defined in Section I of this Convention.

Section I—Rights and freedoms

Article 2—Right to life

1. Everyone's right to life shall be protected by law. No one shall be deprived of his life intentionally save in the execution of a sentence of a court following his conviction of a crime for which this penalty is provided by law.

2. Deprivation of life shall not be regarded as inflicted in contravention of this article when it results from the use of force which is no more than absolutely necessary:
   a. in defence of any person from unlawful violence;
   b. in order to effect a lawful arrest or to prevent the escape of a person lawfully detained;
   c. in action lawfully taken for the purpose of quelling a riot or insurrection.

Article 3—Prohibition of torture

No one shall be subjected to torture or to inhuman or degrading treatment or punishment.

Article 4—Prohibition of slavery and forced labour

1. No one shall be held in slavery or servitude.
2. No one shall be required to perform forced or compulsory labour.
3. For the purpose of this article the term "forced or compulsory labour" shall not include:
   a. any work required to be done in the ordinary course of detention imposed according to the provisions of Article 5 of this Convention or during conditional release from such detention;
   b. any service of a military character or, in case of conscientious objectors in countries where they are recognised, service exacted instead of compulsory military service;
   c. any service exacted in case of an emergency or calamity threatening the life or well-being of the community;
   d. any work or service which forms part of normal civic obligations.

Article 5—Right to liberty and security

1. Everyone has the right to liberty and security of person. No one shall be deprived of his liberty save in the following cases and in accordance with a procedure prescribed by law:
   a. the lawful detention of a person after conviction by a competent court;
   b. the lawful arrest or detention of a person for non-compliance with the lawful order of a court or in order to secure the fulfilment of any obligation prescribed by law;
   c. the lawful arrest or detention of a person effected for the purpose of bringing him before the competent legal authority on reasonable suspicion of having committed an offence or when it is reasonably considered necessary to prevent his committing an offence or fleeing after having done so;
   d. the detention of a minor by lawful order for the purpose of educational supervision or his lawful detention for the purpose of bringing him before the competent legal authority;
   e. the lawful detention of persons for the prevention of the spreading of infectious diseases, of persons of unsound mind, alcoholics or drug addicts or vagrants;
   f. the lawful arrest or detention of a person to prevent his effecting an unauthorised entry into the country or of a person against whom action is being taken with a view to deportation or extradition.
3. Everyone who is arrested shall be informed promptly, in a language which he understands, of the reasons for his arrest and of any charge against him.
4. Everyone arrested or detained in accordance with the provisions of paragraph 1.c of this article shall be brought promptly before a judge or other officer authorised by law to exercise judicial power and shall be entitled to trial within a reasonable time or to release pending trial. Release may be conditioned by guarantees to appear for trial.
5. Everyone who is deprived of his liberty by arrest or detention shall be entitled to take proceedings by which the lawfulness of his detention shall be decided speedily by a court and his release ordered if the detention is not lawful.

6. Everyone who has been the victim of arrest or detention in contravention of the provisions of this article shall have an enforceable right to compensation.

Article 6—Right to a fair trial

1. In the determination of his civil rights and obligations or of any criminal charge against him, everyone is entitled to a fair and public hearing within a reasonable time by an independent and impartial tribunal established by law. Judgment shall be pronounced publicly but the press and public may be excluded from all or part of the trial in the interests of morals, public order or national security in a democratic society, where the interests of juveniles or the protection of the private life of the parties so require, or to the extent strictly necessary in the opinion of the court in special circumstances where publicity would prejudice the interests of justice.
2. Everyone charged with a criminal offence shall be presumed innocent until proved guilty according to law.
3. Everyone charged with a criminal offence has the following minimum rights:
   a. to be informed promptly, in a language which he understands and in detail, of the nature and cause of the accusation against him;
   b. to have adequate time and facilities for the preparation of his defence;
   c. to defend himself in person or through legal assistance of his own choosing or, if he has not sufficient means to pay for legal assistance, to be given it free when the interests of justice so require;
   d. to examine or have examined witnesses against him and to obtain the attendance and examination of witnesses on his behalf under the same conditions as witnesses against him;
   e. to have the free assistance of an interpreter if he cannot understand or speak the language used in court.

Article 7—No punishment without law

1. No one shall be held guilty of any criminal offence on account of any act or omission which did not constitute offence under national or international law at the time when it was committed. Nor shall a heavier penalty be imposed than the one that was applicable at the time the criminal offence was committed.
2. This article shall not prejudice the trial and punishment of any person for any act or omission which, at the time when it was committed, was criminal according to the general principles of law recognised by civilised nations.

Article 8—Right to respect for private and family life

1. Everyone has the right to respect for his private and family life, his home and his correspondence.
2. There shall be no interference by a public authority with the exercise of this right except such as is in accordance with the law and is necessary in a democratic society in the interests of national security, public safety or the economic well-being of the country, for the prevention of disorder or crime, for the protection of health or morals, or for the protection of the rights and freedoms of others.

Article 9—Freedom of thought, conscience and religion

1. Everyone has the right to freedom of thought, conscience and religion; this right includes freedom to change his religion or belief and freedom, either alone or in community with others and in public or private, to manifest his religion or belief, in worship, teaching, practice and observance.
2. Freedom to manifest one's religion or beliefs shall be subject only to such limitations as are prescribed by law and are necessary in a democratic society in the interests of public safety, for the protection of public order, health or morals, or for the protection of the rights and freedoms of others.

Article 10—Freedom of expression

1. Everyone has the right to freedom of expression. This right shall include freedom to hold opinions and to receive and impart information and ideas without interference by public authority and regardless of frontiers. This article shall not prevent States from requiring the licensing of broadcasting, television or cinema enterprises.
2. The exercise of these freedoms, since it carries with it duties and responsibilities, may be subject to such formalities, conditions, restrictions or penalties as are prescribed by law and are necessary in a democratic society, in the interests of national security, territorial integrity or public safety, for the prevention of disorder or crime, for the protection of health or morals, for the protection of the reputation or rights of others, for preventing the disclosure of information received in confidence, or for maintaining the authority and impartiality of the judiciary.

Article 11—Freedom of assembly and association

1. Everyone has the right to freedom of peaceful assembly and to freedom of association with others, including the right to form and to join trade unions for the protection of his interests.
2. No restrictions shall be placed on the exercise of these rights other than such as are prescribed by law and are necessary in a democratic society in the interests of national security or public safety, for the prevention of disorder or crime, for the protection of health or morals or for the protection of the reputation or rights of others. This article shall not prevent the imposition of lawful restrictions on the exercise of these rights by members of the armed forces, of the police or of the administration of the State.

Article 12—Right to marry

Men and women of marriageable age have the right to marry and to found a family, according to the national laws governing the exercise of this right.

Article 13—Right to an effective remedy

Everyone whose rights and freedoms as set forth in this Convention are violated shall have an effective remedy before a national authority notwithstanding that the violation has been committed by persons acting in an official capacity.

Article 14—Prohibition of discrimination

The enjoyment of the rights and freedoms set forth in this Convention shall be secured without discrimination on any ground such as sex, race, colour, language, religion, political or other opinion, national or social origin, association with a national minority, property, birth or other status.

Article 15—derogation in time of emergency

1. In time of war or other public emergency threatening the life of the nation any High Contracting Party may take measures derogating from its obligations under this Convention to the extent strictly required by the exigencies of the situation, provided that such measures are not inconsistent with its other obligations under international law.
2. No derogation from Article 2, except in respect of deaths resulting from lawful acts of war, or from Articles 2, 4 (paragraph 1) and 7 shall be made under this provision.
3. Any High Contracting Party availing itself of this right of derogation shall keep the Secretary General of the Council of Europe fully informed of the measures which it has taken and the reasons therefor. It shall also inform the Secretary General of the Council of Europe when such measures have ceased to operate and the provisions of the Convention are again being fully executed.

Article 16—Restrictions on political activity of aliens

Nothing in Articles 10, 11 and 14 shall be regarded as preventing the High Contracting Parties from imposing restrictions on the political activity of aliens.

Article 17—Prohibition of abuse of rights

Nothing in this Convention may be interpreted as implying for any State, group or person any right to engage in any activity or perform any act aimed at the destruction of any of the rights and freedoms set forth herein or at their limitation to a greater extent than is provided for in the Convention.

Article 18—Limitation on use of restrictions on rights

The restrictions permitted under this Convention to the said rights and freedoms shall not be applied for any purpose other than those for which they have been prescribed.

Section II—European Court of Human Rights

Article 19—Establishment of the Court

To ensure the observance of the engagements undertaken by the High Contracting Parties in the Convention and the Protocols thereto, there shall be set up a European Court of Human Rights, hereinafter referred to as "the Court". It shall function on a permanent basis.

Article 20—Number of judges

The Court shall consist of a number of judges equal to that of the High Contracting Parties.

Article 21—Criteria for office

1. The judges shall be of high moral character and must either possess the qualifications required for appointment to high judicial office or be jurisconsults of recognised competence.
2. The judges shall sit on the Court in their individual capacity.
3. During their term of office the judges shall not engage in any activity which is incompatible with their independence, impartiality or with the demands of a full-time office; all questions arising from the application of this paragraph shall be decided by the Court.

Article 22—Election of judges

1. The judges shall be elected by the Parliamentary Assembly with respect to each High Contracting Party by a majority of votes cast from a list of three candidates nominated by the High Contracting Party.
2. The same procedure shall be followed to complete the Court in the event of the accession of new High Contracting Parties and in filing casual vacancies.

Article 23—Terms of office

1. The judges shall be elected for a period of six years. They may be re-elected. However, the terms of office of one-half of the judges elected at the first election shall expire at the end of three years.
2. The judges whose terms of office are to expire at the end of the initial period of three years shall be chosen by lot by the Secretary General of the Council of Europe immediately after their election.
3. In order to ensure that, as far as possible, the terms of office of one-half of the judges are renewed every three years, the Parliamentary Assembly may decide, before proceeding to any subsequent election, that the term or terms of office of one or more judges to be elected shall be for a period other than six years but not more than nine and not less than three years.

4. In cases where more than one term of office is involved and where the Parliamentary Assembly applies the preceding paragraph, the allocation of the terms of office shall be effected by a drawing of lots by the Secretary General of the Council of Europe immediately after the election.
5. A judge elected to replace a judge whose term of office has not expired shall hold office for the remainder of his predecessor's term.
6. The terms of office of judges shall expire when they reach the age of 70.
7. The judges shall hold office until replaced. They shall, however, continue to deal with such cases as they already have under consideration.

Article 24—Dismissal

No judge may be dismissed from his office unless the other judges decide by a majority of two-thirds that he has ceased to fulfil the required conditions.

Article 25—Registry and legal secretaries

The Court shall have a registry, the functions and organisation of which shall be laid down in the rules of the Court. The Court shall be assisted by legal secretaries.

Article 26—Plenary Court

The plenary Court shall:

a. elect its President and one or two Vice-Presidents for a period of three years; they may be re-elected;
b. set up Chambers, constituted for a fixed period of time;
c. elect the Presidents of the Chambers of the Court; they may be re-elected;
d. adopt the rules of the Court, and
e. elect the Registrar and one or more Deputy Registrars.

Article 27—Committees, Chambers and Grand Chamber

1. To consider cases brought before it, the Court shall sit in committees of three judges, in Chambers of seven judges and in a Grand Chamber of seventeen judges. The Court's Chambers shall set up committees for a fixed period of time.
2. There shall sit as an *ex officio* member of the Chamber and the Grand Chamber the judge elected in respect of the State Party concerned or, if there is none or if he is unable to sit, a person of its choice who shall sit in the capacity of judge.
3. The Grand Chamber shall also include the President of the Court, the Vice-Presidents, the Presidents of the Chambers and other judges chosen in accordance with the rules of the Court. When a case is referred to the Grand Chamber under Article 43, no judge from the Chamber which rendered the judgment shall sit in the Grand Chamber, with the exception of the President of the Chamber and the judge who sat in respect of the State Party concerned.

Article 28—Declarations of inadmissibility by committees

A committee may, by a unanimous vote, declare inadmissible or strike out of its list of cases an application submitted under Article 34 where such a decision can be taken without further examination. The decision shall be final.

Article 29—Decisions by Chambers on admissibility and merits

1. If no decision is taken under Article 28, a Chamber shall decide on the admissibility and merits of individual applications submitted under Article 34.
2. A Chamber shall decide on the admissibility and merits of inter-State applications submitted under Article 33.

3. The decision on admissibility shall be taken separately unless the Court, in exceptional cases, decides otherwise.

Article 30—Relinquishment of jurisdiction to the Grand Chamber

Where a case pending before a Chamber raises a serious question affecting the interpretation of the Convention or the protocols thereto, or where the resolution of a question before the Chamber might have a result inconsistent with a judgment previously delivered by the Court, the Chamber may, at any time before it has rendered its judgment, relinquish jurisdiction in favour of the Grand Chamber, unless one of the parties to the case objects.

Article 31—Powers of the Grand Chamber

The Grand Chamber shall:

    a. determine applications submitted either under Article 33 or Article 34 when a Chamber has relinquished jurisdiction under Article 30 or when the case has been referred to it under Article 43; and

    b. consider requests for advisory opinions submitted under Article 47.

Article 32—Jurisdiction of the Court

1. The jurisdiction of the Court shall extend to all matters concerning the interpretation and application of the Convention and the protocols thereto which are referred to it as provided in Articles 33, 34 and 47.
2. In the event of dispute as to whether the Court has jurisdiction, the Court shall decide.

Article 33—Inter-State cases

Any High Contracting Party may refer to the Court any alleged breach of the provisions of the Convention and the protocols thereto by another High Contracting Party.

Article 34—Individual applications

The Court may receive applications from any person, non-governmental organisation or group of individuals claiming to be the victim of a violation by one of the High Contracting Parties of the rights set forth in the Convention or the protocols thereto. The High Contracting Parties undertake not to hinder in any way the effective exercise of this right.

Article 35—Admissibility criteria

1. The Court may only deal with the matter after all domestic remedies have been exhausted, according to the generally recognised rules of international law, and within a period of six months from the date on which the final decision was taken.
2. The Court shall not deal with any application submitted under Article 34 that:
    a. is anonymous; or
    b. is substantially the same as a matter that has already been examined by the Court or has already been submitted to another procedure of international investigation or settlement and contains no relevant new information.
3. The Court shall declare inadmissible any individual application submitted under Article 34 which it considers incompatible with the provisions of the Convention or the protocols thereto, manifestly ill-founded, or an abuse of the right of application.
4. The Court shall reject any application which it considers inadmissible under this Article. It may do so at any stage of the proceedings.

Article 36—Third party intervention

1. In all cases before a Chamber or the Grand Chamber, a High Contracting Party one of whose nationals is an applicant shall have the right to submit written comments and to take part in hearings.
2. The President of the Court may, in the interests of the proper administration of justice, invite any High Contracting Party which is not a party to the proceedings or any person concerned who is not the applicant to submit written comments or take part in hearings.

Article 37—Striking out applications

1. The Court may at any stage of the proceedings decide to strike an application out of its list of cases where the circumstances lead to the conclusion that:
   a. the applicant does not intend to pursue his application; or
   b. the matter has been resolved; or
   c. for any other reason established by the Court, it is no longer justified to continue the examination of the application.
   However, the Court shall continue the examination of the application if respect for human rights as defined in the Convention and the protocols thereto so requires.
2. The Court may decide to restore an application to its list of cases if it considers that the circumstances justify such a course.

Article 38—Examination of the case and friendly settlement proceedings

1. If the Court declares the application admissible, it shall:
   a. pursue the examination of the case, together with the representatives of the parties, and if need be, undertake an investigation, for the effective conduct of which the States concerned shall furnish all necessary facilities;
   b. place itself at the disposal of the parties concerned with a view to securing a friendly settlement of the matter on the basis of respect for human rights as defined in the Convention and the protocols thereto.
2. Proceedings conducted under paragraph 1.b shall be confidential.

Article 39—Finding of a friendly settlement

If a friendly settlement is effected, the Court shall strike the case out of its list by means of a decision which shall be confined to a brief statement of the facts and of the solution reached.

Article 40—Public hearings and access to documents

1. Hearings shall be in public unless the Court in exceptional circumstances decides otherwise.
2. Documents deposited with the Registrar shall be accessible to the public unless the President of the Court decides otherwise.

Article 41—Just satisfaction

If the Court finds that there has been a violation of the Convention or the protocols thereto, and if the internal law of the High Contracting Party concerned allows only partial reparation to be made, the Court shall, if necessary, afford just satisfaction to the injured party.

Article 42—Judgments of Chambers

Judgments of Chambers shall become final in accordance with the provisions of Article 44, paragraph 2.

Article 43—Referral to the Grand Chamber

1. Within a period of three months from the date of the judgment of the Chamber, any party to the case may, in exceptional cases, request that the case be referred to the Grand Chamber.

2. A panel of five judges of the Grand Chamber shall accept the request if the case raises a serious question affecting the interpretation or application of the Convention or the protocols thereto, or a serious issue of general importance.
3. If the panel accepts the request, the Grand Chamber shall decide the case by means of a judgment.

Article 44—Final judgments

1. The judgment of the Grand Chamber shall be final.
2. The judgment of a Chamber shall become final:
   a. when the parties declare that they will not request that the case be referred to the Grand Chamber; or
   b. three months after the date of the judgment, if reference of the case to the Grand Chamber has not been requested; or
   c. when the panel of the Grand Chamber rejects the request to refer under Article 43.
3. The final judgment shall be published.

Article 45—Reasons for judgments and decisions

1. Reasons shall be given for judgments as well as for decisions declaring applications admissible or inadmissible.
2. If a judgment does not represent, in whole or in part, the unanimous opinion of the judges, any judge shall be entitled to deliver a separate opinion.

Article 46—Binding force and execution of judgments

1. The High Contracting Parties undertake to abide by the final judgment of the Court in any case to which they are parties.
2. The final judgment of the Court shall be transmitted to the Committee of Ministers, which shall supervise its execution.

Article 47—Advisory opinions

1. The Court may, at the request of the Committee of Ministers, give advisory opinions on legal questions concerning the interpretation of the Convention and the protocols thereto.
2. Such opinions shall not deal with any question relating to the content or scope of the rights or freedoms defined in Section I of the Convention and the protocols thereto, or with any other question which the Court or the Committee of Ministers might have to consider in consequence of any such proceedings as could be instituted in accordance with the Convention.
3. Decisions of the Committee of Ministers to request an advisory opinion of the Court shall require a majority vote of the representatives entitled to sit on the Committee.

Article 48—Advisory jurisdiction of the Court

The Court shall decide whether a request for an advisory opinion submitted by the Committee of Ministers is within its competence as defined in Article 47.

Article 49—Reasons for advisory opinions

1. Reasons shall be given for advisory opinions of the Court.
2. If the advisory opinion does not represent, in whole or in part, the unanimous opinion of the judges, any judge shall be entitled to deliver a separate opinion.
3. Advisory opinions of the Court shall be communicated to the Committee of Ministers.

Article 50—Expenditure on the Court

The expenditure on the Court shall be borne by the Council of Europe.

Article 51—Privileges and immunities of judges

The judges shall be entitled, during the exercise of their functions, to the privileges and immunities provided for in Article 40 of the Statute of the Council of Europe and in the agreements made thereunder.

Section III—Miscellaneous provisions

Article 52—Inquiries by the Secretary General

On receipt of a request from the Secretary General of the Council of Europe any High Contracting Party shall furnish an explanation of the manner in which its internal law ensures the effective implementation of any of the provisions of the Convention.

Article 53—Safeguard for existing human rights

Nothing in this Convention shall be construed as limiting or derogating from any of the human rights and fundamental freedoms which may be ensured under the laws of any High Contracting Party or under any other agreement to which it is a Party.

Article 54—Powers of the Committee of Ministers

Nothing in this Convention shall prejudice the powers conferred on the Committee of Ministers by the Statute of the Council of Europe.

Article 55—Exclusion of other means of dispute settlement

The High Contracting Parties agree that, except by special agreement, they will not avail themselves of treaties, conventions or declarations in force between them for the purpose of submitting, by way of petition, a dispute arising out of the interpretation or application of this Convention to a means of settlement other than those provided for in this Convention.

Article 56—Territorial application

1. Any State may at the time of its ratification or at any time thereafter declare by notification addressed to the Secretary General of the Council of Europe that the present Convention shall, subject to paragraph 4 of this Article, extend to all or any of the territories for whose international relations it is responsible.
2. The Convention shall extend to the territory or territories named in the notification as from the thirtieth day after the receipt of this notification by the Secretary General of the Council of Europe.
3. The provisions of this Convention shall be applied in such territories with due regard, however, to local requirements.
4. Any State which has made a declaration in accordance with paragraph 1 of this article may at any time thereafter declare on behalf of one or more of the territories to which the declaration relates that it accepts the competence of the Court to receive applications from individuals, non-governmental organisations or groups of individuals as provided by Article 34 of the Convention.

Article 57—Reservations

1. Any State may, when signing this Convention or when depositing its instrument of ratification, make a reservation in respect of any particular provision of the Convention to the extent that any law then in force in its territory is not in conformity with the provision. Reservations of a general character shall not be permitted under this article.
2. Any reservation made under this article shall contain a brief statement of the law concerned.

Article 58—Denunciation

1. A High Contracting Party may denounce the present Convention only after the expiry of five years from the date on which it became a party to it and after six

months' notice contained in a notification addressed to the Secretary General of the Council of Europe, who shall inform the other High Contracting Parties.

2. Such a denunciation shall not have the effect of releasing the High Contracting Party concerned from its obligations under this Convention in respect of any act which, being capable of constituting a violation of such obligations, may have been performed by it before the date at which the denunciation became effective.

3. Any High Contracting Party which shall cease to be a member of the Council of Europe shall cease to be a Party to this Convention under the same conditions.

4. The Convention may be denounced in accordance with the provisions of the preceding paragraphs in respect of any territory to which it has been declared to extend under the terms of Article 56.

Article 59—Signature and ratification

1. This Convention shall be open to the signature of the members of the Council of Europe. It shall be ratified. Ratifications shall be deposited with the Secretary General of the Council of Europe.

2. The present Convention shall come into force after the deposit of ten instruments of ratification.

3. As regards any signatory ratifying subsequently, the Convention shall come into force at the date of the deposit of its instrument of ratification.

4. The Secretary General of the Council of Europe shall notify all the members of the Council of Europe of the entry into force of the Convention, the names of the High Contracting Parties who have ratified it, and the deposit of all instruments of ratification which may be effected subsequently.

Done at Rome this 4th day of November 1950, in English and French, both texts being equally authentic, in a single copy which shall remain deposited in the archives of the Council of Europe. The Secretary General shall transmit certified copies to each of the signatories.

Protocol No. 1
to the Convention for the Protection
of Human Rights and Fundamental Freedoms

PARIS, 20.III.1952

The governments signatory hereto, being members of the Council of Europe,

Being resolved to take steps to ensure the collective enforcement of certain rights and freedoms other than those already included in Section 1 of the Convention for the Protection of Human Rights and Fundamental Freedoms signed at Rome on 4 November 1950 (hereinafter referred to as 'the Convention'),

Have agreed as follows:

Article 1—Protection of property

Every natural or legal person is entitled to the peaceful enjoyment of his possessions. No one shall be deprived of his possessions except in the public interest and subject to the conditions provided for by law and by the general principles of international law.

The preceding provisions shall not, however, in any way impair the right of a State to enforce such laws as it deems necessary to control the use of property in accordance with the general interest or to secure the payment of taxes or other contributions or penalties.

Article 2—Right to education

No person shall be denied the right to education. In the exercise of any functions which it assumes in relation to education and to teaching, the State shall respect the right of parents to ensure such education and teaching in conformity with their own religious and philosophical convictions.

Article 3—Right to free elections

The High Contracting Parties undertake to hold free elections at reasonable intervals by secret ballot, under conditions which will ensure the free expression of the opinion of the people in the choice of the legislature.

Article 4—Territorial application

Any High Contracting Party may at the time of signature or ratification or at any time thereafter communicate to the Secretary General of the Council of Europe a declaration stating the extent to which it undertakes that the provisions of the present Protocol shall apply to such of the territories for the international relations of which it is responsible as are named therein.

Any High Contracting Party which has communicated a declaration in virtue of the preceding paragraph may from time to time communicate a further declaration modifying the terms of any former declaration or terminating the application of the provisions of this Protocol in respect of any territory.

A declaration made in accordance with this article shall be deemed to have been made in accordance with paragraph 1 of Article 56 of the Convention.

Article 5—Relationship to the Convention

As between the High Contracting Parties the provisions of Articles 1, 2, 3 and 4 of this Protocol shall be regarded as additional articles to the Convention and all the provisions of the Convention shall apply accordingly.

Article 6—Signature and ratification

This Protocol shall be open for signature by the members of the Council of Europe, who are the signatories of the Convention; it shall be ratified at the same time as or after the ratification of the Convention. It shall enter into force after the deposit of ten instruments of ratification. As regards any signatory ratifying subsequently, the Protocol shall enter into force at the date of the deposit of its instrument of ratification.

The instruments of ratification shall be deposited with the Secretary General of the Council of Europe, who will notify all members of the names of those who have ratified.

Done at Paris on the 20th day of March 1952, in English and French, both texts being equally authentic, in a single copy which shall remain deposited in the archives of the Council of Europe. The Secretary General shall transmit certified copies to each of the signatory governments.

Protocol No. 4
to the Convention for the Protection
of Human Rights and Fundamental Freedoms
securing certain rights and freedoms
other than those already included in the Convention
and in the First Protocol thereto

STRASBOURG, 16.IX.1963

The governments signatory hereto, being members of the Council of Europe,

Being resolved to take steps to ensure the collective enforcement of certain rights and freedoms other than those already included in Section 1 of the Convention for the Protection of Human Rights and Fundamental Freedoms signed at Rome on 4th November 1950 (hereinafter referred to as 'the Convention') and in Articles 1 to 3 of the First Protocol to the Convention, signed at Paris on 20th March 1952,

Have agreed as follows:

Article 1—Prohibition of imprisonment for debt

No one shall be deprived of his liberty merely on the ground of inability to fulfil a contractual obligation.

Article 2—Freedom of movement

1. Everyone lawfully within the territory of a State shall, within that territory, have the right to liberty of movement and freedom to choose his residence.
2. Everyone shall be free to leave any country, including his own.
3. No restrictions shall be placed on the exercise of these rights other than such as are in accordance with law and are necessary in a democratic society in the interests of national security or public safety, for the maintenance of public order, for the prevention of crime, for the protection of health or morals, or for the protection of the rights and freedoms of others.
4. The rights set forth in paragraph 1 may also be subject, in particular areas, to restrictions imposed in accordance with law and justified by the public interest in a democratic society.

Article 3—Prohibition of expulsion of nationals

1. No one shall be expelled, by means either of an individual or of a collective measure, from the territory of the State of which he is a national.
2. No one shall be deprived of the right to enter the territory of the state of which he is a national.

Article 4—Prohibition of collective expulsion of aliens

Collective expulsion of aliens is prohibited.

Article 5—Territorial application

1. Any High Contracting Party may, at the time of signature or ratification of this Protocol, or at any time thereafter, communicate to the Secretary General of the Council of Europe a declaration stating the extent to which it undertakes that the provisions of this Protocol shall apply to such of the territories for the international relations of which it is responsible as are named therein.
2. Any High Contracting Party which has communicated a declaration in virtue of the preceding paragraph may, from time to time, communicate a further declaration modifying the terms of any former declaration or terminating the application of the provisions of this Protocol in respect of any territory.
3. A declaration made in accordance with this article shall be deemed to have been made in accordance with paragraph 1 of Article 56 of the Convention.
4. The territory of any State to which this Protocol applies by virtue of ratification or acceptance by that State, and each territory to which this Protocol is applied by virtue of a declaration by that State under this article, shall be treated as separate territories for the purpose of the references in Articles 2 and 3 to the territory of a State.
5. Any State which has made a declaration in accordance with paragraph 1 or 2 of this Article may at any time thereafter declare on behalf of one or more of the territories to which the declaration relates that it accepts the competence of the Court to receive applications from individuals, non-governmental organisations or groups of individuals as provided in Article 34 of the Convention in respect of all or any of Articles 1 to 4 of this Protocol.

Article 6—Relationship to the Convention

As between the High Contracting Parties the provisions of Articles 1 to 5 of this Protocol shall be regarded as additional Articles to the Convention, and all the provisions of the Convention shall apply accordingly.

Article 7—Signature and ratification

1. This Protocol shall be open for signature by the members of the Council of Europe who are the signatories of the Convention; it shall be ratified at the same time as or after the ratification of the Convention. It shall enter into force after the deposit of five instruments of ratification. As regards any signatory ratifying subsequently, the Protocol shall enter into force at the date of the deposit of its instrument of ratification.
2. The instruments of ratification shall be deposited with the Secretary General of the Council of Europe, who will notify all members of the names of those who have ratified.

In witness whereof the undersigned, being duly authorised thereto, have signed this Protocol.

Done at Strasbourg on the 16th day of September 1963, in English and French, both texts being equally authoritative, in a single copy which shall remain deposited in the archives of the Council of Europe. The Secretary General shall transmit certified copies to each of the signatory states.

**Protocol No. 6
to the Convention for the Protection
of Human Rights and Fundamental Freedoms
concerning the Abolition of the Death Penalty**

STRASBOURG, 28.IV.1983

The member States of the Council of Europe, signatory to this Protocol to the Convention for the Protection of Human Rights and Fundamental Freedoms, signed at Rome on 4 November 1950 (hereinafter referred to as 'the Convention'),

Considering that the evolution that has occurred in several member States of the Council of Europe expresses a general tendency in favour of abolition of the death penalty;

Have agreed as follows:

Article 1—Abolition of the death penalty

The death penalty shall be abolished. No-one shall be condemned to such penalty or executed.

Article 2—Death penalty in time of war

A State may make provision in its law for the death penalty in respect of acts committed in time of war or of imminent threat of war; such penalty shall be applied only in the instances laid down in the law and in accordance with its provisions. The State shall communicate to the Secretary General of the Council of Europe the relevant provisions of that law.

Article 3—Prohibition of derogations

No derogation from the provisions of this Protocol shall be made under Article 15 of the Convention.

Article 4—Prohibition of reservations

No reservation may be made under Article 57 of the Convention in respect of the provisions of this Protocol.

Article 5—Territorial application

1. Any State may at the time of signature or when depositing its instrument of ratification, acceptance or approval, specify the territory or territories to which this Protocol shall apply.
2. Any State may at any later date, by a declaration addressed to the Secretary General of the Council of Europe, extend the application of this Protocol to any other territory specified in the declaration. In respect of such territory the Protocol shall enter into force on the first day of the month following the date of receipt of such declaration by the Secretary General.
3. Any declaration made under the two preceding paragraphs may, in respect of any territory specified in such declaration, be withdrawn by a notification addressed to the Secretary General. The withdrawal shall become effective on the first day of the month following the date of receipt of such notification by the Secretary General.

Article 6—Relationship to the Convention

As between the States Parties the provisions of Articles 1 and 5 of this Protocol shall be regarded as additional articles to the Convention and all the provisions of the Convention shall apply accordingly.

Article 7—Signature and ratification

The Protocol shall be open for signature by the member States of the Council of Europe, signatories to the Convention. It shall be subject to ratification, acceptance or approval. A member State of the Council of Europe may not ratify, accept or approve this Protocol unless it has, simultaneously or previously, ratified the Convention. Instruments of ratification, acceptance or approval shall be deposited with the Secretary General of the Council of Europe.

Article 8—Entry into force

1. This Protocol shall enter into force on the day of the month following the date on which five member States of the Council of Europe have expressed their consent to be bound by the Protocol in accordance with the provisions of Article 7.
2. In respect of any member State which subsequently expresses its consent to be bound by it, the Protocol shall enter into force on the first day of the month following the date of the deposit of the instrument of ratification, acceptance or approval.

Article 9—Depositary functions

The Secretary General of the Council of Europe shall notify the member States of the Council of:

    a. any signature;

    b. the deposit of any instrument of ratification, acceptance or approval;

    c. any date of entry into force of this Protocol in accordance with Articles 5 and 8;

    d. any other act, notification or communication relating to this Protocol.

In witness whereof the undersigned, being duly authorised thereto, have signed this Protocol.

Done at Strasbourg, this 28th day of April 1983, in English and in French, both texts being equally authentic, in a single copy which shall be deposited in the archives of the Council of Europe. The Secretary General of the Council of Europe shall transmit certified copies to each member State of the Council of Europe.

Protocol No. 7
to the Convention for the Protection
of Human Rights and Fundamental Freedoms

STRASBOURG, 22.XI.1984

The member States of the Council of Europe signatory hereto,

Being resolved to take further steps to ensure the collective enforcement of certain rights and freedoms by means of the Convention for the Protection of Human Rights and Fundamental Freedoms signed at Rome on 4 November 1950 (hereinafter referred to as 'the Convention'),

Have agreed as follows:

Article 1—Procedural safeguards relating to expulsion of aliens

1. An alien lawfully resident in the territory of a State shall not be expelled therefrom except in pursuance of a decision reach in accordance with law and shall be allowed:
   a. to submit reasons against his expulsion;
   b. to have his case reviewed, and
   c. to be represented for these purposes before the competent authority or a person or persons designated by that authority.
2. An alien may be expelled before the exercise of his rights under paragraph 1.a., b. and c. of this Article, when such expulsion is necessary in the interests of public order or is grounded on reasons of national security.

Article 2—Right of appeal in criminal matters

1. Everyone convicted of a criminal offence by a tribunal shall have the right to have his conviction or sentence reviewed by a higher tribunal. The exercise of this right, including the grounds on which it may be exercised, shall be governed by law.
2. This right may be subject to exceptions in regard to offences of a minor character, as prescribed by law, or in cases in which the person concerned was tried in the first instance by the highest tribunal or was convicted following an appeal against acquittal.

Article 3—Compensation for wrongful conviction

When a person has by a final decision been convicted of a criminal offence and when subsequently his conviction has been reversed, or he has been pardoned, on the ground that a new or newly discovered fact shows conclusively that there has been a miscarriage of justice, the person who has suffered punishment as a result of such conviction shall be compensated according to the law or the practice of the state concerned, unless it is proved that the nondisclosure of the unknown fact in time is wholly or partly attributable to him.

Article 4—Right not to be tried or punished twice

1. No one shall be liable to be tried or punished again in criminal proceedings under the jurisdiction of the same state for an offence for which he has already been finally acquitted or convicted in accordance with the law and penal procedure of that state.
2. The provisions of the preceding paragraph shall not prevent the reopening of the case in accordance with the law and penal procedure of the State concerned, if there is evidence of new or newly discovered facts, or if there has

been a fundamental defect in the previous proceedings, which could affect the outcome of the case.

3. No derogation from this Article shall be made under Article 15 of the Convention.

Article 5—Equality between spouses

Spouses shall enjoy equality of rights and responsibilities of a private law character between them, and in their relations with their children, as to marriage, during marriage and in the event of its dissolution. This Article shall not prevent States from taking such measures as are necessary in the interests of the children.

Article 6—Territorial applications

1. Any State may at the time of signature or when depositing its instrument of ratification, acceptance or approval, specify the territory or territories to which this Protocol shall apply and state the extent to which it undertakes that the provisions of this Protocol shall apply to this or these territories.

2. Any state may at any later date, by a declaration addressed to the Secretary-General of the Council of Europe, extend the application of this Protocol to any other territory specified in the declaration. In respect of such territory the protocol shall enter into force on the first day of the month following the expiration of a period of two months after the date of receipt of such notification by the Secretary-General of such declaration.

3. Any declaration made under the two preceding paragraphs may, in respect of any territory specified in such declaration, be withdrawn or modified by a notification addressed to the Secretary-General. The withdrawal or modification shall become effective on the first day of the month following the expiration of a period of two months after the date of receipt of such notification by the Secretary-General.

4. A declaration made in accordance with this Article shall be deemed to have been made in accordance with paragraph 1 of Article 56 of the Convention.

5. The territory of any State to which this Protocol applies by virtue of ratification, acceptance or approval by that State, and each territory to which this Protocol is applied by virtue of a declaration by that State under this Article, may be treated as separate territories for the purpose of the reference in Article 1 to the territory of a State.

6. Any State which has made a declaration in accordance with paragraph 1 or 2 of this Article may at any time thereafter declare on behalf of one or more of the territories to which the declaration relates that it accepts the competence of the Court to receive applications from individuals, non-governmental organisations or groups of individuals as provided in Article 34 of the Convention in respect of Articles 1 to 5 of this Protocol.

Article 7—Relationship to the Convention

As between the States Parties, the provisions of Article 1 to 6 of this Protocol shall be regarded as additional Articles to the Convention, and all the provisions of the Convention shall apply accordingly.

Article 8—Signature and ratification

This Protocol shall be open for signature by member States of the Council of Europe which have signed the Convention. It is subject to ratification, acceptance or approval. A member State of the Council of Europe may not ratify, accept or approve this Protocol without previously or simultaneously ratifying the Convention. Instruments of ratification, acceptance or approval shall be deposited with the Secretary General of the Council of Europe.

Article 9—Entry into force

1. This Protocol shall enter into force on the first day of the month following the expiration of a period of two months after the date on which seven member

States of the Council of Europe have expressed their consent to be bound by the Protocol in accordance with the provisions of Article 8.

2. In respect of any member State which subsequently expresses its consent to be bound by it, the Protocol shall enter into force on the first day of the month following the expiration of a period of two months after the date of the deposit of the instrument of ratification, acceptance or approval.

Article 10—Depositary functions

The Secretary General of the Council of Europe shall notify the member States of the Council of:

    a. any signature;

    b. the deposit of any instrument of ratification, acceptance or approval;

    c. any date of entry into force of this Protocol in accordance with Articles 6 and 9;

    d. any other act, notification or communication relating to this Protocol.

In witness whereof the undersigned, being duly authorised thereto, have signed this Protocol.

Done at Strasbourg, this 22nd day of November 1984, in English and in French, both texts being equally authentic, in a single copy which shall be deposited in the archives of the Council of Europe. The Secretary General of the Council of Europe shall transmit certified copies to each member State of the Council of Europe.

APPENDIX C

Universal Declaration of Human Rights 1948

PREAMBLE

Whereas recognition of the inherent dignity and of the equal and inalienable rights of all members of the human family is the foundation of freedom, justice and peace in the world,

Whereas disregard and contempt for human rights have resulted in barbarous acts which have outraged the conscience of mankind, and the advent of a world in which human beings shall enjoy freedom of speech and belief and freedom from fear and want has been proclaimed as the highest aspiration of the common people,

Whereas it is essential, if man is not to be compelled to have recourse, as a last resort, to rebellion against tyranny and oppression, that human rights should be protected by the rule of law,

Whereas it is essential to promote the development of friendly relations between nations,

Whereas the peoples of the United Nations have in the Charter reaffirmed their faith in fundamental human rights, in the dignity and worth of the human person and in the equal rights of men and women and have determined to promote social progress and better standards of life in larger freedom,

Whereas Member States have pledged themselves to achieve, in co-operation with the United Nations, the promotion of universal respect for and observance of human rights and fundamental freedoms,

Whereas a common understanding of these rights and freedoms is of the greatest importance for the full realization of this pledge.

Now, Therefore,

The General Assembly

Proclaims

This universal declaration of human rights as a common standard of achievement for all peoples and all nations, to the end that every individual and every organ of society, keeping this Declaration constantly in mind, shall strive by teaching and education to promote respect for these rights and freedoms and by progressive measures, national and international, to secure their universal and effective recognition and observance, both among the peoples of Member States themselves and among the peoples of territories under their jurisdiction.

All human beings are born free and equal in dignity and rights. They are endowed with reason and conscience and should act towards one another in a spirit of brotherhood.

Article 2

Everyone is entitled to all the rights and freedoms set forth in this Declaration, without distinction of any kind, such as race, colour, sex, language, religion, political or other opinion, national or social origin, property, birth or other status.

Furthermore, no distinction shall be made on the basis of the political, jurisdictional or international status of the country or territory to which a person belongs, whether it be independent, trust, non-self-governing or under any other limitation of sovereignty.

Article 3

Everyone has the right to life, liberty and security of person.

Article 4

No one shall be held in slavery or servitude: slavery and the slave trade shall be prohibited in all their forms.

Article 5

No one shall be subjected to torture or cruel, inhuman or degrading treatment or punishment.

Article 6

Everyone has the right to recognition everywhere as a person before the law.

Article 7

All are equal before the law and are entitled without any discrimination to equal protection of the law. All are entitled to equal protection against any discrimination in violation of this Declaration and against any incitement to such discrimination.

Article 8

Everyone has the right to an effective remedy by the competent national tribunals for acts violating the fundamental rights granted him by the constitution or by law.

Article 9

No one shall be subjected to arbitrary arrest, detention or exile.

Article 10

Everyone is entitled in full equality to a fair and public hearing by an independent and impartial tribunal, in the determination of his rights and obligations and of any criminal charge against him.

Article 11

1. Everyone charged with a penal offence has the right to be presumed innocent until proved guilty according to law in a public trial at which he has had all the guarantees necessary for his defence.
2. No one shall be held guilty of any penal offence on account of any act or omission which did not constitute a penal offence, under national or inter-national law, at the time when it was committed. Nor shall a heavier penalty be imposed than the one that was applicable at the time the penal offence was committed.

Article 12

No one shall be subjected to arbitrary interference with his privacy, family, home or correspondence, nor to attacks upon his honour and reputation. Everyone has the right to the protection of the law against such interference or attacks.

Article 13

1. Everyone has the right to freedom of movement and residence within the borders of each state.
2. Everyone has the right to leave any country, including his own, and to return to his country.

Article 14

1. Everyone has the right to seek and to enjoy in other countries asylum from persecution.
2. This right may not be invoked in the case of prosecutions genuinely arising from non-political crimes or from acts contrary to the purposes and principles of the United Nations.

Article 15

1. Everyone has the right to a nationality.
2. No one shall be arbitrarily deprived of his nationality nor denied the right to change his nationality.

Article 16

1. Men and women of full age, without any limitation due to race, nationality or religion, have the right to marry and to found a family. They are entitled to equal rights as to marriage, during marriage and at its dissolution.

2. Marriage shall be entered into only with the free and full consent of the intending spouses.
3. The family is the natural and fundamental group unit of society and is entitled to protection by society and the State.

Article 17

1. Everyone has the right to own property alone as well as in association with others.
2. No one shall be arbitrarily deprived of his property.

Article 18

Everyone has the right to freedom of thought, conscience and religion; this right includes freedom to change his religion or belief, and freedom, either alone or in community with others and in public or private, to manifest his religion or belief in teaching, practice, worship and observance.

Article 19

Everyone has the right to freedom of opinion and expression; this right includes freedom to hold opinions without interference and to seek, receive and impart information and ideas through any media and regardless of frontiers.

Article 20

1. Everyone has the right to freedom of peaceful assembly and association.
2. No one may be compelled to belong to an association.

Article 21

1. Everyone has the right to take part in the government of his country, directly or through freely chosen representatives.
2. Everyone has the right of equal access to public service in his country.
3. The will of the people shall be the basis of the authority of the government; this will shall be expressed in periodic and genuine elections which shall be by universal and equal suffrage and shall be held by secret vote or by equivalent free voting procedures

Article 22

Everyone, as a member of society, has the right to social security and is entitled to realization, through national effort and international co-operation and in accordance with the organization and resources of each State, of the economic, social and cultural rights indispensable for his dignity and the free development of his personality.

Article 23

1. Everyone has the right to work, to free choice of employment, to just and favourable conditions of work and to protection against unemployment.
2. Everyone, without any discrimination, has the right to equal pay for equal work.
3. Everyone who works has the right to just and favourable remuneration ensuring for himself and his family an existence worthy of human dignity, and supplemented, if necessary, by other means of social protection.
4. Everyone has the right to form and to join trade unions for the protection of his interests.

Article 24

Everyone has the right to rest and leisure, including reasonable limitation of working hours and periodic holidays with pay.

Article 25

1. Everyone has the right to a standard of living adequate for the health and well-being of himself and of his family, including food, clothing, housing and medical care and necessary social services, and the right to security in the event of unemployment, sickness, disability, widowhood, old age or other lack of livelihood in circumstances beyond his control.
2. Motherhood and childhood are entitled to special care and assistance. All children, whether born in or out of wedlock, shall enjoy the same social protection.

Article 26

1. Everyone has the right to education. Education shall be free, at least in the elementary and fundamental stages. Elementary education shall be compulsory. Technical and professional education shall be made generally available and higher education shall be equally accessible to all on the basis of merit.
2. Education shall be directed to the full development of the human personality and to the strengthening of respect for human rights and fundamental freedoms. It shall promote understanding, tolerance and friendship among all nations, racial or religious groups, and shall further the activities of the United Nations for the maintenance of peace.
3. Parents have a prior right to choose the kind of education that shall be given to their children.

Article 27

1. Everyone has the right freely to participate in the cultural life of the community, to enjoy the arts and to share in scientific advancement and its benefits.
2. Everyone has the right to the protection of the moral and material interests resulting from any scientific, literary or artistic production of which he is the author.

Article 28

Everyone is entitled to a social and international order in which the rights and freedoms set forth in this Declaration can be fully realized.

Article 29

1. Everyone has duties to the community in which alone the free and full development of his personality is possible.
2. In the exercise of his rights and freedoms, everyone shall be subject only to such limitations as are determined by law solely for the purpose of securing due recognition and respect for the rights and freedoms of others and of meeting the just requirements of morality, public order and the general welfare in a democratic society.
3. These rights and freedoms may in no case be exercised contrary to the purposes and principles of the United Nations.

Article 30

Nothing in this Declaration may be interpreted as implying for any State, group or person any right to engage in any activity or to perform any act aimed at the destruction of any of the rights and freedoms set forth herein.

APPENDIX D

International Covenant
on Civil and Political Rights 1996

PREAMBLE

The States Parties to the present Covenant,

Considering that, in accordance with the principles proclaimed in the Charter of the United Nations, recognition of the inherent dignity and of the equal and inalienable rights of all members of the human family is the foundation of freedom, justice and peace in the world.

Recognizing that these rights derive from the inherent dignity of the human person,

Recognizing that, in accordance with the Universal Declaration of Human Rights, the ideal of free human beings enjoying civil and political freedom and freedom from fear and want can only be achieved if conditions are created whereby everyone may enjoy his civil and political rights, as well as his economic, social and cultural rights,

Considering the obligation of States under the Charter of the United Nations to promote universal respect for, and observance of, human rights and freedoms,

Realizing that the individual, having duties to other individuals and to the community to which he belongs, is under a responsibility to strive for the promotion and observance of the rights recognized in the present Covenant,

Agree upon the following articles:

PART I

Article 1

1. All peoples have the right of self-determination. By virtue of that right they freely determine their political status and freely pursue their economic, social and cultural development.
2. All peoples may, for their own ends, freely dispose of their natural wealth and resources without prejudice to any obligations arising out of international economic co-operation, based upon the principle of mutual benefit, and international law. In no case may a people be deprived of its own means of subsistence.
3. The States Parties to the present Covenant, including those having responsibility for the administration of Non-Self-Governing and Trust Territories, shall promote the realization of the right of self-determination, and shall respect that right, in conformity with the provisions of the Charter of the United Nations.

PART II

Article 2

1. Each State Party to the present Covenant undertakes to respect and to ensure to all individuals within its territory and subject to its jurisdiction the rights recognized in the present Covenant, without distinction of any kind, such as race, colour, sex, language, religion, political or other opinion, national or social origin, property, birth or other status.
2. Where not already provided for by existing legislative or other measures, each State Party to the present Covenant undertakes to take the necessary steps, in accordance with its constitutional processes and with the provisions of the present Covenant, to adopt such legislative or other measures as may be necessary to give effect to the rights recognized in the present Covenant.
3. Each State Party to the present Covenant undertakes:
   (a) To ensure that any person whose rights or freedoms as herein recognized are violated shall have an effective remedy, notwithstanding that the violation has been committed by persons acting in an official capacity;
   (b) To ensure that any person claiming such a remedy shall have his right thereto determined by competent judicial, administrative or legislative authorities, or by any other competent authority provided for by the legal system of the State, and to develop the possibilities of judicial remedy;
   (c) To ensure that the competent authorities shall enforce such remedies when granted.

Article 3

The States Parties to the present Covenant undertake to ensure the equal right of men and women to the enjoyment of all civil and political rights set forth in the present Covenant.

Article 4

1. In time of public emergency which threatens the life of the nation and the existence of which is officially proclaimed, the State Parties to the present Covenant may take measures derogating from their obligations under the present Covenant to the extent strictly required by the exigencies of the situation, provided that such measures are not inconsistent with their other obligations under international law and do not involve discrimination solely on the ground of race, colour, sex, language, religion or social origin.
2. No derogation from Articles 6, 7, 8 (paragraphs 1 and 2), 11, 15, 16 and 18 may be made under this provision.
3. Any State Party to the present Covenant availing itself of the right of derogation shall immediately inform the other States Parties to the present Covenant, through the intermediary of the Secretary-General of the United Nations of the provisions from which it has derogated and of the reasons by which it was actuated. A further communication shall be made, through the same intermediary on the date on which it terminates such derogation.

Article 5

1. Nothing in the present Covenant may be interpreted as implying for any State, group or person any right to engage in any activity or perform any act aimed

at the destruction of any of the rights and freedoms recognized herein or at their limitation to a greater extent than is provided for in the present Covenant.

2. There shall be no restriction upon or derogation from any of the fundamental human rights recognized or existing in any State Party to the present Covenant pursuant to law, conventions, regulations or custom on the pretext that the present Covenant does not recognize such rights or that it recognizes them to a lesser extent.

PART III

Article 6

1. Every human being has the inherent right to life. This right shall be protected by law. No one shall be arbitrarily deprived of his life.
2. In countries which have not abolished the death penalty, sentence of death may be imposed only for the most serious crimes in accordance with the law in force at the time of the commission of the crime and not contrary to the provisions of the present Covenant and to the Convention on the Prevention and Punishment of the Crime of Genocide. This penalty can only be carried out pursuant to a final judgment rendered by a competent court.
3. When deprivation of life constitutes the crime of genocide, it is understood that nothing in this Article shall authorize any State Party to the present Covenant to derogate in any way from any obligation assumed under the provisions of the Convention on the Prevention and Punishment of the Crime of Genocide.
4. Anyone sentenced to death shall have the right to seek pardon or commutation of the sentence. Amnesty, pardon or commutation of the sentence of death may be granted in all cases.
5. Sentence of death shall not be imposed for crimes committed by persons below eighteen years of age and shall not be carried out on pregnant women.
6. Nothing in this Article shall be invoked to delay or to prevent the abolition of capital punishment by any State Party to the present Covenant.

Article 7

1. No one shall be held in slavery; slavery and the slave-trade in all their forms shall be prohibited.
2. No one shall be held in servitude.
3. (a) No one shall be required to perform forced or compulsory labour.
   (b) Paragraph 3 (a) shall not be held to preclude, in countries where imprisonment with hard labour may be imposed as a punishment for a crime, the performance of hard labour in pursuance of a sentence to such punishment by a competent court;
   (c) For the purpose of this paragraph the term 'forced or compulsory labour' shall not include:
   (i) Any work or service, not referred to in sub-paragraph (b), normally required of a person who is under detention in consequence of a lawful order of a court, or of a person during conditional release from such detention;
   (ii) Any service of a military character and, in countries where conscientious objection is recognized, any national service required by law of conscientious objectors;
   (iii) Any service exacted in cases of emergency or calamity threatening the life or well-being of the community;

(iv) Any work or service which forms part of normal civil obligations.

Article 9

1. Everyone has the right to liberty and security of person. No one shall be subjected to arbitrary arrest or detention. No one shall be deprived of his liberty except on such grounds and in accordance with such procedures as are established by law.
2. Anyone who is arrested shall be informed, at the time of arrest, of the reasons for his arrest and shall be promptly informed of any charges against him.
3. Anyone arrested or detained on a criminal charge shall be brought promptly before a judge or other officer authorized by law to exercise judicial power and shall be entitled to trial within a reasonable time or to release. It shall not be the general rule that persons awaiting trial shall be detained in custody, but release may be subject to guarantees to appear for trial, at any other stage of the judicial proceedings, and, should occasion arise, for execution of the judgment.
4. Anyone who is deprived of his liberty by arrest or detention shall be entitled to take proceedings before a court, in order that that court may decide without delay on the lawfulness of his detention and order his release if the detention is not lawful.
5. Anyone who has been the victim of unlawful arrest or detention shall have an enforceable right to compensation.

Article 10

1. All persons deprived of their liberty shall be treated with humanity and with respect for the inherent dignity of the human person.
2. (a) Accused persons shall, save in exceptional circumstances, be segregated from convicted persons and shall be subject to separate treatment appropriate to their status as unconvicted persons;
   (b) Accused juvenile persons shall be separated from adults and brought as speedily as possible for adjudication.
3. The penitentiary system shall comprise treatment of prisoners the essential aim of which shall be their reformation and social rehabilitation. Juvenile offenders shall be segregated from adults and be accorded treatment appropriate to their age and legal status.

Article 11

No one shall be imprisoned merely on the ground of inability to fulfil a contractual obligation.

Article 12

1. Everyone lawfully within the territory of a State shall, within that territory, have the right to liberty of movement and freedom to choose his residence.
2. Everyone shall be free to leave any country, including his own.
3. The above-mentioned rights shall not be subject to any restrictions except those which are provided by law, are necessary to protect national security, public order ordre public), public health or morals or the rights and freedoms of others, and are consistent with the other rights recognized in the present Covenant.

4. No one shall be arbitrarily deprived of the right to enter his own country.

Article 13

An alien lawfully in the territory of a State Party to the present Covenant may be expelled therefrom only in pursuance of a decision reached in accordance with law and shall, except where compelling reasons of national security otherwise require, be allowed to submit the reasons against his expulsion and to have his case reviewed by, and be represented for the purpose before, the competent authority or a person or persons especially designated by the competent authority.

Article 14

1. All persons shall be equal before the courts and tribunals. In the determination of any criminal charge against him, or of his rights and obligations in a suit at law, everyone shall be entitled to a fair and public hearing by a competent, independent and impartial tribunal established by law. The Press and the public may be excluded from all or part of a trial for reasons of morals, public order *(ordre public)* or national security in a democratic society, or when the interest of the private lives of the parties so requires, or to the extent strictly necessary in the opinion of the court in special circumstances where publicity would prejudice the interests of justice; but any judgement rendered in a criminal case or in a suit at law shall be made public except where the interest of juvenile persons otherwise requires or the proceedings concern matrimonial disputes or the guardianship of children.
2. Everyone charged with a criminal offence shall have the right to be presumed innocent until proved guilty according to law.
3. In the determination of any criminal charge against him, everyone shall be entitled to the following minimum guarantees, in full equality:
   (a) To be informed promptly and in detail in a language which he understands of the nature and cause of the charge against him;
   (b) To have adequate time and facilities for the preparation of his defence and to communicate with counsel of his own choosing;
   (c) To be tried without undue delay;
   (d) To be tried in his presence, and to defend himself in person or through legal assistance of his own choosing; to be informed, if he does not have legal assistance, of this right; and to have legal assistance assigned to him, in any case where the interests of justice so require, and without payment by him in any such case if he does not have sufficient means to pay for it;
   (e) To examine, or have examined, the witnesses against him and to obtain the attendance and examination of witnesses on his behalf under the same conditions as witnesses against him;
   (f) To have the free assistance of an interpreter if he cannot understand or speak the language used in court;
   (g) Not to be compelled to testify against himself or to confess guilt.
4. In the case of juvenile persons, the procedure shall be such as will take account of their age and the desirability of promoting their rehabilitation.
5. Everyone convicted of a crime shall have the right to his conviction and sentence being reviewed by a higher tribunal according to law.
6. When a person has by a final decision been convicted of a criminal offence and when subsequently his conviction has been reversed or he has been pardoned on the ground that a new or newly discovered fact shows conclusively that there has been a miscarriage of justice, the person who has suffered punishment as a result of such conviction shall be compensated according to law, unless it is proved that the non-disclosure of the unknown fact in time is wholly or partly attributable to him.

7. No one shall be liable to be tried or punished again for an offence for which he has already been finally convicted or acquitted in accordance with the law and penal procedure of each country.

Article 15

1. No one shall be held guilty of any criminal offence on account of any act or omission which did not constitute a criminal offence, under national or international law, at the time when it was committed. Nor shall a heavier penalty be imposed than the one that was applicable at the time when the criminal offence was committed. If, subsequent to the commission of the offence, provision is made by law for the imposition of a lighter penalty, the offender shall benefit thereby.
2. Nothing in this article shall prejudice the trial and punishment of any person for any act or omission which, at the time when it was committed, was criminal according to the general principles of law recognized by the community of nations.

Article 16

Everyone shall have the right to recognition everywhere as a person before the law.

Article 17

1. No one shall be subjected to arbitrary or unlawful interference with his privacy, family, home or correspondence, nor to unlawful attacks on his honour and reputation.
2. Everyone has the right to the protection of the law against such interference or attacks.

Article 18

1. Everyone shall have the right to freedom of thought, conscience and religion. This right shall include freedom to have or to adopt a religion or belief of his choice, and freedom, either individually or in community with others and in public or private, to manifest his religion or belief in worship, observance, practice and teaching.
2. No one shall be subject to coercion which would impair his freedom to have or to adopt a religion or belief of his choice.
3. Freedom to manifest one's religion or beliefs may be subject only to such limitations as are prescribed by law and are necessary to protect public safety, order, health, or morals or the fundamental rights and freedoms of others.
4. The States Parties to the present Covenant undertake to have respect for the liberty of parents and, when applicable, legal guardians to ensure the religious and moral education of their children in conformity with their own convictions.

Article 19

1. Everyone shall have the right to hold opinions without interference.
2. Everyone shall have the right to freedom of expression; this right shall include freedom to seek, receive and impart information and ideas of all kinds,

regardless of frontiers, either orally, in writing or in print, in the form of art, or through any other media of his choice.

3. The exercise of the rights provided for in paragraph 2 of this article carries with it special duties and responsibilities. It may therefore be subject to certain restrictions, but these shall only be such as are provided by law and are necessary:
   (a) For respect of the rights or reputations of others;
   (b) For the protection of national security or of public order *(ordre public)*, or of public health or morals.

Article 20

1. Any propaganda for war shall be prohibited by law.
2. Any advocacy of national, racial or religious hatred that constitutes incitement to discrimination, hostility or violence shall be prohibited by law.

Article 21

The right of peaceful assembly shall be recognized. No restrictions may be placed on the exercise of this right other than those imposed in conformity with the law and which are necessary in a democratic society in the interests of national security or public safety, public order *(ordre public)*, the protection of public health or morals or the protection of the rights and freedoms of others.

Article 22

1. Everyone shall have the right to freedom of association with others, including the right to form and join trade unions for the protection of his interests.
2. No restrictions may be placed on the exercise of this right other than those which are prescribed by law and which are necessary in a democratic society in the interests of national security or public safety, public order *(ordre public)*, the protection of public health or morals or the protection of the rights and freedoms of others. This Article shall not prevent the imposition of lawful restrictions on members of the armed forces and of the police in their exercise of this right.
3. Nothing in this article shall authorize States Parties to the International Labour Organization Convention of 1948 concerning Freedom of Association and Protection of the Right to Organize to take legislative measures which would prejudice, or to apply the law in such a manner as to prejudice, the guarantees provided for in that Convention.

Article 23

1. The family is the natural and fundamental group unit of society and is entitled to protection by society and the State.
2. The right of men and women of marriageable age to marry and to found a family shall be recognized.
3. No marriage shall be entered into without the free and full consent of the intending spouses.
4. States Parties to the present Covenant shall take appropriate steps to ensure equality of rights and responsibilities of spouses as to marriage, during marriage and at its dissolution. In the case of dissolution, provision shall be made for the necessary protection of any children.

Article 24

1. Every child shall have, without any discrimination as to race, colour, sex, language, religion, national or social origin, property or birth, the right to such measures of protection as are required by his status as a minor, on the part of his family, society and the State.
2. Every child shall be registered immediately after birth and shall have a name.
3. Every child has the right to acquire a nationality.

Article 25

Every citizen shall have the right and the opportunity, without any of the distinctions mentioned in Article 2 and without unreasonable restrictions:

(a) To take part in the conduct of public affairs, directly or through freely chosen representatives;

(b) To vote and to be elected at genuine periodic elections which shall be by universal and equal suffrage and shall be held by secret ballot, guaranteeing the free expression of the will of the electors;

(c) To have access, on general terms of equality, to public service in his country.

Article 26

All persons are equal before the law and are entitled without any discrimination to the equal protection of the law. In this respect, the law shall prohibit any discrimination and guarantee to all persons equal and effective protection against discrimination on any ground such as race, colour, sex, language, religion, political or other opinion, national or social origin, property, birth or other status.

Article 27

In those States in which ethnic, religious or linguistic minorities exist, persons belonging to such minorities shall not be denied the right, in community with the other members of their group, to enjoy their own culture, to profess and practise their own religion, or to use their own language.

Part IV

Article 28

1. There shall be established a Human Rights Committee (hereafter referred to in the present Covenant as the Committee). It shall consist of eighteen members and shall carry out the functions hereinafter provided.
2. The Committee shall be composed of nationals of the States Parties to the present Covenant who shall be persons of high moral character and recognized competence in the field of human rights, consideration being given to the usefulness of the participation of some persons having legal experience.

3. The members of the Committee shall be elected and shall serve in their personal capacity.

Article 29

1. The members of the Committee shall be elected by secret ballot from a list of persons possessing the qualifications prescribed in Article 28 and nominated for the purpose by the States Parties to the present Covenant.
2. Each State Party to the present Covenant may nominate not more than two persons. These persons shall be nationals of the nominating State.
3. A person shall be eligible for renomination.

Article 30

1. The initial election shall be held no later than six months after the date of the entry into force of the present Covenant.
2. At least four months before the date of each election to the Committee, other than an election to fill a vacancy declared in accordance with Article 34, the Secretary-General of the United Nations shall address a written invitation to the States Parties to the present Covenant to submit their nominations for membership of the Committee within three months.
3. The Secretary-General of the United Nations shall prepare a list in alphabetical order of all the persons thus nominated, with an indication of the States Parties which have nominated them, and shall submit it to the States Parties to the present Covenant no later than one month before the date of each election.
4. Elections of the members of the Committee shall be held at a meeting of the States Parties to the present Covenant convened by the Secretary-General of the United Nations at the Headquarters of the United Nations. At that meeting, for which two thirds of the States Parties to the present Covenant shall constitute a quorum, the persons elected to the Committee shall be those nominees who obtain the largest number of votes and an absolute majority of the votes of the representatives of States Parties present and voting.

Article 31

1. The Committee may not include more than one national of the same State.
2. In the election of the Committee, consideration shall be given to equitable geographical distribution of membership and to the representation of the different forms of civilization and of the principal legal systems.

Article 32

1. The members of the Committee shall be elected for a term of four years. They shall be eligible for re-election if renominated. However, the terms of nine of the members elected at the first election shall expire at the end of two years; immediately after the first election, the names of these nine members shall be chosen by lot by the Chairman of the meeting referred to in Article 30, paragraph 4.
2. Elections at the expiry of office shall be held in accordance with the preceding Articles of this part of the present Covenant.

Article 33

1. If, in the unanimous opinion of the other members, a member of the Committee has ceased to carry out his functions for any cause other than absence of a temporary character, the Chairman of the Committee shall notify the Secretary-General of the United Nations, who shall then declare the seat of that member to be vacant.
2. In the event of the death or the resignation of a member of the Committee, the Chairman shall immediately notify the Secretary-General of the United Nations, who shall declare the seat vacant from the date of death or the date on which the resignation takes effect.

Article 34

1. When a vacancy is declared in accordance with Article 33 and if the term of office of the member to be replaced does not expire within six months of the declaration of the vacancy, the Secretary-General of the United Nations shall notify each of the States Parties to the present Covenant, which may within two months submit nominations in accordance with Article 29 for the purpose of fulfilling the vacancy.
2. The Secretary-General of the United Nations shall prepare a list in alphabetical order of the persons thus nominated and shall submit it to the States Parties to the present Covenant. The election to fill the vacancy shall then take place in accordance with the relevant provisions of this part of the present Covenant.
3. A member of the Committee elected to fill a vacancy declared in accordance with Article 33 shall hold office for the remainder of the term of the member who vacated the seat of the Committee under the provisions of that Article.

Article 35

The members of the Committee shall, with the approval of the General Assembly of the United Nations, receive emoluments from United Nations resources on such terms and conditions as the General Assembly may decide, having regard to the importance of the Committee's responsibilities.

Article 36

The Secretary-General of the United Nations shall provide the necessary staff and facilities for the effective performance of the functions of the Committee under the present Covenant.

Article 37

1. The Secretary-General of the United Nations shall convene the initial meeting of the Committee at the Headquarters of the United Nations.
2. After its initial meeting, the Committee shall meet at such times as shall be provided in its rules of procedure.
3. The Committee shall normally meet at the Headquarters of the United Nations or at the United Nations Office at Geneva.

Article 38

Every member of the Committee shall, before taking up his duties, make a solemn declaration in open committee that he will perform his functions impartially and conscientiously.

Article 39

1. The Committee shall elect its officers for a term of two years. They may be re-elected.
2. The Committee shall establish its own rules of procedure, but these rules shall provide, *inter alia*, that:
   (a) Twelve members shall constitute a quorum;
   (b) Decisions of the Committee shall be made by a majority vote of the members present.

Article 40

1. The States Parties to the present Covenant undertake to submit reports on the measures they have adopted which give effect to the rights recognized herein and on the progress made in the enjoyment of those rights:
   (a) Within one year of the entry into force of the present Covenant for the States Parties concerned;
   (b) Thereafter whenever the Committee so requests.
2. All reports shall be submitted to the Secretary-General of the United Nations, who shall transmit them to the Committee for consideration. Reports shall indicate the factors and difficulties, if any, affecting the implementation of the present Covenant.
3. The Secretary-General of the United Nations may, after consultation with the Committee, transmit to the specialized agencies concerned copies of such parts of the reports as may fall within their field of competence.
4. The Committee shall study the reports submitted by the States Parties to the present Covenant. It shall transmit its reports, and such general comments as it may consider appropriate, to the States Parties. The Committee may also transmit to the Economic and Social Council these comments along with the copies of the reports it has received from States Parties to the present Covenant.
5. The States Parties to the present Covenant may submit to the Committee observations on any comments that may be made in accordance with paragraph 4 of this Article.

Article 41

1. A State Party to the present Covenant may at any time declare under this article that it recognizes the competence of the Committee to receive and consider communications to the effect that a State Party claims that another State Party is not fulfilling its obligations under the present Covenant. Communications under this article may be received and considered only if submitted by a State Party which has made a declaration recognizing in regard to itself the competence of the Committee. No communication shall be received by the Committee if it concerns a State Party which has not made such a declaration. Communications received under this Article shall be dealt with in accordance with the following procedure:
   (a) If a State Party to the present Covenant considers that another State Party is not giving effect to the provisions of the present Covenant, it may, by

written communication, bring the matter to the attention of that State Party. Within three months after the receipt of the communication, the receiving State shall afford the State which sent the communication an explanation or any other statement in writing clarifying the matter, which should include, to the extent possible and pertinent, reference to domestic proce- dures and remedies taken, pending, or available in the matter.

(b) If the matter is not adjusted to the satisfaction of both States Parties concerned within six months after the receipt by the receiving State of the initial communication, either State shall have the right to refer the matter to the Committee, by notice given to the Committee and to the other State.

(c) The Committee shall deal with a matter referred to it only after it has ascertained that all available domestic remedies have been invoked and exhausted in the matter, in conformity with the generally recognized principles of international law. This shall not be the rule where the applica- tion of the remedies is unreasonably prolonged.

(d) The Committee shall hold closed meetings when examining communica- tions under this article.

(e) Subject to the provisions of sub-paragraph (c), the Committee shall make available its good offices to the States Parties concerned with a view to a friendly solution of the matter on the basis of respect for human rights and fundamental freedoms as recognized in the present Covenant.

(f) In any matter referred to it, the Committee may call upon the States Parties concerned, referred to in sub-paragraph (b), to supply any relevant information.

(g) The States Parties concerned, referred to in sub-paragraph (b), shall have the right to be represented when the matter is being considered in the Committee and to make submissions orally and/or in writing.

(h) The Committee shall, within twelve months after the date of receipt of notice under sub-paragraph (b), submit a report:

(i) If a solution within the terms of sub-paragraph (e) is reached, the Committee shall confine its report to a brief statement of the facts and of the solution reached;

(ii) If a solution within the terms of sub-paragraph (e) is not reached, the Committee shall confine its report to a brief statement of the facts; the written submissions and record of the oral submissions made by the States Parties concerned shall be attached to the report.

In every matter, the report shall be communicated to the States Parties concerned.

2. The provisions of this Article shall come into force when ten States Parties to the present Covenant have made declarations under paragraph 1 of this Article. Such declarations shall be deposited by the States Parties with the Secretary-General of the United Nations, who shall transmit copies thereof to the other States Parties. A declaration may be withdrawn at any time by notification to the Secretary-General. Such a withdrawal shall not prejudice the consideration of any matter which is the subject of a communication already transmitted under this Article; no further communication by any State Party shall be received after the notification of withdrawal of the declaration has been received by the Secretary-General, unless the State Party con- cerned has made a new declaration.

Article 42

1. (a) If a matter referred to the Committee in accordance with Article 41 is not resolved to the satisfaction of the States Parties concerned, the Commit- tee may, with the prior consent of the States Parties concerned, appoint an *ad hoc* Conciliation Commission (hereinafter referred to as the Commis- sion). The good offices of the Commission shall be made available to the

States Parties concerned with a view to an amicable solution of the matter on the basis of respect for the present Covenant.

   (b) The Commission shall consist of five persons acceptable to the States Parties concerned. If the States Parties concerned fail to reach agreement within three months on all or part of the composition of the Commission the members of the Commission concerning whom no agreement has been reached shall be elected by secret ballot by a two-thirds majority vote of the Committee from among its members.

2. The members of the Commission shall serve in their personal capacity. They shall not be nationals of the States Parties concerned, or of a State not party to the present Covenant, or of a State Party which has not made a declaration under Article 41.

3. The Commission shall elect its own Chairman and adopt its own rules of procedure.

4. The meetings of the Commission shall normally be held at the Headquarters of the United Nations or at the United Nations Office at Geneva. However, they may be held at such other convenient places as the Commission may determine in consultation with the Secretary-General of the United Nations and the States Parties concerned.

5. The secretariat provided in accordance with Article 36 shall also service the commissions appointed under this article.

6. The information received and collated by the Committee shall be made available to the Commission and the Commission may call upon the States Parties concerned to supply any other relevant information.

7. When the Commission has fully considered the matter, but in any event not later than twelve months after having been seized of the matter, it shall submit to the Chairman of the Committee a report for communication to the States Parties concerned.

   (a) If the Commission is unable to complete its consideration of the matter within twelve months, it shall confine its report to a brief statement of the status of its consideration of the matter.

   (b) If an amicable solution to the matter on the basis of respect for human rights as recognized in the present Covenant is reached, the Commission shall confine its report to a brief statement of the facts and of the solution reached.

   (c) If a solution within the terms of sub-paragraph (b) is not reached, the Commission's report shall embody its findings on all questions of fact relevant to the issues between the States Parties concerned, and its views on the possibilities of an amicable solution of the matter. This report shall also contain the written submissions and a record of the oral submissions made by the States Parties concerned.

   (d) If the Commission's report is submitted under sub-paragraph (c), the States Parties concerned shall, within three months of the receipt of the report, notify the Chairman of the Committee whether or not they accept the contents of the report of the Commission.

8. The provisions of this Article are without prejudice to the responsibilities of the Committee under Article 41.

9. The States Parties concerned shall share equally all the expenses of the members of the Commission in accordance with estimates to be provided by the Secretary-General of the United Nations.

10. The Secretary-General of the United Nations shall be empowered to pay the expenses of the members of the Commission, if necessary, before reimbursement by the States Parties concerned, in accordance with paragraph 9 of this Article.

Article 43

The members of the Committee, and of the *ad hoc* conciliation commissions which may be appointed under Article 42, shall be entitled to the facilities, privileges and immunities of experts on mission for the United Nations as laid down in the relevant sections of the Convention on the Privileges and Immunities of the United Nations.

Article 44

The provisions for the implementation of the present Covenant shall apply without prejudice to the procedures prescribed in the field of human rights by or under the constituent instruments and the conventions of the United Nations and of the specialized agencies and shall not prevent the States Parties to the present Covenant from having recourse to other procedures for settling a dispute in accordance with general or special international agreements in force between them.

Article 45

The Committee shall submit to the General Assembly of the United Nations through the Economic and Social Council, an annual report on its activities.

PART V

Article 46

Nothing in the present Covenant shall be interpreted as impairing the provisions of the Charter of the United Nations and of the constitutions of the specializing agencies which define the respective responsibilities of the various organs of the United Nations and of the specialized agencies in regard to the matters dealt with in the present Covenant.

Article 47

Nothing in the present Covenant shall be interpreted as impairing the inherent right of all peoples to enjoy and utilize fully and freely their natural wealth and resources.

Article 48

1. The present Covenant is open for signature by any State Member of the United Nations or member of any of its specialized agencies, by any State Party to the Statute of the International Court of Justice, and by any other State which has been invited by the General Assembly of the United Nations to become a party to the present Covenant.
2. The present Covenant is subject to ratification. Instruments of ratification shall be deposited with the Secretary-General of the United Nations.
3. The present Covenant shall be open to accession by any State referred to in paragraph 1 of this article.
4. Accession shall be effected by the deposit of an instrument of accession with the Secretary-General of the United Nations.
5. The Secretary-General of the United Nations shall inform all States which have signed this Covenant or acceded to it of the deposit of each instrument of ratification or accession.

Article 49

1. The present Covenant shall enter into force three months after the date of the deposit with the Secretary-General of the United Nations of the thirty-fifth instrument of ratification or instrument of accession.
2. For each State ratifying the present Covenant or acceding to it after the deposit of the thirty-fifth instrument of ratification or instrument of accession, the present Covenant shall enter into force three months after the date of the deposit of its own instrument of ratification or instrument of accession.

Article 50

The provisions of the present Covenant shall extend to all parts of federal States without any limitations or exceptions.

Article 51

1. Any State Party to the present Covenant may propose an amendment and file it with the Secretary-General of the United Nations. The Secretary-General of the United Nations shall thereupon communicate any proposed amendments to the States Parties to the present Covenant with a request that they notify him whether they favour a conference of States Parties for the purpose of considering and voting upon the proposals. In the event that at least one-third of the States Parties favours such a conference, the Secretary-General shall convene the conference under the auspices of the United Nations. Any amendment adopted by a majority of the States Parties present and voting at the conference shall be submitted to the General Assembly of the United Nations for approval.
2. Amendments shall come into force when they have been approved by the General Assembly of the United Nations and accepted by a two-thirds majority of the States Parties to the present Covenant in accordance with their respective constitutional processes.
3. When amendments come into force, they shall be binding on those States Parties which have accepted them, other States Parties still being bound by the provisions of the present Covenant and any earlier amendment which they have accepted.

Article 52

Irrespective of the notifications made under Article 48, paragraph 5, the Secretary-General of the United Nations shall inform all States referred to in paragraph 1 of the same Article of the following particulars:

(a) Signatures, ratifications and accessions under Article 48;

(b) The date of the entry into force of the present Covenant under Article 49 and the date of the entry into force of any amendments under Article 51.

Article 53

1. The present Covenant, of which the Chinese, English, French, Russian and Spanish texts are equally authentic, shall be deposited in the archives of the United Nations.

2. The Secretary-General of the United Nations shall transmit certified copies of the present Covenant to all States referred to in Article 48.

Second Optional Protocol to the International Covenant on Civil and Political Rights, Aiming at the abolition of the death penalty

Adopted and proclaimed by General Assembly resolution 44/128 of 15 December 1989

The States Parties to the present Protocol,

Believing that abolition of the death penalty contributes to enhancement of human dignity and progressive development of human rights,

Recalling article 3 of the Universal Declaration on Human Rights, adopted on 10 December 1948, and article 6 of the International Covenant on Civil and Political Rights, adopted on 16 December 1966,

Noting that article 6 of the International Covenant on Civil and Political Rights refers to abolition of the death penalty in terms that strongly suggest that abolition is desirable,

Convinced that all measures of abolition of the death penalty should be considered as progress in the enjoyment of the right to life,

Desirous to undertake hereby an international commitment to abolish the death penalty,

Have agreed as follows:

Article 1

1. No one within the jurisdiction of a State Party to the present Protocol shall be executed.
2. Each State party shall take all necessary measures to abolish the death penalty within its jurisdiction.

Article 2

1. No reservation is admissible to the present Protocol, except for a reservation made at the time of ratification or accession that provides for the application of the death penalty in time of war pursuant to a conviction for a most serious crime of a military nature committed during wartime.
2. The State party making such a reservation shall at the time of ratification or accession communicate to the Secretary-General of the United Nations the relevant provisions of its national legislation applicable during wartime.
3. The State Party having made such a reservation shall notify the Secretary-General of the United Nations of any beginning or ending of a state of war applicable to its territory.

Article 3

The States Parties to the present Protocol shall include in the reports they submit to the Human Rights Committee, in accordance with article 40 of the Covenant, information on the measures that they have adopted to give effect to the present Protocol.

Article 4

With respect to the States Parties to the Covenant that have made a declaration under article 41, the competence of the Human Rights Committee to receive and consider communications when a State Party claims that another State Party is not fulfilling its obligations shall extend to the provisions of the present Protocol, unless the State Party concerned has made a statement to the contrary at the moment of ratification or accession.

Article 5

With respect to the States Parties to the first Optional Protocol to the International Covenant on Civil and Political Rights adopted on 16 December 1966, the competence of the Human Rights Committee to receive and consider communications from individuals subject to its jurisdiction shall extend to the provisions of the present Protocol, unless the State Party concerned has made a statement to the contrary at the moment of ratification or accession.

Article 6

1. The provisions of the present Protocol shall apply as additional provisions to the Covenant.
2. Without prejudice to the possibility of a reservation under article 2 of the present Protocol, the right guaranteed in article 1, paragraph 1, of the present Protocol shall not be subject to any derogation under article 4 of the Covenant.

Article 7

1. The present Protocol is open for signature by any State that has signed the Covenant.
2. The present Protocol is subject to ratification by any State that has ratified the Covenant or acceded to it. Instruments of ratification shall be deposited with the Secretary-General of the United Nations.
3. The present Protocol shall be open to accession by any State that has ratified the Covenant or acceded to it.
4. Accession shall be effected by the deposit of an instrument of accession with the Secretary-General of the United Nations.
5. The Secretary-General of the United Nations shall inform all States that have signed the present Protocol or acceded to it of the deposit of each instrument of ratification or accession.

Article 8

1. The present Protocol shall enter into force three months after the date of the deposit with the Secretary-General of the United Nations of the tenth instrument of ratification or accession.
2. For each State ratifying the present Protocol or acceding to it after the deposit of the tenth instrument of ratification or accession, the present Protocol shall enter into force three months after the date of the deposit of its own instrument of ratification or accession.

Article 9

The provisions of the present Protocol shall extend to all parts of federal States without any limitations or exceptions.

Article 10

The Secretary-General of the United Nations shall inform all States referred to in article 48, paragraph 1, of the Covenant of the following particulars:

(a) Reservation, communications and notifications under article 2 of the present Protocol;

(b) Statements made under articles 4 or 5 of the present Protocol;

(c) Signatures, ratifications and accessions under article 7 of the present Protocol;

(d) The date of the entry into force of the present Protocol under article 8 thereof.

Article 11

1. The present Protocol, of which the Arabic, Chinese, English, French, Russian and Spanish texts are equally authentic, shall be deposited in the archives of the United Nations.
2. The Secretary-General of the United Nations shall transmit certified copies of the present Protocol to all States referred to in article 48 of the Covenant.

APPENDIX E

International Covenant on
Economic, Social and Cultural Rights 1966

This appears in the annex to a resolution adopted by the United Nations General Assembly on 16 December 1966. The Covenant entered into force on 3 January 1976; and ninety-nine States have become parties.

PREAMBLE

The States Parties to the present Covenant,

Considering the obligation of States under the Charter of the United Nations to promote universal respect for, and observance of, human rights and freedoms,

Realizing that the individual, having duties to other individuals and to the community to which he belongs, is under a responsibility to strive for the promotion and observance of the rights recognized in the present Covenant,

Agree upon the following articles:

PART I

Article 1

1. All peoples have the right of self-determination. By virtue of that right they freely determine their political status and freely pursue their economic, social and cultural development.
2. All peoples may, for their own ends, freely dispose of their natural wealth and resources without prejudice to any obligations arising out of international economic co-operation, based upon the principle of mutual benefit, and international law. In no case may a people be deprived of its own means of subsistence.
3. The States Parties to the present Covenant, including those having responsibility for the administration of Non-Self-Governing and Trust Territories, shall promote the realization of the right of self-determination, and shall respect that right, in conformity with the provisions of the Charter of the United Nations.

PART II

Article 2

1. Each State Party to the present Covenant undertakes to take steps, individually and through international assistance and co-operation, especially economic and technical, to the maximum of its available resources, with a view to achieving progressively the full realization of the rights recognized in the

present Covenant by all appropriate means, including particularly the adoption of legislative measures.

2. The States Parties to the present Covenant undertake to guarantee that the rights enunciated in the present Covenant will be exercised without discrimination of any kind as to race, colour, sex, language, religion, political or other opinion, national or social origin, property, birth or other status.

3. Developing countries, with due regard to human rights and their national economy, may determine to what extent they would guarantee the economic rights recognized in the present Covenant to non-nationals.

Article 3

The States Parties to the present Covenant undertake to ensure the equal right of men and women to the enjoyment of all economic, social and cultural rights set forth in the present Covenant.

Article 4

The States Parties to the present Covenant recognize that, in the enjoyment of those rights provided by the State in conformity with the present Covenant, the State may subject such rights only to such limitations as are determined by law only in so far as this may be compatible with the nature of these rights and solely for the purpose of promoting the general welfare in a democratic society.

Article 5

1. Nothing in the present Covenant may be interpreted as implying for any State, group or person any right to engage in any activity or to perform any act aimed at the destruction of any of the rights or freedoms recognized herein, or at their limitation to a greater extent than is provided for in the present Covenant.

2. No restriction upon or derogation from any of the fundamental human rights recognized or existing in any country in virtue of law, conventions, regulations or custom shall be admitted on the pretext that the present Covenant does not recognize such rights or that it recognizes them to a lesser extent.

PART III

Article 6

1. The States Parties to the present Covenant recognize the right to work, which includes the right of everyone to the opportunity to gain his living by work which he freely chooses or accepts, and will take appropriate steps to safeguard this right.

2. The steps to be taken by a State Party to the present Covenant to achieve the full realization of this right shall include technical and vocational guidance and training programmes, policies and techniques to achieve steady economic, social and cultural development and full and productive employment under conditions safeguarding fundamental political and economic freedoms to the individual.

Article 7

The States Parties to the present Covenant recognize the right of everyone to the enjoyment of just and favourable conditions of work, which ensure, in particular:

    (a) Remuneration which provides all workers, as a minimum with:

        (i) Fair wages and equal remuneration for work of equal value without distinction of any kind, in particular women being guaranteed conditions of work not inferior to those enjoyed by men, with equal pay for equal work;

        (ii) A decent living for themselves and their families in accordance with the provisions of the present Covenant;

    (b) Safe and healthy working conditions;

    (c) Equal opportunity for everyone to be promoted in his employment to an appropriate higher level, subject to no considerations other than those of seniority and competence;

    (d) Rest, leisure and reasonable limitation of working hours and periodic holidays with pay, as well as remuneration for public holidays.

Article 8

1. The States Parties to the present Covenant undertake to ensure:
    (a) The right of everyone to form trade unions and join the trade union of his choice, subject only to the rules of the organization concerned, for the promotion and protection of his economic and social interests. No restrictions may be placed on the exercise of this right other than those prescribed by law and which are necessary in a democratic society in the interests of national security or public order or for the protection of the rights and freedoms of others;
    (b) The right of trade unions to establish national federations or confederations and the right of the latter to form or join international trade union organizations;
    (c) The right of trade unions to function freely subject to no limitations other than those prescribed by law and which are necessary in a democratic society in the interests of national security or public order or for the protection of the rights and freedoms of others;
    (d) The right to strike, provided that it is exercised in conformity with the laws of the particular country.
2. This Article shall not prevent the imposition of lawful restrictions on the exercise of these rights by members of the armed forces or of the police or of the administration of the State.
3. Nothing in this Article shall authorize States Parties to the International Labour Organization Convention of 1948 concerning Freedom of Association and Protection of the Right to Organize to take legislative measures which would prejudice, or apply the law in such a manner as would prejudice, the guarantees provided for in that Convention.

Article 9

The States Parties to the present Covenant recognize the right of everyone to social security, including social insurance.

Article 10

The States Parties to the present Covenant recognize that:
1. The widest possible protection and assistance should be accorded to the family, which is the natural and fundamental group unit of society, particularly for its establishment and while it is responsible for the care and education of dependent children. Marriage must be entered into with the free consent of the intending spouses.
2. Special protection should be accorded to mothers during a reasonable period before and after childbirth. During such period working mothers should be accorded paid leave or leave with adequate social security benefits.
3. Special measures of protection and assistance should be taken on behalf of all children and young persons without any discrimination for reasons of parentage or other conditions. Children and young persons should be protected from economic and social exploitation. Their employment in work harmful to their morals or health or dangerous to life or likely to hamper their normal development should be punishable by law. States should also set age limits below which the paid employment of child labour should be prohibited and punishable by law.

Article 11

1. The States Parties to the present Covenant recognize the right of everyone to an adequate standard of living for himself and his family, including adequate food, clothing and housing, and to the continuous improvement of living conditions. The States Parties will take appropriate steps to ensure the realization of this right, recognizing to this effect the essential importance of international co-operation based on free consent.
2. The States Parties to the present Covenant, recognizing the fundamental right of everyone to be free from hunger, shall take, individually and through international co-operation, the measures, including specific programmes, which are needed:
   (a) To improve methods of production, conservation and distribution of food by making full use of technical and scientific knowledge, by disseminating knowledge of the principles of nutrition and by developing or reforming agrarian systems in such a way as to achieve the most efficient development and utilization of natural resources;
   (b) Taking into account the problems of both food-importing and food-exporting countries, to ensure an equitable distribution of world food supplies in relation to need.

Article 12

1. The States Parties to the present Covenant recognize the right of everyone to the enjoyment of the highest attainable standard of physical and mental health.
2. The steps to be taken by the States Parties to the present Covenant to achieve the full realization of this right shall include those necessary for:
   (a) The provision for the reduction of the stillbirth-rate and of infant mortality and for the healthy development of the child;
   (b) The improvement of all aspects of environmental and industrial hygiene;
   (c) The prevention, treatment and control of epidemic, endemic, occupational and other diseases;
   (d) The creation of conditions which would assure to all medical service and medical attention in the event of sickness.

Article 13

1. The States Parties to the present Covenant recognize the right of everyone to education. They agree that education shall be directed to the full development of the human personality and the sense of its dignity, and shall strengthen the respect for human rights and fundamental freedoms. They further agree that education shall enable all persons to participate effectively in a free society, promote understanding, tolerance and friendship among all nations and all racial, ethnic or religious groups, and further the activities of the United Nations for the maintenance of peace.

2. The States Parties to the present Covenant recognize that, with a view to achieving the full realization of this right:
   (a) Primary education shall be compulsory and available free to all;
   (b) Secondary education in its different forms, including technical and vocational secondary education, shall be made generally available and accessible to all by every appropriate means, and in particular by the progressive introduction of free education;
   (c) Higher education shall be made equally accessible to all, on the basis of capacity, by every appropriate means, and in particular by the progressive introduction of free education;
   (d) Fundamental education shall be encouraged or intensified as far as possible for those persons who have not received or completed the whole period of their primary education;
   (e) The development of a system of schools at all levels shall be actively pursued, an adequate fellowship system shall be established, and the material conditions of teaching staff shall be continuously improved.

3. The States Parties to the present Covenant undertake to have respect for the liberty of parents and, when applicable, legal guardians, to choose for their children schools, other than those established by the public authorities, which conform to such minimum educational standards as may be laid down or approved by the State and to ensure the religious and moral education of their children in conformity with their own convictions.

4. No part of this Article shall be construed so as to interfere with the liberty of individuals and bodies to establish and direct educational institutions, subject always to the observance of the principles set forth in paragraph 1 of this Article and to the requirement that the education given in such institutions shall conform to such minimum standards as may be laid down by the State.

Article 14

Each State Party to the present Covenant which, at the time of becoming a Party, has not been able to secure in its metropolitan territory or other territories under its jurisdiction compulsory primary education, free of charge, undertakes, within two years, to work out and adopt a detailed plan of action for the progressive implementation, within a reasonable number of years, to be fixed in the plan, of the principle of compulsory education free of charge for all.

Article 15

1. The States Parties to the present Covenant recognize the right of everyone:
   (a) To take part in cultural life;
   (b) To enjoy the benefits of scientific progress and its applications;
   (c) To benefit from the protection of the moral and material interests resulting from any scientific, literary or artistic production of which he is the author.

2. The steps to be taken by the States Parties to the present Covenant to achieve the full realization of this right shall include those necessary for the conservation, the development and the diffusion of science and culture.
3. The States Parties to the present Covenant undertake to respect the freedom indispensable for scientific research and creative activity.
4. The States Parties to the present Covenant recognize the benefits to be derived from the encouragement and development of international contacts and co-operation in the scientific and cultural fields.

PART IV

Article 16

1. The States Parties to the present Covenant undertake to submit in conformity with this part of the Covenants reports on the measures which they have adopted and the progress made in achieving the observance of the rights recognized herein.
2. (a) All reports shall be submitted to the Secretary-General of the United Nations, who shall transmit copies to the Economic and Social Council for consideration in accordance with the provisions of the present Covenant.
   (b) The Secretary-General of the United Nations shall also transmit to the specialized agencies copies of the reports, or any relevant parts therefrom, from States Parties to the present Covenant which are also members of these specialized agencies in so far as these reports, or parts therefrom, relate to any matters which fall within the responsibilities of the said agencies in accordance with their constitutional instruments.

Article 17

1. The States Parties to the present Covenant shall furnish their reports in stages, in accordance with a programme to be established by the Economic and Social Council within one year of the entry into force of the present Covenant after consultation with the States Parties and the specialized agencies concerned.
2. Reports may indicate factors and difficulties affecting the degree of fulfilment of obligations under the present Covenant.
3. Where relevant information has previously been furnished to the United Nations or to any specialized agency by any State Party to the present Covenant, it will not be necessary to reproduce that information, but a precise reference to the information so furnished will suffice.

Article 18

Pursuant to its responsibilities under the Charter of the United Nations in the field of human rights and fundamental freedoms, the Economic and Social Council may make arrangements with the specialized agencies in respect of their reporting to it on the progress made in achieving the observance of the provisions of the present Covenant falling within the scope of their activities. These reports may include particulars of decisions and recommendations on such implementation adopted by their competent organs.

Article 19

The Economic and Social Council may transmit to the Commission on Human Rights for study and general recommendation or as appropriate for information the reports concerning human rights submitted by States in accordance with Articles 16 and 17, and those concerning human rights submitted by the specialized agencies in accordance with Article 18.

Article 20

The States Parties to the present Covenant and the specialized agencies concerned may submit comments to the Economic and Social Council on any general recommendation under Article 19 or reference to such general recommendation in any report of the Commission on Human Rights or any documentation referred to therein.

Article 21

The Economic and Social Council may submit from time to time to the General Assembly reports with recommendations of a general nature and a summary of the information received from the States Parties to the present Covenant and the specialized agencies on the measures taken and the progress made in achieving general observance of the rights recognized in the present Covenant.

Article 22

The Economic and Social Council may bring to the attention of other organs of the United Nations, their subsidiary organs and specialized agencies concerned with furnishing technical assistance any matters arising out of the reports referred to in this part of the present Covenant which may assist such bodies in deciding, each within its field of competence, on the advisability of international measures likely to contribute to the effective progressive implementation of the present Covenant.

Article 23

The States Parties to the present Covenant agree that international action for the achievement of the rights recognized in the present Covenant includes such methods as the conclusion of conventions, the adoption of recommendations, the furnishing of technical assistance and the holding of regional meetings and technical meetings for the purpose of consultation and study organized in conjunction with the Governments concerned.

Article 24

Nothing in the present Covenant shall be interpreted as impairing the provisions of the Charter of the United Nations and of the constitutions of the specialized agencies which define the respective responsibilities of the various organs of the United Nations and of the specialized agencies in regard to the matters dealt with in the present Covenant.

Article 25

Nothing in the present Covenant shall be interpreted as impairing the inherent right of all peoples to enjoy and utilize fully and freely their natural wealth and resources.

PART V

Article 26

1. The present Covenant is open for signature by any State Member of the United Nations or member of any of its specialized agencies, by any State Party to the Statute of the International Court of Justice, and by any other State which has been invited by the General Assembly of the United Nations to become a party to the present Covenant.
2. The present Covenant is subject to ratification. Instruments of ratification shall be deposited with the Secretary-General of the United Nations.
3. The present Covenant shall be open to accession by any State referred to in paragraph 1 of this Article.
4. Accession shall be effected by the deposit of an instrument of accession with the Secretary-General of the United Nations.
5. The Secretary-General of the United Nations shall inform all States which have signed the present Covenant or acceded to it of the deposit of each instrument of ratification or accession.

Article 27

1. The present Covenant shall enter into force three months after the date of the deposit with the Secretary-General of the United Nations of the thirty-fifth instrument of ratification or instrument of accession.
2. For each State ratifying the present Covenant or acceding to it after the deposit of the thirty-fifth instrument of ratification or instrument of accession, the present Covenant shall enter into force three months after the date of the deposit of its own instrument of ratification or instrument of accession.

Article 28

The provisions of the present Covenant shall extend to all parts of federal States without any limitations or exceptions.

Article 29

1. Any State Party to the present Covenant may propose an amendment and file it with the Secretary-General of the United Nations. The Secretary-General shall thereupon communicate any proposed amendments to the States Parties to the present Covenant with a request that they notify him whether they favour a conference of States Parties for the purpose of considering and voting upon the proposals. In the event that at least one third of the States Parties favours such a conference, the Secretary-General shall convene the conference under the auspices of the United Nations. Any amendment

adopted by a majority of the States Parties present and voting at the conference shall be submitted to the General Assembly of the United Nations for approval.

2. Amendments shall come into force when they have been approved by the General Assembly of the United Nations and accepted by a two-thirds majority of the State Parties to the present Covenant in accordance with their respective constitutional processes.

3. When amendments come into force they shall be binding on those State Parties which have accepted them, other States Parties still being bound by the provisions of the present Covenant and any earlier amendment which they have accepted.

Article 30

Irrespective of the notifications made under Article 26, paragraph 5, the Secretary-General of the United Nations shall inform all States referred to in paragraph 1 of the same Article of the following particulars:

(a) Signatures, ratifications and accessions under Article 26;

(b) The date of the entry into force of the present Covenant under Article 27 and the date of the entry into force of any amendments under Article 29.

Article 31

1. The present Covenant, of which the Chinese, English, French, Russian and Spanish texts are equally authentic, shall be deposited in the archives of the United Nations.

2. The Secretary-General of the United Nations shall transmit certified copies of the present Covenant to all States referred to in Article 26.

APPENDIX F

Canada Act 1982

U.K., 1982, c.11

An Act to give effect to a request by the Senate and House of Commons in Canada.

Whereas Canada has requested and consented to the enactment of an Act of the Parliament of the United Kingdom to give effect to the provisions hereinafter set forth and the Senate and the House of Commons of Canada in Parliament assembled have submitted an address to Her Majesty requesting that Her Majesty may graciously be pleased to cause a Bill to be laid before the Parliament of the United Kingdom for that purpose.

Be it therefore enacted by the Queen's Most Excellent Majesty, by and with the advice and consent of the Lords Spiritual and Temporal, and Commons, in this present Parliament assembled, and by the authority of the same as follows:

Constitution Act, 1982 enacted

1. *The Constitution Act, 1982* set out in Schedule B to this Act is hereby enacted for and shall have the force of law in Canada and shall come into force as provided in that Act.

Termination of power to legislate for Canada

2. No Act of the Parliament of the United Kingdom passed after the *Constitution Act, 1982* comes into force shall extend to Canada as part of its law.

French version

3. So far as it is not contained in Schedule B, the French version of this Act is set out in Schedule A to this Act and has the same authority in Canada as the English version thereof.

Short title

4. This Act may be cited as the *Canada Act 1982*.

Constitution Act, 1982

Schedule B to Canada Act 1982 (U.K.)

PART I

CANADIAN CHARTER OF RIGHTS AND FREEDOMS

Whereas Canada is founded upon principles that recognize the supremacy of God and the rule of law:

Guarantee of Rights and Freedoms

Rights and freedoms in Canada

1. The *Canadian Charter of Rights and Freedoms* guarantees the rights and freedoms set out in it subject only to such reasonable limits prescribed by law as can be demonstrably justified in a free and democratic society.

Fundamental Freedoms

Fundamental freedoms

2. Everyone has the following fundamental freedoms:
   (a) Freedom of conscience and religion;
   (b) Freedom of thought, belief, opinion and expression, including freedom of the press and other media of communication;
   (c) Freedom of peaceful assembly; and
   (d) Freedom of association.

Democratic Rights

Democratic rights of citizens

3. Every citizen of Canada has the right to vote in an election of members of the House of Commons or of a legislative assembly and to be qualified for membership therein.

Maximum duration of legislative bodies

4 (1) No House of Commons and no legislative assembly shall continue for longer than five years from the date fixed for the return of the writs at a general election of its members.[1]

Continuation in special circumstances

(2) In time of real or apprehended war, invasion or insurrection, a House of Commons may be continued by Parliament and a legislative assembly may be continued by the legislature beyond five years if such continuation is not opposed by the votes of more than one-third of the members of the House of Commons or the legislative assembly, as the case may be.[2]

Annual sitting of legislative bodies

5. There shall be a sitting of Parliament and of each legislature at least once every twelve months.[3]

Mobility of citizens

6 (1) Every citizen of Canada has the right to enter, remain in and leave Canada.

Rights to move and gain livelihood

(2) Every citizen of Canada and every person who has the status of a permanent resident of Canada has the right

---

[1] See section 50 and the footnotes to sections 85 and 88 of the *Constitution Act, 1867*.
[2] Replaces part of Class 1 of section 91 of the *Constitution Act, 1867*, which was repealed as set out in subitem 1(3) of the Schedule to this Act.
[3] See the footnotes to sections 20, 86 and 88 of the *Constitution Act, 1867*.

(a) to move to and take up residence in any province;

(b) to pursue the gaining of a livelihood in any province.

Limitation

(3) The rights specified in subsection (2) are subject to

(a) any laws or practices of general application in force in a province other than those that discriminate among persons primarily on the basis of province of present or previous residence;

and

(b) any laws providing for reasonable residency requirements as a qualification for the receipt of publicly provided social services.

Affirmative action programs

(4) Subsections (2) and (3) do not preclude any law, program or activity that has as its object the amelioration in a province of conditions of individuals in that province who are socially or economically disadvantaged if the rate of employment in that province is below the rate of employment in Canada.

Legal rights

Life, liberty and security of person

7 Everyone has the right to life, liberty and security of the person and the right not to be deprived thereof except in accordance with the principles of fundamental justice.

Search or seizure

8 Everyone has the right to be secure against unreasonable search or seizure.

Detention or imprisonment

9 Everyone has the right not to be arbitrarily detained or imprisoned.

Arrest or detention

10 Everyone has the right on arrest or detention

(a) to be informed promptly of the reasons therefor;

(b) to retain and instruct counsel without delay and to be informed of that right; and

(c) to have the validity of the detention determined by way of *habeas corpus* and to be released if the detention is not lawful.

Proceedings in criminal and penal matters

11 Any person charged with an offence has the right

(a) to be informed without unreasonable delay of the specific offence;

(b) to be tried within a reasonable time;

(c) not to be compelled to be a witness in proceedings against that person in respect of the offence;

(d) to be presumed innocent until proven guilty according to law in a fair and public hearing by an independent and impartial tribunal;

(e) not to be denied reasonable bail without just cause;

(f)　except in the case of an offence under military law tried before a military tribunal, to the benefit of trial by jury where the maximum punishment for the offence is imprisonment for five years or a more severe punishment;

(g)　not to be found guilty on account of any act or omission unless, at the time of the act or omission, it constituted an offence under Canadian or international law or was criminal according to the general principles of law recognized by the community of nations;

(h)　if finally acquitted of the offence, not to be tried for it again and, if finally found guilty and punished for the offence, not to be tried or punished for it again; and

(i)　if found guilty of the offence and if the punishment for the offence has been varied between the time of commission and the time of sentencing, to the benefit of the lesser punishment.

Treatment or punishment

12 Everyone has the right not to be subjected to any cruel and unusual treatment or punishment.

Self-incrimination

13 A witness who testifies in any proceedings has the right not to have any incriminating evidence so given used to incriminate that witness in any other proceedings, except in a prosecution for perjury or for the giving of contradictory evidence.

Interpreter

14 A party or witness in any proceedings who does not understand or speak the language in which the proceedings are conducted or who is deaf has the right to the assistance of an interpreter.

Equality Rights

Equality before and under law and equal protection and benefit of law

15 (1) Every individual is equal before and under the law and has the right to the equal protection and equal benefit of the law without discrimination and, in particular, without discrimination based on race, national or ethnic origin, colour, religion, sex, age or mental or physical disability.

Affirmative action programs

(2) Subsection (1) does not preclude any law, program or activity that has as its object the amelioration of conditions of disadvantaged individuals or groups including those that are disadvantaged because of race, national or ethnic origin, colour, religion, sex, age or mental or physical disability.[4]

Official Languages of Canada

Official languages of Canada

16 (1) English and French are the official languages of Canada and have equality of status and equal rights and privileges as to their use in all institutions of the Parliament and government of Canada.

---

[4] Subsection 32(2) provides that section 15 shall not have effect until three years after section 32 comes into force. Section 32 came into force on April 17, 1982; therefore, section 15 had effect on April 17, 1985.

Official languages of New Brunswick

(2) English and French are the official languages of New Brunswick and have equality of status and equal rights and privileges as to their use in all institutions of the legislature and government of New Brunswick.

Advancement of status and use

(3) Nothing in this Charter limits the authority of Parliament or a legislature to advance the equality of status or use of English and French.

English and French linguistic communities in New Brunswick

16.1 (1) The English linguistic community and the French linguistic community in New Brunswick have equality of status and equal rights and privileges, including the right to distinct educational institutions and such distinct cultural institutions as are necessary for the preservation and promotion of those communities.

Role of the legislature and government of New Brunswick

(2) The role of the legislature and government of New Brunswick to preserve and promote the status, rights and privileges referred to in sub-section (1) is affirmed.[5]

Proceedings of Parliament

17 (1) Everyone has the right to use English or French in any debates and other proceedings of Parliament.[6]

Proceedings of New Brunswick legislature

(2) Everyone has the right to use English or French in any debates and other proceedings of the legislature of New Brunswick.[7]

Parliamentary statute and records

18 (1) The statutes, records and journals of Parliament shall be printed and published in English and French and both language versions are equally authoritative.[8]

New Brunswick statutes and records

(2) The statutes, records and journals of the legislature of New Brunswick shall be printed and published in English and French and both language versions are equally authoritative.[9]

Proceedings in courts established by Parliament

19 (1) Either English or French may be used by any person in, or in any pleading in or process issuing from, any court established by Parliament.[10]

Proceedings in New Brunswick courts

(2) Either English or French may be used by any person in, or in any pleading in or process issuing from, any court of New Brunswick.[11]

---

[5] Section 16.1 was added by *Constitution Amendment, 1993 (New Brunswick)*. See S1/93–54.
[6] See section 1.33 of the *Constitution Act, 1967*, and the footnote thereto.
[7] *Id.*
[8] *Id.*
[9] *Id.*
[10] *Id.*
[11] *Id.*

Communications by public with federal institutions

20 (1) Any member of the public in Canada has the right to communicate with, and to receive available services from, any head or central office of an institution of the Parliament or government of Canada in English or French, and has the same right with respect to any other office of any such institution where

(a) there is a significant demand for communications with and services from that office in such language; or

(b) due to the nature of the office, it is reasonable that communications with and services from that office be available in both English and French.

Communications by public with New Brunswick institutions

(2) Any member of the public in New Brunswick has the right to communicate with, and to receive available services from, any office of an institution of the legislature or government of New Brunswick in English or French.

Continuation of existing constitutional provisions

21 Nothing in sections 16 to 20 abrogates or derogates from any right, privilege or obligation with respect to the English and French languages, or either of them, that exists or is continued by virtue of any other provision of the Constitution in Canada.[12]

Rights and privileges preserved

22 Nothing in sections 16 to 20 abrogates or derogates from any legal or customary right or privilege acquired or enjoyed either before or after the coming into force of this Charter with respect to any language that is not English or French.

Minority Language

Educational Rights

Language of instruction

23 (1) Citizens of Canada

(a) whose first language learned and still understood is that of the English or French linguistic minority population of the province in which they reside, or

(b) who have received their primary school instruction in Canada in English or French and reside in a province where the language in which they received that instruction is the language of the English or French linguistic minority population of the province,

have the right to have their children receive primary and secondary school instruction in that language in that province.[13]

Continuity of language instruction

(2) Citizens of Canada of whom any child has received or is receiving primary or secondary school instruction in English or French in Canada, have the right to

---

[12] See, for example, section 133 of the *Constitution Act, 1867*, and the *Manitoba Act, 1870*, in the footnote thereto.

[13] Paragraph 23(1)(a) is not in force in respect of Quebec. See section 59 *infra*.

have all their children receive primary and secondary school instruction in the same language.

Application where numbers warrant

(3) The right of citizens of Canada under subsections (1) and (2) to have their children receive primary and secondary school instruction in the language of the English or French linguistic minority population of a province

(a) applies whenever in the province the number of children of citizens who have such a right is sufficient to warrant the provision to them out of public funds of minority language instruction; and

(b) includes, where the number of those children so warrants, the right to have them receive that instruction in minority language educational facilities provided out of public funds.

Enforcement

Enforcement of guaranteed rights and freedoms

24 (1) Anyone whose rights or freedoms, as guaranteed by this Charter, have been infringed or denied may apply to a court of competent jurisdiction to obtain such remedy as the court considers appropriate and just in the circumstances.

Exclusion of evidence bringing administration of justice into disrepute

(2) Where, in proceedings under subsection (1), a court concludes that evidence was obtained in a manner that infringed or denied any rights or freedoms guaranteed by this Charter, the evidence shall be excluded if it is established that, having regard to all the circumstances, the admission of it in the proceedings would bring the administration of justice into disrepute.

General

Aboriginal rights and freedoms not affected by Charter

25 The guarantee in this Charter of certain rights and freedoms shall not be construed so as to abrogate or derogate from any aboriginal, treaty or other rights or freedoms that pertain to the aboriginal peoples of Canada including

(a) any rights or freedoms that have been recognized by the Royal Proclamation of October 7, 1763; and

(b) any rights or freedoms that now exist by way of land claims agreements or may be so acquired.[14]

Other rights and freedoms not affected by Charter

26 The guarantee in this Charter of certain rights and freedoms shall not be construed as denying the existence of any other rights or freedoms that exist in Canada.

---

[14] Paragraph 25(b) was repealed and re-enacted by the *Constitution Amendment Proclamation, 1983. See* S1/84–102.
Paragraph 25(b) as originally enacted read as follows:

"(b) any rights or freedoms that may be acquired by Canada by way of land claim settlement."

Multicultural heritage

27 This Charter shall be interpreted in a manner consistent with the preservation and enhancement of the multicultural heritage of Canadians.

Rights guaranteed equally to both sexes

28 Notwithstanding anything in this Charter, the rights and freedoms referred to in it are guaranteed equally to male and female persons.

Rights respecting certain schools preserved

29 Nothing in this Charter abrogates or derogates from any rights or privileges guaranteed by or under the Constitution of Canada in respect of denominational, separate or dissentient schools.[15]

Application to territories and territorial authorities

30 A reference in this Charter to a province or to the legislative assembly or legislature of a province shall be deemed to include a reference to the Yukon Territory and the Northwest Territories, or to the appropriate legislative authority thereof, as the case may be.

Legislative powers not extended

31 Nothing in this Charter extends the legislative powers of any body or authority.

Application of Charter

Application of Charter

32 (1) This Charter applies

    (a) to the Parliament and government of Canada in respect of all matters within the authority of Parliament including all matters relating to the Yukon Territory and Northwest Territories; and

    (b) to the legislature and government of each province in respect of all matters within the authority of the legislature of each province.

Exception

(2) Notwithstanding subsection (1), section 15 shall not have effect until three years after this section comes into force.

Exception where express declaration

33 (1) Parliament or the legislature of a province may expressly declare in an Act of Parliament or of the legislature, as the case may be, that the Act or a provision thereof shall operate notwithstanding a provision included in section 2 or sections 7 to 15 of this Charter.

Operation of exception

(2) An Act or a provision of an Act in respect of which a declaration made under this section is in effect shall have such operation as it would have but for the provision of this Charter referred to in the declaration.

Five year limitation

(3) A declaration made under subsection (1) shall cease to have effect five years after it comes into force or on such earlier date as may be specified in the declaration.

---

[15] See section 93 of the *Constitution Act, 1867*, and the footnote thereto.

Re-enactment

(4) Parliament or the legislature of a province may re-enact a declaration made under subsection (1).

Five year limitation

(5) Subsection (3) applies in respect of a re-enactment made under subsection (4).

Citation

Citation

34 This Part may be cited as the *Canadian Charter of Rights and Freedoms.*

APPENDIX G

New Zealand Bill of Rights Act 1990

PREAMBLE

An Act—

(a) To affirm, protect, and promote human rights and fundamental freedoms in New Zealand; and

(b) To affirm New Zealand's commitment to the International Covenant on Civil and Political Rights

[28 AUGUST 1990]

PART 0
SHORT TITLE

BE IT ENACTED by the Parliament of New Zealand as follows:

1 Short Title and commencement—(1) This Act may be cited as the New Zealand Bill of Rights Act 1990.

(2) This Act shall come into force on the 28th day after the date on which it receives the Royal assent.

PART I

GENERAL PROVISIONS

2 Rights affirmed—The rights and freedoms contained in this Bill of Rights are affirmed.

3 Application—This Bill of Rights applies only to acts done—

(a) By the legislative, executive, or judicial branches of the government of New Zealand; or

(b) By any person or body in the performance of any public function, power, or duty conferred or imposed on that person or body by or pursuant to law.

4 Other enactments not affected—No court shall, in relation to any enactment (whether passed or made before or after the commencement of this Bill of Rights),—

(a) Hold any provision of the enactment to be impliedly repealed or revoked, or to be in any way invalid or ineffective; or

(b) Decline to apply any provision of the enactment—

by reason only that the provision is inconsistent with any provision of this Bill of Rights.

5 Justified limitations—Subject to section 4 of this Bill of Rights, the rights and freedoms contained in this Bill of Rights may be subject only to such reasonable limits prescribed by law as can be demonstrably justified in a free and democratic society.

6 Interpretation consistent with Bill of Rights to be preferred—Wherever an enactment can be given a meaning that is consistent with the rights and freedoms contained in this Bill of Rights, that meaning shall be preferred to any other meaning.

7 Attorney-General to report to Parliament where Bill appears to be inconsistent with Bill of Rights—Where any Bill is introduced into the House of Representatives, the Attorney-General shall, —

    (a) In the case of a Government Bill, on the introduction of that Bill; or

    (b) In any other case, as soon as practicable after the introduction of the Bill,
    —

bring to the attention of the House of Representatives any provision in the Bill that appears to be inconsistent with any of the rights and freedoms contained in this Bill of Rights.

PART II

CIVIL AND POLITICAL RIGHTS

TITLE I

Life and Security of the Person

8 Right not to be deprived of life—No one shall be deprived of life except on such grounds as are established by law and are consistent with the principles of fundamental justice.

9 Right not to be subjected to torture or cruel treatment—Everyone has the right not to be subjected to torture or to cruel, degrading, or disproportionately severe treatment or punishment.

10 Right not to be subjected to medical or scientific experimentation—Every person has the right not to be subjected to medical or scientific experimentation without that person's consent.

11 Right to refuse to undergo medical treatment—Everyone has the right to refuse to undergo medical treatment.

Democratic and Civil Rights

12 Electoral rights—Every New Zealand citizen who is of or over the age of 18 years—

(a) Has the right to vote in genuine periodic elections of members of the House of Representatives, which elections shall be by equal suffrage and by secret ballot; and

(b) Is qualified for membership of the House of Representatives.

13 Freedom of thought, conscience and religion—Everyone has the right to freedom of thought, conscience, religion, and belief, including the right to adopt and to hold opinions without interference.

14 Freedom of expression—Everyone has the right to freedom of expression, including the freedom to seek, receive, and impart information and opinions of any kind in any form.

15 Manifestation of religion and belief—Every person has the right to manifest that person's religion or belief in worship, observance, practice, or teaching, either individually or in community with others, and either in public or in private.

16 Freedom of peaceful assembly—Everyone has the right to freedom of peaceful assembly.

17 Freedom of association—Everyone has the right to freedom of association.

18 Freedom of movement—(1) Everyone lawfully in New Zealand has the right to freedom of movement and residence in New Zealand.

(2) Every New Zealand citizen has the right to enter New Zealand.

(3) Everyone has the right to leave New Zealand.

(4) No one who is not a New Zealand citizen and who is lawfully in New Zealand shall be required to leave New Zealand except under a decision taken on grounds prescribed by law.

Non-Discrimination and Minority Rights

19 Freedom from discrimination—(1) Everyone has the right to freedom from discrimination on the ground of colour, race, ethnic or national origins, sex, marital status, or religious or ethical belief.

(2) Measures taken in good faith for the purpose of assisting or advancing persons or groups of persons disadvantaged because of colour, race, ethnic or national origins, sex, marital status, or religious or ethical belief do not constitute discrimination.

20 Rights of minorities—A person who belongs to an ethnic, religious or linguistic minority in New Zealand shall not be denied the right, in community with other members of that minority, to enjoy the culture, to profess and practise the religion, or to use the language, of that minority.

Search, Arrest, and Detention

21 Unreasonable search and seizure—Everyone has the right to be secure against unreasonable search or seizure, whether of the person, property, or correspondence or otherwise.

22 Liberty of the person—Everyone has the right not to be arbitrarily arrested or detained.

23 Rights of persons arrested or detained—(1) Everyone who is arrested or who is detained under any enactment—

(a) Shall be informed at the time of the arrest or detention of the reason for it; and

(b) Shall have the right to consult and instruct a lawyer without delay and to be informed of that right; and

(c) Shall have the right to have the validity of the arrest or detention determined without delay by way of *habeas corpus* and to be released if the arrest or detention is not lawful.

(2) Everyone who is arrested for an offence has the right to be charged promptly or to be released.

(3) Everyone who is arrested for an offence and is not released shall be brought as soon as possible before a court or competent tribunal.

(4) Everyone who is—

(a) Arrested; or

(b) Detained under any enactment—

for any offence or suspected offence shall have the right to refrain from making any statement and to be informed of that right.

(5) Everyone deprived of liberty shall be treated with humanity and with respect for the inherent dignity of the person.

24 Rights of persons charged—Everyone who is charged with an offence—

(a) Shall be informed promptly and in detail of the nature and cause of the charge; and

(b) Shall be released on reasonable terms and conditions unless there is just cause for continued detention; and

(c) Shall have the right to consult and instruct a lawyer; and

(d) Shall have the right to adequate time and facilities to prepare a defence; and

(e) Shall have the right, except in the case of an offence under military law tried before a military tribunal, to the benefit of a trial by jury when the penalty for the offence is or includes imprisonment for more than 3 months; and

(f) Shall have the right to receive legal assistance without cost if the interests of justice so require and the person does not have sufficient means to provide for that assistance; and

(g) Shall have the right to have free assistance of an interpreter if the person cannot understand or speak the language used in court.

25 Minimum standards of criminal procedure—Everyone who is charged with an offence has, in relation to the determination of the charge, the following minimum rights:

(a) The right to a fair and public hearing by an independent and impartial court:

(b) The right to be tried without undue delay:

(c) The right to be presumed innocent until proved guilty according to law:

(d) The right not to be compelled to be a witness or to confess guilt:

(e) The right to be present at the trial and to present a defence:

(f) The right to examine the witnesses for the prosecution and to obtain the attendance and examination of witnesses for the defence under the same conditions as the prosecution:

(g) The right, if convicted of an offence in respect of which the penalty has been varied between the commission of the offence and sentencing, to the benefit of the lesser penalty;

(h) The right, if convicted of the offence, to appeal according to law to a higher court against the conviction or against the sentence or against both:

(i) The right, in the case of a child, to be dealt with in a manner that takes account of the child's age.

26 Retroactive penalties and double jeopardy—(1) No one shall be liable to conviction of any offence on account of any act or omission which did not constitute an offence by such person under the law of New Zealand at the time it occurred.

(2) No one who has been finally acquitted or convicted of, or pardoned for, an offence shall be tried or punished for it again.

27 Right to justice—(1) Every person has the right to the observance of the principles of natural justice by any tribunal or other public authority which has the power to make a determination in respect of that person's rights, obligations, or interests protected or recognised by law.

(2) Every person whose rights, obligations, or interests protected or recognised by law have been affected by a determination of any tribunal or other public authority has the right to apply, in accordance with law, for judicial review of that determination.

(3) Every person has the right to bring civil proceedings against, and to defend civil proceedings brought by, the Crown, and to have those proceedings heard, according to law, in the same way as civil proceedings between individuals.

PART III

MISCELLANEOUS PROVISIONS

28 Other rights and freedoms not affected—An existing right or freedom shall not be held to be abrogated or restricted by reason only that the right or freedom is not included in this Bill of Rights or is included only in part.

29 Application to legal persons—Except where the provisions of this Bill of Rights otherwise provide, the provisions of this Bill of rights apply, so far as practicable, for the benefit of all legal persons as well as for the benefit of all natural persons.

This Act is administered in the Department of Justice

[New Zealand Bill of Rights Act 1990, No. 109
s 19—Subs 1993 No 82, s 145 and Second Schedule. (On 1 February 1994)
The new section provides:

"**19 Freedom from discrimination**—(1) Everyone has the right to freedom from discrimination on the grounds of discrimination in the Human Rights Act 1993.
(2) Measures taken in good faith for the purpose of assisting or advancing persons or groups of persons disadvantaged because of discrimination that is unlawful by virtue of Part II of the Human Rights Act 1993 do not constitute discrimination."]

Appendix H

South African Constitution 1996

Chapter 2

Bill of Rights

Index of Sections

Rights

7 (1) This Bill of Rights is a cornerstone of democracy in South Africa. It enshrines the rights of all people in our country and affirms the democratic values of human dignity, equality and freedom.

(2) The state must respect, protect, promote and fulfil the rights in the Bill of Rights.

(3) The rights in the Bill of Rights are subject to the limitations contained or referred to in section 36, or elsewhere in the Bill.

Application

8 (1) The Bill of Rights applies to all law, and binds the legislature, the executive, the judiciary and all organs of state.

(2) A provision of the Bill of Rights binds a natural or a juristic person if, and to the extent that, it is applicable, taking into account the nature of the right and the nature of any duty imposed by the right.

(3) When applying a provision of the Bill of Rights to a natural or juristic person in terms of subsection (2), a court

    a. in order to give effect to a right in the Bill, must apply, or if necessary develop, the common law to the extent that legislation does not give effect to that right; and

    b. may develop rules of the common law to limit the right, provided that the limitation is in accordance with section 36(1).

(4) A juristic person is entitled to the rights in the Bill of Rights to the extent required by the nature of the rights and the nature of that juristic person.

Equality

9 (1) Everyone is equal before the law and has the right to equal protection and benefit of the law.

(2) Equality includes the full and equal enjoyment of all rights and freedoms. To promote the achievement of equality, legislative and other measures designed to protect or advance persons, or categories of persons, disadvantaged by unfair discrimination may be taken.

(3) The state may not unfairly discriminate directly or indirectly against anyone on one or more grounds, including race, gender, sex, pregnancy, marital status, ethnic or social origin, colour, sexual orientation, age, disability, religion, conscience, belief, culture, language and birth.

(4) No person may unfairly discriminate directly or indirectly against anyone on one or more grounds in terms of subsection (3). National legislation must be enacted to prevent or prohibit unfair discrimination.

(5) Discrimination on one or more of the grounds listed in subsection (3) is unfair unless it is established that the discrimination is fair.

Human dignity

10 Everyone has inherent dignity and the right to have their dignity respected and protected.

Life

11 Everyone has the right to life.

Freedom and security of the person

12 (1) Everyone has the right to freedom and security of the person, which includes the right

    a. not to be deprived of freedom arbitrarily or without just cause;

    b. not to be detained without trial;

    c. to be free from all forms of violence from either public or private sources;

    d. not to be tortured in any way; and

    e. not to be treated or punished in a cruel, inhuman or degrading way.

(2) Everyone has the right to bodily and psychological integrity, which includes the right

    a. to make decisions concerning reproduction;

    b. to security in and control over their body; and

    c. not to be subjected to medical or scientific experiments without their informed consent.

Slavery, servitude and forced labour

13 No one may be subjected to slavery, servitude or forced labour.

Privacy

14 Everyone has the right to privacy, which includes the right not to have

    a. their person or home searched;
    b. their property searched;
    c. their possessions seized; or
    d. the privacy of their communications infringed.

Freedom of religion, belief and opinion

15 (1) Everyone has the right to freedom of conscience, religion, thought, belief and opinion.

(2) Religious observances may be conducted at state or state-aided institutions, provided that

    a. those observances follow rules made by the appropriate public author-
       ities;
    b. they are conducted on an equitable basis; and
    c. attendance at them is free and voluntary.

(3) a. This Section does not prevent legislation recognising
       i. marriages concluded under any tradition, or a system of religious, personal or family law; or
       ii. systems of personal and family law under any tradition, or adhered to by persons professing a particular religion.
     b. Recognition in terms of paragraph (a) must be consistent with this sec-
       tion and the other provisions of the Constitution.

Freedom of expression

16 (1) Everyone has the right to freedom of expression, which includes

    a. freedom of the press and other media;
    b. freedom to receive or impart information or ideas;
    c. freedom of artistic creativity; and
    d. academic freedom and freedom of scientific research.

(2) The right in subsection (1) does not extend to

    a. propaganda for war;
    b. incitement of imminent violence; or
    c. advocacy of hatred that is based on race, ethnicity, gender or religion, and that constitutes incitement to cause harm.

Assembly, demonstration, picket and petition

17 Everyone has the right, peacefully and unarmed, to assemble, to demonstrate, to picket and to present petitions.

Freedom of association

18 Everyone has the right to freedom of association.

Political rights

19 (1) Every citizen is free to make political choices, which includes the right

    a. to form a political party;
    b. to participate in the activities of, or recruit members for, a political party; and
    c. to campaign for a political party or cause.

(2) Every citizen has the right to free, fair and regular elections for any legislative body established in terms of the Constitution.

(3) Every adult citizen has the right

    a. to vote in elections for any legislative body established in terms of the Constitution, and to do so in secret; and
    b. to stand for public office and, if elected, to hold office.

Citizenship

20 No citizen may be deprived of citizenship.

Freedom of movement and residence

21 (1) Everyone has the right to freedom of movement.
(2) Everyone has the right to leave the Republic.
(3) Every citizen has the right to enter, to remain in and to reside anywhere in, the Republic.
(4) Every citizen has the right to a passport.

Freedom of trade, occupation and profession

22 Every citizen has the right to choose their trade, occupation or profession freely. The practice of a trade, occupation or profession may be regulated by law.

Labour relations

23 (1) Everyone has the right to fair labour practices.
(2) Every worker has the right

    a. to form and join a trade union;
    b. to participate in the activities and programmes of a trade union; and
    c. to strike.

(3) Every employer has the right

    a. to form and join an employers' organisation; and
    b. to participate in the activities and programmes of an employer's organisation.

(4) Every trade union and every employers' organisation has the right

    a. to determine its own administration, programmes and activities;
    b. to organise; and
    c. to form and join a federation.

(5) Every trade union, employers' organisation and employer has the right to engage in collective bargaining. National legislation may be enacted to regulate collective bargaining. To the extent that the legislation may limit a right in this Chapter, the limitation must comply with section 36(1).
(6) National legislation may recognise union security arrangements contained in collective agreements. To the extent that the legislation may limit a right in this Chapter, the limitation must comply with section 36(1).

Environment

24 Everyone has the right

    a. to an environment that is not harmful to their health or well-being; and
    b. to have the environment protected, for the benefit of present and future generations, through reasonable legislative and other measures that
        i. prevent pollution and ecological degradation;
        ii. promote conservation; and
        iii. secure ecologically sustainable development and use of natural resources while promoting justifiable economic and social development.

Property

25 (1) No one may be deprived of property except in terms of law of general application, and no law may permit arbitrary deprivation of property.

(2) Property may be expropriated only in terms of law of general application

a. for a public purpose or in the public interest; and
b. subject to compensation, the amount of which and the time and manner of payment of which have either been agreed to by those affected or decided or approved by a court.

(3) The amount of the compensation and the time and manner of payment must be just and equitable, reflecting an equitable balance between the public interest and the interests of those affected, having regard to all relevant circumstances, including

a. the current use of the property;
b. the history of the acquisition and use of the property;
c. the market value of the property;
d. the extent of direct state investment and subsidy in the acquisition and beneficial capital improvement of the property; and
e. the purpose of the expropriation.

(4) For the purposes of this section

a. the public interest includes the nation's commitment to land reform, and to reforms to bring about equitable access to all South Africa's natural resources; and
b. property is not limited to land.

(5) The state must take reasonable legislative and other measures, within its available resources, to foster conditions which enable citizens to gain access to land on an equitable basis.

(6) A person or community whose tenure of land is legally insecure as a result of past racially discriminatory laws or practices is entitled, to the extent provided by an Act of Parliament, either to tenure which is legally secure or to comparable redress.

(7) A person or community dispossessed of property after 19 June 1913 as a result of past racially discriminatory laws or practices is entitled, to the extent provided by an Act of Parliament, either to restitution of that property or to equitable redress.

(8) No provision of this section may impede the state from taking legislative and other measures to achieve land, water and related reform, in order to redress the results of past racial discrimination, provided that any departure from the provisions of this section is in accordance with the provisions of section 36(1).

(9) Parliament must enact the legislation referred to in subsection (6).

Housing

26 (1) Everyone has the right to have access to adequate housing.

(2) The state must take reasonable legislative and other measures, within its available resources, to achieve the progressive realisation of this right.

(3) No one may be evicted from their home, or have their home demolished, without an order of court made after considering all the relevant circumstances. No legislation may permit arbitrary evictions.

Health care, food, water and social security

27 (1) Everyone has the right to have access to

a. health care services, including reproductive health care;
b. sufficient food and water; and

   c. social security, including, if they are unable to support themselves and their dependants, appropriate social assistance.

(2) The state must take reasonable legislative and other measures, within its available resources, to achieve the progressive realisation of each of these rights.

(3) No one may be refused emergency medical treatment.

Children

28 (1) Every child has the right

   a. to a name and a nationality from birth;
   b. to family care or parental care, or to appropriate alternative care when removed from the family environment;
   c. to basic nutrition, shelter, basic health care services and social services;
   d. to be protected from maltreatment, neglect, abuse or degradation;
   e. to be protected from exploitative labour practices;
   f. not to be required or permitted to perform work or provide services that
      i. are inappropriate for a person of that child's age; or
     ii. place at risk the child's well-being, education, physical or mental health or spiritual, moral or social development;
   g. not to be detained except as a measure of last resort, in which case, in addition to the rights a child enjoys under sections 12 and 35, the child may be detained only for the shortest appropriate period of time, and has the right to be
      i. kept separately from detained persons over the age of 18 years; and
     ii. treated in a manner, and kept in conditions, that take account of the child's age;
   h. to have a legal practitioner assigned to the child by the state, and at state expense, in civil proceedings affecting the child, if substantial injustice would otherwise result; and
   i. not to be used directly in armed conflict, and to be protected in times of armed conflict.

(2) A child's best interests are of paramount importance in every matter concerning the child.

(3) In this section "child" means a person under the age of 18 years.

Education

29 (1) Everyone has the right

   a. to a basic education, including adult basic education; and
   b. to further education, which the state, through reasonable measures, must make progressively available and accessible.

(2) Everyone has the right to receive education in the official language or languages of their choice in public educational institutions where that education is reasonably practicable. In order to ensure the effective access to, and implementation of, this right, the state must consider all reasonable educational alternatives, including single medium institutions, taking into account

   a. equity;
   b. practicability; and
   c. the need to redress the results of past racially discriminatory laws and practices.

(3) Everyone has the right to establish and maintain, at their own expense, independent educational institutions that

   a. do not discriminate on the basis of race;

b. are registered with the state; and
c. maintain standards that are not inferior to standards at comparable public educational institutions.

(4) Subsection (3) does not preclude state subsidies for independent educational institutions.

Language and culture

30 Everyone has the right to use the language and to participate in the cultural life of their choice, but no one exercising these rights may do so in a manner inconsistent with any provision of the Bill of Rights.

Cultural, religious and linguistic communities

31 (1) Persons belonging to a cultural, religious or linguistic community may not be denied the right, with other members of that community

a. to enjoy their culture, practise their religion and use their language; and
b. to form, join and maintain cultural, religious and linguistic associations and other organs of civil society.

(2) The rights in subsection (1) may not be exercised in a manner inconsistent with any provision of the Bill of Rights.

Access to information

32 (1) Everyone has the right of access to

a. any information held by the state; and
b. any information that is held by another person and that is required for the exercise or protection of any rights.

(2) National legislation must be enacted to give effect to this right, and may provide for reasonable measures to alleviate the administrative and financial burden on the state.

Just administrative action

33 (1) Everyone has the right to administrative action that is lawful, reasonable and procedurally fair.
(2) Everyone whose rights have been adversely affected by administrative action has the right to be given written reasons.
(3) National legislation must be enacted to give effect to these rights, and must

a. provide for the review of administrative action by a court or, where appropriate, an independent and impartial tribunal;
b. impose a duty on the state to give effect to the rights in subsections (1) and (2); and
c. promote an efficient administration.

Access to courts

34 Everyone has the right to have any dispute that can be resolved by the application of law decided in a fair public hearing before a court or, where appropriate, another independent and impartial tribunal or forum.

Arrested, detained and accused persons

35 (1) Everyone who is arrested for allegedly committing an offence has the right

a. to remain silent;

    b. to be informed promptly
       i. of the right to remain silent; and
      ii. of the consequences of not remaining silent;
    c. not to be compelled to make any confession or admission that could be used in evidence against that person;
    d. to be brought before a court as soon as reasonably possible, but not later than
       i. 48 hours after the arrest; or
      ii. the end of the first court day after the expiry of the 48 hours, if the 48 hours expire outside ordinary court hours or on a day which is not an ordinary court day;
    e. at the first court appearance after being arrested, to be charged or to be informed of the reason for the detention to continue, or to be released; and
    f. to be released from detention if the interests of justice permit, subject to reasonable conditions.

(2) Everyone who is detained, including every sentenced prisoner, has the right

    a. to be informed promptly of the reason for being detained;
    b. to choose, and to consult with, a legal practitioner, and to be informed of this right promptly;
    c. to have a legal practitioner assigned to the detained person by the state and at state expense, if substantial injustice would otherwise result, and to be informed of this right promptly;
    d. to challenge the lawfulness of the detention in person before a court and, if the detention is unlawful, to be released;
    e. to conditions of detention that are consistent with human dignity, including at least exercise and the provision, at state expense, of adequate accommodation, nutrition, reading material and medical treatment; and
    f. to communicate with, and be visited by, that person's
       i. spouse or partner;
      ii. next of kin;
      iv. chosen religious counsellor; and
      v. chosen medical practitioner.

(3) Every accused person has a right to a fair trial, which includes the right

    a. to be informed of the charge with sufficient detail to answer it;
    b. to have adequate time and facilities to prepare a defence;
    c. to a public trial before an ordinary court;
    d. to have their trial begin and conclude without unreasonable delay;
    e. to be present when being tried;
    f. to choose, and be represented by, a legal practitioner, and to be informed of this right promptly;
    g. to have a legal practitioner assigned to the accused person by the state and at state expense, if substantial injustice would otherwise result, and to be informed of this right promptly;
    h. to be presumed innocent, to remain silent, and not to testify during the proceedings;
    i. to adduce and challenge evidence;
    j. not to be compelled to give self-incriminating evidence;
    k. to be tried in a language that the accused person understands or, if that is not practicable, to have the proceedings interpreted in that language;
    l. not to be convicted for an act or omission that was not an offence under either national or international law at the time it was committed or omitted;
    m. not to be tried for an offence in respect of an act or omission for which that person has previously been either acquitted or convicted;

n. to the benefit of the least severe of the prescribed punishments if the prescribed punishment for the offence has been changed between the time that the offence was committed and the time of sentencing; and

o. of appeal to, or review by, a higher court.

(4) Whenever this section requires information to be given to a person, that information must be given in a language that the person understands.

(5) Evidence obtained in a manner that violates any right in the Bill of Rights must be excluded if the admission of that evidence would render the trial unfair or otherwise be detrimental to the administration of justice.

Limitation of rights

36 (1) The rights in the Bill of Rights may be limited only in terms of law of general application to the extent that the limitation is reasonable and justifiable in an open and democratic society based on human dignity, equality and freedom, taking into account all relevant factors, including

a. the nature of the right;

b. the importance of the purpose of the limitation;

c. the nature and extent of the limitation;

d. the relation between the limitation and its purpose; and

e. less restrictive means to achieve the purpose.

(2) Except as provided in subsection (1) or in any other provision of the Constitution, no law may limit any right entrenched in the Bill of rights.

States of emergency

37 (1) A state of emergency may be declared only in terms of an Act of Parliament, and only when

a. the life of the nation is threatened by war, invasion, general insurrection, disorder, natural disaster or other public emergency; and

b. the declaration is necessary to restore peace and order.

(2) A declaration of a state of emergency, and any legislation enacted or other action taken in consequence of that declaration, may be effective only

a. prospectively; and

b. for no more than 21 days from the date of the declaration, unless the National Assembly resolves to extend the declaration. The Assembly may extend a declaration of a state of emergency for no more than three months at a time. The first extension of the state of emergency must be by a resolution adopted with a supporting vote of a majority of the members of the Assembly. Any subsequent extension must be by a resolution adopted with a supporting vote of at least 60 per cent of the members of the Assembly. A resolution in terms of this paragraph may be adopted only following a public debate in the Assembly.

(3) Any competent court may decide on the validity of

a. a declaration of a state of emergency;

b. any extension of a declaration of a state of emergency; or

c. any legislation enacted, or other action taken, in consequence of a declaration of a state of emergency.

(4) Any legislation enacted in consequence of a declaration of a state of emergency may derogate from the Bill of Rights only to the extent that

a. the derogation is strictly required by the emergency; and

b. the legislation

    i. is consistent with the Republic's obligations under international law applicable to states of emergency;

    vi. conforms to subsection (5); and

    vii. is published in the national Government Gazette as soon as reasonably possible after being enacted.

(5) No Act of Parliament that authorises a declaration of a state of emergency, and no legislation enacted or other action taken in consequence of a declaration, may permit or authorise

    a. indemnifying from the state, or any person, in respect of any unlawful act;

    b. any derogation from this section; or

    c. any derogation from a section mentioned in column 1 of the Table of Non-Derogable Rights, to the extent indicated opposite that section in column 3 of the Table.

Table of Non-Derogable Rights

1 Section Number	2 Section Title	3 Extent to which the right is protected
9	Equality	With respect to *unfair discrimination solely on the grounds of* race, *colour, ethnic or social origin*, sex, religion or language
10	Human Dignity	Entirely
11	Life	Entirely
12	Freedom and Security of the person	With respect to subsections (1)(d) and (e) and (2)(c).
13	Slavery, servitude and forced labour	With respect to slavery and servitude.
28	Children	With respect to: • subsection (1)(d) and (e): • the rights in subparagraphs (i) and (ii) *of subsection (1)(g); and* • *subsection 1(i) in respect of children of 15 years and younger*
35	Arrested, detained and accused persons	With respect to: • subsections (1)(a), (b) and (c) and (2)(d): • *the rights in paragraphs (a) to (o) of subsection (3), excluding paragraph (d);* • *subsection (4); and* • *subsection (5) with respect to the exclusion of evidence if the admission of that evidence would render the trial unfair.*

(6) Whenever anyone is detained without trial in consequence of a derogation of rights resulting from a declaration of a state of emergency, the following conditions must be observed:

    a. An adult family member or friend of the detainee must be contacted as soon as reasonably possible, and informed that the person has been detained.

    b. A notice must be published in the national Government Gazette within five days of the person being detained, stating the detainee's name and place of detention and referring to the emergency measure in terms of which that person has been detained.

c. The detainee must be allowed to choose, and be visited at any reasonable time by, a medical practitioner.

d. The detainee must be allowed to choose, and be visited at any reasonable time by, a legal representative.

e. A court must review the detention as soon as reasonably possible, but no later than 10 days after the date the person was detained, and the court must release the detainee unless it is necessary to continue the detention to restore peace and order.

f. A detainee who is not released in terms of a review under paragraph (e), or who is not released in terms of a review under this paragraph, may apply to a court for a further review of the detention at any time after 10 days have passed since the previous review, and the court must release the detainee unless it is still necessary to continue the detention to restore peace and order.

g. The detainee must be allowed to appear in person before any court considering the detention, to be represented by a legal practitioner at those hearings, and to make representations against continued detention.

h. The state must present written reasons to the court to justify the continued detention of the detainee, and must give a copy of those reasons to the detainee at least two days before the court reviews the detention.

(7) If a court releases a detainee, that person may not be detained again on the same grounds unless the state first shows a court good cause for re-detaining that person.

(8) Subsections (6) and (7) do not apply to persons who are not South African citizens and who are detained in consequence of an international armed conflict. Instead, the state must comply with the standards binding on the Republic under international humanitarian law in respect of the detention of such persons.

Enforcement of rights

38 Anyone listed in this section has the right to approach a competent court, alleging that a right in the Bill of Rights has been infringed or threatened, and the court may grant appropriate relief, including a declaration of rights. The persons who may approach a court are—

a. anyone acting in their own interest;

b. anyone acting on behalf of another person who cannot act in their own name;

c. anyone acting as a member of, or in the interest of, a group or class of persons;

d. anyone acting in the public interest; and

e. an association acting in the interest of its members.

Interpretation of Bill of Rights

39 (1) When interpreting the Bill of Rights, a court, tribunal or forum

a. must promote the values that underlie an open and democratic society based on human dignity, equality and freedom;

b. must consider international law; and

c. may consider foreign law.

(2) When interpreting any legislation, and when developing the common law or customary law, every court, tribunal or forum must promote the spirit, purport and objects of the Bill of Rights.

(3) The Bill of Rights does not deny the existence of any other rights or freedoms that are recognised or conferred by common law, customary law or legislation, to the extent that they are consistent with the Bill.

Appendix I

American Bill of Rights

First Ten Amendments passed by Congress September 25, 1789.
Ratified by three-fourths of the States December 15, 1791.

Amendment I

Congress shall make no law respecting an establishment of religion, or prohibiting the free exercise thereof; or abridging the freedom of speech, or of the press; or the right of the people peaceably to assemble, and to petition the government for a redress of grievances.

Amendment II

A well regulated militia, being necessary to the security of a free State, the right of the people to keep and bear arms, shall not be infringed.

Amendment III

No soldier shall, in time of peace be quartered in any house, without the consent of the owner, nor in time of war, but in a manner to be prescribed by law.

Amendment IV

The right of the people to be secure in their persons, houses, papers, and effects, against unreasonable searches and seizures, shall not be violated, and no warrants shall issue, but upon probable cause, supported by oath or affirmation, and particularly describing the place to be searched, and the persons or things to be seized.

Amendment V

No person shall be held to answer for a capital, or otherwise infamous crime, unless on a presentment or indictment of a grand jury, except in cases arising in the land or naval forces, or in the militia, when in actual service in time of war or public danger; nor shall any person be subject for the same offense to be twice put in jeopardy of life or limb; nor shall be compelled in any criminal case to be a witness against himself, nor be deprived of life, liberty, or property, without due process of law; nor shall private property be taken for public use without just compensation.

AMENDMENT VI

In all criminal prosecutions, the accused shall enjoy the right to a speedy and public trial, by an impartial jury of the State and district wherein the crime shall have been committed, which district shall have been previously ascertained by law, and to be informed of the nature and cause of the accusation; to be confronted with the witnesses against him; to have compulsory process for obtaining witnesses in his favour, and to have the assistance of counsel for his defense.

AMENDMENT VII

In suits at common law, where the value in controversy shall exceed twenty dollars, the right of trial by jury shall be preserved, and no fact tried by a jury shall be otherwise reexamined in any court of the United States, than according to the rules of the common law.

AMENDMENT VIII

Excessive bail shall not be required, nor excessive fines imposed, nor cruel and unusual punishments inflicted.

AMENDMENT IX

The enumeration in the Constitution of certain rights shall not be construed to deny or disparage others retained by the people.

AMENDMENT X

The powers not delegated to the United States by the Constitution, nor prohibited by it to the States, are reserved to the States respectively, or to the people.

AMENDMENT XIII

Passed by Congress January 31, 1865. Ratified December 6, 1865.

SECTION 1. Neither slavery nor involuntary servitude, except as punishment for crime whereof the party shall have been duly convicted, shall exist within the United States, or any place subject to their jurisdiction.
SECTION 2. Congress shall have power to enforce this article by appropriate legislation.

AMENDMENT XIV

Passed by Congress June 13, 1866. Ratified July 9, 1868.

SECTION 1. All persons born or naturalized in the United States, and subject to the jurisdiction thereof, are citizens of the United States and of the State wherein they reside. No State shall make or enforce any law which shall abridge the privileges or immunities of citizens of the United States; nor shall any State deprive any person of life, liberty, or property, without due process of law; nor deny to any person within its jurisdiction the equal protection of the laws . . .

SECTION 5. The Congress shall have power to enforce, by appropriate legislation, the provisions of this article.

AMENDMENT XV

Passed by Congress February 26, 1869. Ratified February 3, 1870.

SECTION 1. The right of citizens of the United States to vote shall not be denied or abridged by the United States or by any State on account of race, colour, or previous condition of servitude.

SECTION 2. The Congress shall have power to enforce this article by appropriate legislation.

AMENDMENT XIX

Passed by Congress June 4, 1919. Ratified August 18, 1920.

The right of citizens of the United States to vote shall not be denied or abridged by the United States or by any State on account of sex.

The Congress shall have power by appropriate legislation to enforce the provisions of this article.

AMENDMENT XXIV

Passed by Congress August 27, 1962. Ratified January 23, 1964.

SECTION 1. The right of citizens of the United States to vote in any primary or other election for President or Vice President, for electors for President or Vice President, or for Senator or Representative in Congress, shall not be denied or abridged by the United States or any State by reason of failure to pay any poll tax or other tax.

SECTION 2. The Congress shall have the power to enforce this article by appropriate legislation.

AMENDMENT XXVI

Passed by Congress March 23, 1971. Ratified June 30, 1971.

SECTION 1. The right of citizens of the United States, who are eighteen years of age or older, to vote shall not be denied or abridged by the United States or any State on account of age.

SECTION 2. The Congress shall have the power to enforce this article by appropriate legislation.

APPENDIX J

Hong Kong Bill of Rights Ordinance 1991

HONG KONG

ORDINANCE No. 59 OF 1991

I assent
(L.S.)
David WILSON,
Governor.
6 June 1991

An Ordinance to provide for the incorporation into law of Hong Kong of provisions
of the International Covenant on Civil and Political Rights as applied to Hong Kong;
and for ancillary and connected matters.

[8 June 1991]

Enacted by the Governor of Hong Kong, with the advice and consent of the Legislative Council thereof.

CONTENTS

PART I—PRELIMINARY

PART II—THE HONG KONG BILL OF RIGHTS

Article 18 Freedom of association
Article 19 Rights in respect of marriage and family
Article 20 Rights of children
Article 21 Right to participate in public life
Article 22 Equality before and equal protection of law
Article 23 Rights of minorities

PART III—EXCEPTIONS AND SAVINGS

PART I

PRELIMINARY

1. Short title and commencement

   i. This Ordinance may be cited as the Hong Kong Bill of Rights Ordinance 1991.

   ii. This Ordinance shall come into operation on 8 June 1991.

2. Interpretation

   i. In this Ordinance, unless the context otherwise requires –

   "*article*" means an article of the Bill of Rights;
   "*Bill of Rights*" means the Hong Kong Bill of Rights set out in Part II;
   "*commencement date*" means the date on which this Ordinance comes into operation;
   "*legislation*" means legislation that can be amended by an Ordinance;
   "*pre-existing legislation*" means legislation enacted before the commencement date.

   ii. The Bill of Rights is subject to Part III.

   iii. In interpreting and applying this Ordinance, regard shall be had to the fact that the purpose of this Ordinance is to provide for the incorporation into the law of Hong Kong of provisions of the International Covenant on Civil and Political Rights as applied to Hong Kong, and for ancillary and connected matters.

   iv. Nothing in this Ordinance shall be interpreted as implying for the Government or any authority, group or person any right to engage in any activity or perform any act aimed at the destruction of any of the rights and freedoms recognized in the Bill of Rights or at their limitation to a greater extent than is provided for in the Bill. [cf. ICCPR Art. 5.1]

   v. There shall be no restriction upon or derogation from any of the fundamental human rights recognized or existing in Hong Kong pursuant to law, conventions, regulations or custom on the pretext that the Bill of Rights does not recognize such rights or that it recognizes them to a lesser extent. [cf. ICCPR Art. 5.2]

   vi. A heading to any article does not have any legislative effect and does not in any way vary, limit or extend the meaning of the article.

3. Effect on pre-existing legislation

   i. All pre-existing legislation that admits of a construction consistent with this Ordinance shall be given such a construction.

   ii. All pre-existing legislation that does not admit of a construction consistent with this Ordinance is, to the extent of the inconsistency, repealed.

4. Interpretation of subsequent legislation

All legislation enacted on or after the commencement date shall, to the extent that it admits of such a construction, be constructed so as to be consistent with the International Covenant on Civil and Political Rights as applied to Hong Kong.

5. Public emergencies

i. In time of public emergency which threatens the life of the nation and the existence of which is officially proclaimed, measures may be taken derogating from the Bill of Rights to the extent strictly required by the exigencies of the situation, but these measures shall be taken in accordance with law.

ii. No measure shall be taken under subsection (1) that—

a. is inconsistent with any obligation under international law that applies to Hong Kong (other than an obligation under the International Covenant on Civil and Political Rights);

b. involves discrimination solely on the ground of race, colour, sex, language, religion or social origin; or

c. derogates from article 2, 3, 4(1) and (2), 7, 12, 13 and 15. [cf. ICCPR Art. 4]

6. Remedies for contravention of Bill of Rights

i. A court or tribunal—

a. in proceeding within its jurisdiction in an action for breach of this Ordinance; and

b. in other proceedings within its jurisdiction in which a violation or threatened violation of the Bill of Rights is relevant,

may grant such remedy or relief, or make such order, in respect of such a breach, violation or threatened violation as it has power to grant or make in those proceedings and as it considers appropriate and just in the circumstances.

ii. No proceedings shall be held to be outside the jurisdiction of any court or tribunal on the ground that they relate to the Bill of Rights.

7. Binding effect of Ordinance

i. This Ordinance binds only—

a. the Government and all public authorities; and

b. any person acting on behalf of the Government or a

c. public authority.

ii. In this section— "*person*" includes any body of persons, corporate or unincorporate.

Part II

The Hong Kong Bill of Rights

8. Hong Kong Bill of Rights

The Hong Kong Bill of Rights is as follows.

Article 1
Entitlement to rights without distinction

i. The rights recognized in this Bill of Rights shall be enjoyed without distinction of any kind, such as race, colour, sex, language, religion, political or other opinion, national or social origin, property, birth or other status.
ii. Men and women shall have an equal right to the enjoyment of all civil and political rights set forth in this Bill of Rights.
[cf. ICCPR Arts. 2 & 3]

Article 2
Right to life

i. Every human being has the inherent right to life. This right shall be protected by law. No one shall be arbitrarily deprived of his life.
ii. Sentence of death may be imposed only for the most serious crimes in accordance with the law in force at the time of the commission of the crime and not contrary to the provisions of this Bill of Rights and to the Convention on the Prevention and Punishment of the Crime of Genocide. This penalty can only be carried out pursuant to a final judgment rendered by a competent court.
iii. When deprivation of life constitutes the crime of genocide, nothing in this article shall authorize the derogation in any way from any obligation assumed under the provisions of the Convention on the Prevention and Punishment of the Crime of Genocide.
iv. Anyone sentenced to death shall have the right to seek pardon or commutation of the sentence. Amnesty, pardon or commutation of the sentence of death may be granted in all cases.
v. Sentence of death shall not be imposed for crimes committed by persons below 18 years of age and shall not be carried out on pregnant women.
vi. Nothing in this article shall be invoked to delay or to prevent the abolition of capital punishment in Hong Kong.
[cf. ICCPR Art.6]

Article 3
No torture or inhuman treatment and
No experimentation without consent

No one shall be subject to torture or to cruel, inhuman or degrading treatment or punishment. In particular, no one shall be subjected without his free consent to medical or scientific experimentation.
[cf. ICCPR Art. 7]

Article 4
No slavery or servitude

i. No one shall be held in slavery; slavery and the slave-trade in all their forms shall be prohibited.
ii. No one shall be held in servitude.
iii. a. no one shall be required to perform forced or compulsory labour.
    b. For the purpose of this paragraph the term "forced or compulsory labour" shall not include—
        1. any work or service normally required of a person who is under detention in consequence of a lawful order of a court, or of a person during conditional release from such detention;

2. any service of a military character and, where conscientious objection is recognized, any national service required by law of conscientious objectors;
3. any service exacted in cases of emergency or calamity threatening the life or well-being of the community;
4. any work or service which forms part of normal civil obligations.

[cf. ICCPR Art. 8]

Article 5
Liberty and security of person

i. Everyone has the right to liberty and security of person. No one shall be subjected to arbitrary arrest or detention. No one shall be deprived of his liberty except on such grounds and in accordance with such procedure as are established by law.
ii. Anyone who is arrested shall be informed, at the time of arrest, of the reasons for his arrest and shall be promptly informed of any charges against him.
iii. Anyone arrested or detained on a criminal charge shall be brought promptly before a judge or other officer authorized by law to exercise judicial power and shall be entitled to trial within a reasonable time or to release. It shall not be the general rule that persons awaiting trial shall be detained in custody, but release may be subject to guarantees to appear for trial, at any other stage of the judicial proceedings, and, should occasion arise, for execution of the judgment.
iv. Anyone who is deprived of his liberty by arrest or detention shall be entitled to take proceedings before a court, in order that that court may decide without delay on the lawfulness of his detention and order his release if the detention is not lawful.
v. Anyone who has been the victim of unlawful arrest or detention shall have an enforceable right to compensation.

[cf. ICCPR Art. 9]

Article 6
Rights of persons deprived of their liberty

i. All persons deprived of their liberty shall be treated with humanity and with respect for the inherent dignity of the human person.
ii. a. Accused persons shall, save in exceptional circumstances, be segregated from convicted persons and shall be subject to separate treatment appropriate to their status as unconvicted persons.
b. Accused juvenile persons shall be separated from adults
c. and brought as speedily as possible for adjudication.
iii. The penitentiary system shall comprise treatment of prisoners the essential aim of which shall be their reformation and social rehabilitation. Juvenile offenders shall be segregated from adults and be accorded treatment appropriate to their age and legal status.

[cf. ICCPR Art. 10]

Article 7
No imprisonment for breach of contract

No one shall be imprisoned merely on the ground of inability to fulfil a contractual obligation.

[cf. ICCPR Art. 11]

Article 8
Liberty of movement

i. Everyone lawfully within Hong Kong shall, within Hong Kong, have the right to liberty of movement and freedom to choose his residence.
ii. Everyone shall be free to leave Hong Kong.
iii. The above-mentioned rights shall not be subject to any restrictions except those which are provided by law, are necessary to protect national security, public order (ordre public), public health or morals or the rights and freedoms of others, and are consistent with the other rights recognized in this Bill of Rights.
iv. No one who has the right of abode in Hong Kong shall be arbitrarily deprived of the right to enter Hong Kong.
[cf. ICCPR Art. 12]

Article 9
Restriction on expulsion from Hong Kong

A person who does not have the right of abode in Hong Kong but who is lawfully in Hong Kong may be expelled therefrom only in pursuance of a decision reached in accordance with law and shall, except where compelling reasons of national security otherwise require, be allowed to submit the reasons against his expulsion and to have his case reviewed by, and be represented for the purpose before, the competent authority or a person or persons especially designated by the competent authority.
[cf. ICCPR Art. 13]

Article 10
Equality before courts and right to fair and public hearing

All persons shall be equal before the courts and tribunals. In the determination of any criminal charge against him, or of his rights and obligations in a suit at law, everyone shall be entitled to a fair and public hearing by a competent, independent and impartial tribunal established by law. The press and the public may be excluded from all or part of a trial for reasons of morals, public order (ordre public) or national security in a democratic society, or when the interest of the private lives of the parties so requires, or to the extent strictly necessary in the opinion of the court in special circumstances where publicity would prejudice the interests of justice, but any judgment rendered in a criminal case or in a suit at law shall be made public except where the interest of juvenile persons otherwise requires or the proceedings concern matrimonial disputes or the guardianship of children.
[cf. ICCPR Art. 14]

Article 11
Rights of persons charged with or convicted of criminal offence

i. Everyone charged with a criminal offence shall have the right to be presumed innocent until proved guilty according to law.
ii. In the determination of any criminal charge against him, everyone shall be entitled to the following minimum guarantees, in full equality—

a. to be informed promptly and in detail in a language which he understands of the nature and cause of the charge against him;
b. to have adequate time and facilities for the preparation of his defence and to communicate with counsel of his own choosing;
c. to be tried without undue delay;
d. to be tried in his presence, and to defend himself in person or through legal assistance of his own choosing; to be informed, if he does not have legal assistance, of this right; and to have legal assistance assigned to him, in any case where the interests of justice so require, and without payment by him in any such case if he does not have sufficient means to pay for it;
e. to examine, or have examined, the witnesses against him and to obtain the attendance and examination of witnesses on his behalf under the same conditions as witnesses against him;
f. to have the free assistance of an interpreter if he cannot understand or speak the language used in court;
g. not to be compelled to testify against himself or to confess guilt.
iii. In the case of juvenile persons, the procedure shall be such as will take account of their age and the desirability of promoting their rehabilitation.
iv. Everyone convicted of a crime shall have the right to his conviction and sentence being reviewed by a higher tribunal according to law.
v. When a person has by a final decision been convicted of a criminal offence and when subsequently his conviction has been reversed or he has been pardoned on the ground that a new or newly discovered fact shows con-clusively that there has been miscarriage of justice, the person who has suffered punishment as a result of such conviction shall be compensated according to law, unless it is proved that the non-disclosure of the unknown fact in time is wholly or partly attributable to him.
vi. No one shall be liable to be tried or punished again for an offence for which he already been finally convicted or acquitted in accordance with the law and penal procedure of Hong Kong.
[cf. ICCPR Art. 14.2 to 7]

Article 12
No retrospective criminal offences or penalties

i. No one shall be held guilty of any criminal offence on account of any act or omission which did not constitute a criminal offence, under Hong Kong or international law, at the time when it was committed. Nor shall a heavier penalty be imposed than the one that was applicable at the time when the criminal offence was committed. If, subsequent to the commission of the offence, provision is made by law for the imposition of a lighter penalty, the offender shall benefit thereby.
ii. Nothing in this article shall prejudice the trial and punishment of any person for any act or omission which, at the time when it was committed, was criminal according to the general principles of law recognized by the commu-nity of nations.
[cf. ICCPR Art. 15]

Article 13
Right to recognition as person before law

Everyone shall have the right to recognition everywhere as a person before the law.
[cf. ICCPR Art. 16]

Article 14
Protection of privacy, family, home, Correspondence, honour and reputation

i. No one shall be subjected to arbitrary or unlawful interference with his privacy.
v. Everyone has the right to protection of the law against such interference or attacks.
[cf. ICCPR Art. 17]

Article 15
Freedom of thought, conscience and religion

i. Everyone shall have the right to freedom of thought, conscience and religion. This right shall include freedom to have or to adopt a religion or belief of his choice, and freedom, either individually or in community with others and in public or private, to manifest his religion or belief in worship, observance, practice and teaching.
ii. No one shall be subject to coercion which would impair his freedom to have or to adopt a religion or belief of his choice.
iii. Freedom to manifest one's religion or beliefs may be subject only to such limitations as are prescribed by law and are necessary to protect public safety, order, health, or morals or the fundamental rights and freedoms of others.
iv. The liberty of parents and, when applicable, legal guardians to ensure the religious and moral education of their children in conformity with their own convictions shall be respected.
[cf. ICCPR Art. 18]

Article 16
Freedom of opinion and expression

i. Everyone shall have the right to hold opinions without interference.
ii. Everyone shall have the right to freedom of expression; this right shall include freedom to seek, receive and impart information and ideas of all kinds, regardless of frontiers, either orally, in writing or in print, in the form of art, or through any other media of his choice.
iii. The exercise of the rights provided for in paragraph (2) of this article carries with it special duties and responsibilities. It may therefore be subject to certain restrictions, but these shall only be such as are provided by law and are necessary—
    a. for respect of the rights or reputations of others;
    b. for the protection of national security or of public order (ordre public), or of public health or morals.
[cf. ICCPR Art. 19]

Article 17
Right of peaceful assembly

The right of peaceful assembly shall be recognized. No restrictions may be placed on the exercise of this right other than those imposed in conformity with the law and which are necessary in a democratic society in the interests of national security or public safety, public order (ordre public), the protection of public health or morals or the protection the rights and freedoms of others. [cf. ICCPR Art. 21]

Article 18
Freedom of association

i. Everyone shall have the right to freedom of association with others, including the right to form and join trade unions for the protection of his interests.
ii. No restrictions may be placed on the exercise of this right other than those which are prescribed by law and which are necessary in such a manner as to prejudice the guarantees provided for in the International Labour Organization Convention of 1948 concerning Freedom of Association and Protection of the Right to Organize as it applies to Hong Kong.
[cf. ICCPR Art. 22]

Article 19
Rights in respect of marriage and family

i. The family is the natural and fundamental group unit of society and is entitled to protection by society and the State.
ii. The right of men and women of marriageable age to marry and to found a family shall be recognized.
iii. No marriage shall be entered into without the free and full consent of the intending spouses.
iv. Spouses shall have equal rights and responsibility as to marriage, during marriage and at its dissolution. In the case of dissolution, provision shall be made for the necessary protection of any children.
[cf. ICCPR Art.23]

Article 20
Rights of children

i. Every child shall have, without any discrimination as to race, colour, sex, language, religion, national or social origin, property or birth, the right to such measures of protection as are required by his status as a minor, on the part of his family society and the State.
ii. Every child shall be registered immediately after birth and shall have a name.
[cf. ICCPR Art. 24]

Article 21
Right to participate in public life

Every permanent resident shall have the right and the opportunity, without any of the distinctions mentioned in article 1(1) and without unreasonable restrictions—
    a. to take part in the conduct of public affairs, directly or through freely chosen representatives;
    b. to vote and to be elected at genuine periodic elections which shall be by universal and equal suffrage and shall be held by secret ballot, guaranteeing the free expression of the will of the electors;

    c. to have access, on general terms of equality, to public service in Hong Kong.
[cf. ICCPR Art. 25]

Article 22
Equality before and equal protection of law

All persons are equal before the law and are entitled without any discrimination to the equal protection of the law. In this respect, the law shall prohibit any discrimination and guarantee to all persons equal and effective protection against discrimination on any ground such as race, colour, sex, language, religion, political or other opinion, national or social origin, property, birth or other status.
[cf. ICCPR Art. 26]

Article 23
Rights of minorities

Persons belonging to ethnic, religious or linguistic minorities shall not be denied the right, in community with the other members of their group, to enjoy their own culture, to profess and practise their own religion, or to use their own language.
[cf. ICCPR Art. 27]

PART III

EXCEPTIONS AND SAVINGS

9. Armed forces and persons detained in penal establishments
Members of and persons serving with the armed forces of the government responsible for the foreign affairs of Hong Kong and persons lawfully detained in penal establishments of whatever character are subject to such restrictions as may from time to time be authorized by law for the preservation of service and custodial discipline.
10. Juveniles under detention
Where at any time there is a lack of suitable prison facilities or where the mixing of adults and juveniles is mutually beneficial, article 6(2)(b) and (3) does not require juveniles who are detained to be accommodated separately from adults.
11. Immigration legislation
As regards persons not having the right to enter and remain in Hong Kong, this Ordinance does not affect any immigration legislation governing entry into, stay in and departure from Hong Kong, or the application of any such legislation.
12. Persons not having the right of abode
Article 9 does not confer a right of review in respect of a decision to deport a person not having the right of abode in Hong Kong or a right to be represented for this purpose before the competent authority.
13. Executive and Legislative Councils
Article 21 does not require the establishment of an elected Executive or Legislative Council in Hong Kong.
14. Temporary savings
i. For a period of 1 year beginning, on the commencement date, this Ordinance is subject to the Ordinances listed in the Schedule.
ii. This Ordinance does not affect—
    a. any act done (including any act done in the exercise of a discretion); or

b. any omission authorized or required, or occurring in the exercise of a discretion,

before the first anniversary of the commencement date, under or by any Ordinance listed in the Schedule.

iii. The Legislative Council may before the first anniversary of the commencement date by resolution amend this section for all or any of the following purposes—

a. to provide that, for a period of 1 year beginning on the first anniversary of the commencement date, this Ordinance is subject to such of the Ordinances listed in the Schedule as are specified in the amendment;

b. to provide that this Ordinance does not affect—
1. any act done (including any act done in the exercise of a discretion); or
2. any omission authorized or required, or occurring in the exercise of a discretion, before the second anniversary of the commencement date, under or by any Ordinance listed in the Schedule that is specified in the amendment; and

c. to repeal this subsection.

iv. In this section, a reference to an Ordinance includes a reference to any subsidiary legislation made under that Ordinance.

v. This section operates notwithstanding section 3.

SCHEDULE

PROVISIONS TO WHICH SECTION 14(1) AND (2) APPLIES

Immigration Ordinance (Cap. 115)
Societies Ordinance (Cap. 151)
Crimes Ordinance (Cap. 200)
Prevention of Bribery Ordinance (Cap. 201)
Independent Commission Against Corruption Ordinance (Cap. 204)
Police Force Ordinance (Cap. 232)

APPENDIX K

Constitution of India

PART III

FUNDAMENTAL RIGHTS

General

Rights to Equality

Right to Freedom

Rights against Exploitation

Right to Freedom of Religion

Cultural and Educational Rights

General

12. Definition.

In this part, unless the context otherwise requires, "the State" includes the Government and Parliament of India and the Government and the Legislature of each of the States and all local or other authorities within the territory of India or under the control of the Government of India.

13. Laws inconsistent with or in derogation of the fundamental rights.

(1) All laws in force in the territory of India immediately before the commencement of this Constitution, in so far as they are inconsistent with the provisions of this Part, shall, to the extent of such inconsistency, be void.

(2) The State shall not make any law which takes away or abridges the rights conferred by this Part and any law made in contravention of this clause shall, to the extent of the contravention, be void.

(3) In this article, unless the context otherwise requires,

(a) "law" includes any Ordinance, order, bye-law, rule, regulation, notification, custom or usage having in the territory of India the force of law;

(b) "laws in force" includes laws passed or made by a Legislature or other competent authority in the territory of India before the commencement of this Constitution and not previously repealed, notwithstanding that any such law or any part thereof may not be then in operation either at all or in particular areas.

[(4) Nothing in this article shall apply to any amendment of this Constitution made under article 368.]

Right to Equality

14. Equality before law.

The State shall not deny to any person equality before the law or the equal protection of the laws within the territory of India.

15. Prohibition of discrimination on grounds of religion, race, caste, sex or place of birth.

(1) The State shall not discriminate against any citizen on grounds only of religion, race, caste, sex, place of birth or any of them.

(2) No citizen shall, on grounds only of religion, race, caste, sex, place of birth or any of them, be subject to any disability, liability, restriction or condition with regard to—

(a) access to shops, public restaurants, hotels and places of public entertainment; or

(b) the use of wells, tanks, bathing ghats, roads and places of public resort maintained wholly or partly out of State funds or dedicated to the use of the general public.

(3) Nothing in this article shall prevent the State from making any special provision for women and children.

[(4) Nothing in this article or in clause (2) of article 29 shall prevent the State from making any special provision for the advancement of any socially and educationally backward classes of citizens or for the Scheduled Castes and the Schedule Tribes.]

16. Equality of opportunity in matters of public employment.

(1) There shall be equality of opportunity for all citizens in matters relating to employment or appointment to any office under the State.

(2) No citizen shall, on grounds only of religion, race, caste, sex, descent, place of birth, residence or any of them, be ineligible for, or discriminated against in respect of, any employment or office under the State.

(3) Nothing in this article shall prevent Parliament from making any law prescribing, in regard to a class or classes of employment or appointment to an office [under the Government of, or any local or other authority within, a State or Union territory, any requirement as to residence within that State or Union territory] prior to such employment or appointment.

[(4A) Nothing in this article shall prevent the State from making any provision for reservation in matters of promotion to any class or classes of posts in the services under the State in favour of the Scheduled Castes and the Schedule Tribes which, in the opinion of the State, are not adequately represented in the services under the State.]

[(4B) Nothing in this article shall prevent the State from considering any unfilled vacancies of a year which are reserved for being filled up in that year in accordance with any provision for reservation made under clause (4) or clause (4A) as a separate class of vacancies to be filled up in any succeeding year or years and such class of vacancies shall not be considered together with the vacancies of the year in which they are being filled up for determining the ceiling of fifty per cent reservation on total number of vacancies of that year.]

(5) Nothing in this article shall affect the operation of any law which provides that the incumbent of an office in connection with the affairs of any religious or denominational institution or any member of the governing body thereof shall be a person professing a particular religion or belonging to a particular denomination.

17. Abolition of Untouchability.

"Untouchability" is abolished and its practice in any form is forbidden. The enforcement of any disability rising out of "Untouchability" shall be an offence punishable in accordance with law.

18. Abolition of titles.

(1) No title, not being a military or academic distinction, shall be conferred by the State.

(2) No citizen of India shall accept any title from any foreign State.

(3) No person who is not a citizen of India shall, while he holds any office of profit or trust under the State, accept without the consent of the President any title from any foreign State.

(4) No person holding any office of profit or trust under the State shall, without the consent of the President, accept any present, emolument, or office of any kind from or under any foreign State.

Right to Freedom

19. Protection of certain rights regarding freedom of speech, etc.

(1) All citizens shall have the right—

(a) to freedom of speech and expression;

(b) to assemble peaceably and without arms;

(c) to form associations or unions;

(d) to move freely throughout the territory of India;

(e) to reside and settle in any part of the territory of India; [and]

(g) to practise any profession, or to carry on any occupation, trade or business.

(2) Nothing in sub-clause (a) of clause (1) shall affect the operation of any existing law, or prevent the State from making any law, in so far as such law imposes reasonable restrictions on the exercise of the right conferred by the said sub-clause in the interests of the sovereignty and integrity of India, the security of the State, friendly relations with foreign States, public order, decency or morality, or in relation to contempt of court, defamation or incitement to an offence.

(3) Nothing in sub-clause (b) of the said clause shall affect the operation of any existing law in so far as it imposes, or prevents the State from making any law imposing, in the interests of the sovereignty and integrity of India or public order, reasonable restrictions on the exercise of the right conferred by the said sub-clause.

(4) Nothing in sub-clause (c) of the said clause shall affect the operation of any existing law in so far as it imposes, or prevents the State from making any law imposing, in the interests of the sovereignty and integrity of India or public or morality, reasonable restrictions on the exercise of the right conferred by the said sub-clause.

(5) Nothing in sub-clauses (d) and (e) of the said clause shall affect the operation of any existing law in so far as it imposes, or prevents the State from making any law imposing, reasonable restrictions on the exercise of any of the rights conferred by the said sub-clauses either in the interests of the general public or for the protection of the interests of any Scheduled Tribe.

(6) Nothing in sub-clause (g) of the said clause shall affect the operation of any existing law in so far as it imposes, or prevents the State from making any law imposing, in the interests of the general public, reasonable restrictions on the exercise of the right conferred by the said sub-clause, and, in particular, nothing in the said sub-clause shall affect the operation of any existing law in so far as it relates to, or prevents the State from making any law relating to—

(i) the professional or technical qualifications necessary for practising any profession or carrying on any occupation, trade or business, or

(ii) the carrying on by the State, or by a corporation owned or controlled by the State, of any trade, business, industry or service, whether to the exclusion, complete or partial, of citizens or otherwise.

20. Protection in respect of conviction for offences.

(1) No person shall be convicted of any offence except for violation of a law in force at the time of the commission of the act charged as an offence, nor be subjected to a penalty greater than that which might have been inflicted under the law in force at the time of the commission of the offence.

(2) No person shall be prosecuted and punished for the same offence more than once.

(3) No person accused of any offence shall be compelled to be a witness against himself.

21. Protection of life and personal liberty.

No person shall be deprived of his life or personal liberty except according to procedure established by law.

22. Protection against arrest and detention in certain cases.

(1) No person who is arrested shall be detained in custody without being informed, as soon as may be, of the grounds for such arrest nor shall he be denied the right to consult, and to be defended by, a legal practitioner of his choice.

(2) Every person who is arrested and detained in custody shall be produced before the nearest magistrate within a period of twenty-four hours of such arrest excluding the time necessary for the journey from the place of arrest to the court of the magistrate and no such person shall be detained in custody beyond the said period without the authority of a magistrate.

(3) Nothing in clauses (1) and (2) shall apply—

(a) to any person who for the time being is an enemy alien; or

(b) to any person who is arrested or detained under any law providing for preventive detention.

(4) No law providing for preventive detention shall authorise the detention of a person for a longer period than three months unless—

(a) an Advisory Board consisting of persons who are, or have been, or are qualified to be appointed as, Judges of a High Court has reported before the expiration of the said period of three months that there is in its opinion sufficient cause for such detention: Provided that nothing in this sub-clause shall authorise the detention of any person beyond the maximum period prescribed by any law made by Parliament under sub-clause (b) of clause (7); or

(b) such person is detained in accordance with the provisions of any law made by Parliament under sub-clauses (a) and (b) of clause (7).

(5) When any person is detained in pursuance of an order made under any law providing for preventive detention, the authority making the order shall, as soon as may be, communicate to such person the grounds on which the order has been made and shall afford him the earliest opportunity of making a representation against the order.

(6) Nothing in clause (5) shall require the authority making any such order as is referred to in that clause to disclose facts which such authority considers to be against the public interest to disclose.

(7) Parliament may by law prescribe—

(a) the circumstances under which, and the class or classes of cases in which, a person may be detained for a period longer than three months under any law providing for preventive detention without obtaining the opinion of an Advisory Board in accordance with the provisions of sub-clause (a) of clause (4);

(b) the maximum period for which any person may in any class or classes of cases be detained under any law providing for preventive detention; and

(c) the procedure to be followed by an Advisory Board in an inquiry under sub-clause (a) of clause (4).

Right against Exploitation

23. Prohibition of traffic in human beings and forced labour.

(1) Traffic in human beings and beggars and other similar forms of forced labour are prohibited and any contravention of this provision shall be an offence punishable in accordance with law.

(2) Nothing in this article shall prevent the State from imposing compulsory service for public purposes, and in imposing such service the State shall not make any discrimination on grounds only of religion, race, caste or class or any of them.

24. Prohibition of employment of children in factories, etc.

No child below the age of fourteen years shall be employed to work in any factory or mine or engaged in any other hazardous employment.

Right to Freedom of Religion

25. Freedom of conscience and free profession, practice and propagation of religion.

(1) Subject to public order, morality and health and to the other provisions of this Part, all persons are equally entitled to freedom of conscience and the right freely to profess, practise and propagate religion.

(2) Nothing in this article shall affect the operation of any existing law or prevent the State from making any law—

(a) regulating or restricting any economic, financial, political or other secular activity which may be associated with religious practice;

(b) providing for social welfare and reform or the throwing open of Hindu religious institutions of a public character to all classes and sections of Hindus.

Explanation I.—The wearing and carrying of kirpans shall be deemed to be included in the profession of the Sikh religion.

Explanation II.—In sub-clause (b) of clause (2), the reference to Hindus shall be construed as including a reference to persons professing the Sikh, Jaina or Buddhist religion, and the reference to Hindu religious institutions shall be construed accordingly.

26. Freedom to manage religious affairs.

Subject to public order, morality and health, every religious denomination or any section thereof shall have the right—

(a) to establish and maintain institutions for religious and charitable purposes;

(b) to manage its own affairs in matters of religion;

(c) to own and acquire movable and immovable property; and

(d) to administer such property in accordance with law.

27. Freedom as to payment of taxes for promotion of any particular religion.

No person shall be compelled to pay any taxes, the proceeds of which are specifically appropriated in payment of expenses for the promotion or main-tenance of any particular religion or religious denomination.

28. Freedom as to attendance at religious instruction or religious worship in certain educational institutions.

(1) No religious instruction shall be provided in any educational institution wholly maintained out of State funds.

(2) Nothing in clause (1) shall apply to an educational institution which is administered by the State but has been established under any endowment or trust which requires that religious instruction shall be imparted in such institution.

(3) No person attending any educational institution recognised by the State or receiving aid out of State funds shall be required to take part in any religious instruction that may be imparted in such institution or to attend any religious worship that may be conducted in such institution or in any premises attached thereto unless such person or, if such person is a minor, his guardian has given his consent thereto.

Cultural and Educational Rights

29. Protection of interests and minorities.

(1) Any section of the citizens residing in the territory of India or any part thereof having a distinct language, script or culture of its own shall have the right to conserve the same.

(2) No citizen shall be denied admission into any educational institution main-tained by the State or receiving aid out of State funds on grounds only of religion, race, caste, language or any of them.

30. Right of minorities to establish and administer educational institutions.

(1) All minorities, whether based on religion or language, shall have the right to establish and administer educational institutions of their choice.

(1A) In making any law providing for the compulsory acquisition of any property of any educational institution established and administered by a minority, referred to in clause (1), the State shall ensure that the amount fixed by or determined under such law for the acquisition of such property is such as would not restrict or abrogate the right guaranteed under that clause.

(2) The State shall not, in granting aid to educational institutions, discriminate against any educational institution on the ground that it is under the management of a minority, whether based on religion or language.

[31. Compulsory acquisition of property.

Rep. by the Constitution (Forty-fourth Amendment) Act, 1978, s.6 (w.e.f. 20–6–1979)].

Savings of Certain Laws

31A. Saving of laws providing for acquisition of estates, etc.

(1) Notwithstanding anything contained in article 13, no law providing for—

  (a) the acquisition by the State of any estate or of any rights therein or the extinguishment or modification of any such rights, or

(b) the taking over of the management of any property by the State for a limited period either in the public interest or in order to secure the proper management of the property, or

(c) the amalgamation of two or more corporations either in the public interest or in order to secure the proper management of any of the corporations, or

(d) the extinguishment or modification of any rights of managing agents, secretaries and treasurers, managing directors, directors or managers of corporations, or of any voting rights of shareholders thereof, or

(e) the extinguishment or modification of any rights accruing by virtue of any agreement, lease or licence for the purpose of searching for, or winning, any mineral or mineral oil, or the premature termination or cancellation of any such agreement, lease or licence, shall be deemed to be void on the ground that it is inconsistent with, or takes away or abridges any of the rights conferred by article 14 or article 19: Provided that where such law is a law made by the Legislature of a State, the provisions of this article shall not apply thereto unless such law, having been reserved for the consideration of the President, has received his assent: Provided further that where any law makes any provision for the acquisition by the State of any estate and where any land comprised therein is held by a person under his personal cultivation, it shall not be lawful for the State to acquire any portion of such land as is within the ceiling limit applicable to him under any law for the time being in force or any building or structure standing thereon or appurtenant thereto, unless the law relating to the acquisition of such land, building or structure, provides for payment of compensation at a rate which shall not be less than the market value thereof.

(2) In this article—

(a) the expression "estate" shall, in relation to any local area, having the same meaning as that expression or its local equivalent has in the existing law relating to land tenures in force in that areas and shall also include—

(i) any jagir, inam or muafi or other similar grant and in the States of Tamil Nadu and Kerala, any janmam right;
(ii) any land held under ryotwari settlement;
(iii) any land held or let for purposes of agriculture or for purposes ancillary thereto, including waste land, forest land, land for pasture or sites of buildings and other structures occupied by cultivators of land, agricultural labourers and village artisans;

(b) the expression "rights", in relation to an estate, shall include any rights vesting in a proprietor, sub-proprietor, under-proprietor, tenure-holder, raiyat, under-raiyat or other intermediary and any rights or privileges in respect of land revenue.

31B. Validation of certain Acts and Regulations.

Without prejudice to the generality of the provisions contained in article 31A, none of the Acts and Regulations specified in the Ninth Schedule nor any of the provisions thereof shall be deemed to be void, or ever to have become void, on the ground that such Act, Regulation or provision is inconsistent with, or takes away or abridges any of the rights conferred by, any provisions of this Part, and notwithstanding any judgment, decree or order of any court or Tribunal to the contrary, each of the said Acts and Regulations shall, subject to the power of any competent Legislature to repeal or amend it, continue in force.

31C. Saving of laws giving effect to certain directive principles.

Notwithstanding anything contained in article 13, no law giving effect to the policy of the State towards securing all or any of the principles laid down in Part IV shall be deemed to be void on the ground that it is inconsistent with, or takes away or abridges any of the rights conferred by article 14 or article 19; and no law containing a declaration that it is for giving effect to such policy shall be called in question in any court on the ground that it does not give effect to such policy:

Provided that where such law is made by the Legislature of a State, the provisions of this article shall not apply thereto unless such law, having been reserved for the consideration of the President, has received his assent.

[31D. Saving of laws in respect of anti-national activities.

Rep. by the Constitution (Forty-third Amendment) Act, 1977, s.2 (w.e.f. 13–4–1978)].

Right to Constitutional Remedies

32. Remedies for enforcement of rights conferred by this Part.

(1) The right to move the Supreme Court by appropriate proceedings for the enforcement of the rights conferred by this Part is guaranteed.

(2) The Supreme Court shall have power to issue directions or orders or writs, including writs in the nature of habeas corpus, mandamus, prohibition, quo warranto and certiorari, whichever may be appropriate, for the enforcement of any of the rights conferred by this part.

(3) Without prejudice to the powers conferred on the Supreme Court by clauses (1) and (2), Parliament may by law empower any other court to exercise within the local limits of its jurisdiction all or any of the powers exercisable by the Supreme Court under clause (2).

(4) The right guaranteed by this article shall not be suspended except as otherwise provided for by this Constitution.

[32A. Constitutional validity of State laws not to be considered in proceeding under article 32.]

Rep. by the Constitution (Forty-third Amendment) Act, 1977, s.3 (w.e.f. 13–4–1978)].

33. Power of Parliament to modify the rights conferred by this Part in their application to Forces, etc.

Parliament may, by law, determine to what extent any of the rights conferred by this Part shall, in their application to—

(a) the members of the Armed Forces; or

(b) the members of the Forces charged with the maintenance of public order; or

(c) persons employed in any bureau or other organisation established by the State for purposes of intelligence or counter intelligence; or

(d) persons employed in, or in connection with, the telecommunication systems set up for the purposes of any Force, bureau or organisation referred to in clauses (a) to (c),

be restricted or abrogated so as to ensure the proper discharge of their duties and the maintenance of discipline among them.

34. Restriction on rights conferred by this Part while martial law is in force in any area.

Notwithstanding anything in the foregoing provisions of this Part, Parliament may by law indemnify any person in the service of the Union or of a State or any other person in respect of any act done by him in connection with the maintenance or restoration of order in any area within the territory of India where martial law was in force or validate any sentence passed, punishment inflicted, forfeiture ordered or other act done under martial law in such area.

35. Legislation to give effect to the provisions of this Part.

Notwithstanding anything in this Constitution—

   (a) Parliament shall have, and the Legislature of a State shall not have, power to make laws—

      (i) with respect to any of the matters which under clause (3) of article 16, clause (3) of article 32, article 33 and article 34 may be provided for by law made by Parliament; and

      (ii) for prescribing punishment for those acts which are declared to be offences under this Part; and Parliament shall, as soon as may be after the commencement of this Constitution, make laws for prescribing punishment for the acts referred to in sub-clause (ii);

   (b) any law in force immediately before the commencement of this Constitution in the territory of India with respect to any of the matters referred to in sub-clause (i) of clause (a) or providing for punishment for any act referred to in sub-clause (ii) of that clause shall, subject to the terms thereof and to any adaptations and modifications that may be made therein under article 372, continue in force until altered or repealed or amended by Parliament.

Explanation—In this article, the expression "law in force" has the same meaning as in article 372.

Index